Directory of Financial Aids for Women 2017-2019 Edition

Gail Ann Schlachter
R. David Weber
Foreword by: Eric Goldman

A Listing of Scholarships, Fellowships, Grants, Awards, Internships, and Other Sources of Free Money Available Primarily or Exclusively to Women, Plus a Set of Six Indexes (Program Title, Sponsoring Organization, Residency, Tenability, Subject, and Deadline Date)

AdmitHub
Boston, Massachusetts

Library of Congress Cataloging in Publication Data

Schlachter, Gail A.
    Directory of financial aids for women, 2017-2019
    Includes indexes.
    1. Women - United States - Scholarships, fellowships, etc. - Directories. 2. Grants-in-aid - United States - Directories. 3. Credit - United States - Directories. I. Title.

AdmitHub
Harvard Innovation Launch Lab
114 Western Ave.
Boston, MA 02134
    (617) 575-9369
    Email: rsp@admithub.com
Visit our web site: www.admithub.com

Manufactured in the United States of America
Price: $40

Contents

Foreword

About Dr. Gail Schlachter and Reference Service Press

Dr. Gail Ann Schlachter (1943-2015), original founder of Reference Service Press, was working as a librarian in the mid-1970s when she recognized that women applying for college faced significant obstacles finding information about financial aid resources designed to help them. This challenge inspired her to publish her ground-breaking book, *Directory of Financial Aids for Women*, in 1977. The book's success prompted additional financial aid directories for other underserved communities, including minorities, the disabled and our nation's military personnel and veterans.

By 1985, the business had become so successful that she left her job as a publishing company executive to run her company, Reference Service Press, full-time. Over the years, the company's offerings expanded to over two dozen financial aid titles covering many different types of students—law students, business students, students studying abroad, and many more. The company's success was driven by its database of tens of thousands of financial aid programs, laboriously hand-built over the decades and kept current to exacting specifications. In 1995, Reference Service Press once again broke new ground by launching one of the first-ever searchable electronic databases of financial aid resources (initially through America Online). For more background about the founding and success of Reference Service Press, see Katina Strauch's 1997 "Against the Grain" interview with Dr. Schlachter, available at http://docs.lib.purdue.edu/cgi/viewcontent.cgi?article=2216&context=atg.

Dr. Schlachter was also a major figure in the library community for nearly five decades. She served: as reference book review editor for *RQ* (now *Reference and User Services Quarterly*) for 10 years; as president of the American Library Association's Reference and User Services Association; as editor of the *Reference and User Services Association Quarterly*; seven terms on the American Library Association's governing council; and on the association's Executive Board. She was posthumously inducted into the California Library Association Hall of Fame. The University of Wisconsin School of Library and Information Studies named Dr. Schlachter an "Alumna of the Year," and she was recognized with both the Isadore Gilbert Mudge Citation and the Louis Shores/Oryx Press Award.

Dr. Schlachter will be remembered for how her financial aid directories helped thousands of students achieve their educational and professional dreams. She also will be remembered for her countless contributions to the library profession. And, as an American Library Association Executive Board resolution from June 2015 says, she will be remembered, "most importantly, for her mentorship, friendship, and infectious smile." Yet, despite her impressive lifetime of professional accomplishments, Dr. Schlachter always was most proud of her family, including her husband Stuart Hauser, her daughter Dr. Sandy Hirsh (and Jay Hirsh) and son Eric Goldman (and Lisa Goldman), and her grandchildren Hayley, Leah, Jacob, and Dina.

Introduction

HOW THE DIRECTORY GOT ITS START

This directory began in 1977 when Dr. Gail Schlachter founded Reference Service Press and published the first edition of *Directory of Financial Aids for Women*. To complete its 300 programs on 200 pages, she laboriously photocopied program information, cut and pasted the draft, and then produced the final "camera-ready" version on an IBM Selectric typewriter. If you look carefully at the first edition, you'll be able to see where she used White-Out and correction tape!

HOW THE DIRECTORY HAS GROWN IN THE PAST 40 YEARS

In 1977 and 1978, while she was furiously researching, writing, editing, and updating entries for the very first edition of the *Directory of Financial Aids for Women*, major events were occurring that would have a lasting effect on the role of women in American society:

- The first National Women's Conference was held in Houston, Texas, attended by 20,000 women who passed the landmark National Plan of Action.

- The National Coalition Against Domestic Violence was established.

- The Air Force graduated its first women pilots.

- Congress passed the Pregnancy Discrimination Act, prohibiting discrimination against pregnant women in all areas of employment.

- Congress allocated $5 million to the Department of Labor to set up centers for displaced homemakers.

- The Philadelphia Mint began stamping the Susan B. Anthony dollar.

- Dianne Feinstein became the first female mayor of San Francisco, replacing the assassinated George Moscone.

- Margaret Thatcher was chosen to become Britain's first female prime minister.

- Hanna Gray was named president of the University of Chicago, becoming the first woman to lead a major American university.

But, for her, the most significant development occurred in the field of higher education. In 1978, for the first time ever, more women than men entered American colleges and universities. She knew these women would face many challenges, particularly financial ones. Numerous studies had shown that, historically, when women competed against men for college aid, they were notably unsuccessful. She believed she could help to level this funding playing field by compiling the first-ever listing of financial aid opportunities open primarily or exclusively to women. And, so, the *Directory of Financial Aids for Women* was launched. Finally, women could find out about the hundreds of funding opportunities that were available just for them!

She was right. The directory did make a difference. Orders poured in. Women wrote about their successes. The book was featured in numerous magazines, television shows, bibliographic guides, and reviewing sources. It became clear to Reference Service Press that there was a continuing need for this type of compilation. So, in 1980, the company made a commitment to collect, organize, and disseminate - on an on-going basis - the most current and accurate information available on all types of funding opportunities open to women.

To accomplish this goal over the years, RSP staff had to become sophisticated information sleuths, tracking down all possible leads, identifying even the slightest changes to existing programs, finding new sources of funding opportunities for women, and constantly expanding and updating the electronic database used to prepare each new biennial edition of the *Directory of Financial Aids for Women*. In the past 40 years, the directory has increased fivefold in size, growing to the staggering 1,443 opportunities described in the 2017-2019 edition's more than 400 pages. Those entries have been carefully selected from the RSP database of 35,000 unique funding records, formatted using a layout and font chosen specifically for maximum utility, and produced simultaneously in both book and electronic versions. Access to the information has advanced significantly as well, going beyond the simple program title listing in the first edition (with basic subject, geographic, and sponsor indexes) to a user-friendly grouping of records by recipient category (undergraduates, graduate students, and professionals/postdoctorates) and six detailed and sub-divided indexes in the latest edition, making it possible to search the information by all current, variant, and former program titles; every sponsor and administering organization; each location where an applicant must live; every place where the money can be spent; hundreds of specific subject fields; and month-by-month deadline dates.

One thing that hasn't changed during the past 40 years, however, is the passionate commitment to making a difference. Little did Dr. Schlachter realize, when she first published the *Directory of Financial Aids for Women* in 1978, that she had taken the initial steps on what would become a life-long search for unique funding opportunities available specifically to special needs groups. Her dedication is possibly why *The Simba Report on Directory Publishing* called Reference Service Press "a true success in the world of independent directory publishers" and why both Kaplan Educational Centers and Military.com have hailed the company as "the leading authority on scholarships."

Following Dr. Schlachter's untimely death in 2015 and the acquisition of RSP by AdmitHub, the commitment to quality has remained unabated. In the capable hands of the AdmitHub staff, the work of gathering and disseminating, through book and electronic formats, data on financial aid opportunities will continue.

WHY THIS DIRECTORY IS NEEDED

Currently, billions of dollars in financial aid are available primarily or exclusively for women. In fact, more money is available today than ever before. This funding is open to applicants at any level (high school through postdoctoral and professional) for study, research, travel, training, career development, or innovative efforts. While numerous directories have been prepared to identify and describe general financial aid programs (those open to both men and women), they have never been covered more than a small portion of the programs designed primarily or exclusively for women. As a result, many advisors, librarians, scholars, researchers, and students have not been aware of the impressive array of financial aid programs established with women in mind. Now, with the 2017-2019 edition of the *Directory of Financial Aids for Women*, up-to-date and comprehensive information is available in a single source about the special resources set aside for women. No other source, in print or online, comes anywhere close to matching the extensive coverage provided by this publication.

The unique value of the *Directory* has been highly praised by the reviewers. Here are just some of the rave reviews:

- "The title is a must-purchase guide." --*American Reference Books Annual*
- "Nobody does a better job...a great resource and highly recommended." --*College Spotlight*
- "The only current source of information on financial aid specifically for women... an essential and reasonably priced purchase." --*Reference Books Bulletin*
- "The quintessential acquisition for public libraries of all sizes...feminists, homemakers, and women everywhere will welcome this book, since it is so well- done and simple to use." --*Small Press*
- "The variety of programs is amazing...an essential purchase...has become the standard source of information on scholarships, fellowships, loans, grants, awards, and internships available primarily to women." --*Library Journal*

SAMPLE ENTRY

[1] **[95]**

[2] **BEATRICE WARDE SCHOLARSHIP**

[3] Type Directors Club
347 West 36th Street, Suite 603
New York, NY 10018
(212) 633-8943
Fax: (212) 633-8944
E-mail: director@tdc.org
Web: www.tdc.rg/beatrice-warde

[4] **Summary** To provide financial assistance to women working on an undergraduate degree in typography.

[5] **Eligibility** This program is open to women entering their senior year with a major related to typography, ranging from design criticism to type design and graphic design. Applicants must have a GPA of 3.0 or higher. Along with their application, they must submit 3 samples of their work and letters of recommendation. Selection is based on merit, including talent, sophistication, and skill in the use of typography.

[6] **Financial data** The stipend is $5,000. Funds are sent directly to the recipient's college or university.

[7] **Duration** 1 year.

[8] **Additional information** This program began in 2016 with support from the Monotone Corporation, the long-time employer of the program's namesake.

[9] **Number awarded** 1 each year.

[10] **Deadline** February of each year.

DEFINITION

[1] **Entry number:** The consecutive number assigned to the references and used to index the entry.

[2] **Program title:** Title of the scholarship, fellowship, grant or other source of free money described in the directory.

[3] **Sponsoring organization:** Name, address, telephone number, toll-free number, fax number, email address, and/or web site (if information was supplied) for organization sponsoring the program.

[4] **Summary:** Identifies the major program requirements; read the rest of the entry for additional detail.

[5] **Eligibility:** Qualifications required of applicants, plus information on application procedure and selection process.

[6] **Financial data:** Financial details of the program, including fixed sum, average amount, or range of funds offered; expenses for which funds may or may not be applied, and cash-related benefits applied (e.g., room and board).

[7] **Duration:** Period for which support is provided; renewal prospects.

[8] **Additional information:** Any unusual (generally nonmonetary) benefits, features, restrictions, or limitations associated with the program.

[9] **Number awarded:** Total number of recipients each year or other specified period.

[10] **Deadline:** The month by which applications must be submitted.

Previous editions of the directory were selected as the "cream of the crop" in *School Library Journal's* "Reference Round-Up;" were included in *Recommended Reference Books for Small and Medium-sized Libraries and Media Centers*; were featured in *Glamour, Good Housekeeping, New Women,* and *Teen* magazines; and were selected as the "Best of the Best" in education and career information print materials by members of the National Education Information Center Advisory Committee. In the view of The Grantsmanship Center, "No organization interested in serving women should be without this directory!" Want to read more reviews? Go to www.rspfunding.com/reviews.html.

WHAT'S UPDATED?

The preparation of each new edition of *Directory of Financial Aids for Women* involves extensive updating and revision. To make sure that the information included here is both reliable and current, the editors at Reference Service Press 1) updated all relevant programs currently in our funding database and 2) collected information on all programs open primarily or exclusively to women that were added to Reference Service Press' funding database since the last edition of the directory, and then 3) searched extensively for new program leads in a variety of sources, including printed directories, news reports, journals, newsletters, house organs, annual reports, and sites on the Internet. We only include program descriptions in the directory that are written directly from information supplied by the sponsoring organization or posted on their web sites (no information was ever taken from secondary sources), we sent up to four collection letters (followed by up to three telephone inquiries, if necessary) to each sponsor identified in the process. Despite our best efforts, however, some sponsoring organizations still failed to respond and, as a result, their programs are not included in this edition of the directory.

The 2017-2019 edition of *Directory of Financial Aids for Women* completely revises and updates the previous (17th) edition. Programs that have ceased operation have been dropped. Similarly, programs that have broadened their focus to include men have also been removed from the listing. Profiles of continuing programs have been rewritten to reflect operations in 2017-2019; more than 70 percent of the continuing programs reported subsequent changes in their locations, requirements (particularly application deadline), benefits, or eligibility requirements since 2012. In addition, more than 450 new entries have been added to the program section of the directory. The resulting listing describes the close to 1,500 biggest and best sources of free money available to women, including scholarships, fellowships, grants, awards, and internships.

WHAT MAKES THIS DIRECTORY UNIQUE?

The 2017-2019 edition of the *Directory of Financial Aids for Women* identifies billions of dollars available for study, research, creative activities, past accomplishments, future projects, professional development, and work experience. The listings cover every major subject area, are sponsored by more than 900 different private and public agencies and organizations, and are open to women at any level - from high school through postdoctorates and professional. This approach is unique. No other source, in print or online, provides this type of comprehensive and current coverage of funding opportunities available primarily or exclusively to women.

Not only does the *Directory of Financial Aids for Women* provide the most comprehensive coverage of available funding (1,443 entries), but it also displays the most informative program descriptions (on the average, more than twice the detail found in any other listing). In addition to this extensive and focused coverage, the directory also offers several other unique features. First of all, hundreds of funding opportunities listed here have never been covered in any other source. So, even if you have checked elsewhere, you will want to look at the *Directory of Financial Aids for Women* for additional leads. And, here's another plus: all of the funding programs in this edition of the directory offer "free" money; not one of the programs will ever require you to pay anything back (provided, of course, that you meet the program requirements).

Further, unlike other funding directories, which generally follow a straight alphabetical arrangement, the

Directory of Financial Aids for Women groups entries by intended recipients (undergraduate, graduate students, or professionals/postdoctorates), to make it easy for you to search for appropriate programs.

This same convenience is offered in the indexes, where program title, sponsoring organization, geographic, subject, and deadline date entries are each subdivided by recipient group.

Finally, we have tried to anticipate all the ways you might wish to search for funding. The volume is organized so you can identify programs not only by intended recipient, but also by subject focus, sponsoring organization, program title, residency requirements, where the money can be spent, and even deadline date. Plus, we've included all the information you'll need to decide if a program is right for you: purpose, eligibility requirements, financial data, duration, special features, limitations, number awarded, and application. You can even get fax numbers, toll-free numbers, email addresses, and websites (when available), along with complete contact information.

WHAT'S EXCLUDED?

While this book is intended to be the most comprehensive source of information of funding available to women, there are some programs we've specifically excluded from the directory.

- Programs that do not accept applications from U.S. citizens or residents: If a funding opportunity is open only to foreign nationals or excludes American from applying, it is not covered.

- Programs that are open equally to men and women: Only funding opportunities set aside primarily or exclusively for women are included here.

- Money for study outside the United States: Since there are comprehensive and up-to-date directories that describe available funding for study, research, or other activities abroad (see the list of Reference Service Press publications opposite the directory's title page), only programs that fund activities in the United States are covered here.

- Very restrictive programs: The emphasis here is on the biggest and best funding available. In general, programs are excluded if they are open only to a limited geographic area (less than a state) or offer limited financial support (less than $1,000). Note, however, that the majority of programs award considerably more than $1,000 minimum requirement, paying up to full tuition or stipends that exceed $25,000 a year!

- Programs administered by individual academic institutions solely for their own students: The directory identifies "portable" programs - ones that can be used at any number of schools. Financial aid administered by individual schools specifically for their own students is not covered. Write directly to the schools you are considering to get information on their offerings.

- Money that must be repaid: Only "free money" is identified here. If a program requires repayment or charges interest, it's not listed. Now you can find out about billions of dollars in aid and know (if you meet the program requirements) that not one dollar of that will ever need to be repaid.

HOW THE DIRECTORY IS ORGANIZED

The *Directory* is divided into two sections: 1) a detailed list of funding opportunities open to women and 2) a set of six indexes to help you pinpoint appropriate funding programs.

Financial Aid Programs Open Primarily or Exclusively to Women. The first section of the directory describes the nearly 1,500 biggest and best sources of free money aimed primarily or exclusively at women. These programs are sponsored by government agencies, professional organizations, corporations, sororities and social groups, foundations, religious groups, educational associations, and military/veterans organizations. They are open to women at any level (high school through postdoctoral) for study, research, travel, training, career development, personal needs, or creative activities. All areas of the sciences, social sciences, and humanities are covered in the awards listed. The focus is on programs tenable in the United States that are open to women who are U.S. citizens or permanent residents.

To help you focus your search, the entries in this section are grouped in the following three chapters:

- **Undergraduates**. Included here are more than 700 scholarships, grants, awards, internships, and other sources of free money that support women's undergraduate study, training, research, or creative activities. These programs are open to high school seniors, high school graduates, currently-enrolled college students, and students returning to college after an absence. Money is available to support these students in any type of public or private postsecondary institution, ranging from technical schools and community colleges to major universities in the United States.

- **Graduate Students**. Described here are nearly 500 fellowships, grants, awards, internships, and other sources of free money that support women's post- baccalaureate study, training, research, and creative activities. These programs are available to students applying to, currently enrolled in, or returning to a master's, doctoral, professional, or specialist program in public or private graduate schools in the United States.

- **Professionals/Postdoctorates**. Included here are more than 275 funding programs for women who are U.S. citizens or residents and 1) are in professional positions (e.g. artists, writers), whether or not they have an advanced degree; 2) are master's or professional degree recipients; 3) have earned a doctoral degree or its equivalent (e.g. Ph.D., Ed.D., M.D.); or 4) have recognized stature as established scientists, scholars, academicians, or researchers.

Within each chapter in the Directory, entries appear alphabetically by program title. Since some of the programs supply assistance to more than one specific group, those are listed in all relevant chapters. For example, the Amelia Earhart Memorial Academic Scholarship supports both undergraduate or graduate study, so the program is described in both the Undergraduate and Graduate Students chapters.

Each program entry has been designed to give you a concise profile that, as the sample on page 7 illustrates, includes information (when available) on organization address and telephone numbers (including toll-free and fax numbers), email addresses and website, purpose, eligibility, money awarded, duration, special features, limitations, number of awards, and application deadline.

The information reported for each of the programs in this section was gathered from research conducted through the end of 2016. While the listing is intended to cover as comprehensively as possible the biggest and best sources of free money to women, some sponsoring organizations did not post information online or respond to our research inquiries and, consequently, are not included in this edition of the directory.

Indexes.

To help you find the aid you need, we have constructed indexes for program title, sponsoring organization, residency, tenability, subject focus, and deadline date. Note: numbers in the index refer to entry numbers, not to page numbers in the book.

Program Title Index. If you know the name of a particular funding program and want to find out where it is covered in the Directory, use the Program Title Index. To assist you in your search, every program is listed by all its known names, former names, and abbreviations. Since one program can be included in more than one place (e.g., a program providing assistance to both undergraduate and graduate students is described in both the first and second chapter), each entry number in the index has been coded to indicate the intended recipient group ("U" = Undergraduate; "G" = Graduate Students; "P" = Professionals/Postdoctorates). By using this coding system, you can avoid duplicate entries and turn directory to the programs that match your eligibility characteristics.

Sponsoring Organization Index.This index makes it easy to identify agencies that offer funding primarily or exclusively to women. More than 900 organizations are listed alphabetically, word by word.

As in the Program Title Index, we've used a code to help you determine which organizations sponsor programs that match your education level.

Residency Index. Some programs listed in this book are restricted to women in a particular state, region, or other geographic location. Others are open to women wherever they live. This index help you identify programs available only to residents in your area as well as programs that have no residency restrictions. Further, to assist you in your search, we've also indicated the recipient level for the funding offered to residents in each of the areas listed in the index.

Tenability Index. This index identifies the geographic locations where the funding described in the Directory may be used. Index entries (city, county, state, province, region) are arranged alphabetically (word by word) and subdivided by recipient group. Use this index when you are looking for money to support your activities in a particular geographic area.

Subject Index. This index allows you to identify the subject focus of each of the financial aid opportunities described in the Directory. More than 250 different subject terms are listed. Extensive "see" and "see also" references, as well as recipient group subdivisions, will help you in your search for appropriate funding opportunities.

Calendar Index. Since most financial aid programs have specific deadline dates, some may have closed by the time you begin to look for funding. You can use the Calendar Index to determine which programs are still open. This index is arranged by student group (Undergraduate, Graduate Students, and Professionals/Postdoctorates) and subdivided by month during which the deadline falls. Filing dates can and quite often do vary from year to year; consequently, the dates in this index should be used only as a guide for deadlines beyond the end of 2017.

HOW TO USE THE DIRECTORY

Here are some tips to help you get the most out of the financial aid listings in *Directory of Financial Aids for Women*:

To Locate Funding by Recipient Group. To bring together programs with a similar educational focus, this directory is divided into three chapters: Undergraduate, Graduate Students, and Professionals/Postdoctorates. If you want to get an overall picture of the sources of free money available to women in any of these categories, turn to the appropriate chapter and then review the entries there. Since each of these chapters functions as a self-contained entity, you can browse through any of them without having to first consult an index.

To Locate a Particular Women's Financial Aid Program. If you know the name of a particular financial aid program, and the group eligible for that award, then go directly to the appropriate chapter in the directory (e.g., Undergraduate, Graduate Students), where you will find the program profiles arranged alphabetically by title. To save time, though, you should always check the Program Title Index first if you know the name of a specific award but are not sure in which chapter it has been listed. Plus, since we index each program by all its known names and abbreviations, you'll also be able to track down a program where you only know the popular rather than the official name.

To Locate Financial Aid Programs Sponsored by a Particular Organization. The Sponsoring Organization Index makes it easy to identify agencies that provide financial assistance to women or to target specific financial aid programs for women offered by a particular organization. Each entry number in the index coded to identify recipient group (Undergraduate, Graduate Students, Professionals/Postdoctorates), so that you can easily target appropriate entries.

To Browse Quickly Through the Listings. Look at the listings in the chapter that relates to you (Undergraduates, Graduate Students, or Professionals/Postdoctorates) and read the "Summary" paragraph in each entry. In seconds, you'll know if this is an opportunity that you might want to pursue. If it is, be sure to read the rest of the information in the entry, to make sure you meet all of the program requirements before writing or going online for an application form. Please save your time and energy. Don't apply if you don't qualify!

To Locate Funding Open to Women from or Tenable in a Particular Geographic Location. The Residency Index identifies financial aid programs open to women in a particular geographic location.

The Tenability Index shows where the money can be spent. In both indexes, "see" and "see also" references are used liberally, and index entries for a particular geographic area are subdivided by recipient group (Undergraduates, Graduate Students, and Professionals/Postdoctorates) to help you identify the funding that's right for you. When using these indexes, always check the listings under the term "United States", since the programs indexed there have no geographic restrictions and can be used in any area.

To Locate Financial Aid for Women in a Particular Subject Area. Turn to the Subject Index first if you are interested in identifying financial aid programs for women in a particular subject area (more than 250 different subject fields are listed there). To make your search easier, the intended recipient groups (Undergraduate, Graduate Students, Professionals/Postdoctorates) are clearly labeled in each of the subject listings. Extensive cross-references are also provided. As part of your search, be sure to check the listings in the index under the heading "General Programs;" those programs provide funding in any subject area (although they may be restricted in other ways).

To Locate Financial Aid for Women by Deadline Date. If you are working with specific time constraints and want to weed out financial aid programs whose filing dates you won't be able to meet, turn first to the Calendar Index and check the program references listed under the appropriate recipient group and month. Note: not all sponsoring organizations supplied deadline information; those programs are listed under the "Deadline not specified" entries in the index. To identify every relevant financial aid program, regardless of filing date, go to the appropriate chapter and read through all the entries there that match your educational level.

To Locate Financial Aid Programs Open to Both Men and Women. Only programs designed with women in mind are listed in this publication. There are thousands of other programs that are open equally to men and women. To identify these programs, talk to your local librarian, check with your campus financial aid office, look at the list of RSP print resources on the page opposite the title page in this directory, or see if your library subscribes to Reference Service Press' interactive online funding database (for more information on that resource, go online to: www.rspfunding.com/esubscriptions.html

PLANS TO UPDATE THE DIRECTORY

This volume, covering 2017-2019, is the 18th edition of the *Directory of Financial Aids for Women*. The next biennial edition will cover the years 2019-2021 and will be released in the Fall of 2019.

ACKNOWLEDGEMENTS

A debt of gratitude is owed all the organizations that contributed information to the 2017-2019 edition of the *Directory of Financial Aids for Women*. Their generous cooperation has helped to make this publication the most current and comprehensive survey of awards.

ABOUT THE AUTHORS

Dr. Gail Ann Schlachter (1943-2015) worked for more than three decades as a library administrator, a library educator, and an administrator of library-related publishing companies. Among the reference books to her credit are the biennially-issued *College Student's Guide to Merit and Other No-Need Funding* (named by *Choice* as one of the outstanding reference titles of the year) and two award-winning bibliographic guides: *Minorities and Women: A Guide to Reference Literature in the Social Sciences* (which also was chosen as an "Outstanding Reference Book of the Year" by *Choice*) and *Reference Sources in Library and Information Services* (which won the first Knowledge Industry Publications "Award for Library Literature"). She was the reference book review editor for *RQ* (now *Reference and User Services Quarterly*) for 10 years, was a past president of the American Library Association's Reference and User Services Association, was the former editor-in-chief of the *Reference and User Services Association Quarterly*, and served five terms on the American Library Association's governing council. In recognition of her outstanding contributions to reference service, Dr. Schlachter was named the University of Wisconsin School of Library and Information Studies "Alumna of the Year" and received both the Isadore Gilbert Mudge Citation and the Louis Shores/Oryx Press Award.

Dr. R. David Weber taught history and economics at Los Angeles Harbor College (in Wilmington, California) for many years and continues to teach history as an emeritus professor. During his years of full-time teaching there, and at East Los Angeles College, he directed the Honors Program and was frequently chosen the "Teacher of the Year." He is the author of a number of critically-acclaimed reference works, including *Dissertations in Urban History* and the three-volume *Energy Information Guide*. With Gail Schlachter, he is the author of Reference Service Press's award-winning *High School Senior's Guide to Merit and other No-Need Funding* and a number of other financial aid titles, including *Financial Aid for Veterans, Military Personnel, and Their Families* and *Financial Aid for the Disabled and Their Families*, which was selected as one of the "Best Reference Books of the Year" by *Library Journal*.

ABOUT THE FOREWORD AUTHOR

Professor Eric Goldman, who served as a consultant in the research process and wrote the foreword for this edition of *Directory of Financial Aid for Women*, teaches intellectual property and cyberlaw at Santa Clara University Law School, where he is also the co-director of the High Tech Law Institute. Previously, he was general counsel for Epinions.com and an attorney at the Silicon Valley law firm of Cooley Godward. Professor Goldman knows first-hand the value of financial aid. Thanks in part to the scholarships he received, he was able to graduate from law school debt free!

Financial Aid Programs Primarily or Exclusively for Women

Undergraduates ●

Graduate Students ●

Professionals/Postdoctorates ●

Undergraduates

Listed alphabetically by program title and described in detail here are 716 scholarships, grants, awards, internships, and other sources of "free money" set aside for females who are college-bound high school seniors, high school graduates who haven't started college yet, and continuing or returning undergraduate students. This funding is available to support study, training, research, and/or creative activities in the United States.

[1]
1,000 DREAMS SCHOLARSHIP FUND

Greater Kansas City Community Foundation
Attn: Scholarship Coordinator
1055 Broadway Boulevard, Suite 130
Kansas City, MO 64105-1595
(816) 842-0944   Fax: (816) 842-8079
E-mail: scholarships@growyourgiving.org
Web: www.growyourgiving.org

Summary To provide funding for educational expenses to women currently enrolled in high school or college.

Eligibility This program is open to women who are currently enrolled in high school or at a 2- or 4-year college or university. Applicants must be seeking funding for education-related expenses such as instructional programs related to creative or artistic pursuits, graduate examination application fees, educational conferences, textbooks, or tuition. Along with their application, they must submit 2 letters of recommendation and an essay explaining how the grant would be used. Selection is based on application contents, information in letters of recommendation, and financial need.

Financial data The stipend is $1,000 per year.

Duration 1 year; recipients may reapply.

Number awarded Up to 5 each semester.

Deadline February of each year for fall; August of each year for spring.

[2]
AAPT-ALPHA AWARD

American Association of Physics Teachers
Attn: Awards Committee
One Physics Ellipse
College Park, MD 20740-3845
(301) 209-3311   Fax: (301) 209-0845
E-mail: awards@aapt.org
Web: www.aapt.org

Summary To recognize and reward undergraduate students who build and develop an advanced laboratory experiment for their school's advanced laboratory program.

Eligibility This award is available to undergraduate students, acting individually or in a group, who have built (and possibly developed) an advanced laboratory experiment that will become a new part of their school's program. The experiment must be new to the home department, either based on the literature or being used at other institutions. It may have been carried out as a senior project, senior thesis, or equivalent. Nominations of women and members of underrepresented minority groups are especially encouraged.

Financial data The award includes an honorarium of $4,000, a citation, reimbursement of travel expenses to the meeting of the American Association of Physics Teachers (AAPT) at which the award is presented, and the opportunity to present a talk at that meeting. The faculty supervisor receives a citation and travel expenses to the same AAPT meeting. For groups of students, the honorarium is shared among all those involved.

Duration The award is presented annually.

Additional information This program began in 2014 with support from TeachSpin, Inc. It is jointly administered by AAPT and the Advanced Laboratory Physics Association (ALPhA).

Number awarded 1 each year.

Deadline August of each year.

[3]
AAU HIGH SCHOOL SULLIVAN SCHOLARSHIP AWARD

Amateur Athletic Union of the United States
1910 Hotel Plaza Boulevard
P.O. Box 22409
Lake Buena Vista, FL 32830
(407) 934-7200   Toll Free: (800) AAU-4USA
Fax: (407) 934-7242   E-mail: pam@aausports.org
Web: www.aausports.org/Sullivan

Summary To provide financial assistance for college to outstanding high school athletes (females and males judged separately).

Eligibility This program is open to seniors graduating from high schools in the United States and planning to attend a college or university. Applicants must have a record of outstanding participation in sports. Men and women are judged separately. Selection is based on athletic accomplishments, leadership, character, and academic performance.

Financial data Stipends are $10,000 for winners and $2,500 for other finalists.

Duration 1 year.

Additional information This program, which began in 2011, is sponsored by Eastbay.

Number awarded 8 each year: 1 male winner, 1 female winner, 3 male finalists, and 3 female finalists.

Deadline February of each year.

[4]
AAUW CAREER DEVELOPMENT GRANTS

American Association of University Women
Attn: AAUW Educational Foundation
1111 16th Street, N.W.
Washington, DC 20036-4873
(202) 785-7700   Toll Free: (800) 326-AAUW
Fax: (202) 872-1425   TDD: (202) 785-7777
E-mail: aauw@applyists.com
Web: www.aauw.org

Summary To provide financial assistance to women who are seeking career advancement, career change, or reentry into the workforce.

Eligibility This program is open to women who are U.S. citizens or permanent residents, have earned a bachelor's degree, received their most recent degree more than 4 years ago, and are making career changes, seeking to advance in current careers, or reentering the workforce. Applicants must be interested in working toward a master's degree, second bachelor's or associate degree, professional degree (e.g., M.D., J.D.), certification program, or technical school certificate. They must be planning to undertake course work at an accredited 2- or 4-year college or university (or a technical school that is licensed, accredited, or approved by the U.S. Department of Education). Primary consideration is given to women of color and women pursuing their first advanced degree or credentials in nontraditional fields. Support is not provided for prerequisite course work or for Ph.D. course work or dissertations. Selection is based on demonstrated commitment to education and equity for women and girls, reason for seeking higher education or technical training, degree to which study plan is consistent with career objectives, potential for success in chosen field, documentation of opportunities in chosen field, feasibility of study plans and proposed time schedule, validity of proposed budget and budget narrative (including sufficient outside support), and quality of written proposal.

Financial data Grants range from $2,000 to $12,000. Funds may be used for tuition, fees, books, supplies, local transportation, dependent child care, or purchase of a computer required for the study program.

Duration 1 year, beginning in July; nonrenewable.

Additional information The filing fee is $35.

Number awarded Varies each year; recently, 63 of these grants, with a value of $670,000, were awarded.

Deadline December of each year.

[5]
ACCELERATOR APPLICATIONS DIVISION SCHOLARSHIP

American Nuclear Society
Attn: Scholarship Coordinator
555 North Kensington Avenue
La Grange Park, IL 60526-5535
(708) 352-6611   Toll Free: (800) 323-3044
Fax: (708) 352-0499   E-mail: outreach@ans.org
Web: www.ans.org/honors/scholarships/aad

Summary To provide financial assistance to undergraduate students who are interested in preparing for a career dealing with accelerator applications aspects of nuclear science or nuclear engineering.

Eligibility This program is open to students entering their junior year in physics, engineering, or materials science at an accredited institution in the United States. Applicants must submit a description of their long- and short-term professional objectives, including their research interests related to accelerator aspects of nuclear science and engineering. Selection is based on that statement, faculty recommendations, and academic performance. Special consideration is given to members of underrepresented groups (women and minorities), students who can demonstrate financial need, and applicants who have a record of service to the American Nuclear Society (ANS).

Financial data The stipend is $1,000 per year.

Duration 1 year (the junior year); may be renewed for the senior year.

Additional information This program is offered by the Accelerator Applications Division (AAD) of the ANS.

Number awarded 1 each year.

Deadline January of each year.

[6]
ACXIOM DIVERSITY SCHOLARSHIP PROGRAM

Acxiom Corporation
601 East Third Street
P.O. Box 8190
Little Rock, AR 72203-8190
(501) 342-1000   Toll Free: (877) 314-2049
E-mail: Candice.Davis@acxiom.com
Web: www.acxiom.com/about-acxiom/careers

Summary To provide financial assistance and possible work experience to upper-division and graduate students who are members of a diverse population that historically has been underrepresented in the information technology work force.

Eligibility This program is open to juniors, seniors, and graduate students who are working full time on a degree in a field of information technology, including computer science, computer information systems, management information systems, information quality, information systems, engineering, mathematics, statistics, or related areas of study. Women, veterans, minorities, and individuals with disabilities are encouraged to apply. Applicants must have a GPA of 3.0 or higher. Along with their application, they must submit a 500-word essay describing how the scholarship will help them achieve their academic, professional, and personal goals. Selection is based on academic achievement, relationship of field of study to information technology, and relationship of areas of professional interest to the sponsor's business needs.

Financial data The stipend is $5,000 per year.

Duration 1 year; may be renewed 1 additional year, provided the recipient remains enrolled full time, maintains a GPA of 3.0 or higher, and (if offered an internship) continues to meet internship expectations.

Additional information Recipients may be offered an internship (fall, spring, summer, year-round) at 1 of the sponsor's offices in Austin (Texas), Conway (Arkansas), Downers Grove (Illinois), Little Rock (Arkansas), Nashville (Tennessee), New York (New York), or Redwood City (California).

Number awarded Up to 5 each year.

Deadline December of each year.

[7]
ADA I. PRESSMAN SCHOLARSHIP

Society of Women Engineers
Attn: Scholarship Selection Committee
203 North LaSalle Street, Suite 1675
Chicago, IL 60601-1269
(312) 596-5223   Toll Free: (877) SWE-INFO
Fax: (312) 644-8557   E-mail: scholarships@swe.org
Web: societyofwomenengineers.swe.org

Summary To provide financial assistance to women working on an undergraduate or graduate degree in engineering or computer science.

Eligibility This program is open to women who will be sophomores, juniors, seniors, or graduate students at ABET-accredited colleges and universities. Applicants must be U.S. citizens working full time on a degree in computer science or engineering. Selection is based on merit.

Financial data The stipend is $5,000 per year.

Duration 1 year; may be renewed up to 4 additional years.

Additional information This program began in 2004.

Number awarded 9 each year.

Deadline February of each year.

[8] ADMIRAL GRACE MURRAY HOPPER MEMORIAL SCHOLARSHIPS

Society of Women Engineers
Attn: Scholarship Selection Committee
203 North LaSalle Street, Suite 1675
Chicago, IL 60601-1269
(312) 596-5223   Toll Free: (877) SWE-INFO
Fax: (312) 644-8557   E-mail: scholarships@swe.org
Web: societyofwomenengineers.swe.org

Summary To provide financial assistance to women who will be entering college as freshmen and are interested in studying engineering or computer science.

Eligibility This program is open to women who are entering college as full-time freshmen at an ABET-accredited 4-year college or university. Applicants must be planning to major in computer science or computer engineering. Selection is based on merit. Preference is given to students in computer-related engineering.

Financial data The stipend is $1,500.

Duration 1 year.

Additional information This program, established in 1992, is named for the "mother of computerized data automation in the naval service."

Number awarded 3 each year.

Deadline May of each year.

[9] ADULT STUDENTS IN SCHOLASTIC TRANSITION (ASIST) PROGRAM

Executive Women International
Attn: Scholarship Coordinator
3860 South 2300 East
Salt Lake City, UT 84109
(801) 355-2800   Toll Free: (877) 4EWI-NOW
Fax: (801) 355-2852   E-mail: ewi@ewiconnect.com
Web: www.ewiconnect.com/?page_id=3949

Summary To provide financial assistance to adults who are interested in pursuing additional education to improve their life status.

Eligibility This program is open to adult students at transitional points in their lives. Applicants may be persons who are 1) past high school age and entering a college, university, trade school, and/or the workforce for the first time; 2) already enrolled in a college, university, or trade program as nontraditional students; 3) re-training due to changes in the workplace; or 4) otherwise finished with high school but not the traditional college or trade school student. They must utilize reentry programs available through colleges and universities, community agencies, and service groups or career professionals; be 18 years of age or older; have clearly defined career goals and objectives; specify the educational requirements to attain their goals and objectives; and reside within the boundaries of a participating chapter of Executive Women International (EWI). Priority is given to applicants who are responsible for small children; are socially, physically, or economically challenged adults; and can demonstrate financial need. Interested students submit their application to a participating EWI chapter; each chapter selects outstanding applicants and forwards their forms to the corporate level for consideration for these scholarships.

Financial data The stipend at the corporate level ranges from $2,000 to $10,000.

Duration 1 year.

Additional information Currently, 38 EWI chapters participate in this program. For a list of those chapters and the counties they serve, contact EWI.

Number awarded 13 each year: 1 at $10,000, 2 at $5,000, and 10 at $2,000. In addition, 42 chapters awarded scholarships. A total of $250,000 is distributed through this program each year.

Deadline Each participating chapter sets its own application deadline.

[10] ADVANCING ASPIRATIONS GLOBAL SCHOLARSHIPS

Womenetics
Attn: Advancing Aspirations Global Scholarships
99 West Paces Ferry Road, N.W., Suite 200
Atlanta, GA 30305
(404) 816-7224   E-mail: scholarships@womenetics.com
Web: www.womenetics.com/Events/Scholarships

Summary To recognize and reward undergraduates who submit outstanding essays on topics related to the global advancement of women.

Eligibility This competition is open to U.S. citizens and permanent residents who are currently enrolled as undergraduates at accredited colleges and universities. Applicants must submit an essay of up to 2,500 words on assigned topics; recently, those were 1) career growth and flexible workplace initiatives; 2) men in the game: how to make gender diversity an enterprise-wide effort; 3) when employees thrive, businesses thrive; 4) developing key competencies in the next generation of leaders; and 5) P&L responsibility gap among female leaders. They must also submit a "works cited" page to document any research they conducted to write the essay and a 200-word essay on what they plan to do with the prize money if they win.

Financial data For each topic, the winner receives a $5,000 prize and other essayists each receive $2,500 prizes. Funds may be used to finance education, travel, or other opportunities that may lead to further understanding of the global issues raised in the essays.

Duration The competition is held annually.

Additional information Recently, prizes were sponsored by Discover. Winners are also invited to conferences of the sponsor, which covers all expenses of the first-place winners.

Number awarded 5 each year: 1 first-place winner and 4 additional essayists.

Deadline August of each year.

[11] ADVANCING WOMEN IN ACCOUNTING SCHOLARSHIP

Illinois CPA Society
Attn: CPA Endowment Fund of Illinois
550 West Jackson, Suite 900
Chicago, Il 60661-5716
(312) 993-0407   Toll Free: (800) 993-0407 (within IL)
Fax: (312) 993-9954
Web: www.icpas.org/hc-endowment.aspx?id=3906

Summary To provide financial assistance to female residents of Illinois who will be enrolled as seniors or graduate students in an accounting program in the state.

Eligibility This program is open to women in Illinois who plan to enroll as seniors or graduate students in an accounting program at a college or university in the state. Applicants must be planning to complete the educational requirements needed to sit for the C.P.A. examination in Illinois within 3 years. They must have at least a 3.0 GPA and be able to demonstrate financial need or special circumstances. U.S. citizenship or permanent resident status is required. Selection is based on academic achievement and financial need.

Financial data The maximum stipend is $4,000 for payment of tuition and fees. Awards include up to $500 in expenses for books and required classroom materials.

Duration 1 year (fifth year for accounting students planning to become a C.P.A.).

Additional information This program was established by the Women's Executive Committee of the Illinois CPA Society. The scholarship does not cover the cost of C.P.A. examination review courses. Recipients may not receive a full graduate assistantship, fellowship, or scholarship from a college or university, participate in a full-tuition reimbursement cooperative education or internship program, or participate in an employee full-tuition reimbursement program during the scholarship period.

Number awarded Varies each year; recently, 3 were awarded.

Deadline March of each year.

[12]
ADVANCING WOMEN IN STEM SCHOLARSHIPS

Zenefits FTW Insurance Services
303 Second Street
North Tower, Suite 401
San Francisco, CA 94107
Toll Free: (888) 249-3263   E-mail: advisor@zenefits.com
Web: www.zenefits.com/scholarship

Summary To provide financial assistance to women who are working on a college degree in a field of science, technology, engineering, or mathematics (STEM).

Eligibility This program is open to women who have completed at least 1 academic year of full-time study at a college or university. Applicants must be working on an undergraduate degree in a field of STEM. They must have a GPA of 3.0 or higher and be able to demonstrate financial need. Along with their application, they must submit a 500-word essay on who or what inspired them to study their chosen field and what they find most exciting about it. Selection is based on that essay (50%) and financial need (50%).

Financial data The stipend is $6,000.

Duration 1 year.

Number awarded 1 each year.

Deadline December of each year.

[13]
AFRICAN WOMEN'S EDUCATION FUND OF UTAH

Community Foundation of Utah
423 West 800 South, Suite A101
Salt Lake City, UT 84101
(801) 559-3005   Fax: (866) 935-2353
E-mail: scholarships@utahcf.org
Web: www.utahcf.org

Summary To provide financial assistance for higher education in Utah to women refugees or asylees from Africa.

Eligibility This program is open to women refugees or asylees from Africa who wish to enroll in educational or technical training or certification through qualified schools or programs in Utah. The institution must be an accredited public nonprofit 2- or 4-year college or university or a vocational/technical school or training program. Students at academic institutions should have a GPA of 2.0 or higher; students at vocational institutions should be able to demonstrate progress as reported by teachers and administrators. Selection is based on academic progress and achievement, desire and intent to achieve education or training, and financial need.

Financial data A stipend is awarded (amount not specified).

Duration 1 year.

Additional information This program began in 2013.

Number awarded Varies each year.

Deadline April of each year.

[14]
AGNES F. VAGHI SCHOLARSHIP

National Italian American Foundation
Attn: Education Director
1860 19th Street, N.W.
Washington, DC 20009
(202) 387-0600   Fax: (202) 387-0800
E-mail: scholarships@niaf.org
Web: niaf.awardspring.com/Home/ScholarshipDetails/9300

Summary To provide financial assistance to women of Italian ancestry who are majoring in designated fields.

Eligibility This program is open to Italian American women (defined as having at least 1 ancestor who has immigrated from Italy) who are U.S. citizens or permanent residents. Applicants must be members, or have a parent or guardian who is a member, of the National Italian American Foundation (NIAF). They must be undergraduates majoring in Italian studies, English, literature, or journalism and have a GPA of 3.5 or higher. Selection is based on academic merit.

Financial data The stipend is $2,500.

Duration 1 year. Recipients are encouraged to reapply.

Number awarded 1 or more each year.

Deadline February of each year.

[15]
AGNES MORRIS EDUCATION SCHOLARSHIP

Louisiana Federation of Business and Professional
  Women's Clubs, Inc.
c/o Linda Burns
1424 Evangeline Road
Glenmora, LA 71433
(318) 748-7603   E-mail: amesfchair@bpwlouisiana.org
Web: lafbpw.wildapricot.org/page-924449

Summary To provide financial assistance to members of the Louisiana Federation of Business and Professional Women's Clubs (BPW/LA) who are interested in attending college in any state.

Eligibility This program is open to women who are 25 years of age or older and members of the BPW/LA and a BPW local organization in Louisiana. Applicants must be enrolled at or entering an accredited university, college, technical school, or program of course work for licensed or career advancement in any state. Along with their application, they must submit transcripts from their high school and any institution of higher education they have attended, entrance examination scores, 3 letters of recommendation, and a 250-word statement on why they want this scholarship and their plans for using it. Financial need is not considered in the selection process.

Financial data The stipend is $1,000 per year. Funds are issued jointly to the student and the institution.

Duration 1 year; may be renewed, provided the recipient completes at least 6 hours per semester and maintains a GPA of 2.0 or higher.

Additional information This program originated as the Agnes Morris Educational Loan Fund.

Number awarded 1 or more each year.

Deadline March of each year.

[16] AHIMA FOUNDATION DIVERSITY SCHOLARSHIPS

American Health Information Management Association
Attn: AHIMA Foundation
233 North Michigan Avenue, 21st Floor
Chicago, IL 60601-5809
(312) 233-1137   Fax: (312) 233-1537
E-mail: info@ahimafoundation.org
Web: www.ahimafoundation.org

Summary To provide financial assistance to members of the American Health Information Management Association (AHIMA) who are interested in working on an undergraduate or graduate degree in health information management (HIM) or health information technology (HIT) and who will contribute to diversity in the profession.

Eligibility This program is open to AHIMA members who are enrolled at least half time in an accredited program. Applicants must be working on a degree in HIM or HIT at the associate, bachelor's, post-baccalaureate, master's, or doctoral level. They must have a GPA of 3.5 or higher and at least 6 credit hours remaining after the date of the award. To qualify for this support, applicants must demonstrate how they will contribute to diversity in the health information management profession; diversity is defined as differences in race, ethnicity, nationality, gender, sexual orientation, socioeconomic status, age, physical capabilities, or religious beliefs. Along with their application, they must submit essays on assigned topics related to their involvement in the HIM profession. Selection is based on the clarity and completeness of thought in the essays; cumulative GPA; volunteer, work, and/or leadership experience; honors, awards, or recognitions; commitment to the HIM profession; and references.

Financial data Stipends are $1,000 for associate degree students, $1,500 for bachelor's degree or post-baccalaureate certificate students, $2,000 for master's degree students, or $2,500 for doctoral degree students.

Duration 1 year.

Number awarded 1 or more each year.

Deadline September of each year.

[17] AIET MINORITIES AND WOMEN EDUCATIONAL SCHOLARSHIP PROGRAM

Appraisal Institute
Attn: Appraisal Institute Education Trust
200 West Madison Street, Suite 1500
Chicago, IL 60606
(312) 335-4133   Fax: (312) 335-4134
E-mail: educationtrust@appraisalinstitute.org
Web: www.appraisalinstitute.org

Summary To provide financial assistance to women and minority undergraduate students majoring in real estate or allied fields.

Eligibility This program is open to members of groups underrepresented in the real estate appraisal profession. Those groups include women, American Indians, Alaska Natives, Asians and Pacific Islanders, Blacks or African Americans, and Hispanics. Applicants must be full- or part-time students enrolled in real estate courses within a degree-granting college, university, or junior college. They must have a GPA of 2.5 or higher and be able to demonstrate financial need. U.S. citizenship is required.

Financial data The stipend is $1,000. Funds are paid directly to the recipient's institution to be used for tuition and fees.

Duration 1 year.

Number awarded At least 1 each year.

Deadline April of each year.

[18] AIR PRODUCTS WOMEN OF GASES AND WELDING SCHOLARSHIP

American Welding Society
Attn: AWS Foundation, Inc.
8669 N.W. 36th Street, Suite 130
Doral, FL 33166-6672
(305) 443-9353   Toll Free: (800) 443-9353, ext. 250
Fax: (305) 443-7559   E-mail: nprado-pulido@aws.org
Web: app.aws.org

Summary To provide financial assistance to women interested in attending college to study a field related to welding.

Eligibility This program is open to women who are enrolled or planning to enroll full time in a 2- or 4-year welding-related educational or engineering program. Applicants must have a GPA of 2.5 or higher. Financial need is not required, but priority is given to applicants who can demonstrate a financial need. U.S. citizenship is required.

Financial data The stipend is $2,500; funds are paid directly to the educational institution.

Duration 1 year; nonrenewable.

Additional information This program, which began in 2013, is sponsored by Air Products and Chemicals.

Number awarded 1 each year.

Deadline February of each year.

[19]
AIRBUS LEADERSHIP GRANT

Women in Aviation International
Attn: Scholarships
Morningstar Airport
3647 State Route 503 South
West Alexandria, OH 45381-9354
(937) 839-4647   Fax: (937) 839-4645
E-mail: scholarships@wai.org
Web: www.wai.org

Summary To provide financial assistance for college to members of Women in Aviation International (WAI).

Eligibility This program is open to WAI members who are college sophomores or higher working on a degree in an aviation-related field. Applicants must have a GPA of 3.0 or higher and be able to demonstrate leadership potential. Along with their application, they must submit 1) a 500-word essay and professional resume that include their aviation history and goals, what they have done for themselves to achieve their goals, where they see themselves in 5 and 10 years, involvement in aviation activities, how the scholarship will help them achieve their objectives, and their present financial need; and 2) a 500-word essay that addresses their career aspirations with clear, concise examples of how they have exhibited leadership in their academic, work, and personal life.

Financial data The stipend is $5,000.

Duration 1 year.

Additional information WAI is a nonprofit professional organization dedicated to encouraging women to consider an aviation career and to providing educational outreach activities and networking resources to women active in the industry.

Number awarded 1 each year.

Deadline November of each year.

[20]
AIRBUS MANUFACTURING GRANT

Women in Aviation International
Attn: Scholarships
Morningstar Airport
3647 State Route 503 South
West Alexandria, OH 45381-9354
(937) 839-4647   Fax: (937) 839-4645
E-mail: scholarships@wai.org
Web: www.wai.org

Summary To provide financial assistance to members of Women in Aviation International (WAI) who are working on a license or degree in a field related to aviation manufacturing.

Eligibility This program is open to WAI members who are enrolled at a college, university, or trade/technical school in a program related to aviation manufacturing. Applicants must have a GPA of 3.0 or higher in their field of study Along with their application, they must submit 1) a 500-word essay and professional resume that include their aviation history and goals, what they have done for themselves to achieve their goals, where they see themselves in 5 and 10 years, involvement in aviation activities, how the scholarship will help them achieve their objectives, and their present financial need; and 2) a 500-word essay that addresses their career aspirations with clear, concise examples of how they are exhibiting or will

exhibit behaviors that promote a safe, productive, and engaged manufacturing workplace.

Financial data The stipend is $5,000.

Duration 1 year.

Additional information WAI is a nonprofit professional organization dedicated to encouraging women to consider an aviation career and to providing educational outreach activities and networking resources to women active in the industry.

Number awarded 1 each year.

Deadline November of each year.

[21]
ALABAMA GOLF ASSOCIATION WOMEN'S SCHOLARSHIP FUND

Alabama Golf Association
Attn: Adam Powell
1025 Montgomery Highway, Suite 210
Birmingham, AL 35216
(205) 979-1234   Toll Free: (800) 783-4446
Fax: (205) 803-6518   E-mail: adam@bamagolf.com
Web: www.alabamagolf.org

Summary To provide financial assistance to female high school seniors in Alabama who can demonstrate an interest in golf and plan to attend college in the state.

Eligibility This program is open to women who are graduating from high schools in Alabama and planning to enroll full time at a 4-year college or university in the state. Applicants must be able to demonstrate an interest in the game of golf and financial need. They must have an ACT score of 22 or higher. Along with their application, they must submit a 200-word statement on why a college education is important to them, their goals, and how they hope to achieve those goals. Selection is based on academic excellence, citizenship, sportsmanship, community involvement, and financial need.

Financial data The stipend is $4,000 per year.

Duration 1 year; may be renewed up to 3 additional years if the recipient maintains a GPA of 2.4 or higher during her freshman year and 2.8 or higher during subsequent years.

Additional information This program, established in 1993, includes the Stone Hodo Scholarship and the Ann Samford Upchurch Scholarship.

Number awarded 1 each year.

Deadline March of each year.

[22]
ALBERTA E. CROWE STAR OF TOMORROW AWARD

United States Bowling Congress
Attn: Youth Department
621 Six Flags Drive
Arlington, TX 76011
(817) 385-8426   Toll Free: (800) 514-BOWL, ext. 8426
Fax: (817) 385-8412   E-mail: tournaments@ibcyouth.com
Web: www.bowl.com

Summary To provide financial assistance for college to outstanding women bowlers.

Eligibility This program is open to women amateur bowlers who are current members in good standing of the United States Bowling Congress (USBC) Youth organization and competitors in its sanctioned events. Applicants must be high school seniors or college students and have a GPA of 3.0 or higher. They may not have competed in a professional bowling tournament. Along with their application, they must submit a 500-word essay on how the lessons they have learned through academics, community involvement, and bowling have influenced their life and their goals for the future. Selection is based on bowling performances on local, regional, state, and national levels; academic achievement; and extracurricular involvement.

Financial data The stipend is $1,500 per year.

Duration 1 year; may be renewed for 3 additional years.

Number awarded 1 each year.

Deadline November of each year.

[23]
ALCOA CHUCK MCLANE SCHOLARSHIP

Girl Scouts of the United States of America
420 Fifth Avenue
New York, NY 10018-2798
Toll Free: (800) GSUSA-4-U
Web: www.girlscouts.org

Summary To provide financial assistance to Girl Scouts who complete a Gold Award in fields of science, technology, engineering, and mathematics (STEM) and plan to study those fields in college.

Eligibility This program is open to members of Girl Scouts who are in their senior year of high school and had a GPA of 3.0 or higher through their sophomore year. Applicants must have earned their Gold Award with a project in STEM. They must be planning to enroll as a freshman at a 4-year college or university and major in a field of STEM. Along with their application, they must submit 1) a 200-word essay describing their Take Action project and used STEM for that project; 2) a 300-word essay describing how that project was innovative and its impact on the community and sustainability; and 3)) a 300-word essay on how they intend to use STEM for their studies and/or career.

Financial data The stipend is $5,000 per year.

Duration 2 years: the freshman and junior year of college. Recipients must earn a GPA of 3.0 or higher and continue to major in a field of STEM in order to receive the second year of funding.

Additional information This program was established by Alcoa Foundation in 2013. It is currently sponsored by Arconic Foundation.

Number awarded 2 each year.

Deadline February of each year.

[24]
ALICE T. SCHAFER MATHEMATICS PRIZE

Association for Women in Mathematics
11240 Waples Mill Road, Suite 200
Fairfax, VA 22030
(703) 934-0163   Fax: (703) 359-7562
E-mail: awm@awm-math.org
Web: sites.google.com

Summary To recognize and reward undergraduate women who have demonstrated excellence in mathematics.

Eligibility Women may not apply for this award; they must be nominated by a member of the mathematical community. The nominee may be at any level in her undergraduate

career. She must be a U.S. citizen or attending school in the United States. Selection is based on the quality of the student's performance in advanced mathematics courses and special programs, demonstration of real interest in mathematics, ability for independent work in mathematics, and performance in mathematical competitions at the local or national level.

Financial data The prize is $1,000.

Duration The prize is presented annually.

Additional information This prize was first presented in 1990.

Number awarded 1 each year.

Deadline Nominations must be submitted by September of each year.

[25]
ALPHA KAPPA ALPHA ENDOWMENT AWARDS

Alpha Kappa Alpha Sorority, Inc.
Attn: Educational Advancement Foundation
5656 South Stony Island Avenue
Chicago, IL 60637
(773) 947-0026   Toll Free: (800) 653-6528
Fax: (773) 947-0277   E-mail: akaeaf@akaeaf.net
Web: www.akaeaf.org/fellowships_endowments.htm

Summary To provide financial assistance to undergraduate and graduate students (especially African American women) who meet designated requirements.

Eligibility This program is open to undergraduate and graduate students who are enrolled full time as sophomores or higher in an accredited degree-granting institution and are planning to continue their program of education. Applicants may apply for scholarships that include specific requirements established by the donor of the endowment that supports it. Along with their application, they must submit 1) a list of honors, awards, and scholarships received; 2) a list of organizations in which they have memberships, especially minority organizations; and 3) a statement of their personal and career goals, including how this scholarship will enhance their ability to attain those goals. The sponsor is a traditionally African American women's sorority.

Financial data Award amounts are determined by the availability of funds from the particular endowment. Recently, stipends averaged more than $1,700 per year.

Duration 1 year or longer.

Additional information Each endowment establishes its own requirements. Examples of requirements include residence of the applicant, major field of study, minimum GPA, attendance at an Historically Black College or University (HBCU) or member institution of the United Negro College Fund (UNCF), or other personal feature. For further information on all endowments, contact the sponsor.

Number awarded Varies each year; recently, 49 were awarded.

Deadline April of each year.

[26]
ALPHA KAPPA ALPHA UNDERGRADUATE SCHOLARSHIPS

Alpha Kappa Alpha Sorority, Inc.
Attn: Educational Advancement Foundation
5656 South Stony Island Avenue
Chicago, IL 60637
(773) 947-0026   Toll Free: (800) 653-6528
Fax: (773) 947-0277   E-mail: akaeaf@akaeaf.net
Web: www.akaeaf.org/undergraduate_scholarships.htm

Summary To provide financial assistance to students (especially African American women) who are working on an undergraduate degree in any field.

Eligibility This program is open to undergraduate students who are enrolled full time as sophomores or higher in an accredited degree-granting institution and are planning to continue their program of education. Applicants may apply either for a scholarship based on merit (requires a GPA of 3.0 or higher) or on financial need (requires a GPA of 2.5 or higher). Along with their application, they must submit 1) a list of honors, awards, and scholarships received; 2) a list of organizations in which they have memberships, especially minority organizations; and 3) a statement of their personal and career goals, including how this scholarship will enhance their ability to attain those goals. The sponsor is a traditionally African American women's sorority.

Financial data Stipends range up to $2,500.

Duration 1 year; nonrenewable.

Number awarded Varies each year; recently, 133 were awarded.

Deadline April of each year.

[27]
ALPHA PHI/BETTY MULLINS JONES SCHOLARSHIP

National Panhellenic Conference
Attn: NPC Foundation
3901 West 86th Street, Suite 398
Indianapolis, IN 46268
(317) 872-3185   Fax: (317) 872-3192
E-mail: npccentral@npcwomen.org
Web: www.npcwomen.org/foundation/scholarships.aspx

Summary To provide financial assistance to undergraduate women who are members of Greek-letter societies.

Eligibility This program is open to Greek-affiliated women at colleges and universities in the United States. Applicants must be able to demonstrate that they have worked to further their fraternal community's reputation on their campus. Along with their application, they must submit a 500-word essay on why they should receive a scholarship. Selection is based on financial need, academic standing, and service to campus, chapter, and community.

Financial data The stipend is $1,000.

Duration 1 year.

Number awarded 1 each year.

Deadline April of each year.

[28]
ALPHA STATE ASPIRING EDUCATOR AWARDS

Delta Kappa Gamma Society International-Alpha State Organization
Attn: Alpha State Texas Educational Foundation
6220 Campbell Road, Suite 204
P.O. Box 797787
Dallas, TX 75379-7787
(972) 930-9945   Toll Free: (800) 305-3525
Fax: (972) 447-0471   E-mail: astef3256x@sbcglobal.net
Web: www.astef.org/forms.html

Summary To provide financial assistance to female residents of Texas who are working on an undergraduate degree or certificate in education at a school in any state.

Eligibility This program is open to female residents of Texas who are attending a college or university in any state and working on an undergraduate degree in education or taking courses for certification. Applicants may not be members of Delta Kappa Gamma (an honorary society for women educators), but they must be recommended by a member of its Alpha State Organization. Along with their application, they must submit a statement of their specific goals, how they plan to achieve their goals, why they want to pursue those goals, and where they aspire to teach after completing certification. Financial need is not considered in the selection process.

Financial data Stipends are $1,000 for students enrolled in at least 6 hours or $500 for students enrolled in at least 3 hours.

Duration 1 year.

Number awarded Varies each year; recently, 5 were awarded.

Deadline February of each year.

[29]
AMAC MEMBER AWARD

Airport Minority Advisory Council
Attn: AMAC Foundation
2001 Jefferson Davis Highway, Suite 500
Arlington, VA 22202
(703) 414-2622   Fax: (703) 414-2686
E-mail: terrifrierson@palladiumholdingsco.com
Web: amac-org.com/amac-foundation/scholarships

Summary To provide financial assistance to minority and female high school seniors and undergraduates who are preparing for a career in the aviation industry and are connected to Airport Minority Advisory Council (AMAC).

Eligibility This program is open to minority and female high school seniors and current undergraduates who have a GPA of 2.5 or higher and a record of involvement in community and extracurricular activities. Applicants must be interested in working on a bachelor's degree in accounting, architecture, aviation, business administration, engineering, or finance as preparation for a career in the aviation or airport industry. They must be AMAC members, family of members, or mentees of member. Along with their application, they must submit a 750-word essay on how they have overcome barriers in life to achieve their academic and/or career goals; their dedication to succeed in the aviation industry and how AMAC can help them achieve their goal; and the most important issues that the aviation industry is facing today and how they see themselves changing those. Financial need is not considered in the selection process. U.S. citizenship is required.

Financial data The stipend is $2,000 per year.

Duration 1 year; recipients may reapply.

Number awarded 4 each year.

Deadline May of each year.

[30]
AMELIA EARHART MEMORIAL ACADEMIC SCHOLARSHIPS

Ninety-Nines, Inc.
4300 Amelia Earhart Road, Suite A
Oklahoma City, OK 73159
(405) 685-7969   Toll Free: (800) 994-1929
Fax: (405) 685-7985   E-mail: AEChair@ninety-nines.org
Web: www.ninety-nines.org/scholarships.htm

Summary To provide funding to members of the Ninety-Nines (an organization of women pilots) who are enrolled in academic study related to aviation or aerospace.

Eligibility This program is open to women from any country who have been members of the organization for at least 1 year. Applicants must be currently enrolled at an accredited college or university and working on an associate, bachelor's, master's, or doctoral degree in such fields as aerospace engineering, aviation technology, aviation business management, air traffic management, or professional pilot. They must have a GPA of 3.0 or higher and be able to demonstrate financial need. Along with their application, they must submit a 1-page essay about their activities in aviation, their participatin in the Ninety-Nines, their goals in aviation or aerospace, how they have financed their training and education so far, their financial need to complete their training, and how awarding them this scholarship will benefit the Ninety-Nines and the aviation community.

Financial data The stipend is $5,000 per year.

Duration 1 year; may be renewed.

Additional information This program began in 1941.

Number awarded Varies each year; recently, 3 were awarded: 2 to undergraduates and 1 to a graduate student.

Deadline November of each year.

[31]
AMELIA EARHART MEMORIAL SCHOLARSHIPS

Ninety-Nines, Inc.
4300 Amelia Earhart Road, Suite A
Oklahoma City, OK 73159
(405) 685-7969   Toll Free: (800) 994-1929
Fax: (405) 685-7985   E-mail: AEChair@ninety-nines.org
Web: www.ninety-nines.org/scholarships.htm

Summary To provide funding to members of the Ninety-Nines (an organization of women pilots) who are interested in advanced flight training or other technical study related to aviation.

Eligibility This program is open to women from any country who have been members of the organization for at least 1 year. They must be interested in 1 of the following 4 types of scholarships: 1) flight training, to complete an additional pilot certificate or rating or pilot training course; 2) jet type rating, to complete type rating certification in any jet; 3) technical training, to complete an aviation or aerospace technical training or certification course. Applicants for flight training schol-

arships must be a current pilot with the appropriate medical certification and approaching the flight time requirement for the rating or certificate. Applicants for jet type rating scholarships must be a current airline transport pilot with a first-class medical certificate and at least 100 hours of multi-engine flight time or combined multi-engine and turbine time. Applicants for technical training scholarships must be enrolled in a course (e.g., airframe and/or powerplant (A&P) mechanic certificate, dispatcher certificate, air traffic control training program, government or manufacturer's safety training) that is not part of a college degree program. All applicants must submit a 1-page essay about their activities in aviation, their participatin in the Ninety-Nines, their goals in aviation or aerospace, how they have financed their training and education so far, their financial need to complete their training, and how awarding them this scholarship will benefit the Ninety-Nines and the aviation community.

Financial data These scholarships provide payment of all costs to complete the appropriate rating or certificate.

Duration Support is provided until completion of the rating or certificate.

Additional information This program began in 1941.

Number awarded Varies each year; recently, 22 were awarded.

Deadline November of each year.

[32]
AMELIA KEMP MEMORIAL SCHOLARSHIP

Women of the Evangelical Lutheran Church in America
Attn: Scholarships
8765 West Higgins Road
Chicago, IL 60631-4101
(773) 380-2741   Toll Free: (800) 638-3522, ext. 2741
Fax: (773) 380-2419   E-mail: valora.starr@elca.org
Web: www.womenoftheelca.org

Summary To provide financial assistance to lay women of color who are members of Evangelical Lutheran Church of America (ELCA) congregations and who wish to study on the undergraduate, graduate, professional, or vocational school level.

Eligibility This program is open to ELCA lay women of color who are at least 21 years of age and have experienced an interruption of at least 2 years in their education since high school. Applicants must have been admitted to an educational institution to prepare for a career in other than ordained ministry. U.S. citizenship is required.

Financial data The maximum stipend is $1,000 per year.

Duration 1 year; recipients may reapply for 1 additional year.

Number awarded 1 or more each year.

Deadline February of each year.

[33]
AMERICAN AIRLINES AIRCRAFT MAINTENANCE TECHNICIAN SCHOLARSHIP

Women in Aviation International
Attn: Scholarships
Morningstar Airport
3647 State Route 503 South
West Alexandria, OH 45381-9354
(937) 839-4647   Fax: (937) 839-4645
E-mail: scholarships@wai.org
Web: www.wai.org

Summary To provide financial assistance to members of Women in Aviation International (WAI) who are interested in earning a degree or certificate in a field related to aviation maintenance.

Eligibility This program is open to WAI members who are interested in preparing for a career in aviation maintenance, engineering, or technical management. Applicants must be enrolled or planning to enroll in an aviation maintenance technician program or a degree program in aviation maintenance technology. They must have a GPA of 3.0 or higher and be U.S. citizens or permanent residents. Along with their application, they must submit a 500-word essay and professional resume that include their aviation history and goals, what they have done for themselves to achieve their goals, where they see themselves in 5 and 10 years, involvement in aviation activities, how the scholarship will help them achieve their objectives, and their present financial need. Selection is based on academic standing, personal accomplishments, teamwork, leadership skills, and community service involvement.

Financial data The stipend is $5,000. Recipients are also reimbursed for up to $2,000 in travel, conference fee, and hotel expenses to attend the WAI annual conference.

Duration Funds must be used within 1 year.

Additional information WAI is a nonprofit professional organization dedicated to encouraging women to consider an aviation career and to providing educational outreach activities and networking resources to women active in the industry. This program was established in 2012 by American Airlines.

Number awarded 1 each year.

Deadline November of each year.

[34]
AMERICAN AIRLINES ENGINEERING SCHOLARSHIP

Women in Aviation International
Attn: Scholarships
Morningstar Airport
3647 State Route 503 South
West Alexandria, OH 45381-9354
(937) 839-4647   Fax: (937) 839-4645
E-mail: scholarships@wai.org
Web: www.wai.org

Summary To provide financial assistance to members of Women in Aviation International (WAI) who are studying aeronautical, electrical, or mechanical engineering in college.

Eligibility This program is open to WAI members who are currently enrolled in an accredited U.S. engineering program and have "a passion to work in the airline/aviation industry."

Applicants must be working on a degree in aeronautical, electrical, or mechanical engineering. They must be U.S. citizens or permanent residents and have a GPA of 3.0 or higher. Along with their application, they must submit a 500-word essay and professional resume that include their aviation history and goals, what they have done for themselves to achieve their goals, where they see themselves in 5 and 10 years, involvement in aviation activities, how the scholarship will help them achieve their objectives, and their present financial need. Selection is based on academic standing, personal accomplishments, teamwork, leadership skills, community service involvement, and future career aspirations.

Financial data The stipend is $5,000. Recipients are also reimbursed for up to $2,000 in travel, conference fee, and hotel expenses to attend the WAI annual conference.

Duration 1 year.

Additional information WAI is a nonprofit professional organization dedicated to encouraging women to consider an aviation career and to providing educational outreach activities and networking resources to women active in the industry. This program is sponsored by American Airlines.

Number awarded 1 each year.

Deadline November of each year.

[35]
AMERICAN AIRLINES VETERAN'S INITIATIVE SCHOLARSHIP

Women in Aviation International
Attn: Scholarships
Morningstar Airport
3647 State Route 503 South
West Alexandria, OH 45381-9354
(937) 839-4647   Fax: (937) 839-4645
E-mail: scholarships@wai.org
Web: www.wai.org

Summary To provide financial assistance to members of Women in Aviation International (WAI) who are also veterans and interested in earning a degree or certificate in a field related to aviation maintenance.

Eligibility This program is open to WAI members who served honorably in the U.S. armed services and are interested in aviation or aeronautical education or training. Applicants must be enrolled or planning to enroll in an accredited flight school, institution, or college. Along with their application, they must submit a 500-word essay and professional resume that include their aviation history and goals, what they have done for themselves to achieve their goals, where they see themselves in 5 and 10 years, involvement in aviation activities, how the scholarship will help them achieve their objectives, and their present financial need. Selection is based on achievements, teamwork, leadership skills, motivation, and community service involvement.

Financial data The stipend is $5,000.

Duration Funds must be used within 1 year.

Additional information WAI is a nonprofit professional organization dedicated to encouraging women to consider an aviation career and to providing educational outreach activities and networking resources to women active in the industry. This program was established in 2012 by American Airlines.

Number awarded 1 each year.

Deadline November of each year.

[36]
AMERICAN ASSOCIATION OF JAPANESE UNIVERSITY WOMEN SCHOLARSHIP PROGRAM

American Association of Japanese University Women
Attn: Scholarship Committee
3543 West Boulevard
Los Angeles, CA 90016
E-mail: aajuwcholar@gmail.com
Web: www.aajuw.org/new-page-3

Summary To provide financial assistance to female students currently enrolled in upper-division or graduate classes in California.

Eligibility This program is open to women enrolled at accredited colleges or universities in California as juniors, seniors, or graduate students. Applicants must be involved in U.S.-Japan relations, cultural exchanges, and leadership development in the areas of their designated field of study. Along with their application, they must submit a current resume, an official transcript of the past 2 years of college work, 2 letters of recommendation, and an essay (up to 2 pages in English or 1,200 characters in Japanese) on what they hope to accomplish in their field of study and how that will contribute to better U.S.-Japan relations.

Financial data The stipend is $2,000.

Duration 1 year.

Additional information The association was founded in 1970 to promote the education of women as well as to contribute to U.S.-Japan relations, cultural exchanges, and leadership development.

Number awarded 1 to 3 each year. Since this program was established, it has awarded nearly $100,000 worth of scholarships to 110 women.

Deadline September of each year.

[37]
AMERICAN BAPTIST CHURCHES OF WISCONSIN ADULT WOMEN IN SEMINARY EDUCATION SCHOLARSHIPS

American Baptist Churches of Wisconsin
Attn: American Baptist Women of Wisconsin
15330 Watertown Plank Road
Elm Grove, WI 53122-2340
(262) 782-3140   Toll Free: (800) 311-3140
Fax: (262) 782-7573   E-mail: email@abcofwi.org
Web: www.abcofwi.org/abwinfo.htm

Summary To provide financial assistance for seminary education to adult women in Wisconsin who are members of the American Baptist Church.

Eligibility This program is open to adult women who are residents of Wisconsin and have been active members of an American Baptist Church for at least 3 years. Applicants must be attending a college or seminary affiliated with the American Baptist Church and preparing for a career in ministry. They must be able to demonstrate financial need.

Financial data The stipend is awarded (amount not specified).

Duration 1 year.

Number awarded 1 or more each year.

Deadline February of each year.

[38]
AMERICAN BAPTIST CHURCHES OF WISCONSIN CONTINUING EDUCATION FOR ADULT WOMEN SCHOLARSHIPS

American Baptist Churches of Wisconsin
Attn: American Baptist Women of Wisconsin
15330 Watertown Plank Road
Elm Grove, WI 53122-2340
(262) 782-3140   Toll Free: (800) 311-3140
Fax: (262) 782-7573   E-mail: email@abcofwi.org
Web: www.abcofwi.org/abwinfo.htm

Summary To provide financial assistance for seminary education to adult women in Wisconsin who are members of the American Baptist Church.

Eligibility This program is open to adult women who are residents of Wisconsin and have been active members of an American Baptist Church for at least 3 years. Applicants must be attending a college, university, or other institution of higher education in any state. Their school does not need to be affiliated with the American Baptist Church and applicants may be majoring in any field. They must be able to demonstrate financial need.

Financial data The stipend is awarded (amount not specified).

Duration 1 year; may be renewed 1 or 3 additional years.

Number awarded 1 or more each year.

Deadline February of each year.

[39]
AMERICAN BAPTIST WOMEN'S MINISTRIES OF NEW YORK STATE SCHOLARSHIPS

American Baptist Women's Ministries of New York State
c/o Jackie Lottermoser, Scholarship Committee
9 West Fifth Street
Oneida, NY 13421
(315) 363-1224   E-mail: choralmom@verizon.net
Web: www.abwm-nys.org/abwm-of-nys-scholarship

Summary To provide financial assistance to women who are members of American Baptist Churches in New York and interested in attending college in any state.

Eligibility This program is open to women who are residents of New York and active members of an American Baptist Church. Applicants must be enrolled or planning to enroll full time at a college or university in any state. While in college, they must maintain Christian fellowship, preferably with the American Baptist Church (although any Protestant church or campus ministry is acceptable). Along with their application, they must submit a 1-page essay on an event that occurred in their life during the past year and how it has impacted their faith. Women may be of any age; graduate students are considered on an individual basis. Financial need is considered in the selection process.

Financial data A stipend is awarded (amount not specified).

Duration 1 year.

Number awarded Varies each year.

Deadline May of each year.

[40]
AMERICAN BAPTIST WOMEN'S MINISTRIES OF WISCONSIN CONTINUING EDUCATION FOR ADULT WOMEN SCHOLARSHIP

American Baptist Women's Ministries of Wisconsin
c/o Rev. Jackie Colbert, Scholarship Committee Chair
3101 Ashford Lane
Madison, WI 53713
Web: www.abcofwi.org/abwinfo.htm

Summary   To provide financial assistance to adult female members of American Baptist Churches in Wisconsin who are interested in attending college in any state.

Eligibility   This program is open to adult women who are residents of Wisconsin and attending or planning to attend college in any state. Applicants must have been an active member of an American Baptist Church in Wisconsin for the preceding 3 years. The college does not need to be affiliated with the American Baptist Churches USA. Financial need is considered in the selection process. Preference is given to women working on a degree in nursing.

Financial data   A stipend is awarded (amount not specified).

Duration   2 or 4 years.

Number awarded   1 or more each year.

Deadline   March of each year.

[41]
AMERICAN BUSINESS WOMEN'S ASSOCIATION PRESIDENT'S SCHOLARSHIP

American Business Women's Association
Attn: Stephen Bufton Memorial Educational Fund
9820 Metcalf Avenue, Suite 110
Overland Park, KS 66212
Toll Free: (800) 228-0007
Web: www.sbmef.org

Summary   To provide financial assistance to upper-division women who are working on a degree in a specified field (the field changes each year).

Eligibility   This program is open to women who are entering their junior or senior year of college and have a cumulative GPA of 3.0 or higher. Applicants are not required to be members of the American Business Women's Association. Along with their application, they must submit a 250-word biographical sketch that includes information about their background, activities, honors, work experience, and long-term educational and professional goals. Financial need is not considered in the selection process. Each year, the trustees designate an academic discipline for which the scholarship will be presented that year. U.S. citizenship is required.

Financial data   The stipend is $10,000. Funds are paid directly to the recipient's institution to be used only for tuition, books, and fees.

Duration   1 year.

Additional information   This program was created in 1969 as part of ABWA's Stephen Bufton Memorial Education Fund.

Number awarded   1 each year.

Deadline   May of each year.

[42]
AMERICAN LEGION AUXILIARY EMERGENCY FUND

American Legion Auxiliary
Attn: AEF Program Case Manager
8945 North Meridian Street
Indianapolis, IN 46260
(317) 569-4544   Fax: (317) 569-4502
E-mail: aef@alaforveterans.org
Web: www.alaforveterans.org

Summary   To provide funding to members of the American Legion Auxiliary who are facing temporary emergency needs.

Eligibility   This program is open to members of the American Legion Auxiliary who have maintained their membership for the immediate past 2 consecutive years and have paid their dues for the current year. Applicants must need emergency assistance for the following purposes: 1) food, shelter, and utilities during a time of financial crisis; 2) food and shelter because of weather-related emergencies and natural disasters; or 3) educational training for eligible members who lack the necessary skills for employment or to upgrade competitive workforce skills. They must have exhausted all other sources of financial assistance, including funds and/or services available through the local Post and/or Unit, appropriate community welfare agencies, or state and federal financial aid for education. Grants are not available to settle already existing or accumulated debts, handle catastrophic illness, resettle disaster victims, or other similar problems.

Financial data   The maximum grant is $2,400. Payments may be made directly to the member or to the mortgage company or utility. Educational grants may be paid directly to the educational institution.

Duration   Grants are expended over no more than 3 months.

Additional information   This program began in 1969. In 1981, it was expanded to include the Displaced Homemaker Fund (although that title is no longer used).

Number awarded   Varies each year.

Deadline   Applications may be submitted at any time.

[43]
AMERICAN METEOROLOGICAL SOCIETY NAMED SCHOLARSHIPS

American Meteorological Society
Attn: Development and Student Program Manager
45 Beacon Street
Boston, MA 02108-3693
(617) 227-2426, ext. 3907   Fax: (617) 742-8718
E-mail: dFernandez@ametsoc.org
Web: www2.ametsoc.org

Summary   To provide financial assistance to undergraduates majoring in meteorology or an aspect of atmospheric sciences.

Eligibility   This program is open to full-time students entering their final year of undergraduate study and majoring in meteorology or an aspect of the atmospheric or related oceanic and hydrologic sciences. Applicants must intend to make atmospheric or related sciences their career. They must be U.S. citizens or permanent residents enrolled at a U.S. institution and have a cumulative GPA of 3.25 or higher. Along with their application, they must submit 200-word essays on

1) their most important attributes and achievements that qualify them for this scholarship; and 2) their career goals in the atmospheric or related sciences. Financial need is considered in the selection process. The sponsor specifically encourages applications from women, minorities, and students with disabilities who are traditionally underrepresented in the atmospheric and related sciences.

Financial data Stipend amounts vary each year.

Duration 1 year.

Additional information All scholarships awarded through this program are named after individuals who have assisted the sponsor in various ways.

Number awarded Varies each year; recently, 22 were awarded.

Deadline February of each year.

[44]
AMERICAN TRANSMISSION COMPANY SCHOLARSHIPS

Society of Women Engineers
Attn: Scholarship Selection Committee
203 North LaSalle Street, Suite 1675
Chicago, IL 60601-1269
(312) 596-5223   Toll Free: (877) SWE-INFO
Fax: (312) 644-8557   E-mail: scholarships@swe.org
Web: societyofwomenengineers.swe.org

Summary To provide financial assistance to women from designated states working on an undergraduate degree in civil or electrical engineering.

Eligibility This program is open to women who are entering their sophomore, junior, or senior year at a 4-year ABET-accredited college or university. Applicants must be working full time on a degree in computer science or civil or electrical engineering and have a GPA of 3.0 or higher. They must be residents of and attending college in Illinois, Indiana, Iowa, Michigan, Minnesota, or Wisconsin. Selection is based on merit.

Financial data The stipend is $1,500.

Duration 1 year.

Additional information This program is sponsored by American Transmission Company.

Number awarded 2 each year.

Deadline February of each year.

[45]
AMERICA'S NATIONAL TEENAGER SCHOLARSHIP PROGRAM

America's National Teenager Scholarship Organization
5153 Fredericksburg Way East
Brentwood, TN 37027
(615) 405-5107   Toll Free: (866) NAT-TEEN
Fax: (888) 370-2075   E-mail: info@nationalteen.com
Web: www.nationalteen.com/pageants

Summary To recognize (locally and nationally) the scholastic and leadership achievements of America's teenage girls and to provide cash, tuition scholarships, and awards to the participants.

Eligibility Girls who are 13 to 15 years of age are eligible to enter the Miss Junior National Teenager competition and girls who are 16 to 18 may enter the Miss National Teenager competition. Entrants must have no children and never have been married. Selection is based on academic excellence (15%), school and community involvement (15%), social and conversational skills in an interview (30%), poise and personality in an evening gown (15%), personal expression (15%), and response to an on-stage question (10%). There is no swimsuit or talen competition.

Financial data This program awards approximately $100,000 in scholarships at state and national levels each year.

Duration The contest is held annually.

Additional information The contest began in 1971, to recognize the leadership achievements of America's teenagers and to provide travel, entertainment, and scholarships for their college education. The application fee is $25.

Number awarded Varies each year.

Deadline Deadline dates vary. Check with the sponsors of your local and state pageant.

[46]
AMS FRESHMAN UNDERGRADUATE SCHOLARSHIPS

American Meteorological Society
Attn: Development and Student Program Manager
45 Beacon Street
Boston, MA 02108-3693
(617) 227-2426, ext. 3907   Fax: (617) 742-8718
E-mail: dFernandez@ametsoc.org
Web: www2.ametsoc.org

Summary To provide financial assistance to high school seniors planning to attend college to prepare for a career in the atmospheric or related oceanic or hydrologic sciences.

Eligibility This program is open to high school seniors entering their freshman year of college to work on a bachelor's degree in the atmospheric or related oceanic or hydrologic sciences. Applicants must be U.S. citizens or permanent residents planning to enroll full time. Along with their application, they must submit a 500-word essay on how they believe their college education, and what they learn in the atmospheric and related sciences, will help them to serve society during their professional career. Selection is based on performance in high school, including academic records, recommendations, scores from a national examination, and the essay. Financial need is not considered. The sponsor specifically encourages applications from women, minorities, and students with disabilities who are traditionally underrepresented in the atmospheric and related oceanic sciences.

Financial data The stipend is $2,500 per academic year.

Duration 1 year; may be renewed for the second year of college study.

Number awarded Varies each year; recently, 13 were awarded.

Deadline February of each year.

[47]
AMVETS NATIONAL LADIES AUXILIARY SCHOLARSHIPS

AMVETS National Ladies Auxiliary
Attn: Scholarship Officer
4647 Forbes Boulevard
Lanham, MD 20706-4380
(301) 459-6255   Fax: (301) 459-5403
E-mail: auxhdqs@amvets.org
Web: www.amvetsaux.org/scholarships.html

Summary   To provide financial assistance to members and certain dependents of members of AMVETS National Ladies Auxiliary who are already enrolled in college.

Eligibility   Applicants must belong to AMVETS Auxiliary or be the child or grandchild of a member. They must be in at least the second year of undergraduate study at an accredited college or university. Applications must include 3 letters of recommendation and an essay (from 200 to 500 words) about their past accomplishments, career and educational goals, and objectives for the future. Selection is based on the letters of reference (15%), academic record (15%), the essay (25%), and financial need (45%).

Financial data   Scholarships are $1,000 or $750 each.

Duration   1 year.

Number awarded   Up to 7 each year: 2 at $1,000 and 5 at $750.

Deadline   June of each year.

[48]
ANN GRIFFEL SCHOLARSHIP

Iowa Golf Association
Attn: Scholarship Selection Committee
1605 North Ankeny Boulevard, Suite 210
Ankeny, IA 50023
(515) 207-1062   Toll Free: (888) 388-4442
Fax: (515) 207-1065
Web: www.iowagolf.org/Foundation/scholarships.html

Summary   To provide financial assistance to female high school seniors in Iowa who have been active in golf and plan to attend college in the state.

Eligibility   This program is open to women graduating from high schools in Iowa and planning to attend a college, university, or trade school in the state. Applicants must submit transcripts with GPA and ACT/SAT results and 2 letters of recommendation. They must also submit statements on what the game of golf has meant to them and the role it will play in their future, awards received, participation in extracurricular activities in school and community, plans for college, career expectations, work experience, and financial need. Selection is based on academic performance, extracurricular activities, and leadership qualities, not on golf accomplishments or ability.

Financial data   The stipend is $2,000.

Duration   1 year.

Additional information   This program began in 1963.

Number awarded   Varies each year; recently, 5 were awarded. Since the program was established, it has awarded 218 scholarships.

Deadline   March of each year.

[49]
ANN LIGUORI FOUNDATION SPORTS MEDIA SCHOLARSHIP

New York Women in Communications, Inc.
Attn: NYWICI Foundation
355 Lexington Avenue, 15th Floor
New York, NY 10017-6603
(212) 297-2133   Fax: (212) 370-9047
E-mail: nywicipr@nywici.org
Web: www.nywici.org/foundation/scholarships

Summary   To provide financial assistance to female residents of designated eastern states who are enrolled at a college in any state and preparing for a career in sports journalism.

Eligibility   This program is open to women who are residents of New York, New Jersey, Connecticut, or Pennsylvania and currently enrolled as juniors, seniors or graduate students at a college or university in any state. Also eligible are women who reside outside the 4 states but are currently enrolled at a college or university within 1 of the 5 boroughs of New York City. Applicants must be interested in preparing for a career in sports broadcasting, reporting, programming, or production. They must have a GPA of 3.2 or higher. Graduate students must be members of New York Women in Communications, Inc. (NYWICI). Along with their application, they must submit a 2-page resume; a personal essay of 300 words on an assigned topic that changes annually; 2 letters of recommendation; and an official transcript. Selection is based on academic record, need, demonstrated leadership, participation in school and community activities, honors and other awards or recognition, work experience, goals and aspirations, and unusual personal and/or family circumstances. U.S. citizenship or permanent resident status is required.

Financial data   The stipend ranges up to $10,000.

Duration   1 year.

Number awarded   1 each year.

Deadline   January of each year.

[50]
ANN WOOD-KELLY MEMORIAL SCHOLARSHIP

Ninety-Nines, Inc.-Eastern New England Chapter
c/o Vanessa Blakeley, Scholarship Chair
77 Corey Street
West Roxbury, MA 02132
E-mail: blakeley.vanessa@gmail.com
Web: www.womenpilotsene.org/scholarships.htm

Summary   To provide financial assistance to female residents of New England who are interested in preparing for a career in aviation.

Eligibility   This program is open to women who are at least of high school age and reside or study in 1 of the following states: Maine, New Hampshire, Rhode Island, Vermont, Massachusetts, or Connecticut. Applicants must be studying or planning to study in an area of aviation at an accredited college or university, at a college or other flight school, or with a private instructor. They must have at least a private pilot certificate. Along with their application, they must submit a personal letter describing their aviation-related goals, including descriptions of all their aviation-related activities. Selection is based on academic achievement, interest and dedication to a career in aviation, recommendations, involvement in aviation activities (e.g., flying, aviation employment, model airplane building, science fair projects), and financial need.

Financial data The stipend is $1,500.

Duration 1 year.

Number awarded 1 each year.

Deadline January of each year.

[51]
ANNALEY NAEGLE REDD STUDENT AWARD IN WOMEN'S HISTORY

Brigham Young University
Attn: Charles Redd Center for Western Studies
954 Spencer W. Kimball Tower
Provo, UT 84602
(801) 422-4048   Fax: (801) 422-0035
E-mail: redd_center@byu.edu
Web: reddcenter.byu.edu

Summary To provide funding to undergraduate and graduate students interested in conducting research on women in the West.

Eligibility This program is open to undergraduate and graduate students who are interested in conducting a research project related to women in the American West (defined as west of the Mississippi). Applicants may be proposing any kind of project, including seminar papers, theses, or dissertations. Along with their application, they must submit brief statements on the central research question and conceptual framework, how the project will increase understanding of the American West, where they plan to conduct research and the resources available there, other research that has been conducted on the topic, what makes this study and approach unique and important, the planned use of the research, and a detailed budget.

Financial data The grant is $1,500. Funds may be used for research support (supplies, travel, etc.) but not for salary or capital equipment.

Duration Normally work is to be undertaken during the summer.

Number awarded 1 each year.

Deadline March of each year.

[52]
ANNE B. ANSTINE SCHOLARSHIP

Pennsylvania Federation of Republican Women
Attn: Scholarship Committee
806 North Second Street
Harrisburg, PA 17102-3212
(717) 234-5914   E-mail: pfrw@comcast.net
Web: www.pfrw.org/Programs.php

Summary To provide financial assistance to female high school seniors who are children or grandchildren of members of the Pennsylvania Federation of Republican Women (PFRW) and interested in attending college in any state.

Eligibility This program is open to women graduating from high schools in Pennsylvania whose parents, grandparents, or legal guardians have been PFRW members for at least 3 years. Applicants must submit transcripts that include SAT scores, a list of high school extracurricular activities, and information on work and other outside activities. Financial need is not considered in the selection process.

Financial data A stipend is awarded (amount not specified).

Duration 1 year.

Number awarded 1 each year.

Deadline April of each year.

[53]
ANNE MAUREEN WHITNEY BARROW MEMORIAL SCHOLARSHIP

Society of Women Engineers
Attn: Scholarship Selection Committee
203 North LaSalle Street, Suite 1675
Chicago, IL 60601-1269
(312) 596-5223   Toll Free: (877) SWE-INFO
Fax: (312) 644-8557   E-mail: scholarships@swe.org
Web: societyofwomenengineers.swe.org

Summary To provide financial assistance to women interested in studying engineering or computer science in college.

Eligibility This program is open to women who are enrolled or planning to enroll full time at an ABET-accredited 4-year college or university. Applicants must be planning to major in engineering or computer science. Selection is based on merit.

Financial data The stipend is $7,000 per year.

Duration 1 year; may be renewed for 4 additional years.

Additional information This program began in 1991.

Number awarded 1 every 5 years.

Deadline May of the years in which it is offered.

[54]
ANNE SHEN SMITH ENDOWED SCHOLARSHIP

Society of Women Engineers
Attn: Scholarship Selection Committee
203 North LaSalle Street, Suite 1675
Chicago, IL 60601-1269
(312) 596-5223   Toll Free: (877) SWE-INFO
Fax: (312) 644-8557   E-mail: scholarships@swe.org
Web: societyofwomenengineers.swe.org

Summary To provide financial assistance to women, especially those from underrepresented groups, working on an undergraduate degree in engineering at colleges in California.

Eligibility This program is open to women who are entering their sophomore, junior, or senior year at a 4-year ABET-accredited college or university in California. Applicants must be working full time on a degree in computer science or any field of engineering. Preference is given to members of groups underrepresented in engineering. U.S. citizenship is required. Selection is based on merit.

Financial data The stipend is $1,000.

Duration 1 year.

Additional information This program began in 2015.

Number awarded 1 each year.

Deadline February of each year.

[55]
ANNE TRABUE SCHOLARSHIP

Women's Southern California Golf Association
Attn: Foundation
402 West Arrow Highway, Suite 10
San Dimas, CA 91773
(909) 592-1281, ext. 212   Fax: (909) 592-7542
E-mail: info@wscgafoundation.org
Web: www.wscgafoundation.com/scholarships.php

Summary To provide financial assistance to women in southern California who play golf and are interested in working on an undergraduate degree in English or journalism at a college in any state.

Eligibility This program is open to female residents of southern California who play golf and are enrolled or planning to enroll full time at an accredited college or university in any state. Applicants must be interested in working on an associate or bachelor's degree in English or journalism. They must have a GPA of 3.2 or higher. Along with their application, they must submit information on their family financial situation and an essay of up to 1,000 words on why they selected their major, their relevant academic and professional experience to date, and how golf and other sports (if applicable) will remain an integral part of their undergraduate experience.

Financial data A stipend is awarded (amount not specified).

Duration 1 year.

Number awarded 1 or more each year.

Deadline May of each year.

[56]
ANNIE L. ADAIR SCHOLARSHIP

Native Daughters of the Golden West
Attn: Education and Scholarships
543 Baker Street
San Francisco, CA 94117-1405
(415) 563-9091   Toll Free: (800) 994-NDGW
Fax: (415) 563-5230   E-mail: ndgwgpo@att.net
Web: www.ndgw.org/edu.htm

Summary To provide financial assistance to members of the Native Daughters of the Golden West (NDGW) in California and their families who are interested in working on a degree in business or social welfare at a college in the state.

Eligibility This program is open to members and their children who are attending or planning to attend an accredited university, college, or vocational school in California and major in business or social welfare. Applicants must be high school seniors or undergraduates who have completed the first year of college with a GPA of 3.0 or higher. They must have been born in the state and be sponsored by a local parlor of the NDGW.

Financial data The stipend is $1,300 per year.

Duration 1 year; may be renewed if the recipient maintains a GPA of 3.0 or higher.

Number awarded 2 each year.

Deadline April of each year.

[57]
AOPA STUDENT PILOT SCHOLARSHIP

Women in Aviation International
Attn: Scholarships
Morningstar Airport
3647 State Route 503 South
West Alexandria, OH 45381-9354
(937) 839-4647   Fax: (937) 839-4645
E-mail: scholarships@wai.org
Web: www.wai.org

Summary To provide funding to members of Women in Aviation International (WAI) who are interested in working on an additional license or certificate.

Eligibility This program is open to women who are WAI members and have obtained a student pilot certificate. Applicants must be interested in earning a recreational, sport pilot, or private pilot certificate. Along with their application, they must submit 1) a 500-word essay and professional resume that include their aviation history and goals, what they have done for themselves to achieve their goals, where they see themselves in 5 and 10 years, involvement in aviation activities, how the scholarship will help them achieve their objectives, and their present financial need; and 2) a 300-word essay on their thoughts on general aviation's role in supporting the nation and local communities. Preference is given to full-time students who have a cumulative GPA of 3.0 or higher and are enrolled in high school, an accredited college or university, or an accredited flight school. U.S. citizenship is required. Selection is based on merit, including previous accomplishments, ability to set and achieve goals, involvement in general aviation, and commitment to completing flight training.

Financial data The stipend is $3,000. Funds are paid directly to the flight school.

Duration Training must be completed within 1 year.

Additional information WAI is a nonprofit professional organization dedicated to encouraging women to consider an aviation career and to providing educational outreach activities and networking resources to women active in the industry. This program is sponsored by the Aircraft Owners and Pilots Association (AOPA).

Number awarded 1 each year.

Deadline November of each year.

[58]
APIQWTC SCHOLARSHIP

Asian Pacific Islander Queer Women and Transgender
  Community
c/o Amy Sueyoshi
San Francisco State University
College of Ethnic Studies
1600 Holloway Avenue
San Francisco, CA 94132
(415) 405-0774   E-mail: sueyoshi@sfsu.edu
Web: www.apiqwtc.org/resources/apiqwtc-scholarship

Summary To provide financial assistance to Asian Pacific Islander (API) lesbian and bisexual women and transgender individuals who are high school seniors, undergraduates, or graduate students interested in working on a degree in any field at a college in any state.

Eligibility This program is open to API high school seniors and current undergraduate or graduate students in any field. Applicants must identify as a lesbian, bisexual, or queer woman or a transgender individual. Along with their application, they must submit a 2-page personal statement that covers their community involvement and future goals; how their cultural heritage, sexual orientation, and/or gender identity has influenced their life; any activities in which they have been involved; any relevant experiences up to the present; and how they see themselves involved in the community in the future, either through their career or otherwise.

Financial data The stipend is $1,000.

Duration 1 year.

Additional information The Asian Pacific Islander Queer Women and Transgender Community (APIQWTC) is a community of more than 10 organizations in the San Francisco Bay area provide support and community for queer Asian and Pacific Islander individuals, but its scholarships are available to students from any state.

Number awarded 2 each year.

Deadline February of each year.

[59]
APS/IBM RESEARCH INTERNSHIP FOR UNDERGRADUATE WOMEN

American Physical Society
Attn: Committee on the Status of Women in Physics
One Physics Ellipse
College Park, MD 20740-3844
(301) 209-3232   Fax: (301) 209-0865
E-mail: apsibmin@us.ibm.com
Web: www.aps.org

Summary To provide an opportunity for undergraduate women to participate in a summer research internship in science or engineering at facilities of IBM.

Eligibility This program is open to women currently enrolled as sophomores or juniors and majoring in biology, chemistry, chemical engineering, computer science or engineering, electrical engineering, materials science or engineering, mechanical engineering, or physics. Applicants are not required to be U.S. citizens, but they must be enrolled at a college or university in the United States. They must be interested in working as a research intern at a participating IBM laboratory. A GPA of at least 3.0 is required. Selection is based on commitment to and interest in their major field of study.

Financial data Interns receive a competitive salary of approximately $8,000 for the summer.

Duration 10 weeks during the summer.

Additional information Participating IBM laboratories are the Almaden Research Center in San Jose, California, the Watson Research Center in Yorktown Heights, New York, or the Austin Research Laboratory in Austin, Texas.

Number awarded 1 each year.

Deadline February of each year.

[60]
AQUA FOUNDATION FOR WOMEN SCHOLARSHIPS

Aqua Foundation for Women
4500 Biscayne Boulevard, Suite 340
Miami, FL 33137
(305) 576-AQUA   E-mail: scholars@aquafoundation.org
Web: www.aquafoundation.org/scholarships

Summary To provide financial assistance for college to lesbian, bisexual, and transgender (LBT) women who have ties to Florida.

Eligibility This program is open to LBT women who are 1) residents of any state attending college in south Florida; or 2) residents of Florida attending college in any state. Applicants must have a history of leadership in the LBT community and plans to remain a leader in that committee. They must have a GPA of 3.0 or higher.

Financial data Stipends range up to $5,000 per year.

Duration 1 year; may be renewed, provided the recipient maintains a GPA of 3.0 or higher.

Number awarded Varies each year; recently, 12 were awarded.

Deadline April of each year.

[61]
ARCELORMITTAL EMERGING LEADER SCHOLARSHIPS

Society of Women Engineers
Attn: Scholarship Selection Committee
203 North LaSalle Street, Suite 1675
Chicago, IL 60601-1269
(312) 596-5223   Toll Free: (877) SWE-INFO
Fax: (312) 644-8557   E-mail: scholarships@swe.org
Web: societyofwomenengineers.swe.org

Summary To provide financial assistance to members of the Society of Women Engineers (SWE) who are interested in studying specified fields of engineering at designated universities.

Eligibility This program is open to SWE members who are entering their junior year at Ohio State University, Indiana University, Purdue University, Michigan State University, Michigan Technological University, Pennsylvania State University, Rose-Hulman Institute of Technology, Purdue University Northwest (formerly Purdue University-Calumet), Missouri University of Science and Technology, Iowa State University, or University of Illinois at Urbana-Champaign. Applicants must be enrolled full time and majoring in computer science or computer, electrical, or materials engineering. They must be U.S. citizens. Preference is given to members of underrepresented groups, including veterans. Selection is based on merit and financial need.

Financial data The stipend is $1,000.

Duration 1 year.

Additional information This program is sponsored by ArcelorMittal.

Number awarded 1 each year.

Deadline February of each year.

[62]
AREMA PRESIDENTIAL SPOUSE SCHOLARSHIP

American Railway Engineering and Maintenance-of-Way
Association
Attn: AREMA Educational Foundation Scholarship
Review Committee
4501 Forbes Boulevard, Suite 130
Lanham, MD 20706
(301) 459-3200, ext. 708   Fax: (301) 459-8077
E-mail: abell@arema.org
Web: www.aremafoundation.org/scholarships.html

Summary To provide financial assistance to female undergraduate students who are interested in majoring in engineering or engineering technology and preparing for a career in
railway engineering.

Eligibility This program is open to women who have completed at least 1 quarter or semester at an ABET-accredited
4- or 5-year program (or a comparably accredited program in
Canada or Mexico). Applicants must be working on a bachelor's degree in engineering or engineering technology and
have a GPA of 2.0 or higher. They must be interested in a
career in railway engineering. Along with their application,
they must submit a 350-word cover letter explaining why they
believe they are deserving of this scholarship and identifying
the areas of railroading in which they are particularly interested. Financial need is not considered in the selection process.

Financial data The stipend is $1,000.

Duration 1 year.

Number awarded 1 each year.

Deadline December of each year.

[63]
ARFORA/HELEN MUNTEAN EDUCATION SCHOLARSHIP FOR WOMEN

Association of Romanian Orthodox Ladies Auxiliaries of
North America
c/o Corina Phillips, Scholarship Committee
8190 Buffham Road
Lodi, OH 44254
(330) 241-4775   E-mail: corina5dan@aol.com
Web: www.roea.org/helenmuntean.html

Summary To provide financial assistance to women who
are members of a parish of the Romanian Orthodox Episcopate of America and interested in working on a degree in education in college.

Eligibility This program is open to women who have been
voting communicant members of a parish of the Romanian
Orthodox Episcopate of America for at least 1 year or are
daughters of a communicant member. Applicants must have
completed at least 1 year of work on a baccalaureate degree
in education at a college or university. Along with their application, they must submit a 300-word statement describing
their personal goals; high school, university, church, and
community involvement; honors and awards; and why they
should be considered for this award. Selection is based on
academic achievement, character, worthiness, and participation in religious life.

Financial data The stipend is $1,000.

Duration 1 year; nonrenewable.

Additional information The Association of Romanian
Orthodox Ladies Auxiliaries (ARFORA) was established in
1938 as a women's organization within the Romanian Orthodox Episcopate of America.

Number awarded 1 or more each year.

Deadline May of each year.

[64]
ARFORA UNDERGRADUATE SCHOLARSHIP FOR WOMEN

Association of Romanian Orthodox Ladies Auxiliaries of
North America
c/o Corina Phillips, Scholarship Committee
8190 Buffham Road
Lodi, OH 44254
(330) 241-4775   E-mail: corina5dan@aol.com
Web: www.roea.org/arforaundergrad.html

Summary To provide financial assistance to women who
are members of a parish of the Romanian Orthodox Episcopate of America and currently enrolled in college.

Eligibility This program is open to women who have been
voting communicant members of a parish of the Romanian
Orthodox Episcopate of America for at least 1 year or are
daughters of a communicant member. Applicants must have
completed at least 1 year of undergraduate study at a college
or university. Along with their application, they must submit a
300-word statement describing their personal goals; high
school, university, church, and community involvement; honors and awards; and why they should be considered for this
award. Selection is based on academic achievement, character, worthiness, and participation in religious life.

Financial data The stipend is $1,000.

Duration 1 year; nonrenewable.

Additional information This program began in 1994. The
Association of Romanian Orthodox Ladies Auxiliaries
(ARFORA) was established in 1938 as a women's organiza-
tion within the Romanian Orthodox Episcopate of America.

Number awarded 1 or more each year.

Deadline May of each year.

[65]
ARIZONA BPW FOUNDATION SCHOLARSHIPS

Arizona Business and Professional Women's Foundation
Attn: Administrator
P.O. Box 32596
Phoenix, AZ 85064
Web: www.arizonabpwfoundation.com/scholarships.html

Summary To provide financial assistance to women in Arizona who are attending or interested in attending a community college in the state.

Eligibility This program is open to women, at least 25
years of age, who are attending a community college or trade
school in Arizona. Applicants must fall into 1 of the following
categories: women who have been out of the workforce and
wish to upgrade their skills; women with no previous experience in the workforce who are seeking a marketable skill; and
women who are currently employed who are interested in
career advancement or change. Along with their application,
they must submit 2 letters of recommendation, a statement of
financial need (latest income tax return must be provided), a
career goal statement, and their most recent transcript (when

available). Selection is based on financial need, field of study, and possibility of success.

Financial data The stipend is $1,000 per year.

Duration 1 year; renewable for up to 3 consecutive semesters if the recipient maintains a GPA of 2.0 or higher.

Additional information In addition to the general scholarship, there are 3 named endowments: Dr. Dorine Chancellor (established in 1990 and open to students at any community college in Arizona, although 1 is set aside specifically for a student at Eastern Arizona College), Lynda Crowell (established in 1999 and open to students at community colleges in Maricopa County), and Muriel Lothrop-Ely (established in 2006 and open to students at any community college in Arizona).

Number awarded Varies each year; recently, 10 were awarded.

Deadline March of each year.

[66]
ARKANSAS SINGLE PARENT SCHOLARSHIPS

Arkansas Single Parent Scholarship Fund
Attn: Executive Director
614 East Emma Avenue, Suite 119
Springdale, AR 72764
(479) 927-1402   Fax: (479) 927-0755
E-mail: rhill@aspsf.org
Web: www.aspsf.org/scholarships/how-to-apply

Summary To provide financial assistance to single parents in Arkansas who plan to attend college in any state.

Eligibility This program is open to single parents in Arkansas who have custodial care of 1 or more children younger than 18 years of age. Applicants must reside in 1 of the 70 counties in which a Single Parent Scholarship Fund has been established; for a list of these counties, contact the sponsor. They must be planning to attend a college or university in any state. Financial need is considered in the selection process in most counties, and students are expected to qualify for a federal Pell Grant.

Financial data Each participating county organization establishes its own stipend. Most are in the range of $500 per semester.

Additional information This program was established in 1990.

Number awarded Varies each year; recently, approximately 2,300 were awarded. Since the program was established, it has awarded more than $23 million in scholarships.

Deadline Each participating county organization establishes its own deadline.

[67]
ARLENE JOHNS MEMORIAL GOLD AWARD SCHOLARSHIP

Girl Scouts of Oregon and Southwest Washington
Attn: Shannon Shea, Portland Service Center Office
9620 S.W. Barbur Boulevard
Portland, OR 97219
(503) 977-6813   Toll Free: (800) 338-5248
Fax: (503) 977-6801   E-mail: sshea@girlscoutsosw.org
Web: www.girlscoutsosw.org

Summary To provide financial assistance to high school seniors in Oregon and southwestern Washington who are

Ambassador Girl Scouts and planning to attend college in any state.

Eligibility This program is open to seniors graduating from high schools in Oregon and southwestern Washington who are Ambassador Girl Scouts and have earned their Gold Award. Applicants must be planning to enroll at an accredited university, college, technical school, vocational school, or trade school in any state. Along with their application, they must submit 1) a 1,000-word essay on how Girl Scouts has impacted their life and how that will impact them in the future; 2) a 500-word description of their Gold Award project; and 3) a 500-word essay on how they have made the world a better place by being a Girl Scout.

Financial data A stipend is awarded (amount not specified).

Duration 1 year.

Number awarded 1 each year.

Deadline May of each year.

[68]
ARMENIAN INTERNATIONAL WOMEN'S ASSOCIATION SCHOLARSHIPS

Armenian International Women's Association
65 Main Street, Room 3A
Watertown, MA 02472
(617) 926-0171   E-mail: aiwainc@aol.com
Web: www.aiwainternational.org/initiatives/scholarships

Summary To provide financial assistance to Armenian women who are upper-division and graduate students.

Eligibility This program is open to full-time women students of Armenian descent attending an accredited college or university. Applicants must be full-time juniors, seniors, or graduate students with a GPA of 3.2 or higher. They must submit an essay, up to 500 words, describing their planned academic program, their career goals, and the reasons why they believe they should be awarded this scholarship. Selection is based on financial need and merit.

Financial data Stipends are $1,000 or $500.

Duration 1 year.

Additional information This program includes the following named scholarships: the Ethel Jafarian Duffett Scholarships, the Zarouhi Y. Getsoyan Scholarship, the Rose "Azad" Hovannesian Scholarship, the Agnes Missirian Scholarship, and the Dr. Carolann S. Najarian Scholarships.

Number awarded Varies each year; recently, 18 were awarded: 17 at $1,000 and ' at $500.

Deadline April of each year.

[69]
ARMY WOMEN'S FOUNDATION LEGACY SCHOLARSHIPS

Army Women's Foundation
Attn: Scholarship Committee
P.O. Box 5030
Fort Lee, VA 23801-0030
(804) 734-3078   E-mail: info@awfdn.org
Web: www.awfdn.org/scholarships.shtml

Summary To provide financial assistance for college or graduate school to women who are serving or have served in the Army and their children.

Eligibility This program is open to 1) women who have served or are serving honorably in the U.S. Army, U.S. Army Reserve, or Army National Guard; and 2) children of those women. Applicants must be 1) high school graduates or GED recipients enrolled at a community college or technical certificate program who have a GPA of 2.5 or higher; 2) sophomores or higher at an accredited college or university who have a GPA of 3.0 or higher; or 3) students enrolled in or accepted to a graduate program who have a GPA of 3.0 or higher. Along with their application, they must submit a 2-page essay on why they should be considered for this scholarship; their future plans as related to their program of study; their community service, activities, and work experience; and how the Army has impacted their life and/or goals. Selection is based on merit, academic potential, community service, and financial need.

Financial data The stipend is $2,500 for college and graduate students or $1,000 for community college and certificate students.

Duration 1 year.

Number awarded Varies each year; recently, 19 soldiers (3 community college and certificate students, 9 4-year college students, and 7 graduate students) and 16 children (1 community college or certificate student, 13 4-year college students, and 2 graduate students) received these scholarships.

Deadline January of each year.

[70]
ARTHUR H. GOODMAN MEMORIAL SCHOLARSHIP

San Diego Foundation
Attn: Community Scholarships
2508 Historic Decatur Road, Suite 200
San Diego, CA 92106
(619) 814-1343   Fax: (619) 239-1710
E-mail: scholarships@sdfoundation.org
Web: www.sdfoundation.org

Summary To provide financial assistance to female and minority community college students in California or Arizona planning to transfer to a 4-year school in any state to prepare for a career in economic development.

Eligibility This program is open to women and minorities currently enrolled at a community college in California or Arizona and planning to transfer as a full- or part-time student at a 4-year school in any state. Applicants must submit information on their long-term career goal, a list of volunteer and extracurricular activities, documentation of financial need, and a 3-page personal statement on their commitment to community involvement and desire to prepare for a career in the field of economic development.

Financial data Stipends range from $1,500 to $3,000.

Duration 1 year.

Additional information This program was established in 1998 by the CDC Small Business Finance Corporation.

Number awarded Varies each year; recently, 5 were awarded.

Deadline April of each year.

[71]
ARTTABLE MENTORED INTERNSHIPS FOR DIVERSITY IN THE VISUAL ARTS PROFESSIONS

ArtTable Inc.
1 East 53rd Street, Fifth Floor
New York, NY 10022
(212) 343-1735   Fax: (866) 363-4188
E-mail: info@arttable.org
Web: www.arttable.org/summermentoredinternship

Summary To provide an opportunity for women who are from diverse backgrounds to gain mentored work experience during the summer and to prepare for a career as an art professional.

Eligibility This program is open to women who are college seniors, recent graduates, or graduate students and interested in preparing for a career as a visual arts professional (including administrative director, art adviser, art appraiser, art critic, art dealer, art librarian, arts funder, arts lawyer, conservator, curator, editor, educator, fundraiser, management consultant, public relations consultant, writer). Applicants must be from a cultural or ethnic background that is underrepresented in the field. They must be interested in working during the summer with a mentor at an art museum or similar facility. U.S. citizenship or permanent resident status is required.

Financial data The stipend is $3,000. The hosting institution or mentor receives $500 for administrative and other costs.

Duration 8 weeks during the summer.

Additional information This program began in 2000. Support is provided by the Samuel H. Kress Foundation.

Number awarded Varies each year; recently, 5 of these internships were awarded.

Deadline February of each year.

[72]
ASIAN WOMEN IN BUSINESS SCHOLARSHIP FUND

Asian Women in Business
42 Broadway, Suite 1748
New York, NY 10004
(212) 868-1368   Fax: (877) 686-6870
E-mail: info@awib.org
Web: www.awib.org

Summary To provide financial assistance for college to Asian women who have demonstrated community leadership or entrepreneurial achievement.

Eligibility This program is open to women who are of Asian or Pacific Island ancestry and are U.S. citizens or permanent residents. Applicants must be enrolled full time at an accredited 4-year undergraduate institution in the United States and have a GPA of 3.0 or higher. They must be able to demonstrate either 1) a leadership role in a community endeavor; and/or 2) a record of entrepreneurial achievement (e.g., founded their own business). Additional funding is available to applicants who can demonstrate financial need.

Financial data The stipend is $2,500. Funds are paid directly to the recipient.

Duration 1 year; nonrenewable.

Additional information This program began in 2006.

Number awarded 4 each year.

Deadline September of each year.

[73]
ASSE DIVERSITY COMMITTEE UNDERGRADUATE SCHOLARSHIP

American Society of Safety Engineers
Attn: ASSE Foundation
Scholarship Award Program
1800 East Oakton Street
Des Plaines, IL 60018
(847) 768-3412   Fax: (847) 768-3434
E-mail: foundation@asse.org
Web: www.asse.org/foundation/scholarships/award-listing

Summary To provide financial assistance to upper-division students who come from diverse groups and are working on a degree related to occupational safety.

Eligibility This program is open to students who are working on an undergraduate degree in occupational safety, health, environment, industrial hygiene, occupational health nursing, or a closely-related field (e.g., industrial or environmental engineering). Applicants must be full-time students who have completed at least 60 semester hours and have a GPA of 3.0 or higher. A goal of this program is to support individuals regardless of race, ethnicity, gender, religion, personal beliefs, age, sexual orientation, physical challenges, geographic location, university, or specific area of study. U.S. citizenship is not required. Membership in the American Society of Safety Engineers (ASSE) is not required, but preference is given to members.

Financial data The stipend is $1,000 per year.

Duration 1 year; recipients may reapply.

Number awarded 1 each year.

Deadline November of each year.

[74]
ASSOCIATION FOR WOMEN GEOSCIENTISTS MINORITY SCHOLARSHIP

Association for Women Geoscientists
Attn: AWG Foundation
12000 North Washington Street, Suite 285
Thornton, CO 80241
(303) 412-6219   Fax: (303) 253-9220
E-mail: office@awg.org
Web: www.awg.org/eas/minority.htm

Summary To provide financial assistance to underrepresented minority women who are interested in working on an undergraduate degree in the geosciences.

Eligibility This program is open to women who are African American, Hispanic, or Native American (including Eskimo, Hawaiian, Samoan, or American Indian). Applicants must be full-time students working on, or planning to work on, an undergraduate degree in the geosciences (including geology, geophysics, geochemistry, hydrology, meteorology, physical oceanography, planetary geology, or earth science education). They must submit a 500-word essay on their academic and career goals, 2 letters of recommendation, high school and/or college transcripts, and SAT or ACT scores. Financial need is not considered in the selection process. U.S. citizenship is required.

Financial data A total of $6,000 is available for this program each year.

Duration 1 year; may be renewed.

Additional information This program, first offered in 2004, is supported by ExxonMobil Foundation.

Number awarded 1 or more each year.

Deadline June of each year.

[75]
ASSOCIATION FOR WOMEN IN ARCHITECTURE FOUNDATION SCHOLARSHIPS

Association for Women in Architecture and Design
Attn: Scholarship Chair
1315 Storm Parkway
Torrance, CA 90501
(310) 534-8466   Fax: (310) 257-1942
E-mail: scholarships@awa-la.org
Web: www.awaplusd.org/scholarships

Summary To provide financial assistance to women undergraduates in California who are interested in preparing for a career in architecture.

Eligibility This program is open to women who have completed at least 18 college units of study in any of the following fields: architecture; civil, structural, mechanical, or electrical engineering as related to environmental design; landscape architecture; urban and/or land planning; interior design; architectural rendering and illustration; or environmental design. Applicants must be residents of California or attending school in the state. Students in their final year of study are also eligible and may use the funds for special projects (such as a trip abroad). Selection is based on grades, a personal statement, recommendations, and the quality and organization of materials submitted; financial need is not considered.

Financial data The stipend is $1,000.

Duration 1 year.

Number awarded 5 each year.

Deadline April of each year.

[76]
ASSOCIATION FOR WOMEN IN AVIATION MAINTENANCE SCHOLARSHIP PROGRAM

Association for Women in Aviation Maintenance
Attn: World Headquarters
2330 Kenlee Drive
Cincinnati, OH 45230
(386) 416-0248   Fax: (386) 236-0517
E-mail: scholarships@awam.org
Web: www.awam.org/scholarships

Summary To provide financial assistance to members of the Association for Women in Aviation Maintenance (AWAM) who are interested in preparing for a career as an aviation mechanic.

Eligibility Applicants for all awards included in this program must be AWAM members (membership in the association is open to both men and women). Some awards specify that applicants must be women, and others impose additional requirements. Most provide support for study at a particular aviation maintenance school or training program, although some offer cash awards that recipients can use at the school or program of their choice. All applicants must submit a resume describing their education, work experience, qualifications, and honors; a 200-word essay on their interest in aviation; and at least 2 letters of recommendation.

Financial data Cash awards are $1,500, $1,000, or $500. Other awards provide full or partial payment of tuition and/or other program expenses.

Duration Awards are offered annually.

Additional information The cash awards offered through this program include the Aircraft Electronics Association Avionics Technician Scholarship, Aviation Student Entrepreneur Scholarship, the "Bowling for Success" Scholarship, the "Helping Hand" from Rice Family Scholarships, the "Searching for Success" Scholarship, the "Taking it to the Sky at WAI" Scholarship, and the "Tools Beneath Your Wings" Scholarship. Other programs are offered by Abaris Training Resources, Airbus Helicopters, Baker School of Aeronautics, Bombardier Aerospace, Delta Airlines, DME Services, FedEx, FlightSafety International, JetBlue Airways, Pratt & Whitney, Southwest Airlines, and UPS.

Number awarded Varies each year; recently, 36 scholarships with a value in excess of $120,000 were awarded, but most of those were for specified schools or training programs. The cash awards for use at any maintenance or other training program were 1 at $1,500, 1 at $1,000, and 5 at $500.

Deadline December of each year.

[77]
ASSOCIATION FOR WOMEN IN SPORTS MEDIA SCHOLARSHIP/INTERNSHIP PROGRAM

Association for Women in Sports Media
Attn: Scholarship and Internship Coordinator
7742 Spalding Drive, Suite 377
Norcross, GA 30092
E-mail: awsminternship@gmail.com
Web: www.awsmonline.org/internship-scholarship

Summary To provide financial assistance and work experience to women undergraduate and graduate students who are interested in preparing for a career in sports writing.

Eligibility This program is open to women who are enrolled in college or graduate school full time and preparing for a career in sports media, including print/online, magazine, broadcast reporting, broadcast projection, or public relations. Applicants must submit a 750-word essay describing their most memorable experience in sports or sports media, a 1-page resume highlighting their journalism experience, a letter of recommendation, up to 5 samples of their work, and a $20 application fee. They must apply for and accept an internship with a sports media organization.

Financial data Winners receive a stipend up to $1,000 and placement in a paid internship.

Duration 1 year; nonrenewable.

Additional information This program, which began in 1990, includes the "Sophie Scholarship," the Jim Brennan Scholarship, the Betty Brennan Scholarship, the Mary Garber Scholarship, the Mike Roberts Memorial Scholarship, and the Leah Siegel Scholarship.

Number awarded Varies each year; recently, 7 students received support from this program.

Deadline October of each year.

[78]
ASSOCIATION OF WOMEN CONTRACTORS SCHOLARSHIPS

Association of Women Contractors
1337 St. Clair Avenue, Suite 4
St. Paul, MN 55105
(651) 489-2221   E-mail: awcmn@awcmn.org
Web: www.awcmn.org/programs/scholarship

Summary To provide financial assistance to women from Minnesota who are attending college to prepare for a career in the construction industry.

Eligibility This program is open to women who are either 1) residents of Minnesota attending a 4-year college or university, community or technical college, construction trade school, or construction industry apprenticeship program in any state; or 2) residents of other states enrolled in such a program in Minnesota. Applicants must be majoring in a construction-related field, including (but not limited to) architecture, carpentry, construction management, engineering (civil, construction, electrical, mechanical), interior design, or landscape design. Applicants must submit a brief statement addressing the selection priorities: (in order) financial need, personal information (involvement in student and community activity and organizations, honors, awards, family responsibility), and short and/or long-term career goals.

Financial data Stipends are $1,500 or $1,000.

Duration 1 year.

Additional information This program began in 2007. The highest-ranked applicant receives the Helen Baker Memorial Scholarship (established in 2010).

Number awarded Varies each year; recently, 8 were awarded: 1 at $1,500 (the Helen Baker Memorial Scholarship) and 7 at $1,000.

Deadline April of each year.

[79]
ASSOCIATION ON AMERICAN INDIAN AFFAIRS DISPLACED HOMEMAKER SCHOLARSHIPS

Association on American Indian Affairs, Inc.
Attn: Director of Scholarship Programs
966 Hungerford Drive, Suite 12-B
Rockville, MD 20850
(240) 314-7155   Fax: (240) 314-7159
E-mail: general.aaia@indian-affairs.org
Web: www.indian-affairs.org

Summary To provide financial assistance to Native American displaced homemakers who are trying to complete their college education.

Eligibility This program is open to full-time college students who are Native Americans and have special needs because of family responsibilities. Examples of displaced homemakers include students who are attending college for the first time, usually 35 years of age or older, because they have put off higher education to raise their children, students who are entering or returning to college after their children enter elementary school, and men or women who have been divorced and had to leave college to care for children and are now returning. Applicants must submit proof of tribal enrollment and an essay of 2 to 3 pages on 1 of the following topics: 1) why the sponsor's International Repatriation Project is important and how they would inform others about it; 2) the

Annie E. Casey Foundation's Juvenile Detention Alternatives Initiative and tribal and community-based alternatives to detention for juveniles; or 3) how tribal leaders can promote higher education in their family and community. They must have a GPA of 2.5 or higher. Selection is based on merit and need.

Financial data The stipend is $1,500. Awards are intended to assist recipients with child care, transportation, and some basic living expenses as well as educational costs.

Duration 1 year; recipients may reapply.

Number awarded Varies each year; recently, 2 were awarded.

Deadline May of each year.

[80]
ATP GENERAL AVIATION MAINTENANCE SCHOLARSHIP

Women in Aviation International
Attn: Scholarships
Morningstar Airport
3647 State Route 503 South
West Alexandria, OH 45381-9354
(937) 839-4647   Fax: (937) 839-4645
E-mail: scholarships@wai.org
Web: www.wai.org

Summary To provide financial assistance to members of Women in Aviation International (WAI) who are interested in a career in general aviation maintenance.

Eligibility This program is open to WAI members who are enrolled at an aviation maintenance technician school and working on an airframe and powerplant (A&P) license. They must have a cumulative GPA of 3.0 or higher. Along with their application, they must submit a 500-word essay and professional resume that include their aviation history and goals, what they have done for themselves to achieve their goals, where they see themselves in 5 and 10 years, involvement in aviation activities, how the scholarship will help them achieve their objectives, their ambitions and interest in general aviation, and their present financial need. Selection is based on academic performance, personal accomplishments, involvement in the general aviation community, future career aspirations, and enthusiasm for general aviation.

Financial data The stipend is $1,000. Funds may be used for tuition, books, and fees.

Duration 1 year.

Additional information WAI is a nonprofit professional organization dedicated to encouraging women to consider an aviation career and to providing educational outreach activities and networking resources to women active in the industry. This program was established by Aircraft Technical Publishers (ATP) in 2014.

Number awarded 1 each year.

Deadline November of each year.

[81]
AUDRE LORDE SCHOLARSHIP AWARD

ZAMI NOBLA
Attn: Audre Lorde Scholarship Fund
P.O. Box 90986
Atlanta, GA 30364
(404) 647-4754   E-mail: zami@zami.org
Web: www.zami.org/audrelordescholar.html

Summary To provide financial assistance to mature out Black lesbians who are interested in entering or continuing in college or graduate school.

Eligibility This program is open to Black lesbians who are at least 40 years of age and out to themselves and their family, friends, and community. Applicants must be enrolled or planning to enroll full or part time at a technical, undergraduate, or graduate school in any state. They must have a cumulative GPA in high school, college, or technical school of 3.0 or higher. Along with their application, they must submit an essay of 2 to 3 pages on their choice of 2 of 5 assigned topics that relate to their experience as a Black lesbian.

Financial data The stipend is $1,000.

Duration 1 year.

Additional information From 1995 to 2008, the Audre Lorde Scholarship Fund was maintained by an organization named ZAMI: Atlanta's Premiere Organization for Lesbians of African Descent. The fund was reestablished in 2013 by the current sponsor, which stands for ZAMI National Organization of Black Lesbians on Aging.

Number awarded 1 each year.

Deadline April of each year.

[82]
AURA NEELY-GARY MEMORIAL SCHOLARSHIP

Community Foundation of Greater Jackson
525 East Capitol Street, Suite 5B
Jackson, MS 39201
(601) 974-6044   Fax: (601) 974-6045
E-mail: info@cfgj.org
Web: www.cfgj.org/scholarships.html

Summary To provide financial assistance to students at colleges and universities in Mississippi who have resumed their studies after an absence.

Eligibility This program is open to residents of any state who are enrolled or planning to enroll at a college or university in Mississippi. Preference is given to students who desire to resume their education following a period of personal difficulties. Special consideration is given to young women who had previously dropped out of school and are now enrolled at a postsecondary institution. Applicants must be able to demonstrate financial need and potential contribution to society.

Financial data The stipend is $2,000.

Duration 1 year.

Additional information This program began in 2007.

Number awarded Varies each year; recently, 3 were awarded.

Deadline April of each year.

[83]
AUTOMOTIVE WOMEN'S ALLIANCE FOUNDATION SCHOLARSHIPS

Automotive Women's Alliance Foundation
Attn: Scholarship
P.O. Box 4305
Troy, MI 48099
Toll Free: (877) 393-AWAF   Fax: (248) 239-0291
E-mail: admin@AWAFoundation.org
Web: www.awafoundation.org/pages/Scholarships

Summary To provide financial assistance to women who are interested in attending college or graduate school to prepare for a career in the automotive industry.

Eligibility This program is open to women who are entering or enrolled in an undergraduate or graduate program that will prepare them for a career in the automotive industry. Applicants must be citizens of Canada or the United States. They must have a GPA of 3.0 or higher. Along with their application, they must submit a 1-page cover letter explaining their automotive-related career aspirations.

Financial data The stipend is $2,500.

Duration 1 year.

Additional information This program began in 2001.

Number awarded Varies each year; recently, 21 were awarded.

Deadline Deadline not specified.

[84]
AUXILIARY LEGACY SCHOLARSHIP

National Society of Professional Engineers
Attn: NSPE Educational Foundation
1420 King Street
Alexandria, VA 22314-2794
(703) 684-2833   Toll Free: (888) 285-NSPE
Fax: (703) 684-2821   E-mail: education@nspe.org
Web: www.nspe.org

Summary To provide financial assistance to female members of the National Society of Professional Engineers (NSPE) who are entering their junior year at a college or university in any state.

Eligibility This program is open to women who are NSPE student members entering their junior year in an ABET-accredited engineering program. Applicants must submit a 500-word essay on their engineering career goals and aspirations and their plans to achieve those. Selection is based on that essay, GPA, internship and co-op experience, involvement in other activities, 2 faculty recommendations, and honors and awards since high school. U.S. citizenship is required.

Financial data The stipend is $2,000; funds are paid directly to the recipient's institution.

Duration 1 year.

Number awarded 1 each year.

Deadline February of each year.

[85]
AVIATION AND PROFESSIONAL DEVELOPMENT SCHOLARSHIP

Airport Minority Advisory Council
Attn: AMAC Foundation
2001 Jefferson Davis Highway, Suite 500
Arlington, VA 22202
(703) 414-2622   Fax: (703) 414-2686
E-mail: terrifrierson@palladiumholdingsco.com
Web: amac-org.com/amac-foundation/scholarships

Summary To provide financial assistance to minority and female high school seniors and undergraduates who are preparing for a career in the aviation industry and interested in participating in activities of the Airport Minority Advisory Council (AMAC).

Eligibility This program is open to minority and female high school seniors and current undergraduates who have a GPA of 2.5 or higher and a record of involvement in community and extracurricular activities. Applicants must be interested in working on a bachelor's degree in accounting, architecture, aviation, business administration, engineering, or finance as preparation for a career in the aviation or airport industry. They must be interested in participating in the AMAC program, including becoming a member if they are awarded a scholarship, and communicating with AMAC once each semester during the term of the scholarship. Along with their application, they must submit a 750-word essay on how they have overcome barriers in life to achieve their academic and/or career goals; their dedication to succeed in the aviation industry and how AMAC can help them achieve their goal; and the most important issues that the aviation industry is facing today and how they see themselves changing those. Financial need is not considered in the selection process. U.S. citizenship is required.

Financial data The stipend is $2,000 per year.

Duration 1 year; recipients may reapply.

Number awarded 4 each year.

Deadline May of each year.

[86]
AWC SCHOLARSHIP FUND FOR WOMEN IN COMPUTING

Ann Arbor Area Community Foundation
Attn: Scholarships
301 North Main Street, Suite 300
Ann Arbor, MI 48104
(734) 663-0401   Fax: (734) 663-3514
Web: www.aaacf.org

Summary To provide financial assistance to women undergraduates from any state working on a degree in a computer- or technology-related field at institutions in Washtenaw County, Michigan.

Eligibility This program is open to undergraduate women from any state enrolled at institutions of higher education in Washtenaw County, Michigan. Applicants must be preparing for a career in a field related to computers or technology and have at least 2 semesters of course work remaining. Along with their application, they must submit essays of 300 to 600 words on 1) their most fulfilling computer-related project or experience; 2) what intrigued them most about their chosen course of study; and 3) how they would encourage other women to join the field. Financial need is not considered in the selection process.

Financial data The stipend is $1,000.

Duration 1 year.

Additional information The Ann Arbor chapter of the Association for Women in Computing (AWC) established this program in 2003.

Number awarded 2 each year.

Deadline March of each year.

[87]
B. JUNE WEST RECRUITMENT GRANT

Delta Kappa Gamma Society International-Theta State
  Organization
c/o Sharron Stepro, Committee on Professional Affairs
  Chair
10038 San Marcos Court
Las Cruces, NM 88007-8954
(575) 541-8922   E-mail: jsrhett@comcast.net
Web: thetastatenmdkg.weebly.com

Summary To provide financial assistance to women in New Mexico who are interested in preparing for a career as a teacher.

Eligibility This program is open to women residents of New Mexico who are 1) graduating high school seniors planning to go into education; 2) college students majoring in education; or 3) teachers needing educational assistance. Applicants must submit a list of activities in which they are involved, 3 letters of recommendation, a list of achievements and awards, and a statement of their educational goal and how this grant would be of assistance to them. Financial need is not considered in the selection process.

Financial data A stipend is awarded (amount not specified).

Duration 1 year.

Number awarded 1 or more each year.

Deadline February of each year.

[88]
BALTIMORE-WASHINGTON CONFERENCE UNITED METHODIST WOMEN SCHOLARSHIP

United Methodist Church-Baltimore-Washington
  Conference
Attn: Associate Director, Young Adult and Campus
  Ministry
11711 East Market Place
Fulton, MD 20759
(410) 309-3446   Toll Free: (800) 492-2525, ext. 446
Fax: (410) 309-9794   E-mail: ccook@bwcumc.com
Web: www.bwcumc.org/finance/college-scholarships

Summary To provide financial assistance for college to female Methodists from the Baltimore-Washington Conference.

Eligibility This program is open to full-time female undergraduate students at accredited colleges and universities in any state who have been members of a United Methodist Church in the Baltimore-Washington Conference for at least 1 year. Applicants must have a GPA of 2.5 or higher. Selection is based on academic merit, involvement in the church, service as a leader, and financial need.

Financial data The stipend ranges from $400 to $1,000 per year.

Duration 1 year; may be renewed.

Number awarded Varies each year.

Deadline March of each year.

[89]
BANNER ENGINEERING MINNESOTA SWE SCHOLARSHIP

Society of Women Engineers-Minnesota Section
Attn: Scholarship Committee
P.O. Box 18481
Minneapolis, MN 55418
E-mail: scholarships@swe-mn.org
Web: www.swe-mn.org/scholarships.html

Summary To provide financial assistance to women from any state working on an undergraduate or graduate degree in electrical or mechanical engineering at colleges and universities in Minnesota, North Dakota, and South Dakota.

Eligibility This program is open to female undergraduate and graduate students at ABET-accredited engineering programs in Minnesota, North Dakota, or South Dakota. Applicants must be working full time on a degree in electrical or mechanical engineering. Along with their application, they must submit a 250-word essay describing how they plan to utilize their engineering knowledge and skills after they graduate. Selection is based on potential to succeed as an engineer (20 points), communication skills (10 points), extracurricular or community involvement and leadership skills (10 points), demonstration of work experience and successes (10 points), and academic success (5 points).

Financial data The stipend is $2,000.

Duration 1 year.

Additional information This program is sponsored by Banner Engineering Corporation.

Number awarded 1 each year.

Deadline March of each year.

[90]
BARBARA ALICE MOWER MEMORIAL SCHOLARSHIP

Barbara Alice Mower Memorial Scholarship Committee
c/o Nancy A. Mower
1536 Kamole Street
Honolulu, HI 96821-1424
(808) 373-2901   E-mail: nmower@hawaii.edu

Summary To provide financial assistance to female residents of Hawaii who are interested in women's studies and are attending college on the undergraduate or graduate level in the United States or abroad.

Eligibility This program is open to female residents of Hawaii who are at least juniors in college, are interested in and committed to women's studies, and have worked or studied in the field. Selection is based on interest in studying about and commitment to helping women, previous work and/or study in that area, previous academic performance, character, personality, and future plans to help women (particularly women in Hawaii). If there are several applicants who meet all these criteria, then financial need may be taken into consideration.

Financial data The stipend ranges from $1,000 to $3,500.

Duration 1 year; may be renewed.

Additional information Recipients may use the scholarship at universities in Hawaii, on the mainland, or in foreign countries. They must focus on women's studies or topics that relate to women in school.

Number awarded 1 or more each year.

Deadline April of each year.

[91]
BARBARA JEAN BARKER MEMORIAL SCHOLARSHIP FOR A DISPLACED HOMEMAKER

General Federation of Women's Clubs of Vermont
c/o Madge Tucker, Scholarship Chair
4246 Route 100
Plymouth, VT 05056

Summary To provide financial assistance to displaced homemakers in Vermont who are interested in attending college in any state.

Eligibility Applicants must be Vermont residents who have been homemakers (primarily) for at least 15 years and have lost their main means of support through death, divorce, separation, spouse's long-time illness, or spouse's long-time unemployment. Applicants must be interested in upgrading their skills so they can work outside the home. As part of the application process, they must submit a completed application form and a letter of recommendation (from a personal friend or their postsecondary school). Selection is based on the information provided in the application form and a personal interview (finalists only).

Financial data The stipend ranges from $500 to $1,500.

Duration 1 year.

Additional information This program began in 1993.

Number awarded 3 or 4 each year.

Deadline March of each year.

[92]
BARBARA LEPPE HAWAI'I SCHOLARSHIP FUND

Hawai'i Community Foundation
Attn: Scholarship Department
827 Fort Street Mall
Honolulu, HI 96813
(808) 566-5570   Toll Free: (888) 731-3863
Fax: (808) 521-6286
E-mail: scholarships@hcf-hawaii.org
Web: hcf.scholarships.ngwebsolutions.com

Summary To provide financial assistance to women from Hawaii who are interested in working on an undergraduate degree in any field at a school in any state.

Eligibility This program is open to female residents of Hawaii who are enrolled full time at a 2- or 4-year college or university in any state. Applicants may be working on a degree in any field They must be able to demonstrate academic achievement (GPA of 2.7 or higher), good moral character, and financial need. Along with their application, they must submit a short statement indicating their reasons for attending college, their planned course of study, their career goals, and what community service means to them. Preference is given to 1) students from rural areas within Hawaii; and 2) at-risk youth.

Financial data The amounts of the awards depend on the availability of funds and the need of the recipient. Recently, the average value of the scholarships awarded by the foundation was $2,800.

Duration 1 year; may be renewed.

Number awarded 1 or more each year.

Deadline February of each year.

[93]
BARBARA MCBRIDE MEMORIAL ENDOWED SCHOLARSHIP FUND

Society of Exploration Geophysicists
Attn: SEG Foundation
8801 South Yale, Suite 500
P.O. Box 702740
Tulsa, OK 74170-2740
(918) 497-5500   Fax: (918) 497-5557
E-mail: scholarships@seg.org
Web: www.seg.org

Summary To provide financial assistance to women who are interested in studying applied geophysics or a related field on the undergraduate or graduate school level.

Eligibility This program is open to women who are 1) high school students planning to enter college in the fall; or 2) undergraduate or graduate students whose grades are above average. Applicants must intend to work on a degree directed toward a career in applied geophysics or a closely-related field (e.g., earth and environmental sciences, geology, geosciences, or physics). Along with their application, they must submit a 250-word essay on their interest in geophysics. Financial need is not considered in the selection process.

Financial data Stipends provided by this sponsor range from $500 to $14,000 and average approximately $2,500 per year.

Duration 1 academic year; may be renewable, based on scholastic standing, availability of funds, and continuance of a course of study leading to a career in applied geophysics.

Additional information This program began in 2001.

Number awarded 1 each year.

Deadline February of each year.

[94]
BAYER SCHOLARSHIPS

Society of Women Engineers
Attn: Scholarship Selection Committee
203 North LaSalle Street, Suite 1675
Chicago, IL 60601-1269
(312) 596-5223   Toll Free: (877) SWE-INFO
Fax: (312) 644-8557   E-mail: scholarships@swe.org
Web: societyofwomenengineers.swe.org

Summary To provide financial assistance to women, especially those from underrepresented groups, working on an undergraduate degree in designated fields of engineering at colleges in Pennsylvania and Texas.

Eligibility This program is open to women who are entering their sophomore, junior, or senior year at a 4-year ABET-accredited college or university in Pennsylvania or Texas. Applicants must be working full time on a degree in computer science or chemical, electrical, materials, or mechanical engineering. Preference is given to members of groups underrepresented in engineering, including veterans. Selection is based on financial need and merit.

Financial data The stipend is $2,500.

Duration 1 year.

Additional information This program, which began in 2015, is sponsored by Bayer.

Number awarded 2 each year.

Deadline February of each year.

[95]
BEATRICE WARDE SCHOLARSHIP

Type Directors Club
347 West 36th Street, Suite 603
New York, NY 10018
(212) 633-8943   Fax: (212) 633-8944
E-mail: director@tdc.org
Web: www.tdc.org/beatrice-warde

Summary To provide financial assistance to women working on an undergraduate degree in typography.

Eligibility This program is open to women entering their senior year with a major related to typography, ranging from design criticism to type design and graphic design. Applicants must have a GPA of 3.0 or higher. Along with their application, they must submit 3 samples of their work and letters of recommendation. Selection is based on merit, including talent, sophistication, and skill in the use of typography.

Financial data The stipend is $5,000. Funds are sent directly to the recipient's college or university.

Duration 1 year.

Additional information This program began in 2016 with support from the Monotype Corporation, the long-time employer of the program's namesake.

Number awarded 1 each year.

Deadline February of each year.

[96]
BECHTEL CORPORATION SCHOLARSHIP

Society of Women Engineers
Attn: Scholarship Selection Committee
203 North LaSalle Street, Suite 1675
Chicago, IL 60601-1269
(312) 596-5223   Toll Free: (877) SWE-INFO
Fax: (312) 644-8557   E-mail: scholarships@swe.org
Web: societyofwomenengineers.swe.org

Summary To provide financial assistance to undergraduate women who are members of the Society of Women Engineers and majoring in engineering.

Eligibility This program is open to SWE members who are entering their sophomore, junior, or senior year at an ABET-accredited college or university. Applicants must be working full time on a degree in computer science or architectural, civil, electrical, environmental, or mechanical engineering or equivalent fields of engineering technology. They must have a GPA of 3.0 or higher. Selection is based on merit.

Financial data The stipend is $1,400.

Duration 1 year.

Additional information This program, established in 2000, is sponsored by Bechtel Group Foundation.

Number awarded 2 each year.

Deadline February of each year.

[97]
BEE WINKLER WEINSTEIN FUND

Stonewall Community Foundation
Attn: Grants
446 West 33rd Street, Sixth Floor
New York, NY 10001
(212) 367-1155   Fax: (212) 367-1157
E-mail: grants@stonewallfoundation.org
Web: www.stonewallfoundation.org/grants/scholarships

Summary To provide funding to lesbians and other women who wish to become self-sufficient but face obstacles because of their sexual identity.

Eligibility This program is open to lesbians, female bisexuals, and transgender individuals (male to female). Applicants must be between 18 and 25 years of age and able to demonstrate financial need. They must be striving to become self-sufficient but lack funding and other support from their family because of sexual or gender identity. Examples of eligible needs include GED tutoring, work uniforms, legal name changes, college application fees, domestic needs (e.g., bedding, rental security deposits), and licensing and testing fees. Support for tuition for vocational or technical training is available, but the cost of academic tuition for college or graduate school is not covered.

Financial data Grants have ranged from $35 to $1,500. Funds are made payable to 501(C)3 organizations.

Duration These are 1-time grants.

Number awarded Varies each year.

Deadline Applications may be submitted at any time.

[98]
BELLES OF THE AMERICAN ROYAL (BOTAR) ORGANIZATION AFA SCHOLARSHIPS

Agriculture Future of America
P.O. Box 414838
Kansas City, MO 64141
(816) 472-4232   Toll Free: (888) 472-4232
Fax: (816) 472-4239   E-mail: scholarship@agfuture.org
Web: www.agfuture.org

Summary To provide financial assistance to female high school seniors and current undergraduates from the Midwest who are interested in studying agriculture in college.

Eligibility This program is open to women who are graduating high school seniors or current undergraduates attending or planning to attend a 4-year college or university in the Midwest. Applicants must have a major in an agriculture-related field and a GPA of 3.0 or higher. Along with their application, they must submit an essay of 300 to 500 words on their personal vision for agriculture, including why they are interested in an agricultural career. Selection is based on that essay, leader and community involvement, and financial need.

Financial data The stipend is $3,200 per year. Funds are paid at the beginning of the second semester of the freshman year, provided the recipient attends the sponsor's Leaders Conference during the fall of the freshman year. The program provides a grant of $1,000 to help defray costs of attending the conference and a $200 travel stipend for attendance at the general membership meeting of the Belles of the American Royal (BOTAR) Organization.

Duration 1 year; may be renewed up to 3 additional years.

Additional information This program is sponsored by the Belles of the American Royal Organization as part of the Leader and Academic Scholarships program of Agriculture Future of America (AFA).

Number awarded 4 each year.

Deadline March of each year.

[99]
BERNICE F. ELLIOTT MEMORIAL SCHOLARSHIP

Baptist Convention of New Mexico
Attn: Woman's Missionary Union
c/o Connie Dixon
P.O. Box 119
Elida, NM 88116
(575) 760-1603   E-mail: cdixon@bcnm.com
Web: www.bcnm.com/scholarships

Summary To provide financial assistance to women who are Southern Baptists from New Mexico and interested in attending a college or seminary in any state.

Eligibility This program is open to women college and seminary students who are members of churches affiliated with the Baptist Convention of New Mexico. Preference is given to applicants who are committed to full-time Christian service, have a background in the Woman's Missionary Union, and can demonstrate financial need.

Financial data A stipend is awarded (amount not specified).

Duration 1 year; may be renewed.

Number awarded 1 or more each year.

Deadline March of each year.

[100]
BERNICE MURRAY SCHOLARSHIP

Vermont Student Assistance Corporation
Attn: Scholarship Programs
10 East Allen Street
P.O. Box 2000
Winooski, VT 05404-2601
(802) 654-3798   Toll Free: (888) 253-4819
Fax: (802) 654-3765   TDD: (800) 281-3341 (within VT)
E-mail: info@vsac.org
Web: services.vsac.org

Summary To provide financial assistance for child care to single parents in Vermont who wish to improve their education or skills.

Eligibility Applicants must be Vermont residents, single parents with primary custody of at least 1 child 12 years of age or younger, able to demonstrate financial need, and enrolled in a full- or part-time degree program at an approved postsecondary school. Along with their application, they must submit 1) a 100-word essay on any significant barriers that limit their access to education; 2) a 250-word essay on their short- and long-term academic, educational, career, vocational, and/or employment goals; and 3) a 100-word essay on how the program in which they will be enrolled will enhance their career or vocation. Selection is based on their essays, a letter of recommendation, financial need (expected family contribution of $23,760 or less), and a personal interview.

Financial data The maximum stipend is $2,000; funds must be used to pay for child care services while the recipient attends an approved postsecondary institution.

Duration 1 year; recipients may reapply.

Additional information This program is sponsored by U.S. Senator James Jeffords and the Federal Executives' Association.

Number awarded 1 or 2 each year.

Deadline March of each year.

[101]
BERTA LEE WHITE SCHOLARSHIPS

Mississippi Farm Bureau Federation
Attn: Coordinator of Women's Programs
6311 Ridgewood Road
P.O. Box 1972
Jackson, MS 39215-1972
(601) 977-4245   Toll Free: (800) 227-8244
E-mail: cbilbo@msfb.com
Web: www.msfb.org/Member_Benefits/scholarships.aspx

Summary To provide financial assistance to female members of the Mississippi Farm Bureau who are majoring in agriculture at a community college or university in Mississippi.

Eligibility This program is open to female members of the Farm Bureau (and members of Farm Bureau families) who have already completed their freshman year in an agriculture major at a university or community college in Mississippi. Applicants must submit 1) an essay of 250 to 300 words on what they will contribute to the field of agriculture; and 2) an essay of 150 to 200 words on why they need a scholarship. Selection is based on the essays (10%), financial need (40%), academic performance (20%), school and community activities (10%), leadership qualities (10%), and letters of recommendation (10%).

Financial data The stipend is $3,000. Funds are paid directly to the recipient's school in 2 installments; the second payment is released only if the recipient maintains a GPA of 2.5 or higher in the first semester.

Duration 1 year.

Number awarded 4 each year.

Deadline May of each year.

[102]
BERTHA PITTS CAMPBELL SCHOLARSHIP PROGRAM

Delta Sigma Theta Sorority, Inc.
Attn: Scholarship and Standards Committee Chair
1707 New Hampshire Avenue, N.W.
Washington, DC 20009
(202) 986-2400   Fax: (202) 986-2513
E-mail: dstemail@deltasigmatheta.org
Web: www.deltasigmatheta.org

Summary To provide financial assistance to members of Delta Sigma Theta who are working on an undergraduate or graduate degree in education.

Eligibility This program is open to current undergraduate and graduate students who are working on a degree in education. Applicants must be active, dues-paying members of Delta Sigma Theta. Selection is based on meritorious achievement.

Financial data The stipends range from $1,000 to $2,000. The funds may be used to cover tuition, fees, and living expenses.

Duration 1 year; may be renewed for 1 additional year.

Additional information This sponsor is a traditionally-African American social sorority. The application fee is $20.

Number awarded 1 or more each year.

Deadline March of each year.

[103]
BESSIE BARROW MEMORIAL FOUNDATION SCHOLARSHIPS

Baptist Convention of Maryland/Delaware
Attn: United Baptist Women of Maryland, Inc.
10255 Old Columbia Road
Columbia, MD 21046
(410) 290-5290   Toll Free: (800) 466-5290
E-mail: gparker@bcmd.org
Web: www.bcmd.org/wmu

Summary To provide financial assistance to women who are members of Baptist churches associated with an affiliate of United Baptist Women of Maryland and interested in working on an undergraduate degree at a college in any state.

Eligibility This program is open to women who are enrolled or planning to enroll full time at an accredited college or university in any state to work on an undergraduate degree in any field. Applicants must be a member in good standing of a Baptist church associated with an affiliate of United Baptist Women of Maryland. They must have a grade average of "C" or higher and be able to demonstrate financial need. Along with their application, they must submit brief statements on their Christian experience, school activities, church and community activities, and career goals.

Financial data A stipend is awarded (amount not specified).

Duration 1 year.

Number awarded Varies each year.

Deadline June of each year.

[104]
BETTY HANSEN NATIONAL SCHOLARSHIPS

Danish Sisterhood of America
c/o Connie Schell, Scholarship Chair
246 Foster Road
Fort Covington, NY 12937
(518) 358-4686
E-mail: vicepresident@danishsisterhood.com
Web: www.danishsisterhood.org/scholarships-grants.html

Summary To provide financial assistance for educational purposes in the United States or Denmark to members or relatives of members of the Danish Sisterhood of America.

Eligibility This program is open to members or the family of members of the sisterhood who are interested in attending an accredited 4-year college or university as a full-time undergraduate or graduate student. Members must have belonged to the sisterhood for at least 1 year. They must have a GPA of 2.5 or higher. Selection is based on academics (including ACT or SAT scores), academic awards or honors, other special recognition and awards, employment record, special talents or hobbies, and participation in Danish Sisterhood and other civic activities. Upon written request, the scholarship may be used for study in Denmark.

Financial data The stipend is $1,000 per year.

Duration 1 year; may be renewed 1 additional year.

Number awarded Up to 8 each year.

Deadline February of each year.

[105]
BETTY LOU BAILEY SWE REGION F SCHOLARSHIP

Society of Women Engineers
Attn: Scholarship Selection Committee
203 North LaSalle Street, Suite 1675
Chicago, IL 60601-1269
(312) 596-5223   Toll Free: (877) SWE-INFO
Fax: (312) 644-8557   E-mail: scholarships@swe.org
Web: societyofwomenengineers.swe.org

Summary To provide financial assistance to members of the Society of Women Engineers (SWE) working on an undergraduate or graduate degree in engineering or computer science at a school in its Region F (New England and upstate New York).

Eligibility This program is open to members of the society who will be sophomores, juniors, seniors, or graduate students at ABET-accredited colleges and universities. First preference is given to applicants who attend college or graduate school in the New England states or upstate New York; second preference is given to students who reside in New England or upstate New York. Applicants must be working full time on a degree in computer science or engineering and have a GPA of 3.0 or higher. Financial need is considered in the selection process. U.S. citizenship is required.

Financial data The stipend is $1,500.

Duration 1 year.

Number awarded 1 each year.

Deadline February of each year.

[106]
BETTY MCKERN SCHOLARSHIP

Association for Iron and Steel Technology-Midwest
  Chapter
c/o Leroy Campbell, Scholarship Chair
ArcelorMittal Indiana Harbor
3210 Watling Street
East Chicago, IN 46312
(219) 399-5767 E-mail: leroy.campbell@arcelormittal.com
Web: www.aist.org

Summary To provide financial assistance to women who are members or dependents of members of the Midwest Chapter of the Association for Iron and Steel Technology (AIST) and plan to study engineering at a college in any state to prepare for a career in the iron and steel industry.

Eligibility This program is open to women who are members or dependents of members of the AIST Midwest Chapter and are graduating high school seniors or currently enrolled full time in the first, second, or third year at an accredited college or university in any state. Applicants must be studying or planning to study engineering and have an interest in preparing for a career in the iron and steel industry. Along with their application, they must submit a letter of recommendation, a current transcript (including SAT/ACT scores), a resume that includes their work experience and extracurricular activities, and a 1- to 2-page essay describing their objectives for college and career. Selection is based on merit.

Financial data The stipend is $3,000.

Duration   1 year.

Additional information   The AIST was formed in 2004 by the merger of the Iron and Steel Society (ISS) and the Association of Iron and Steel Engineers (AISE). The Midwest Chapter replaced the former AISE Chicago Section in northern Illinois and northwestern Indiana and includes the states of Wisconsin, Minnesota, Iowa, Nebraska, South Dakota, and North Dakota.

Number awarded   1 each year.

Deadline   March of each year.

[107]
BETTY RENDEL SCHOLARSHIPS

National Federation of Republican Women
Attn: Scholarship Coordinator
124 North Alfred Street
Alexandria, VA 22314-3011
(703) 548-9688   Fax: (703) 548-9836
E-mail: mail@nfrw.org
Web: www.nfrw.org/rendel

Summary   To provide financial assistance to undergraduate Republican women who are majoring in political science, government, or economics.

Eligibility   This program is open to women who have completed at least 2 years of college. Applicants must be majoring in political science, government, or economics. Along with their application, they must submit 3 letters of recommendation, an official transcript, a 1-page essay on why they should be considered for the scholarship, and a 1-page essay on career goals. Applications must be submitted to the Republican federation president in the applicant's state. Each president chooses 1 application from her state to submit for scholarship consideration. Financial need is not a factor in the selection process. U.S. citizenship is required.

Financial data   The stipend is $1,000.

Duration   1 year; nonrenewable.

Additional information   This program began in 1995.

Number awarded   3 each year.

Deadline   Applications must be submitted to the state federation president by May of each year.

[108]
BETTYE MOSS POWERS SCHOLARSHIP

Tennessee Baptist Convention
Attn: WMU Scholarships
330 Seven Springs Way
P.O. Box 728
Brentwood, TN 37024-9728
(615) 371-7919   Toll Free: (800) 558-2090, ext. 7919
Fax: (615) 371-2014   E-mail: jheath@tnbaptist.org
Web: www.tnbaptist.org

Summary   To provide financial assistance to members of Baptist churches in Tennessee who have been active in Baptist mission programs and are enrolled as upper-division students at a college in the state.

Eligibility   This program is open to members and active participants in a Tennessee Baptist church who are enrolled full time as upper-division undergraduates at a college or university in the state to prepare for a career in missions. Applicants must show evidence of participation in Tennessee Baptist missions programs, Baptist collegiate ministries, and Ten-

nessee Baptist ministry. They must have a GPA of 2.6 or higher and be able to demonstrate financial need. Preference is given to women, but men may be considered if no women apply.

Financial data   A stipend is awarded (amount not specified).

Duration   1 year.

Number awarded   1 or more each year.

Deadline   January of each year.

[109]
BEV GRANGER SCHOLARSHIP

Women's Southern California Golf Association
Attn: Foundation
402 West Arrow Highway, Suite 10
San Dimas, CA 91773
(909) 592-1281, ext. 212   Fax: (909) 592-7542
E-mail: info@wscgafoundation.org
Web: www.wscgafoundation.com/scholarships.php

Summary   To provide financial assistance to women in southern California who play golf and are interested in working on an undergraduate degree in biology, nursing, or premedicine at a college in any state.

Eligibility   This program is open to female residents of southern California who play golf and are enrolled or planning to enroll full time at an accredited college or university in any state. Applicants must be interested in working on an associate or bachelor's degree in biological sciences, nursing, or a pre-medical field. They must have a GPA of 3.2 or higher. Along with their application, they must submit information on their family financial situation and an essay of up to 1,000 words on why they selected their major, their relevant academic and professional experience to date, and how golf and other sports (if applicable) will remain an integral part of their undergraduate experience.

Financial data   A stipend is awarded (amount not specified).

Duration   1 year.

Number awarded   1 or more each year.

Deadline   May of each year.

[110]
BILL HUNSBERGER SCHOLARSHIP FUND

Community Foundation of Greater Jackson
525 East Capitol Street, Suite 5B
Jackson, MS 39201
(601) 974-6044   Fax: (601) 974-6045
E-mail: info@cfgj.org
Web: www.cfgj.org/scholarships.html

Summary   To provide financial assistance to women studying journalism or political science at designated universities in Mississippi.

Eligibility   This program is open to women entering their junior or senior year of full-time study. The award rotates among students majoring in journalism at the University of Southern Mississippi, journalism at the University of Mississippi, and political science involved with student media at Mississippi State University.

Financial data   The stipend is $2,000.

Duration   1 year.

Number awarded 1 each year.
Deadline April of each year.

[111]
BILLINGS CHAPTER AFWA WOMEN IN TRANSITION SCHOLARSHIP

Accounting and Financial Women's Alliance-Billings
Chapter
Attn: Scholarship Chair
P.O. Box 20593
Billings, MT 59104-0593
E-mail: aswabillings@gmail.com
Web: www.billingsafwa.org/scholarship

Summary To provide financial assistance to women who are returning to colleges or universities in Montana to work on a degree in accounting.

Eligibility This program is open to women who have a gap of at least 4 years between high school and college or in college attendance. Applicants must be working on a degree in accounting or finance at a college or university in Montana. They must have a GPA of 3.0 or higher. Along with their application, they must submit an essay of 150 to 250 words on their career goals and objectives, the impact they want to have on the accounting world, their community involvement, extracurricular activities, applicable and current work experience, and leadership. Selection is based on that essay, leadership, character, scholastic average, communication skills, community service, extracurricular activities, and financial need.

Financial data A stipend is awarded (amount not specified).

Duration 1 year.

Number awarded 1 each year.

Deadline February of each year.

[112]
BIRMINGHAM SECTION SWE SCHOLARSHIP

Society of Women Engineers-Birmingham Section
c/o Shunna Cannon, Outreach Chair
P.O. Box 361311
Birmingham, AL 35236
E-mail: smcannon@southernco.com
Web: www.swebham.org/page-979915

Summary To provide financial assistance to female high school seniors planning to study engineering at a college or university in Alabama.

Eligibility This program is open to women graduating from high schools in any state and planning to enter a college or university in Alabama that has an ABET-accredited engineering program. Applicants must submit an essay about their career goals and why they need this scholarship. Selection is based on that essay (10 points); SAT or ACT test scores (10 points); GPA, honors received, and early college courses completed (10 points); high school science and mathematics courses completed by date of graduation (10 points); leadership and extracurricular activities (10 points); community and civic activities and employment (10 points); communication skills (10 points); and financial need (5 points). U.S. citizenship or permanent resident status is required.

Financial data The stipend is $1,000.

Duration 1 year.

Number awarded Varies each year; recently, 3 were awarded.

Deadline July of each year.

[113]
B.J. HARROD SCHOLARSHIPS

Society of Women Engineers
Attn: Scholarship Selection Committee
203 North LaSalle Street, Suite 1675
Chicago, IL 60601-1269
(312) 596-5223   Toll Free: (877) SWE-INFO
Fax: (312) 644-8557   E-mail: scholarships@swe.org
Web: societyofwomenengineers.swe.org

Summary To provide financial assistance to women who will be entering college as freshmen and are interested in studying engineering or computer science.

Eligibility This program is open to women who are entering college as freshmen. Applicants must be planning to enroll full time at an ABET-accredited 4-year college or university and major in computer science, engineering technology, or engineering. Selection is based on merit.

Financial data The stipend is $1,500.

Duration 1 year.

Additional information This program began in 1998.

Number awarded 2 each year.

Deadline May of each year.

[114]
B.K. KRENZER MEMORIAL REENTRY SCHOLARSHIP

Society of Women Engineers
Attn: Scholarship Selection Committee
203 North LaSalle Street, Suite 1675
Chicago, IL 60601-1269
(312) 596-5223   Toll Free: (877) SWE-INFO
Fax: (312) 644-8557   E-mail: scholarships@swe.org
Web: societyofwomenengineers.swe.org

Summary To provide financial assistance to women interested in returning to college or graduate school to study engineering or computer science.

Eligibility This program is open to women who are planning to enroll at an ABET-accredited 4-year college or university. Applicants must have been out of the engineering workforce and school for at least 2 years and must be planning to return as an undergraduate or graduate student to work on a degree in computer science or engineering. Selection is based on merit. Preference is given to engineers who already have a degree and are planning to reenter the engineering workforce after a period of temporary retirement.

Financial data The stipend is $2,500.

Duration 1 year.

Additional information This program began in 1996.

Number awarded 1 each year.

Deadline February of each year.

[115]
BMBG/JANIE WULKAN MEMORIAL SCHOLARSHIP

American Public Transportation Association
Attn: American Public Transportation Foundation
1666 K Street, N.W., Suite 1100
Washington, DC 20006
(202) 496-4803   Fax: (202) 496-4323
E-mail: pboswell@apta.com
Web: www.aptfd.org/Pages/default.aspx

Summary   To provide financial assistance to undergraduate and graduate women who are preparing for a career in the public transportation industry.

Eligibility   This program is open to female sophomores, juniors, seniors, and graduate students who are preparing for a career in the transit industry. Any member organization of the American Public Transportation Association (APTA) can nominate and sponsor candidates for this scholarship. Nominees must be enrolled in a fully-accredited institution, have and maintain at least a 3.0 GPA, and be either employed by or demonstrate a strong interest in entering the business administration or management area of the public transportation industry. They must submit a 1,000-word essay on the topic, "In what segment of the public transportation industry will you make a career and why?" Selection is based on demonstrated interest in the transit field as a career, need for financial assistance, academic achievement, essay content and quality, and involvement in extracurricular citizenship and leadership activities.

Financial data   The stipend is $2,500.

Duration   1 year; may be renewed.

Additional information   This program is sponsored by the Business Member Board of Governors (BMBG) of the American Public Transportation Association.

Number awarded   1 each year.

Deadline   June of each year.

[116]
BOB RAPP MEMORIAL ASA SCHOLARSHIP

Oregon Amateur Softball Association
c/o Marissa Boman, Scholarship Committee Chair
14160 S.E. Oatfield Road
Milwaukie, OR 97267
(503) 709-1642   E-mail: Marissaboman18@gmail.com
Web: www.oregon-asa.com/rapp

Summary   To provide financial assistance to female high school seniors in Oregon who have played softball and plan to attend college in any state.

Eligibility   This program is open to female seniors graduating from high schools in Oregon who plan to attend a college or university in any state. Applicants must have played for an American Softball Association (ASA) team at some time. Along with their application, they must submit an essay on how ASA softball impacted their life. Financial need is not considered in the selection process.

Financial data   Stipends are $1,000 or $500.

Duration   1 year.

Number awarded   4 each year: 2 at $1,000 and 2 at $500.

Deadline   June of each year.

[117]
BOBBI MCCALLUM MEMORIAL SCHOLARSHIP

Seattle Foundation
Attn: Scholarship Administrator
1200 Fifth Avenue, Suite 1300
Seattle, WA 98101-3151
(206) 515-2119   Fax: (206) 622-7673
E-mail: scholarships@seattlefoundation.org
Web: www.washboard.org

Summary   To provide financial assistance to women college students in Washington who are interested in preparing for a career in journalism.

Eligibility   This program is open to female residents of Washington who are entering their junior or senior year and studying print journalism at a 4-year public college or university in the state. Applicants must submit 5 samples of news writing (published or unpublished); brief essays on topics related to their interest in journalism; 2 letters of recommendation; and documentation of financial need. Selection is based on need, talent, and motivation to prepare for a career in print journalism.

Financial data   The stipend is $5,000 per year.

Duration   1 year; may be renewed.

Additional information   This scholarship was established in 1970 by the late Dr. Walter Scott Brown in memory of Bobbi McCallum, a prizewinning reporter and columnist for the *Seattle Post-Intelligencer* who died in 1969 at age 25 while a patient of Dr. Brown. The scholarship was administered by the newspaper until it suspended publication in 2010 and the program was transferred to the Seattle Foundation.

Number awarded   6 each year.

Deadline   March of each year.

[118]
BOEING COMPANY CAREER ENHANCEMENT SCHOLARSHIP

Women in Aviation International
Attn: Scholarships
Morningstar Airport
3647 State Route 503 South
West Alexandria, OH 45381-9354
(937) 839-4647   Fax: (937) 839-4645
E-mail: scholarships@wai.org
Web: www.wai.org

Summary   To provide financial assistance to members of Women in Aviation International (WAI) who are active in aerospace and need financial support to advance their career.

Eligibility   This program is open to WAI members who wish to advance their career in the aerospace industry in the fields of engineering, technology development, or management. Applicants may be 1) full-time or part-time employees working in the aerospace industry or a related field; or 2) students working on an aviation-related degree who are at least sophomores and have a GPA of 2.5 or higher. Along with their application, they must submit a 500-word essay and professional resume that include their aviation history and goals, what they have done for themselves to achieve their goals, where they see themselves in 5 and 10 years, involvement in aviation activities, how the scholarship will help them achieve their objectives, and their present financial need.

Financial data   The stipend is $2,500.

Duration 1 year.

Additional information WAI is a nonprofit professional organization dedicated to encouraging women to consider an aviation career and to providing educational outreach activities and networking resources to women active in the industry. This program is sponsored by the Boeing Company.

Number awarded 2 each year.

Deadline November of each year.

[119]
BONITA JEAN OLSON MEMORIAL SCHOLARSHIP

Women in Aviation International
Attn: Scholarships
Morningstar Airport
3647 State Route 503 South
West Alexandria, OH 45381-9354
(937) 839-4647   Fax: (937) 839-4645
E-mail: scholarships@wai.org
Web: www.wai.org

Summary To provide financial assistance to members of Women in Aviation International (WAI) who are working on a college degree in a field related to science, technology, engineering, or mathematics (STEM).

Eligibility This program is open to WAI members who are currently enrolled at an accredited 2- or 4-year college or university, technical institute, or certificate program. Applicants must be preparing for a career in a field of STEM related to aviation or aerospace. They must have experience volunteering in STEM or aviation-related events and/or WAI activities in the previous year. Along with their application, they must submit a 500-word essay and professional resume that include their aviation history and goals, what they have done for themselves to achieve their goals, where they see themselves in 5 and 10 years, involvement in aviation activities, how the scholarship will help them achieve their objectives, and their present financial need. The sponsor defines STEM fields to include air traffic controller, avionics technician, dispatch certification, aircraft mechanic, meteorologist, or educator for STEM. Preference is given to applicants from the Seattle area of Washington, but all WAI members are eligible.

Financial data The stipend is $3,000. Funds are paid directly to an accredited program or institution and may be applied to tuition, books, or laboratory fees. They may not be used for housing, transportation, flight training, meals, or incidental expenses.

Duration 1 year.

Additional information WAI is a nonprofit professional organization dedicated to encouraging women to consider an aviation career and to providing educational outreach activities and networking resources to women active in the industry.

Number awarded 1 each year.

Deadline November of each year.

[120]
BOSTON SCIENTIFIC SCHOLARSHIPS

Society of Women Engineers
Attn: Scholarship Selection Committee
203 North LaSalle Street, Suite 1675
Chicago, IL 60601-1269
(312) 596-5223   Toll Free: (877) SWE-INFO
Fax: (312) 644-8557   E-mail: scholarships@swe.org
Web: societyofwomenengineers.swe.org

Summary To provide financial assistance to upper-division women majoring in computer science or designated engineering specialties at designated universities.

Eligibility This program is open to women who are entering their senior year at a designated ABET-accredited college or university. Applicants must be working full time on a degree in computer science or chemical, computer, electrical, industrial, manufacturing, materials, or mechanical engineering and have a GPA of 3.5 or higher. Selection is based on merit.

Financial data The stipend is $5,000.

Duration 1 year.

Additional information This program, established in 2004, is supported by Boston Scientific Corporation. The designated colleges and universities are California Polytechnic State University at San Luis Obispo, Case Western Reserve, Duke, Florida A&M, Iowa State, M.I.T., and Michigan Technological University.

Number awarded 2 each year.

Deadline February of each year.

[121]
BOX ENGINEERING DIVERSITY SCHOLARSHIP

Box, Inc.
Attn: Scholarship
4440 El Camino Real
Los Altos, CA 94022
Toll Free: (877) 729-4269   E-mail: scholarship@box.com
Web: www.boxdiversityscholarship.com

Summary To provide financial assistance to college students majoring in designated fields of technology who are members of groups underrepresented in those fields.

Eligibility This program is open to U.S. citizens currently enrolled as sophomores or juniors at a 4-year college or university who are majoring in science, engineering, information technology, mathematics, or a related field. Applicants must identify with an underrepresented minority (e.g., female, LGBT, Hispanic, African American, or Native American). Finalists are invited to the sponsor's headquarters in Los Altos, California.

Financial data Stipends are $20,000 or $4,000.

Duration 1 year.

Number awarded 1 at $20,000 and 4 at $4,000 each year.

Deadline October of each year.

[122]
BPW/MAINE CONTINUING EDUCATION SCHOLARSHIP

Maine Federation of Business and Professional Women's Clubs
Attn: BPW/Maine Futurama Foundation
c/o Marilyn V. Ladd, Office Manager
103 County Road
Oakland, ME 04963
Web: www.bpwmefoundation.org/scholarship-program

Summary To provide financial assistance to women in Maine who are attending college in any state.

Eligibility This program is open to women who are residents of Maine. Applicants must have completed at least 1 year of college or an accredited training program in any state requiring attendance for more than a year. They must have a definite plan to complete the educational program, regardless of whether it leads to an associate or bachelor's degree or other certificate. Along with their application, they must submit a statement describing their educational, personal, and career goals, including their financial need. Preference is given to members of Maine Federation of Business and Professional Women's Clubs.

Financial data The stipend is $1,200.

Duration 1 year.

Number awarded 1 or more each year.

Deadline April of each year.

[123]
BPW/WA MEMBER SCHOLARSHIP

Washington State Business and Professional Women's Foundation
Attn: Sue Tellock, Scholarship Committee Chair
1914 N.W. 87th Circle
Vancouver, WA 98665
Web: www.bpwwafoundation.org/scholarships

Summary To provide financial assistance to members of the Washington State Federation of Business and Professional Women (BPW/WA) who are interested in further education to enhance their career or potential.

Eligibility This program is open to women who have been residents of Washington for 2 or more years and have been accepted into a program or course of study at an accredited school in the state. Applicants must be current BPW/WA members. They must be able to demonstrate scholastic ability and financial need. Along with their application, they must submit a 500-word essay on their specific short-term goals and how the proposed training will help them accomplish those goals and make a difference in their professional career. U.S. citizenship is required.

Financial data The stipend is $1,000.

Duration 1 year.

Number awarded 1 or more each year.

Deadline May of each year.

[124]
BPW/WA PAST PRESIDENT MEMORIAL SCHOLARSHIP

Washington State Business and Professional Women's Foundation
Attn: Sue Tellock, Scholarship Committee Chair
1914 N.W. 87th Circle
Vancouver, WA 98665
Web: www.bpwwafoundation.org/scholarships

Summary To provide financial assistance to mature women in Washington who are interested in continuing their education.

Eligibility This program is open to women who have been residents of Washington for 2 or more years and have been accepted into a program or course of study at an accredited school in the state. Applicants must be 30 years of age or older. They must be able to demonstrate scholastic ability and financial need. Along with their application, they must submit a 500-word essay on their specific short-term goals and how the proposed training will help them accomplish those goals and make a difference in their professional career. U.S. citizenship is required.

Financial data The stipend is $1,000.

Duration 1 year.

Number awarded 1 or more each year.

Deadline May of each year.

[125]
BPW-IOWA FOUNDATION SCHOLARSHIP

Business and Professional Women of Iowa Foundation
c/o DiAnne Lerud-Chubb, Scholarship Chair
2429 Gnahn Street
Burlington, IA 52601
(319) 759-3896   E-mail: lerud2@mchsi.com
Web: www.bpw-iowa.org/bpw-iowa-foundation-scholarship

Summary To provide financial assistance for college to nontraditional students who reside in Iowa.

Eligibility Applicants must be Iowa residents (although they may be currently attending school in another state) who have completed at least 1 year of education beyond high school. They must be nontraditional students who 1) have been out of the workforce and need additional education to go back to work or 2) completed high school 5 or more years ago and now want to restart their college education. Along with their application, they must submit essays on why they think they should receive this scholarship and how they expect to use the training. Selection is based on academic ability, leadership skills, career goals, and financial need. U.S. citizenship is required.

Financial data The stipend is $1,000. Funds are sent directly to the recipient's school.

Duration 1 year.

Number awarded Varies each year; recently, 4 were awarded.

Deadline March of each year.

[126]
BRADFORD GRANT-IN-AID

Delta Kappa Gamma Society International-Delta State
 Organization
c/o Gwen Simmons, Scholarship Committee Chair
P.O. Box 277
Point Lookout, MO 65726
E-mail: gwensimmons@suddenlink.net
Web: www.dkgmissouri.com/resources.html

Summary To provide financial assistance to upper-division women who are residents of Missouri and attending college in any state to prepare for a career in education.

Eligibility This program is open to female residents of Missouri who are preparing for a career in education through a teacher preparation program at a college or university in any state. Applicants must have completed at least 75 college hours. Preference is given to relatives (e.g., daughter, granddaughter, niece, sister) of members of Delta Kappa Gamma (an honorary society of women educators). Financial need is not considered in the selection process.

Financial data The stipend is $1,000.

Duration 1 year.

Number awarded Up to 2 each year.

Deadline February of each year.

[127]
BRILL FAMILY SCHOLARSHIP

Society of Women Engineers
Attn: Scholarship Selection Committee
203 North LaSalle Street, Suite 1675
Chicago, IL 60601-1269
(312) 596-5223   Toll Free: (877) SWE-INFO
Fax: (312) 644-8557   E-mail: scholarships@swe.org
Web: societyofwomenengineers.swe.org

Summary To provide financial assistance to undergraduate women majoring in designated engineering specialties.

Eligibility This program is open to women who are entering their sophomore, junior, or senior year at an ABET-accredited 4-year college or university. Applicants must be working full time on a degree in computer science or aeronautical or biomedical engineering. Selection is based on merit.

Financial data The stipend is $1,500.

Duration 1 year.

Number awarded 1 each year.

Deadline February of each year.

[128]
BUFTON FAMILY MEMORIAL SCHOLARSHIP

American Business Women's Association
Attn: Stephen Bufton Memorial Educational Fund
9820 Metcalf Avenue, Suite 110
Overland Park, KS 66212
Toll Free: (800) 228-0007
Web: www.sbmef.org

Summary To provide financial assistance to women who are interested in working on an undergraduate degree in a field of science, technology, engineering, or mathematics (STEM).

Eligibility This program is open to women who are entering at least their sophomore year with a major in a field of STEM at an accredited college or university. Applicants must submit a 250-word biographical sketch that includes information about their background, activities, honors, work experience, and long-term educational and professional goals. They must have a GPA of 3.0 or higher. Financial need is not considered in the selection process. U.S. citizenship is required.

Financial data The stipend is $6,500. Funds are paid directly to the recipient's institution to be used only for tuition, books, and fees.

Duration 1 year; nonrenewable.

Number awarded 1 each year.

Deadline May of each year.

[129]
BUICK ACHIEVERS SCHOLARSHIP PROGRAM

Scholarship America
Attn: Scholarship Management Services
One Scholarship Way
P.O. Box 297
St. Peter, MN 56082
(507) 931-1682   Toll Free: (866) 243-4644
Fax: (507) 931-9168
E-mail: buickachievers@scholarshipamerica.org
Web: www.buickachievers.com

Summary To provide financial assistance to entering and continuing college students planning to major in specified fields related to engineering, design, or business.

Eligibility This program is open to high school seniors and graduates who are enrolled or planning to enroll full time at an accredited 4-year college or university as first-time freshmen or continuing undergraduates. Applicants must be interested in majoring in fields of engineering (chemical, computer, controls, electrical, energy, environmental, industrial, manufacturing, materials, mechanical, plastic/polymers, or software); technology (automotive technology, computer information systems, computer science, engineering technology, information technology, mechatronics); design (automotive, fine arts, graphic, industrial, product, transportation); or business (accounting, business administration, economics, ergonomics, finance, human resources, industrial hygiene, international business, labor and industrial relations, management information systems, marketing, mathematics, occupational health and safety, production management, statistics, or supply chain/logistics). U.S. citizenship or permanent resident status is required. Selection is based on academic achievement, financial need, participation and leadership in community and school activities, work experience, and interest in preparing for a career in the automotive or related industry. Special consideration is given to first-generation college students, women, minorities, military veterans, and dependents of military personnel.

Financial data Stipends are $25,000 per year.

Duration 1 year; may be renewed up to 3 additional years (and 1 additional year for students in a 5-year engineering program), provided the recipient remains enrolled full time, maintains a GPA of 3.0 or higher, and continues to major in an eligible field.

Additional information This program, which began in 2011, is funded by the General Motors Foundation.

Number awarded 100 each year.

Deadline February of each year.

[130]
BUSINESS AND PROFESSIONAL WOMEN'S FOUNDATION OF MARYLAND SCHOLARSHIP

Business and Professional Women of Maryland
Attn: BPW Foundation of Maryland
c/o Joyce Draper, Chief Financial Officer
615 Fairview Avenid
Frederick, MD 21701
Web: www.bpwmaryland.org/bpwmd.asp

Summary To provide financial assistance for college to mature women in Maryland.

Eligibility This program is open to women who are at least 25 years of age and who are interested in working on undergraduate studies to upgrade their skills for career advancement, to train for a new career field, or to reenter the job market. Applicants must be residents of Maryland or, if a resident of another state, a member of Business and Professional Women of Maryland. They must be U.S. citizens and have been accepted into an accredited program or course of study at a Maryland academic institution. Along with their application, they must submit a 200-word statement on how they expect the proposed training or education to add to their opportunities for advancement or employment. Selection is based on that statement, academic performance, work experience, community service, volunteer experience, and financial need.

Financial data The stipend is $1,400.

Duration 1 year.

Number awarded 1 or more each year.

Deadline April of each year.

[131]
BUSINESS WOMEN OF MISSOURI SCHOLARSHIPS

Business Women of Missouri Foundation, Inc.
Attn: Scholarship Committee Chair
P.O. Box 28243
Kansas City, MO 64188
(816) 333-6959   Fax: (816) 333-6959
E-mail: jo.mofedbpw@gmail.com
Web: www.businesswomenmo.org

Summary To provide financial assistance to women in Missouri who plan to attend college in any state.

Eligibility This program is open to women in Missouri who have been accepted into an accredited program or course of study in any state to upgrade their skills and/or complete education for career advancement. Along with their application, they must submit brief statements on the following: their achievements and/or specific recognitions in their field of endeavor; professional and/or civic affiliations; present and long-range career goals; how they plan to participate in and contribute to their community upon completion of their program of study; why they feel they would make a good recipient; and any special circumstances that may have influenced their ability to continue or complete their education. They must also demonstrate financial need and U.S. citizenship.

Financial data The stipend is $1,000.

Duration 1 year.

Additional information This program includes the Elizabeth Halpin Scholarship, the Hazel R. Kohring Women in Transition Scholarship, the Judge Hazel Palmer Memorial Scholarship, the Sue Panetti-Lee Scholarship, and the Phyllis Sanders Scholarship.

Number awarded Varies each year; recently, 11 were awarded.

Deadline January of each year.

[132]
BX "EXCELLENCE" WOMEN IN CONSTRUCTION SCHOLARSHIP

Associated General Contractors of South Dakota
Attn: Highway-Heavy-Utilities Chapter
300 East Capitol Avenue, Suite 1
Pierre, SD 57501
(605) 224-8689   Toll Free: (800) 242-6373
Fax: (605) 224-9915
Web: www.sdagc.org/workforce-development/scholarships

Summary To provide financial assistance to female residents of South Dakota who are interested in attending a college, university, or technical institute in any state to prepare for a career in a construction-related field.

Eligibility This program is open to female residents of South Dakota who are graduating high school seniors or students already enrolled at a college, university, or technical institute in any state. Applicants must be preparing for a career in a construction-related field. Along with their application, they must submit a brief essay that covers why they are interested in a career in the construction industry, the event or series of events that led them to that decision, and their career objectives. They must be sponsored by a member of the Associated General Contractors of South Dakota. Financial need is considered in the selection process.

Financial data The stipend is $1,000 or $1,500.

Duration 1 year.

Number awarded Varies each year; recently, 2 were awarded: 1 at $1,500 and 1 at $1,000.

Deadline April of each year.

[133]
CABELA'S WOMEN IN LEADERSHIP SCHOLARSHIP

Harry and Reba Huge Foundation
25 East Battery Street
Charleston, SC 29401-2740
(843) 718-3119
E-mail: jack.siemsen@thehugefoundation.org
Web: www.thehugefoundation.org/scholarships

Summary To provide financial assistance to female high school seniors in Nebraska who plan to attend college in any state.

Eligibility This program is open to women graduating from high schools in Nebraska and planning to enroll at a college or university in any state. Applicants must submit 1-page essays on the following topics: 1) the single most important event in their lives; and 2) what they regard as the most pressing problem facing Nebraska today and why. The program includes some scholarships for women who are eligible for federal Pell Grants.

Financial data The stipend is $2,500 per year.

Duration 1 year; may be renewed up to 3 additional years, provided the recipient maintains a GPA of 3.0 or higher.

Additional information This program is sponsored by Cabela's Incorporated, World's Foremost Bank, and the Harry and Reba Huge Foundation.

Number awarded 4 each year, of which 2 are reserved for students who are eligible for federal Pell Grants.

Deadline January of each year.

[134]
CADY McDONNELL MEMORIAL SCHOLARSHIP

National Society of Professional Surveyors
Attn: Scholarships
5119 Pegasus Court, Suite Q
Frederick, MD 21704
(240) 439-4615, ext. 105   Fax: (240) 439-4952
E-mail: trisha.milbun@nsps.us.com
Web: www.nsps.us.com/?page=Scholarships

Summary To provide financial assistance for undergraduate study in surveying to female members of the National Society of Professional Surveyors (NSPS) from designated western states.

Eligibility This program is open to women who are NSPS members and enrolled full or part time at a 2- or 4-year college or university in any state. Applicants must be residents of Alaska, Arizona, California, Colorado, Hawaii, Idaho, Montana, Nevada, New Mexico, Oregon, Utah, Washington, or Wyoming. They must be majoring in surveying or a closely-related program (e.g., mapping, surveying engineering, geographic information systems, geodetic science). Along with their application, they must submit a statement describing their educational objectives, future plans for study or research, professional activities, and financial need. Selection is based on that statement (30%), academic record (30%), letters of recommendation (20%), and professional activities (20%); if 2 or more applicants are judged equal based on those criteria, financial need might be considered.

Financial data The stipend is $2,000.

Duration 1 year.

Additional information This program was previously offered by the American Congress on Surveying and Mapping (ACSM), which merged with the NSPS in 2012.

Number awarded 1 each odd-numbered year.

Deadline April of each odd-numbered year.

[135]
CALIFORNIA JOB'S DAUGHTERS FOUNDATION SCHOLARSHIPS

California Job's Daughters Foundation
303 West Lincoln, Suite 210
Anaheim, CA 92805-2928
(714) 491-4994   Fax: (714) 991-6798
E-mail: Secretary@cajdfoundation.org
Web: www.cajdfoundation.org/Scholarships.html

Summary To provide financial assistance to members of the International Order of Job's Daughters in California who plan to attend college in any state.

Eligibility This program is open to members of Job's Daughters in good standing, active or majority, in California. Applicants may indicate their choice of an academic or vocational scholarship. Selection is based on scholastic standing,

Job's Daughters activities, the applicant's self-help plan, recommendations from the Executive Bethel Guardian Council, faculty recommendations, achievements outside of Job's Daughters, and financial need.

Financial data Stipends are $1,500, $1,000 or $500.

Duration 1 year; some of the scholarships may be renewed up to 3 additional years, but most are nonrenewable.

Number awarded Varies each year; recently, 18 were awarded: 4 at $1,500, 12 at $1,000 (of which 1 was renewable), and 2 at $500.

Deadline March of each year.

[136]
CALIFORNIA LEGION AUXILIARY PAST DEPARTMENT PRESIDENT'S JUNIOR SCHOLARSHIP

American Legion Auxiliary
Department of California
401 Van Ness Avenue, Suite 319
San Francisco, CA 94102-4570
(415) 861-5092   Fax: (415) 861-8365
E-mail: calegionaux@calegionaux.org
Web: www.calegionaux.org/scholarships.htm

Summary To provide financial assistance for college to the daughters and other female descendants of California veterans who are active in the American Legion Junior Auxiliary.

Eligibility This program is open to the daughters, granddaughters, and great- granddaughters of veterans who served during wartime. Applicants must be in their senior year at an accredited high school, must have been members of the Junior Auxiliary for at least 3 consecutive years, and must be residents of California (if eligibility for Junior Auxiliary membership is by a current member of the American Legion or Auxiliary in California, the applicant may reside elsewhere). They must be planning to attend college in California. Selection is based on scholastic merit (20%); active participation in Junior Auxiliary (15%); record of service or volunteerism within the applicant's community, school, and/or unit (35%); a brief description of the applicant's desire to pursue a higher education (15%); and 3 letters of reference (15%).

Financial data The stipend depends on the availability of funds but ranges from $300 to $1,000.

Duration 1 year.

Number awarded 1 each year.

Deadline April of each year.

[137]
CALIFORNIA P.E.O. SELECTED SCHOLARSHIPS

P.E.O. Foundation-California State Chapter
c/o Dee Zasio, Scholarship Selection Committee
21916 Strawberry Drive
Canyon Lake, CA 92587
E-mail: peoca.ssc@gmail.com
Web: www.peocalifornia.org

Summary To provide financial assistance to female residents of California attending college or graduate school in any state.

Eligibility This program is open to female residents of California who have completed 4 years of high school (or the equivalent); are enrolled at or accepted by an accredited college, university, vocational school, or graduate school in any state; and have an excellent academic record. Selection is based on financial need, character, academic ability, and school and community activities. Some awards include additional requirements. U.S. citizenship is required.

Financial data Stipends recently ranged from $400 to $2,500.

Duration 1 year; may be renewed for up to 3 additional years.

Additional information This program includes the following named scholarships: the Barbara Furse Mackey Scholarship (for women whose education has been interrupted); the Beverly Dye Anderson Scholarship (for the fields of teaching or health care); the Marjorie M. McDonald P.E.O. Scholarship (for women who are continuing their education after a long hiatus from school); the Ora Keck Scholarship (for women who are preparing for a career in music or the fine arts); the Phyllis J. Van Deventer Scholarship (for women who are preparing for a career in music performance or music education); the Jean Gower Scholarship (for women preparing for a career in education); the Helen D. Thompson Memorial Scholarship (for women studying music or fine arts); the Stella May Nau Scholarship (for women who are interested in reentering the job market); the Linda Jones Memorial Fine Arts Scholarship (for women studying fine arts); the Polly Thompson Memorial Music Scholarship (for women studying music); the Ruby W. Henry Scholarship; the Jean W. Gratiot Scholarship; the Pearl Prime Scholarship; the Helen Beardsley Scholarship; the Chapter GA Scholarship; and the Nearly New Scholarship.

Number awarded Varies each year; recently, 43 were awarded.

Deadline January of each year.

[138] CALTECH AMGEN SCHOLARS PROGRAM

California Institute of Technology
Attn: Student-Faculty Programs
1200 East California Boulevard
MailCode 330-87
Pasadena, CA 91125
(626) 395-2885   Fax: (626) 389-5467
E-mail: sfp@clatech.edu
Web: sfp.caltech.edu/programs/amgen_scholars

Summary To provide an opportunity for undergraduate students, especially those from diverse populations, to participate in biological and chemical summer research at the California Institute of Technology (Caltech).

Eligibility This program is open to sophomores, juniors, and non-graduating seniors at 4-year colleges and universities in the United States, Puerto Rico, and other U.S. territories. Applicants must be U.S. citizens or permanent residents who have a cumulative GPA of 3.2 or higher and an interest in preparing for a Ph.D. or M.D./Ph.D. They must be interested in working on a summer research project at Caltech in biology, chemistry, or biotechnical-related fields. Applications are encouraged from, but not limited to, underrepresented minorities, women, first-generation college students, geographically underrepresented students, educationally and financially disadvantaged students, and students with disabilities.

Financial data Scholars receive a stipend of $6,000, campus housing, a modest board allowance, and travel to and from Pasadena.

Duration 10 weeks during the summer.

Additional information This program serves as the Cal Tech component of the Amgen Scholars Program, which operates at 8 other U.S. universities (and the National Institutes of Health) and is funded by the Amgen Foundation.

Number awarded Varies each year.

Deadline February of each year.

[139] CAMMER-HILL GRANT

Wisconsin Women of Color Network, Inc.
c/o P.E. Kiram
756 North 35th Street, Suite 101
Milwaukee, WI 53208
(414) 899-2329   E-mail: pekiram64@gmail.com

Summary To provide financial assistance for vocation/technical school or community college to adult women of color from Wisconsin.

Eligibility This program is open to residents of Wisconsin who are adult women of color planning to continue their education at a vocational/technical school or community college in any state. Applicants must be a member of 1 of the following groups: African American, Asian, American Indian, or Hispanic. They must be able to demonstrate financial need. Along with their application, they must submit a 1-page essay on how this scholarship will help them accomplish their educational goal. U.S. citizenship is required.

Financial data A stipend is awarded (amount not specified).

Duration 1 year.

Additional information This program began in 1994.

Number awarded 1 each year.

Deadline May of each year.

[140] CAPTAIN FARIAH PETERSON SCHOLARSHIP

Organization of Black Aerospace Professionals, Inc.
Attn: Scholarship Coordinator
One Westbrook Corporate Center, Suite 300
Westchester, IL 60154
(708) 449-7755   Toll Free: (800) JET-OBAP
Fax: (708) 449-7754 E-mail: obapscholarships@obap.org
Web: www.obap.org/fariah-peterson-scholarship

Summary To provide financial assistance to female members of the Organization of Black Aerospace Professionals (OBAP) who are enrolled in a flight training program.

Eligibility This program is open to African American females who are OBAP members enrolled or entering a flight program to advance a rating, certificate, or degree. Applicants must have a GPA of 2.5 or higher. Along with their application, they must submit a 500-word essay on how this scholarship will help them achieve their goals.

Financial data The stipend is $7,000. Funds are paid directly to the recipient's college.

Duration 1 year.

Additional information The OBAP was originally established in 1976 as the Organization of Black Airline Pilots to make certain Blacks and other minorities had a group that would keep them informed about opportunities for advancement within commercial aviation.

Number awarded 1 each year.

Deadline May of each year.

[141]
CAPTAIN SALLY TOMPKINS NURSING AND APPLIED HEALTH SCIENCES SCHOLARSHIP

United Daughters of the Confederacy-Virginia Division
c/o Patt Graves, Second Vice President
838 Crymes Road
Keysville, VA 23947-2815
(434) 696-2202   E-mail: thebargthree@aol.com
Web: www.vaudc.org

Summary To provide financial assistance for college to women who are Confederate descendants from Virginia and working on a degree in nursing at a school in the state.

Eligibility This program is open to women residents of Virginia interested in working on a degree in nursing at a school in the state. Applicants must be 1) lineal descendants of Confederates; or 2) collateral descendants and members of the Children of the Confederacy or the United Daughters of the Confederacy. They must submit proof of the Confederate military record of at least 1 ancestor, with the company and regiment in which he served. They must also submit a personal letter pledging to make the best possible use of the scholarship; describing their health, social, family, religious, and fraternal connections within the community; and reflecting on what a Southern heritage means to them (using the term "War Between the States" in lieu of "Civil War"). They must have a GPA of 3.0 or higher and be able to demonstrate financial need.

Financial data The amount of the stipend depends on the availability of funds. Payment is made directly to the college or university the recipient attends.

Duration 1 year; may be renewed up to 3 additional years if the recipient maintains a GPA of 3.0 or higher.

Number awarded This scholarship is offered whenever a prior recipient graduates or is no longer eligible.

Deadline March of the years in which a scholarship is available.

[142]
CAR CARE COUNCIL WOMEN'S BOARD SCHOLARSHIPS

Car Care Council
Attn: Women's Board
7101 Wisconsin Avenue, Suite 1300
Bethesda, MD 20814
(301) 654-6664, ext. 1019
Web: www.automotivescholarships.com

Summary To provide financial assistance to women who are high school seniors or current technical students interested in studying automotive technology.

Eligibility This program is open to women interested in preparing for a career in the automotive technology industry. Applicants must be high school seniors planning to attend an ASE-certified postsecondary training program or students who have completed 1 year at an ASE-certified postsecondary training program. They must have a GPA of 2.5 or higher.

Financial data Stipends range from $1,000 to $5,000.

Duration 1 year.

Additional information This program includes 2 named $5,000 scholarship for current technical school students: the Becky Babcox Women's Board Scholarship and the Continental Female Leadership Scholarship.

Number awarded 8 each year: 4 to high school seniors (3 at $3,000 and 1 at $1,000) and 4 to students in technical schools (2 at $5,000, 1 at $4,000, and 1 at $3,000).

Deadline Deadline not specified.

[143]
CAREER EAGLES AVIATION SCHOLARSHIPS

Women in Aviation International
Attn: Scholarships
Morningstar Airport
3647 State Route 503 South
West Alexandria, OH 45381-9354
(937) 839-4647   Fax: (937) 839-4645
E-mail: scholarships@wai.org
Web: www.wai.org

Summary To provide financial assistance to members of Women in Aviation International (WAI) who are high school seniors working on a degree to prepare for a career as a professional pilot.

Eligibility This program is open to WAI members who are high school seniors planning to enroll in a baccalaureate program to prepare for a career as a professional pilot. Applicants must have a GPA of 3.0 or higher. Along with their application, they must submit 1) a 500-word essay and professional resume that include their aviation history and goals, what they have done for themselves to achieve their goals, where they see themselves in 5 and 10 years, involvement in aviation activities, how the scholarship will help them achieve their objectives, and their present financial need; and 2) an essay of 500 to 1,000 words on what has inspired them to prepare for a career as a professional pilot, their greatest life challenge and how it has enriched them, and why they are the most qualified candidate for this scholarship.

Financial data The stipend is $5,000. Funds are paid directly to the recipient's institution.

Duration Training must be completed within 1 year.

Additional information WAI is a nonprofit professional organization dedicated to encouraging women to consider an aviation career and to providing educational outreach activities and networking resources to women active in the industry. This program is sponsored by Career Eagles, the Ohio State University Center for Aviation Studies, the Knowlton Foundation, Youth Aviation Adventure, and the Experimental Aircraft Association.

Number awarded 2 each year.

Deadline November of each year.

[144]
CARLOZZI FAMILY SCHOLARSHIP

New York Women in Communications, Inc.
Attn: NYWICI Foundation
355 Lexington Avenue, 15th Floor
New York, NY 10017-6603
(212) 297-2133   Fax: (212) 370-9047
E-mail: nywicipr@nywici.org
Web: www.nywici.org/foundation/scholarships

Summary To provide financial assistance to female residents of designated eastern states who are working on an undergraduate degree in communications at a college in any state.

Eligibility This program is open to women who are residents of New York, New Jersey, Connecticut, or Pennsylvania and currently enrolled as undergraduates at a college or university in any state. Also eligible are women who reside outside the 4 states but are currently enrolled at a college or university within 1 of the 5 boroughs of New York City. All applicants must be working on a degree in a communications-related field (e.g., advertising, broadcasting, communications, digital media, English, film, journalism, marketing, public relations, publishing) and be an accomplished writer. They must have a GPA of 3.2 or higher. Along with their application, they must submit a 2-page resume; a personal essay of 300 words on an assigned topic that changes annually; 2 letters of recommendation; and an official transcript. Selection is based on academic record, need, demonstrated leadership, participation in school and community activities, honors and other awards or recognition, work experience, goals and aspirations, and unusual personal and/or family circumstances. U.S. citizenship or permanent resident status is required.

Financial data The stipend ranges up to $10,000.

Duration 1 year.

Number awarded 1 each year.

Deadline January of each year.

[145]
CAROL STEPHENS SWE REGION F SCHOLARSHIP

Society of Women Engineers
Attn: Scholarship Selection Committee
203 North LaSalle Street, Suite 1675
Chicago, IL 60601-1269
(312) 596-5223   Toll Free: (877) SWE-INFO
Fax: (312) 644-8557   E-mail: scholarships@swe.org
Web: societyofwomenengineers.swe.org

Summary To provide financial assistance to members of the Society of Women Engineers (SWE) working on an undergraduate or graduate degree in engineering or computer science at a school in its Region F (New England and upstate New York).

Eligibility This program is open to members of the society who will be sophomores, juniors, seniors, or graduate students at ABET-accredited colleges and universities. First preference is given to applicants who attend college or graduate school in the New England states or upstate New York; second preference is given to students who reside in New England or upstate New York. Applicants must be working full time on a degree in computer science or engineering. Financial need is considered in the selection process. U.S. citizenship is required.

Financial data The stipend is $1,250.

Duration 1 year.

Additional information This program began in 2012.

Number awarded 1 each year.

Deadline February of each year.

[146]
CAROLYN B. ELMAN NATIONAL UNDERGRADUATE SCHOLARSHIP

American Business Women's Association
Attn: Stephen Bufton Memorial Educational Fund
9820 Metcalf Roe Avenue, Suite 110
Overland Park, KS 66212
Toll Free: (800) 228-0007
Web: www.sbmef.org/National/index.cfm

Summary To provide financial assistance to female undergraduate students who are working on a degree in a specified field (the field changes each year).

Eligibility This program is open to women who have completed at least 60 credit hours of work on an undergraduate degree. Applicants are not required to be members of the American Business Women's Association. Along with their application, they must submit a 250-word biographical sketch that includes information about their background, activities, honors, work experience, and long-term educational and professional goals. Financial need is not considered in the selection process. Annually, the trustees designate an academic discipline for which the scholarship will be presented that year. U.S. citizenship is required.

Financial data The stipend is $10,000 per year. Funds are paid directly to the recipient's institution to be used only for tuition, books, and fees.

Duration 2 years.

Additional information This program began in 2011 as part of ABWA's Stephen Bufton Memorial Education Fund.

Number awarded 1 each odd-numbered year.

Deadline May of each odd-numbered year.

[147]
CATHOLIC DAUGHTERS OF THE AMERICAS CAMPUS COURT SCHOLARSHIP

Catholic Daughters of the Americas
Attn: Scholarship Chair
10 West 71st Street
New York, NY 10023
(212) 877-3041   Fax: (212) 724-5923
E-mail: CDofANatl@aol.com
Web: www.catholicdaughters.org

Summary To provide financial assistance for college to members of a Campus Court (local chapter) of the Catholic Daughters of the Americas.

Eligibility This program is open to students who are of the Catholic faith and enrolled at a college or university. Applicants must be a member of a Campus Court of the Catholic Daughters of the Americas. Along with their application, they must submit an autobiography, a list of their reasons for applying for this scholarship, and a letter from the advisor of their Campus Court verifying their membership. Financial need is not considered in the selection process.

Financial data The stipend is $2,000.

Duration 1 year.

Number awarded 1 each year.

Deadline April of each year.

[148]
CECELIA CONNELLY MEMORIAL SCHOLARSHIPS IN UNDERWATER ARCHAEOLOGY

Women Divers Hall of Fame
43 MacKey Avenue
Port Washington, NY 11050-3628
E-mail: scholarships@wdhof.org
Web: www.wdhof.org/scholarships/scholarships.shtml

Summary To provide financial assistance to women who are working on an undergraduate or graduate degree in underwater archaeology.

Eligibility This program is open to women of any age who are enrolled in an accredited undergraduate or graduate course of study in the field of underwater archaeology. Applicants must be seeking funding to assist with college tuition and fees or field study costs.

Financial data The stipend is $2,000 for graduate students or $750 for undergraduates.

Duration 1 year.

Number awarded 2 each year: 1 undergraduate and 1 graduate student.

Deadline November of each year.

[149]
CHARLIE ADAMS ENDOWED SCHOLARSHIPS

North Carolina High School Athletic Association
Attn: Director of Grants and Fundraising
222 Finley Golf Course Road
P.O. Box 3216
Chapel Hill, NC 27515-3216
(919) 240-7371   Fax: (919) 240-7399
E-mail: mary@nchsaa.org
Web: www.nchsaa.org

Summary To provide financial assistance to high school seniors in North Carolina who have participated in male wresting or female cross country and plan to attend college in any state.

Eligibility This program is open to seniors graduating from high schools that are members of the North Carolina High School Athletic Association (NCHSAA). Males must have participated on their varsity wrestling team; females must have participated on their varsity cross country team. Applicants must have a clean disciplinary record (both school and athletics related) and demonstrated athletic success. They must be planning to attend an accredited college, university, or community college in any state. Along with their application, they must submit a 2-page essay addressing how athletic participation has influenced their decision-making and the importance of athletics in teaching independence, unselfishness, and honesty. Financial need is not considered in the selection process.

Financial data The stipend is $1,500.

Duration 1 year; nonrenewable.

Additional information This program began in 2010.

Number awarded 2 each year: 1 to a male and 1 to a female.

Deadline February of each year.

[150]
CHERYL A. RUGGIERO SCHOLARSHIP

Rhode Island Society of Certified Public Accountants
40 Sharpe Drive, Unit 5
Cranston, RI 02920
(401) 331-5720   Fax: (401) 454-5780
E-mail: info@riscpa.org
Web: www.riscpa.org/careers/become-a-cpa

Summary To provide financial assistance to female undergraduate and graduate students from Rhode Island who are working on a degree in accounting at a school in any state.

Eligibility This program is open to female residents of Rhode Island who are working on an undergraduate or graduate degree in public accounting at a school in any state. Applicants must be U.S. citizens who have a GPA of 3.0 or higher. Selection is based on demonstrated potential to become a valued member of the public accounting profession. Finalists are interviewed.

Financial data The stipend is $1,550.

Duration 1 year.

Additional information This program began in 2005.

Number awarded 1 each year.

Deadline January of each year.

[151]
CHERYL DANT HENNESY SCHOLARSHIP

National FFA Organization
Attn: Scholarship Office
6060 FFA Drive
P.O. Box 68960
Indianapolis, IN 46268-0960
(317) 802-4419   Fax: (317) 802-5419
E-mail: scholarships@ffa.org
Web: www.ffa.org/participate/scholarships

Summary To provide financial assistance to female FFA members from Kentucky, Georgia, or Tennessee who plan to attend college in any state.

Eligibility This program is open to female members who are seniors graduating from high schools in Kentucky, Georgia, or Tennessee. Applicants must be interested in working on a 2- or 4-year degree in any area of study at a college or university in any state. They must demonstrate financial need and personal motivation. Selection is based on academic achievement, FFA involvement, community service, and leadership skills. U.S. citizenship is required.

Financial data The stipend is $1,250 per year.

Duration 1 year; may be renewed up to 3 additional years, provided the recipient maintains a GPA of 2.0 or higher.

Number awarded Approximately 3 each year.

Deadline January of each year.

[152]
CHERYL KRAFF-COOPER, M.D. GIRAFFE FUND EMERGENCY GRANTS FOR UNDERGRADUATES

Alpha Epsilon Phi
Attn: AEPhi Foundation
11 Lake Avenue Extension, Suite 1A
Danbury, CT 06811
(203) 748-0029   Fax: (203) 748-0039
E-mail: aephifoundation@aephi.org
Web: www.aephi.org/foundation/scholarships

Summary To provide assistance to undergraduate members of Alpha Epsilon Phi who are facing severe financial emergencies.

Eligibility This program is open to undergraduate members of the sorority who can demonstrate that they will be forced to withdraw from school if they do not receive emergency assistance. Applicants must submit statements on their career and professional objectives, academic or professional honors, other honors received, scholarships and loans received, Alpha Epsilon Phi activities, college and community activities, work experience, and why they need emergency assistance.

Financial data Stipends are $1,000; funds may be used only for tuition, fees, and books.

Duration These are 1-time grants.

Number awarded Several each year.

Deadline Applications may be submitted at any time.

[153]
CHEVRON SWE SCHOLARSHIPS

Society of Women Engineers
Attn: Scholarship Selection Committee
203 North LaSalle Street, Suite 1675
Chicago, IL 60601-1269
(312) 596-5223   Toll Free: (877) SWE-INFO
Fax: (312) 644-8557   E-mail: scholarships@swe.org
Web: societyofwomenengineers.swe.org

Summary To provide financial assistance to women who are interested in studying specified fields of engineering at designated universities.

Eligibility This program is open to women who are entering their freshman, sophomore, or junior year at Colorado School of Mines, University of Michigan, California Polytechnic State University at San Luis Obispo, Pennsylvania State University, or Massachusetts Institute of Technology. Applicants must be enrolled full time and interested in majoring in computer science, safety science, cybersecurity, MIS, or chemical, civil, computer, electrical, environmental, manufacturing, materials, mechanical, or petroleum engineering. They must have a GPA of 3.2 or higher. Selection is based on merit.

Financial data The stipend is $5,000.

Duration 1 year.

Additional information This program is sponsored by Chevron.

Number awarded 18 each year.

Deadline May of each year for entering freshmen; February of each year for continuing undergraduates.

[154]
CHOBANI SCHOLARSHIP

New York Women in Communications, Inc.
Attn: NYWICI Foundation
355 Lexington Avenue, 15th Floor
New York, NY 10017-6603
(212) 297-2133   Fax: (212) 370-9047
E-mail: nywicipr@nywici.org
Web: www.nywici.org/foundation/scholarships

Summary To provide financial assistance to female residents of designated eastern states who are enrolled at a college in any state and preparing for a culinary communications career.

Eligibility This program is open to women who are residents of New York, New Jersey, Connecticut, or Pennsylvania and currently enrolled as sophomores, juniors, or seniors at a college or university in any state. Also eligible are women who reside outside the 4 states but are currently enrolled at a college or university within 1 of the 5 boroughs of New York City. Applicants must have demonstrated an interest in 1) communications; and 2) food and its positive impact on life. They must be currently enrolled, or planning to enroll, at a culinary school and have a GPA of 3.2 or higher. Along with their application, they must submit a 2-page resume; a personal essay of 300 words on an assigned topic that changes annually; 2 letters of recommendation; and an official transcript. Selection is based on academic record, need, demonstrated leadership, participation in school and community activities, honors and other awards or recognition, work experience, goals and aspirations, and unusual personal and/or family circumstances. U.S. citizenship or permanent resident status is required.

Financial data The stipend ranges up to $10,000.

Duration 1 year.

Number awarded 1 each year.

Deadline January of each year.

[155]
CHUNGHI HONG PARK SCHOLARSHIPS

Korean-American Scientists and Engineers Association
Attn: Scholarship Committee
1952 Gallows Drive, Suite 300
Vienna, VA 22182
(703) 748-1221   Fax: (703) 748-1331
E-mail: hq@ksea.org
Web: scholarship.ksea.org/InfoUndergraduate.aspx

Summary To provide financial assistance to women who are undergraduate student members of the Korean-American Scientists and Engineers Association (KSEA).

Eligibility This program is open to women who are Korean American undergraduate students, are KSEA members, have completed at least 2 semesters as a college student, and are majoring in science, engineering, or a related field. Along with their application, they must submit an essay of 600 to 800 words on a topic that changes annually but relates to science or engineering; recently, students were asked how this scholarship would make a difference in their studies in science and engineering. Selection is based on the essay (25%), KSEA activities and community service (25%), recommendation letters (20%), and academic performance (30%).

Financial data The stipend is $1,000.

Duration 1 year.

Number awarded 2 each year.

Deadline March of each year.

[156]
CLAES NOBEL WOMEN OF TOMORROW LEADERSHIP AWARDS

National Society of High School Scholars Foundation
Attn: Scholarships
1936 North Druid Hills Road
Atlanta, GA 30319
(404) 235-5500　　　　　Toll Free: (866) 343-1800
Fax: (404) 235-5510
E-mail: scholarships@nshssfoundation.org
Web: www.nhss.org/member-benefits/scholarships

Summary To provide financial assistance to female high school senior members of the National Society of High School Scholars (NSHSS) who have demonstrated outstanding leadership.

Eligibility This program is open to women who are NSHSS high school senior members planning to enroll at a college or university. Applicants must have a GPA of 3.5 or higher and a record of outstanding leadership skills in their schools and communities. Along with their application, they must submit a 500-word essay explaining how they possess the mindset and skills to succeed as a leader in the field of their dreams.

Financial data A stipend is awarded (amount not specified).

Duration 1 year.

Number awarded 1 or more each year.

Deadline March of each year.

[157]
CLAY FORD MINORITY SCHOLARSHIPS

Florida Board of Accountancy
Florida Department of Business and Professional Regulation
Attn: Division of Certified Public Accounting
240 N.W. 76th Drive, Suite A
Gainesville, FL 32607-6656
(352) 333-2505　　　　　Fax: (352) 333-2508
E-mail: CPA.Applications@dbpr.state.fl.us
Web: www.myfloridalicense.com

Summary To provide financial assistance to female and minority residents of Florida who are entering the fifth year of an accounting program.

Eligibility This program is open to Florida residents who have completed at least 120 credit hours at a college or university in the state and have a GPA of 2.5 or higher. Applicants must be planning to remain in school as a full-time student for the fifth year required to sit for the C.P.A. examination. They must be members of a minority group, defined to include African Americans, Hispanic Americans, Asian Americans, Native Americans, or women. Selection is based on scholastic ability and performance and financial need.

Financial data Stipends range from $3,000 to $6,000 per semester.

Duration 1 semester; may be renewed 1 additional semester.

Number awarded Varies each year; a total of $200,000 is available for this program annually.

Deadline May of each year.

[158]
COLLABORATIVE RESEARCH EXPERIENCES FOR UNDERGRADUATES

Computing Research Association
1828 L Street, N.W., Suite 800
Washington, DC 20036-4632
(202) 234-2111　　　　　Fax: (202) 667-1066
E-mail: creu@cra.org
Web: www.cra.org/cra-w/creu

Summary To provide funding to underrepresented undergraduate students who are interested in conducting a research project in computer science or engineering.

Eligibility This program is open to teams of 2 or 4 undergraduates who have completed 2 years of study, including at least 4 courses in computer science or computer engineering, at a college or university in the United States. Applicants must be interested in conducting a research project directly related to computer science or computer engineering. They must apply jointly with 1 or 2 sponsoring faculty members. Teams consisting of underrepresented groups (women, African Americans, Mexican-Americans, American Indians, Alaska Natives, Native Hawaiians, Pacific Islanders, mainland Puerto Ricans, individuals who identify as part of the LGBTQI community, and persons with disabilities) are especially encouraged to apply; teams may also include students from non-underrepresented groups, but financial support is available only to underrepresented students. U.S. citizenship or permanent resident status is required.

Financial data The program provides a stipend of $3,000 for the academic year. Students who wish to participate in an optional summer extension receive an additional stipend of $4,000. Additional funding up to $1,500 per team may be available for purchase of supporting materials and/or travel to conferences to present the work.

Duration 1 academic year plus an optional summer extension.

Additional information This program is sponsored by the Computing Research Association's Committee on the Status of Women in Computing Research (CRA-W) and the Coalition to Diversify Computing (CDC) in cooperation with the National Science Foundation.

Number awarded Varies each year; recently, 14 teams of students received support from this program.

Deadline May of each year.

[159]
COLLEEN CONLEY MEMORIAL SCHOLARSHIP

New Mexico Engineering Foundation
Attn: Scholarship Chair
P.O. Box 3828
Albuquerque, NM 87190-3828
(505) 615-1800　　　　　E-mail: info@nmef.net
Web: www.nmef.net/?section=scholarship

Summary To provide financial assistance to female high school seniors in New Mexico who plan to study engineering at a college or university in any state.

Eligibility This program is open to female seniors graduating from high schools in New Mexico who are planning to enroll at a college or university in any state and major in engineering, engineering technology, or a related field (including scientific disciplines). Applicants must have a GPA of 3.0 or higher. Along with their application, they must submit a 300-word letter discussing their interest in science or engineering and their future plans. Financial need is not considered in the selection process. Preference is given to applicants who are the first member of their family to attend college.

Financial data The stipend is $1,000.

Duration 1 year; may be renewed up to 3 additional years, provided the recipient remains enrolled at least half time and maintains a GPA of 2.5 or higher.

Additional information This program is sponsored by the Central New Mexico Section of the Society of Women Engineers.

Number awarded 1 each year.

Deadline February of each year.

[160]
COLORADO FIESTA PAGEANT QUEEN

Colorado State Fair
Attn: Fiesta Committee
c/o Brian Montez
1001 Beulah Avenue
Pueblo, CO 81004
(719) 778-4350   E-mail: pageant@fiestacommittee.org
Web: sites.google.com

Summary To recognize and reward, with college scholarships, Hispanic women who participate in the Colorado State Fair Fiesta Pageant.

Eligibility This competition is open to women of Hispanic descent who have been residents of Colorado for at least 6 months and are U.S. citizens or eligible non-citizens. Applicants must be between 18 and 22 years of age and enrolled or planning to enroll full time at a college or university in Colorado. They must have a GPA of 3.0 or higher. During the Colorado State Fair Fiesta in June, they participate in the Queen Pageant, with the Queen and Attendants selected on the basis of personal interviews (30%), a 3- to 5-minute speech (30%), talent (20%), evening gown (10%), and an impromptu question (10%).

Financial data Awards are $2,500 for the Fiesta Queen, $1,500 to the First Attendant, $1,250 to the Second Attendant, and $1,000 to the Third Attendant. Funds are disbursed directly to the college each recipient attends, upon proof of full-time enrollment.

Duration The competition is held annually.

Number awarded 4 each year.

Deadline May of each year.

[161]
COLORADO LEGION AUXILIARY DEPARTMENT PRESIDENT'S SCHOLARSHIP FOR JUNIOR AUXILIARY MEMBERS

American Legion Auxiliary
Department of Colorado
7465 East First Avenue, Suite D
Denver, CO 80230
(303) 367-5388   Fax: (303) 367-5388
E-mail: dept-sec@alacolorado.com
Web: www.alacolorado.com/scholarships.html

Summary To provide financial assistance to junior members of the American Legion Auxiliary in Colorado who plan to attend college in the state.

Eligibility This program is open to seniors at high schools in Colorado who have been junior members of the auxiliary for the past 3 years. Applicants must be Colorado residents planning to attend college in the state. Along with their application, they must submit a 1,000-word essay on a topic that changes annually; recently, students were asked to write on, "How Military Families Are Keeping the Promise to Preserve our Freedom." Selection is based on character (20%), Americanism (20%), leadership (20%), scholarship (20%), and financial need (20%).

Financial data The stipend is $1,000.

Duration 1 year; nonrenewable.

Number awarded 2 each year.

Deadline Applications must be submitted to the unit president by February of each year.

[162]
COLORADO SECTION COLLEGE SCHOLARSHIP FOR JEWISH WOMEN

National Council of Jewish Women-Colorado Section
Attn: Scholarship Program
6018 South Lima Way
Englewood, CO 80111
(303) 290-6655   E-mail: gmkern@comcast.net
Web: www.ncjwcolorado.org

Summary To provide financial assistance to Jewish women from Colorado who are interested in attending college or graduate school in any state.

Eligibility This program is open to Jewish residents of Colorado who are women at least 16 years of age. Applicants must be enrolled or planning to enroll at an accredited college, university, junior college, community college, technical school, or graduate school in any state. Along with their application, they must submit a 1-page essay about their personal and educational goals and why they feel they deserve this scholarship, information about their academic record, documentation of their involvement in the community, and documentation of financial need.

Financial data The stipend is $2,000.

Duration 1 year.

Number awarded Several each year.

Deadline March of each year.

[163]
COLORADO WOMEN'S EDUCATION FOUNDATION SCHOLARSHIPS

Colorado Federation of Business and Professional
  Women
Attn: Colorado Women's Education Foundation
P.O. Box 1189
Boulder, CO 80306-1189
(303) 443-2573   Fax: (720) 564-0397
E-mail: office@cwef.org
Web: www.cwef.org/scholarships/how-to-apply

Summary To provide financial assistance for college to mature women residing in Colorado.

Eligibility This program is open to women 25 years of age and older who are enrolled at an accredited Colorado college, university, or vocational school. Applicants must be U.S. citizens who have resided in Colorado for at least 12 months. Along with their application, they must submit a copy of their most recent high school or college transcript, proof of Colorado residency and U.S. citizenship, a statement of their educational and career goals, 2 letters of recommendation, and documentation of financial need.

Financial data Stipends range from $250 to $1,000 per year. Funds are sent directly to the recipient's institution to be used for tuition, fees, or books.

Duration 1 year; recipients may reapply.

Number awarded Varies each year; recently, 22 were awarded.

Deadline May of each year.

[164]
CONNECTICUT ELKS ASSOCIATION GIRL SCOUT GOLD AWARD SCHOLARSHIP

Girl Scouts of Connecticut
Attn: Program Department
340 Washington Street
Hartford, CT 06106
(860) 522-0163   Toll Free: (800) 922-2770 (within CT)
E-mail: general@gsofct.org
Web: www.gsofct.org/pages/goldaward.php

Summary To provide financial assistance to Girl Scouts in Connecticut who plan to attend college in any state.

Eligibility This program is open to high school seniors who are registered Girl Scouts in Connecticut and planning to attend college in any state. Applicants must have earned the Gold Award. They must be able to demonstrate leadership ability and a strong record of participation in activities in and outside of Girl Scouts. Selection is based on leadership (30 points), community and religious service (30 points), classroom and extracurricular activities (15 points), scholastic achievements or awards (10 points), individual interests and/or hobbies (5 points), and overall review by Elks Committee (10 points).

Financial data The stipend is $1,000.

Duration 1 year.

Additional information This program is sponsored by the Connecticut Elks Association.

Number awarded 1 each year.

Deadline March of each year.

[165]
CONNIE SETTLES SCHOLARSHIP

American Legion Auxiliary
Department of California
401 Van Ness Avenue, Suite 319
San Francisco, CA 94102-4570
(415) 861-5092   Fax: (415) 861-8365
E-mail: calegionaux@calegionaux.org
Web: www.calegionaux.org/scholarships.htm

Summary To provide financial assistance to members of the American Legion Auxiliary in California who are attending college or graduate school in the state.

Eligibility This program is open to residents of California who are currently working on an undergraduate or graduate degree at a college or university in the state. Applicants must have been members of the American Legion Auxiliary for at least the 2 preceding years and be current members. Each unit of the Auxiliary may nominate only 1 member. Selection is based on transcripts, 2 letters of recommendation, a letter from the applicant about themselves and their goals, and financial need. Support is not provided for programs of study deemed to be nonessential (e.g., sewing classes, aerobics, sculpting).

Financial data The stipend is $5,000. Funds are paid directly to the recipient's college or university.

Duration 1 year.

Number awarded 1 each year.

Deadline Applications must be submitted to Auxiliary units by February of each year.

[166]
CONSTANCE K. RIFE SCHOLARSHIP

Simply Golf
1323 N.W. Fairway Circle
Blue Springs, MO 64014-2246
(402) 305-5370   E-mail: mark@simplygolf.us.com
Web: www.simplygolf.us.com

Summary To provide financial assistance to female high school seniors in Nebraska who have played golf and plan to attend college in any state.

Eligibility This program is open to women graduating from high schools in Nebraska and planning to enroll full time at a college or university in any state. Applicants must be an active member of a Nebraska School Activities Association recognized high school golf team. They must have a GPA of 3.0 or higher.

Financial data The stipend is $1,000.

Duration 1 year.

Additional information This program began in 2010.

Number awarded 1 each year.

Deadline March of each year.

[167]
CORAL JEAN COTTERELL ACHIEVEMENT SCHOLARSHIPS

Society of Women Engineers-Columbia River Section
c/o Jennifer Bly, Scholarship Chair
Intel
2501 N.W. 229th Avenue
Hillsboro, OR 97124
(503) 696-8080   E-mail: scholarships-crs@swe.org
Web: columbiariver.swe.org/scholarships.html

Summary To provide financial assistance to members of the Society of Women Engineers (SWE) who are working on an undergraduate degree in engineering at designated colleges in Oregon.

Eligibility This program is open to women from any state currently enrolled full time at Oregon Institute of Technology at Wilsonville, Oregon Institute of Technology at Klamath Falls, George Fox University, Portland State University, or the University of Portland. Applicants must be working on an undergraduate degree in engineering and have a GPA of 3.0 or higher. They must be SWE Collegiate members in good standing and active within an existing SWE Collegiate or Collegiate Interest Section.

Financial data The stipend is $1,000.

Duration 1 year.

Number awarded 4 each year.

Deadline April of each year.

[168]
CORINNE JEANNINE SCHILLINGS FOUNDATION ACADEMIC SCHOLARSHIPS

Corinne Jeannine Schillings Foundation
10645 Nebraska Street
Frankfort, IL 60423-2223
(815) 534-5598   E-mail: dschillings1@comcast.net
Web: www.cjsfoundation.org/html/academic_study.html

Summary To provide financial assistance to Girl Scouts who plan to study a foreign language in college.

Eligibility This program is open to members of the Girl Scouts who have earned the Silver or Gold Award. Applicants must be enrolled or planning to enroll full time at a 4-year college or university and major or minor in a foreign language. They must have a GPA of 3.0 or higher. Along with their application, they must submit a 5-page essay about themselves, including the impact of Girl Scouting on their life, why they have chosen to major or minor in a foreign language, how they plan to utilize their language skills, and why they feel they should receive this scholarship. Financial need is not considered in the selection process.

Financial data The stipend is $1,500 per year.

Duration 1 year; may be renewed up to 3 additional years, provided the recipient maintains a GPA of 3.0 or higher, both overall and in foreign language classes.

Additional information This program began in 2005.

Number awarded Varies each year; recently, this program awarded 12 new and renewal scholarships.

Deadline May of each year.

[169]
CPCHEM SCHOLARSHIPS FOR WOMEN IN ENGINEERING

Society of Women Engineers
Attn: Scholarship Selection Committee
203 North LaSalle Street, Suite 1675
Chicago, IL 60601-1269
(312) 596-5223   Toll Free: (877) SWE-INFO
Fax: (312) 644-8557   E-mail: scholarships@swe.org
Web: societyofwomenengineers.swe.org

Summary To provide financial assistance to women who are residents of Oklahoma or Texas and studying chemical, electrical, or mechanical engineering at universities in those states.

Eligibility This program is open to female residents of Oklahoma or Texas who are entering their junior year at the University of Texas at Austin, University of Houston, Texas A&M University, University of Oklahoma, or Oklahoma State University. Applicants must be enrolled full time and majoring in computer, electrical, or mechanical engineering. They must have a GPA of 3.25 or higher. Selection is based on merit.

Financial data The stipend is $7,500.

Duration 1 year.

Additional information This program is sponsored by Chevron Phillips Chemical (CPChem).

Number awarded 3 each year.

Deadline February of each year.

[170]
CREW NETWORK FOUNDATION SCHOLARSHIP PROGRAM

Commercial Real Estate Women (CREW) Network
Attn: Foundation
1201 Wakarusa Drive, Suite D
Lawrence, KS 66049
(785) 832-1808   Fax: (785) 832-1551
E-mail: crewnetwork@crewnetwork.org
Web: www.crewnetwork.org/scholarship.aspx

Summary To provide financial assistance to women who are attending college to prepare for a career in commercial real estate.

Eligibility This program is open to women who are enrolled as full-time juniors, seniors, or graduate students at a college or university that has an accredited real estate program. If their institution does not have a real estate program, they may be studying another field, as long as they are preparing for a career in commercial real estate. They must have a GPA of 3.0 or higher and be U.S. or Canadian citizens. Along with their application, undergraduates must submit a brief statement about their interest in commercial real estate and their career objectives; graduate students must submit a statement that explains why they are interested in the commercial real estate industry, their experiences and insights into that industry and how those have impacted them, the impact they expect to make in the commercial real estate industry, and how their long-term career objectives make them uniquely qualified for this scholarship. Selection is based on those statements, academic record, commitment to a career within the commercial real estate industry, extracurricular activities, history of employment, personal and professional references, practical experience in the field, and accomplishments.

Financial data The stipend is $5,000.

Duration 1 year.

Additional information This program includes the Jane Ayers Wooley Memorial Scholarship, the Goldie B. Wolfe Miller Women Leaders in Real Estate Initiative Scholarship, and the Prudential Real Estate Investors Scholarship.

Number awarded 10 each year.

Deadline April of each year.

[171]
CUBA WADLINGTON, JR. AND MICHAEL P. JOHNSON SCHOLARSHIP

Tulsa Community Foundation
Attn: Scholarships
7030 South Yale Avenue, Suite 600
Tulsa, OK 74136
(918) 494-8823   Fax: (918) 494-9826
E-mail: scholarships@tulsacf.org
Web: www.tulsacf.org/whatwedo/education/scholarships

Summary To provide financial assistance to upper-division students at colleges in any state who are members of an underrepresented group in the energy industry.

Eligibility This program is open to students entering their junior or senior year at a college or university in any state and preparing for a career in the energy industry with a major in accounting, engineering, finance, or technology. Applicants must be members of a group underrepresented in the energy industry (women and ethnic minorities). They must have a GPA of 3.0 or higher. Along with their application, they must submit a 2-page personal essay that includes their future or academic career goals, any adversity or challenge they have overcome or anticipate in pursuit of their educational goals, and the importance of diversity in the workplace and how dealing with diversity in their own life has shaped them. Financial need is not considered in the selection process.

Financial data The stipend is $2,000. Funds are paid directly to the university.

Duration 1 year; nonrenewable.

Additional information This program is supported by the Williams Companies of Tulsa, Oklahoma.

Number awarded Varies each year.

Deadline June of each year.

[172]
CUMMINS SCHOLARSHIPS

Society of Women Engineers
Attn: Scholarship Selection Committee
203 North LaSalle Street, Suite 1675
Chicago, IL 60601-1269
(312) 596-5223   Toll Free: (877) SWE-INFO
Fax: (312) 644-8557   E-mail: scholarships@swe.org
Web: societyofwomenengineers.swe.org

Summary To provide financial assistance to women working on an undergraduate degree in computer science or designated engineering specialties.

Eligibility This program is open to women who are sophomores, re-entry, or nontraditional students at 4-year ABET-accredited colleges and universities. Applicants must be working full time on a degree in computer science, industrial

systems, metrology, metallurgy, or automotive, chemical, computer, electrical, industrial, manufacturing, materials, or mechanical engineering and have a GPA of 3.0 or higher. Preference is given to members of groups underrepresented in engineering or computer science and to students interested in an internship with the sponsor. Selection is based on merit.

Financial data The stipend is $2,500.

Duration 1 year.

Additional information This program is sponsored by Cummins, Inc.

Number awarded 2 each year.

Deadline February of each year.

[173]
CYNTHIA HUNT-LINES SCHOLARSHIP

Minnesota Nurses Association
Attn: Minnesota Nurses Association Foundation
345 Randolph Avenue, Suite 200
St. Paul, MN 55102-3610
(651) 414-2822   Toll Free: (800) 536-4662, ext. 122
Fax: (651) 695-7000   E-mail: linda.owens@mnnurses.org
Web: www.mnnurses.org

Summary To provide financial assistance to members of the Minnesota Nurses Association (MNA) and the Minnesota Student Nurses Association (MSNA) who are single parents and interested in working on a baccalaureate or master's degree in nursing.

Eligibility This program is open to MNA and MSNA members who are enrolled or entering a baccalaureate or master's program in nursing in Minnesota or North Dakota. Applicants must be single parents, at least 21 years of age, with at least 1 dependent. Along with their application, they must submit: a current transcript; a short essay describing their interest in nursing, their long-range career goals, and how their continuing education will have an impact on the profession of nursing in Minnesota; a description of their financial need; and 2 letters of support.

Financial data The stipend is $5,000 per year.

Duration 1 year; may be renewed 1 additional year.

Number awarded 1 each year.

Deadline May of each year.

[174]
D. ANITA SMALL SCIENCE AND BUSINESS SCHOLARSHIP

Business and Professional Women of Maryland
Attn: BPW Foundation of Maryland
c/o Joyce Draper, Chief Financial Officer
615 Fairview Avenue
Frederick, MD 21701
Web: www.bpwmaryland.org/bpwmd.asp

Summary To provide financial assistance to women in Maryland who are interested in working on an undergraduate or graduate degree in a science or business-related field.

Eligibility This program is open to women who are at least 21 years of age and have been accepted to a bachelor's or advanced degree program at an accredited Maryland academic institution. Applicants must be preparing for a career in 1 of the following or a related field: business administration, computer sciences, engineering, mathematics, medical sciences (including nursing, laboratory technology, therapy, etc.), or physical sciences. They must have a GPA of 3.0 or higher. Along with their application, they must submit a 200-word statement on how they expect the proposed training or education to add to their opportunities for advancement or employment. Selection is based on that statement, academic performance, work experience, community service, volunteer experience, and financial need.

Financial data The stipend is $1,500.

Duration 1 year.

Number awarded 1 or more each year.

Deadline April of each year.

[175]
DAGMAR JEPPESON GRANT

Delta Kappa Gamma Society International-Alpha Rho
  State Organization
c/o Martha Nicoloff, State Scholarship Chair
242 Muirfield Avenue, S.E.
Salem, OR 97306
(503) 999-20698   E-mail: nicoloff2@comcast.net
Web: www.deltakappagamma.org

Summary To provide financial assistance to women from Oregon who are enrolled as upper-division students at a college in any state and preparing for a career in early childhood or elementary education.

Eligibility This program is open to female residents of Oregon who are at least juniors at a college in any state and interested in preparing for a career in early childhood or elementary education. Applicants may not be members of Delta Kappa Gamma (an honorary society of women educators), but they must be sponsored by a local chapter of the society. Along with their application, they must submit a summary of their education from high school through the present, high school and college activities and achievements, community service, employment history, career goals, and financial need.

Financial data A stipend is awarded (amount not specified).

Duration 1 year.

Number awarded 1 or more each year.

Deadline January of each year.

[176]
DASSAULT FALCON SCHOLARSHIP

Women in Aviation International
Attn: Scholarships
Morningstar Airport
3647 State Route 503 South
West Alexandria, OH 45381-9354
(937) 839-4647   Fax: (937) 839-4645
E-mail: scholarships@wai.org
Web: www.wai.org

Summary To provide financial assistance to women who are working on an undergraduate or graduate degree in a field related to aviation.

Eligibility This program is open to women who are working on an undergraduate or graduate degree in an aviation-related field. Applicants must be U.S. citizens, be fluent in English, and have a GPA of 3.0 or higher. Along with their application, they must submit a 500-word essay and profes-

sional resume that include their aviation history and goals, what they have done for themselves to achieve their goals, where they see themselves in 5 and 10 years, involvement in aviation activities, how the scholarship will help them achieve their objectives, and their present financial need.

Financial data The stipend is $1,000.

Duration 1 year.

Additional information Women in Aviation International is a nonprofit professional organization dedicated to encouraging women to consider an aviation career and to providing educational outreach activities and networking resources to women active in the industry. This program is sponsored by Dassault Falcon Jet Corporation.

Number awarded 1 each year.

Deadline November of each year.

[177]
DAUGHTERS OF PENELOPE KELLIE STATHEROS RE-ENTRY SCHOLARSHIP

American Hellenic Educational Progressive Association-
  District 11
Attn: AHEPA Buckeye Scholarship Foundation
c/o Tony Capranica, Chair
601 Tall Pines Drive
Toledo, OH 43615
(330) 372-1869   E-mail: tony.capranica@gmail.com
Web: www.bsf.buckeyedistrict11.org/?page_id=386

Summary To provide financial assistance to women who wish to reenter the workforce and are members of the Daughters of Penelope in its District 11 (Kentucky, Ohio, and parts of Pennsylvania and West Virginia).

Eligibility This program is open to residents of Kentucky, Ohio, and parts of Pennsylvania and West Virginia who have been members of the Daughters of Penelope for the past 2 years and the current year. Applicants must be women entering an accredited college, vocational school, or university in any state to obtain training necessary to prepare for a career in the field of her choice. Financial need is considered in the selection process.

Financial data The stipend is $1,000.

Duration 1 year.

Additional information This program began in 1987.

Number awarded 1 each year.

Deadline March of each year.

[178]
DAUGHTERS OF PENELOPE UNDERGRADUATE SCHOLARSHIPS

Daughters of Penelope
Attn: Daughters of Penelope Foundation, Inc.
1909 Q Street, N.W., Suite 500
Washington, DC 20009-1007
(202) 234-9741   Fax: (202) 483-6983
E-mail: president@dopfoundationinc.com
Web: www.dopfoundationinc.com/scholarships/apply

Summary To provide financial assistance for college to women of Greek descent.

Eligibility This program is open to women who have been members of the Daughters of Penelope or the Maids of Athena for at least 2 years, or whose parents or grandparents have been members of the Daughters of Penelope or the

Order of AHEPA for at least 2 years. Applicants must be 1) high school seniors or recent high school graduates applying to a college, university, or accredited technical school; or 2) current undergraduates at the college level. They must have taken the SAT or ACT (or Canadian, Greek, or Cypriot equivalent) and must write an essay (in English) about their educational and vocational goals. Selection is based on academic merit only.

Financial data Stipends are $1,500 or $1,000.

Duration 1 year; nonrenewable.

Additional information This program includes the following endowed awards: the Daughters of Penelope Past Grand Presidents' Memorial Scholarship, the Alexandra Apostolides Sonenfeld Scholarship, the Helen J. Beldecos Scholarship, the Hopewell Agave Chapter 224 Scholarship, the Kottis Family Scholarship, the Mary M. Verges Scholarship, the Joanne V. Hologgitas Ph.D. Scholarship, the Eos #1 Mother Lodge Chapter Scholarship, the Barbara Edith Quincey Thorndyke Memorial Scholarship, and the Paula J. Alexander Memorial Scholarship.

Number awarded Varies each year; recently, 22 were awarded: 5 at $1,500 and 17 at $1,000.

Deadline May of each year.

[179]
DAUGHTERS OF THE CINCINNATI SCHOLARSHIP PROGRAM

Daughters of the Cincinnati
Attn: Scholarship Administrator
20 West 44th Street, Suite 508
New York, NY 10036
(212) 991-9945 E-mail: scholarships@daughters1894.org
Web: www.daughters1894.org/scholarship

Summary To provide financial assistance for college to high school seniors who are the daughters of active-duty, deceased, or retired military officers.

Eligibility This program is open to high school seniors who are the daughters of career commissioned officers of the regular Army, Navy, Air Force, Coast Guard, or Marine Corps on active duty, deceased, or retired. Applicants must be planning to enroll in an undergraduate program at a college or university in any state. Along with their application, they must submit an official school transcript, SAT or ACT scores, a letter of recommendation, an essay on their choice of 3 assigned topics, and documentation of financial need.

Financial data Scholarship amounts have ranged from $4,000 to $5,000 per year. Funds are paid directly to the college of the student's choice.

Duration 1 year; may be renewed up to 3 additional years, provided the recipient remains in good academic standing.

Additional information This program was originally established in 1906.

Number awarded Approximately 12 each year.

Deadline March of each year.

[180]
DAVIS & DAVIS SCHOLARSHIP

National Naval Officers Association-Washington, D.C.
   Chapter
c/o LCDR Stephen Williams
P.O. Box 30784
Alexandria, VA 22310
(703) 566-3840   Fax: (703) 566-3813
E-mail: Stephen.Williams@navy.mil
Web: dcnnoa.memberlodge.com/page-309002

Summary To provide financial assistance to female African American high school seniors from the Washington, D.C. area who are interested in attending college in any state.

Eligibility This program is open to female African American seniors graduating from high schools in the Washington, D.C. metropolitan area who plan to enroll full time at an accredited 2- or 4-year college or university in any state. Applicants must have a GPA of 2.5 or higher and be U.S. citizens or permanent residents. Selection is based on academic achievement, community involvement, and financial need.

Financial data The stipend is $1,000.

Duration 1 year; nonrenewable.

Additional information Recipients are not required to join or affiliate with the military in any way.

Number awarded Varies each year; recently, 2 were awarded.

Deadline March of each year.

[181]
DAVIS SCHOLARSHIP FOR WOMEN IN STEM

United Negro College Fund
Attn: Scholarships and Grants Department
1805 Seventh Street, N.W.
Washington, DC 20001
(202) 810-0258   Toll Free: (800) 331-2244
E-mail: scholarships@uncf.org
Web: www.scholarships.uncf.org

Summary To provide financial assistance to women who are majoring in fields of science, technology, engineering, or mathematics (STEM) at colleges and universities that are members of the United Negro College Fund (UNCF).

Eligibility This program is open to women who are U.S. citizens, nationals, or permanent residents and currently enrolled as freshmen, sophomores, or juniors at UNCF institutions. Applicants must be majoring in a field of STEM. They must have a GPA of 3.0 or higher and be able to document financial need. Along with their application, they must submit an essay about women who have been innovators in a STEM field, their contributions, and their impact in their field.

Financial data Stipends range up to $10,000.

Duration 1 year.

Number awarded 1 or more each year.

Deadline June of each year.

[182]
DEAN WEESE SCHOLARSHIP

University Interscholastic League
Attn: Texas Interscholastic League Foundation
1701 Manor Road
P.O. Box 151027
Austin, TX 78715-1027
(512) 382-0916   Fax: (512) 382-0377
E-mail: info@tilfoundation.org
Web: www.tilfoundation.org/scholarships/list

Summary To provide financial assistance to high school seniors who participate in programs of the Texas Interscholastic League Foundation (TILF), have competed in girls' high school varsity basketball, and plan to attend college in the state.

Eligibility This program is open to seniors graduating from high schools in Texas who have competed in a University Interscholastic League (UIL) academic state meet and have participated in girls' high school varsity basketball. Applicants must be planning to attend a college or university in the state and major in any field. Along with their application, they must submit high school transcripts that include SAT and/or ACT scores and documentation of financial need.

Financial data The stipend is $1,000.

Duration 1 year; nonrenewable.

Additional information This program is sponsored by Whataburger Inc. and Southwest Shootout Inc.

Number awarded 1 each year.

Deadline May of each year.

[183]
DEGENRING SCHOLARSHIP FUND

American Baptist Women's Ministries of New Jersey
c/o Gail Gillespie, Treasurer
125 Oak Street
East Orange, NJ 07018
(973) 820-8405   E-mail: gillespiegail@yahoo.com
Web: www.abwminnj.org/news-events

Summary To provide financial assistance to Baptist women in New Jersey who are interested in attending college in any state to prepare for a career in Christian service.

Eligibility This program is open to Baptist women in New Jersey who are at least sophomores at postsecondary institutions in any state and preparing for a career involving Christian work. Applicants must be members of an American Baptist Church in New Jersey. Selection is based on financial need and career goals.

Financial data The amount awarded varies, depending upon the need of the recipient and her career goals in Christian work.

Duration 1 year.

Number awarded 1 or more each year.

Deadline February of each year.

[184]
DELAYED EDUCATION SCHOLARSHIP FOR WOMEN

American Nuclear Society
Attn: Scholarship Coordinator
555 North Kensington Avenue
La Grange Park, IL 60526-5535
(708) 352-6611   Toll Free: (800) 323-3044
Fax: (708) 352-0499   E-mail: outreach@ans.org
Web: committees.ans.org/need/apply.html

Summary To provide financial assistance to mature women whose formal studies in nuclear science or nuclear engineering have been delayed or interrupted.

Eligibility Applicants must be mature women who have experienced at least a 1-year delay or interruption of their undergraduate studies and are returning to school to work on an undergraduate or graduate degree in nuclear science or nuclear engineering. They must be members of the American Nuclear Society (ANS), but they may be citizens of any country. Along with their application, they must submit an essay on their academic and professional goals, experiences that have affected those goals, and other relevant information. Selection is based on that essay, academic achievement, letters of recommendation, and financial need.

Financial data The stipend is $5,000. Funds may be used by the student to cover any educational expense, including tuition, books, room, and board.

Duration 1 year; nonrenewable.

Number awarded 1 each year.

Deadline January of each year.

[185]
DELLA VAN DEUREN MEMORIAL SCHOLARSHIPS

American Legion Auxiliary
Department of Wisconsin
Attn: Education Chair
2930 American Legion Drive
P.O. Box 140
Portage, WI 53901-0140
(608) 745-0124   Toll Free: (866) 664-3863
Fax: (608) 745-1947   E-mail: alawi@amlegionauxwi.org
Web: www.amlegionauxwi.org/Scholarships.htm

Summary To provide financial assistance to Wisconsin residents who are members or children of members of the American Legion Auxiliary and interested in attending college in any state.

Eligibility This program is open to members and children of members of the American Legion Auxiliary in Wisconsin. Applicants must be high school seniors or graduates attending or planning to attend a college or university in any state. They must have a GPA of 3.5 or higher and be able to demonstrate financial need. Along with their application, they must submit a 300-word essay on "Education—An Investment in the Future."

Financial data The stipend is $1,000.

Duration 1 year; nonrenewable.

Number awarded 2 each year.

Deadline March of each year.

[186]
DELMAR PENINSULA SECTION SWE SCHOLARSHIP

Society of Women Engineers-DelMar Peninsula Section
c/o Lynn Srivastava, Scholarship Chair
Pepco Holdings
701 Ninth Street, N.W.
Washington, DC 20068
(202) 872-2000
E-mail: lynn.srivastava@pepcoholdings.com
Web: swedelmar.weebly.com/scholarship.html

Summary To provide financial assistance to female high school seniors in the DelMar area who are interested in majoring in engineering at a college in any state.

Eligibility This program is open to female high school seniors in Delaware and Maryland who will be enrolling in an engineering program at an ABET-accredited college or university in any state. Applicants must have SAT scores of 600 or higher in mathematics, 500 or higher in critical reading, and 500 or higher in writing (or ACT scores of 29 or higher in mathematics and 25 or higher in English). They must submit an essay (up to 500 words) on their interest in engineering, their major area of study and area of specialization, the occupation they propose to pursue after graduation, their long-term goals, and how they hope to achieve those. Selection is based on the essay, academic record, honors and scholarships, volunteer activities, work experience, and letters of recommendation. Financial need is not required.

Financial data The stipend is at least $1,000.

Duration 1 year (freshman year); nonrenewable.

Number awarded At least 5 each year.

Deadline December of each year.

[187]
DELTA AIR LINES AIRCRAFT MAINTENANCE TECHNOLOGY SCHOLARSHIPS

Women in Aviation International
Attn: Scholarships
Morningstar Airport
3647 State Route 503 South
West Alexandria, OH 45381-9354
(937) 839-4647   Fax: (937) 839-4645
E-mail: scholarships@wai.org
Web: www.wai.org

Summary To provide financial assistance to members of Women in Aviation International (WAI) who are interested in a career in aviation maintenance.

Eligibility This program is open to WAI members who are full-time students with at least 2 semesters of study remaining. Applicants must be preparing for an aviation maintenance technician license in airframe and powerplant (A&P) or a degree in aviation maintenance technology. They must have a cumulative GPA of 3.0 or higher and be U.S. citizens or eligible noncitizens. Along with their application, they must submit an essay of 500 to 1,000 words on who or what inspired them to prepare for a career in aviation maintenance technology, their greatest life challenge, their greatest strength and strongest characteristic, their most memorable academic experience, and why they are the most qualified candidate for this scholarship.

Financial data The stipend is $5,000. Recipients are also reimbursed for up to $2,000 in travel, conference fee, and hotel expenses to attend the WAI annual conference.

Duration 1 year.

Additional information WAI is a nonprofit professional organization dedicated to encouraging women to consider an aviation career and to providing educational outreach activities and networking resources to women active in the industry. This program is sponsored by Delta Air Lines.

Number awarded 1 each year.

Deadline November of each year.

[188]
DELTA AIR LINES AVIATION MAINTENANCE MANAGEMENT/AVIATION BUSINESS MANAGEMENT SCHOLARSHIPS

Women in Aviation International
Attn: Scholarships
Morningstar Airport
3647 State Route 503 South
West Alexandria, OH 45381-9354
(937) 839-4647   Fax: (937) 839-4645
E-mail: scholarships@wai.org
Web: www.wai.org

Summary To provide financial assistance to members of Women in Aviation International (WAI) who are interested in a career in aviation management.

Eligibility This program is open to WAI members who are full-time students with at least 2 semesters of study remaining. Applicants must be working on an associate or baccalaureate degree in aviation maintenance management or aviation business management and have a cumulative GPA of 3.0 or higher. They must be U.S. citizens or eligible noncitizens. Along with their application, they must submit an essay of 500 to 1,000 words on who or what inspired them to prepare for a career in aviation maintenance management or aviation business management, their greatest life challenge, their greatest strength and strongest characteristic, their most memorable academic experience, and why they are the most qualified candidate for this scholarship. Selection is based on achievements, attitude toward self and others, commitment to success, dedication to career, financial need, motivation, reliability, responsibility, and teamwork.

Financial data The stipend is $5,000. Recipients are also reimbursed for up to $2,000 in travel, conference fee, and hotel expenses to attend the WAI annual conference.

Duration 1 year.

Additional information WAI is a nonprofit professional organization dedicated to encouraging women to consider an aviation career and to providing educational outreach activities and networking resources to women active in the industry. This program is sponsored by Delta Air Lines.

Number awarded 1 each year.

Deadline November of each year.

[189]
DELTA AIR LINES ENGINEERING SCHOLARSHIP

Women in Aviation International
Attn: Scholarships
Morningstar Airport
3647 State Route 503 South
West Alexandria, OH 45381-9354
(937) 839-4647   Fax: (937) 839-4645
E-mail: scholarships@wai.org
Web: www.wai.org

Summary   To provide financial assistance to members of Women in Aviation International (WAI) who are studying engineering in college.

Eligibility   This program is open to WAI members who are full-time juniors or seniors with at least 2 semesters of study remaining. Applicants must be working on a baccalaureate degree in aerospace, aeronautical, electrical, or mechanical engineering and have a cumulative GPA of 3.0 or higher. They must be U.S. citizens or eligible noncitizens. Along with their application, they must submit an essay of 500 to 1,000 words on who or what inspired them to prepare for a career in engineering, their greatest life challenge, their greatest strength and strongest characteristic, their most memorable academic experience, and why they are the most qualified candidate for this scholarship. Selection is based on achievements, attitude toward self and others, commitment to success, dedication to career, financial need, motivation, reliability, responsibility, and teamwork.

Financial data   The stipend is $5,000. Recipients are also reimbursed for up to $2,000 in travel, conference fee, and hotel expenses to attend the WAI annual conference.

Duration   1 year.

Additional information   WAI is a nonprofit professional organization dedicated to encouraging women to consider an aviation career and to providing educational outreach activities and networking resources to women active in the industry. This program is sponsored by Delta Air Lines.

Number awarded   1 each year.

Deadline   November of each year.

[190]
DELTA SIGMA THETA SORORITY GENERAL SCHOLARSHIPS

Delta Sigma Theta Sorority, Inc.
Attn: Scholarship and Standards Committee Chair
1707 New Hampshire Avenue, N.W.
Washington, DC 20009
(202) 986-2400   Fax: (202) 986-2513
E-mail: dstemail@deltasigmatheta.org
Web: www.deltasigmatheta.org

Summary   To provide financial assistance to members of Delta Sigma Theta who are working on an undergraduate or graduate degree in any field.

Eligibility   This program is open to active, dues-paying members of Delta Sigma Theta who are currently enrolled in college or graduate school. Applicants must submit an essay on their major goals and educational objectives, including realistic steps they foresee as necessary for the fulfillment of their plans. Financial need is considered in the selection process.

Financial data   The stipends range from $1,000 to $2,000. The funds may be used to cover tuition, fees, and living expenses.

Duration   1 year; may be renewed for 1 additional year.

Additional information   This sponsor is a traditionally-African American social sorority. The application fee is $20.

Number awarded   Varies each year.

Deadline   March of each year.

[191]
DENVER CHAPTER AFWA SCHOLARSHIPS

Accounting and Financial Women's Alliance-Denver
   Chapter
c/o Mary Tatman, Scholarship Trust Chair
P.O. Box 2234
Denver, CO 80201-2234
(303) 234-9150   E-mail: marytat@questoffice.net
Web: www.afwadenver.org/scholarship.php

Summary   To provide financial assistance to women working on a degree in accounting at a college or university in Colorado.

Eligibility   This program is open to women who have completed at least 60 semester hours toward a degree in accounting with a GPA of 3.0 or higher. Applicants must be attending a college or university in Colorado. Membership in the Accounting and Financial Women's Alliance (AFWA) is not required. Selection is based on academic achievement, extracurricular activities and honors, a statement of career goals and objectives, 3 letters of recommendation, and financial need.

Financial data   A stipend is awarded (amount not specified).

Duration   1 year.

Number awarded   Several each year; a total of $7,000 is available for this program annually.

Deadline   June of each year.

[192]
DETROIT SECTION SWE SCHOLARSHIPS

Society of Women Engineers-Detroit Section
Attn: Scholarship Chair
P.O. Box 2978
Southfield, MI 48037-2978
E-mail: lisa.purvis@swe.org
Web: www.swedetroit.org/outreach—scholarships.html

Summary   To provide financial assistance to female high school seniors in Michigan who are interested in studying engineering at a school in any state.

Eligibility   This program is open to female seniors at high schools in Michigan who are planning to enroll the following fall at a university or college in any state that has an ABET-accredited engineering program. Along with their application, they must submit a 1-page essay on the type of engineering that interests them and why. Selection is based on that essay (40%); awards and honors received in high school (20%); leadership, activities (community, church, school, etc.), and employment (30%); and academic performance (10%).

Financial data   The stipend is $1,000.

Duration   1 year.

Number awarded Varies each year; recently, 2 were awarded.

Deadline February of each year.

[193]
DIAMONDS IN THE ROUGH MINISTRY SCHOLARSHIP

Diamonds in the Rough Ministry International
Attn: Scholarship Fund
4209 Samuell Boulevard
Dallas, TX 75228
(972) 288-0112   E-mail: a.moses523@gmail.com
Web: www.diamondsntherough.org/scholarship.html

Summary To provide financial assistance to female high school seniors from Texas who are allowing God to develop them into precious diamonds by attending college in any state.

Eligibility This program is open to women who are graduating from high schools in Texas and planning to attend college in any state. Applicants must be able to demonstrate that they understand the goal of the sponsoring organization to "empower women down the road of self-discovery and self-worth in Jesus Christ." They must have a GPA of 2.5 or higher. Along with their application, they must submit a 500-word essay on how they have allowed God to use their life as a testimony to His grace.

Financial data A stipend is awarded (amount not specified).

Duration 1 year.

Additional information This program began in 2011.

Number awarded 1 or 2 each year.

Deadline April of each year.

[194]
DINAH SHORE SCHOLARSHIP

Ladies Professional Golf Association
Attn: LPGA Foundation
100 International Golf Drive
Daytona Beach, FL 32124-1082
(386) 274-6200   Fax: (386) 274-1099
E-mail: foundation.scholarships@lpga.com
Web: www.lpga.com

Summary To provide financial assistance for college to female graduating high school seniors who played golf in high school.

Eligibility This program is open to female high school seniors who have a GPA of 3.2 or higher. Applicants must have played in at least 50% of their high school golf team's scheduled events or have played golf "regularly" for the past 2 years. They must be planning to enroll full time at a college or university in the United States, but they must not be planning to play collegiate golf. Along with their application, they must submit a letter that describes how golf has been an integral part of their lives and includes their personal, academic, and professional goals; chosen discipline of study; and how this scholarship will be of assistance. Financial need is not considered in the selection process.

Financial data The stipend is $5,000.

Duration 1 year.

Additional information This program, established in 1994, is supported by Kraft Foods, Inc.

Number awarded 1 each year.

Deadline May of each year.

[195]
DISTINGUISHED YOUNG WOMEN SCHOLARSHIPS

Distinguished Young Women
Attn: Foundation Administrator
751 Government Street
Mobile, AL 36602
(251) 438-3621   Fax: (251) 431-0063
E-mail: foundation@distinguishedyw.org
Web: www.distinguishedyw.org

Summary To recognize and reward, with college scholarships, female high school seniors who participate in the Distinguished Young Women competition.

Eligibility This competition is open to girls who are seniors in high school, are U.S. citizens, have never been married, and have never been pregnant. Contestants first enter local competitions, from which winners advance to the state level. The winner in each state is invited to the national competition, held in Mobile, Alabama in June of each year. Prior to the contestants' arrival for the national competition, the judges evaluate their high school academic records and test scores for the scholastics score (20% of the overall score). At the competition, girls are given scores on the basis of their personality, ability to relate to others, maturity, and ability to express themselves in an interview (25% of overall score); their performing arts talent presented during a 90-second audition on stage in front of an audience (25% of overall score); their fitness as demonstrated during a choreographed group aerobic routine (15% of overall score); and their self-expression, grace, poise, demeanor, carriage, posture, and speaking ability (15% of overall score). The girls with the highest scores in each of the 5 categories receive awards. Overall scores are used for selection of 13 finalists, from whom the "Distinguished Young Woman of America" and 2 runners-up are selected. Category awards are presented in the 5 categories of scholastics, interview, talent, self-expression, and fitness. In addition, "satellite awards" are presented to girls who excel in special activities.

Financial data The "Distinguished Young Woman of America" receives a $40,000 scholarship; other scholarships are $15,000 for the first runner-up, $10,000 for the second runner-up, $2,500 for each of the 10 other finalists, $2,000 for the Joy Mitchell Grodnick Distinguished Spirit Award, $2,500 for the 5 category overall winners, $1,000 for each of the category winners, and "satellite awards" ranging from $500 to $2,000 for other activities.

Duration The competition is held annually.

Additional information This program began in 1958 as America's Junior Miss. It acquired its current name in 2010.

Number awarded Varies each year; recently, 3 awards were presented for the "Distinguished Young Woman of America" and 2 runners-up, 10 other finalists, 1 Joy Mitchell Grodnick Distinguished Spirit Award, 5 category overall winners, 20 category winners (4 for each category), and 7 satellite awards.

Deadline Each local competition sets its own deadline.

[196]
DISTRICT OF COLUMBIA AREA AFWA CHAPTER SCHOLARSHIPS

Accounting and Financial Women's Alliance-District of
  Columbia Area Chapter
c/o Rebecca Boland, Programs Committee Chair
Hertzbach & Company
1803 Research Boulevard, Suite 215
Rockville, MD 20850
(301) 315-2150   E-mail: rboland@hertzbach.com
Web: www.dcchapterafwa.org/scholarship-information

Summary To provide financial assistance to women from
any state working on an undergraduate degree in accounting
or finance at a college or university in the Washington, D.C.
area.

Eligibility This program is open to female residents of any
state who are working on a bachelor's degree in accounting
or finance at a college or university in the Washington, D.C.
area. Applicants must be entering their third, fourth, or fifth
year of study and have a GPA of 3.0 or higher. Along with their
application, they must submit an essay of 150 to 250 words
on their career goals and objectives, the impact they want to
have on the accounting world, community involvement, and
leadership examples. Membership in the Accounting and
Financial Women's Alliance (AFWA) is required. Selection is
based on leadership, character, communication skills, scholastic average, and financial need.

Financial data The stipend is $1,500.

Duration 1 year.

Number awarded 1 each year.

Deadline March of each year.

[197]
DIXIE SOFTBALL SCHOLARSHIPS

Dixie Softball, Inc.
Attn: President
1101 Skelton Drive
Birmingham, AL 35224
(205) 785-2255   Fax: (205) 785-2258
E-mail: OBIEDSI@aol.com
Web: softball.dixie.org/site/ClientSite/article/1064923

Summary To provide financial assistance for college to
high school senior women who have participated in the Dixie
Softball program.

Eligibility This program is open to high school senior
women who played in the Dixie Softball program for at least 2
seasons. Applicants must submit academic data (GPA, SAT/
ACT scores, class rank), a letter explaining why they are
seeking this assistance, verification from a Dixie Softball local
official of the number of years the applicant participated in the
program, and documentation of financial need. Ability as an
athlete is not considered in the selection process.

Financial data The stipend is $1,500.

Duration 1 year.

Additional information This program, established in
1979, includes the following named scholarships: the Billy
Adkins Memorial Scholarship, the Frank L. Baxter Honorary
Scholarship, the R.T. Adams Memorial Scholarship, the
Helen Louise Jordan Memorial Scholarship, the George D.
Matthews, Sr. Memorial Scholarship, the Tim Neely Memorial
Scholarship, the Aubrey Tapley Memorial Scholarship, and

the Charles "Buddy" Wade Memorial Scholarship. Dixie Softball operates in Alabama, Arkansas, Florida, Georgia, Louisiana, Mississippi, North Carolina, South Carolina, Tennessee,
Texas, and Virginia.

Number awarded 8 each year.

Deadline January of each year.

[198]
DOMINIQUE LISA PANDOLFO SCHOLARSHIP

Community Foundation of New Jersey
Attn: Chief Operating Officer
35 Knox Hill Road
P.O. Box 338
Morristown, NJ 07963-0338
(973) 267-5533, ext. 227   Toll Free: (800) 659-5533
Fax: (973) 267-2903   E-mail: fkrueger@cfnj.org
Web: www.cfnj.org/current-funds/student-scholarships

Summary To provide financial assistance to female residents of New Jersey who demonstrate outstanding scholarship, character, personality, and leadership qualities.

Eligibility This program is open to women graduating from
high schools in New Jersey who have already been accepted
at a postsecondary educational institution in any state. Applicants may not necessarily be the top student in their class,
but they must have shown outstanding potential, merit, and/or
improvement. Selection is based primarily on financial need,
but academic performance, extracurricular activities, and
work experience are also considered.

Financial data The stipend is $1,250 per year. Funds are
made payable jointly to the recipient and her educational
institution.

Duration 4 years, provided the recipient maintains a GPA
of 2.8 or higher.

Additional information This program was established
after September 11, 2001 to honor a student who was killed
in the attack on the World Trade Center.

Number awarded 1 each year.

Deadline March of each year.

[199]
DONALD AND ITASKER THORNTON MEMORIAL SCHOLARSHIP

Thornton Sisters Foundation
P.O. Box 21
Atlantic Highlands, NJ 07716-0021
(732) 872-1353   E-mail: tsfoundation2001@yahoo.com
Web: www.thornton-sisters.com/ttsf.htm

Summary To provide financial assistance for college to
women of color in New Jersey.

Eligibility This program is open to women of color (defined
as African Americans, Latino Americans, Caribbean Americans, and Native Americans) who are graduating from high
schools in New Jersey. Applicants must have a grade average
of "C+" or higher and be able to document financial need.
They must be planning to attend an accredited 4-year college
or university. Along with their application, they must submit a
500-word essay describing their family background, personal
and financial hardships, honors or academic distinctions, and
community involvement and activities.

Financial data A stipend is awarded (amount not specified). Funds are to be used for tuition and/or books.

Duration 1 year; nonrenewable.
Number awarded 1 or more each year.
Deadline May of each year.

[200]
DOREEN MCMULLAN MCCARTHY MEMORIAL ACADEMIC SCHOLARSHIP FOR WOMEN WITH BLEEDING DISORDERS

National Hemophilia Foundation
Attn: Victory for Women Program
7 Penn Plaza
370 Seventh Avenue, Suite 1204
New York, NY 10001
(212) 328-3700   Toll Free: (800) 42-HANDI, ext. 2
Fax: (212) 328-3777   E-mail: sroger@hemophilia.org
Web: www.hemophilia.org

Summary To provide financial assistance for college or graduate school to women who have a bleeding disorder.

Eligibility This program is open to women who are entering or already enrolled in an undergraduate or graduate program at a university, college, or accredited vocational school. Applicants must have von Willebrand Disease, hemophilia or other clotting factor deficiency, platelet disorder, or carrier status. Along with their application, they must submit a 250-word essay that describes how their education and future career plans will benefit others in the bleeding disorders community. Selection is based on that essay, achievements, and community service to the bleeding disorders community.

Financial data The stipend is $2,500.

Duration 1 year.

Additional information The program, known also as V4W, was established in 2005 as the Project Red Flag Academic Scholarship for Women with Bleeding and later named the Victory for Women Academic Scholarship for Women with Bleeding Disorders.

Number awarded 1 each year.

Deadline March of each year.

[201]
DORIS HERTSGAARD SCHOLARSHIP

Fargo-Moorhead Area Foundation
Attn: Finance/Program Assistant
502 First Avenue North, Suite 202
Fargo, ND 58102-4804
(701) 234-0756   Fax: (701) 234-9724
E-mail: Cher@areafoundation.org
Web: www.areafoundation.org/index.php/scholarships

Summary To provide financial assistance to women from any state who are working on an undergraduate or graduate degree in a mathematics-related field at specified colleges and universities in Minnesota or North Dakota.

Eligibility This program is open to women from any state who are currently enrolled at Concordia University, Minnesota State University at Moorhead, or North Dakota State University. Applicants must be working on an undergraduate or graduate degree with a mathematics component (e.g., computer science, engineering, mathematics, physical science, statistics). Along with their application, they must submit a 2-page essay on their professional goals and how those relate to their academic interest in their mathematical field of study. Financial need is considered in the selection process, but

greater emphasis is placed on academic achievement. Preference is given to women who are single parents with preteenage children.

Financial data A stipend is awarded (amount not specified).

Duration 1 year.

Number awarded 1 or more each year.

Deadline April of each year.

[202]
DORIS M. GERRISH SCHOLARSHIPS

Native Daughters of the Golden West
Attn: Education and Scholarships
543 Baker Street
San Francisco, CA 94117-1405
(415) 563-9091   Toll Free: (800) 994-NDGW
Fax: (415) 563-5230   E-mail: ndgwgpo@att.net
Web: www.ndgw.org/edu.htm

Summary To provide financial assistance to female residents of California who are preparing for a teaching career.

Eligibility This program is open to women from California who are working on a teaching credential at an accredited university, college, or vocational school in the state. Applicants must be undergraduates who have completed the first year of college with a GPA of 3.0 or higher. They must have been born in the state and be sponsored by a local parlor of the Native Daughters of the Golden West (NDGW). Preference is given to members of NDGW.

Financial data The stipend is $1,500.

Duration 1 year; nonrenewable.

Number awarded 3 each year.

Deadline April of each year.

[203]
DOROTHEA DEITZ ENDOWED MEMORIAL SCHOLARSHIP

Women's Sports Foundation
Attn: Award and Grant Programs Manager
Eisenhower Park
1899 Hempstead Turnpike, Suite 400
East Meadow, NY 11554-1000
(516) 307-3915   Toll Free: (800) 227-3988
E-mail: lflores@womenssportsfoundation.org
Web: www.womenssportsfoundation.org

Summary To provide financial assistance to women who are high school seniors in New York and planning to attend college in any state to prepare for a career as a physical education teacher.

Eligibility This program is open to female seniors graduating from high schools in New York and planning to enroll full time at a college or university in any state. Applicants must be planning to prepare for a career in the physical education teaching profession. They must have a GPA of 3.0 or higher. Selection is based on academic achievement, character, physical education competence, participation in athletics, quality of leadership, community service, and financial need.

Financial data The stipend is $1,000.

Duration 1 year; nonrenewable.

Additional information This program began in 2015.

Number awarded 3 to 9 each year.

Deadline May of each year.

[204]
DOROTHY C. WISNER SCHOLARSHIP

P.E.O. Foundation-California State Chapter
c/o Holly Harris, White Scholarship Fund
56 Cottage court
Sonora, CA 95370
E-mail: peoca.rgw@gmail.com
Web: www.peocalifornia.org

Summary To provide financial assistance to women from California who are interested in working on an undergraduate degree in the medical field at a school in any state.

Eligibility This program is open to female residents of California who have completed at least their first year of undergraduate work in the broad field of medicine. Graduate students are not eligible. Applicants may be studying in any state. They must submit a personal narrative that describes their background, interests, scholastic achievements, extracurricular activities, service, talents, and goals. Selection is based on character, integrity, academic excellence, and financial need. U.S. citizenship is required.

Financial data The stipend ranges from $500 to $1,000 per year.

Duration 1 year; recipients may reapply.

Additional information This fund was established in 1990.

Number awarded 1 each year.

Deadline January of each year.

[205]
DOROTHY CAMPBELL MEMORIAL SCHOLARSHIP

Oregon Office of Student Access and Completion
Attn: Scholarship Processing Coordinator
1500 Valley River Drive, Suite 100
Eugene, OR 97401-2146
(541) 687-7422   Toll Free: (800) 452-8807, ext. 7422
Fax: (541) 687-7414   TDD: (800) 735-2900
E-mail: cheryl.a.connolly@state.or.us
Web: app.oregonstudentaid.gov/Catalog/Default.aspx

Summary To provide financial assistance to women in Oregon who are interested in golf and planning to attend college in the state.

Eligibility This program is open to residents of Oregon who are U.S. citizens or permanent residents. Applicants must be female high school seniors who have a cumulative GPA of 2.75 or higher and a record of participation on their high school golf team (including an intramural team). They must be planning to enroll full-time at an Oregon 4-year college. Along with their application, they must submit a 1-page essay on the contribution that golf has made to their development. Financial need is considered in the selection process.

Financial data Stipends for scholarships offered by the Oregon Office of Student Access and Completion (OSAC) range from $1,000 to $10,000 but recently averaged $4,368.

Duration 1 year; may be renewed up to 3 additional years.

Additional information This program is administered by the OSAC with funds provided by the Oregon Community Foundation.

Number awarded Varies each year; recently, 2 were awarded.

Deadline February of each year.

[206]
DOROTHY COOKE WHINERY MUSIC BUSINESS/ TECHNOLOGY SCHOLARSHIP

Sigma Alpha Iota Philanthropies, Inc.
One Tunnel Road
Asheville, NC 28805
(828) 251-0606   Fax: (828) 251-0644
E-mail: nh@sai-national.org
Web: app.smarterselect.com

Summary To provide financial assistance to members of Sigma Alpha Iota (an organization of women musicians) working on a degree in music, business, or technology.

Eligibility This program is open to members of the organization enrolled as undergraduate or graduate students. Applicants must be working on a degree in the field of music business or music technology, including music marketing, music business administration, entertainment industry, commercial music, recording and production, music management, or other related fields. They must have a GPA of 3.0 or higher. Along with their application, they must submit a statement of purpose that includes their career goals.

Financial data The stipend is $2,000.

Duration 1 year.

Additional information This program began in 2003.

Number awarded 1 each year.

Deadline March of each year.

[207]
DOROTHY E. SCHOELZEL MEMORIAL SCHOLARSHIP

General Federation of Women's Clubs of Connecticut
c/o Joan Duffy, President
2 Quincy Close
Ridgefield, CT 06877
E-mail: duffy-gfwc@appsolutions.com
Web: www.gfwcct.org

Summary To provide financial assistance to women in Connecticut who are working on an undergraduate or graduate degree in education.

Eligibility This program is open to female residents of Connecticut who have completed at least 3 years of college. Applicants must have a GPA of 3.0 or higher and be working on a bachelor's or master's degree in education. They must be U.S. citizens. Selection is based on academic ability, future promise, and financial need.

Financial data The stipend is $2,000.

Duration 1 year.

Number awarded 1 each year.

Deadline February of each year.

[208]
DOROTHY L. WELLER PEO SCHOLARSHIP

P.E.O. Foundation-California State Chapter
c/o Marilyn Bauriedel, Weller Scholarship Fund
3673 South Court
Palo Alto, CA 94306
E-mail: peoca.dlw@gmail.com
Web: www.peocalifornia.org

Summary To provide financial assistance for law school or paralegal studies to women in California.

Eligibility This program is open to female residents of California who have been admitted to an accredited law school or a licensed paralegal school. Applicants must have completed 4 years of high school and be able to demonstrate excellence in academic ability, character, integrity, and school activities. Financial need is also considered in the selection process. U.S. citizenship is required.

Financial data Recently, the stipend was $2,500.

Duration 1 year.

Number awarded Varies each year; recently, 4 were awarded.

Deadline January of each year.

[209]
DOROTHY LEMKE HOWARTH MEMORIAL SCHOLARSHIPS

Society of Women Engineers
Attn: Scholarship Selection Committee
203 North LaSalle Street, Suite 1675
Chicago, IL 60601-1269
(312) 596-5223   Toll Free: (877) SWE-INFO
Fax: (312) 644-8557   E-mail: scholarships@swe.org
Web: societyofwomenengineers.swe.org

Summary To provide financial assistance to lower-division women majoring in computer science or engineering.

Eligibility This program is open to women who are entering their sophomore year at a 4-year ABET-accredited college or university. Applicants must be U.S. citizens who are working full time on a degree in computer science or engineering. Selection is based on merit.

Financial data The stipend is $3,000.

Duration 1 year.

Additional information This program began in 1992.

Number awarded 6 each year.

Deadline February of each year.

[210]
DOROTHY M. AND EARL S. HOFFMAN SCHOLARSHIPS

Society of Women Engineers
Attn: Scholarship Selection Committee
203 North LaSalle Street, Suite 1675
Chicago, IL 60601-1269
(312) 596-5223   Toll Free: (877) SWE-INFO
Fax: (312) 644-8557   E-mail: scholarships@swe.org
Web: societyofwomenengineers.swe.org

Summary To provide financial assistance to women who will be entering college as freshmen and are interested in studying engineering or computer science.

Eligibility This program is open to women who are entering college as freshmen with a GPA of 3.5 or higher. Applicants must be planning to enroll full time at an ABET-accredited 4-year college or university and major in computer science or engineering. Selection is based on merit. Preference is given to students at Bucknell University and Rensselaer Polytechnic Institute.

Financial data The stipend is $3,000 per year.

Duration 1 year; may be renewed for up to 2 additional years, provided the recipient maintains a GPA of 3.0 or higher.

Additional information This program began in 1999.

Number awarded Varies each year; recently, 8 were awarded.

Deadline May of each year.

[211]
DOROTHY P. MORRIS SCHOLARSHIP

Society of Women Engineers
Attn: Scholarship Selection Committee
203 North LaSalle Street, Suite 1675
Chicago, IL 60601-1269
(312) 596-5223   Toll Free: (877) SWE-INFO
Fax: (312) 644-8557   E-mail: scholarships@swe.org
Web: societyofwomenengineers.swe.org

Summary To provide financial assistance to undergraduate women majoring in computer science or engineering.

Eligibility This program is open to women who are entering their sophomore, junior, or senior year at a 4-year ABET-accredited college or university. Applicants must be U.S. citizens working full time on a degree in computer science or engineering. Financial need is considered in the selection process.

Financial data The stipend is $1,500.

Duration 1 year.

Number awarded 1 each year.

Deadline February of each year.

[212]
DOROTHY YOTHERS "SECOND CHANCES" SCHOLARSHIP

Washington State Elks Association
4512 South Pine Street
P.O. Box 110760
Tacoma, WA 98411-0760
(253) 472-6223   Toll Free: (800) 825-ELKS
Fax: (253) 472-6217
Web: www.waelks.org/forms.htm

Summary To provide financial assistance to mature women in Washington state who are interested in pursuing vocational training.

Eligibility This program is open to women older than 25 years of age who are residents of Washington. Applicants must be U.S. citizens and planning to enroll in a course of vocational/technical training that does not exceed 2 years in length. Students seeking education that requires a 4-year degree are ineligible. Along with their application, they must submit a statement of 200 to 300 words describing their activities, accomplishments, needs, and objectives that they believe qualify them for this grant. Selection is based on motivation, skills, and financial need.

Financial data   Stipends range up to $1,000 per quarter.

Duration   1 quarter; may be renewed until completion of the program, provided the recipient maintains a GPA of 3.0 or higher.

Number awarded   The Washington State Elks Association awards 60 scholarships each year.

Deadline   May of each year.

[213]
DR. BEA OKWU GIRL SCOUT GOLD AWARD SCHOLARSHIP

Girl Scouts of Connecticut
Attn: Program Department
340 Washington Street
Hartford, CT 06106
(860) 522-0163   Toll Free: (800) 922-2770 (within CT)
E-mail: general@gsofct.org
Web: www.gsofct.org/pages/goldaward.php

Summary   To provide financial assistance to Girl Scouts in Connecticut who plan to attend college in any state.

Eligibility   This program is open to high school seniors who are registered Girl Scouts in Connecticut and planning to attend college in any state. Applicants must have earned the Gold Award. Along with their application, they must submit brief essays on 1) how their overall Girl Scout experience has empowered them; and 2) how their Gold Award project addressed a community issue and how, as a result of accomplishing their Gold Award, they have grown personally. Selection is based primarily on achievement in the completion of the Gold Award requirements.

Financial data   The stipend is $1,000.

Duration   1 year.

Number awarded   1 each year.

Deadline   March of each year.

[214]
DR. BLANCA MOORE-VELEZ WOMAN OF SUBSTANCE SCHOLARSHIP

National Association of Negro Business and Professional
   Women's Clubs
Attn: Scholarship Committee
1806 New Hampshire Avenue, N.W.
Washington, DC 20009-3206
(202) 483-4206   Fax: (202) 462-7253
E-mail: arlucas48@gmail.com
Web: www.nanbpwc.org/index-11.html

Summary   To provide financial assistance to mature African American women who are interested in working on an undergraduate degree at a college in any state.

Eligibility   This program is open to African American women over 35 years of age who are working on an undergraduate degree at an accredited college or university in any state. They must have a GPA of 3.0 or higher. Along with their application, they must submit a 500-word essay on "Challenges to the Mature Student and How I Overcame Them." Financial need is not considered in the selection process. U.S. citizenship is required.

Financial data   A stipend is awarded (amount not specified).

Duration   1 year.

Number awarded   1 each year.

Deadline   February of each year.

[215]
DR. CELESTE BELCASTRO SCHOLARSHIP

Society of Women Engineers-Hampton Roads Section
Attn: Scholarship Committee Chair
P.O. Box 5020
Virginia Beach, VA 23471
Web: www.hr-swe.org/scholarships

Summary   To provide financial assistance to women working on an undergraduate degree in engineering.

Eligibility   This program is open to full-time undergraduate female engineering student enrolled at a college, university, or community college in any state. Applicants must be U.S. citizens or permanent residents. Along with their application, they must submit a 250-word essay on why they should be considered for this scholarship.

Financial data   The stipend is $1,000.

Duration   1 year.

Number awarded   1 each year.

Deadline   May of each year.

[216]
DR. IVY M. PARKER MEMORIAL SCHOLARSHIP

Society of Women Engineers
Attn: Scholarship Selection Committee
203 North LaSalle Street, Suite 1675
Chicago, IL 60601-1269
(312) 596-5223   Toll Free: (877) SWE-INFO
Fax: (312) 644-8557   E-mail: scholarships@swe.org
Web: societyofwomenengineers.swe.org

Summary   To provide financial assistance to upper-division women majoring in computer science or engineering.

Eligibility   This program is open to women who are entering their junior or senior year at an ABET-accredited college or university. Applicants must be working full time on a degree in computer science, engineering technology, or engineering. Financial need is considered in the selection process.

Financial data   The stipend is $1,500.

Duration   1 year; students who receive the scholarship as a junior may renew it for their senior year.

Additional information   This program began in 1987.

Number awarded   1 each year.

Deadline   February of each year.

[217]
DR. JULIANNE MALVEAUX SCHOLARSHIP

National Association of Negro Business and Professional
   Women's Clubs
Attn: Scholarship Committee
1806 New Hampshire Avenue, N.W.
Washington, DC 20009-3206
(202) 483-4206   Fax: (202) 462-7253
E-mail: arlucas48@gmail.com
Web: www.nanbpwc.org/index-11.html

Summary   To provide financial assistance to African American women studying journalism, economics, or a related field in college.

Eligibility This program is open to African American women enrolled at an accredited college or university as a sophomore or junior. Applicants must have a GPA of 3.0 or higher and be majoring in journalism, economics, or a related field. Along with their application, they must submit an essay, up to 1,000 words in length, on their career plans and their relevance to the theme of the program: "Black Women's Hands Can Rock the World." U.S. citizenship is required.

Financial data The stipend is $1,000.

Duration 1 year.

Number awarded 1 or more each year.

Deadline February of each year.

[218]
DR. SHARON WIBER YOUNG CAREERIST SCHOLARSHIP

Kansas Federation of Business & Professional Women's Clubs, Inc.
Attn: Kansas BPW Educational Foundation, Inc.
c/o Kathy Niehoff, Executive Secretary
605 East 15th
Ottawa, KS 66067
(785) 242-9319   Fax: (785) 242-1047
E-mail: kathyniehoff@sbcglobal.net
Web: kansasbpw.memberlodge.org/page-450103?

Summary To provide financial assistance for college to residents of Kansas who have participated in the Young Careerist Program of the Kansas BPW Educational Foundation.

Eligibility This program is open to members of the Kansas BPW between 21 and 35 years of age who have represented their local BPW organization in district, regional, or state Young Careerist competitions and are majoring in a subject that will increase their employable skills. Applicants must submit 1) proof of participation in the Young Careerist program; and 2) a 3-page personal biography in which they express their career goals, the direction they want to take in the future, their proposed field of study, their reason for selecting that field, the institutions they plan to attend and why, their circumstances for reentering school (if a factor), and what makes them uniquely qualified for this scholarship. They must also be able to document financial need. Applications must be submitted through a local unit of the sponsor.

Financial data A stipend is awarded (amount not specified).

Duration 1 year.

Number awarded 1 or more each year.

Deadline December of each year.

[219]
DRIVE TO SUCCEED SCHOLARSHIP

General Motors Corporation
Women's Retail Network
c/o Charitable Management Systems, Inc.
P.O. Box 648
Naperville, IL 60566
(630) 428-2412   Fax: (630) 428-2695
E-mail: wrnscholarshipinfo@gmsac.com
Web: www.gmsac.com

Summary To provide financial assistance to women attending college or graduate school to prepare for a retail automotive career.

Eligibility This program is open to women who are enrolled full time in undergraduate, graduate, and nontraditional continuing education institutions that offer degrees in the automotive retail and/or automotive service field. Applicants must be interested in preparing for a career in automotive retail and/or service management. They may also be currently employees of an automotive dealership and enrolled in an educational institution that offers formal programs or certifications that advance their career within automotive retail. Applicants must be citizens of the United States or have the ability to accept permanent employment in the United States without the need for visa sponsorship now or in the future. Along with their application, they must submit an essay of 500 to 750 words on their interest and motivation for a career in the automotive retail and/or automotive service sector. Selection is based on that statement, academic performance, leadership and participation in school and community activities, work experience, career and educational aspirations, and financial need.

Financial data The stipend is $5,000 per year.

Duration 1 year; recipients may reapply.

Additional information This program began in 2011.

Number awarded Varies each year; recently, 6 were awarded.

Deadline April of each year.

[220]
DUPONT SCHOLARSHIPS

Society of Women Engineers
Attn: Scholarship Selection Committee
203 North LaSalle Street, Suite 1675
Chicago, IL 60601-1269
(312) 596-5223   Toll Free: (877) SWE-INFO
Fax: (312) 644-8557   E-mail: scholarships@swe.org
Web: societyofwomenengineers.swe.org

Summary To provide financial assistance to women interested in studying chemical or mechanical engineering at a college or university in the East or Midwest.

Eligibility This program is open to women entering their sophomore, junior, or senior year as a full-time student at an ABET-accredited 4-year college or university in an eastern or midwestern state. Applicants must have a GPA of 3.0 or higher and be planning to major in chemical or mechanical engineering or related engineering technology. Selection is based on merit.

Financial data The stipend is $1,000.

Duration 1 year.

Additional information This program, established in 2000, is sponsored by E.I. duPont de Nemours and Company.

Number awarded 2 each year.

Deadline February of each year.

[221]
E. WAYNE COOLEY SCHOLARSHIP AWARD

Iowa Girls High School Athletic Union
Attn: Scholarships
5000 Westown Parkway, Suite 150
West Des Moines, IA 50266
(515) 288-9741   Fax: (515) 284-1969
E-mail: mail@ighsau.org
Web: www.ighsau.org

Summary   To provide financial assistance to female high school seniors in Iowa who have participated in athletics and plan to attend college in the state.

Eligibility   This program is open to women graduating from high schools in Iowa who have a GPA of 3.75 or higher and an ACT score of 23 or higher. Applicants must have earned a varsity letter in at least 2 different sports and have participated in at least 2 sports each year of high school. They must be planning to attend a college or university in Iowa. Each high school in the state may nominate 1 student. Selection is based on academic achievements, athletic accomplishments, non-sports extracurricular activities, and community involvement.

Financial data   The winner's stipend is $3,750 per year. Finalists receive a $1,000 scholarship.

Duration   4 years for the winner, provided she maintains at least a 2.5 GPA while enrolled in college. The scholarships for finalists are for 1 year.

Additional information   This program began in 1993.

Number awarded   6 each year: 1 winner and 5 finalists.

Deadline   November of each year.

[222]
EDITH GREEN GRANT

Delta Kappa Gamma Society International-Alpha Rho
   State Organization
c/o Martha Nicoloff, State Scholarship Chair
242 Muirfield Avenue, S.E.
Salem, OR 97306
(503) 999-20698   E-mail: nicoloff2@comcast.net
Web: www.deltakappagamma.org

Summary   To provide financial assistance to women from Oregon who are enrolled as upper-division students at a college in any state and preparing for a career in secondary education.

Eligibility   This program is open to female residents of Oregon who are at least juniors at a college in any state and interested in preparing for a career in secondary education. Applicants may not be members of Delta Kappa Gamma (an honorary society of women educators), but they must be sponsored by a local chapter of the society. Along with their application, they must submit a summary of their education from high school through the present, high school and college activities and achievements, community service, employment history, career goals, and financial need.

Financial data   A stipend is awarded (amount not specified).

Duration   1 year.

Number awarded   1 or more each year.

Deadline   January of each year.

[223]
EDUCATIONAL FOUNDATION FOR WOMEN IN ACCOUNTING IMA UNDERGRADUATE SCHOLARSHIP

Educational Foundation for Women in Accounting
Attn: Foundation Administrator
136 South Keowee Street
Dayton, OH 45402
(937) 424-3391   Fax: (937) 222-5749
E-mail: info@efwa.org
Web: www.efwa.org/scholarships_undergraduate.php

Summary   To provide financial support to women who are working on an undergraduate accounting degree.

Eligibility   This program is open to women who are enrolled at any stage in an accounting bachelor's degree program at an accredited college or university. Selection is based on aptitude for accounting and business, commitment to the goal of working on a degree in accounting (including evidence of continued commitment after receiving this award), clear evidence that the candidate has established goals and a plan for achieving those goals (both personal and professional), and financial need. U.S. citizenship is required.

Financial data   The stipend is $2,000. Winners also receive a CMA Learning System kit (worth $745) and a complimentary 1-year student membership to the Institute of Management Accountants (IMA).

Duration   1 year.

Additional information   This program is funded by the IMA.

Number awarded   2 each year.

Deadline   April of each year.

[224]
EDWIN G. AND LAURETTA M. MICHAEL SCHOLARSHIP

Christian Church (Disciples of Christ)
Attn: Disciples Home Missions
130 East Washington Street
P.O. Box 1986
Indianapolis, IN 46206-1986
(317) 713-2652   Toll Free: (888) DHM-2631
Fax: (317) 635-4426   E-mail: mail@dhm.disciples.org
Web: www.discipleshomemissions.org

Summary   To provide financial support to ministers' wives whose basic education was interrupted to enable their husbands to complete their theological education.

Eligibility   This program is open to ministers' wives who are working on an undergraduate degree and whose husbands have completed their basic theological education, are employed full time in ministry, and hold standing in the ministry of the Christian Church (Disciples of Christ) in the United States or Canada. Primary consideration is given to ministers' wives who will be in institutions of higher education accredited by 1 of the major regionally accrediting bodies for secondary schools and colleges. Evidence of financial need is required.

Financial data   The stipend is $1,000.

Duration   1 year.

Number awarded   A limited number are awarded each year.

Deadline   March of each year.

[225]
ELIZABETH AHLEMEYER QUICK/GAMMA PHI BETA SCHOLARSHIP

National Panhellenic Conference
Attn: NPC Foundation
3901 West 86th Street, Suite 398
Indianapolis, IN 46268
(317) 872-3185   Fax: (317) 872-3192
E-mail: npcfoundation@npcwomen.org
Web: www.npcwomen.org/foundation/scholarships.aspx

Summary   To provide financial assistance to undergraduate women who are members of Greek-letter societies.

Eligibility   This program is open to women enrolled full time as juniors or seniors at colleges and universities in the United States. Applicants must have a GPA of 3.0 or higher and be able to demonstrate financial need. They must be nominated by their college Panhellenic and have demonstrated outstanding service to that organization. Along with their application, they must submit a 500-word essay on why they should receive a scholarship. Selection is based on financial need, academic standing, and service to campus, chapter, and community.

Financial data   The stipend is $2,000.

Duration   1 year.

Number awarded   1 each year.

Deadline   April of each year.

[226]
ELIZABETH GREENHALGH MEMORIAL SCHOLARSHIP

Women Divers Hall of Fame
43 MacKey Avenue
Port Washington, NY 11050-3628
E-mail: scholarships@wdhof.org
Web: www.wdhof.org/scholarships/scholarships.shtml

Summary   To provide financial assistance to women divers who are working on an undergraduate degree in journalism, graphic arts, or photography.

Eligibility   This program is open to women divers who are working on an undergraduate degree in journalism, graphic arts, or photography to better serve the ocean environment or ocean community. Applicants must be seeking funding to assist with college tuition and fees or to support a research internship program at an accredited university.

Financial data   The stipend is $1,500.

Duration   1 year.

Number awarded   1 each year.

Deadline   November of each year.

[227]
ELIZABETH LOWELL PUTNAM PRIZE

Mathematical Association of America
1529 18th Street, N.W.
Washington, DC 20036-1358
(202) 387-5200   Toll Free: (800) 741-9415
Fax: (202) 265-2384   E-mail: maahq@maa.org
Web: www.maa.org

Summary   To recognize and reward outstanding women participants in a mathematics competition.

Eligibility   This program is open to women at colleges and universities in Canada and the United States. Entrants participate in an examination containing mathematics problems designed to test originality as well as technical competence. The woman with the highest score receives this prize.

Financial data   The prize is $1,000.

Duration   The competition is held annually.

Additional information   This program began in 1992.

Number awarded   1 each year.

Deadline   Deadline not specified.

[228]
ELIZABETH MCLEAN MEMORIAL SCHOLARSHIP

Society of Women Engineers
Attn: Scholarship Selection Committee
203 North LaSalle Street, Suite 1675
Chicago, IL 60601-1269
(312) 596-5223   Toll Free: (877) SWE-INFO
Fax: (312) 644-8557   E-mail: scholarships@swe.org
Web: societyofwomenengineers.swe.org

Summary   To provide financial assistance to undergraduate women majoring in civil engineering.

Eligibility   This program is open to women who are entering their sophomore, junior, or senior year at an ABET-accredited 4-year college or university. Applicants must be working full time on a degree in civil engineering. Selection is based on merit.

Financial data   The stipend is $1,500.

Duration   1 year.

Additional information   This program began in 2004.

Number awarded   1 each year.

Deadline   February of each year.

[229]
ELLA JEAN MORGAN MEMORIAL DIVE TRAINING GRANTS

Women Divers Hall of Fame
43 MacKey Avenue
Port Washington, NY 11050-3628
E-mail: scholarships@wdhof.org
Web: www.wdhof.org/scholarships/scholarships.shtml

Summary   To provide financial assistance to young women who are interested in beginning dive training.

Eligibility   This program is open to women between 15 and 21 years of age who are interested in dive training. Applicants must be interested in a course that consists of at least 12 hours of classroom training, 12 hours of pool/confined-water training, and at least 5 open-water dives. It must culminate in certification from a nationally recognized diver-training agency.

Financial data   The grant is $1,000, including $500 for training and $500 for equipment.

Duration   Training must be completed within 1 year.

Number awarded   2 each year.

Deadline   November of each year.

[230]
ELLEN HIPPELI MEMORIAL SCHOLARSHIP

Society of Women Engineers
Attn: Scholarship Selection Committee
203 North LaSalle Street, Suite 1675
Chicago, IL 60601-1269
(312) 596-5223   Toll Free: (877) SWE-INFO
Fax: (312) 644-8557   E-mail: scholarships@swe.org
Web: societyofwomenengineers.swe.org

Summary To provide financial assistance to women who are entering freshmen at a college in any state to study nuclear engineering.

Eligibility This program is open to women who are entering freshmen at an ABET-accredited college or university in any state. Applicants must be planning to work on a degree in nuclear engineering. They must be U.S. citizens. Selection is based on merit.

Financial data The stipend is $1,000.

Duration 1 year.

Additional information This program, which began in 2015, is sponsored by the Central New Mexico section of SWE, but women from any state are eligible.

Number awarded 1 each year.

Deadline May of each year.

[231]
ELOISE CAMPBELL MEMORIAL SCHOLARSHIPS

United Daughters of the Confederacy
Attn: Second Vice President General
328 North Boulevard
Richmond, VA 23220-4009
(804) 355-1636   Fax: (804) 353-1396
E-mail: udc@hqudc.org
Web: www.hqudc.org/scholarships

Summary To provide financial assistance for college to women, particularly in selected areas of Arkansas or Texas, who are lineal descendants of Confederate veterans.

Eligibility Eligible to apply for these scholarships are lineal descendants of worthy Confederates or collateral descendants who are members of the Children of the Confederacy or the United Daughters of the Confederacy. Applicants must be female and have at least a 3.0 GPA in high school. Preference is given to candidates from Bowie County, Texas and Miller County, Arkansas. Applications must be accompanied by a family financial report and certified proof of the Confederate military record of 1 ancestor, with the company and regiment in which he served.

Financial data The amount of the scholarship depends on the availability of funds.

Duration 1 year; may be renewed up to 3 additional years, provided the recipient remains enrolled full time with a GPA of 3.0 or higher.

Number awarded 1 each year.

Deadline April of each year.

[232]
ELSIE G. RIDDICK SCHOLARSHIP

Business and Professional Women of North Carolina
Attn: North Carolina Business and Professional Women's
  Foundation, Inc.
c/o Carol Ambrose, Scholarship Chair
2300 Cloister Drive
Charlotte, NC 28211
(704) 362-2066   E-mail: mcarolambrose65@gmail.com
Web: www.bpw-nc.org/Educational_Scholarship

Summary To provide financial assistance to women attending North Carolina colleges, community colleges, or graduate schools.

Eligibility This program is open to women who are currently enrolled in a community college, 4-year college, or graduate school in North Carolina. Applicants must be endorsed by a local BPW unit and have a GPA of 2.5 or higher. Along with their application, they must submit a 1-page statement that summarizes their career goals, previous honors, or community activities and justifies their need for this scholarship. U.S. citizenship is required.

Financial data The stipend is $1,000. Funds are paid directly to the recipient's school.

Duration 1 year; recipients may reapply.

Additional information This program began in 1925 as a loan fund. Since 1972 it has been administered as a scholarship program.

Number awarded 1 each year.

Deadline April of each year.

[233]
EMERGE SCHOLARSHIPS

Emerge Scholarships, Inc.
3525 Piedmont Road, Building 5, Suite 300
Atlanta, GA 30305
(404) 760-2887   E-mail: info@emergescholarships.org
Web: www.emergescholarships.org

Summary To provide financial assistance to women in Georgia interested in returning to college or graduate school after a delay or interruption.

Eligibility This program is open to female residents of Georgia who are at least 25 years of age and who have interrupted or delayed their education because they are changing careers, seeking advancement in their career or work life, looking for personal growth, or returning to school after caring for children. Applicants must have been accepted as an undergraduate or graduate student at an educational institution. Along with their application, they must submit a 2-page essay on how beginning or continuing their education will positively impact their life. Selection is based on that essay, leadership and participation in community activities, honors and awards received, career and life goals, financial need, and other funding received.

Financial data Stipends range from $2,000 to $5,000.

Duration 1 year.

Additional information This program began in 2001. Winners are invited to Atlanta to accept their scholarships; the sponsor pays all travel expenses.

Number awarded Varies each year; recently, 7 were awarded.

Deadline May of each year.

[234]
EMERINE MEMORIAL SCHOLARSHIP

Columbus Foundation
Attn: Scholarship Manager
1234 East Broad Street
Columbus, OH 43205-1453
(614) 251-4000   Fax: (614) 251-4009
E-mail: aszempruch@columbusfoundation.org
Web: tcfapp.org

Summary To provide financial assistance to women working on an undergraduate or graduate degree at a college or university in Ohio.

Eligibility This program is open to women currently attending an accredited 4-year college or university in Ohio. Applicants may be residents of any state, although preference may be given to Ohio residents. They must meet 1 of the following stipulations: 1) returned to college as an undergraduate or graduate student after an extended absence of at least 2 years; 2) 23 years of age or older and in college for the first time or applying for graduate school for the first time with a GPA of 3.0 or higher; or 3) has completed the freshman year with a GPA of 3.0 or higher. Along with their application, they must submit their most recent transcript, 2 letters of recommendation, a list of volunteer activities, a list of extracurricular activities, a personal essay on how volunteering has impacted their life, and information on financial need.

Financial data The stipend is $1,500.

Duration 1 year.

Number awarded 1 or more each year.

Deadline March of each year.

[235]
EMILY CHAISON GOLD AWARD SCHOLARSHIP

Girl Scouts of Connecticut
Attn: Program Department
340 Washington Street
Hartford, CT 06106
(860) 522-0163   Toll Free: (800) 922-2770 (within CT)
E-mail: general@gsofct.org
Web: www.gsofct.org/pages/goldaward.php

Summary To provide financial assistance to Girl Scouts in Connecticut who plan to attend college in any state.

Eligibility This program is open to high school seniors who are registered Girl Scouts in Connecticut and planning to attend college in any state. Applicants must have earned the Gold Award. Along with their application, they must submit brief essays on 1) how their overall Girl Scout experience has empowered them; and 2) how they will embody Girl Scout values in the future and the involvement they intend to have with Girl Scouts and why. Selection is based on the essays, community service, and commitment to Girl Scouting.

Financial data The stipend is $1,000.

Duration 1 year.

Additional information This program began in 1985.

Number awarded 1 each year.

Deadline March of each year.

[236]
EMILY SANNEBECK SCHOLARSHIP

Asbury United Methodist Church
Attn: Scholarship Committee
10000 Candelaria, N.E.
Albuquerque, NM 87112
(505) 299-0643   Fax: (505) 299-4954
E-mail: church@asburyabq.org
Web: www.asburyabq.org/sannebeck-scholarship

Summary To provide financial assistance to residents of New Mexico, especially single women, who are interested in attending college or seminary in any state.

Eligibility This program is open to residents of New Mexico who are enrolled or planning to enroll at a college, university, vocational/technical school, or seminary in any state. Applicants must submit a letter that explains their educational plans, need for assistance, school of interest, past academic record, and background information. Preference is given to single women, especially single parents seeking to improve their ability to support themselves. Membership in the sponsoring organization or the United Methodist Church is not required.

Financial data The stipend is $2,000.

Duration 1 year.

Number awarded 1 each year.

Deadline May of each year.

[237]
ESPERANZA SCHOLARSHIP

New York Women in Communications, Inc.
Attn: NYWICI Foundation
355 Lexington Avenue, 15th Floor
New York, NY 10017-6603
(212) 297-2133   Fax: (212) 370-9047
E-mail: nywicipr@nywici.org
Web: www.nywici.org/foundation/scholarships

Summary To provide financial assistance to Hispanic women who are residents of designated eastern states and interested in preparing for a career in communications at a college or graduate school in any state.

Eligibility This program is open to Hispanic women who are seniors graduating from high schools in New York, New Jersey, Connecticut, or Pennsylvania or undergraduate or graduate students who are permanent residents of those states; they must be attending or planning to attend a college or university in any state. Graduate students must be members of New York Women in Communications, Inc. (NYWICI). Also eligible are Hispanic women who reside outside the 4 states but are currently enrolled at a college or university within 1 of the 5 boroughs of New York City. All applicants must be working on a degree in a communications-related field (e.g., advertising, broadcasting, communications, digital media, English, film, journalism, marketing, public relations, publishing) and have a GPA of 3.2 or higher. Along with their application, they must submit a 2-page resume; a personal essay of 300 words on an assigned topic that changes annually; 2 letters of recommendation; and an official transcript. Selection is based on academic record, need, demonstrated leadership, participation in school and community activities, honors and other awards or recognition, work experience, goals and aspirations, and unusual personal and/or family circumstances. U.S. citizenship or permanent resident status is required.

Financial data The stipend ranges up to $10,000.

Duration 1 year.

Additional information This program is funded by Macy's and Bloomingdale's.

Number awarded 1 each year.

Deadline January of each year.

[238]
ETHEL LEE HOOVER ELLIS SCHOLARSHIP

National Association of Negro Business and Professional Women's Clubs
Attn: Scholarship Committee
1806 New Hampshire Avenue, N.W.
Washington, DC 20009-3206
(202) 483-4206   Fax: (202) 462-7253
E-mail: arlucas48@gmail.com
Web: www.nanbpwc.org/index-11.html

Summary To provide financial assistance to African American women from designated southern states studying business at a college in any state.

Eligibility This program is open to African Americans women who are residents of Alabama, Florida, Georgia, Mississippi, North Carolina, South Carolina, Tennessee, or West Virginia. Applicants must be enrolled at an accredited college or university in any state as a sophomore or junior. They must have a GPA of 3.0 or higher and be majoring in business. Along with their application, they must submit an essay, up to 750 words in length, on the topic, "Business and Community United." U.S. citizenship is required.

Financial data A stipend is awarded (amount not specified).

Duration 1 year.

Number awarded 1 or more each year.

Deadline February of each year.

[239]
ETHEL O. GARDNER PEO SCHOLARSHIP

P.E.O. Foundation-California State Chapter
c/o Pat Lachman, Gardner Scholarship Fund
4400 Hessel Road
Sebastopol, CA 95472
E-mail: peoca.eog@gmail.com
Web: www.peocalifornia.org

Summary To provide financial assistance to women from California who are upper-division or graduate students at a school in any state.

Eligibility This program is open to female residents of California who have completed at least 2 years at a college or university in any state. Applicants must be enrolled as full-time undergraduate or graduate students. Selection is based on financial need, character, and a record of academic and extracurricular activities achievement. U.S. citizenship is required.

Financial data Stipends range from $500 to $1,500.

Duration 1 year.

Number awarded Varies each year; recently, 69 were awarded.

Deadline January of each year.

[240]
EUGENIA VELLNER FISCHER AWARD FOR THE PERFORMING ARTS

Miss America Organization
Attn: Director of Scholarships
Park Place and Boardwalk
P.O. Box 1919
Atlantic City, NJ 08404
(609) 653-8700, ext. 127   Fax: (609) 653-8740
E-mail: info@missamerica.org
Web: www.missamerica.org

Summary To provide financial assistance to women who are working on an undergraduate or graduate degree in the performing arts and who, in the past, competed at some level in the Miss America competition.

Eligibility This program is open to women who are working on an undergraduate, master's, or higher degree in the performing arts and who competed at the local, state, or national level in a Miss America competition within the past 10 years. Applicants may be studying dance, instrumental, monologue, or vocal. They must submit an essay, up to 500 words, on the factors that influenced their decision to enter the field of performing arts, what they consider to be their major strengths in the field, and how they plan to use their degree in the field. Selection is based on GPA, class rank, extracurricular activities, financial need, and level of participation within the system.

Financial data The stipend is $2,000.

Duration 1 year; renewable.

Additional information This scholarship was established in 1999.

Number awarded 1 each year.

Deadline June of each year.

[241]
EUNICE RIGGINS MEMORIAL SCHOLARSHIP

Alpha Delta Kappa-North Carolina Chapter
c/o Erna Brown, Scholarship Chair
3645 Moose Road
Kannapolis, NC 28083
(704) 857-1988   E-mail: jamesbrown@ctc.net
Web: www.alphadeltakappa.org

Summary To provide financial assistance to female high school seniors in North Carolina who plan to attend college in the state.

Eligibility This program is open to women graduating from high schools in North Carolina and planning to enroll at a 4-year college or university in the state. Applicants must rank in the top 10% of their class and have scores of at least 1740 on the SAT or 25 on the ACT. Along with their application, they must submit a personal statement on their plans, career goals, and reasons for wanting this scholarship. Selection is based on character and participation in extracurricular activities; financial need is not considered.

Financial data The stipend is $2,000.

Duration 1 year; nonrenewable.

Number awarded 1 each year.

Deadline January of each year.

[242]
EXELON SCHOLARSHIPS

Society of Women Engineers
Attn: Scholarship Selection Committee
203 North LaSalle Street, Suite 1675
Chicago, IL 60601-1269
(312) 596-5223   Toll Free: (877) SWE-INFO
Fax: (312) 644-8557   E-mail: scholarships@swe.org
Web: societyofwomenengineers.swe.org

Summary To provide financial assistance to women who will be entering their freshman, sophomore, or junior year and are interested in studying engineering or computer science.

Eligibility This program is open to women who are enrolling full time in their freshman, sophomore, or junior year at an ABET-accredited 4-year college or university. Preference is given to students at Bradley University, Illinois Institute of Technology, University of Illinois at Chicago, University of Illinois at Urbana-Champaign, University of Maryland-Baltimore County, University of Maryland at College Park, Morgan State University, Pennsylvania State University, or Purdue University. Applicants must be planning to major in computer science or computer, electrical, or mechanical engineering. U.S. citizenship is required. Preference is given to members of groups underrepresented in engineering and computer science, including ethnic and racial minorities, persons with disabilities, and veterans. Selection is based on merit.

Financial data The stipend is $1,000.

Duration 1 year.

Additional information This program is sponsored by Exelon Corporation, parent of ComEd and PECO, the electric utilities for northern Illinois and southeastern Pennsylvania, respectively.

Number awarded 5 each year.

Deadline May of each year for entering freshmen; February of each year for continuing sophomores and juniors.

[243]
FANNIE WILDER EDUCATIONAL FUND SCHOLARSHIP

Center for Scholarship Administration, Inc.
4320 Wade Hampton Boulevard, Suite G
Taylors, SC 29687-0031
(864) 268-3363   Fax: (864) 268-7160
E-mail: allisonleewagoner@bellsouth.net
Web: www.csascholars.org/wilder/index.php?&cff=wilder

Summary To provide financial assistance to women from Georgia who plan to attend college in any state.

Eligibility This program is open to female residents of Georgia who have a cumulative GPA of 2.5 or higher. Applicants must be high school seniors or undergraduates currently enrolled full time at an accredited 4-year college or university in any state. Selection is based on academic ability, educational goals, participation in extracurricular activities, career ambitions, and financial need.

Financial data A stipend is awarded (amount not specified).

Duration 1 year; may be renewed up to 3 additional years or until completion of a bachelor's degree (whichever comes first).

Number awarded 1 or more each year.

Deadline March of each year.

[244]
FAY H. SPENCER MEMORIAL SCHOLARSHIPS IN ARCHITECTURE

Texas Society of Architects
Attn: Texas Architectural Foundation
500 Chicon Street
Austin, TX 78702
(512) 478-7386   Fax: (512) 478-0528
E-mail: foundation@texasarchitect.org
Web: www.texasarchitects.org/v/scholarships

Summary To provide financial assistance to women from any state who are entering their fifth or sixth year of study at designated schools of architecture in Texas.

Eligibility This program is open to women from any state who are entering their fifth or sixth year of study at the school of architecture at the University of Houston, Rice University, Texas A&M University, or the University of Texas. Applicants must submit their application to the office of the dean of their school. Along with their application, they must submit essays on 1) the principal architectural areas or practice categories in which they are most interested, excel, or desire to develop their proficiency; and 2) career plans, short/long-range goals, vision, or other topic about which they are passionate. Financial need is considered in the selection process.

Financial data A stipend is awarded (amount not specified).

Duration 1 year.

Number awarded 2 each year.

Deadline February of each year.

[245]
FCA WOMEN IN ENGINEERING SCHOLARSHIPS

Society of Women Engineers
Attn: Scholarship Selection Committee
203 North LaSalle Street, Suite 1675
Chicago, IL 60601-1269
(312) 596-5223   Toll Free: (877) SWE-INFO
Fax: (312) 644-8557   E-mail: scholarships@swe.org
Web: societyofwomenengineers.swe.org

Summary To provide financial assistance to women working on a degree in computer science or designated fields of engineering.

Eligibility This program is open to women who are entering full-time freshmen, sophomores, juniors, seniors or graduate students at an ABET-accredited 4-year college or university. Applicants must be interested in studying computer science or automotive, chemical, civil, computer, electrical, industrial, manufacturing, materials, or mechanical engineering and have a GPA of 3.0 or higher. Selection is based on merit.

Financial data The stipend is $2,500.

Duration 1 year.

Additional information This program is supported by the Fellowship of Christian Athletes.

Number awarded 20 each year.

Deadline February of each year for continuing students; May of each year for entering freshmen.

[246]
FEDERATION OF HOUSTON PROFESSIONAL WOMEN EDUCATIONAL FOUNDATION SCHOLARSHIPS

Federation of Houston Professional Women
Attn: Educational Foundation
P.O. Box 27621
Houston, TX 77227-7621
E-mail: ef@fhpw.org
Web: www.fhpw.org/fhpw-ef-scholarship

Summary To provide financial assistance for college or graduate school to women from Texas.

Eligibility This program is open to women who are residents of Texas and have completed at least 30 semesters hours of work on an associate, bachelor's, or graduate degree at an accredited college or university in the state. Applicants must be U.S. citizens or permanent residents and have a GPA of 3.0 or higher. Along with their application, they must submit 1) a 200-word statement on their short- and long-term goals; 2) a 400-word essay on either the experiences that have helped determine their goals or the avenues that can help determine their goals; and 3) a 100-word biographical sketch. Financial need is considered in the selection process.

Financial data Stipends are $2,000 for students at 4-year colleges and universities or $1,000 for students at community colleges. Funds are issued payable jointly to the student and the educational institution.

Duration 1 year.

Additional information This program began in 2000.

Number awarded Varies each year; recently, 18 were awarded. Since this program began, it has awarded more than $275,000 in scholarships.

Deadline March of each year.

[247]
FEMALE COLLEGE ATHLETE UNDERGRADUATE SCHOLARSHIP

North Carolina Alliance for Athletics, Health, Physical Education, Recreation, Dance, and Sport Management
Attn: Executive Director
3434 Edwards Mill Road, Suite 112-183
Raleigh, NC 27605
(919) 833-1219   Toll Free: (888) 840-6500
Fax: (888) 840-6FAX E-mail: awards@ncaahperd-sm.org
Web: www.ncaahperd-sm.org

Summary To provide financial assistance to women who are undergraduates involved in sports at an institution that is a member of the former North Carolina Association of Intercollegiate Athletics for Women (NCAIAW).

Eligibility This program is open to women who are members of the North Carolina Alliance for Athletics, Health, Physical Education, Recreation, Dance, and Sport Management (NCAAHPERD-SM) and have participated on 1 or more varsity athletic teams either as a player or in the support role of manager, trainer, etc. Applicants must be attending 1 of the following former NCAIAW colleges or universities in North Carolina: Appalachian State, Belmont Abbey, Bennett, Campbell, Davidson, Duke, East Carolina, Gardner-Webb, High Point, Mars Hill, Meredith, North Carolina A&T, North Carolina State, Pembroke State, Salem, University of North Carolina at Ashville, University of North Carolina at Chapel Hill, University of North Carolina at Charlotte, University of North Carolina at Wilmington, Wake Forest, or Western Carolina. They must be majoring in health education, physical education, recreation, dance, and/or sports management; be able to demonstrate high standards of scholarship; and show evidence of leadership potential (as indicated by participation in school and community activities).

Financial data The stipend is $1,000. Funds are sent to the recipient's school.

Duration 1 year.

Additional information This scholarship was established in 1983 when the NCAIAW dissolved and transferred its assets to the North Carolina Alliance for Athletics, Health, Physical Education, Recreation, Dance, and Sport Management.

Number awarded 1 each year.

Deadline June of each year.

[248]
FINANCIAL WOMEN OF SAN FRANCISCO SCHOLARSHIPS

Financial Women of San Francisco
Attn: Scholarships
P.O. Box 26143
San Francisco, CA 94126
(415) 586-8599   Fax: (415) 586-6606
E-mail: info@financialwomensf.org
Web: www.financialwomensf.org/scholarships

Summary To provide financial assistance to women who are working on an undergraduate or graduate degree in a field related to finance at a college in the San Francisco Bay area.

Eligibility This program is open to women who are entering their junior or senior year or are entering or enrolled as graduate students. Applicants must be attending a college or university located in the San Francisco Bay area (Alameda, Contra Costa, Marin, Napa, San Francisco, San Mateo, Santa Clara, Solano, Sonoma counties); they may be enrolled at an institution outside that area if they are attending a satellite campus located within 1 of those counties and taking at least 80% of their classes at the satellite campus. They must be working on a degree and preparing for a career in finance or in the financial services industry and have a GPA of 3.4 or higher. Along with their application, they must submit a 1,000-word essay on their interest in finance and their reasons for choosing that field. Selection is based on demonstrated leadership skills (both academic and community), communication skills, alignment with the sponsor's goals of supporting women with careers in finance, and financial need.

Financial data Stipends are $5,000 for undergraduates or $10,000 for graduate students.

Duration 1 year.

Additional information This program began in 1985.

Number awarded Varies each year; recently 11 were awarded (2 undergraduates and 9 graduate students). Since the program was established, it has awarded more than $2 million in scholarships to more than 200 women.

Deadline March of each year.

[249]
FLORENCE A. COOK RECRUITMENT GRANTS

Delta Kappa Gamma Society International-Lambda State
  Organization
c/o Kammie Richter, Recruitment Grant Committee Chair
Oakwood CUSD 76
12190 US Route 150
Oakwood, IL 61858
(217) 443-2883   Fax: (217) 446-6218
E-mail: kmrcht93@yahoo.com
Web: www.deltakappagamma.org/IL/profaffairs.htm

Summary To provide financial assistance to female residents of Illinois who are studying education at a college in any state.

Eligibility This program is open to female residents of Illinois who are enrolled in a certified teacher education program at a college or university in any state. Each chapter of the sponsoring organization in Illinois may nominate 1 student for this scholarship. Nominees must submit a 2-page personal essay on their career goals and interests within the field of education. Selection is based on the essay, academic excellence, leadership qualities, participation in school activities, contribution to the community and church, and letters of recommendation.

Financial data The stipend is $1,500.

Duration 1 year.

Additional information The sponsor is an honorary society of women educators.

Number awarded 6 each year: 1 in each area of the state.

Deadline January of each year.

[250]
FLORENCE ALLEN SCHOLARSHIPS

The Allen Endowment
c/o Holly S. Goodyear
3500 Granger Road
Medina, OH 44256-8602
(330) 725-3333   E-mail: allenendowmen@gmail.com

Summary To provide financial assistance to women from Ohio who are interested in attending college in any state.

Eligibility This program is open to women from Ohio who are either traditional students (graduating high school seniors or recent GED recipients) or nontraditional students (at least 30 years of age). Traditional students must be enrolled or planning to enroll full time at a 4-year college or university in any state; nontraditional students must also attend a 4-year college or university, but they are not required to enroll full time. All applicants must submit an essay describing their plans for enrollment in the educational program, career goals, and financial need. U.S. citizenship is required.

Financial data Stipends range from $500 to $1,000.

Duration 1 year.

Additional information This program was originally established in 1924, but became a tax-exempt endowment fund in 1988; since that time, it has awarded more than $86,200 in scholarships.

Number awarded 1 or more each year.

Deadline March of each year.

[251]
FLORIDA ALPHA DELTA KAPPA PAST STATE PRESIDENTS' SCHOLARSHIP AWARD

Alpha Delta Kappa-Florida Chapter
c/o Vivian Bowden
1843 Shadyhill Terrace
Winter Park, FL 32792

Summary To provide financial assistance to women working on an undergraduate or graduate degree in education at a college or university in Florida.

Eligibility This program is open to women currently enrolled at a community college or 4-year college or university in Florida. Applicants must have a GPA of 3.0 or higher and be working on an undergraduate or graduate degree in education. Selection is based on academic ability and performance, character, leadership, and participation in extracurricular activities on campus and in the community.

Financial data The stipend is $1,000.

Duration 1 year.

Number awarded 1 each year.

Deadline December of each year.

[252]
FLORIDA GOLDCOAST CHAPTER 75TH ANNIVERSARY SCHOLARSHIP

Ninety-Nines, Inc.-Florida Goldcoast Chapter
c/o Kimberley Lowe
100 Edgewater Drive, Unit 342
Coral Gables, FL 33133-6980
(305) 984-0561   E-mail: flynlowe@comcast.net
Web: www.flgoldcoast99s.org/scholarships.html

Summary To provide financial assistance to female pilots in Florida who are interested in an aviation training program at a college or flight school in the state.

Eligibility This program is open to women who have a private pilot's certificate and are either residents of Florida or students currently enrolled in an aviation training program in the state. Applicants must be interested in acquiring an additional rating or certificate, attending a college program, or engaging in another aviation endeavor. Along with their application, they must submit a statement describing their education, aviation training and experience, aviation organizations, and employment history; another statement covering their educational purpose and/or aviation goals, their goals, why they chose aviation, and the pilot certificate or rating, college degree, or other goal they plan to attain using this scholarship; and 2 letters of reference. Selection is based on financial need, desire to prepare for a career in aviation, ability to represent women in aviation, likelihood of success in reaching goals, and neatness and completeness of application package.

Financial data The stipend is $2,000.

Duration 1 year.

Number awarded 1 or more each year.

Deadline November of each year.

[253]
FLORIDA LEGION AUXILIARY MEMORIAL SCHOLARSHIP

American Legion Auxiliary
Department of Florida
1912A Lee Road
P.O. Box 547917
Orlando, FL 32854-7917
(407) 293-7411   Toll Free: (866) 710-4192
Fax: (407) 299-6522   E-mail: contact@alafl.org
Web: www.alafl.org/resources/scholarships

Summary To provide financial assistance to members and female dependents of members of the Florida American Legion Auxiliary who are interested in attending college in any state.

Eligibility Applicants must be members of the Florida Auxiliary or daughters or granddaughters of members who have at least 3 years of continuous membership. They must be sponsored by their local units, be Florida residents, and be enrolled or planning to enroll full time at a college, university, community college, or vocational/technical school in any state. Selection is based on academic record and financial need.

Financial data The stipends are up to $2,000 for a 4-year university or up to $1,000 for a community college or vocational/technical school. All funds are paid directly to the institution.

Duration 1 year; may be renewed if the recipient needs further financial assistance and has maintained at least a 2.5 GPA.

Number awarded Varies each year, depending on the availability of funds.

Deadline January of each year.

[254]
FLORIDA P.E.O. SCHOLARSHIPS

P.E.O. Sisterhood-Florida Chapters
c/o Donna Beckwith
2 Holly Circle
Indialantic, FL 32903-4112
(321) 723-1813   E-mail: FLPEOS@gmail.com
Web: www.peoflorida.org

Summary To provide financial assistance to women from Florida who will be entering their freshman year at a college in the state.

Eligibility This program is open to women who are residents of Florida and entering their freshman year as full-time students at an accredited college or university in the state. Applicants must be planning to work on a bachelor's or associate degree. They must be sponsored by a Florida P.E.O. chapter. Selection is based on scholarship, character, and financial need.

Financial data Stipends range up to $2,500.

Duration 1 year; may be renewed 1 additional year, provided the recipient maintains a GPA of 2.5 or higher.

Additional information This program began in 1994.

Number awarded Varies each year.

Deadline Students must apply to their local P.E.O. chapter by January of each year.

[255]
FORD EMERGING VOICES SCHOLARSHIPS

Alliance for Women in Media
Attn: Foundation
2365 Harrodsburg Road, Suite A325
Lexington, KY 40504
(202) 750-3664   E-mail: info@allwomeninmedia.org
Web: www.allwomeninmedia.org/foundation/scholarships

Summary To provide financial assistance to women who are working on an undergraduate or graduate degree in a media-related field and submit outstanding essays on media topics.

Eligibility This program is open to women currently enrolled in an undergraduate or graduate degree program at a college or university in any state. Applicants must be preparing for a media career and working on a degree in such fields as cable, communications, television, radio, digital media, publishing, journalism, advertising, production, creative design, or related areas. Along with their application, they must submit an essay of 300 to 500 words on 1 of the following topics: 1) the most impactful media event in their lifetime and why; 2) in the current political landscape, do they feel that the media is a reflection of the masses or influences the mass public; or 3) a woman in a media that they consider personally influential.

Financial data The stipend is $2,500, paid directly to the recipient's institution. The winners are also invited to write 4 blog posts for the sponsor's web site.

Duration 1 year.

Additional information This program is sponsored by the Ford Motor Company Fund.

Number awarded 2 each year.

Deadline April.

[256]
FORD EMPOWERING AMERICA SCHOLARSHIPS

Alliance for Women in Media
Attn: Foundation
2365 Harrodsburg Road, Suite A325
Lexington, KY 40504
(202) 750-3664   E-mail: info@allwomeninmedia.org
Web: www.allwomeninmedia.org/foundation/scholarships

Summary To provide financial assistance to women who are working on an undergraduate or graduate degree in a media-related field and submit outstanding videos on a female leader in their community.

Eligibility This program is open to women currently enrolled in an undergraduate or graduate degree program at a college or university in any state. Applicants must be preparing for a media career and working on a degree in such fields as cable, communications, television, radio, digital media, publishing, journalism, advertising, production, creative design, or related areas. Along with their application, they must submit a video of 3 to 5 minutes in length on a female leader in their community, which may be defined as family, school, city, or personal network. The leader can be in the media industry, a small business owner, community volunteer, or anyone who especially inspires the applicant.

Financial data The winner receives a stipend of $3,000, payable to her educational institution, and up to $350 to reimburse expenses for her and the person she highlights to attend the sponsor's Women in Media event in New York. The runner-up receives a $2,000 stipend, payable to her educational institution.

Duration 1 year.

Additional information This program is sponsored by the Ford Motor Company Fund.

Number awarded 2 each year.

Deadline April.

[257]
FORD MOTOR COMPANY SWE SCHOLARSHIPS

Society of Women Engineers
Attn: Scholarship Selection Committee
203 North LaSalle Street, Suite 1675
Chicago, IL 60601-1269
(312) 596-5223   Toll Free: (877) SWE-INFO
Fax: (312) 644-8557   E-mail: scholarships@swe.org
Web: societyofwomenengineers.swe.org

Summary To provide financial assistance to undergraduate women majoring in designated engineering specialties.

Eligibility This program is open to women who are entering their sophomore or junior year at a 4-year ABET-accredited college or university. Juniors must be working full time on a degree in automotive, electrical, or mechanical engineering; sophomores may be studying those specialties or industrial or manufacturing engineering. All applicants must have a GPA of 3.5 or higher and be able to demonstrate leadership potential. Selection is based on merit and leadership potential.

Financial data The stipend is $1,250.

Duration 1 year.

Additional information This program, established in 2003, is sponsored by the Ford Motor Company.

Number awarded 3 each year: 1 to a sophomore and 2 to juniors.

Deadline February of each year.

[258]
FORD OPPORTUNITY PROGRAM SCHOLARSHIP

Ford Family Foundation
Attn: Scholarship Office
44 Club Road, Suite 100
Eugene, OR 97401
(541) 485-6211   Toll Free: (877) 864-2872
Fax: (541) 485-6223   E-mail: fordscholarships@tfff.org
Web: www.tfff.org

Summary To provide financial assistance to residents of Oregon and Siskiyou County, California who are single parents working on a college degree at a school in Oregon or California.

Eligibility This program is open to residents of Oregon and Siskiyou County, California who are U.S. citizens or permanent residents. Applicants must be single heads of household with custody of a dependent child or children. They must have a cumulative high school or college GPA of 3.0 or higher or a GED score of 680 or higher, and they must be planning to earn a bachelor's degree. Students from Oregon must attend a college or university in the state; students from Siskiyou County, California must attend a college or university in California. Selection is based on initiative and commitment to roles in school, home, and/or community activities; concern

for others through contributions to volunteer projects and/or family needs; work ethic through paid or unpaid work experiences; ability to succeed academically in college; character; ability to communicate personal strengths and goals clearly; and financial need.

Financial data This program provides up to 90% of a recipient's unmet financial need, to a maximum of $25,000 per year.

Duration 1 year; may be renewed for up to 3 additional years.

Additional information This program, managed by the Oregon Office of Student Access and Completion, began in 1996.

Number awarded 50 each year.

Deadline February of each year.

[259]
FORGING INDUSTRY WOMEN'S SCHOLARSHIP

Forging Industry Association
Attn: Forging Industry Educational & Research
  Foundation
1111 Superior Avenue, Suite 615
Cleveland, OH 44114
(216) 781-5040   Fax: (216) 781-0102
E-mail: info@forgings.org
Web: sms.scholarshipamerica.org/forgingw

Summary To provide financial assistance to women who are working on an undergraduate or graduate degree in a field that will prepare them for a career in the forging industry.

Eligibility This program is open to women who are currently enrolled full time at a 2- or 4-year college or university in North America and working on an associate, bachelor's, or master's degree in computer science, engineering (electrical, industrial, materials science, mechanical, or metallurgical), industrial management, management information systems, manufacturing, marketing, or related field that will prepare them for a career in the forging industry. Applicants must be willing to consider a compensated internship at a forging industry company after the successful completion of each academic year. They must be citizens of the United States, Canada, or Mexico. Selection is based on academic record, demonstrated leadership and participation in school and community activities, honors, work experience, a statement of goals and aspirations, unusual personal or family circumstances, and an outside appraisal; financial need is not considered.

Financial data The stipend is $5,000 per year (or up to 50% of combined fees for tuition, room, and board).

Duration 1 year; may be renewed 1 additional year (provided the recipient maintains a GPA of 2.75 or higher) and recipients may reapply for up to 2 more years of support.

Additional information This program is administered by Scholarship Management Services, a division of Scholarship America.

Number awarded 1 or more each year.

Deadline April of each year.

[260]
FRAMELINE COMPLETION FUND

Frameline
Attn: Completion Fund
145 Ninth Street, Suite 300
San Francisco, CA 94103
(415) 703-8650   Fax: (415) 861-1404
E-mail: info@frameline.org
Web: frameline.org

Summary To provide funding to lesbian, gay, bisexual, and transgender (LGBT) film/video artists.

Eligibility This program is open to LGBT artists who are in the last stages of the production of documentary, educational, narrative, animated, or experimental projects about or of interest to LGBT people and their communities. Applicants may be independent artists, students, producers, or nonprofit corporations. They must be interested in completion work and must have 90% of the production completed; projects in development, script-development, pre-production, or production are not eligible. Student projects are eligible only if the student maintains artistic and financial control of the project. Women and people of color are especially encouraged to apply. Selection is based on financial need, the contribution the grant will make to completing the project, assurances that the project will be completed, and the statement the project makes about LGBT people and/or issues of concern to them and their communities.

Financial data Grants range from $1,000 to $5,000.

Duration These are 1-time grants.

Additional information This program began in 1990.

Number awarded Varies each year; recently, 5 were awarded. Since this program was established, it has provided $464,200 in support to 136 films.

Deadline October of each year.

[261]
FRAN O'SULLIVAN WOMEN IN LENOVO LEADERSHIP (WILL) SCHOLARSHIP

Society of Women Engineers
Attn: Scholarship Selection Committee
203 North LaSalle Street, Suite 1675
Chicago, IL 60601-1269
(312) 596-5223   Toll Free: (877) SWE-INFO
Fax: (312) 644-8557   E-mail: scholarships@swe.org
Web: societyofwomenengineers.swe.org

Summary To provide financial assistance to women working on an undergraduate or graduate degree in computer science or engineering.

Eligibility This program is open to women who are entering full-time freshmen, sophomores, juniors, seniors, or graduate students at an ABET-accredited 4-year college or university. Applicants must be interested in studying computer science, computer engineering, electrical engineering, or engineering technology. Selection is based on merit.

Financial data The stipend is $5,000. The award includes a travel grant for the recipient to attend the national conference of the Society of Women Engineers.

Duration 1 year.

Additional information This program began in 2011.

Number awarded 1 each year.

Deadline February of each year for continuing students; May of each year for entering freshmen.

[262]
FRAN SARGENT SCHOLARSHIP

Ninety-Nines, Inc.-Florida Goldcoast Chapter
c/o Kimberley Lowe
100 Edgewater Drive, Unit 342
Coral Gables, FL 33133-6980
(305) 984-0561   E-mail: flynlowe@comcast.net
Web: www.flgoldcoast99s.org/scholarships.html

Summary To provide financial assistance to female pilots in Florida who are interested in an aviation training program at a college or flight school in the state.

Eligibility This program is open to women who have a private pilot's certificate and are either residents of Florida or students currently enrolled in an aviation training program in the state. Applicants must be interested in acquiring an additional rating or certificate, attending a college program, or engaging in another aviation endeavor. Along with their application, they must submit a statement describing their education, aviation training and experience, aviation organizations, and employment and/or educational history; another statement covering their educational purpose and/or aviation goals, their goals, why they chose aviation, and the pilot certificate or rating, college degree, or other goal they plan to attain using this scholarship; and 2 letters of reference. Selection is based on financial need, desire to prepare for a career in aviation, ability to represent women in aviation, likelihood of success in reaching goals, and neatness and completeness of application package.

Financial data The stipend is $2,500.

Duration 1 year.

Number awarded 1 or more each year.

Deadline October of each year.

[263]
FRANCIS M. KEVILLE MEMORIAL SCHOLARSHIP

Construction Management Association of America
Attn: CMAA Foundation
7926 Jones Branch Drive, Suite 800
McLean, VA 22101-3303
(703) 677-3361   E-mail: foundation@cmaanet.org
Web: www.cmaafoundation.org

Summary To provide financial assistance to minority and female undergraduate and graduate students working on a degree in construction management.

Eligibility This program is open to women and members of minority groups who are enrolled as full-time undergraduate or graduate students. Applicants must have completed at least 1 year of study and have at least 1 full year remaining for a bachelor's or master's degree in construction management or a related field. Along with their application, they must submit essays on why they are interested in a career in construction management and why they should be awarded this scholarship. Selection is based on that essay (20%), academic performance (40%), recommendation of the faculty adviser (15%), and extracurricular activities (25%); a bonus of

5% is given to student members of the Construction Management Association of America (CMAA).

Financial data The stipend is $5,000. Funds are disbursed directly to the student's university.

Duration 1 year.

Number awarded 1 each year.

Deadline April of each year.

[264]
FRESH START SCHOLARSHIP

Wilmington Women in Business
Attn: Fresh Start Scholarship Foundation, Inc.
P.O. Box 7784
Wilmington, DE 19803
(302) 397-3440 E-mail: FSSF@freshstartscholarship.org
Web: www.freshstartscholarship.org/apply

Summary To provide financial assistance to women from Delaware who have experienced an interruption in their education and are interested in attending college in the state.

Eligibility This program is open to women who are residents of Delaware or have been employed in the state for at least the past 12 months, are at least 20 years of age, have a high school diploma or GED, and have been admitted to an accredited Delaware college in a 2- or 4-year undergraduate degree program. Applicants must have had at least a 2-year break in education either after completing high school or during college studies. They must have at least a "C" average if currently enrolled in college and be recommended by a social service agency (or a college representative if a social service agency is not available). U.S. citizenship or permanent resident status is required. Selection is based on academic qualifications, personal challenges, and financial need.

Financial data The stipend varies annually, depending on the availability of funds, but recently averaged approximately $2,500. Awards are paid to the college at the beginning of each semester.

Duration 1 year.

Additional information This program began in 1996.

Number awarded Varies each year; recently, the program awarded 20 returning and 14 new scholarships. Since the program was established, it has awarded more than $830,000 to 186 women.

Deadline May of each year.

[265]
GAIL BRISTOL SCHOLARSHIP

Society of Plastics Engineers
Attn: SPE Foundation
6 Berkshire Boulevard, Suite 306
Bethel, CT 06801
(203) 740-5457   Fax: (203) 775-8490
E-mail: foundation@4spe.org
Web: old.4spe.org/forms/spe-foundation-scholarship-form

Summary To provide financial assistance to undergraduate students, especially women, who have a career interest in the plastics industry.

Eligibility This program is open to full-time undergraduate students at 4-year colleges and 2-year technical programs. Preference is given to women . Applicants must be majoring in or taking courses that would be beneficial to a career in the plastics or polymer industry (e.g., plastics engineering, poly-

mer sciences, chemistry, physics, chemical engineering, mechanical engineering, industrial engineering). Along with their application, they must submit 3 letters of recommendation; a high school and/or college transcript; a 1- to 2-page statement telling why they are applying for the scholarship, their qualifications, and their educational and career goals in the plastics industry; their employment history; and a list of current and past school activities and community activities and honors. Financial need is considered in the selection process. U.S. citizenship is required.

Financial data The stipend is $3,000. Funds are paid directly to the recipient's school.

Duration 1 year.

Number awarded 1 each year.

Deadline April of each year.

[266]
GAIL BURNS-SMITH "DARE TO DREAM" SCHOLARSHIPS

Connecticut Sexual Assault Crisis Services, Inc.
96 Pitkin Street
East Hartford, CT 06108
(860) 292-9881   Toll Free: (888) 999-5545
Fax: (860) 291-9335   E-mail: info@connsacs.org
Web: www.connsacs.org

Summary To provide financial assistance to students from Connecticut who have participated in sexual violence prevention activities and are interested in attending college to continue their involvement in the field.

Eligibility This program is open to Connecticut residents who are attending college in any state and to residents of other states attending college in Connecticut. Applicants must have paid or volunteer work experience in the field of women's issues or sexual violence prevention or advocacy. They must be planning to continue work in the field of sexual violence prevention or advocacy, either on behalf of individual victims or via public policy advocacy.

Financial data The stipend is $1,000.

Duration 1 year.

Additional information This program began in 2004.

Number awarded 1 each year.

Deadline March of each year.

[267]
GE WOMEN'S NETWORK ENGINEERING SCHOLARSHIP

Society of Women Engineers-Minnesota Section
Attn: Scholarship Committee
P.O. Box 18481
Minneapolis, MN 55418
E-mail: scholarships@swe-mn.org
Web: www.swe-mn.org/scholarships.html

Summary To provide financial assistance to women from any state working on an undergraduate or graduate degree in computer science or specified fields of engineering at colleges and universities in Minnesota, North Dakota, and South Dakota.

Eligibility This program is open to female undergraduate and graduate students at ABET-accredited engineering programs in Minnesota, North Dakota, or South Dakota. Applicants must be working full time on a degree in computer science or aerospace/aeronautical, computer, electrical, or mechanical engineering. Along with their application, they must submit a 250-word essay describing how they plan to utilize their engineering knowledge and skills after they graduate. Selection is based on potential to succeed as an engineer (20 points), communication skills (10 points), extracurricular or community involvement and leadership skills (10 points), demonstration of work experience and successes (10 points), and academic success (5 points).

Financial data The stipend is $2,500.

Duration 1 year.

Additional information This program is sponsored by the General Electric Women's Network.

Number awarded 1 each year.

Deadline March of each year.

[268]
GE WOMEN'S NETWORK SCHOLARSHIPS

Society of Women Engineers
Attn: Scholarship Selection Committee
203 North LaSalle Street, Suite 1675
Chicago, IL 60601-1269
(312) 596-5223   Toll Free: (877) SWE-INFO
Fax: (312) 644-8557   E-mail: scholarships@swe.org
Web: societyofwomenengineers.swe.org

Summary To provide financial assistance to female undergraduate students majoring in computer science or specified fields of engineering.

Eligibility This program is open women who are entering their sophomore or junior year at a 4-year ABET-accredited college or university. Applicants must be working full time on a degree in computer science or aeronautical, computer, electrical, industrial, or mechanical engineering and have a GPA of 3.0 or higher. Along with their application, they must submit an essay on why they want to be an engineer or computer scientist, how they believe they will make a difference as an engineer or computer scientist, and what influenced them to study engineering or computer science. Selection is based on merit. Preference is given to students attending selected schools; for a list, contact the sponsor.

Financial data The stipend is $5,000.

Duration 1 year.

Additional information This program, established in 2002, is sponsored by the General Electric Women's Network of the General Electric Company.

Number awarded 43 each year.

Deadline February of each year.

[269]
GENERATION GOOGLE SCHOLARSHIPS FOR HIGH SCHOOL SENIORS

Google Inc.
Attn: Scholarships
1600 Amphitheatre Parkway
Mountain View, CA 94043-8303
(650) 253-0000   Fax: (650) 253-0001
E-mail: generationgoogle@google.com
Web: www.google.com

Summary To provide financial assistance to members of underrepresented groups planning to work on a bachelor's degree in a computer-related field.

Eligibility This program is open to high school seniors planning to enroll full time at a college or university in the United States or Canada. Applicants must be members of a group underrepresented in computer science: African Americans, Hispanics, American Indians, Filipinos/Native Hawaiians/Pacific Islanders, women, or people with a disability. They must be interested in working on a bachelor's degree in computer science, computer engineering, or a closely-related field. Selection is based on academic achievement, leadership, and passion for computer science and technology.

Financial data The stipend is $10,000 per year for U.S. students or $C5,000 for Canadian students.

Duration 1 year; may be renewed for up to 3 additional years or until graduation, whichever comes first.

Additional information Recipients are required to attend Google's Computer Science Summer Institute at Mountain View, California, Seattle, Washington, or Cambridge, Massachusetts in the summer.

Number awarded Varies each year.

Deadline February of each year.

[270]
GET IT GIRL COLLEGE TECHNOLOGY SCHOLARSHIP PROGRAM

Michigan Council of Women in Technology Foundation
Attn: Scholarship Committee
P.O. Box 214585
Auburn Hills, MI 48321
(248) 654-3697   Fax: (248) 281-5391
E-mail: info@mcwt.org
Web: www.mcwt.org/Scholarships_196.html

Summary To provide financial assistance to female high school seniors from Michigan who have participated in the GET IT Girl program and are interested in working on a degree in a field related to information technology at a school in any state.

Eligibility This program is open to women graduating from high schools in Michigan who have participated in the sponsor's GET IT Girl program and are planning to enroll at a college or university in any state. Applicants must be planning to work on a degree in a field related to information technology, including business analytics for information science, business applications, computer science, computer engineering, computer information systems, digital forensics, information assurance, information systems, or software engineering. They must have a GPA of 3.0 or higher. Programs in which technology is a secondary element (such as architecture, biomedical engineering, computer aided design, finance, library science, marketing, mechanical engineering, or psychology) are not eligible. Financial need is not considered in the selection process. U.S. citizenship is required.

Financial data The stipend is $5,000 per year; funds are sent directly to the financial aid office at the college or university where the recipient is enrolled.

Duration 1 year; may be renewed for up to 3 additional years, provided the recipient maintains a GPA of 3.0 or higher.

Number awarded 1 each year.

Deadline January of each year.

[271]
GFWC/MFWC HEBRON MEMORIAL SCHOLARSHIP

GFWC/Mississippi Federation of Women's Clubs, Inc.
c/o Darlene G. Adams, President
3004 The Woods Road
Picayune, MS 39466
E-mail: info@gfwc-mfwc.org
Web: www.gfwc-mfwc.org

Summary To provide financial assistance to women in Mississippi who are interested in attending college or graduate school in the state.

Eligibility This program is open to women who are residents of Mississippi and are high school seniors, high school graduates, or graduates of a college in the state. Applicants must be planning to enroll at a Mississippi institution of higher learning as an undergraduate or graduate student. They may be planning to work on a degree in any field, but preference is given to applicants in areas of service where it is felt there is a need in the state.

Financial data The stipend is $1,000. Funds are sent directly to the recipient's institution.

Duration 1 year.

Number awarded 1 each year.

Deadline January of each year.

[272]
GFWC/OHIO FEDERATION OF WOMEN'S CLUBS CLUBWOMAN SCHOLARSHIP

GFWC/Ohio Federation of Women's Clubs
c/o Sharon Pervo, Scholarship Chair
208 Cherry Lane
Avon Lake, OH 44012
E-mail: pervo208@oh.rr.com
Web: www.angelfire.com

Summary To provide financial assistance members of the GFWC/Ohio Federation of Women's Clubs who wish to return to college.

Eligibility This program is open to members of a federated club who wish to return to college in Ohio. Applicants must be able to demonstrate that they need additional education or training in order to join the work force or to help to provide for themselves and/or their families.

Financial data A stipend is awarded (amount not specified).

Duration 1 year.

Number awarded 1 each year.

Deadline February of each year.

[273]
GFWC RI ARTS SCHOLARSHIP PROGRAM

General Federation of Women's Clubs of Rhode Island
Attn: VP Membership
821 West Shore Road
Warwick, RI 02889
(401) 365-4392   E-mail: sackett159@aol.net
Web: www.gfwcri.org/#!gfwc-ri-art-scholarship/x5z92

Summary To recognize and reward high school students in Rhode Island who submit art work that depicts women.

Eligibility This competition is open to students at all public and private high schools in Rhode Island. Applicants participate in the Scholastic Art Awards program sponsored by Scholastic Inc. and the Rhode Island Art Education Association, which accepts works in a variety of media. This sponsor limits awards to paintings that depict women in today's world.

Financial data Cash prizes are awarded (amount not specified).

Duration The competition is held annually.

Number awarded 3 each year.

Deadline January of each year.

[274]
GILDA MURRAY SCHOLARSHIPS

Texas Business Women
Attn: Texas Business and Professional Women's
     Foundation
P.O. Box 70
Round Rock, TX 78680-0070
E-mail: info@tbwconnect.com
Web: www.texasbpwfoundation.org/scholarships.php

Summary To provide financial assistance to members of Texas Business Women (TBW) who are interested in career advancement.

Eligibility This program is open to members of TBW who are interested in pursuing education or training necessary to prepare for employment or to advance in a business or profession. Applicants must be at least 25 years of age and have a record of active participation in the association. Along with their application, they must submit a 1-page description of the course and its benefits to them. Selection is based on merit and need.

Financial data Funding covers 50% of the cost of the training, to a maximum of $1,000 per year.

Duration 1 year; may be renewed.

Additional information This program began in 1998 when Texas Business Women was named Texas Federation of Business and Professional Women's Clubs.

Number awarded 1 or more each year.

Deadline Applications may be submitted at any time.

[275]
G.I.R.L. SCHOLARSHIP PROGRAM

Daybreak Game Company, LLC
8928 Terman Court
San Diego, CA 92121
(858) 577-3100   Fax: (858) 230-0852
Web: www.daybreakgames.com/girl

Summary To provide financial assistance to undergraduates, especially women, interested in preparing for a career in the video games industry.

Eligibility This program, which stands for Games in Real Life, is open to undergraduates working on a degree in a field related to video games (including video game art, design, animation, production, programming, or visual effects). All students who are legal U.S. residents are eligible, but a goal of the program is to increase the number of women in the video games industry. The program includes 2 categories. Students interested in the art and design category must submit 2 pieces of concept art inspired by games of the sponsor. Students interested in the programming and engineering category must submit an original game feature for a game of the sponsor. Applicants for both categories must also submit a 500-word essay about why they want to work in the video game industry and how their unique perspective and imagination will contribute to the future of gaming.

Financial data   The stipend is $5,000.

Duration   1 year.

Additional information   Recipients also have an opportunity to be hired for a paid summer internship at the sponsor's headquarters in San Diego, California. This program, which began in 2008, is sponsored by Daybreak Game Company, formerly known as Sony Online Entertainment, and administered by Scholarship Management Services, a division of Scholarship America.

Number awarded   2 each year: 1 for each category.

Deadline   April of each year.

[276]
GIRL SCOUTS NATION'S CAPITAL GOLD AWARD SCHOLARSHIPS

Girl Scout Council of the Nation's Capital
Attn: Gold Award Scholarship Committee
4301 Connecticut Avenue, N.W.
Washington, DC 20008
(202) 534-3776   Fax: (202) 274-2161
E-mail: goldaward@gscnc.org
Web: www.gscnc.org

Summary   To provide financial assistance to high school seniors in the Washington, D.C. area who are Girl Scouts and planning to attend college in any state.

Eligibility   This program is open to seniors graduating from high schools in the Washington, D.C. area and planning to attend a college or university in any state. Applicants must be Girl Scouts who have earned their Gold Award. Along with their application, they must submit essays describing their activities in Girl Scouts and other community organizations.

Financial data   The stipend is $1,000.

Duration   1 year.

Additional information   This program includes the Sara and Lawrence Phillips Girl Scout Gold Award Scholarships and the Gold Award Scholarship in Honor of Marilynn Carr.

Number awarded   14 each year.

Deadline   March of each year.

[277]
GIRL SCOUTS OF NEW MEXICO TRAILS GOLD AWARD SCHOLARSHIP

Girl Scouts of New Mexico Trails
Attn: Gold Award Committee
4000 Jefferson Plaza N.E.
Albuquerque, NM 87109
(505) 343-1040   Fax: (505) 343-1050
E-mail: goldsilverbronze@gs-nmtrails.org
Web: www.nmgirlscouts.org

Summary   To provide financial assistance to Girl Scouts in New Mexico who have received the highest award and are interested in attending college in any state.

Eligibility   This program is open to Girl Scouts in New Mexico who have received the highest award, including Golden Eagle of Merit, Golden Eaglet, Curved Bar, First Class, or Gold Award. Applicants must be interested in enrolling at an

institution of higher education in any state at any stage of their life or educational career. Selection is based on the impact of their award project on the community beyond Girl Scouting (30%); impact of their project on themselves (30%); evidence of active involvement in community service (20%); evidence of intent for continued, ongoing community service (10%); and letters of reference (10%).

Financial data   A stipend is awarded (amount not specified).

Duration   1 year.

Number awarded   Varies each year.

Deadline   Applications may be submitted at any time.

[278]
GLADYS ANDERSON EMERSON SCHOLARSHIP

Iota Sigma Pi
c/o Kathryn A. Thomasson, National Director for Student Awards
University of North Dakota
Department of Chemistry
Abbott Hall, Room 322
151 Cornell Street, Stop 9024
Grand Forks, ND 58202-9024
(701) 777-3199   E-mail: kthomasson@und.edu
Web: www.iotasigmapi.info/awards/studentawards.html

Summary   To provide financial assistance to women undergraduates who have achieved excellence in the study of chemistry or biochemistry.

Eligibility   The nominee must be a female chemistry or biochemistry student who has attained at least junior standing but has at least 1 semester of work to complete. Both the nominator and the nominee must be members of Iota Sigma Pi, although students who are not members but wish to apply for the scholarship may be made members by National Council action. Selection is based on transcripts; a list of all academic honors and professional memberships; a short essay by the nominee describing herself, her goals in chemistry, any hobbies or talents, and her financial need; and letters of recommendation.

Financial data   The stipend is $2,000.

Duration   1 year.

Additional information   This program began in 1987.

Number awarded   1 or 2 each year.

Deadline   February of each year.

[279]
GLADYS BALES SCHOLARSHIP FOR MATURE WOMEN

Idaho State Business and Professional Women
Attn: Scholarship Committee
P.O. Box 790
Emmett, ID 83617
E-mail: idahostatebpw@yahoo.com
Web: www.idahostatebpw.org/Scholarhip_Instructions.html

Summary   To provide financial assistance to mature women in Idaho who are interested in majoring in any field at a college in any state.

Eligibility   This program is open to women in Idaho who are 25 years of age or older. Applicants must be enrolled or planning to enroll full or part time at a community college, technical school, or 4-year university in any state. They must have a

GPA of 2.5 or higher. Along with their application, they must submit brief essays on 1) their career objectives; 2) why the sponsor should consider them for this scholarship, including their financial need; and 3) the challenges they anticipate in reaching their career goal and their plan to address those challenges. Priority is given to women who are 1) returning to the workforce; 2) unemployed or in a job with limited pay, limited growth opportunities, and limited benefits; or 3) raising another family member's child (e.g., grandparents raising grandchildren). U.S. citizenship is required.

Financial data The stipend is $1,000. Funds are issued payable to both the educational institution and the recipient and are to be used for tuition, fees, and books.

Duration 1 year.

Number awarded 3 each year.

Deadline June of each year.

[280]
GLADYS C. ANDERSON MEMORIAL SCHOLARSHIP

American Foundation for the Blind
Attn: Information Center
1000 Fifth Avenue, Suite 350
Huntington, WV 25701
Toll Free: (800) AFB-LINE   E-mail: tannis@afb.net
Web: www.afb.org/scholarships.asp

Summary To provide financial assistance to legally blind women who are studying classical or religious music on the undergraduate or graduate school level.

Eligibility This program is open to women who are legally blind, U.S. citizens, and enrolled in an undergraduate or graduate degree program in classical or religious music. Along with their application, they must submit 200-word essays on 1) their past and recent achievements and accomplishments; 2) their intended field of study and why they have chosen it; and 3) the role their visual impairment has played in shaping their life. They must also submit a sample performance tape or CD of up to 30 minutes. Financial need is considered in the selection process.

Financial data The stipend is $1,000.

Duration 1 academic year.

Number awarded 1 each year.

Deadline May of each year.

[281]
GLADYS L. MERSEREAU GRANTS-IN-AID

Delta Kappa Gamma Society International-Pi State Organization
c/o Deborah Bedard, Grants-in-Aid Committee Chair
P.O. Box 782
Glens Falls, NY 12801-0782
E-mail: dmbedard29@yahoo.com
Web: www.deltakappagamma.org/NY

Summary To provide financial assistance to women in New York whose education was interrupted and who now need help to become teachers.

Eligibility This program is open to women in New York who are interested in completing teacher certification requirements but whose education has been interrupted. Along with their application, they must submit a statement on their educational philosophy, documentation of their financial need,

and 3 letters of recommendation (including at least 1 from a member of the sponsoring organization). Members of that organization are not eligible.

Financial data The amounts of the grants depend on the availability of funds.

Duration 1 year.

Additional information This program began in 1975.

Number awarded Varies each year; recently, 5 were awarded.

Deadline February of each year.

[282]
GLAMOUR'S TOP TEN COLLEGE WOMEN COMPETITION

Glamour Magazine
4 Times Square, 16th Floor
New York, NY 10036-6593
Toll Free: (800) 244-GLAM   Fax: (212) 286-6922
E-mail: TTCW@glamour.com
Web: www.glamour.com

Summary To recognize and reward outstanding college women.

Eligibility This competition is open to women enrolled full time in their junior or senior year at accredited colleges and universities in the United States and Canada. Applications must be approved and signed by the appropriate members of the school's faculty and administration (i.e., faculty adviser, the director of public relations, the director of student activities, or the dean of students). There is no limit on the number of applicants from any 1 school. Applicants must submit an essay (up to 500 words) describing their most meaningful achievements and how those relate to their field of study and future goals. Selection is based on leadership experience (34%), personal involvement in campus and community affairs (33%), and academic excellence (33%).

Financial data The grand prize is $20,000 and other prizes are $3,000. Each winner also receives a trip to New York City and recognition in the October issue of *Glamour* magazine.

Duration The competition is held annually.

Additional information The first competition was held in 1990.

Number awarded 10 each year: 1 grand prize and 9 other prizes.

Deadline September of each year.

[283]
GO ON GIRL ASPIRING WRITER SCHOLARSHIP

Go On Girl! Book Club, Inc.
P.O. Box 3368
New York, NY 10185
E-mail: writingawards@goongirl.org
Web: www.goongirl.org/scholarships/index.php

Summary To provide financial assistance to women majoring in a field related to writing at an Historically Black College or University (HBCU).

Eligibility This program is open to female U.S. citizens of African descent who are full-time freshmen, sophomores, or juniors at HBCUs majoring in a writing-related field (e.g., English, literature, journalism). Applicants must have a GPA of 2.5

or higher. Along with their application, they must submit an 800-word essay on "The Power of the Written Word."

Financial data The stipend is $1,000.

Duration 1 year.

Additional information Go On Girl! Book Club was founded in 1991 and is currently the largest reading group for Black women in the country. It first awarded this scholarship in 2001.

Number awarded 1 each year.

Deadline March of each year.

[284]
GO RED MULTICULTURAL SCHOLARSHIP FUND

American Heart Association
Attn: Go Red for Women
7272 Greenville Avenue
Dallas, TX 75231-4596
Toll Free: (800) AHA-USA1
E-mail: GoRedScholarship@heart.org
Web: www.goredforwomen.org

Summary To provide financial assistance to women from multicultural backgrounds who are preparing for a career in a field of health care.

Eligibility This program is open to women who are currently enrolled at an accredited college, university, health care institution, or program and have a GPA of 3.0 or higher. Applicants must be U.S. citizens or permanent residents of Hispanic, African American, Asian/Pacific Islander, or other minority origin. They must be working on an undergraduate or graduate degree as preparation for a career as a nurse, physician, or allied health care worker. Selection is based on community involvement, a personal essay, transcripts, and 2 letters of recommendation.

Financial data The stipend is $2,500.

Duration 1 year.

Additional information This program, which began in 2012, is supported by Macy's.

Number awarded 16 each year.

Deadline December of each year.

[285]
GOOGLE ANITA BORG MEMORIAL SCHOLARSHIPS

Google Inc.
Attn: Scholarships
1600 Amphitheatre Parkway
Mountain View, CA 94043-8303
(650) 253-0000   Fax: (650) 253-0001
E-mail: anitaborgscholarship@google.com
Web: www.google.com/anitaborg/us

Summary To provide financial assistance to women working on a bachelor's or graduate degree in a computer-related field.

Eligibility This program is open to women who are entering their senior year of undergraduate study or are enrolled in a graduate program in computer science, computer engineering, or a closely-related field. Applicants must be full-time students at a university in the United States and have a GPA of 3.5 or higher. They must submit essays of 400 to 600 words on 1) a significant technical project on which they have worked; 2) their leadership abilities; 3) what they would do if

someone gave them the funding and resources for a 3- to 12-month project to investigate a technical topic of their choice; and 4) what they would do if someone gave them $1,000 to plan an event or project to benefit women in technical fields. Citizens, permanent residents, and international students are eligible. Selection is based on academic background and demonstrated leadership.

Financial data The stipend is $10,000 per year.

Duration 1 year; recipients may reapply.

Additional information These scholarships were first offered in 2004.

Number awarded Varies each year; recently, 19 were awarded.

Deadline November of each year.

[286]
GRANDMA MOSES SCHOLARSHIP

Western Art Association
Attn: Foundation
13730 Loumont Street
Whittier, CA 90601

Summary To provide financial assistance for art school to female high school seniors whose art demonstrates a "congruence with the art of Grandma Moses."

Eligibility This program is open to female graduating high school seniors. Applicants must be planning to study art in a college, university, or specialized school of art. Preference is given to applicants from the western United States. Candidates must submit samples of their art work; selection is based on the extent to which their work "manifests a congruence with the work of the famed folk artist, Grandma Moses." Financial need is not considered.

Financial data The stipend is $3,000 per year.

Duration 1 year; may be renewed up to 3 additional years.

Additional information Requests for applications should be accompanied by a self-addressed stamped envelope, the student's e-mail address, and the source where they found the scholarship information.

Number awarded 1 each year.

Deadline March of each year.

[287]
GREATER ROCHESTER CHAPTER NAWIC SCHOLARSHIP

National Association of Women in Construction-Greater
   Rochester Chapter 314
c/o Pat Hynes, Treasurer
Hynes Concrete Contractor, Inc.
1599 Wayneport Road
P.O. Box 607
Macedon, NY 14502
(315) 986-2415   E-mail: hccipat@rochester.rr.com
Web: www.nawicrochester.org

Summary To provide financial assistance to women from New York who are interested in preparing for a career in construction at a college in any state.

Eligibility This program is open to women who are graduating from high schools in New York or currently enrolled full time at an accredited college or university in any state. Applicants must be working on a degree in a construction-related field, including architecture, construction management, or engineering (civil, electrical, mechanical, or structural). Along with their application, they must submit a 1-page essay on their accomplishments, achievements, awards, aspirations, and why they feel they qualify to receive this award. Selection is based on that essay, grades, extracurricular activities, employment experience, recommendations, and interest in construction. A personal interview may be required.

Financial data A stipend is awarded (amount not specified).

Duration 1 year; nonrenewable.

Number awarded 1 or more each year.

Deadline April of each year.

[288]
GREATLAND SWE SECTION SCHOLARSHIPS

Society of Women Engineers-Greatland Section
c/o Ellen Hamel, Scholarship Chair
PND Engineers
1506 West 36th Avenue
Anchorage, AK 99503
(907) 561-1011 E-mail: akswescholarship@hotmail.com
Web: www.swealaska.org/programs.html

Summary To provide financial assistance to female high school seniors in Alaska who plan to major in engineering at a college in any state.

Eligibility This program is open to women graduating from high schools in Alaska and planning to enroll in an ABET-accredited engineering program at a 4-year college or university in any state. Applicants must submit a 2-page essay discussing their interest in engineering, the specific engineering field in which they wish to major, and their experiences that have led them to choose engineering as a career. Selection is based on that essay, academic performance, activities and honors, recommendations, work and technical experience, application presentation, and financial need.

Financial data The stipend is $2,000 or $1,500.

Duration 1 year.

Number awarded 1 at $2,000 and 2 at $1,500 each year.

Deadline February of each year.

[289]
HAL DAVIS MEMORIAL SCHOLARSHIP

California Land Surveyors Association
Attn: CLSA Education Foundation
2520 Venture Oaks Way, Suite 150
Sacramento, CA 95833
(916) 239-4083 Fax: (916) 924-7323
E-mail: clsa@californiasurveyors.org
Web: www.californiasurveyors.org/scholarhaldavis.html

Summary To provide financial assistance to residents of any state, especially women, who are studying fields related to surveying at a college in California.

Eligibility This program is open to students currently enrolled in an ABET-accredited program in surveying or geomatics in California. Preference is given to applicants in the following order: 1) women in surveying; 2) students who have demonstrated a commitment to professional activities, including membership in the California Land Surveyors Association (CLSA); and 3) students who are involved in leadership. Along with their application, they must submit an essay on their educational objectives, future plans for study, profes-

sional activities, how they have promoted the profession, surveying-related work experience, and financial need.

Financial data The stipend is $2,000.

Duration 1 year.

Number awarded 1 each year.

Deadline December of each year.

[290]
HARVARD AMGEN SCHOLARS PROGRAM

Harvard College
Attn: Office of Undergraduate Research and Fellowships
77 Dunster Street, Second Floor
Cambridge, MA 02138
(617) 496-6220 E-mail: amgenscholars@harvard.edu
Web: uraf.harvard.edu/amgen-scholars

Summary To provide an opportunity for undergraduates, especially those from underrepresented groups, to participate in summer research projects in the biological sciences at Columbia University.

Eligibility This program is open to sophomores, juniors, and non-graduating seniors at 4-year colleges and universities in the United States, Puerto Rico, and other U.S. territories. Applicants must be U.S. citizens or permanent residents who have a cumulative GPA of 3.2 or higher and an interest in preparing for a Ph.D. or M.D./Ph.D. They must be interested in working on a summer research project at Harvard in fields of biotechnology. Applications are encouraged from members of groups traditionally underrepresented in fields of biotechnology: African American/Black, Chicano/Latino/Hispanic, Puerto Rican, American Indian/Alaskan Native, Pacific Islander, women, and those with disabilities, as well as students who come from rural or inner-city areas and individuals whose backgrounds and experiences would bring diversity to the biotechnology fields.

Financial data Scholars receive a stipend of $4,000, a meal allowance of $500, housing in a residential River House of Harvard, and, for non-Harvard students, travel to and from Boston.

Duration 10 weeks during the summer.

Additional information This program serves as the Harvard component of the Amgen Scholars Program, which operates at 8 other U.S. universities (and the National Institutes of Health) and is funded by the Amgen Foundation.

Number awarded Approximately 20 each year.

Deadline January of each year.

[291]
HASMIK MGRDICHIAN SCHOLARSHIP

Armenian International Women's Association-Los
 Angeles Affiliate
c/o Lily Ring Balian
2311 Roscomare Road, Number 10
Los Angeles, CA 90077
(310) 472-2454 E-mail: info@aiwala.org
Web: www.aiwala.org/index.php/projects

Summary To provide financial assistance to Armenian women from California who are interested in attending college in any state.

Eligibility This program is open to female residents of California who are of Armenian descent. Applicants must be enrolled or planning to enroll full time at an accredited college or university in any state. They must have a GPA of 3.5 or higher and be able to demonstrate financial need. Along with their application, they must submit a 500-word statement describing their planned academic program, their career goals, and the reasons why they believe they should be awarded this scholarship.

Financial data The stipend is $5,000.

Duration 1 year.

Additional information This program began in 2011.

Number awarded 4 each year.

Deadline March of each year.

[292]
HATTIE J. HILLIARD SCHOLARSHIP

Wisconsin Women of Color Network, Inc.
c/o P.E. Kiram
756 North 35th Street, Suite 101
Milwaukee, WI 53208
(414) 899-2329   E-mail: pekiram64@gmail.com

Summary To provide financial assistance to women of color from Wisconsin who are interested in studying art at a school in any state.

Eligibility This program is open to residents of Wisconsin who are women of color enrolled or planning to enroll at a college, university, or vocational/technical school in any state. Applicants must be a member of 1 of the following groups: African American, Asian, American Indian, or Hispanic. Their field of study must be art, graphic art, commercial art, or a related area. They must be able to demonstrate financial need. Along with their application, they must submit a 1-page essay on how this scholarship will help them accomplish their educational goal. U.S. citizenship is required.

Financial data A stipend is awarded (amount not specified).

Duration 1 year.

Additional information This program began in 1995.

Number awarded 1 each year.

Deadline May of each year.

[293]
HAWAI'I'S DAUGHTERS GUILD OF CALIFORNIA SCHOLARSHIPS

Hawai'i's Daughters Guild of California
P.O. Box 3305
Gardena, CA 90247
E-mail: HDG.Scholarship@gmail.com
Web: www.hawaiidaughtersguild.webs.com

Summary To provide financial assistance for college or graduate school to women of Polynesian ancestry from California.

Eligibility This program is open to California residents who are women of Polynesian ancestry and graduating high school seniors, full-time undergraduates, or full-time graduate students. Applicants must have a GPA of 3.0 or higher and be able to demonstrate financial need. Along with their application, they must submit transcripts, 3 letters of recommendation, an autobiographical essay, and proof of ancestry. Selection is based on goals as described in the autobiographical essay, academic achievement, extracurricular activities, community service, and financial need.

Financial data A stipend is awarded (amount not specified).

Duration 1 year.

Number awarded Varies each year.

Deadline March of each year.

[294]
HEARST SCHOLARSHIP OF NEW YORK WOMEN IN COMMUNICATIONS

New York Women in Communications, Inc.
Attn: NYWICI Foundation
355 Lexington Avenue, 15th Floor
New York, NY 10017-6603
(212) 297-2133   Fax: (212) 370-9047
E-mail: nywicipr@nywici.org
Web: www.nywici.org/foundation/scholarships

Summary To provide financial assistance to female residents of designated eastern states who are enrolled as undergraduates at a college in any state and preparing for a career in magazines or digital media.

Eligibility This program is open to women who are residents of New York, New Jersey, Connecticut, or Pennsylvania and currently enrolled as sophomores, juniors, or seniors at a college or university in any state. Also eligible are women who reside outside the 4 states but are currently enrolled at a college or university within 1 of the 5 boroughs of New York City. Applicants must be able to demonstrate a commitment to a career in magazines (editorial or advertising sales) or digital media. They must have a GPA of 3.2 or higher. Along with their application, they must submit a 2-page resume; a personal essay of 300 words on an assigned topic that changes annually; 2 letters of recommendation; and an official transcript. Selection is based on academic record, need, demonstrated leadership, participation in school and community activities, honors and other awards or recognition, work experience, goals and aspirations, and unusual personal and/or family circumstances. U.S. citizenship or permanent resident status is required.

Financial data The stipend ranges up to $10,000.

Duration 1 year.

Additional information This program is sponsored by the Hearst Corporation, which may invite the recipient to apply for a summer internship at its New York City headquarters.

Number awarded 1 each year.

Deadline January of each year.

[295]
HEATHER WESTPHAL MEMORIAL SCHOLARSHIP AWARD

International Association of Fire Chiefs
Attn: IAFC Foundation
4025 Fair Ridge Drive, Suite 300
Fairfax, VA 22033-2868
(703) 896-4822   Fax: (703) 273-9363
E-mail: Sbaroncelli@iafc.org
Web: www.iafcf.org/Scholarship.htm

Summary To provide financial assistance to female firefighters, especially members of the International Association of Fire Chiefs, who wish to further their academic education.

Eligibility This program is open to women who are active members of state, county, provincial, municipal, community, industrial, or federal fire departments in the United States or Canada and have demonstrated proficiency as members for at least 2 years of paid or 3 years of volunteer service. Dependents of members are not eligible. Applicants must be planning to work on an associate or bachelor's degree at a recognized institution of higher education. Along with their application, they must submit a 250-word essay that includes a brief description of the course work, how the course work will benefit their fire service career and department and improve the fire service, and their financial need. Preference is given to members of the International Association of Fire Chiefs (IAFC).

Financial data A stipend is awarded (amount not specified).

Duration Up to 1 year.

Additional information This program began in 2009 with support from the International Association of Women in Fire and Emergency Service.

Number awarded 1 each year.

Deadline April of each year.

[296]
HECKSEL-SUTHERLAND SCHOLARSHIP

Ninety-Nines, Inc.-Michigan Chapter
c/o Rosemary Sieracki, Administrator
41490 Hanford Road
Canton, MI 48187-3512
(734) 981-4787　　　　　E-mail: sierackr@att.net
Web: www.michigan99s.info/node/6

Summary To provide financial assistance to women in Michigan who are interested in attending a school in any state to prepare for a career in aviation.

Eligibility This program is open to women who live in Michigan and are interested in preparing for a career in aviation or aeronautics. Applicants must be enrolled or planning to enroll in private pilot training, additional pilot certificate or rating, college education in aviation, technical training in aviation, or other aviation-related training. Along with their application, they must submit 1) a 1-page essay on how the money will be used; 2) documentation from the training or academic institution verifying the cost of the training; 3) copies of all aviation and medical certificates and the last 3 pages of the pilot logbook (if applicable); and 4) an essay that covers their aviation history, short- and long-term goals, how the scholarship will help them achieve those goals, any educational awards and honors they have received, their significant or unique achievements, where training would be received and the costs involved, their involvement in aviation activities, and their community involvement. Selection is based on motivation, willingness to accept responsibility, reliability, and commitment to success.

Financial data The stipend is $2,000.

Duration 1 year.

Additional information This program began in 2012.

Number awarded 1 each year.

Deadline October of each year.

[297]
HELEN LAUGHLIN AM MODE MEMORIAL SCHOLARSHIP

American Radio Relay League
Attn: ARRL Foundation
225 Main Street
Newington, CT 06111-1494
(860) 594-0348　　　　　Toll Free: (888) 277-5289
Fax: (860) 594-0259　　　　E-mail: foundation@arrl.org
Web: www.arrl.org/scholarship-descriptions

Summary To provide financial assistance to radio amateurs, especially women, from designated states who are interested in working on an undergraduate degree in any field at a college in any state.

Eligibility This program is open to radio amateurs of general class or higher who are residents of Texas. If there is no qualified applicant from Texas, second preference is given to residents of Arkansas. If no qualified resident of Arkansas applies, third preference is given to residents of Louisiana, Mississippi, Oklahoma, or Tennessee. Applicants must be interested in attending an accredited 4-year college or university in any state to major in any field. They must submit an essay on the role amateur radio has played in their lives and provide documentation of financial need. Further preference is given to 1) women amateur radio operators who are performing at a high academic level; and 2) applicants who have made a contact in the AM mode.

Financial data The stipend is $1,000.

Duration 1 year.

Number awarded 1 each year.

Deadline January of each year.

[298]
HELEN TRUEHEART COX ART SCHOLARSHIP FOR A NATIVE AMERICAN WOMAN

National League of American Pen Women
1300 17th Street, N.W.
Washington, DC 20036-1973
(202) 785-1997　　　　　Fax: (202) 452-8868
E-mail: contact@nlapw.org
Web: www.nlapw.org/grants-and-scholarships

Summary To provide financial assistance to Native American women interested in studying art in college.

Eligibility This program is open to women between 18 and 25 years of age who are members of a Native American tribe. Applicants must be interested in attending a college, university, or trade school in any state and majoring in art. They must submit 3 prints (4 by 6 inches) in any media (e.g., oil, water color, original works on paper, sculpture, acrylic) or 3 prints (8 by 10 inches) of photographic works. Financial need is considered in the selection process.

Financial data The stipend is $1,000.

Duration 1 year.

Additional information A fee of $20 must accompany each application.

Number awarded 1 each even-numbered year.

Deadline October of odd-numbered years.

[299]
HELOISE WERTHAN KUHN SCHOLARSHIP

Community Foundation of Middle Tennessee
Attn: Scholarship Coordinator
3833 Cleghorn Avenue, Suite 400
Nashville, TN 37215-2519
(615) 321-4939, ext. 116   Toll Free: (888) 540-5200
Fax: (615) 327-2746   E-mail: pcole@cfmt.org
Web: www.cfmt.org/request/scholarships/allscholarships

Summary To provide financial assistance to residents of Tennessee who are pregnant or parenting teens and interested in attending college in any state.

Eligibility This program is open to residents of middle Tennessee who are pregnant or parenting teens. Applicants must be attending or planning to attend an accredited college, university, junior college, technical school, or job training program in any state to increase their job skills and become more employable. Along with their application, they must submit an essay describing their educational plans and how those plans will help them reach their career goals. Financial need is considered in the selection process.

Financial data Stipends range from $500 to $2,500 per year. Funds are paid to the recipient's school and must be used for tuition, fees, books, supplies, room, board, or miscellaneous expenses.

Duration 1 year; recipients may reapply.

Additional information This program began in 2001.

Number awarded 1 or more each year.

Deadline March of each year.

[300]
HELPING HANDS OF WSC ENDOWMENT SCHOLARSHIP

Epsilon Sigma Alpha International
Attn: ESA Foundation
363 West Drake Road
Fort Collins, CO 80526
(970) 223-2824   Fax: (970) 223-4456
Web: www.epsilonsigmaalpha.org

Summary To provide financial assistance for college to members of the Western States Council (WSC) of Epsilon Sigma Alpha (ESA).

Eligibility This program is open to ESA members and their families from its WSC (Alaska, Arizona, Australia, California, Oregon, or Washington). Applicants must be 1) graduating high school seniors with a GPA of 3.0 or higher or with minimum scores of 22 on the ACT or 1030 on the combined critical reading and mathematics SAT; 2) enrolled in college with a GPA of 3.0 or higher; 3) enrolled at a technical school or returning to school after an absence for retraining of job skills or obtaining a degree; or 4) engaged in online study through an accredited college, university, or vocational school. They may be majoring or planning to major in any field at an institution in any state or in Australia. U.S. or Australian citizenship is required. Selection is based on service and leadership (30 points), financial need (30 points), and scholastic ability (30 points). A $5 processing fee is required.

Financial data The stipend is $1,400.

Duration 1 year; nonrenewable.

Additional information Epsilon Sigma Alpha (ESA) is a women's service organization. This program began in 2006.

Completed applications must be submitted to the ESA state counselor who then verifies the information before forwarding them to the scholarship director.

Number awarded 1 each year.

Deadline January of each year.

[301]
HERMINE DALKOWITZ TOBOLOWSKY SCHOLARSHIP

Texas Business Women
Attn: Texas Business and Professional Women's
  Foundation
P.O. Box 70
Round Rock, TX 78680-0070
E-mail: info@tbwconnect.com
Web: www.texasbpwfoundation.org/scholarships.php

Summary To provide financial assistance to women from any state who are attending college in Texas to prepare for a career in selected professions.

Eligibility This program is open to women from any state who are interested in preparing for a career in law, public service, government, political science, or women's history. Applicants must have completed at least 2 semesters of study at an accredited college or university in Texas, have a GPA of 3.0 or higher, and be U.S. citizens. Along with their application, they must submit a 2-page essay on 1 of the following topics: the importance of women in the workforce, the importance of women in public services, or the importance of the study of women in history. Selection is based on academic achievement and financial need.

Financial data The stipend is $3,000.

Duration 1 year.

Additional information This program began in 1995 when Texas Business Women was named Texas Federation of Business and Professional Women's Clubs.

Number awarded 1 or more each year.

Deadline December of each year.

[302]
HONDA SWE SCHOLARSHIPS

Society of Women Engineers
Attn: Scholarship Selection Committee
203 North LaSalle Street, Suite 1675
Chicago, IL 60601-1269
(312) 596-5223   Toll Free: (877) SWE-INFO
Fax: (312) 644-8557   E-mail: scholarships@swe.org
Web: societyofwomenengineers.swe.org

Summary To provide financial assistance to undergraduate women from designated states, especially members of underrepresented groups, who are majoring in designated engineering specialties.

Eligibility This program is open to SWE members who are entering their junior or senior year at a 4-year ABET-accredited college or university. Preference is given to members of underrepresented ethnic or racial groups, candidates with disabilities, and veterans. Applicants must be U.S. citizens working full time on a degree in automotive engineering, chemical engineering, computer science, electrical engineering, engineering technology, manufacturing engineering, materials science and engineering, or mechanical engineering. They must be residents of or attending college in Illinois,

Indiana, Michigan, Ohio, Pennsylvania, or Wisconsin. Financial need is considered in the selection process.

Financial data The stipend is $1,000.

Duration 1 year.

Additional information This program is sponsored by American Honda Motor Company.

Number awarded 5 each year.

Deadline February of each year.

[303]
HONEYWELL SCHOLARSHIPS

Society of Women Engineers
Attn: Scholarship Selection Committee
203 North LaSalle Street, Suite 1675
Chicago, IL 60601-1269
(312) 596-5223   Toll Free: (877) SWE-INFO
Fax: (312) 644-8557   E-mail: scholarships@swe.org
Web: societyofwomenengineers.swe.org

Summary To provide financial assistance to members of the Society of Women Engineers (SWE) from designated states, especially members of underrepresented groups, interested in studying specified fields of engineering in college.

Eligibility This program is open to SWE members who are rising college sophomores, juniors, or seniors and have a GPA of 3.5 or higher. Applicants must be enrolled full time at an ABET-accredited 4-year college or university and major in computer science or aerospace, automotive, chemical, computer, electrical, industrial, manufacturing, materials, mechanical, or petroleum engineering. They must reside or attend college in Arizona, California, Florida, Indiana, Kansas, Minnesota, New Mexico, Puerto Rico, Texas, or Washington. Preference is given to members of groups underrepresented in computer science and engineering who can demonstrate financial need. U.S. citizenship is required.

Financial data The stipend is $5,000.

Duration 1 year.

Additional information This program is sponsored by Honeywell International Inc.

Number awarded 3 each year.

Deadline February of each year for current college students; May of each year for high school seniors.

[304]
HONOLULU ALUMNAE PANHELLENIC ASSOCIATION COLLEGIATE SCHOLARSHIPS

Honolulu Alumnae Panhellenic Association
c/o Hazel Tagatac, Vice President of Scholarship
6401 101st Street
Ewa Beach, HI 96706
E-mail: hapascholarship@gmail.com
Web: hawaiipanhellenic.net

Summary To provide financial assistance to female college students from Hawaii who are members of a National Panhellenic Conference (NPC) sorority.

Eligibility This program is open to women who are initiated and active members of an NPC-affiliated sorority at a college or university in any state where they are working on an undergraduate degree. Their permanent home address or college address must be in Hawaii. Along with their application, they must submit brief essays on how membership in their sorority

has impacted their life, how they have contributed to their sorority and the Panhellenic community, and how this scholarship will benefit them. Financial need is not considered in the selection process.

Financial data The stipend ranges from $500 to $1,000.

Duration 1 year.

Additional information This program includes the Jacque Law Scholarship and the Leah Rowland Scholarship.

Number awarded Varies each year; recently, 2 were awarded.

Deadline March of each year.

[305]
HONOLULU ALUMNAE PANHELLENIC ASSOCIATION HIGH SCHOOL SCHOLARSHIPS

Honolulu Alumnae Panhellenic Association
c/o Hazel Tagatac, Vice President of Scholarship
6401 101st Street
Ewa Beach, HI 96706
E-mail: hapascholarship@gmail.com
Web: hawaiipanhellenic.net

Summary To provide financial assistance to female high school seniors in Hawaii who are interested in going to a college with National Panhellenic Conference (NPC) sororities on campus.

Eligibility This program is open to women graduating from high schools in Hawaii. Applicants must be interested in attending a 4-year college or university that has NPC sororities, although they are not required to join a sorority. Along with their application, they must submit 1) a brief essay on how this scholarship would benefit them and, if they are considering joining a sorority, what they hope to gain from membership; 2) transcripts; 3) a list of all class and school offices, other offices and responsibilities, school and athletic activities, extracurricular and community activities, honors, and awards; and 4) letters of recommendation from a teacher, counselor, or other mentor. Financial need is not considered in the selection process.

Financial data The stipend ranges from $500 to $1,000.

Duration 1 year.

Additional information This program includes the Rebecca B. Hall Memorial Scholarship.

Number awarded Varies each year; recently, 3 were awarded.

Deadline March of each year.

[306]
HONOLULU BRANCH AAUW SCHOLARSHIPS

Hawai'i Community Foundation
Attn: Scholarship Department
827 Fort Street Mall
Honolulu, HI 96813
(808) 566-5570   Toll Free: (888) 731-3863
Fax: (808) 521-6286
E-mail: scholarships@hcf-hawaii.org
Web: hcf.scholarships.ngwebsolutions.com

Summary To provide financial assistance to women in Hawaii who are working on an undergraduate or graduate degree at a school in the state.

Eligibility This program is open to female residents of Hawaii who are currently enrolled at an accredited university in the state. Applicants must be working full time on an undergraduate degree or full or part time on a graduate degree in any field. They must have a GPA of 3.0 or higher. All fields of study are eligible, but preference is given to students working on a degree in a field of science, technology, engineering, or mathematics (STEM). Along with their application, they must submit a brief curriculum vitae or resume highlighting their academic achievements. Financial need is considered in the selection process.

Financial data The amounts of the awards depend on the availability of funds and the need of the recipient. Recently, the average value of the scholarships awarded by the foundation was $2,800.

Duration 1 year.

Additional information This program is sponsored by the Honolulu Branch of the American Association of University Women (AAUW).

Number awarded 1 or more each year.

Deadline February of each year.

[307]
HONOLULU CHAPTER ADULT STUDENTS IN SCHOLASTIC TRANSITION (ASIST) SCHOLARSHIP PROGRAM

Executive Women International-Honolulu Chapter
Attn: Roseann Freitas
P.O. Box 2295
Honolulu, HI 96804-2295
(808) 263-8894 E-mail: roseann@archipelagohawaii.com
Web: www.ewihonolulu.org/scholarships/asist.html

Summary To provide financial assistance to nontraditional students from Hawaii who wish to attend college in any state.

Eligibility This program is open to adult residents of Hawaii at transitional points in their lives. Applicants may be persons who are 1) past high school age and entering a college, university, trade school, and/or the workforce for the first time; 2) already enrolled in a college, university, or trade program as nontraditional students; 3) re-training due to changes in the workplace; or 4) otherwise finished with high school but not the traditional college or trade school student. They must utilize reentry programs available through colleges and universities, community agencies, and service groups or career professionals; be 18 years of age or older; have clearly defined career goals and objectives; and specify the educational requirements to attain their goals and objectives. Priority is given to applicants who are responsible for small children; are socially, physically, or economically challenged adults; and can demonstrate financial need. U.S. citizenship or permanent resident status is required.

Financial data Stipends range from $1,500 to $4,000.

Duration 1 year.

Number awarded Varies each year; recently, 7 were awarded: 1 at $4,000, 1 at $3,000, 1 at $2,000, and 4 at $1,500.

Deadline May of each year.

[308]
HORIZONS FOUNDATION SCHOLARSHIP PROGRAM

Women in Defense
c/o National Defense Industrial Association
2111 Wilson Boulevard, Suite 400
Arlington, VA 22201-3061
(703) 522-1820   Fax: (703) 522-1885
E-mail: wid@ndia.org
Web: www.womenindefense.net

Summary To provide financial assistance to members of Women in Defense (WID) who are upper-division or graduate students engaged in or planning careers related to the national security interests of the United States.

Eligibility This program is open to WID members who are already working in national security fields as well as women planning such careers. Applicants must 1) be currently enrolled at an accredited college or university, either full or part time, as graduate students or upper-division undergraduates; 2) demonstrate financial need; 3) be U.S. citizens; 4) have a GPA of 3.25 or higher; and 5) demonstrate interest in preparing for a career related to national security or defense. The preferred fields of study include business (as it relates to national security or defense), computer science, cyber security, economics, engineering, government relations, international relations, law (as it relates to national security or defense), mathematics, military history, political science, physics, and security studies; others are considered if the applicant can demonstrate relevance to a career in national security or defense. Selection is based on academic achievement, participation in defense and national security activities, field of study, work experience, statements of objectives, recommendations, and financial need.

Financial data The stipend ranges up to $10,000.

Duration 1 year; renewable.

Additional information This program began in 1988.

Number awarded Varies each year; recently, 3 worth $16,000 were awarded.

Deadline July of each year.

[309]
HORIZONS-MICHIGAN SCHOLARSHIP

Women in Defense-Michigan Chapter
Attn: Scholarship Director
P.O. Box 4744
Troy, MI 48099
E-mail: scholarships@wid-mi.org
Web: www.wid-mi.org

Summary To provide financial assistance to women in Michigan who are upper-division or graduate students working on a degree related to national defense.

Eligibility This program is open to women who are residents of Michigan and enrolled either full or part time at a college or university in the state. Applicants must be juniors, seniors, or graduate students and have a GPA of 3.25 or higher. They must be interested in preparing for a career related to national security or defense. Relevant fields of study include security studies, military history, government relations, engineering, computer science, physics, mathematics, business (as related to national security or defense), law (as related to national security or defense), international relations, political science, or economics; other fields may be considered if the applicant can demonstrate relevance to a career in national security or defense. Along with their application, they must submit brief statements on their interest in a career in national security or defense, the principal accomplishments in their life that relate to their professional goals, and the objectives of their educational program. Selection is based on those statements, academic achievement, participation in defense and national security activities, field of study, work experience, recommendations, and financial need. U.S. citizenship is required.

Financial data Stipends have averaged at least $3,000.

Duration 1 year.

Additional information This program began in 2009.

Number awarded Varies each year; recently, 6 were awarded.

Deadline September of each year.

[310]
HORMEL FOODS MINNESOTA SECTION SWE SCHOLARSHIPS

Society of Women Engineers-Minnesota Section
Attn: Scholarship Committee
P.O. Box 18481
Minneapolis, MN 55418
E-mail: scholarships@swe-mn.org
Web: www.swe-mn.org/scholarships.html

Summary To provide financial assistance to women from any state working on an undergraduate or graduate degree in industrial technology or specified fields of engineering at colleges and universities in Minnesota, North Dakota, and South Dakota.

Eligibility This program is open to female undergraduate and graduate students at ABET-accredited engineering programs in Minnesota, North Dakota, or South Dakota. Applicants must be working full time on a degree in industrial technology or agricultural, civil, electrical, industrial, manufacturing, or mechanical engineering. Along with their application, they must submit a 250-word essay describing how they plan to utilize their engineering knowledge and skills after they graduate. Selection is based on potential to succeed as an engineer (20 points), communication skills (10 points), extracurricular or community involvement and leadership skills (10 points), demonstration of work experience and successes (10 points), and academic success (5 points).

Financial data The stipend is $1,000.

Duration 1 year.

Additional information This program is sponsored by Hormel Foods.

Number awarded 2 each year.

Deadline March of each year.

[311]
HOUSTON AREA SECTION FIRST SCHOLARSHIP

Society of Women Engineers-Houston Area Section
Attn: Vice President External
P.O. Box 1355
Houston, TX 77251-1355
E-mail: vp_external@swehouston.org
Web: societyofwomenengineers.swe.org

Summary To provide financial assistance to high school women, especially those in Texas, interested in studying engineering at a college in any state.

Eligibility This program is open to female high school seniors planning to attend an ABET-accredited 4-year college or university to major in engineering. Preference is given to students attending high school in Texas, but applicants may be planning to enroll at a college in any state. They must have completed at least 1 regional FIRST (For Inspiration and Recognition of Science and Technology) competition. Along with their application, they must submit transcripts; a 1-page essay on why they would like to be an engineer, how they believe they will make a difference as an engineer, and what influenced them to study engineering; a letter of reference regarding their scholastic ability, general character, attitude, ambition, motivation, and leadership characteristics; and a resume. Information on financial situation is purely voluntary and is not used in the selection process.

Financial data The stipend is $1,000.

Duration 1 year; nonrenewable.

Number awarded 1 each year.

Deadline February of each year.

[312]
HUMBLE ARTESIAN ABWA SCHOLARSHIP

American Business Women's Association-Humble
  Artesian Chapter
c/o Dee Driscoll, Education Committee
7810 FM 1960 E, Suite 104
Humble, TX 77346
(281) 852-3667   Fax: (281) 852-3663
E-mail: driscolldee@yahoo.com
Web: www.abwahumble.org/scholarship

Summary To provide financial assistance to women from any state who have completed at least the sophomore year of college.

Eligibility This program is open to all women who are U.S. citizens. Applicants must be enrolled as juniors, seniors, or graduate students at a college or university in any state and have a GPA of 2.5 or higher.

Financial data The stipend is $1,500.

Duration 1 year.

Number awarded 1 each year.

Deadline January of each year.

[313]
HUNTSVILLE CHAPTER AFWA SCHOLARSHIPS

Accounting and Financial Women's Alliance-Huntsville
  Chapter
c/o Sylvia Ayers, Education Chair
COLSA Corporation
6728 Odyssey Drive, N.W.
Huntsville, AL 35806
(256) 964-5555   E-mail: sayers@colsa.com
Web: www.huntsvilleafwa.org/wordpress/scholarship

Summary To provide financial assistance to women working on an undergraduate or graduate degree in accounting at a college or university in Alabama.

Eligibility This program is open to women working full or part time on a bachelor's or master's degree in accounting at a college, university, or professional school of accounting in

Alabama. Applicants must have completed at least 60 semester hours. They are not required to be members of the Accounting and Financial Women's Alliance (AFWA). Along with their application, they must submit a 250-word essay on how they plan to incorporate into their strategic career goals the sponsor's philosophy of achieving balance among life priorities, including career, personal development, family, friendships, and community and societal needs. Selection is based on that essay, academic record, extracurricular activities and honors, employment history, a statement of career goals and objectives, and financial need.

Financial data The stipend ranges from $500 to $2,500.

Duration 1 year.

Number awarded Varies each year; recently, 4 were awarded.

Deadline March of each year.

[314]
HWNT AUSTIN SCHOLARSHIP

Hispanic Scholarship Consortium
Attn: Scholarship Selection Committee
7703 North Lamar Boulevard, Suite 310
Austin, TX 78752
(512) 368-2956   Fax: (512) 692-1831
E-mail: scholarships@hispanicscholar.org
Web: hispanicscholar.academicworks.com

Summary To provide financial assistance and work experience to female high school seniors and college seniors of Hispanic heritage from Texas who plan to attend college or graduate school in any state.

Eligibility This program is open to female residents of Texas of Hispanic heritage who are either 1) seniors graduating from high schools in Texas; or 2) seniors graduating from colleges in any state. High school seniors must be planning to enroll full time at an accredited 2- or 4-year college or university in any state; college seniors must be planning to enroll in graduate school. Applicants must have a GPA of 3.0 or higher. Selection is based on academic achievement, community service, personal strengths, leadership, and financial need. U.S. citizenship is not required; students may qualify under Texas Senate Bill 1528.

Financial data The stipend is $2,000 per year.

Duration 1 year; may be renewed up to 3 additional years, provided the recipient remains enrolled full time, maintains a GPA of 3.0 or higher, and participates in at least 25 hours of community service per semester.

Additional information This program is sponsored by the Austin chapter of Hispanic Women's Network of Texas (HWNT). Scholarship winners must also participate in a year-long internship with the magazine.

Number awarded Varies each year; recently, 2 were awarded.

Deadline April of each year.

[315]
IBM LINDA SANFORD WOMEN'S TECHNICAL ADVANCEMENT SCHOLARSHIP

Society of Women Engineers
Attn: Scholarship Selection Committee
203 North LaSalle Street, Suite 1675
Chicago, IL 60601-1269
(312) 596-5223   Toll Free: (877) SWE-INFO
Fax: (312) 644-8557   E-mail: scholarships@swe.org
Web: societyofwomenengineers.swe.org

Summary To provide financial assistance to women returning to college to work on a degree in computer or electrical engineering.

Eligibility This program is open to women who have been absent from college for a period of years and are returning to study at a 4-year ABET-accredited college or university. Applicants must be working on a degree in computer science, mathematical analysis, or electrical or computer engineering and have a GPA of 3.5 or higher. Selection is based on merit.

Financial data The stipend is $1,000.

Duration 1 year.

Additional information This program is sponsored by the IBM Corporation.

Number awarded 1 each year.

Deadline Deadline not specified.

[316]
IDA M. POPE MEMORIAL SCHOLARSHIPS

Hawai'i Community Foundation
Attn: Scholarship Department
827 Fort Street Mall
Honolulu, HI 96813
(808) 566-5570   Toll Free: (888) 731-3863
Fax: (808) 521-6286
E-mail: scholarships@hcf-hawaii.org
Web: hcf.scholarships.ngwebsolutions.com

Summary To provide financial assistance to Native Hawaiian women who are interested in working on an undergraduate or graduate degree in designated fields at a school in any state.

Eligibility This program is open to female residents of Hawaii who are Native Hawaiian, defined as a descendant of the aboriginal inhabitants of the Hawaiian islands prior to 1778. Applicants must be enrolled full time at a 2- or 4-year college or university in any state and working on an undergraduate or graduate degree in health, science, mathematics, or education (including counseling and social work). They must be able to demonstrate academic achievement (GPA of 3.5 or higher), good moral character, and financial need. Along with their application, they must submit a short statement indicating their reasons for attending college, their planned course of study, their career goals, and what community service means to them.

Financial data The amounts of the awards depend on the availability of funds and the need of the recipient. Recently, the average value of the scholarships awarded by the foundation was $2,800.

Duration 1 year; may be renewed.

Number awarded Varies each year; recently, 61 were awarded.

Deadline February of each year.

[317]
ILLINOIS SCHOLARSHIPS FOR JUNIOR MEMBERS

American Legion Auxiliary
Department of Illinois
2720 East Lincoln Street
P.O. Box 1426
Bloomington, IL 61702-1426
(309) 663-9366   Fax: (309) 663-5827
E-mail: karen.boughan@ilala.org
Web: www.ilala.org/education.html

Summary To provide financial assistance to high school seniors or graduates in Illinois who are junior members of the American Legion Auxiliary and planning to attend college in any state.

Eligibility This program is open to junior members of the Illinois American Legion Auxiliary who are daughters, granddaughters, great-granddaughters, or sisters of veterans who served during eligibility dates for membership in the American Legion. Applicants must have been members for at least 3 years. They must be high school seniors or graduates who have not yet attended an institution of higher learning and are planning to attend college in any state. Along with their application, they must submit a 1,000-word essay on "The Veteran in My Life." Selection is based on that essay (25%) character and leadership (25%), scholarship (25%), and financial need (25%).

Financial data The stipend is $1,000.

Duration 1 year.

Number awarded Varies each year.

Deadline March of each year.

[318]
INDIANA AMERICAN LEGION GOLD AWARD GIRL SCOUT OF THE YEAR SCHOLARSHIP ACHIEVEMENT AWARD

American Legion
Department of Indiana
777 North Meridian Street, Suite 104
Indianapolis, IN 46204
(317) 630-1200   Fax: (317) 630-1277
Web: www.indianalegion.org/scholarships—awards.html

Summary To recognize and reward, with scholarships to attend college in any state, members of the Girl Scouts in Indiana who have received the Gold Award.

Eligibility This program is open to high school seniors in Indiana who plan to attend college in any state. Applicants must be registered Girl Scouts who have received the Gold Award; are active members of their religious institution and have received the appropriate religious emblem at the Ambassador or Senior Scout level; have demonstrated good and practical citizenship in their Girl Scouting, school, religious institution, and community; are U.S. citizens; and submit letters of recommendation from a leader in each of the following groups: Scouting, school, religious institution, and community.

Financial data The awards are a $1,000 scholarship for the state winner and $200 scholarships for each district winner.

Duration The awards are presented annually.

Additional information Winners must utilize their awards within 1 year of graduating from high school as full-time students at an accredited institution of higher education in the United States.

Number awarded 12 each year: 1 state winner and 11 district winners.

Deadline April of each year.

[319]
INDIANA WOMEN IN PUBLIC FINANCE SCHOLARSHIP

Indiana Women in Public Finance
c/o Katie Aeschliman, Scholarship Committee
BMO Harris Bank
135 North Pennsylvania Street, Ninth Floor
Indianapolis, IN 46204
(317) 269-1376   E-mail: indianawpf@gmail.com
Web: www.indianawpf.com/scholarship

Summary To provide financial assistance to women from Indiana who are working on a degree in a field related to public finance at a college in the state.

Eligibility This program is open to women who are residents of Indiana and currently enrolled as juniors at a college or university in the state. Applicants must be majoring in finance, public finance, law, government accounting, public policy, public management, or a closely-related field. Along with their application, they must submit 500-word essays on 1) any extracurricular activities in which they have participated; and 2) their post-collegiate work plans.

Financial data The stipend is $1,500.

Duration 1 year.

Additional information Indiana Women in Public Finance was organized in 2009.

Number awarded 2 each year.

Deadline September of each year.

[320]
INDIANA WOMEN IN TRANSITION SCHOLARSHIP

Indiana Women's Education Foundation, Inc.
510 East Silver Street
Knightstown, IN 46148
(317) 442-2620   E-mail: bmofield@centurylink.net
Web: www.inwomeneducation.org/index.php/scholarships

Summary To provide financial assistance for college to mature women in Indiana.

Eligibility This program is open to women who are 30 years of age or older and have been an Indiana resident for at least 1 year. Applicants must be reentering the workforce, be changing careers, or be a displaced worker. They must have applied to a postsecondary institution for at least part-time attendance. Along with their application, they must submit 1) a statement (up to 200 words) on their career goals and how their education relates to those goals; and 2) documentation of financial need.

Financial data The stipend is $1,000. Funds are paid directly to the recipient's school.

Duration 1 year; recipients may reapply.

Additional information This program began in 1995, when the Indiana Women's Education Foundation was named the Indiana Business and Professional Women's Foundation.

Number awarded 1 each year.

Deadline February of each year.

[321]
INDIANA WORKING WOMAN SCHOLARSHIP

Indiana Women's Education Foundation, Inc.
510 East Silver Street
Knightstown, IN 46148
(317) 442-2620   E-mail: bmofield@centurylink.net
Web: www.inwomeneducation.org/index.php/scholarships

Summary To provide financial assistance for college to women in Indiana who are also working at least part time.

Eligibility This program is open to women who are 25 years of age or older and have been an Indiana resident for at least 1 year. Applicants must be employed at least 20 hours per week and must have applied to or be attending a postsecondary institution on at least a part-time basis. Along with their application, they must submit 1) a statement (up to 200 words) on their career goals and how their education relates to those goals; and 2) documentation of financial need.

Financial data The stipend is $1,000. Funds are paid directly to the recipient's school.

Duration 1 year; recipients may reapply.

Additional information This program began in 1995, when the Indiana Women's Education Foundation was named the Indiana Business and Professional Women's Foundation.

Number awarded 1 each year.

Deadline February of each year.

[322]
INTERMOUNTAIN SECTION AWWA DIVERSITY SCHOLARSHIP

American Water Works Association-Intermountain
  Section
Attn: Member Services Coordinator
3430 East Danish Road
Sandy, UT 84093
(801) 712-1619, ext. 2   Fax: (801) 487-6699
E-mail: nicoleb@ims-awwa.org
Web: ims-awwa.site-ym.com/group/StudentPO

Summary To provide financial assistance to female and minority undergraduate and graduate students working on a degree in the field of water quality, supply, and treatment at a university in the Intermountain West.

Eligibility This program is open to 1) women; and 2) students who identify as Hispanic or Latino, Black or African American, Native Hawaiian or other Pacific Islander, Asian, or American Indian or Alaska Native. Applicants must be entering or enrolled in an undergraduate or graduate program at a college or university in the Intermountain West (defined to include all or portions of Arizona, Colorado, Idaho, Montana, Nevada, New Mexico, Utah, or Wyoming) that relates to water quality, supply, or treatment. Along with their application, they must submit a 2-page essay on their academic interests and career goals and how those relate to water quality, supply, or treatment. Selection is based on that essay, letters of recommendation, and potential to contribute to the field of water quality, supply, and treatment in the Intermountain West.

Financial data The stipend is $1,000. The winner also receives a 1-year student membership in the Intermountain Section of the American Water Works Association (AWWA).

Duration 1 year; nonrenewable.

Number awarded 1 each year.

Deadline November of each year.

[323]
INTERPUBLIC GROUP SCHOLARSHIP AND INTERNSHIP

New York Women in Communications, Inc.
Attn: NYWICI Foundation
355 Lexington Avenue, 15th Floor
New York, NY 10017-6603
(212) 297-2133   Fax: (212) 370-9047
E-mail: nywicipr@nywici.org
Web: www.nywici.org/foundation/scholarships

Summary To provide financial assistance and work experience to women from ethnically diverse groups who are residents of designated eastern states and enrolled as juniors at a college in any state to prepare for a career in advertising or public relations.

Eligibility This program is open to female residents of New York, New Jersey, Connecticut, or Pennsylvania who are from ethnically diverse groups and currently enrolled as juniors at a college or university in any state. Also eligible are women who reside outside the 4 states but are currently enrolled at a college or university within 1 of the 5 boroughs of New York City. Applicants must be preparing for a career in advertising or public relations and have a GPA of 3.2 or higher. They must be available for a summer internship with Interpublic Group (IPG) in New York City. Along with their application, they must submit a 2-page resume; a personal essay of 300 words on an assigned topic that changes annually; 2 letters of recommendation; and an official transcript. Selection is based on academic record, need, demonstrated leadership, participation in school and community activities, honors and other awards or recognition, work experience, goals and aspirations, and unusual personal and/or family circumstances. U.S. citizenship or permanent status is required.

Financial data The scholarship stipend ranges up to $10,000; the internship is salaried (amount not specified).

Duration 1 year.

Additional information This program is sponsored by IPG, a holding company for a large number of firms in the advertising industry.

Number awarded 2 each year.

Deadline January of each year.

[324]
IOTA SIGMA PI MEMBERS-AT-LARGE REENTRY AWARD

Iota Sigma Pi
c/o Gail Blaustein, MAL National Coordinator
Benedictine College
Department of Chemistry and Biochemistry
Westerman 406A
1020 North Second Street
Atchison, KS 66002
(913) 360-7515   E-mail: MAL.IotaSigmaPi@gmail.com
Web: www.ispmembersatlarge.com

Summary To provide financial assistance to women who are reentering college to work on an undergraduate or graduate degree in chemistry.

Eligibility This program is open to women who have returned to academic studies after an absence of 3 or more years and have completed at least 1 academic year of college chemistry since returning. Students must be working on an undergraduate or graduate degree in chemistry or a related field at a 4-year college or university. They must be nominated by a member of Iota Sigma Pi or by a member of the faculty at their institution. Nominees must submit a short essay describing their goals, pertinent experiences that influenced their choice of major, any interests or talents that will assist them in succeeding in their professional career, and how the scholarship will benefit them in meeting their goals. Financial need is not considered in the selection process.

Financial data The winner receives a stipend of $1,500, a certificate, and a 1-year waiver of Iota Sigma Pi dues.

Duration 1 year.

Additional information This award was first presented in 1991.

Number awarded 1 each year.

Deadline February of each year.

[325]
IRENE AND LEETA WAGY MEMORIAL SCHOLARSHIP

Daughters of the American Revolution-Missouri State
  Society
Attn: State Scholarship Chair
821 Main Street
P.O. Box 297
Boonville, MO 65233
(660) 882-5320   E-mail: missouridar@gmail.com
Web: www.mssdar.org/statepages/education.html

Summary To provide financial assistance to female high school seniors in Missouri who plan to study education at a college or university in the state.

Eligibility This program is open to female seniors graduating from high schools in Missouri in the top 10% of their class. Applicants must be planning to attend an accredited college or university in Missouri to major in education. Selection is based on academic skills, character, and financial need. U.S. citizenship is required.

Financial data The stipend is $1,000.

Duration 1 year.

Number awarded 1 or more each year.

Deadline December of each year.

[326]
ISABEL M. HERSON SCHOLARSHIP IN EDUCATION

Zeta Phi Beta Sorority, Inc.
Attn: National Educational Foundation
1734 New Hampshire Avenue, N.W.
Washington, DC 20009
(202) 387-3103   Fax: (202) 232-4593
E-mail: info@zetaphibetasororityhq.org
Web: www.zpbnef1975.org/scholarships-and-descriptions

Summary To provide financial assistance to undergraduate and graduate students interested in preparing for a career in education.

Eligibility This program is open to students enrolled full time in an undergraduate or graduate program leading to a degree in either elementary or secondary education. Proof of enrollment is required. Along with their application, they must submit a 150-word essay on their educational goals and professional aspirations, how this award will help them to achieve those goals, and why they should receive the award. Financial need is not considered in the selection process.

Financial data The stipend ranges from $500 to $1,000.

Duration 1 academic year.

Additional information Zeta Phi Beta is a traditionally African American sorority.

Number awarded 1 or more each year.

Deadline January of each year.

[327]
ISO NEW ENGLAND SCHOLARSHIPS

Society of Women Engineers
Attn: Scholarship Selection Committee
203 North LaSalle Street, Suite 1675
Chicago, IL 60601-1269
(312) 596-5223   Toll Free: (877) SWE-INFO
Fax: (312) 644-8557   E-mail: scholarships@swe.org
Web: societyofwomenengineers.swe.org

Summary To provide financial assistance to women who have ties to New England and are interested in working on an undergraduate or graduate degree in computer or electrical engineering.

Eligibility This program is open to women who are sophomores, juniors, seniors, or graduate students and working full time on an undergraduate or graduate degree in computer or electrical engineering with a power focus. Applicants must be residents of New England or attending an ABET-accredited college or university in that region. They must have a GPA of 3.5 or higher. Selection is based on merit.

Financial data The stipend is $2,500.

Duration 1 year.

Additional information This program began in 2014 with support from ISO New England.

Number awarded 2 each year.

Deadline February of each year.

[328]
ITW SCHOLARSHIPS

Society of Women Engineers
Attn: Scholarship Selection Committee
203 North LaSalle Street, Suite 1675
Chicago, IL 60601-1269
(312) 596-5223   Toll Free: (877) SWE-INFO
Fax: (312) 644-8557   E-mail: scholarships@swe.org
Web: societyofwomenengineers.swe.org

Summary To provide financial assistance to undergraduate women majoring in designated engineering specialties.

Eligibility This program is open to women who are entering their junior year at a 4-year ABET-accredited college or university. Applicants must be working full time on a degree in computer science, electrical or mechanical engineering, or polymer science. Preference is given to 1) members of groups underrepresented in engineering or computer science; 2) students interested in an internship with the sponsor; 3) residents of Illinois, Ohio, Texas, or Wisconsin; and 4) students attending the University of Illinois at Chicago, Georgia Institute of Technology, Ohio State University, Northwestern University, or Pennsylvania State University. Selection is based on merit. U.S. citizenship is required.

Financial data The stipend is $2,500 per year.

Duration 1 year; may be renewed 1 additional year.

Additional information This program is sponsored by Illinois Tool Works, Inc.

Number awarded 2 each year.

Deadline February of each year.

[329]
JAN GWATNEY SCHOLARSHIP

United Daughters of the Confederacy
Attn: Second Vice President General
328 North Boulevard
Richmond, VA 23220-4009
(804) 355-1636   Fax: (804) 353-1396
E-mail: udc@hqudc.org
Web: www.hqudc.org/scholarships

Summary To provide financial assistance to female lineal descendants of Confederate Veterans, especially those from designated southern states.

Eligibility Eligible to apply for these scholarships are female lineal descendants of worthy Confederates or collateral descendants who are current or former members of the Children of the Confederacy or current members of the United Daughters of the Confederacy. Applicants must submit a family financial report and certified proof of the Confederate record of 1 ancestor, with the company and regiment in which he served. They must have at least a 3.0 GPA in high school. Preference is given to residents of Georgia, Louisiana, or Texas.

Financial data The amount of this scholarship depends on the availability of funds.

Duration 1 year; may be renewed up to 3 additional years, provided the recipient remains enrolled full time with a GPA of 3.0 or higher.

Number awarded 1 each year.

Deadline April of each year.

[330]
JANE CHAMBERS PLAYWRITING AWARD

Association for Theatre in Higher Education
Attn: Women and Theatre Program
P.O. Box 1290
Boulder, CO 80306-1290
(303) 530-2167   Toll Free: (888) 284-3737
Fax: (303) 530-2168   E-mail: vpawards@athe.org
Web: www.womenandtheatreprogram.com

Summary To recognize and reward outstanding plays and performance texts that were created by women and have a majority of parts for women performers.

Eligibility Women are invited to submit plays and performance texts that reflect a feminist perspective and contain significant opportunities for women performers. Scripts may be produced or unproduced. There is no limitation on length, style, or subject. Current undergraduate and graduate students may enter the student category of the competition.

Financial data The general award consists of $1,000, free registration to attend the Women and Theatre Conference (early August), and a rehearsed reading of the winning piece at that conference. The student award is $150 and a year's membership in Women and Theatre.

Duration The competition is held annually.

Number awarded 1 general award and 1 student award are presented each year.

Deadline February of each year.

[331]
JANE LORING JONES SCHOLARSHIPS

American Baptist Churches of the Rocky Mountains
Attn: American Baptist Women's Ministries
9085 East Mineral Circle, Suite 170
Centennial, CO 80112
(303) 988-3900   E-mail: web@abcrm.org
Web: www.abcrm.org/ministries/abwm/colorado

Summary To provide financial assistance to women who are members of churches affiliated with the American Baptist Churches (ABC) USA in Colorado, New Mexico, and Utah and interested in attending an ABC college in any state.

Eligibility This program is open to women under 26 years of age who are active members of churches cooperating with ABC in Colorado, New Mexico, or Utah. Applicants must be enrolled or planning to enroll full time at an ABC college or university in any state. They are not required to enter Christian service as a vocation, but they must have a real desire to prepare themselves for Christian leadership in the home, church, and community. Along with their application, they must submit a personal letter describing their Christian experience; their participation in the life of their church, school, and community; and their goals for the future. Selection is based on academic performance, Christian participation in church and school, and financial need. Preference is given to women entering their first or second year at an ABC school.

Financial data For students attending an ABC-related college or university and living on campus, the stipend is $3,000 per year. For students at those colleges and universities but living off campus, the stipend is $1,500 per year. For students at other colleges and universities and living on campus, the stipend is $2,000 per year. For students at such colleges and universities and living off campus, the stipend is $1,000 per year.

Duration 1 year; recipients may reapply.

Number awarded 1 or more each year.

Deadline May of each year.

[332]
JANE M. KLAUSMAN WOMEN IN BUSINESS SCHOLARSHIPS

Zonta International
Attn: Foundation
1211 West 22nd Street, Suite 900
Oak Brook, IL 60523-3384
(630) 928-1400   Fax: (630) 928-1559
E-mail: programs@zonta.org
Web: www.zonta.org

Summary To provide financial assistance to women working on an undergraduate or master's degree in business at a school in any country.

Eligibility This program is open to women who are working on a business-related degree at a college or university anywhere in the world at the level of the second year of an undergraduate program through the final year of a master's degree program. Applicants first compete at the club level, and then advance to district and international levels. Along with their application, they must submit a 500-word essay that describes their academic and professional goals, the relevance of their program to the business field, and how this scholarship will assist them in reaching their goals. Selection is based on that essay, academic record, demonstrated intent to complete a program in business, achievement in business-related subjects, and 2 letters of recommendation.

Financial data District winners receive a $1,000 scholarship; the international winners receive a $7,000 scholarship.

Duration 1 year.

Additional information This program began in 1998.

Number awarded Up to 32 district winners and 12 international winners are selected each year. Since this program was established, it has awarded 441 of these scholarships, worth more than $1 million, to 335 women from 50 countries.

Deadline Clubs set their own deadlines but must submit their winners to the district governor by May of each year.

[333]
JANE WALKER SCHOLARSHIP

United Methodist Church-Alabama-West Florida
Conference
Attn: Commission on the Status and Role of Women
4719 Windmere Boulevard
Montgomery, AL 36106
(334) 356-8014   Toll Free: (888) 873-3127
Fax: (334) 356-8029   E-mail: awfcrc@awfumc.org
Web: www.awfumc.org/janewalkerscholarship

Summary To provide financial assistance to female residents of the Alabama-West Florida Conference of the United Methodist Church (UMC) who are undergraduate or seminary students preparing for a church-related career.

Eligibility This program is open to women who are residents of the Alabama-West Florida Conference of the UMW and who affirm, represent, and advocate women's leadership in the church. Applicants must be accepted or enrolled at an approved UMC seminary or working on an undergraduate degree in Christian education at an approved UMC institution in any state. They must be a candidate for ministry or preparing for a UMC church-related career. Along with their application, they must submit a 500-word essay on why they are preparing for full-time Christian ministry and how they can promote the cause of women through this ministry. Financial need is considered in the selection process.

Financial data The stipend is $1,000.

Duration 1 year.

Number awarded 1 each year.

Deadline May of each year.

[334]
JANET CULLEN TANAKA SCHOLARSHIP

Association for Women Geoscientists
Attn: AWG Foundation
12000 North Washington Street, Suite 285
Thornton, CO 80241
(303) 412-6219   Fax: (303) 253-9220
E-mail: scholarship@awg-ps.org
Web: www.awg.org/eas/pugetsound.htm

Summary To provide financial assistance to women from any state who are working on an undergraduate degree in geoscience at a college or university in Oregon or Washington.

Eligibility This program is open to undergraduate women from any state who are working on a bachelor's degree and committed to preparing for a career or graduate work in the geosciences, including geology, environmental or engineering geology, geochemistry, geophysics, hydrogeology, or hydrology. Applicants must be currently enrolled at a 2- or 4-year college or university in Oregon or Washington and have a GPA of 3.2 or higher. Selection is based on potential for professional success, academic achievements, and financial need.

Financial data The stipend is $1,000.

Duration 1 year.

Additional information This program is sponsored by the Pacific Northwest Chapter of the Association for Women Geoscientists.

Number awarded 1 each year.

Deadline December of each year.

[335]
JANET H. GRISWOLD PEO SCHOLARSHIP

P.E.O. Foundation-California State Chapter
c/o Pat Lachman, Gardner Scholarship Fund
4400 Hessel Road
Sebastopol, CA 95472
E-mail: peoca.eog@gmail.com
Web: www.peocalifornia.org

Summary To provide financial assistance to women from California who are undergraduate or graduate students at a school in any state.

Eligibility This program is open to female residents of California who are attending an accredited college or university in any state. Applicants must be enrolled as full-time undergraduate or graduate students. Selection is based on financial need, character, and a record of academic and extracurricular activities achievement. U.S. citizenship is required.

Financial data Stipends range from $500 to $1,500.

Duration 1 year.

Number awarded Varies each year.

Deadline January of each year.

[336]
JAZZ PERFORMANCE AWARDS

Sigma Alpha Iota Philanthropies, Inc.
One Tunnel Road
Asheville, NC 28805
(828) 251-0606   Fax: (828) 251-0644
E-mail: nh@sai-national.org
Web: www.sai-national.org

Summary To provide financial assistance to members of Sigma Alpha Iota (an organization of women musicians) who are interested in working on an undergraduate or graduate degree in jazz performance.

Eligibility This program is open to members of the organization who are enrolled in an undergraduate or graduate degree program in jazz performance or studies. Applicants must be younger than 32 years of age. Along with their application, they must submit a CD recording of a performance "set" of 30 to 45 minutes.

Financial data Stipends are $2,000 for the winner or $1,500 for the runner-up.

Duration 1 year.

Additional information These awards were first presented in 2006.

Number awarded 2 every 3 years.

Deadline March of the year of the awards (2018, 2021, etc.).

[337]
JEAN BARTEL AWARDS FOR MILITARY AWARENESS

The Miss America Foundation
1432 K Street, N.W., Suite 900
Washington, DC 20005
(609) 344-1800
Web: www.missamericafoundation.org/scholarships

Summary To recognize and reward women who have participated in the Miss America Pageant at any level and have conducted projects to honor members of the armed forces.

Eligibility This program is open to women who have competed at any level of the Miss America Pageant within the past 10 years. Applicants must submit an essay describing how they have fulfilled a legitimate need in their community through the creation, development, and/or participation in a community-based project or event to raise awareness of the work of members of the armed forces. Selection is based on that essay, GPA (high school and undergraduate), class rank, extracurricular activities, financial aid requirements, household income, and level of participation within the Miss America system.

Financial data The awards are college scholarships of $6,000 for the winner, $4,000 for the first runner-up, and $3,000 for the second runner-up.

Duration The awards are presented annually.

Number awarded 3 each year.

Deadline Deadline not specified.

[338]
JEAN BARTEL QUALITY OF LIFE AWARDS

The Miss America Foundation
1432 K Street, N.W., Suite 900
Washington, DC 20005
(609) 344-1800
Web: www.missamericafoundation.org/scholarships

Summary To recognize and reward, with college scholarships, women who participate in the Miss America Pageant at the national level and demonstrate outstanding community service.

Eligibility This program is open to women who compete at the national level of the Miss America Pageant and demonstrate a commitment to enhancing the quality of life for others through volunteerism and community service. Applicants must demonstrate that they have fulfilled a legitimate need in their community through the creation, development, and/or participation in a community service project. Selection is based on the depth of service, creativity of the project, and effects on the lives of others.

Financial data The awards are college scholarships of $6,000 for the winner, $4,000 for the first runner-up, and $2,000 for the second runner-up.

Duration The awards are presented annually.

Additional information This program began in 1988.

Number awarded 3 each year.

Deadline Deadline not specified.

[339]
JEAN E. LYONS MEMORIAL SCHOLARSHIP

New Hampshire Women's Golf Association
c/o Mary Jane Cormier, Scholarship Committee
4 Wyndmere Drive
Londonderry, NH 03053
(603) 867-0606   E-mail: info@nhwga.org
Web: www.nhwga.org/juniors/scholarship-info

Summary To provide financial assistance to women in New Hampshire who have played golf and are interested in attending college in any state.

Eligibility This program is open to women who are residents of New Hampshire or playing members at New Hampshire golf clubs. Applicants must be enrolled or planning to enroll at a college or university in any state; preference is given to candidates enrolled in a 4-year undergraduate program. They must play golf; preference is given to applicants who play golf competitively in high school and/or who plan to play golf competitively in college. Along with their application, they must submit an essay describing their education and career goals, why they have chosen their course of study, and the job or career they are considering. Selection is based on academic success (as measured by grades and test scores) and character (as measured by extracurricular activities).

Financial data The stipend is $1,500. Funds are sent directly to the recipient's school.

Duration 1 year.

Additional information This scholarship, first awarded in 2009, is endowed through the New Hampshire Charitable Foundation.

Number awarded 1 each year.

Deadline April of each year.

[340]
JEAN FITZGERALD SCHOLARSHIP

Hawai'i Community Foundation
Attn: Scholarship Department
827 Fort Street Mall
Honolulu, HI 96813
(808) 566-5570   Toll Free: (888) 731-3863
Fax: (808) 521-6286
E-mail: scholarships@hcf-hawaii.org
Web: hcf.scholarships.ngwebsolutions.com

Summary To provide financial assistance to women tennis players in Hawaii who are entering freshmen at a college in any state.

Eligibility This program is open to female Hawaiian residents who are active tennis players entering their freshman year at a college or university in any state as full-time students. Preference may be given to members of the Hawai'i Pacific Section of the United States Tennis Association (USTA). Applicants must be able to demonstrate academic achievement (GPA of 2.7 or higher), good moral character, and financial need. Along with their application, they must submit a short statement indicating their reasons for attending college, their planned course of study, their career goals, and what community service means to them.

Financial data The amounts of the awards depend on the availability of funds and the need of the recipient. Recently, the average value of the scholarships awarded by the foundation was $2,800.

Duration 1 year.

Number awarded Varies each year; recently, 2 were awarded.

Deadline February of each year.

[341]
JEAN IBENDAHL SCHOLARSHIP

American Agri-Women
Daughters of American Agriculture
c/o Ardath DeWall
11841 North Mount Vernon Road
Shannon, IL 61078
E-mail: info@americanagriwomen.org
Web: www.americanagriwomen.org

Summary To provide financial assistance for college to young women involved in an aspect of agriculture.

Eligibility This program is open to women who are farmers, ranchers, or the wife, daughter, or other close relative of a farmer, rancher, or other person employed in agriculture. Applicants must be between 18 and 23 years of age and interested in working on a degree in agribusiness, agricultural leadership, communications, education, technology, rural sociology, medicine, or other fields directly related to agriculture and the needs of agricultural communities. Selection is based on financial need, knowledge of or work experience in agriculture, GPA, and test scores.

Financial data The stipend is $1,000.

Duration 1 year; nonrenewable.

Additional information This program began in 1991.

Number awarded 1 each year.

Deadline May of each year.

[342]
JEANNE L. HAMMOND MEMORIAL SCHOLARSHIP

Maine Federation of Business and Professional Women's
  Clubs
Attn: BPW/Maine Futurama Foundation
c/o Marilyn V. Ladd, Office Manager
103 County Road
Oakland, ME 04963
Web: www.bpwmefoundation.org/scholarship-program

Summary To provide financial assistance to female high school seniors and recent graduates in Maine who plan to attend college in any state.

Eligibility This program is open to women who are seniors graduating from high schools in Maine or recent graduates of those schools. Applicants must be planning to enroll at least half time for their first year of postsecondary study at an accredited college or university in any state. They must have a realistic goal for the educational plans. Along with their application, they must submit a statement describing their educational and personal goals, including their financial need. First priority is given to women who can demonstrate a record of school and/or community involvement. Second priority is given to applicants who are interested in working on a journalism degree, members of the Maine Federation of Business and Professional Women's Clubs (BPW/Maine) and their female dependents, and members of the American Association of University Women (AAUW) and their female dependents.

Financial data The stipend is $1,200. Funds are paid directly to the recipient's school.

Duration 1 year.

Number awarded 1 or more each year.

Deadline April of each year.

[343]
JEANNETTE RANKIN AWARD

Jeannette Rankin Foundation, Inc.
1 Huntington Road, Suite 701
Athens, GA 30606
(706) 208-1211   Fax: (706) 548-0202
E-mail: info@rankinfoundation.org
Web: www.rankinfoundation.org

Summary To provide financial assistance for college to women who are 35 years of age or older.

Eligibility This program is open to women who are 35 years of age or older and working on a technical or vocational certificate, associate degree, or first bachelor's degree. Applicants must meet standards of a low-income household, currently defined as net income less than $18,662 for a family of 1, rising to $71,506 for a family of 6. Along with their application, they must submit a 2-page essay that includes a description of their academic and career goals, what they have done of which they are the most proud, and how their education will benefit themselves, their family, and their community. Selection is based on the applicants' goals, plan for reaching those goals, and how they will use their education to give back to the community. U.S. citizenship or permanent resident status is required.

Financial data The stipend is $2,000.

Duration 1 year; nonrenewable.

Additional information This program began in 1978. Awards are not given to students enrolled in graduate courses or working on a second undergraduate degree.

Number awarded Varies each year; recently, 60 were awarded. Since the program began, it has awarded more than $2.3 million in scholarships to more than 800 women.

Deadline March of each year.

[344]
JENNIFER DUNN-THOMSON SCHOLARSHIP

Washington Policy Center
Attn: Operations Manager
P.O. Box 3643
Seattle, WA 98124
E-mail: bgoodwin@washingtonpolicy.org
Web: washingtonpolicy.org/jenniferdunn

Summary To provide funding for undergraduate or graduate study or for an internship to women who are preparing for a career in public service.

Eligibility This program is open to women who are currently enrolled as an undergraduate or graduate student. Applicants must have an above-average GPA and good oral and written communication skills. They must be able to demonstrate leadership and a commitment to public service and free-market principles.

Financial data The grant is $5,000. Funds may be used for tuition or to provide support for an internship on Capitol Hill in Washington, D.C.

Duration 1 year.

Additional information This program began in 2005.

Number awarded 1 each year.

Deadline April of each year.

[345]
JESSICA POWELL LOFTIS SCHOLARSHIP FOR ACTEENS

Woman's Missionary Union
Attn: WMU Foundation
100 Missionary Ridge
Birmingham, AL 35242
(205) 408-5525   Toll Free: (877) 482-4483
Fax: (205) 408-5508   E-mail: wmufoundation@wmu.org
Web: www.wmufoundation.com/?q=content/scholarships

Summary To provide financial assistance for college or other activities to female high school seniors who have been active in the Southern Baptist Convention's Acteens (Academic/Events/Training).

Eligibility This program is open to female high school seniors who are members of a Baptist church and active in Acteens. Applicants must 1) be planning to attend college and have completed *Quest for Vision* in the MissionsQuest program or StudiAct; 2) have been an Acteen for at least 1 year and be planning to attend an Acteens event; or 3) be an Acteens leader who is pursuing academic or leadership training to lead an Acteens group. Along with their application, they must submit an essay listing their major accomplishments and mission activities.

Financial data A stipend is awarded (amount not specified).

Duration 1 year.

Additional information This program began in 1995 by Woman's Missionary Union, an Auxiliary to Southern Baptist Convention.

Number awarded 1 or more each year.

Deadline February of each year.

[346]
JESSICA REDFIELD GHAWI SCHOLARSHIP

San Antonio Area Foundation
Attn: Scholarship Funds Program Officer
303 Pearl Parkway, Suite 114
San Antonio, TX 78215-1285
(210) 228-3759   Fax: (210) 225-1980
E-mail: buresti@ssafdn.org
Web: www.saafdn.org

Summary To provide financial assistance to upper-division women from any state working on a degree in sports journalism or broadcasting.

Eligibility This program is open to women entering their junior or senior year of full-time study at a college or university in any state. Applicants must be preparing for a career in journalism, preferable sports journalism or broadcasting. They must have a GPA of 2.5 or higher. Along with their application, they must submit brief statements on what sports provides to society, their short-term career goals in the field of journalism, an experience from their own life and how it has influenced them, and their favorite sport or sports personality.

Financial data Stipends vary; recently, they averaged $2,000.

Duration 1 year; may be renewed.

Additional information This program began in 2012 to honor a woman killed in the Aurora, Colorado theater shooting of July 20 of that year.

Number awarded 1 each year.

Deadline March of each year.

[347]
JILL S. TIETJEN P.E. SCHOLARSHIP

Society of Women Engineers
Attn: Scholarship Selection Committee
203 North LaSalle Street, Suite 1675
Chicago, IL 60601-1269
(312) 596-5223   Toll Free: (877) SWE-INFO
Fax: (312) 644-8557   E-mail: scholarships@swe.org
Web: societyofwomenengineers.swe.org

Summary To provide financial assistance to women working on an undergraduate degree in engineering or computer science.

Eligibility This program is open to women who will be sophomores, juniors, or seniors at ABET-accredited colleges and universities. Applicants must be U.S. citizens working full time on a degree in computer science, engineering technology, or engineering. Selection is based on merit.

Financial data The stipend is $1,750.

Duration 1 year.

Additional information This program began in 2004.

Number awarded 1 each year.

Deadline February of each year.

[348]
JOHN CURRAN NON-FINALIST INTERVIEW AWARD

The Miss America Foundation
1432 K Street, N.W., Suite 900
Washington, DC 20005
(609) 344-1800
Web: www.missamericafoundation.org/scholarships

Summary To recognize and reward, with scholarships for college study of journalism or communications, women who compete in the interview phase of the Miss America Pageant at the national level.

Eligibility This program is open to women who compete at the national level of the Miss America Pageant. The award is presented to the non-finalist competitor who has the highest score in the interview phase of the competition. They must be majoring in journalism or communications in college.

Financial data The award is a $1,000 scholarship.

Duration 1 year.

Number awarded 1 each year.

Deadline Varies, depending upon the date of local pageants leading to the state and then national finals.

[349]
JOHN DEERE SCHOLARSHIP FOR FEMALE AND MINORITY STUDENTS

American Welding Society
Attn: AWS Foundation, Inc.
8669 N.W. 36th Street, Suite 130
Doral, FL 33166-6672
(305) 443-9353   Toll Free: (800) 443-9353, ext. 250
Fax: (305) 443-7559   E-mail: nprado-pulido@aws.org
Web: www.aws.org/foundation/page/john-deere-scholarship

Summary To provide financial assistance to female and minority undergraduate students, especially those from designated states, who are working on a degree in welding engineering or welding engineering technology at a university in any state.

Eligibility This award is available to U.S. citizens who are women or members of minority groups. Preference is given to residents of Illinois, Iowa, Kansas Minnesota, Missouri, Nebraska, North Dakota, South Dakota, or Wisconsin. Applicants must have completed at least 1 semester of full-time study in a 4-year undergraduate program of welding engineering, welding engineering technology, or mechanical or manufacturing engineering with a welding emphasis. They must have a GPA of 3.0 or higher. Along with their application, they must submit a statement of unmet financial need (although financial need is not required to apply), transcripts, 2 letters of recommendation, and a personal statement that provides their personal objectives and values, their career objectives with a statement of why they want to prepare for a career in welding, participation and leadership in campus and outside organizations, participation in American Welding Society (AWS) student and section activities, and general background information.

Financial data The stipend is $2,500.

Duration 1 year; nonrenewable.

Additional information This program is sponsored by John Deere.

Number awarded 1 each year.

Deadline February of each year.

[350]
JOHN DEERE SWE SCHOLARSHIPS

Society of Women Engineers
Attn: Scholarship Selection Committee
203 North LaSalle Street, Suite 1675
Chicago, IL 60601-1269
(312) 596-5223   Toll Free: (877) SWE-INFO
Fax: (312) 644-8557   E-mail: scholarships@swe.org
Web: societyofwomenengineers.swe.org

Summary To provide financial assistance to women from designated states working on an undergraduate or graduate degree in selected engineering specialties.

Eligibility This program is open to women who are sophomores, juniors, seniors, or graduate students at a 4-year ABET-accredited college or university. Applicants must be working full time on a degree in computer science or agricultural, aeronautical, chemical, computer, electrical, industrial, manufacturing, materials, or mechanical engineering. Preference is given to residents or students in Georgia, Illinois, Indiana, Iowa, Kansas, Louisiana, Michigan, Minnesota, Missouri, Montana, Nebraska, North Carolina, North Dakota, Ohio, Oklahoma, South Dakota, or Tennessee. They must have a GPA of 3.0 or higher. Selection is based on merit.

Financial data The stipend is $2,000.

Duration 1 year.

Additional information This program is sponsored by John Deere.

Number awarded 2 each year.

Deadline February of each year.

[351]
JOHN EDGAR THOMSON FOUNDATION AID

John Edgar Thomson Foundation
Attn: Director
201 South 18th Street, Suite 318
Philadelphia, PA 19103
(215) 545-6083   Toll Free: (800) 888-1278
Fax: (215) 545-5102   E-mail: sjethomson@aol.com
Web: www.brs.org

Summary To provide financial assistance for education or maintenance to daughters of railroad employees who died while employed by a railroad in the United States.

Eligibility This program is open to women whose parent died in the active employ of a railroad in the United States, although the cause of death need not be work related. Applicants must live in the home of the surviving parent or guardian (unless attending college full time and living on campus), be in good health, and receive satisfactory academic grades. Eligibility of the daughter is also dependent upon the parent's remaining unmarried. Consideration is given to other factors as well, including the financial status of the family.

Financial data Payments are made on a monthly basis to assist with the education or maintenance of eligible daughters. The payment is available from infancy to age 18 or, under certain circumstances, to age 24 (for pursuit of higher education). This supplement to family income is to be used in its entirety for the benefit of the recipient. The grant may be terminated at any time if the financial need ceases or the daughter or surviving parent is either unable or fails to meet the eligibility requirements.

Duration Monthly payments may be made up to 24 years.

Additional information This foundation was established in 1882. Grantees are encouraged to participate in religious services of their faith.

Number awarded Varies; generally, 100 or more each year.

Deadline Deadline not specified.

[352]
JUDGE WILLIAM F. COOPER SCHOLARSHIP

Center for Scholarship Administration, Inc.
4320 Wade Hampton Boulevard, Suite G
Taylors, SC 29687-0031
(864) 268-3363   Fax: (864) 268-7160
E-mail: allisonleewagoner@bellsouth.net
Web: www.csascholars.org/copr/index.php?&cff=copr

Summary To provide financial assistance to female high school seniors in Georgia, especially residents of Chatham County, who plan to attend college in any state.

Eligibility This program is open to female seniors graduating from high schools in Georgia. Preference is given to residents of Chatham County. Applicants must be planning to enroll full time at an accredited 2- or 4-year college, university, or technical college in any state to study any field except law, theology, or medicine. They must be able to demonstrate financial need and an acceptable GPA. Selection is based on academic ability, educational goals, career ambitions, and financial need.

Financial data A stipend is awarded (amount not specified).

Duration 1 year; may be renewed up to 3 additional years or until completion of a bachelor's degree, whichever comes first.

Number awarded 1 or more each year.

Deadline December of each year.

[353]
JUDITH MCMANUS PRICE SCHOLARSHIPS

American Planning Association
Attn: Leadership Affairs Associate
205 North Michigan Avenue, Suite 1200
Chicago, IL 60601
(312) 431-9100   Fax: (312) 786-6700
E-mail: mgroh@planning.org
Web: www.planning.org/scholarships/apa

Summary To provide financial assistance to women and underrepresented minority students enrolled in undergraduate or graduate degree programs at recognized planning schools.

Eligibility This program is open to undergraduate and graduate students in urban and regional planning who are women or members of the following minority groups: African American, Hispanic American, or Native American. Applicants must be citizens of the United States and able to document financial need. They must intend to work as practicing planners in the public sector. Along with their application, they must submit a 2-page personal and background statement describing how their education will be applied to career goals and why they chose planning as a career path. Selection is

based (in order of importance), on: 1) commitment to planning as reflected in their personal statement and on their resume; 2) academic achievement and/or improvement during the past 2 years; 3) letters of recommendation; 4) financial need; and 5) professional presentation.

Financial data Stipends range from $2,000 to $4,000 per year. The money may be applied to tuition and living expenses only. Payment is made to the recipient's university and divided by terms in the school year.

Duration 1 year; recipients may reapply.

Additional information This program began in 2002.

Number awarded Varies each year; recently, 3 were awarded.

Deadline April of each year.

[354]
JUDITH RESNIK SWE MEMORIAL SCHOLARSHIP

Society of Women Engineers
Attn: Scholarship Selection Committee
203 North LaSalle Street, Suite 1675
Chicago, IL 60601-1269
(312) 596-5223   Toll Free: (877) SWE-INFO
Fax: (312) 644-8557   E-mail: scholarships@swe.org
Web: societyofwomenengineers.swe.org

Summary To provide financial assistance to undergraduate members of the Society of Women Engineers (SWE) who are majoring in designated engineering specialties.

Eligibility This program is open to society members who are entering their sophomore, junior, or senior year at an ABET-accredited 4-year college or university. Applicants must be working full time on a degree in aerospace, aeronautical, astronautical, or other space-related field of engineering and have a GPA of 3.0 or higher. Selection is based on merit.

Financial data The stipend is $3,500.

Duration 1 year.

Additional information This award was established in 1990 to honor society member Judith Resnik, who was killed aboard the Challenger space shuttle.

Number awarded 1 each year.

Deadline February of each year.

[355]
JUDY CORMAN MEMORIAL SCHOLARSHIP AND INTERNSHIP

New York Women in Communications, Inc.
Attn: NYWICI Foundation
355 Lexington Avenue, 15th Floor
New York, NY 10017-6603
(212) 297-2133   Fax: (212) 370-9047
E-mail: nywicipr@nywici.org
Web: www.nywici.org/foundation/scholarships

Summary To provide financial assistance and work experience to female residents of designated eastern states who are interested in preparing for a career in communications and media relations at a college or graduate school in any state.

Eligibility This program is open to women who are seniors graduating from high schools in New York, New Jersey, Connecticut, or Pennsylvania or undergraduate or graduate students who are permanent residents of those states; they must be attending or planning to attend a college or university in any state. Graduate students must be members of New York Women in Communications, Inc. (NYWICI). Also eligible are women who reside outside the 4 states but are currently enrolled at a college or university within 1 of the 5 boroughs of New York City. Applicants must be preparing for a career in communications and media relations and be interested in a summer internship with Scholastic. They must have a GPA of 3.2 or higher. Along with their application, they must submit a 2-page resume; a personal essay of 300 words on an assigned topic that changes annually; 2 letters of recommendation; and an official transcript. Selection is based on academic record, need, demonstrated leadership, participation in school and community activities, honors and other awards or recognition, work experience, goals and aspirations, and unusual personal and/or family circumstances. U.S. citizenship or permanent resident status is required.

Financial data The scholarship stipend ranges up to $10,000; the internship is salaried (amount not specified).

Duration 1 year.

Additional information This program is sponsored by Scholastic, Inc.

Number awarded 1 each year.

Deadline January of each year.

[356]
JULIA H. DODDS JUNIOR GIRL'S AWARD

Illinois Women's Golf Association
c/o Marlene Miller
11683 Wimbledon Circle
Wellington, FL 33414
(561) 333-3014   E-mail: mememiller@aol.com
Web: www.iwga.org/charitable-activities/scholarships

Summary To provide financial assistance to women in Illinois who have participated in golf and are interested in attending college in any state.

Eligibility This program is open to female high school seniors in Illinois who have played in the Illinois Women's Golf Association (IWGA) State Junior Tournament. Nominations may be submitted by anyone with knowledge of qualified girls. Nominees must arrange for 2 letters of recommendation, 1 from their high school golf coach and 1 from a teacher or principal at their high school. Selection is based on character, scholarship, leadership, sportsmanship, and love for the game of golf.

Financial data The stipend is $2,000. Funds are paid directly to the recipient's college.

Duration 1 year.

Additional information This program began in 1992.

Number awarded 1 each year.

Deadline March of each year.

[357]
JULIETTE MATHER SCHOLARSHIP

Woman's Missionary Union
Attn: WMU Foundation
100 Missionary Ridge
Birmingham, AL 35242
(205) 408-5525   Toll Free: (877) 482-4483
Fax: (205) 408-5508   E-mail: wmufoundation@wmu.org
Web: www.wmufoundation.com/?q=content/scholarships

Summary To provide financial assistance to female Southern Baptist undergraduate or graduate students preparing for a career in Christian ministry.

Eligibility This program is open to female Southern Baptist undergraduate and graduate students who are preparing for a career in Christian ministry and service. They must be interested in preparing to become the Baptist leaders of the future.

Financial data A stipend is awarded (amount not specified).

Duration 1 year.

Number awarded Varies each year.

Deadline January of each year.

[358]
JUNE P. GALLOWAY UNDERGRADUATE SCHOLARSHIP

North Carolina Alliance for Athletics, Health, Physical
    Education, Recreation, Dance, and Sport Management
Attn: Executive Director
3434 Edwards Mill Road, Suite 112-183
Raleigh, NC 27605
(919) 833-1219   Toll Free: (888) 840-6500
Fax: (888) 840-6FAX E-mail: awards@ncaahperd-sm.org
Web: www.ncaahperd-sm.org

Summary To provide financial assistance for college to female members of the North Carolina Alliance for Athletics, Health, Physical Education, Recreation, Dance, and Sport Management (NCAAHPERD-SM).

Eligibility This program is open to rising female seniors majoring in health education, physical education, recreation, dance, and/or sport management who are members of NCAAHPERD-SM. Applicants must have a GPA of 2.0 or higher for all college work and 3.0 or higher for their major. Selection is based two-thirds on academic achievement and one-third on leadership and contributions to the profession. Financial need is not considered.

Financial data The stipend is $1,000.

Duration 1 year.

Additional information This program began in 1974.

Number awarded 1 each year.

Deadline June of each year.

[359]
JUNIOR GIRLS' GOLF SCHOLARSHIP FOUNDATION SCHOLARSHIPS

Florida State Golf Association
Attn: Junior Girls' Golf Scholarship Foundation
c/o Sisi Hedges
110 Country Club Lane
Mulberry, FL 33860
E-mail: hedgesh@aol.com
Web: www.jggsf.org

Summary To provide financial assistance to female high school seniors in Florida who have an interest in golf and are interested in attending college in the state.

Eligibility This program is open to women who are graduating seniors at high schools in Florida and have an interest or association with the game of golf. Applicants must be planning to attend a junior college, college, university, or technical school in the state but not be eligible for a golf scholarship.

They must have a GPA of 3.0 or higher and be able to document financial need. Along with their application, they must submit a brief statement on the extent of their participation in golf, transcripts that include SAT and ACT scores, and 3 letters of recommendation.

Financial data Stipends are $10,000, $2,000, or $1,500. Funds are paid directly to the recipient's school.

Duration 1 year.

Additional information This program consists of the Marcia Mileti Scholarship (established in 2014), the Peggy Brass Scholarship (established in 2014), and the Peg and Bill Roberts Scholarship (established in 2015).

Number awarded 3 each year.

Deadline May of each year.

[360]
JUNIOR GIRLS SCHOLARSHIPS

Ladies Auxiliary to the Veterans of Foreign Wars
Attn: Director of Programs
406 West 34th Street, Tenth Floor
Kansas City, MO 64111
(816) 561-8655   Fax: (816) 931-4753
E-mail: info@ladiesauxvfw.org
Web: www.ladiesauxvfw.org/programs-page/scholarships

Summary To provide financial assistance for college to outstanding members of a Junior Girls Unit of the Ladies Auxiliary to the Veterans of Foreign Wars.

Eligibility Applicants must have been active members of a unit for 1 year, have held an office in the unit, and be between 13 and 16 years of age. Previous winners are not eligible, although former applicants who did not receive scholarships may reapply. Selection is based on participation in the Junior Girls Unit (40 points), school activities (30 points), and academic achievement (30 points).

Financial data The winner receives a $7,500 scholarship. Funds are paid directly to the college of the recipient's choice. In addition, $100 is awarded to each Junior Girl who is selected as the department winner and entered in the national competition.

Duration 1 year.

Number awarded 1 each year.

Deadline March of each year.

[361]
KA'IULANI HOME FOR GIRLS TRUST SCHOLARSHIP

Hawai'i Community Foundation
Attn: Scholarship Department
827 Fort Street Mall
Honolulu, HI 96813
(808) 566-5570   Toll Free: (888) 731-3863
Fax: (808) 521-6286
E-mail: scholarships@hcf-hawaii.org
Web: hcf.scholarships.ngwebsolutions.com

Summary To provide financial assistance to women of Native Hawaiian ancestry who are attending college in any state.

Eligibility This program is open to women of Native Hawaiian ancestry who are full-time freshmen or sophomores at an accredited 2- or 4-year college or university in any state. Applicants must demonstrate academic achievement (GPA of

3.3 or higher), good moral character, and financial need. Along with their application, they must submit a short statement indicating their reasons for attending college, their planned course of study, their career goals, and what community service means to them.

Financial data The amounts of the awards depend on the availability of funds and the need of the recipient. Recently, the average value of the scholarships awarded by the foundation was $2,800.

Duration 1 year; may be renewed.

Additional information This fund was established in 1963 when the Ka'iulani Home for Girls, formerly used to provide boarding home facilities for young women of Native Hawaiian ancestry, was demolished and the property sold.

Number awarded Varies each year.

Deadline February of each year.

[362]
KANSAS WOMEN'S GOLF ASSOCIATION SCHOLARSHIP

Kansas Women's Golf Association
c/o Jan Knuth, Scholarship Chair
6120 East Murdock
Wichita, KS 67208
(316) 619-3550   E-mail: KWGAScholarship@gmail.com
Web: www.kwga.org/#!kwga-scholarship/clfy

Summary To provide financial assistance to women in Kansas who are members of the Kansas Women's Golf Association (KWGA) and interested in attending college in any state.

Eligibility This program is open to women in Kansas who are graduating or have graduated from a high school in the state. Applicants must be members, junior associate, or associate KWGA members. They must be enrolled or planning to enroll full time at an accredited collegiate institution in any state. Along with their application, they must submit a 1-page essay describing why they merit this scholarship, how they have benefited from KWGA membership, and their goals. Selection is based on that essay, academic record, character, leadership and community service, letters of recommendation, and participation in KWGA.

Financial data A stipend is awarded (amount not specified). Funds are paid directly to the recipient's collegiate institution.

Duration 1 year; nonrenewable.

Additional information This program was formerly named the Natasha Matson Fife Scholarship.

Number awarded 1 each year.

Deadline March of each year.

[363]
KATE GLEASON SCHOLARSHIP

ASME International
Attn: Scholarships
Two Park Avenue, Floor 7
New York, NY 10016-5618
(212) 591-7790   Toll Free: (800) THE-ASME
Fax: (212) 591-7143   E-mail: LefeverB@asme.org
Web: www.asme.org

Summary To provide financial assistance to female undergraduate and graduate students from any country who are working on a degree in mechanical engineering.

Eligibility This program is open to women who are enrolled in an ABET-accredited or equivalent mechanical engineering, mechanical engineering technology, or related undergraduate or graduate program. Applicants must submit a nomination from their department head, a recommendation from a faculty member, and an official transcript. Only 1 nomination may be submitted per department. There are no citizenship requirements, but study must be conducted in the United States. Selection is based on academic ability and potential contribution to the mechanical engineering profession.

Financial data The stipend is $3,000.

Duration 1 year.

Number awarded 1 each year.

Deadline February of each year.

[364]
KATHLEEN BARRA MEMORIAL SCHOLARSHIP

American Association of University Women-Northern
   Ocean County Branch
P.O. Box 1994
Brick, NJ 08723
E-mail: AAUWNOCBNJ@gmail.com
Web: northernocean-nj.aauw.net/scholarships

Summary To provide financial assistance to women who are friends or relatives of members of the American Association of University Women (AAUW) in New Jersey and working on a degree in a business-related field at a school in any state.

Eligibility This program is open to women who are a friend or relative of a current member of the AAUW in any of the New Jersey branches. Applicants must be enrolled or planning to enroll full time at a college or university in any state and working on a degree in a business-related field (e.g., marketing, economics, business). Along with their application, they must submit a 2-page essay on their educational and career goals and personal ambitions. Financial need is not considered in the selection process.

Financial data The stipend is $1,000.

Duration 1 year.

Number awarded 1 each year.

Deadline May of each year.

[365]
KATHY KARDISH WILSON MEMORIAL
EDUCATIONAL FUND

Chautauqua Region Community Foundation
Attn: Scholarship Coordinator
418 Spring Street
Jamestown, NY 14701
(716) 661-3394   Fax: (716) 488-0387
E-mail: llynde@crcfonline.org
Web: www.crcfonline.org/providing/scholarships

Summary To provide financial assistance to married women in New York, Ohio, and Pennsylvania who are interested in returning to school to complete an undergraduate or graduate degree.

Eligibility This program is open to women who live and attend college or graduate school in New York, Ohio, or Pennsylvania. Applicants must be mothers of school-aged children, part of a 2-income family in which tuition would be a burden on the family, able to complete the educational and career goals set for themselves, community-minded and considerably involved in at least 1 community organization, and giving of themselves and their talents to help others reach their potential. Along with their application, they must submit a 1-page essay describing their past achievements, career goals, and reasons for returning to school or training.

Financial data A stipend is awarded (amount not specified).

Duration 1 year.

Number awarded 1 or more each year.

Deadline May of each year.

[366]
KATHY LOUDAT MUSIC SCHOLARSHIP

New Mexico Baptist Foundation
5325 Wyoming Boulevard, N.E.
P.O. Box 16560
Albuquerque, NM 87191-6560
(505) 332-3777   Toll Free: (877) 841-3777
Fax: (505) 332-2777   E-mail: foundation@nmbf.com
Web: www.nmbf.com

Summary To provide financial assistance to female members of Southern Baptist churches in New Mexico who are attending college in any state to prepare for a career in church music.

Eligibility This program is open to full-time female college, university, and seminary students who are preparing for a career in church music. Applicants must have a GPA of 3.0 or higher and be able to demonstrate financial need. They must be members of Southern Baptist churches in New Mexico or former members in good standing with the Southern Baptist Convention.

Financial data A stipend is awarded (amount not specified).

Duration 1 year.

Number awarded 1 or more each year.

Deadline April of each year.

[367]
KATIE ROSE MARTIN SCHOLARSHIP

Community Foundation of Middle Tennessee
Attn: Scholarship Coordinator
3833 Cleghorn Avenue, Suite 400
Nashville, TN 37215-2519
(615) 321-4939, ext. 116   Toll Free: (888) 540-5200
Fax: (615) 327-2746   E-mail: pcole@cfmt.org
Web: www.cfmt.org/request/scholarships/allscholarships

Summary To provide financial assistance to female residents of any state attending a school of cosmetology in Tennessee.

Eligibility This program is open to women who are high school graduates or second career adults. Applicants must be attending an accredited cosmetology school in Tennessee. Along with their application, they must submit an essay describing their educational plans and how those plans will help them reach their career goals. Financial need is considered in the selection process.

Financial data Stipends range from $500 to $2,500 per year. Funds are paid to the recipient's school and must be used for tuition, fees, books, supplies, room, board, or miscellaneous expenses.

Duration 1 year.

Additional information This program began in 2010.

Number awarded 1 or more each year.

Deadline March of each year.

[368]
KATZ-WARD FAMILY SCHOLARSHIP

Philadelphia Foundation
1234 Market Street, Suite 1800
Philadelphia, PA 19107-3794
(215) 563-6417   Fax: (215) 563-6882
E-mail: scholarships@philafound.org
Web: www.philafound.org

Summary To provide financial assistance to single mothers who are residents of Pennsylvania and attending college in any state.

Eligibility This program is open to residents of Pennsylvania who are single mothers with at least 1 dependent child living in their care. Applicants must be enrolled as a sophomore at a 4-year college or university in any state. They must have a GPA of 1.67 or higher and be able to demonstrate financial need. Along with their application, they must submit an essay on their career goals after college, what they learned about themselves in their first year of college, and how they plan to meet any unmet expenses.

Financial data The stipend is $1,000.

Duration 1 year; nonrenewable.

Number awarded 1 each year.

Deadline June of each year.

[369]
KELLOGG COMPANY SCHOLARSHIPS

Society of Women Engineers
Attn: Scholarship Selection Committee
203 North LaSalle Street, Suite 1675
Chicago, IL 60601-1269
(312) 596-5223   Toll Free: (877) SWE-INFO
Fax: (312) 644-8557   E-mail: scholarships@swe.org
Web: societyofwomenengineers.swe.org

Summary To provide financial assistance to undergraduate members of the Society of Women Engineers (SWE) who are majoring in designated engineering specialties.

Eligibility This program is open to society members who are entering their sophomore or junior year at an ABET-accredited 4-year college or university. Applicants must be working full time on a degree in computer science or biosystems, chemical, or mechanical engineering and have a GPA of 3.2 or higher. Preference is given to students attending designated universities in Michigan and to those who can demonstrate financial need.

Financial data The stipend is $3,000 or $1,000.

Duration 1 year.

Additional information This program is sponsored by the Kellogg Company. For a list of the designated universities, contact SWE.

Number awarded 3 each year: 1 at $3,000 and 2 at $1,000.

Deadline February of each year.

[370]
KENNEDY CENTER SUMMER INTERNSHIP

Sigma Alpha Iota Philanthropies, Inc.
One Tunnel Road
Asheville, NC 28805
(828) 251-0606   Fax: (828) 251-0644
E-mail: nh@sai-national.org
Web: app.smarterselect.com

Summary To provide summer internships at the Kennedy Center to members of Sigma Alpha Iota (an organization of women musicians).

Eligibility This program is open to student members of the organization who are interested in a summer internship at the DeVos Institute for Arts Management at the John F. Kennedy Center for the Performing Arts in Washington, D.C. Applicants must be juniors, seniors, graduate students, or graduates out of school for less than 2 years.

Financial data The stipend is $2,400.

Duration 10 weeks during the summer.

Additional information Assignments are full time, with possible college credit available.

Number awarded 1 or more each year.

Deadline February of each year.

[371]
KENTUCKY COLONELS BETTER LIFE SCHOLARSHIPS

Kentucky Community and Technical College System
Attn: Financial Aid
300 North Main Street
Versailles, KY 40383
(859) 256-3100   Toll Free: (877) 528-2748 (within KY)
Web: www.kctcs.edu

Summary To provide financial assistance to single parents attending or planning to attend 1 of the schools within the Kentucky Community and Technical College System (KCTCS).

Eligibility This program is open to Kentucky residents who are single working parents with at least 1 child under 12 years of age. Applicants must be attending or planning to attend a KCTCS institution and able to demonstrate unmet financial need. Selection is based on demonstrated enthusiasm for learning and potential for academic success.

Financial data The stipend is $2,500 per year.

Duration 1 year; may be renewed 1 additional year if the recipient maintains full-time enrollment and satisfactory academic progress.

Additional information This program began in 2004.

Number awarded 32 each year: 2 in each of the KCTCS districts.

Deadline Deadline not specified.

[372]
KENTUCKY WOMEN IN AGRICULTURE SCHOLARSHIP

Kentucky Women in Agriculture
Attn: Scholarship
P.O. Box 4409
Lexington, KY 40544-4409
Toll Free: (877) 266-8823
E-mail: info@kywomeninag.com
Web: www.kywomeninag.com/index.html

Summary To provide financial assistance to female residents of Kentucky enrolled as upper-division or graduate students at colleges in the state and working on a degree in agriculture.

Eligibility This program is open to women who are residents of Kentucky and enrolled full time as juniors, seniors, or graduate students at a college or university in the state. Applicants must be working on a degree in a field related to agriculture and have a GPA of 2.5 or higher. Along with their application, they must submit a 500-word essay on their career goals for working in agriculture and how this scholarship will support them in their academic pursuits. Selection is based on desire to work in the field of agriculture (40 points), financial need (30 points), academic record (20 points), and extracurricular activities (10 points).

Financial data The stipend is $1,000.

Duration 1 year.

Number awarded 1 each year.

Deadline June of each year.

[373]
KIM MILLER SYNCHRONIZED SWIMMING SCHOLARSHIP

Community Foundation of Greater New Britain
Attn: Scholarship Manager
74A Vine Street
New Britain, CT 06052-1431
(860) 229-6018, ext. 305   Fax: (860) 225-2666
E-mail: cfarmer@cfgnb.org
Web: www.cfgnb.org

Summary To provide financial assistance for college to high school seniors who are registered members of United States Synchronized Swimming (USSS) East Zone.

Eligibility This program is open to graduating high school seniors who are members of USSS East Zone. Applicants must be planning to attend a college or university in any state and participate in synchronized swimming at the collegiate level. They must have a GPA of 3.0 or higher. Along with their application, they must submit an essay explaining why they feel they should be awarded this scholarship.

Financial data A stipend is awarded (amount not specified).

Duration 1 year.

Additional information This program began in 2007 by the Hamden Heronettes Synchronized Swim Team of Hamden, Connecticut.

Number awarded 1 each year.

Deadline February of each year.

[374]
KIRSTEN R. LORENTZEN AWARD

Society of Physics Students
c/o American Institute of Physics
One Physics Ellipse
College Park, MD 20740-3843
(301) 209-3007   Fax: (301) 209-0839
E-mail: sps@aip.org
Web: www.spsnational.org

Summary To provide financial assistance to women undergraduates majoring in physics or geoscience.

Eligibility This program is open to women who are college sophomores or juniors at institutions in the United States. Applicants must be working on a bachelor's degree in physics (including space physics and geophysics) or geoscience. They must demonstrate excellence in their studies as well as outdoor activities, service, sports, music, or other non-academic pursuits. Selection is based on academic performance both in physics and overall studies, potential and intention for continued academic development in physics, a statement of career objectives, a statement of participation in activities of the Society of Physics Students (SPS), and 2 letters of recommendation. U.S. citizenship or permanent resident status is required.

Financial data The stipend is $2,000.

Duration 1 year.

Additional information This award was established in 2004 with support from the Association for Women in Science.

Number awarded 1 each year.

Deadline February of each year.

[375]
KOCH DISCOVERY SCHOLARSHIPS

Society of Women Engineers
Attn: Scholarship Selection Committee
203 North LaSalle Street, Suite 1675
Chicago, IL 60601-1269
(312) 596-5223   Toll Free: (877) SWE-INFO
Fax: (312) 644-8557   E-mail: scholarships@swe.org
Web: societyofwomenengineers.swe.org

Summary To provide financial assistance to women interested in studying specified fields of engineering at universities in designated states.

Eligibility This program is open to women who are entering their sophomore or junior year at an ABET-accredited 4-year college or university in Alabama, Arkansas, Florida, Georgia, Illinois, Indiana, Iowa, Kansas, Michigan, Minnesota, Mississippi, Missouri, Nebraska, North Carolina, North Dakota, Oklahoma, Oregon, South Carolina, South Dakota, Tennessee, Texas, Utah, Virginia, or Wisconsin. Applicants must be majoring in computer science or chemical, electrical, environmental, industrial, manufacturing, materials, or mechanical engineering. They must be enrolled full time. U.S. citizenship is required. Selection is based on merit.

Financial data The stipend is $2,500.

Duration 1 year.

Additional information This program began in 2013.

Number awarded 5 each year.

Deadline February of each year.

[376]
KPMG FUTURE LEADERS PROGRAM

Stanford University
Hoover Institution
Attn: Office of Condoleezza Rice
434 Galvez Mall
Stanford, CA 94305-6003
(650) 723-1754
E-mail: CRice_FutureLeaders@Stanford.edu
Web: womensleadership.kpmg.us

Summary To provide financial assistance to women who are high school seniors interested in studying business or a field of science, technology, engineering, or mathematics (STEM) at a college in any state.

Eligibility This program is open to female high school seniors who plan to enroll at a 4-year college or university and major in business or a field of STEM. Applicants must have a GPA of 3.5 or higher and be able to demonstrate financial need (household income less than $75,000 per year). Along with their application, they must submit essays of 250 to 500 words on the following topics: 1) the challenges they have had to overcome to achieve their goals and complete their high school education; 2) their financial need and how this scholarship will help them financially to achieve their dreams of going to college; and 3) how this award will help them achieve their goals. U.S. citizenship or permanent resident status is required.

Financial data The stipend is $10,000 per year.

Duration 4 years.

Additional information This program was established in 2016 by KPMG LLP with proceeds from the KPMG Women's Leadership Summit and the KPMG Women's PGA Championship, a collaboration between KPMG, the Professional Golfers' Association (PGA) of America, and the Ladies Professional Golf Association (LPGA). Former Secretary of State Condoleezza Rice has agreed to facilitate the program. Recipients must attend the 3-day KPMG Future Leaders Retreat in July at Stanford University, focused on leadership training, career development skills, and an introduction to golf. They are also paired with a woman leader participating in the KPMG Women's Leadership Summit as a mentor. The PGA of America and LPGA provide the golf instruction.

Number awarded 16 each year.

Deadline January of each year.

[377]
LA FRA SCHOLARSHIP

Ladies Auxiliary of the Fleet Reserve Association
c/o Sandra Robbins, National Scholarship Chair
2712 Holly Ridge Road
Orange Park, FL 32073
(904) 269-2136   E-mail: slgr@bellsouth.net
Web: www.la-fra.org/scholarship.html

Summary To provide financial assistance for college to the daughters and granddaughters of naval personnel.

Eligibility Eligible to apply for these scholarships are the daughters and granddaughters of Navy, Marine, Coast Guard, active Fleet Reserve, Fleet Marine Corps Reserve, and Coast Guard Reserve personnel on active duty, retired with pay, or deceased while on active duty or retired with pay. Applicants must submit an essay on their life experiences,

career objectives, and what motivated them to select those objectives. Selection is based on academic record, financial need, extracurricular activities, leadership skills, and participation in community activities. U.S. citizenship is required.

Financial data The stipend is $2,500.

Duration 1 year; may be renewed.

Number awarded 1 each year.

Deadline April of each year.

[378]
LA JOLLA LASIK NATIONAL SCHOLARSHIP

American Business Women's Association
Attn: Stephen Bufton Memorial Educational Fund
9820 Metcalf Avenue, Suite 110
Overland Park, KS 66212
Toll Free: (800) 228-0007
Web: www.sbmef.org

Summary To provide financial assistance to women who are interested in working on an undergraduate degree in any field.

Eligibility This program is open to women who are entering at least their freshman year at an accredited college or university with a major in any field. Applicants must submit a 250-word biographical sketch that includes information about their background, activities, honors, work experience, and long-term educational and professional goals. They must have a GPA of 3.0 or higher. Financial need is not considered in the selection process. U.S. citizenship is required.

Financial data The stipend is $2,000. Funds are paid directly to the recipient's institution to be used only for tuition, books, and fees.

Duration 1 year; nonrenewable.

Number awarded 1 each year.

Deadline May of each year.

[379]
LAO AMERICAN WOMEN ASSOCIATION OF WASHINGTON D.C. METROPOLITAN AREA VOCATIONAL TRAINING/GED SCHOLARSHIP FUND

Lao American Women Association
Attn: Scholarship Committee
3908 Carroll Court
Chantilly, VA 20151
(703) 283-8698   E-mail: info@lawadc.org
Web: www.lawadc.org/em-schol.htm

Summary To provide financial assistance to women of Lao ancestry in the Washington, D.C. area who need additional training to find a job.

Eligibility This program is open to women in the Washington, D.C. metropolitan area who are of Lao parentage. Applicants must be in need of additional training to find a job, to obtain work at a higher level, or to complete a GED certificate. They must provide information on their personal situation, proposed training program, work experience, family and community activities, and financial situation. They must also submit a 150-word personal statement on their family and community activities. Financial need is considered in the selection process (must have family income less than $75,000 per year).

Financial data The stipend is $1,000 for vocational training or $500 for GED completion.
Duration 1 year.
Number awarded Either 1 scholarship for vocational training or 2 for GED completion are awarded each year.
Deadline April of each year.

[380]
LAUREN LOVE MEMORIAL SCHOLARSHIP

American Academy of Physician Assistants
Attn: Physician Assistant Foundation
2318 Mill Road, Suite 1300
Alexandria, VA 22314-6868
(703) 836-2272   Fax: (703) 684-1924
E-mail: pafoundation@aapa.org
Web: www.pa-foundation.org
Summary To provide financial assistance to student members of the American Academy of Physician Assistants (AAPA), especially women, who are from Arizona.
Eligibility This program is open to Arizona-based AAPA student members attending a physician assistant program accredited by the Commission on Accreditation of Allied Health Education Programs. Applicants must have overcome a challenge (e.g., medical condition, poverty) to succeed in their college studies. They must have completed at least 1 semester of PA studies. Preference is given to women.
Financial data The stipend is $3,500.
Duration 1 year; nonrenewable.
Number awarded 1 each year.
Deadline January of each year.

[381]
LCDR EIFFERT FOSTER STUDENT SCHOLARSHIP

National Naval Officers Association-Washington, D.C.
  Chapter
c/o LCDR Stephen Williams
P.O. Box 30784
Alexandria, VA 22310
(703) 566-3840   Fax: (703) 566-3813
E-mail: Stephen.Williams@navy.mil
Web: dcnnoa.memberlodge.com/page-309002
Summary To provide financial assistance to female African American high school seniors from the Washington, D.C. area who have been in foster care and are interested in attending college in any state.
Eligibility This program is open to female African American seniors graduating from high schools in the Washington, D.C. metropolitan area who plan to enroll full time at an accredited 2- or 4-year college or university in any state. Applicants must have lived in a foster home. They must have a GPA of 2.5 or higher and be U.S. citizens or permanent residents. Selection is based on academic achievement, community involvement, and financial need.
Financial data The stipend is $1,000.
Duration 1 year; nonrenewable.
Additional information Recipients are not required to join or affiliate with the military in any way.
Number awarded 1 each year.
Deadline March of each year.

[382]
LCDR JANET COCHRAN AND CDR CONNIE GREENE SCHOLARSHIP

National Naval Officers Association-Washington, D.C.
  Chapter
c/o LCDR Stephen Williams
P.O. Box 30784
Alexandria, VA 22310
(703) 566-3840   Fax: (703) 566-3813
E-mail: Stephen.Williams@Navy.mil
Web: dcnnoa.memberlodge.com/page-309002
Summary To provide financial assistance to female minority high school seniors from the Washington, D.C. area who are interested in attending college in any state.
Eligibility This program is open to female minority seniors graduating from high schools in the Washington, D.C. metropolitan area who plan to enroll full time at an accredited 2- or 4-year college or university in any state. Applicants must have a GPA of 2.5 or higher and be U.S. citizens or permanent residents. Selection is based on academic achievement, community involvement, and financial need.
Financial data The stipend is $1,500.
Duration 1 year; nonrenewable.
Additional information Recipients are not required to join or affiliate with the military in any way.
Number awarded 1 each year.
Deadline March of each year.

[383]
LEANNA DORWORTH MEMORIAL SCHOLARSHIP

Society of Manufacturing Engineers
Attn: SME Education Foundation
One SME Drive
P.O. Box 930
Dearborn, MI 48121-0930
(313) 425-3300   Toll Free: (866) 547-6333
Fax: (313) 425-3411   E-mail: foundation@sme.org
Web: www.smeef.org
Summary To provide financial assistance to women who are members or children of members of the Society of Manufacturing Engineers (SME) and interested in working on a degree in a field of science, technology, engineering, or mathematics (STEM).
Eligibility This program is open to high school seniors and undergraduates who have completed less than 30 credit hours at a North American college or university and have a GPA of 2.5 or higher. Applicants must be working on or planning to work full or part time on an associate or bachelor's degree in a field of STEM, especially industrial or manufacturing engineering. They must be student members of SME or the child or grandchild of a member. Along with their application, they must submit a brief statement about why they chose their major, their career and educational objectives, and how this scholarship will help them attain those objectives. Financial need is not considered in the selection process. Applicants must be U.S. or Canadian citizens or permanent residents or have a valid student visa.
Financial data Stipends range from $1,000 to $6,000 and recently averaged approximately $2,000.
Duration 1 year; may be renewed.

Number awarded 1 each year.

Deadline January of each year.

[384]
LEATRICE GREGORY PENDRAY SCHOLARSHIP

American Institute of Aeronautics and Astronautics
Attn: AIAA Foundation Scholarship Program
1801 Alexander Bell Drive, Suite 500
Reston, VA 20191-4344
(703) 264-7530   Toll Free: (800) 639-AIAA, ext. 530
Fax: (703) 264-7657   E-mail: merries@aiaa.org
Web: www.aiaa.org/Scholarships

Summary To provide financial assistance to women who are undergraduate student members of the American Institute of Aeronautics and Astronautics (AIAA).

Eligibility This program is open to female college students who have completed at least 1 semester or quarter of full-time college work in engineering or science fields that relate to aerospace or aeronautics. Applicants must have a GPA of 3.3 or higher, be student members of the AIAA, and be interested in a career in the aerospace field. They may be of any nationality but studying in the United States or its territories. Selection is based on, in order of importance, GPA, an essay of 500 to 1,000 words on their career objectives and the academic program required to achieve those objectives, 3 letters of recommendation, and extracurricular activities.

Financial data The stipend is $1,250.

Duration 1 year; recipients may reapply if they have a GPA of 3.3 or higher.

Number awarded 1 each year.

Deadline January of each year.

[385]
LEGACY SCHOLARSHIP IN MEMORY OF BELOVED ABWA GOOD GUY, JACK MARLETT

American Business Women's Association
Attn: Stephen Bufton Memorial Educational Fund
9820 Metcalf Avenue, Suite 110
Overland Park, KS 66212
Toll Free: (800) 228-0007
Web: www.sbmef.org

Summary To provide financial assistance to women who are interested in working on an undergraduate degree in business.

Eligibility This program is open to women who are entering at least their freshman year with a major in business at an accredited college or university. Applicants must submit a 250-word biographical sketch that includes information about their background, activities, honors, work experience, and long-term educational and professional goals. They must have a GPA of 3.0 or higher. Financial need is not considered in the selection process. U.S. citizenship is required.

Financial data The stipend is $5,000. Funds are paid directly to the recipient's institution to be used only for tuition, books, and fees.

Duration 1 year; nonrenewable.

Number awarded 1 each year.

Deadline May of each year.

[386]
LEGACY SCHOLARSHIP IN MEMORY OF BELOVED MEMBER, CAROLINE VACLAV

American Business Women's Association
Attn: Stephen Bufton Memorial Educational Fund
9820 Metcalf Avenue, Suite 110
Overland Park, KS 66212
Toll Free: (800) 228-0007
Web: www.sbmef.org

Summary To provide financial assistance to women who are interested in working on a degree in nursing or other medical field.

Eligibility This program is open to women who are entering at least their freshman year in a nursing or other medical program at an accredited college or university. Applicants must submit a 250-word biographical sketch that includes information about their background, activities, honors, work experience, and long-term educational and professional goals. They must have a GPA of 3.0 or higher. Financial need is not considered in the selection process. U.S. citizenship is required.

Financial data The stipend is $5,000. Funds are paid directly to the recipient's institution to be used only for tuition, books, and fees.

Duration 1 year; nonrenewable.

Number awarded 1 each year.

Deadline May of each year.

[387]
LEMIEUX-LOVEJOY YOUTH SCHOLARSHIP

Maine Federation of Business and Professional Women's Clubs
Attn: BPW/Maine Futurama Foundation
c/o Marilyn V. Ladd, Office Manager
103 County Road
Oakland, ME 04963
Web: www.bpwmefoundation.org/scholarship-program

Summary To provide financial assistance to female high school seniors and recent graduates in Maine who plan to attend college in any state.

Eligibility This program is open to women who are seniors graduating from high schools in Maine or recent graduates of those schools. Applicants must be planning to enroll as freshmen at an accredited college or university in any state. They must have a realistic goal for the educational plans. Along with their application, they must submit a statement describing their educational and personal goals, including their financial need.

Financial data The stipend is $1,200. Funds are paid directly to the recipient's school.

Duration 1 year.

Number awarded 1 or more each year.

Deadline April of each year.

[388]
LESLIE S. PARKER MEMORIAL SCHOLARSHIP

Order of the Eastern Star-Grand Chapter of Oregon
c/o Nancy Harper, Scholarship Committee Chair
1421 Raydean Drive
Grants Pass, OR 97527
E-mail: totemspole@charter.net
Web: www.oregonoes.org/scholarships/index.html

Summary To provide financial assistance to women who are residents of Oregon and attending college or graduate school in the state.

Eligibility This program is open to female residents of Oregon who have completed at least 2 years of undergraduate or graduate study at an accredited non-sectarian college or university in the state. Applicants must be able to demonstrate financial need.

Financial data Stipends recently were $1,140. Funds are sent directly to the recipient's college or university to be used for books, tuition, room and board, clothing, or medical aid.

Duration 1 year.

Number awarded Varies each year; recently, 5 were awarded.

Deadline April of each year.

[389]
LETA ANDREWS SCHOLARSHIP

University Interscholastic League
Attn: Texas Interscholastic League Foundation
1701 Manor Road
P.O. Box 151027
Austin, TX 78715-1027
(512) 382-0916   Fax: (512) 382-0377
E-mail: info@tilfoundation.org
Web: www.tilfoundation.org/scholarships/list

Summary To provide financial assistance to high school seniors who participate in programs of the Texas Interscholastic League Foundation (TILF), have competed in girls' high school varsity basketball, and plan to attend college in the state.

Eligibility This program is open to seniors graduating from high schools in Texas who have competed in a University Interscholastic League (UIL) academic state meet and have participated in girls' high school varsity basketball. Applicants must be planning to attend a college or university in the state and major in any field. Along with their application, they must submit high school transcripts that include SAT and/or ACT scores and documentation of financial need.

Financial data The stipend is $1,000.

Duration 1 year; nonrenewable.

Additional information This program is sponsored by Whataburger Inc. and Southwest Shootout Inc.

Number awarded 1 each year.

Deadline May of each year.

[390]
LILLIAN MOLLER GILBRETH MEMORIAL SCHOLARSHIP

Society of Women Engineers
Attn: Scholarship Selection Committee
203 North LaSalle Street, Suite 1675
Chicago, IL 60601-1269
(312) 596-5223   Toll Free: (877) SWE-INFO
Fax: (312) 644-8557   E-mail: scholarships@swe.org
Web: societyofwomenengineers.swe.org

Summary To provide financial assistance to upper-division women majoring in computer science or engineering.

Eligibility This program is open to women who are entering their junior or senior year at an ABET-accredited 4-year college or university. Applicants must be working full time on a degree in computer science, engineering technology, or engineering. Selection is based on merit.

Financial data The stipend is $14,500 per year.

Duration 1 year; may be renewed 1 additional year.

Additional information This program began in 1958.

Number awarded 1 each year.

Deadline February of each year.

[391]
LILLIAN WALL SCHOLARSHIP

Zonta Club of Bangor
c/o Barbara A. Cardone
P.O. Box 1904
Bangor, ME 04402-1904
Web: www.zontaclubofbangor.org/?area=scholarship

Summary To provide financial assistance to women attending or planning to attend college in Maine and major in special education or a related field.

Eligibility This program is open to women who are attending or planning to attend an accredited 2- or 4-year college in Maine. Applicants must major in special education or a related field. Along with their application, they must submit brief essays on 1) their goals in seeking higher education and their plans for the future; and 2) any school and community activities that have been of particular importance to them and why they found them worthwhile. Financial need may be considered in the selection process.

Financial data The stipend is $1,000.

Duration 1 year.

Number awarded 1 each year.

Deadline March of each year.

[392]
LINDA RIDDLE/SGMA ENDOWED SCHOLARSHIPS

Women's Sports Foundation
Attn: Award and Grant Programs Manager
Eisenhower Park
1899 Hempstead Turnpike, Suite 400
East Meadow, NY 11554-1000
(516) 307-3915   Toll Free: (800) 227-3988
E-mail: lflores@womenssportsfoundation.org
Web: www.womenssportsfoundation.org

Summary To provide financial assistance to female high school seniors who have participated in athletics and plan to attend college in any state.
Eligibility This program is open to women who are graduating high school seniors planning to enroll full-time at an accredited 2- or 4-year college or university. Applicants must have participated on an officially recognized high school athletic team and maintained a GPA of 3.5 or higher. They must be U.S. citizens or permanent residents and able to demonstrate financial need.
Financial data The stipend is $1,500.
Duration 1 year.
Additional information This program, which began in 1996, is sponsored by the Sporting Goods Manufacturers Association (SGMA), which recently changed its name to the Sports and Fitness Industry Association.
Number awarded 1 or more each year.
Deadline March of each year.

[393]
LINLY HEFLIN SCHOLARSHIP

Linly Heflin Unit
c/o Caroline Thomas, Scholarship Committee Co-Chair
13 Office Park Circle, Suite 8
Birmingham, AL 35223-2520
(205) 871-8171 E-mail: linlyheflinscholarship@gmail.com
Web: www.linlyheflin.org/scholarship-information

Summary To provide financial assistance to women attending colleges and universities in Alabama.
Eligibility This program is open to female residents of Alabama entering or attending accredited 4-year colleges in the state. Applicants must have an ACT score of 23 or higher. U.S. citizenship is required. Selection is based on academic proficiency and financial need.
Financial data The stipend is $4,000 per year.
Duration 1 year; may be renewed until completion of an undergraduate degree, provided the recipient remains enrolled full time, continues to demonstrate financial need, and maintains a GPA of 2.5 or higher.
Additional information The Linly Heflin Unit was founded in 1919 as an organization of 125 women who raise funds for these scholarships.
Number awarded Approximately 20 to 25 of these scholarships are awarded each year.
Deadline January of each year.

[394]
LISA SECHRIST MEMORIAL FOUNDATION SCHOLARSHIP

Lisa Sechrist Memorial Foundation
Attn: Kim Mackmin, Scholarship Selection Committee
Brookfield Residential
3201 Jermantown Road, Suite 150
Fairfax, VA 22030
(703) 270-1400
E-mail: Kim.Mackmin@Broodfieldhomes.com
Web: www.lisasechrist.com/scholarship_award.html

Summary To provide financial assistance to female high school seniors from Virginia who come from disadvantaged backgrounds and plan to attend college in any state.
Eligibility This program is open to women graduating from high schools in Virginia who come from a disadvantaged background. Applicants must be planning to attend an accredited college, university, community college, or technical school in any state. Preference is given to applicants who are members of honor societies, participate in sports or other extracurricular activities, demonstrate citizenship and service within the community, and/or exhibit leadership skills within the school or community. Selection is based on merit, integrity, academic potential, and financial need.
Financial data The stipend is $2,500 per year.
Duration 4 years, provided the recipient maintains a GPA of 2.5 or higher.
Number awarded 1 each year.
Deadline March of each year.

[395]
LOCKHEED MARTIN SCHOLARSHIPS

Society of Women Engineers
Attn: Scholarship Selection Committee
203 North LaSalle Street, Suite 1675
Chicago, IL 60601-1269
(312) 596-5223   Toll Free: (877) SWE-INFO
Fax: (312) 644-8557   E-mail: scholarships@swe.org
Web: societyofwomenengineers.swe.org

Summary To provide financial assistance to women working on an undergraduate degree in computer science, computer engineering, or electrical engineering.
Eligibility This program is open to women who are entering full-time freshmen, sophomores, juniors, or seniors at an ABET-accredited 4-year college or university. Applicants must be interested in studying computer science, computer engineering, software engineering, or electrical engineering and have a GPA of 3.2 or higher. Selection is based on merit.
Financial data The stipend is $2,000. The award includes a travel grant for the recipient to attend the national conference of the Society of Women Engineers.
Duration 1 year.
Additional information This program, established in 1996, is supported by Lockheed Martin Corporation.
Number awarded 8 each year.
Deadline February of each year for continuing students; May of each year for entering freshmen.

[396]
LODINE ROBINSON NATIONAL ASSOCIATION OF WOMEN IN CONSTRUCTION SCHOLARSHIP

Arizona Community Foundation
Attn: Director of Scholarships
2201 East Camelback Road, Suite 405B
Phoenix, AZ 85016
(602) 381-1400   Toll Free: (800) 222-8221
Fax: (602) 381-1575
E-mail: scholarship@azfoundation.org
Web: azfoundation.academicworks.com/opportunities/2537

Summary To provide financial assistance to women from Arizona who are working on a degree in a field related to construction at a public university in the state.
Eligibility This program is open to women who are residents of Arizona and enrolled in at construction-related program that will lead to a 2- or 4-year college or university

degree, certificate, or journeyman status. Applicants must be majoring in architecture, construction trade or apprenticeship, engineering (architectural, civil, electrical, or mechanical), building technology or inspection, CADD/BIM, construction management, or surveying. They must have a GPA of 2.5 or higher and a record of participation in volunteer organizations.

Financial data The stipend is $2,000.

Duration 1 year; nonrenewable.

Additional information This program is sponsored by Greater Phoenix Chapter 98 of National Association of Women in Construction.

Number awarded 1 or more each year.

Deadline March of each year.

[397]
LOREEN ARBUS FOUNDATION SCHOLARSHIP

Alliance for Women in Media
Attn: Foundation
2365 Harrodsburg Road, Suite A325
Lexington, KY 40504
(202) 750-3664   E-mail: info@allwomeninmedia.org
Web: www.allwomeninmedia.org/foundation/scholarships

Summary To provide financial assistance to women who are working on an undergraduate or graduate degree in a media-related field and submit outstanding essays on people with disabilities.

Eligibility This program is open to women currently enrolled in an undergraduate or graduate degree program at a college or university in any state. Applicants must be preparing for a media career and working on a degree in such fields as cable, communications, television, radio, digital media, publishing, journalism, advertising, production, creative design, or related areas. Along with their application, they must submit an essay of 750 to 1,000 words on an individual who has a disability (can be the applicant) and how that person has broken the stereotypes that go along with their particular disability.

Financial data The stipend is $2,500, paid directly to the recipient's institution.

Duration 1 year.

Additional information This program is offered in partnership with the Loreen Arbus Foundation.

Number awarded 1 each year.

Deadline April.

[398]
LOS ANGELES SECTION SWE SCHOLARSHIPS

Society of Women Engineers-Los Angeles Section
Attn: Scholarship Chair
291 Del Amo Fashion Square
Box 14322
Torrance, CA 90503
E-mail: julim.lee@swe.org
Web: www.swela.org

Summary To provide financial assistance to women from any state who are working on an undergraduate or graduate degree in engineering at a college or university in Los Angeles County, California.

Eligibility This program is open to women enrolled in an engineering program leading to a bachelor's or graduate

degree at any of the ABET-accredited colleges or universities in Los Angeles County (California State University at Northridge, California State University at Los Angeles, University of California at Los Angeles, California Institute of Technology, Harvey Mudd University, California State Polytechnic University at Pomona, Loyola Marymount University, and University of Southern California). Applicants must be members of the Society of Women Engineers (SWE) section at their university and have a GPA of 3.0 or higher. Along with their application, they must submit 3 500-word essays on 1) why they decided to study engineering; 2) why they have applied for this scholarship; and 3) what they consider their most important achievement to date. Selection is based on those essays, academic ability, engineering interest, job experience, and leadership; special consideration is given to those with unique circumstances and financial need and to reentering women who have been out of the engineering job market for at least 2 years.

Financial data Stipends range from $500 to $1,500.

Duration 1 year.

Number awarded Varies each year; recently, 5 were awarded.

Deadline February of each year.

[399]
LOUISE MORITZ MOLITORIS LEADERSHIP AWARD

Women's Transportation Seminar
Attn: WTS Foundation
1701 K Street, N.W., Suite 800
Washington, DC 20006
(202) 955-5085   Fax: (202) 955-5088
E-mail: wts@wtsinternational.org
Web: www.wtsinternational.org/education/scholarships

Summary To provide financial assistance to undergraduate women interested in a career in transportation.

Eligibility This program is open to women who are working on an undergraduate degree in transportation or a transportation-related field (e.g., transportation engineering, planning, finance, or logistics). Applicants must have a GPA of 3.0 or higher. Along with their application, they must submit a 500-word statement about their career goals after graduation and why they think they should receive the scholarship award; their statement should specifically address the issue of leadership. Applications must be submitted first to a local chapter; the chapters forward selected applications for consideration on the national level. Minority women are especially encouraged to apply. Selection is based on transportation involvement and goals, job skills, academic record, and leadership potential; financial need is not considered.

Financial data The stipend is $5,000.

Duration 1 year.

Additional information Local chapters may also award additional funding to winners for their area.

Number awarded 1 each year.

Deadline Applications must be submitted by November to a local WTS chapter.

[400]
LP GUERRA NATIONAL SCHOLARSHIP

American Business Women's Association
Attn: Stephen Bufton Memorial Educational Fund
9820 Metcalf Avenue, Suite 110
Overland Park, KS 66212
Toll Free: (800) 228-0007
Web: www.sbmef.org/National/index.cfm

Summary To provide financial assistance to women who are interested in working on a baccalaureate degree in any field.

Eligibility This program is open to women who are entering at least their freshman year at an accredited college or university that offers a baccalaureate degree. Applicants must submit 1) a 250-word biographical sketch that includes information about their background, activities, honors, work experience, and long-term educational and professional goals; and 2) an essay of 500 to 700 words on how they have overcome challenges in academic, personal or business environments that have equipped them with the knowledge and skills to succeed in their specific area of study or industry. They must have a GPA of 3.0 or higher. Financial need is not considered in the selection process. U.S. citizenship is required.

Financial data The stipend is $2,000. Funds are paid directly to the recipient's institution to be used only for tuition, books, and fees.

Duration 1 year; nonrenewable.

Additional information This program is sponsored by the law firm of Luis P. Guerra, L.L.C. of Phoenix as part of ABWA's Stephen Bufton Memorial Education Fund.

Number awarded 1 each year.

Deadline May of each year.

[401]
LUCILE B. KAUFMAN WOMEN'S SCHOLARSHIPS

Society of Manufacturing Engineers
Attn: SME Education Foundation
One SME Drive
P.O. Box 930
Dearborn, MI 48121-0930
(313) 425-3300   Toll Free: (866) 547-6333
Fax: (313) 425-3411   E-mail: foundation@sme.org
Web: www.smeef.org

Summary To provide financial assistance to undergraduate women enrolled in a degree program in manufacturing engineering or manufacturing engineering technology.

Eligibility This program is open to women enrolled full time at a degree-granting institution in North America and preparing for a career in manufacturing engineering. Applicants must have completed at least 30 units in a manufacturing engineering or manufacturing engineering technology curriculum and have a GPA of 3.0 or higher. Along with their application, they must submit a brief statement about why they chose their major, their career and educational objectives, and how this scholarship will help them attain those objectives. Financial need is not considered in the selection process. Applicants must be U.S. or Canadian citizens or permanent residents or have a valid student visa.

Financial data Stipends range from $1,000 to $6,000 and recently averaged approximately $2,000.

Duration 1 year; may be renewed.

Number awarded Varies each year; recently, 3 were awarded.

Deadline January of each year.

[402]
LUCILE MILLER WRIGHT SCHOLARS PROGRAM

Girls Incorporated
Attn: Scholarships and Awards
120 Wall Street, Third Floor
New York, NY 10005-3902
(212) 509-2000   Toll Free: (800) 374-4475
Fax: (212) 509-8708
E-mail: communications@girlsinc.org
Web: www.girlsinc.org/about/national-scholars.html

Summary To provide financial assistance for college to Girls Incorporated members.

Eligibility This program is open to members of Girls Incorporated affiliates who are currently in high school (in grades 11 or 12) and have been members of the association for at least 2 years. They must have a GPA of 2.8 or higher. Selection is based on extracurricular activities, goals and objectives, soundness of ideas, motivation, communication skills, and presentation. Financial need is not considered. Academic record is of secondary importance.

Financial data The scholarships are either $15,000 or $2,500. Funds are held in escrow and paid directly to the recipient's college, professional school, or technical institute.

Duration Up to 5 years.

Additional information This program began in 1992. Funds may not be used for education at a vocational or technical school.

Number awarded Varies each year; recently, 15 were awarded. Since this program was established, it has awarded $4.2 million in scholarships to 413 high school women.

Deadline Deadline not specified.

[403]
LUCY KASPARIAN AHARONIAN SCHOLARSHIPS

Armenian International Women's Association
65 Main Street, Room 3A
Watertown, MA 02472
(617) 926-0171   E-mail: aiwainc@aol.com
Web: www.aiwainternational.org/initiatives/scholarships

Summary To provide financial assistance to Armenian women who are upper-division or graduate students working on a degree in specified fields.

Eligibility This program is open to full-time women students of Armenian descent attending an accredited college or university. Applicants must be full-time juniors, seniors, or graduate students with a GPA of 3.2 or higher. They must be working on a degree in architecture, computer science, engineering, mathematics, science, or technology. Selection is based on financial need and merit.

Financial data The stipend is $1,000.

Duration 1 year.

Additional information This program, established in 2008, is offered in conjunction with the Boston Section of the Society of Women Engineers.

Number awarded Varies each year; recently, 3 were awarded: 2 to undergraduates and 1 to a graduate student.

Deadline April of each year.

[404]
LUELLA AND GEORGE SHAVER FAMILY SCHOLARSHIP

Girl Scouts of Oregon and Southwest Washington
Attn: Shannon Shea, Portland Service Center Office
9620 S.W. Barbur Boulevard
Portland, OR 97219
(503) 977-6813   Toll Free: (800) 338-5248
Fax: (503) 977-6801   E-mail: sshea@girlscoutsosw.org
Web: www.girlscoutsosw.org

Summary To provide financial assistance to high school seniors in Oregon and southwestern Washington who are Ambassador Girl Scouts and planning to attend college in any state.

Eligibility This program is open to seniors graduating from high schools in Oregon and southwestern Washington who are Ambassador Girl Scouts and have earned their Gold Award. Applicants must be planning to enroll at an accredited college, vocational training program, or apprenticeship program in any state. Along with their application, they must submit 1) a 1,000-word essay on how Girl Scouts has impacted their life and how that will impact them in the future; and 2) a 500-word essay on how they have made the world a better place by being a Girl Scout.

Financial data A stipend is awarded (amount not specified).

Duration 1 year.

Number awarded 1 each year.

Deadline April of each year.

[405]
LYDIA CRUZ AND SANDRA MARIE RAMOS SCHOLARSHIP

Delta Tau Lambda Sorority
P.O. Box 7714
Ann Arbor, MI 48107
E-mail: DTL-info@deltataulambda.org
Web: www.deltataulambda.org/dtl_scholarship.html

Summary To provide financial assistance for college to Latina high school seniors.

Eligibility This program is open to Latinas who are graduating from high schools in any state and planning to enroll at a 2- or 4-year college or university. Applicants must submit 500-word essays on 1) the extracurricular activities with which they have been involved; and 2) the social or personal issue about which they are most passionate and how earning a higher education degree will help them resolve those issues or bring awareness to them. Selection is based on academic excellence and community service.

Financial data A stipend is awarded (amount not specified).

Duration 1 year.

Additional information Delta Tau Lambda was established in 1994 as a social sorority for Latinas. It established this scholarship in 1995.

Number awarded 1 or more each year.

Deadline Deadline not specified.

[406]
LYDIA PICKUP MEMORIAL SCHOLARSHIP

Society of Women Engineers-Pacific Northwest Section
Attn: Scholarship Committee
P.O. Box 1601
Bellevue, WA 98009
(425) 418-8244
E-mail: SWEPNWScholarship@gmail.com
Web: www.swe-pnw.org/scholarships.html

Summary To provide financial assistance to women from any state studying engineering at a university in Montana or western Washington.

Eligibility This program is open to women from any state who have, at the time of application, completed at least 50% of the requirements toward college graduation in an engineering field. Applicants must be attending an ABET-accredited engineering school in Montana or western Washington. They must have a GPA of 3.0 or higher. Along with their application, they must submit 1) a 300-word essay on their educational and career goals; and 2) a 500-word essay describing why they have chosen their particular field of engineering; the person, event, or job experience influencing their decision to work on an engineering degree; and the most and least favorite courses they have taken and which course they are most looking forward to and why. Selection is based on the essays, academic achievement, extracurricular and community service activities, and financial need.

Financial data The stipend is $1,000.

Duration 1 year.

Number awarded 1 each year.

Deadline December of each year.

[407]
LYNN G. BELLENGER ENGINEERING TECHNOLOGY SCHOLARSHIP

American Society of Heating, Refrigerating and Air-
    Conditioning Engineers
Attn: Scholarship Administrator
1791 Tullie Circle, N.E.
Atlanta, GA 30329-2305
(404) 539-1120   Fax: (404) 539-2120
E-mail: lbenedict@ashrae.org
Web: www.ashrae.org

Summary To provide financial assistance to female engineering technology students interested in heating, ventilating, air conditioning, and refrigeration (HVAC&R).

Eligibility This program is open to female engineering technology students enrolled full time in a program leading to an associate or bachelor's degree. Applicants must be engaged in a course of study that traditionally has been preparatory for the profession of HVAC&R. They must have a GPA of 3.0 or higher and a standing in the top 30% of their class. Selection is based on potential service to the HVAC&R profession, financial need, leadership ability, recommendations from instructors, and work ethics.

Financial data The stipend is $5,000.

Duration 1 year.

Number awarded 1 each year.

Deadline April of each year.

[408]
LYNN G. BELLENGER SCHOLARSHIP

American Society of Heating, Refrigerating and Air-
Conditioning Engineers
Attn: Scholarship Administrator
1791 Tullie Circle, N.E.
Atlanta, GA 30329-2305
(404) 539-1120 Fax: (404) 539-2120
E-mail: lbenedict@ashrae.org
Web: www.ashrae.org

Summary To provide financial assistance to female undergraduate engineering students interested in heating, ventilating, air conditioning, and refrigeration (HVAC&R).

Eligibility This program is open to female undergraduate
engineering students working on a bachelor's degree in a
program recognized as accredited by the American Society of
Heating, Refrigerating and Air-Conditioning Engineers
(ASHRAE). Applicants must be enrolled full time in a course
of study that has traditionally been preparatory for the profession of HVAC&R. They must have a GPA of 3.0 or higher and
a standing in the top 30% of their class. Selection is based on
potential service to the HVAC&R profession, financial need,
leadership ability, recommendations from instructors, and
work ethics.

Financial data The stipend is $5,000.

Duration 1 year.

Number awarded 1 each year.

Deadline November of each year.

[409]
M. JOSEPHINE O'NEIL ARTS AWARD

Delta Kappa Gamma Society International-Lambda State
Organization
c/o Mary Stayner
3045 Fairway Road
Stockton, IL 61085
E-mail: jmstayner@gmail.com
Web: www.deltakappagamma.org/IL/forms.html

Summary To provide financial assistance to female residents of Illinois who are studying an arts-related field at a college in any state.

Eligibility This program is open to female residents of Illinois who are in or approaching junior standing at an accredited college or university in any state. Applicants must be
majoring in 1 or more areas of the arts, including music,
visual arts, dance, or drama. Along with their application, they
must submit 1) evidence of the quality and extent of accomplishment in the arts, such as programs of performances, cat-
alogs, articles from the media, published reviews of their
work, listings of awards and prizes, or other recognition; 2)
samples of their work on DVD, 35mm slides, CD, videotapes,
or audio tapes; 3) college transcripts; 4) letters of recommendation; 5) a statement on the use of the award for continued
involvement in their selected area of the arts; and 6) a personal essay on their family, personal interests, awards,
achievements, goals (short- and long-term), and philosophy.

Selection is based on evidence from applicant's essay concerning goals, leadership, activities, and philosophy; evidence from all sources of potential for contribution to the society with emphasis on college work; academic background;
recommendation letters; and appearance and clarity of cover
page information and application.

Financial data The stipend ranges up to $6,000.

Duration 1 year.

Additional information The sponsor is an honorary society of women educators.

Number awarded 1 each year.

Deadline February of each year.

[410]
M. LOUISE CARPENTER GLOECKNER, M.D.
SUMMER RESEARCH FELLOWSHIP

Drexel University College of Medicine
Attn: Archives and Special Collections
2900 West Queen Lane
Philadelphia, PA 19129
(215) 991-8340 Fax: (215) 991-8172
E-mail: archives@drexelmed.edu
Web: archives.drexelmed.edu/fellowship.php

Summary To provide funding to scholars and students
interested in conducting research during the summer on the
history of women in medicine at the Archives and Special
Collections on Women in Medicine at Drexel University in
Philadelphia.

Eligibility This program is open to students at all levels,
scholars, and general researchers. Applicants must be interested in conducting research utilizing the archives, which
emphasize the history of women in medicine, nursing, medical missionaries, the American Medical Women's Association, American Women's Hospital Service, and other women
in medical organizations. Selection is based on research
background of the applicant, relevance of the proposed
research project to the goals of the applicant, overall quality
and clarity of the proposal, appropriateness of the proposal to
the holdings of the collection, and commitment of the applicant to the project.

Financial data The grant is $4,000.

Duration 4 to 6 weeks during the summer.

Number awarded 1 each year.

Deadline March of each year.

[411]
MABEL HEIL SCHOLARSHIP

United Methodist Church-Wisconsin Conference
Attn: United Methodist Women
750 Windsor Street
P.O. Box 620
Sun Prairie, WI 53590-0620
(608) 837-7328 Toll Free: (888) 240-7328
Fax: (608) 837-8547
Web: www.wisconsinumc.org

Summary To provide financial assistance to United Methodist women from Wisconsin who are interested in attending
college or graduate school in any state.

Eligibility This program is open to women who are members of congregations affiliated with the Wisconsin Conference of the United Methodist Church and attending or plan-

ning to attend college or graduate school in any state. Applicants must submit an essay on why they consider themselves a worthy student and a letter of recommendation from their pastor or the president of the local United Methodist Women. Preference is given to women who are responsible for others and are returning to the employment field. Lowest priority is given to recent high school graduates.

Financial data A stipend is awarded (amount not specified).

Duration 1 semester; recipients may reapply.

Number awarded 1 or more each year.

Deadline April of each year for the first semester; September of each year for the second semester.

[412]
MAHINDRA USA WOMEN IN AG SCHOLARSHIPS

National FFA Organization
Attn: Scholarship Office
6060 FFA Drive
P.O. Box 68960
Indianapolis, IN 46268-0960
(317) 802-4419   Fax: (317) 802-5419
E-mail: scholarships@ffa.org
Web: www.ffa.org/participate/scholarships

Summary To provide financial assistance to female FFA members interested in studying fields related to agriculture in college.

Eligibility This program is open to female members from 24 designated states who are graduating high school seniors or currently-enrolled college students. Applicants must be working on or planning to work on a 2- or 4-year degree in agriculture in any state. They must have a GPA of 3.0 or higher and be able to demonstrate strong leadership skills, participation in community service, and financial need. Selection is based on academic achievement, FFA involvement, community service, and leadership skills. U.S. citizenship is required.

Financial data The stipend is $2,500. Funds are paid directly to the recipient.

Duration 1 year; nonrenewable.

Additional information This program is sponsored by Mahindra USA, Inc. The designated states are Alabama, Arizona, Arkansas, California, Connecticut, Florida, Georgia, Illinois, Indiana, Iowa, Kansas, Kentucky, Louisiana, Maine, Maryland, Massachusetts, Michigan, Missouri, New York, Oklahoma, Tennessee, Texas, Virginia, and West Virginia.

Number awarded 4 each year.

Deadline January of each year.

[413]
MAIDS OF ATHENA SCHOLARSHIPS

Maids of Athena
1909 Q Street, N.W., Suite 500
Washington, DC 20009-1007
(202) 232-6300   Fax: (202) 232-2145
E-mail: MOAHeadquarters@gmail.com
Web: www.maidsofathena.org/scholarships.html

Summary To provide financial assistance for undergraduate and graduate education to women of Greek descent.

Eligibility This program is open to women who are members of the Maids of Athena. Applicants may be a graduating

high school senior, an undergraduate student, or a graduate student. Along with their application, they must submit a 250-word essay on their involvement in the Maids of Athena and how they perpetuate the goals and values of the Order. Selection is based on academic merit, financial need, and participation in the organization.

Financial data The stipend is $1,000.

Duration 1 year.

Additional information Membership in Maids of Athena is open to unmarried women between 14 and 24 years of age who are of Greek descent from either parent.

Number awarded At least 2 each year.

Deadline May of each year.

[414]
MAINE MEDIA WOMEN SCHOLARSHIP

Maine Media Women
Attn: Scholarship Committee
P.O. Box 175
Round Pond, ME 04564-0175
(207) 529-5304

Summary To provide financial assistance to female high school seniors in Maine who are interested in attending college in any state to prepare for a career in communications media.

Eligibility This program is open to female seniors graduating from high schools in Maine who plan to attend college in any state. Applicants must be planning to prepare for a career in communications media, including art, photography, design and marketing, creative writing, desktop publishing, photojournalism, videography, or communications. Along with their application, they must submit a letter that includes why they wish to be considered for this scholarship, why they wish to go into a specific communications field, high school activities and honors, and any work or volunteer experience. Selection is based on merit.

Financial data The stipend is $1,000.

Duration 1 year.

Number awarded 1 each even-numbered year.

Deadline March of each even-numbered year.

[415]
MAKING A DIFFERENCE LEADER SCHOLARSHIP

Royal Neighbors of America
Attn: Fraternal Services
230 16th Street
Rock Island, IL 61201-8645
(309) 788-4561   Toll Free: (800) 627-4762
E-mail: contact@royalneighbors.org
Web: www.royalneighbors.org

Summary To provide financial assistance to female members of the Royal Neighbors of America (RNA) who are high school seniors planning to attend college.

Eligibility This program is open to female high school seniors who are beneficial members of RNA and rank in the top quarter of their senior class. Applicants must have an outstanding record of volunteerism. They must be planning to enroll full time at an accredited college, university, or junior college to work eventually on a bachelor's degree.

Financial data The stipend is $5,000 per year.

Duration 1 year; may be renewed up to 3 additional years.
Number awarded 1 each year.
Deadline February of each year.

[416]
MANAHAN-BOHAN AWARD

Philanthrofund Foundation
Attn: Scholarship Committee
1409 Willow Street, Suite 109
Minneapolis, MN 55403-2241
(612) 870-1806   Toll Free: (800) 435-1402
Fax: (612) 871-6587   E-mail: info@PfundOnline.org
Web: www.pfundonline.org/scholarships.html

Summary To provide financial assistance to lesbian students from rural Minnesota.

Eligibility This program is open to residents of Madelia, Minnesota; if no resident of Madelia applies, the award is available to residents of any rural area in Minnesota. Applicants must be self-identified as lesbian. They may be attending or planning to attend trade school, technical college, college, or university in any state (as an undergraduate or graduate student). Selection is based on the applicant's 1) affirmation of GLBT or allied identity; 2) evidence of experience and skills in service and leadership; and 3) evidence of service, leading, and working for change in GLBT communities, including serving as a role model, mentor, and/or adviser.

Financial data The stipend is $1,000. Funds must be used for tuition, books, fees, or dissertation expenses.

Duration 1 year.
Number awarded 1 each year.
Deadline January of each year.

[417]
MANUELA NEHLS RE-ENTRY SCHOLARSHIPS

American GI Forum Colorado State Women
Attn: Kathleen Clenin, Scholarship Committee Chair
P.O. Box 11784
Denver, CO 80211
(303) 458-1700   Toll Free: (866) 244-3628
Fax: (303) 458-1634   E-mail: kathyclenin@comcast.net
Web: www.agifusa.org/women

Summary To provide financial assistance to women from Colorado who are members of the American GI Forum and interested in attending college.

Eligibility This program is open to female residents of Colorado who have been members of the American GI Forum for at least 18 months. Applicants must be enrolled or planning to enroll in a certificate, vocational, or degree program at a school in any state. Along with their application, they must submit an essay of 250 to 500 words on their educational and career goals, why they should be selected to receive this award, and what they know about the American GI Forum. Selection is based on that essay, academic goals, extracurricular activities, and community service.

Financial data A stipend is awarded (amount not specified).

Duration 1 year; recipients may reapply.

Additional information The American GI Forum is the largest federally-chartered Hispanic veterans' organization in the United States.

Number awarded 1 or more each year.
Deadline April of each year.

[418]
MARA CRAWFORD PERSONAL DEVELOPMENT SCHOLARSHIP

Kansas Federation of Business & Professional Women's Clubs, Inc.
Attn: Kansas BPW Educational Foundation, Inc.
c/o Kathy Niehoff, Executive Secretary
605 East 15th
Ottawa, KS 66067
(785) 242-9319   Fax: (785) 242-1047
E-mail: kathyniehoff@sbcglobal.net
Web: kansasbpw.memberlodge.org/page-450103?

Summary To provide financial assistance to women in Kansas who are already in the workforce but are interested in pursuing additional education.

Eligibility This program is open to women residents of Kansas who graduated from high school more than 5 years previously and are already in the workforce. Applicants may be seeking a degree in any field of study and may be attending a 2-year, 4-year, vocational, or technological program. They must submit a 3-page personal biography in which they express their career goals, the direction they want to take in the future, their proposed field of study, their reason for selecting that field, the institutions they plan to attend and why, their circumstances for reentering school (if a factor), and what makes them uniquely qualified for this scholarship. Preference is given to applicants who demonstrate they have serious family responsibilities and obligations. Applications must be submitted through a local unit of the sponsor.

Financial data A stipend is awarded (amount not specified).

Duration 1 year.
Number awarded 1 or more each year.
Deadline December of each year.

[419]
MARGARET ABEL SCHOLARSHIP

Delta Kappa Gamma Society International-Alpha Zeta State Organization
c/o Faith Steinfort, State Scholarship Chair
1509 Glenview Drive
Cinnaminson, NJ 08077-2156
E-mail: fsseagull@comcast.net
Web: dkgalphazetastate-nj.weebly.com

Summary To provide financial assistance to women who are residents of New Jersey working on an undergraduate or graduate degree in education at a school in the state.

Eligibility This program is open to women who residents of New Jersey and enrolled as juniors, seniors, or graduate students at a 4-year college or university in the state. Applicants must be preparing for a career as a teacher and have a GPA of 3.0 or higher. They must be U.S. citizens. Along with their application, they must submit a 500-word essay on their desire to become a teacher and the attributes that make them worthy to receive this scholarship.

Financial data The stipend is $1,000.

Duration 1 year; recipients may reapply.

Number awarded 1 or more each year.
Deadline December of each year.

[420]
MARILYNN SMITH SCHOLARSHIP

Ladies Professional Golf Association
Attn: LPGA Foundation
100 International Golf Drive
Daytona Beach, FL 32124-1082
(386) 274-6200 Fax: (386) 274-1099
E-mail: foundation.scholarships@lpga.com
Web: www.lpga.com

Summary To provide financial assistance to female graduating high school seniors who played golf in high school and plan to continue playing in college.

Eligibility This program is open to female high school seniors who have a GPA of 3.2 or higher. Applicants must have played in at least 50% of their high school golf team's scheduled events or have played golf "regularly" for the past 2 years. They must be planning to enroll full time at a college or university in the United States and play competitive golf. Along with their application, they must submit a letter that describes how golf has been an integral part of their lives and includes their personal, academic, and professional goals; their chosen discipline of study; and how this scholarship will be of assistance. Financial need is not considered in the selection process.

Financial data The stipend is $5,000.
Duration 1 year.
Additional information This program began in 1999.
Number awarded 20 each year.
Deadline May of each year.

[421]
MARION J. BAGLEY SCHOLARSHIP

American Legion Auxiliary
Department of New Hampshire
Attn: Department Auxiliary Secretary
121 South Fruit Street, Room A131
Concord, NH 03301
(603) 856-8942 E-mail: nhalasec@legionnh.org
Web: www.legionnh.org

Summary To provide financial assistance to members of the New Hampshire American Legion Auxiliary who plan to attend college in any state.

Eligibility This program is open to graduating high school seniors, graduates of a high school or equivalent, or students currently attending an institution of higher learning in any state. Applicants must be a resident of New Hampshire or have been a member of a unit of the American Legion Auxiliary in that state for at least 3 years. Along with their application, they must submit 3 letters of recommendation; a list of school, church, and community activities or organizations in which they have participated; transcripts; and a 1,000-word essay on "My Obligations as an American." Financial need is considered in the selection process.

Financial data The stipend is $1,000.
Duration 1 year.
Number awarded 1 each year.
Deadline March of each year.

[422]
MARION REID SCHOLARSHIPS

United Methodist Church-Rocky Mountain Conference
Attn: Board of Higher Education and Campus Ministry
6110 Greenwood Plaza Boulevard
Greenwood Village, CO 80111-4803
(303) 733-3736 Toll Free: (800) 536-3736
Fax: (303) 733-1730
Web: www.rmcumc.org/scholarships

Summary To provide financial assistance to women who are members of a United Methodist Church (UMC) in its Rocky Mountain Conference and interested in attending college in any state.

Eligibility This program is open to who are members of a UMC congregation in the Rocky Mountain Conference (which serves Colorado, Utah, and Wyoming). Applicants must be enrolled or planning to enroll at a college or university in any state to study any field. They must have a GPA of 2.8 or higher. Along with their application, they must submit essays on their field of study and their interest in it, plans after graduation, involvement in the UMC, involvement in service and mission outside the church, and financial need.

Financial data The stipend is $2,500.
Duration 1 year.
Number awarded 3 each year.
Deadline July of each year.

[423]
MARJORIE BOWENS-WHEATLEY SCHOLARSHIPS

Unitarian Universalist Association
Attn: UU Women's Federation
258 Harvard Street
Brookline, MA 02446
(617) 838-6989 E-mail: uuwf@uua.org
Web: www.uuwf.org

Summary To provide financial assistance to women of color who are working on an undergraduate or graduate degree to prepare for Unitarian Universalist ministry or service.

Eligibility This program is open to women of color who are either 1) aspirants or candidates for the Unitarian Universalist ministry; or 2) candidates in the Unitarian Universalist Association's professional religious education or music leadership credentialing programs. Applicants must submit a 1- to 2-page narrative that covers their call to UU ministry, religious education, or music leadership; their passions; how their racial/ethnic/cultural background influences their goals for their calling; and how the work of the program's namesake relates to their dreams and plans for their UU service.

Financial data The stipend is $1,500.
Duration 1 year.
Additional information This program began in 2009.
Number awarded Varies each year; recently, 2 were awarded.
Deadline March of each year.

[424]
MARJORIE PEARSON MEMORIAL AWARD

Maine State Society of Washington, D.C.
c/o Jessica Strelitz Stewart, Scholarship Committee Chair
4718 Columbia Road
Annandale, VA 22003-6110
(703) 256-4524　　E-mail: mssfscholarship@gmail.com
Web: www.mainestatesociety.org/foundation

Summary To provide financial assistance to women who are currently enrolled full time at a university within Maine.

Eligibility This program is open to full-time female students enrolled at a 4-year degree-granting, nonprofit institution of higher learning in Maine. High school seniors are not eligible. Applicants must have been legal residents of Maine for at least 4 years (or have at least 1 parent who has been a resident of Maine for at least 4 years). They must be under 25 years of age, be enrolled in at least 12 semester hours or the equivalent, have a GPA of 3.2 or higher, and be working on a baccalaureate degree. Along with their application, they must submit a 750-word essay on 1 of 3 topics that are assigned annually; recently, students could write on 1) how they plan to give back to the state of Maine; 2) the Maine resident, living or dead, who has inspired them and why; or 3) the class or job that has inspired them to pursue their current career goals. Selection is based on academic performance, volunteer leadership, and "a passion for the State of Maine."

Financial data The stipend is $1,500.

Duration 1 year; nonrenewable.

Number awarded 1 each year.

Deadline March of each year.

[425]
MARTHA GUERRA-ARTEAGA SCHOLARSHIP

National Organization of Professional Hispanic Natural Resources Conservation Service Employees
c/o Angel M. Domenech, Scholarship Committee Co-Chair
Natural Resources Conservation Service
Soil Survey Office
3100 Alvey Park Drive West
Owensboro, KY 42303-2191
(270) 685-1707, ext. 118
E-mail: scholarships@nophnrcse.org
Web: www.nophnrcse.org

Summary To provide financial assistance to Hispanic women interested in working on a bachelor's degree in a field related to public affairs or natural resources conservation.

Eligibility This program is open to Hispanic women who are graduating high school seniors or current full-time college students with at least 1 year remaining before graduation. Applicants must be interested in working on a bachelor's degree in public affairs, communications, or natural resources conservation. They must have a GPA of 2.75 or higher. Along with their application, they must submit a personal statement (in English) of 350 to 500 words on their background, name of school they attend or plan to attend, personal and career goals, extracurricular activities, and interest in preparing for a career related to natural resources conservation. Financial need is not considered in the selection process. U.S. citizenship is required.

Financial data The stipend is $1,000.

Duration 1 year.

Additional information The National Organization of Professional Hispanic Natural Resources Conservation Service Employees (NOPRNRCSE) is comprised of Hispanic employees of the Natural Resources Conservation Service of the U.S. Department of Agriculture (USDA-NRCS).

Number awarded 1 each year.

Deadline May of each year.

[426]
MARY BARRETT MARSHALL SCHOLARSHIP

American Legion Auxiliary
Department of Kentucky
134 Walnut Street
Frankfort, KY 40601
(502) 352-2380　　　　　　　　　Fax: (502) 352-2381
E-mail: aladeptaux@yahoo.com
Web: www.kyamlegionaux.org/scholarships

Summary To provide financial assistance to female dependents of veterans in Kentucky who plan to attend college in the state.

Eligibility This program is open to the daughters, wives, sisters, widows, granddaughters, or great-granddaughters of veterans eligible for membership in the American Legion who are high school seniors or graduates and 5-year residents of Kentucky. Applicants must be planning to attend a college or university in Kentucky.

Financial data The stipend is $1,000. The funds may be used for tuition, registration fees, laboratory fees, and books, but not for room and board.

Duration 1 year.

Number awarded 1 each year.

Deadline March of each year.

[427]
MARY BLACKWELL BARNES MEMORIAL SCHOLARSHIPS

Women in Public Finance-Virginia Chapter
Attn: Scholarship Committee
P.O. Box 129
Richmond, VA 23219
E-mail: info@virginiawpf.org
Web: www.virginiawpf.org/index.php/scholarships

Summary To provide financial assistance to women from any state who are working on an undergraduate or graduate degree in a field related to public finance at a college in Virginia or Washington, D.C.

Eligibility This program is open to women from any state who are enrolled at a college or university in Virginia or Washington, D.C. as a sophomore or higher undergraduate or a graduate student. Applicants must be preparing for a career in public finance, including work in government, nonprofits, law, or finance. Along with their application, they must submit a 500-word career essay on either 1) their career and educational goals and what has influenced those goals; or 2) their favorite work experience and how it has helped shape or change their thoughts about possible career options. They must also submit a 500-word personal essay on 1 of the following: 1) an interest they have pursued outside of their college classes; 2) a goal they set for themselves and achieved; or 3) an experience, achievement, or risk they have taken or ethical dilemma they have faced. Financial need is not considered.

Financial data   Stipends range from $1,000 to $5,000.

Duration   1 year.

Additional information   This program began in 2009.

Number awarded   Up to 5 each year.

Deadline   May of each year.

[428]
MARY ELLEN RUSSELL MEMORIAL SCHOLARSHIP

Society of Women Engineers-Pacific Northwest Section
Attn: Scholarship Committee
P.O. Box 1601
Bellevue, WA 98009
(425) 418-8244
E-mail: SWEPNWScholarship@gmail.com
Web: www.swe-pnw.org/scholarships.html

Summary   To provide financial assistance to women from any state studying engineering at a university in Montana or western Washington.

Eligibility   This program is open to women from any state who, at the time of application, have completed at least 50% of the requirements toward college graduation in an engineering field. Applicants must be attending an ABET-accredited engineering school in Montana or western Washington. They must have a GPA of 3.0 or higher. Along with their application, they must submit 1) a 300-word essay on their educational and career goals; and 2) a 500-word essay describing why they have chosen their particular field of engineering; the person, event, or job experience influencing their decision to work on an engineering degree; and the most and least favorite courses they have taken and which course they are most looking forward to and why. Selection is based on the essays, academic achievement, extracurricular and community service activities, and financial need.

Financial data   The stipend is $1,000.

Duration   1 year.

Number awarded   1 each year.

Deadline   December of each year.

[429]
MARY GUNTHER MEMORIAL SCHOLARSHIP

Society of Women Engineers
Attn: Scholarship Selection Committee
203 North LaSalle Street, Suite 1675
Chicago, IL 60601-1269
(312) 596-5223   Toll Free: (877) SWE-INFO
Fax: (312) 644-8557   E-mail: scholarships@swe.org
Web: societyofwomenengineers.swe.org

Summary   To provide financial assistance to women interested in studying engineering or computer science in college.

Eligibility   This program is open to women who are enrolled or planning to enroll full time at an ABET-accredited 4-year college or university. Applicants must be planning to major in engineering or computer science; preference is given to students majoring in architectural or environmental engineering. Entering freshmen must have a GPA of 3.5 or higher; current undergraduates must have a GPA of 3.0 or higher. Selection is based on merit.

Financial data   The stipend is $3,000.

Duration   1 year.

Additional information   This program began in 2011.

Number awarded   4 each year: 2 for entering freshmen and 2 for continuing undergraduates.

Deadline   February of each year for continuing undergraduates; May of each year for entering freshmen.

[430]
MARY LILY RESEARCH GRANTS

Duke University
David M. Rubenstein Rare Book and Manuscript Library
Attn: Sallie Bingham Center for Women's History and
    Culture
P.O. Box 90185
Durham, NC 27708-0185
(919) 660-5828   Fax: (919) 660-5934
E-mail: cwhc@duke.edu
Web: library.duke.edu/rubenstein/bingham/grants

Summary   To provide funding to scholars at all levels who wish to use the resources of the Sallie Bingham Center for Women's History and Culture in the Special Collections Library at Duke University.

Eligibility   This program is open to undergraduates, graduate students, faculty members, and independent scholars in any academic field who wish to use the resources of the center for their research in women's studies. Writers, creative and performing artists, filmmakers, and journalists are also eligible. Applicants must reside outside a 100-mile radius of Durham, North Carolina. Undergraduate and graduate students must be currently enrolled, be working on a degree, and enclose a letter of recommendation from their adviser or thesis director. Faculty members must be working on a research project and enclose a curriculum vitae. Independent scholars must be working on a nonprofit project and enclose a curriculum vitae. Research topics should be strongly supported by the collections of the center.

Financial data   Grants up to $1,000 are available; funds may be used for travel, accommodations, meals, and photocopying and reproduction expenses.

Additional information   The library's collections are especially strong in the history of feminist activism and theory, prescriptive literature, girls' literature, artists' books by women, lay and ordained church women, gender expression, women's sexuality, and the history and culture of women in the South. A number of prominent women writers have placed their personal and professional papers in the collections.

Number awarded   Varies each year; recently, 11 were awarded.

Deadline   January of each year.

[431]
MARY MACON MCGUIRE SCHOLARSHIP

General Federation of Women's Clubs of Virginia
Attn: Scholarship Committee
513 Forest Avenue
P.O. Box 8750
Richmond, VA 23226
(804) 288-3724   Toll Free: (800) 699-8392
Fax: (804) 288-0341
E-mail: scholarships@gfwcvirginia.org
Web: www.gfwcvirginia.org/forms.htm

Summary   To provide financial assistance to women heads of households in Virginia who have returned to school.

Eligibility   This program is open to women residents of Virginia who are heads of households. Applicants must be currently enrolled in a course of study (vocational or academic) at an accredited Virginia school. They must have returned to school to upgrade their education and employment skills in order to better provide for their families. Selection is based on 3 letters of recommendation; a resume of educational and employment history, financial circumstances, and community activities; and an essay up to 2,000 words that outlines the financial need for the grant as well as the reasons for entering the field of study selected.

Financial data   The stipend is $2,500. Funds are paid directly to the recipient's college or university.

Duration   1 year.

Additional information   This program began in 1929 as a loan fund. It was converted to its current form in 2000.

Number awarded   2 each year.

Deadline   March of each year.

[432]
MARY PAOLOZZI MEMBER'S SCHOLARSHIP

Navy Wives Clubs of America
c/o NSA Mid-South
P.O. Box 54022
Millington, TN 38054-0022
Toll Free: (866) 511-NWCA
E-mail: nwca@navywivesclubsofamerica.org
Web: www.navywivesclubsofamerica.org/scholarships

Summary   To provide financial assistance for undergraduate or graduate study to members of the Navy Wives Clubs of America (NWCA).

Eligibility   This program is open to NWCA members who can demonstrate financial need. Applicants must be 1) a high school graduate or senior planning to attend college full time next year; 2) currently enrolled in an undergraduate program and planning to continue as a full-time undergraduate; 3) a college graduate or senior planning to be a full-time graduate student next year; or 4) a high school graduate or GED recipient planning to attend vocational or business school next year. Along with their application, they must submit a brief statement on why they feel they should be awarded this scholarship and any special circumstances (financial or other) they wish to have considered. Financial need is also considered in the selection process.

Financial data   Stipends range from $500 to $1,000 each year (depending upon the donations from the NWCA chapters).

Duration   1 year.

Additional information   Membership in the NWCA is open to spouses of enlisted personnel serving in the Navy, Marine Corps, Coast Guard, and the active Reserve units of those services; spouses of enlisted personnel who have been honorably discharged, retired, or transferred to the Fleet Reserve on completion of duty; and widows of enlisted personnel in those services.

Number awarded   1 or more each year.

Deadline   May of each year.

[433]
MARY R. NORTON MEMORIAL SCHOLARSHIP AWARD FOR WOMEN

ASTM International
100 Barr Harbor Drive
P.O. Box C700
West Conshohocken, PA 19428-2959
(610) 832-9500
Web: www.astm.org/studentmember/Student_Awards.html

Summary   To provide financial assistance to female undergraduate and graduate students working on a degree related to physical metallurgy.

Eligibility   This program is open to women entering their senior year of college or first year of graduate study. Applicants must be working on a degree in physical metallurgy or materials science, with an emphasis on relationship of microstructure and properties.

Financial data   The stipend is $1,000.

Duration   1 year.

Additional information   This program, established in 1975, is administered by ASTM Committee CO4 on Metallography. ASTM International was formerly the American Society for Testing and Materials.

Number awarded   1 or more each year.

Deadline   Deadline not specified.

[434]
MARY RUBIN AND BENJAMIN M. RUBIN SCHOLARSHIP FUND

Central Scholarship Bureau
6 Park Center Court, Suite 221
Owings Mills, MD 21117
(410) 415-5558   Toll Free: (855) 276-0239
Fax: (410) 415-5501
E-mail: gohigher@central-scholarship.org
Web: www.central-scholarship.org/scholarships/overview

Summary   To provide financial assistance to women in Maryland who plan to attend college in any state.

Eligibility   This program is open to women residents of Maryland who are attending or planning to attend a college or university in any state. Applicants must have been out of high school for at least 12 months. They must have a GPA of 3.0 or higher and a family income of less than $90,000 per year. Selection is based on academic achievement, extracurricular activities, and financial need. U.S. citizenship or permanent resident status is required.

Financial data   Stipends range up to $2,500 per year. Funds may be used to pay tuition only.

Duration   1 year. May be renewed up to 4 additional years. Renewal applicants who maintain a GPA of 3.0 or higher are given preference over new applicants.

Additional information This non-sectarian fund, established in 1988, is administered by the Central Scholarship Bureau for the Jewish Community Federation of Baltimore.

Number awarded 1 or more each year.

Deadline March of each year.

[435]
MARY V. MUNGER MEMORIAL SCHOLARSHIPS

Society of Women Engineers
Attn: Scholarship Selection Committee
203 North LaSalle Street, Suite 1675
Chicago, IL 60601-1269
(312) 596-5223 Toll Free: (877) SWE-INFO
Fax: (312) 644-8557 E-mail: scholarships@swe.org
Web: societyofwomenengineers.swe.org

Summary To provide financial assistance to undergraduate members of the Society of Women Engineers (SWE) who are majoring in computer science or engineering.

Eligibility This program is open to members of the society who are juniors, seniors, or reentry students at a 4-year ABET-accredited college or university. Applicants must be majoring in computer science or engineering. Selection is based on merit. U.S. citizenship is required.

Financial data The stipend is $2,750.

Duration 1 year.

Number awarded 2 each year.

Deadline February of each year.

[436]
MARY VON MACH SCHOLARSHIP

Ninety-Nines, Inc.-Michigan Chapter
c/o Rebecca Duggan
Michigan Aviation Education Foundation
22436 Mylls Street
St. Clair Shores, MI 48081-2619
(586) 441-4531 E-mail: rebdpilot@wideopenwest.com
Web: www.michigan99s.info/node/6

Summary To provide financial assistance to women who are cadets in the Civil Air Patrol (CAP) in Michigan and plan to study aviation at a college in any state.

Eligibility This program is open to women in Michigan who have been CAP cadets for at least 1 year. Applicants must be planning to attend a college in any state to prepare for a career in aviation. They must be able to attend Flight Encampment and be prepared to take and pass a Third Class Flight Physical before encampment. Along with their application, they must submit a narrative that covers how they became interested in the Flight Encampment, how it will fit their career goals, how they define a pilot's responsibilities, how they heard about this scholarship, and the activities (school, community, CAP) in which they are involved. Selection is based on attitude, appearance, CPA and academic achievements, demonstrated potential, commitment to personal development, and future career goals.

Financial data A stipend is awarded (amount not specified).

Duration 1 year.

Number awarded 2 each year.

Deadline October of each year.

[437]
MARY VOSWINKEL MEMORIAL SCHOLARSHIP

International Association of Campus Law Enforcement
 Administrators
Attn: Association Administrator
342 North Main Street
West Hartford, CT 06117-2507
(860) 586-7517 Fax: (860) 586-7550
E-mail: awards@iaclea.org
Web: www.iaclea.org

Summary To provide financial assistance to female undergraduate and graduate students who are working for campus security at their school.

Eligibility This program is open to women working on an undergraduate or graduate degree at a college or university that is a member of the International Association of Campus Law Enforcement Administrators (IACLEA). Applicants must be employed in some capacity by the campus security, public safety, or police department at their institution. They must have a GPA of 3.0 or higher and be able to demonstrate financial need.

Financial data The stipend is $1,000.

Duration 1 year.

Number awarded 1 each year.

Deadline March of each year.

[438]
MARYLAND LEGION AUXILIARY CHILDREN AND YOUTH FUND SCHOLARSHIP

American Legion Auxiliary
Department of Maryland
1589 Sulphur Spring Road, Suite 105
Baltimore, MD 21227
(410) 242-9519 Fax: (410) 242-9553
E-mail: hq@alamd.org
Web: www.alamd.org/Scholarships.html

Summary To provide financial assistance for college to the daughters of veterans who are Maryland residents and wish to study designated fields at a school in the state.

Eligibility This program is open to Maryland senior high school girls with a veteran parent who wish to study arts, sciences, business, public administration, education, or a medical field other than nursing at a college or university in the state. Preference is given to children of members of the American Legion or American Legion Auxiliary. Selection is based on character (30%), Americanism (20%), leadership (10%), scholarship (20%), and financial need (20%). U.S. citizenship is required.

Financial data The stipend is $2,000.

Duration 1 year; may be renewed up to 3 additional years.

Number awarded 1 each year.

Deadline April of each year.

[439]
MARYLAND LEGION AUXILIARY PAST PRESIDENTS' PARLEY NURSING SCHOLARSHIP

American Legion Auxiliary
Department of Maryland
1589 Sulphur Spring Road, Suite 105
Baltimore, MD 21227
(410) 242-9519   Fax: (410) 242-9553
E-mail: hq@alamd.org
Web: www.alamd.org/Scholarships.html

Summary To provide financial assistance to the female descendants of Maryland veterans who wish to study nursing at a school in any state.

Eligibility This program is open to Maryland residents who are the daughters, granddaughters, great-granddaughters, step-daughters, step-granddaughters, or step-great-grand-daughters of ex-servicewomen (or of ex-servicemen, if there are no qualified descendants of ex-servicewomen). Applicants must be interested in attending a school in any state to become a registered nurse and be able to show financial need. They must submit a 300-word essay on the topic "What a Nursing Career Means to Me."

Financial data The stipend is $2,000. Funds are sent directly to the recipient's school.

Duration 1 year; may be renewed for up to 3 additional years if the recipient remains enrolled full time.

Number awarded 1 each year.

Deadline April of each year.

[440]
MASWE SCHOLARSHIPS

Society of Women Engineers
Attn: Scholarship Selection Committee
203 North LaSalle Street, Suite 1675
Chicago, IL 60601-1269
(312) 596-5223   Toll Free: (877) SWE-INFO
Fax: (312) 644-8557   E-mail: scholarships@swe.org
Web: societyofwomenengineers.swe.org

Summary To provide financial assistance to undergraduate women majoring in computer science or engineering.

Eligibility This program is open to women who are entering their sophomore, junior, or senior year at a 4-year ABET-accredited college or university. Applicants must be working full time on a degree in computer science, engineering technology, or engineering. Financial need is considered in the selection process.

Financial data The stipend is $1,500.

Duration 1 year.

Additional information These scholarships were established by the Men's Auxiliary of the Society of Women Engineers (MASWE) in 1971 and are continued through a fund established by the organization when it disbanded in 1976 (effective with the opening of Society of Women Engineer's membership to men).

Number awarded 4 each year.

Deadline February of each year.

[441]
MEDTRONIC SWENET SCHOLARSHIP

Society of Women Engineers-Minnesota Section
Attn: Scholarship Committee
P.O. Box 18481
Minneapolis, MN 55418
E-mail: scholarships@swe-mn.org
Web: www.swe-mn.org/scholarships.html

Summary To provide financial assistance to women from any state working on an undergraduate or graduate degree in specified fields of engineering at colleges and universities in Minnesota, North Dakota, and South Dakota.

Eligibility This program is open to female undergraduate and graduate students at ABET-accredited engineering programs in Minnesota, North Dakota, or South Dakota. Applicants must be working full time on a degree in biomedical, chemical, electrical, or mechanical engineering. Along with their application, they must submit a 250-word essay describing how they plan to utilize their engineering knowledge and skills after they graduate. Selection is based on potential to succeed as an engineer (20 points), communication skills (10 points), extracurricular or community involvement and leadership skills (10 points), demonstration of work experience and successes (10 points), and academic success (5 points).

Financial data The stipend is $1,000.

Duration 1 year.

Additional information This program is sponsored by Medtronic, Inc.

Number awarded 3 each year.

Deadline March of each year.

[442]
MEREDITH CORPORATION SCHOLARSHIP

New York Women in Communications, Inc.
Attn: NYWICI Foundation
355 Lexington Avenue, 15th Floor
New York, NY 10017-6603
(212) 297-2133   Fax: (212) 370-9047
E-mail: nywicipr@nywici.org
Web: www.nywici.org/foundation/scholarships

Summary To provide financial assistance and work experience to female residents of designated eastern states who are interested in preparing for a career in publishing at a college or graduate school in any state.

Eligibility This program is open to women who are residents of New York, New Jersey, Connecticut, or Pennsylvania and enrolled as sophomores, juniors, seniors, or graduate students at a college or university in any state. Graduate students must be members of New York Women in Communications, Inc. (NYWICI). Also eligible are women who reside outside the 4 states but are currently enrolled at a college or university within 1 of the 5 boroughs of New York City. Applicants must be preparing for a career in publishing (print, digital, and/or marketing) and be interested in a summer internship with Meredith Corporation. They must have a GPA of 3.2 or higher. Along with their application, they must submit a 2-page resume; a personal essay of 300 words on an assigned topic that changes annually; 2 letters of recommendation; and an official transcript. Selection is based on academic record, need, demonstrated leadership, participation in school and community activities, honors and other awards or recognition, work experience, goals and aspirations, and unusual personal and/or family circumstances. U.S. citizenship or permanent resident status is required.

Financial data The scholarship stipend ranges up to $10,000; the internship is salaried (amount not specified).

Duration 1 year.

Additional information This program is sponsored by Meredith Corporation.

Number awarded 1 each year.

Deadline January of each year.

[443]
MEREDITH THOMS MEMORIAL SCHOLARSHIPS

Society of Women Engineers
Attn: Scholarship Selection Committee
120 South LaSalle Street, Suite 1515
Chicago, IL 60603-3572
(312) 596-5223   Toll Free: (877) SWE-INFO
Fax: (312) 644-8557
E-mail: scholarshipapplication@swe.org
Web: societyofwomenengineers.swe.org

Summary To provide financial assistance to undergraduate women majoring in computer science or engineering.

Eligibility This program is open to women who are entering their sophomore, junior, or senior year at a 4-year ABET-accredited college or university. Applicants must be working full time on a degree in computer science, engineering technology, or engineering and have a GPA of 3.0 or higher. Selection is based on merit.

Financial data The stipend is $2,700.

Duration 1 year.

Additional information This program began in 2001.

Number awarded 5 each year.

Deadline February of each year.

[444]
MICHAEL BAKER SCHOLARSHIP FOR DIVERSITY IN ENGINEERING

Association of Independent Colleges and Universities of
  Pennsylvania
101 North Front Street
Harrisburg, PA 17101-1404
(717) 232-8649   Fax: (717) 233-8574
E-mail: info@aicup.org
Web: www.aicup.org/Foundation-Scholarships

Summary To provide financial assistance to women and minority students from any state enrolled at member institutions of the Association of Independent Colleges and Universities of Pennsylvania (AICUP) who are majoring in designated fields of engineering.

Eligibility This program is open to full-time undergraduate students from any state enrolled at designated AICUP colleges and universities who are women and/or members of the following minority groups: American Indians, Alaska Natives, Asians, Blacks/African Americans, Hispanics/Latinos, Native Hawaiians, or Pacific Islanders. Applicants must be juniors majoring in architectural, civil, or environmental engineering with a GPA of 3.0 or higher. Along with their application, they must submit a 2-page essay on what they believe will be the greatest challenge facing the engineering profession over the next decade, and why.

Financial data The stipend is $2,500 per year.

Duration 1 year; may be renewed 1 additional year if the recipient maintains appropriate academic standards.

Additional information This program, sponsored by the Michael Baker Corporation, is available at the 88 private colleges and universities in Pennsylvania that comprise the AICUP.

Number awarded 1 each year.

Deadline April of each year.

[445]
MICHELE L. MCDONALD SCHOLARSHIP

Educational Foundation for Women in Accounting
Attn: Foundation Administrator
136 South Keowee Street
Dayton, OH 45402
(937) 424-3391   Fax: (937) 222-5749
E-mail: info@efwa.org
Web: www.efwa.org/scholarships_undergraduate.php

Summary To provide financial support to women who are returning to college from the workforce or after raising their family to work on a degree in accounting.

Eligibility This program is open to women who are returning to college from the workforce or after raising children. Applicants must be planning to begin a program of study for a college degree in accounting. Selection is based on aptitude for accounting and business, commitment to the goal of working on a degree in accounting (including evidence of continued commitment after receiving this award), clear evidence that the candidate has established goals and a plan for achieving those goals (both personal and professional), and financial need. U.S. citizenship is required.

Financial data The stipend is $1,000 per year.

Duration 1 year; may be renewed 1 additional year if the recipient completes at least 12 hours each semester.

Additional information This program was established by the Albuquerque Chapter of the American Society of Women Accountants (ASWA) and transferred to the Educational Foundation for Women in Accounting in 2006.

Number awarded 1 each year.

Deadline April of each year.

[446]
MICHIGAN COUNCIL OF WOMEN IN TECHNOLOGY FOUNDATION SCHOLARSHIPS

Michigan Council of Women in Technology Foundation
Attn: Scholarship Committee
P.O. Box 214585
Auburn Hills, MI 48321
(248) 654-3697   Fax: (248) 281-5391
E-mail: info@mcwt.org
Web: www.mcwt.org/Scholarships_196.html

Summary To provide financial assistance to women from Michigan who are interested in working on an undergraduate or graduate degree in a field related to information technology at a school in any state.

Eligibility This program is open to female residents of Michigan who are graduating high school seniors, current undergraduates, or graduate students and enrolled or planning to enroll at a college or university in any state. Applicants must be planning to work on a degree in a field related to information technology, including business analytics for information science, business applications, computer science, computer engineering, computer information systems, digital forensics, information assurance, information systems, or software engineering. They must have a GPA of 3.0 or higher. Programs in which technology is a secondary element (such as architecture, biomedical engineering, computer aided design, finance, library science, marketing, mechanical engineering, or psychology) are not eligible. Financial need is not considered in the selection process. U.S. citizenship is required.

Financial data The stipend is $5,000 per year; funds are sent directly to the financial aid office at the college or university where the recipient is enrolled.

Duration 1 year; may be renewed for up to 3 additional years for high school seniors or 2 additional years for undergraduate and graduate students. Renewal requires the recipient to maintain a GPA of 3.0 or higher.

Number awarded Varies each year: recently, 4 were awarded: 1 to a high school senior, 2 to undergraduates, and 1 to a graduate student.

Deadline January of each year.

[447]
MICHIGAN JOB'S DAUGHTERS SCHOLARSHIPS

International Order of Job's Daughters-Grand Guardian
  Council of Michigan
c/o Tammy Felch, Educational Trustee Board Chair
2055 Pagel Avenue
Lincoln Park, MI 48146
Web: www.michiganiojd.org/scholarships.htm

Summary To provide financial assistance to members of Job's Daughters in Michigan who are interested in attending college in any state.

Eligibility This program is open to members of Job's Daughters in Michigan who are high school seniors or graduates under 25 years of age. Applicants must be attending or planning to attend a college or university in any state. Along with their application, they must submit a brief summary of their personal goals and financial situation.

Financial data A stipend is awarded (amount not specified).

Duration 1 year; may be renewed.

Number awarded Varies each year.

Deadline April of each year.

[448]
MILLIE GONZALEZ MEMORIAL SCHOLARSHIPS

Matrix Health Group
Attn: Memorial Scholarship Program
2202 Brownstone Court
Champaign, IL 61822
(217) 840-1033
E-mail: maria.vetter@matrixhealthgroup.com
Web: www.factorsupportnetwork.com

Summary To provide financial assistance for college to women who have a bleeding disorder.

Eligibility This program is open to graduating female high school seniors and students currently enrolled full time at an accredited college, university, or technical school. Applicants must have von Willebrand's disease or other bleeding disor-

der. They must have a GPA of 2.0 or higher for their senior year in high school or their current year in college. Along with their application, they must submit transcripts, ACT or SAT test scores, 2 letters of recommendation, information on their work and school activities, and an essay of 300 to 400 words on 1 of the following topics: 1) the experiences that have influenced their decision to pursue their educational goals or career choice; 2) how they feel their life has been influenced by having a bleeding disorder; or 3) their biggest challenge in having a bleeding disorder and how they have or are working through it. Selection is based on that essay, academic merit, and reference letters.

Financial data The stipend is $1,000.

Duration 1 year.

Additional information This program is supported by Factor Support Network Pharmacy and administered by Matrix Health Group.

Number awarded 1 each year.

Deadline July of each year.

[449]
MILWAUKEE CHAPTER AFWA SCHOLARSHIPS

Accounting and Financial Women's Alliance-Milwaukee
  Chapter
c/o Wendy Menzel, Scholarship Chair
Northwestern Mutual
500 West Silver Spring Drive, Suite K-290
Glendale, WI 53217-5057
(414) 358-5105 E-mail: scholarship@milwaukeeafwa.org
Web: www.milwaukeeafwa.org/scholarship

Summary To provide financial assistance to women from any state who are majoring in accounting or finance at a college in Wisconsin.

Eligibility This program is open to women who are entering their second year at a 2-year college or their senior year at a 4-year college or university in Wisconsin. Applicants must be majoring in accounting or finance. Along with their application, they must submit an essay of 150 to 250 words on their career goals and objectives, the impact they want to have on the accounting world, community involvement, and leadership examples. Selection is based on the essay, grades, extracurricular activities, life experience, and financial need.

Financial data The stipend is $2,000 for students in a 4-year program or $750 for students in a 2-year program.

Duration 1 year.

Number awarded 2 each year: 1 to a woman at a 2-year college and 1 to a woman at a 4-year college or university.

Deadline November of each year.

[450]
MINERVA NATIONAL SCHOLARSHIP

American Business Women's Association
Attn: Stephen Bufton Memorial Educational Fund
9820 Metcalf Avenue, Suite 110
Overland Park, KS 66212
Toll Free: (800) 228-0007
Web: www.sbmef.org

Summary To provide financial assistance to women who are interested in working on a baccalaureate degree in any field.

Eligibility This program is open to women who are entering at least their freshman year at an accredited college or university that offers a baccalaureate degree with a major in any field. Applicants must submit 1) a 250-word biographical sketch that includes information about their background, activities, honors, work experience, and long-term educational and professional goals; and 2) an essay of 500 to 700 words on the most creative way they have overcome prejudice in a school, social, work or professional setting. They must have a GPA of 3.0 or higher. Financial need is not considered in the selection process. U.S. citizenship is required.

Financial data The stipend is $2,000. Funds are paid directly to the recipient's institution to be used only for tuition, books, and fees.

Duration 1 year; nonrenewable.

Additional information This program is sponsored by the warehouse management software company Minerva Associates as part of ABWA's Stephen Bufton Memorial Education Fund.

Number awarded 1 each year.

Deadline May of each year.

[451]
MINNESOTA CHILD CARE GRANT PROGRAM

Minnesota Office of Higher Education
Attn: Manager of State Financial Aid Programs
1450 Energy Park Drive, Suite 350
St. Paul, MN 55108-5227
(651) 642-0567   Toll Free: (800) 657-3866
Fax: (651) 642-0675   TDD: (800) 627-3529
E-mail: info.ohe@state.mn.us
Web: www.ohe.state.mn.us/mPg.cfm?pageID=140

Summary To provide financial assistance for child care to students in Minnesota who are not receiving Minnesota Family Investment Program (MFIP) benefits.

Eligibility Minnesota residents who are working on an undergraduate degree or vocational certificate in the state and who have children age 12 and under (14 and under if disabled) may receive this assistance to help pay child care expenses. They must demonstrate financial need but must not be receiving Minnesota Family Investment Program (MFIP) benefits. U.S. citizenship or eligible noncitizen status is required.

Financial data The amount of the assistance depends on the income of applicant and spouse, number of day care hours necessary to cover education and work obligations, student's enrollment status, and number of eligible children in applicant's family. The maximum available is $2,800 per eligible child per academic year.

Duration 1 year; may be renewed as long as the recipient remains enrolled on at least a half-time basis in an undergraduate program.

Additional information Assistance may cover up to 40 hours per week per eligible child.

Number awarded Varies each year; recently, a total of $1.1 million was provided for this program.

Deadline Deadline not specified.

[452]
MINNESOTA LEGION AUXILIARY PAST PRESIDENTS PARLEY HEALTH CARE SCHOLARSHIP

American Legion Auxiliary
Department of Minnesota
State Veterans Service Building
20 West 12th Street, Room 314
St. Paul, MN 55155-2069
(651) 224-7634   Toll Free: (888) 217-9598
Fax: (651) 224-5243   E-mail: deptoffice@mnala.org
Web: www.mnala.org/Scholarships.aspx

Summary To provide financial assistance for education in health care fields to members of the American Legion Auxiliary in Minnesota.

Eligibility This program is open to residents of Minnesota who have been members of the American Legion Auxiliary for at least 3 years. Applicants must have a GPA of 2.0 or higher and be planning to study in Minnesota. They must be preparing for a career in a phase of health care, including nursing assistant, registered nurse, licensed practical nurse, X-ray or other technician, dietician, physical or other therapist, dental hygienist, or dental assistant.

Financial data The stipend is $1,000. Funds are sent directly to the recipient's school after satisfactory completion of the first quarter.

Duration 1 year.

Number awarded Up to 10 each year.

Deadline March of each year.

[453]
MINNESOTA SECTION SWE BOSTON SCIENTIFIC SCHOLARSHIP

Society of Women Engineers-Minnesota Section
Attn: Scholarship Committee
P.O. Box 18481
Minneapolis, MN 55418
E-mail: scholarships@swe-mn.org
Web: www.swe-mn.org/scholarships.html

Summary To provide financial assistance to women from any state working on an undergraduate or graduate degree in computer science or specified fields of engineering at colleges and universities in Minnesota, North Dakota, and South Dakota.

Eligibility This program is open to female undergraduate and graduate students at ABET-accredited engineering programs in Minnesota, North Dakota, or South Dakota. Applicants must be working full time on a degree in computer science or biomedical, chemical, electrical, or mechanical engineering. Along with their application, they must submit a 250-word essay describing how they plan to utilize their engineering knowledge and skills after they graduate. Selection is based on potential to succeed as an engineer (20 points), communication skills (10 points), extracurricular or community involvement and leadership skills (10 points), demonstration of work experience and successes (10 points), and academic success (5 points).

Financial data The stipend is $1,000.

Duration 1 year.

Additional information This program is sponsored by Boston Scientific.

Number awarded 1 each year.

Deadline March of each year.

[454]
MINNESOTA SECTION SWE SCHOLARSHIP

Society of Women Engineers-Minnesota Section
Attn: Scholarship Committee
P.O. Box 18481
Minneapolis, MN 55418
E-mail: scholarships@swe-mn.org
Web: www.swe-mn.org/scholarships.html

Summary To provide financial assistance to upper-division women from any state studying engineering or computer science at colleges and universities in Minnesota, North Dakota, and South Dakota.

Eligibility This program is open to women entering their junior or senior year at an ABET-accredited engineering or computer science program in Minnesota, North Dakota, or South Dakota. Applicants must be full-time students majoring in engineering or computer science. Along with their application, they must submit a 250-word essay describing how they plan to utilize their engineering knowledge and skills after they graduate. Selection is based on potential to succeed as an engineer (20 points), communication skills (10 points), extracurricular or community involvement and leadership skills (10 points), demonstration of work experience and successes (10 points), and academic success (5 points).

Financial data The stipend is $1,500.

Duration 1 year.

Number awarded 1 each year.

Deadline March of each year.

[455]
MINNESOTA WOMEN'S GOLF ASSOCIATION SCHOLARSHIP

Minnesota Women's Golf Association
Attn: MWGA Charitable Foundation
6550 York Avenue South, Suite 211
Edina, MN 55435-2333
(952) 927-4643, ext. 11   Fax: (952) 927-9642
E-mail: paula@mwga-online.org
Web: www.mwga-online.org

Summary To provide financial assistance to female high school seniors in Minnesota who are interested in golf and plan to attend college in any state.

Eligibility This program is open to women who are graduating seniors at high schools in Minnesota planning to enroll full time at a 4-year college or university in any state. Applicants must be U.S. citizens who have an interest or involvement in the sport of golf, although skill or excellence in the game is not considered in the selection process. They must have a GPA of 3.2 or higher and be able to demonstrate financial need.

Financial data The stipend is $3,000 per year.

Duration 1 year; may be renewed up to 3 additional years.

Number awarded Varies each year; recently, 4 were awarded.

Deadline March of each year.

[456]
MISS AMERICA ACADEMIC ACHIEVEMENT AWARDS

The Miss America Foundation
1432 K Street, N.W., Suite 900
Washington, DC 20005
(609) 344-1800
Web: www.missamericafoundation.org/scholarships

Summary To recognize and reward, with college scholarships, women who participate in the Miss America Pageant at the state level and demonstrate academic excellence.

Eligibility This competition is open to women who compete at the state level of the Miss America Pageant. Selection is based on academic excellence (grades, course content, and academic standing of the institution).

Financial data The stipend is $1,000.

Duration 1 year.

Additional information This program, established in 1998, is administered by Scholarship Management Services, a division of Scholarship America.

Number awarded Up to 52 each year: 1 for each of the states, the District of Columbia, and the Virgin Islands.

Deadline Varies, depending upon the date of local pageants leading to the state finals.

[457]
MISS AMERICA COMMUNITY SERVICE AWARDS

The Miss America Foundation
1432 K Street, N.W., Suite 900
Washington, DC 20005
(609) 344-1800
Web: www.missamericafoundation.org/scholarships

Summary To recognize and reward, with college scholarships, women who participate in the Miss America Pageant at the state level and demonstrate outstanding community service.

Eligibility This competition is open to women who compete at the state level of the Miss America Pageant. Applicants must demonstrate that they have fulfilled a legitimate need in their community through the creation, development, and/or participation in a community service project. Selection is based on excellence of community service.

Financial data The stipend is $1,000.

Duration 1 year.

Additional information This program, established in 1998, is administered by Scholarship Management Services, a division of Scholarship America.

Number awarded Up to 52 each year: 1 for each of the states, the District of Columbia, and the Virgin Islands.

Deadline Varies, depending upon the date of local pageants leading to the state finals.

[458]
MISS AMERICA COMPETITION AWARDS

Miss America Organization
Attn: Director of Scholarships
Park Place and Boardwalk
P.O. Box 1919
Atlantic City, NJ 08404
(609) 653-8700, ext. 127   Fax: (609) 653-8740
E-mail: info@missamerica.org
Web: www.missamerica.org

Summary To provide educational scholarships to participants in the Miss America Pageant on local, state, and national levels.

Eligibility To enter an official Miss America Preliminary Pageant, candidates must meet certain basic requirements and agree to abide by all the rules of the local, state, and national Miss America Pageants. Among the qualifications required are that the applicant be female, between the ages of 17 and 24, a resident of the town or state in which they first compete, in good health, of good moral character, and a citizen of the United States. A complete list of all eligibility requirements is available from each local and state pageant. Separate scholarships are awarded to the winners of the talent competition and the lifestyle and fitness in swimsuit competition. Other special awards may be presented on a 1-time basis.

Financial data More than $45 million in cash and tuition assistance is awarded annually at the local, state, and national Miss America Pageants. At the national level, nearly $500,000 is awarded: Miss America receives $50,000 in scholarship money, the first runner-up $25,000, second runner-up $20,000, third runner-up $15,000, fourth runner-up $10,000, 5 other top 10 finalists $7,000 each, 2 other top 12 semifinalists $5,000 each, 3 other top 15 semifinalists $4,000 each, and other national contestants $3,000 each. Other awards include those for the 3 preliminary talent winners at $2,000 each, the 3 preliminary lifestyle and fitness in swimsuit winners at $1,000 each, the 5 non-finalist talent winners at $1,000 each, and the Miss Congeniality Award of $2,000.

Duration The pageants are held every year.

Additional information The Miss America Pageant has been awarding scholarships since 1945. Scholarships are to be used for tuition, room, board, supplies, and other college expenses. Use of the scholarships must begin within 4 years from the date of the award (5 years if the recipient is Miss America), unless a reasonable extension is requested and granted. Training under the scholarship should be continuous and completed within 10 years from the date the scholarship is activated; otherwise, the balance of the scholarship may be canceled without further notice.

Number awarded At the national level, 52 contestants (1 from each state, the District of Columbia, and the Virgin Islands) share the awards.

Deadline Varies, depending upon the date of local pageants leading to the state and national finals.

[459]
MISS AMERICA STEM SCHOLARSHIPS

The Miss America Foundation
1432 K Street, N.W., Suite 900
Washington, DC 20005
(609) 344-1800
Web: www.missamericafoundation.org/scholarships

Summary To recognize and reward, with college scholarships, women who participate in the Miss America Pageant at the national level and are majoring in a field of science, technology, engineering, or mathematics (STEM).

Eligibility This program is open to women who compete at the national level of the Miss America Pageant. Applicants must be enrolled or planning to enroll in college and major in a field of STEM.

Financial data The stipend is $5,000.

Duration 1 year.

Number awarded 5 each year.

Deadline Varies, depending upon the date of local pageants leading to the state and then national finals.

[460]
MISS AMERICA'S OUTSTANDING TEEN SCHOLARSHIPS

Miss America's Outstanding Teen, Inc.
Attn: Business and Scholarship Manager
12718 DuPont Circle, Suite A5B
Tampa, FL 33626
(813) 510-3237   E-mail: amanda@maoteen.org
Web: www.maoteen.org/scholarships

Summary To recognize and reward, with college scholarships, girls who are selected for the national finals of the Miss America's Outstanding Teen competition.

Eligibility These awards are presented to the girls who participate in the national finals of the Miss America's Outstanding Teen competition. Girls must be U.S. citizens between 13 and 17 years of age. They first enter a competition in their home state. Selection of scholarship winners is based on academic merit and civic and social achievement. Awards are also presented for Preliminary Evening Wear/On State Question, Preliminary Talent, Outstanding Vocal Talent, Outstanding Dance Talent, Outstanding Instrumental Talent, Outstanding Dance Talent, Scholastic Excellence, Outstanding Achievement in Academic Life, and First, Second, and Third Place Ad Sales.

Financial data Stipends are $25,000 for Miss America's Outstanding Teen, $10,000 for first runner-up, $7,500 for second runner-up, $5,000 for third runner-up, and $2,000 for fourth runner-up. Each of the 5 semi-finalists wins a $1,500 scholarship and all non-finalists win $1,000 scholarships. Other scholarships range from $500 to $2,000.

Duration The competition is held annually.

Number awarded All 52 girls (1 from each state plus 1 from the District of Columbia and 1 from the Virgin Islands) who compete in the Miss America's Outstanding Teen National Pageant receive at least 1 scholarship. A total of 76 scholarships is awarded each year.

Deadline Each state organization sets its own deadline; check with the national organization to learn the date in your state.

[461]
MISS TEEN OF AMERICA SCHOLARSHIPS

Miss Teen of America Organization
Attn: National Office
15600 Wayzata Boulevard, Suite 108
Wayzata, MN 55391
(952) 405-8882   E-mail: info@missteenofamerica.com
Web: www.missteenofamerica.com

Summary To recognize and reward, with college scholarships, teenaged girls who are selected as outstanding participants in the Miss Teen of American competition.

Eligibility To participate in the Miss Teen of America competition, girls must be between 13 and 18 years of age, never have been married or had a marriage annulled, or have been pregnant. Girls who win state titles advance to the Miss Teen of America National Pageant. Scholarships are awarded on the basis of academic record (15%), service and achievement to school and community (15%), personal development (15%), general awareness (15%), personality projection and poise in evening wear (15%), and judge's interview (25%).

Financial data Scholarships, presented as cash to the recipients, are $5,000 for Miss Teen of America, $750 for first runner-up, and $250 for second runner-up. Each Miss Teen of America state titleholder receives a $1,000 cash scholarship plus $250 cash to be used for Special Olympics inclusion event at her school in honor of the Miss Teen of America alliance with Special Olympics. Each Distinguished Youth of America state titleholder receives a $1,000 cash scholarship plus $100 cash to be used for Special Olympics inclusion event at her school in honor of the Miss Teen of America alliance with Special Olympics.

Duration The competition is held annually.

Number awarded Varies each year, depending on the number of states that select a local competition.

Deadline Each state pageant sets its own deadline; check with the National Office to learn the date in your state.

[462]
MISSOURI ANGUS AUXILIARY QUEEN PROGRAM

Missouri Angus Association
c/o Greg Connell, General Manager
P.O. Box 109
Eugene, MO 65032
(573) 694-6152   E-mail: connell@missouriangus.org
Web: www.missouriangus.org

Summary To recognize and reward, with college scholarships, young women in Missouri who are involved in the Angus cattle industry.

Eligibility This program is open to female members of the Missouri Junior Angus Association (MJAA) between 16 and 21 years of age. Applicants must be involved in the production and/or promotion of Angus cattle and be committed to the promotion of the breed. They must be willing to commit to attend several promotional events in Missouri (e.g., state fairs, livestock shows) and serve as a spokesperson for the association. Along with their application, they must submit a list of their school activities, a list of their community and/or service activities, information on their involvement in activities of the MJAA and the National Junior Angus Association (NJAA), an explanation of how their MJAA or NJAA experi-

ences positively impacted them and/or another person, and an explanation of why they wish to be selected for this honor.

Financial data The woman chosen as queen receives a $150 clothing allowance, round-trip mileage of 25 cents per mile for each of the required events, and a $50 lodging allowance for each night's stay at each required event. Upon successful completion of all required appearances and submission of a written report on her experience, she receives a $1,000 college scholarship.

Duration A queen is selected each year.

Number awarded 1 each year.

Deadline April of each year.

[463]
MISSOURI JOB'S DAUGHTERS SCHOLARSHIPS

International Order of Job's Daughters-Grand Guardian
   Council of Missouri
c/o Kathy Rodemacher, Scholarship and Loan Committee
   Chair
7836 Germania, Apartment A
St. Louis, MO 63111
(314) 578-1137   E-mail: momkathy54@sbcglobal.net
Web: www.mojdi.org/1/category/ggc

Summary To provide financial assistance to members of Job's Daughters in Missouri who are interested in attending college in any state.

Eligibility This program is open to residents of Missouri who have been an active member of a Missouri Job's Daughter Bethel for at least 1 year or are majority members younger than 25 years of age. Applicants must be attending or planning to attend a college or university in any state. Along with their application, they must submit 1) an essay describing how Job's Daughters has helped them develop leadership abilities and explaining how those relate to their everyday life; 2) an essay on the ways in which Job's Daughters has helped them to grow as an individual; 3) brief statements on their awards and honors in Job's Daughters, high school activities, church activities, community activities, and volunteer work. Their Executive Bethel Council must submit a letter of recommendation on why they are qualified to receive this scholarship and the contributions they have made to their Bethel. Selection is based on the applicant's essays and statements, the letter of recommendation, academic standing in high school or college, and contributions to Bethel and community.

Financial data A stipend is awarded (amount not specified).

Duration 1 year; recipients may reapply.

Number awarded Several each year.

Deadline March of each year.

[464]
MISSOURI WOMEN'S GOLF EDUCATION ASSOCIATION SCHOLARSHIPS

Missouri Women's Golf Association
Attn: Scholarship Director
1616 Oil Well Drive
P.O. Box 104164
Jefferson City, MO 65110
(573) 636-8994   Fax: (573) 636-4225
E-mail: Scholarship@mowomensga.org
Web: www.mowomensga.org/scholarship-application

Summary To provide financial assistance to female high school seniors in Missouri who have been involved in golf and plan to attend college in any state.

Eligibility This program is open to women graduating from high schools in Missouri or Johnson County, Kansas and planning to attend college in any state. Applicants must submit a copy of their high school transcript, a statement of their involvement in golf, a description of their involvement in community and school activities, a statement on their future field of study and educational path to success in that area, a statement of their future goals pertaining to golf, 3 personal references, an essay on the qualities that make them an excellent candidate for this scholarship, and a statement of their financial need. U.S. citizenship is required.

Financial data A stipend is awarded (amount not specified).

Duration 1 year; nonrenewable.

Additional information This program includes the Susan E. Shepherd Memorial Scholarship, funded by the Shepherd Foundation of St. Louis, and the Mary Jane Landreth Scholarship, established in 2006.

Number awarded Varies each year; recently, 8 were awarded.

Deadline March of each year.

[465]
MONTANA STATE WOMEN'S GOLF ASSOCIATION SCHOLARSHIPS

Montana State Women's Golf Association
c/o Carla Berg, Executive Secretary/Director
P.O. Box 52
Sidney, MT 59270
(406) 480-1912   E-mail: 1mswga@gmail.com
Web: www.msgagolf.org

Summary To provide financial assistance to women golfers in Montana who are entering college in any state.

Eligibility This program is open to female residents of Montana who are entering their freshman year at a college or university in any state. Applicants must have been involved with golf sometime (on a high school team or in a junior program), and have an official handicap issued by the Montana State Golf Association (MSGA). They must submit information on their high school golf playing record, amateur playing record, leadership positions, activities and organizations, community and volunteer service, and honors and awards. They must also submit a brief essay on their career aspirations and how they hope to achieve those life goals. Neither financial need nor skill in golf are considered in the selection process.

Financial data The stipend is $1,000.

Duration 1 year.

Additional information This program began in 1990.

Number awarded 1 or more each year.

Deadline March of each year.

[466]
MOSS ADAMS FOUNDATION SCHOLARSHIP

Educational Foundation for Women in Accounting
Attn: Foundation Administrator
136 South Keowee Street
Dayton, OH 45402
(937) 424-3391   Fax: (937) 222-5749
E-mail: info@efwa.org
Web: www.efwa.org/scholarships_graduate.php

Summary To provide financial support to women, including minority women, who are working on an accounting degree.

Eligibility This program is open to women who are enrolled in an accounting degree program at an accredited college or university. Applicants must meet 1 of the following criteria: 1) women pursuing a fifth-year requirement either through general studies or within a graduate program; 2) women returning to school as current or reentry juniors or seniors; or 3) minority women. Selection is based on aptitude for accounting and business, commitment to the goal of working on a degree in accounting (including evidence of continued commitment after receiving this award), clear evidence that the candidate has established goals and a plan for achieving those goals (both personal and professional), financial need, and a demonstration of how the scholarship will impact her life. U.S. citizenship is required.

Financial data The stipend is $1,000.

Duration 1 year.

Additional information This program was established by Rowling, Dold & Associates LLP, a woman-owned C.P.A. firm based in San Diego. It was renamed when that firm merged with Moss Adams LLP.

Number awarded 2 each year: 1 to an undergraduate and 1 to a graduate student.

Deadline April of each year.

[467]
MOTHERS RETURNING TO SCHOOL CAREER STEP SCHOLARSHIPS

Career Step
Attn: Scholarship Committee
4692 North 300 West, Suite 150
Provo, UT 84604
(801) 489-9393   Toll Free: (800) 411-7073
Fax: (801) 491-6645
E-mail: scholarships@careerstep.com
Web: www.careerstep.com/scholarships

Summary To provide financial assistance to mothers who plan to return to college to benefit their family and/or community.

Eligibility This program is open to mothers who are enrolled or planning to enroll at a college, university, or vocational/technical school. There is no age requirement. Applicants must submit an essay and/or video of 800 to 1,000 words on how they plan to use their education to benefit their family and/or community. Essays should cite specific experiences that encouraged them to continue their education or specific situations where they can apply their skills.

Financial data The stipend is $2,000. Funds are sent directly to the recipient's institution.

Duration 1 year.

Number awarded   3 each year: 1 for each cycle.

Deadline   April, August, or December of each year.

[468]
MRS. DEXTER OTIS ARNOLD SCHOLARSHIP

General Federation of Women's Clubs of New Hampshire
c/o Judy McPhail, Scholarship Chair
94 Primrose Lane
Penacook, NH 03303
E-mail: info@gfwcnh.org
Web: www.gfwcnh.org

Summary   To provide financial assistance to female high school seniors in New Hampshire who plan to attend college in the state.

Eligibility   This program is open to female seniors graduating from high schools in New Hampshire and planning to attend an accredited college, university, or technical/specialty school in the state. Applicants must submit a 1-page essay on their reasons for pursuing further education, their intended major, and why they consider themselves a worthy applicant for this scholarship. Selection is based on academic achievement, community service, leadership, individual determination, school activities, and financial need.

Financial data   The stipend is $1,200.

Duration   1 year.

Number awarded   1 each year.

Deadline   March of each year.

[469]
MSCPA WOMEN IN ACCOUNTING SCHOLARSHIP

Massachusetts Society of Certified Public Accountants
Attn: MSCPA Educational Foundation
105 Chauncy Street, Tenth Floor
Boston, MA 02111
(617) 556-4000   Toll Free: (800) 392-6145
Fax: (617) 556-4126   E-mail: info@mscpaonline.org
Web: www.cpatrack.com/scholarships

Summary   To provide financial assistance to women from Massachusetts working on an undergraduate or graduate degree in accounting at a college or university in the state.

Eligibility   This program is open to female Massachusetts residents enrolled at a college or university in the state. Applicants must be undergraduates who have completed the first semester of their junior year or graduate students. They must be able to demonstrate financial need, academic excellence, and an intention to prepare for a career as a Certified Public Accountant (C.P.A.) at a firm in Massachusetts.

Financial data   The stipend is $2,500.

Duration   1 year.

Additional information   This program is sponsored by the Women's Golf Committee of the Massachusetts Society of Certified Public Accountants (MSCPA).

Number awarded   Varies each year; recently, 4 were awarded.

Deadline   March of each year.

[470]
MTS SYSTEMS SCHOLARSHIP

Society of Women Engineers-Minnesota Section
Attn: Scholarship Committee
P.O. Box 18481
Minneapolis, MN 55418
E-mail: scholarships@swe-mn.org
Web: www.swe-mn.org/scholarships.html

Summary   To provide financial assistance to women from any state working on an undergraduate or graduate degree in software or mechanical engineering at colleges and universities in Minnesota, North Dakota, and South Dakota.

Eligibility   This program is open to female undergraduate and graduate students at ABET-accredited engineering programs in Minnesota, North Dakota, or South Dakota. Applicants must be working full time on a degree in software or mechanical engineering. Along with their application, they must submit a 250-word essay describing how they plan to utilize their engineering knowledge and skills after they graduate. Selection is based on potential to succeed as an engineer (20 points), communication skills (10 points), extracurricular or community involvement and leadership skills (10 points), demonstration of work experience and successes (10 points), and academic success (5 points).

Financial data   The stipend is $1,500.

Duration   1 year.

Additional information   This program is sponsored by MTS Systems Corporation.

Number awarded   1 each year.

Deadline   March of each year.

[471]
MUSIC THERAPY SCHOLARSHIP

Sigma Alpha Iota Philanthropies, Inc.
One Tunnel Road
Asheville, NC 28805
(828) 251-0606   Fax: (828) 251-0644
E-mail: nh@sai-national.org
Web: app.smarterselect.com

Summary   To provide financial assistance to members of Sigma Alpha Iota (an organization of women musicians) who are working on an undergraduate or graduate degree in music therapy.

Eligibility   This program is open to members of the organization who have completed at least 2 years of study for an undergraduate or graduate degree in music therapy. Applicants must submit an essay that includes their personal definition of music therapy, their career plans and professional goals as a music therapist, and why they feel they are deserving of this scholarship. Selection is based on music therapy skills, musicianship, fraternity service, community service, leadership, self-reliance, and dedication to the field of music therapy as a career.

Financial data   The stipend is $1,500.

Duration   1 year.

Number awarded   1 each year.

Deadline   March of each year.

[472]
MUSICIANS WITH SPECIAL NEEDS SCHOLARSHIP

Sigma Alpha Iota Philanthropies, Inc.
One Tunnel Road
Asheville, NC 28805
(828) 251-0606   Fax: (828) 251-0644
E-mail: nh@sai-national.org
Web: app.smarterselect.com

Summary To provide financial assistance for college or graduate school to members of Sigma Alpha Iota (an organization of women musicians) who have a disability and are working on a degree in music.

Eligibility This program is open to members of the organization who either 1) have a sensory or physical impairment and are enrolled in a graduate or undergraduate degree program in music; or 2) are preparing to become a music teacher or therapist for people with disabilities. Performance majors must submit a 15-minute DVD of their work; non-performance majors must submit evidence of work in their area of specialization, such as composition, musicology, or research.

Financial data The stipend is $1,500.

Duration 1 year.

Number awarded 1 each year.

Deadline March of each year.

[473]
MWV SCHOLARSHIPS

Society of Women Engineers
Attn: Scholarship Selection Committee
203 North LaSalle Street, Suite 1675
Chicago, IL 60601-1269
(312) 596-5223   Toll Free: (877) SWE-INFO
Fax: (312) 644-8557   E-mail: scholarships@swe.org
Web: societyofwomenengineers.swe.org

Summary To provide financial assistance to members of the Society of Women Engineers (SWE) who are interested in studying specified fields of engineering at designated universities.

Eligibility This program is open to SWE members who are entering their sophomore, junior, or senior year at North Carolina State University, Auburn University, Texas A&M University, Clemson University, Virginia Commonwealth University, Pennsylvania State University, Georgia Institute of Technology, North Carolina A&T State University, or Virginia Polytechnic Institute and State University. Applicants must be enrolled full time and majoring in computer science or chemical, electrical, industrial or mechanical engineering. They must be U.S. citizens. Selection is based on merit.

Financial data The stipend is $3,000.

Duration 1 year.

Additional information This program is sponsored by MWV, formerly MeadWestvaco.

Number awarded 3 each year.

Deadline February of each year.

[474]
MYRT WILLEY SCHOLARSHIP

Zonta Club of Bangor
c/o Barbara A. Cardone
P.O. Box 1904
Bangor, ME 04402-1904
Web: www.zontaclubofbangor.org/?area=scholarship

Summary To provide financial assistance to women attending or planning to attend college in Maine and major in a business-related field.

Eligibility This program is open to women who are attending or planning to attend an accredited 2- or 4-year college in Maine. Applicants must major in a business-related field. Along with their application, they must submit brief essays on 1) their goals in seeking higher education and their plans for the future; and 2) any school and community activities that have been of particular importance to them and why they found them worthwhile. Financial need may be considered in the selection process.

Financial data The stipend is $1,000.

Duration 1 year.

Number awarded 1 each year.

Deadline March of each year.

[475]
MYRTLE CREASMAN SCHOLARSHIP

Tennessee Baptist Convention
Attn: WMU Scholarships
330 Seven Springs Way
P.O. Box 728
Brentwood, TN 37024-9728
(615) 371-7919   Toll Free: (800) 558-2090, ext. 7919
Fax: (615) 371-2014   E-mail: jheath@tnbaptist.org
Web: www.tnbaptist.org

Summary To provide financial assistance to female members of Baptist churches in Tennessee who have been active in Baptist mission programs and are attending college in any state.

Eligibility This program is open to women who are members and active participants in a Tennessee Baptist church and currently enrolled as full-time undergraduates at a college or university in any state. Applicants must be currently serving as a missions volunteer and preparing for a career in missions or a church-related vocation. They must have an "A" average for high school and a GPA of 3.5 or higher for college. Financial need is considered in the selection process.

Financial data A stipend is awarded (amount not specified).

Duration 1 year.

Number awarded 1 each year.

Deadline January of each year.

[476]
NACOPRW NY SCHOLARSHIP

National Conference of Puerto Rican Women-New York
  Chapter
Attn: Scholarship Chair
P.O. Box 469 Lenox Hill Station
New York, NY 10021
(276) 690-9196
E-mail: scholarshipchair@nacoprwnewyork.org
Web: www.nacoprwnewyork.org/scholarships

Summary To provide financial assistance to Puerto Rican women who are residents of New York and interested in attending college in any state.

Eligibility This program is open to women who are residents of New York and of Puerto Rican heritage by birth or descent through maternal lineage. Applicants must be enrolled or planning to enroll at a college, university, or trade/vocational school in any state. They must have a GPA of at least 3.0 in high school, college, or university or 2.5 in trade/vocational school. Along with their application, they must submit a 250-word essay describing their career goals and explaining what this award means to them.

Financial data The stipend is $1,500.

Duration 1 year.

Additional information Recipients must commit to up to 10 hours of community service during the academic year.

Number awarded 1 or more each year.

Deadline June of each year.

[477]
NACOPRW SCHOLARSHIP AWARD

National Conference of Puerto Rican Women-Miami
  Chapter
c/o Zoraida Sequinot, President
1506 East Mowry Drive
Homestead, FL 33033
(305) 247-9925   E-mail: NACOPRW.MIAMI@gmail.com
Web: www.nacoprwmiami.org/category/scholarship-awards

Summary To provide financial assistance for college to Puerto Rican women.

Eligibility This program is open to women who are Puerto Rican by birth or descent. Applicants must have been admitted to an accredited college or university in the United States or Puerto Rico. They must have a GPA of 3.0 or higher and be able to demonstrate financial need.

Financial data The stipend is approximately $1,000.

Duration 1 year.

Additional information The National Conference of Puerto Rican Women (NACOPRW) "promotes the full participation of Puerto Rican and other Hispanic women in the economic, social and political life of the United States and Puerto Rico."

Number awarded 2 each year.

Deadline April of each year.

[478]
NAHB PROFESSIONAL WOMEN IN BUILDING STRATEGIES FOR SUCCESS SCHOLARSHIP

National Housing Endowment
1201 15th Street, N.W.
Washington, DC 20005
(202) 266-8069   Toll Free: (800) 368-5242, ext. 8069
Fax: (202) 266-8177   E-mail: scholarships@nahb.com
Web: www.nationalhousingendowment.org

Summary To provide financial assistance to undergraduate students, especially women, interested in preparing for a career in the building industry.

Eligibility This program is open to current undergraduates who are enrolled full time at a 2- or 4-year college or university or a vocational program. Applicants must be working on or planning to work on a degree in a housing-related program, such as construction management, building, construction technology, civil engineering, architecture, design, or a trade specialty. They must have at least a 2.5 GPA in all courses and at least a 3.0 GPA in core curriculum classes. Preference is given to 1) women; 2) applicants who would be unable to afford college without financial assistance; and 3) students who are current members (or will be members in the upcoming semester) of a student chapter of the National Association of Home Builders (NAHB). Along with their application, they must submit an essay on their reasons for becoming a professional in the housing industry and their career goals. Selection is based on financial need, career goals, academic achievement, employment history, extracurricular activities, and letters of recommendation.

Financial data The stipend is $2,000. Funds are made payable to the recipient and sent to the recipient's school.

Duration 1 year; may be renewed.

Additional information The National Housing Endowment is the philanthropic arm of the National Association of Home Builders (NAHB). Its women's council established this scholarship in 2001.

Number awarded Varies each year; recently, 11 were awarded. Since this program began, it has awarded nearly $30,500 to 32 students.

Deadline March of each year.

[479]
NANCY ANNE WEINSTEIN SCHOLARSHIP

Accounting and Financial Women's Alliance-Richmond
  Chapter
c/o Marie J. Ramkey, Scholarship Committee Chair
Patton Tax Group, LLC
7201 Glen Forest Drive, Suite 205
Richmond, VA 23226
(804) 357-2837   E-mail: MJramkey@comcast.net
Web: www.aswarichmond.org/scholar.htm

Summary To provide financial assistance to nontraditional female students at colleges in the Richmond area of North Carolina working on a degree in accounting or finance.

Eligibility This program is open to women from any state who have had to delay starting or completing a college degree. Applicants must be attending a college, university, or professional school of accounting in the Richmond area. They must be entering their third, fourth, or fifth year of study with a declared major in accounting or finance and a have

GPA of 3.0 or higher. Along with their application, they must submit an essay of 150 to 250 words on their career goals and objectives, the impact they want to have on the accounting and financial world, community involvement, and leadership examples. Selection is based on leadership, character, communication skills, scholastic average, and financial need. Membership in the Accounting and Financial Women's Alliance (AFWA) is not required.

Financial data A stipend is awarded (amount not specified).

Duration 1 year.

Number awarded 2 each year.

Deadline February of each year.

[480]
NANCY KELLY FEMALE WRITER AWARD

Philanthrofund Foundation
Attn: Scholarship Committee
1409 Willow Street, Suite 109
Minneapolis, MN 55403-2241
(612) 870-1806   Toll Free: (800) 435-1402
Fax: (612) 871-6587   E-mail: info@PfundOnline.org
Web: www.pfundonline.org/scholarships.html

Summary To provide financial assistance to female Minnesota students who have supported gay, lesbian, bisexual, and transgender (GLBT) activities and are interested in studying writing.

Eligibility This program is open to female residents of Minnesota and students attending a Minnesota educational institution. Applicants must be self-identified as GLBT or from a GLBT family. They may be attending or planning to attend trade school, technical college, college, or university (as an undergraduate or graduate student) to study writing. Preference is given to students in a liberal arts program or studying writing from a liberal arts perspective. Selection is based on the applicant's 1) affirmation of GLBT or allied identity; 2) evidence of experience and skills in service and leadership; and 3) evidence of service, leading, and working for change in GLBT communities, including serving as a role model, mentor, and/or adviser.

Financial data The stipend is $2,000. Funds must be used for tuition, books, fees, or dissertation expenses.

Duration 1 year.

Number awarded 1 each year.

Deadline January of each year.

[481]
NANCY LORRAINE JENSEN MEMORIAL SCHOLARSHIP FUND

Sons of Norway
Attn: Foundation
1455 West Lake Street
Minneapolis, MN 55408-2666
(612) 827-3611   Toll Free: (800) 945-8851
Fax: (612) 827-0658   E-mail: foundation@sofn.com
Web: www.sofn.com/foundation/grants_and_scholarships

Summary To provide financial assistance to women who have a connection to the Sons of Norway and are interested in studying chemistry, physics, or engineering in college.

Eligibility This program is open to women who are U.S. citizens between 17 and 35 years of age and members (or

daughters or granddaughters of members) of the Sons of Norway; they must have been a member for at least 3 years. Applicants must have a combined SAT score of 1800 or higher, a mathematics score of 600 or higher, or an ACT score of 26 or higher. They must be full-time undergraduate students and have completed at least 1 quarter or semester of study in chemistry, physics, or chemical, electrical, or mechanical engineering. Selection is based on long-term career goals, clarity of study plan, academic potential, evidence of ability to succeed, and letters of recommendation attesting to good character, eagerness, earnestness, and ambition in the field of science or engineering.

Financial data Stipends range from 50% of tuition for 1 quarter or semester to 100% for 1 year. Grants are issued jointly to the recipient and her institution.

Duration Awards are made for either 1 term (quarter or semester) or 1 year; a student may receive up to 3 awards as an undergraduate.

Additional information This fund was established in 1995 by Dr. and Mrs. Arthur S. Jensen in memory of their daughter, a chemical engineer whose work resulted in advances in the field of weather satellite photography and who died at the age of 35.

Number awarded Varies each year; recently, 4 were awarded.

Deadline March of each year.

[482]
NANNIE W. NORFLEET SCHOLARSHIP

American Legion Auxiliary
Department of North Carolina
P.O. Box 25726
Raleigh, NC 27611-5726
(919) 832-4051   Fax: (919) 832-1888
E-mail: ncala@ncrrbiz.com
Web: www.alanorthcarolina.com

Summary To provide financial assistance to members of the American Legion Auxiliary in North Carolina and their children and grandchildren who plan to attend college in any state.

Eligibility This program is open to North Carolina residents who are either adult members of the American Legion Auxiliary or high school seniors (with preference to the children and grandchildren of members). Applicants must be interested in attending college in any state. They must be able to demonstrate financial need.

Financial data The stipend is $1,000.

Duration 1 year.

Number awarded 1 each year.

Deadline March of each year.

[483]
NATHALIE A. PRICE MEMORIAL SCHOLARSHIP

Ocean State Women's Golf Association
P.O. Box 597
Portsmouth, RI 02871-0597
(401) 683-6301   E-mail: oswgari@aol.com
Web: www.oswga.org

Summary To provide financial assistance to women in Rhode Island who have played golf and are interested in attending college in any state.

Eligibility This program is open to women in Rhode Island who are graduating high school seniors or current students under 25 years of age at a college or university in any state. Applicants must have been active in golf, as a member of the Ocean State Women's Golf Association (OSWGA), as a member of another association, or on their school golf team. They must have a GPA of 2.5 or higher. Along with their application, they must submit a transcript, a list of their citizenship and community service activities, and letters of recommendation. Financial need is not considered.

Financial data A stipend is awarded (amount not specified).

Duration 1 year; may be renewed.

Additional information This program began in 1996.

Number awarded Varies each year; recently, 7 were awarded.

Deadline June of each year.

[484]
NATIONAL JCDA SCHOLARSHIP

Catholic Daughters of the Americas
Attn: Scholarship Chair
10 West 71st Street
New York, NY 10023
(212) 877-3041   Fax: (212) 724-5923
E-mail: CDofANatl@aol.com
Web: www.catholicdaughters.org

Summary To provide financial assistance for college to members of the Junior Catholic Daughters of the Americas (JCDA).

Eligibility This program is open to students entering their freshman year of college who have been JCDA members for at least 2 years. Applicants must submit a 500-word essay on a topic that changes annually but relates to their Catholic faith. Financial need is not considered in the selection process.

Financial data The stipend is $1,000.

Duration 1 year.

Number awarded 1 each year.

Deadline April of each year.

[485]
NATIONAL ORGANIZATION OF ITALIAN AMERICAN WOMEN SCHOLARSHIPS

National Organization of Italian American Women
25 West 43rd Street, Suite 1005
New York, NY 10036
(212) 642-2003   Fax: (212) 642-2006
E-mail: noiaw@noiaw.org
Web: www.noiaw.org/scholarships

Summary To provide financial assistance for college or graduate school to women of Italian descent.

Eligibility This program is open to women who have at least 1 parent of Italian American descent and are working on an associate, bachelor's, or master's degree. Applicants must be enrolled full time at a 4-year college or university and have a GPA of 3.5 or higher. Along with their application, they must submit a 2-page essay on how being an Italian American has impacted them personally and professionally. U.S. citizenship is required. Financial need is considered in the selection process. Preference is given to 1) students enrolled at the City

University of New York (CUNY) system; and 2) students majoring in Italian language and/or culture.

Financial data The stipend is $2,000.

Duration 1 year; nonrenewable.

Additional information A processing fee of $25 must accompany the application.

Number awarded 5 each year, including 1 reserved for an undergraduate or graduate student at the CUNY system.

Deadline March of each year.

[486]
NATIONAL PATHFINDER SCHOLARSHIPS

National Federation of Republican Women
Attn: Scholarship Coordinator
124 North Alfred Street
Alexandria, VA 22314-3011
(703) 548-9688   Fax: (703) 548-9836
E-mail: mail@nfrw.org
Web: www.nfrw.org/pathfinder

Summary To provide financial assistance for college or graduate school to Republican women.

Eligibility This program is open to women currently enrolled as college sophomores, juniors, seniors, or master's degree students. Recent high school graduates and first-year college women are not eligible. Applicants must submit 3 letters of recommendation, an official transcript, a 1-page essay on why they should be considered for the scholarship, and a 1-page essay on career goals. Applications must be submitted to the Republican federation president in the applicant's state. Each president chooses 1 application from her state to submit for scholarship consideration. Financial need is not a factor in the selection process. U.S. citizenship is required.

Financial data The stipend is $2,500.

Duration 1 year; nonrenewable.

Additional information This program, previously named the Nancy Reagan Pathfinder Scholarships, was established in 1985.

Number awarded 3 each year.

Deadline Applications must be submitted to the state federation president by May of each year.

[487]
NATIONAL SPACE GRANT COLLEGE AND FELLOWSHIP PROGRAM

National Aeronautics and Space Administration
Attn: Office of Education
300 E Street, S.W.
Mail Suite 6M35
Washington, DC 20546-0001
(202) 358-1069   Fax: (202) 358-7097
E-mail: aleksandra.korobov@nasa.gov
Web: www.nasa.gov

Summary To provide financial assistance to undergraduate and graduate students interested in preparing for a career in a space-related field.

Eligibility This program is open to undergraduate and graduate students at colleges and universities that participate in the National Space Grant program of the U.S. National Aeronautics and Space Administration (NASA) through their state consortium. Applicants must be interested in a program of study and/or research in a field of science, technology, engineering, or mathematics (STEM) related to space. A specific goal of the program is to recruit and train U.S. citizens, especially underrepresented minorities, women, and persons with disabilities, for careers in aerospace science and technology. Financial need is not considered in the selection process.

Financial data Each consortium establishes the terms of the fellowship program in its state.

Additional information NASA established the Space Grant program in 1989. It operates through 52 consortia in each state, the District of Columbia, and Puerto Rico. Each consortium includes selected colleges and universities in that state as well as other affiliates from industry, museums, science centers, and state and local agencies.

Number awarded Varies each year.

Deadline Each consortium sets its own deadlines.

[488]
NATIONAL STRENGTH AND CONDITIONING ASSOCIATION WOMEN'S SCHOLARSHIPS

National Strength and Conditioning Association
Attn: NSCA Foundation
1885 Bob Johnson Drive
Colorado Springs, CO 80906-4000
(719) 632-6722, ext. 152   Toll Free: (800) 815-6826
Fax: (719) 632-6367   E-mail: foundation@nsca.org
Web: www.nsca.com/foundation/nsca-scholarships

Summary To provide financial assistance to women who are interested in working on an undergraduate or graduate degree in strength training and conditioning.

Eligibility This program is open to women who are 17 years of age or older. Applicants must have been accepted into an accredited postsecondary institution to work on an undergraduate or graduate degree in the strength and conditioning field. Along with their application, they must submit a 500-word essay on their personal and professional goals and how receiving this scholarship will assist them in achieving those goals. Selection is based on that essay, academic achievement, strength and conditioning experience, honors and awards, community involvement, letters of recommendation, and involvement in the National Strength and Conditioning Association (NSCA).

Financial data The stipend is $1,500.

Duration 1 year.

Additional information The NSCA is a nonprofit organization of strength and conditioning professionals, including coaches, athletic trainers, physical therapists, educators, researchers, and physicians. This program began in 2003.

Number awarded Varies each year; recently, 9 were awarded.

Deadline March of each year.

[489]
NATIONAL YOUNG WOMEN OF DISTINCTION SCHOLARSHIPS

Girl Scouts of the United States of America
420 Fifth Avenue
New York, NY 10018-2798
Toll Free: (800) GSUSA-4-U
Web: www.girlscouts.org

Summary To provide financial assistance for college to Girl Scouts who complete outstanding Gold Award projects.

Eligibility This program is open to members of Girl Scouts in grades 9-12 who have received their Gold Award. Applicants must be nominated by their local council, each of which may nominate 3 of its Gold Award recipients during the current year. The Gold Award projects must demonstrate extraordinary leadership, have a measurable and sustainable impact, and address a local challenge related to a national and/or global issue.

Financial data The stipend is $5,000.

Duration 1 year (the freshman year of college).

Additional information Funding for this program is provided by the Kappa Delta Foundation, the charitable arm of Kappa Delta Sorority.

Number awarded 10 each year.

Deadline Girls submit their application to local councils, which set their own deadlines. Councils submit their nominations during April.

[490]
NATIVE DAUGHTERS OF THE GOLDEN WEST SCHOLARSHIPS

Native Daughters of the Golden West
Attn: Education and Scholarships
543 Baker Street
San Francisco, CA 94117-1405
(415) 563-9091   Toll Free: (800) 994-NDGW
Fax: (415) 563-5230   E-mail: ndgwgpo@att.net
Web: www.ndgw.org/edu.htm

Summary To provide financial assistance to members of the Native Daughters of the Golden West (NDGW) in California and their families who are interested in attending a campus of the University of California or the California State University system.

Eligibility This program is open to members and their children who are attending or planning to attend a campus of the University of California or the California State University system. Applicants must be high school seniors or undergraduates who have completed the first year of college with a GPA of 3.0 or higher. They must have been born in the state and be sponsored by a local parlor of the NDGW.

Financial data The stipend is $1,350.

Duration 1 year; may be renewed if the recipient maintains a GPA of 3.0 or higher.

Number awarded 3 each year.

Deadline April of each year.

[491]
NAWIC DE CHAPTER 96 SCHOLARSHIP

National Association of Women in Construction-
   Wilmington Chapter 96
Attn: Gladys King, Scholarship Chair
P.O. Box 96
Montchanin, DE 19710
(302) 285-3630   E-mail: mail@nawicde.org
Web: www.nawicde.org/scholarships-block-kids

Summary To provide financial assistance to female residents of Delaware who are interested in attending college in any state to prepare for a career in construction.

Eligibility This program is open to female residents of Delaware who are interested in working full or part time on an associate or bachelor's degree in a construction-related program, including engineering, at a school in any state. Applicants may be high school seniors, high school graduates, or currently-enrolled college students. Selection is based on GPA, interest in construction, extracurricular activities, employment experience, academic adviser evaluation, and financial need.

Financial data Stipends range from $500 to $1,000.

Duration 1 year; may be renewed, provided the recipient maintains a GPA of 2.5 or higher.

Number awarded 1 or more each year.

Deadline March of each year.

[492]
NCTA/AWM JOINT SCHOLARSHIP

Alliance for Women in Media
Attn: Foundation
2365 Harrodsburg Road, Suite A325
Lexington, KY 40504
(202) 750-3664   E-mail: info@allwomeninmedia.org
Web: www.allwomeninmedia.org/foundation/scholarships

Summary To provide financial assistance to women who are working on an undergraduate or graduate degree in a media-related field and submit project concepts on topics related to media.

Eligibility This program is open to women currently enrolled in an undergraduate or graduate degree program at a college or university in any state. Applicants must be preparing for a media career and working on a degree in such fields as cable, communications, television, radio, digital media, publishing, journalism, advertising, production, creative design, or related areas. Along with their application, they must submit a project concept from a list of 3 industry-specific topics. Recently, the topics were 1) the significance in today's society of digital literacy and 21st literacy skills; 2) a forecast of trends in new and digital media as they may affect providers and users of services; or 3) cable industry public policy viewpoints. They must also submit a statement about why they consider the topic to be important.

Financial data The winner receives a stipend of $3,000, payable to her educational institution, and up to $350 to reimburse expenses for her and the person she highlights to attend the sponsor's Women in Media event in New York. The runner-up receives a $2,000 stipend, payable to her educational institution.

Duration 1 year.

Additional information This program in partnership with the National Cable and Telecommunications Association (NCTA).

Number awarded 2 each year.

Deadline April.

[493]
NETWORK OF EXECUTIVE WOMEN SCHOLARSHIP

Network of Executive Women
Attn: Scholarship Program
c/o Accenture
161 North Clark Street, 38th Floor
Chicago, IL 60601
(312) 693-6855   Fax: (312) 726-4704
E-mail: connect@newonline.org
Web: www.newonline.org/page/scholarships

Summary To provide financial assistance to upper-division and graduate student women preparing for a career in the retail, consumer goods, or service industries.

Eligibility This program is open to women enrolled full time as juniors, seniors, or graduate students in a retail, consumer goods, or service industry program at a U.S. college or university. Applicants must have a GPA of 3.0 or higher. Along with their application, they must submit a 1-page essay explaining why they merit this scholarship and outlining their retail, consumer goods, or service industry interests. Selection is based on that essay, a current resume, a transcript, and 2 letters of recommendation; financial need is not considered. U.S. citizenship is required.

Financial data The stipend is $5,000.

Duration 1 year.

Number awarded Varies each year; recently, 5 were awarded.

Deadline April of each year.

[494]
NEW HAMPSHIRE WOMEN'S GOLF ASSOCIATION SCHOLARSHIPS

New Hampshire Women's Golf Association
c/o Mary Jane Cormier, Scholarship Committee
4 Wyndmere Drive
Londonderry, NH 03053
(603) 867-0606   E-mail: info@nhwga.org
Web: www.nhwga.org/juniors/scholarship-info

Summary To provide financial assistance to members of the New Hampshire Women's Golf Association (NHWGA) and their families who are attending college in any state.

Eligibility This program is open to residents of New Hampshire who are enrolled as a full-time undergraduate student at an accredited college or university in any state. Applicants must be members or relatives of members of the NHWGA. Along with their application, they must submit an essay describing their education and career goals, why they have chosen their course of study, and the job or career they are considering. Selection is based on the essay, academic record, extracurricular activities, community and volunteer activities, work experience, and financial need.

Financial data Stipends are at least $1,000.

Duration 1 year.

Additional information This program began in 1970.

Number awarded Varies each year; recently, 9 of these scholarships, worth a total of $12,000, were awarded. Since this program began, it has awarded more than $350,000 in scholarships.

Deadline April of each year.

[495]
NEW HORIZONS LEADER SCHOLARSHIP

Royal Neighbors of America
Attn: Fraternal Services
230 16th Street
Rock Island, IL 61201-8645
(309) 788-4561   Toll Free: (800) 627-4762
E-mail: contact@royalneighbors.org
Web: www.royalneighbors.org

Summary To provide financial assistance to women who are members of the Royal Neighbors of America and interested in attending college.

Eligibility This program is open to female beneficial members of the society who are 18 years of age or older and planning to enroll as a full- or part-time student at an accredited college, university, or junior college. They must have previously graduated from high school.

Financial data The stipend is $5,000 per year.

Duration 1 year; may be renewed up to 3 additional years.

Number awarded 1 each year.

Deadline February of each year.

[496]
NEW JERSEY SCHOOLWOMEN'S CLUB SCHOLARSHIPS

New Jersey Schoolwomen's Club
c/o Judy Jordan
67 Spray Way
Lavalette, NJ 08735

Summary To provide financial assistance to female high school seniors in New Jersey who plan to attend college in any state to prepare for a career in education.

Eligibility This program is open to women graduating from high schools in New Jersey who plan to attend a college or university in any state to work on a baccalaureate degree and certification in education. Applicants must have a GPA of 3.0 or higher and scores of at least 1460 on the SAT or 24 on the ACT. Along with their application, they must submit a 500-word essay on why they have chosen the field of education as a career, what they anticipate their area of concentration will be, and the contributions they expect to make to their students and to the profession during their career. Financial need is not considered in the selection process.

Financial data Stipends are $1,000 or $500.

Duration 1 year.

Additional information This program includes the Jeannette Hodge Scholarship and the Patricia Barber Scholarship.

Number awarded 4 each year: 2 at $1,000 (the 2 named scholarships) and 2 at $500.

Deadline February of each year.

[497]
NEW MEXICO FEDERATION OF REPUBLICAN WOMEN SCHOLARSHIP

New Mexico Federation of Republican Women
c/o Barbara McClain, President
2884 Panorama Heights
Albuquerque, NM 87124
(505) 892-3330   E-mail: barbmcclain70@gmail.com
Web: nmfrw.com

Summary To provide financial assistance for college in New Mexico to women who reside in the state and are Republicans or daughters of Republicans.

Eligibility This program is open to women who are seniors graduating from high schools in New Mexico and planning to enroll at a college, university, or vocational school in the state. Applicants must be registered Republicans or, if younger than 18 years of age, daughters of registered Republicans. Along with their application, they must submit a brief letter outlining their college major, their future goals, and how this scholarship will assist them in realizing those goals.

Financial data The stipend is $1,500.

Duration 1 year.

Number awarded 1 each year.

Deadline March of each year.

[498]
NFWL/NRA SCHOLARSHIP PROGRAM

National Foundation for Women Legislators, Inc.
1727 King Street, Suite 300
Alexandria, VA 22314
(703) 518-7931   E-mail: meghan@womenlegislators.org
Web: www.womenlegislators.org/programs/scholarships

Summary To recognize and reward, with college scholarships, the best essays written by female high school juniors or seniors on a topic related to the Constitution.

Eligibility This competition is open to female high school juniors or seniors. Applicants are invited to write an essay of 400 to 600 words on a topic (changes annually) related to the Constitution; recently, students were given their choice of 4 topics related to the 19th Amendment. In addition to the essay, candidates must submit 2 personal reference letters.

Financial data Each winner receives a $3,000 unrestricted scholarship to use toward college tuition at any U.S. college or university and an all-expense paid trip to the foundation's annual conference.

Duration The competition is held annually.

Additional information This essay competition is sponsored jointly by the National Foundation of Women Legislators (NFWL) and the National Rifle Association (NRA).

Number awarded 6 each year.

Deadline July of each year.

[499]
NINA BELLE REDDITT MEMORIAL SCHOLARSHIP

American Business Women's Association-Pirate Charter Chapter
Attn: Scholarship Program
P.O. Box 20498
Greenville, NC 27858-0498
E-mail: pirateabwascholarship@yahoo.com

Summary To provide financial assistance to female residents of North Carolina interested in working on an undergraduate or graduate degree at a school in the state.

Eligibility This program is open to women who are residents of North Carolina and U.S. citizens. Applicants must be graduating high school seniors, undergraduates, or graduate students and have a GPA of 2.5 or higher. They must be attending or planning to attend an accredited college, university, community college, or vocational/technical school in

North Carolina. Along with their application, they must submit a 2-page biographical sketch that includes information about their background, school activities, outside interests, honors and awards, work experience, community service, and long-term goals. Financial need is not considered in the selection process.

Financial data The stipend is $5,000.

Duration 1 year.

Additional information This program began in 1978.

Number awarded 2 each year.

Deadline May of each year.

[500]
NMC SCHOLARSHIP PROGRAM

National Museum of Women in the Arts-New Mexico
  Committee
Attn: Scholarships
P.O. Box 31314
Santa Fe, NM 87594
E-mail: womenintheartsnm@gmail.com
Web: www.newmexicowomeninthearts.org

Summary To provide financial assistance to women from New Mexico who are currently studying art at a school in any state.

Eligibility This program is open to women who are residents of New Mexico and working on an undergraduate degree in art. Applicants must be enrolled as juniors or seniors at an accredited institution in any state. They must be able to demonstrate exceptional talent and creativity in 1 or more fields of art study. Selection is based on artistic merit, educational achievement, and financial need.

Financial data The stipend is $2,500. Funds are paid directly to the institution to be used to subsidize the costs of tuition, art materials, supplies, equipment, and education-related technology needs.

Duration 1 year.

Number awarded 1 each year.

Deadline Deadline not specified.

[501]
NONDAS HURST VOLL SCHOLARSHIP

The Fund for Community Progress
Attn: Scholarship Committee
90 Jefferson Boulevard, Suite B
Warwick, RI 02888
(401) 941-7100   Fax: (401) 941-7177
E-mail: info@fundcp.org
Web: www.fundcp.org

Summary To provide financial assistance to single mothers in Rhode Island who are transitioning off public assistance and wish to attend college in any state to study social services.

Eligibility This program is open to residents of Rhode Island who are single mothers of a dependent child or children. Applicants must have been involved with The Fund for Community Progress or 1 of its member agencies and be transitioning off public assistance. They must be registered or planning to enroll in a college certificate or degree program in social services or a related field at a school in any state. Along with their application, they must submit a 500-word essay on their reasons for beginning or continuing college

studies, how they chose their intended career training, and how this award can help them achieve their goals. Selection is based on that essay, academic information, employment and community activities, and financial need.

Financial data A stipend is awarded (amount not specified).

Duration 1 year.

Additional information This program began in 2006.

Number awarded 1 or more each year.

Deadline April of each year.

[502]
NORMA ROSS WALTER SCHOLARSHIP PROGRAM

Willa Cather Foundation
Attn: Scholarship Program
413 North Webster
Red Cloud, NE 68970
(402) 746-2653   Toll Free: (866) 731-7304
Fax: (402) 746-2652
Web: www.willacather.org/learn/scholarships

Summary To provide financial assistance to female seniors in Nebraska high schools who plan to major in English at an accredited college or university in any state.

Eligibility This program is open to women graduating from high schools in Nebraska and planning to enter a college or university in any state as a first-year student. Applicants must intend to continue their education as English majors (journalism is not acceptable). Along with their application, they must submit 1) a 1,500-word essay on several of the short stories or a novel written by Willa Cather; and 2) an essay on why they wish to enroll in college as an English major. Selection is based on intellectual promise, creativity, and character.

Financial data Stipends are $2,500, $1,750, or $1,250.

Duration 1 year; nonrenewable.

Additional information This program began in 1987.

Number awarded 3 each year: 1 each at $2,500, $1,750, and $1,250.

Deadline January of each year.

[503]
NORTH CAROLINA BUSINESS AND PROFESSIONAL WOMEN'S FOUNDATION SCHOLARSHIPS

Business and Professional Women of North Carolina
Attn: North Carolina Business and Professional Women's
  Foundation, Inc.
c/o Carol Ambrose, Scholarship Chair
2300 Cloister Drive
Charlotte, NC 28211
(704) 362-2066   E-mail: mcarolambrose65@gmail.com
Web: www.bpw-nc.org/Educational_Scholarship

Summary To provide financial assistance to women attending North Carolina colleges, community colleges, or graduate schools.

Eligibility This program is open to women who are currently enrolled in a community college, 4-year college, or graduate school in North Carolina. Applicants must be endorsed by a local BPW unit and have a GPA of 2.5 or higher. Along with their application, they must submit a 1-

page statement that summarizes their career goals, previous honors, or community activities and justifies their need for this scholarship. U.S. citizenship is required.

Financial data The stipend is $1,000. Funds are paid directly to the recipient's school.

Duration 1 year; recipients may reapply.

Additional information This program began in 1996.

Number awarded 2 each year: 1 for an undergraduate and 1 for a graduate student.

Deadline April of each year.

[504]
NORTH DAKOTA WOMEN'S OPPORTUNITY SCHOLARSHIP FUND

North Dakota Council on Abused Women's Services
Attn: Scholarship Review Committee
525 North Fourth Street
Bismarck, ND 58501
(701) 255-6240   Toll Free: (888) 255-6240
Fax: (701) 255-1904
Web: www.cawsnorthdakota.org

Summary To provide financial assistance to women in North Dakota who are interested in attending a college or university in the state.

Eligibility This program is open to female residents of North Dakota who are enrolled or planning to enroll full time at a college, university, or certification program in the state. Applicants must be able to demonstrate income lower than established financial guidelines for 125% of poverty (currently, $14,850 for a family of 1, rising to $51,113 for a family of 8). Along with their application, they must submit an essay of 500 to 1,000 words on their motivation for attending college and their plans for the future. Priority is given to 1) first-time students and current students in special circumstances that may prevent them from completing a pending degree or program; and 2) students who may not be eligible for sources of funding normally available to low-income applicants.

Financial data A stipend is awarded (amount not specified).

Duration 1 year; may be renewed.

Number awarded Varies each year.

Deadline June of each year.

[505]
NORTHROP GRUMMAN CORPORATION SCHOLARSHIP

Society of Women Engineers
Attn: Scholarship Selection Committee
203 North LaSalle Street, Suite 1675
Chicago, IL 60601-1269
(312) 596-5223   Toll Free: (877) SWE-INFO
Fax: (312) 644-8557   E-mail: scholarships@swe.org
Web: societyofwomenengineers.swe.org

Summary To provide financial assistance to female undergraduates at designated universities who are interested in studying specified fields of engineering.

Eligibility This program is open to women who entering their freshman, sophomore, or junior year as a full-time student at an ABET-accredited 4-year college or university. Applicants must have a GPA of 3.5 or higher and be majoring in computer science or computer, electrical, software, or sys-

tems engineering. They must be enrolled or planning to enroll at 1 of 26 eligible universities; for a list, contact the Society of Women Engineers (SWE). Selection is based on merit.

Financial data The stipend is $5,000.

Duration 1 year.

Additional information This program, established in 1983, is sponsored by Northrup Grumman Corporation.

Number awarded 5 each year.

Deadline February of each year for continuing undergraduates; May of each year for entering freshmen.

[506]
NORTHROP GRUMMAN FOUNDATION SCHOLARSHIP

Society of Women Engineers
Attn: Scholarship Selection Committee
203 North LaSalle Street, Suite 1675
Chicago, IL 60601-1269
(312) 596-5223   Toll Free: (877) SWE-INFO
Fax: (312) 644-8557   E-mail: scholarships@swe.org
Web: societyofwomenengineers.swe.org

Summary To provide financial assistance to female undergraduates at designated universities who are interested in studying specified fields of engineering.

Eligibility This program is open to women who entering their freshman, sophomore, or junior year as a full-time student at an ABET-accredited 4-year college or university. Applicants must be majoring in computer science or computer, electrical, software, or systems engineering. They must be enrolled or planning to enroll at 1 of 53 eligible universities; for a list, contact the Society of Women Engineers (SWE). Selection is based on merit. U.S. citizenship is required.

Financial data The stipend is $5,000.

Duration 1 year.

Additional information This program is sponsored by Northrup Grumman Foundation.

Number awarded 4 each year.

Deadline February of each year for continuing undergraduates; May of each year for entering freshmen.

[507]
NORTHWEST WOMEN IN EDUCATIONAL ADMINISTRATION SCHOLARSHIP

Confederation of Oregon School Administrators
Attn: Youth Development Program
707 13th Street, S.E., Suite 100
Salem, OR 97301-4035
(503) 581-3141   Fax: (503) 581-9840
Web: www.cosa.k12.or.us/members/scholarships

Summary To provide financial assistance to women who are high school seniors in Oregon and interested in preparing for a teaching career at a community college, college, or university in the state.

Eligibility This program is open to women who are graduating from public high schools in Oregon. Applicants must be interested in attending a community college, college, or university in the state to major in education. They must have been active in community and school affairs, have a GPA of 3.5 or higher, and be able to enroll in the fall term after graduating from high school. Along with their application, they must submit a 1-page statement on their background, influences, and goals and the endorsement of a member of the Confederation of Oregon School Administrators (COSA). Financial need is not considered in the selection process.

Financial data The stipend is $1,000. Funds are paid directly to the recipient.

Duration 1 year; nonrenewable.

Additional information This program is offered through Northwest Women in Educational Administration.

Number awarded 2 each year.

Deadline February of each year.

[508]
NYWICI FOUNDATION SCHOLARSHIPS

New York Women in Communications, Inc.
Attn: NYWICI Foundation
355 Lexington Avenue, 15th Floor
New York, NY 10017-6603
(212) 297-2133   Fax: (212) 370-9047
E-mail: nywicipr@nywici.org
Web: www.nywici.org/foundation/scholarships

Summary To provide financial assistance to female residents of designated eastern states who are interested in preparing for a career in communications at a college or graduate school in any state.

Eligibility This program is open to women who are seniors graduating from high schools in New York, New Jersey, Connecticut, or Pennsylvania or undergraduate or graduate students who are permanent residents of those states; they must be attending or planning to attend a college or university in any state. Graduate students must be members of New York Women in Communications, Inc. (NYWICI). Also eligible are women who reside outside the 4 states but are currently enrolled at a college or university within 1 of the 5 boroughs of New York City. All applicants must be working on a degree in a communications-related field (e.g., advertising, broadcasting, communications, digital media, English, film, journalism, marketing, public relations, publishing) and have a GPA of 3.2 or higher. Along with their application, they must submit a 2-page resume; a personal essay of 300 words on an assigned topic that changes annually; 2 letters of recommendation; and an official transcript. Selection is based on academic record, need, demonstrated leadership, participation in school and community activities, honors and other awards or recognition, work experience, goals and aspirations, and unusual personal and/or family circumstances. U.S. citizenship or permanent resident status is required.

Financial data The maximum stipend is $10,000.

Duration 1 year; recipients may reapply.

Number awarded Varies each year; recently, 10 were awarded.

Deadline January of each year.

[509]
O WINES OPPORTUNITY FOR SUCCESS SCHOLARSHIPS

College Success Foundation
1605 N.W. Sammamish Road, Suite 200
Issaquah, WA 98027-5388
(425) 416-2000   Toll Free: (877) 898-2048
Fax: (425) 416-2001
E-mail: scholarshipservices@collegesuccessfoundation. org
Web: www.collegesuccessfoundation.org

Summary To provide financial assistance to women who are high school seniors in any state and planning to enroll at a college or university.

Eligibility This program is open to female seniors graduating from high schools in any state and planning to enroll full time at a 4-year college or university. Applicants must be U.S. citizens or permanent residents and have a GPA of 3.2 or higher. They must have a family income that is less than 50% of the median level for their state.

Financial data The stipend is $5,000 per year.

Duration 1 year; may be renewed up to 3 additional years.

Additional information This program began in 2008 with support from O Wines, which was acquired by Ste. Michelle Wine Estates in 2012.

Number awarded Varies each year; recently, 13 were awarded. Since the program was established, it has awarded 52 scholarships.

Deadline April of each year.

[510]
OKLAHOMA CITY CHAPTER AWC SCHOLARSHIPS

Association for Women in Communications-Oklahoma City Chapter
c/o Tina Evans, Scholarship Committee Chair
1404 Fox View Court
Edmond, OK 73034
(405) 590-8466   E-mail: tina_evans@cox.net
Web: awcokc.org/scholarships

Summary To provide financial assistance to women from any state working on an undergraduate or graduate degree in communications or a related field at a school in Oklahoma.

Eligibility This program is open to women who are residents of any state working full time on an undergraduate or graduate degree in a communications-related field (e.g., public relations, journalism, advertising, photography, graphic design) at a 2- or 4-year college or university in Oklahoma. Applicants must submit a 250-word statement explaining why they are applying for the scholarship, why they chose to study communications, their goals after graduation, and related topics. Selection is based on aptitude, interest in a communications-related career, academic achievement, community service, and financial need.

Financial data Stipends range from $1,000 to $1,500.

Duration 1 year.

Additional information Recipients must enroll full time.

Number awarded Varies each year; recently, 5 were awarded: 1 at $1,500, 2 at $1,250, and 2 at $1,000.

Deadline February of each year.

[511]
OLIVE LYNN SALEMBIER MEMORIAL REENTRY SCHOLARSHIP

Society of Women Engineers
Attn: Scholarship Selection Committee
203 North LaSalle Street, Suite 1675
Chicago, IL 60601-1269
(312) 596-5223   Toll Free: (877) SWE-INFO
Fax: (312) 644-8557   E-mail: scholarships@swe.org
Web: societyofwomenengineers.swe.org

Summary   To provide financial assistance to women interested in returning to college or graduate school to study engineering or computer science.

Eligibility   This program is open to women who are planning to enroll at an ABET-accredited 4-year college or university. Applicants must have been out of the engineering workforce and school for at least 2 years and must be planning to return as an undergraduate or graduate student to major in computer science, engineering technology, or engineering. Selection is based on merit.

Financial data   The award is $1,500.

Duration   1 year; may be renewed up to 3 additional years, provided the recipient maintains a GPA of 3.0 or higher.

Additional information   This program began in 1980.

Number awarded   1 each year.

Deadline   February of each year.

[512]
OLIVE WHITMAN MEMORIAL SCHOLARSHIP

Daughters of the American Revolution-New York State
   Organization
c/o Nancy Goodnough
59 Susquehanna Avenue
Coopertown, NY 13326
(607) 547-8794   E-mail: ngoodnaugh@gmail.com
Web: www.nydar.org

Summary   To provide financial assistance for college or graduate school to Native American women in New York.

Eligibility   This program is open to women who are at least 50% Native American and residents of New York. Applicants must be graduating or have graduated from a high school in the state with a "B+" average. They must be attending or planning to attend an accredited college, university, or graduate school in the state.

Financial data   The stipend is $1,000.

Duration   1 year.

Number awarded   1 each year.

Deadline   April of each year.

[513]
OMAHA CHAPTER AFWA SCHOLARSHIPS

Accounting and Financial Women's Alliance-Omaha
   Chapter
c/o Natalya Walls, President
Bland & Associates, PC
450 Regency Parkway, Suite 120
Omaha, NE 68114
(402)397-8822   E-mail: omahaafwa@gmail.com
Web: www.omahaafwa.org

Summary   To provide financial assistance to women from any state working on an undergraduate or graduate degree in accounting at a school in Nebraska.

Eligibility   This program is open to women from any state enrolled part or full time in a bachelor's or master's degree program in accounting or finance at a college or university in Nebraska. Applicants must have completed at least 60 semester hours of a 4- or 5-year program. They must have a GPA of 3.0 or higher. Membership in the Accounting and Financial Women's Alliance (AFWA) is not required. Along with their application, they must submit an essay of 150 to 250 words on their career goals and objectives, the impact they want to have on the accounting or financial world, community involvement, and leadership examples. Selection is based on leadership, character, communication skills, scholastic average, and financial need.

Financial data   The stipend is $1,000.

Duration   1 year.

Number awarded   Varies each year; recently, 2 were awarded.

Deadline   April of each year.

[514]
ONE FAMILY SCHOLARS PROGRAM

One Family, Inc.
Attn: Director of Programs
800 South Street, Suite 610
Waltham, MA 02453
(617) 423-0504   Fax: (617) 588-0441
E-mail: mmiller@onefamilyinc.org
Web: www.onefamilyscholars.org/scholar-application

Summary   To provide financial assistance to residents of Massachusetts who are single heads of households and interested in attending college in the state.

Eligibility   This program is open to residents of Massachusetts who are single heads of household with dependent children younger than 18 years of age. Applicants must be attempting to enter or reenter college in Massachusetts to work on an associate or bachelor's degree. They must apply through a participating social service organization at sites in Massachusetts. Along with their application, they must submit a personal essay and 3 letters of reference. They must also apply for financial aid and participate in an interview. U.S. citizenship or permanent resident status is required. Selection is based on financial need (family earnings below 200% of the federal poverty level), clear and realistic academic and career goals, potential for success in chosen academic program, and desire to participate actively in all aspects of the program.

Financial data   A stipend is awarded (amount not specified).

Duration   1 year; may be renewed until completion of a degree, provided the scholar successfully completes 6 to 9 credits per semester; participates in mandatory leadership development retreats, seminars, and activities; maintains a GPA of 3.0 or higher; remains a Massachusetts resident; and maintains contact with site coordinators.

Additional information   This program began in 2000 by the Paul and Phyllis Fireman Charitable Foundation.

Number awarded Varies each year; recently, 23 scholars received support from this program.

Deadline June of each year for fall; October of each year for spring.

[515]
ONIPA'A CHAPTER ABWA SCHOLARSHIPS

American Business Women's Association-Onipa'a
   Chapter
c/o Julie Dugan, Education Committee Chair
P.O. Box 43
Waimanalo, HI 96795
(808) 259-6051   E-mail: Dugan.Julie@jobcorps.org
Web: abwaonipaa.weebly.com/scholarships.html

Summary To provide financial assistance to female residents of Hawaii who are working on an undergraduate degree at a college or university in the state.

Eligibility This program is open to residents of Hawaii who have completed at least 2 semesters as a full-time undergraduate student at an accredited university, community college, or business school in the state. Applicants must have a GPA of 3.0 or higher. Along with their application, they must submit a 1-page biographical summary that includes educational background and career objective. Financial need is also considered in the selection process. U.S. citizenship is required.

Financial data The stipend is $1,000.

Duration 1 year.

Number awarded 1 each year.

Deadline April of each year.

[516]
ORDER OF THE AMARANTH IN PENNSYLVANIA SCHOLARSHIP PROGRAM

Pennsylvania Masonic Youth Foundation
Attn: Educational Endowment Fund
1244 Bainbridge Road
Elizabethtown, PA 17022-9423
(717) 367-1536   Toll Free: (800) 266-8424 (within PA)
Fax: (717) 367-0616   E-mail: pmyf@pagrandlodge.org
Web: www.pmyf.org/scholarships

Summary To provide financial assistance to women in Pennsylvania who have a connection to Masonry and are interested in attending college in any state.

Eligibility This program is open to 1) daughters and granddaughters of members of the Order of the Amaranth in Pennsylvania; and 2) active Pennsylvania Rainbow Girls and Job's Daughters. Applicants must be between 18 and 21 years of age, high school graduates, and enrolled at an institution of higher learning in any state.

Financial data The stipend depends on the availability of funds.

Duration 1 year.

Additional information This program is sponsored by the Grand Court of Pennsylvania of the Order of the Amaranth.

Number awarded 1 or more each year.

Deadline January of each year.

[517]
OREGON BPW FOUNDATION SCHOLARSHIPS

Oregon Business and Professional Women's Foundation
Attn: Scholarship Program
P.O. Box 133
Roseburg, OR 97470
(541) 672-5820
Web: www.bpworegon.org

Summary To provide financial assistance to women in Oregon who are interested in returning to college.

Eligibility This program is open to women in Oregon who have been accepted into a program of study at an accredited U.S. institution. Applicants must be planning to work on a degree or certificate that will give them marketable skills to increase their economic security and enable them to enter the work force. They must be full-time students; part-time students may be eligible if they have completed at least 45 hours in their program of study. Along with their application, they must submit an essay on their short-term career goals, how this proposed training will help them to accomplish those goals, and how those apply to their long-range career goals. Financial need is considered in the selection process. U.S. citizenship is required.

Financial data A stipend is awarded (amount not specified). Funds are intended to cover tuition, fees, and other related expenses such as books.

Duration 1 year.

Number awarded Varies each year.

Deadline April of each year for summer and fall terms; September of each year for winter term; January of each year for spring term.

[518]
OREGON EASTERN STAR TRAINING AWARDS FOR RELIGIOUS LEADERSHIP

Order of the Eastern Star-Grand Chapter of Oregon
c/o Holly Austin, ESTARL Scholarship Selection
   Committee
14726 Albers Way N.E.
Aurora, OR 97002
(503) 678-1905   E-mail: hollydell@gmail.com
Web: www.oregonoes.org/Scholarships.html

Summary To provide financial assistance to female residents of Oregon who are attending college or seminary in any state to work on an undergraduate or graduate degree that will prepare them for a career in church service.

Eligibility This program is open to female residents of Oregon who are attending a school in any state that is accredited by the Accrediting Association of Bible Colleges, American Association of Schools of Religious Education, American Association of Theological School, National Association of Schools of Music, or similar association. Applicants must be working on an undergraduate or graduate degree that will prepare them for a full-time church vocation. They must submit a letter of reference from a denominational leader who can describe their relationship or prospect for full-time church service. Membership in the Order of the Eastern Star (OES) or other Masonic organization is not required, but applicants must be sponsored by an Oregon OES chapter. Financial need is considered in the selection process.

Financial data Stipends range from $500 to $5,000.

Duration 1 year.
Number awarded Varies each year; recently, 2 at $5,000, 1 at $1,500, and 2 at $500 were awarded.
Deadline April of each year.

[519]
OREGON LEGION AUXILIARY DEPARTMENT NURSES SCHOLARSHIP FOR WIDOWS

American Legion Auxiliary
Department of Oregon
30450 S.W. Parkway Avenue
P.O. Box 1730
Wilsonville, OR 97070-1730
(503) 682-3162   Fax: (503) 685-5008
E-mail: alaor@alaoregon.com
Web: www.alaoregon.org/scholarships.php

Summary To provide financial assistance to the widows of Oregon veterans who are interested in studying nursing at a school in any state.

Eligibility This program is open to Oregon residents who are the widows of deceased veterans. Applicants must have been accepted by an accredited hospital or university school of nursing in any state. Along with their application, they must submit a 500-word essay on, "How Military Families Are Keeping the Promise to Preserve our Freedom." Selection is based on ability, aptitude, character, determination, seriousness of purpose, and financial need.

Financial data The stipend is $1,500.
Duration 1 year; may be renewed.
Number awarded 1 each year.
Deadline April of each year.

[520]
OREGON LEGION AUXILIARY DEPARTMENT SCHOLARSHIPS FOR CHILDREN AND WIDOWS OF VETERANS

American Legion Auxiliary
Department of Oregon
30450 S.W. Parkway Avenue
P.O. Box 1730
Wilsonville, OR 97070-1730
(503) 682-3162   Fax: (503) 685-5008
E-mail: alaor@alaoregon.com
Web: www.alaoregon.org/scholarships.php

Summary To provide financial assistance to the children and widows of Oregon veterans who are interested in attending college in any state.

Eligibility This program is open to Oregon residents who are children or widows of veterans. Applicants must be interested in obtaining education beyond the high school level at a college, university, business school, vocational school, or any other accredited postsecondary school in any state. Along with their application, they must submit a 500-word essay on, "How Military Families Are Keeping the Promise to Preserve our Freedom." Selection is based on ability, aptitude, character, seriousness of purpose, and financial need.

Financial data The stipend is $1,000.
Duration 1 year; nonrenewable.
Number awarded 1 or more each year.
Deadline February of each year.

[521]
OREGON LEGION AUXILIARY DEPARTMENT SCHOLARSHIPS FOR WIVES OF DISABLED VETERANS

American Legion Auxiliary
Department of Oregon
30450 S.W. Parkway Avenue
P.O. Box 1730
Wilsonville, OR 97070-1730
(503) 682-3162   Fax: (503) 685-5008
E-mail: alaor@alaoregon.com
Web: www.alaoregon.org/scholarships.php

Summary To provide financial assistance to the wives of disabled Oregon veterans who are interested in attending college in any state.

Eligibility This program is open to Oregon residents who are wives of disabled veterans. Applicants must be interested in obtaining education beyond the high school level at a college, university, business school, vocational school, or any other accredited postsecondary school in any state. Along with their application, they must submit a 500-word essay on, "How Military Families Are Keeping the Promise to Preserve our Freedom." Selection is based on ability, aptitude, character, seriousness of purpose, and financial need.

Financial data The stipend is $1,000.
Duration 1 year; nonrenewable.
Number awarded 1 or more each year.
Deadline February of each year.

[522]
OUTPUTLINKS WOMAN OF DISTINCTION AWARD

Electronic Document Systems Foundation
Attn: EDSF Scholarship Awards
1845 Precinct Line Road, Suite 212
Hurst, TX 76054
(817) 849-1145   Fax: (817) 849-1185
E-mail: info@edsf.org
Web: www.edsf.org/what_we_do/scholarships/index.html

Summary To provide financial assistance to female undergraduate and graduate students from any country interested in preparing for a career in document management and graphic communications.

Eligibility This program is open to full-time female undergraduate and graduate students from any country who demonstrate a strong interest in preparing for a career in the document management and graphic communications industry, including computer science and engineering (e.g., web design, webmaster, software development, materials engineer, applications specialist, information technology designer, database manager); graphic and media communications (e.g., graphic designer, art director, illustrator, color scientist, print production, prepress imaging specialist, workflow specialist, document preparation, production and/or document distribution, content management, e-commerce, imaging science, printing, web authoring, electronic publishing, archiving, security); or business (e.g., sales, marketing, trade shows, customer service, project or product development, management). Preference is given to graduate students and upper-division undergraduates, but freshmen and sophomores who can show interest, experience, and/or commitment to the document management and graphic communication industry are encouraged to apply. Applicants must have a GPA of 3.0 or higher. Along with their application, they must submit 2 essays on assigned topics that change annually but relate to the document management and graphic communication industries. Selection is based on the essays, academic achievement, participation in school activities, community service, honors and organizational affiliations, education objectives, and recommendations; financial need is not considered.

Financial data   The stipend is $5,000.

Duration   1 year.

Additional information   This program is sponsored by OutputLinks Communications Group.

Number awarded   1 each year.

Deadline   April of each year.

[523]
OWANAH ANDERSON SCHOLARSHIPS

Association on American Indian Affairs, Inc.
Attn: Director of Scholarship Programs
966 Hungerford Drive, Suite 12-B
Rockville, MD 20850
(240) 314-7155   Fax: (240) 314-7159
E-mail: general.aaia@indian-affairs.org
Web: www.indian-affairs.org

Summary   To provide financial assistance to female Native American upper-division students.

Eligibility   This program is open to female Native American students enrolled as full-time juniors and majoring in any field. Applicants must submit proof of tribal enrollment and an essay of 2 to 3 pages on 1 of the following topics: 1) why the sponsor's International Repatriation Project is important and how they would inform others about it; 2) the Annie E. Casey Foundation's Juvenile Detention Alternatives Initiative and tribal and community-based alternatives to detention for juveniles; or 3) how tribal leaders can promote higher education in their family and community. They must have a GPA of 2.5 or higher. Selection is based on merit and need.

Financial data   The stipend is $1,500 per year.

Duration   2 years.

Number awarded   Varies each year; recently, 3 were awarded.

Deadline   May of each year.

[524]
PA BPW FOUNDATION SCHOLARSHIP

Business and Professional Women of Pennsylvania
c/o Catherine E. Collins, Foundation Vice Chair
475 Gallitzin Road
Cresson, PA 16630
(814) 886-7024   E-mail: cathcollins1@aol.com
Web: bpwpa.wildapricot.org

Summary   To provide financial assistance for continuing education to women in Pennsylvania.

Eligibility   This program is open to women in Pennsylvania who have been accepted into an accredited educational institution. Applicants must be able to demonstrate financial need. They must submit an essay that discusses their specific short-term career goals, how the proposed education will

help them to accomplish those goals, and why their goals are important to them in making a difference in todays' world.

Financial data   The stipend is $2,500.

Duration   1 year.

Number awarded   6 each year: 3 in fall and 3 in spring.

Deadline   April of each year for fall semester; October of each year for spring semester.

[525]
PAST PRESIDENTS SCHOLARSHIPS OF THE SOCIETY OF WOMEN ENGINEERS

Society of Women Engineers
Attn: Scholarship Selection Committee
203 North LaSalle Street, Suite 1675
Chicago, IL 60601-1269
(312) 596-5223   Toll Free: (877) SWE-INFO
Fax: (312) 644-8557   E-mail: scholarships@swe.org
Web: societyofwomenengineers.swe.org

Summary   To provide financial assistance to women working on an undergraduate or graduate degree in engineering or computer science.

Eligibility   This program is open to women who will be sophomores, juniors, seniors, or graduate students at ABET-accredited colleges and universities. Applicants must be U.S. citizens working full time on a degree in computer science or engineering. Along with their application, they must submit a 1-page essay on why they want to be an engineer or computer scientist, how they believe they will make a difference as an engineer or computer scientist, and what influenced them to study engineering or computer science. Selection is based on merit.

Financial data   The stipend is $2,000.

Duration   1 year.

Additional information   This program began in 1999 by an anonymous donor to honor the commitment and accomplishments of past presidents of the Society of Women Engineers (SWE).

Number awarded   2 each year.

Deadline   February of each year.

[526]
PATRICIA CREED SCHOLARSHIP

Connecticut Women's Golf Association
c/o Linda Kaye, Scholarship Committee
27 Hunter Road
Avon, CT 06001
(860) 678-0380   E-mail: scholarships@cwga.org
Web: www.cwga.org/PME_CWGA_Scholarships

Summary   To provide financial assistance to women high school seniors from Connecticut who are golfers and planning to attend college in any state.

Eligibility   This program is open to female high school seniors who are residents of Connecticut planning to attend a public college or university in any state. Applicants must be active golfers with a handicap. Along with their application, they must submit a 250-word essay on how golf has made an impact on their life. Selection is based on character, academic achievement, interest in golf, and financial need.

Financial data   A stipend is awarded (amount not specified).

Duration   1 year.

Additional information This program began in 1997.

Number awarded 1 or 2 each year.

Deadline April of each year.

[527]
PATSY TAKEMOTO MINK EDUCATION FOUNDATION EDUCATION SUPPORT AWARD

Patsy Takemoto Mink Education Foundation for Low-Income Women and Children
P.O. Box 769
Granby, MA 01033
Web: www.patsyminkfoundation.org/edsupport.html

Summary To provide financial assistance for college or graduate school to low-income mothers.

Eligibility This program is open to women who are at least 17 years of age and are from a low-income family (less than $20,000 annually for a family of 2, $24,000 for a family of 3, or $28,000 for a family of 4). Applicants must be mothers with minor children. They must be 1) enrolled in a skills training, ESL, or GED program; or 2) working on a vocational/technical, associate, bachelor's, master's, professional, or doctoral degree. Along with their application, they must submit brief essays on what this award will help them accomplish, the program in which they are or will be enrolled, how they decided on that educational pursuit, their educational goals, their educational experience, and their personal and educational history.

Financial data The stipend is $5,000.

Duration 1 year.

Additional information This program began in 2003.

Number awarded Up to 5 each year.

Deadline July of each year.

[528]
PAULA LORING SIMON SCHOLARSHIP

Society of Women Engineers
Attn: Scholarship Selection Committee
203 North LaSalle Street, Suite 1675
Chicago, IL 60601-1269
(312) 596-5223   Toll Free: (877) SWE-INFO
Fax: (312) 644-8557   E-mail: scholarships@swe.org
Web: societyofwomenengineers.swe.org

Summary To provide financial assistance to women who will be entering college as freshmen and are interested in studying electrical engineering or computer science or engineering.

Eligibility This program is open to women who are entering college as freshmen with a GPA of 3.0 or higher. Applicants must be planning to enroll full time at an ABET-accredited 4-year college or university and major in computer science or computer or electrical engineering. Selection is based on merit.

Financial data The stipend is $1,000.

Duration 1 year.

Number awarded 1 each year.

Deadline May of each year.

[529]
PAULINA HAYES SCHOLARSHIP

General Federation of Women's Clubs of Wyoming
c/o Wendy Owen
2700 Carey Avenue
Cheyenne, WY 82009
(307) 631-5547   E-mail: sewbusy3@gmail.com

Summary To provide financial assistance to women in Wyoming who are nontraditional students at colleges in the state.

Eligibility This program is open to women older than 18 years of age who are residents of Wyoming and attending or planning to attend the University of Wyoming, a Wyoming community college, or any licensed, accredited technical, vocational, or trade school in the state. Applicants must be nontraditional students, defined to include women who did not attend an institution of higher education immediately after high school (although they may be current enrolled), women who did not attend an institution of higher education immediately after completing a GED, or women who left an institution of higher education for any reason without completing a degree or certificate. Along with their application, they must submit a 350-word essay on themselves, including why they are applying for this scholarship, their financial circumstances, their family and work situation, any and all special circumstances, any financial aid they are receiving, any specific degree they are pursuing, and their school and extracurricular activities.

Financial data A stipend is awarded (amount not specified).

Duration 1 year.

Additional information This program began in 2009.

Number awarded Varies each year.

Deadline March of each year.

[530]
PAYSCALE'S WOMEN IN STEM SCHOLARSHIP

Payscale, Inc.
1000 First Avenue South, Suite 500
Seattle, WA 98134
Web: www.payscale.com/education/scholarship

Summary To provide financial assistance to women interested in working on an undergraduate or graduate degree in a field of science, technology, engineering, or mathematics (STEM).

Eligibility This program is open to women enrolled or planning to enroll at an accredited college or university. Applicants must be interested in working on an associate, bachelor's, or graduate degree in a field of STEM. Selection is based primarily on an essay of 300 to 500 words on why they want to work on a STEM degree, what inspires them, and what they want to do with their degree.

Financial data The stipend is $2,000.

Duration 1 year.

Additional information This program began in 2016.

Number awarded 1 each year.

Deadline February of each year.

[531]
PENNSYLVANIA FEDERATION OF DEMOCRATIC WOMEN MEMORIAL SCHOLARSHIP

Pennsylvania Federation of Democratic Women
c/o Bonita Hannis, Scholarship Chair
36 Betts Lane
Lock Haven, PA 17745
(570) 769-7175   E-mail: behannis@kcnet.org
Web: www.pfdw.org/Scholarship/tabid/101/Default.aspx

Summary To provide financial assistance to women from Pennsylvania who are registered Democrats and attending college in any state.

Eligibility This program is open to women who are residents of Pennsylvania and currently enrolled as juniors at an accredited college or university in any state. Applicants must be registered Democrats and an active participant in the Democratic Party with a Democratic Party family background. Along with their application, they must submit a 1-page essay describing their need for this scholarship, their professional goals, their Democratic Party activities, and their family Democratic Party involvement.

Financial data The stipend is $5,000.

Duration 1 year (the senior year of college).

Number awarded 2 to 5 each year.

Deadline March of each year.

[532]
P.E.O. PROGRAM FOR CONTINUING EDUCATION

P.E.O. Sisterhood
Attn: Scholar Awards Office
3700 Grand Avenue
Des Moines, IA 50312-2899
(515) 255-3153   Fax: (515) 255-3820
E-mail: psa@peodsm.org
Web: www.peointernational.org

Summary To provide financial assistance to mature women interested in resuming or continuing their academic or technical education.

Eligibility This program is open to mature women who are citizens of the United States or Canada and have experienced an interruption in their education that has lasted at least 24 consecutive months during their adult life. Applicants are frequently single parents who must acquire marketable skills to support their families. They must be within 2 years of completing an academic or technical course of study and be sponsored by a local P.E.O. chapter. Students enrolled in a doctoral degree program are not eligible.

Financial data The maximum stipend is $3,000.

Duration 1 year; nonrenewable.

Additional information This program was established in 1973 by the Women's Philanthropic Educational Organization (P.E.O.).

Number awarded Varies each year; for a recent biennium, 3,242 of these awards, with a total value of nearly $4.3 million, were granted.

Deadline Applications may be submitted at any time.

[533]
P.E.O. STAR SCHOLARSHIPS

P.E.O. Sisterhood
Attn: Scholar Awards Office
3700 Grand Avenue
Des Moines, IA 50312-2899
(515) 255-3153   Fax: (515) 255-3820
E-mail: psa@peodsm.org
Web: www.peointernational.org

Summary To provide financial assistance for college to female high school seniors in the United States or Canada.

Eligibility This program is open to women who are graduating from high schools in the United States or Canada and planning to enroll full or part time at an accredited postsecondary educational institution. Applicants must have an unweighted GPA of 3.0 or higher. They must be sponsored by a local P.E.O. chapter. Selection is based on academic excellence, leadership, extracurricular activities, community service, and potential for success; financial need is not considered. U.S. or Canadian citizenship or permanent resident status is required.

Financial data The stipend is $2,500.

Duration 1 year; nonrenewable.

Additional information This program was established in 2009 by the Women's Philanthropic Educational Organization (P.E.O.).

Number awarded Varies each year.

Deadline October of each year.

[534]
PEPPY MOLDOVAN SCHOLARSHIP

Illinois Society of Professional Engineers
Attn: ISPE Foundation, Inc.
100 East Washington Street
Springfield, IL 62701
(217) 544-7424   Fax: (217) 528-6545
E-mail: info@IllinoisEngineer.com
Web: www.illinoisengineer.com

Summary To provide financial assistance to women who are working on an engineering degree at from selected colleges in Illinois.

Eligibility This program is open to women currently enrolled as sophomore engineering students at the following institutions: Illinois Central College, Kaskaskia Community College, Rend Lake Community College, Bradley University, Southern Illinois University (SIU) at Carbondale, Southern Illinois University (SIU) at Edwardsville, or the University of Illinois at Urbana-Champaign (UIUC). Applicants must have been accepted for enrollment in an ABET-accredited engineering program at Bradley University, SIU Carbondale, SIU Edwardsville, UIUC. or the University of Illinois at Chicago. Along with their application, they must submit a 500-word essay on their interest in engineering, their major area of study and specialization, the occupation they propose to pursue after graduation, their long-term goals, and how they hope to achieve those. Selection is based on the essay, transcripts, work experience, extracurricular activities, honors and scholarships, and 2 letters of reference.

Financial data The stipend is $1,000.

Duration 1 year.

Number awarded 1 each year.

Deadline March of each year.

[535]
PGA OF AMERICA DIVERSITY SCHOLARSHIP PROGRAM

Professional Golfers' Association of America
Attn: PGA Foundation
100 Avenue of the Champions
Palm Beach Gardens, FL 33418
Toll Free: (888) 532-6662   E-mail: sjubb@pgahq.com
Web: www.pgafoundation.com

Summary To provide financial assistance to women and minorities interested in attending a designated college or university to prepare for a career as a golf professional.

Eligibility This program is open to women and minorities interested in becoming a licensed PGA Professional. Applicants must be interested in attending 1 of 20 colleges and universities that offer the Professional Golf Management (PGM) curriculum sanctioned by the PGA.

Financial data The stipend is $3,000 per year.

Duration 1 year; may be renewed.

Additional information This program began in 1993. Programs are offered at the following universities: Arizona State University (Tempe), Campbell University (Buies Creek, North Carolina), Clemson University (Clemson, South Carolina), Coastal Carolina University (Conway, South Carolina), Eastern Kentucky University (Richmond), Ferris State University (Big Rapids, Michigan), Florida State University (Tallahassee), Florida Gulf Coast University (Fort Myers), Methodist University (Fayetteville, North Carolina), Mississippi State University (Mississippi State), New Mexico State University (Las Cruces), North Carolina State University (Raleigh), Pennsylvania State University (University Park), Sam Houston State University (Huntsville), University of Central Oklahoma (Edmond), University of Colorado at Colorado Springs, University of Idaho (Moscow), University of Maryland Eastern Shore (Princess Anne), University of Nebraska at Lincoln, and University of Nevada at Las Vegas.

Number awarded Varies each year; recently, 20 were awarded.

Deadline Deadline not specified.

[536]
PHIPPS MEMORIAL SCHOLARSHIP

General Federation of Women's Clubs of Connecticut
c/o Joan Duffy, President
2 Quincy Close
Ridgefield, CT 06877
E-mail: duffy-gfwc@appsolutions.com
Web: www.gfwcct.org

Summary To provide financial assistance to women in Connecticut who are working on an undergraduate or graduate degree.

Eligibility This program is open to female residents of Connecticut who have completed at least 2 years of college. Applicants must have a GPA of 3.0 or higher and be working on a bachelor's or master's degree in any field. They must be U.S. citizens. Selection is based on academic ability, future promise, and financial need.

Financial data The stipend is $1,000.

Duration 1 year.

Number awarded 1 each year.

Deadline February of each year.

[537]
PHOENIX SECTION SWE SCHOLARSHIPS

Society of Women Engineers-Phoenix Section
c/o Stephanie Kinsey, Scholarship Chair
Total Networks
4201 North 24th Street, Suite 230
Phoenix, AZ 85016
(602) 567-1910, ext. 121   E-mail: azkinsey@cox.net
Web: www.swephoenix.com/programs

Summary To provide financial assistance to women working on an undergraduate or graduate degree in engineering at designated colleges in Arizona.

Eligibility This program is open to women from any state currently enrolled at Arizona State University, DeVry, Northern Arizona University, or Embry Riddle University. Applicants must be working on an undergraduate or graduate degree in a field of engineering. Selection is based on an essay, academics, employment history, and participation in the Society of Women Engineers (SWE) and other activities.

Financial data The stipend is $1,000.

Duration 1 year.

Number awarded 2 or 3 each year.

Deadline Deadline not specified.

[538]
PHYLLIS DOBBYN HOLT SCHOLARSHIPS

Sigma Alpha Iota Philanthropies, Inc.
One Tunnel Road
Asheville, NC 28805
(828) 251-0606   Fax: (828) 251-0644
E-mail: nh@sai-national.org
Web: app.smarterselect.com

Summary To provide financial assistance for undergraduate study to members of Sigma Alpha Iota (an organization of women musicians).

Eligibility This program is open to members of the organization in the first 3 years of undergraduate study. Candidates must be nominated by their chapter and their chapter adviser must submit a letter of recommendation. Nominees must submit a brief statement of career goals and aspirations. Selection is based on financial need, musical ability, scholarship, potential leadership, contribution to campus and community life, and exemplification of the ideals of the organization.

Financial data The stipend is $2,000.

Duration 1 year.

Number awarded 3 each year.

Deadline March of each year.

[539]
PHYLLIS G. MEEKINS SCHOLARSHIP

Ladies Professional Golf Association
Attn: LPGA Foundation
100 International Golf Drive
Daytona Beach, FL 32124-1082
(386) 274-6200   Fax: (386) 274-1099
E-mail: foundation.scholarships@lpga.com
Web: www.lpga.com

Summary To provide financial assistance to minority female graduating high school seniors who played golf in high school and plan to continue to play in college.

Eligibility This program is open to female high school seniors who are members of a recognized minority group. Applicants must have a GPA of 3.0 or higher and a background in golf. They must be planning to enroll full time at a college or university in the United States and play competitive golf. Along with their application, they must submit a letter that describes how golf has been an integral part of their lives and includes their personal, academic, and professional goals; their chosen discipline of study; and how this scholarship will be of assistance. Financial need is considered in the selection process. U.S. citizenship or legal resident status is required.

Financial data The stipend is $1,250.

Duration 1 year.

Additional information This program began in 2006.

Number awarded 1 each year.

Deadline May of each year.

[540]
PI STATE NATIVE AMERICAN GRANTS-IN-AID

Delta Kappa Gamma Society International-Pi State
  Organization
c/o Arlene Ida, Native American Committee Chair
3 Sherwood Park Drive
Burnt Hills, NY 12027
E-mail: aiddski@nucap.rr.com
Web: www.deltakappagamma.org/NY

Summary To provide funding to Native American women from New York who plan to work in education or another service field.

Eligibility This program is open to Native American women from New York who are attending a 2- or 4-year college in the state. Applicants must be planning to work in education or another service field, but preference is given to those majoring in education. Both undergraduate and graduate students are eligible.

Financial data The grant is $500 per semester ($1,000 per year). Funds may be used for any career-related purpose, including purchase of textbooks.

Duration 1 semester; may be renewed for a total of 5 years and a total of $5,000 over a recipient's lifetime.

Number awarded Up to 5 each year.

Deadline May of each year for fall; January of each year for winter or spring.

[541]
PINK TRACTOR SCHOLARSHIP

National FFA Organization
Attn: Scholarship Office
6060 FFA Drive
P.O. Box 68960
Indianapolis, IN 46268-0960
(317) 802-4419   Fax: (317) 802-5419
E-mail: scholarships@ffa.org
Web: www.ffa.org/participate/scholarships

Summary To provide financial assistance to female FFA members interested in studying fields related to farm management in college.

Eligibility This program is open to female members who are graduating high school seniors, live on a family farm in the continental United States, and plan to work on a 4-year degree. Applicants must be planning to major in agricultural business management, farm and ranch management, livestock management, or agricultural sales and marketing. They must have a GPA of 3.0 or higher and be able to demonstrate an interest in managing a farm. Selection is based on academic achievement, FFA involvement, community service, and leadership skills. U.S. citizenship is required.

Financial data The stipend is $1,000. Funds are paid directly to the recipient.

Duration 1 year; nonrenewable.

Additional information This program is sponsored by PinkTractor.com.

Number awarded 1 each year.

Deadline January of each year.

[542]
P.O. PISTILLI SCHOLARSHIPS

Design Automation Conference
c/o Andrew B. Kahng, Scholarship Director
University of California at San Diego-Jacobs School of
  Engineering
Jacobs Hall, EBU3B, Rpp, 2134
9500 Gilman Drive
La Jolla, CA 92093-0404
(858) 822-4884   Fax: (858) 534-7029
E-mail: abk@cs.ucsd.edu
Web: www.dac.com

Summary To provide financial assistance to female, minority, or disabled high school seniors who are interested in preparing for a career in computer science or electrical engineering.

Eligibility This program is open to graduating high school seniors who are members of underrepresented groups: women, African Americans, Hispanics, Native Americans, and students with disabilities. Applicants must be interested in preparing for a career in electrical engineering, computer engineering, or computer science. They must have at least a 3.0 GPA, have demonstrated high achievements in math and science courses, have demonstrated involvement in activities associated with the underrepresented group they represent, and be able to demonstrate significant financial need. U.S. citizenship is not required, but applicants must be U.S. residents when they apply and must plan to attend an accredited U.S. college or university. Along with their application, they must submit 3 letters of recommendation, official transcripts,

ACT/SAT and/or PSAT scores, a personal statement outlining future goals and why they think they should receive this scholarship, and documentation of financial need.

Financial data Stipends are $4,000 per year. Awards are paid each year in 2 equal installments.

Duration 1 year; may be renewed up to 4 additional years.

Additional information This program is funded by the Design Automation Conference of the Association for Computing Machinery's Special Interest Group on Design Automation.

Number awarded 2 to 7 each year.

Deadline January of each year.

[543]
PRATT & WHITNEY CANADA WOMEN IN ENGINEERING SCHOLARSHIP

Experimental Aircraft Association
Attn: Education Department
3000 Poberezny Road
Oshkosh, WI 54902
(920) 426-6823   Toll Free: (800) 564-6322
Fax: (800) 564-6322   E-mail: scholarships@eaa.org
Web: www.eaa.org

Summary To provide financial assistance to women from any country who are interested in studying aerospace engineering in college.

Eligibility This program is open to women from any country who are enrolled or accepted for full-time enrollment at an accredited college or university. Applicants must be planning to major in engineering; special consideration is given to students majoring in aerospace engineering. They must have a GPA of 3.3 or higher. Along with their application, they must submit an essay of 500 to 1,000 words highlighting their passion for the aerospace industry and what they hope to accomplish in the next 5 years.

Financial data The stipend is $10,000. Funds are paid directly to the recipient's college or university.

Duration 1 year.

Additional information This program is sponsored by Pratt & Whitney Canada.

Number awarded 1 each year.

Deadline February of each year.

[544]
PRESIDENT RONALD REAGAN SCHOLARSHIP

California Federation of Republican Women
Attn: Advocacy Office
770 L Street, Suite 950
Sacramento, CA 95814
(916) 442-4084   E-mail: scholarship@cfrw.org
Web: www.cfrw.org/index.cfm/scholarships.htm

Summary To provide financial assistance to women who are registered Republican residents of California studying political science, communications, or law at a college in any state.

Eligibility This program is open to women who are residents of California and registered Republicans. Applicants must have completed at least 2 years at a college or university in any state with a major in political science, communications, or a field directed toward law. They must be U.S. citizens.

Financial data The stipend is $2,000.

Duration 1 year.

Number awarded 1 each year.

Deadline August of each year.

[545]
PRISCILLA CARNEY JONES SCHOLARSHIP

American Chemical Society
Attn: Department of Diversity Programs
1155 16th Street, N.W.
Washington, DC 20036
(202) 872-6334   Toll Free: (800) 227-5558, ext. 6334
Fax: (202) 776-8003   E-mail: diversity@acs.org
Web: www.acs.org

Summary To provide financial assistance to female upper-division students majoring in chemistry.

Eligibility This program is open to women entering their junior or senior year of full-time study with a major in chemistry or chemistry-related science. Students in pre-med programs who intend to go to medical school are not eligible. Applicants must have a GPA of 3.25 or higher and be able to demonstrate financial need. They must have completed research or plan to conduct research during their undergraduate years. Along with their application, they must submit brief statements on why they are a good candidate to receive this scholarship, their community service activities and related responsibilities, the key leadership roles they have fulfilled, any research presentations or publications, and their future plans and goals. U.S. citizenship or permanent resident status is required.

Financial data The stipend is at least $1,500.

Duration 1 year.

Number awarded 1 each year.

Deadline April of each year.

[546]
PRISCILLA MAXWELL ENDICOTT SCHOLARSHIPS

Connecticut Women's Golf Association
c/o Linda Kaye, Scholarship Committee
27 Hunter Road
Avon, CT 06001
(860) 678-0380   E-mail: scholarships@cwga.org
Web: www.cwga.org/PME_CWGA_Scholarships

Summary To provide financial assistance to women golfers from Connecticut who are interested in attending college in any state.

Eligibility This program is open to high school seniors and college students who are residents of Connecticut attending or planning to attend a 4-year college or university in any state. Applicants must be active women golfers with a handicap. Along with their application, they must submit a 250-word essay on how golf has made an impact on their life. Selection is based on participation in golf programs, academic achievement, and financial need.

Financial data The maximum stipend is $3,000 per year.

Duration Up to 4 years.

Additional information This program began in 1977.

Number awarded Varies each year; recently, 5 were awarded.

Deadline April of each year.

[547]
PROFESSIONAL BUSINESS WOMEN OF CALIFORNIA ACADEMIC SCHOLARSHIPS

Professional Business Women of California
Attn: Community Director
2977 Ygnacio Valley Road, Suite 179
Walnut Creek, CA 94598
(415) 857-2923   E-mail: carolyn@pbwc.org
Web: www.pbwc.org/join/scholarships

Summary To provide financial assistance to female high school seniors in California who plan to attend college in any state.

Eligibility This program is open to women who are graduating from high schools in California and planning to enroll as an undergraduate at an accredited college or university in any state. Applicants must submit a 2-page essay on their career plans, future goals, and why they believe they are a worthy recipient of this scholarship.

Financial data A stipend is awarded (amount not specified). Funds are sent directly to the recipient's institution.

Duration 1 year.

Number awarded At least 3 each year.

Deadline January of each year.

[548]
PROVIDENCE ALUMNAE CHAPTER SCHOLASTIC ACHIEVEMENT AWARD

Delta Sigma Theta Sorority, Inc.-Providence Alumnae
   Chapter
Attn: Scholarship Committee
P.O. Box 40175
Providence, RI 02940-0175
E-mail: PACScholarship@hotmail.com
Web: www.dstprovidencealumnae.org/scholarship.html

Summary To provide financial assistance to female African American residents of Rhode Island who are attending college in any state.

Eligibility This program is open to African American women who are residents of Rhode Island. Applicants must be attending a 4-year college or university in any state and have a GPA of 3.0 or higher. Along with their application, they must submit a current official transcript that includes ACT and/or SAT scores; documentation of financial need; a description of their career goals, community service activities, educational accomplishments, and personal interests and talents; and a 650-word essay on a topic that changes annually but relates to their personal development.

Financial data The stipend is $1,000.

Duration 1 year.

Number awarded 1 or more each year.

Deadline February of each year.

[549]
PROVIDENCE ALUMNAE IN MEMORIUM AWARD

Delta Sigma Theta Sorority, Inc.-Providence Alumnae
   Chapter
Attn: Scholarship Committee
P.O. Box 40175
Providence, RI 02940-0175
E-mail: PACScholarship@hotmail.com
Web: www.dstprovidencealumnae.org/scholarship.html

Summary To provide financial assistance to African American female high school seniors from Rhode Island who are planning to attend college in any state.

Eligibility This program is open to African American women who are seniors graduating from high schools in Rhode Island. Applicants must be planning to enroll at a college in any state. Along with their application, they must submit a current official transcript that includes ACT and/or SAT scores; documentation of financial need; a description of their career goals, community service activities, educational accomplishments, and personal interests and talents; and a 650-word essay on a topic that changes annually but relates to their personal development.

Financial data The stipend is $1,250.

Duration 1 year.

Number awarded 1 or more each year.

Deadline February of each year.

[550]
PUBLIC BROADCASTING SERVICE (PBS) SCHOLARSHIP OF NEW YORK WOMEN IN COMMUNICATIONS

New York Women in Communications, Inc.
Attn: NYWICI Foundation
355 Lexington Avenue, 15th Floor
New York, NY 10017-6603
(212) 297-2133   Fax: (212) 370-9047
E-mail: nywicipr@nywici.org
Web: www.nywici.org/foundation/scholarships

Summary To provide financial assistance to female residents of designated eastern states who are enrolled as undergraduates at a college in any state and preparing for a communications career in the nonprofit sector.

Eligibility This program is open to women who are residents of New York, New Jersey, Connecticut, or Pennsylvania and currently enrolled as sophomores, juniors, or seniors at a college or university in any state. Also eligible are women who reside outside the 4 states but are currently enrolled at a college or university within 1 of the 5 boroughs of New York City. Applicants must be studying communications (e.g., advertising, marketing, public relations) and preparing for a career in the nonprofit sector. They must have a GPA of 3.2 or higher. Along with their application, they must submit a 2-page resume; a personal essay of 300 words on an assigned topic that changes annually; 2 letters of recommendation; and an official transcript. Selection is based on academic record, need, demonstrated leadership, participation in school and community activities, honors and other awards or recognition, work experience, goals and aspirations, and unusual personal and/or family circumstances. U.S. citizenship or permanent resident status is required.

Financial data The stipend ranges up to $10,000.

Duration 1 year.

Additional information This program is sponsored by the Public Broadcasting Service (PBS).

Number awarded 1 each year.

Deadline January of each year.

[551]
RAE LEE SIPORIN SCHOLARSHIP FOR WOMEN

Albuquerque Community Foundation
Attn: Scholarship Program
624 Tijeras Avenue, N.W.
P.O. Box 25266
Albuquerque, NM 87125-5266
(505) 883-6240   Fax: (505) 883-3629
E-mail: foundation@albuquerquefoundation.org
Web: www.albuquerquefoundation.org

Summary To provide financial assistance to women who are residents of New Mexico entering their senior year at a college in the state with a major in any field.

Eligibility This program is open to women who are residents of New Mexico and are continuing or returning to a college or university in the state to complete the final year for their first undergraduate degree. Applicants must enroll full time unless they need fewer hours to graduate. Along with their application, they must submit a personal essay on their educational goals and what they plan to do after graduation. Financial need is considered in the selection process.

Financial data The stipend is $1,500.

Duration 1 year.

Number awarded 1 to 3 each year.

Deadline June of each year.

[552]
REV. LLOYD ELLIS AND MR. RICHARD CORLEY SCHOLARSHIP

National Naval Officers Association-Washington, D.C.
  Chapter
c/o LCDR Stephen Williams
P.O. Box 30784
Alexandria, VA 22310
(703) 566-3840   Fax: (703) 566-3813
E-mail: Stephen.Williams@navy.mil
Web: dcnnoa.memberlodge.com/page-309002

Summary To provide financial assistance to female African American high school seniors from the Washington, D.C. area who are interested in attending an Historically Black College or University (HBCU) in any state.

Eligibility This program is open to female African American seniors graduating from high schools in the Washington, D.C. metropolitan area who plan to enroll full time at an HBCU in any state. Applicants must have a GPA of 2.5 or higher and be U.S. citizens or permanent residents. Selection is based on academic achievement, community involvement, and financial need.

Financial data The stipend is $1,000.

Duration 1 year; nonrenewable.

Additional information Recipients are not required to join or affiliate with the military in any way.

Number awarded 1 each year.

Deadline March of each year.

[553]
RHODA D. HOOD MEMORIAL SCHOLARSHIP

Northwest Baptist Convention
Attn: Woman's Missionary Union
3200 N.E. 109th Avenue
Vancouver, WA 98682-7749
(360) 882-2101   Fax: (360) 882-2295
E-mail: linda@nwbaptist.org
Web: www.nwbaptist.org

Summary To provide financial assistance to women from the Northwest who are attending college or seminary in any state to prepare for a career in vocational ministry, preferably with a Southern Baptist Convention church.

Eligibility This program is open to women who have been active members of a church affiliated with the Northwest Baptist Convention and a member of the Woman's Missionary Union within their church. Special consideration is given to children of ministers from the Northwest. Applicants must be attending or planning to attend an accredited college, university, or Southern Baptist seminary in any state with the intention of serving in a vocational ministry position through a church or denomination; priority is given to applicants going into a mission vocation affiliated with the Southern Baptist Convention. Along with their application, they must submit 1) a written account of their conversion experience and their call to vocational ministry; and 2) a written endorsement from their church.

Financial data A stipend is awarded (amount not specified).

Duration 1 year; may be renewed if the recipient maintains a GPA of 2.5 or higher.

Additional information The Northwest Baptist Convention serves Oregon, Washington, and northern Idaho.

Number awarded 1 or more each year.

Deadline May of each year for fall term; October of each year for spring term.

[554]
RHODE ISLAND COMMISSION ON WOMEN/ FREDA H. GOLDMAN EDUCATION AWARDS

Rhode Island Foundation
Attn: Donor Services Administrator
One Union Station
Providence, RI 02903
(401) 427-4011   Fax: (401) 331-8085
E-mail: rbogert@rifoundation.org
Web: www.rifoundation.org

Summary To provide supplemental funding to women in Rhode Island who are working on a degree or job training beyond high school.

Eligibility This program is open to women in Rhode Island who are 1) preparing for a nontraditional job or career through an educational program; 2) needing skills to reenter the job market; 3) seeking skills to improve their job status; 4) ex-offenders wishing to undertake vocational or career education and training; or 5) displaced homemakers and single mothers wishing to further their education. Applicants must be enrolled or registered in an educational or job skills training program and be able to demonstrate financial need. Preference is given to highly motivated, self-supporting, low-income women who are completing their first undergraduate degree or certificate program. Along with their application, they must submit an essay (up to 300 words) in which they explain their reasons for returning to school, how they chose their intended career or job training, how this scholarship can help them achieve their goals, and specifically how the money will be used.

Financial data Stipends range from $500 to $1,000; funds may be used for transportation, child care, introductory courses to a program, tutoring, educational materials, and related costs (not including tuition).

Duration 1 year; may be renewed.

Additional information This program, established in 1983 and transferred to the foundation in 1997, is supported by the Rhode Island Commission on Women.

Number awarded 2 each year.

Deadline June of each year.

[555]
RHONDA J.B. O'LEARY MEMORIAL SCHOLARSHIP

Educational Foundation for Women in Accounting
Attn: Foundation Administrator
136 South Keowee Street
Dayton, OH 45402
(937) 424-3391   Fax: (937) 222-5749
E-mail: info@efwa.org
Web: www.efwa.org/scholarships_graduate.php

Summary To provide financial support to women who are enrolled in an undergraduate or graduate accounting degree program at a school in Washington.

Eligibility This program is open to women from any state who are working on a bachelor's or master's degree in accounting at an accredited school in Washington. Selection is based on aptitude for accounting and business, commitment to the goal of working on a degree in accounting (including evidence of continued commitment after receiving this award), clear evidence that the candidate has established goals and a plan for achieving those goals (both personal and professional), and financial need. U.S. citizenship is required.

Financial data The stipend is $2,000 per year.

Duration 1 year; may be renewed 1 additional year if the recipient completes at least 12 hours each semester.

Additional information This program began in 2007 with funds provided by the Seattle Chapter of the American Society of Women Accountants (ASWA).

Number awarded 2 each year: 1 to an undergraduate and 1 to a graduate student.

Deadline April of each year.

[556]
R.L. GILLETTE SCHOLARSHIPS

American Foundation for the Blind
Attn: Information Center
1000 Fifth Avenue, Suite 350
Huntington, WV 25701
Toll Free: (800) AFB-LINE   E-mail: tannis@afb.net
Web: www.afb.org/scholarships.asp

Summary To provide financial assistance to legally blind undergraduate women who are studying literature or music.

Eligibility This program is open to women who are legally blind, U.S. citizens, and enrolled full time in a 4-year baccalaureate degree program in literature or music. Along with

their application, they must submit 200-word essays on 1) their past and recent achievements and accomplishments; 2) their intended field of study and why they have chosen it; and 3) the role their visual impairment has played in shaping their life. They must also submit a sample performance tape or CD (not to exceed 30 minutes) or a creative writing sample. Financial need is considered in the selection process.

Financial data The stipend is $1,000.

Duration 1 academic year.

Number awarded 2 each year.

Deadline May of each year.

[557]
ROBERT G. AND ANNETTE H. PALI SCHOLARSHIP

American Welding Society
Attn: AWS Foundation, Inc.
8669 N.W. 36th Street, Suite 130
Doral, FL 33166-6672
(305) 443-9353   Toll Free: (800) 443-9353, ext. 250
Fax: (305) 443-7559   E-mail: nprado-pulido@aws.org
Web: app.aws.org/foundation/scholarships/pali.html

Summary To provide financial assistance to students, especially women, working on a bachelor's degree in special fields of science or engineering.

Eligibility This program is open to U.S. citizens enrolled in a bachelor's degree program in chemistry, engineering, mathematics, or physics. Applicants must have a GPA of 3.0 or higher. Preference is given to women and to students at Lafayette College.

Financial data The stipend is $2,500; funds are paid directly to the educational institution.

Duration 1 year.

Number awarded 1 each year.

Deadline February of each year.

[558]
ROBERT SMILEY SCHOLARSHIP

Iowa Girls High School Athletic Union
Attn: Scholarships
5000 Westown Parkway, Suite 150
West Des Moines, IA 50266
(515) 288-9741   Fax: (515) 284-1969
E-mail: mail@ighsau.org
Web: www.ighsau.org

Summary To provide financial assistance to female high school seniors in Iowa who have participated in athletics and plan to attend college in the state.

Eligibility This program is open to women graduating from high schools in Iowa who have lettered in 1 varsity sport sponsored by the Iowa Girls High School Athletic Union (IGHSAU) each year of high school and have a GPA of 2.5 or higher. Applicants must be planning to attend a college or university in Iowa. Each high school in the state may nominate 1 student. Selection is based on academic achievements, athletic accomplishments, non-sports extracurricular activities, and community involvement.

Financial data The stipend is $1,000.

Duration 1 year.

Number awarded 1 each year.

Deadline March of each year.

[559]
ROBERTA BANASZAK GLEITER—ENGINEERING ENDEAVOR SCHOLARSHIP

Society of Women Engineers
Attn: Scholarship Selection Committee
203 North LaSalle Street, Suite 1675
Chicago, IL 60601-1269
(312) 596-5223   Toll Free: (877) SWE-INFO
Fax: (312) 644-8557   E-mail: scholarships@swe.org
Web: societyofwomenengineers.swe.org

Summary To provide financial assistance to members of the Society of Women Engineers (SWE) who will be entering their sophomore or junior year of a program in aeronautical or chemical engineering.

Eligibility This program is open to SWE members who are U.S. citizens entering their sophomore or junior year of full-time study at an ABET-accredited 4-year college or university. Applicants must be studying aeronautical or chemical engineering. Preference is given to members of underrepresented groups, reentry candidates, and students who can demonstrate financial need.

Financial data The stipend is $1,250 per year.

Duration 1 year; may be renewed, provided the recipient continues to meet eligibility requirements.

Additional information This program began in 2013.

Number awarded 1 each year.

Deadline February of each year.

[560]
ROCHELLE NICOLETTE PERRY MEMORIAL SCHOLARSHIP

Society of Women Engineers
Attn: Scholarship Selection Committee
203 North LaSalle Street, Suite 1675
Chicago, IL 60601-1269
(312) 596-5223   Toll Free: (877) SWE-INFO
Fax: (312) 644-8557   E-mail: scholarships@swe.org
Web: societyofwomenengineers.swe.org

Summary To provide financial assistance to members of the Society of Women Engineers (SWE) who are working on an undergraduate or graduate degree in electrical engineering or engineering technology.

Eligibility This program is open to SWE members who are full-time sophomores, juniors, seniors, or graduate student at an ABET-accredited 4-year college or university. Applicants must be studying electrical engineering or engineering technology at schools in SWE Region E (Delaware, District of Columbia, eastern Pennsylvania, Maryland, New Jersey, New York, and Virginia) or Region H (Illinois, Indiana, Iowa, Michigan, Minnesota, North Dakota, South Dakota, and Wisconsin). Preference is given to applicants who can demonstrate a high level of dedication and passion for their own community, organizations, and engineering in general. Selection is based on merit.

Financial data The stipend is $1,000.

Duration 1 year.

Additional information This program began in 2014.

Number awarded 1 each year.

Deadline February of each year.

[561]
ROCKWELL AUTOMATION SCHOLARSHIPS

Society of Women Engineers
Attn: Scholarship Selection Committee
203 North LaSalle Street, Suite 1675
Chicago, IL 60601-1269
(312) 596-5223   Toll Free: (877) SWE-INFO
Fax: (312) 644-8557   E-mail: scholarships@swe.org
Web: societyofwomenengineers.swe.org

Summary To provide financial assistance to women majoring in computer science or selected engineering specialties.

Eligibility This program is open to women who are entering their sophomore year at an ABET-accredited college or university. Applicants must be working full time on a degree in computer science, computer engineering, or software engineering. Selection is based on merit. Preference is given to students attending 14 designated universities.

Financial data The stipend is $2,500.

Duration 1 year.

Additional information This program, established in 1991, is supported by Rockwell Automation, Inc. For a list of the preferred universities, check the web site of the Society of Women Engineers (SWE).

Number awarded 2 each year.

Deadline February of each year.

[562]
ROCKWELL COLLINS SWE SCHOLARSHIPS

Society of Women Engineers
Attn: Scholarship Selection Committee
203 North LaSalle Street, Suite 1675
Chicago, IL 60601-1269
(312) 596-5223   Toll Free: (877) SWE-INFO
Fax: (312) 644-8557   E-mail: scholarships@swe.org
Web: societyofwomenengineers.swe.org

Summary To provide financial assistance to undergraduate members of the Society of Women Engineers (SWE) majoring in computer science or selected engineering specialties.

Eligibility This program is open to members of the society who are entering their sophomore, junior, or senior year at a 4-year ABET-accredited college or university. Applicants must be working full time on a degree in computer science or aeronautical, computer, or electrical engineering. They must be available to accept 1 Rockwell Collins co-op or internship prior to completing their degree. Selection is based on merit.

Financial data The stipend is $2,500.

Duration 1 year.

Additional information This program, established in 1991, is supported by Rockwell Collins, Inc.

Number awarded 3 each year.

Deadline February of each year.

[563]
ROCKY MOUNTAIN SECTION COLLEGE SCHOLARSHIPS

Society of Women Engineers-Rocky Mountain Section
c/o Christi Wisleder, College Scholarship Chair
Merrick & Company
5970 Greenwood Plaza Boulevard
Greenwood Village, CO 80111
(303) 751-0741   Toll Free: (800) 544-1714
Fax: (303) 751-2581   E-mail: christi.wisleder@gmail.com
Web: www.swe-rms.org/scholarships.html

Summary   To provide financial assistance to women from any state who are working on an undergraduate or graduate degree in engineering or computer science at colleges and universities in Colorado and Wyoming.

Eligibility   This program is open to women from any state who are enrolled as an undergraduate or graduate engineering student in an ABET-accredited engineering, computer science, or engineering technology program in Colorado or Wyoming (excluding zip codes 80800-81599). Applicants must have a GPA of 3.0 or higher. Along with their application, they must submit an essay on why they have chosen an engineering major, what they will accomplish or how they believe they will make a difference as an engineer, and who or what influenced them to study engineering. Selection is based on merit.

Financial data   The stipend is at least $1,000.

Duration   1 year.

Additional information   This program includes the following named scholarships: the Dorolyn Lines Scholarship, the Lottye Miner Scholarship, and the Rocky Mountain Section Pioneer Scholarship.

Number awarded   3 each year.

Deadline   January of each year.

[564]
ROSE SCHOLARSHIP

Zonta International District 10 Foundation
c/o Lisa LeBlanc
175 Antigua Drive
Lafayette, LA 70503
(337) 984-4197   E-mail: lisa.leblanc@lusfiber.net
Web: www.zontadistrict10.org

Summary   To provide financial assistance to female nontraditional college students in designated states.

Eligibility   This program is open to residents of Arkansas, Louisiana, New Mexico, Oklahoma, or Texas who are nontraditional students, female heads of households, and primary wage earners of their family. Applicants must be attending an accredited educational institution to obtain postsecondary training or certification in a program that does not require a baccalaureate degree. They must be able to document financial need, but other factors considered in the selection process include good citizenship, character, reputation, and moral and ethical standing. U.S. citizenship is required.

Financial data   The stipend is $1,000. Funds are paid directly to the institution providing the certification or training.

Duration   1 year.

Number awarded   1 each year.

Deadline   February of each year.

[565]
ROSENFELD INJURY LAWYERS' SINGLE MOTHERS SCHOLARSHIPS

Rosenfeld Injury Lawyers
33 North Dearborn Street, Suite 1930
Chicago, IL 60602
(847) 835-8895
E-mail: jonathan@rosenfeldinjurylawyers.com
Web: www.rosenfeldinjurylawyers.com

Summary   To recognize and reward, with funding for college or law school, single mothers who submit outstanding essays.

Eligibility   This program is open to single mothers who are enrolled or planning to enroll at an accredited college, university, community college, or law school in any state. Applicants must have a GPA of 3.0 or higher. They must submit a 500-word essay on the advantages of going back to school while caring for their children as a mother. Staff at the sponsoring law firm select 5 finalists and post their essays on its website. The essays that receive the most support on social media are awarded the scholarships.

Financial data   The award is a $1,000 scholarship.

Duration   1 year.

Number awarded   2 each year: 1 to an undergraduate student and 1 to a law student.

Deadline   December of each year.

[566]
RUTH EDELMAN/PRSSA AWARD FOR ACHIEVEMENT IN WOMEN'S LEADERSHIP DEVELOPMENT

Public Relations Student Society of America
Attn: Vice President of Member Services
33 Maiden Lane, 11th Floor
New York, NY 10038-5150
(212) 460-1474   Fax: (212) 995-0757
E-mail: prssa@prsa.org
Web: www.prssa.prsa.org

Summary   To provide financial assistance and work experience to female members of the Public Relations Student Society of America (PRSSA).

Eligibility   This program is open to women who are members of the society and currently enrolled in a full-time program of study at an accredited 4-year college or university. Applicants must submit 2 letters of recommendation and 10 samples of their individual public relations work. Selection is based on leadership, demonstrated interest in women's studies and issues, contributions to the field of public relations as related to women's issues, and recommendations from faculty members and/or industry professionals. Financial need is not considered.

Financial data   The winner receives a cash award of $1,500, of which $1,000 is paid upon winning the award and $500 at the start of a 3-month paid internship at an Edelman Worldwide office in the United States.

Duration   1 year.

Additional information   This program was established by Edelman in 2014.

Number awarded   1 each year.

Deadline   February of each year.

[567]
RUTH WHITNEY SCHOLARSHIP

New York Women in Communications, Inc.
Attn: NYWICI Foundation
355 Lexington Avenue, 15th Floor
New York, NY 10017-6603
(212) 297-2133   Fax: (212) 370-9047
E-mail: nywicipr@nywici.org
Web: www.nywici.org/foundation/scholarships

Summary   To provide financial assistance to female residents of designated eastern states who are interested in preparing for a career in magazine journalism or publishing at a college or graduate school in any state.

Eligibility   This program is open to women who are residents of New York, New Jersey, Connecticut, or Pennsylvania and enrolled as undergraduate or graduate students at a college or university in any state. Graduate students must be members of New York Women in Communications, Inc. (NYWICI). Also eligible are women who reside outside the 4 states but are currently enrolled at a college or university within 1 of the 5 boroughs of New York City. Applicants must have some experience in writing, reporting, or design and be preparing for a career in magazine journalism or publishing. Along with their application, they must submit a 2-page resume; a personal essay of 300 words on an assigned topic that changes annually; 2 letters of recommendation; and an official transcript. Selection is based on academic record, need, demonstrated leadership, participation in school and community activities, honors and other awards or recognition, work experience, goals and aspirations, and unusual personal and/or family circumstances. U.S. citizenship or permanent resident status is required.

Financial data   The stipend ranges up to $10,000.

Duration   1 year.

Additional information   This program is sponsored by *Glamour* magazine, which invites the recipient to visit its offices and spend a week with its editorial team.

Number awarded   1 each year.

Deadline   January of each year.

[568]
RUTHANN FAIRBAIRN SCHOLARSHIP

Oklahoma Society of Certified Public Accountants
Attn: OSCPA Educational Foundation
1900 N.W. Expressway, Suite 910
Oklahoma City, OK 73118-1898
(405) 841-3806
Toll Free: (800) 522-8261, ext. 3806 (within OK)
Fax: (405) 841-3801   E-mail: awelch@oscpa.com
Web: www.oscpa.com/Content/60229.aspx

Summary   To provide financial assistance to female members of the Oklahoma Society of Certified Public Accountants (OSCPA) working on a degree in accounting in Oklahoma.

Eligibility   This program is open to female OSCPA members who are nominated by an accounting program at an Oklahoma college or university. Nominees must be enrolled in a 4- or 5-year degree program in accounting and have successfully completed at least 6 hours of principles of accounting. As part of the selection process, they must submit a resume, a transcript, standardized test scores, and 3 letters of reference.

Financial data   The stipend ranges from $250 to $1,500.
Duration   1 year.
Number awarded   1 each year.
Deadline   March of each year.

[569]
S. EVELYN LEWIS MEMORIAL MEDICAL HEALTH SCIENCE SCHOLARSHIP

Zeta Phi Beta Sorority, Inc.
Attn: National Educational Foundation
1734 New Hampshire Avenue, N.W.
Washington, DC 20009
(202) 387-3103   Fax: (202) 232-4593
E-mail: info@zetaphibetasororityhq.org
Web: www.zpbnef1975.org/scholarships-and-descriptions

Summary   To provide financial assistance to women interested in studying medicine or health sciences on the undergraduate or graduate school level.

Eligibility   This program is open to women enrolled full time in a program on the undergraduate or graduate school level leading to a degree in medicine or health sciences. Proof of enrollment is required. Applicants need not be members of Zeta Phi Beta Sorority. Along with their application, they must submit a 150-word essay on their educational goals and professional aspirations, how this award will help them to achieve those goals, and why they should receive the award. Financial need is not considered in the selection process.

Financial data   The stipend ranges from $500 to $1,000. Funds are paid directly to the college or university.

Duration   1 academic year.

Additional information   Zeta Phi Beta is a traditionally African American sorority.

Number awarded   1 or more each year.

Deadline   January of each year.

[570]
SAN DIEGO CHAPTER AWIS SCHOLARSHIP PROGRAM

Association for Women in Science-San Diego Chapter
Attn: Scholarship Committee
P.O. Box 178096
San Diego, CA 92177
E-mail: scholarship@awissd.org
Web: www.awissd.org/index.php/opportunities/scholarships

Summary   To provide financial assistance to women who are working on an undergraduate or graduate degree in a field of science, technology, engineering, or mathematics (STEM) at a college in San Diego County, California.

Eligibility   This program is open to women from any state currently enrolled at a college, university, or community college in San Diego County, California. Applicants must be working on an undergraduate or graduate degree in a field of STEM and have a GPA of 3.0 or higher. They must be U.S. citizens or permanent residents. Along with their application, they must submit a 750-word personal statement describing their career aspirations and scientific interests, including research experience and relevant extracurricular activities. Financial need is not considered in the selection process.

Financial data   The stipend is $1,000.

Duration   1 year; nonrenewable.

Number awarded Varies each year; recently, 8 were awarded: 1 to a community college student, 3 to undergraduates, and 4 to graduate students.
Deadline February of each year.

[571]
SARA EIKENBERRY VOICE SCHOLARSHIPS

Mu Phi Epsilon Fraternity
Attn: Mu Phi Epsilon Foundation
c/o Liana Sandin, Voice Scholarship Chair
6321 A Street
Lincoln, NE 68510-5010
(402) 560-7126   E-mail: liana.sandin@gmail.com
Web: www.mpefoundation.org

Summary To provide financial assistance to undergraduate or graduate student members of Mu Phi Epsilon who are studying mezzo-soprano or contralto voice.

Eligibility This program is open to undergraduate and graduate student members of Mu Phi Epsilon, a professional music fraternity, who are mezzo-sopranos or contraltos studying voice. Applicants must submit college transcripts; a current resume (including Mu Phi Epsilon participation); 2 letters of recommendation; a high quality compact disc recording that includes 3 art songs or arias of contrasting styles, 1 of which is in English; a list of the recorded repertoire with exact titles, opus numbers, composers' names, and timings; and recent reviews and programs.

Financial data The stipend is $1,000.

Duration 1 year.

Additional information The application submission fee is $25.

Number awarded 2 each year: 1 to an undergraduate and 1 to a graduate student.

Deadline February of each year.

[572]
SARA SCHOLARSHIP

Henry and Sara Sheehan Foundation
310 North Kensington Avenue
LaGrange Park, IL 60526
Web: www.sarascholarship.org

Summary To provide financial assistance to female high school seniors who have played golf and plan to attend college in any state.

Eligibility This program is open to women who are graduating from high school and entering an accredited college or university in any state. Applicants must have been involved in the sport of golf, although skill in golf is not considered in the selection process. They must have a GPA of 3.1 or higher and be able to demonstrate financial need. Along with their application, they must submit 1) a brief description of how they are involved in the sport of golf and what they enjoy about the experience; and 2) a personal essay about themselves, why they want to go to college, and their goals at this time.

Financial data The stipend is $2,000 per year.

Duration 1 year; may be renewed up to 3 additional years, provided the recipient remains enrolled full time, maintains a GPA of 2.1 or higher for the first year and 3.0 or higher for subsequent years, continues to demonstrate financial need, and receives no disciplinary actions from her college.

Additional information This program began in 2012.

Number awarded At least 12 each year.
Deadline May of each year.

[573]
SARAH E. HUNEYCUTT SCHOLARSHIP

Florida State Golf Association
Attn: Junior Girls' Golf Scholarship Foundation
c/o Sisi Hedges
110 Country Club Lane
Mulberry, FL 33860
E-mail: hedgesh@aol.com
Web: www.jggsf.org

Summary To provide financial assistance to female high school seniors in Florida who have an interest in golf and are interested in attending college in the state.

Eligibility This program is open to women who are graduating seniors at high schools in Florida and have an interest or association with the game of golf. Applicants must be planning to attend a junior college, college, university, or technical school in the state but not be eligible for a golf scholarship. They must have a GPA of 3.0 or higher and be able to document financial need. Along with their application, they must submit a brief statement on the extent of their participation in golf, transcripts that include SAT and ACT scores, and 3 letters of recommendation.

Financial data Stipends range up to $5,000 per year. Funds are paid directly to the recipient's school.

Duration 4 years.

Additional information This program was established by the Florida Women's State Golf Association (FWSGA) in 2005. When that organization merged with the Florida State Golf Association in 2012, the scholarship fund remained independent.

Number awarded 1 renewable scholarship at $5,000 per year and a varying number of nonrenewable smaller scholarships are awarded each year.

Deadline May of each year.

[574]
SARAH PEUGH BUTTERFLY SCHOLARSHIP

GFWC/Mississippi Federation of Women's Clubs, Inc.
c/o Darlene G. Adams, President
3004 The Woods Road
Picayune, MS 39466
E-mail: info@gfwc-mfwc.org
Web: www.gfwc-mfwc.org

Summary To provide financial assistance to high school seniors in Mississippi who are members of a Juniorette club affiliated with the GFWC/Mississippi Federation of Women's Clubs and plan to attend college in any state.

Eligibility This program is open to women who are seniors graduating from high schools in Mississippi and members of a GFWC-MFWC Juniorette club. Applicants must be planning to major in any field at a college or university in any state. They must submit a list of their leadership activities, ACT score, and a letter of recommendation from a GFWS-MWFC sponsoring club.

Financial data The stipend is $1,000. Funds are sent directly to the recipient's institution.

Duration 1 year.

Number awarded 1 each year.

Deadline February of each year.

[575]
SCCAWS EDUCATION SCHOLARSHIP

South Carolina Coaches Association of Women's Sports
c/o Amy Boozer, Secretary/Treasurer
P.O. Box 261
Newberry, SC 29108
(803) 321-9274   E-mail: amy_caws@yahoo.com
Web: www.sccaws.org/scholarships.html

Summary To provide financial assistance to female high school senior athletes in South Carolina who plan to study education at a college in any state.

Eligibility This program is open to women graduating from high schools in South Carolina who have participated on at least 1 athletic team. Applicants must be planning to attend a college or university in any state to prepare for a career as a teacher. They must have minimum scores of 1000 on the SAT and/or 22 on the ACT. Along with their application, they must submit a 1-page essay on why they want to be a teacher and where they envision themselves in the teaching field in 10 years. Selection is based on that essay, academic achievement, participation in athletic and non-athletic extracurricular activities, and financial need.

Financial data A stipend is awarded (amount not specified).

Duration 1 year; nonrenewable.

Number awarded 1 each year.

Deadline March of each year.

[576]
SCCAWS MEDICAL SCHOLARSHIP

South Carolina Coaches Association of Women's Sports
c/o Amy Boozer, Secretary/Treasurer
P.O. Box 261
Newberry, SC 29108
(803) 321-9274   E-mail: amy_caws@yahoo.com
Web: www.sccaws.org/scholarships.html

Summary To provide financial assistance to female high school senior athletes in South Carolina who plan to study a medical field at a college in any state.

Eligibility This program is open to women graduating from high schools in South Carolina who have participated on at least 1 athletic team. Applicants must be planning to attend a college or university in any state to prepare for a career in medicine. They must have minimum scores of 1000 on the SAT and/or 22 on the ACT. Along with their application, they must submit a 1-page essay on why they want to enter the medical field and the area of specialization they plan to pursue. Selection is based on that essay, academic achievement, participation in athletic and non-athletic extracurricular activities, and financial need.

Financial data The stipend is $1,000.

Duration 1 year; nonrenewable.

Additional information Support for this program is provided by Trophies by "M."

Number awarded 1 each year.

Deadline March of each year.

[577]
SCHOLARSHIP PROGRAM FOR WIFLE MEMBERS ONLY

Women in Federal Law Enforcement
Attn: Scholarship Coordinator
2200 Wilson Boulevard, Suite 102
PMB 204
Arlington, VA 22201-3324
(301) 805-2180   Fax: (301) 560-8836
E-mail: WIFLE@comcast.net
Web: www.wifle.org/scholarshipprogram.htm

Summary To provide financial assistance for college or graduate school to women who are interested in preparing for a career in law enforcement and are members of Women in Federal Law Enforcement (WIFLE) or sponsored by a member.

Eligibility This program is open to women who are members of WIFLE or sponsored by a member and have completed at least 1 academic year of full-time study at an accredited 4-year college or university (or at a community college with the intention of transferring to a 4-year school). Applicants must be majoring in criminal justice or a related field (e.g., social sciences, public administration, computer science, finance, linguistic arts, chemistry, physics). They must have a GPA of 3.0 or higher. Students in graduate and postgraduate programs are also eligible, but those working on an associate degree are not. Along with their application, they must submit a letter demonstrating their financial need and describing their career objectives. U.S. citizenship is required.

Financial data The stipend is $1,500 per year.

Duration 1 year; may be renewed automatically for 1 additional year.

Number awarded 1 each year.

Deadline April of each year.

[578]
SCHOLARSHIPS FOR ELCA SERVICE ABROAD

Women of the Evangelical Lutheran Church in America
Attn: Scholarships
8765 West Higgins Road
Chicago, IL 60631-4101
(773) 380-2741   Toll Free: (800) 638-3522, ext. 2741
Fax: (773) 380-2419   E-mail: valora.starr@elca.org
Web: www.womenoftheelca.org

Summary To provide financial assistance to lay women who are members of Evangelical Lutheran Church of America (ELCA) congregations and who wish to pursue postsecondary education for service abroad, either in general or in health fields.

Eligibility This program is open to ELCA lay women who are at least 21 years of age and have experienced an interruption of at least 2 years in their education since high school. Applicants must have been admitted to an academic institution to prepare for a career other than the ordained ministry. This program is available only to women studying for ELCA service abroad, either in general or in health professions associated with ELCA projects abroad. U.S. citizenship is required.

Financial data The stipend ranges from $800 to $1,000 per year.

Duration 1 year; recipients may reapply for 1 additional year.

Additional information This program includes the following named scholarships: the Belmer Scholarship, the Flora Prince Scholarship, the Kahler Scholarship, the Vickers/Raup Scholarship, and the Emma Wettstein Scholarship.

Number awarded 1 or more each year.

Deadline February of each year.

[579]
SCHOLARSHIPS FOR WOMEN RESIDENTS OF THE STATE OF DELAWARE

American Association of University Women-Wilmington
　　Branch
Attn: Scholarship Committee
1800 Fairfax Boulevard
Wilmington, DE 19803-3106
(302) 428-0939　　　　　E-mail: aauwwilm@gmail.com
Web: wilmington-de.aauw.net/scholarships

Summary To provide financial assistance to female residents of Delaware who plan to attend college in any state.

Eligibility This program is open to women who are U.S. citizens and 1) a Delaware resident and a high school graduate; 2) a Delaware resident and a senior at a high school in New Castle County; or 3) a resident of New Castle County, Delaware and a home-schooled student who can meet the admission requirements of the University of Delaware. Applicants must be attending or planning to attend a college or university in any state. Along with their application, they must submit a 150-word essay on what they plan to study and why. High school seniors must also submit a 150-word essay on either 1) what they would do and where they would do it if they had 4 hours to spend any place, either now or in history; or 2) the famous person, past or present, they would like to meet and why. Selection is based on scholastic standing, contributions to school and community, SAT or ACT scores, and financial need. An interview is required.

Financial data A stipend is awarded (amount not specified).

Duration 1 year.

Number awarded Varies each year; recently, 17 of these scholarships, worth $55,000, were awarded.

Deadline February of each year.

[580]
SCHOLARSHIPS FOR WOMEN STUDYING INFORMATION SECURITY

Applied Computer Security Association
Attn: Director of Scholarship Programs
2906 Covington Road
Silver Spring, MD 20910
(703) 989-8907　　　　　E-mail: swsis@swsis.org
Web: swsis.wordpress.com/applying-for-scholarships

Summary To provide financial assistance to women who are working on an undergraduate or graduate degree in a field related to information security.

Eligibility This program is open to women who are entering their junior or senior year of undergraduate study or first year of a master's degree program. Applicants must be working on a degree in a field related to information security (e.g., network security, software security/assurance, operating sys-

tems security, database security, applications security, formal methods, forensics, cybersecurity, security usability). Along with their application, they must submit an essay describing their interest in the field, letters of reference, a resume or curriculum vitae, and transcripts. Preference is given to U.S. citizens and permanent residents.

Financial data Stipends range from $5,000 to $10,000 per year. Funds are paid directly to the recipient's institution.

Duration 1 year; may be renewed 1 additional year.

Additional information This program, which began in 2011, is managed by the Applied Computer Security Association (ACSA) and the Computing Research Association (CRA) Committee on the Status of Women in Computing Research. Additional funding is provided by Hewlett Packard.

Number awarded 16 each year.

Deadline January of each year.

[581]
SCIENCE AMBASSADOR SCHOLARSHIP

Cards Against Humanity
Attn: Jenn Bane
1917 North Elston Avenue
Chicago, IL 60641
(312) 756-0834　E-mail: jenn@cardsagainsthumanity.com
Web: www.scienceambassadorscholarship.org

Summary To provide financial assistance to women who are interested in working on an undergraduate degree in a field of science, technology, engineering, or mathematics (STEM).

Eligibility This program is open to women who are enrolled or planning to enroll full time at a college or university and major in a field of STEM. Applicants must submit a video of themselves explaining a topic in science about which they are passionate. U.S. citizenship or permanent resident status is required.

Financial data The scholarship provides full payment of tuition at the college or university of the winner's choice.

Duration Up to 4 years.

Additional information This program began in 2015 with funding from sales of the Cards Against Humanity Science Pack.

Number awarded 1 each year.

Deadline November of each year.

[582]
SEATTLE CHAPTER AWIS SCHOLARSHIPS

Association for Women in Science-Seattle Chapter
c/o Fran Solomon, Scholarship Committee Chair
5805 16th Avenue, N.E.
Seattle, WA 98105
(206) 522-6441　　　　E-mail: scholarship@seattleawis.org
Web: www.seattleawis.org/award/scholarships

Summary To provide financial assistance to women undergraduates from any state majoring in science, mathematics, or engineering at colleges and universities in Washington.

Eligibility This program is open to women from any state entering their junior or senior year at a 4-year college or university in Washington. Applicants must have a declared major in science (e.g., biological sciences, environmental science, biochemistry, chemistry, pharmacy, geology, computer science, physics), mathematics, or engineering. Along with their application, they must submit essays on the events that led to their choice of a major, their current career plans and long-term goals, and their volunteer and community activities. Selection is based on academic excellence, motivation to prepare for a science-based career, record of giving back to their communities, and financial need. At least 1 scholarship is reserved for a woman from a group that is underrepresented in science, mathematics, and engineering careers, including Native American Indians and Alaska Natives, Black/African Americans, Mexican Americans/Chicanas/Latinas, Native Pacific Islanders (Polynesians, Melanesians, and Micronesians), adult learners (returning students), and women with disabilities.

Financial data Stipends range from $1,000 to $5,000.

Duration 1 year.

Additional information This program includes the following named awards: the Virginia Badger Scholarship, the Angela Paez Memorial Scholarship, and the Fran Solomon Scholarship. Support for the program is provided by several sponsors, including the American Chemical Society, Iota Sigma Pi, Rosetta Inpharmatics, and ZymoGenetics, Inc.

Number awarded Varies each year; recently 2 at $5,000, 1 at $1,500, and 1 at $1,000 were awarded.

Deadline March of each year.

[583]
SEATTLE PROFESSIONAL CHAPTER AWC SCHOLARSHIPS

Association for Women in Communications-Seattle
  Professional Chapter
Attn: Tina Christiansen, Vice-President, Finance
P.O. Box 60262
Shoreline, WA 98160
E-mail: tina@writeasrain.com
Web: www.seattleawc.org/scholarships-and-awards

Summary To provide financial assistance to female upper-division and graduate students in Washington who are preparing for a career in the communications industry.

Eligibility This program is open to female residents of any state who are enrolled at a 4-year college or university in Washington as a junior, senior, or graduate student. Applicants must be working on or planning to work on a degree in a communications program, including print and broadcast journalism, television and radio production, video or film, advertising, public relations, marketing, graphic or multimedia design, photography, speech communications, or technical communication. Selection is based on demonstrated excellence in communications, goals and progress toward a career in communications, contributions made to communications on campus and/or in the community, scholastic achievement, and financial need.

Financial data The stipend is $1,500. Funds are paid directly to the recipient's school and must be used for tuition and fees.

Duration 1 year.

Number awarded 2 each year.

Deadline March of each year.

[584]
SEHAR SALEHA AHMAD AND ABRAHIM EKRAMULLAH ZAFAR FOUNDATION SCHOLARSHIP

Oregon Office of Student Access and Completion
Attn: Scholarship Processing Coordinator
1500 Valley River Drive, Suite 100
Eugene, OR 97401-2146
(541) 687-7422   Toll Free: (800) 452-8807, ext. 7422
Fax: (541) 687-7414   TDD: (800) 735-2900
E-mail: cheryl.a.connolly@state.or.us
Web: app.oregonstudentaid.gov/Catalog/Default.aspx

Summary To provide financial assistance to female high school seniors in Oregon who are interested in studying mathematics or science at a college in the state.

Eligibility This program is open to women who are graduating seniors from high schools in Oregon (including GED recipients and home-schooled students). Applicants must be planning to major in mathematics or science at a 4-year college or university in the state. They must have a GPA of 3.8 or higher and be able to demonstrate financial need.

Financial data Stipends for scholarships offered by the Oregon Office of Student Access and Completion (OSAC) range from $1,000 to $10,000 but recently averaged $4,368.

Duration 1 year; may be renewed if the recipient shows satisfactory academic progress and continued financial need.

Number awarded 1 or more each year.

Deadline February of each year.

[585]
SENATOR SCOTT WHITE MEMORIAL SCHOLARSHIP

Women's Transportation Seminar-Puget Sound Chapter
c/o Laurie Thomsen, Scholarship Co-Chair
Osborn Consulting, Inc.
1800 112th Avenue N.E.
Bellevue, WA 98004
(425) 451-4009   Fax: (888) 391-8517
E-mail: laurie@osbornconsulting.com
Web: www.wtsinternational.org

Summary To provide financial assistance to women undergraduate and graduate students from Washington working on a degree related to public policy or public administration in transportation.

Eligibility This program is open to women who are residents of Washington, studying at a college in the state, or working as an intern in the state. Applicants must be currently enrolled in an undergraduate or graduate degree program in public policy or public administration in a transportation-related field. They must have a GPA of 3.0 or higher and plans to prepare for a career in their field of study. Minority women are especially encouraged to apply. Along with their application, they must submit a 500-word statement about their career goals after graduation, how their goals are related to public policy or public administration, and why they think they should receive this scholarship award. Selection is based on that statement, academic record, financial need, and transportation-related activities or job skills.

Financial data The stipend is $2,500.

Duration 1 year.

Additional information This program began in 2012.

Number awarded 1 each year.

Deadline November of each year.

[586]
SHANNON FUND

Episcopal Diocese of Bethlehem
c/o Diocesan House
333 Wyandotte Street
Bethlehem, PA 18015
(610) 691-5655, ext. 222
Toll Free: (800) 358-5655 (within PA)
E-mail: rick@diobeth.org
Web: www.diobeth.org

Summary To provide financial assistance to residents of Pennsylvania who are daughters of Episcopal clergy and interested in working on a degree at a college in any state.

Eligibility Applicants must be 1) residents of 1 of the 5 dioceses of Pennsylvania; 2) daughters of an Episcopal priest; 3) younger than 20 years of age; and 4) interested in working on a degree at a college in any state. The clergy parent must live in Pennsylvania and must be canonically resident in 1 of its dioceses. Financial need is considered in the selection process.

Financial data A stipend is awarded (amount not specified). Funds are paid directly to the recipient's college or university.

Duration 1 year.

Number awarded 5 each year.

Deadline April of each year.

[587]
SHARON D. BANKS MEMORIAL UNDERGRADUATE SCHOLARSHIP

Women's Transportation Seminar
Attn: WTS Foundation
1701 K Street, N.W., Suite 800
Washington, DC 20006
(202) 955-5085   Fax: (202) 955-5088
E-mail: wts@wtsinternational.org
Web: www.wtsinternational.org/education/scholarships

Summary To provide financial assistance to undergraduate women interested in a career in transportation.

Eligibility This program is open to women who are working on an undergraduate degree in transportation or a transportation-related field (e.g., transportation engineering, planning, finance, or logistics). Applicants must have a GPA of 3.0 or higher and be interested in a career in transportation. Along with their application, they must submit a 500-word statement about their career goals after graduation and why they think they should receive the scholarship award. Applications must be submitted first to a local chapter; the chapters forward selected applications for consideration on the national level. Minority women are especially encouraged to apply. Selection is based on transportation involvement and goals, job skills, and academic record; financial need is not considered.

Financial data The stipend is $5,000.

Duration 1 year.

Additional information This program began in 1992. Local chapters may also award additional funding to winners in their area.

Number awarded 1 each year.

Deadline Applications must be submitted by November to a local WTS chapter.

[588]
SHARON JUNOD MCKIMPSON SCHOLARSHIP

Iowa United Methodist Foundation
2301 Rittenhouse Street
Des Moines, IA 50321
(515) 974-8927
Web: www.iumf.org/scholarships/general

Summary To provide financial assistance to female Methodists from Iowa, who are interested in working on a degree in mathematics or science at a college in any state.

Eligibility This program is open to women who are members of a United Methodist church in Iowa who are enrolled at a college or university in any state. Applicants must be working on an undergraduate or graduate degree in mathematics or science. They must submit transcripts, 3 letters of recommendation, ACT and/or SAT scores, and documentation of financial need.

Financial data Recently, the stipend was $1,650.

Duration 1 year.

Number awarded 1 each year.

Deadline February of each year.

[589]
SHELLY SZEPANSKI MEMORIAL FLIGHT SCHOLARSHIP

Alaska Community Foundation
Attn: Scholarships
3201 C Street, Suite 110
Anchorage, AK 99503
(907) 334-6700   Toll Free: (855) 336-6701
Fax: (907) 334-5780   E-mail: info@alaskacf.org
Web: www.alaskacf.org/scholarships

Summary To provide financial assistance to female residents of Alaska who are interested in learning to fly as preparation for a science-related career.

Eligibility This program is open to women who are residents of Alaska and currently enrolled in a science-related degree program, preferably in wildlife biology or natural resources. Applicants must have passed their FAA written flight test and medical examination and be planning to earn a private or commercial/instrument rating, including a float rating, as part of a career in a science-related field. Along with their application, they must submit a 1,000-word essay describing their background, educational and professional goals, how flying is relevant to those goals, and specific qualifications for this scholarship. Preference is given to applicants attending college in Alaska and to those who can demonstrate financial need.

Financial data The stipend is $5,000 per year.

Duration 1 year; recipients may reapply.

Number awarded 1 or more each year.

Deadline May of each year.

[590]
SHIPLEY ROSE BUCKNER MEMORIAL SCHOLARSHIP

Funeral Service Foundation
Attn: Executive Director
13625 Bishop's Drive
Brookfield, WI 53005-6607
(262) 789-1880   Toll Free: (877) 402-5900
Fax: (262) 789-6977
E-mail: info@funeralservicefoundation.org
Web: www.funeralservicefoundation.org

Summary To provide financial assistance to female mortuary science students.

Eligibility This program is open to women who are currently enrolled full or part time or accepted for enrollment in a program of mortuary science accredited by the American Board of Funeral Service Education. Applicants must submit an essay of 500 to 1,000 words on a topic that changes annually but relates to the funeral profession; recently, students were asked to explain why they chose to enter the funeral service profession and to discuss why they think memorialization is essential in today's society. Selection is based primarily on that essay and academic achievement; financial need is not considered.

Financial data The stipend is $5,000 or $2,500; funds are sent directly to the school.

Duration 1 year; nonrenewable.

Additional information This program began in 2012.

Number awarded Either 1 at $5,000 or 2 at $2,500 each are awarded each year.

Deadline June of each year.

[591]
SIGMA ALPHA IOTA SUMMER MUSIC SCHOLARSHIPS

Sigma Alpha Iota Philanthropies, Inc.
One Tunnel Road
Asheville, NC 28805
(828) 251-0606   Fax: (828) 251-0644
E-mail: nh@sai-national.org
Web: app.smarterselect.com

Summary To provide financial assistance for summer study in music, in the United States or abroad, to members of Sigma Alpha Iota (an organization of women musicians).

Eligibility This program is open to undergraduate and graduate student members of the organization who are planning to study at a summer music program in the United States or abroad. Applicants must submit a complete resume (including musical studies and activities, academic GPA, community service record, and record of participation in Sigma Alpha Iota), supporting materials (recital and concert programs, reviews, repertoire list, etc.), a statement of why they chose this program and how it will aid their musical growth, a full brochure of information on the program (including cost and payment due dates), a copy of the completed summer school application and acceptance letter (when available), and a letter of recommendation from their major teacher.

Financial data The stipend is $1,000. Funds for study in the United States are applied directly to the recipient's tuition; funds for study abroad are mailed directly to the recipient.

Duration Summer months.

Number awarded 5 each year.

Deadline March of each year.

[592]
SIGMA ALPHA IOTA UNDERGRADUATE PERFORMANCE AWARDS

Sigma Alpha Iota Philanthropies, Inc.
One Tunnel Road
Asheville, NC 28805
(828) 251-0606   Fax: (828) 251-0644
E-mail: nh@sai-national.org
Web: www.sai-national.org

Summary To recognize and reward, with scholarships for additional study, outstanding performances in vocal and instrumental categories by undergraduate members of Sigma Alpha Iota (an organization of women musicians).

Eligibility This competition is open to undergraduate student members of the organization who are vocalists or instrumentalists. Entrants must be younger than 25 years of age. Selection is based on taped auditions in 4 categories: voice, keyboard or percussion, strings, and winds or brass.

Financial data The awards are $1,500. Funds must be used for continued study.

Duration The competition is held triennially.

Additional information This program includes the Blanche Z. Hoffman Memorial Award for Voice and the Mary Ann Starring Memorial Award for Woodwinds or Brass.

Number awarded 4 every 3 years: 1 in each of the 4 categories.

Deadline March of the year of the awards (2018, 2021, etc.).

[593]
SIGMA ALPHA IOTA UNDERGRADUATE SCHOLARSHIPS

Sigma Alpha Iota Philanthropies, Inc.
One Tunnel Road
Asheville, NC 28805
(828) 251-0606   Fax: (828) 251-0644
E-mail: nh@sai-national.org
Web: app.smarterselect.com

Summary To provide financial assistance for undergraduate study to members of Sigma Alpha Iota (an organization of women musicians).

Eligibility This program is open to members of the organization in the first 3 years of undergraduate study. Candidates must be nominated by their chapter and their chapter adviser must submit a letter of recommendation. Nominees must submit a brief statement of career goals and aspirations. Selection is based on financial need, musical ability, scholarship, potential leadership, contribution to campus and community life, and exemplification of the ideals of the organization.

Financial data The stipend is $1,500.

Duration 1 year.

Number awarded 10 each year.

Deadline March of each year.

[594]
SIGMA GAMMA RHO SCHOLARSHIPS/ FELLOWSHIPS

Sigma Gamma Rho Sorority, Inc.
Attn: National Education Fund
1000 Southhill Drive, Suite 200
Cary, NC 27513
(919) 678-9720 Toll Free: (888) SGR-1922
Fax: (919) 678-9721
E-mail: customerservice@sgrho1922.org
Web: www.sgrho1922.org/nef

Summary To provide financial assistance for undergraduate or graduate study to applicants who can demonstrate financial need.

Eligibility This program is open to high school seniors, undergraduates, and graduate students who can demonstrate financial need. The sponsor is a traditionally African American sorority, but support is available to males and females of all races. Applicants must have a GPA of "C" or higher.

Financial data A stipend is awarded (amount not specified).

Duration 1 year.

Additional information This program includes the following named awards: the Lorraine A. Williams Scholarship, the Philo Sallie A. Williams Scholarship, the Cleo W. Higgins Scholarship (limited to doctoral students), the Lillie and Carnell VanLandingham Scholarship, the Minnie and William Blakely Book Scholarship, the Inez Colson Memorial Scholarship (limited to students majoring in education or mathematics at Savannah State University), and the Philo Geneva Young Scholarship. A processing fee of $20 is required.

Number awarded Varies each year.

Deadline April of each year.

[595]
SIGNATURE FLIGHT SUPPORT CORPORATION SCHOLARSHIP

Women in Aviation International
Attn: Scholarships
Morningstar Airport
3647 State Route 503 South
West Alexandria, OH 45381-9354
(937) 839-4647 Fax: (937) 839-4645
E-mail: scholarships@wai.org
Web: www.wai.org

Summary To provide financial assistance for college to members of Women in Aviation International (WAI).

Eligibility This program is open to WAI members who are undergraduate or graduate students working on a degree in a field related to aviation, preferably FBO management. Applicants must have a GPA of 3.0 or higher and be a U.S. citizen. Along with their application, they must submit 1) a 500-word essay and professional resume that include their aviation history and goals, what they have done for themselves to achieve their goals, where they see themselves in 5 and 10 years, involvement in aviation activities, how the scholarship will help them achieve their objectives, and their present financial need; and 2) an essay of 500 to 1,000 words on their current educational status, why they chose a career in avia-

tion, their experience in aviation, and their aspirations in the field.

Financial data The stipend is $1,500.

Duration 1 year.

Additional information This program was established in 2014 by Signature Flight Support Corporation.

Number awarded 1 each year.

Deadline November of each year.

[596]
SIMSBURY WOMAN'S CLUB ADULT WOMEN'S SCHOLARSHIP

Simsbury Woman's Club
Attn: Patty Crawford, Scholarship Chair
P.O. Box 903
Simsbury, CT 06070
E-mail: SWCScholarshp@gmail.com
Web: www.simsburywomansclub.org

Summary To provide financial assistance to female residents of Connecticut enrolled at a college in any state.

Eligibility This program is open to female residents of Connecticut who are currently enrolled at an institution of higher learning in any state. Applicants must have completed at least 60 credits of undergraduate work and have a GPA of 3.0 or higher. They must be U.S. citizens. Selection is based on future promise, academic ability, and financial need.

Financial data The stipend is $2,000.

Duration 1 year.

Number awarded 1 each year.

Deadline February of each year.

[597]
SISTER ELIZABETH CANDON SCHOLARSHIP

Vermont Student Assistance Corporation
Attn: Scholarship Programs
10 East Allen Street
P.O. Box 2000
Winooski, VT 05404-2601
(802) 654-3798 Toll Free: (888) 253-4819
Fax: (802) 654-3765 TDD: (800) 281-3341 (within VT)
E-mail: info@vsac.org
Web: services.vsac.org

Summary To provide financial assistance to single mothers in Vermont who plan to attend college in any state.

Eligibility This program is open to female residents of Vermont who are single parents with primary custody of at least 1 child 12 years of age or younger. Applicants must be enrolled at least half time in an accredited undergraduate degree program in any state. Along with their application, they must submit 1) a 250-word essay on their short- and long-term academic, educational, career, vocational, and/or employment goals; 2) a 100-word essay on how the program in which they will be enrolled will enhance their career or vocation; and 3) a 250-word essay on what they believe distinguishes their application from others that may be submitted. Selection is based on those essays, a letter of recommendation, and financial need (expected family contribution less than $23,760).

Financial data The stipend is $1,000 per year.

Duration 1 year; may be renewed up to 3 additional years.

Number awarded 1 each year.

Deadline March of each year.

[598]
SISTER THOMAS MORE BERTELS SCHOLARSHIP

American Agri-Women
Daughters of American Agriculture
c/o Ardath DeWall
11841 North Mount Vernon Road
Shannon, IL 61078
E-mail: info@americanagriwomen.org
Web: www.americanagriwomen.org

Summary To provide financial assistance for college to mature women involved in agriculture.

Eligibility This program is open to women who are farmers, ranchers, or the wife, daughter, or other close relative of a farmer, rancher, or other person employed in agriculture. Applicants must be 24 years of age or older and be interested in working on a degree in agribusiness, agricultural leadership, communications, education, technology, rural sociology, medicine, or other courses directly related to agriculture and the needs of agricultural communities. Selection is based on financial need, knowledge of or work experience in agriculture, GPA, and test scores.

Financial data The stipend is $1,000.

Duration 1 year; nonrenewable.

Additional information This program began in 1991.

Number awarded 1 each year.

Deadline May of each year.

[599]
SOCCERLOCO NATIONAL SCHOLARSHIP

American Business Women's Association
Attn: Stephen Bufton Memorial Educational Fund
9820 Metcalf Avenue, Suite 110
Overland Park, KS 66212
Toll Free: (800) 228-0007
Web: www.sbmef.org

Summary To provide financial assistance to women who have participated in athletics and are interested in working on a baccalaureate degree in any field.

Eligibility This program is open to women who are entering at least their freshman year at a college or university that offers a baccalaureate degree and have a cumulative GPA of 3.0 or higher. Applicants must submit 1) a 150-word biographical sketch that includes information about their background, activities, honors, work experience, and long-term educational and professional goals; and 2) an essay of 500 to 700 words on how their athletic career has helped them to become a better teammate, leader and person. Financial need is not considered in the selection process.

Financial data The stipend is $2,000. Funds are paid directly to the recipient's institution to be used only for tuition, books, and fees.

Duration 1 year; nonrenewable.

Additional information This program was begun in 2014 with support from the women's soccer equipment and apparel firm Soccerloco as part of ABWA's Stephen Bufton Memorial Education Fund.

Number awarded 1 each year.

Deadline May of each year.

[600]
SOCIETY OF DAUGHTERS OF THE UNITED STATES ARMY SCHOLARSHIPS

Society of Daughters of the United States Army
c/o Mary P. Maroney, Scholarship Chair
11804 Grey Birch Place
Reston, VA 20191

Summary To provide financial assistance for college to daughters and granddaughters of active, retired, or deceased career Army warrant and commissioned officers.

Eligibility This program is open to the daughters, adopted daughters, stepdaughters, or granddaughters of career commissioned officers or warrant officers of the U.S. Army (active, regular, or Reserve) who 1) are currently on active duty; 2) retired after 20 years of service; 3) was medically retired before 20 years of service; 4) died while on active duty; or 5) died after retiring from active duty with 20 or more years of service. Applicants must have at least a 3.0 GPA and be enrolled or planning to enroll full time at the undergraduate level. Selection is based on depth of character, leadership, seriousness of purpose, academic achievement, and financial need.

Financial data Scholarships, to a maximum of $1,000, are paid directly to the college or school for tuition, laboratory fees, books, or other expenses.

Duration 1 year; may be renewed up to 4 additional years if the recipient maintains at least a 3.0 GPA.

Additional information Recipients may attend any accredited college, professional, or vocational school. This program includes named scholarships from the following funds: the Colonel Hayden W. Wagner Memorial Fund, the Eugenia Bradford Roberts Memorial Fund, the Daughters of the U.S. Army Scholarship Fund, the Gladys K. and John K. Simpson Scholarship Fund, and the Margaret M. Prickett Scholarship Fund.

Number awarded Up to 10 each year.

Deadline February of each year.

[601]
SOROPTIMIST LIVE YOUR DREAM AWARDS

Soroptimist International of the Americas
Attn: Program Department
1709 Spruce Street
Philadelphia, PA 19103-6103
(215) 893-9000   Fax: (215) 893-5200
E-mail: siahq@soroptimist.org
Web: www.soroptimist.org

Summary To provide financial assistance to women reentering the job market to upgrade their employment status through education.

Eligibility This program is open to women who provide the primary financial support for their family. Applicants must have been accepted to a vocational/skills training program or an undergraduate degree program. They must reside in 1 of the 20 countries or territories (divided into 28 regions) that are part of Soroptimist International of the Americas. Along with their application, they must submit 1) a 300-word description of their career goals and how their education and/

or skills training support those goals; 2) a 750-word essay on the challenges they have faced and how this award could help them to live their dreams; and 3) documentation of financial need.

Financial data Each region grants an award of $5,000; most regions grant additional $3,000 awards. From among the regional winners, additional awards of $10,000 are presented to the most outstanding applicants.

Duration The awards are issued each year and are nonrenewable.

Additional information This program, established in 1972, was originally known as the Training Awards Program and subsequently as the Women's Opportunity Awards Program. The awards may not be used for graduate study or international travel. Applications are to be processed through the local Soroptimist club. Countries that are part of Soroptimist International of the Americas include Argentina, Bolivia, Brazil, Canada, Chile, Colombia, Ecuador, Guam, Japan, Republic of Korea, Mexico, Northern Mariana Islands, Panama, Paraguay, Peru, Philippines, Puerto Rico, Taiwan, United States, and Venezuela.

Number awarded Awards are presented in each of the 28 regions. From among the regional winners, 3 receive an additional award from Soroptimist International of the Americas. A total of approximately $1.6 million is awarded annually to more than 1,200 women. Since the program was established, it has awarded approximately $30 million in scholarships to more than 30,000 women.

Deadline Applications must be submitted to regional contacts by November of each year.

[602]
SOUTH DAKOTA JOB'S DAUGHTERS SCHOLARSHIPS

International Order of Job's Daughters-Grand Guardian
  Council of South Dakota
c/o Carrie Bunkowske, Education Scholarship Committee
  Chair
909 Park Street
Sturgis, SD 57785
(605) 347-1464   E-mail: slimecarebear@msn.com
Web: www.sdjd.org/?page_id=29

Summary To provide financial assistance to members of Job's Daughters in South Dakota who are interested in attending college in any state.

Eligibility This program is open to members of Job's Daughters in South Dakota who are graduating high school seniors or students currently attending college or technical school in any state. Applicants must submit a brief statement on why they chose their planned field of study and a resume that includes extracurricular activities, honors they have received, church and community activities and honors, and involvement in Job's Daughters. They must also submit a 500-word essay on how being in Job's Daughters has affected their life and what receiving this scholarship means to them. Selection is based on academics, merit, community involvement, work history, and participation in Job's Daughters.

Financial data A stipend is awarded (amount not specified).

Duration 1 year.

Number awarded Varies each year; recently, 4 were awarded.

Deadline March of each year.

[603]
SOUTHWEST AIRLINES FLIGHT TRAINING SCHOLARSHIP

Women in Aviation International
Attn: Scholarships
Morningstar Airport
3647 State Route 503 South
West Alexandria, OH 45381-9354
(937) 839-4647   Fax: (937) 839-4645
E-mail: scholarships@wai.org
Web: www.wai.org

Summary To provide financial assistance to members of Women in Aviation International (WAI) who are working on a degree to prepare for a career as a professional pilot.

Eligibility This program is open to WAI members who are currently enrolled in an accredited collegiate 4-year degree program to work on a commercial, multiengine, and/or flight instructor certificate. Applicants must have a GPA of 3.0 or higher, an FAA private and instrument rating, and a current FAA first-class medical certificate. Along with their application, they must submit an essay on how this scholarship will help them reach their professional career goals, 2 letters of recommendation (1 regarding their career aspirations and 1 regarding their flying ability), their most recent transcript, and a list of WAI volunteer functions they have performed.

Financial data The stipend is $5,000. Funds are paid directly to the recipient's institution.

Duration Training must be completed within 1 year.

Additional information WAI is a nonprofit professional organization dedicated to encouraging women to consider an aviation career and to providing educational outreach activities and networking resources to women active in the industry. This program is sponsored by Southwest Airlines.

Number awarded 6 each year.

Deadline November of each year.

[604]
SOUTHWEST IDAHO SECTION SWE SCHOLARSHIPS

Society of Women Engineers-Southwest Idaho Section
c/o Scholarship Committee Chair
11548 West Rader Drive
Boise, ID 83713
(208) 396-4458   E-mail: idahoswe@gmail.com
Web: www.swiswe.org/scholarships.html

Summary To provide financial assistance to female high school seniors in Idaho planning to enter an engineering school in any state.

Eligibility This program is open to women graduating from high schools in Idaho and planning to attend an ABET-accredited 4- or 5-year engineering program in any state. Applicants must submit an essay of 500 to 1,000 words on their desire to enter an engineering or engineering-related field, transcripts, SAT/ACT scores, and a letter of recommendation from a high school science or mathematics teacher. Selection is based on that essay, academic accomplishments (especially in science and mathematics), extracurricular accomplishments, and the letter of recommendation. Financial need is not considered.

Financial data Stipends are generally $2,000.

Duration 1 year.

Number awarded Varies each year; recently, 6 were awarded.

Deadline February of each year.

[605]
SPACE COAST CHAPTER WOMEN IN DEFENSE SCHOLARSHIP PROGRAM

Women in Defense-Space Coast Chapter
Attn: Scholarship Program
P.O. Box 410832
Melbourne, FL 32941-0832
E-mail: stem@scwid.org
Web: www.scwid.org

Summary To provide financial assistance to women in Florida who are interested in working on an undergraduate or graduate degree in national security, defense, or a field related to science, technology, engineering, or mathematics (STEM) at a college in the state.

Eligibility This program is open to female residents of Florida who are graduating high school seniors, undergraduates, or graduate students enrolled or planning to enroll full or part time at an accredited college or university in the state. Applicants must be preparing for a career related to national security, defense, or a STEM-related field. They must be U.S. citizens and have a GPA of 3.0 or higher. Along with their application, they must submit an essay of 500 to 600 words that covers their career interest, prior accomplishments, and proposed program or course emphasis. Selection is based on that essay (25%), academic ability and field of study (15%), professional or academic recommendations (15%), defense and national security activities (15%), employment (10%), awards and honors (10%), and financial need (10%).

Financial data The stipend is $1,000.

Duration 1 year.

Number awarded At least 1 each year.

Deadline April of each year.

[606]
SPENCER-WILKINSON AWARDS

Virginia State Golf Association
Attn: VSGA-VIP Scholarship Foundation
2400 Dovercourt Drive
Midlothian, VA 23113
(804) 378-2300, ext. 11   Fax: (804) 378-8216
E-mail: contact@vsga.org
Web: www.vsga.org

Summary To provide financial assistance to female high school seniors in Virginia who have an interest in golf and plan to attend college in the state.

Eligibility This program is open to female high school seniors in Virginia who are interested in golf and wish to attend a college or university in the state. Applicants must submit an essay of 500 words or less on how golf has influenced their life, the role it will play in their future plans, why they are applying for this scholarship, and their career plans following graduation. Selection is based on the essay, interest in golf (excellence and ability are not considered), academic

achievement, citizenship, character, and financial need. Applications must be made on behalf of the candidate by a member club of the Virginia State Golf Association (VSGA).

Financial data Stipends range from $1,000 to $7,000. Funds may be used only for tuition, room, and other approved educational expenses.

Duration 1 year.

Additional information This program began in 1996.

Number awarded Varies each year; recently, 2 were awarded. Since the program was established, it has awarded 42 scholarships worth more than $150,000.

Deadline February of each year.

[607]
SPIRIT OF YOUTH SCHOLARSHIP FOR JUNIOR MEMBERS

American Legion Auxiliary
8945 North Meridian Street
Indianapolis, IN 46260
(317) 569-4500   Fax: (317) 569-4502
E-mail: alahq@alaforveterans.org
Web: www.alaforveterans.org

Summary To provide financial assistance for college to junior members of the American Legion Auxiliary.

Eligibility Applicants for this scholarship must have been junior members of the Auxiliary for at least the past 3 years. They must be seniors at an accredited high school in the United States, have a GPA of 3.0 or higher, and be planning to enroll full time at an accredited 4-year institution of higher education. Along with their application, they must submit a 1,000-word essay on a topic that changes annually; recently, students were asked to write on "How Military Families Are Keeping the Promise to Preserve our Freedom." Selection is based on that essay (30%), character and leadership (30%), and academic record (40%). Each unit of the Auxiliary may select a candidate for application to the department level, and each department submits a candidate for the national award.

Financial data The stipend is $1,250 per year.

Duration 4 years.

Additional information Applications are available from the president of the candidate's own unit or from the secretary or education chair of the department.

Number awarded 5 each year: 1 in each division of the American Legion Auxiliary.

Deadline Applications must be submitted to the unit president by February of each year.

[608]
STACIE LYNN HAYS MEMORIAL SCHOLARSHIP

Chickasaw Foundation
2020 Arlington, Suite 4
P.O. Box 1726
Ada, OK 74821-1726
(580) 421-9030   Fax: (580) 421-9031
E-mail: ChickasawFoundation@chickasaw.net
Web: www.chickasawfoundation.org/Scholarships.aspx

Summary To provide financial assistance to members of the Chickasaw Nation, especially women, who are working on an undergraduate degree in business administration.

Eligibility This program is open to Chickasaw students who are currently enrolled full time at a 2- or 4-year college or university and working on an undergraduate degree in business administration. Preference is given to women and students who can demonstrate financial need. Applicants must have a GPA of 2.75 or higher. Along with their application, they must submit high school or college transcripts; 2 letters of recommendation; a copy of their Chickasaw Nation citizenship card; documentation of financial need; a 2-page list of honors, achievements, awards, club memberships, societies, and civic involvement; and a 1-page essay on their long-term goals and plans for achieving those.

Financial data A stipend is awarded (amount not specified).

Duration 1 year.

Number awarded 1 each year.

Deadline June of each year.

[609]
STEPHANIE HUSEK SCHOLARSHIP

First Catholic Slovak Union of the United States and
  Canada
Attn: Scholarship Program
6611 Rockside Road, Suite 300
Independence, OH 44131
(216) 642-9406   Toll Free: (800) JEDNOTA
Fax: (216) 642-4310   E-mail: scholarship@fcsu.com
Web: www.fcsu.com/scholarships

Summary To provide financial assistance for college to female high school seniors who are members of the First Catholic Slovak Union of the United States and Canada (FCSU).

Eligibility This program is open to women graduating from high schools in the United States and Canada and planning to attend an approved institution of higher education. Applicants must be of Slovak descent and Catholic faith. They must be FCSU members who have had for at least 4 years $5,000 or more of reserve insurance, $10,000 or more of JEP single premium policy, or $25,000 or more of annual premium JEP policy. Along with their application, they must submit brief essays on their career plans, what they hope to achieve in life, how their career plan will help them achieve their goals, and why they think they should receive this scholarship. Selection is based on those essays, a transcript of grades that includes ACT or SAT scores, extracurricular school activities, volunteer community activities, work experience, and financial need.

Financial data The stipend is $1,250. The winner also receives a $3,000 single premium life insurance policy upon proof of graduation from college.

Duration 1 year; nonrenewable.

Number awarded 1 each year.

Deadline March of each year.

[610]
STEPHEN BUFTON MEMORIAL EDUCATION FUND OUTRIGHT GRANTS PROGRAM

American Business Women's Association
Attn: Stephen Bufton Memorial Educational Fund
11050 Roe Avenue, Suite 200
Overland Park, KS 66211
Toll Free: (800) 228-0007
Web: www.sbmef.org/Opportunities.cfm

Summary To provide financial assistance to women undergraduate and graduate students in any field who are sponsored by a chapter of the American Business Women's Association (ABWA).

Eligibility This program is open to women who are at least juniors at an accredited college or university. Applicants must be working on an undergraduate or graduate degree and have a GPA of 2.5 or higher. They are not required to be ABWA members, but they must be sponsored by an ABWA chapter that has contributed to the fund in the previous chapter year. U.S. citizenship is required.

Financial data The maximum grant is $1,500. Funds are paid directly to the recipient's institution to be used only for tuition, books, and fees.

Duration 1 year. Grants are not automatically renewed, but recipients may reapply.

Additional information This program began in 1953. The ABWA does not provide the names and addresses of local chapters; it recommends that applicants check with their local Chamber of Commerce, library, or university to see if any chapter has registered a contact's name and number.

Number awarded Varies each year; since the inception of this program, it has awarded more than $14 million to more than 14,000 students.

Deadline May of each year.

[611]
SUCCESS FOR SURVIVORS SCHOLARSHIPS

General Federation of Women's Clubs
Attn: Programs Department
1734 N Street, N.W.
Washington, DC 20036-2990
(202) 347-3168   Fax: (202) 835-0246
E-mail: programs@gfwc.org
Web: www.gfwc.org

Summary To provide financial assistance for college to victims of domestic violence.

Eligibility This program is open to U.S. citizens and permanent residents who have survived intimate partner abuse. Applicants must be enrolled or planning to enroll at an accredited postsecondary or vocational institution. They must be recommended by a licensed or accredited domestic violence agency and/or counselor or social worker. Along with their application, they must submit 3 essays up to 500 words each on 1) their educational goals and how this scholarship will help them achieve those; 2) their career goals; and 3) a challenge they have faced and the steps they took to overcome that challenge.

Financial data The stipend is $2,500.

Duration 1 year.

Additional information This program began in 2011.

Number awarded Varies each year; recently, 8 were awarded.

Deadline February of each year.

[612]
SUE J. IRWIN SCHOLARSHIP

Native Daughters of the Golden West
Attn: Education and Scholarships
543 Baker Street
San Francisco, CA 94117-1405
(415) 563-9091   Toll Free: (800) 994-NDGW
Fax: (415) 563-5230   E-mail: ndgwgpo@att.net
Web: www.ndgw.org/edu.htm

Summary   To provide financial assistance for college to members of the Native Daughters of the Golden West (NDGW) in California and their families.

Eligibility   This program is open to members and their children who are attending or planning to attend an accredited university, college, or vocational school in California. Applicants must be high school seniors or undergraduates who have completed the first year of college with a GPA of 3.0 or higher. They must have been born in the state and be sponsored by a local parlor of the NDGW.

Financial data   The stipend is $1,000.

Duration   1 year; may be renewed if the recipient maintains a GPA of 3.0 or higher.

Number awarded   4 each year.

Deadline   April of each year.

[613]
SUSAN AND MARVIN WHATLEY SCHOLARSHIP

Society of Women Engineers
Attn: Scholarship Selection Committee
203 North LaSalle Street, Suite 1675
Chicago, IL 60601-1269
(312) 596-5223   Toll Free: (877) SWE-INFO
Fax: (312) 644-8557   E-mail: scholarships@swe.org
Web: societyofwomenengineers.swe.org

Summary   To provide financial assistance to reentry women who are interested in studying computer science or engineering at designated universities.

Eligibility   This program is open to women who are reentry or nontraditional students. Applicants must be enrolled full time and majoring in computer science or engineering at University of Tennessee, University of Virginia, Louisiana State University, Iowa State University, Clemson University, or Middle Tennessee State University. Selection is based on merit.

Financial data   The stipend is $1,000 per year.

Duration   1 year; may be renewed, provided the recipient maintains a GPA of 3.0 or higher.

Number awarded   1 each year.

Deadline   February of each year.

[614]
SUSAN EKDALE MEMORIAL FIELD CAMP SCHOLARSHIP

Association for Women Geoscientists-Salt Lake Chapter
c/o Janae Wallace
Utah Geological Survey
1594 West North Temple
Salt Lake City, Utah 84114-6100
(801) 537-3387   Fax: (801) 537-3400
E-mail: janaewallace@utah.gov
Web: www.awg.org/eas/ekdale.htm

Summary   To provide financial assistance for a summer field camp to women who have a Utah connection and are majoring in geoscience.

Eligibility   This program is open to women majoring in geoscience at a college or university in Utah who must attend a summer field camp as part of their graduation requirements. Women geoscience students from Utah attending college in other states are also eligible. Applicants must submit a 1- to 2-page essay in which they describe their personal and academic highlights, their reasons for applying for the scholarship, and what they, as women, can contribute to the geosciences. Selection is based on merit and need.

Financial data   The stipend is $2,000. Funds must be used to help pay field camp expenses.

Duration   Summer months.

Number awarded   1 each year.

Deadline   March of each year.

[615]
SUSAN MISZKOWICZ SEPTEMBER 11 MEMORIAL SCHOLARSHIP

Society of Women Engineers
Attn: Scholarship Selection Committee
203 North LaSalle Street, Suite 1675
Chicago, IL 60601-1269
(312) 596-5223   Toll Free: (877) SWE-INFO
Fax: (312) 644-8557   E-mail: scholarships@swe.org
Web: societyofwomenengineers.swe.org

Summary   To provide financial assistance to undergraduate women majoring in computer science or engineering.

Eligibility   This program is open to women who are entering their sophomore, junior, or senior year at a 4-year ABET-accredited college or university. Applicants must be working full time on a degree in computer science or engineering. Selection is based on merit.

Financial data   The stipend is $1,500.

Duration   1 year.

Additional information   This program began in 2002 to honor a member of the Society of Women Engineers who was killed in the New York World Trade Center on September 11, 2001.

Number awarded   1 each year.

Deadline   February of each year.

[616]
SUSAN W. CODA MEMORIAL SCHOLARSHIP

P.E.O. Sisterhood-Utah State Chapter
c/o Kathy Tall, Scholarship Committee
1972 West 4335 South
Roy, UT 84067-2729
(801) 390-4461   E-mail: peoutah.coda@gmail.com
Web: www.peoutah.org

Summary   To provide financial assistance to women from Utah who are attending college outside the state.

Eligibility   This program is open to women who are residents of Utah and currently attending a 4-year college or university outside the state. Applicants must have a GPA of at least 3.8 and high SAT/ACT scores. Along with their application, they must submit an essay expanding on their educational goals and reasons for attending college outside the state of Utah. Selection is based on academic accomplishment, leadership abilities, participation in extracurricular school activities, and involvement in community affairs.

Financial data A stipend is awarded (amount not specified).

Duration 1 year; nonrenewable.

Additional information This program began in 1988.

Number awarded 1 each year.

Deadline February of each year.

[617]
SUSIE HOLMES MEMORIAL SCHOLARSHIP

International Order of Job's Daughters
c/o Judy Burl, Supreme Scholarship Chair
121 Byrd Street
Hopewell, VA 23860
(804) 458-5552   E-mail: jgburl@aol.com
Web: www.jobsdaughtersinternational.org

Summary To provide financial assistance for college to members of Job's Daughters.

Eligibility This program is open to high school graduates who are members of Job's Daughters. Applicants must be able to demonstrate dedicated, continuous, and joyful service to Job's Daughters; regular attendance at Supreme and/or Grand Sessions; participation in competitions at Supreme and/or Grand Sessions; friendship and impartiality in their Bethel; good character and integrity; and a GPA of 2.5 or higher.

Financial data The stipend is $1,000.

Duration 1 year.

Number awarded 1 or more each year.

Deadline April of each year.

[618]
SWE BOSTON SECTION SCHOLARSHIP

Society of Women Engineers
Attn: Scholarship Selection Committee
203 North LaSalle Street, Suite 1675
Chicago, IL 60601-1269
(312) 596-5223   Toll Free: (877) SWE-INFO
Fax: (312) 644-8557   E-mail: scholarships@swe.org
Web: societyofwomenengineers.swe.org

Summary To provide financial assistance to women from Massachusetts who are working on an undergraduate degree in computer science or engineering, preferably at a school in the Boston metropolitan area.

Eligibility This program is open to women who are residents of Massachusetts entering their junior or senior year at an ABET-accredited 4-year college or university. Applicants must be working full time on a degree in computer science or engineering and have a GPA of 3.5 or higher. Financial need is considered in the selection process. Preference is given to students attending designated universities in the Boston metropolitan area.

Financial data The stipend is $1,250.

Duration 1 year.

Additional information The designated universities are Boston University, Massachusetts Institute of Technology, University of Massachusetts at Dartmouth, University of Massachusetts at Lowell, Northeastern University, Tufts University, Wentworth Institute of Technology, Worcester Polytechnic Institute, Suffolk University, and Merrimack College. This program, which began in 2009, is sponsored by the Boston Section of the Society of Women Engineers.

Number awarded 1 each year.

Deadline February of each year.

[619]
SWE CENTRAL NEW MEXICO PIONEERS SCHOLARSHIP

Society of Women Engineers
Attn: Scholarship Selection Committee
203 North LaSalle Street, Suite 1675
Chicago, IL 60601-1269
(312) 596-5223   Toll Free: (877) SWE-INFO
Fax: (312) 644-8557   E-mail: scholarships@swe.org
Web: societyofwomenengineers.swe.org

Summary To provide financial assistance to members of the Society of Women Engineers (SWE) from any state interested in working on an undergraduate degree in engineering or computer science at a college or university in New Mexico.

Eligibility This program is open to women who are sophomores, juniors, or seniors at an ABET-accredited college, university, or 4-year engineering technology program in New Mexico. Applicants must be working on a degree in computer science or engineering and have a GPA of 3.0 or higher. They must be U.S. citizens and members of the society. Selection is based on merit.

Financial data The stipend is $1,500 per year.

Duration 1 year; may be renewed up to 2 additional years.

Additional information This program, which began in 2004, is sponsored by the Central New Mexico section of SWE.

Number awarded 1 each year.

Deadline February of each year.

[620]
SWE CENTRAL NEW MEXICO RE-ENTRY SCHOLARSHIP

Society of Women Engineers
Attn: Scholarship Selection Committee
203 North LaSalle Street, Suite 1675
Chicago, IL 60601-1269
(312) 596-5223   Toll Free: (877) SWE-INFO
Fax: (312) 644-8557   E-mail: scholarships@swe.org
Web: societyofwomenengineers.swe.org

Summary To provide financial assistance to members of the Society of Women Engineers (SWE) from any state who are reentering college or graduate school in New Mexico to work on a degree in engineering or computer science.

Eligibility This program is open to members of the society who are sophomores, juniors, seniors, or graduate students at an ABET-accredited college, university, or 4-year engineering technology program in New Mexico. Applicants must be returning to college or graduate school after an absence of several years to work on a degree in computer science or engineering. They must have a GPA of 3.0 or higher. Selection is based on merit. U.S. citizenship is required.

Financial data The stipend is $1,500 per year.

Duration 1 year; may be renewed up to 5 additional years.

Additional information This program, which began in 2005, is sponsored by the Central New Mexico section of SWE.

Number awarded 1 each year.

Deadline February of each year.

[621]
SWE NEW JERSEY SECTION SCHOLARSHIP

Society of Women Engineers
Attn: Scholarship Selection Committee
203 North LaSalle Street, Suite 1675
Chicago, IL 60601-1269
(312) 596-5223   Toll Free: (877) SWE-INFO
Fax: (312) 644-8557   E-mail: scholarships@swe.org
Web: societyofwomenengineers.swe.org

Summary To provide financial assistance to women from New Jersey who will be entering freshmen at a college in any state and are interested in studying engineering technology, engineering, computer science.

Eligibility This program is open to women who are entering college in any state as freshmen. Applicants must be residents of New Jersey planning to enroll full time at an ABET-accredited 4-year college or university in any state and major in computer science or engineering. Selection is based on merit.

Financial data The stipend is $2,000.

Duration 1 year.

Additional information This program began in 2008 with support from the New Jersey Section of the Society of Women Engineers (SWE).

Number awarded 1 each year.

Deadline May of each year.

[622]
SWE PHOENIX SECTION SCHOLARSHIP

Society of Women Engineers
Attn: Scholarship Selection Committee
203 North LaSalle Street, Suite 1675
Chicago, IL 60601-1269
(312) 596-5223   Toll Free: (877) SWE-INFO
Fax: (312) 644-8557   E-mail: scholarships@swe.org
Web: societyofwomenengineers.swe.org

Summary To provide financial assistance to members of the Society of Women Engineers (SWE) working on an undergraduate degree in engineering or computer science at a school in Arizona.

Eligibility This program is open to members of the society who will be sophomores, juniors, or seniors at ABET-accredited colleges and universities in Arizona. Applicants must be working full time on a degree in computer science or engineering. Selection is based on merit.

Financial data The stipend is $3,000.

Duration 1 year.

Additional information This program, which began in 2011, is sponsored by the Phoenix Section of SWE.

Number awarded 1 each year.

Deadline February of each year.

[623]
SWE REGION E SCHOLARSHIP

Society of Women Engineers
Attn: Scholarship Selection Committee
203 North LaSalle Street, Suite 1675
Chicago, IL 60601-1269
(312) 596-5223   Toll Free: (877) SWE-INFO
Fax: (312) 644-8557   E-mail: scholarships@swe.org
Web: societyofwomenengineers.swe.org

Summary To provide financial assistance to members of the Society of Women Engineers (SWE) working on an undergraduate or graduate degree in engineering or computer science at a school in the mid-Atlantic (Region E).

Eligibility This program is open to members of the society who will be sophomores, juniors, seniors, or graduate students at ABET-accredited colleges and universities in Delaware, Maryland, New Jersey, New York, eastern Pennsylvania, Virginia, or Washington, D.C. Applicants must be working full time on a degree in computer science or engineering. Selection is based on merit.

Financial data The stipend is $1,500.

Duration 1 year.

Additional information This program began in 2014.

Number awarded 1 each year.

Deadline February of each year.

[624]
SWE REGION G-JUDY SIMMONS MEMORIAL SCHOLARSHIP

Society of Women Engineers
Attn: Scholarship Selection Committee
203 North LaSalle Street, Suite 1675
Chicago, IL 60601-1269
(312) 596-5223   Toll Free: (877) SWE-INFO
Fax: (312) 644-8557   E-mail: scholarships@swe.org
Web: societyofwomenengineers.swe.org

Summary To provide financial assistance to members of the Society of Women Engineers (SWE) working on an undergraduate or graduate degree in engineering or computer science at a school in the Ohio Valley (Region G).

Eligibility This program is open to members of the society who will be sophomores, juniors, seniors, or graduate students at ABET-accredited colleges and universities in Kentucky, Ohio, western Pennsylvania, or West Virginia. Applicants must be working full time on a degree in computer science or engineering. Selection is based on merit.

Financial data The stipend is $1,250.

Duration 1 year.

Additional information This program, which began in 2014, is sponsored by Region G of SWE.

Number awarded 1 each year.

Deadline February of each year.

[625]
SWE REGION H SCHOLARSHIP

Society of Women Engineers
Attn: Scholarship Selection Committee
203 North LaSalle Street, Suite 1675
Chicago, IL 60601-1269
(312) 596-5223   Toll Free: (877) SWE-INFO
Fax: (312) 644-8557   E-mail: scholarships@swe.org
Web: societyofwomenengineers.swe.org

Summary   To provide financial assistance to members of the Society of Women Engineers (SWE) working on an undergraduate or graduate degree in engineering or computer science at a school in the upper Midwest (Region H).

Eligibility   This program is open to members of the society who will be sophomores, juniors, seniors, or graduate students at ABET-accredited colleges and universities in Illinois, Indiana, Iowa, Michigan, Minnesota, North Dakota, South Dakota, or Wisconsin. Applicants must have a record of active involvement in SWE, based on the amount of time spent volunteering, level of commitment, and years of service. They must be working full time on a degree in computer science or engineering. Selection is based on merit and participation in SWE activities.

Financial data   The stipend is $1,500 or $1,250.

Duration   1 year.

Additional information   This program began in 2008.

Number awarded   2 each year: 1 at $1,500 and 1 at $1,250.

Deadline   February of each year.

[626]
SWE REGION J SCHOLARSHIP

Society of Women Engineers
Attn: Scholarship Selection Committee
203 North LaSalle Street, Suite 1675
Chicago, IL 60601-1269
(312) 596-5223   Toll Free: (877) SWE-INFO
Fax: (312) 644-8557   E-mail: scholarships@swe.org
Web: societyofwomenengineers.swe.org

Summary   To provide financial assistance to reentry members of the Society of Women Engineers (SWE) working on a degree in engineering or computer science at a school in the Northwest (Region J).

Eligibility   This program is open to members of the society who are reentry or nontraditional students at ABET-accredited colleges and universities in Alaska, Idaho, Montana, Oregon, or Washington. Applicants must be working full time on a degree in computer science or engineering. Selection is based on merit.

Financial data   The stipend is $1,000 per year.

Duration   1 year; may be renewed up to 4 additional years.

Additional information   This program began in 2015.

Number awarded   1 each year.

Deadline   February of each year.

[627]
SYLVIA FORMAN PRIZE COMPETITION

American Anthropological Association
Attn: Association for Feminist Anthropology
2300 Clarendon Boulevard, Suite 1301
Arlington, VA 22201
(703) 528-1902   Fax: (703) 528-3546
Web: www.aaanet.org/sections/afa/sylvia-forman-prize

Summary   To recognize and reward the best student essays in feminist anthropology.

Eligibility   This award is available to graduate and undergraduate students who submit essays (up to 35 pages) in any subfield of anthropology that focus on such topics as feminist analysis of women's work, reproduction, sexuality, religion, language and expressive culture, family and kin relations, economic development, gender and material culture, gender and biology, women and development, globalization, or race and class. Essays that have been submitted for publication but have not yet been accepted may be eligible as entries. Already accepted or published articles may not be submitted. Only 1 submission per student is accepted. Selection is based on the use of feminist theory to analyze a particular issue; organization, quality, and clarity of writing; effective use of both theory and data; significance to feminist scholarship; timeliness and relevance of the topic; and originality of research topic.

Financial data   The prize is $1,000 for a graduate student or $500 for an undergraduate.

Duration   The competition is held annually.

Additional information   The winning essays are published in the association's *Anthropology Newsletter*. This competition began in 1995.

Number awarded   At least 2 each year: 1 for an undergraduate and 1 for a graduate student.

Deadline   May of each year.

[628]
SYMANTEC SCHOLARSHIP

Society of Women Engineers-Minnesota Section
Attn: Scholarship Committee
P.O. Box 18481
Minneapolis, MN 55418
E-mail: scholarships@swe-mn.org
Web: www.swe-mn.org/scholarships.html

Summary   To provide financial assistance to women from any state working on an undergraduate or graduate degree in computer science or software engineering at colleges and universities in Minnesota, North Dakota, and South Dakota.

Eligibility   This program is open to female undergraduate and graduate students at ABET-accredited engineering programs in Minnesota, North Dakota, or South Dakota. Applicants must be working full time on a degree in computer science or software engineering. Along with their application, they must submit a 250-word essay describing how they plan to utilize their engineering knowledge and skills after they graduate. Selection is based on potential to succeed as an engineer (20 points), communication skills (10 points), extracurricular or community involvement and leadership skills (10 points), demonstration of work experience and successes (10 points), and academic success (5 points).

Financial data   The stipend is $1,500.

Duration 1 year.

Additional information This program is sponsored by Symantec Corporation.

Number awarded 1 each year.

Deadline March of each year.

[629]
T & T HIKE SCHOLARSHIP

International Order of Job's Daughters
c/o Judy Burl, Supreme Scholarship Chair
121 Byrd Street
Hopewell, VA 23860
(804) 458-5552   E-mail: jgburl@aol.com
Web: www.jobsdaughtersinternational.org

Summary To provide financial assistance to members of Job's Daughters who are working on a degree related to speech disabilities.

Eligibility This program is open to Job's Daughters in good standing in their Bethels and unmarried majority members under 30 years of age. Applicants must be entering their junior year of college or higher in audiology, speech pathology, or deaf education. Selection is based on scholastic standing, Job's Daughters activities, recommendation by the Executive Bethel Guardian Council, faculty recommendations, and achievements outside Job's Daughters.

Financial data The stipend is $1,000.

Duration 1 year.

Number awarded 1 or more each year.

Deadline April of each year.

[630]
TCW COLLEGIATE CATTLEWOMEN SCHOLARSHIP

Texas CattleWomen, Inc.
Attn: Erin Worrell, Scholarship Chair
657 Blue Oak Trail
Harper, TX 78631-6371
(512) 413-1616   E-mail: worrellerin@gmail.com
Web: www.txcattlewomen.org/scholarship.html

Summary To provide financial assistance to members of Texas CattleWomen (TCW) who are majoring in an agriculture-related field at a college in the state.

Eligibility This program is open to members of TCW who are currently enrolled at the sophomore through senior level at a 4-year college or university in the state. They must have a GPA of 3.0 or higher and be majoring in an agricultural field. Along with their application, they must submit 1) a 750-word essay on an issue or concern they see ranchers facing and how they feel the industry and their generation can address it and gain from it; 2) a 500-word essay about themselves, their interest in and willingness to support the production and consumption of beef, their career goals, and how they intend to make an impact in the beef industry; and 3) a 1-page resume on their education and collegiate work experience, collegiate extracurricular activities, and collegiate level special honors and awards. Selection is based on evidence of potential for continuing education, participation in student activities, evidence of leadership qualities, ability to relate well with others, financial need, and interest in and willingness to support the production and consumption of beef.

Financial data The stipend is $1,000 per year. Funds may be used for any educational expense.

Duration 1 year; recipients may reapply.

Number awarded 1 each year.

Deadline March of each year.

[631]
TECHNICAL WOMEN'S ORGANIZATION SCHOLARSHIP

Technical Women's Organization
c/o Brenda Smith-Keene, Education Chair
P.O. Box 47126
Kansas City, MO 64188
(816) 329-2967   E-mail: Brenda.Smith-Keene@faa.gov
Web: www.technicalwomen.org/scholorship

Summary To provide financial assistance to members of the Technical Women's Organization (TWO) within the Federal Aviation Administration (FAA) who are interested in studying a technical field related to aviation safety.

Eligibility This program is open to 1) FAA employees who are TWO members; and 2) non-FAA employees who are sponsored by a TWO member. Applicants must be interested in working on an aviation-related technical degree. Along with their application, they must submit a list of extracurricular activities, a statement of personal and technical goals, a job history for the past 3 years, information on formal training during the past 3 years, 2 letters of recommendation (plus a third letter from a TWO member for non-FAA employees), and (for non-FAA applicants) transcripts. Financial need is not considered in the selection process.

Financial data The stipend is $1,000.

Duration 1 year.

Number awarded 3 each year: 2 for TWO members and 1 for non-members sponsored by a member.

Deadline May of each year.

[632]
TED AND RUTH NEWARD SCHOLARSHIPS

Society of Plastics Engineers
Attn: SPE Foundation
6 Berkshire Boulevard, Suite 306
Bethel, CT 06801
(203) 740-5457   Fax: (203) 775-8490
E-mail: foundation@4spe.org
Web: old.4spe.org/forms/spe-foundation-scholarship-form

Summary To provide financial assistance to undergraduate and graduate students, especially women, who have a career interest in the plastics industry.

Eligibility This program is open to full-time undergraduate students at 4-year colleges and 2-year technical programs and to graduate students. Preference is given to women for 1 of the scholarships. Applicants must be majoring in or taking courses that would be beneficial to a career in the plastics or polymer industry (e.g., plastics engineering, polymer sciences, chemistry, physics, chemical engineering, mechanical engineering, industrial engineering). Along with their application, they must submit 3 letters of recommendation; a high school and/or college transcript; a 1- to 2-page statement telling why they are applying for the scholarship, their qualifications, and their educational and career goals in the plastics industry; their employment history; and a list of current and past school activities and community activities and honors. Financial need is considered in the selection process. U.S. citizenship is required.

Financial data The stipend is $3,000. Funds are paid directly to the recipient's school.

Duration 1 year.

Number awarded 4 each year.

Deadline April of each year.

[633]
TENNESSEE ACTEENS SCHOLARSHIP

Tennessee Baptist Convention
Attn: WMU Scholarships
330 Seven Springs Way
P.O. Box 728
Brentwood, TN 37024-9728
(615) 371-7919   Toll Free: (800) 558-2090, ext. 7919
Fax: (615) 371-2014   E-mail: jheath@tnbaptist.org
Web: www.tnbaptist.org

Summary To provide financial assistance to members of Baptist churches in Tennessee who have been active in the Acteens program for girls and plan to attend college in any state.

Eligibility This program is open to high school seniors who are members and active participants in mission programs and ministry of a Tennessee Baptist church. Applicants must be able to demonstrate active involvement in Acteens in at least 2 of the following ways: 1) participation in local ministry for at least 2 years; 2) completion of at least 2 levels of the Acteens individual achievement plan; 3) selection as a state or national Acteen advisory panelist or Top Teen; or 4) service for 2 summers as an Acteens Activator. They must have a GPA of 2.6 or higher and be planning to enroll full time at a college or university in any state.

Financial data The stipend is $2,500.

Duration 1 year.

Number awarded 1 each year.

Deadline January of each year.

[634]
TEXAS ANGUS ASSOCIATION ENDOWMENT SCHOLARSHIP FUND

Texas Angus Association
Attn: Scholarship Chair
131 East Exchange Avenue, Suite 116
Fort Worth, TX 76164
(817) 740-0778   Fax: (817) 740-0877
E-mail: taa@texasangus.com
Web: www.texasangus.com/scholarships.html

Summary To provide financial assistance to female members of the Texas Junior Angus Association (TJAA) who participate in the Fort Worth Stock Show.

Eligibility This program is open to members of the TJAA who exhibit heifers in the Fort Worth Stock Show. Judges select the Grand Champion Female and the Reserve Grand Champion Female of the show. If those winners are TJAA members, they receive these scholarships. If the winners are not TJAA members, the next highest qualifiers who are members receive the scholarships.

Financial data The Grand Champion Female receives a $5,000 scholarship and the Reserve Grand Champion Female receives a $2,500 scholarship.

Duration 1 year.

Number awarded 2 each year.

Deadline March of each year.

[635]
TEXAS DISTRICT LUTHERAN WOMEN'S MISSIONARY LEAGUE SCHOLARSHIP

Lutheran Women in Mission-Texas District
Attn: Scholarship Committee Chair
7900 East Highway 290
Austin, TX 78724
(903) 983-3979   E-mail: info@txlcms.org
Web: www.lwmltxdist.org/scholarships.html

Summary To provide financial assistance to female members of the Lutheran Church-Missouri Synod (LCMS) in Texas who are interested in preparing for a career within the denomination.

Eligibility This program is open to women who are communicant members of a congregation of the Texas District of the LCMS. Applicants must be full-time undergraduate students enrolled or planning to enroll at a recognized institution of higher learning in a course of study leading to full-time professional church work in the LCMS. Selection is based primarily on overall aptitude for professional church work. Financial need is also considered.

Financial data A stipend is awarded (amount not specified).

Duration 1 year.

Additional information This program began in 1990.

Number awarded 1 or more each year. Since the program began, it has awarded 76 scholarships.

Deadline March of each year.

[636]
TEXAS ELKS STATE ASSOCIATION GIRL SCOUT GOLD AWARD SCHOLARSHIP

Texas Elks State Association
c/o Patricia Smith, State Scholarship Chair
1813 Evergreen Court
Harlingen, TX 78550-4479
(956) 428-0262   Fax: (956) 428-1546
E-mail: harotti@aol.com
Web: www.texaselks.org/Scholarships_3.html

Summary To provide financial assistance to high school seniors in Texas who earned the Girl Scout Gold Award and plan to attend college in the state.

Eligibility This program is open to seniors at high schools in Texas who have earned a Girl Scout Gold Award. Applicants must be planning to attend a college, university, or trade/vocational school in the state. Selection is based on leadership, achievement, recommendations, and financial need.

Financial data The stipend is $2,500. Funds are paid directly to the recipient's school.

Duration 1 year.

Number awarded 1 each year.

Deadline Applications must be submitted to local lodges by March of each year.

[637]
TEXAS FEDERATION OF REPUBLICAN WOMEN STATE SCHOLARSHIPS

Texas Federation of Republican Women
Attn: Scholarship Chair
13740 North Highway 183, Suite J4
Austin, TX 78750-1832
(512) 477-1615　　　　　E-mail: pam@acefences.com
Web: www.tfrw.org/programs/scholarships

Summary To provide financial assistance to women in Texas who are registered Republicans and attending college in any state.

Eligibility This program is open to women who have been residents of Texas for at least 2 years and have completed at least 12 hours of undergraduate study at an institution of higher learning in any state. Applicants must be U.S. citizens who are registered to vote and have a record of Republican party activity. They must have a GPA of 2.5 or higher. Financial need is not considered in the selection process.

Financial data A stipend is awarded (amount not specified).

Duration 1 year.

Number awarded 1 or more each year.

Deadline September of each year.

[638]
THADDEUS COLSON AND ISABELLE SAALWAECHTER FITZPATRICK MEMORIAL SCHOLARSHIP

Community Foundation of Louisville
Attn: Program Officer, Mission and Impact
Waterfront Plaza, West Tower
325 West Main Street, Suite 1110
Louisville, KY 40202-4251
(502) 855-6971　　　　　Fax: (502) 855-6173
E-mail: ebonyo@cflouisville.org
Web: cflouisville.academicworks.com/opportunities/599

Summary To provide financial assistance to women from Kentucky studying fields related to the environment at colleges and universities in the state.

Eligibility This program is open to female residents of Kentucky who are entering their sophomore, junior, or senior year at a 4-year public college or university in the state. Applicants must be majoring in an environmentally-related program (e.g., agriculture, biology, horticulture, environmental studies, environmental engineering). They must be enrolled full time with a GPA of 3.0 or higher. Along with their application, they must submit a 200-word essay describing their interest, leadership, volunteer efforts, and work experience in the environmental field; their future plans and goals in the environmental field; and what they hope to accomplish with their college degree. Financial need is also considered in the selection process.

Financial data The stipend ranges up to $4,500. Funds are paid directly to the college or university.

Duration 1 year; nonrenewable.

Number awarded 1 each year.

Deadline March of each year.

[639]
TIFFANY PHILLIPS SCHOLAR-ATHLETE AWARD

The Miss America Foundation
1432 K Street, N.W., Suite 900
Washington, DC 20005
(609) 344-1800
Web: www.missamericafoundation.org/scholarships

Summary To provide financial assistance to female scholar-athletes who are interested in working on an undergraduate degree and who competed at some level in the Miss America competition of the current year.

Eligibility This program is open to women who have competed at the local, state, or national level in the Miss America competition of the current year, regardless of whether or not they won a title, and are attending or planning to attend a college or university. Applicants must 1) be a participant in and demonstrate good sportsmanship in an athletic sport at the high school or university they attend; 2) have a GPA of 3.5 or higher; and 3) be involved in an activity that benefits their community or campus. Along with their application, they must submit brief statements on their greatest achievement as an athlete and a synopsis of their extracurricular or community service activities. Financial need is not considered in the selection process.

Financial data The stipend is $2,000.

Duration 1 year; renewable.

Additional information This scholarship was established in 1998.

Number awarded 1 each year.

Deadline June of each year.

[640]
TRAUB-DICKER RAINBOW SCHOLARSHIPS

Stonewall Community Foundation
Attn: Grants
446 West 33rd Street, Sixth Floor
New York, NY 10001
(212) 367-1155　　　　　Fax: (212) 367-1157
E-mail: grants@stonewallfoundation.org
Web: stonewallfoundation.org/grants/scholarships

Summary To provide financial assistance to undergraduate and graduate students who identify as lesbians.

Eligibility This program is open to lesbian-identified students who are 1) graduating high school seniors planning to attend a recognized college or university; 2) currently-enrolled undergraduates; and 3) graduate students. Applicants must submit 400-word essays on 1) their personal history, including a significant challenge or achievement in terms of community service, academic excellence, or dynamic leadership; 2) a particularly important experience they have had as a lesbian and how it has affected them; and 3) their plans or goals to give back to or focus on the lesbian, gay, bisexual, and transgender (LGBT) community while in school or after graduating. Selection is based on academic excellence, community service, and commitment to impacting LGBT issues. Financial need is not considered.

Financial data The stipend is $3,000. Funds are paid directly to the recipient's school to help pay for tuition, books, or room and board.

Duration 1 year.

Additional information This program began in 2004.

Number awarded 3 each year.

Deadline April of each year.

[641]
TREWA SCHOLARSHIPS

Texas Rural Electric Women's Association
c/o Karen Culpepper, Scholarship Chair
Wise Electric Cooperative
P.O. Box 269
Decatur, TX 76234
(940) 626-3003   E-mail: kculpepper@wiseec.com
Web: www.trewa.org/content/scholarships-0

Summary To provide financial assistance to members and children of members of the Texas Rural Electric Women's Association (TREWA) who plan to study a field related to energy or electricity at a college in any state.

Eligibility This program is open to current members of the association and their children who are graduating high school seniors, current full-time college students, or adults. Applicants may be enrolled or planning to enroll full time at an accredited college, university, junior or community college, trade/technical school, or business school in any state to work on a degree, certificate, diploma, or license. Along with their application, they must submit a 250-word essay on their planned field of study and how it relates to energy or electricity, their goals (educational, professional, and personal), their plans for the future, and why they have chosen their particular field of study. Grades received in high school are not the deciding factor in the selection process; leadership qualities, career focus, energy awareness, the essay, general knowledge of the rural electric program, and financial need are considered.

Financial data The stipend is $1,500. Funds are paid directly to the recipient's institution, half at the beginning of the first semester and half upon verification of completion of the first semester with passing grades.

Duration 1 year; nonrenewable.

Additional information This scholarship is sponsored by TREWA and administered by Texas Electric Cooperatives, Inc. Membership in TREWA is open to rural electric employees, directors, and co-op members. The organization is run by women, but men are also eligible to join.

Number awarded 20 each year.

Deadline March of each year.

[642]
TULSA CHAPTER AFWA SCHOLARSHIPS

Accounting and Financial Women's Alliance-Tulsa
  Chapter
c/o Hilary Penrod, Scholarship Chair
Grant Thornton LLP
2431 East 61st Street, Suite 500
Tulsa, OK 74136
(918) 877-0800   Fax: (918) 877=0805
E-mail: afwatulsa@gmail.com
Web: sites.google.com/site/tulsaafwa/scholarship

Summary To provide financial assistance to nontraditional students, especially women and single parents, interested in studying accounting or finance at a college or university in the Tulsa area of Oklahoma.

Eligibility This program is open to nontraditional students, defined as those who have had a break in their academic career due to unforeseen life circumstances and/or unique personal and academic challenges. Applicants must have decided to further their education after a life changing event or overcoming an obstacle. They must be enrolled at a college or university in the Tulsa area of Oklahoma and be majoring in accounting or finance with a GPA of 3.0 or higher. Students at 2-year colleges must have completed at least 30 semester hours and students at 4-year colleges and universities must have completed at least 60 hours. Priority is given to women, single parents, and students working part time while attending college full time. Along with their application, they must submit an essay of 500 to 1,000 words describing 1) their educational and personal background, including any details relevant to this scholarship, their experiences, and their financial situation; and 2) the career goals and objectives, community involvement, and leadership examples. Selection is based on academic average, leadership, character, communication skills, and financial need.

Financial data Stipends may range up to $3,000.

Duration 1 year.

Number awarded Varies each year; recently, 1 at $2,500 and 1 at $500 were awarded.

Deadline May of each year.

[643]
TURNER CONSTRUCTION SCHOLARSHIPS

Society of Women Engineers
Attn: Scholarship Selection Committee
203 North LaSalle Street, Suite 1675
Chicago, IL 60601-1269
(312) 596-5223   Toll Free: (877) SWE-INFO
Fax: (312) 644-8557   E-mail: scholarships@swe.org
Web: societyofwomenengineers.swe.org

Summary To provide financial assistance to members of the Society of Women Engineers (SWE) who will be entering their sophomore year of a program in a field related to civil, construction management, or mechanical engineering.

Eligibility This program is open to SWE members who are U.S. citizens entering their sophomore year of full-time study at an ABET-accredited 4-year college or university. Applicants must be studying civil engineering, construction engineering or management, or mechanical engineering. Selection is based on merit.

Financial data The stipend is $2,500.

Duration 1 year.

Number awarded 2 each year.

Deadline February of each year.

[644]
TWEET COLEMAN AVIATION SCHOLARSHIP

American Association of University Women-Honolulu
  Branch
Attn: Scholarship Committee
1888 Kalakaua Avenue, Suite C312-359
Honolulu, HI 96815
Web: honolulu-hi.aauw.net

Summary To provide financial assistance to women in Hawaii who are interested in a career in aviation.

Eligibility This program is open to women who have completed at least an associate degree and are residents of Hawaii, stationed in the military in the state, or attending an accredited college in the state (including those from out of state). Applicants must be interested in obtaining a private pilot license. Along with their application, they must submit essays of 250 to 300 words on 1) their goals in aviation; and 2) how they plan to use the money from the scholarship.

Financial data The stipend is $2,000. Funds may be used for flight training, ground school training, and aviation study manuals.

Duration 1 year.

Additional information This program began in 1990.

Number awarded 1 each year.

Deadline April of each year.

[645]
TWISTER SCHOLARSHIP

Women in Technology of Tennessee
c/o Julie Foster
330 Franklin Road, Suite 135A-538
Brentwood, TN 37027
(615) 587-3019   E-mail: Julie.foster@asurion.com
Web: www.wittn.org/Nashville-T.W.I.S.T.E.R.Event

Summary To provide financial assistance to female high school seniors in Tennessee who are interested in attending college in any state to prepare for a career in science, technology, engineering, or research.

Eligibility This program is open to women who are graduating from a Tennessee public high school, approved private high school, or home school and participate in the TWISTER (Tennessee Women in Science, Technology, Engineering & Research) conference. Applicants must be interested in attending college in any state to prepare for a career in science, technology, engineering, or research. They must have a GPA of 3.0 or higher. Along with their application, they must submit a 2-page essay on a topic that changes annually but relates to science, technology, engineering, or mathematics (STEM); recently, students were asked to write on their goals for STEM and their inspiration. Selection is based on that essay (50%), transcripts (25%), memberships and honors in academic or service clubs (15%), and 2 letters of recommendation (10%).

Financial data Stipends are $5,000 or $1,000.

Duration 1 year.

Additional information This program, established in 2006, is offered in partnership with the Adventure Science Center of Nashville.

Number awarded 2 each year: 1 at $5,000 and 1 at $1,000.

Deadline January of each year.

[646]
TYLER J. VINEY MEMORIAL SCHOLARSHIP

Texas Society of Architects
Attn: Texas Architectural Foundation
500 Chicon Street
Austin, TX 78702
(512) 478-7386   Fax: (512) 478-0528
E-mail: foundation@texasarchitect.org
Web: www.texasarchitects.org/v/scholarships

Summary To provide financial assistance to residents of any state who are entering their fourth or fifth year of study at a school of architecture in Texas.

Eligibility This program is open to residents of any state who are entering their fourth or fifth year of study at 1 of the 8 schools of architecture in Texas. Applicants must submit their application to the office of the dean of their school. Along with their application, they must submit essays on 1) the principal architectural areas or practice categories in which they are most interested, excel, or desire to develop their proficiency; and 2) career plans, short/long-range goals, vision, or other topic about which they are passionate. Selection is based on potential architectural talent, demonstrated interest in photography, and financial need. Priority is given to female and minority students.

Financial data The stipend ranges up to $2,000.

Duration 1 year.

Number awarded 1 each year.

Deadline February of each year.

[647]
UNITED AIRLINES PILOT SCHOLARSHIPS OF WOMEN IN AVIATION INTERNATIONAL

Women in Aviation International
Attn: Scholarships
Morningstar Airport
3647 State Route 503 South
West Alexandria, OH 45381-9354
(937) 839-4647   Fax: (937) 839-4645
E-mail: scholarships@wai.org
Web: www.wai.org

Summary To provide financial assistance to members of Women in Aviation International (WAI) who are working on an undergraduate or graduate degree to prepare for a career as a professional airline pilot.

Eligibility This program is open to WAI members who are currently enrolled as full-time juniors, seniors, or graduate students in an accredited collegiate aviation or aeronautical science program. Applicants must have a GPA of 3.0 or higher and an FAA instrument rating; preference is given to those with an FAA commercial certificate and/or an FAA multiengine rating. Along with their application, they must submit academic transcripts, copies of pilot and medical certificates, and an essay describing career aspirations and goals, achievements and honors, aviation development to date, involvement with WAI, volunteerism, leadership, and planned use of scholarship funds. Selection is based on merit, career aspirations, dedication, contributions to community, and service with WAI.

Financial data The stipend is $5,000. Funds are paid directly to the recipient's institution. The award includes round-trip airfare, accommodations, and registration to attend the WAI annual conference.

Duration Training must be completed within 1 year.

Additional information WAI is a nonprofit professional organization dedicated to encouraging women to consider an aviation career and to providing educational outreach activities and networking resources to women active in the industry. This program is sponsored by United Airlines.

Number awarded 2 each year.

Deadline November of each year.

[648]
UNITED AIRLINES TECH OPS-WOMEN IN AVIATION SCHOLARSHIP

Women in Aviation International
Attn: Scholarships
Morningstar Airport
3647 State Route 503 South
West Alexandria, OH 45381-9354
(937) 839-4647   Fax: (937) 839-4645
E-mail: scholarships@wai.org
Web: www.wai.org

Summary To provide financial assistance to members of Women in Aviation International (WAI) who are working on a degree or certificate to prepare for a career in aviation.

Eligibility This program is open to WAI members who are currently enrolled or accepted for enrollment in an aerospace/aeronautical engineering program, aviation maintenance technology program, or aviation technician program at an accredited college, university, or AMT school. Applicants must have a GPA of 3.0 or higher and be U.S. citizens or eligible non-citizens. Along with their application, they must submit an essay of 500 to 1,000 on what WAI means to them, their greatest strength, and why they are the most qualified candidate for this scholarship.

Financial data The stipend is $1,500. Funds are paid directly to the recipient's institution.

Duration Training must be completed within 1 year.

Additional information WAI is a nonprofit professional organization dedicated to encouraging women to consider an aviation career and to providing educational outreach activities and networking resources to women active in the industry. This program is sponsored by United Airlines.

Number awarded 2 each year.

Deadline November of each year.

[649]
UNITED PARCEL SERVICE SCHOLARSHIP FOR FEMALE STUDENTS

Institute of Industrial and Systems Engineers
Attn: Scholarship Coordinator
3577 Parkway Lane, Suite 200
Norcross, GA 30092
(770) 449-0461, ext. 105   Toll Free: (800) 494-0460
Fax: (770) 441-3295   E-mail: bcameron@iisenet.org
Web: www.iienet2.org/Details.aspx?id=857

Summary To provide financial assistance to female undergraduates who are studying industrial engineering at a school in the United States, Canada, or Mexico.

Eligibility Eligible to be nominated are female undergraduate students enrolled at any school in the United States or its

territories, Canada, or Mexico, provided the school's engineering program is accredited by an agency recognized by the Institute of Industrial and Systems Engineers (IISE) and the student is pursuing a full-time course of study in industrial engineering with a GPA of at least 3.4. Nominees must have at least 5 full quarters or 3 full semesters remaining until graduation. Students may not apply directly for these awards; they must be nominated by the head of their industrial engineering department. Nominees must be IISE members. Selection is based on scholastic ability, character, leadership, and potential service to the industrial engineering profession.

Financial data The stipend is $4,000.

Duration 1 year.

Additional information Funding for this program is provided by the UPS Foundation.

Number awarded 1 each year.

Deadline Schools must submit nominations by November of each year.

[650]
UTC AEROSPACE SYSTEMS SCHOLARSHIP

Society of Women Engineers-Minnesota Section
Attn: Scholarship Committee
P.O. Box 18481
Minneapolis, MN 55418
E-mail: scholarships@swe-mn.org
Web: www.swe-mn.org/scholarships.html

Summary To provide financial assistance to women from any state working on an undergraduate or graduate degree in specified fields of engineering at colleges and universities in Minnesota, North Dakota, and South Dakota.

Eligibility This program is open to female undergraduate and graduate students at ABET-accredited engineering programs in Minnesota, North Dakota, or South Dakota. Applicants must be working full time on a degree in aerospace, electrical, industrial, manufacturing, or mechanical engineering. Along with their application, they must submit a 250-word essay describing how they plan to utilize their engineering knowledge and skills after they graduate. Selection is based on potential to succeed as an engineer (20 points), communication skills (10 points), extracurricular or community involvement and leadership skills (10 points), demonstration of work experience and successes (10 points), and academic success (5 points).

Financial data The stipend is $1,500.

Duration 1 year.

Additional information This program is sponsored by UTC Aerospace Systems.

Number awarded 1 each year.

Deadline March of each year.

[651]
VALERIE RUSSELL SCHOLARSHIP

United Church of Christ
Attn: Associate Director, Grant and Scholarship
  Administration
700 Prospect Avenue East
Cleveland, OH 44115-1100
(216) 736-2166   Toll Free: (866) 822-8224, ext. 2166
Fax: (216) 736-3783   E-mail: scholarships@ucc.org
Web: www.ucc.org/russell_scholarship

Summary To provide financial assistance to African American laywomen who are members of a United Church of Christ (UCC) congregation and working on an undergraduate or graduate degree to advance the justice ministries of the denomination.

Eligibility This program is open to African American laywomen who have a strong theologically-grounded commitment to the justice ministries of the UCC but are not a member in discernment, licensed, commissioned, or ordained. Applicants must be 1) working on an undergraduate or graduate degree in a field that will affirm the values of the UCC and promote its justice commitments; or 2) already professionally engaged in justice work either in the church or in a secular organization and seeking funds for continuing education activities (e.g., classes, workshops, travel) that will assist in personal skill building.

Financial data Stipends range from $1,500 to $2,000 per year. Funds may be used for tuition for undergraduate or graduate study or for continuing education activities.

Duration 1 year; may be renewed.

Additional information This program began in 1997.

Number awarded 1 or more each year.

Deadline February of each year.

[652]
VALLIERE/GIROUX SCHOLARSHIP FOR SINGLE WORKING MOMS

Wisconsin Indian Education Association
Attn: Scholarship Coordinator
P.O. Box 910
Keshena, WI 54135
(715) 799-5110   Fax: (715) 799-5102
E-mail: vnuske@mitw.org
Web: www.wiea.org/index.php/About/Scholarships

Summary To provide financial assistance to members of Wisconsin Indian tribes who are single mothers and interested in attending college in any state.

Eligibility This program is open to residents of Wisconsin who can provide proof of tribal enrollment. Applicants must be single mothers with children whom they are supporting financially. Applicants must have been accepted at a 4-year college or university in any state for enrollment in at least 6 credits per semester. They must have a GPA of 2.5 or higher. Along with their application, they must submit a 1-page personal essay on how they will apply their education and their educational goals. Selection is based on that essay (20 points), letters of recommendation (15 points), and GPA (15 points if 3.5 or higher, 10 points if 3.00 to 3.49, 5 points if 2.50 to 2.99). Financial need is not considered.

Financial data The stipend is $1,000.

Duration 1 year; nonrenewable.

Additional information Eligible tribes include Menominee, Oneida, Stockbridge-Munsee, Forest County Potowatomi, Ho-Chunk, Bad River Chippewa, Lac Courte Oreilles Ojibwe, St. Croix Chippewa, Red Cliff Chippewa, Sakoagon (Mole Lake) Chippewa, Brotherton, and Lac du Flambeau Chippewa.

Number awarded 1 each year.

Deadline March of each year.

[653]
VERIZON SWE SCHOLARSHIP

Society of Women Engineers
Attn: Scholarship Selection Committee
203 North LaSalle Street, Suite 1675
Chicago, IL 60601-1269
(312) 596-5223   Toll Free: (877) SWE-INFO
Fax: (312) 644-8557   E-mail: scholarships@swe.org
Web: societyofwomenengineers.swe.org

Summary To provide financial assistance to women who are interested in studying specified fields of engineering at designated universities.

Eligibility This program is open to women who are entering their sophomore, junior, or senior year at Pennsylvania State University, Cornell University, University of Puerto Rico, Rutgers University, New Jersey Institute of Technology, Georgia Institute of Technology, University of South Florida, University of Massachusetts, University of Texas at Austin, University of Texas at Dallas, CUNY-City College, Stevens Institute of Technology, or Virginia Polytechnic Institute and State University. Applicants must be enrolled full time and majoring in computer information systems, computer science or computer, electrical, or industrial engineering. They must be U.S. citizens. Selection is based on merit.

Financial data The stipend is $3,000.

Duration 1 year.

Additional information This program is sponsored by Verizon.

Number awarded 1 each year.

Deadline February of each year.

[654]
VICKIE CLARK-FLAHERTY SCHOLARSHIP

North Carolina Restaurant and Lodging Association
Attn: NC Hospitality Education Foundation
6036 Six Forks Road
Raleigh, NC 27609
(919) 844-0098   Toll Free: (800) 582-8750
Fax: (919) 844-0190   E-mail: info@ncrla.org
Web: www.ncrla.org/?page=NCHEFScholarships

Summary To provide financial assistance to female residents of North Carolina who are interested in attending college in any state to major in a hospitality-related field.

Eligibility This program is open to female residents of North Carolina who are high school seniors, high school graduates, or undergraduates enrolled or planning to enroll full time at an accredited 2- or 4-year college, university, or vocational/technical school in the United States. Preference is given to students majoring in a hospitality-related field. Selection is based on academic achievement, community involvement, student leadership, extracurricular activities, employment and/or school references, and financial need.

Financial data The stipend ranges from $1,500 to $2,500 per year.

Duration 1 year; recipients may reapply.

Number awarded 1 or more each year.

Deadline February of each year.

[655]
VIP WOMEN IN TECHNOLOGY SCHOLARSHIPS

Visionary Integration Professionals
Attn: WITS Program
80 Iron Point Circle, Suite 100
Folsom, CA 95630
(916) 985-9625   Toll Free: (800) 434-2673
Fax: (916) 985-9632   E-mail: WITS@trustvip.com
Web: www.trustvip.com/community-support-service

Summary To provide financial assistance to women preparing for a career in information technology or a related field.

Eligibility This program is open to women who are enrolled at or accepted into a 2- or 4-year college or university to prepare for a career in information technology, computer science, management information systems, computer engineering, or a related field. Applicants must have a cumulative GPA of 3.0 or higher. Along with their application, they must submit a 1,000-word essay in which they define a specific problem that they see in their community related to information technology and recommend a solution that is thoughtful and likely to make an impact on the problem. Selection is based on that essay, academic performance, and participation in community service and/or extracurricular activities.

Financial data The stipend is $2,500.

Duration 1 year.

Additional information This program began in 2007.

Number awarded Varies each year; recently, 9 were awarded. Since this program was established, it has awarded more than $120,000 in support to more than 70 women.

Deadline March of each year.

[656]
VIRGINIA JOB'S DAUGHTERS PAST GRAND'S SCHOLARSHIP

International Order of Job's Daughters-Grand Guardian
  Council of Virginia
c/o J. Stan Boren, Past Grand's Scholarship Chair
2733 Luther Catlett Circle
Sevierville, TN 37876
(865) 429-8998
Web: www.jdiva.org/forms

Summary To provide financial assistance to members of Job's Daughters in Virginia who are currently attending college in any state.

Eligibility This program is open to students currently enrolled at colleges in any state who are Virginia residents and members of Job's Daughters. Applicants must submit official copies of all their high school and college transcripts, 2 letters of recommendation, a letter signed by each of the Executive Members of their Bethel Guardian Council, and a short essay on why they want or need this scholarship.

Financial data A stipend is awarded (amount not specified).

Duration 1 year.

Number awarded 1 or more each year.

Deadline April of each year.

[657]
VIRGINIA M. WAGNER EDUCATIONAL GRANT

Soroptimist International of the Americas-Midwestern
  Region
c/o Kris Armstrong, Governor
607 West Hamilton Road
Bloomington, IL 61704-8616
E-mail: soroptimist@simwr.org
Web: www.simwr.org/virginia-wagner-award

Summary To provide financial assistance to women working on an undergraduate or graduate degree at a college or university in midwestern states.

Eligibility This program is open to women who reside in Illinois, Indiana, Kentucky, Michigan, Ohio, or Wisconsin and are attending college or graduate school in any state. Applicants must be working on a bachelor's, master's, or doctoral degree in the field of their choice. Awards are first presented at the club level, then in districts, and finally for the entire region. Selection is based on the effort toward education by the applicant and her family, cumulative GPA, extracurricular activities, general impression, and financial need.

Financial data Club level awards vary at the discretion of the club. District finalists receive a $500 award and are then judged at the regional level. The regional winner receives a $2,500 award.

Duration 1 year.

Additional information This program began in 1972 and given its current name in 2004.

Number awarded 4 district winners are selected each year; 1 of those receives the regional award.

Deadline January of each year.

[658]
VOICE OF WORKING WOMEN CAREER DEVELOPMENT AWARDS

Business and Professional Women/New Jersey
c/o Penny Miller
267 Serpent Lane
Manahawkin, NJ 08050-2039
(609) 978-8638   E-mail: momlbi@yahoo.com
Web: www.businessandprofessionalwomennj.org

Summary To provide financial assistance for further education to mature women in New Jersey.

Eligibility This program is open to women in New Jersey who are 25 years of age or older. Applicants must be seeking funding to advance their careers, reenter the workforce, or make a career change.

Financial data The stipend is $1,000.

Duration 1 year.

Additional information This program includes the Mildred A. Butler Career Development Award and the Mary L. Johnston Scholarship Award.

Number awarded 1 or more each year.

Deadline April of each year.

[659]
WALDO AND ALICE AYER MUSIC SCHOLARSHIP

New Hampshire Charitable Foundation
37 Pleasant Street
Concord, NH 03301-4005
(603) 225-6641   Toll Free: (800) 464-6641
Fax: (603) 225-1700   E-mail: info@nhcf.org
Web: www.nhcf.org/page.aspx?pid=487

Summary To provide financial assistance to residents of New Hampshire (especially women) who are interested in majoring in music or music education at a college in any state.

Eligibility This program is open to residents of New Hampshire who are attending or planning to attend a college or university in any state to become a professional musician or music teacher. Applicants must have a GPA of 2.5 or higher and be able to demonstrate financial need. Preference is given to female applicants.

Financial data The stipend ranges from $500 to $3,500 and averages $1,800.

Duration 1 year.

Additional information This program was previously sponsored by the Citizens Bank Foundation but is currently administered as part of the Statewide Student Aid Program of the New Hampshire Charitable Foundation.

Number awarded 1 or more each year.

Deadline April of each year.

[660]
WALTER REED SMITH SCHOLARSHIP PROGRAM

United Daughters of the Confederacy
Attn: Second Vice President General
328 North Boulevard
Richmond, VA 23220-4009
(804) 355-1636   Fax: (804) 353-1396
E-mail: udc@hqudc.org
Web: www.hqudc.org/scholarships

Summary To provide financial assistance to mature women who are lineal descendants of Confederate veterans and plan to major in selected fields in college.

Eligibility Eligible to apply for these scholarships are women over the age of 30 who are lineal descendants of worthy Confederates or collateral descendants and members of the Children of the Confederacy or the United Daughters of the Confederacy. Applicants must intend to study business administration, computer science, home economics, nutrition, or nursing. They must submit certified proof of the Confederate record of 1 ancestor, with the company and regiment in which he served, and must have had at least a 3.0 GPA in high school.

Financial data The amount of this scholarship depends on the availability of funds.

Duration 1 year; may be renewed up to 3 additional years, provided the recipient remains enrolled full time with a GPA of 3.0 or higher.

Number awarded 1 each year.

Deadline April of each year.

[661]
WANDA MUNN SCHOLARSHIP

Society of Women Engineers
Attn: Scholarship Selection Committee
203 North LaSalle Street, Suite 1675
Chicago, IL 60601-1269
(312) 596-5223   Toll Free: (877) SWE-INFO
Fax: (312) 644-8557   E-mail: scholarships@swe.org
Web: societyofwomenengineers.swe.org

Summary To provide financial assistance to women from selected northwestern states interested in returning to college or graduate school to study engineering or computer science.

Eligibility This program is open to women who are planning to enroll at an ABET-accredited 4-year college or university. Applicants must have been out of the engineering workforce and school for at least 2 years and must be planning to return as an undergraduate or graduate student to work on a degree in computer science or engineering. They must be residents of or attending school in Alaska, Idaho, Montana, Oregon, or Washington and have a GPA of 3.0 or higher. Selection is based on merit. Preference is given to engineers who already have a degree and are planning to reenter the engineering workforce after a period of temporary retirement.

Financial data The stipend is $1,500.

Duration 1 year.

Additional information This program is sponsored by the Eastern Washington Section of the Society of Women Engineers.

Number awarded 1 each year.

Deadline February of each year.

[662]
WASHINGTON STATE BUSINESS AND PROFESSIONAL WOMEN'S FOUNDATION MATURE WOMAN EDUCATIONAL SCHOLARSHIP

Washington State Business and Professional Women's Foundation
Attn: Sue Tellock, Scholarship Committee Chair
1914 N.W. 87th Circle
Vancouver, WA 98665
Web: www.bpwwafoundation.org/scholarships

Summary To provide financial assistance to mature women from Washington interested in attending postsecondary school in the state for retraining or continuing education.

Eligibility This program is open to women over 30 years of age who have been residents of Washington for at least 2 years. Applicants must be planning to enroll at a college or university in the state for a program of retraining or continuing education. Along with their application, they must submit a 500-word essay on their specific short-term goals and how the proposed training will help them accomplish those goals and make a difference in their professional career. Financial need is considered in the selection process. U.S. citizenship is required.

Financial data The stipend is $1,000.

Duration 1 year.

Number awarded Varies each year; recently, 3 were awarded.

Deadline May of each year.

[663]
WASHINGTON STATE BUSINESS AND PROFESSIONAL WOMEN'S FOUNDATION SINGLE PARENT SCHOLARSHIP

Washington State Business and Professional Women's
  Foundation
Attn: Sue Tellock, Scholarship Committee Chair
1914 N.W. 87th Circle
Vancouver, WA 98665
Web: www.bpwwafoundation.org/scholarships

Summary To provide financial assistance to women from Washington who are single parents interested in returning to college to continue their education.

Eligibility This program is open to women of any age who have been residents of Washington for at least 2 years. Applicants must have at least 1 dependent child, under 18 years of age, living at home. They must be interested in returning to school in the state to continue their education beyond the high school level. Along with their application, they must submit a 500-word essay on their specific short-term goals and how the proposed training will help them accomplish those goals and make a difference in their professional career. Financial need is considered in the selection process. U.S. citizenship is required.

Financial data The stipend is $1,000.

Duration 1 year.

Number awarded 1 or more each year.

Deadline May of each year.

[664]
WASHINGTON WOMEN IN NEED EDUCATIONAL GRANTS

Washington Women in Need
Attn: Programs
232 Fifth Avenue South, Suite 201
Kirkland, WA 98004
(425) 451-8838   Toll Free: (888) 440-WWIN
Fax: (425) 451-8845   E-mail: wwininfo@wwin.org
Web: www.wwin.org/apply-for-an-education-grant

Summary To provide financial assistance to low-income women who reside in Washington and are interested in attending college in the state.

Eligibility This program is open to women who are at least 18 years of age and have resided in Washington for at least the past 12 months. Their income must be less than $16,243 for a family of 1, ranging up to $56,428 for a family of 8. Applicants must be interested in attending an accredited institution in the state to work on a vocational or technical certificate, associate degree, or bachelor's degree. They must first apply for all available federal and private grants and scholarships. If all available assistance does not fully cover the costs of tuition and books, they may apply for these grants. Only U.S. citizens, permanent residents, refugees, or asylees are eligible.

Financial data Stipends range up to $5,000 per year.

Duration 1 year; renewal is possible if the recipient maintains a GPA of 2.5 or higher and remains eligible for in-state tuition at their institution.

Number awarded Approximately 55 each year.

Deadline April or October of each year.

[665]
WCA FOUNDATION SCHOLARSHIP

Minnesota Private College Council
445 Minnesota Street, Suite 500
St. Paul, MN 55101-2903
(651) 228-9061   Toll Free: (800) 774-2655
Fax: (651) 228-0379
E-mail: colleges@mnprivatecolleges.org
Web: www.mnprivatecolleges.org

Summary To provide financial assistance to women attending private colleges and universities in Minnesota who are interested in developing and implementing a service project.

Eligibility This program is open to women currently enrolled at the member colleges of the Minnesota Private College. Applicants must have a GPA of 2.5 or higher and be able to demonstrate financial need.

Financial data The stipend is $1,000.

Duration 1 year.

Additional information The member colleges are Augsburg College, Bethany Lutheran College, Carleton College, College of Saint Benedict, The College of St. Scholastica, Concordia College (Moorhead), Concordia University (St. Paul), Gustavus Adolphus College, Hamline College, Macalester College, Minneapolis College of Art and Design, Saint John's University, Saint Mary's University of Minnesota, St. Catherine University, St. Olaf College, and University of St. Thomas. This program is supported by the WCA Foundation.

Number awarded 1 or more each year.

Deadline Deadline not specified.

[666]
WCA FOUNDATION SCHOLARSHIPS

Minnesota Private College Council
Attn: Minnesota Private College Fund
445 Minnesota Street, Suite 500
St. Paul, MN 55101-2903
(651) 228-9061   Toll Free: (888) PRI-FUND
Fax: (651) 228-0379
E-mail: cjones@mnprivatecolleges.org
Web: www.mnprivatecolleges.org

Summary To provide financial assistance to women enrolled at designated private colleges and universities in Minnesota.

Eligibility This program is open to women currently enrolled at any of 16 private colleges and universities in Minnesota. Applicants must have a GPA of 2.5 or higher and be able to demonstrate financial need.

Financial data The stipend is $1,000.

Duration 1 year.

Additional information This program is sponsored by the WCA Foundation, a benevolent nonprofit organization founded in Minnesota in 1866. The member institutions of the Minnesota Private College Council are Augsburg College, Bethany Lutheran College, Carleton College, College of St. Benedict, College of St. Scholastica, Concordia College (Moorhead), Concordia College (St. Paul), Gustavus Adolphus College, Hamline University, Macalester College, Minneapolis College of Art and Design, St. John's University, St. Mary's University of Minnesota, St. Catherine University, St. Olaf College, and University of St. Thomas.

Number awarded Varies each year.

Deadline Deadline not specified.

[667]
WEBBER GROUP CAREER ADVANCEMENT SCHOLARSHIP

Maine Federation of Business and Professional Women's Clubs
Attn: BPW/Maine Futurama Foundation
c/o Marilyn V. Ladd, Office Manager
103 County Road
Oakland, ME 04963
Web: www.bpwmefoundation.org/scholarship-program

Summary To provide financial assistance to Maine women over 30 years of age who are continuing a program of higher education.

Eligibility This program is open to women who are older than 30 years of age and residents of Maine. Applicants must be continuing in, or returning to, an accredited program of higher education or job-related training, either full or part time. They must have a definite plan to use the desired training in a practical and immediate way to improve chances for advancement, train for a new career field, or enter or reenter the job market. Along with their application, they must submit a statement describing their educational, personal, and career goals, including financial need, expectations of training, and future plans for using this educational program.

Financial data The stipend is $1,200. Funds are paid directly to the school.

Duration 1 year.

Number awarded 1 or more each year.

Deadline April of each year.

[668]
WESTROCK SCHOLARSHIPS

Society of Women Engineers
Attn: Scholarship Selection Committee
203 North LaSalle Street, Suite 1675
Chicago, IL 60601-1269
(312) 596-5223   Toll Free: (877) SWE-INFO
Fax: (312) 644-8557   E-mail: scholarships@swe.org
Web: societyofwomenengineers.swe.org

Summary To provide financial assistance to women who are interested in studying specified fields of engineering at designated universities.

Eligibility This program is open to women who are entering their sophomore, junior, or senior year at North Carolina State University, Purdue University, Miami University of Ohio, Auburn University, State University of New York College of Environmental Science and Forestry, Georgia Institute of Technology, University of Washington, or Virginia Polytechnic Institute and State University. Applicants must be enrolled full time and majoring in computer science or chemical, electrical, industrial or mechanical engineering. They must have a GPA of 3.0 or higher. Selection is based on merit.

Financial data The stipend is $3,000.

Duration 1 year.

Additional information This program is sponsored by Westrock Company.

Number awarded 3 each year.

Deadline February of each year.

[669]
WICHITA CHAPTER AFWA SCHOLARSHIPS

Accounting and Financial Women's Alliance-Wichita Chapter
c/o Kate Grant, Scholarship Chair
Kirkpatrick, Sprecker & Company, LLP
311 South Hillside Street
Wichita, KS 67211
(316) 685-1411, ext. 305   Toll Free: (877) 299-1532
Fax: (316) 685-4575   E-mail: ekgrant1215@gmail.com
Web: www.wichitaafwa.org/Scholarship_Requirements

Summary To provide financial assistance to women working on an undergraduate or graduate degree in accounting or finance at a college or university in Kansas.

Eligibility This program is open to women working full or part time on an associate, bachelor's, or master's degree in accounting or finance at a college or university in Kansas. Applicants must have completed at least 15 semester hours in a 2-year program or 60 semester hours in a 4-year program. They must have a cumulative GPA of 3.0 or higher. Membership in the Accounting and Financial Women's Alliance (AFWA) is not required. Along with their application, they must submit an essay of 150 to 250 words on their career goals and objectives, the impact they want to have on the accounting and financial world, community involvement, and leadership examples. Selection is based on leadership, character, communication skills, GPA, and financial need.

Financial data The stipend is $1,000.

Duration 1 year.

Additional information The highest-ranked recipient is entered into the national competition for scholarships that range from $1,500 to $4,500.

Number awarded Varies each year; recently, 3 were awarded.

Deadline February of each year.

[670]
WIFLE ANNUAL SCHOLARSHIP PROGRAM

Women in Federal Law Enforcement
Attn: Scholarship Coordinator
2200 Wilson Boulevard, Suite 102
PMB 204
Arlington, VA 22201-3324
(301) 805-2180   Fax: (301) 560-8836
E-mail: WIFLE@comcast.net
Web: www.wifle.org/scholarshipprogram.htm

Summary To provide financial assistance for college or graduate school to women interested in preparing for a career in law enforcement.

Eligibility This program is open to women who have completed at least 1 academic year of full-time study at an accredited 4-year college or university (or at a community college with the intention of transferring to a 4-year school). Applicants must be majoring in criminal justice or a related field (e.g., social sciences, public administration, computer science, finance, linguistic arts, chemistry, physics). They must have a GPA of 3.0 or higher. Students in graduate and postgraduate programs are also eligible, but those working on an associate degree are not. Along with their application, they must submit a 500-word essay describing a community project in which they have been involved and the results or impact to the community. Selection is based on academic potential, achievement, and commitment to serving communities in the field of law enforcement. U.S. citizenship is required.

Financial data The stipend is $2,500.

Duration 1 year; may be renewed.

Number awarded Varies each year; recently, 6 were awarded.

Deadline April of each year.

[671]
WIFTA STUDENT TUITION SCHOLARSHIP PROGRAM

Women in Film and Television Atlanta
P.O. Box 52726
Atlanta, GA 30355
(770) 621-5071   E-mail: executivedirector@wifta.org
Web: www.wifta.org

Summary To provide financial assistance to members of Women in Film and Television Atlanta (WIFTA) who are working on an undergraduate degree in film or video at a college in Georgia.

Eligibility This program is open to women who are members of WIFTA and majoring in (or having a primary field of study in) film or video at an accredited 4-year college or university in Georgia. Applicants must have a GPA of 2.75 or higher. Along with their application, they must submit a 5-minute sample of their work on DVD and a 1,000-word essay highlighting their accomplishments and explaining their career goals. Selection is based on academic standing, artistic talents, and commitment to a film-based curriculum.

Financial data The stipend is $1,500.

Duration 1 year.

Number awarded 1 or more each year.

Deadline May of each year.

[672]
WILLIAM A. RICE FAMILY, WOMEN IN WELDING SCHOLARSHIP

American Welding Society
Attn: AWS Foundation, Inc.
8669 N.W. 36th Street, Suite 130
Doral, FL 33166-6672
(305) 443-9353   Toll Free: (800) 443-9353, ext. 250
Fax: (305) 443-7559   E-mail: nprado-pulido@aws.org
Web: app.aws.org/foundation/scholarships/rice.html

Summary To provide financial assistance to women working on a bachelor's degree in welding-related fields at designated universities.

Eligibility This program is open to women enrolled in a bachelor's degree program in welding engineering, welding engineering technology, materials joining engineering, or materials joining technology. Applicants must be attending Ferris State University, Ohio State University, LeTourneau University, Pennsylvania College of Technology, or Montana Tech of the University of Montana. U.S. citizenship is required.

Financial data The stipend is $5,000; funds are paid directly to the educational institution.

Duration 1 year.

Number awarded 1 each year.

Deadline February of each year.

[673]
WILLIAM BRIDGE SCHOLARSHIP

Ninety-Nines, Inc.-Eastern New England Chapter
c/o Vanessa Blakeley, Scholarship Chair
77 Corey Street
West Roxbury, MA 02132
E-mail: blakeley.vanessa@gmail.com
Web: www.womenpilotsene.org/scholarships.htm

Summary To provide financial assistance to female residents of New England who are interested in preparing for a career in aviation.

Eligibility This program is open to women who are at least of high school age and reside or study in 1 of the following states: Maine, New Hampshire, Rhode Island, Vermont, Massachusetts, or Connecticut. Applicants must be studying or planning to study in an area of aviation at an accredited college or university, at a college or other flight school, or with a private instructor. They must have at least a private pilot certificate. Along with their application, they must submit a personal letter describing their aviation-related goals, including descriptions of all their aviation-related activities. Selection is based on academic achievement, interest and dedication to a career in aviation, recommendations, involvement in aviation activities (e.g., flying, aviation employment, model airplane building, science fair projects), and financial need.

Financial data The stipend is $1,500.

Duration 1 year.

Number awarded 1 each year.

Deadline January of each year.

[674]
WILLIAM RUCKER GREENWOOD SCHOLARSHIP

Association for Women Geoscientists-Potomac Chapter
Attn: Scholarships
P.O. Box 6644
Arlington, VA 22206-0644
E-mail: awgpotomacschol@hotmail.com
Web: www.awg.org/members/po_scholarships.htm

Summary To provide financial assistance to minority women from any state working on an undergraduate or graduate degree in the geosciences at a college in the Potomac Bay region.

Eligibility This program is open to minority women who are residents of any state and currently enrolled as full-time undergraduate or graduate geoscience majors at an accredited, degree-granting college or university in Delaware, the District of Columbia, Maryland, Virginia, or West Virginia. Selection is based on the applicant's 1) participation in geoscience or earth science educational activities; and 2) potential for leadership as a future geoscience professional.

Financial data The stipend is $1,000. The recipient also is granted a 1-year membership in the Association for Women Geoscientists (AWG).

Duration 1 year.

Number awarded 1 each year.

Deadline April of each year.

[675]
WISCONSIN LEGION AUXILIARY DEPARTMENT PRESIDENT'S SCHOLARSHIP

American Legion Auxiliary
Department of Wisconsin
Attn: Education Chair
2930 American Legion Drive
P.O. Box 140
Portage, WI 53901-0140
(608) 745-0124   Toll Free: (866) 664-3863
Fax: (608) 745-1947   E-mail: alawi@amlegionauxwi.org
Web: www.amlegionauxwi.org/Scholarships.htm

Summary To provide financial assistance to Wisconsin residents who are members or children of members of the American Legion Auxiliary and interested in attending college in any state.

Eligibility This program is open to members and children of members of the American Legion Auxiliary in Wisconsin. Applicants must be high school seniors or graduates and attending or planning to attend a college or university in any state. They must have a GPA of 3.5 or higher and be able to demonstrate financial need. Along with their application, they must submit a 300-word essay on "Education—An Investment in the Future."

Financial data The stipend is $1,000.

Duration 1 year.

Number awarded 3 each year.

Deadline March of each year.

[676]
WISCONSIN WOMEN IN GOVERNMENT UNDERGRADUATE SCHOLARSHIPS

Wisconsin Women in Government, Inc.
Attn: Scholarship Committee
P.O. Box 2543
Madison, WI 53701
(608) 848-2321
E-mail: info@wiscwomeningovernment.org
Web: www.wiscwomeningovernment.org/scholarships.cfm

Summary To provide financial assistance to women in Wisconsin interested in attending a college or university in the state to prepare for a career in public service.

Eligibility This program is open to women in Wisconsin who are enrolled full or part time at an institution that is a member of the University of Wisconsin system, the Wisconsin Technical College System, or the Wisconsin Association of Independent Colleges and Universities. Applicants must have a grade average of "C" or higher and be able to demonstrate financial need. They must possess leadership potential, initiative, and excellent communication skills and have an interest in public service, government, and/or the political process. Juniors and seniors must have declared a major. Selection is based on leadership, demonstrated ability to handle responsibility, initiative, communication skills, academic achievement, community involvement, and commitment to public service.

Financial data The stipend is $3,000 per year. Funds may be used for tuition, school supplies, child care, or to reduce loan burden.

Duration 1 year; may be renewed.

Number awarded Varies each year; recently, 3 were awarded.

Deadline May of each year.

[677]
WISCONSIN WOMEN'S ALLIANCE FOUNDATION SCHOLARSHIP

Community Foundation for the Fox Valley Region, Inc.
Attn: Scholarships
4455 West Lawrence Street
Appleton, WI 54914
(920) 830-1290   Fax: (920) 830-1293
E-mail: scholarships@cffoxvalley.org
Web: www.cffoxvalley.org/page.aspx?pid=1313

Summary To provide financial assistance to mature women in Wisconsin who are working full time on an undergraduate or graduate degree at a school in any state.

Eligibility This program is open to Wisconsin women who are 25 years of age or older. Applicants must be attending an accredited 2- or 4-year college, university, or technical college to work on an undergraduate or graduate degree. Selection is based on career path and goals, employment history, volunteer activities, professional and community activities, and financial need.

Financial data The stipend ranges up to $1,000.

Duration 1 year.

Number awarded Normally, 3 each year.

Deadline March of each year.

[678]
WOKSAPE OYATE: "WISDOM OF THE PEOPLE" KEEPERS OF THE NEXT GENERATION AWARD

American Indian College Fund
Attn: Scholarship Department
8333 Greenwood Boulevard
Denver, CO 80221
(303) 426-8900   Toll Free: (800) 776-FUND
Fax: (303) 426-1200
E-mail: scholarships@collegefund.org
Web: www.collegefund.org

Summary To provide financial assistance to Native Americans who are single parents and attending or planning to attend a Tribal College or University (TCU).

Eligibility This program is open to American Indians or Alaska Natives who are single parents and enrolled or planning to enroll full time at an eligible TCU. Applicants must have a GPA of 2.0 or higher. Applications are available only online and include required essays on specified topics. Selection is based on exceptional academic achievement. U.S. citizenship is required.

Financial data The stipend is $8,000.

Duration 1 year.

Additional information This program began in 2006 with an endowment grant from the Lilly Endowment.

Number awarded 1 each year.

Deadline May of each year.

[679]
WOMEN CHEFS AND RESTAURATEURS SCHOLARSHIP PROGRAM

Women Chefs and Restaurateurs
Attn: Scholarship Program Coordinator
115 South Patrick Street, Suite 101
Alexandria, VA 22314
(630) 396-8339   Toll Free: (877) 927-7787
E-mail: Scholarship@womenchefs.org
Web: www.womenchefs.org/career-development

Summary To provide financial assistance to members of Women Chefs and Restaurateurs (WCR) who are interested in preparing for a culinary or related career.

Eligibility This program is open to women who are members of WCR, interested in attending a culinary or related school, and at least 18 years of age (21 for the wine scholarships). Recently, support was offered at the Italian culinary experience, the classic culinary arts program, and the classic pastry arts program at the International Culinary Center (New York, New York); the Italian Culinary Experience, the classic pastry arts program, and the intensive sommelier program at the International Culinary Center (Campbell, California); the Barbara Lazaroff WCR Future Leader in Hospitality Scholarship; the Master the Art and Science of Sous-Vide Scholarship at the Culinary Research and Education Academy in Sterling, Virginia; the Trial Celebrity Chef Anita Lo Scholarship at Annisa in New York; a scholarship in the culinary program at Southern Alberta Institute of Technology (SAIT) in Calgary; and Ann Cooper's "Healthy School Lunch" Scholarship in Boulder, Colorado. Applicants must submit a 1-page essay about their food service career, their culinary interests, what inspires them professionally, and how the scholarship will contribute to their career.

Financial data In general, scholarships provide payment of full or partial tuition, or stipends of $5,000 to $7,500 per year.

Duration Program lengths vary; scholarships must be used during the calendar year in which they are awarded.

Additional information Students may apply for only 1 program on a single application; the fee is $25 for the first application $40 for multiple applications (to a maximum of 3).

Number awarded Varies each year.

Deadline July of each year.

[680]
WOMEN DIVERS HALL OF FAME MARINE CONSERVATION UNDERGRADUATE SCHOLARSHIP

Women Divers Hall of Fame
43 MacKey Avenue
Port Washington, NY 11050-3628
E-mail: scholarships@wdhof.org
Web: www.wdhof.org/scholarships/scholarships.shtml

Summary To provide financial assistance to women who are working on an undergraduate degree in marine conservation.

Eligibility This program is open to women of any age who are enrolled in an accredited undergraduate academic or research program in the field of marine conservation. Applicants must be seeking funding to assist with college tuition

and fees, to support independent research, or to support a research internship program at an accredited university.

Financial data The stipend is $1,000.

Duration 1 year.

Number awarded 1 each year.

Deadline November of each year.

[681]
WOMEN DIVERS HALL OF FAME UNDERGRADUATE MARINE RESEARCH INTERNSHIP

Women Divers Hall of Fame
43 MacKey Avenue
Port Washington, NY 11050-3628
E-mail: scholarships@wdhof.org
Web: www.wdhof.org/scholarships/scholarships.shtml

Summary To provide financial assistance to undergraduate women who are interested in a marine research internship.

Eligibility This program is open to women who have completed at least 60 credits of undergraduate study or are classified as juniors by their institution. Applicants must be seeking funding to participate in a research internship in marine biology.

Financial data The stipend is $1,000.

Duration 1 year.

Number awarded 1 each year.

Deadline November of each year.

[682]
WOMEN IN FILM DALLAS UNDERGRADUATE STUDENT TUITION SCHOLARSHIP

Women in Film Dallas
Attn: Scholarships and Grants
5930 Royal Lane, Suite E
PMB 236
Dallas, TX 75230
(214) 379-1171   Toll Free: (800) 724-0767
Fax: (214) 379-1172   E-mail: scholarships@wifdallas.org
Web: www.wifdallas.org/page-950618

Summary To provide financial assistance to women from any state who are studying film, television, or video at colleges and universities in north Texas.

Eligibility This program is open to women who are residents of any state working full time on an undergraduate degree in film, television, or video at an accredited college or university in the following Texas counties: Collin, Dallas, Denton, Ellis, Kaufman, Rockwall, or Tarrant. Applicants must have consistently maintained a GPA of 3.0 or higher. Along with their application, they must submit a 1,000-word essay on their interest and experiences in motion picture arts and sciences, 2 letters of recommendation, and a short sample of their work. Financial need is not considered in the selection process.

Financial data The stipend is $1,000.

Duration 1 year.

Number awarded 1 each year.

Deadline June of each year.

[683]
WOMEN IN LEADERSHIP SCHOLARSHIP OF BROWN AND CALDWELL

Brown and Caldwell
Attn: HR/Scholarship Program
1527 Cole Boulevard, Suite 300
Lakewood, CO 80401
(303) 239-5400 Fax: (303) 239-5454
E-mail: scholarships@brwncald.com
Web: www.brownandcaldwell.com/Scholarships.asp?id=4

Summary To provide financial assistance to female upper-division and graduate students working on a degree in an environmental or engineering field.

Eligibility This program is open to female U.S. citizens and permanent residents enrolled as full-time juniors, seniors, or graduate students at an accredited college or university. Applicants must identify as a woman who demonstrates leadership within the community. They must have a GPA of 3.0 or higher with a declared major in civil, chemical, or environmental engineering or an environmental science (e.g., biology, geology, hydrogeology, ecology). Along with their application, they must submit an essay (up to 250 words) on a topic that changes annually but relates to their personal development. Financial need is not considered in the selection process.

Financial data The stipend is $5,000.

Duration 1 year.

Additional information This program began in 1999.

Number awarded 1 each year.

Deadline May of each year.

[684]
WOMEN IN NEED SCHOLARSHIP

Educational Foundation for Women in Accounting
Attn: Foundation Administrator
136 South Keowee Street
Dayton, OH 45402
(937) 424-3391 Fax: (937) 222-5749
E-mail: info@efwa.org
Web: www.efwa.org/scholarships_undergraduate.php

Summary To provide financial support to women who are the sole source of support for themselves and their families and are in the junior year of an accounting degree program.

Eligibility This program is open to women who, either through divorce or death of a spouse, have become the sole source of support for themselves and their families. Women who are single parents as a result of other circumstances are also considered. Applicants must be working on a degree in accounting as incoming, current, or reentry juniors. Selection is based on aptitude for accounting and business, commitment to the goal of working on a degree in accounting (including evidence of continued commitment after receiving this award), clear evidence that the candidate has established goals and a plan for achieving those goals (both personal and professional), and financial need. U.S. citizenship is required.

Financial data The stipend is $2,000 per year.

Duration 1 year; may be renewed 1 additional year if the recipient completes at least 12 hours each semester.

Additional information This program began in 2000.

Number awarded 1 or more each year.

Deadline April of each year.

[685]
WOMEN IN PUBLIC FINANCE SCHOLARSHIP PROGRAM

Women in Public Finance
Attn: Scholarship Committee
P.O. Box 1195
Chicago, IL 60690-1195
(312) 340-9484 E-mail: scholarship@wpfc.com
Web: www.wpfc.com

Summary To provide financial assistance to women who are high school seniors and interested in attending college to prepare for a career in public finance or related fields.

Eligibility This program is open to female graduating high school seniors who have exhibited academic achievement, preferably with a demonstrated aptitude in mathematics and demonstrated leadership skills. Applicants must be planning to enroll in college to prepare for a career in finance, especially public finance, or related fields (e.g., government, non-profits, law). They must have a GPA of 3.0 or higher. Along with their application, they must submit 1) a 250-word essay on their favorite subjects in school and why those are their favorites; and 2) an essay of 350 to 500 words on their choice of 4 topics related to their interests and goals. Financial need is not considered in the selection process.

Financial data The stipend is $1,000.

Duration 1 year.

Number awarded Up to 14 each year.

Deadline June of each year.

[686]
WOMEN IN TRANSITION ACCOUNTING SCHOLARSHIP

Educational Foundation for Women in Accounting
Attn: Foundation Administrator
136 South Keowee Street
Dayton, OH 45402
(937) 424-3391 Fax: (937) 222-5749
E-mail: info@efwa.org
Web: www.efwa.org/scholarships_undergraduate.php

Summary To provide financial support to women who have become the sole support of their family and wish to begin work on an undergraduate accounting degree.

Eligibility This program is open to women who, either through divorce or death of a spouse, have become the sole source of support for themselves and their family. Women who are single parents as a result of other circumstances are also considered. Applicants should be incoming or current freshmen, or they may be returning to school with sufficient credits to qualify for freshman status. Selection is based on aptitude for accounting, commitment to the goal of working on a degree in accounting (including evidence of continued commitment after receiving this award), clear evidence that the candidate has established goals and a plan for achieving those goals (both personal and professional), and financial need. U.S. citizenship is required.

Financial data The stipend is $4,000 per year.

Duration 1 year; may be renewed 3 additional years if the recipient completes at least 12 hours each semester and maintains a GPA of 3.0 or higher.

Additional information This program, established in 1990, was formerly called the Displaced Homemaker's Scholarship.

Number awarded 1 each year.

Deadline April of each year.

[687]
WOMEN MILITARY AVIATORS DREAM OF FLIGHT SCHOLARSHIP

Women in Aviation International
Attn: Scholarships
Morningstar Airport
3647 State Route 503 South
West Alexandria, OH 45381-9354
(937) 839-4647   Fax: (937) 839-4645
E-mail: scholarships@wai.org
Web: www.wai.org

Summary To provide financial assistance to members of Women in Aviation International (WAI) who have military experience and are interested in flight training or academic study.

Eligibility This program is open to WAI members who have military experience and are enrolled at an accredited academic institution or an FAA Part 141 approved flight school. Applicants must be seeking flight ratings in order to pursue opportunities in aviation. Along with their application, they must submit 1) a 500-word essay and professional resume that include their aviation history and goals, what they have done for themselves to achieve their goals, where they see themselves in 5 and 10 years, involvement in aviation activities, how the scholarship will help them achieve their objectives, and their present financial need; and 2) a narrative addressing their demonstrated persistence and determination to fly, ability to complete their current training program with 1 year, and their interest and/or participation in military aviation.

Financial data The stipend is $2,500. A 1-year membership in Women Military Aviators (WMA) is also provided.

Duration Recipients must be able to complete training within 1 year.

Additional information WAI is a nonprofit professional organization dedicated to encouraging women to consider an aviation career and to providing educational outreach activities and networking resources to women active in the industry. WMA established this program in 2005 to honor the women aviators who were serving or had served in Iraq and Afghanistan.

Number awarded 1 each year.

Deadline November of each year.

[688]
WOMEN OF AT&T SACRAMENTO CHAPTER SCHOLARSHIPS

Women of AT&T-Sacramento Chapter
c/o Virginia Carvalho
3900 Channel Drive
West Sacramento, CA 95691-3432
E-mail: m14119@att.com

Summary To provide financial assistance to female residents of California and Nevada who are interested in attend-

ing college in any state and are sponsored by a member of Women of AT&T (WOA).

Eligibility This program is open to women who are attending or planning to attend a college, university, or vocational/trade school in any state. Applicants must be residents of California or Nevada or have been residents previously for at least 2 years. They must have a GPA of 3.0 or higher. A member of WOA Sacramento Chapter must agree to sponsor them. Along with their application, they must submit 1) a 100-word essay on their educational and long-term career goals; 2) a 250-word essay on why they deserve this scholarship; and 3) a 500-word essay on their choice of 3 topics that relate to the interests of the sponsoring organization. Selection is based on those essays, academic standing (GPA, class rank, SAT/ACT scores), community or school involvement, work experience, and leadership abilities. Some scholarships are reserved for applicants who come from low-income families (less than $17,655 for a family of 1, rising to $61,225 for a family of 8) and for those who plan to major in a field of science, technology, engineering, or mathematics (STEM).

Financial data The stipend is $1,000.

Duration 1 year.

Number awarded 7 each year: 2 reserved for low-income students, 2 reserved for women interested in studying a field of STEM, and 3 with no other restrictions.

Deadline May of each year.

[689]
WOMEN OF THE ELCA SCHOLARSHIP PROGRAM

Women of the Evangelical Lutheran Church in America
Attn: Scholarships
8765 West Higgins Road
Chicago, IL 60631-4101
(773) 380-2741   Toll Free: (800) 638-3522, ext. 2741
Fax: (773) 380-2419   E-mail: valora.starr@elca.org
Web: www.womenoftheelca.org

Summary To provide financial assistance to lay women who are members of Evangelical Lutheran Church of America (ELCA) congregations and who wish to take classes on the undergraduate, graduate, professional, or vocational school level.

Eligibility This program is open to ELCA lay women who are at least 21 years of age and have experienced an interruption of at least 2 years in their education since high school. Applicants must have been admitted to an educational institution to prepare for a career in other than the ordained ministry. They may be working on an undergraduate, graduate, professional, or vocational school degree. U.S. citizenship is required.

Financial data The average stipend is $1,000 per year.

Duration 1 year; recipients may reapply for 1 additional year.

Additional information These scholarships are supported by several endowment funds: the Cronk Memorial Fund, the First Triennial Board Scholarship Fund, the General Scholarship Fund, the Mehring Fund, the Paepke Scholarship Fund, the Piero/Wade/Wade Fund, and the Edwin/Edna Robeck Scholarship.

Number awarded Varies each year; recently, 15 were awarded.

Deadline February of each year.

[690]
WOMEN@MICROSOFT HOPPERS SCHOLARSHIP

Fargo-Moorhead Area Foundation
Attn: Finance/Program Assistant
502 First Avenue North, Suite 202
Fargo, ND 58102-4804
(701) 234-0756   Fax: (701) 234-9724
E-mail: Cher@areafoundation.org
Web: www.areafoundation.org/index.php/scholarships

Summary To provide financial assistance to women who are interested in studying computer science at a college or university in Minnesota or the Dakotas.

Eligibility This program is open to women who are accepted or enrolled at a college or university in Minnesota, North Dakota, or South Dakota. Applicants must be undergraduates with a declared major in computer science or a related discipline and a GPA of 3.0 or higher. Along with their application, they must submit essays, up to 500 words each, on 2 of the following topics: 1) What they see as the computer industry's primary shortcomings? If they were a leader in the technical world today, how would they take the shortcomings and turn them to positive attributes? 2) Describe examples of their leadership experience in which they significantly influenced others, helped resolve disputes, or contributed to group efforts over time; 3) What guidance do they have for organizations in the technology industry as they respond to the social media wave; or 4) What they think the computer/software industry will be like in the next 10 years. Selection is based on the essays, academic achievement, character, qualities of leadership, and financial need.

Financial data The stipend is $1,500.

Duration 1 year.

Additional information This program began in 1990 as part of an effort to make Microsoft a great place for women. In addition to scholarships, other Hoppers committees deal with outreach, technical women, mentoring, program, career development, and diversity. The program is named for Grace Hopper, a computer science pioneer.

Number awarded 1 each year.

Deadline May of each year.

[691]
WOMEN'S ECONOMIC COUNCIL FOUNDATION SCHOLARSHIP AWARDS FOR NON-TRADITIONAL STUDENTS

Tennessee Economic Council on Women
Attn: Women's Economic Council Foundation
405 Westland Drive
Lebanon, TN 37087
(615) 969-2857
Web: www.womenseconomicfoundation.org

Summary To provide financial assistance to women in Tennessee who plan to return to college in any state to improve their economic autonomy after an absence.

Eligibility This program is open to women who are residents of Tennessee and have been out of high school or received a GED 5 years previously or longer. Applicants must

be enrolled or planning to enroll as an undergraduate at a college or university in any state. Along with their application, they must submit a summary of their personal education goals. Selection is based on that summary, participation in community activities, work history, letters of recommendation, and financial need.

Financial data The stipend is $1,000.

Duration 1 year.

Number awarded 3 each year: 1 to a woman in each division of the state (western, central, and eastern).

Deadline September of each year.

[692]
WOMEN'S ECONOMIC COUNCIL FOUNDATION SCHOLARSHIP AWARDS FOR TRADITIONAL HIGH SCHOOL SENIORS

Tennessee Economic Council on Women
Attn: Women's Economic Council Foundation
405 Westland Drive
Lebanon, TN 37087
(615) 969-2857
Web: www.womenseconomicfoundation.org

Summary To provide financial assistance to female high school seniors in Tennessee who plan to attend college in any state to improve their economic autonomy.

Eligibility This program is open to women graduating from high schools in Tennessee and planning to enroll at a college or university in any state. Applicants must submit a copy of their high school transcript that includes their ACT/SAT scores, a description of participation in school and community activities, a general description of employment positions held, 2 letters of recommendation, and a summary of personal education goals. Financial need is not considered in the selection process. The program includes 1 scholarship reserved for a Girl Scout Gold Award recipient.

Financial data The stipend is $1,000.

Duration 1 year.

Number awarded 3 each year, including 1 for an applicant who has received the Girl Scout Gold Award.

Deadline September of each year.

[693]
WOMEN'S GOLF ASSOCIATION OF MASSACHUSETTS JUNIOR SCHOLAR PROGRAM

Women's Golf Association of Massachusetts, Inc.
Attn: WGAM Junior Scholarship Fund, Inc.
William F. Connell Golf House
300 Arnold Palmer Boulevard
Norton, MA 02766
(774) 430-9010   Fax: (774) 430-9011
E-mail: info@wgam.org
Web: www.wgam.org/scholarship-info

Summary To provide financial assistance to high school seniors who have an affiliation with the Women's Golf Association of Massachusetts (WGAM) and are planning to attend college in any state.

Eligibility This program is open to female high school seniors who are members of WGAM, daughters or granddaughters of members, or Massachusetts residents who have an interest in golf. Applicants must be planning to attend a college or university in any state. Along with their application, they must submit an essay of 250 to 500 words on their choice of assigned topics. Selection is based on high school academic record and performance, leadership qualities, community and civic involvement, character, and personality. Applicants who cannot demonstrate financial need may be designated as a scholar but not receive a stipend. An interview is required.

Financial data The stipend depends on the need of the recipient.

Duration 1 year; may be renewed.

Additional information This program began in 1985.

Number awarded Varies each year; recently, 8 were awarded.

Deadline May of each year.

[694]
WOMEN'S INDEPENDENCE SCHOLARSHIP PROGRAM

Women's Independence Scholarship Program, Inc.
Attn: WISP Program
4900 Randall Parkway, Suite H
Wilmington, NC 28403
(910) 397-7742   Toll Free: (866) 255-7742
Fax: (910) 397-0023   E-mail: nancy@wispinc.org
Web: www.wispinc.org/Scholarship/tabid/56/Default.aspx

Summary To provide financial assistance for college or graduate school to women who are victims of partner abuse.

Eligibility This program is open to women who are victims of partner abuse and have worked for at least 6 months with a nonprofit domestic violence victim services provider that is willing to sponsor them. Applicants must be interested in attending a vocational school, community college, 4-year college or university, or (in exceptional circumstances) graduate school as a full- or part-time student. They should have left an abusive partner at least 1 year previously; women who have been parted from their batterer for more than 5 years are also eligible, but funding for such applicants may be limited. Preference is given to single mothers with young children. Special consideration is given to applicants who plan to use their education to further the rights of, and options for, women and girls. Selection is based primarily on financial need. U.S. citizenship or permanent resident status is required.

Financial data Stipends depend on the need of the recipient, but they are at least $250 and average $2,000 per academic term. First priority is given to funding for direct educational expenses (tuition, books, and fees), which is paid directly to the educational institution. Second priority is for assistance in reducing indirect financial barriers to education (e.g., child care, transportation), which is paid directly to the sponsoring agency.

Duration 1 year; may be renewed if the recipient maintains a GPA of 2.75 or higher.

Additional information This program began in 1999 when the sponsor was known as the Sunshine Lady Foundation.

Number awarded Varies each year. Since the program began, it has awarded more than $16 million in scholarships to approximately 2,000 women.

Deadline Applications may be submitted at any time, but they must be received at least 2 months before the start of the intended program.

[695]
WOMEN'S JEWELRY ASSOCIATION STUDENT SCHOLARSHIPS

Women's Jewelry Association
Attn: Scholarship Chair
82 Washington Street, Suite 203A
Poughkeepsie, NY 12601
(212) 687-2722   Fax: (646) 355-0219
E-mail: Jennyo@tbirdjewels.com
Web: www.womensjewelryassociation.com

Summary To provide financial assistance for college to women who are interested in careers in jewelry.

Eligibility This program is open to women who are enrolled at a college or university and taking classes in fine jewelry and watch design. Applicants in the designer category must submit images (e.g., CAD, drawings of finished work they have created. Applicants in the designer/creator category must submit images of finished pieces that they have designed and created. Applicants in the non-designer category must be interested in preparing for a career as a bench jeweler, appraiser, gemologist, watch-maker, or retailer; they must submit a 2-page essay on the program for which they are applying, what motivated them to attend this program, why they think they deserve a scholarship, why they wish to prepare for a career in jewelry or watches, their goals and aspirations for the future, and how the jewelry industry will benefit from their receiving this scholarship. Financial need is not considered in the selection process.

Financial data Stipends range from $500 to $7,000.

Duration 1 year.

Number awarded Varies each year; recently, 11 of these scholarships, with a total value of $30,000, were awarded.

Deadline April of each year.

[696]
WOMEN'S LEADERSHIP IN AGRICULTURE SCHOLARSHIP PROGRAM

Ohio Farm Bureau Federation
Attn: Foundation
280 North High Street, Sixth Floor
P.O. Box 182383
Columbus, OH 43218-2383
(614) 249-2400   Fax: (614) 249-2200
E-mail: foundation@ofbf.org
Web: www.ofbf.org/foundation/scholarships-and-grants

Summary To provide financial assistance to female residents of Ohio who are interested in attending college or graduate school in any state to prepare for a career related to agriculture.

Eligibility This program is open to female Ohio residents who are attending or planning to attend an accredited 2-year technical school, 2- or 4-year college or university, or graduate school in any state. Applicants do not need to be members of the Ohio Farm Bureau Federation, their respective county Farm Bureau, or any other club or organization directly related to vocational agriculture. Nor are they required to be working on a degree directly connected to a school and/or college of agriculture. However, they must submit an explanation of how their career plans involve an aspect of the field of agriculture (e.g., food production, scientific research, education or outreach, technical support, food processing, product distribution, marketing, policymaking, advocacy). Financial need is not considered in the selection process.

Financial data The stipend is at least $1,500.

Duration 1 year.

Additional information This program began in 2006 with a grant from the Charlotte R. Schmidlapp Fund.

Number awarded 1 or more each year.

Deadline February of each year.

[697]
WOMEN'S OVERSEAS SERVICE LEAGUE SCHOLARSHIPS FOR WOMEN

Women's Overseas Service League
Attn: Scholarship Committee
P.O. Box 124
Cedar Knolls, NJ 07927-0124
E-mail: kelsey@openix.com
Web: www.wosl.org/scholarships.htm

Summary To provide financial assistance for college to women who are committed to a military or other public service career.

Eligibility This program is open to women who are committed to a military or other public service career. Applicants must have completed at least 12 semester hours of postsecondary study with a GPA of 2.5 or higher. They must be working on an academic degree (the program may be professional or technical in nature) and must agree to enroll for at least 6 semester hours of study each academic period. Along with their application, they must submit a 250-word essay on their career goals. Financial need is considered in the selection process.

Financial data Stipends range from $500 to $1,000 per year.

Duration 1 year; may be renewed 1 additional year.

Additional information The Women's Overseas Service League is a national organization of women who have served overseas in or with the armed forces.

Number awarded Varies each year.

Deadline February of each year.

[698]
WOMEN'S SECOND CHANCE COLLEGE SCHOLARSHIP

Community Foundation of Louisville
Attn: Program Officer, Mission and Impact
Waterfront Plaza, West Tower
325 West Main Street, Suite 1110
Louisville, KY 40202-4251
(502) 855-6971   Fax: (502) 855-6173
E-mail: ebonyo@cflouisville.org
Web: cflouisville.academicworks.com/opportunities/602

Summary To provide financial assistance for college to mature female residents of Kentucky and southern Indiana.

Eligibility This program is open to women between 25 and 40 years of age who reside in Kentucky or the Indiana counties of Clark, Crawford, Floyd, Harrison, Scott, or Washington. Applicants must have a high school diploma or GED certificate and may have some college credits. They must commit to enroll full or part time at a participating college or university and complete a baccalaureate degree within an agreed upon period of time. Selection is based on financial need and desire to learn.

Financial data The stipend is ranges up to $5,000 per year.

Duration 1 year; renewable until completion of a baccalaureate degree if the recipient maintains a GPA of 2.5 or higher.

Number awarded 1 or more each year.

Deadline March of each year.

[699]
WOMEN'S SOUTHERN CALIFORNIA GOLF FOUNDATION SCHOLARSHIPS

Women's Southern California Golf Association
Attn: Foundation
402 West Arrow Highway, Suite 10
San Dimas, CA 91773
(909) 592-1281, ext. 212   Fax: (909) 592-7542
E-mail: info@wscgafoundation.org
Web: www.wscgafoundation.com/scholarships.php

Summary To provide financial assistance to women in southern California who play golf and are interested in working on an undergraduate degree in any field at a college in any state.

Eligibility This program is open to female residents of southern California who play golf and are enrolled or planning to enroll full time at an accredited college or university in any state. Applicants must be interested in working on an associate or bachelor's degree in any field. They must have a GPA of 3.2 or higher. Along with their application, they must submit information on their family financial situation and an essay of up to 1,000 words on why they selected their major, their relevant academic and professional experience to date, and how golf and other sports (if applicable) will remain an integral part of their undergraduate experience.

Financial data A stipend is awarded (amount not specified).

Duration 1 year.

Additional information This program includes the Flo Scott Scholarship.

Number awarded Varies each year.

Deadline May of each year.

[700]
WOMEN'S SOUTHERN GOLF ASSOCIATION SCHOLARSHIP

Women's Southern Golf Association
c/o Connie Bousquet, Scholarship Committee Chair
105 Mariners Island
Mandeville, LA 70448
(504) 669-3908
E-mail: scholarship@womens-southerngolfassociation. org
Web: www.womens-southerngolfassociation.org

Summary To provide financial assistance to women golfers in the southern states who plan to attend college in any state.
Eligibility This program is open to amateur female golfers who are residents of 1 of the 15 southern states (Alabama, Arkansas, Florida, Georgia, Kentucky, Louisiana, Maryland, Mississippi, North Carolina, Oklahoma, South Carolina, Tennessee, Texas, Virginia, and West Virginia) or the District of Columbia. Applicants must be graduating high school seniors planning to work on an undergraduate degree at an accredited institution of higher learning in any state. Along with their application, they must submit transcripts that include SAT and/or ACT scores, documentation of financial need, and a 200-word personal statement on their goals for college and their future. Selection is based on academic excellence, citizenship, sportsmanship, and financial need. U.S. citizenship is required.
Financial data The stipend is $3,500 per year. Funds are paid directly to the recipient's college.
Duration 1 year; may be renewed up to 3 additional years, provided the recipient maintains a GPA of 3.0 or higher.
Additional information This program began in 1973.
Number awarded 1 each year.
Deadline April of each year.

[701]
WOMEN'S TRANSPORTATION SEMINAR JUNIOR COLLEGE SCHOLARSHIP

Women's Transportation Seminar
Attn: WTS Foundation
1701 K Street, N.W., Suite 800
Washington, DC 20006
(202) 955-5085   Fax: (202) 955-5088
E-mail: wts@wtsinternational.org
Web: www.wtsinternational.org/education/scholarships

Summary To provide financial assistance to women enrolled at a community college or trade school to prepare for a career in transportation.
Eligibility This program is open to women who are working on an associate or technical degree in transportation or a transportation-related field (e.g., transportation engineering, planning, finance, or logistics). Applicants must have a GPA of 3.0 or higher. Along with their application, they must submit a 500-word statement about their career goals after graduation and why they think they should receive the scholarship award. Applications must be submitted first to a local chapter; the chapters forward selected applications for consideration on the national level. Minority women are especially encouraged to apply. Selection is based on transportation involvement and goals, job skills, academic record, and leadership potential; financial need is not considered.
Financial data The stipend is $1,000.
Duration 1 year.
Additional information Local chapters may also award additional funding to winners for their area.
Number awarded 1 each year.
Deadline Applications must be submitted by November to a local WTS chapter.

[702]
WOMEN'S WESTERN GOLF FOUNDATION SCHOLARSHIP

Women's Western Golf Foundation
c/o Mrs. Richard Willis, Scholarship Selection Director
393 Ramsay Road
Deerfield, IL 60015
Web: www.wwga.org

Summary To provide financial assistance to high school senior girls who are interested in the sport of golf and plan to attend college.
Eligibility This program is open to high school senior girls who meet entrance requirements of, and plan to enroll at, an accredited 4-year college or university. Applicants must submit a 150-word essay describing their involvement in the sport of golf. Selection is based on academic achievement, financial need, excellence of character, and involvement with the sport of golf. Skill or excellence in the game is not a criterion. U.S. citizenship is required.
Financial data The stipend is $2,000 per year. The funds are to be used to pay for room, board, tuition, and other university fees or charges.
Duration 1 year; may be renewed up to 3 additional years if the recipient maintains a GPA of 3.0 or higher.
Additional information This program began in 1971.
Number awarded 15 each year. Since this program began, it has awarded more than $3.5 million to more than 530 undergraduates.
Deadline Preliminary applications must be submitted by February of each year.

[703]
WOMEN'S WILDLIFE MANAGEMENT/ CONSERVATION SCHOLARSHIP

National Rifle Association of America
Attn: Women's Policies Committee
11250 Waples Mill Road
Fairfax, VA 22030-7400
(703) 267-1399   Toll Free: (800) 861-1166
E-mail: grantprogram@nrahq.org
Web: wwmcs.nra.org

Summary To provide financial assistance to women who are upper-division students working on a degree in wildlife management or conservation.
Eligibility This program is open to women currently enrolled full time as college juniors or seniors. Applicants must be working on a degree in wildlife management or conservation. They must have a GPA of 3.0 or higher. Financial need is not considered in the selection process.
Financial data The stipend is $1,000 per year.
Duration 1 year; may be renewed 1 additional year.
Additional information This program began in 2006.
Number awarded 1 each year.
Deadline October of each year.

[704]
WTS TRANSPORTATION YOU HIGH SCHOOL SCHOLARSHIP

Women's Transportation Seminar
Attn: WTS Foundation
1701 K Street, N.W., Suite 800
Washington, DC 20006
(202) 955-5085　　　　　　Fax: (202) 955-5088
E-mail: wts@wtsinternational.org
Web: www.wtsinternational.org/education/scholarships

Summary To provide financial assistance to female high school seniors who are studying fields of science, technology, engineering, or mathematics (STEM) and planning to attend college to prepare for a career in transportation.

Eligibility This program is open to women who are high school seniors with a GPA of 3.0 or higher. Applicants must be studying STEM fields in high school and be planning to attend college to prepare for a career in transportation (e.g., civil engineering, city planning, logistics, automotive engineering, truck repair). Along with their application, they must submit a 500-word statement about their career goals after graduation and why they think they should receive the scholarship. Applications must be submitted first to a local chapter; the chapters forward selected applications for consideration on the national level. Minority women are especially encouraged to apply. Selection is based on transportation involvement and goals, job skills, academic record, and leadership potential; financial need is not considered.

Financial data The stipend is $1,000.

Duration 1 year.

Additional information Local chapters may also award additional funding to winners for their area.

Number awarded 1 each year.

Deadline Applications must be submitted by November to a local WTS chapter.

[705]
XI PSI OMEGA CHAPTER SCHOLARSHIPS

Alpha Kappa Alpha Sorority, Inc.-Xi Psi Omega Chapter
Attn: President
P.O. Box 140894
Anchorage, AK 99514
(907) 346-3998　　　　　E-mail: akaxpo@gmail.com
Web: www.xipsiomega.com/scholarship.html

Summary To provide financial assistance to high school seniors (especially African American women) from Alaska who plan to attend college in any state.

Eligibility This program is open to seniors graduating from high schools in Alaska who are planning to attend a 2- or 4-year accredited college or university in any state. Applicants must have a GPA of 2.5 or higher and a record of active participation in school and community activities. Alpha Kappa Alpha (AKA) is currently 1 of the largest social sororities whose membership is predominantly African American women.

Financial data A stipend is awarded (amount not specified).

Duration 1 year; nonrenewable.

Additional information The Xi Psi Omega chapter of AKA serves alumnae members in Alaska.

Number awarded 1 or more each year.

Deadline March of each year.

[706]
YOUNG LADIES' RADIO LEAGUE SCHOLARSHIPS

Foundation for Amateur Radio, Inc.
Attn: Scholarship Committee
P.O. Box 911
Columbia, MD 21044-0911
(410) 552-2652　　　　　　Fax: (410) 981-5146
E-mail: farscholarships@gmail.com
Web: www.farweb.org

Summary To provide funding to female licensed radio amateurs who are interested in earning a bachelor's or graduate degree in the United States.

Eligibility This program is open to female radio amateurs who have at least an FCC Technician Class license or equivalent foreign authorization. Applicants must intend to work full or part time on a bachelor's or graduate degree at a college or university in the United States. There are no restrictions on the course of study or residency location. Non-U.S. amateurs are eligible. Preference is given to students working on a degree in communications, electronics, or related arts and sciences. Financial need is considered in the selection process.

Financial data The stipend is $2,000 or $1,000.

Duration 1 year.

Additional information This program, which is financed by the Young Ladies' Radio League and administered by the Foundation for Amateur Radio, includes the following named scholarships: the Ethel Smith, K4LMB, Memorial Scholarship (established in 2000 and restricted to full-time students), the Mary Lou Brown, NM7N, Memorial Scholarship (established in 2000 and restricted to full-time students), and the Martha "Marte" Wessel, K0EPE, Memorial Scholarship (established in 2014 and open to part-time students working full time).

Number awarded 3 each year: 2 at $2,000 and 1 at $1,000.

Deadline April of each year.

[707]
YOUNG WOMEN'S MINISTRIES SUPPLEMENTAL AWARD FOR UNDERGRADUATE WOMEN

Presbyterian Church (USA)
Attn: Office of Financial Aid for Service
100 Witherspoon Street
Louisville, KY 40202-1396
(502) 569-5224　　　　Toll Free: (888) 728-7228, ext. 5224
Fax: (502) 569-8766　　　　　　TDD: (800) 833-5955
E-mail: finaid@pcusa.org
Web: www.presbyterianmission.org

Summary To provide supplemental financial assistance to undergraduate women who receive National Presbyterian College Scholarships or Student Opportunity Scholarships.

Eligibility This program is open to undergraduate women who apply for National Presbyterian College Scholarships or Student Opportunity Scholarships. Applicants must be active members of the Presbyterian Church (USA) and entering or attending a college or university affiliated with the PCUSA (for the National Presbyterian College Scholarships) or attending any college or university (for the Student Opportunity Scholarships). They must have a GPA of 2.5 or higher and continuing financial need even after the receipt of the other scholarship. Along with their application, they must submit essays of 300 to 500 words on 1) how their faith has empowered them and shaped their studies and/or vocational choices; and 2) how they have worked for the empowerment of women during their lifetime and how they plan to do so in the future.

Financial data The stipend is $1,000.

Duration 1 year; nonrenewable.

Additional information This program is sponsored by the PCUSA Young Women's Ministries and administered by its Office of Financial Aid for Service.

Number awarded 6 each year.

Deadline July of each year.

[708]
YUKIKO HOWELL MEMORIAL STEM SCHOLARSHIP

Women in Aviation International
Attn: Scholarships
Morningstar Airport
3647 State Route 503 South
West Alexandria, OH 45381-9354
(937) 839-4647   Fax: (937) 839-4645
E-mail: scholarships@wai.org
Web: www.wai.org

Summary To provide financial assistance to members of Women in Aviation International (WAI) who are working on a college degree in a field related to science, technology, engineering, or mathematics (STEM).

Eligibility This program is open to WAI members who are currently enrolled at an accredited 2- or 4-year college or university, technical institute, or certificate program. Applicants must be preparing for a career in a field of STEM or taking STEM continuing education classes. They must have experience volunteering in STEM or aviation-related events and/or activities in the previous year. Along with their application, they must submit a 500-word essay and professional resume that include their aviation history and goals, what they have done for themselves to achieve their goals, where they see themselves in 5 and 10 years, involvement in aviation activities, how the scholarship will help them achieve their objectives, and their present financial need. The sponsor defines STEM fields to include air traffic controller, avionics technician, dispatch certification, aircraft mechanic, meteorologist, or educator for STEM.

Financial data The stipend is $1,500.

Duration 1 year.

Additional information WAI is a nonprofit professional organization dedicated to encouraging women to consider an aviation career and to providing educational outreach activities and networking resources to women active in the industry. This program began in 2014.

Number awarded 1 each year.

Deadline November of each year.

[709]
YWAF HIGHER EDUCATION SCHOLARSHIPS

Young Women's Alliance
Attn: Foundation
P.O. Box 684612
Austin, TX 78701
(512) 553-6176
E-mail: development@youngwomensalliance.org
Web: www.youngwomensalliance.org/ywaf_scholarships

Summary To provide financial assistance to women from any state enrolled as upper-division or graduate students at a college or university in central Texas.

Eligibility This program is open to women from any state who are younger than 40 years of age. Applicants must have completed at least 60 undergraduate semester hours or be working on a graduate degree at an accredited institution of higher learning in central Texas. They must have devoted at least 40 hours of work on a Community Impact Project during the current semester. Along with their application, they must submit a description of their Community Impact Project and a personal statement about why they should be chosen to receive this scholarship. Selection is based on academic achievement, demonstrated leadership, commitment to both past community service and the Community Impact Project, and financial need.

Financial data The stipend is $2,500.

Duration 1 year.

Additional information This foundation was established in 1997.

Number awarded 1 or more each year.

Deadline March of each year.

[710]
ZETA PHI BETA GENERAL UNDERGRADUATE SCHOLARSHIPS

Zeta Phi Beta Sorority, Inc.
Attn: National Educational Foundation
1734 New Hampshire Avenue, N.W.
Washington, DC 20009
(202) 387-3103   Fax: (202) 232-4593
E-mail: info@zetaphibetasororityhq.org
Web: www.zpbnef1975.org/scholarships-and-descriptions

Summary To provide financial assistance to students interested in postsecondary education.

Eligibility This program is open to high school seniors or college students enrolled or planning to enroll in a postsecondary institution of higher learning in the United States. Applicants must be enrolled or planning to enroll on a full-time basis. Along with their application, they must submit a 150-word essay on their educational goals and professional aspirations, how this award will help them to achieve those goals, and why they should receive the award. Financial need is not considered in the selection process.

Financial data The stipend ranges from $500 to $1,000 per year; funds are paid directly to the recipient's college or university to be applied to tuition or other fees.

Duration 1 academic year; may be renewed.

Additional information Zeta Phi Beta is a traditionally African American sorority.

Number awarded Varies each year.

Deadline January of each year.

[711]
ZOE CAVALARIS OUTSTANDING FEMALE ATHLETE AWARD

Daughters of Penelope
Attn: Athletics Chair
1909 Q Street, N.W., Suite 500
Washington, DC 20009-1007
(202) 234-9741   Fax: (202) 483-6983
E-mail: dophq@ahepa.org
Web: www.daughtersofpenelope.org

Summary To recognize and reward women of Greek descent who demonstrate excellence in high school or college athletics.

Eligibility This award is presented to a young woman of Hellenic descent who has unusually high quality athletic ability and a record of accomplishment in any sport or any series of sports. Nominees must be outstanding high school or college amateur female athletes recognized for their accomplishments during their high school and/or college years. Along with a letter of nomination from a sponsoring chapter of Daughters of Penelope, they must submit documentation of their current overall GPA, academic honors, other honors, participation in sports activities, extracurricular activities (other than sports), church and/or community activities, and special achievements (other than sports).

Financial data The award includes a college scholarship (amount not specified), an engraved plaque, public recognition through Daughters of Penelope events and publications, and reimbursement of transportation and hotel accommodations to attend the organization's national convention.

Duration The award is presented annually.

Number awarded 1 each year.

Deadline May of each year.

[712]
ZONTA CLUB OF BANGOR SCHOLARSHIPS

Zonta Club of Bangor
c/o Barbara A. Cardone
P.O. Box 1904
Bangor, ME 04402-1904
Web: www.zontaclubofbangor.org/?area=scholarship

Summary To provide financial assistance to women attending or planning to attend college in Maine and major in any field.

Eligibility This program is open to women who are attending or planning to attend an accredited 2- or 4-year college in Maine. Applicants may major in any field. Along with their application, they must submit brief essays on 1) their goals in seeking higher education and their plans for the future; and 2) any school and community activities that have been of particular importance to them and why they found them worthwhile. Financial need may be considered in the selection process.

Financial data The stipend is $1,000.

Duration 1 year.

Number awarded 2 each year.

Deadline March of each year.

[713]
ZONTA CLUB OF LAFAYETTE WOMAN'S SCHOLARSHIP

Zonta Club of Lafayette
c/o Lisa LeBlanc
175 Antigua Drive
Lafayette, LA 70503
(337) 984-4197   E-mail: lisa.leblanc@lusfiber.net
Web: /www.zontalafayette.com/scholarships.html

Summary To provide financial assistance to female residents of Louisiana who are attending college in the state.

Eligibility This program is open to female residents of Louisiana who are the major wage earner of their family. Applicants must be enrolled at a Louisiana university, college, or vocational/technical school in non-remedial courses and have minimum ACT scores of 18 in English and 19 in mathematics or SAT scores of at least 450 in critical reading and 460 in mathematics. U.S. citizenship and evidence of financial need are required.

Financial data The stipend is $1,250.

Duration 1 year.

Number awarded 1 each year.

Deadline September of each year.

[714]
ZONTA CLUB OF MILWAUKEE WOMEN IN STEM SCHOLARSHIP

Zonta Club of Milwaukee
c/o Missy Creevy, Scholarship Chair
18850-C Stonehedge Drive
Brookfield, WI 53045
(262) 794-0083
E-mail: zcscholarship@zontamilwaukee.org
Web: www.zontamilwaukee.org/?page_id=185

Summary To provide financial assistance to women with ties to southeastern Wisconsin who are upper-division students working on a degree in a field of science, technology, engineering, or mathematics (STEM).

Eligibility This program is open to women who are entering the third or fourth year of an undergraduate degree program in a STEM-related field at a college, university, or institute. Applicants must be residents of or attending college in southeastern Wisconsin (Kenosha, Milwaukee, Ozaukee, Racine, Washington, or Waukesha counties). Along with their application, they must submit a 500-word essay that describes their academic and professional goals, the relevance of their program of study to STEM, and how the scholarship will assist them in reaching their goals. Financial need is not considered in the selection process.

Financial data The stipend is $1,000.

Duration 1 year.

Additional information This program began in 2005.

Number awarded 1 each year.

Deadline June of each year.

[715]
ZONTA CLUB OF WASHINGTON UNDERGRADUATE SCHOLARSHIPS

Zonta Club of Washington, D.C.
Attn: Scholarship Committee
P.O. Box 9753
Washington, DC 20016
E-mail: ScholarshipUndergrad@zontawashingtondc.org
Web: www.zontawashingtondc.org

Summary   To provide financial assistance to women from any state who are attending college in Washington, D.C.

Eligibility   This program is open to women undergraduates from any state who are enrolled full or part time at universities in the Washington, D.C. area. Applicants must have a GPA of 3.0 or higher. Selection is based on GPA, community involvement and leadership, relevant personal circumstances, an essay on academic and career interests, letters of recommendation, commitment to professional excellence in future career, and financial need.

Financial data   The amount awarded varies; recently, stipends averaged $4,000.

Duration   1 year.

Number awarded   Varies each year; recently, 5 were awarded.

Deadline   March of each year.

[716]
ZONTA INTERNATIONAL YOUNG WOMEN IN PUBLIC AFFAIRS AWARDS

Zonta International
Attn: Foundation
1211 West 22nd Street, Suite 900
Oak Brook, IL 60523-3384
(630) 928-1400   Fax: (630) 928-1559
E-mail: programs@zonta.org
Web: www.zonta.org

Summary   To recognize and reward women in secondary schools who are interested in a career in fields related to public affairs.

Eligibility   This program is open to young women, 16 to 19 years of age, who are currently living or studying in a district or region of Zonta International. Applicants must be interested in preparing for a career in government, public policy, or volunteer organizations. Along with their application, they must submit essays on their student activities and leadership roles (200 words), their community service activities (200 words), their efforts to understand other countries (150 words), and the status of women in their country and worldwide (300 words). Selection is based on commitment to volunteerism, experience in local or student government, volunteer leadership achievements, knowledge of Zonta International and its programs, and advocating in Zonta International's mission of advancing the status of women worldwide. Winners are selected at the club level and forwarded for a district competition; district winners are entered in the international competition.

Financial data   District awardees receive $1,000 and international awardees receive an additional $3,000.

Duration   The competition is held annually.

Number awarded   Varies each year; recently, 32 district winners were selected, of whom 10 were chosen as international awardees. Since the program began, it has presented 763 awards, totaling nearly $700,000, to 661 young women from 53 countries.

Deadline   Clubs set their own deadlines but must submit their winners to the district governor by March of each year.

Additional information   This program began in 1990.

Graduate Students

Listed alphabetically by program title and described in detail here are 450 fellowships, grants, awards, internships, and other sources of "free money" set aside for women who are incoming, continuing, or returning graduate students working on a master's. doctoral, or professional degree. This funding is available to support study, training, research, and/or creative activities in the United States.

[717]
AAUW CAREER DEVELOPMENT GRANTS

American Association of University Women
Attn: AAUW Educational Foundation
1111 16th Street, N.W.
Washington, DC 20036-4873
(202) 785-7700   Toll Free: (800) 326-AAUW
Fax: (202) 872-1425   TDD: (202) 785-7777
E-mail: aauw@applyists.com
Web: www.aauw.org

Summary To provide financial assistance to women who are seeking career advancement, career change, or reentry into the workforce.

Eligibility This program is open to women who are U.S. citizens or permanent residents, have earned a bachelor's degree, received their most recent degree more than 4 years ago, and are making career changes, seeking to advance in current careers, or reentering the workforce. Applicants must be interested in working toward a master's degree, second bachelor's or associate degree, professional degree (e.g., M.D., J.D.), certification program, or technical school certificate. They must be planning to undertake course work at an accredited 2- or 4-year college or university (or a technical school that is licensed, accredited, or approved by the U.S. Department of Education). Primary consideration is given to women of color and women pursuing their first advanced degree or credentials in nontraditional fields. Support is not provided for prerequisite course work or for Ph.D. course work or dissertations. Selection is based on demonstrated commitment to education and equity for women and girls, reason for seeking higher education or technical training, degree to which study plan is consistent with career objectives, potential for success in chosen field, documentation of opportunities in chosen field, feasibility of study plans and proposed time schedule, validity of proposed budget and budget narrative (including sufficient outside support), and quality of written proposal.

Financial data Grants range from $2,000 to $12,000. Funds may be used for tuition, fees, books, supplies, local transportation, dependent child care, or purchase of a computer required for the study program.

Duration 1 year, beginning in July; nonrenewable.

Additional information The filing fee is $35.

Number awarded Varies each year; recently, 63 of these grants, with a value of $670,000, were awarded.

Deadline December of each year.

[718]
ACC NATIONAL CAPITAL REGION CORPORATE SCHOLARS PROGRAM

Association of Corporate Counsel-National Capital
  Region
Attn: Executive Director
P.O. Box 2147
Rockville, MD 20847-2147
(301) 881-3018   E-mail: Ilene.Reid-NCR@accglobal.com
Web: m.acc.com/chapters/ncr/scholars.cfm

Summary To provide an opportunity for summer work experience in the metropolitan Washington, D.C. area to students at law schools in the area who will contribute to the diversity of the profession.

Eligibility This program is open to students entering their second or third year of part- or full-time study at law schools in the Washington, D.C. metropolitan area (including suburban Maryland and all of Virginia). Applicants must be able to demonstrate how they contribute to diversity in the legal profession, based not only on ideas about gender, race, and ethnicity, but also concepts of socioeconomic background and their individual educational and career path. They must be interested in working during the summer at a sponsoring private corporation and nonprofit organizations in the Washington, D.C. area. Along with their application, they must submit a personal statement of 250 to 500 words explaining why they qualify for this program, a writing sample, their law school transcript, and a resume.

Financial data The stipend is at least $9,000.

Duration 10 weeks during the summer.

Additional information The sponsor is the local chapter of the Association of Corporate Counsel (ACC). It established this program in 2004 with support from the Minority Corporate Counsel Association (MCCA).

Number awarded Varies each year; recently, 13 of these internships were awarded.

Deadline January of each year.

[719]
ACCESS TO JUSTICE FELLOWSHIPS OF THE OREGON STATE BAR

Oregon State Bar
Attn: Diversity and Inclusion Department
16037 S.W. Upper Boones Ferry Road
P.O. Box 231935
Tigard, OR 97281-1935
(503) 620-0222
Toll Free: (800) 452-8260, ext. 338 (within OR)
Fax: (503) 684-1366   TDD: (503) 684-7416
E-mail: cling@osbar.org
Web: www.osbar.org/diversity/programs.html#access

Summary To provide summer work experience to law students in Oregon who have encountered barriers and will help the Oregon State Bar achieve its diversity and inclusion objectives.

Eligibility This program is open to students at law schools in Oregon who have experienced economic, social, or other barriers; who have a demonstrated commitment to increasing access to justice; who have personally experienced discrimination or oppression; and who will contribute to the Oregon State Bar's diversity and inclusion program, defined to include age, culture, disability, ethnicity, gender and gender identity or expression, geographic location, national origin, race, religion, sex, sexual orientation, and socio-economic status. They must be interested in working for a public employer or nonprofit organization in Oregon during the summer. Preference is given to students who indicate an intention to practice in Oregon. Along with their application, they must submit a 500-word personal statement on either 1) how their status as a person of diversity has influenced their decision to become a lawyer and how will it influence them throughout their legal professional career; or 2) a challenge they have faced, how they met the challenge, and how that experience will affect the decisions they will make as a legal professional. They must also submit a sample of their legal writing. Selection is based on the personal statement (35%), legal writing ability

(25%), academic achievement (15%), work experience and honors (10%), and financial need (15%).

Financial data   Fellows receive a stipend of $5,000.

Duration   3 months during the summer.

Number awarded   2 each year.

Deadline   January of each year.

[720]
ACM/IEEE-CS GEORGE MICHAEL MEMORIAL HPC FELLOWSHIPS

Association for Computing Machinery
Attn: Awards Committee Liaison
2 Penn Plaza, Suite 701
New York, NY 10121-0701
(212) 626-0561   Toll Free: (800) 342-6626
Fax: (212) 944-1318   E-mail: acm-awards@acm.org
Web: awards.acm.org/hpcfell/nominations.cfm

Summary   To provide financial assistance to doctoral students from any country who are working on a degree in high performance computing (HPC) and will contribute to diversity in the field.

Eligibility   This program is open to students from any country who have completed at least 1 year full-time study in a Ph.D. program in HPC and have at least 1 year remaining before graduating. Applications from women, minorities, international students, and all who contribute to diversity are especially encouraged. Selection is based on overall potential for research excellence, degree to which technical interests align with those of the HPC community, demonstration of current and planned future use of HPC resources, evidence of a plan of student to enhance HPC-related skills, evidence of academic progress to date (including presentations and publications), and recommendation by faculty adviser.

Financial data   The stipend is $5,000. Fellows also receive reimbursement of travel expenses to attend the conference of the Association for Computing Machinery (ACM).

Duration   1 year.

Additional information   This program, which began in 2007, is sponsored by the IEEE Computer Society.

Number awarded   Up to 6 each year.

Deadline   April of each year.

[721]
ACM SIGHPC/INTEL COMPUTATIONAL AND DATA SCIENCE FELLOWSHIPS

Association for Computing Machinery
Attn: Special Interest Group on High Performance
   Computing (SIGHPC)
Office of SIG Services
2 Penn Plaza, Suite 701
New York, NY 10121-0701
(212) 626-0606   Toll Free: (800) 342-6626
Fax: (212) 944-1318   E-mail: cappo@hq.acm.org
Web: www.sighpc.org/fellowships

Summary   To provide financial assistance to female and underrepresented minority graduate students in any country who are working on a degree in computational or data science.

Eligibility   This program is open to women and members of racial or ethnic backgrounds that have not traditionally participated in the computing field. Applicants must be enrolled as

graduate students at a college or university in any country and working on a graduate degree in computational or data science. They must have completed less than half of their planning program of study; preference is given to students who are still early in their studies. Selection is based on overall potential for excellence in data science and/or computational science, likelihood of successfully completing a graduate degree, and extent to which applicants will increase diversity in the workplace.

Financial data   The stipend is $15,000.

Duration   1 year.

Additional information   This program was established in 2016 by Intel Corporation.

Number awarded   Varies each year; recently, 14 were presented.

Deadline   April of each year.

[722]
ACXIOM DIVERSITY SCHOLARSHIP PROGRAM

Acxiom Corporation
601 East Third Street
P.O. Box 8190
Little Rock, AR 72203-8190
(501) 342-1000   Toll Free: (877) 314-2049
E-mail: Candice.Davis@acxiom.com
Web: www.acxiom.com/about-acxiom/careers

Summary   To provide financial assistance and possible work experience to upper-division and graduate students who are members of a diverse population that historically has been underrepresented in the information technology work force.

Eligibility   This program is open to juniors, seniors, and graduate students who are working full time on a degree in a field of information technology, including computer science, computer information systems, management information systems, information quality, information systems, engineering, mathematics, statistics, or related areas of study. Women, veterans, minorities, and individuals with disabilities are encouraged to apply. Applicants must have a GPA of 3.0 or higher. Along with their application, they must submit a 500-word essay describing how the scholarship will help them achieve their academic, professional, and personal goals. Selection is based on academic achievement, relationship of field of study to information technology, and relationship of areas of professional interest to the sponsor's business needs.

Financial data   The stipend is $5,000 per year.

Duration   1 year; may be renewed 1 additional year, provided the recipient remains enrolled full time, maintains a GPA of 3.0 or higher, and (if offered an internship) continues to meet internship expectations.

Additional information   Recipients may be offered an internship (fall, spring, summer, year-round) at 1 of the sponsor's offices in Austin (Texas), Conway (Arkansas), Downers Grove (Illinois), Little Rock (Arkansas), Nashville (Tennessee), New York (New York), or Redwood City (California).

Number awarded   Up to 5 each year.

Deadline   December of each year.

[723]
ADA I. PRESSMAN SCHOLARSHIP

Society of Women Engineers
Attn: Scholarship Selection Committee
203 North LaSalle Street, Suite 1675
Chicago, IL 60601-1269
(312) 596-5223   Toll Free: (877) SWE-INFO
Fax: (312) 644-8557   E-mail: scholarships@swe.org
Web: societyofwomenengineers.swe.org

Summary   To provide financial assistance to women working on an undergraduate or graduate degree in engineering or computer science.

Eligibility   This program is open to women who will be sophomores, juniors, seniors, or graduate students at ABET-accredited colleges and universities. Applicants must be U.S. citizens working full time on a degree in computer science or engineering. Selection is based on merit.

Financial data   The stipend is $5,000 per year.

Duration   1 year; may be renewed up to 4 additional years.

Additional information   This program began in 2004.

Number awarded   9 each year.

Deadline   February of each year.

[724]
ADVANCING WOMEN IN ACCOUNTING SCHOLARSHIP

Illinois CPA Society
Attn: CPA Endowment Fund of Illinois
550 West Jackson, Suite 900
Chicago, Il 60661-5716
(312) 993-0407   Toll Free: (800) 993-0407 (within IL)
Fax: (312) 993-9954
Web: www.icpas.org/hc-endowment.aspx?id=3906

Summary   To provide financial assistance to female residents of Illinois who will be enrolled as seniors or graduate students in an accounting program in the state.

Eligibility   This program is open to women in Illinois who plan to enroll as seniors or graduate students in an accounting program at a college or university in the state. Applicants must be planning to complete the educational requirements needed to sit for the C.P.A. examination in Illinois within 3 years. They must have at least a 3.0 GPA and be able to demonstrate financial need or special circumstances. U.S. citizenship or permanent resident status is required. Selection is based on academic achievement and financial need.

Financial data   The maximum stipend is $4,000 for payment of tuition and fees. Awards include up to $500 in expenses for books and required classroom materials.

Duration   1 year (fifth year for accounting students planning to become a C.P.A.).

Additional information   This program was established by the Women's Executive Committee of the Illinois CPA Society. The scholarship does not cover the cost of C.P.A. examination review courses. Recipients may not receive a full graduate assistantship, fellowship, or scholarship from a college or university, participate in a full-tuition reimbursement cooperative education or internship program, or participate in an employee full-tuition reimbursement program during the scholarship period.

Number awarded   Varies each year; recently, 3 were awarded.

Deadline   March of each year.

[725]
AFA DISSERTATION AWARD

American Anthropological Association
Attn: Association for Feminist Anthropology
2300 Clarendon Boulevard, Suite 1301
Arlington, VA 22201
(703) 528-1902   Fax: (703) 528-3546
Web: www.aaanet.org/sections/afa/scholarship-grant

Summary   To provide funding to doctoral candidates completing a dissertation on a topic related to feminist anthropology.

Eligibility   This program is open to doctoral candidates who are in the writing phase of a dissertation that makes a significant contribution to feminist anthropology. Applicants must be members of the Association for Feminist Anthropology (AFA) of the American Anthropological Association. They may be working in any of the subfields of anthropology (archaeology, biological anthropology, cultural anthropology, or linguistics).

Financial data   The grant is $2,000.

Duration   1 year.

Number awarded   1 each year.

Deadline   April of each year.

[726]
AFRL/DAGSI OHIO STUDENT-FACULTY RESEARCH FELLOWSHIP PROGRAM

Dayton Area Graduate Studies Institute
3155 Research Boulevard, Suite 205
Kettering, OH 45420
(937) 781-4001   Fax: (937) 781-4005
E-mail: kelam@dagsi.org
Web: www.dagsi.org/pages/osrfp_proinforeq.html

Summary   To provide funding to faculty and graduate students from any state who are enrolled at universities in Ohio that participate in the Dayton Area Graduate Studies Institute (DAGSI) and are interested in conducting research in aerospace technologies of interest to the U.S. Air Force.

Eligibility   This program is open to research teams of full-time graduate students and faculty at 18 designated Ohio universities that participate in DAGSI. Applicants must be interested in conducting research that will utilize the facilities of the Air Force Research Laboratory (AFRL) at Wright-Patterson Air Force Base. All 4 directorates at the AFRL (sensors, materials and manufacturing, human effectiveness, and aerospace systems) participate in this program. Applications from Ph.D. candidates must be developed and written largely by the student, with support, guidance, and input as necessary from the faculty partner. For master's projects, the proposal can be developed and written jointly by the faculty member and the student. All participants (faculty and student) must be U.S. citizens. Underrepresented minorities, women, and persons with disabilities are strongly urged to apply.

Financial data   Grants provide stipends of $23,500 for students who have a master's degree and are working on a Ph.D. or $18,500 for students who have a bachelor's degree and are working on a master's; student's tuition for 1 academic year; a faculty stipend of $11,000; student and faculty allowances of $3,000 each for program-related travel or other approved expenses; and overhead at a maximum off-campus rate of 26% of student and faculty stipends and miscellaneous allowances. The maximum DAGSI contribution is $51,000 for Ph.D. programs or $43,500 for master's programs; a cost-share commitment equal to one-third of the DAGSI contribution must be provided by the university, industry, AFRL, or other allowable government source.

Duration 1 year; master's awards are nonrenewable but Ph.D. awards may be renewed for 2 additional years. Students are expected to spend 8 consecutive weeks conducting research at AFRL and faculty members are expected to spend at least 3 weeks over the year conducting research at AFRL.

Additional information DAGSI was established in 1994 as a consortium of graduate engineering schools at the University of Dayton, Wright State University, and the Air Force Institute of Technology. The Ohio State University and the University of Cincinnati joined as affiliated members in 1996 and Miami University and Ohio University joined as associate members in 2001. Students from the following universities are also eligible to participate in this program: University of Akron, Bowling Green State University, Central State University, Cleveland State University, Kent State University, Shawnee State University, University of Toledo, Youngstown State University, Medical College of Ohio, Northeastern Ohio Universities College of Medicine, and Case Western Reserve University.

Number awarded At least 10 each year.

Deadline January of each year.

[727]
AHIMA FOUNDATION DIVERSITY SCHOLARSHIPS

American Health Information Management Association
Attn: AHIMA Foundation
233 North Michigan Avenue, 21st Floor
Chicago, IL 60601-5809
(312) 233-1137   Fax: (312) 233-1537
E-mail: info@ahimafoundation.org
Web: www.ahimafoundation.org

Summary To provide financial assistance to members of the American Health Information Management Association (AHIMA) who are interested in working on an undergraduate or graduate degree in health information management (HIM) or health information technology (HIT) and who will contribute to diversity in the profession.

Eligibility This program is open to AHIMA members who are enrolled at least half time in an accredited program. Applicants must be working on a degree in HIM or HIT at the associate, bachelor's, post-baccalaureate, master's, or doctoral level. They must have a GPA of 3.5 or higher and at least 6 credit hours remaining after the date of the award. To qualify for this support, applicants must demonstrate how they will contribute to diversity in the health information management profession; diversity is defined as differences in race, ethnicity, nationality, gender, sexual orientation, socioeconomic status, age, physical capabilities, or religious beliefs. Along with their application, they must submit essays on assigned topics related to their involvement in the HIM profession. Selection is based on the clarity and completeness of thought in the essays; cumulative GPA; volunteer, work, and/or leadership

experience; honors, awards, or recognitions; commitment to the HIM profession; and references.

Financial data Stipends are $1,000 for associate degree students, $1,500 for bachelor's degree or post-baccalaureate certificate students, $2,000 for master's degree students, or $2,500 for doctoral degree students.

Duration 1 year.

Number awarded 1 or more each year.

Deadline September of each year.

[728]
ALEXANDRA KIRKLEY, MD TRAVELING FELLOWSHIP

Ruth Jackson Orthopaedic Society
9400 West Higgins Road, Suite 500
Rosemont, IL 60018
(847) 698-1626   Fax: (847) 268-9461
E-mail: rjos@aaos.org
Web: www.rjos.org/category/research-grant-opportunities

Summary To provide funding to female orthopedic medical students who are interested in traveling to enrich their academic career.

Eligibility This program is open to female medical students who are members of the Ruth Jackson Orthopaedic Society (RJOS). Applicants must be Board Eligible orthopedic surgeons and citizens of the United States or Canada. They must be interested in a program of travel to enrich their academic career.

Financial data Grants up to $5,000 are available.

Number awarded 1 each year.

Deadline October of each year.

[729]
ALICE WILKEY POYNTER SCHOLARSHIP

Kappa Alpha Theta Foundation
Attn: Manager of Programs
8740 Founders Road
Indianapolis, IN 46268-1337
(317) 876-1870   Toll Free: (800) KAO-1870
Fax: (317) 876-1925
E-mail: gmerritt@kappaalphatheta.org
Web: www.kappaalphathetafoundation.org

Summary To provide financial assistance to members of Kappa Alpha Theta in Indiana who are planning to work on a graduate degree in journalism.

Eligibility This program is open to members of Kappa Alpha Theta who are currently enrolled as seniors at colleges or universities in Indiana. Applicants must be planning to attend graduate school, preferably to work on a degree in journalism. Selection is based on GPA, demonstrated commitment to Kappa Alpha Theta service, demonstrated commitment to non-Theta activities, personal statements on assigned topics related to their involvement in Kappa Alpha Theta, and recommendations.

Financial data The stipend is $1,150.

Duration 1 year.

Number awarded 1 each year.

Deadline March of each year.

[730]
ALPHA DELTA KAPPA REGIONAL PROFESSIONAL DEVELOPMENT SCHOLARSHIPS

Alpha Delta Kappa
Attn: Scholarships
1615 West 92nd Street
Kansas City, MO 64114
(816) 363-5525   Toll Free: (800) 247-2311
Fax: (816) 363-4010
E-mail: headquarters@alphadeltakappa.org
Web: www.alphadeltakappa.org

Summary To provide funding for advanced study or a project in connection with a degree program to members of Alpha Delta Kappa, an honor society of women educators.

Eligibility This program is open to Alpha Delta Kappa members who desire to pursue a planned program of study supportive of the purposes of the organization. Their proposed program may involve 1) meeting partial requirements for a degree, certification, or endorsements; 2) planning, research, or study through course work; or 3) setting up guidelines for evaluation. Applicants must submit a brief description of their professional development plan, a statement of the reasons for applying for this scholarship, and a description of how the scholarship will help them meet their professional goals and enrich the lives of their students.

Financial data Stipends average $1,500.

Duration The program normally should be completed within 1 year, although more time may be allowed through consultation between the recipient and her Regional Scholarship Programs committee.

Number awarded 14 each year: 2 in each Alpha Delta Kappa region.

Deadline Members must submit duplicate copies of their application to their Regional Scholarship Programs committee chair and to international headquarters by January of each year.

[731]
ALPHA KAPPA ALPHA ENDOWMENT AWARDS

Alpha Kappa Alpha Sorority, Inc.
Attn: Educational Advancement Foundation
5656 South Stony Island Avenue
Chicago, IL 60637
(773) 947-0026   Toll Free: (800) 653-6528
Fax: (773) 947-0277   E-mail: akaeaf@akaeaf.net
Web: www.akaeaf.org/fellowships_endowments.htm

Summary To provide financial assistance to undergraduate and graduate students (especially African American women) who meet designated requirements.

Eligibility This program is open to undergraduate and graduate students who are enrolled full time as sophomores or higher in an accredited degree-granting institution and are planning to continue their program of education. Applicants may apply for scholarships that include specific requirements established by the donor of the endowment that supports it. Along with their application, they must submit 1) a list of honors, awards, and scholarships received; 2) a list of organizations in which they have memberships, especially minority organizations; and 3) a statement of their personal and career goals, including how this scholarship will enhance their

ability to attain those goals. The sponsor is a traditionally African American women's sorority.

Financial data Award amounts are determined by the availability of funds from the particular endowment. Recently, stipends averaged more than $1,700 per year.

Duration 1 year or longer.

Additional information Each endowment establishes its own requirements. Examples of requirements include residence of the applicant, major field of study, minimum GPA, attendance at an Historically Black College or University (HBCU) or member institution of the United Negro College Fund (UNCF), or other personal feature. For further information on all endowments, contact the sponsor.

Number awarded Varies each year; recently, 49 were awarded.

Deadline April of each year.

[732]
ALPHA KAPPA ALPHA GRADUATE SCHOLARSHIPS

Alpha Kappa Alpha Sorority, Inc.
Attn: Educational Advancement Foundation
5656 South Stony Island Avenue
Chicago, IL 60637
(773) 947-0026   Toll Free: (800) 653-6528
Fax: (773) 947-0277   E-mail: akaeaf@akaeaf.net
Web: www.akaeaf.org/graduate_scholarships.htm

Summary To provide financial assistance for study or research to graduate students (especially African American women).

Eligibility This program is open to students who are working full time on a graduate degree in any state. Applicants may apply either for a scholarship based on merit (requires a GPA of 3.0 or higher) or on financial need (requires a GPA of 2.5 or higher). Along with their application, they must submit 1) a list of honors, awards, and scholarships received; 2) a list of organizations in which they have memberships, especially minority organizations; 3) a description of the project or research on which they are currently working, or (if they are not involved in a project or research) the aspects of their field that interest them; and 4) a statement of their personal and career goals, including how this scholarship will enhance their ability to attain those goals. The sponsor is a traditionally African American women's sorority.

Financial data Stipends range up to $3,000.

Duration 1 year; nonrenewable.

Number awarded Varies each year; recently, 147 were awarded.

Deadline August of each year.

[733]
AMELIA EARHART FELLOWSHIP AWARDS

Zonta International
Attn: Foundation
1211 West 22nd Street, Suite 900
Oak Brook, IL 60523-3384
(630) 928-1400   Fax: (630) 928-1559
E-mail: programs@zonta.org
Web: www.zonta.org

Summary To provide financial assistance to women interested in doctoral study in scientific or engineering areas related to aerospace.

Eligibility This program is open to women who have a bachelor's degree in an area of science or engineering related to aerospace. Applicants must be registered as a full-time student at an accredited Ph.D. program at a recognized institution of higher learning and be able to provide evidence of a well-defined research and development program. They may be citizens of any country and studying in any country. Along with their application, they must submit a 500-word statement on their academic research program, their professional goals, and the relevance of their research program to aerospace-related sciences or engineering.

Financial data The stipend is $10,000, paid in 2 installments. Funds may be used for tuition, books, and fees.

Duration 1 year; renewable.

Additional information The fellowship may be used at any institution offering accredited courses in the applicant's field of study in the United States or abroad. Fellows may receive financial assistance from other programs. This program, established in 1938, is named for Amelia Earhart, famed air pioneer and Zontian, who disappeared over the Pacific in 1937.

Number awarded 35 each year. Since the program began, it has awarded more than 1,000 of these fellowships, worth $9.3 million, to women from 70 countries.

Deadline November of each year.

[734]
AMELIA EARHART MEMORIAL ACADEMIC SCHOLARSHIPS

Ninety-Nines, Inc.
4300 Amelia Earhart Road, Suite A
Oklahoma City, OK 73159
(405) 685-7969   Toll Free: (800) 994-1929
Fax: (405) 685-7985   E-mail: AEChair@ninety-nines.org
Web: www.ninety-nines.org/scholarships.htm

Summary To provide funding to members of the Ninety-Nines (an organization of women pilots) who are enrolled in academic study related to aviation or aerospace.

Eligibility This program is open to women from any country who have been members of the organization for at least 1 year. Applicants must be currently enrolled at an accredited college or university and working on an associate, bachelor's, master's, or doctoral degree in such fields as aerospace engineering, aviation technology, aviation business management, air traffic management, or professional pilot. They must have a GPA of 3.0 or higher and be able to demonstrate financial need. Along with their application, they must submit a 1-page essay about their activities in aviation, their participatin in the Ninety-Nines, their goals in aviation or aerospace, how they have financed their training and education so far, their financial need to complete their training, and how awarding them this scholarship will benefit the Ninety-Nines and the aviation community.

Financial data The stipend is $5,000 per year.

Duration 1 year; may be renewed.

Additional information This program began in 1941.

Number awarded Varies each year; recently, 3 were awarded: 2 to undergraduates and 1 to a graduate student.

Deadline November of each year.

[735]
AMELIA EARHART RESEARCH SCHOLAR GRANT

Ninety-Nines, Inc.
Attn: Chair, Research Scholar Grants
4300 Amelia Earhart Road, Suite A
Oklahoma City, OK 73159
(405) 685-7969   Toll Free: (800) 994-1929
Fax: (405) 685-7985   E-mail: AEChair@ninety-nines.org
Web: www.ninety-nines.org/scholarships.htm

Summary To provide funding to scholars interested in expanding knowledge about women in aviation and space.

Eligibility This program is open to scholars who are conducting research on the role of women in aviation and space. Disciplines may include, but are not limited to, biology, business administration, economics, ergonomics, history, human engineering, psychology, or sociology. Applicants may be seeking funding to be used in conjunction with other research activities, such as completion of requirements for an advanced degree or matching funds with other grants to support a program larger than either grant could sponsor independently.

Financial data The amount awarded varies; generally, the grant is at least $1,000.

Duration The grant is awarded periodically.

Number awarded 1 each granting period.

Deadline Deadline not specified.

[736]
AMELIA KEMP MEMORIAL SCHOLARSHIP

Women of the Evangelical Lutheran Church in America
Attn: Scholarships
8765 West Higgins Road
Chicago, IL 60631-4101
(773) 380-2741   Toll Free: (800) 638-3522, ext. 2741
Fax: (773) 380-2419   E-mail: valora.starr@elca.org
Web: www.womenoftheelca.org

Summary To provide financial assistance to lay women of color who are members of Evangelical Lutheran Church of America (ELCA) congregations and who wish to study on the undergraduate, graduate, professional, or vocational school level.

Eligibility This program is open to ELCA lay women of color who are at least 21 years of age and have experienced an interruption of at least 2 years in their education since high school. Applicants must have been admitted to an educational institution to prepare for a career in other than ordained ministry. U.S. citizenship is required.

Financial data The maximum stipend is $1,000 per year.

Duration 1 year; recipients may reapply for 1 additional year.

Number awarded 1 or more each year.

Deadline February of each year.

[737]
AMERICAN ASSOCIATION OF JAPANESE UNIVERSITY WOMEN SCHOLARSHIP PROGRAM

American Association of Japanese University Women
Attn: Scholarship Committee
3543 West Boulevard
Los Angeles, CA 90016
E-mail: aajuwcholar@gmail.com
Web: www.aajuw.org/new-page-3

Summary To provide financial assistance to female students currently enrolled in upper-division or graduate classes in California.

Eligibility This program is open to women enrolled at accredited colleges or universities in California as juniors, seniors, or graduate students. Applicants must be involved in U.S.-Japan relations, cultural exchanges, and leadership development in the areas of their designated field of study. Along with their application, they must submit a current resume, an official transcript of the past 2 years of college work, 2 letters of recommendation, and an essay (up to 2 pages in English or 1,200 characters in Japanese) on what they hope to accomplish in their field of study and how that will contribute to better U.S.-Japan relations.

Financial data The stipend is $2,000.

Duration 1 year.

Additional information The association was founded in 1970 to promote the education of women as well as to contribute to U.S.-Japan relations, cultural exchanges, and leadership development.

Number awarded 1 to 3 each year. Since this program was established, it has awarded nearly $100,000 worth of scholarships to 110 women.

Deadline September of each year.

[738]
AMERICAN ASSOCIATION OF UNIVERSITY WOMEN DISSERTATION FELLOWSHIPS

American Association of University Women
Attn: AAUW Educational Foundation
1111 16th Street, N.W.
Washington, DC 20036-4873
(202) 785-7700   Toll Free: (800) 326-AAUW
Fax: (202) 872-1425   TDD: (202) 785-7777
E-mail: aauw@applyists.com
Web: www.aauw.org

Summary To provide funding to women in the final year of writing their dissertation.

Eligibility This program is open to U.S. citizens and permanent residents who are women and intend to pursue professional careers in the United States. They should have successfully completed all required course work for their doctorate, passed all preliminary examinations, and received written acceptance of their prospectus. Applicants may propose research in any field. Selection is based on scholarly excellence, quality of project design, originality of project, scholarly significance of project to discipline, feasibility of project and proposed schedule, qualifications of applicant, potential of applicant to make a significant contribution to field, applicant's teaching experience, applicant's commitment to women's issues in profession and community, and applicant's mentoring of other women.

Financial data The stipend is $20,000.

Duration 1 year, beginning in July.

Additional information The filing fee is $40. It is expected that the fellowship will be used for the final year of doctoral work and that the degree will be received at the end of the fellowship year. The fellowship is not intended to fund extended field research. The recipient should be prepared to devote full time to the dissertation during the fellowship year.

Number awarded Varies each year; recently, 60 were awarded.

Deadline November of each year.

[739]
AMERICAN BAPTIST CHURCHES OF WISCONSIN ADULT WOMEN IN SEMINARY EDUCATION SCHOLARSHIPS

American Baptist Churches of Wisconsin
Attn: American Baptist Women of Wisconsin
15330 Watertown Plank Road
Elm Grove, WI 53122-2340
(262) 782-3140   Toll Free: (800) 311-3140
Fax: (262) 782-7573   E-mail: email@abcofwi.org
Web: www.abcofwi.org/abwinfo.htm

Summary To provide financial assistance for seminary education to adult women in Wisconsin who are members of the American Baptist Church.

Eligibility This program is open to adult women who are residents of Wisconsin and have been active members of an American Baptist Church for at least 3 years. Applicants must be attending a college or seminary affiliated with the American Baptist Church and preparing for a career in ministry. They must be able to demonstrate financial need.

Financial data The stipend is awarded (amount not specified).

Duration 1 year.

Number awarded 1 or more each year.

Deadline February of each year.

[740]
AMERICAN BAPTIST WOMEN'S MINISTRIES OF NEW YORK STATE SCHOLARSHIPS

American Baptist Women's Ministries of New York State
c/o Jackie Lottermoser, Scholarship Committee
9 West Fifth Street
Oneida, NY 13421
(315) 363-1224   E-mail: choralmom@verizon.net
Web: www.abwm-nys.org/abwm-of-nys-scholarship

Summary To provide financial assistance to women who are members of American Baptist Churches in New York and interested in attending college in any state.

Eligibility This program is open to women who are residents of New York and active members of an American Baptist Church. Applicants must be enrolled or planning to enroll full time at a college or university in any state. While in college, they must maintain Christian fellowship, preferably with the American Baptist Church (although any Protestant church or campus ministry is acceptable). Along with their application, they must submit a 1-page essay on an event that occurred in their life during the past year and how it has impacted their faith. Women may be of any age; graduate students are considered on an individual basis. Financial need is considered in the selection process.

Financial data A stipend is awarded (amount not specified).

Duration 1 year.

Number awarded Varies each year.

Deadline May of each year.

[741]
AMERICAN BAPTIST WOMEN'S MINISTRIES OF WISCONSIN ADULT WOMEN SEMINARY SCHOLARSHIP

American Baptist Women's Ministries of Wisconsin
c/o Rev. Jackie Colbert, Scholarship Committee Chair
3101 Ashford Lane
Madison, WI 53713
Web: www.abcofwi.org/abwinfo.htm

Summary To provide financial assistance to female members of American Baptist Churches in Wisconsin who are interested in attending a seminary in any state that is affiliated with the denomination.

Eligibility This program is open to adult women who are residents of Wisconsin and attending or planning to attend an American Baptist seminary in any state. Applicants must have been an active member of an American Baptist Church in Wisconsin for the preceding 3 years. They must have graduated from a college affiliated with the American Baptist Churches USA. Financial need is considered in the selection process.

Financial data A stipend is awarded (amount not specified).

Duration 1 year; may be renewed up to 3 additional years.

Number awarded 1 or more each year.

Deadline March of each year.

[742]
AMERICAN EPILEPSY SOCIETY PREDOCTORAL RESEARCH FELLOWSHIPS

American Epilepsy Society
135 South LaSalle Street, Suite 2850
Chicago, IL 60603
(312) 883-3800   Fax: (312) 896-5784
E-mail: info@aesnet.org
Web: www.aesnet.org

Summary To provide funding to doctoral candidates who are interested in conducting dissertation research related to epilepsy.

Eligibility This program is open full-time doctoral students conducting dissertation research with an epilepsy-related theme under the guidance of a mentor with expertise in epilepsy research. Applicants must have a defined research plan and access to institutional resources to conduct the proposed project. Selection is based on the applicant's potential and commitment to develop as an independent and productive epilepsy researcher, academic record, and research experience; the mentor's research qualifications; the research training plan; and the quality of the research facilities, resources, and training opportunities. Applications are especially encouraged from women, members of minority groups, and people with disabilities. U.S. citizenship is not required, but all research must be conducted in the United States.

Financial data Grants range up $30,000, including $29,000 as stipend and $1,000 for travel support and complimentary registration to attend the sponsor's annual meeting.

Duration 1 year; nonrenewable.

Additional information In addition to the funding provided by the American Epilepsy Society, support is available from the TESS Research Foundation for applications focused on epilepsy due to SLC13A5 mutations; the LGS Foundation for applications focused on Lennox-Gastaut-Syndrome; the PCDH19 Alliance for applications focused on epilepsy due to PCDH19 mutations; the Dravet Syndrome Foundation for applications focused on Dravet Syndrome; Wishes for Elliott for applications focused on epilepsy due to SCN8A mutations; and the TS Alliance for applications focused on epilepsy associated with tuberous sclerosis complex (TSC).

Number awarded Varies each year.

Deadline Letters of intent must be submitted by October of each year; final proposals are due in January.

[743]
AMERICAN METEOROLOGICAL SOCIETY GRADUATE FELLOWSHIP IN THE HISTORY OF SCIENCE

American Meteorological Society
Attn: Development and Student Program Manager
45 Beacon Street
Boston, MA 02108-3693
(617) 227-2426, ext. 3907   Fax: (617) 742-8718
E-mail: dFernandez@ametsoc.org
Web: www2.ametsoc.org

Summary To provide funding to graduate student members of the American Meteorological Society (AMS) interested in conducting dissertation research on the history of meteorology.

Eligibility This program is open to AMS members and student members who are planning to complete a doctoral dissertation on the history of the atmospheric or related oceanic or hydrologic sciences. Applicants must be U.S. citizens or permanent residents and working on a degree at a U.S. institution. Fellowships may be used to support research at a location away from the student's institution, provided the plan is approved by the student's thesis adviser. In such an instance, an effort is made to place the student into a mentoring relationship with a member of the society at an appropriate institution. The sponsor specifically encourages applications from women, minorities, and students with disabilities who are traditionally underrepresented in the atmospheric and related oceanic sciences.

Financial data The stipend is $15,000.

Duration 1 year.

Number awarded 1 each year.

Deadline February of each year.

[744]
AMERICAN MUSEUM OF NATURAL HISTORY GRADUATE STUDENT FELLOWSHIP PROGRAM

American Museum of Natural History
Attn: Richard Gilder Graduate School
Central Park West at 79th Street
New York, NY 10024-5192
(212) 769-5055   E-mail: Fellowships-rggs@amnh.org
Web: www.amnh.org

Summary To provide financial assistance to doctoral students in selected programs at designated universities who are interested in utilizing the resources of the American Museum of Natural History in their training and research program.

Eligibility This program is open to doctoral students in scientific disciplines practiced at the museum. The applicant's university exercises educational jurisdiction over the program and awards the degree; the museum curator serves as a graduate adviser, co-major professor, or major professor. Both U.S. citizens and noncitizens are eligible to apply. Candidates for a master's degree are not eligible. The museum encourages women, minorities, persons with disabilities, and Vietnam Era and disabled veterans to apply.

Financial data Fellowships provide a stipend and health insurance.

Duration 1 year; may be renewed up to 3 additional years.

Additional information The cooperating universities (and their relevant programs) are Columbia University, in anthropology, vertebrate and invertebrate paleontology, earth and planetary sciences, and evolutionary, ecological, and environmental biology; Cornell University in entomology; the Graduate Center of City University of New York in earth and planetary sciences, paleontology, and evolutionary biology; New York University in molecular biology; and Stony Brook University in astronomy and astrophysics. Students must apply simultaneously to the museum and to 1 of the cooperating universities.

Number awarded Varies each year.

Deadline December of each year.

[745]
AMS GRADUATE FELLOWSHIPS

American Meteorological Society
Attn: Development and Student Program Manager
45 Beacon Street
Boston, MA 02108-3693
(617) 227-2426, ext. 3907   Fax: (617) 742-8718
E-mail: dFernandez@ametsoc.org
Web: www2.ametsoc.org

Summary To encourage students entering their first year of graduate school to work on an advanced degree in the atmospheric and related oceanic and hydrologic sciences.

Eligibility This program is open to students entering their first year of graduate study and planning to work on an advanced degree in the atmospheric or related oceanic or hydrologic sciences. Applicants must be U.S. citizens or permanent residents and have a GPA of 3.25 or higher. Along with their application, they must submit 200-word essays on 1) their most important achievements that qualify them for this scholarship; and 2) their career goals in the atmospheric or related sciences. Selection is based on academic record as an undergraduate. The sponsor specifically encourages applications from women, minorities, and students with disabilities who are traditionally underrepresented in the atmospheric and related sciences.

Financial data The stipend is $25,000 per academic year.

Duration 9 months.

Additional information This program was initiated in 1991. It is funded by high-technology firms and government agencies.

Number awarded Varies each year; recently, 8 were awarded.

Deadline January of each year.

[746]
AMWA MEDICAL EDUCATION SCHOLARSHIPS

American Medical Women's Association
Attn: National Student Leadership
12100 Sunset Hills Road, Suite 130
Reston, VA 20190
(703) 234-4069   Toll Free: (866) 564-2483
Fax: (703) 435-4390   E-mail: awards@amwa-student.org
Web: www.amwa-doc.org

Summary To provide financial assistance for medical education to student members of the American Medical Women's Association (AMWA).

Eligibility This program is open to student members of the association currently enrolled in medical school. Applicants must submit brief statements on a situation in which they demonstrated leadership, their involvement in AMWA, their plans for future AMWA involvement, and their goals for women in medicine. Financial need is considered but is not required.

Financial data The stipend is $1,000.

Duration 1 year.

Number awarded 4 each year.

Deadline January or September of each year.

[747]
ANARCHA, BETSY AND LUCY MEMORIAL SCHOLARSHIP AWARD

National Medical Fellowships, Inc.
Attn: Scholarship Program
347 Fifth Avenue, Suite 510
New York, NY 10016
(212) 483-8880   Toll Free: (877) NMF-1DOC
Fax: (212) 483-8897   E-mail: scholarships@nmfonline.org
Web: www.nmfonline.org

Summary To provide financial assistance to African American women who are attending medical school.

Eligibility This program is open to African American women who are enrolled in the first or second year of an accredited medical school in the United States. Applicants must be known descendants of slaves. Selection is based on leadership, commitment to serving medically underserved communities, and financial need.

Financial data The stipend is $5,000.

Duration 1 year; nonrenewable.

Additional information This program is named after 3 slaves who served as subjects of experimentation that helped shape advances in current clinical and surgical knowledge and are recognized as the Mothers of Gynecology.

Number awarded　1 or more each year.
Deadline　September of each year.

[748]
ANITA BENEDETTI MEMORIAL SCHOLARSHIP
Spencer Educational Foundation, Inc.
c/o Risk Insurance and Management Society
1065 Avenue of the Americas, 13th Floor
New York, NY 10018
(212) 655-6223　　E-mail: asabatino@spencered.org
Web: www.spencered.org/students/graduate-scholarships
Summary　To provide financial assistance to female full-time graduate students who are preparing for a career in risk management.
Eligibility　This program is open to women who are enrolled as a full-time master's degree candidate or a teaching-oriented pre-dissertation Ph.D. candidate. Applicants must be working on a degree in a risk management discipline and be preparing for a career in that field. They must have a GPA of 3.0 or higher and relevant work experience. Along with their application, they must submit a 500-word essay on their chosen career path and goals. Selection is based on merit.
Financial data　The stipend is $10,000.
Duration　1 year.
Number awarded　1 or more each year.
Deadline　January of each year.

[749]
ANL LABORATORY–GRADUATE RESEARCH APPOINTMENTS
Argonne National Laboratory
Division of Educational Programs
Attn: Graduate Student Program Office
9700 South Cass Avenue/DEP 223
Argonne, IL 60439-4845
(630) 252-3366　　　　Fax: (630) 252-3193
E-mail: education@anl.gov
Web: www.anl.gov
Summary　To offer opportunities for qualified graduate students to carry out their master's or doctoral thesis research at the Argonne National Laboratory (ANL).
Eligibility　Appointments are available for graduate students at U.S. universities who wish to carry out their thesis research under the co-sponsorship of an Argonne National Laboratory staff member and a faculty member. Research may be conducted in the basic physical and life sciences, mathematics, computer science, and engineering, as well as in a variety of applied areas relating to energy, conservation, environmental impact and technology, nanomaterials, and advanced nuclear energy systems. Applicants must be U.S. citizens or permanent residents. The laboratory encourages applications from all qualified persons, especially women and members of underrepresented minority groups.
Financial data　Support consists of a stipend, tuition payments up to $5,000 per year, and payment of certain travel expenses. In addition, the student's faculty sponsor may receive payment for limited travel expenses.
Duration　1 year; may be renewed.
Additional information　This program, which is also referred to as the Lab–Grad Program, is sponsored by the

U.S. Department of Energy. In certain cases, students may be awarded support for pre-thesis studies on campus, provided that they intend to carry out their thesis research at Argonne.
Number awarded　Varies each year.
Deadline　Applications may be submitted at any time, but a complete application should be submitted at least 2 months prior to the proposed starting date.

[750]
ANN E. DICKERSON SCHOLARSHIPS
Christian Church (Disciples of Christ)
Attn: Higher Education and Leadership Ministries
734 West Port Plaza, Suite 270
St. Louis, MO 63146
(314) 991-3000　　　　Fax: (314) 485-1714
E-mail: helm@helmdisciples.org
Web: www.helmdisciples.org
Summary　To provide financial assistance to female members of the Christian Church (Disciples of Christ) who are working on a Ph.D. degree in religion.
Eligibility　This program is open to women working on a Ph.D. degree in religion. Applicants must members of the Christian Church (Disciples of Christ). Along with their application, they must submit a 300-word essay describing their vocational goals, their academic interests, and how they envision being of service to the church.
Financial data　The stipend is $2,000.
Duration　1 year.
Number awarded　3 each year.
Deadline　April of each year.

[751]
ANNALEY NAEGLE REDD STUDENT AWARD IN WOMEN'S HISTORY
Brigham Young University
Attn: Charles Redd Center for Western Studies
954 Spencer W. Kimball Tower
Provo, UT 84602
(801) 422-4048　　　　Fax: (801) 422-0035
E-mail: redd_center@byu.edu
Web: reddcenter.byu.edu
Summary　To provide funding to undergraduate and graduate students interested in conducting research on women in the West.
Eligibility　This program is open to undergraduate and graduate students who are interested in conducting a research project related to women in the American West (defined as west of the Mississippi). Applicants may be proposing any kind of project, including seminar papers, theses, or dissertations. Along with their application, they must submit brief statements on the central research question and conceptual framework, how the project will increase understanding of the American West, where they plan to conduct research and the resources available there, other research that has been conducted on the topic, what makes this study and approach unique and important, the planned use of the research, and a detailed budget.
Financial data　The grant is $1,500. Funds may be used for research support (supplies, travel, etc.) but not for salary or capital equipment.

Duration Normally work is to be undertaken during the summer.

Number awarded 1 each year.

Deadline March of each year.

[752]
ANNE C. CARTER GLOBAL HEALTH FELLOWSHIP

American Medical Women's Association
Attn: National Student Leadership
12100 Sunset Hills Road, Suite 130
Reston, VA 20190
(703) 234-4069   Toll Free: (866) 564-2483
Fax: (703) 435-4390
E-mail: global.health@amwa-student.org
Web: www.amwa-doc.org

Summary To funding to student members of the American Medical Women's Association (AMWA) who are interested in developing a global health project and then implementing it in Uganda.

Eligibility This program is open to student members of the association who are currently enrolled in medical school. Applicants must propose to conduct a 2-year project related to global health under the mentorship of a faculty member at their school. The first year focuses on a global health curriculum, local project development, and mentorship. The second year focuses on in-depth planning and preparation for a medical service learning trip to Engeye Clinic in Uganda, culminating in a capstone global health project in Engeye. Along with their application, they must submit 4 brief essays on 1) their interest and past experiences in global health; 2) a problem they saw in their community and what they personally did to address the problem; 3) a project idea for AMWA local or national branches that promotes global health awareness; and 4) what they hope to accomplish through this fellowship and how they think it will impact their future career path.

Financial data Fellows receive a grant of $1,000 to fund their local planning project and to subsidize expenses for their international global health project and trip to Uganda.

Duration This is a 2-year fellowship.

Additional information This program began in 2011.

Number awarded 4 each year.

Deadline September of each year.

[753]
ANNE C. CARTER STUDENT LEADERSHIP AWARD

American Medical Women's Association
Attn: National Student Leadership
12100 Sunset Hills Road, Suite 130
Reston, VA 20190
(703) 234-4069   Toll Free: (866) 564-2483
Fax: (703) 435-4390
E-mail: associatedirector@amwa-doc.org
Web: www.amwa-doc.org

Summary To recognize and reward student members of the American Medical Women's Association (AMWA) who have demonstrated exceptional leadership skills.

Eligibility This program is open to student members of the association who are nominated by their chapter. Nominees must have demonstrated exceptional leadership skills

through vision, inspiration, innovation, and coordination of local projects that further the mission of AMWA by improving women's health and/or supporting women in medicine.

Financial data The award is $1,000. The nominating chapter also receives an award of $500 to be used at its discretion.

Duration The award is presented annually.

Additional information This award was first presented in 2004.

Number awarded 1 each year.

Deadline January of each year.

[754]
ANNETTE URSO RICKEL FOUNDATION DISSERTATION AWARD FOR PUBLIC POLICY

American Psychological Foundation
750 First Street, N.E.
Washington, DC 20002-4242
(202) 336-5843   Fax: (202) 336-5812
E-mail: foundation@apa.org
Web: www.apa.org/apf/funding/rickel-foundation.aspx

Summary To provide funding to psychology doctoral candidates who wish to conduct dissertation research on public policy.

Eligibility This program is open to full-time psychology doctoral students at universities in the United States or Canada who have completed candidacy (including dissertation approval). Applicants must be planning to conduct dissertation research on public policy that has the potential to improve services for children and families facing psychosocial issues such as prevention of child abuse, school programs for children with psychological issues, services for youth in the criminal justice system, healthy parenting, math and science education, and contributing to the adoption of sound policy affecting children, youth and families. Selection is based on conformance with stated program goals, magnitude of incremental contribution, quality of proposed work, and applicant's demonstrated scholarship and research competence. The sponsor encourages applications from individuals who represent diversity in race, ethnicity, gender, age, disability, and sexual orientation.

Financial data The grant is $1,000.

Duration 1 year.

Additional information This program began in 2008.

Number awarded 1 each year.

Deadline September of each year.

[755]
APA/DIVISION 39 GRANT

American Psychological Foundation
750 First Street, N.E.
Washington, DC 20002-4242
(202) 336-5843   Fax: (202) 336-5812
E-mail: foundation@apa.org
Web: www.apa.org/apf/funding/division-39.aspx

Summary To provide funding to psychologists who wish to conduct psychoanalytical research related to underserved populations.

Eligibility This program is open to psychologists who have a demonstrated knowledge of psychoanalytical principles. Applicants may be, but are not required to be, practicing psychoanalytic therapists. Preference is given to graduate students involved in dissertation research, early-career professionals, and/or those who demonstrate a long-term interest in research related to underserved populations. The research may be of an empirical, theoretical, or clinical nature. Selection is based on conformance with stated program goals and qualifications; quality and potential impact of both previous and proposed research projects; originality, innovation, and contribution to the field with both previous and proposed research projects; and applicant's demonstrated interest in research related to underserved populations. The sponsor encourages applications from individuals who represent diversity in race, ethnicity, gender, age, disability, and sexual orientation.

Financial data The grant is $4,000.

Duration 1 year.

Additional information This program, which began in 2014, is sponsored by the American Psychological Association's Division 39 (Psychoanalysis).

Number awarded 1 each year.

Deadline July of each year.

[756]
APF GRADUATE STUDENT SCHOLARSHIPS

American Psychological Foundation
750 First Street, N.E.
Washington, DC 20002-4242
(202) 336-5843   Fax: (202) 336-5812
E-mail: foundation@apa.org
Web: www.apa.org/apf/funding/cogdop.aspx

Summary To provide funding for research to graduate students in psychology.

Eligibility Each department of psychology that is a member in good standing of the Council of Graduate Departments of Psychology (COGDOP) may nominate up to 3 candidates for these scholarships. Nominations must include a completed application form, a letter of nomination from the department chair or director of graduate studies, a letter of recommendation from the nominee's graduate research adviser, a transcript of all graduate course work completed by the nominee, a curriculum vitae, and a brief outline of the nominee's thesis or dissertation research project. Selection is based on the context for the research, the clarity and comprehensibility of the research question, the appropriateness of the research design, the general importance of the research, and the use of requested funds. The sponsor encourages applications from individuals who represent diversity in race, ethnicity, gender, age, disability, and sexual orientation.

Financial data Awards range from $1,000 to $5,000 per year. A total of $28,000 is available for these scholarships each year.

Duration 1 year.

Additional information The highest rated nominees receive the Charles and Carol Spielberger Scholarship of $5,000, the Harry and Miriam Levinson Scholarship of $5,000 and the William and Dorothy Bevan Scholarship of $5,000. The next highest rated nominee receives the Ruth G. and Joseph D. Matarazzo Scholarship of $3,000. The next highest rated nominee receives the Clarence J. Rosecrans Scholarship of $2,000. The next highest rated nominees receive the William C. Howell Scholarship, the Dr. Judy Kuriansky Scholarship, and the Peter and Malina James and Dr. Louis P.

James Legacy Scholarship of $1,000 each. Another 8 scholarships of $1,000 each, offered by the COGDOP, are also awarded.

Number awarded 16 each year: 3 at $5,000, 1 at $3,000, 1 at $2,000, and 11 at $1,000.

Deadline June of each year.

[757]
APIQWTC SCHOLARSHIP

Asian Pacific Islander Queer Women and Transgender
  Community
c/o Amy Sueyoshi
San Francisco State University
College of Ethnic Studies
1600 Holloway Avenue
San Francisco, CA 94132
(415) 405-0774   E-mail: sueyoshi@sfsu.edu
Web: www.apiqwtc.org/resources/apiqwtc-scholarship

Summary To provide financial assistance to Asian Pacific Islander (API) lesbian and bisexual women and transgender individuals who are high school seniors, undergraduates, or graduate students interested in working on a degree in any field at a college in any state.

Eligibility This program is open to API high school seniors and current undergraduate or graduate students in any field. Applicants must identify as a lesbian, bisexual, or queer woman or a transgender individual. Along with their application, they must submit a 2-page personal statement that covers their community involvement and future goals; how their cultural heritage, sexual orientation, and/or gender identity has influenced their life; any activities in which they have been involved; any relevant experiences up to the present; and how they see themselves involved in the community in the future, either through their career or otherwise.

Financial data The stipend is $1,000.

Duration 1 year.

Additional information The Asian Pacific Islander Queer Women and Transgender Community (APIQWTC) is a community of more than 10 organizations in the San Francisco Bay area provide support and community for queer Asian and Pacific Islander individuals, but its scholarships are available to students from any state.

Number awarded 2 each year.

Deadline February of each year.

[758]
ARFORA/MARTHA GAVRILA SCHOLARSHIP FOR WOMEN

Association of Romanian Orthodox Ladies Auxiliaries of
  North America
c/o Corina Phillips, Scholarship Committee
8190 Buffham Road
Lodi, OH 44254
(330) 241-4775   E-mail: corina5dan@aol.com
Web: www.roea.org/arforagavrila.html

Summary To provide financial assistance to women who are members of a parish of the Romanian Orthodox Episcopate of America and interested in working on a graduate degree.

Eligibility This program is open to women who have been voting communicant members of a parish of the Romanian

Orthodox Episcopate of America for at least 1 year. Applicants must have completed a baccalaureate degree and been accepted as a graduate student at a college or university in any state. Along with their application, they must submit a 300-word statement describing their personal goals; high school, university, church, and community involvement; honors and awards; and why they should be considered for this award. Selection is based on academic achievement, character, worthiness, and participation in religious life.

Financial data The stipend is $1,000.

Duration 1 year.

Additional information This program began in 1985. The Association of Romanian Orthodox Ladies Auxiliaries (ARFORA) was established in 1938 as a women's organization within the Romanian Orthodox Episcopate of America.

Number awarded 1 each year.

Deadline May of each year.

[759]
ARMENIAN INTERNATIONAL WOMEN'S ASSOCIATION SCHOLARSHIPS

Armenian International Women's Association
65 Main Street, Room 3A
Watertown, MA 02472
(617) 926-0171   E-mail: aiwainc@aol.com
Web: www.aiwainternational.org/initiatives/scholarships

Summary To provide financial assistance to Armenian women who are upper-division and graduate students.

Eligibility This program is open to full-time women students of Armenian descent attending an accredited college or university. Applicants must be full-time juniors, seniors, or graduate students with a GPA of 3.2 or higher. They must submit an essay, up to 500 words, describing their planned academic program, their career goals, and the reasons why they believe they should be awarded this scholarship. Selection is based on financial need and merit.

Financial data Stipends are $1,000 or $500.

Duration 1 year.

Additional information This program includes the following named scholarships: the Ethel Jafarian Duffett Scholarships, the Zarouhi Y. Getsoyan Scholarship, the Rose "Azad" Hovannesian Scholarship, the Agnes Missirian Scholarship, and the Dr. Carolann S. Najarian Scholarships.

Number awarded Varies each year; recently, 18 were awarded: 17 at $1,000 and ' at $500.

Deadline April of each year.

[760]
ARMONICA LAW STUDENT GRANT PROGRAM

Oregon Women Lawyers Foundation
P.O. Box 82522
Portland, OR 97282
(503) 841-5720   E-mail: info@owlsfoundation.org
Web: www.owlsfoundation.org

Summary To provide financial assistance to law students in Oregon, especially minorities and women.

Eligibility This program is open to residents of any state entering their third or fourth year at a law school in Oregon. Applicants must be able to demonstrate, through their personal, volunteer, or education experience, a commitment to the goals of the sponsoring foundation: increasing diversity in

the legal profession through grants and scholarships, promoting pro bono legal work, encouraging child care in Oregon's courthouses, promoting access to justice for low-income Oregonians, and providing education about domestic violence and abuse. Ethnic minorities and women are especially encouraged to apply.

Financial data The stipend is $1,000.

Duration 1 year.

Additional information This program began in 2007 to honor Armonica Gilford, the first African American female assistant attorney general for the Oregon Department of Justice. Each recipient is matched with an ethnic minority female judge or attorney to serve as the student's mentor for the year.

Number awarded 6 each year.

Deadline September of each year.

[761]
ARMY WOMEN'S FOUNDATION LEGACY SCHOLARSHIPS

Army Women's Foundation
Attn: Scholarship Committee
P.O. Box 5030
Fort Lee, VA 23801-0030
(804) 734-3078   E-mail: info@awfdn.org
Web: www.awfdn.org/scholarships.shtml

Summary To provide financial assistance for college or graduate school to women who are serving or have served in the Army and their children.

Eligibility This program is open to 1) women who have served or are serving honorably in the U.S. Army, U.S. Army Reserve, or Army National Guard; and 2) children of those women. Applicants must be 1) high school graduates or GED recipients enrolled at a community college or technical certificate program who have a GPA of 2.5 or higher; 2) sophomores or higher at an accredited college or university who have a GPA of 3.0 or higher; or 3) students enrolled in or accepted to a graduate program who have a GPA of 3.0 or higher. Along with their application, they must submit a 2-page essay on why they should be considered for this scholarship; their future plans as related to their program of study; their community service, activities, and work experience; and how the Army has impacted their life and/or goals. Selection is based on merit, academic potential, community service, and financial need.

Financial data The stipend is $2,500 for college and graduate students or $1,000 for community college and certificate students.

Duration 1 year.

Number awarded Varies each year; recently, 19 soldiers (3 community college and certificate students, 9 4-year college students, and 7 graduate students) and 16 children (1 community college or certificate student, 13 4-year college students, and 2 graduate students) received these scholarships.

Deadline January of each year.

[762]
ARTTABLE MENTORED INTERNSHIPS FOR DIVERSITY IN THE VISUAL ARTS PROFESSIONS

ArtTable Inc.
1 East 53rd Street, Fifth Floor
New York, NY 10022
(212) 343-1735   Fax: (866) 363-4188
E-mail: info@arttable.org
Web: www.arttable.org/summermentoredinternship

Summary To provide an opportunity for women who are from diverse backgrounds to gain mentored work experience during the summer and to prepare for a career as an art professional.

Eligibility This program is open to women who are college seniors, recent graduates, or graduate students and interested in preparing for a career as a visual arts professional (including administrative director, art adviser, art appraiser, art critic, art dealer, art librarian, arts funder, arts lawyer, conservator, curator, editor, educator, fundraiser, management consultant, public relations consultant, writer). Applicants must be from a cultural or ethnic background that is underrepresented in the field. They must be interested in working during the summer with a mentor at an art museum or similar facility. U.S. citizenship or permanent resident status is required.

Financial data The stipend is $3,000. The hosting institution or mentor receives $500 for administrative and other costs.

Duration 8 weeks during the summer.

Additional information This program began in 2000. Support is provided by the Samuel H. Kress Foundation.

Number awarded Varies each year; recently, 5 of these internships were awarded.

Deadline February of each year.

[763]
ASME GRADUATE TEACHING FELLOWSHIP

ASME International
Attn: Education Manager
Two Park Avenue, Floor 7
New York, NY 10016-5618
(212) 591-7559   Toll Free: (800) THE-ASME
Fax: (212) 591-7856   E-mail: lawreya@asme.org
Web: www.asme.org

Summary To provide funding to members of the American Society of Mechanical Engineers (ASME) who are working on a doctorate in mechanical engineering.

Eligibility This program is open to U.S. citizens or permanent residents who have an undergraduate degree from an ABET-accredited program, belong to the society as a student member, are currently employed as a teaching assistant with lecture responsibility, and are working on a Ph.D. in mechanical engineering. Along with their application, they must submit a statement about their interest in a faculty career. Applications from women and minorities are particularly encouraged.

Financial data Fellowship stipends are $5,000 per year.

Duration Up to 2 years.

Additional information Recipients must teach at least 1 lecture course.

Number awarded Up to 4 each year.

Deadline February of each year.

[764]
ASP GRADUATE STUDENT VISITOR PROGRAM

National Center for Atmospheric Research
Attn: Advanced Study Program
3090 Center Green Drive
P.O. Box 3000
Boulder, CO 80307-3000
(303) 497-1328   Fax: (303) 497-1646
E-mail: paulad@ucar.edu
Web: www.asp.ucar.edu/graduate/graduate_visitor.php

Summary To provide an opportunity for graduate students to conduct research at the National Center for Atmospheric Research (NCAR) in Boulder, Colorado under the supervision of a staff member.

Eligibility This program is open to advanced M.S. and Ph.D. students in the atmospheric and related sciences, engineering, and scientific computing. Interdisciplinary studies utilizing the NCAR resources in climate, weather, and related disciplines are also welcome. Applicants should consult with an NCAR staff member who will agree to serve as a host for the research project. Students may not apply directly for this program; the application must be submitted by the NCAR staff member in collaboration with the student's thesis adviser. Selection is based on 1) the programmatic fit and need to visit NCAR as part of the thesis or final project work; and 2) the commitment to student mentoring by the NCAR host and the student's adviser. The program encourages applications from members of groups historically underrepresented in the atmospheric and related sciences, including Blacks or African Americans, Hispanics or Latinos, American Indians and Alaska Natives, women, first-generation college students, LGBT students, and students with disabilities.

Financial data Support is limited to travel expenses for the student and a per diem allowance of $2,000 per month. Travel expenses are also supported for the student's thesis adviser for visits up to 2 weeks. The student's university must provide all support for the student's salary and benefits.

Duration Visits may extend from a few months to a year, but most are 3 to 6 months.

Additional information NCAR is operated by the University Corporation for Atmospheric Research (a consortium of more than 100 North American universities and research institutes) and sponsored by the National Science Foundation. This program was established in 2006.

Number awarded Varies each year; recently, 24 students received support from this program.

Deadline October of each year.

[765]
ASSE DIVERSITY COMMITTEE GRADUATE SCHOLARSHIP

American Society of Safety Engineers
Attn: ASSE Foundation
Scholarship Award Program
1800 East Oakton Street
Des Plaines, IL 60018
(847) 768-3412   Fax: (847) 768-3434
E-mail: foundation@asse.org
Web: www.asse.org/foundation/scholarships/award-listing

Summary To provide financial assistance to graduate students who come from diverse groups and are working on a degree related to occupational safety.

Eligibility This program is open to students who are working on a graduate degree in occupational safety, health, environment, industrial hygiene, occupational health nursing, or a closely-related field (e.g., industrial or environmental engineering). Applicants must be full-time students who have completed at least 9 semester hours and have a GPA of 3.5 or higher. A goal of this program is to support individuals regardless of race, ethnicity, gender, religion, personal beliefs, age, sexual orientation, physical challenges, geographic location, university, or specific area of study. U.S. citizenship is not required. Membership in the American Society of Safety Engineers (ASSE) is not required, but preference is given to members.

Financial data The stipend is $1,000 per year.

Duration 1 year; recipients may reapply.

Number awarded 1 each year.

Deadline November of each year.

[766]
ASSOCIATION FOR WOMEN IN SPORTS MEDIA SCHOLARSHIP/INTERNSHIP PROGRAM

Association for Women in Sports Media
Attn: Scholarship and Internship Coordinator
7742 Spalding Drive, Suite 377
Norcross, GA 30092
E-mail: awsminternship@gmail.com
Web: www.awsmonline.org/internship-scholarship

Summary To provide financial assistance and work experience to women undergraduate and graduate students who are interested in preparing for a career in sports writing.

Eligibility This program is open to women who are enrolled in college or graduate school full time and preparing for a career in sports media, including print/online, magazine, broadcast reporting, broadcast projection, or public relations. Applicants must submit a 750-word essay describing their most memorable experience in sports or sports media, a 1-page resume highlighting their journalism experience, a letter of recommendation, up to 5 samples of their work, and a $20 application fee. They must apply for and accept an internship with a sports media organization.

Financial data Winners receive a stipend up to $1,000 and placement in a paid internship.

Duration 1 year; nonrenewable.

Additional information This program, which began in 1990, includes the "Sophie Scholarship," the Jim Brennan Scholarship, the Betty Brennan Scholarship, the Mary Garber Scholarship, the Mike Roberts Memorial Scholarship, and the Leah Siegel Scholarship.

Number awarded Varies each year; recently, 7 students received support from this program.

Deadline October of each year.

[767]
ASSOCIATION FOR WOMEN LAWYERS FOUNDATION SCHOLARSHIP

Association for Women Lawyers
Attn: Foundation Scholarship Committee
3322 North 92nd Street
Milwaukee, WI 53222-3507
(414) 750-4404   Fax: (414) 255-3615
E-mail: dana@barefoot-marketing.com
Web: www.associationforwomenlawyers.org/scholarships

Summary To provide financial assistance to women enrolled at law schools in Wisconsin.

Eligibility This program is open to women who have completed the first or second year at a law school in Wisconsin. Applicants must be able to meet 1 or more of the following criteria: service to others, diversity, academic achievement, unique life experience or circumstance, advancement of women in the profession, or compelling financial need.

Financial data The stipend varies; recently, awards averaged $2,500.

Duration 1 year.

Additional information This program began in 1998.

Number awarded Varies each year; recently, 2 were awarded.

Deadline June of each year.

[768]
ASSOCIATION OF BLACK WOMEN LAWYERS OF NEW JERSEY SCHOLARSHIPS

Association of Black Women Lawyers of New Jersey, Inc.
Attn: Scholarship Committee
P.O. Box 22524
Trenton, NJ 08607
E-mail: law860@verizon.net
Web: abwl-nj.org/scholarship-applicationluncheon

Summary To provide financial assistance to African American women from New Jersey attending law school in any state.

Eligibility This program is open to African American women who are 1) residents of New Jersey and currently enrolled in their first, second, or third year at an accredited law school in any state; or 2) residents of other states enrolled at a law school in New Jersey. Applicants must submit either a sample of their legal writing or an essay of 2 to 3 pages on a topic that changes annually; recently, students were asked to write on the use of excessive force in minority and immigrant communities. Selection is based on that writing sample or essay, academic achievement, demonstrated community service and civic involvement, and financial need.

Financial data Stipends range from $1,000 to $2,000.

Duration 1 year.

Number awarded At least 3 each year.

Deadline February of each year.

[769]
AUDRE LORDE SCHOLARSHIP AWARD

ZAMI NOBLA
Attn: Audre Lorde Scholarship Fund
P.O. Box 90986
Atlanta, GA 30364
(404) 647-4754   E-mail: zami@zami.org
Web: www.zami.org/audrelordescholar.html

Summary To provide financial assistance to mature out Black lesbians who are interested in entering or continuing in college or graduate school.

Eligibility This program is open to Black lesbians who are at least 40 years of age and out to themselves and their family, friends, and community. Applicants must be enrolled or planning to enroll full or part time at a technical, undergraduate, or graduate school in any state. They must have a cumulative GPA in high school, college, or technical school of 3.0 or higher. Along with their application, they must submit an essay of 2 to 3 pages on their choice of 2 of 5 assigned topics that relate to their experience as a Black lesbian.

Financial data The stipend is $1,000.

Duration 1 year.

Additional information From 1995 to 2008, the Audre Lorde Scholarship Fund was maintained by an organization named ZAMI: Atlanta's Premiere Organization for Lesbians of African Descent. The fund was reestablished in 2013 by the current sponsor, which stands for ZAMI National Organization of Black Lesbians on Aging.

Number awarded 1 each year.

Deadline April of each year.

[770]
AUTOMOTIVE WOMEN'S ALLIANCE FOUNDATION SCHOLARSHIPS

Automotive Women's Alliance Foundation
Attn: Scholarship
P.O. Box 4305
Troy, MI 48099
Toll Free: (877) 393-AWAF   Fax: (248) 239-0291
E-mail: admin@AWAFoundation.org
Web: www.awafoundation.org/pages/Scholarships

Summary To provide financial assistance to women who are interested in attending college or graduate school to prepare for a career in the automotive industry.

Eligibility This program is open to women who are entering or enrolled in an undergraduate or graduate program that will prepare them for a career in the automotive industry. Applicants must be citizens of Canada or the United States. They must have a GPA of 3.0 or higher. Along with their application, they must submit a 1-page cover letter explaining their automotive-related career aspirations.

Financial data The stipend is $2,500.

Duration 1 year.

Additional information This program began in 2001.

Number awarded Varies each year; recently, 21 were awarded.

Deadline Deadline not specified.

[771]
AWHONN NOVICE RESEARCHER AWARD

Association of Women's Health, Obstetric and Neonatal Nurses
Attn: Research Grants Program
1800 M Street, N.W., Suite 740S
Washington, DC 20036
(202) 261-2402   Toll Free: (800) 673-8499, ext. 2402
Fax: (202) 728-0575
E-mail: researchprograms@awhonn.org
Web: www.awhonn.org/?AvailableGrants

Summary To provide funding for small research projects to members of the Association of Women's Health, Obstetric and Neonatal Nurses (AWHONN) who qualify as novice researchers.

Eligibility This program is open to members of the association who have at least a master's degree or are currently enrolled in a master's program and completing a thesis or clinical research project. Applicants must be interested in beginning areas of study, investigating clinical issues, and/or launching a pilot study. They must identify a senior researcher who has agreed to serve as mentor and who submits a letter of support describing the role he or she will be implementing.

Financial data The grant is $5,000. Funds may not be used for indirect costs, tuition, computer hardware or printers, conference attendance, or salary for the principal investigator or other investigators.

Duration 1 year.

Number awarded 1 each year.

Deadline November of each year.

[772]
BANNER ENGINEERING MINNESOTA SWE SCHOLARSHIP

Society of Women Engineers-Minnesota Section
Attn: Scholarship Committee
P.O. Box 18481
Minneapolis, MN 55418
E-mail: scholarships@swe-mn.org
Web: www.swe-mn.org/scholarships.html

Summary To provide financial assistance to women from any state working on an undergraduate or graduate degree in electrical or mechanical engineering at colleges and universities in Minnesota, North Dakota, and South Dakota.

Eligibility This program is open to female undergraduate and graduate students at ABET-accredited engineering programs in Minnesota, North Dakota, or South Dakota. Applicants must be working full time on a degree in electrical or mechanical engineering. Along with their application, they must submit a 250-word essay describing how they plan to utilize their engineering knowledge and skills after they graduate. Selection is based on potential to succeed as an engineer (20 points), communication skills (10 points), extracurricular or community involvement and leadership skills (10 points), demonstration of work experience and successes (10 points), and academic success (5 points).

Financial data The stipend is $2,000.

Duration 1 year.

Additional information This program is sponsored by Banner Engineering Corporation.

Number awarded   1 each year.
Deadline   March of each year.

[773]
BAPTIST WOMEN IN MINISTRY OF NORTH CAROLINA STUDENT SCHOLARSHIPS

Baptist Women in Ministry of North Carolina
c/o Esther Soud Parker, Treasurer
7913 Ocoee Court
Raleigh, NC 27612
Web: www.bwimnc.org/scholarships

Summary   To provide financial assistance to women ministerial students enrolled at North Carolina Baptist institutions.

Eligibility   This program is open to women working on a graduate degree in theological education at North Carolina Baptist institutions. Applicants must be able to demonstrate a clear call and commitment to vocational Christian ministry, academic excellence, leadership skills, and expressed support of inclusiveness in all dimensions of life.

Financial data   The stipend is $2,000.

Duration   1 year.

Additional information   The eligible schools include Duke Divinity School, Campbell University Divinity School, M. Christopher White School of Divinity at Gardner-Webb University, and the Wake Forest University Divinity School.

Number awarded   4 each year: 1 at each of the eligible schools.

Deadline   Deadline not specified.

[774]
BARBARA ALICE MOWER MEMORIAL SCHOLARSHIP

Barbara Alice Mower Memorial Scholarship Committee
c/o Nancy A. Mower
1536 Kamole Street
Honolulu, HI 96821-1424
(808) 373-2901   E-mail: nmower@hawaii.edu

Summary   To provide financial assistance to female residents of Hawaii who are interested in women's studies and are attending college on the undergraduate or graduate level in the United States or abroad.

Eligibility   This program is open to female residents of Hawaii who are at least juniors in college, are interested in and committed to women's studies, and have worked or studied in the field. Selection is based on interest in studying about and commitment to helping women, previous work and/or study in that area, previous academic performance, character, personality, and future plans to help women (particularly women in Hawaii). If there are several applicants who meet all these criteria, then financial need may be taken into consideration.

Financial data   The stipend ranges from $1,000 to $3,500.

Duration   1 year; may be renewed.

Additional information   Recipients may use the scholarship at universities in Hawaii, on the mainland, or in foreign countries. They must focus on women's studies or topics that relate to women in school.

Number awarded   1 or more each year.

Deadline   April of each year.

[775]
BARBARA GIBSON FROEMMING SCHOLARSHIP

Kappa Delta Sorority
Attn: Foundation Project Coordinator
3205 Players Lane
Memphis, TN 38125
(901) 748-1897   Toll Free: (800) 536-1897
Fax: (901) 748-0949   E-mail: katie.boyd@kappadelta.org
Web: www.kappadelta.org/opportunities/scholarships

Summary   To provide financial assistance to members of Kappa Delta Sorority who are working on a graduate degree in education.

Eligibility   This program is open to graduate members of Kappa Delta Sorority. Applicants must submit a personal statement giving their reasons for applying for this scholarship, official undergraduate and graduate transcripts, and 2 letters of recommendation. They must be working on a graduate degree in education. Selection is based on academic excellence; service to the chapter, alumnae association, or national Kappa Delta; service to the campus and community; personal objectives and goals; potential; recommendations; and financial need.

Financial data   The stipend is $2,000 per year. Funds may be used only for tuition, fees, and books, not for room and board.

Duration   1 year; may be renewed.

Additional information   This program began in 2007.

Number awarded   1 each year.

Deadline   January of each year.

[776]
BARBARA MCBRIDE MEMORIAL ENDOWED SCHOLARSHIP FUND

Society of Exploration Geophysicists
Attn: SEG Foundation
8801 South Yale, Suite 500
P.O. Box 702740
Tulsa, OK 74170-2740
(918) 497-5500   Fax: (918) 497-5557
E-mail: scholarships@seg.org
Web: www.seg.org

Summary   To provide financial assistance to women who are interested in studying applied geophysics or a related field on the undergraduate or graduate school level.

Eligibility   This program is open to women who are 1) high school students planning to enter college in the fall; or 2) undergraduate or graduate students whose grades are above average. Applicants must intend to work on a degree directed toward a career in applied geophysics or a closely-related field (e.g., earth and environmental sciences, geology, geosciences, or physics). Along with their application, they must submit a 250-word essay on their interest in geophysics. Financial need is not considered in the selection process.

Financial data   Stipends provided by this sponsor range from $500 to $14,000 and average approximately $2,500 per year.

Duration   1 academic year; may be renewable, based on scholastic standing, availability of funds, and continuance of a course of study leading to a career in applied geophysics.

Additional information   This program began in 2001.

Number awarded   1 each year.

Deadline   February of each year.

[777]
BARBARA ROSENBLUM CANCER DISSERTATION SCHOLARSHIP

Sociologists for Women in Society
Attn: Administrative Officer
University of Kansas
Department of Sociology
1415 Jayhawk Boulevard, Room 716
Lawrence, KS 66045
(785) 864-9405   E-mail: swsao@outlook.com
Web: www.socwomen.org

Summary   To provide funding to women interested in conducting doctoral research on the social science aspects of women and cancer.

Eligibility   This program is open to women doctoral students with a feminist orientation who are interested in studying breast cancer and its impact on diverse groups of women, including those of diverse social classes and cultural backgrounds, socioeconomic status, sexual orientation, language, religion, geographical area, and other cultural perspectives. The research may be conducted in the areas of sociology, anthropology, psychology, or other social science fields concerned with women's experiences with breast cancer and the prevention of breast cancer. Priority is given to research that is not only useful academically but will have pragmatic and practical applications such as informing and empowering women, demystifying the disease, and/or having implications for the breast cancer epidemic more broadly.

Financial data   The grant is $1,500.

Duration   1 year.

Additional information   This program began in 1991.

Number awarded   1 each year.

Deadline   March of each year.

[778]
BAY AREA MINORITY LAW STUDENT SCHOLARSHIPS

Bar Association of San Francisco
Attn: Diversity Pipeline Programs Manager
301 Battery Street, Third Floor
San Francisco, CA 94111-3203
(415) 782-8914   Fax: (415) 477-2388
E-mail: emcgriff@sfbar.org
Web: www.sfbar.org

Summary   To provide financial assistance to underrepresented students from any state who are interested in attending law school in northern California.

Eligibility   This program is open to underrepresented students (women, racial and ethnic minorities, students with disabilities, LGBT students) who accept offers of admission from designated law schools in northern California. Applicants must submit a 500-word essay on obstacles they have overcome in pursuing their education and the qualities and talents they would bring to the legal profession. Financial need is considered in the selection process.

Financial data   The stipend is $10,000 per year.

Duration   3 years.

Additional information   This program began in 1998. Since then, more than $1.7 million in scholarships have been awarded to 93 students. The designated law schools are the Berkeley School of Law at the University of California, University of California at Davis School of Law, Golden Gate University School of Law, Hastings College of the Law at the University of California, McGeorge School of Law of University of the Pacific, University of San Francisco School of Law, Santa Clara University School of Law, and Stanford Law School.

Number awarded   Varies each year; recently, 4 were awarded.

Deadline   April of each year.

[779]
BENTON-MEIER SCHOLARSHIPS

American Psychological Foundation
750 First Street, N.E.
Washington, DC 20002-4242
(202) 336-5843   Fax: (202) 336-5812
E-mail: foundation@apa.org
Web: www.apa.org/apf/funding/benton-meier.aspx

Summary   To provide research funding to graduate students completing a dissertation related to neuropsychology.

Eligibility   This program is open to students who have been admitted to candidacy for a doctoral degree in the area of neuropsychology. Applicants must submit statements documenting their research competence and area commitment, a budget and justification, and how the scholarship money will be used. Selection is based on conformance with stated program goals and the applicant's demonstrated scholarship and research competence. The sponsor encourages applications from individuals who represent diversity in race, ethnicity, gender, age, disability, and sexual orientation.

Financial data   The grant is $2,500.

Duration   1 year.

Additional information   This program replaces the Henry Hécaen Scholarship, first awarded in 1994, and the Manfred Meier Scholarship, first awarded in 1997.

Number awarded   2 each year.

Deadline   May of each year.

[780]
BERNICE F. ELLIOTT MEMORIAL SCHOLARSHIP

Baptist Convention of New Mexico
Attn: Woman's Missionary Union
c/o Connie Dixon
P.O. Box 119
Elida, NM 88116
(575) 760-1603   E-mail: cdixon@bcnm.com
Web: www.bcnm.com/scholarships

Summary   To provide financial assistance to women who are Southern Baptists from New Mexico and interested in attending a college or seminary in any state.

Eligibility   This program is open to women college and seminary students who are members of churches affiliated with the Baptist Convention of New Mexico. Preference is given to applicants who are committed to full-time Christian service, have a background in the Woman's Missionary Union, and can demonstrate financial need.

Financial data   A stipend is awarded (amount not specified).

Duration 1 year; may be renewed.

Number awarded 1 or more each year.

Deadline March of each year.

[781]
BERTHA PITTS CAMPBELL SCHOLARSHIP PROGRAM

Delta Sigma Theta Sorority, Inc.
Attn: Scholarship and Standards Committee Chair
1707 New Hampshire Avenue, N.W.
Washington, DC 20009
(202) 986-2400   Fax: (202) 986-2513
E-mail: dstemail@deltasigmatheta.org
Web: www.deltasigmatheta.org

Summary To provide financial assistance to members of Delta Sigma Theta who are working on an undergraduate or graduate degree in education.

Eligibility This program is open to current undergraduate and graduate students who are working on a degree in education. Applicants must be active, dues-paying members of Delta Sigma Theta. Selection is based on meritorious achievement.

Financial data The stipends range from $1,000 to $2,000. The funds may be used to cover tuition, fees, and living expenses.

Duration 1 year; may be renewed for 1 additional year.

Additional information This sponsor is a traditionally-African American social sorority. The application fee is $20.

Number awarded 1 or more each year.

Deadline March of each year.

[782]
BESSIE BELLAMY PARKER SCHOLARSHIPS

South Carolina United Methodist Foundation
4908 Colonial Drive
P.O. Box 5087
Columbia, SC 29250-5087
(803) 786-9486   Fax: (803) 691-0220
E-mail: scumf@bellsouth.net
Web: www.umcsc.org

Summary To provide financial assistance to female Methodist seminary students from South Carolina.

Eligibility This program is open to women from South Carolina who are certified candidates for ministry in the United Methodist Church. Applicants must have completed at least 1 year of full-time enrollment in an approved United Methodist seminary with a grade average of "C" or higher. They must be planning to work in a local church setting. Selection is based (in descending order of importance) on self-understanding of ministry and intended future direction, promise for ministry, financial need, and academic performance in seminary.

Financial data A stipend is awarded (amount not specified).

Duration 1 year.

Additional information This scholarship was established by the South Carolina Conference of the United Methodist Church in 1986.

Number awarded 1 or more each year.

Deadline March of each year.

[783]
BETH E. MARCUS SCHOLARSHIP FUND

Reformed Church in America
Attn: Scholarship Fund
4500 60th Street S.E.
Grand Rapids, MI 49512
(616) 698-7071   Toll Free: (800) 968-3943
Fax: (616) 698-6606   E-mail: women@rca.org
Web: www.rca.org/women/beth-e-marcus-scholarship-fund

Summary To provide financial assistance to women attending a seminary of the Reformed Church in America (RCA) to prepare for a career in ministry.

Eligibility This program is open to women who are members of an RCA church and currently attending 1 of its seminaries: New Brunswick Theological Seminary (New Brunswick, New Jersey), Western Theological Seminary (Holland, Michigan), or the Ministerial Formation Certification Agency (Grand Rapids, Michigan). Applicants must "intend to serve Christ in ministry and mission." They must be working on an M.Div., M.A., M.T.S., or equivalent degree and have a GPA of 3.0 or higher.

Financial data Stipends are $500 per year for part-time students or $1,000 per year for full-time students.

Duration 1 year; recipients may reapply.

Number awarded 6 each year: 1 full-time student and 1 part-time student at each of the 3 RCA seminaries.

Deadline April of each year.

[784]
BETTY HANSEN NATIONAL SCHOLARSHIPS

Danish Sisterhood of America
c/o Connie Schell, Scholarship Chair
246 Foster Road
Fort Covington, NY 12937
(518) 358-4686
E-mail: vicepresident@danishsisterhood.com
Web: www.danishsisterhood.org/scholarships-grants.html

Summary To provide financial assistance for educational purposes in the United States or Denmark to members or relatives of members of the Danish Sisterhood of America.

Eligibility This program is open to members or the family of members of the sisterhood who are interested in attending an accredited 4-year college or university as a full-time undergraduate or graduate student. Members must have belonged to the sisterhood for at least 1 year. They must have a GPA of 2.5 or higher. Selection is based on academics (including ACT or SAT scores), academic awards or honors, other special recognition and awards, employment record, special talents or hobbies, and participation in Danish Sisterhood and other civic activities. Upon written request, the scholarship may be used for study in Denmark.

Financial data The stipend is $1,000 per year.

Duration 1 year; may be renewed 1 additional year.

Number awarded Up to 8 each year.

Deadline February of each year.

[785]
BETTY LOU BAILEY SWE REGION F SCHOLARSHIP

Society of Women Engineers
Attn: Scholarship Selection Committee
203 North LaSalle Street, Suite 1675
Chicago, IL 60601-1269
(312) 596-5223   Toll Free: (877) SWE-INFO
Fax: (312) 644-8557   E-mail: scholarships@swe.org
Web: societyofwomenengineers.swe.org

Summary To provide financial assistance to members of the Society of Women Engineers (SWE) working on an undergraduate or graduate degree in engineering or computer science at a school in its Region F (New England and upstate New York).

Eligibility This program is open to members of the society who will be sophomores, juniors, seniors, or graduate students at ABET-accredited colleges and universities. First preference is given to applicants who attend college or graduate school in the New England states or upstate New York; second preference is given to students who reside in New England or upstate New York. Applicants must be working full time on a degree in computer science or engineering and have a GPA of 3.0 or higher. Financial need is considered in the selection process. U.S. citizenship is required.

Financial data The stipend is $1,500.

Duration 1 year.

Number awarded 1 each year.

Deadline February of each year.

[786]
BIRDELLA ROSS SCHOLARSHIP

Delta Kappa Gamma Society International-Tau State
   Organization
c/o Mary Kay Feltes, Scholarship Committee Chair
P.O. Box 51
Owatonna, MN 55060
Web: dkgmn.weebly.com/forms.html

Summary To provide financial assistance to members of Delta Kappa Gamma Society International in Minnesota who are interested in pursuing advanced study or training.

Eligibility This program is open to residents of Minnesota who have been members of Delta Kappa Gamma (an honorary society of women educators) for at least 2 years. Applicants must be interested in working on a graduate degree, obtaining licensure, or attending a special workshop. Along with their application, they must submit a 100-word essay describing their short- and long-term goals and a short outline of the proposed program for which they are seeking this scholarship.

Financial data The stipend is $4,000. Funds are paid directly to the college or university.

Duration 1 year.

Number awarded 1 each odd-numbered year.

Deadline February of each odd-numbered year.

[787]
BISHOP MURPHY SCHOLARSHIPS

Women's Ordination Conference
Attn: Scholarship Committee
P.O. Box 15058
Washington, DC 20003
(202) 675-1006   Fax: (202) 675-1008
E-mail: woc@womensordination.org
Web: www.womensordination.org

Summary To provide financial assistance to members of the Women's Ordination Conference (WOC) who are working on a graduate degree to prepare for Catholic ministry.

Eligibility This program is open to women who are members of the WOC. Applicants must be enrolled or accepted in a graduate program at a seminary or a diocesan certificate program preparing for Catholic priestly ministry. They must submit a letter of recommendation from a mentor who can testify to their commitment to WOC's goals, a personal statement of how their future ministry supports WOC's mission, a resume or curriculum vitae, and proof of enrollment.

Financial data The stipend is $1,000. Funds must be used for educational expenses.

Duration 1 year.

Additional information The WOC is an organization "working locally and nationally in collaboration with the worldwide movement for women's ordination." In pursuit of its goals, it "works for justice and equality for women in our church; strives to eliminate all forms of domination and discrimination in the Catholic church; advocates inclusive church structures; supports and affirms women's talents, gifts and calls to ministry." Recipients are required to submit a report at the end of the grant period explaining how the award impacted their study and growth.

Number awarded 1 or 2 each year.

Deadline January of each year.

[788]
B.J. DEAN SCHOLARSHIP

Community Foundation of Middle Tennessee
Attn: Scholarship Coordinator
3833 Cleghorn Avenue, Suite 400
Nashville, TN 37215-2519
(615) 321-4939, ext. 116   Toll Free: (888) 540-5200
Fax: (615) 327-2746   E-mail: pcole@cfmt.org
Web: www.cfmt.org/request/scholarships/allscholarships

Summary To provide financial assistance to women from Tennessee or Texas preparing for a career in the ministry at a seminary in any state.

Eligibility This program is open to women from Tennessee or Texas interested in entering the ministry; students enrolled at Yale Divinity School are also eligible. Applicants must be preparing for full-time ministry but not necessarily seeking ordination. They must be planning to enroll full time at a seminary in any state. There are no denominational restrictions. Along with their application, they must submit an essay describing their educational plans and how those plans will help them reach their career goals. Financial need is considered in the selection process.

Financial data Stipends range from $500 to $2,500 per year. Funds are paid to the recipient's school and must be used for tuition, fees, books, supplies, room, board, or miscellaneous expenses.

Duration 1 year; recipients may reapply.

Additional information This program began in 1995.

Number awarded 1 or more each year.

Deadline March of each year.

[789]
B.K. KRENZER MEMORIAL REENTRY SCHOLARSHIP

Society of Women Engineers
Attn: Scholarship Selection Committee
203 North LaSalle Street, Suite 1675
Chicago, IL 60601-1269
(312) 596-5223   Toll Free: (877) SWE-INFO
Fax: (312) 644-8557   E-mail: scholarships@swe.org
Web: societyofwomenengineers.swe.org

Summary To provide financial assistance to women interested in returning to college or graduate school to study engineering or computer science.

Eligibility This program is open to women who are planning to enroll at an ABET-accredited 4-year college or university. Applicants must have been out of the engineering workforce and school for at least 2 years and must be planning to return as an undergraduate or graduate student to work on a degree in computer science or engineering. Selection is based on merit. Preference is given to engineers who already have a degree and are planning to reenter the engineering workforce after a period of temporary retirement.

Financial data The stipend is $2,500.

Duration 1 year.

Additional information This program began in 1996.

Number awarded 1 each year.

Deadline February of each year.

[790]
BMBG/JANIE WULKAN MEMORIAL SCHOLARSHIP

American Public Transportation Association
Attn: American Public Transportation Foundation
1666 K Street, N.W., Suite 1100
Washington, DC 20006
(202) 496-4803   Fax: (202) 496-4323
E-mail: pboswell@apta.com
Web: www.aptfd.org/Pages/default.aspx

Summary To provide financial assistance to undergraduate and graduate women who are preparing for a career in the public transportation industry.

Eligibility This program is open to female sophomores, juniors, seniors, and graduate students who are preparing for a career in the transit industry. Any member organization of the American Public Transportation Association (APTA) can nominate and sponsor candidates for this scholarship. Nominees must be enrolled in a fully-accredited institution, have and maintain at least a 3.0 GPA, and be either employed by or demonstrate a strong interest in entering the business administration or management area of the public transportation industry. They must submit a 1,000-word essay on the topic, "In what segment of the public transportation industry will you make a career and why?" Selection is based on demonstrated interest in the transit field as a career, need for finan-

cial assistance, academic achievement, essay content and quality, and involvement in extracurricular citizenship and leadership activities.

Financial data The stipend is $2,500.

Duration 1 year; may be renewed.

Additional information This program is sponsored by the Business Member Board of Governors (BMBG) of the American Public Transportation Association.

Number awarded 1 each year.

Deadline June of each year.

[791]
BOBBIE BURK CONDUCTING SCHOLARSHIP FOR GRADUATE STUDENTS

Sigma Alpha Iota Philanthropies, Inc.
One Tunnel Road
Asheville, NC 28805
(828) 251-0606   Fax: (828) 251-0644
E-mail: nh@sai-national.org
Web: app.smarterselect.com

Summary To provide financial assistance to members of Sigma Alpha Iota (an organization of women musicians) who are working on a graduate degree in conducting.

Eligibility This program is open to members of the organization who are currently enrolled in a graduate degree program with an emphasis on conducting. Applicants must include a videotape of a performance they conducted.

Financial data The stipend is $2,500.

Duration 1 year.

Number awarded 1 each year.

Deadline March of each year.

[792]
BOEING COMPANY CAREER ENHANCEMENT SCHOLARSHIP

Women in Aviation International
Attn: Scholarships
Morningstar Airport
3647 State Route 503 South
West Alexandria, OH 45381-9354
(937) 839-4647   Fax: (937) 839-4645
E-mail: scholarships@wai.org
Web: www.wai.org

Summary To provide financial assistance to members of Women in Aviation International (WAI) who are active in aerospace and need financial support to advance their career.

Eligibility This program is open to WAI members who wish to advance their career in the aerospace industry in the fields of engineering, technology development, or management. Applicants may be 1) full-time or part-time employees working in the aerospace industry or a related field; or 2) students working on an aviation-related degree who are at least sophomores and have a GPA of 2.5 or higher. Along with their application, they must submit a 500-word essay and professional resume that include their aviation history and goals, what they have done for themselves to achieve their goals, where they see themselves in 5 and 10 years, involvement in aviation activities, how the scholarship will help them achieve their objectives, and their present financial need.

Financial data The stipend is $2,500.

Duration 1 year.

Additional information WAI is a nonprofit professional organization dedicated to encouraging women to consider an aviation career and to providing educational outreach activities and networking resources to women active in the industry. This program is sponsored by the Boeing Company.

Number awarded 2 each year.

Deadline November of each year.

[793]
C200 SCHOLAR AWARDS

Committee of 200
Attn: C200 Foundation
980 North Michigan Avenue, Suite 1575
Chicago, IL 60611-7540
(312) 255-0296   Fax: (312) 255-0789
E-mail: info@c200.org
Web: www.c200.org

Summary To provide financial assistance to women working on an M.B.A. degree at universities that host Reachout seminars conducted by the Committee of 200 (C200).

Eligibility Twice each year, C200 co-sponsors 1-day outreach seminars for women M.B.A. students. Seminars rotate among the outstanding business schools in the country. These scholarships are available to first-year women students at each of the schools where a Reachout is held. The schools select finalists on the basis of work experience, GPA, recommendations, and essays. Members of C200 interview the finalists and select the winners.

Financial data The stipend is $10,000.

Duration 1 year.

Additional information Scholars also receive an internship at a C200 member's company.

Number awarded 3 each year.

Deadline Deadline not specified.

[794]
CALIFORNIA P.E.O. SELECTED SCHOLARSHIPS

P.E.O. Foundation-California State Chapter
c/o Dee Zasio, Scholarship Selection Committee
21916 Strawberry Drive
Canyon Lake, CA 92587
E-mail: peoca.ssc@gmail.com
Web: www.peocalifornia.org

Summary To provide financial assistance to female residents of California attending college or graduate school in any state.

Eligibility This program is open to female residents of California who have completed 4 years of high school (or the equivalent); are enrolled at or accepted by an accredited college, university, vocational school, or graduate school in any state; and have an excellent academic record. Selection is based on financial need, character, academic ability, and school and community activities. Some awards include additional requirements. U.S. citizenship is required.

Financial data Stipends recently ranged from $400 to $2,500.

Duration 1 year; may be renewed for up to 3 additional years.

Additional information This program includes the following named scholarships: the Barbara Furse Mackey Scholarship (for women whose education has been interrupted); the Beverly Dye Anderson Scholarship (for the fields of teaching or health care); the Marjorie M. McDonald P.E.O. Scholarship (for women who are continuing their education after a long hiatus from school); the Ora Keck Scholarship (for women who are preparing for a career in music or the fine arts); the Phyllis J. Van Deventer Scholarship (for women who are preparing for a career in music performance or music education); the Jean Gower Scholarship (for women preparing for a career in education); the Helen D. Thompson Memorial Scholarship (for women studying music or fine arts); the Stella May Nau Scholarship (for women who are interested in reentering the job market); the Linda Jones Memorial Fine Arts Scholarship (for women studying fine arts); the Polly Thompson Memorial Music Scholarship (for women studying music); the Ruby W. Henry Scholarship; the Jean W. Gratiot Scholarship; the Pearl Prime Scholarship; the Helen Beardsley Scholarship; the Chapter GA Scholarship; and the Nearly New Scholarship.

Number awarded Varies each year; recently, 43 were awarded.

Deadline January of each year.

[795]
CAROL STEPHENS SWE REGION F SCHOLARSHIP

Society of Women Engineers
Attn: Scholarship Selection Committee
203 North LaSalle Street, Suite 1675
Chicago, IL 60601-1269
(312) 596-5223   Toll Free: (877) SWE-INFO
Fax: (312) 644-8557   E-mail: scholarships@swe.org
Web: societyofwomenengineers.swe.org

Summary To provide financial assistance to members of the Society of Women Engineers (SWE) working on an undergraduate or graduate degree in engineering or computer science at a school in its Region F (New England and upstate New York).

Eligibility This program is open to members of the society who will be sophomores, juniors, seniors, or graduate students at ABET-accredited colleges and universities. First preference is given to applicants who attend college or graduate school in the New England states or upstate New York; second preference is given to students who reside in New England or upstate New York. Applicants must be working full time on a degree in computer science or engineering. Financial need is considered in the selection process. U.S. citizenship is required.

Financial data The stipend is $1,250.

Duration 1 year.

Additional information This program began in 2012.

Number awarded 1 each year.

Deadline February of each year.

[796]
CAROL TYLER AWARD

International Precious Metals Institute
5101 North 12th Avenue, Suite C
Pensacola, FL 32504
(850) 476-1156   Fax: (850) 476-1548
E-mail: mail@ipmi.org
Web: www.ipmi.org/awards/index.cfm

Summary To recognize and reward women who have a record of outstanding achievement in the science and technology of precious metals.

Eligibility This award is available to women who are graduate students or currently employed in industry or academia. Nominees must have made outstanding theoretical and experimental contributions to the science and technology of precious metals. They may be residents of any country.

Financial data The award is $5,000 and a certificate.

Duration The award is presented annually.

Additional information This award was first presented in 2011.

Number awarded 1 each year.

Deadline January of each year.

[797]
CAROL WILLIAMS-NICKELSON AWARD FOR WOMEN'S LEADERSHIP AND SCHOLARSHIP IN WOMEN'S ISSUES

American Psychological Association
Attn: American Psychological Association of Graduate
  Students
750 First Street, N.E.
Washington, DC 20002-4242
(202) 336-6014   Fax: (202) 336-5694
E-mail: apags@apa.org
Web: www.apa.org

Summary To recognize and reward female psychology doctoral students who are members of the American Psychological Association of Graduate Students (APAGS) and have advanced women's issues.

Eligibility This program is open to women who are working on a doctoral degree in psychology and are members of APAGS. Applicants must have demonstrated exceptional leadership by serving in 1 or more leadership roles locally, regionally, and/or nationally while also advancing women's issues through their writing, publications, research, advocacy, or other scholarly activities. Examples of relevant issues include personal and professional balance, barriers to women's achievement, challenges to advancement in academia or other environments, inequities in pay, different career opportunities, health disparities, dual-career family issues, combining family and child-rearing with a career, mentoring, or other issues that are important to or impact women. Along with their application, they must submit a 1,500-word essay that describes their future educational and professional goals and how their research, advocacy, or other scholarly work advances women and women's issues.

Financial data The award is $1,000.

Duration 1 year.

Additional information This program began in 2008.

Number awarded 1 each year.

Deadline May of each year.

[798]
CAROLYN HELMAN LICHTENBERG GRADUATE FELLOWSHIP

Pi Beta Phi
Attn: Pi Beta Phi Foundation
1154 Town and Country Commons Drive
Town and Country, MO 63017
(636) 256-1357   Fax: (636) 256-8124
E-mail: fndn@pibetaphi.org
Web: www.pibetaphifoundation.org/programs/scholarships

Summary To provide financial assistance for graduate school to members of Pi Beta Phi, especially those working on a master's degree in education.

Eligibility This program is open to women who are dues-paying members in good standing of Pi Beta Phi (as a graduating senior or alumna) and graduated no more than 4 years previously. Applicants must be planning full-time graduate work at an accredited college, university, or technical professional school. They must have a GPA of 3.0 or higher for all undergraduate and graduate study. First preference is given to members working on a master's degree in education. Selection is based on financial need, academic record, and service to the sorority, campus, and community.

Financial data Stipends range from $1,500 to $6,500.

Duration 1 year.

Number awarded 1 each year.

Deadline February of each year.

[799]
CAROLYN WEATHERFORD SCHOLARSHIP FUND

Woman's Missionary Union
Attn: WMU Foundation
100 Missionary Ridge
Birmingham, AL 35242
(205) 408-5525   Toll Free: (877) 482-4483
Fax: (205) 408-5508   E-mail: wmufoundation@wmu.org
Web: www.wmufoundation.com/?q=content/scholarships

Summary To provide an opportunity for women to work on a graduate degree or an internship so they can engage in activities of the Woman's Missionary Union (WMU).

Eligibility This program is open to women who are members of the Baptist Church and are attending or planning to attend a Southern Baptist seminary or divinity school at the graduate level or participate in an internship. Applicants must be interested in 1) field work experience as interns or in women's missionary work in the United States; or 2) service in women's missionary work in the United States. They must arrange for 3 letters of endorsement, from a recent professor, a state or associational WMU official, and a recent pastor. Selection is based on current active involvement in WMU, previous activity in WMU, plans for long-term involvement in WMU and/or home missions, academic strength, leadership skills, and personal and professional characteristics.

Financial data A stipend is awarded (amount not specified).

Duration 1 year.

Number awarded 1 or more each year.

Deadline February of each year.

[800]
CARRIE CHAPMAN CATT PRIZE FOR RESEARCH ON WOMEN AND POLITICS

Iowa State University
Attn: Carrie Chapman Catt Center for Women and Politics
309 Carrie Chapman Catt Hall
2224 Osborn Drive
Ames, IA 50011-4009
(515) 294-3181   Fax: (515) 294-3741
E-mail: cattcntr@iastate.edu
Web: cattcenter.las.iastate.edu

Summary To recognize and reward outstanding research in the area of women and politics.

Eligibility This competition is open to scholars at all levels, including graduate students and junior faculty, who are planning to conduct research in the area of women and politics. Applicants must submit a detailed description of their research project, including 1) its purpose and content; 2) a discussion of relevant theory, contributions to literature in the field, and methodology; 3) a statement on how this prize will contribute to the research project; 4) a timetable for completion of the project; and 5) a bibliography. They also must submit a 1-page biographical statement. Research projects can address the annual conference theme or any other topic related to women and politics.

Financial data Prizes are $2,000 for winners or $1,000 for honorable mention. All prize-winners may also receive travel expenses to Des Moines, Iowa where awards are presented at the annual conference of the Carrie Chapman Catt Center for Women and Politics.

Duration The prizes are awarded annually.

Number awarded Up to 4 winners and up to 2 honorable mentions are selected each year.

Deadline November of each year.

[801]
CATHERINE PRELINGER AWARD

Coordinating Council for Women in History
c/o Sandra Dawson, Executive Director
Northern Illinois University
Department of History and Women's Studies
715 Zulauf Hall
DeKalb, IL 60115
(815) 895-2624   E-mail: Prelingeraward@theccwh.org
Web: www.theccwh.org

Summary To provide funding to members of the Coordinating Council for Women in History (CCWH) for a project that focuses on women's roles in history.

Eligibility This program is open to members of CCWH whose academic path has not followed the traditional pattern of uninterrupted study. Applicants must hold either A.B.D. status or a Ph.D. and be engaged in scholarship that is historical in nature, although their degree may be in related fields. They must submit a description of a project they propose to undertake with this award, including the work they intend to complete, the schedule they have developed, the sources they intend to use, and the contribution the work will make to women in history. Independent and non-academic scholars are encouraged to apply.

Financial data The grant is $20,000.

Duration 1 year.

Additional information This program began in 1998.

Number awarded 1 each year.

Deadline May of each year.

[802]
CCWH/BERKS GRADUATE STUDENT FELLOWSHIP

Coordinating Council for Women in History
c/o Sandra Dawson, Executive Director
Northern Illinois University
Department of History and Women's Studies
715 Zulauf Hall
DeKalb, IL 60115
(815) 895-2624 E-mail: CCWHBerksAward@theccwh.org
Web: www.theccwh.org

Summary To provide funding to women graduate students in history for completion of their doctoral dissertations.

Eligibility This program is open to women graduate students in history departments at U.S. institutions who are members of the Coordinating Council for Women in History (CCWH). Applicants must have passed to A.B.D. status. They may be specializing in any field of history.

Financial data The grant is $1,000.

Duration 1 year.

Additional information This program, established in 1991, is administered by the CCWH and the Berkshire Conference of Women Historians. The award is presented at the CCWH luncheon at the annual meeting of the American Historical Association, although the recipient does not need to be present to accept the award.

Number awarded 1 each year.

Deadline May of each year.

[803]
CECELIA CONNELLY MEMORIAL SCHOLARSHIPS IN UNDERWATER ARCHAEOLOGY

Women Divers Hall of Fame
43 MacKey Avenue
Port Washington, NY 11050-3628
E-mail: scholarships@wdhof.org
Web: www.wdhof.org/scholarships/scholarships.shtml

Summary To provide financial assistance to women who are working on an undergraduate or graduate degree in underwater archaeology.

Eligibility This program is open to women of any age who are enrolled in an accredited undergraduate or graduate course of study in the field of underwater archaeology. Applicants must be seeking funding to assist with college tuition and fees or field study costs.

Financial data The stipend is $2,000 for graduate students or $750 for undergraduates.

Duration 1 year.

Number awarded 2 each year: 1 undergraduate and 1 graduate student.

Deadline November of each year.

[804]
CELIA M. HOWARD FELLOWSHIP

Illinois Federation of Business Women's Clubs
c/o Fayrene Wright, Howard Fellowship Fund Committee
   Chair
804 East Locust Street
Robinson, IL 62454
(618) 546-1233   E-mail: fayrene26@gmail.com
Web: www.celiamhowardfellowship.com

Summary To provide funding to women in Illinois who are interested in working on a graduate degree in specified fields at eligible universities.

Eligibility This program is open to Illinois women who are U.S. citizens; have been Illinois residents for at least the past 2 years; have earned a bachelor's degree with at least 12 hours of undergraduate work in economics, history, and/or political science; and have a GPA of 3.0 or higher. A personal interview may be required. Applicants must be planning to study for a master's degree in administration of justice at Southern Illinois University at Carbondale or Edwardsville; a J.D. degree at the University of Illinois College of Law at Urbana-Champaign; a master's degree in diplomacy at the Fletcher School of Law and Diplomacy in Medford, Massachusetts; or a master's degree in international studies, modern languages, or world business at the Garvin School of International Management in Glendale, Arizona. Selection is based on financial need, previous graduate study, practical business experience in government, and leadership experience.

Financial data Awards normally pay full tuition and recently averaged $16,250 per year. Funds are paid directly to the recipient's school.

Duration 1 year; renewable.

Additional information This program began in 1948.

Number awarded Varies each year; recently, 8 were awarded.

Deadline November of each year.

[805]
CH2M HILL PARTNERSHIP SCHOLARSHIP

Women's Transportation Seminar
Attn: WTS Foundation
1701 K Street, N.W., Suite 800
Washington, DC 20006
(202) 955-5085   Fax: (202) 955-5088
E-mail: wts@wtsinternational.org
Web: www.wtsinternational.org/education/scholarships

Summary To provide financial assistance to women graduate students interested in preparing for a career in transportation.

Eligibility This program is open to women who are enrolled in a graduate degree program in a transportation-related field (e.g., transportation engineering, planning, finance, or logistics). Applicants must have at least a 3.0 GPA and be interested in a career in transportation. Along with their application, they must submit a 750-word statement about their career goals after graduation and why they think they should receive the scholarship award. Applications must be submitted first to a local chapter; the chapters forward selected applications for consideration on the national level. Minority women are particularly encouraged to apply. Selec-

tion is based on transportation involvement and goals, job skills, and academic record.

Financial data The stipend is $10,000.

Duration 1 year.

Additional information This program is sponsored by CH2M Hill. Local chapters may also award additional funding to winners in their area.

Number awarded 1 each year.

Deadline Applications must be submitted by November to a local WTS chapter.

[806]
CHARLES TIMOTHY STONER LAW SCHOLARSHIP

Women's Basketball Coaches Association
Attn: Manager of Events, Awards and Office
   Administration
4646 Lawrenceville Highway
Lilburn, GA 30047-3620
(770) 279-8027, ext. 110   Fax: (770) 279-8473
E-mail: dtrujillo@wbca.org
Web: wbca.org

Summary To provide financial assistance for law school to women's basketball players.

Eligibility This program is open to women's college basketball players who are seniors planning to attend law school. Applicants must be nominated by a member of the Women's Basketball Coaches Association (WBCA). Selection is based on a letter of recommendation, academic major and GPA, basketball statistics for all 4 years of college, academic and athletic honors, and campus activities.

Financial data The stipend is $1,000.

Duration 1 year; nonrenewable.

Additional information This program began in 1996.

Number awarded 1 each year.

Deadline Deadline not specified.

[807]
CHARLOTTE BRENT MEMORIAL SCHOLARSHIP

United Methodist Church-Louisiana Conference
Attn: Coordinator, Conference Board of Ordained Ministry
527 North Boulevard
Baton Rouge, LA 70802-5700
(225) 346-1646, ext. 230
Toll Free: (888) 239-5286, ext. 230
Fax: (225) 383-2652
E-mail: JohnEdddHarper@la-umc.org
Web: www.la-umc.org/boardofordainedministry

Summary To provide financial assistance to women from Louisiana who are attending a Methodist seminary in any state to prepare for a career in ordained ministry.

Eligibility This program is open to female members of United Methodist Churches in Louisiana who are enrolled or planning to enroll full time at a Methodist seminary in any state. Applicants must be beginning a second career as an ordained minister. Along with their application, they must submit an essay on their vocational goals and plans for ministry.

Financial data The stipend is $1,000.

Duration 1 year.

Number awarded 1 each year.

Deadline February of each year.

[808]
CHERYL A. RUGGIERO SCHOLARSHIP

Rhode Island Society of Certified Public Accountants
40 Sharpe Drive, Unit 5
Cranston, RI 02920
(401) 331-5720　　　　　　　　Fax: (401) 454-5780
E-mail: info@riscpa.org
Web: www.riscpa.org/careers/become-a-cpa

Summary To provide financial assistance to female undergraduate and graduate students from Rhode Island who are working on a degree in accounting at a school in any state.

Eligibility This program is open to female residents of Rhode Island who are working on an undergraduate or graduate degree in public accounting at a school in any state. Applicants must be U.S. citizens who have a GPA of 3.0 or higher. Selection is based on demonstrated potential to become a valued member of the public accounting profession. Finalists are interviewed.

Financial data The stipend is $1,550.

Duration 1 year.

Additional information This program began in 2005.

Number awarded 1 each year.

Deadline January of each year.

[809]
CHI OMEGA FOUNDATION ALUMNAE EDUCATIONAL GRANTS

Chi Omega Fraternity
Attn: Chi Omega Foundation
3395 Players Club Parkway
Memphis, TN 38125
(901) 748-8600　　　　　　　　Fax: (901) 748-8686
E-mail: foundation@chiomega.com
Web: www.chiomega.com/wemakeadifference/scholarships

Summary To provide financial assistance for graduate school to women who are members of Chi Omega Fraternity and have been out of college for a period of time.

Eligibility This program is open to women over 24 years of age who are alumnae members of Chi Omega Fraternity. Applicants must be planning to enter graduate school as a full- or part-time student for career qualification or advancement. Along with their application, they must submit a personal letter describing their reasons and need for the grant. Selection is based on academic achievement, aptitude, service to Chi Omega, contributions to the university and community, personal and professional goals, and financial need.

Financial data The stipend is $1,000.

Duration 1 year.

Additional information This program began in 1997.

Number awarded 10 each year.

Deadline January of each year.

[810]
CHRYSALIS SCHOLARSHIP

Association for Women Geoscientists
Attn: AWG Foundation
12000 North Washington Street, Suite 285
Thornton, CO 80241
(303) 412-6219　　　　　　　　Fax: (303) 253-9220
E-mail: chrysalis@awg.org
Web: www.awg.org/AWGFoundation/chrysalis.htm

Summary To provide assistance to women who have returned to graduate school to earn a degree in the geosciences and need funding to complete their thesis.

Eligibility This program is open to women geoscience graduate students whose education has been significantly interrupted by life circumstances. Applicants must submit a letter describing their background, career goals and objectives, how the scholarship will be used, and nature and length of the interruption to their education.

Financial data The stipend is $2,000. The funds may be used for typing, drafting, child care, or anything necessary to allow a degree candidate to finish her thesis and enter a geoscience profession.

Duration 1 year.

Number awarded 1 or more each year.

Deadline March of each year.

[811]
CHURCH TRAINING AND DEACONESS HOUSE SCHOLARSHIP

Episcopal Diocese of Pennsylvania
Attn: Church Training and Deaconess House Scholarship Fund
3717 Chestnut Street, Suite 300
Philadelphia, PA 19104
(215) 627-6434, ext. 101　　　　　Fax: (267) 900-2928
E-mail: nevin-field@stpetersphila.org
Web: www.diopa.org/deaconess-training

Summary To provide financial assistance for graduate school to women preparing for a career in religious or benevolent work for the Episcopal Church.

Eligibility This program is open to women who are seeking to be ordained to the ministry of the Episcopal Church or to work on a graduate degree that would further their lay ministry. Preference is given to women in the Diocese of Pennsylvania. Applicants must submit a 250-word essay on how they expect to use this graduate educational training to advance their ordained or lay ministry within the Episcopal Church or the church at large. Selection is based on the quality of the essay, academic record, and financial need.

Financial data Stipends range from $2,000 to $3,000.

Duration 1 year; may be renewed up to 2 additional years.

Number awarded 1 or more each year.

Deadline March of each year.

[812]
CLAIRE BARRETT MEMORIAL SCHOLARSHIP

Women's Transportation Seminar-Boston Chapter
c/o Susie Bailey
HDR, Inc.
695 Atlantic Avenue
Boston, MA 0211-2626
(617) 357-7700   Fax: (617) 357-7759
E-mail: susie.bailey@hdrinc.com
Web: www.wtsinternational.org/boston/scholarships

Summary To provide financial assistance to women from any state who have an interest in public policy issues and are working on a transportation-related graduate degree at a college or university in Massachusetts.

Eligibility This program is open to women enrolled at colleges and universities in Massachusetts who are working on a graduate degree in a transportation-related field, including transportation engineering, planning, finance, or logistics. Applicants must be able to demonstrate 1) plans to prepare for a career in a transportation-related field; 2) excellent communication skills; 3) a belief in the power of public dialogue in communicating and improving the goals of public institutions and public projects; and 4) current involvement in a research or thesis project that incorporates use of public transportation, environmental awareness, use of public art, awareness of diversity, and use of landscape architecture. Along with their application, they must submit a 750-word personal statement about their career goals after graduation, a link between their passion and the purpose of this scholarship, why they think they should receive this scholarship, and a description of their research or thesis project. Selection is based on the applicant's specific transportation involvement and goals, job skills, and academic record. Minority women are especially encouraged to apply.

Financial data The stipend is $6,000.

Duration 1 year.

Additional information This program began in 2005.

Number awarded 1 or more each year.

Deadline October of each year.

[813]
CLAUDIA STEELE BAKER GRADUATE FELLOWSHIP

Alpha Chi Omega Foundation
Attn: Foundation Coordinator
5939 Castle Creek Parkway North Drive
Indianapolis, IN 46250-4343
(317) 579-5050   Fax: (317) 579-5051
E-mail: rhaley@alphachiomega.org
Web: www.alphachiomega.org

Summary To provide financial assistance to Alpha Chi Omega members who are interested in studying social services in graduate school.

Eligibility Women college seniors and graduates who are members of the sorority are eligible to apply if they have majored in a social service field, are committed to peace and understanding, and plan to attend graduate school. Selection is based on campus, community, and chapter service.

Financial data A stipend is awarded (amount not specified).

Duration 1 year.

Number awarded 1 each year.

Deadline February of each year.

[814]
COLORADO SECTION COLLEGE SCHOLARSHIP FOR JEWISH WOMEN

National Council of Jewish Women-Colorado Section
Attn: Scholarship Program
6018 South Lima Way
Englewood, CO 80111
(303) 290-6655   E-mail: gmkern@comcast.net
Web: www.ncjwcolorado.org

Summary To provide financial assistance to Jewish women from Colorado who are interested in attending college or graduate school in any state.

Eligibility This program is open to Jewish residents of Colorado who are women at least 16 years of age. Applicants must be enrolled or planning to enroll at an accredited college, university, junior college, community college, technical school, or graduate school in any state. Along with their application, they must submit a 1-page essay about their personal and educational goals and why they feel they deserve this scholarship, information about their academic record, documentation of their involvement in the community, and documentation of financial need.

Financial data The stipend is $2,000.

Duration 1 year.

Number awarded Several each year.

Deadline March of each year.

[815]
CONNIE SETTLES SCHOLARSHIP

American Legion Auxiliary
Department of California
401 Van Ness Avenue, Suite 319
San Francisco, CA 94102-4570
(415) 861-5092   Fax: (415) 861-8365
E-mail: calegionaux@calegionaux.org
Web: www.calegionaux.org/scholarships.htm

Summary To provide financial assistance to members of the American Legion Auxiliary in California who are attending college or graduate school in the state.

Eligibility This program is open to residents of California who are currently working on an undergraduate or graduate degree at a college or university in the state. Applicants must have been members of the American Legion Auxiliary for at least the 2 preceding years and be current members. Each unit of the Auxiliary may nominate only 1 member. Selection is based on transcripts, 2 letters of recommendation, a letter from the applicant about themselves and their goals, and financial need. Support is not provided for programs of study deemed to be nonessential (e.g., sewing classes, aerobics, sculpting).

Financial data The stipend is $5,000. Funds are paid directly to the recipient's college or university.

Duration 1 year.

Number awarded 1 each year.

Deadline Applications must be submitted to Auxiliary units by February of each year.

[816]
COSROW SCHOLARSHIP

United Methodist Church-Oklahoma Conference
Attn: Commission on the Status and Role of Women
1501 N.W. 24th Street
Oklahoma, OK 73106-3635
(405) 530-2000   Toll Free: (800) 231-4166
Fax: (405) 525-4164
Web: www.okumc.org/awards

Summary To provide financial assistance to Methodist women from Oklahoma interested in preparing for full-time ministry.

Eligibility This program is open to women who are members of the Oklahoma Conference of the United Methodist Church (UMC). Applicants must be interested in full-time ministry in the UMC as a seminary student, by taking pre-seminary courses, or by pursuing ministerial education through the Course of Study program.

Financial data A stipend is awarded (amount not specified).

Duration 1 year.

Number awarded 1 or more each year.

Deadline August of each year.

[817]
CREDIT SUISSE MBA FELLOWSHIP

Credit Suisse
Attn: Diversity and Inclusion Programs
Eleven Madison Avenue
New York, NY 10010-3629
(212) 325-2000   Fax: (212) 325-6665
E-mail: campus.diversity@credit-suisse.com
Web: www.credit-suisse.com

Summary To provide financial assistance and work experience at offices of Credit Suisse to women and underrepresented minority graduate students working on a master's degree as preparation for a career in investment banking.

Eligibility This program is open to students entering their first year of a full-time M.B.A. program who are female, Black/African American, Hispanic/Latino, or Native American. Applicants must be able to demonstrate a strong interest in a career in investment banking. Selection is based on academic excellence, leadership ability, and interest in the financial services industry.

Financial data The stipend is $15,000 for the first year; for the second year, students may elect to have $30,000 paid directly to their university or to have $15,000 paid to them for tuition and for academic and living expenses.

Duration 1 year (the first year of graduate school), followed by a summer internship at 1 of the offices of Credit Suisse. Students who successfully complete the internship and accept an office of full-time employment with the firm are eligible for a second year of funding.

Additional information Offices of Credit Suisse are located in Chicago, Houston, Los Angeles, New York, and San Francisco.

Number awarded 1 or more each year.

Deadline November of each year.

[818]
CREW NETWORK FOUNDATION SCHOLARSHIP PROGRAM

Commercial Real Estate Women (CREW) Network
Attn: Foundation
1201 Wakarusa Drive, Suite D
Lawrence, KS 66049
(785) 832-1808   Fax: (785) 832-1551
E-mail: crewnetwork@crewnetwork.org
Web: www.crewnetwork.org/scholarship.aspx

Summary To provide financial assistance to women who are attending college to prepare for a career in commercial real estate.

Eligibility This program is open to women who are enrolled as full-time juniors, seniors, or graduate students at a college or university that has an accredited real estate program. If their institution does not have a real estate program, they may be studying another field, as long as they are preparing for a career in commercial real estate. They must have a GPA of 3.0 or higher and be U.S. or Canadian citizens. Along with their application, undergraduates must submit a brief statement about their interest in commercial real estate and their career objectives; graduate students must submit a statement that explains why they are interested in the commercial real estate industry, their experiences and insights into that industry and how those have impacted them, the impact they expect to make in the commercial real estate industry, and how their long-term career objectives make them uniquely qualified for this scholarship. Selection is based on those statements, academic record, commitment to a career within the commercial real estate industry, extracurricular activities, history of employment, personal and professional references, practical experience in the field, and accomplishments.

Financial data The stipend is $5,000.

Duration 1 year.

Additional information This program includes the Jane Ayers Wooley Memorial Scholarship, the Goldie B. Wolfe Miller Women Leaders in Real Estate Initiative Scholarship, and the Prudential Real Estate Investors Scholarship.

Number awarded 10 each year.

Deadline April of each year.

[819]
CYNTHIA HUNT-LINES SCHOLARSHIP

Minnesota Nurses Association
Attn: Minnesota Nurses Association Foundation
345 Randolph Avenue, Suite 200
St. Paul, MN 55102-3610
(651) 414-2822   Toll Free: (800) 536-4662, ext. 122
Fax: (651) 695-7000   E-mail: linda.owens@mnnurses.org
Web: www.mnnurses.org

Summary To provide financial assistance to members of the Minnesota Nurses Association (MNA) and the Minnesota Student Nurses Association (MSNA) who are single parents and interested in working on a baccalaureate or master's degree in nursing.

Eligibility This program is open to MNA and MSNA members who are enrolled or entering a baccalaureate or master's program in nursing in Minnesota or North Dakota. Applicants must be single parents, at least 21 years of age, with at least

1 dependent. Along with their application, they must submit: a current transcript; a short essay describing their interest in nursing, their long-range career goals, and how their continuing education will have an impact on the profession of nursing in Minnesota; a description of their financial need; and 2 letters of support.

Financial data The stipend is $5,000 per year.

Duration 1 year; may be renewed 1 additional year.

Number awarded 1 each year.

Deadline May of each year.

[820]
D. ANITA SMALL SCIENCE AND BUSINESS SCHOLARSHIP

Business and Professional Women of Maryland
Attn: BPW Foundation of Maryland
c/o Joyce Draper, Chief Financial Officer
615 Fairview Avenue
Frederick, MD 21701
Web: www.bpwmaryland.org/bpwmd.asp

Summary To provide financial assistance to women in Maryland who are interested in working on an undergraduate or graduate degree in a science or business-related field.

Eligibility This program is open to women who are at least 21 years of age and have been accepted to a bachelor's or advanced degree program at an accredited Maryland academic institution. Applicants must be preparing for a career in 1 of the following or a related field: business administration, computer sciences, engineering, mathematics, medical sciences (including nursing, laboratory technology, therapy, etc.), or physical sciences. They must have a GPA of 3.0 or higher. Along with their application, they must submit a 200-word statement on how they expect the proposed training or education to add to their opportunities for advancement or employment. Selection is based on that statement, academic performance, work experience, community service, volunteer experience, and financial need.

Financial data The stipend is $1,500.

Duration 1 year.

Number awarded 1 or more each year.

Deadline April of each year.

[821]
DASSAULT FALCON SCHOLARSHIP

Women in Aviation International
Attn: Scholarships
Morningstar Airport
3647 State Route 503 South
West Alexandria, OH 45381-9354
(937) 839-4647   Fax: (937) 839-4645
E-mail: scholarships@wai.org
Web: www.wai.org

Summary To provide financial assistance to women who are working on an undergraduate or graduate degree in a field related to aviation.

Eligibility This program is open to women who are working on an undergraduate or graduate degree in an aviation-related field. Applicants must be U.S. citizens, be fluent in English, and have a GPA of 3.0 or higher. Along with their application, they must submit a 500-word essay and professional resume that include their aviation history and goals,

what they have done for themselves to achieve their goals, where they see themselves in 5 and 10 years, involvement in aviation activities, how the scholarship will help them achieve their objectives, and their present financial need.

Financial data The stipend is $1,000.

Duration 1 year.

Additional information Women in Aviation International is a nonprofit professional organization dedicated to encouraging women to consider an aviation career and to providing educational outreach activities and networking resources to women active in the industry. This program is sponsored by Dassault Falcon Jet Corporation.

Number awarded 1 each year.

Deadline November of each year.

[822]
DAUGHTERS OF PENELOPE GRADUATE STUDENT SCHOLARSHIPS

Daughters of Penelope
Attn: Daughters of Penelope Foundation, Inc.
1909 Q Street, N.W., Suite 500
Washington, DC 20009-1007
(202) 234-9741   Fax: (202) 483-6983
E-mail: president@dopfoundationinc.com
Web: www.dopfoundationinc.com/scholarships/apply

Summary To provide financial assistance for graduate school to women of Greek descent.

Eligibility This program is open to women who have been members of the Daughters of Penelope or the Maids of Athena for at least 2 years, or whose parents or grandparents have been members of the Daughters of Penelope or the Order of AHEPA for at least 2 years. Applicants must be accepted or currently enrolled for a minimum of 9 units per academic year in an M.A., M.S., M.B.A., Ph.D., D.D.S., M.D., or other graduate degree program. They must have taken the GRE or other entrance examination (or Canadian, Greek, or Cypriot equivalent) and must write an essay (in English) about their educational and vocational goals. Selection is based on academic merit.

Financial data Stipends are $2,500 or $1,000.

Duration 1 year; nonrenewable.

Additional information This program includes the Dorothy Lillian Quincey Memorial Graduate Scholarship, the Big Five Graduate Scholarship, and the Sonja Stefanadis Graduate Scholarship.

Number awarded Varies each year; recently, 3 of these scholarships (1 at $2,500 and 2 at $1,000) were awarded.

Deadline May of each year.

[823]
DAVE CALDWELL SCHOLARSHIP

American Water Works Association
Attn: Scholarship Coordinator
6666 West Quincy Avenue
Denver, CO 80235-3098
(303) 794-7771   Toll Free: (800) 926-7337
Fax: (303) 347-0804   E-mail: scholarships@awwa.org
Web: www.awwa.org

Summary To provide financial assistance to outstanding minority and female students interested in working on a graduate degree in the field of water supply and treatment.

Eligibility This program is open to minority and female students working on a graduate degree in the field of water supply and treatment at a college or university in Canada, Guam, Mexico, Puerto Rico, or the United States. Students who have been accepted into graduate school but have not yet begun graduate study are encouraged to apply. Applicants must submit a 2-page resume, official transcripts, 3 letters of recommendation, a proposed curriculum of study, a 1-page statement of educational plans and career objectives demonstrating an interest in the drinking water field, and a 3-page proposed plan of research. Selection is based on academic record and potential to provide leadership in applied research and consulting in the drinking water field.

Financial data The stipend is $10,000.

Duration 1 year; nonrenewable.

Additional information Funding for this program comes from the engineering firm Brown and Caldwell.

Number awarded 1 each year.

Deadline January of each year.

[824]
DAVID EATON SCHOLARSHIP

Unitarian Universalist Association
Attn: Ministerial Credentialing Office
24 Farnsworth Street
Boston, MA 02210-1409
(617) 948-6403   Fax: (617) 742-2875
E-mail: mcoadministrator@uua.org
Web: www.uua.org

Summary To provide financial assistance to minority women preparing for the Unitarian Universalist (UU) ministry.

Eligibility This program is open to women from historically marginalized groups who are currently enrolled or planning to enroll full or at least half time in a UU ministerial training program with aspirant or candidate status. Applicants must be citizens of the United States or Canada. Priority is given first to those who have demonstrated outstanding ministerial ability and secondarily to students with the greatest financial need (especially persons of color).

Financial data The stipend ranges from $1,000 to $15,000 per year.

Duration 1 year.

Number awarded 1 or 2 each year.

Deadline April of each year.

[825]
DELAYED EDUCATION SCHOLARSHIP FOR WOMEN

American Nuclear Society
Attn: Scholarship Coordinator
555 North Kensington Avenue
La Grange Park, IL 60526-5535
(708) 352-6611   Toll Free: (800) 323-3044
Fax: (708) 352-0499   E-mail: outreach@ans.org
Web: committees.ans.org/need/apply.html

Summary To provide financial assistance to mature women whose formal studies in nuclear science or nuclear engineering have been delayed or interrupted.

Eligibility Applicants must be mature women who have experienced at least a 1-year delay or interruption of their undergraduate studies and are returning to school to work on

an undergraduate or graduate degree in nuclear science or nuclear engineering. They must be members of the American Nuclear Society (ANS), but they may be citizens of any country. Along with their application, they must submit an essay on their academic and professional goals, experiences that have affected those goals, and other relevant information. Selection is based on that essay, academic achievement, letters of recommendation, and financial need.

Financial data The stipend is $5,000. Funds may be used by the student to cover any educational expense, including tuition, books, room, and board.

Duration 1 year; nonrenewable.

Number awarded 1 each year.

Deadline January of each year.

[826]
DELTA KAPPA GAMMA SCHOLARSHIP PROGRAM

Delta Kappa Gamma Society International
Attn: Scholarships Committee
416 West 12th Street
P.O. Box 1589
Austin, TX 78767-1589
(512) 478-5748   Toll Free: (888) 762-4685
Fax: (512) 478-3961   E-mail: societyoper@dkg.org
Web: www.dkg.org/category/committee/scholarship

Summary To provide financial assistance to members of Delta Kappa Gamma Society International from any country interested in graduate study or research.

Eligibility Applicants must have been members in good standing of the Delta Kappa Gamma Society International (an honorary society of women educators) for at least 3 years, have completed a bachelor's degree or equivalent, and have been accepted and enrolled in a graduate program at a nationally accredited institution of higher education, preferably working on a doctoral degree. Along with their application, they must submit a 500-word impact statement that describes the area of their intended study or major interest, the potential benefits of the degree to them professionally, and the potential benefits of the degree to Delta Kappa Gamma. Selection is based on that statement (30 points), active participation and demonstrated leadership in Delta Kappa Gamma (20 points), recognitions for achievement (10 points), professional work experience (10 points), current status of program (10 points), prior education (10 points), and recommendations (10 points).

Financial data The stipend is $6,000 for master's degree students or $10,000 for doctoral students.

Duration 1 year.

Additional information Delta Kappa Gamma Society International has 170,000 members in 13 countries and is the largest organization of its kind. This program includes the following named awards: the Marjorie Jeanne Allen Scholarship, the Mamie Sue Bastian Scholarship, the Annie Webb Blanton Scholarship, the Blanton Centennial Scholarship, the A. Margaret Boyd Scholarship, the Edna McGuire Boyd Scholarship, the Eula Lee Carter Scholarship, the Delta Kappa Gamma Founders Scholarship, the Delta Kappa Gamma Golden Anniversary Scholarship, the Delta Kappa Gamma 60th Anniversary Scholarship, the Delta Kappa Gamma 70th Anniversary Scholarship, the Zora Ellis Scholarship, the Emma Giles Scholarship, the Carolyn Guss Scholarship, the Ola B. Hiller Scholarship, the Eunah Temple Holden Scholarship, the Dr. Evelyn L. Milam Scholarships, the Berneta Minkwitz Scholarship, the Lois and Marguerite Morse Scholarship, the Catherine Nutterville Scholarship, the Alida W. Parker Scholarship, the J. Maria Pierce Scholarship, the Emma Reinhart Scholarship, the Norma Bristow Salter Scholarship, the Maycie K. Southall Scholarship, the M. Margaret Stroh Scholarship, the Letti P. Trefz Scholarship, the Mary Frances White Scholarship, the Hazel Johnson Memorial Scholarship (even-numbered years only), and the Mary Katherine Shoup Scholarship (odd-numbered years only). Recipients must remain active members of Delta Kappa Gamma, work full time on the study or research outlined in their applications, submit reports requested by the society, and acknowledge assistance of the society in any publication that results from data gathered while the award was being used.

Number awarded Up to 30 each year.

Deadline January of each year.

[827]
DELTA SIGMA THETA SORORITY GENERAL SCHOLARSHIPS

Delta Sigma Theta Sorority, Inc.
Attn: Scholarship and Standards Committee Chair
1707 New Hampshire Avenue, N.W.
Washington, DC 20009
(202) 986-2400   Fax: (202) 986-2513
E-mail: dstemail@deltasigmatheta.org
Web: www.deltasigmatheta.org

Summary To provide financial assistance to members of Delta Sigma Theta who are working on an undergraduate or graduate degree in any field.

Eligibility This program is open to active, dues-paying members of Delta Sigma Theta who are currently enrolled in college or graduate school. Applicants must submit an essay on their major goals and educational objectives, including realistic steps they foresee as necessary for the fulfillment of their plans. Financial need is considered in the selection process.

Financial data The stipends range from $1,000 to $2,000. The funds may be used to cover tuition, fees, and living expenses.

Duration 1 year; may be renewed for 1 additional year.

Additional information This sponsor is a traditionally-African American social sorority. The application fee is $20.

Number awarded Varies each year.

Deadline March of each year.

[828]
DOCTORAL DISSERTATION IMPROVEMENT GRANTS IN THE DIRECTORATE FOR BIOLOGICAL SCIENCES

National Science Foundation
Directorate for Biological Sciences
Attn: Division of Environmental Biology
4201 Wilson Boulevard
Arlington, VA 22230
(703) 292-8480   TDD: (800) 281-8749
E-mail: ddig-deb@nsf.gov
Web: www.nsf.gov

Summary To provide partial support for dissertation research in selected areas supported by the National Science Foundation (NSF) Directorate for Biological Sciences (DBS).

Eligibility Applications may be submitted through regular university channels by dissertation advisers on behalf of graduate students who have advanced to candidacy and have begun or are about to begin dissertation research. Students must be enrolled at U.S. institutions but need not be U.S. citizens. Proposals should focus on the ecology, ecosystems, systematics, or population biology programs in the DBS Division of Environmental Biology, or the animal behavior programs in the DBS Division of Integrative Organismal Systems. In the selection process, consideration is given to the achievement of societally relevant outcomes, including full participation of women, persons with disabilities, and underrepresented minorities.

Financial data Grants range up to $13,000; funds may be used for travel to specialized facilities or field research locations, specialized research equipment, purchase of supplies and services not otherwise available, fees for computerized or other forms of data, and rental of environmental chambers or other research facilities. Funding is not provided for stipends, tuition, textbooks, journals, allowances for dependents, travel to scientific meetings, publication costs, dissertation preparation or reproduction, or indirect costs.

Duration Normally 2 years.

Number awarded 100 to 120 each year; approximately $1,600,000 is available for this program each year.

Deadline October of each year.

[829]
DONNA HIEKEN DOCTORAL GRANT

Sigma Alpha Iota Philanthropies, Inc.
One Tunnel Road
Asheville, NC 28805
(828) 251-0606   Fax: (828) 251-0644
E-mail: nh@sai-national.org
Web: app.smarterselect.com

Summary To provide funding for doctoral research in music to members of Sigma Alpha Iota (an organization of women musicians).

Eligibility This program is open to members of the organization who are enrolled in a program leading to a doctoral degree. They must be conducting doctoral research on music education, music therapy, musicology, ethnomusicology, music theory, psychology of music, or applied research (including performance or pedagogy).

Financial data The grant is $2,500 per year.

Duration 1 year.

Number awarded 1 each year.

Deadline March of each year.

[830]
DOREEN MCMULLAN MCCARTHY MEMORIAL ACADEMIC SCHOLARSHIP FOR WOMEN WITH BLEEDING DISORDERS

National Hemophilia Foundation
Attn: Victory for Women Program
7 Penn Plaza
370 Seventh Avenue, Suite 1204
New York, NY 10001
(212) 328-3700   Toll Free: (800) 42-HANDI, ext. 2
Fax: (212) 328-3777   E-mail: sroger@hemophilia.org
Web: www.hemophilia.org

Summary To provide financial assistance for college or graduate school to women who have a bleeding disorder.

Eligibility This program is open to women who are entering or already enrolled in an undergraduate or graduate program at a university, college, or accredited vocational school. Applicants must have von Willebrand Disease, hemophilia or other clotting factor deficiency, platelet disorder, or carrier status. Along with their application, they must submit a 250-word essay that describes how their education and future career plans will benefit others in the bleeding disorders community. Selection is based on that essay, achievements, and community service to the bleeding disorders community.

Financial data The stipend is $2,500.

Duration 1 year.

Additional information The program, known also as V4W, was established in 2005 as the Project Red Flag Academic Scholarship for Women with Bleeding and later named the Victory for Women Academic Scholarship for Women with Bleeding Disorders.

Number awarded 1 each year.

Deadline March of each year.

[831]
DORIS BALLANCE ORMAN, '25, FELLOWSHIP

Gallaudet University Alumni Association
Attn: Graduate Fellowship Fund Committee
Peikoff Alumni House
Gallaudet University
800 Florida Avenue, N.E.
Washington, DC 20002-3695
(202) 651-5060   Fax: (202) 651-5062
TDD: (202) 651-5060
E-mail: alumni.relations@gallaudet.edu
Web: www.gallaudet.edu

Summary To provide financial assistance to deaf women who wish to work on a graduate degree at universities for people who hear normally.

Eligibility This program is open to deaf or hard of hearing women graduates of Gallaudet University or other accredited academic institutions who have been accepted for graduate study at colleges or universities for people who hear normally. Applicants must be working full time on a doctorate or other terminal degree. They must have a particular interest in the arts, the humanities, or community leadership. Financial need is considered in the selection process.

Financial data The amount awarded varies, depending upon the needs of the recipient and the availability of funds.

Duration 1 year; may be renewed.

Additional information This program is 1 of 12 designated funds within the Graduate Fellowship Fund of the Gallaudet University Alumni Association.

Number awarded Up to 1 each year.

Deadline April of each year.

[832]
DORIS HERTSGAARD SCHOLARSHIP

Fargo-Moorhead Area Foundation
Attn: Finance/Program Assistant
502 First Avenue North, Suite 202
Fargo, ND 58102-4804
(701) 234-0756   Fax: (701) 234-9724
E-mail: Cher@areafoundation.org
Web: www.areafoundation.org/index.php/scholarships

Summary To provide financial assistance to women from any state who are working on an undergraduate or graduate degree in a mathematics-related field at specified colleges and universities in Minnesota or North Dakota.

Eligibility This program is open to women from any state who are currently enrolled at Concordia University, Minnesota State University at Moorhead, or North Dakota State University. Applicants must be working on an undergraduate or graduate degree with a mathematics component (e.g., computer science, engineering, mathematics, physical science, statistics). Along with their application, they must submit a 2-page essay on their professional goals and how those relate to their academic interest in their mathematical field of study. Financial need is considered in the selection process, but greater emphasis is placed on academic achievement. Preference is given to women who are single parents with pre-teenage children.

Financial data A stipend is awarded (amount not specified).

Duration 1 year.

Number awarded 1 or more each year.

Deadline April of each year.

[833]
DOROTHY COOKE WHINERY MUSIC BUSINESS/ TECHNOLOGY SCHOLARSHIP

Sigma Alpha Iota Philanthropies, Inc.
One Tunnel Road
Asheville, NC 28805
(828) 251-0606   Fax: (828) 251-0644
E-mail: nh@sai-national.org
Web: app.smarterselect.com

Summary To provide financial assistance to members of Sigma Alpha Iota (an organization of women musicians) working on a degree in music, business, or technology.

Eligibility This program is open to members of the organization enrolled as undergraduate or graduate students. Applicants must be working on a degree in the field of music business or music technology, including music marketing, music business administration, entertainment industry, commercial music, recording and production, music management, or other related fields. They must have a GPA of 3.0 or higher. Along with their application, they must submit a statement of purpose that includes their career goals.

Financial data The stipend is $2,000.

Duration 1 year.

Additional information This program began in 2003.
Number awarded 1 each year.
Deadline March of each year.

[834]
DOROTHY E. SCHOELZEL MEMORIAL SCHOLARSHIP

General Federation of Women's Clubs of Connecticut
c/o Joan Duffy, President
2 Quincy Close
Ridgfield, CT 06877
E-mail: duffy-gfwc@appsolutions.com
Web: www.gfwcct.org

Summary To provide financial assistance to women in Connecticut who are working on an undergraduate or graduate degree in education.

Eligibility This program is open to female residents of Connecticut who have completed at least 3 years of college. Applicants must have a GPA of 3.0 or higher and be working on a bachelor's or master's degree in education. They must be U.S. citizens. Selection is based on academic ability, future promise, and financial need.

Financial data The stipend is $2,000.

Duration 1 year.

Number awarded 1 each year.

Deadline February of each year.

[835]
DOROTHY L. WELLER PEO SCHOLARSHIP

P.E.O. Foundation-California State Chapter
c/o Marilyn Bauriedel, Weller Scholarship Fund
3673 South Court
Palo Alto, CA 94306
E-mail: peoca.dlw@gmail.com
Web: www.peocalifornia.org

Summary To provide financial assistance for law school or paralegal studies to women in California.

Eligibility This program is open to female residents of California who have been admitted to an accredited law school or a licensed paralegal school. Applicants must have completed 4 years of high school and be able to demonstrate excellence in academic ability, character, integrity, and school activities. Financial need is also considered in the selection process. U.S. citizenship is required.

Financial data Recently, the stipend was $2,500.

Duration 1 year.

Number awarded Varies each year; recently, 4 were awarded.

Deadline January of each year.

[836]
DOYNE M. GREEN SCHOLARSHIP

Seattle Foundation
Attn: Scholarship Administrator
1200 Fifth Avenue, Suite 1300
Seattle, WA 98101-3151
(206) 515-2119   Fax: (206) 622-7673
E-mail: scholarships@seattlefoundation.org
Web: www.washboard.org

Summary To provide financial assistance to women in Washington working on a graduate degree in law, medicine, or social and public services at a school in any state.

Eligibility This program is open to female residents of Washington who have completed the first year of a graduate program in law, medicine, or social and public services at a school in any state. Applicants must be able to demonstrate financial need. Along with their application, they must submit a brief statement on their plans as they relate to their educational and career objectives and long-term goals.

Financial data The stipend is $4,000.

Duration 1 year; nonrenewable.

Number awarded 8 each year.

Deadline February of each year.

[837]
DR. B. OLIVE COLE GRADUATE EDUCATIONAL GRANT

Lambda Kappa Sigma Pharmacy Fraternity
Attn: Educational Trust
S77 W16906 Casey Drive
P.O. Box 570
Muskego, WI 53150-0570
Toll Free: (800) LKS-1913   Fax: (262) 679-4558
E-mail: lks@lks.org
Web: www.lks.org

Summary To provide financial assistance to members of Lambda Kappa Sigma who are interested in working on an advanced degree.

Eligibility This program is open to members of Lambda Kappa Sigma who are enrolled in a program of graduate study and research that will advance their career. Eligible programs include master's or doctoral degrees (e.g., M.S., M.A., M.B.A., M.P.H., Ph.D., J.D., Dr.P.H.) as well as joint degree programs that combine the Pharm.D. degree with master's or doctoral studies. Applicants must have an initial degree in pharmacy. They must rank in the upper half of their class and be able to demonstrate financial need. Studies may be at institutions that do not offer the Pharm.D. or have a chapter of Lambda Kappa Sigma.

Financial data The stipend is $1,000.

Duration 1 year.

Additional information This program began in 1972. Lambda Kappa Sigma was founded in 1913 to promote the profession of pharmacy among women. Although some of its chapters are now coeducational, it still emphasizes women's health issues.

Number awarded 1 each year.

Deadline January of each year.

[838]
DR. BESSIE ELIZABETH DELANEY FELLOWSHIP

National Dental Association
Attn: National Dental Association Foundation, Inc.
3517 16th Street, N.W.
Washington, DC 20010
(734) 544-1336   E-mail: admin@ndaonline.org
Web: www.ndafoundation.org

Summary To provide financial assistance to women who are members of minority groups and interested in working on a postdoctoral degree in fields related to dentistry.

Eligibility This program is open to female members of minority groups who are working on a postdoctoral degree in an area related to dentistry, such as public health, administration, pediatrics, research, or law. Students working on a master's degree beyond their residency may be considered. Applicants must be members of the National Dental Association (NDA) and U.S. citizens or permanent residents. Along with their application, they must submit a letter explaining why they should be considered for this scholarship, 2 letters of recommendation, a curriculum vitae, a description of the program, nomination by their program director, and documentation of financial need.

Financial data The stipend is $10,000.

Duration 1 year.

Additional information This program, established in 1990, is supported by the Colgate-Palmolive Company.

Number awarded 1 each year.

Deadline May of each year.

[839]
DR. DAVID B. ALLMAN MEDICAL SCHOLARSHIPS

The Miss America Foundation
1432 K Street, N.W., Suite 900
Washington, DC 20005
(609) 344-1800
Web: www.missamericafoundation.org/scholarships

Summary To provide financial assistance to medical students who have competed or are competing in the Miss America contest at any level.

Eligibility This program is open to women who have competed in the Miss America competition at least once, at any level of competition, within the past 10 years. Applicants do not have to apply during the year they competed; they may apply any year following as long as they are attending or accepted by a medical school and plan to become a medical doctor. They must submit an essay, up to 500 words, on why they wish to become a medical doctor and how this scholarship can help them attain that goal. Selection is based on GPA, class rank, MCAT score, extracurricular activities, financial need, and level of participation within the system.

Financial data The stipend is $7,500.

Duration 1 year.

Additional information This scholarship was established in 1974.

Number awarded 1 each year.

Deadline June of each year.

[840]
DR. DORRI PHIPPS FELLOWSHIPS

Alpha Kappa Alpha Sorority, Inc.
Attn: Educational Advancement Foundation
5656 South Stony Island Avenue
Chicago, IL 60637
(773) 947-0026   Toll Free: (800) 653-6528
Fax: (773) 947-0277   E-mail: akaeaf@akaeaf.net
Web: www.akaeaf.org/fellowships_endowments.htm

Summary To provide financial assistance to students (especially African American women) working on a degree in medicine or conducting research related to lupus.

Eligibility This program is open to students currently enrolled in a medical or related program in any state. Applicants must be working on a degree in medicine or conducting research related to lupus. Along with their application, they must submit 1) a list of honors, awards, and scholarships received; 2) a list of organizations in which they have memberships, especially minority organizations; 3) a description of the project or research on which they are currently working, of (if they are not involved in a project or research) the aspects of their field that interest them; and 4) a statement of their personal and career goals, including how this scholarship will enhance their ability to attain those goals. The sponsor is a traditionally African American women's sorority.

Financial data A stipend is awarded (amount not specified).

Duration 1 year.

Number awarded Varies each even-numbered year; recently, 5 were awarded.

Deadline April of each even-numbered year.

[841]
DR. JOAN SHELLEY W. FERNANDEZ POINT SCHOLARSHIP

Point Foundation
Attn: Selections and Scholar Support Manager
5055 Wilshire Boulevard, Suite 501
Los Angeles, CA 90036
(323) 933-1234   Toll Free: (866) 33-POINT
Fax: (866) 39-POINT
E-mail: applications@pointfoundation.org
Web: www.pointfoundation.org/currentnamedscholarships

Summary To provide financial assistance to lesbians interested in working on a master's degree to prepare for a career as a theater director.

Eligibility This program is open to lesbians of any age who are interested in working on a master's degree to prepare for a career as a theater director. There are no citizenship requirements; both international and undocumented students are eligible. Selection is based on academic achievement, personal merit, leadership, involvement in the LGBTQ community, professional experiences, personal and future goals, and financial need.

Financial data Stipends recently averaged more than $30,000.

Duration 1 year; may be renewed.

Number awarded 1 in years when funding is available.

Deadline January of each year.

[842]
DR. MARIE E. ZAKRZEWSKI MEDICAL SCHOLARSHIP

Kosciuszko Foundation
Attn: Grants Department
15 East 65th Street
New York, NY 10021-6595
(212) 734-2130, ext. 210   Fax: (212) 628-4552
E-mail: addy@thekf.org
Web: www.thekf.org/scholarships/tuition/mzms

Summary To provide financial assistance to women of Polish ancestry studying medicine.

Eligibility This program is open to young women of Polish ancestry entering their first, second, or third year of study at an accredited medical school in the United States. Applicants must be U.S. citizens of Polish descent or Polish citizens with permanent resident status in the United States. They must have a GPA of 3.0 or higher. First preference is given to residents of Massachusetts. If no candidates from Massachusetts apply, qualified residents of New England are considered. Selection is based on academic excellence; the applicant's academic achievements, interests, and motivation; the applicant's interest in Polish subjects or involvement in the Polish American community; and financial need.

Financial data The stipend is $3,500.

Duration 1 year; nonrenewable.

Additional information This program is funded by the Massachusetts Federation of Polish Women's Clubs but administered by the Kosciuszko Foundation. The application fee is $35.

Number awarded 1 each year.

Deadline January of each year.

[843]
DR. MARY FEENEY BONAWITZ SCHOLARSHIP

Accounting and Financial Women's Alliance
Attn: Educational Foundation
2365 Harrodsburg Road, A325
Lexington, KY 40504
(859) 219-3532   Toll Free: (800) 326-2163
Fax: (859) 219-3577   E-mail: foundation@afwa.org
Web: www.afwa.org/foundation/scholarships

Summary To provide funding for research to members of the Accounting and Financial Women's Alliance (AFWA) working on a doctoral degree in accounting.

Eligibility This program is open to AFWA members who are currently enrolled in an AASCB-accredited Ph.D. program in accounting. Applicants must be seeking funding for research costs (such as measurement instruments and analysis, uses of financial databases, copying, and telecommunications expenses). Along with their application, they must submit an essay of 150 to 250 words on their reasons for working on a Ph.D. in accounting and how they would advocate for women in the accounting profession if they receive this scholarship. Selection is based on leadership, character, communication skills, scholastic average, and financial need. Applications must be submitted to a local AFWA chapter.

Financial data The grant is $1,000.

Duration 1 year.

Number awarded 1 each year.

Deadline Local chapters must submit their candidates to the national office by February of each year.

[844]
DR. NANCY FOSTER SCHOLARSHIP PROGRAM

National Oceanic and Atmospheric Administration
Attn: Office of National Marine Sanctuaries
1305 East-West Highway
N/ORM 6 SSMC4, Room 11146
Silver Spring, MD 20910
(301) 713-7245   Fax: (301) 713-9465
E-mail: fosterscholars@noaa.gov
Web: fosterscholars.noaa.gov/aboutscholarship.html

Summary To provide financial assistance to graduate students, especially minorities and women, who are interested in working on a degree in fields related to marine sciences.

Eligibility This program is open to U.S. citizens, particularly women and members of minority groups, currently working on or intending to work on a master's or doctoral degree in oceanography, marine biology, or maritime archaeology, including all science, engineering, and resource management of ocean and coastal areas. Applicants must submit a description of their academic, research, and career goals, and how their proposed course of study or research will help them to achieve those goals. They must be enrolled full time and have a GPA of 3.3 or higher. As part of their program, they must be interested in participating in a summer research collaboration at a facility of the National Oceanic and Atmospheric Administration (NOAA). Selection is based on academic record and a statement of career goals and objectives (20%); quality of project and applicability to program priorities (30%); recommendations and/or endorsements (15%); additional relevant experience related to diversity of education, extracurricular activities, honors and awards, written and oral communication skills, and interpersonal skills (20%); and financial need (15%).

Financial data The program provides a stipend of $30,000 per academic year, a tuition allowance of up to $12,000 per academic year, and up to $10,000 of support for a 4- to 6-week research collaboration at a NOAA facility is provided.

Duration Master's degree students may receive up to 2 years of stipend and tuition support and 1 research collaboration (for a total of $94,000). Doctoral students may receive up to 4 years of stipend and tuition support and 2 research collaborations (for a total of $188,000).

Additional information This program began in 2001.

Number awarded Varies each year; recently, 3 were awarded.

Deadline December of each year.

[845]
DR. ROSE M. GREEN THOMAS ACADEMIC MEDICINE SCHOLARSHIP AWARD

Black Women Physicians Educational and Research
   Foundation
Attn: Scholars Fund
P.O. Box 4502
Gary, IN 46404
(219) 616-3912
Web: www.aacom.org

Summary To provide financial assistance to minority female medical students interested in a career in academic medicine.

Eligibility This program is open to minority women currently enrolled at an accredited medical school in any state. Applicants must submit an essay of 500 to 650 words on their career goals in academic medicine. Selection is based on academic achievement, motivation for a career in academic medicine, leadership activities, and community involvement.

Financial data The stipend is $1,000.

Duration 1 year.

Number awarded 1 each year.

Deadline May of each year.

[846]
DRIVE TO SUCCEED SCHOLARSHIP

General Motors Corporation
Women's Retail Network
c/o Charitable Management Systems, Inc.
P.O. Box 648
Naperville, IL 60566
(630) 428-2412   Fax: (630) 428-2695
E-mail: wrnscholarshipinfo@gmsac.com
Web: www.gmsac.com

Summary To provide financial assistance to women attending college or graduate school to prepare for a retail automotive career.

Eligibility This program is open to women who are enrolled full time in undergraduate, graduate, and nontraditional continuing education institutions that offer degrees in the automotive retail and/or automotive service field. Applicants must be interested in preparing for a career in automotive retail and/or service management. They may also be currently employees of an automotive dealership and enrolled in an educational institution that offers formal programs or certifications that advance their career within automotive retail. Applicants must be citizens of the United States or have the ability to accept permanent employment in the United States without the need for visa sponsorship now or in the future. Along with their application, they must submit an essay of 500 to 750 words on their interest and motivation for a career in the automotive retail and/or automotive service sector. Selection is based on that statement, academic performance, leadership and participation in school and community activities, work experience, career and educational aspirations, and financial need.

Financial data The stipend is $5,000 per year.

Duration 1 year; recipients may reapply.

Additional information This program began in 2011.

Number awarded Varies each year; recently, 6 were awarded.

Deadline April of each year.

[847]
EDITH SEVILLE COALE SCHOLARSHIPS

Zonta Club of Washington, D.C.
Attn: Scholarship Committee
P.O. Box 9753
Washington, DC 20016
E-mail: Foundation@zontawashingtondc.org
Web: www.zontawashingtondc.org

Summary To provide financial assistance to women who have completed the first year of medical school in the Washington, D.C. area.

Eligibility This program is open to women from any state who are in the second, third, or fourth year of medical school in the Washington, D.C. area. Selection is based on financial need and scholastic achievement.

Financial data Stipends range from $5,000 to $8,000.

Duration 1 year.

Additional information The trust fund contains limited funds. Awards are not made for the first year of medical school. Preference is given to women students nominated by medical school faculty members.

Number awarded Varies each year; recently, 6 were awarded.

Deadline March of each year.

[848]
EDNA FURBUR FELLOWSHIP

American Indian Graduate Center
Attn: Executive Director
3701 San Mateo Boulevard, N.E., Suite 200
Albuquerque, NM 87110-1249
(505) 881-4584   Toll Free: (800) 628-1920
Fax: (505) 884-0427   E-mail: fellowships@aigc.com
Web: www.aigcs.org/scholarships/graduate-fellowships

Summary To provide financial assistance to female Native American graduate students interested in working on a degree related to the arts.

Eligibility This program is open to women who are enrolled members of federally-recognized American Indian tribes and Alaska Native groups or who can document one-fourth degree federally-recognized Indian blood. Applicants must be enrolled full time in a graduate program in the creative fine arts, visual works, crafts, music, performing, dance, literary arts, creative writing, or poetry. Along with their application, they must submit a 500-word essay on how receiving this fellowship will enable them to continue to build, promote, and honor self-sustaining American Indian and Alaska Native communities. Financial need is also considered in the selection process.

Financial data Stipends range from $500 to $5,000 per academic year, depending on the availability of funds and the recipient's unmet financial need.

Duration 1 year; may be renewed.

Number awarded 1 each year.

Deadline May of each year.

[849]
EDUCATIONAL FOUNDATION FOR WOMEN IN ACCOUNTING IMA GRADUATE SCHOLARSHIP

Educational Foundation for Women in Accounting
Attn: Foundation Administrator
136 South Keowee Street
Dayton, OH 45402
(937) 424-3391   Fax: (937) 222-5749
E-mail: info@efwa.org
Web: www.efwa.org/scholarships_graduate.php

Summary To provide financial support to women who are entering a graduate program in accounting.

Eligibility This program is open to women who are entering a master's degree program in accounting at an accredited college or university. Selection is based on aptitude for accounting and business, commitment to the goal of working on a degree in accounting (including evidence of continued commitment after receiving this award), clear evidence that the candidate has established goals and a plan for achieving those goals (both personal and professional), and financial need. U.S. citizenship is required.

Financial data The stipend is $1,000. Winners also receive a CMA Learning System kit (worth $745) and a complimentary 1-year student membership to the Institute of Management Accountants (IMA).

Duration 1 year.

Additional information This program is funded by the IMA.

Number awarded 1 each year.

Deadline April of each year.

[850]
E.K. WISE SCHOLARSHIP FUND

American Occupational Therapy Association
Attn: Membership Department
4720 Montgomery Lane, Suite 200
Bethesda, MD 20824-3449
(301) 652-6611, ext. 2769   Fax: (240) 762-5150
TDD: (800) 377-8555   E-mail: ekwise@aota.org
Web: www.aota.org

Summary To provide financial assistance to female members of the American Occupational Therapy Association (AOTA) who are working on a professional master's degree in occupational therapy.

Eligibility This program is open to women who are AOTA members working full time on a professional post-baccalaureate occupational therapy degree. Applicants must be able to demonstrate a sustained record of outstanding scholastic performance, demonstrated leadership, and community service. Along with their application, they must submit an essay (up to 1,000 words) on how they can contribute to meeting the AOTA objective of developing a well-prepared, diverse workforce. Financial need is considered in the selection process. U.S. citizenship or permanent resident status is required.

Financial data The stipend is $2,500 per year.

Duration 1 year; may be renewed 1 additional year.

Additional information This fund was established in 1969 as the E.K. Wise Loan Program. In 2008, the AOTA converted it to a scholarship program.

Number awarded 3 each year.

Deadline May of each year.

[851]
ELIZABETH MUNSTERBERG KOPPITZ CHILD PSYCHOLOGY GRADUATE FELLOWSHIPS

American Psychological Foundation
750 First Street, N.E.
Washington, DC 20002-4242
(202) 336-5843   Fax: (202) 336-5812
E-mail: foundation@apa.org
Web: www.apa.org/apf/funding/koppitz.aspx

Summary To provide funding to doctoral students interested in conducting research in child psychology.

Eligibility This program is open to graduate students who have progressed academically through the qualifying examinations, usually after the third or fourth year of doctoral study. Applicants must be interested in conducting psychological research that promotes the advancement of knowledge and learning in the field of child psychology. Selection is based on conformance with stated program goals, magnitude of incremental contribution, quality of proposed work, and applicant's demonstrated scholarship and research competence. The sponsor encourages applications from individuals who represent diversity in race, ethnicity, gender, age, disability, and sexual orientation.

Financial data The grant is $25,000.

Duration 1 year.

Additional information This fellowship was first awarded in 2003.

Number awarded Varies each year; recently, 6 were selected.

Deadline November of each year.

[852]
ELLEN CUSHING SCHOLARSHIPS

American Baptist Churches USA
Attn: American Baptist Home Mission Societies
Office of Financial Aid for Studies
P.O. Box 851
Valley Forge, PA 19482-0851
(610) 768-2067   Toll Free: (800) ABC-3USA, ext. 2067
Fax: (610) 768-2470
E-mail: communications@abhms.org
Web: www.abhms.org

Summary To provide financial assistance to Baptist women interested in working on a graduate degree in human service fields.

Eligibility This program is open to female Baptists in graduate programs who are preparing for a human service career in the secular world. Applicants must be U.S. citizens who have been a member of a church affiliated with American Baptist Churches USA for at least 1 year. M.Div. and D.Min. students are not eligible. Preference is given to students active in their school, church, or region.

Financial data The stipend is $2,000.

Duration 1 year.

Number awarded Up to 3 each year.

Deadline May of each year.

[853]
ELLIOTT G. HEARD JR. MEMORIAL SCHOLARSHIP

Elliott G. Heard Jr. Memorial Scholarship Committee
P.O. Box 214
Mullica Hill, NJ 08062
(609) 202-0061   Fax: (703) 903-3690
E-mail: yhbautista@yahoo.com

Summary To provide financial assistance to students enrolled or planning to enroll at an accredited law school.

Eligibility This program is open to college seniors who have been accepted to an accredited law school and students currently enrolled in law school who are not in their final semester. Applicants must be U.S. citizens. Along with their application, they must submit a 500-word essay describing why they should be considered for this scholarship and why they decided on a career in the law. Minorities, women, and the physically challenged are especially encouraged to apply. Finalists are invited to an interview. Selection is based on academic achievement, community service, leadership, citizenship, and financial need.

Financial data The stipend is $1,000.

Duration 1 year; nonrenewable.

Additional information This program is named after the first African American jurist in Gloucester County, New Jersey.

Number awarded 2 each year.

Deadline October of each year.

[854]
ELSIE G. RIDDICK SCHOLARSHIP

Business and Professional Women of North Carolina
Attn: North Carolina Business and Professional Women's
 Foundation, Inc.
c/o Carol Ambrose, Scholarship Chair
2300 Cloister Drive
Charlotte, NC 28211
(704) 362-2066   E-mail: mcarolambrose65@gmail.com
Web: www.bpw-nc.org/Educational_Scholarship

Summary   To provide financial assistance to women attending North Carolina colleges, community colleges, or graduate schools.

Eligibility   This program is open to women who are currently enrolled in a community college, 4-year college, or graduate school in North Carolina. Applicants must be endorsed by a local BPW unit and have a GPA of 2.5 or higher. Along with their application, they must submit a 1-page statement that summarizes their career goals, previous honors, or community activities and justifies their need for this scholarship. U.S. citizenship is required.

Financial data   The stipend is $1,000. Funds are paid directly to the recipient's school.

Duration   1 year; recipients may reapply.

Additional information   This program began in 1925 as a loan fund. Since 1972 it has been administered as a scholarship program.

Number awarded   1 each year.

Deadline   April of each year.

[855]
EMERGE SCHOLARSHIPS

Emerge Scholarships, Inc.
3525 Piedmont Road, Building 5, Suite 300
Atlanta, GA 30305
(404) 760-2887   E-mail: info@emergescholarships.org
Web: www.emergescholarships.org

Summary   To provide financial assistance to women in Georgia interested in returning to college or graduate school after a delay or interruption.

Eligibility   This program is open to female residents of Georgia who are at least 25 years of age and who have interrupted or delayed their education because they are changing careers, seeking advancement in their career or work life, looking for personal growth, or returning to school after caring for children. Applicants must have been accepted as an undergraduate or graduate student at an educational institution. Along with their application, they must submit a 2-page essay on how beginning or continuing their education will positively impact their life. Selection is based on that essay, leadership and participation in community activities, honors and awards received, career and life goals, financial need, and other funding received.

Financial data   Stipends range from $2,000 to $5,000.

Duration   1 year.

Additional information   This program began in 2001. Winners are invited to Atlanta to accept their scholarships; the sponsor pays all travel expenses.

Number awarded   Varies each year; recently, 7 were awarded.

Deadline   May of each year.

[856]
EMERINE MEMORIAL SCHOLARSHIP

Columbus Foundation
Attn: Scholarship Manager
1234 East Broad Street
Columbus, OH 43205-1453
(614) 251-4000   Fax: (614) 251-4009
E-mail: aszempruch@columbusfoundation.org
Web: tcfapp.org

Summary   To provide financial assistance to women working on an undergraduate or graduate degree at a college or university in Ohio.

Eligibility   This program is open to women currently attending an accredited 4-year college or university in Ohio. Applicants may be residents of any state, although preference may be given to Ohio residents. They must meet 1 of the following stipulations: 1) returned to college as an undergraduate or graduate student after an extended absence of at least 2 years; 2) 23 years of age or older and in college for the first time or applying for graduate school for the first time with a GPA of 3.0 or higher; or 3) has completed the freshman year with a GPA of 3.0 or higher. Along with their application, they must submit their most recent transcript, 2 letters of recommendation, a list of volunteer activities, a list of extracurricular activities, a personal essay on how volunteering has impacted their life, and information on financial need.

Financial data   The stipend is $1,500.

Duration   1 year.

Number awarded   1 or more each year.

Deadline   March of each year.

[857]
EMPOWERING WOMEN IN LAW SCHOLARSHIP

The Pearce Law Firm
1429 Walnut Street, 14th Floor
Philadelphia, PA 19102
(215) 557-8686
Web: www.thepearcelawfirm.com/empowering-scholarship

Summary   To provide financial assistance to women who are currently attending law school.

Eligibility   This program is open to women who have completed at least 1 semester of law school and have a GPA of 3.0 or higher. Selection is based on essays on topics related to women in the legal community, academic achievement, school and community activities, demonstrated leadership abilities, and financial need.

Financial data   The stipend is $2,000.

Duration   1 year; nonrenewable.

Number awarded   1 each year.

Deadline   December of each year.

[858]
ENVIRONMENT AND NATURAL RESOURCES FELLOWSHIPS

Harvard University
John F. Kennedy School of Government
Belfer Center for Science and International Affairs
Attn: STPP Fellowship Coordinator
79 John F. Kennedy Street, Mailbox 53
Cambridge, MA 02138
(617) 495-1498   Fax: (617) 495-8963
E-mail: patricia_mclaughlin@hks.harvard.edu
Web: belfercenter.ksg.harvard.edu

Summary To provide funding to professionals, postdoctorates, and doctoral students interested in conducting research on environmental and natural resource issues at the Belfer Center for Science and International Affairs at Harvard University in Cambridge, Massachusetts.

Eligibility The postdoctoral fellowship is open to recent recipients of the Ph.D. or equivalent degree, university faculty members, and employees of government, military, international, humanitarian, and private research institutions who have appropriate professional experience. Applicants for predoctoral fellowships must have passed their general examinations. Scholars from a wide range of disciplinary and multi-disciplinary fields and those holding a Ph.D. in engineering or in the natural sciences are strongly encouraged to apply. The program especially encourages applications from women, minorities, and citizens of all countries. All applicants must be interested in conducting research on projects of the Environment and Natural Resources (ENRP) Program. Recently, those included projects on energy technology innovation, sustainable energy development in China, managing the atom, and the geopolitics of energy.

Financial data The stipend is $37,500 for postdoctoral research fellows or $25,000 for predoctoral research fellows. Fellows who renew their grant receive a monthly stipend of $3,750 for postdoctoral fellows or $2,500 for predoctoral fellows. Stipends for advanced research fellows vary. Health insurance is also provided.

Duration 10 months; may be renewed on a month-by-month basis.

Additional information Fellows are expected to devoted some portion of their time to collaborative endeavors, as arranged by the appropriate program or project director. Predoctoral fellows are expected to contribute to the program's research activities, as well as work on (and ideally complete) their dissertations. Postdoctoral research fellows are also expected to complete a book, monograph, or other significant publication during their period of residence.

Number awarded A limited number each year.

Deadline January of each year.

[859]
ESPERANZA SCHOLARSHIP

New York Women in Communications, Inc.
Attn: NYWICI Foundation
355 Lexington Avenue, 15th Floor
New York, NY 10017-6603
(212) 297-2133   Fax: (212) 370-9047
E-mail: nywicipr@nywici.org
Web: www.nywici.org/foundation/scholarships

Summary To provide financial assistance to Hispanic women who are residents of designated eastern states and interested in preparing for a career in communications at a college or graduate school in any state.

Eligibility This program is open to Hispanic women who are seniors graduating from high schools in New York, New Jersey, Connecticut, or Pennsylvania or undergraduate or graduate students who are permanent residents of those states; they must be attending or planning to attend a college or university in any state. Graduate students must be members of New York Women in Communications, Inc. (NYWICI). Also eligible are Hispanic women who reside outside the 4 states but are currently enrolled at a college or university within 1 of the 5 boroughs of New York City. All applicants must be working on a degree in a communications-related field (e.g., advertising, broadcasting, communications, digital media, English, film, journalism, marketing, public relations, publishing) and have a GPA of 3.2 or higher. Along with their application, they must submit a 2-page resume; a personal essay of 300 words on an assigned topic that changes annually; 2 letters of recommendation; and an official transcript. Selection is based on academic record, need, demonstrated leadership, participation in school and community activities, honors and other awards or recognition, work experience, goals and aspirations, and unusual personal and/or family circumstances. U.S. citizenship or permanent resident status is required.

Financial data The stipend ranges up to $10,000.

Duration 1 year.

Additional information This program is funded by Macy's and Bloomingdale's.

Number awarded 1 each year.

Deadline January of each year.

[860]
ESTHER EDWARDS GRADUATE SCHOLARSHIP

United Methodist Church
Attn: General Board of Higher Education and Ministry
Office of Loans and Scholarships
1001 19th Avenue South
P.O. Box 340007
Nashville, TN 37203-0007
(615) 340-7344   Fax: (615) 340-7367
E-mail: umscholar@gbhem.org
Web: www.gbhem.org

Summary To provide financial assistance to female graduate students who are working on a degree in higher education administration to prepare for a career with a United Methodist school.

Eligibility This program is open to women who are working on a graduate degree to prepare for an executive management career in higher education administration with a United Methodist school, college, or university. Applicants must have been active, full members of a United Methodist Church for at least 1 year prior to applying. They must have a GPA of 3.0 or higher. First preference is given to students currently employed by a United Methodist school, college, or university and to full-time students.

Financial data The stipend is $5,000.

Duration 1 year; nonrenewable.

Number awarded 1 each year.

Deadline February of each year.

[861]
ESTHER KATZ ROSEN FUND GRANTS

American Psychological Foundation
750 First Street, N.E.
Washington, DC 20002-4242
(202) 336-5843   Fax: (202) 336-5812
E-mail: foundation@apa.org
Web: www.apa.org/apf/funding/rosen.aspx

Summary To provide funding to graduate students and early-career psychologists interested in conducting research or other projects on psychological issues relevant to giftedness in children.

Eligibility This program is open to 1) graduate students at universities in the United States and Canada who have advanced to candidacy; and 2) psychologists who completed their doctoral degree within the past 10 years. Applicants must be interested in engaging in activities related to identified gifted and talented children and adolescents, including research, pilot projects, research-based programs, or projects aimed at improving the quality of education in psychological science and its application in secondary schools for high ability students. Selection is based on conformance with stated program goals and qualifications, quality and impact of proposed work, innovation and contribution to the field, and applicant's demonstrated competence and capability to execute the proposed work. The sponsor encourages applications from individuals who represent diversity in race, ethnicity, gender, age, disability, and sexual orientation.

Financial data Grants range from $1,000 to $50,000.

Duration 1 year.

Additional information The Esther Katz Rosen Fund was established in 1974. In 2013, the sponsor combined the Rosen Graduate Student Fellowship, the Rosen Early Career Research Grant, and the Pre-College Grant program into this single program.

Number awarded Varies each year; recently, 2 were awarded.

Deadline February of each year.

[862]
ESTHER NGAN-LING CHOW AND MAREYJOYCE GREEN SCHOLARSHIP

Sociologists for Women in Society
Attn: Administrative Officer
University of Kansas
Department of Sociology
1415 Jayhawk Boulevard, Room 716
Lawrence, KS 66045
(785) 864-9405   E-mail: swsao@outlook.com
Web: www.socwomen.org

Summary To provide funding to women of color who are conducting dissertation research in sociology.

Eligibility This program is open to women from a racial/ethnic group that faces discrimination in the United States. Applicants must be in the early stages of writing a doctoral dissertation in sociology on a topic relating to the concerns that women of color face domestically and/or internationally. They must be able to demonstrate financial need. Both domestic and international students are eligible to apply. Along with their application, they must submit a personal statement that details their short- and long-term career and research goals; a resume or curriculum vitae; 2 letters of recommendation; and a 5-page dissertation proposal that includes the purpose of the research, the work to be accomplished through support from this scholarship, and a time line for completion.

Financial data The stipend is $15,000. An additional grant of $500 is provided to enable the recipient to attend the winter meeting of Sociologists for Women in Society (SWS), and travel expenses to attend the summer meeting are reimbursed.

Duration 1 year.

Additional information This program began in 2007 and was originally named the Women of Color Dissertation Scholarship.

Number awarded 1 each year.

Deadline March of each year.

[863]
ETHEL F. LORD AWARD

Soroptimist International of the Americas-North Atlantic Region
c/o Peggy Gentile-Van Meter, Chair
47 Roberts Road
Bridgeton, NJ 08302
(609) 381-5254   E-mail: peggyvanmeter@aol.com
Web: www.soroptimistnar.org/forms-documents

Summary To provide financial assistance to women who reside in the north Atlantic region and are working on a graduate degree in gerontology at a university in the region.

Eligibility This program is open to female residents of Delaware, New Jersey, New York, Pennsylvania, and the panhandle area of West Virginia who are enrolled full time at a college or university in the region. Applicants must be working on a master's or doctoral degree in gerontology. Selection is based on academic excellence and financial need.

Financial data The stipend is $5,000.

Duration 1 year.

Number awarded 1 each year.

Deadline January of each year.

[864]
ETHEL O. GARDNER PEO SCHOLARSHIP

P.E.O. Foundation-California State Chapter
c/o Pat Lachman, Gardner Scholarship Fund
4400 Hessel Road
Sebastopol, CA 95472
E-mail: peoca.eog@gmail.com
Web: www.peocalifornia.org

Summary To provide financial assistance to women from California who are upper-division or graduate students at a school in any state.

Eligibility This program is open to female residents of California who have completed at least 2 years at a college or university in any state. Applicants must be enrolled as full-time undergraduate or graduate students. Selection is based on financial need, character, and a record of academic and extracurricular activities achievement. U.S. citizenship is required.

Financial data Stipends range from $500 to $1,500.

Duration 1 year.

Number awarded Varies each year; recently, 69 were awarded.

Deadline January of each year.

[865]
EUGENIA VELLNER FISCHER AWARD FOR THE PERFORMING ARTS

Miss America Organization
Attn: Director of Scholarships
Park Place and Boardwalk
P.O. Box 1919
Atlantic City, NJ 08404
(609) 653-8700, ext. 127   Fax: (609) 653-8740
E-mail: info@missamerica.org
Web: www.missamerica.org

Summary To provide financial assistance to women who are working on an undergraduate or graduate degree in the performing arts and who, in the past, competed at some level in the Miss America competition.

Eligibility This program is open to women who are working on an undergraduate, master's, or higher degree in the performing arts and who competed at the local, state, or national level in a Miss America competition within the past 10 years. Applicants may be studying dance, instrumental, monologue, or vocal. They must submit an essay, up to 500 words, on the factors that influenced their decision to enter the field of performing arts, what they consider to be their major strengths in the field, and how they plan to use their degree in the field. Selection is based on GPA, class rank, extracurricular activities, financial need, and level of participation within the system.

Financial data The stipend is $2,000.

Duration 1 year; renewable.

Additional information This scholarship was established in 1999.

Number awarded 1 each year.

Deadline June of each year.

[866]
FCA WOMEN IN ENGINEERING SCHOLARSHIPS

Society of Women Engineers
Attn: Scholarship Selection Committee
203 North LaSalle Street, Suite 1675
Chicago, IL 60601-1269
(312) 596-5223   Toll Free: (877) SWE-INFO
Fax: (312) 644-8557   E-mail: scholarships@swe.org
Web: societyofwomenengineers.swe.org

Summary To provide financial assistance to women working on a degree in computer science or designated fields of engineering.

Eligibility This program is open to women who are entering full-time freshmen, sophomores, juniors, seniors or graduate students at an ABET-accredited 4-year college or university. Applicants must be interested in studying computer science or automotive, chemical, civil, computer, electrical, industrial, manufacturing, materials, or mechanical engineering and have a GPA of 3.0 or higher. Selection is based on merit.

Financial data The stipend is $2,500.

Duration 1 year.

Additional information This program is supported by the Fellowship of Christian Athletes.

Number awarded 20 each year.

Deadline February of each year for continuing students; May of each year for entering freshmen.

[867]
FEDERATION OF HOUSTON PROFESSIONAL WOMEN EDUCATIONAL FOUNDATION SCHOLARSHIPS

Federation of Houston Professional Women
Attn: Educational Foundation
P.O. Box 27621
Houston, TX 77227-7621
E-mail: ef@fhpw.org
Web: www.fhpw.org/fhpw-ef-scholarship

Summary To provide financial assistance for college or graduate school to women from Texas.

Eligibility This program is open to women who are residents of Texas and have completed at least 30 semesters hours of work on an associate, bachelor's, or graduate degree at an accredited college or university in the state. Applicants must be U.S. citizens or permanent residents and have a GPA of 3.0 or higher. Along with their application, they must submit 1) a 200-word statement on their short- and long-term goals; 2) a 400-word essay on either the experiences that have helped determine their goals or the avenues that can help determine their goals; and 3) a 100-word biographical sketch. Financial need is considered in the selection process.

Financial data Stipends are $2,000 for students at 4-year colleges and universities or $1,000 for students at community colleges. Funds are issued payable jointly to the student and the educational institution.

Duration 1 year.

Additional information This program began in 2000.

Number awarded Varies each year; recently, 18 were awarded. Since this program began, it has awarded more than $275,000 in scholarships.

Deadline March of each year.

[868]
FELLOWSHIP ON WOMEN AND PUBLIC POLICY

University at Albany
Center for Women in Government and Civil Society
Attn: Fellowship Program Coordinator
135 Western Avenue, Draper 302
Albany, NY 12222
(518) 591-8762   Fax: (518) 442-3877
E-mail: cwgcs@albany.edu
Web: www.albany.edu

Summary To provide an opportunity for women graduate students in New York to contribute to the improvement of the status of women and underrepresented populations through work experience and course work.

Eligibility This program is open to women graduate students at all accredited colleges and universities within New York who have completed 12 graduate credit hours with a GPA of 3.0 or higher. Applicants must have demonstrated an interest in studies, research, employment, or voluntary activities designed to improve the status of women and underrepresented populations. They must be available to accept an assignment to a policy-making office, such as the legislature, a state agency, or a nonprofit organization, while earning graduate credits from the Rockefeller College of Public Affairs and Policy at the University at Albany, SUNY. Along with their application, they must submit a 1,500-word essay on why they are interested in becoming a fellow.

Financial data Fellows receive a $10,000 stipend plus free tuition for 9 graduate credits of related academic work.

Duration 7 months.

Additional information This program was initiated in 1983. Fellows work 30 hours a week at their assignment and complete 12 credits of graduate coursework.

Number awarded Varies each year; recently, 15 of these fellows were appointed.

Deadline August of each year.

[869]
FINANCIAL WOMEN OF SAN FRANCISCO SCHOLARSHIPS

Financial Women of San Francisco
Attn: Scholarships
P.O. Box 26143
San Francisco, CA 94126
(415) 586-8599   Fax: (415) 586-6606
E-mail: info@financialwomensf.org
Web: www.financialwomensf.org/scholarships

Summary To provide financial assistance to women who are working on an undergraduate or graduate degree in a field related to finance at a college in the San Francisco Bay area.

Eligibility This program is open to women who are entering their junior or senior year or are entering or enrolled as graduate students. Applicants must be attending a college or university located in the San Francisco Bay area (Alameda, Contra Costa, Marin, Napa, San Francisco, San Mateo, Santa Clara, Solano, Sonoma counties); they may be enrolled at an institution outside that area if they are attending a satellite campus located within 1 of those counties and taking at least 80% of their classes at the satellite campus. They must be working on a degree and preparing for a career in finance or in the financial services industry and have a GPA of 3.4 or higher. Along with their application, they must submit a 1,000-word essay on their interest in finance and their reasons for choosing that field. Selection is based on demonstrated leadership skills (both academic and community), communication skills, alignment with the sponsor's goals of supporting women with careers in finance, and financial need.

Financial data Stipends are $5,000 for undergraduates or $10,000 for graduate students.

Duration 1 year.

Additional information This program began in 1985.

Number awarded Varies each year; recently 11 were awarded (2 undergraduates and 9 graduate students). Since the program was established, it has awarded more than $2 million in scholarships to more than 200 women.

Deadline March of each year.

[870]
F.J. MCGUIGAN DISSERTATION AWARD

American Psychological Foundation
750 First Street, N.E.
Washington, DC 20002-4242
(202) 336-5843   Fax: (202) 336-5812
E-mail: foundation@apa.org
Web: www.apa.org/apf/funding/mcguigan-dissertation.aspx

Summary To provide funding to doctoral candidates interested in conducting research on the materialistic understanding of the human mind.

Eligibility This program is open to graduate students enrolled full time in a psychology program at an accredited college or university in the United States or Canada. Applicants must be interested in conducting dissertation research that addresses an aspect of mental function (e.g., cognition, affect, motivation) and seeks to understand the mind from both a neural and behavioral perspective. Selection is based on conformance with stated program goals, quality of proposed work, and applicant's demonstrated scholarship and research competence. The sponsor encourages applications from individuals who represent diversity in race, ethnicity, gender, age, disability, and sexual orientation.

Financial data The grant is $2,000.

Duration 1 year.

Additional information This grant was first awarded in 2009.

Number awarded 1 each year.

Deadline May of each year.

[871]
FLORENCE GAYNOR AWARD

National Association of Health Services Executives
Attn: Educational Assistance Program
1050 Connecticut Avenue, N.W., Tenth Floor
Washington, DC 20036
(202) 772-1030   Fax: (202) 772-1072
E-mail: nahsehg@nahse.org
Web: www.nahse.org/student-scholarships.html

Summary To provide financial assistance to African American women who are members of the National Association of Health Services Executives (NAHSE) and interested in preparing for a career in health care administration.

Eligibility This program is open to African American women who are either enrolled or accepted at an accredited college or university to work on a master's or doctoral degree in health care administration. Applicants must be members of NAHSE and able to demonstrate financial need. They must have a GPA of 2.5 or higher as undergraduates or 3.0 or higher as graduate students. Along with their application, they must submit a 3-page essay that describes themselves and their career goals, commitment and interest in health care management, and financial need.

Financial data The stipend is $2,500. Funds are sent to the recipient's institution.

Duration 1 year.

Number awarded 1 each year.

Deadline May of each year.

[872]
FLORIDA ALPHA DELTA KAPPA PAST STATE PRESIDENTS' SCHOLARSHIP AWARD

Alpha Delta Kappa-Florida Chapter
c/o Vivian Bowden
1843 Shadyhill Terrace
Winter Park, FL 32792

Summary To provide financial assistance to women working on an undergraduate or graduate degree in education at a college or university in Florida.

Eligibility This program is open to women currently enrolled at a community college or 4-year college or university in Florida. Applicants must have a GPA of 3.0 or higher and be working on an undergraduate or graduate degree in education. Selection is based on academic ability and performance, character, leadership, and participation in extracurricular activities on campus and in the community.

Financial data The stipend is $1,000.

Duration 1 year.

Number awarded 1 each year.

Deadline December of each year.

[873]
FLORIDA LEGION AUXILIARY MASTER'S PROGRAM GRANT

American Legion Auxiliary
Department of Florida
1912A Lee Road
P.O. Box 547917
Orlando, FL 32854-7917
(407) 293-7411   Toll Free: (866) 710-4192
Fax: (407) 299-6522   E-mail: contact@alafl.org
Web: www.alafl.org/resources/scholarships

Summary To provide financial assistance to members of the Florida American Legion Auxiliary who are interested in working on a master's degree in any field at a university in any state.

Eligibility This program is open to residents of Florida who have been members of the American Legion Auxiliary for at least 5 consecutive years. Applicants must be planning to enroll in an accredited master's degree program in any field at a college or university in any state. They must be sponsored by the local American Legion Auxiliary unit. Selection is based on academic record and financial need.

Financial data The stipend is $2,500 per year. All funds are paid directly to the institution.

Duration 1 year; may be renewed 1 additional year if the recipient needs further financial assistance and has maintained at least a 2.5 GPA.

Number awarded 1 each year.

Deadline January of each year.

[874]
FORD EMERGING VOICES SCHOLARSHIPS

Alliance for Women in Media
Attn: Foundation
2365 Harrodsburg Road, Suite A325
Lexington, KY 40504
(202) 750-3664   E-mail: info@allwomeninmedia.org
Web: www.allwomeninmedia.org/foundation/scholarships

Summary To provide financial assistance to women who are working on an undergraduate or graduate degree in a media-related field and submit outstanding essays on media topics.

Eligibility This program is open to women currently enrolled in an undergraduate or graduate degree program at a college or university in any state. Applicants must be preparing for a media career and working on a degree in such fields as cable, communications, television, radio, digital media, publishing, journalism, advertising, production, creative design, or related areas. Along with their application, they must submit an essay of 300 to 500 words on 1 of the following topics: 1) the most impactful media event in their lifetime and why; 2) in the current political landscape, do they feel that the media is a reflection of the masses or influences the mass public; or 3) a woman in a media that they consider personally influential.

Financial data The stipend is $2,500, paid directly to the recipient's institution. The winners are also invited to write 4 blog posts for the sponsor's web site.

Duration 1 year.

Additional information This program is sponsored by the Ford Motor Company Fund.

Number awarded 2 each year.

Deadline April.

[875]
FORD EMPOWERING AMERICA SCHOLARSHIPS

Alliance for Women in Media
Attn: Foundation
2365 Harrodsburg Road, Suite A325
Lexington, KY 40504
(202) 750-3664   E-mail: info@allwomeninmedia.org
Web: www.allwomeninmedia.org/foundation/scholarships

Summary To provide financial assistance to women who are working on an undergraduate or graduate degree in a media-related field and submit outstanding videos on a female leader in their community.

Eligibility This program is open to women currently enrolled in an undergraduate or graduate degree program at a college or university in any state. Applicants must be preparing for a media career and working on a degree in such fields as cable, communications, television, radio, digital media, publishing, journalism, advertising, production, creative design, or related areas. Along with their application, they must submit a video of 3 to 5 minutes in length on a female leader in their community, which may be defined as family, school, city, or personal network. The leader can be in the media industry, a small business owner, community volunteer, or anyone who especially inspires the applicant.

Financial data The winner receives a stipend of $3,000, payable to her educational institution, and up to $350 to reimburse expenses for her and the person she highlights to attend the sponsor's Women in Media event in New York. The runner-up receives a $2,000 stipend, payable to her educational institution.

Duration 1 year.

Additional information This program is sponsored by the Ford Motor Company Fund.

Number awarded 2 each year.

Deadline April.

[876]
FORGING INDUSTRY WOMEN'S SCHOLARSHIP

Forging Industry Association
Attn: Forging Industry Educational & Research
  Foundation
1111 Superior Avenue, Suite 615
Cleveland, OH 44114
(216) 781-5040   Fax: (216) 781-0102
E-mail: info@forgings.org
Web: sms.scholarshipamerica.org/forgingw

Summary   To provide financial assistance to women who are working on an undergraduate or graduate degree in a field that will prepare them for a career in the forging industry.

Eligibility   This program is open to women who are currently enrolled full time at a 2- or 4-year college or university in North America and working on an associate, bachelor's, or master's degree in computer science, engineering (electrical, industrial, materials science, mechanical, or metallurgical), industrial management, management information systems, manufacturing, marketing, or related field that will prepare them for a career in the forging industry. Applicants must be willing to consider a compensated internship at a forging industry company after the successful completion of each academic year. They must be citizens of the United States, Canada, or Mexico. Selection is based on academic record, demonstrated leadership and participation in school and community activities, honors, work experience, a statement of goals and aspirations, unusual personal or family circumstances, and an outside appraisal; financial need is not considered.

Financial data   The stipend is $5,000 per year (or up to 50% of combined fees for tuition, room, and board).

Duration   1 year; may be renewed 1 additional year (provided the recipient maintains a GPA of 2.75 or higher) and recipients may reapply for up to 2 more years of support.

Additional information   This program is administered by Scholarship Management Services, a division of Scholarship America.

Number awarded   1 or more each year.

Deadline   April of each year.

[877]
FOUNDATION FOR THE HISTORY OF WOMEN IN MEDICINE FELLOWSHIPS

Foundation for the History of Women in Medicine
c/o Archives for Women in Medicine
Francis A. Countway Library of Medicine
10 Shattuck Street
Boston, MA 02115
(617) 432-2170   E-mail: chm@hms.harvard.edu
Web: www.fhwim.org/fellowships/foundation-fellowships

Summary   To provide funding to students and scholars interested in short-term use of resources in the Boston area to conduct research on the history of women and medicine.

Eligibility   This program is open to doctoral candidates and other advanced scholars interested in using the Archives for Women in Medicine at the Countway Library's Center for the History of Medicine in Boston. Applicants must be interested in conducting research on the history of women in medicine. Preference is given to projects that deal specifically with women as physicians, health workers, or medical scientists,

but proposals dealing with the history of women's health issues are also considered. Preference is given to applicants who live beyond commuting distance of the Countway.

Financial data   The grant is $5,000.

Duration   Recipients may conduct research on a flexible schedule during 1 academic year.

Additional information   The Francis A. Countway Library of Medicine, the largest academic medical library in the United States, was established in 1960 as the result of an alliance between the Boston Medical Library and the Harvard Medical School Library.

Number awarded   1 or 2 each year.

Deadline   March of each year.

[878]
FRAMELINE COMPLETION FUND

Frameline
Attn: Completion Fund
145 Ninth Street, Suite 300
San Francisco, CA 94103
(415) 703-8650   Fax: (415) 861-1404
E-mail: info@frameline.org
Web: frameline.org

Summary   To provide funding to lesbian, gay, bisexual, and transgender (LGBT) film/video artists.

Eligibility   This program is open to LGBT artists who are in the last stages of the production of documentary, educational, narrative, animated, or experimental projects about or of interest to LGBT people and their communities. Applicants may be independent artists, students, producers, or nonprofit corporations. They must be interested in completion work and must have 90% of the production completed; projects in development, script-development, pre-production, or production are not eligible. Student projects are eligible only if the student maintains artistic and financial control of the project. Women and people of color are especially encouraged to apply. Selection is based on financial need, the contribution the grant will make to completing the project, assurances that the project will be completed, and the statement the project makes about LGBT people and/or issues of concern to them and their communities.

Financial data   Grants range from $1,000 to $5,000.

Duration   These are 1-time grants.

Additional information   This program began in 1990.

Number awarded   Varies each year; recently, 5 were awarded. Since this program was established, it has provided $464,200 in support to 136 films.

Deadline   October of each year.

[879]
FRANCES C. ALLEN FELLOWSHIPS

Newberry Library
Attn: Committee on Awards
60 West Walton Street
Chicago, IL 60610-3305
(312) 255-3666   Fax: (312) 255-3513
E-mail: research@newberry.org
Web: www.newberry.org/short-term-fellowships

Summary   To provide funding to Native American women graduate students who wish to use the resources of the

D'Arcy McNickle Center for the History of the American Indian at the Newberry Library.

Eligibility This program is open to women of American Indian heritage who are interested in using the library for a project appropriate to its collections. Applicants must be enrolled in a graduate or pre-professional program, especially in the humanities or social sciences. Recommendations are required; at least 2 must come from academic advisers or instructors who can comment on the significance of the applicant's proposed project and explain how it will help in the achievement of professional goals.

Financial data The basic stipend is $2,500 per month; supplemental funding may be available on a case by case basis.

Duration From 1 month to 1 year.

Additional information These grants were first awarded in 1983. Fellows must spend a significant portion of their time at the library's D'Arcy McNickle Center.

Number awarded Varies each year; recently, 2 were awarded.

Deadline December of each year.

[880]
FRANCES LEWIS FELLOWSHIPS IN GENDER AND WOMEN'S STUDIES

Virginia Historical Society
Attn: Chair, Research Fellowships and Awards Committee
428 North Boulevard
P.O. Box 7311
Richmond, VA 23221-0311
(804) 342-9686   Fax: (804) 355-2399
E-mail: fpollard@vahistorical.org
Web: www.vahistorical.org/research/fellowships.htm

Summary To offer short-term financial assistance to pre- and postdoctoral scholars interested in conducting research in women's studies at the Virginia Historical Society.

Eligibility This program is open to doctoral candidates, faculty, or independent scholars interested in conducting research in women's studies. Applicants whose research promises to result in a significant publication, such as in the society's documents series of edited texts or in the *Virginia Magazine of History and Biography,* receive primary consideration. Along with their application, they must submit a resume, 2 letters of recommendation, a description of the research project (up to 2 pages), and a cover letter. Because the program is designed to help defray research travel expenses, residents of the Richmond metropolitan area are not eligible. Also ineligible are undergraduates, master's students, and graduate students not yet admitted to Ph.D. candidacy. Selection is based on the applicants' scholarly qualifications, the merits of their research proposals, and the appropriateness of their topics to the holdings of the Virginia Historical Society.

Financial data A few small grants (up to $150 per week) are awarded for mileage to researchers who live at least 50 miles from Richmond. The majority of the awards are $500 per week and go to researchers who live further away and thus incur greater expenses.

Duration Up to 3 weeks a year. Recipients may reapply in following years up to these limits: a maximum of 3 weeks in a 5-year period for doctoral candidates; a maximum of 6 weeks in a 5-year period for faculty or independent scholars.

Additional information The society's library contains 7 million manuscripts and thousands of books, maps, broadsides, newspapers, and historical objects. This program was formerly known as the Sydney and Frances Lewis Fellowships. Recipients are expected to work on a regular basis in the society's reading room during the period of the award.

Number awarded Varies each year; recently, the society awarded a total of 20 research fellowships.

Deadline January of each year.

[881]
FRANCIS M. KEVILLE MEMORIAL SCHOLARSHIP

Construction Management Association of America
Attn: CMAA Foundation
7926 Jones Branch Drive, Suite 800
McLean, VA 22101-3303
(703) 677-3361   E-mail: foundation@cmaanet.org
Web: www.cmaafoundation.org

Summary To provide financial assistance to minority and female undergraduate and graduate students working on a degree in construction management.

Eligibility This program is open to women and members of minority groups who are enrolled as full-time undergraduate or graduate students. Applicants must have completed at least 1 year of study and have at least 1 full year remaining for a bachelor's or master's degree in construction management or a related field. Along with their application, they must submit essays on why they are interested in a career in construction management and why they should be awarded this scholarship. Selection is based on that essay (20%), academic performance (40%), recommendation of the faculty adviser (15%), and extracurricular activities (25%); a bonus of 5% is given to student members of the Construction Management Association of America (CMAA).

Financial data The stipend is $5,000. Funds are disbursed directly to the student's university.

Duration 1 year.

Number awarded 1 each year.

Deadline April of each year.

[882]
GABWA FOUNDATION SCHOLARSHIPS

Georgia Association of Black Women Attorneys
Attn: GABWA Foundation
P.O. Box 7381
Atlanta, GA 30309
(678) 825-5675   E-mail: contact@gabwa.org
Web: www.gabwa.org/foundation.php

Summary To provide financial assistance to Black women from any state enrolled at law schools in Georgia.

Eligibility This program is open to Black women from any state enrolled in the second or third year at a law school in Georgia. Applicants must be able to demonstrate academic achievement, leadership, and commitment to the profession and their community. Along with their application, they must submit a 300-word personal statement that discusses their experience as a Black woman law student, how they expect their legal career to benefit the community at large, and how this scholarship will benefit their quest for a legal education and future career goals. Financial need is considered in the selection process but is not required.

Financial data Stipend amounts vary, depending on the availability of funds; recently, they averaged $5,000.

Duration 1 year.

Additional information This program began in 2002.

Number awarded Varies each year; recently, 10 were awarded. Since the program was established, it has awarded more than $250,000 to more than 50 African American women law students.

Deadline October of each year.

[883]
GAIUS CHARLES BOLIN DISSERTATION AND POST-MFA FELLOWSHIPS

Williams College
Attn: Dean of the Faculty
880 Main Street
Hopkins Hall, Third Floor
P.O. Box 141
Williamstown, MA 01267
(413) 597-4351   Fax: (413) 597-3553
E-mail: gburda@williams.edu
Web: faculty.williams.edu

Summary To provide financial assistance to members of underrepresented groups who are interested in teaching courses at Williams College while working on their doctoral dissertation or building their post-M.F.A. professional portfolio.

Eligibility This program is open to members of underrepresented groups, including ethnic minorities, first-generation college students, women in predominantly male fields, and scholars with disabilities. Applicants must be 1) doctoral candidates in any field who have completed all work for a Ph.D. except for the dissertation; or 2) artists who completed an M.F.A. degree within the past 2 years and are building their professional portfolio. They must be willing to teach a course at Williams College. Along with their application, they must submit a full curriculum vitae, a graduate school transcript, 3 letters of recommendation, a copy of their dissertation prospectus or samples of their artistic work, and a description of their teaching interests within a department or program at Williams College. U.S. citizenship or permanent resident status is required.

Financial data Fellows receive $38,000 for the academic year, plus housing assistance, office space, computer and library privileges, and a research allowance of up to $4,000.

Duration 2 years.

Additional information Bolin fellows are assigned a faculty adviser in the appropriate department. This program was established in 1985. Fellows are expected to teach a 1-semester course each year. They must be in residence at Williams College for the duration of the fellowship.

Number awarded 2 each year.

Deadline November of each year.

[884]
GE WOMEN'S NETWORK ENGINEERING SCHOLARSHIP

Society of Women Engineers-Minnesota Section
Attn: Scholarship Committee
P.O. Box 18481
Minneapolis, MN 55418
E-mail: scholarships@swe-mn.org
Web: www.swe-mn.org/scholarships.html

Summary To provide financial assistance to women from any state working on an undergraduate or graduate degree in computer science or specified fields of engineering at colleges and universities in Minnesota, North Dakota, and South Dakota.

Eligibility This program is open to female undergraduate and graduate students at ABET-accredited engineering programs in Minnesota, North Dakota, or South Dakota. Applicants must be working full time on a degree in computer science or aerospace/aeronautical, computer, electrical, or mechanical engineering. Along with their application, they must submit a 250-word essay describing how they plan to utilize their engineering knowledge and skills after they graduate. Selection is based on potential to succeed as an engineer (20 points), communication skills (10 points), extracurricular or community involvement and leadership skills (10 points), demonstration of work experience and successes (10 points), and academic success (5 points).

Financial data The stipend is $2,500.

Duration 1 year.

Additional information This program is sponsored by the General Electric Women's Network.

Number awarded 1 each year.

Deadline March of each year.

[885]
GEIS MEMORIAL AWARD

American Psychological Association
Attn: Division 35 (Psychology of Women)
750 First Street, N.E.
Washington, DC 20002-4242
(202) 216-7602   Fax: (202) 336-5953
TDD: (202) 336-6123 E-mail: martha.bergen@gmail.com
Web: www.apadivisions.org/division-35/awards/geis.aspx

Summary To provide funding to psychology doctoral students interested in conducting feminist research.

Eligibility This program is open to advanced doctoral students interested in conducting dissertation research on the psychology of women. The research must be feminist, address a feminist/womanist issue, use social psychology research methods, and make a significant contribution to social psychology theory and practice. Selection is based on basis of theoretical and methodological soundness, relevance to feminist goals, and relevance of future goals to a career that furthers feminist social psychology and research.

Financial data The grant is $15,000.

Duration 1 academic year.

Number awarded 1 each year.

Deadline April of each year.

[886]
GEOGRAPHY AND SPATIAL SCIENCES DOCTORAL DISSERTATION RESEARCH IMPROVEMENT AWARDS

National Science Foundation
Directorate for Social, Behavioral, and Economic Sciences
Attn: Geography and Spatial Sciences Program
4201 Wilson Boulevard
Arlington, VA 22230
(703) 292-7301   TDD: (800) 281-8749
E-mail: tbaerwal@nsf.gov
Web: www.nsf.gov

Summary To provide funding for dissertation research to doctoral candidates in geography and spatial sciences.

Eligibility This program is open to doctoral candidates at U.S. universities in fields related to geography and spatial sciences who are conducting dissertation research. Applicants are encouraged to propose plans for research about the nature, causes, and consequences of human activity and natural environmental processes across a range of scales. Proposals should offer promise of contributing to scholarship by enhancing geographical knowledge, concepts, theories, methods, and their application to societal problems and concerns. In the selection process, the sponsor values the advancement of scientific knowledge and activities that contribute to societally relevant outcomes, such as full participation of women, persons with disabilities, and underrepresented minorities in science, technology, engineering, or mathematics (STEM).

Financial data Grants are $16,000, including both direct and indirect costs. Funds may be used only for research and related costs; support is not provided for a stipend or salary for the student or for tuition.

Duration 1 year.

Number awarded 30 to 40 each year.

Deadline February or August of each year.

[887]
GEOLOGICAL SOCIETY OF AMERICA GRADUATE STUDENT RESEARCH GRANTS

Geological Society of America
Attn: Program Officer-Grants, Awards and Recognition
3300 Penrose Place
P.O. Box 9140
Boulder, CO 80301-9140
(303) 357-1060   Toll Free: (888) 443-4472, ext. 1060
Fax: (303) 357-1070   E-mail: awards@geosociety.org
Web: www.geosociety.org/grants/gradgrants.htm

Summary To provide funding to graduate student members of the Geological Society of America (GSA) interested in conducting research at universities in the United States, Canada, Mexico, or Central America.

Eligibility This program is open to GSA members working on a master's or doctoral degree at a university in the United States, Canada, Mexico, or Central America. Applicants must be interested in conducting geological research. Minorities, women, and persons with disabilities are strongly encouraged to apply. Selection is based on the scientific merits of the proposal, the capability of the investigator, and the reasonableness of the budget.

Financial data Grants range up to $2,500 and recently averaged $1,851. Funds can be used for the cost of travel, room and board in the field, services of a technician or field assistant, funding of chemical and isotope analyses, or other expenses directly related to the fulfillment of the research contract. Support is not provided for the purchase of ordinary field equipment, for maintenance of the families of the grantees and their assistants, as reimbursement for work already accomplished, for institutional overhead, for adviser participation, or for tuition costs.

Duration 1 year.

Additional information In addition to general grants, GSA awards a number of specialized grants.

Number awarded Varies each year; recently, the society awarded nearly 400 grants worth more than $723,000 through this and all of its specialized programs.

Deadline January of each year.

[888]
GEOPHYSICAL FLUID DYNAMICS FELLOWSHIPS

Woods Hole Oceanographic Institution
Attn: Academic Programs Office
Clark Laboratory, MS 31
266 Woods Hole Road
Woods Hole, MA 02543-1541
(508) 289-2950   Fax: (508) 457-2188
E-mail: gfd@whoi.edu
Web: www.whoi.edu/main/gfd/fellowships

Summary To provide summer research and study opportunities at Woods Hole Oceanographic Institution (WHOI) to pre- and postdoctoral scholars interested in geophysical fluid dynamics.

Eligibility This program is open to pre- and postdoctorates who are interested in pursuing research or study opportunities in a field that involves non-linear dynamics of rotating, stratified fluids. Fields of specialization include classical fluid dynamics, physical oceanography, meteorology, geophysical fluid dynamics, astrophysics, planetary atmospheres, hydromagnetics, physics, and applied mathematics. Applications from women and members of underrepresented groups are particularly encouraged.

Financial data Participants receive a stipend of $6,284 and an allowance for travel expenses within the United States.

Duration 10 weeks during the summer.

Additional information Each summer, the program at WHOI revolves around a central theme. A recent theme related to shear turbulence. The main components of the summer program are a series of principal lectures, a set of supplementary research seminars, and research projects conducted by the student fellows with the active support of the staff. Funding for this program, which began in 1959, is provided by the National Science Foundation and Office of Naval Research.

Number awarded Up to 10 graduate students are supported each year.

Deadline February of each year.

[889]
GEORGIA ASSOCIATION FOR WOMEN LAWYERS SCHOLARSHIPS

Georgia Association for Women Lawyers
Attn: GAWL Foundation, Inc.
P.O. Box 79308
Atlanta, GA 30357
(404) 496-5358   E-mail: gawlscholarships@gmail.com
Web: www.gawl.org/cpages/scholarships

Summary To provide financial assistance to women enrolled at law schools in Georgia.

Eligibility This program is open to women enrolled in the second or third year at a law school in Georgia. Applicants must submit an essay that covers 1) why they are a deserving candidate for this scholarship; 2) their involvement in social, civic, religious, professional, or other community groups working to support or advance women's issues; 3) how this scholarship would benefit them personally; and 4) their career objectives and expectations with respect to the practice of law. Selection is based on academic achievement, leadership, involvement in programs that affect and/or promote the advancement of women in the profession and in the community, participation in community outreach activities and/or philanthropic endeavors, and commitment to the legal profession.

Financial data Stipends range from $1,000 to $5,000.

Duration 1 year.

Number awarded 2 to 4 each year.

Deadline February of each year.

[890]
GEORGIA HARKNESS SCHOLARSHIP AWARDS

United Methodist Church
Attn: General Board of Higher Education and Ministry
Office of Loans and Scholarships
1001 19th Avenue South
P.O. Box 340007
Nashville, TN 37203-0007
(615) 340-7342   Fax: (615) 340-7367
E-mail: umscholar@gbhem.org
Web: www.gbhem.org

Summary To provide financial assistance to women over 35 years of age who are preparing for a second career in ordained ministry as an elder in the United Methodist Church.

Eligibility This program is open to women over 35 years of age who have a bachelor's degree. Applicants must be enrolled full time in a school of theology approved by the University Senate of the United Methodist Church and working on an M.Div. degree. They must be currently certified as candidates for ordained ministry as an elder in the United Methodist Church. The award is not available for undergraduate, D.Min., or Ph.D. work. Selection is based on financial need, academic scholarship, spiritual leadership, and commitment to social justice.

Financial data The stipend is $5,000.

Duration 1 year; recipients may reapply.

Number awarded Varies each year; recently, 11 were awarded.

Deadline February of each year.

[891]
GERTRUDE BOYD CRANE SCHOLARSHIP

United Methodist Church-Oregon-Idaho Conference
Attn: United Methodist Women
1505 S.W. 18th Avenue
Portland, OR 97201-2524
(503) 226-7031   Toll Free: (800) J-WESLEY
E-mail: cjoh1@frontier.com
Web: www.umoi.org/scholarships

Summary To provide financial assistance to female Methodists from Oregon and Idaho who are interested in attending graduate school or seminary in any state to prepare for a church-related career.

Eligibility This program is open to women who are members of congregations affiliated with the Oregon-Idaho Conference of the United Methodist Church (UMC). Applicants must be enrolled or planning to enroll at an accredited graduate school or seminary in any state to prepare for a church-related vocation within the Conference. Selection is based primarily on financial need.

Financial data The stipend, which depends on the availability of funds, has ranged from $200 to $1,900.

Duration 1 year.

Number awarded Varies each year; recently, 4 were awarded.

Deadline April of each year.

[892]
GERTRUDE M. COX SCHOLARSHIP IN STATISTICS

American Statistical Association
Attn: Awards Liaison
732 North Washington Street
Alexandria, VA 22314-1914
(703) 684-1221, ext. 1860   Toll Free: (888) 231-3473
Fax: (703) 684-2037   E-mail: awards@amstat.org
Web: www.amstat.org/awards/coxscholarship.cfm

Summary To provide funding to women who wish to earn a graduate degree in order to enter statistically-oriented professions.

Eligibility This program is open to women who are citizens or permanent residents of the United States or Canada and admitted to full-time study in a graduate statistics (including biostatistics and other statistical sciences) program. Women in or entering the early stages of graduate training are especially encouraged to apply. Applicants must submit a 1-page personal essay on why they are enrolled in their present academic program and how they intend to use their technical training, along with examples of acts of leadership, community service, and/or mentoring they have performed. Selection is based on academic record, employment history, references, and a personal statement of interest.

Financial data The stipend is $2,000.

Duration 1 year.

Additional information This program began in 1989.

Number awarded 2 each year: 1 to a woman in or entering the early stages of graduate training and 1 to a woman in a more advanced stage of training.

Deadline February of each year.

[893]
GFWC/MFWC HEBRON MEMORIAL SCHOLARSHIP

GFWC/Mississippi Federation of Women's Clubs, Inc.
c/o Darlene G. Adams, President
3004 The Woods Road
Picayune, MS 39466
E-mail: info@gfwc-mfwc.org
Web: www.gfwc-mfwc.org

Summary To provide financial assistance to women in Mississippi who are interested in attending college or graduate school in the state.

Eligibility This program is open to women who are residents of Mississippi and are high school seniors, high school graduates, or graduates of a college in the state. Applicants must be planning to enroll at a Mississippi institution of higher learning as an undergraduate or graduate student. They may be planning to work on a degree in any field, but preference is given to applicants in areas of service where it is felt there is a need in the state.

Financial data The stipend is $1,000. Funds are sent directly to the recipient's institution.

Duration 1 year.

Number awarded 1 each year.

Deadline January of each year.

[894]
GILDA MURRAY SCHOLARSHIPS

Texas Business Women
Attn: Texas Business and Professional Women's
  Foundation
P.O. Box 70
Round Rock, TX 78680-0070
E-mail: info@tbwconnect.com
Web: www.texasbpwfoundation.org/scholarships.php

Summary To provide financial assistance to members of Texas Business Women (TBW) who are interested in career advancement.

Eligibility This program is open to members of TBW who are interested in pursuing education or training necessary to prepare for employment or to advance in a business or profession. Applicants must be at least 25 years of age and have a record of active participation in the association. Along with their application, they must submit a 1-page description of the course and its benefits to them. Selection is based on merit and need.

Financial data Funding covers 50% of the cost of the training, to a maximum of $1,000 per year.

Duration 1 year; may be renewed.

Additional information This program began in 1998 when Texas Business Women was named Texas Federation of Business and Professional Women's Clubs.

Number awarded 1 or more each year.

Deadline Applications may be submitted at any time.

[895]
GLADYS C. ANDERSON MEMORIAL SCHOLARSHIP

American Foundation for the Blind
Attn: Information Center
1000 Fifth Avenue, Suite 350
Huntington, WV 25701
Toll Free: (800) AFB-LINE   E-mail: tannis@afb.net
Web: www.afb.org/scholarships.asp

Summary To provide financial assistance to legally blind women who are studying classical or religious music on the undergraduate or graduate school level.

Eligibility This program is open to women who are legally blind, U.S. citizens, and enrolled in an undergraduate or graduate degree program in classical or religious music. Along with their application, they must submit 200-word essays on 1) their past and recent achievements and accomplishments; 2) their intended field of study and why they have chosen it; and 3) the role their visual impairment has played in shaping their life. They must also submit a sample performance tape or CD of up to 30 minutes. Financial need is considered in the selection process.

Financial data The stipend is $1,000.

Duration 1 academic year.

Number awarded 1 each year.

Deadline May of each year.

[896]
GLORINE TUOHEY MEMORIAL SCHOLARSHIP

American Business Women's Association
Attn: Stephen Bufton Memorial Educational Fund
9820 Metcalf Avenue, Suite 110
Overland Park, KS 66212
Toll Free: (800) 228-0007
Web: www.sbmef.org/National/index.cfm

Summary To provide financial assistance to female graduate students who are working on a degree in a specified field (the field changes each year).

Eligibility This program is open to women who are working on a graduate degree and have a cumulative GPA of 3.0 or higher. Applicants are not required to be members of the American Business Women's Association. Along with their application, they must submit a 250-word biographical sketch that includes information about their background, activities, honors, work experience, and long-term educational and professional goals. Financial need is not considered in the selection process. Annually, the trustees designate an academic discipline for which the scholarship will be presented that year. U.S. citizenship is required.

Financial data The stipend is $3,000. Funds are paid directly to the recipient's institution to be used only for tuition, books, and fees.

Duration 1 year.

Additional information This program was created in 1997 as part of ABWA's Stephen Bufton Memorial Education Fund.

Number awarded 1 each year.

Deadline May of each year.

[897]
GO RED MULTICULTURAL SCHOLARSHIP FUND

American Heart Association
Attn: Go Red for Women
7272 Greenville Avenue
Dallas, TX 75231-4596
Toll Free: (800) AHA-USA1
E-mail: GoRedScholarship@heart.org
Web: www.goredforwomen.org

Summary To provide financial assistance to women from multicultural backgrounds who are preparing for a career in a field of health care.

Eligibility This program is open to women who are currently enrolled at an accredited college, university, health care institution, or program and have a GPA of 3.0 or higher. Applicants must be U.S. citizens or permanent residents of Hispanic, African American, Asian/Pacific Islander, or other minority origin. They must be working on an undergraduate or graduate degree as preparation for a career as a nurse, physician, or allied health care worker. Selection is based on community involvement, a personal essay, transcripts, and 2 letters of recommendation.

Financial data The stipend is $2,500.

Duration 1 year.

Additional information This program, which began in 2012, is supported by Macy's.

Number awarded 16 each year.

Deadline December of each year.

[898]
GOOGLE ANITA BORG MEMORIAL SCHOLARSHIPS

Google Inc.
Attn: Scholarships
1600 Amphitheatre Parkway
Mountain View, CA 94043-8303
(650) 253-0000   Fax: (650) 253-0001
E-mail: anitaborgscholarship@google.com
Web: www.google.com/anitaborg/us

Summary To provide financial assistance to women working on a bachelor's or graduate degree in a computer-related field.

Eligibility This program is open to women who are entering their senior year of undergraduate study or are enrolled in a graduate program in computer science, computer engineering, or a closely-related field. Applicants must be full-time students at a university in the United States and have a GPA of 3.5 or higher. They must submit essays of 400 to 600 words on 1) a significant technical project on which they have worked; 2) their leadership abilities; 3) what they would do if someone gave them the funding and resources for a 3- to 12-month project to investigate a technical topic of their choice; and 4) what they would do if someone gave them $1,000 to plan an event or project to benefit women in technical fields. Citizens, permanent residents, and international students are eligible. Selection is based on academic background and demonstrated leadership.

Financial data The stipend is $10,000 per year.

Duration 1 year; recipients may reapply.

Additional information These scholarships were first offered in 2004.

Number awarded Varies each year; recently, 19 were awarded.

Deadline November of each year.

[899]
GRADUATE FELLOWSHIP IN THE HISTORY OF SCIENCE

American Geophysical Union
Attn: History of Geophysics
2000 Florida Avenue, N.W.
Washington, DC 20009-1277
(202) 777-7522   Toll Free: (800) 966-2481
Fax: (202) 328-0566
E-mail: HistoryofGeophysics@agu.org
Web: education.agu.org

Summary To provide funding to doctoral candidates conducting dissertation research in the history of geophysics.

Eligibility This program is open to doctoral candidates at U.S. institutions who have passed all preliminary examinations. Applicants must be completing a dissertation in the history of the geophysical sciences, including topics related to atmospheric sciences, biogeosciences, geodesy, geomagnetism and paleomagnetism, hydrology, ocean sciences, planetary sciences, seismology, space physics, aeronomy, tectonophysics, volcanology, geochemistry, and petrology. They must submit a cover letter with a curriculum vitae, undergraduate and graduate transcripts, a 10-page description of the dissertation topic and proposed research plan, and 3 letters of recommendation. U.S. citizenship or permanent resident status is required. Applications are encouraged from women, minorities, and students with disabilities who are traditionally underrepresented in the geophysical sciences.

Financial data The grant is $5,000; funds are to be used to assist with the costs of travel to obtain archival or research materials.

Duration 1 year.

Number awarded 1 each year.

Deadline September of each year.

[900]
GRADUATE RESEARCH FELLOWSHIP PROGRAM OF THE NATIONAL SCIENCE FOUNDATION

National Science Foundation
Directorate for Education and Human Resources
Attn: Division of Graduate Education
4201 Wilson Boulevard, Room 875S
Arlington, VA 22230
(703) 331-3542   Toll Free: (866) NSF-GRFP
Fax: (703) 292-9048   E-mail: info@nsfgrfp.org
Web: www.nsf.gov/funding/pgm_summ.jsp?pims_id=6201

Summary To provide financial assistance to graduate students interested in working on a master's or doctoral degree in fields supported by the National Science Foundation (NSF).

Eligibility This program is open to U.S. citizens, nationals, and permanent residents who wish to work on research-based master's or doctoral degrees in a field of science, technology, engineering, or mathematics (STEM) supported by NSF (including astronomy, chemistry, computer and information sciences and engineering, geosciences, engineering, life sciences, materials research, mathematical sciences, physics, psychology, social sciences, or STEM education and learning). Other work in medical, dental, law, public health, or practice-oriented professional degree programs, or in joint science-professional degree programs, such as M.D./Ph.D. and J.D./Ph.D. programs, is not eligible. Applications normally should be submitted during the senior year in college or in the first year of graduate study; eligibility is limited to those who have completed no more than 12 months of graduate study since completion of a baccalaureate degree. Applicants who have already earned an advanced degree in science, engineering, or medicine (including an M.D., D.D.S., or D.V.M.) are ineligible. Selection is based on 1) intellectual merit of the proposed activity: strength of the academic record, proposed plan of research, previous research experience, references, appropriateness of the choice of institution; and 2) broader impacts of the proposed activity: how well does the activity advance discovery and understanding, how well does it broaden the participation of underrepresented groups (e.g., women, minorities, persons with disabilities, veterans), to what extent will it enhance the infrastructure for research and education, will the results be disseminated broadly to enhance scientific and technological understanding, what may be the benefits of the proposed activity to society).

Financial data The stipend is $32,000 per year; an additional $12,000 cost-of-education allowance is provided to the recipient's institution.

Duration Up to 3 years, usable over a 5-year period.

Number awarded Approximately 2,000 each year.

Deadline October of each year.

[901]
GRETCHEN L. BLECHSCHMIDT AWARD

Geological Society of America
Attn: Program Officer-Grants, Awards and Recognition
3300 Penrose Place
P.O. Box 9140
Boulder, CO 80301-9140
(303) 357-1060   Toll Free: (888) 443-4472, ext. 1060
Fax: (303) 357-1070   E-mail: awards@geosociety.org
Web: www.geosociety.org/grants/gradgrants.htm

Summary To provide support to female members of the Geological Society of America (GSA) interested in conducting doctoral research in geology.

Eligibility This program is open to GSA members working on a doctoral degree at a university in the United States, Canada, Mexico, or Central America. Applicants must be women interested in a career in academic research. Their proposals must be in the fields of 1) biostratigraphy and/or paleoceanography; or 2) sequence stratigraphy analysis, particularly in conjunction with research in deep-sea sedimentology. Disabled and minority women are particularly encouraged to submit research proposals. Selection is based on the scientific merits of the proposal, the capability of the investigator, and the reasonableness of the budget.

Financial data Grants range up to $2,500. Funds can be used for the cost of travel, room and board in the field, services of a technician or field assistant, funding of chemical and isotope analyses, or other expenses directly related to the fulfillment of the research contract. Support is not provided for the purchase of ordinary field equipment, for maintenance of the families of the grantees and their assistants,

as reimbursement for work already accomplished, for institutional overhead, for adviser participation, or for tuition costs.

Duration 1 year.

Number awarded 1 each year.

Deadline January of each year.

[902]
HADASSAH-BRANDEIS INSTITUTE RESEARCH AWARDS

Brandeis University
Hadassah-Brandeis Institute
Attn: Program Manager
515 South Street
Mailstop 079
Waltham, MA 02454-9110
(781) 736-8113   Fax: (781) 736-2078
E-mail: dolins@brandeis.edu
Web: www.brandeis.edu/hbi/grants/research.html

Summary To provide funding to scholars, graduate students, writers, activists, and artists conducting research in the field of Jewish women's studies.

Eligibility This program offers senior grants (for established scholars and professionals) and junior grants (for graduate students and scholars within 3 years of receiving a Ph.D.). All applicants must be interested in conducting interdisciplinary research on Jewish women and gender issues, although there are no gender or religious limitations. Graduate students in recognized master's and Ph.D. programs are encouraged to apply. Applications from outside the United States are welcome. Grants are awarded in 10 categories: history; the Yishuv and Israel; Diaspora studies; families, children, and the Holocaust; gender, culture, religion, and the law; women's health; Judaism; biography; the arts (performance arts, visual arts, creative writing); and film and video. Applications must specify the category and may be for only 1 category. Selection is based on excellence.

Financial data Senior grants are $5,000 and junior grants are $2,000.

Duration 1 year.

Additional information The Hadassah-Brandeis Institute was formerly the Hadassah International Research Institute on Jewish Women at Brandeis University.

Number awarded Between 20 and 30 each year.

Deadline September of each year.

[903]
HARRIET EVELYN WALLACE SCHOLARSHIP

American Geosciences Institute
Attn: Scholarship Coordinator
4220 King Street
Alexandria, VA 22302-1502
(703) 379-2480   Fax: (703) 379-7563
E-mail: wallacescholarship@agiweb.org
Web: www.americangeosciences.org

Summary To provide financial assistance to women interested in working on a graduate degree in the geosciences.

Eligibility This program is open to women who are entering or currently enrolled in a graduate program in the geosciences. Applications must have at least 1 year remaining in their graduate program and be members of at least 1 of the 51 professional member societies of the American Geosciences Institute. They must have an undergraduate GPA of 3.25 or higher and a graduate GPA of 3.0 or higher. Along with their application, they must submit a 500-word abstract about their research interests. Selection is based on the probability of successfully completing a geoscience graduate program and transitioning into the geoscience profession following graduation.

Financial data   The stipend is $5,000 per year.

Duration   1 year; may be renewed 1 additional year.

Additional information   This program began in 2013.

Number awarded   2 each year: 1 for a master's degree student and 1 for a doctoral student.

Deadline   January of each year.

[904]
HAWAI'I'S DAUGHTERS GUILD OF CALIFORNIA SCHOLARSHIPS

Hawai'i's Daughters Guild of California
P.O. Box 3305
Gardena, CA 90247
E-mail: HDG.Scholarship@gmail.com
Web: www.hawaiidaughtersguild.webs.com

Summary   To provide financial assistance for college or graduate school to women of Polynesian ancestry from California.

Eligibility   This program is open to California residents who are women of Polynesian ancestry and graduating high school seniors, full-time undergraduates, or full-time graduate students. Applicants must have a GPA of 3.0 or higher and be able to demonstrate financial need. Along with their application, they must submit transcripts, 3 letters of recommendation, an autobiographical essay, and proof of ancestry. Selection is based on goals as described in the autobiographical essay, academic achievement, extracurricular activities, community service, and financial need.

Financial data   A stipend is awarded (amount not specified).

Duration   1 year.

Number awarded   Varies each year.

Deadline   March of each year.

[905]
HELEN ANN MINS ROBBINS FELLOWSHIP

University of Rochester
Attn: Rossell Hope Robbins Library
Rush Rhees 416
Rochester, NY 14627-0055
(585) 275-4471   E-mail: mturner@library.rochester.edu
Web: www.library.rochester.edu/robbins/fellowship

Summary   To provide funding to women interested in using the resources of the Rossell Hope Robbins Library at the University of Rochester to conduct research for a dissertation in medieval studies.

Eligibility   This program is open to women working on a doctoral dissertation in medieval studies, especially English literature, British history and culture, and the relations between England and France in the Middle Ages. Applicants must be interested in using the resources of the Rossell Hope Robbins Library while remaining in residence in Rochester, New York for the academic year. Along with their application, they must submit a narrative of 750 to 1,000 words describing

their dissertation, outlining the appropriateness of the library to the work they are doing, and commenting on the benefit of the period of research free of other obligations that the fellowship would allow.

Financial data   The grant is $24,000.

Duration   1 academic year (up to 12 months).

Additional information   The fellow is expected to engage in the academic life of the university and, towards the end of her residency, to give a lecture based on her research.

Number awarded   1 each even-numbered year.

Deadline   March of each even-numbered year.

[906]
HELEN W. NIES SCHOLARSHIP

Federal Circuit Bar Association
1620 I Street, N.W., Suite 900
Washington, DC 20006
(202) 466-3923   Fax: (202) 833-1061
E-mail: fcbascholarships@fedcirbar.org
Web: www.fedcirbar.org

Summary   To provide financial assistance to female law students who are interested in intellectual property law.

Eligibility   This program is open to women who are currently enrolled in ABA-accredited law schools and are interested in intellectual property law. Applicants must submit a 450-word essay on their financial need, interest in particular areas of the law, and any other qualifications for this particular scholarship. Selection is based on academic excellence, financial need, and interest in intellectual property law.

Financial data   The stipend is $10,000.

Duration   1 year.

Additional information   This scholarship was first presented in 2007.

Number awarded   1 each year.

Deadline   April of each year.

[907]
HELEN WOODRUFF NOLOP SCHOLARSHIP IN AUDIOLOGY AND ALLIED FIELDS

Delta Zeta Sorority
Attn: Foundation Coordinator
202 East Church Street
Oxford, OH 45056
(513) 523-7597   Fax: (513) 523-1921
E-mail: DZFoundation@dzshq.com
Web: www.deltazeta.org/aboutus/foundation/scholarships

Summary   To provide financial assistance to women who are working on a graduate degree in audiology or a related field.

Eligibility   This program is open to women working on a graduate degree in audiology or a related field of speech and hearing. Membership in Delta Zeta Sorority is not required. Applicants must submit an official transcript, a statement of their career goals, documentation of campus activities and/or community involvement, a list of academic honors, and an explanation of their financial need.

Financial data   The stipend ranges from $1,000 to $15,000, depending on the availability of funds.

Duration   1 year; nonrenewable.

Number awarded 1 each year.

Deadline February of each year.

[908]
HELENE M. OVERLY MEMORIAL GRADUATE SCHOLARSHIP

Women's Transportation Seminar
Attn: WTS Foundation
1701 K Street, N.W., Suite 800
Washington, DC 20006
(202) 955-5085   Fax: (202) 955-5088
E-mail: wts@wtsinternational.org
Web: www.wtsinternational.org/education/scholarships

Summary To provide financial assistance to women graduate students interested in preparing for a career in transportation.

Eligibility This program is open to women who are enrolled in a graduate degree program in a transportation-related field (e.g., transportation engineering, planning, finance, or logistics). Applicants must have at least a 3.0 GPA and be interested in a career in transportation. Along with their application, they must submit a 750-word statement about their career goals after graduation and why they think they should receive the scholarship award. Applications must be submitted first to a local chapter; the chapters forward selected applications for consideration on the national level. Minority women are particularly encouraged to apply. Selection is based on transportation involvement and goals, job skills, and academic record.

Financial data The stipend is $10,000.

Duration 1 year.

Additional information This program began in 1981. Local chapters may also award additional funding to winners in their area.

Number awarded 1 each year.

Deadline Applications must be submitted by November to a local WTS chapter.

[909]
HENRY P. DAVID GRANTS FOR RESEARCH AND INTERNATIONAL TRAVEL IN HUMAN REPRODUCTIVE BEHAVIOR AND POPULATION STUDIES

American Psychological Foundation
750 First Street, N.E.
Washington, DC 20002-4242
(202) 336-5843   Fax: (202) 336-5812
E-mail: foundation@apa.org
Web: www.apa.org/apf/funding/david.aspx

Summary To provide funding to young psychologists who are interested in conducting research on reproductive behavior.

Eligibility This program is open to doctoral students in psychology working on a dissertation and young psychologists who have no more than 10 years of postgraduate experience. Applicants must be interested in conducting research on human reproductive behavior or an area related to population concerns. Along with their application, they must submit a current curriculum vitae, 2 letters of recommendation, and an essay of 1 to 2 pages on their interest in human reproductive behavior or in population studies. The sponsor encourages

applications from individuals who represent diversity in race, ethnicity, gender, age, disability, and sexual orientation.

Financial data The grant is $1,500.

Duration The grant is presented annually.

Additional information Every third year (2017, 1020), the program also provides support for a non-U.S. reproductive health/population science professional to travel to and participate in the Psychosocial Workshop, held in conjunction with the Population Association of America annual meeting.

Number awarded 2 in the years when the program offers support to a non-U.S. professional to travel to the United States; 1 in other years.

Deadline November of each year.

[910]
HERBERT AND BETTY CARNES FUND

American Ornithologists' Union
c/o Brian D. Peer, Research Awards Chair
Western Illinois University
Department of Biological Sciences
Waggoner Hall 333
Macomb, IL 61455
(309) 298-2336   E-mail: BD_peer@wiu-edu
Web: www.americanornithology.org

Summary To provide funding to female graduate students and scholars who are members of the American Ornithologists' Union (AOU) and interested in conducting research on avian biology.

Eligibility This program is open to female AOU members who are graduate students, postdoctorates, or other researchers without access to major funding agencies. Applicants must be interested in conducting research on avian biology. They must be nonsmokers (have not smoked in at least the previous 6 months). Along with their application, they should send a cover letter (about 5 pages) describing their proposed project, a budget, and 1 letter of reference. Selection is based on significance and originality of the research question, clarity of the objectives, feasibility of the plan of research, and appropriateness of the budget.

Financial data The maximum award is $2,500 per year.

Duration 1 year; recipients may reapply for 1 additional award.

Number awarded The sponsor awards a total of 28 to 30 grants each year.

Deadline January of each year.

[911]
HERBERT W. AND CORRINE CHILSTROM SCHOLARSHIP FOR WOMEN PREPARING FOR ORDAINED MINISTRY

Women of the Evangelical Lutheran Church in America
Attn: Scholarships
8765 West Higgins Road
Chicago, IL 60631-4101
(773) 380-2741   Toll Free: (800) 638-3522, ext. 2741
Fax: (773) 380-2419   E-mail: women.elca@elca.org
Web: www.womenoftheelca.org

Summary To provide financial assistance to mature women who are studying for a second career in the ordained ministry in the Evangelical Lutheran Church of America (ELCA).

Eligibility Applicants for this scholarship must be women who have experienced an interruption of at least 5 years in their education since college graduation and are currently entering the final year of an M.Div. program at an ELCA seminary. They must have been endorsed by the Synodical Candidacy Committee. Selection is based on academic achievement, personal commitment and determination to serve as a pastor in the ELCA, and financial need. U.S. citizenship is required.

Financial data The maximum stipend is $1,000 per year.

Duration 1 year; recipients may reapply for 1 additional year.

Additional information This scholarship was established in 1996 to honor Rev. Herbert W. Chilstrom and Rev. Corrine Chilstrom during the 25th anniversary year of the ordination of women in the predecessor bodies of the ELCA. Recipients must agree to serve for at least 3 years as an ELCA pastor after graduation from seminary.

Number awarded 1 each year.

Deadline February of each year.

[912]
HERMINE DALKOWITZ TOBOLOWSKY SCHOLARSHIP

Texas Business Women
Attn: Texas Business and Professional Women's
 Foundation
P.O. Box 70
Round Rock, TX 78680-0070
E-mail: info@tbwconnect.com
Web: www.texasbpwfoundation.org/scholarships.php

Summary To provide financial assistance to women from any state who are attending college in Texas to prepare for a career in selected professions.

Eligibility This program is open to women from any state who are interested in preparing for a career in law, public service, government, political science, or women's history. Applicants must have completed at least 2 semesters of study at an accredited college or university in Texas, have a GPA of 3.0 or higher, and be U.S. citizens. Along with their application, they must submit a 2-page essay on 1 of the following topics: the importance of women in the workforce, the importance of women in public services, or the importance of the study of women in history. Selection is based on academic achievement and financial need.

Financial data The stipend is $3,000.

Duration 1 year.

Additional information This program began in 1995 when Texas Business Women was named Texas Federation of Business and Professional Women's Clubs.

Number awarded 1 or more each year.

Deadline December of each year.

[913]
HILARY A. BUFTON JR. SCHOLARSHIP

American Business Women's Association
Attn: Stephen Bufton Memorial Educational Fund
9820 Metcalf Avenue, Suite 110
Overland Park, KS 66212
Toll Free: (800) 228-0007
Web: www.sbmef.org/National/index.cfm

Summary To provide financial assistance to female graduate students who are working on a degree in a specified field (the field changes each year).

Eligibility This program is open to women who are working on a graduate degree and have a cumulative GPA of 3.0 or higher. Applicants are not required to be members of the American Business Women's Association. Along with their application, they must submit a 250-word biographical sketch that includes information about their background, activities, honors, work experience, and long-term educational and professional goals. Financial need is not considered in the selection process. Annually, the trustees designate an academic discipline for which the scholarship will be presented that year. U.S. citizenship is required.

Financial data The stipend is $10,000 (paid over a 2-year period). Funds are paid directly to the recipient's institution to be used only for tuition, books, and fees.

Duration 2 years.

Additional information This program was created in 1986 as part of ABWA's Stephen Bufton Memorial Education Fund.

Number awarded 1 each even-numbered year.

Deadline May of each even-numbered year.

[914]
HOLLY A. CORNELL SCHOLARSHIP

American Water Works Association
Attn: Scholarship Coordinator
6666 West Quincy Avenue
Denver, CO 80235-3098
(303) 794-7771   Toll Free: (800) 926-7337
Fax: (303) 347-0804   E-mail: scholarships@awwa.org
Web: www.awwa.org

Summary To provide financial assistance to outstanding minority and female students interested in working on an master's degree in the field of water supply and treatment.

Eligibility This program is open to minority and female students working on a master's degree in the field of water supply and treatment at a college or university in Canada, Guam, Mexico, Puerto Rico, or the United States. Students who have been accepted into graduate school but have not yet begun graduate study are encouraged to apply. Applicants must submit a 2-page resume, official transcripts, 3 letters of recommendation, a proposed curriculum of study, a 1-page statement of educational plans and career objectives demonstrating an interest in the drinking water field, and a 3-page proposed plan of research. Selection is based on academic record and potential to provide leadership in the field of water supply and treatment.

Financial data The stipend is $7,500.

Duration 1 year; nonrenewable.

Additional information Funding for this program, which began in 1990, comes from the consulting firm CH2M Hill.

Number awarded 1 each year.

Deadline January of each year.

[915]
HONOLULU ALUMNAE PANHELLENIC ASSOCIATION GRADUATE SCHOLARSHIPS

Honolulu Alumnae Panhellenic Association
c/o Hazel Tagatac, Vice President of Scholarship
6401 101st Street
Ewa Beach, HI 96706
E-mail: hapascholarship@gmail.com
Web: hawaiipanhellenic.net

Summary To provide financial assistance to women from Hawaii who are alumnae members of a National Panhellenic Conference (NPC) sorority and interested in working on a graduate degree.

Eligibility This program is open to women who are alumnae members of an NPC-affiliated sorority and enrolled or planning to enroll at a college or university in any state to work on a graduate degree. Their permanent home address or college address must be in Hawaii. Along with their application, they must submit brief essays on how membership in their sorority impacted their life, how they have contributed to their sorority and the Panhellenic community, and how this scholarship will benefit them. Financial need is not considered in the selection process.

Financial data The stipend ranges from $500 to $1,000.

Duration 1 year.

Number awarded Varies each year.

Deadline March of each year.

[916]
HONOLULU BRANCH AAUW SCHOLARSHIPS

Hawai'i Community Foundation
Attn: Scholarship Department
827 Fort Street Mall
Honolulu, HI 96813
(808) 566-5570   Toll Free: (888) 731-3863
Fax: (808) 521-6286
E-mail: scholarships@hcf-hawaii.org
Web: hcf.scholarships.ngwebsolutions.com

Summary To provide financial assistance to women in Hawaii who are working on an undergraduate or graduate degree at a school in the state.

Eligibility This program is open to female residents of Hawaii who are currently enrolled at an accredited university in the state. Applicants must be working full time on an undergraduate degree or full or part time on a graduate degree in any field. They must have a GPA of 3.0 or higher. All fields of study are eligible, but preference is given to students working on a degree in a field of science, technology, engineering, or mathematics (STEM). Along with their application, they must submit a brief curriculum vitae or resume highlighting their academic achievements. Financial need is considered in the selection process.

Financial data The amounts of the awards depend on the availability of funds and the need of the recipient. Recently, the average value of the scholarships awarded by the foundation was $2,800.

Duration 1 year.

Additional information This program is sponsored by the Honolulu Branch of the American Association of University Women (AAUW).

Number awarded 1 or more each year.

Deadline February of each year.

[917]
HORIZONS FOUNDATION SCHOLARSHIP PROGRAM

Women in Defense
c/o National Defense Industrial Association
2111 Wilson Boulevard, Suite 400
Arlington, VA 22201-3061
(703) 522-1820   Fax: (703) 522-1885
E-mail: wid@ndia.org
Web: www.womenindefense.net

Summary To provide financial assistance to members of Women in Defense (WID) who are upper-division or graduate students engaged in or planning careers related to the national security interests of the United States.

Eligibility This program is open to WID members who are already working in national security fields as well as women planning such careers. Applicants must 1) be currently enrolled at an accredited college or university, either full or part time, as graduate students or upper-division undergraduates; 2) demonstrate financial need; 3) be U.S. citizens; 4) have a GPA of 3.25 or higher; and 5) demonstrate interest in preparing for a career related to national security or defense. The preferred fields of study include business (as it relates to national security or defense), computer science, cyber security, economics, engineering, government relations, international relations, law (as it relates to national security or defense), mathematics, military history, political science, physics, and security studies; others are considered if the applicant can demonstrate relevance to a career in national security or defense. Selection is based on academic achievement, participation in defense and national security activities, field of study, work experience, statements of objectives, recommendations, and financial need.

Financial data The stipend ranges up to $10,000.

Duration 1 year; renewable.

Additional information This program began in 1988.

Number awarded Varies each year; recently, 3 worth $16,000 were awarded.

Deadline July of each year.

[918]
HORIZONS-MICHIGAN SCHOLARSHIP

Women in Defense-Michigan Chapter
Attn: Scholarship Director
P.O. Box 4744
Troy, MI 48099
E-mail: scholarships@wid-mi.org
Web: www.wid-mi.org

Summary To provide financial assistance to women in Michigan who are upper-division or graduate students working on a degree related to national defense.

Eligibility This program is open to women who are residents of Michigan and enrolled either full or part time at a college or university in the state. Applicants must be juniors, seniors, or graduate students and have a GPA of 3.25 or higher. They must be interested in preparing for a career related to national security or defense. Relevant fields of study include security studies, military history, government relations, engineering, computer science, physics, mathematics, business (as related to national security or defense), law (as related to national security or defense), international relations, political science, or economics; other fields may be considered if the applicant can demonstrate relevance to a career in national security or defense. Along with their application, they must submit brief statements on their interest in a career in national security or defense, the principal accomplishments in their life that relate to their professional goals, and the objectives of their educational program. Selection is based on those statements, academic achievement, participation in defense and national security activities, field of study, work experience, recommendations, and financial need. U.S. citizenship is required.

Financial data Stipends have averaged at least $3,000.

Duration 1 year.

Additional information This program began in 2009.

Number awarded Varies each year; recently, 6 were awarded.

Deadline September of each year.

[919]
HORMEL FOODS MINNESOTA SECTION SWE SCHOLARSHIPS

Society of Women Engineers-Minnesota Section
Attn: Scholarship Committee
P.O. Box 18481
Minneapolis, MN 55418
E-mail: scholarships@swe-mn.org
Web: www.swe-mn.org/scholarships.html

Summary To provide financial assistance to women from any state working on an undergraduate or graduate degree in industrial technology or specified fields of engineering at colleges and universities in Minnesota, North Dakota, and South Dakota.

Eligibility This program is open to female undergraduate and graduate students at ABET-accredited engineering programs in Minnesota, North Dakota, or South Dakota. Applicants must be working full time on a degree in industrial technology or agricultural, civil, electrical, industrial, manufacturing, or mechanical engineering. Along with their application, they must submit a 250-word essay describing how they plan to utilize their engineering knowledge and skills after they graduate. Selection is based on potential to succeed as an engineer (20 points), communication skills (10 points), extracurricular or community involvement and leadership skills (10 points), demonstration of work experience and successes (10 points), and academic success (5 points).

Financial data The stipend is $1,000.

Duration 1 year.

Additional information This program is sponsored by Hormel Foods.

Number awarded 2 each year.

Deadline March of each year.

[920]
HUMBLE ARTESIAN ABWA SCHOLARSHIP

American Business Women's Association-Humble
  Artesian Chapter
c/o Dee Driscoll, Education Committee
7810 FM 1960 E, Suite 104
Humble, TX 77346
(281) 852-3667   Fax: (281) 852-3663
E-mail: driscolldee@yahoo.com
Web: www.abwahumble.org/scholarship

Summary To provide financial assistance to women from any state who have completed at least the sophomore year of college.

Eligibility This program is open to all women who are U.S. citizens. Applicants must be enrolled as juniors, seniors, or graduate students at a college or university in any state and have a GPA of 2.5 or higher.

Financial data The stipend is $1,500.

Duration 1 year.

Number awarded 1 each year.

Deadline January of each year.

[921]
HUNTSVILLE CHAPTER AFWA SCHOLARSHIPS

Accounting and Financial Women's Alliance-Huntsville
  Chapter
c/o Sylvia Ayers, Education Chair
COLSA Corporation
6728 Odyssey Drive, N.W.
Huntsville, AL 35806
(256) 964-5555   E-mail: sayers@colsa.com
Web: www.huntsvilleafwa.org/wordpress/scholarship

Summary To provide financial assistance to women working on an undergraduate or graduate degree in accounting at a college or university in Alabama.

Eligibility This program is open to women working full or part time on a bachelor's or master's degree in accounting at a college, university, or professional school of accounting in Alabama. Applicants must have completed at least 60 semester hours. They are not required to be members of the Accounting and Financial Women's Alliance (AFWA). Along with their application, they must submit a 250-word essay on how they plan to incorporate into their strategic career goals the sponsor's philosophy of achieving balance among life priorities, including career, personal development, family, friendships, and community and societal needs. Selection is based on that essay, academic record, extracurricular activities and honors, employment history, a statement of career goals and objectives, and financial need.

Financial data The stipend ranges from $500 to $2,500.

Duration 1 year.

Number awarded Varies each year; recently, 4 were awarded.

Deadline March of each year.

[922]
HWNT AUSTIN SCHOLARSHIP

Hispanic Scholarship Consortium
Attn: Scholarship Selection Committee
7703 North Lamar Boulevard, Suite 310
Austin, TX 78752
(512) 368-2956   Fax: (512) 692-1831
E-mail: scholarships@hispanicscholar.org
Web: hispanicscholar.academicworks.com

Summary   To provide financial assistance and work experience to female high school seniors and college seniors of Hispanic heritage from Texas who plan to attend college or graduate school in any state.

Eligibility   This program is open to female residents of Texas of Hispanic heritage who are either 1) seniors graduating from high schools in Texas; or 2) seniors graduating from colleges in any state. High school seniors must be planning to enroll full time at an accredited 2- or 4-year college or university in any state; college seniors must be planning to enroll in graduate school. Applicants must have a GPA of 3.0 or higher. Selection is based on academic achievement, community service, personal strengths, leadership, and financial need. U.S. citizenship is not required; students may qualify under Texas Senate Bill 1528.

Financial data   The stipend is $2,000 per year.

Duration   1 year; may be renewed up to 3 additional years, provided the recipient remains enrolled full time, maintains a GPA of 3.0 or higher, and participates in at least 25 hours of community service per semester.

Additional information   This program is sponsored by the Austin chapter of Hispanic Women's Network of Texas (HWNT). Scholarship winners must also participate in a year-long internship with the magazine.

Number awarded   Varies each year; recently, 2 were awarded.

Deadline   April of each year.

[923]
IADES FELLOWSHIP AWARD

International Alumnae of Delta Epsilon Sorority
c/o Virginia Borggaard
2453 Bear Den Road
Frederick, MD 21701-9321
Fax: (301) 663-3231   TDD: (301) 663-9235
E-mail: vborggaard@juno.com
Web: www.iades1957.org/scholarships

Summary   To provide financial assistance to deaf women who are working on a doctoral degree.

Eligibility   This program is open to deaf women who have completed 12 or more units in a doctoral-level program and have a GPA of 3.0 or more. They need not be members of Delta Epsilon. Along with their application, they must submit official transcripts, a recent copy of their audiogram, and 2 letters of recommendation.

Financial data   The stipend is $2,000.

Duration   1 year.

Number awarded   1 or more each year.

Deadline   September of each year.

[924]
IBM PHD FELLOWSHIP PROGRAM

IBM Corporation
Attn: University Relations
1133 Westchester Avenue
White Plains, NY 10604
Toll Free: (800) IBM-4YOU   TDD: (800) IBM-3383
E-mail: phdfellow@us.ibm.com
Web: www.research.ibm.com

Summary   To provide funding and work experience to students from any country working on a Ph.D. in a research area of broad interest to IBM.

Eligibility   Students nominated for this fellowship should be enrolled full time at an accredited college or university in any country and should have completed at least 1 year of graduate study in computer science or engineering, electrical or mechanical engineering, physical sciences (chemistry, material sciences, physics), mathematical sciences, public sector and business sciences, or service science, management, and engineering (SSME). Focus areas that receive special consideration include technology that creates new business or social value, cognitive computing research, cloud and distributed computing technology and solutions, or fundamental science and technology. Applicants should be planning a career in research. Nominations must be made by a faculty member and endorsed by the department head. The program values diversity, and encourages nominations of women, minorities, and others who contribute to that diversity. Selection is based on the applicants' potential for research excellence, the degree to which their technical interests align with those of IBM, and academic progress to date. Preference is given to students who have had an IBM internship or have closely collaborated with technical or services people from IBM.

Financial data   Fellowships pay tuition, fees, and a stipend of $17,500 per year.

Duration   1 year; may be renewed up to 2 additional years, provided the recipient is renominated, interacts with IBM's technical community, and demonstrates continued progress and achievement.

Additional information   Recipients are offered an internship at 1 of the IBM Research Division laboratories and are given an IBM computer.

Number awarded   Varies each year; recently, 57 were awarded.

Deadline   October of each year.

[925]
IDA B. WELLS GRADUATE STUDENT FELLOWSHIP

Coordinating Council for Women in History
c/o Sandra Dawson, Executive Director
Northern Illinois University
Department of History and Women's Studies
715 Zulauf Hall
DeKalb, IL 60115
(815) 895-2624   E-mail: Wellsaward@theccwh.org
Web: www.theccwh.org

Summary   To provide funding to women graduate students for completion of their doctoral dissertations on an historical topic.

Eligibility This program is open to women graduate students in history departments at U.S. institutions who are members of the Coordinating Council for Women in History (CCWH). Applicants must have passed to A.B.D. status. They may be specializing in any field, but they must be working on an historical project. Preference is given to applicants working on a project involving issues of race.

Financial data The grant is $1,000.

Duration 1 year.

Additional information This program, established in 1999, is administered by the CCWH and the Berkshire Conference of Women Historians. The award is presented at the CCWH luncheon at the annual meeting of the American Historical Association, although the recipient does not need to be present to accept the award.

Number awarded 1 each year.

Deadline May of each year.

[926]
IDA M. POPE MEMORIAL SCHOLARSHIPS

Hawai'i Community Foundation
Attn: Scholarship Department
827 Fort Street Mall
Honolulu, HI 96813
(808) 566-5570   Toll Free: (888) 731-3863
Fax: (808) 521-6286
E-mail: scholarships@hcf-hawaii.org
Web: hcf.scholarships.ngwebsolutions.com

Summary To provide financial assistance to Native Hawaiian women who are interested in working on an undergraduate or graduate degree in designated fields at a school in any state.

Eligibility This program is open to female residents of Hawaii who are Native Hawaiian, defined as a descendant of the aboriginal inhabitants of the Hawaiian islands prior to 1778. Applicants must be enrolled full time at a 2- or 4-year college or university in any state and working on an undergraduate or graduate degree in health, science, mathematics, or education (including counseling and social work). They must be able to demonstrate academic achievement (GPA of 3.5 or higher), good moral character, and financial need. Along with their application, they must submit a short statement indicating their reasons for attending college, their planned course of study, their career goals, and what community service means to them.

Financial data The amounts of the awards depend on the availability of funds and the need of the recipient. Recently, the average value of the scholarships awarded by the foundation was $2,800.

Duration 1 year; may be renewed.

Number awarded Varies each year; recently, 61 were awarded.

Deadline February of each year.

[927]
INGEBORG HASELTINE SCHOLARSHIP FUND FOR WOMEN

Unitarian Universalist Association
Attn: Ministerial Credentialing Office
24 Farnsworth Street
Boston, MA 02210-1409
(617) 948-6403   Fax: (617) 742-2875
E-mail: mcoadministrator@uua.org
Web: www.uua.org

Summary To provide financial assistance to women preparing for the Unitarian Universalist (UU) ministry.

Eligibility This program is open to women currently enrolled or planning to enroll full time in a UU ministerial training program with aspirant or candidate status. Financial need is considered in the selection process.

Financial data The stipend ranges from $1,000 to $15,000 per year.

Duration 1 year.

Number awarded Varies each year; recently, 5 were awarded.

Deadline April of each year.

[928]
INTELLECTUAL PROPERTY LAW SECTION WOMEN AND MINORITY SCHOLARSHIP

State Bar of Texas
Attn: Intellectual Property Law Section
c/o Bhaveeni D. Parmar, Scholarship Selection
    Committee
Law Office of Bhaveeni Parmar PLLC
4447 North Central Expressway, Suite 110-295
Dallas, Texas 75205
E-mail: bhaveeni@parmarlawoffice.com
Web: www.texasbariplaw.org

Summary To provide financial assistance to female and minority students at law schools in Texas who plan to practice intellectual property law.

Eligibility This program is open to women and members of minority groups (African Americans, Hispanics, Asian Americans, and Native Americans) from any state who are currently enrolled at an ABA-accredited law school in Texas. Applicants must be planning to practice intellectual property law in Texas. Along with their application, they must submit a 2-page essay explaining why they plan to prepare for a career in intellectual property law in Texas, any qualifications they believe are relevant for their consideration for this scholarship, and (optionally) any issues of financial need they wish to have considered.

Financial data The stipend is $5,000.

Duration 1 year.

Number awarded 2 each year: 1 to a women and 1 to a minority.

Deadline May of each year.

[929]
INTERMOUNTAIN SECTION AWWA DIVERSITY SCHOLARSHIP

American Water Works Association-Intermountain
  Section
Attn: Member Services Coordinator
3430 East Danish Road
Sandy, UT 84093
(801) 712-1619, ext. 2   Fax: (801) 487-6699
E-mail: nicoleb@ims-awwa.org
Web: ims-awwa.site-ym.com/group/StudentPO

Summary To provide financial assistance to female and minority undergraduate and graduate students working on a degree in the field of water quality, supply, and treatment at a university in the Intermountain West.

Eligibility This program is open to 1) women; and 2) students who identify as Hispanic or Latino, Black or African American, Native Hawaiian or other Pacific Islander, Asian, or American Indian or Alaska Native. Applicants must be entering or enrolled in an undergraduate or graduate program at a college or university in the Intermountain West (defined to include all or portions of Arizona, Colorado, Idaho, Montana, Nevada, New Mexico, Utah, or Wyoming) that relates to water quality, supply, or treatment. Along with their application, they must submit a 2-page essay on their academic interests and career goals and how those relate to water quality, supply, or treatment. Selection is based on that essay, letters of recommendation, and potential to contribute to the field of water quality, supply, and treatment in the Intermountain West.

Financial data The stipend is $1,000. The winner also receives a 1-year student membership in the Intermountain Section of the American Water Works Association (AWWA).

Duration 1 year; nonrenewable.

Number awarded 1 each year.

Deadline November of each year.

[930]
INTERNATIONAL SECURITY AND COOPERATION PREDOCTORAL FELLOWSHIPS

Stanford University
Center for International Security and Cooperation
Attn: Fellowships Coordinator
Encina Hall, Room C206-10
616 Serra Street
Stanford, CA 94305-6165
(650) 723-9625   Fax: (650) 724-5683
E-mail: CISACfellowship@stanford.edu
Web: cisac.fsi.stanford.edu/docs/cisac_fellowship_program

Summary To provide funding to doctoral students who are interested in working on a dissertation on international security problems at Stanford University's Center for International Security and Cooperation.

Eligibility This program is open to students currently enrolled in doctoral programs at academic institutions in the United States who would benefit from access to the facilities offered by the center. Applicants may be working in any discipline of the social sciences, humanities, natural sciences, law, or engineering that relates to international security problems. Relevant topics include nuclear weapons policy and nonproliferation; nuclear energy; cybersecurity, cyberwarfare, and the future of the Internet; war and civil conflict; global governance, migration and transnational flows, from norms to criminal trafficking; biosecurity and global health; implications of geostrategic shifts; insurgency, terrorism, and homeland security; and consolidating peace after conflict. The sponsor welcomes applications from women, minorities, and citizens of all countries.

Financial data The stipend ranges from $25,000 to $28,000. Medical insurance is available for those who do not have coverage.

Duration 9 to 11 months.

Additional information Fellows are expected to complete dissertation chapters or their dissertation during their fellowship. They should not plan to spend any time conducting research abroad or in other parts of the country.

Number awarded Varies each year; recently, 9 were awarded.

Deadline January of each year.

[931]
IOTA SIGMA PI MEMBERS-AT-LARGE REENTRY AWARD

Iota Sigma Pi
c/o Gail Blaustein, MAL National Coordinator
Benedictine College
Department of Chemistry and Biochemistry
Westerman 406A
1020 North Second Street
Atchison, KS 66002
(913) 360-7515   E-mail: MAL.IotaSigmaPi@gmail.com
Web: www.ispmembersatlarge.com

Summary To provide financial assistance to women who are reentering college to work on an undergraduate or graduate degree in chemistry.

Eligibility This program is open to women who have returned to academic studies after an absence of 3 or more years and have completed at least 1 academic year of college chemistry since returning. Students must be working on an undergraduate or graduate degree in chemistry or a related field at a 4-year college or university. They must be nominated by a member of Iota Sigma Pi or by a member of the faculty at their institution. Nominees must submit a short essay describing their goals, pertinent experiences that influenced their choice of major, any interests or talents that will assist them in succeeding in their professional career, and how the scholarship will benefit them in meeting their goals. Financial need is not considered in the selection process.

Financial data The winner receives a stipend of $1,500, a certificate, and a 1-year waiver of Iota Sigma Pi dues.

Duration 1 year.

Additional information This award was first presented in 1991.

Number awarded 1 each year.

Deadline February of each year.

[932]
IRENE AND DAISY MACGREGOR MEMORIAL SCHOLARSHIP

Daughters of the American Revolution-National Society
Attn: Committee Services Office, Scholarships
1776 D Street, N.W.
Washington, DC 20006-5303
(202) 628-1776
Web: www.dar.org

Summary To provide financial assistance to graduate students working on a degree in medicine or psychiatric nursing.

Eligibility This program is open to students who have been accepted into or are enrolled in an approved program of graduate psychiatric nursing or medicine. Pre-medicine, osteopathic, veterinary, and physician assistant students are not eligible. Applicants must be U.S. citizens and attend an accredited medical school, college, or university in the United States. They must obtain a letter of sponsorship from a local Daughters of the American Revolution (DAR) chapter. Preference is given to women applicants, provided they are "equally qualified." Selection is based on academic excellence, commitment to the field of study, and financial need.

Financial data The stipend is $5,000 per year.

Duration 1 year; may be renewed for up to 3 additional years, provided the recipient maintains a GPA of 3.25 or higher.

Number awarded 1 or more each year.

Deadline February of each year.

[933]
IRENE DRINKALL FRANKE/MARY SEELEY KNUDSTRUP SCHOLARSHIP

Women of the Evangelical Lutheran Church in America
Attn: Scholarships
8765 West Higgins Road
Chicago, IL 60631-4101
(773) 380-2741   Toll Free: (800) 638-3522, ext. 2741
Fax: (773) 380-2419   E-mail: valora.starr@elca.org
Web: www.womenoftheelca.org

Summary To provide financial assistance to lay women who are members of Evangelical Lutheran Church of America (ELCA) congregations and who wish to pursue graduate studies.

Eligibility This program is open to ELCA lay women who are at least 21 years of age and have experienced an interruption of at least 2 years in their education since high school. Applicants must have been admitted to a graduate program at an academic institution to prepare for a career of Christian service but not in the ordained ministry. U.S. citizenship is required.

Financial data The maximum stipend is $1,000 per year.

Duration 1 year; recipients may reapply for 1 additional year.

Number awarded 1 or more each year.

Deadline February of each year.

[934]
ISAAC J. "IKE" CRUMBLY MINORITIES IN ENERGY GRANT

American Association of Petroleum Geologists
  Foundation
Attn: Grants-in-Aid Program
1444 South Boulder Avenue
P.O. Box 979
Tulsa, OK 74101-0979
(918) 560-2644   Toll Free: (855) 302-2743
Fax: (918) 560-2642   E-mail: foundation@aapg.org
Web: foundation.aapg.org

Summary To provide funding to minority and female graduate students who are interested in conducting research related to earth science aspects of the petroleum industry.

Eligibility This program is open to women and ethnic minorities (Black, Hispanic, Asian, or Native American, including American Indian, Eskimo, Hawaiian, or Samoan) who are working on a master's or doctoral degree. Applicants must be interested in conducting research related to the search for and development of petroleum and energy-minerals resources and to related environmental geology issues. Selection is based on student's academic and employment history (10 points), scientific merit of proposal (30 points), suitability to program objectives (30 points), financial merit of proposal (20 points), and endorsement by faculty or department adviser (10 points).

Financial data Grants range from $500 to $3,000. Funds are to be applied to research-related expenses (e.g., a summer of field work). They may not be used to purchase capital equipment or to pay salaries, tuition, room, or board.

Duration 1 year. Doctoral candidates may receive a 1-year renewal.

Number awarded 1 each year.

Deadline February of each year.

[935]
ISABEL M. HERSON SCHOLARSHIP IN EDUCATION

Zeta Phi Beta Sorority, Inc.
Attn: National Educational Foundation
1734 New Hampshire Avenue, N.W.
Washington, DC 20009
(202) 387-3103   Fax: (202) 232-4593
E-mail: info@zetaphibetasororityhq.org
Web: www.zpbnef1975.org/scholarships-and-descriptions

Summary To provide financial assistance to undergraduate and graduate students interested in preparing for a career in education.

Eligibility This program is open to students enrolled full time in an undergraduate or graduate program leading to a degree in either elementary or secondary education. Proof of enrollment is required. Along with their application, they must submit a 150-word essay on their educational goals and professional aspirations, how this award will help them to achieve those goals, and why they should receive the award. Financial need is not considered in the selection process.

Financial data The stipend ranges from $500 to $1,000.

Duration 1 academic year.

Additional information Zeta Phi Beta is a traditionally African American sorority.

Number awarded 1 or more each year.

Deadline January of each year.

[936]
ISO NEW ENGLAND SCHOLARSHIPS

Society of Women Engineers
Attn: Scholarship Selection Committee
203 North LaSalle Street, Suite 1675
Chicago, IL 60601-1269
(312) 596-5223 Toll Free: (877) SWE-INFO
Fax: (312) 644-8557 E-mail: scholarships@swe.org
Web: societyofwomenengineers.swe.org

Summary To provide financial assistance to women who have ties to New England and are interested in working on an undergraduate or graduate degree in computer or electrical engineering.

Eligibility This program is open to women who are sophomores, juniors, seniors, or graduate students and working full time on an undergraduate or graduate degree in computer or electrical engineering with a power focus. Applicants must be residents of New England or attending an ABET-accredited college or university in that region. They must have a GPA of 3.5 or higher. Selection is based on merit.

Financial data The stipend is $2,500.

Duration 1 year.

Additional information This program began in 2014 with support from ISO New England.

Number awarded 2 each year.

Deadline February of each year.

[937]
J. FRANCES ALLEN SCHOLARSHIP AWARD

American Fisheries Society
Attn: Equal Opportunities Section
425 Barlow Place, Suite 110
Bethesda, MD 20814-2144
(301) 897-8616, ext. 205 Fax: (301) 897-8096
E-mail: jsewell@fisheries.org
Web: www.fisheries.org

Summary To provide financial assistance for doctoral studies to female members of the American Fisheries Society (AFS).

Eligibility This program is open to women Ph.D. students who are AFS members. Applicants must be studying a branch of fisheries science, including but not limited to aquatic biology, engineering, fish culture, limnology, oceanography, or sociology. Selection is based on research promise, scientific merit, and academic achievement.

Financial data The stipend is $2,500, paid directly to the student. Funds may be used for any aspect of doctoral education, including tuition, textbooks, equipment, travel, or living expenses.

Duration 1 year; nonrenewable.

Additional information This program began in 1986.

Number awarded 1 each year.

Deadline March of each year.

[938]
JANE CHAMBERS PLAYWRITING AWARD

Association for Theatre in Higher Education
Attn: Women and Theatre Program
P.O. Box 1290
Boulder, CO 80306-1290
(303) 530-2167 Toll Free: (888) 284-3737
Fax: (303) 530-2168 E-mail: vpawards@athe.org
Web: www.womenandtheatreprogram.com

Summary To recognize and reward outstanding plays and performance texts that were created by women and have a majority of parts for women performers.

Eligibility Women are invited to submit plays and performance texts that reflect a feminist perspective and contain significant opportunities for women performers. Scripts may be produced or unproduced. There is no limitation on length, style, or subject. Current undergraduate and graduate students may enter the student category of the competition.

Financial data The general award consists of $1,000, free registration to attend the Women and Theatre Conference (early August), and a rehearsed reading of the winning piece at that conference. The student award is $150 and a year's membership in Women and Theatre.

Duration The competition is held annually.

Number awarded 1 general award and 1 student award are presented each year.

Deadline February of each year.

[939]
JANE M. KLAUSMAN WOMEN IN BUSINESS SCHOLARSHIPS

Zonta International
Attn: Foundation
1211 West 22nd Street, Suite 900
Oak Brook, IL 60523-3384
(630) 928-1400 Fax: (630) 928-1559
E-mail: programs@zonta.org
Web: www.zonta.org

Summary To provide financial assistance to women working on an undergraduate or master's degree in business at a school in any country.

Eligibility This program is open to women who are working on a business-related degree at a college or university anywhere in the world at the level of the second year of an undergraduate program through the final year of a master's degree program. Applicants first compete at the club level, and then advance to district and international levels. Along with their application, they must submit a 500-word essay that describes their academic and professional goals, the relevance of their program to the business field, and how this scholarship will assist them in reaching their goals. Selection is based on that essay, academic record, demonstrated intent to complete a program in business, achievement in business-related subjects, and 2 letters of recommendation.

Financial data District winners receive a $1,000 scholarship; the international winners receive a $7,000 scholarship.

Duration 1 year.

Additional information This program began in 1998.

Number awarded Up to 32 district winners and 12 international winners are selected each year. Since this program was established, it has awarded 441 of these scholarships, worth more than $1 million, to 335 women from 50 countries.

Deadline Clubs set their own deadlines but must submit their winners to the district governor by May of each year.

[940]
JANE WALKER SCHOLARSHIP

United Methodist Church-Alabama-West Florida Conference
Attn: Commission on the Status and Role of Women
4719 Windmere Boulevard
Montgomery, AL 36106
(334) 356-8014   Toll Free: (888) 873-3127
Fax: (334) 356-8029   E-mail: awfcrc@awfumc.org
Web: www.awfumc.org/janewalkerscholarship

Summary To provide financial assistance to female residents of the Alabama-West Florida Conference of the United Methodist Church (UMC) who are undergraduate or seminary students preparing for a church-related career.

Eligibility This program is open to women who are residents of the Alabama-West Florida Conference of the UMW and who affirm, represent, and advocate women's leadership in the church. Applicants must be accepted or enrolled at an approved UMC seminary or working on an undergraduate degree in Christian education at an approved UMC institution in any state. They must be a candidate for ministry or preparing for a UMC church-related career. Along with their application, they must submit a 500-word essay on why they are preparing for full-time Christian ministry and how they can promote the cause of women through this ministry. Financial need is considered in the selection process.

Financial data The stipend is $1,000.

Duration 1 year.

Number awarded 1 each year.

Deadline May of each year.

[941]
JANET H. GRISWOLD PEO SCHOLARSHIP

P.E.O. Foundation-California State Chapter
c/o Pat Lachman, Gardner Scholarship Fund
4400 Hessel Road
Sebastopol, CA 95472
E-mail: peoca.eog@gmail.com
Web: www.peocalifornia.org

Summary To provide financial assistance to women from California who are undergraduate or graduate students at a school in any state.

Eligibility This program is open to female residents of California who are attending an accredited college or university in any state. Applicants must be enrolled as full-time undergraduate or graduate students. Selection is based on financial need, character, and a record of academic and extracurricular activities achievement. U.S. citizenship is required.

Financial data Stipends range from $500 to $1,500.

Duration 1 year.

Number awarded Varies each year.

Deadline January of each year.

[942]
JAZZ PERFORMANCE AWARDS

Sigma Alpha Iota Philanthropies, Inc.
One Tunnel Road
Asheville, NC 28805
(828) 251-0606   Fax: (828) 251-0644
E-mail: nh@sai-national.org
Web: www.sai-national.org

Summary To provide financial assistance to members of Sigma Alpha Iota (an organization of women musicians) who are interested in working on an undergraduate or graduate degree in jazz performance.

Eligibility This program is open to members of the organization who are enrolled in an undergraduate or graduate degree program in jazz performance or studies. Applicants must be younger than 32 years of age. Along with their application, they must submit a CD recording of a performance "set" of 30 to 45 minutes.

Financial data Stipends are $2,000 for the winner or $1,500 for the runner-up.

Duration 1 year.

Additional information These awards were first presented in 2006.

Number awarded 2 every 3 years.

Deadline March of the year of the awards (2018, 2021, etc.).

[943]
JENNIFER DUNN-THOMSON SCHOLARSHIP

Washington Policy Center
Attn: Operations Manager
P.O. Box 3643
Seattle, WA 98124
E-mail: bgoodwin@washingtonpolicy.org
Web: washingtonpolicy.org/jenniferdunn

Summary To provide funding for undergraduate or graduate study or for an internship to women who are preparing for a career in public service.

Eligibility This program is open to women who are currently enrolled as an undergraduate or graduate student. Applicants must have an above-average GPA and good oral and written communication skills. They must be able to demonstrate leadership and a commitment to public service and free-market principles.

Financial data The grant is $5,000. Funds may be used for tuition or to provide support for an internship on Capitol Hill in Washington, D.C.

Duration 1 year.

Additional information This program began in 2005.

Number awarded 1 each year.

Deadline April of each year.

[944]
JIM MCKAY SCHOLARSHIP PROGRAM

National Collegiate Athletic Association
Attn: Jim McKay Scholarship Program Staff Liaison
700 West Washington Street
P.O. Box 6222
Indianapolis, IN 46206-6222
(317) 917-6683   Fax: (317) 917-6888
E-mail: lthomas@ncaa.org
Web: www.ncaa.org/jim-mckay-scholarship-program

Summary To provide financial assistance to student-athletes interested in attending graduate school to prepare for a career in sports communications.

Eligibility This program is open to college seniors planning to enroll full time in a graduate degree program and to students already enrolled full time in graduate study at an institution that is a member of the National Collegiate Athletic Association (NCAA). Applicants must have competed in intercollegiate athletics as a member of a varsity team at an NCAA member institution and have an overall undergraduate cumulative GPA of 3.5 or higher. They must be preparing for a career in the sports communications industry. Women and minorities are especially encouraged to apply. Neither financial need nor U.S. citizenship are required. Nominations must be submitted by the faculty athletics representative or chief academic officer at the institution in which the student is or was an undergraduate.

Financial data The stipend is $10,000.

Duration 1 year; nonrenewable.

Additional information This program began in 2008.

Number awarded 2 each year: 1 female and 1 male.

Deadline January of each year.

[945]
JOAN F. GIAMBALVO FUND FOR THE ADVANCEMENT OF WOMEN

American Medical Association
Attn: AMA Foundation
330 North Wabash Avenue, Suite 39300
Chicago, IL 60611-5885
(312) 464-4743   Fax: (312) 464-4142
E-mail: wpc@ama-assn.org
Web: www.ama-assn.org

Summary To provide funding to physicians and medical students who are interested in conducting a research project related to women in the medical profession.

Eligibility This program is open to investigators or teams of investigators of whom at least 1 member is a medical student or physician. Applicants must be interested in conducting a research project that will advance the progress of women in the medical profession and strengthen the ability of the American Medical Association (AMA) to identify and address the needs of women physicians and medical students.

Financial data The grant is $10,000.

Duration 1 year.

Additional information This program, which began in 2006, is offered by the AMA Foundation in collaboration with the AMA Women Physicians Section (WPS) and with support from Pfizer.

Number awarded 2 each year.

Deadline July of each year.

[946]
JOHN DEERE SWE SCHOLARSHIPS

Society of Women Engineers
Attn: Scholarship Selection Committee
203 North LaSalle Street, Suite 1675
Chicago, IL 60601-1269
(312) 596-5223   Toll Free: (877) SWE-INFO
Fax: (312) 644-8557   E-mail: scholarships@swe.org
Web: societyofwomenengineers.swe.org

Summary To provide financial assistance to women from designated states working on an undergraduate or graduate degree in selected engineering specialties.

Eligibility This program is open to women who are sophomores, juniors, seniors, or graduate students at a 4-year ABET-accredited college or university. Applicants must be working full time on a degree in computer science or agricultural, aeronautical, chemical, computer, electrical, industrial, manufacturing, materials, or mechanical engineering. Preference is given to residents or students in Georgia, Illinois, Indiana, Iowa, Kansas, Louisiana, Michigan, Minnesota, Missouri, Montana, Nebraska, North Carolina, North Dakota, Ohio, Oklahoma, South Dakota, or Tennessee. They must have a GPA of 3.0 or higher. Selection is based on merit.

Financial data The stipend is $2,000.

Duration 1 year.

Additional information This program is sponsored by John Deere.

Number awarded 2 each year.

Deadline February of each year.

[947]
JOSEPH B. GITTLER AWARD OF THE AMERICAN PSYCHOLOGICAL FOUNDATION

American Psychological Foundation
750 First Street, N.E.
Washington, DC 20002-4242
(202) 336-5843   Fax: (202) 336-5812
E-mail: foundation@apa.org
Web: www.apa.org/apf/funding/gittler.aspx

Summary To recognize and reward scholars in psychology who have made outstanding contributions to the philosophical foundations of the discipline.

Eligibility This award is available to psychologists who have an Ed.D., Psy.D., or Ph.D. degree and who are making and will continue to make scholarly contributions to the philosophical foundations of psychological knowledge. Self-nominations are welcome. Selection is based on conformance with stated program goals and magnitude of contributions The sponsor encourages nominations of individuals who represent diversity in race, ethnicity, gender, age, disability, and sexual orientation.

Financial data The award is $7,500.

Duration The award is presented annually.

Additional information This award was first presented in 2008.

Number awarded 1 each year.

Deadline Nominations must be submitted by May of each year.

[948]
JOSEPH H. FICHTER RESEARCH GRANT COMPETITION

Association for the Sociology of Religion
Attn: Executive Officer
University of South Florida
Department of Sociology
4202 East Fowler Avenue, CPR 107
Tampa, FL 33620
(813) 974-2633   Fax: (813) 974-6455
E-mail: jcavendi@usf.edu
Web: www.sociologyofreligion.com

Summary To provide funding to scholars interested in conducting research on women and religion.

Eligibility This program is open to scholars involved in research on women and religion or on the intersection between religion and gender or religion and sexualities. Scholars at the beginning of their careers are particularly encouraged to apply; dissertation research qualifies for funding. Applicants must be members of the association at the time the application is submitted. The proposal should outline the rationale and plan of the research, previous research, methodology proposed, timeline, and budget; a curriculum vitae should also be included. Simultaneous submissions to other grant competitions are permissible if the applicant is explicit about which budget items in the Fichter grant proposal do not overlap items in other submitted proposals.

Financial data Each year, a total of $24,000 is available to be awarded.

Duration 1 year.

Number awarded Varies each year; recently, 6 were awarded.

Deadline April of each year.

[949]
JOSEPHINE CARROLL NORWOOD MEMORIAL SCHOLARSHIPS

Baptist Convention of Maryland/Delaware
Attn: United Baptist Women of Maryland, Inc.
10255 Old Columbia Road
Columbia, MD 21046
(410) 290-5290   Toll Free: (800) 466-5290
E-mail: gparker@bcmd.org
Web: www.bcmd.org/wmu

Summary To provide financial assistance to women who are members of Baptist churches associated with an affiliate of United Baptist Women of Maryland and interested in attending seminary or graduate school in any state to prepare for a Christian vocation.

Eligibility This program is open to women who are enrolled or planning to enroll full time at a seminary or graduate school in any state to prepare for a Christian vocation. Applicants must be a member in good standing of a Baptist church associated with an affiliate of United Baptist Women of Maryland. They must have a grade average of "C" or higher and be able to demonstrate financial need. Along with their application, they must submit brief statements on their Christian experience, school activities, church and community activities, and career goals.

Financial data A stipend is awarded (amount not specified).

Duration 1 year.

Number awarded Varies each year.

Deadline June of each year.

[950]
JUDITH MCMANUS PRICE SCHOLARSHIPS

American Planning Association
Attn: Leadership Affairs Associate
205 North Michigan Avenue, Suite 1200
Chicago, IL 60601
(312) 431-9100   Fax: (312) 786-6700
E-mail: mgroh@planning.org
Web: www.planning.org/scholarships/apa

Summary To provide financial assistance to women and underrepresented minority students enrolled in undergraduate or graduate degree programs at recognized planning schools.

Eligibility This program is open to undergraduate and graduate students in urban and regional planning who are women or members of the following minority groups: African American, Hispanic American, or Native American. Applicants must be citizens of the United States and able to document financial need. They must intend to work as practicing planners in the public sector. Along with their application, they must submit a 2-page personal and background statement describing how their education will be applied to career goals and why they chose planning as a career path. Selection is based (in order of importance), on: 1) commitment to planning as reflected in their personal statement and on their resume; 2) academic achievement and/or improvement during the past 2 years; 3) letters of recommendation; 4) financial need; and 5) professional presentation.

Financial data Stipends range from $2,000 to $4,000 per year. The money may be applied to tuition and living expenses only. Payment is made to the recipient's university and divided by terms in the school year.

Duration 1 year; recipients may reapply.

Additional information This program began in 2002.

Number awarded Varies each year; recently, 3 were awarded.

Deadline April of each year.

[951]
JUDY CORMAN MEMORIAL SCHOLARSHIP AND INTERNSHIP

New York Women in Communications, Inc.
Attn: NYWICI Foundation
355 Lexington Avenue, 15th Floor
New York, NY 10017-6603
(212) 297-2133   Fax: (212) 370-9047
E-mail: nywicipr@nywici.org
Web: www.nywici.org/foundation/scholarships

Summary To provide financial assistance and work experience to female residents of designated eastern states who are interested in preparing for a career in communications and media relations at a college or graduate school in any state.

Eligibility This program is open to women who are seniors graduating from high schools in New York, New Jersey, Connecticut, or Pennsylvania or undergraduate or graduate students who are permanent residents of those states; they must be attending or planning to attend a college or university in any state. Graduate students must be members of New York Women in Communications, Inc. (NYWICI). Also eligible are women who reside outside the 4 states but are currently enrolled at a college or university within 1 of the 5 boroughs of New York City. Applicants must be preparing for a career in communications and media relations and be interested in a summer internship with Scholastic. They must have a GPA of 3.2 or higher. Along with their application, they must submit a 2-page resume; a personal essay of 300 words on an assigned topic that changes annually; 2 letters of recommendation; and an official transcript. Selection is based on academic record, need, demonstrated leadership, participation in school and community activities, honors and other awards or recognition, work experience, goals and aspirations, and unusual personal and/or family circumstances. U.S. citizenship or permanent resident status is required.

Financial data The scholarship stipend ranges up to $10,000; the internship is salaried (amount not specified).

Duration 1 year.

Additional information This program is sponsored by Scholastic, Inc.

Number awarded 1 each year.

Deadline January of each year.

[952]
JULIETTE MATHER SCHOLARSHIP

Woman's Missionary Union
Attn: WMU Foundation
100 Missionary Ridge
Birmingham, AL 35242
(205) 408-5525   Toll Free: (877) 482-4483
Fax: (205) 408-5508   E-mail: wmufoundation@wmu.org
Web: www.wmufoundation.com/?q=content/scholarships

Summary To provide financial assistance to female Southern Baptist undergraduate or graduate students preparing for a career in Christian ministry.

Eligibility This program is open to female Southern Baptist undergraduate and graduate students who are preparing for a career in Christian ministry and service. They must be interested in preparing to become the Baptist leaders of the future.

Financial data A stipend is awarded (amount not specified).

Duration 1 year.

Number awarded Varies each year.

Deadline January of each year.

[953]
JUSTICE JANIE L. SHORES SCHOLARSHIP

Alabama Law Foundation
415 Dexter Avenue
P.O. Box 4129
Montgomery, AL 36101
(334) 387-1600
E-mail: tdaniel@alabamalawfoundation.org
Web: www.alabamalawfoundation.org

Summary To provide financial assistance to female residents of Alabama who are attending law school in the state.

Eligibility This program is open to women who are residents of Alabama and enrolled at a law school in the state.

Applicants must submit documentation of financial need and an essay on their career plans.

Financial data The stipend is $3,500.

Duration 1 year.

Additional information This program began in 2006.

Number awarded 1 or more each year.

Deadline March of each year.

[954]
KATE GLEASON SCHOLARSHIP

ASME International
Attn: Scholarships
Two Park Avenue, Floor 7
New York, NY 10016-5618
(212) 591-7790   Toll Free: (800) THE-ASME
Fax: (212) 591-7143   E-mail: LefeverB@asme.org
Web: www.asme.org

Summary To provide financial assistance to female undergraduate and graduate students from any country who are working on a degree in mechanical engineering.

Eligibility This program is open to women who are enrolled in an ABET-accredited or equivalent mechanical engineering, mechanical engineering technology, or related undergraduate or graduate program. Applicants must submit a nomination from their department head, a recommendation from a faculty member, and an official transcript. Only 1 nomination may be submitted per department. There are no citizenship requirements, but study must be conducted in the United States. Selection is based on academic ability and potential contribution to the mechanical engineering profession.

Financial data The stipend is $3,000.

Duration 1 year.

Number awarded 1 each year.

Deadline February of each year.

[955]
KATHARINE C. BRYAN GRADUATE SCHOLARSHIP

Tennessee Baptist Convention
Attn: WMU Scholarships
330 Seven Springs Way
P.O. Box 728
Brentwood, TN 37024-9728
(615) 371-7919   Toll Free: (800) 558-2090, ext. 7919
Fax: (615) 371-2014   E-mail: jheath@tnbaptist.org
Web: www.tnbaptist.org

Summary To provide financial assistance to female members of Baptist churches in Tennessee who are interested in attending graduate school in any state.

Eligibility This program is open to women who are members of Tennessee Baptist churches or have Tennessee Baptist ties. Applicants must be active in missions and ministries of their local church. They must be enrolled in full-time graduate study in any state and have a GPA of 2.6 or higher. Financial need is not considered in the selection process.

Financial data A stipend is awarded (amount not specified).

Duration 1 year; may be renewed if the recipient maintains a GPA of 3.5 or higher.

Number awarded 1 or more each year.

Deadline January of each year.

[956]
KATHERINE J. SCHUTZE MEMORIAL SCHOLARSHIP

Christian Church (Disciples of Christ)
Attn: Disciples Home Missions
130 East Washington Street
P.O. Box 1986
Indianapolis, IN 46206-1986
(317) 713-2652   Toll Free: (888) DHM-2631
Fax: (317) 635-4426   E-mail: mail@dhm.disciples.org
Web: www.discipleshomemissions.org

Summary To provide financial assistance to female semi-nary students affiliated with the Christian Church (Disciples of Christ).

Eligibility This program is open to female seminary students who are members of a Christian Church (Disciples of Christ) congregation in the United States or Canada. Applicants must plan to prepare for the ordained ministry, be working on an M.Div. or equivalent degree, provide evidence of financial need, be enrolled full time in an accredited school or seminary, provide a transcript of academic work, and be under the care of a regional Commission on the Ministry or in the process of coming under care.

Financial data A stipend is awarded (amount not specified).

Duration 1 year; recipients may reapply.

Number awarded 1 or more each year.

Deadline March of each year.

[957]
KATHY KARDISH WILSON MEMORIAL EDUCATIONAL FUND

Chautauqua Region Community Foundation
Attn: Scholarship Coordinator
418 Spring Street
Jamestown, NY 14701
(716) 661-3394   Fax: (716) 488-0387
E-mail: llynde@crcfonline.org
Web: www.crcfonline.org/providing/scholarships

Summary To provide financial assistance to married women in New York, Ohio, and Pennsylvania who are interested in returning to school to complete an undergraduate or graduate degree.

Eligibility This program is open to women who live and attend college or graduate school in New York, Ohio, or Pennsylvania. Applicants must be mothers of school-aged children, part of a 2-income family in which tuition would be a burden on the family, able to complete the educational and career goals set for themselves, community-minded and considerably involved in at least 1 community organization, and giving of themselves and their talents to help others reach their potential. Along with their application, they must submit a 1-page essay describing their past achievements, career goals, and reasons for returning to school or training.

Financial data A stipend is awarded (amount not specified).

Duration 1 year.

Number awarded 1 or more each year.

Deadline May of each year.

[958]
KATHY LOUDAT MUSIC SCHOLARSHIP

New Mexico Baptist Foundation
5325 Wyoming Boulevard, N.E.
P.O. Box 16560
Albuquerque, NM 87191-6560
(505) 332-3777   Toll Free: (877) 841-3777
Fax: (505) 332-2777   E-mail: foundation@nmbf.com
Web: www.nmbf.com

Summary To provide financial assistance to female members of Southern Baptist churches in New Mexico who are attending college in any state to prepare for a career in church music.

Eligibility This program is open to full-time female college, university, and seminary students who are preparing for a career in church music. Applicants must have a GPA of 3.0 or higher and be able to demonstrate financial need. They must be members of Southern Baptist churches in New Mexico or former members in good standing with the Southern Baptist Convention.

Financial data A stipend is awarded (amount not specified).

Duration 1 year.

Number awarded 1 or more each year.

Deadline April of each year.

[959]
KENNEDY CENTER SUMMER INTERNSHIP

Sigma Alpha Iota Philanthropies, Inc.
One Tunnel Road
Asheville, NC 28805
(828) 251-0606   Fax: (828) 251-0644
E-mail: nh@sai-national.org
Web: app.smarterselect.com

Summary To provide summer internships at the Kennedy Center to members of Sigma Alpha Iota (an organization of women musicians).

Eligibility This program is open to student members of the organization who are interested in a summer internship at the DeVos Institute for Arts Management at the John F. Kennedy Center for the Performing Arts in Washington, D.C. Applicants must be juniors, seniors, graduate students, or graduates out of school for less than 2 years.

Financial data The stipend is $2,400.

Duration 10 weeks during the summer.

Additional information Assignments are full time, with possible college credit available.

Number awarded 1 or more each year.

Deadline February of each year.

[960]
KENNETH B. AND MARNIE P. CLARK FUND

American Psychological Foundation
750 First Street, N.E.
Washington, DC 20002-4242
(202) 336-5843   Fax: (202) 336-5812
E-mail: foundation@apa.org
Web: www.apa.org/apf/funding/clark-fund.aspx

Summary To provide funding to psychologists who wish to conduct a project related to academic achievement in children.

Eligibility This program is open to psychologists who wish to conduct research or development activities that promote the understanding of the relationship between self-identity and academic achievement with an emphasis on children in grade levels K-8. Eligibility alternates between graduate students in odd-numbered years and early-career (within 10 years of completion of postdoctoral work) psychologists. Selection is based on conformance with stated program goals and qualifications; quality and potential impact of proposed work; originality, innovation, and contribution to the field with the proposed project; and applicant's demonstrated competence and capability to execute the proposed work. The sponsor encourages applications from individuals who represent diversity in race, ethnicity, gender, age, disability, and sexual orientation.

Financial data The grant is $10,000.

Duration 1 year.

Additional information This program began in 2012.

Number awarded 1 each year.

Deadline June of each year.

[961]
KENTUCKY WOMEN IN AGRICULTURE SCHOLARSHIP

Kentucky Women in Agriculture
Attn: Scholarship
P.O. Box 4409
Lexington, KY 40544-4409
Toll Free: (877) 266-8823
E-mail: info@kywomeninag.com
Web: www.kywomeninag.com/index.html

Summary To provide financial assistance to female residents of Kentucky enrolled as upper-division or graduate students at colleges in the state and working on a degree in agriculture.

Eligibility This program is open to women who are residents of Kentucky and enrolled full time as juniors, seniors, or graduate students at a college or university in the state. Applicants must be working on a degree in a field related to agriculture and have a GPA of 2.5 or higher. Along with their application, they must submit a 500-word essay on their career goals for working in agriculture and how this scholarship will support them in their academic pursuits. Selection is based on desire to work in the field of agriculture (40 points), financial need (30 points), academic record (20 points), and extracurricular activities (10 points).

Financial data The stipend is $1,000.

Duration 1 year.

Number awarded 1 each year.

Deadline June of each year.

[962]
LAMBDA KAPPA SIGMA GRANTS

Lambda Kappa Sigma Pharmacy Fraternity
Attn: Educational Trust
S77 W16906 Casey Drive
P.O. Box 570
Muskego, WI 53150-0570
Toll Free: (800) LKS-1913   Fax: (262) 679-4558
E-mail: lks@lks.org
Web: www.lks.org

Summary To provide financial assistance to members of Lambda Kappa Sigma who are interested in working on a Pharm.D. degree and can demonstrate leadership.

Eligibility This program is open to collegiate or alumnae members of Lambda Kappa Sigma who are enrolled in a licensure-eligible pharmacy degree program. (In the United States, the Pharm.D. degree is the only qualifying program at schools or colleges of pharmacy recognized by the Accreditation Council on Pharmacy Education.) Applicants must rank in the top half of their class and be able to demonstrate financial need. Along with their application, they must submit a brief essay on their leadership qualities and the importance of leadership.

Financial data The stipend is $1,000.

Duration 1 year.

Additional information Lambda Kappa Sigma was founded in 1913 to promote the profession of pharmacy among women. Although some of its chapters are now coeducational, it still emphasizes women's health issues. This program includes the following named awards: the Cora E. Craven Educational Grant, the Mary Connolly Livingston Educational Grant, the Adele Lobracio Lowe Leadership Grant, the Marilyn and Joe E. Haberle Educational Grant, and the Norma Chipman Wells Loyalty Grant.

Number awarded Varies each year; recently, 8 were awarded.

Deadline January of each year.

[963]
LAURELS FUND SCHOLARSHIPS

Educational Foundation for Women in Accounting
Attn: Foundation Administrator
136 South Keowee Street
Dayton, OH 45402
(937) 424-3391   Fax: (937) 222-5749
E-mail: info@efwa.org
Web: www.efwa.org/scholarships_postgraduate.php

Summary To provide financial support to women working on a doctoral degree in accounting.

Eligibility This program is open to women who are working on a Ph.D. degree in accounting and have completed their comprehensive examinations. Applicants must submit a statement of personal and career goals and objectives. Selection is based on 1) scholarship, including academic achievements in course work and research activities; 2) service, including volunteer work to which the applicant has made significant or long-term commitments; and 3) financial need. U.S. citizenship is required.

Financial data The stipend ranges from $1,000 to $5,000.

Duration 1 year; nonrenewable.

Additional information This program began in 1978.

Number awarded 1 or more each year.
Deadline May of each year.

[964]
LAUREN LOVE MEMORIAL SCHOLARSHIP
American Academy of Physician Assistants
Attn: Physician Assistant Foundation
2318 Mill Road, Suite 1300
Alexandria, VA 22314-6868
(703) 836-2272   Fax: (703) 684-1924
E-mail: pafoundation@aapa.org
Web: www.pa-foundation.org
Summary To provide financial assistance to student members of the American Academy of Physician Assistants (AAPA), especially women, who are from Arizona.
Eligibility This program is open to Arizona-based AAPA student members attending a physician assistant program accredited by the Commission on Accreditation of Allied Health Education Programs. Applicants must have overcome a challenge (e.g., medical condition, poverty) to succeed in their college studies. They must have completed at least 1 semester of PA studies. Preference is given to women.
Financial data The stipend is $3,500.
Duration 1 year; nonrenewable.
Number awarded 1 each year.
Deadline January of each year.

[965]
LAW AND SOCIAL SCIENCES DOCTORAL DISSERTATION RESEARCH IMPROVEMENT GRANTS
National Science Foundation
Attn: Directorate for Social, Behavioral, and Economic Sciences
Division of Social and Economic Sciences
4201 Wilson Boulevard, Room 995N
Arlington, VA 22230
(703) 292-7023   Fax: (703) 292-9083
TDD: (800) 281-8749   E-mail: hsilvers@nsf.gov
Web: www.nsf.gov
Summary To provide funding for dissertation research to doctoral candidates in fields related to law and social sciences.
Eligibility This program is open to doctoral candidates who have passed their qualifying examinations, completed all course work required for the degree, and had their dissertation topic approved. Fields of study including crime, violence, and punishment; economic issues; governance; legal decision making; legal mobilization and conceptions of justice; and litigation and the legal profession. Applicants must submit a project description that includes the scientific significance of the work, its relationship to other current research, and the design of the project in sufficient detail to permit evaluation. In the selection process, consideration is given to the project's broader impact of contributing to societally relevant outcomes, including full participation of women, persons with disabilities, and underrepresented minorities in science, technology, engineering, and mathematics (STEM).
Financial data Grants range up to $20,000. Funds may be used only for costs directly associated with the conduct of dissertation research.

Duration Up to 12 months.
Number awarded Varies each year.
Deadline January of each year.

[966]
LEADERSHIP LEGACY SCHOLARSHIP FOR GRADUATES
Women's Transportation Seminar
Attn: WTS Foundation
1701 K Street, N.W., Suite 800
Washington, DC 20006
(202) 955-5085   Fax: (202) 955-5088
E-mail: wts@wtsinternational.org
Web: www.wtsinternational.org/education/scholarships
Summary To provide financial assistance to graduate women interested in a career in transportation.
Eligibility This program is open to women who are working on a graduate degree in transportation or a transportation-related field (e.g., transportation engineering, planning, business management, finance, or logistics). Applicants must have a GPA of 3.0 or higher and be interested in a career in transportation. Along with their application, they must submit a 1,000-word statement about their vision of how their education will give them the tools to better serve their community's needs and transportation issues. Applications must be submitted first to a local chapter; the chapters forward selected applications for consideration on the national level. Minority women are especially encouraged to apply. Selection is based on transportation involvement and goals, job skills, and academic record; financial need is not considered.
Financial data The stipend is $5,000.
Duration 1 year.
Additional information This program began in 2008. Each year, it focuses on women with a special interest; recently, it was reserved for women who have a specific interest in addressing the impact of transportation on sustainability, land use, environmental impact, security, and quality of life issues internationally.
Number awarded 1 each year.
Deadline Applications must be submitted by November to a local WTS chapter.

[967]
LEAH J. DICKSTEIN, M.D. AWARD
Association of Women Psychiatrists
Attn: Executive Director
P.O. Box 570218
Dallas, TX 75357-0218
(972) 613-0985   Fax: (972) 613-5532
E-mail: womenpsych@aol.com
Web: www.associationofwomenpsychiatrists.com
Summary To recognize and reward outstanding female medical students.
Eligibility This award is available to female medical students who demonstrate superior academic achievement, creativity, and leadership. Activities that may be recognized include service or clinical aspects of medicine, science research, or excellence in art, music, or literature.
Financial data The award consists of $1,000 and a plaque. Funds may be used to attend the annual meeting of

the Association of Women Psychiatrists, with the balance at the discretion of the recipient.

Duration The award is presented annually.

Additional information The awardee is invited to join the award committee for the following year.

Number awarded 1 each year.

Deadline January of each year.

[968]
LESLIE S. PARKER MEMORIAL SCHOLARSHIP

Order of the Eastern Star-Grand Chapter of Oregon
c/o Nancy Harper, Scholarship Committee Chair
1421 Raydean Drive
Grants Pass, OR 97527
E-mail: totemspole@charter.net
Web: www.oregonoes.org/scholarships/index.html

Summary To provide financial assistance to women who are residents of Oregon and attending college or graduate school in the state.

Eligibility This program is open to female residents of Oregon who have completed at least 2 years of undergraduate or graduate study at an accredited non-sectarian college or university in the state. Applicants must be able to demonstrate financial need.

Financial data Stipends recently were $1,140. Funds are sent directly to the recipient's college or university to be used for books, tuition, room and board, clothing, or medical aid.

Duration 1 year.

Number awarded Varies each year; recently, 5 were awarded.

Deadline April of each year.

[969]
LINDA J. MURPHY SCHOLARSHIPS

Women Lawyers' Association of Greater St. Louis
c/o Jennifer Gustafson, Scholarship Committee Chair
Lewis, Rice & Fingersh, L.C.
600 Washington, Suite 2500
St. Louis, MO 63101
(314) 444-7600   E-mail: jgustafson@lewisrice.com
Web: wlastl.org/scholarships

Summary To provide financial assistance to women from any state who are attending law school in Missouri or southern Illinois.

Eligibility This program is open to women attending 1 of the law schools in Missouri (University of Missouri at Columbia, University of Missouri at Kansas City, Washington University, or St. Louis University) or Southern Illinois University School of Law in Carbondale on a part-time or full-time basis. Applicants must submit a 2-page personal statement on events, decisions, or individuals that have helped to shape their life; short-term and long-term career goals; and/or contributions they would like to make to society in general, their community, women, or the legal profession. Selection is based on that statement, academic achievement, and financial need.

Financial data Stipends range from $1,000 to $6,000.

Duration 1 year.

Additional information This program began in 1996.

Number awarded Varies each year; recently, 4 were awarded.

Deadline March of each year.

[970]
LIZETTE PETERSON-HOMER INJURY PREVENTION GRANT AWARD

American Psychological Foundation
750 First Street, N.E.
Washington, DC 20002-4242
(202) 336-5843   Fax: (202) 336-5812
E-mail: foundation@apa.org
Web: www.apa.org/apf/funding/peterson-homer.aspx

Summary To provide funding to graduate students and faculty interested in conducting research related to the prevention of injuries in children.

Eligibility This program is open to graduate students and faculty interested in conducting research that focuses on the prevention of physical injury in children and young adults through accidents, violence, abuse, or suicide. Applicants must submit a 100-word abstract, description of the project, detailed budget, curriculum vitae, and letter from the supporting faculty supervisor (if the applicant is a student). Selection is based on conformance with stated program goals, magnitude of incremental contribution, quality of proposed work, and applicant's demonstrated scholarship and research competence. The sponsor encourages applications from individuals who represent diversity in race, ethnicity, gender, age, disability, and sexual orientation.

Financial data Grants up to $5,000 are available.

Additional information This program began in 1999 as the Rebecca Routh Coon Injury Research Award. The current name was adopted in 2003. It is supported by Division 54 (Society of Pediatric Psychology) of the American Psychological Association and the American Psychological Foundation.

Number awarded 1 each year.

Deadline September of each year.

[971]
LOREEN ARBUS FOUNDATION SCHOLARSHIP

Alliance for Women in Media
Attn: Foundation
2365 Harrodsburg Road, Suite A325
Lexington, KY 40504
(202) 750-3664   E-mail: info@allwomeninmedia.org
Web: www.allwomeninmedia.org/foundation/scholarships

Summary To provide financial assistance to women who are working on an undergraduate or graduate degree in a media-related field and submit outstanding essays on people with disabilities.

Eligibility This program is open to women currently enrolled in an undergraduate or graduate degree program at a college or university in any state. Applicants must be preparing for a media career and working on a degree in such fields as cable, communications, television, radio, digital media, publishing, journalism, advertising, production, creative design, or related areas. Along with their application, they must submit an essay of 750 to 1,000 words on an individual who has a disability (can be the applicant) and how that person has broken the stereotypes that go along with their particular disability.

Financial data The stipend is $2,500, paid directly to the recipient's institution.

Duration 1 year.

Additional information This program is offered in partnership with the Loreen Arbus Foundation.

Number awarded 1 each year.

Deadline April.

[972]
LOS ANGELES SECTION SWE SCHOLARSHIPS

Society of Women Engineers-Los Angeles Section
Attn: Scholarship Chair
291 Del Amo Fashion Square
Box 14322
Torrance, CA 90503
E-mail: julim.lee@swe.org
Web: www.swela.org

Summary To provide financial assistance to women from any state who are working on an undergraduate or graduate degree in engineering at a college or university in Los Angeles County, California.

Eligibility This program is open to women enrolled in an engineering program leading to a bachelor's or graduate degree at any of the ABET-accredited colleges or universities in Los Angeles County (California State University at Northridge, California State University at Los Angeles, University of California at Los Angeles, California Institute of Technology, Harvey Mudd University, California State Polytechnic University at Pomona, Loyola Marymount University, and University of Southern California). Applicants must be members of the Society of Women Engineers (SWE) section at their university and have a GPA of 3.0 or higher. Along with their application, they must submit 3 500-word essays on 1) why they decided to study engineering; 2) why they have applied for this scholarship; and 3) what they consider their most important achievement to date. Selection is based on those essays, academic ability, engineering interest, job experience, and leadership; special consideration is given to those with unique circumstances and financial need and to reentering women who have been out of the engineering job market for at least 2 years.

Financial data Stipends range from $500 to $1,500.

Duration 1 year.

Number awarded Varies each year; recently, 5 were awarded.

Deadline February of each year.

[973]
LOUISIANA WMU SCHOLARSHIP FOR SEMINARY WOMEN

Louisiana Baptist Convention
Attn: Woman's Missionary Union
1250 MacArthur Drive
P.O. Box 311
Alexandria, LA 71309-0311
(318) 448-3402   Toll Free: (800) 622-6549
E-mail: WMM@louisianabaptists.org
Web: www.louisianabaptists.org

Summary This provide financial assistance to women from Louisiana who are working on a master's degree at a Southern Baptist seminary.

Eligibility This program is open to women who are active members of a Southern Baptist church in Louisiana and have been long-term residents of the state. Applicants must be enrolled full time at 1 of the 6 Southern Baptist seminaries, have a GPA of 2.5 or higher, and be working on a master's degree. They must participate in activities of the Woman's Missionary Union (WMU) and be actively involved in missions education of the church or on campus. Along with their application, they must submit evidence of their "devotion to the Lord and their call to ministry."

Financial data The stipend is $1,600 per year.

Duration Up to 3 years.

Additional information The eligible seminaries are Southeastern Baptist Theological Seminary (Wake Forest, North Carolina); Southern Baptist Theological Seminary (Louisville, Kentucky); Southwestern Baptist Theological Seminary (Fort Worth, Texas); New Orleans Baptist Theological Seminary (New Orleans, Louisiana); Midwestern Baptist Theological Seminary (Kansas City, Missouri); or Golden Gate Baptist Theological Seminary (Mill Valley, California).

Number awarded 1 or more each year.

Deadline June of each year.

[974]
LUCY KASPARIAN AHARONIAN SCHOLARSHIPS

Armenian International Women's Association
65 Main Street, Room 3A
Watertown, MA 02472
(617) 926-0171   E-mail: aiwainc@aol.com
Web: www.aiwainternational.org/initiatives/scholarships

Summary To provide financial assistance to Armenian women who are upper-division or graduate students working on a degree in specified fields.

Eligibility This program is open to full-time women students of Armenian descent attending an accredited college or university. Applicants must be full-time juniors, seniors, or graduate students with a GPA of 3.2 or higher. They must be working on a degree in architecture, computer science, engineering, mathematics, science, or technology. Selection is based on financial need and merit.

Financial data The stipend is $1,000.

Duration 1 year.

Additional information This program, established in 2008, is offered in conjunction with the Boston Section of the Society of Women Engineers.

Number awarded Varies each year; recently, 3 were awarded: 2 to undergraduates and 1 to a graduate student.

Deadline April of each year.

[975]
LYDIA I. PICKUP MEMORIAL SCHOLARSHIP

Society of Women Engineers
Attn: Scholarship Selection Committee
203 North LaSalle Street, Suite 1675
Chicago, IL 60601-1269
(312) 596-5223   Toll Free: (877) SWE-INFO
Fax: (312) 644-8557   E-mail: scholarships@swe.org
Web: societyofwomenengineers.swe.org

Summary To provide financial assistance to women working on a graduate degree in engineering or computer science.

Eligibility This program is open to women who will be full-time graduate students at ABET-accredited colleges and universities. Applicants must be working on a degree in computer science, engineering technology, or engineering and have a GPA of 3.0 or higher. Selection is based on merit.

Financial data The stipend is $1,500.

Duration 1 year.

Additional information This program began in 2000.

Number awarded 2 each year.

Deadline February of each year.

[976]
M. LOUISE CARPENTER GLOECKNER, M.D. SUMMER RESEARCH FELLOWSHIP

Drexel University College of Medicine
Attn: Archives and Special Collections
2900 West Queen Lane
Philadelphia, PA 19129
(215) 991-8340   Fax: (215) 991-8172
E-mail: archives@drexelmed.edu
Web: archives.drexelmed.edu/fellowship.php

Summary To provide funding to scholars and students interested in conducting research during the summer on the history of women in medicine at the Archives and Special Collections on Women in Medicine at Drexel University in Philadelphia.

Eligibility This program is open to students at all levels, scholars, and general researchers. Applicants must be interested in conducting research utilizing the archives, which emphasize the history of women in medicine, nursing, medical missionaries, the American Medical Women's Association, American Women's Hospital Service, and other women in medical organizations. Selection is based on research background of the applicant, relevance of the proposed research project to the goals of the applicant, overall quality and clarity of the proposal, appropriateness of the proposal to the holdings of the collection, and commitment of the applicant to the project.

Financial data The grant is $4,000.

Duration 4 to 6 weeks during the summer.

Number awarded 1 each year.

Deadline March of each year.

[977]
M.A. CARTLAND SHACKFORD MEDICAL FELLOWSHIP

Wellesley College
Center for Work and Service
Attn: Extramural Graduate Fellowships and Scholarships
106 Central Street
Wellesley, MA 02181-8203
(781) 283-3525   Fax: (781) 283-3674
E-mail: cws-fellowships@wellesley.edu
Web: www.wellesley.edu/cws/fellowships/wellesley

Summary To provide financial assistance to women for graduate study in the medical fields.

Eligibility This program is open to women who have graduated from an American academic institution and are interested in general medical practice (but not psychiatry).

Financial data The fellowship of at least $10,000 is tenable at any institution of the recipient's choice.

Duration 1 year.

Additional information The recipient must pursue full-time graduate study.

Number awarded 1 each year.

Deadline January of each year.

[978]
MABEL BIEVER MUSIC EDUCATION SCHOLARSHIP FOR GRADUATE STUDENTS

Sigma Alpha Iota Philanthropies, Inc.
One Tunnel Road
Asheville, NC 28805
(828) 251-0606   Fax: (828) 251-0644
E-mail: nh@sai-national.org
Web: app.smarterselect.com

Summary To provide financial assistance for graduate study in music education to members of Sigma Alpha Iota (an organization of women musicians).

Eligibility This program is open to alumnae members of the organization who have completed an undergraduate degree in music education and are accepted into or currently enrolled in a program leading to a master's or doctoral degree in that field. Applicants should have had at least 1 year of teaching experience in a private or public school. If they do not have teaching experience, they must include a video of student teaching experience and references from their major professor and their student teacher adviser.

Financial data The stipend is $1,500.

Duration 1 year.

Additional information This program is sponsored by the Oak Park Alumnae Chapter of Sigma Alpha Iota.

Number awarded 1 each year.

Deadline March of each year.

[979]
MABEL HEIL SCHOLARSHIP

United Methodist Church-Wisconsin Conference
Attn: United Methodist Women
750 Windsor Street
P.O. Box 620
Sun Prairie, WI 53590-0620
(608) 837-7328   Toll Free: (888) 240-7328
Fax: (608) 837-8547
Web: www.wisconsinumc.org

Summary To provide financial assistance to United Methodist women from Wisconsin who are interested in attending college or graduate school in any state.

Eligibility This program is open to women who are members of congregations affiliated with the Wisconsin Conference of the United Methodist Church and attending or planning to attend college or graduate school in any state. Applicants must submit an essay on why they consider themselves a worthy student and a letter of recommendation from their pastor or the president of the local United Methodist Women. Preference is given to women who are responsible for others and are returning to the employment field. Lowest priority is given to recent high school graduates.

Financial data A stipend is awarded (amount not specified).

Duration 1 semester; recipients may reapply.

Number awarded 1 or more each year.

Deadline April of each year for the first semester; September of each year for the second semester.

[980]
MADELINE KOUNTZE DUGGER-KELLY SCHOLARSHIP

Black Women in Sport Foundation
Attn: Tina Sloan Green, President/Executive Director
4300 Monument Road
Philadelphia, PA 19131
(215) 877-1925, ext. 320   Fax: (215) 877-1942
E-mail: tinabwsf@temple.edu
Web: www.blackwomeninsport.org/scholarships-1

Summary To provide financial assistance to Black female graduate students who have participated in sports.

Eligibility This program is open to Black women who are currently enrolled full time in an accredited graduate program. Applicants must have participated in athletics during their undergraduate studies and have displayed the qualities of the program's namesake.

Financial data The stipend is $1,000.

Duration 1 year.

Number awarded 1 each year.

Deadline March of each year.

[981]
MAIDS OF ATHENA SCHOLARSHIPS

Maids of Athena
1909 Q Street, N.W., Suite 500
Washington, DC 20009-1007
(202) 232-6300   Fax: (202) 232-2145
E-mail: MOAHeadquarters@gmail.com
Web: www.maidsofathena.org/scholarships.html

Summary To provide financial assistance for undergraduate and graduate education to women of Greek descent.

Eligibility This program is open to women who are members of the Maids of Athena. Applicants may be a graduating high school senior, an undergraduate student, or a graduate student. Along with their application, they must submit a 250-word essay on their involvement in the Maids of Athena and how they perpetuate the goals and values of the Order. Selection is based on academic merit, financial need, and participation in the organization.

Financial data The stipend is $1,000.

Duration 1 year.

Additional information Membership in Maids of Athena is open to unmarried women between 14 and 24 years of age who are of Greek descent from either parent.

Number awarded At least 2 each year.

Deadline May of each year.

[982]
MALENA RANCE SCHOLARSHIP FUND

Black Entertainment and Sports Lawyers Association
Attn: Scholarships
P.O. Box 230794
New York, NY 10023
E-mail: scholarship@besla.org
Web: www.besla.org/#!scholarship-fund/qe8of

Summary To provide financial assistance to African American women who are interested in the fields of entertainment and/or sports law.

Eligibility This program is open to African American women who have completed at least 1 year of full-time study at an accredited law school. Applicants must be able to demonstrate an interest in entertainment or sports law by 2 or more of the following: 1) completed an intellectual property, entertainment, or sports law related course; 2) completed an internship or clerkship in the entertainment, sports, or related law field; or 3) membership in their school's sports and entertainment club. They must have a GPA of 3.0 or higher. Along with their application, they must submit a 5-page legal memorandum on an issue facing the entertainment or sports industry.

Financial data The stipend is at least $1,500.

Duration 1 year.

Number awarded 1 or more each year.

Deadline September of each year.

[983]
MANAHAN-BOHAN AWARD

Philanthrofund Foundation
Attn: Scholarship Committee
1409 Willow Street, Suite 109
Minneapolis, MN 55403-2241
(612) 870-1806   Toll Free: (800) 435-1402
Fax: (612) 871-6587   E-mail: info@PfundOnline.org
Web: www.pfundonline.org/scholarships.html

Summary To provide financial assistance to lesbian students from rural Minnesota.

Eligibility This program is open to residents of Madelia, Minnesota; if no resident of Madelia applies, the award is available to residents of any rural area in Minnesota. Applicants must be self-identified as lesbian. They may be attending or planning to attend trade school, technical college, college, or university in any state (as an undergraduate or graduate student). Selection is based on the applicant's 1) affirmation of GLBT or allied identity; 2) evidence of experience and skills in service and leadership; and 3) evidence of service, leading, and working for change in GLBT communities, including serving as a role model, mentor, and/or adviser.

Financial data The stipend is $1,000. Funds must be used for tuition, books, fees, or dissertation expenses.

Duration 1 year.

Number awarded 1 each year.

Deadline January of each year.

[984]
MARGARET ABEL SCHOLARSHIP

Delta Kappa Gamma Society International-Alpha Zeta
  State Organization
c/o Faith Steinfort, State Scholarship Chair
1509 Glenview Drive
Cinnaminson, NJ 08077-2156
E-mail: fsseagull@comcast.net
Web: dkgalphazetastate-nj.weebly.com

Summary To provide financial assistance to women who are residents of New Jersey working on an undergraduate or graduate degree in education at a school in the state.

Eligibility This program is open to women who residents of New Jersey and enrolled as juniors, seniors, or graduate students at a 4-year college or university in the state. Applicants must be preparing for a career as a teacher and have a GPA of 3.0 or higher. They must be U.S. citizens. Along with their application, they must submit a 500-word essay on their desire to become a teacher and the attributes that make them worthy to receive this scholarship.

Financial data The stipend is $1,000.

Duration 1 year; recipients may reapply.

Number awarded 1 or more each year.

Deadline December of each year.

[985]
MARGARET MORSE NICE FUND

American Ornithologists' Union
c/o Brian D. Peer, Research Awards Chair
Western Illinois University
Department of Biological Sciences
Waggoner Hall 333
Macomb, IL 61455
(309) 298-2336   E-mail: BD_peer@wiu-edu
Web: www.americanornithology.org

Summary To provide funding to female graduate students who are members of the American Ornithologists' Union (AOU) and interested in conducting research related to ornithology.

Eligibility This program is open to female graduate students who are AOU members. Applicants must be interested in conducting research related to ornithology. They should send a cover letter (about 5 pages) describing their proposed project, a budget, and 1 letter of reference. Selection is based on significance and originality of the research question, clarity of the objectives, feasibility of the plan of research, appropriateness of the budget, and the letter of recommendation.

Financial data The maximum award is $2,500 per year.

Duration 1 year; recipients may reapply for 1 additional award.

Number awarded The sponsor awards a total of 28 to 30 grants each year.

Deadline January of each year.

[986]
MARGARET YARDLEY FELLOWSHIP

New Jersey State Federation of Women's Clubs
Attn: Fellowship Chair
55 Labor Center Way
New Brunswick, NJ 08901-1593
(732) 249-5474   Toll Free: (800) 465-7392
E-mail: njsfwc@njsfwc.org
Web: www.njsfwc.org/projects.php?id=21

Summary To provide financial assistance to women from New Jersey interested in graduate studies in the state.

Eligibility This program is open to women from New Jersey who are entering or enrolled full time in a master's or doctoral program at a college or university in any state. Applicants must submit a 2-page essay describing their charitable endeavors, future goals, and financial need.

Financial data The stipend is $1,000.

Duration 1 year.

Additional information This program began in 1930. Award recipients must give written assurance of an uninterrupted year of study at an American college of their choice.

Number awarded 6 to 8 each year.

Deadline February of each year.

[987]
MARIAN J. WETTRICK CHARITABLE FOUNDATION MEDICAL SCHOLARSHIPS

Marian J. Wettrick Charitable Foundation
c/o Citizens & Northern Bank
Trust Department
10 North Main Street
P.O. Box 229
Coudersport, PA 16915-0229
(814) 274-9150   Toll Free: (800) 921-9150
Fax: (814) 274-0297   E-mail: eileenb@cnbankpa.com

Summary To provide financial assistance to women who graduated from a college in Pennsylvania and are interested in attending a medical school in the state.

Eligibility This program is open to women who graduated from a college or university in Pennsylvania with a recognized pre-medical major. They must be interested in attending a medical school in the state. Priority is given to applicants who are interested in practicing medicine at Charles Cole Medical Center in Coudersport (although this is not a binding requirement). A personal interview may be required. Financial need is considered in the selection process.

Financial data Stipends range from $5,000 to $35,000 per year.

Duration 1 year; may be renewed.

Additional information This program began in 1996.

Number awarded Varies each year; recently, 9 were awarded. Since the program was established, it has awarded more than $1.2 million in scholarships to more than 30 female medical students.

Deadline March of each year.

[988]
MARIE MORISAWA RESEARCH AWARD

Geological Society of America-Quaternary Geology and
    Geomorphology Division
c/o Tammy Rittenour, Second Vice Chair
Utah State University
Department of Geology
Geology 115
Logan, UT 84322-4505
(435) 213-5756   Fax: (435) 797-1588
E-mail: tammy.rittenour@usu.edu
Web: community.geosociety.org

Summary To provide support to female graduate student members of the Geological Society of America (GSA) interested in conducting research on quaternary geology or geomorphology.

Eligibility This program is open to women who are GSA members working on a master's or doctoral degree at a university in any state. Applicants must be interested in conducting research on quaternary geology or geomorphology. Selection is based on quality of the proposed research.

Financial data The grant is $1,000.

Duration 1 year.

Additional information This program, established in 2008, is sponsored by the Geological Society of America's Quaternary Geology and Geomorphology Division.

Number awarded 1 each year.

Deadline January of each year.

[989]
MARILYNNE GRABOYS WOOL SCHOLARSHIP

Rhode Island Foundation
Attn: Donor Services Administrator
One Union Station
Providence, RI 02903
(401) 427-4011   Fax: (401) 331-8085
E-mail: rbogert@rifoundation.org
Web: www.rifoundation.org

Summary To provide financial assistance to women who are residents of Rhode Island and interested in studying law at a school in any state.

Eligibility This program is open to female residents of Rhode Island who are planning to enroll or are registered in an accredited law school in any state. Applicants must be able to demonstrate financial need. Along with their application, they must submit an essay (up to 300 words) on the impact they would like to have on the legal field.

Financial data The stipend is $2,000.

Duration 1 year; nonrenewable.

Number awarded 1 each year.

Deadline June of each year.

[990]
MARJORIE BOWENS-WHEATLEY SCHOLARSHIPS

Unitarian Universalist Association
Attn: UU Women's Federation
258 Harvard Street
Brookline, MA 02446
(617) 838-6989   E-mail: uuwf@uua.org
Web: www.uuwf.org

Summary To provide financial assistance to women of color who are working on an undergraduate or graduate degree to prepare for Unitarian Universalist ministry or service.

Eligibility This program is open to women of color who are either 1) aspirants or candidates for the Unitarian Universalist ministry; or 2) candidates in the Unitarian Universalist Association's professional religious education or music leadership credentialing programs. Applicants must submit a 1- to 2-page narrative that covers their call to UU ministry, religious education, or music leadership; their passions; how their racial/ethnic/cultural background influences their goals for their calling; and how the work of the program's namesake relates to their dreams and plans for their UU service.

Financial data The stipend is $1,500.

Duration 1 year.

Additional information This program began in 2009.

Number awarded Varies each year; recently, 2 were awarded.

Deadline March of each year.

[991]
MARJORIE COOK SCHOLARS PROGRAM

Central Scholarship Bureau
6 Park Center Court, Suite 221
Owings Mills, MD 21117
(410) 415-5558   Toll Free: (855) 276-0239
Fax: (410) 415-5501
E-mail: gohigher@central-scholarship.org
Web: www.central-scholarship.org/scholarships/overview

Summary To provide financial assistance to women in Maryland who are interested in working on a graduate degree in law or public policy at a school in any state.

Eligibility This program is open to female residents of Maryland who are working on a graduate degree in public policy or law at a college or university in any state. Applicants must be able to demonstrate a passion for and commitment to women's rights and equality, as evidenced by volunteerism, internships, dedicated research, or prior work experience related to advancing women's social and political status. They must have a GPA of 3.0 or higher and a family income of less than $90,000 per year. Selection is based on academic achievement, extracurricular activities, and financial need. U.S. citizenship or permanent resident status is required.

Financial data Stipends range up to $5,000.

Duration 1 year.

Additional information This program began in 2008.

Number awarded 1 or more each year.

Deadline March of each year.

[992]
MARK T. BANNER SCHOLARSHIP FOR LAW STUDENTS

Richard Linn American Inn of Court
c/o Amy Ziegler, Scholarship Chair
Green Burns & Crain
300 South Wacker Drive, Suite 2500
Chicago, IL 60606
(312) 987-2926   Fax: (312) 360-9315
E-mail: marktbannerscholarship@linninn.org
Web: www.linninn.org/Pages/scholarship.shtml

Summary To provide financial assistance to law students who are members of a group historically underrepresented in intellectual property law.

Eligibility This program is open to students at ABA-accredited law schools in the United States who are members of groups historically underrepresented (by race, sex, ethnicity, sexual orientation, or disability) in intellectual property law. Applicants must submit a 3-page statement on how ethics, civility, and professionalism have been their focus; how diversity has impacted them; and their commitment to a career in intellectual property law. Selection is based on academic merit; written and oral communication skills; leadership qualities; community involvement; commitment, qualities and actions toward ethics, civility and professionalism; and commitment to a career in IP law.

Financial data The stipend is $5,000.

Duration 1 year.

Number awarded 1 each year.

Deadline November of each year.

[993]
MARY BALL CARRERA SCHOLARSHIP

National Medical Fellowships, Inc.
Attn: Scholarship Program
347 Fifth Avenue, Suite 510
New York, NY 10016
(212) 483-8880   Toll Free: (877) NMF-1DOC
Fax: (212) 483-8897 E-mail: scholarships@nmfonline.org
Web: www.nmfonline.org

Summary To provide financial assistance to Native American women who are attending medical school.

Eligibility This program is open to Native American women who are enrolled in the first or second year of an accredited medical school in the United States. Applicants must be able to demonstrate academic achievement, leadership, and community service, but selection is based primarily on financial need.

Financial data The stipend is $2,500.

Duration 1 year; nonrenewable.

Number awarded 1 or more each year.

Deadline September of each year.

[994]
MARY BLACKWELL BARNES MEMORIAL SCHOLARSHIPS

Women in Public Finance-Virginia Chapter
Attn: Scholarship Committee
P.O. Box 129
Richmond, VA 23219
E-mail: info@virginiawpf.org
Web: www.virginiawpf.org/index.php/scholarships

Summary To provide financial assistance to women from any state who are working on an undergraduate or graduate degree in a field related to public finance at a college in Virginia or Washington, D.C.

Eligibility This program is open to women from any state who are enrolled at a college or university in Virginia or Washington, D.C. as a sophomore or higher undergraduate or a graduate student. Applicants must be preparing for a career in public finance, including work in government, nonprofits, law, or finance. Along with their application, they must submit a 500-word career essay on either 1) their career and educational goals and what has influenced those goals; or 2) their favorite work experience and how it has helped shape or change their thoughts about possible career options. They must also submit a 500-word personal essay on 1 of the following: 1) an interest they have pursued outside of their college classes; 2) a goal they set for themselves and achieved; or 3) an experience, achievement, or risk they have taken or ethical dilemma they have faced. Financial need is not considered.

Financial data Stipends range from $1,000 to $5,000.

Duration 1 year.

Additional information This program began in 2009.

Number awarded Up to 5 each year.

Deadline May of each year.

[995]
MARY ISABEL SIBLEY FELLOWSHIP FOR FRENCH STUDIES

Phi Beta Kappa Society
Attn: Director of Society Affairs
1606 New Hampshire Avenue, N.W.
Washington, DC 20009
(202) 745-3287   Fax: (202) 986-1601
E-mail: awards@pbk.org
Web: www.pbk.org

Summary To provide funding to women interested in conducting dissertation or advanced research on French studies in the United States or any other country.

Eligibility This program is open to unmarried women between 25 and 35 years of age who have demonstrated their ability to conduct original research. Applicants must be planning to conduct a research project dealing with French language or literature. They must hold the doctorate or have fulfilled all the requirements for the doctorate except the dissertation, and they must be planning to devote full time to their research during the fellowship year. Along with their application, they must submit a statement that includes a description of the project, the present state of the project, where the study would be carried out, and expectations regarding publication of the results of the study. Eligibility is not restricted to members of Phi Beta Kappa or to U.S. citizens.

Financial data The stipend is $20,000.

Duration 1 year (the fellowship is offered in even-numbered years only).

Additional information Periodic progress reports are not required, but they are welcomed. It is the hope of the committee that the results of the year of research will be made available in some form, although no pressure for publication will be put on the recipient.

Number awarded 1 every other year.

Deadline January of even-numbered years.

[996]
MARY ISABEL SIBLEY FELLOWSHIP FOR GREEK STUDIES

Phi Beta Kappa Society
Attn: Director of Society Affairs
1606 New Hampshire Avenue, N.W.
Washington, DC 20009
(202) 745-3287   Fax: (202) 986-1601
E-mail: awards@pbk.org
Web: www.pbk.org

Summary To provide funding to women interested in conducting dissertation or advanced research on Greek studies in the United States or any other country.

Eligibility This program is open to unmarried women between 25 and 35 years of age who have demonstrated their ability to conduct original research. Applicants must be planning to conduct a research project dealing with Greek language, literature, history, or archaeology. They must hold the doctorate or have fulfilled all the requirements for the doctorate except the dissertation, and they must be planning to devote full time to their research during the fellowship year. Along with their application, they must submit a statement that includes a description of the project, the present state of the project, where the study would be carried out, and expectations regarding publication of the results of the study. Eligibility is not restricted to members of Phi Beta Kappa or to U.S. citizens.

Financial data The stipend is $20,000.

Duration 1 year (the fellowship is offered in odd-numbered years only).

Additional information Periodic progress reports are not required, but they are welcomed. It is the hope of the committee that the results of the year of research will be made available in some form, although no pressure for publication will be put on the recipient.

Number awarded 1 every other year.

Deadline January of odd-numbered years.

[997]
MARY JONES BERRY SCHOLARSHIP

Society of Women Engineers
Attn: Scholarship Selection Committee
203 North LaSalle Street, Suite 1675
Chicago, IL 60601-1269
(312) 596-5223   Toll Free: (877) SWE-INFO
Fax: (312) 644-8557   E-mail: scholarships@swe.org
Web: societyofwomenengineers.swe.org

Summary To provide financial assistance to women working on a graduate degree in engineering or computer science.

Eligibility This program is open to women who will be full-time graduate students at ABET-accredited colleges and universities. Applicants must be working on a degree in computer science or aeronautical, manufacturing, materials, or mechanical engineering. Preference is given to students at Virginia Tech, University of Virginia, Pennsylvania State, Georgia Tech, or Purdue. Selection is based on merit.

Financial data The stipend is $1,000 per year.

Duration 1 year; may be renewed 1 additional year.

Additional information This program began in 2014.

Number awarded 1 each year.

Deadline February of each year.

[998]
MARY LILY RESEARCH GRANTS

Duke University
David M. Rubenstein Rare Book and Manuscript Library
Attn: Sallie Bingham Center for Women's History and
  Culture
P.O. Box 90185
Durham, NC 27708-0185
(919) 660-5828   Fax: (919) 660-5934
E-mail: cwhc@duke.edu
Web: library.duke.edu/rubenstein/bingham/grants

Summary To provide funding to scholars at all levels who wish to use the resources of the Sallie Bingham Center for Women's History and Culture in the Special Collections Library at Duke University.

Eligibility This program is open to undergraduates, graduate students, faculty members, and independent scholars in any academic field who wish to use the resources of the center for their research in women's studies. Writers, creative and performing artists, filmmakers, and journalists are also eligible. Applicants must reside outside a 100-mile radius of Durham, North Carolina. Undergraduate and graduate stu-

dents must be currently enrolled, be working on a degree, and enclose a letter of recommendation from their adviser or thesis director. Faculty members must be working on a research project and enclose a curriculum vitae. Independent scholars must be working on a nonprofit project and enclose a curriculum vitae. Research topics should be strongly supported by the collections of the center.

Financial data Grants up to $1,000 are available; funds may be used for travel, accommodations, meals, and photocopying and reproduction expenses.

Additional information The library's collections are especially strong in the history of feminist activism and theory, prescriptive literature, girls' literature, artists' books by women, lay and ordained church women, gender expression, women's sexuality, and the history and culture of women in the South. A number of prominent women writers have placed their personal and professional papers in the collections.

Number awarded Varies each year; recently, 11 were awarded.

Deadline January of each year.

[999]
MARY LOUISE ROLLER/ALPHA OMICRON PI SCHOLARSHIP

National Panhellenic Conference
Attn: NPC Foundation
3901 West 86th Street, Suite 398
Indianapolis, IN 46268
(317) 872-3185   Fax: (317) 872-3192
E-mail: npcfoundation@npcwomen.org
Web: www.npcwomen.org/foundation/scholarships.aspx

Summary To provide financial assistance to women who are members of Greek-letter societies and are entering graduate school.

Eligibility This program is open to women who are college seniors planning to attend graduate school in the following fall. Applicants must be nominated by their college Panhellenic and have demonstrated outstanding service to that organization. Along with their application, they must submit a 500-word essay on why they should receive a scholarship. Selection is based on financial need, academic standing, and service to campus, chapter, and community.

Financial data The stipend is $1,000.

Duration 1 year.

Number awarded 1 each year.

Deadline April of each year.

[1000]
MARY MCEWEN SCHIMKE SCHOLARSHIP

Wellesley College
Center for Work and Service
Attn: Extramural Graduate Fellowships and Scholarships
106 Central Street
Wellesley, MA 02181-8203
(781) 283-3525   Fax: (781) 283-3674
E-mail: cws-fellowships@wellesley.edu
Web: www.wellesley.edu/cws/fellowships/wellesley

Summary To provide financial assistance to women working on a graduate degree who need relief from household or child care responsibilities.

Eligibility Women who have graduated from an American academic institution, are over 30 years of age, are currently engaged in graduate study in literature and/or history (preference is given to American studies), and need relief from household or child care responsibilities while pursuing graduate studies may apply. The award is made on the basis of scholarly ability and financial need.

Financial data The fellowship awards range up to $1,500 and are tenable at the institution of the recipient's choice.

Duration 1 year.

Number awarded 1 each year.

Deadline January of each year.

[1001]
MARY PAOLOZZI MEMBER'S SCHOLARSHIP

Navy Wives Clubs of America
c/o NSA Mid-South
P.O. Box 54022
Millington, TN 38054-0022
Toll Free: (866) 511-NWCA
E-mail: nwca@navywivesclubsofamerica.org
Web: www.navywivesclubsofamerica.org/scholarships

Summary To provide financial assistance for undergraduate or graduate study to members of the Navy Wives Clubs of America (NWCA).

Eligibility This program is open to NWCA members who can demonstrate financial need. Applicants must be 1) a high school graduate or senior planning to attend college full time next year; 2) currently enrolled in an undergraduate program and planning to continue as a full-time undergraduate; 3) a college graduate or senior planning to be a full-time graduate student next year; or 4) a high school graduate or GED recipient planning to attend vocational or business school next year. Along with their application, they must submit a brief statement on why they feel they should be awarded this scholarship and any special circumstances (financial or other) they wish to have considered. Financial need is also considered in the selection process.

Financial data Stipends range from $500 to $1,000 each year (depending upon the donations from the NWCA chapters).

Duration 1 year.

Additional information Membership in the NWCA is open to spouses of enlisted personnel serving in the Navy, Marine Corps, Coast Guard, and the active Reserve units of those services; spouses of enlisted personnel who have been honorably discharged, retired, or transferred to the Fleet Reserve on completion of duty; and widows of enlisted personnel in those services.

Number awarded 1 or more each year.

Deadline May of each year.

[1002]
MARY R. NORTON MEMORIAL SCHOLARSHIP AWARD FOR WOMEN

ASTM International
100 Barr Harbor Drive
P.O. Box C700
West Conshohocken, PA 19428-2959
(610) 832-9500
Web: www.astm.org/studentmember/Student_Awards.html

Summary To provide financial assistance to female undergraduate and graduate students working on a degree related to physical metallurgy.

Eligibility This program is open to women entering their senior year of college or first year of graduate study. Applicants must be working on a degree in physical metallurgy or materials science, with an emphasis on relationship of microstructure and properties.

Financial data The stipend is $1,000.

Duration 1 year.

Additional information This program, established in 1975, is administered by ASTM Committee CO4 on Metallography. ASTM International was formerly the American Society for Testing and Materials.

Number awarded 1 or more each year.

Deadline Deadline not specified.

[1003]
MARY VOSWINKEL MEMORIAL SCHOLARSHIP

International Association of Campus Law Enforcement
   Administrators
Attn: Association Administrator
342 North Main Street
West Hartford, CT 06117-2507
(860) 586-7517   Fax: (860) 586-7550
E-mail: awards@iaclea.org
Web: www.iaclea.org

Summary To provide financial assistance to female undergraduate and graduate students who are working for campus security at their school.

Eligibility This program is open to women working on an undergraduate or graduate degree at a college or university that is a member of the International Association of Campus Law Enforcement Administrators (IACLEA). Applicants must be employed in some capacity by the campus security, public safety, or police department at their institution. They must have a GPA of 3.0 or higher and be able to demonstrate financial need.

Financial data The stipend is $1,000.

Duration 1 year.

Number awarded 1 each year.

Deadline March of each year.

[1004]
MCCONNEL FAMILY SCHOLARSHIP

Epsilon Sigma Alpha International
Attn: ESA Foundation
363 West Drake Road
Fort Collins, CO 80526
(970) 223-2824   Fax: (970) 223-4456
E-mail: esainfo@epsilonsigmaalpha.org
Web: www.epsilonsigmaalpha.org

Summary To provide financial assistance to women interested in studying veterinary medicine.

Eligibility This program is open to female residents of any state who are interested in studying veterinary medicine. Applicants may be attending school in any state. They must have a GPA of 3.0 or higher. Selection is based on service and leadership (20 points), financial need (35 points), and scholastic ability (35 points). A $5 processing fee is required.

Financial data The stipend is $1,000.

Duration 1 year; may be renewed.

Additional information Epsilon Sigma Alpha (ESA) is a women's service organization. This program began in 2002. Completed applications must be submitted to the ESA state counselor who then verifies the information before forwarding them to the scholarship director.

Number awarded 5 each year.

Deadline January of each year.

[1005]
MEDICAL RESEARCH FELLOWS PROGRAM

Howard Hughes Medical Institute
Attn: Department of Science Education
4000 Jones Bridge Road
Chevy Chase, MD 20815-6789
(301) 951-6708   Toll Free: (800) 448-4882, ext. 8889
Fax: (301) 215-8888   E-mail: medfellows@hhmi.org
Web: www.hhmi.org

Summary To provide financial assistance to medical, dental, and veterinary students interested in pursuing research training.

Eligibility Applicants must be enrolled in a medical, dental, or veterinary school in the United States, although they may be citizens of any country with a visa authorizing them to work in this country. They must describe a proposed research project to be conducted at an academic or nonprofit research institution in the United States (other than a facility of the National Institutes of Health or other federal agency) or at the sponsor's Janelia Research Campus in Ashburn, Virginia. Research proposals should reflect the interests of the Howard Hughes Medical Institute (HHMI), especially in biochemistry, bioinformatics, biomedical engineering, biophysics, biostatistics, cell biology, developmental biology, epidemiology, genetics, immunology, mathematical and computational biology, microbiology, molecular biology, neuroscience, pharmacology, physiology, structural biology, or virology. Applications from women and minorities underrepresented in the sciences (Blacks or African Americans, Hispanics, American Indians, Native Alaskans, and Native Pacific Islanders) are especially encouraged. Students enrolled in M.D./Ph.D., Ph.D., or Sc.D. programs and those who have completed a Ph.D. or Sc.D. in a laboratory-based science are not eligible. Selection is based on the applicant's ability and promise for a research career as a physician-scientist and the quality of training that will be provided.

Financial data Fellows receive a stipend of $33,000 per year, an allowance of $5,500 for research-related enrichment activities, and an allowance of $5,500 for health, dental, and vision insurance and education and moving expenses.

Duration 12 months, beginning any time between June and August.

Additional information HHMI has entered into partnership agreements with designated sponsors to support fellows in certain areas; those include the Burroughs Wellcome Fund for veterinary students, the Foundation Fighting Blindness for ophthalmology research (particularly in the area of inherited retinal degenerative diseases), the Duchenne Research Fund for research in a field related to Duchenne Muscular Dystrophy, Citizens United for Research in Epilepsy for epilepsy research, the American Society of Human Genetics for genetics research, the Orthopaedic Research and Education Foundation for orthopaedic research, the Parkinson's Dis-

ease Foundation for Parkinson's Disease research, and the Society of Interventional Radiology Foundation for preclinical research in interventional radiology.

Number awarded Up to 60 each year.

Deadline January of each year.

[1006]
MEDTRONIC SWENET SCHOLARSHIP

Society of Women Engineers-Minnesota Section
Attn: Scholarship Committee
P.O. Box 18481
Minneapolis, MN 55418
E-mail: scholarships@swe-mn.org
Web: www.swe-mn.org/scholarships.html

Summary To provide financial assistance to women from any state working on an undergraduate or graduate degree in specified fields of engineering at colleges and universities in Minnesota, North Dakota, and South Dakota.

Eligibility This program is open to female undergraduate and graduate students at ABET-accredited engineering programs in Minnesota, North Dakota, or South Dakota. Applicants must be working full time on a degree in biomedical, chemical, electrical, or mechanical engineering. Along with their application, they must submit a 250-word essay describing how they plan to utilize their engineering knowledge and skills after they graduate. Selection is based on potential to succeed as an engineer (20 points), communication skills (10 points), extracurricular or community involvement and leadership skills (10 points), demonstration of work experience and successes (10 points), and academic success (5 points).

Financial data The stipend is $1,000.

Duration 1 year.

Additional information This program is sponsored by Medtronic, Inc.

Number awarded 3 each year.

Deadline March of each year.

[1007]
MEMORIAL EDUCATION FUND FELLOWSHIPS

General Federation of Women's Clubs of Massachusetts
Attn: Scholarship Chair
245 Dutton Road
P.O. Box 679
Sudbury, MA 01776-0679
(781) 444-3189   E-mail: mapgfwc@msn.com
Web: www.gfwcma.org/scholarships.html

Summary To provide financial assistance to Massachusetts women interested in working on a graduate degree in designated fields at a school in any state.

Eligibility This program is open to women college graduates who have resided in Massachusetts for at least 5 years. Applicants must be planning to work on a graduate degree in a designated field of study that changes annually. Along with their application, they must submit college and graduate school transcripts, a letter of reference from college department chair or recent employer, and a personal statement of no more than 500 words addressing their professional goals and financial need. An interview is required.

Financial data The stipend is $3,000. Funds are paid directly to the recipient's college or university for tuition only.

Duration 1 year; nonrenewable.

Number awarded   2 each year.
Deadline   February of each year.

[1008]
MEREDITH CORPORATION SCHOLARSHIP
New York Women in Communications, Inc.
Attn: NYWICI Foundation
355 Lexington Avenue, 15th Floor
New York, NY 10017-6603
(212) 297-2133   Fax: (212) 370-9047
E-mail: nywicipr@nywici.org
Web: www.nywici.org/foundation/scholarships

Summary   To provide financial assistance and work experi-ence to female residents of designated eastern states who are interested in preparing for a career in publishing at a col-lege or graduate school in any state.

Eligibility   This program is open to women who are resi-dents of New York, New Jersey, Connecticut, or Pennsylvania and enrolled as sophomores, juniors, seniors, or graduate students at a college or university in any state. Graduate stu-dents must be members of New York Women in Communica-tions, Inc. (NYWICI). Also eligible are women who reside out-side the 4 states but are currently enrolled at a college or uni-versity within 1 of the 5 boroughs of New York City. Applicants must be preparing for a career in publishing (print, digital, and/or marketing) and be interested in a summer internship with Meredith Corporation. They must have a GPA of 3.2 or higher. Along with their application, they must submit a 2-page resume; a personal essay of 300 words on an assigned topic that changes annually; 2 letters of recommendation; and an official transcript. Selection is based on academic record, need, demonstrated leadership, participation in school and community activities, honors and other awards or recognition, work experience, goals and aspirations, and unusual personal and/or family circumstances. U.S. citizen-ship or permanent resident status is required.

Financial data   The scholarship stipend ranges up to $10,000; the internship is salaried (amount not specified).
Duration   1 year.
Additional information   This program is sponsored by Meredith Corporation.
Number awarded   1 each year.
Deadline   January of each year.

[1009]
MICHAEL A. ANDERSON, SR. MEMORIAL SCHOLARSHIP
United Methodist Church-Indiana Conference
Attn: Commission on the Status and Role of Women
301 Pennsylvania Parkway, Suite 300
Indianapolis, IN 46280
(317) 564-3250   Fax: (317) 735-4228
E-mail: questions@inumc.org
Web: www.inumc.org/cosrow

Summary   To provide financial assistance to African Amer-ican Methodist women from Indiana who are attending a seminary in any state.

Eligibility   This program is open to female African Ameri-can seminarians who are preparing for the ordained ministry in the Indiana Conference of the United Methodist Church (UMC) at a seminary in any state. Applicants must submit 1)

a 1-page autobiography; 2) a 1-page summary of their under-standing of their call to ministry and the impact that has on their professional goals; and 3) a financial statement. Selec-tion is based on financial need (50%), clarity of call (20%), recommendations (20%), and academic honors and awards (10%).
Financial data   A stipend is awarded (amount not speci-fied). Funds are sent directly to the seminary attended by the recipient.
Duration   1 year.
Number awarded   1 each year.
Deadline   April of each year.

[1010]
MICHELLE JACKSON SCHOLARSHIP FUND
Christian Church (Disciples of Christ)
Attn: Disciples Home Missions
130 East Washington Street
P.O. Box 1986
Indianapolis, IN 46206-1986
(317) 713-2652   Toll Free: (888) DHM-2631
Fax: (317) 635-4426   E-mail: mail@dhm.disciples.org
Web: www.discipleshomemissions.org

Summary   To provide financial assistance to African Amer-ican women interested in preparing for a career in the minis-try of the Christian Church (Disciples of Christ).

Eligibility   This program is open to female African Ameri-can ministerial students who are members of a Christian Church (Disciples of Christ) congregation in the United States or Canada. Applicants must plan to prepare for the ordained ministry, be working on an M.Div. or equivalent degree, pro-vide evidence of financial need, be enrolled full time in an accredited school or seminary, provide a transcript of aca-demic work, and be under the care of a regional Commission on the Ministry or in the process of coming under care.
Financial data   A stipend is awarded (amount not speci-fied).
Duration   1 year; recipients may reapply.
Number awarded   1 each year.
Deadline   March of each year.

[1011]
MICHIGAN COUNCIL OF WOMEN IN TECHNOLOGY FOUNDATION SCHOLARSHIPS
Michigan Council of Women in Technology Foundation
Attn: Scholarship Committee
P.O. Box 214585
Auburn Hills, MI 48321
(248) 654-3697   Fax: (248) 281-5391
E-mail: info@mcwt.org
Web: www.mcwt.org/Scholarships_196.html

Summary   To provide financial assistance to women from Michigan who are interested in working on an undergraduate or graduate degree in a field related to information technology at a school in any state.

Eligibility   This program is open to female residents of Michigan who are graduating high school seniors, current undergraduates, or graduate students and enrolled or plan-ning to enroll at a college or university in any state. Applicants must be planning to work on a degree in a field related to information technology, including business analytics for information science, business applications, computer science, computer engineering, computer information systems, digital forensics, information assurance, information systems, or software engineering. They must have a GPA of 3.0 or higher. Programs in which technology is a secondary element (such as architecture, biomedical engineering, computer aided design, finance, library science, marketing, mechanical engineering, or psychology) are not eligible. Financial need is not considered in the selection process. U.S. citizenship is required.

Financial data The stipend is $5,000 per year; funds are sent directly to the financial aid office at the college or university where the recipient is enrolled.

Duration 1 year; may be renewed for up to 3 additional years for high school seniors or 2 additional years for undergraduate and graduate students. Renewal requires the recipient to maintain a GPA of 3.0 or higher.

Number awarded Varies each year: recently, 4 were awarded: 1 to a high school senior, 2 to undergraduates, and 1 to a graduate student.

Deadline January of each year.

[1012]
MIKE EIDSON SCHOLARSHIP

American Association for Justice
Attn: AAJ Education
777 Sixth Street, N.W., Suite 200
Washington, DC 20001
(202) 684-9563   Toll Free: (800) 424-2725
Fax: (202) 965-0355   E-mail: education@justice.org
Web: www.justice.org

Summary To provide financial assistance to female law students who are interested in a career as a trial lawyer.

Eligibility This program is open to women entering their third year of law school (or fourth year in a night program). Applicants must submit a brief letter explaining their interest in a career as a trial lawyer, dedication to upholding the principles of the Constitution, and commitment to the concept of a fair trial, the adversary system, and a just result for the injured, the accused, and those whose rights are jeopardized.

Financial data The stipend is $5,000.

Duration 1 year.

Additional information This program began in 2008. The American Association for Justice was formerly the Association of Trial Lawyers of America.

Number awarded 1 or 2 each year.

Deadline April of each year.

[1013]
MILDRED RICHARDS TAYLOR MEMORIAL SCHOLARSHIP

United Daughters of the Confederacy
Attn: Second Vice President General
328 North Boulevard
Richmond, VA 23220-4009
(804) 355-1636   Fax: (804) 353-1396
E-mail: udc@hqudc.org
Web: www.hqudc.org/scholarships

Summary To provide financial assistance to female lineal descendants of Confederate veterans who are interested in working on a graduate degree in business.

Eligibility Eligible to apply for these scholarships are female lineal descendants of worthy Confederates or collateral descendants who intend to enroll full time and study business or a business-related field at the graduate level. Applicants must submit certified proof of the Confederate record of 1 ancestor, with the company and regiment in which he served. Preference is given to former members of Children of the Confederacy. They must have a GPA of 3.0 or higher.

Financial data The amount of this scholarship depends on the availability of funds.

Duration 1 year; may be renewed 1 additional year for a master's degree or up to 2 additional years for a doctoral degree.

Number awarded 1 each year.

Deadline April of each year.

[1014]
MINNESOTA SECTION SWE BOSTON SCIENTIFIC SCHOLARSHIP

Society of Women Engineers-Minnesota Section
Attn: Scholarship Committee
P.O. Box 18481
Minneapolis, MN 55418
E-mail: scholarships@swe-mn.org
Web: www.swe-mn.org/scholarships.html

Summary To provide financial assistance to women from any state working on an undergraduate or graduate degree in computer science or specified fields of engineering at colleges and universities in Minnesota, North Dakota, and South Dakota.

Eligibility This program is open to female undergraduate and graduate students at ABET-accredited engineering programs in Minnesota, North Dakota, or South Dakota. Applicants must be working full time on a degree in computer science or biomedical, chemical, electrical, or mechanical engineering. Along with their application, they must submit a 250-word essay describing how they plan to utilize their engineering knowledge and skills after they graduate. Selection is based on potential to succeed as an engineer (20 points), communication skills (10 points), extracurricular or community involvement and leadership skills (10 points), demonstration of work experience and successes (10 points), and academic success (5 points).

Financial data The stipend is $1,000.

Duration 1 year.

Additional information This program is sponsored by Boston Scientific.

Number awarded 1 each year.

Deadline March of each year.

[1015]
MINNIE L. MAFFETT FELLOWSHIPS

Texas Business Women
Attn: Texas Business and Professional Women's Foundation
P.O. Box 70
Round Rock, TX 78680-0070
E-mail: info@tbwconnect.com
Web: www.texasbpwfoundation.org/scholarships.php

Summary To provide financial assistance to women in Texas interested in studying or conducting research in a medical field.

Eligibility This program is open to 1) female graduates of Texas medical schools interested in postgraduate or research work; 2) women who have been awarded a graduate degree in health science or medical science from a Texas university and are seeking certification as a physician assistant or nurse practitioner; 3) women who need financial aid for the first year in establishing a family practice in a rural area of Texas with a population of less than 5,000; and 4) fourth-year female medical students who are completing an M.D. or D.O. degree at an accredited medical school in Texas.

Financial data The stipend recently was $5,000.

Duration 1 year; nonrenewable.

Additional information This program began in 1948 when Texas Business Women was named Texas Federation of Business and Professional Women's Clubs.

Number awarded Varies each year; recently, 3 were awarded.

Deadline December of each year.

[1016]
MORGAN STANLEY MBA FELLOWSHIP

Morgan Stanley
Attn: Diversity Recruiting
1585 Broadway
New York, NY 10036
(212) 762-0211 Toll Free: (888) 454-3965
Fax: (212) 507-4972
E-mail: mbafellowship@morganstanley.com
Web: www.morganstanley.com

Summary To provide financial assistance and work experience to members of underrepresented groups who are working on an M.B.A. degree.

Eligibility This program is open to full-time M.B.A. students who are women, African Americans, Hispanics, Native Americans, or lesbian/gay/bisexual/transgender. Selection is based on assigned essays, academic achievement, recommendations, extracurricular activities, leadership qualities, and on-site interviews.

Financial data The program provides full payment of tuition and fees and a paid summer internship.

Duration 1 year; may be renewed for a second year, providing the student remains enrolled full time in good academic standing and completes the summer internship following the first year.

Additional information The paid summer internship is offered within Morgan Stanley institutional securities (equity research, fixed income, institutional equity, investment banking), investment management, or private wealth management. This program was established in 1999.

Number awarded 1 or more each year.

Deadline December of each year.

[1017]
MOSS ADAMS FOUNDATION SCHOLARSHIP

Educational Foundation for Women in Accounting
Attn: Foundation Administrator
136 South Keowee Street
Dayton, OH 45402
(937) 424-3391 Fax: (937) 222-5749
E-mail: info@efwa.org
Web: www.efwa.org/scholarships_graduate.php

Summary To provide financial support to women, including minority women, who are working on an accounting degree.

Eligibility This program is open to women who are enrolled in an accounting degree program at an accredited college or university. Applicants must meet 1 of the following criteria: 1) women pursuing a fifth-year requirement either through general studies or within a graduate program; 2) women returning to school as current or reentry juniors or seniors; or 3) minority women. Selection is based on aptitude for accounting and business, commitment to the goal of working on a degree in accounting (including evidence of continued commitment after receiving this award), clear evidence that the candidate has established goals and a plan for achieving those goals (both personal and professional), financial need, and a demonstration of how the scholarship will impact her life. U.S. citizenship is required.

Financial data The stipend is $1,000.

Duration 1 year.

Additional information This program was established by Rowling, Dold & Associates LLP, a woman-owned C.P.A. firm based in San Diego. It was renamed when that firm merged with Moss Adams LLP.

Number awarded 2 each year: 1 to an undergraduate and 1 to a graduate student.

Deadline April of each year.

[1018]
MSCPA WOMEN IN ACCOUNTING SCHOLARSHIP

Massachusetts Society of Certified Public Accountants
Attn: MSCPA Educational Foundation
105 Chauncy Street, Tenth Floor
Boston, MA 02111
(617) 556-4000 Toll Free: (800) 392-6145
Fax: (617) 556-4126 E-mail: info@mscpaonline.org
Web: www.cpatrack.com/scholarships

Summary To provide financial assistance to women from Massachusetts working on an undergraduate or graduate degree in accounting at a college or university in the state.

Eligibility This program is open to female Massachusetts residents enrolled at a college or university in the state. Applicants must be undergraduates who have completed the first semester of their junior year or graduate students. They must be able to demonstrate financial need, academic excellence, and an intention to prepare for a career as a Certified Public Accountant (C.P.A.) at a firm in Massachusetts.

Financial data The stipend is $2,500.

Duration 1 year.

Additional information This program is sponsored by the Women's Golf Committee of the Massachusetts Society of Certified Public Accountants (MSCPA).

Number awarded Varies each year; recently, 4 were awarded.

Deadline March of each year.

[1019]
MTS SYSTEMS SCHOLARSHIP

Society of Women Engineers-Minnesota Section
Attn: Scholarship Committee
P.O. Box 18481
Minneapolis, MN 55418
E-mail: scholarships@swe-mn.org
Web: www.swe-mn.org/scholarships.html

Summary To provide financial assistance to women from any state working on an undergraduate or graduate degree in software or mechanical engineering at colleges and universities in Minnesota, North Dakota, and South Dakota.

Eligibility This program is open to female undergraduate and graduate students at ABET-accredited engineering programs in Minnesota, North Dakota, or South Dakota. Applicants must be working full time on a degree in software or mechanical engineering. Along with their application, they must submit a 250-word essay describing how they plan to utilize their engineering knowledge and skills after they graduate. Selection is based on potential to succeed as an engineer (20 points), communication skills (10 points), extracurricular or community involvement and leadership skills (10 points), demonstration of work experience and successes (10 points), and academic success (5 points).

Financial data The stipend is $1,500.

Duration 1 year.

Additional information This program is sponsored by MTS Systems Corporation.

Number awarded 1 each year.

Deadline March of each year.

[1020]
MUSIC THERAPY SCHOLARSHIP

Sigma Alpha Iota Philanthropies, Inc.
One Tunnel Road
Asheville, NC 28805
(828) 251-0606   Fax: (828) 251-0644
E-mail: nh@sai-national.org
Web: app.smarterselect.com

Summary To provide financial assistance to members of Sigma Alpha Iota (an organization of women musicians) who are working on an undergraduate or graduate degree in music therapy.

Eligibility This program is open to members of the organization who have completed at least 2 years of study for an undergraduate or graduate degree in music therapy. Applicants must submit an essay that includes their personal definition of music therapy, their career plans and professional goals as a music therapist, and why they feel they are deserving of this scholarship. Selection is based on music therapy skills, musicianship, fraternity service, community service, leadership, self-reliance, and dedication to the field of music therapy as a career.

Financial data The stipend is $1,500.

Duration 1 year.

Number awarded 1 each year.

Deadline March of each year.

[1021]
MUSICIANS WITH SPECIAL NEEDS SCHOLARSHIP

Sigma Alpha Iota Philanthropies, Inc.
One Tunnel Road
Asheville, NC 28805
(828) 251-0606   Fax: (828) 251-0644
E-mail: nh@sai-national.org
Web: app.smarterselect.com

Summary To provide financial assistance for college or graduate school to members of Sigma Alpha Iota (an organization of women musicians) who have a disability and are working on a degree in music.

Eligibility This program is open to members of the organization who either 1) have a sensory or physical impairment and are enrolled in a graduate or undergraduate degree program in music; or 2) are preparing to become a music teacher or therapist for people with disabilities. Performance majors must submit a 15-minute DVD of their work; non-performance majors must submit evidence of work in their area of specialization, such as composition, musicology, or research.

Financial data The stipend is $1,500.

Duration 1 year.

Number awarded 1 each year.

Deadline March of each year.

[1022]
MYRNA F. BERNATH FELLOWSHIP AWARD

Society for Historians of American Foreign Relations
Attn: Amy Sayward, Executive Director
Middle Tennessee State University
Department of History
MTSU Box 23
Peck Hall, Room 279
Murfreesboro, TN 37132
(615) 898-2569   E-mail: amy.sayward@mtsu.edu
Web: www.shafr.org

Summary To provide funding to women who are members of the Society for Historians of American Foreign Relations (SHAFR) and interested in conducting research on the history of U.S. foreign relations in the United States or any other country.

Eligibility This program is open to women at U.S. universities who wish to conduct historically-based research in the United States or abroad and to women from other countries who wish to conduct research in the United States. The proposed study should focus on U.S. foreign relations, transnational history, international history, peace studies, cultural interchange, or defense or strategic studies. Preference is given to applications from graduate students and those who completed their Ph.D. within the past 5 years. Applicants must submit a project narrative that includes the purpose of the study, significance and scholarly contribution, sources and methods, and timeline for completion.

Financial data The grant is $5,000.

Duration The grant is presented biennially, in odd-numbered years.

Additional information This grant was first presented in 1992.

Number awarded 1 each odd-numbered year.

Deadline September of each even-numbered year.

[1023]
NANCY KELLY FEMALE WRITER AWARD

Philanthrofund Foundation
Attn: Scholarship Committee
1409 Willow Street, Suite 109
Minneapolis, MN 55403-2241
(612) 870-1806   Toll Free: (800) 435-1402
Fax: (612) 871-6587   E-mail: info@PfundOnline.org
Web: www.pfundonline.org/scholarships.html

Summary To provide financial assistance to female Minnesota students who have supported gay, lesbian, bisexual, and transgender (GLBT) activities and are interested in studying writing.

Eligibility This program is open to female residents of Minnesota and students attending a Minnesota educational institution. Applicants must be self-identified as GLBT or from a GLBT family. They may be attending or planning to attend trade school, technical college, college, or university (as an undergraduate or graduate student) to study writing. Preference is given to students in a liberal arts program or studying writing from a liberal arts perspective. Selection is based on the applicant's 1) affirmation of GLBT or allied identity; 2) evidence of experience and skills in service and leadership; and 3) evidence of service, leading, and working for change in GLBT communities, including serving as a role model, mentor, and/or adviser.

Financial data The stipend is $2,000. Funds must be used for tuition, books, fees, or dissertation expenses.

Duration 1 year.

Number awarded 1 each year.

Deadline January of each year.

[1024]
NASA EDUCATION AERONAUTICS SCHOLARSHIP AND ADVANCED STEM TRAINING AND RESEARCH FELLOWSHIP

National Aeronautics and Space Administration
Attn: National Scholarship Deputy Program Manager
Office of Education and Public Outreach
Ames Research Center
Moffett Field, CA 94035
(650) 604-6958   E-mail: elizabeth.a.cartier@nasa.gov
Web: nspires.nasaprs.com

Summary To provide financial assistance to members of underrepresented groups interested in working on a graduate degree in fields of science, technology, engineering, and mathematics (STEM) of interest to the U.S. National Aeronautics and Space Administration (NASA).

Eligibility This program (identified as AS&ASTAR) is open to students who have a bachelor's degree and have historically been underrepresented in NASA-related fields (women, minorities, persons with disabilities, and veterans). Applicants must be working on a research-based master's or doctoral degree in a NASA-related field of STEM, including chemistry, computer and information science and engineering, geosciences (e.g., geophysics, hydrology, oceanography, paleontology, planetary science), engineering (e.g., aeronautical, aerospace, biomedical, chemical, civil, computer, electrical, electronic, environmental, industrial, materials, mechanical, nuclear, ocean, optical, systems), life sciences (e.g., biochemistry, cell biology, environmental biology, genetics, neurosciences, physiology), materials research, mathematical

sciences, or physics and astronomy). They must arrange with a researcher at a NASA Center to serve as a technical adviser in collaboration with the student's faculty adviser. Research must be conducted at a NASA Center as a team project involving the student, the faculty adviser, and the NASA technical adviser. In the selection process, consideration is given to the proposed use of NASA facilities, content, and people. Applications must include a plan for a Center-Based Research Experience (CBRE) to be conducted during the summer at the NASA facility. Students must be U.S. citizens and have a GPA of 3.0 or higher.

Financial data Grants provide a stipend of $25,000 for master's degree students or $30,000 for doctoral candidates, $10,000 for tuition offset and fees, $8,000 as a CBRE allowance, $1,000 as a health insurance allowance, $4,500 as a faculty adviser allowance, and $1,500 as a fellow professional development allowance.

Duration 1 year; may be renewed up to 2 additional years.

Additional information The participating NASA facilities are Ames Research Center (Moffett Field, California), Armstrong Flight Research Center (Edwards, California), Glenn Research Center (Cleveland, Ohio), Goddard Space Flight Center (Greenbelt, Maryland), Jet Propulsion Laboratory (Pasadena, California), Johnson Space Center (Houston, Texas), Kennedy Space Center (Kennedy Space Center, Florida), Langley Research Center (Hampton, Virginia), Marshall Space Flight Center (Marshall Space Flight Center, Alabama), and Stennis Space Center (Stennis Space Center, Mississippi).

Number awarded At least 13 each year.

Deadline June of each year.

[1025]
NATALIE HOPKINS AWARDS

California Native Plant Society
Attn: Educational Grants Committee
2707 K Street, Suite 1
Sacramento, CA 95816-5113
(916) 447-2677   Fax: (916) 447-2727
E-mail: cnps@cnps.org
Web: www.cnps.org/cnps/education/grants.php

Summary To provide funding to female graduate students and scholars interested in conducting research on California's native plants.

Eligibility This program is open to women who are graduate students or other researchers interested in conducting a project related to California native plant studies. There is no standardized application form. Applicants should submit a proposal that contains the following information: title of the project, description of the project (e.g., purpose, objectives, hypotheses, methodology, significance), estimated date of completion, description of the final project, budget, academic status, and personal qualifications.

Financial data Grants recently have ranged from $300 to $1,000.

Additional information This program began in 2007.

Number awarded Varies each year; recently, 6 were awarded.

Deadline September of each year.

[1026]
NATIONAL ASSOCIATION OF UNIVERSITY WOMEN FELLOWSHIPS

National Association of University Women
Attn: Fellowship Chair
1001 E Street, S.E.
Washington, DC 20003
(202) 547-3967   Fax: (202) 547-5226
E-mail: info@nauw1910.org
Web: www.nauw1910.org

Summary To provide financial assistance to members of the National Association of University Women (NAUW) and other women who are working on a doctoral degree.

Eligibility This program is open to women who already have a master's degree and are enrolled in a program leading to a doctoral degree. They should be close to completing their degree. Along with their application, they must submit an outline of their proposed study with reasons for their choice and a developmental outline of their future educational plan. Preference is given to members of NAUW, an organization that historically has served African American women.

Financial data The stipend is $3,000.

Duration 1 year; nonrenewable.

Number awarded 2 each year: 1 to a member of NAUW and 1 to a non-member.

Deadline April of each year.

[1027]
NATIONAL COLLEGIATE ATHLETIC ASSOCIATION POSTGRADUATE SCHOLARSHIP PROGRAM

National Collegiate Athletic Association
Attn: Postgraduate Scholarship Program
700 West Washington Street
P.O. Box 6222
Indianapolis, IN 46206-6222
(317) 917-6683   Fax: (317) 917-6888
E-mail: lthomas@ncaa.org
Web: www.ncaa.org

Summary To provide financial support for graduate education in any field to student-athletes.

Eligibility Eligible are student-athletes who have excelled academically and athletically and who are in their final year of intercollegiate athletics competition at member schools of the National Collegiate Athletic Association (NCAA). Candidates must be nominated by the faculty athletic representative or director of athletics and must have a GPA of 3.2 or higher. Nominees must be planning full- or part-time graduate study. Foreign student-athletes are also eligible. For the fall term, scholarships are presented to athletes who participated in men's and women's cross country, men's football, men's and women's soccer, men's water polo, women's volleyball, women's field hockey, women's equestrian, and women's rugby. For the winter term, scholarships are presented to athletes who participated in men's and women's basketball, men's and women's fencing, men's and women's gymnastics, men's and women's ice hockey, men's and women's rifle, men's and women's skiing, men's and women's swimming and diving, men's and women's indoor track and field, men's wrestling, women's bowling, and women's squash. For the spring term, scholarships are presented to athletes who par-

ticipated in men's baseball, men's and women's golf, men's and women's lacrosse, women's rowing, women's softball, men's and women's tennis, men's volleyball, men's and women's outdoor track and field, women's water polo, and women's sand volleyball. Financial need is not considered in the selection process.

Financial data The stipend is $7,500.

Duration These are 1-time, nonrenewable awards.

Number awarded 174 each year: 87 for women and 87 for men. Each term, 29 scholarships are awarded to men and 29 to women.

Deadline January of each year for fall sports; March of each year for winter sports; May of each year for spring sports.

[1028]
NATIONAL DEFENSE SCIENCE AND ENGINEERING GRADUATE FELLOWSHIP PROGRAM

American Society for Engineering Education
Attn: NDSEG Fellowship Program
1818 N Street, N.W., Suite 600
Washington, DC 20036-2479
(202) 649-3831   Fax: (202) 265-8504
E-mail: ndseg@asee.org
Web: ndseg.asee.org/about_ndseg

Summary To provide financial assistance to doctoral students in areas of science and engineering that are of potential military importance.

Eligibility This program is open to U.S. citizens and nationals entering or enrolled in the early stages of a doctoral program in aeronautical and astronautical engineering; biosciences, including toxicology; chemical engineering; chemistry; civil engineering; cognitive, neural, and behavioral sciences; computer and computational sciences; electrical engineering; geosciences, including terrain, water, and air; materials science and engineering; mathematics; mechanical engineering; naval architecture and ocean engineering; oceanography; or physics, including optics. Applicants must be enrolled or planning to enroll as full-time students. Applications are particularly encouraged from women, members of ethnic minority groups (American Indians, African Americans, Hispanics or Latinos, Native Hawaiians and other Pacific Islanders, Alaska Natives, and Asians), and persons with disabilities. Selection is based on all available evidence of ability, including academic records, letters of recommendation, and GRE scores.

Financial data The annual stipend is $30,500 for the first year, $31,000 for the second year; and $31,500 for the third year; the program also pays the recipient's institution full tuition and required fees (not to include room and board). Medical insurance is covered up to $1,000 per year.

Duration 3 years, as long as satisfactory academic progress is maintained.

Additional information This program is sponsored by the High Performance Computing Modernization Program within the Department of Defense, the Army Research Office, the Air Force Office of Scientific Research, and the Office of Naval Research. Recipients do not incur any military or other service obligation.

Number awarded Approximately 200 each year.

Deadline December of each year.

[1029]
NATIONAL ORGANIZATION OF ITALIAN AMERICAN WOMEN SCHOLARSHIPS

National Organization of Italian American Women
25 West 43rd Street, Suite 1005
New York, NY 10036
(212) 642-2003   Fax: (212) 642-2006
E-mail: noiaw@noiaw.org
Web: www.noiaw.org/scholarships

Summary To provide financial assistance for college or graduate school to women of Italian descent.

Eligibility This program is open to women who have at least 1 parent of Italian American descent and are working on an associate, bachelor's, or master's degree. Applicants must be enrolled full time at a 4-year college or university and have a GPA of 3.5 or higher. Along with their application, they must submit a 2-page essay on how being an Italian American has impacted them personally and professionally. U.S. citizenship is required. Financial need is considered in the selection process. Preference is given to 1) students enrolled at the City University of New York (CUNY) system; and 2) students majoring in Italian language and/or culture.

Financial data The stipend is $2,000.

Duration 1 year; nonrenewable.

Additional information A processing fee of $25 must accompany the application.

Number awarded 5 each year, including 1 reserved for an undergraduate or graduate student at the CUNY system.

Deadline March of each year.

[1030]
NATIONAL PATHFINDER SCHOLARSHIPS

National Federation of Republican Women
Attn: Scholarship Coordinator
124 North Alfred Street
Alexandria, VA 22314-3011
(703) 548-9688   Fax: (703) 548-9836
E-mail: mail@nfrw.org
Web: www.nfrw.org/pathfinder

Summary To provide financial assistance for college or graduate school to Republican women.

Eligibility This program is open to women currently enrolled as college sophomores, juniors, seniors, or master's degree students. Recent high school graduates and first-year college women are not eligible. Applicants must submit 3 letters of recommendation, an official transcript, a 1-page essay on why they should be considered for the scholarship, and a 1-page essay on career goals. Applications must be submitted to the Republican federation president in the applicant's state. Each president chooses 1 application from her state to submit for scholarship consideration. Financial need is not a factor in the selection process. U.S. citizenship is required.

Financial data The stipend is $2,500.

Duration 1 year; nonrenewable.

Additional information This program, previously named the Nancy Reagan Pathfinder Scholarships, was established in 1985.

Number awarded 3 each year.

Deadline Applications must be submitted to the state federation president by May of each year.

[1031]
NATIONAL PHYSICAL SCIENCE CONSORTIUM GRADUATE FELLOWSHIPS

National Physical Science Consortium
c/o University of Southern California
3716 South Hope Street, Suite 348
Los Angeles, CA 90007-4344
(213) 821-2409   Toll Free: (800) 854-NPSC
Fax: (213) 821-6329   E-mail: npsc@npsc.org
Web: www.npsc.org

Summary To provide financial assistance and summer work experience to underrepresented minorities and women interested in working on a Ph.D. in designated science and engineering fields.

Eligibility This program is open to U.S. citizens who are seniors graduating from college with a GPA of 3.0 or higher, enrolled in the first year of a doctoral program, completing a terminal master's degree, or returning from the workforce and holding no more than a master's degree. Students currently in the third or subsequent year of a Ph.D. program or who already have a doctoral degree in any field (Ph.D., M.D., J.D., Ed.D.) are ineligible. Applicants must be interested in working on a Ph.D. in fields that vary but emphasize astronomy, chemistry, computer science, engineering (chemical, computer, electrical, environmental, or mechanical), geology, materials science, mathematical sciences, or physics. The program welcomes applications from all qualified students and continues to emphasize the recruitment of underrepresented minority (African American, Hispanic, Native American Indian, Eskimo, Aleut, and Pacific Islander) and women physical science and engineering students. Fellowships are provided to students at more than 100 universities that are members of the consortium. Selection is based on academic standing (GPA), course work taken in preparation for graduate school, university and/or industry research experience, letters of recommendation, and GRE scores.

Financial data The fellowship pays tuition and fees plus an annual stipend of $20,000. It also provides on-site paid summer employment to enhance technical experience. The exact value of the fellowship depends on academic standing, summer employment, and graduate school attended; the total amount generally exceeds $200,000.

Duration Support is initially provided for 2 or 3 years, depending on the employer-sponsor. If the fellow makes satisfactory progress and continues to meet the conditions of the award, support may continue for a total of up to 6 years or completion of the Ph.D., whichever comes first.

Additional information This program began in 1989. Tuition and fees are provided by the participating universities. Stipends and summer internships are provided by sponsoring organizations. Students must submit separate applications for internships, which may have additional eligibility requirements. Internships are currently available at Lawrence Livermore National Laboratory in Livermore, California (astronomy, chemistry, computer science, geology, materials science, mathematics, and physics); National Institute of Standards and Technology in Gaithersburg, Maryland (various fields of STEM); National Security Agency in Fort Meade,

Maryland (astronomy, chemistry, computer science, geology, materials science, mathematics, and physics); Sandia National Laboratory in Livermore, California (biology, chemistry, computer science, environmental science, geology, materials science, mathematics, and physics); and Sandia National Laboratory in Albuquerque, New Mexico (chemical engineering, chemistry, computer science, materials science, mathematics, mechanical engineering, and physics). Fellows must submit a separate application for dissertation support in the year prior to the beginning of their dissertation research program, but not until they can describe their intended research in general terms.

Number awarded Varies each year; recently, 11 were awarded.

Deadline November of each year.

[1032]
NATIONAL SPACE GRANT COLLEGE AND FELLOWSHIP PROGRAM

National Aeronautics and Space Administration
Attn: Office of Education
300 E Street, S.W.
Mail Suite 6M35
Washington, DC 20546-0001
(202) 358-1069   Fax: (202) 358-7097
E-mail: aleksandra.korobov@nasa.gov
Web: www.nasa.gov

Summary To provide financial assistance to undergraduate and graduate students interested in preparing for a career in a space-related field.

Eligibility This program is open to undergraduate and graduate students at colleges and universities that participate in the National Space Grant program of the U.S. National Aeronautics and Space Administration (NASA) through their state consortium. Applicants must be interested in a program of study and/or research in a field of science, technology, engineering, or mathematics (STEM) related to space. A specific goal of the program is to recruit and train U.S. citizens, especially underrepresented minorities, women, and persons with disabilities, for careers in aerospace science and technology. Financial need is not considered in the selection process.

Financial data Each consortium establishes the terms of the fellowship program in its state.

Additional information NASA established the Space Grant program in 1989. It operates through 52 consortia in each state, the District of Columbia, and Puerto Rico. Each consortium includes selected colleges and universities in that state as well as other affiliates from industry, museums, science centers, and state and local agencies.

Number awarded Varies each year.

Deadline Each consortium sets its own deadlines.

[1033]
NATIONAL STRENGTH AND CONDITIONING ASSOCIATION WOMEN'S SCHOLARSHIPS

National Strength and Conditioning Association
Attn: NSCA Foundation
1885 Bob Johnson Drive
Colorado Springs, CO 80906-4000
(719) 632-6722, ext. 152   Toll Free: (800) 815-6826
Fax: (719) 632-6367   E-mail: foundation@nsca.org
Web: www.nsca.com/foundation/nsca-scholarships

Summary To provide financial assistance to women who are interested in working on an undergraduate or graduate degree in strength training and conditioning.

Eligibility This program is open to women who are 17 years of age or older. Applicants must have been accepted into an accredited postsecondary institution to work on an undergraduate or graduate degree in the strength and conditioning field. Along with their application, they must submit a 500-word essay on their personal and professional goals and how receiving this scholarship will assist them in achieving those goals. Selection is based on that essay, academic achievement, strength and conditioning experience, honors and awards, community involvement, letters of recommendation, and involvement in the National Strength and Conditioning Association (NSCA).

Financial data The stipend is $1,500.

Duration 1 year.

Additional information The NSCA is a nonprofit organization of strength and conditioning professionals, including coaches, athletic trainers, physical therapists, educators, researchers, and physicians. This program began in 2003.

Number awarded Varies each year; recently, 9 were awarded.

Deadline March of each year.

[1034]
NATIONAL URBAN FELLOWS PROGRAM

National Urban Fellows, Inc.
Attn: Program Director
1120 Avenue of the Americas, Fourth Floor
New York, NY 10036
(212) 730-1700   Fax: (212) 730-1823
E-mail: info@nuf.org
Web: www.nuf.org/fellows-overview

Summary To provide mid-career public sector professionals, especially people of color and women, with an opportunity to strengthen leadership skills through a master's degree program coupled with a mentorship.

Eligibility This program is open to U.S. citizens who have a bachelor's degree, have at 5 to 7 years of professional work experience with 2 years in a management capacity, have demonstrated leadership capacity with potential for further growth, have a GPA of 3.0 or higher, and can demonstrate a commitment to public service. Applicants must submit a 1-page autobiographical statement, a 2-page personal statement, and a 2-page statement on their career goals. They may be of any racial or ethnic background, but the program's goal is to increase the number of competent administrators from underrepresented ethnic and cultural groups at all levels of public and private urban management organizations. Semifinalists are interviewed.

Financial data The stipend is $25,000. Fellows are required to pay a $500 registration fee and a $7,500 co-investment tuition payment upon acceptance and enrollment in the program.

Duration 14 months.

Additional information The program begins with a summer semester of study at Bernard M. Baruch College of the City University of New York. Following this, fellows spend 9 months in mentorship assignments with a senior administrator in a government agency, a major nonprofit, or a foundation. The final summer is spent in another semester of study at Baruch College. Fellows who successfully complete all requirements are granted a master's of public administration from that college. A $150 processing fee must accompany each application.

Number awarded Approximately 40 to 50 each year.

Deadline December of each year.

[1035]
NATIVE DAUGHTERS OF THE GOLDEN WEST GRADUATE SCHOLARSHIP

Native Daughters of the Golden West
Attn: Education and Scholarships
543 Baker Street
San Francisco, CA 94117-1405
(415) 563-9091   Toll Free: (800) 994-NDGW
Fax: (415) 563-5230   E-mail: ndgwgpo@att.net
Web: www.ndgw.org/edu.htm

Summary To provide financial assistance for graduate school in the state to members of the Native Daughters of the Golden West (NDGW) in California and their families.

Eligibility This program is open to members and their children who are attending or planning to attend a campus of the University of California or the California State University system. Applicants must be working on or planning to work on a graduate degree in any field. They must have been born in the state and be sponsored by a local parlor of the NDGW.

Financial data The stipend is $1,500.

Duration 1 year; nonrenewable.

Number awarded 1 each year.

Deadline April of each year.

[1036]
NCAA WOMEN'S ENHANCEMENT POSTGRADUATE SCHOLARSHIP FOR CAREERS IN ATHLETICS

National Collegiate Athletic Association
Attn: Office for Diversity and Inclusion
700 West Washington Street
P.O. Box 6222
Indianapolis, IN 46206-6222
(317) 917-6683   Fax: (317) 917-6888
E-mail: lthomas@ncaa.org
Web: www.ncaa.org

Summary To provide funding to women who are interested in working on a graduate degree in athletics.

Eligibility This program is open to women who have been accepted into a program at a National Collegiate Athletic Association (NCAA) member institution that will prepare them for a career in intercollegiate athletics (athletics administrator, coach, athletic trainer, or other career that provides a direct service to intercollegiate athletics). Applicants must be U.S. citizens, have performed with distinction as a student body member at their respective undergraduate institution, have a cumulative undergraduate GPA of 3.2 or higher, and be entering the first semester or term of full-time postgraduate study. Selection is based on the applicant's involvement in extracurricular activities, course work, commitment to preparing for a career in intercollegiate athletics, and promise for success in that career. Financial need is not considered.

Financial data The stipend is $7,500; funds are paid to the college or university of the recipient's choice.

Duration 1 year; nonrenewable.

Number awarded 13 each year.

Deadline February of each year.

[1037]
NCTA/AWM JOINT SCHOLARSHIP

Alliance for Women in Media
Attn: Foundation
2365 Harrodsburg Road, Suite A325
Lexington, KY 40504
(202) 750-3664   E-mail: info@allwomeninmedia.org
Web: www.allwomeninmedia.org/foundation/scholarships

Summary To provide financial assistance to women who are working on an undergraduate or graduate degree in a media-related field and submit project concepts on topics related to media.

Eligibility This program is open to women currently enrolled in an undergraduate or graduate degree program at a college or university in any state. Applicants must be preparing for a media career and working on a degree in such fields as cable, communications, television, radio, digital media, publishing, journalism, advertising, production, creative design, or related areas. Along with their application, they must submit a project concept from a list of 3 industry-specific topics. Recently, the topics were 1) the significance in today's society of digital literacy and 21st literacy skills; 2) a forecast of trends in new and digital media as they may affect providers and users of services; or 3) cable industry public policy viewpoints. They must also submit a statement about why they consider the topic to be important.

Financial data The winner receives a stipend of $3,000, payable to her educational institution, and up to $350 to reimburse expenses for her and the person she highlights to attend the sponsor's Women in Media event in New York. The runner-up receives a $2,000 stipend, payable to her educational institution.

Duration 1 year.

Additional information This program in partnership with the National Cable and Telecommunications Association (NCTA).

Number awarded 2 each year.

Deadline April.

[1038]
NELLIE YEOH WHETTEN AWARD

AVS-Science and Technology of Materials, Interfaces,
   and Processing
Attn: Scholarship Committee
125 Maiden Lane, 15th Floor
New York, NY 10038
(212) 248-0200, ext. 221   Fax: (212) 248-0245
E-mail: angela@avs.org
Web: www.avs.org

Summary To provide financial assistance to women interested in studying vacuum science and technology on the graduate school level.

Eligibility This program is open to women of any nationality who are accepted at or enrolled in a graduate school in North America and studying vacuum science and technology. Applicants are normally expected not to graduate before the award selection. They must submit a description of their current research, including its goals and objectives, the scientific and/or technological reasons that motivate the work, their approach for achieving the goals, progress (if any), program plans, and impact the results might have in the advancement of the area of research. Selection is based on research and academic excellence.

Financial data The stipend is $1,500; the winner also receives reimbursement of travel costs to attend the society's international symposium.

Duration 1 year.

Additional information This award was established in 1989. AVS-Science and Technology of Materials, Interfaces, and Processing was formerly the American Vacuum Society.

Number awarded 1 each year.

Deadline May of each year.

[1039]
NESBITT MEDICAL STUDENT FOUNDATION SCHOLARSHIP

Nesbitt Medical Student Foundation
c/o First Midwest Bank
130 West Lincoln Highway
DeKalb, IL 60115
(815) 593-7051
Web: www.firstmidwest.com/wm_scholarships

Summary To provide financial assistance to needy medical students residing in Illinois and to encourage their entry into general practice in the state.

Eligibility Applicants must be U.S. citizens, residents of Illinois, and either accepted for enrollment or a regular full-time student in good standing at an approved college of medicine. Applicants must be interested in entry into general practice either in DeKalb County or in any county in Illinois having a population of less than 50,000 residents. Preference is given to women, persons who are or have been residents of DeKalb County, and students already attending an approved medical school in Illinois. Financial need must be demonstrated.

Financial data Stipends recently averaged $7,500 per year, depending upon the needs of the recipient.

Duration 1 academic year; renewable.

Number awarded Varies each year; recently, 6 were awarded.

Deadline May of each year.

[1040]
NETWORK OF EXECUTIVE WOMEN SCHOLARSHIP

Network of Executive Women
Attn: Scholarship Program
c/o Accenture
161 North Clark Street, 38th Floor
Chicago, IL 60601
(312) 693-6855   Fax: (312) 726-4704
E-mail: connect@newonline.org
Web: www.newonline.org/page/scholarships

Summary To provide financial assistance to upper-division and graduate student women preparing for a career in the retail, consumer goods, or service industries.

Eligibility This program is open to women enrolled full time as juniors, seniors, or graduate students in a retail, consumer goods, or service industry program at a U.S. college or university. Applicants must have a GPA of 3.0 or higher. Along with their application, they must submit a 1-page essay explaining why they merit this scholarship and outlining their retail, consumer goods, or service industry interests. Selection is based on that essay, a current resume, a transcript, and 2 letters of recommendation; financial need is not considered. U.S. citizenship is required.

Financial data The stipend is $5,000.

Duration 1 year.

Number awarded Varies each year; recently, 5 were awarded.

Deadline April of each year.

[1041]
NEW MEXICO MINORITY DOCTORAL LOAN-FOR-SERVICE PROGRAM

New Mexico Higher Education Department
Attn: Financial Aid Division
2048 Galisteo Street
Santa Fe, NM 87505-2100
(505) 476-8460   Toll Free: (800) 279-9777
Fax: (505) 476-8454   E-mail: fin.aid@state.nm.us
Web: www.hed.state.nm.us/students/minoritydoc.aspx

Summary To provide loans-for-service to underrepresented minorities and women who reside in New Mexico and are interested in working on a doctoral degree in selected fields.

Eligibility This program is open to ethnic minorities and women who are residents of New Mexico and have received a baccalaureate degree from a public 4-year college or university in the state in mathematics, engineering, the physical or life sciences, or any other academic discipline in which ethnic minorities and women are demonstrably underrepresented in New Mexico academic institutions. Applicants must have been admitted as a full-time doctoral student at an approved university in any state. They must be sponsored by a New Mexico institution of higher education which has agreed to employ them in a tenure-track faculty position after they obtain their degree. U.S. citizenship is required.

Financial data Loans average $15,000. This is a loan-for-service program; for every year of service as a college faculty member in New Mexico, a portion of the loan is forgiven. If the entire service agreement is fulfilled, 100% of the loan is eligible for forgiveness. Penalties may be assessed if the service agreement is not satisfied.

Duration 1 year; may be renewed up to 3 additional years.
Number awarded Up to 12 each year.
Deadline March of each year.

[1042]
NEW YORK GRACE LEGENDRE ENDOWMENT FUND FELLOWSHIPS

New York Grace LeGendre Endowment Fund, Inc.
c/o Ramona Gallagher, Fellowship Committee Chair
1217 Delaware Avenue, Apartment 807
Buffalo, NY 14209-1432
E-mail: fellowships@gracelegendre.org
Web: www.gracelegendre.org/Fellowships

Summary To provide financial assistance to women in New York who wish to continue their education on the graduate level.

Eligibility This program is open to women who are permanent residents of New York and citizens of the United States, have a bachelor's degree, and are currently registered full time or have completed 1 semester in an advanced graduate degree program at a recognized college or university in New York. Applicants must show evidence of scholastic ability and need for financial assistance. They should be within 2 years of completing their degree.

Financial data The stipend is $2,000.
Duration 1 year; recipients may reapply.
Additional information This program began in 1989.
Number awarded Varies each year; recently, 3 were awarded. Since the program began, it has awarded $156,000 in fellowships to 147 women.
Deadline February of each year.

[1043]
NINA BELLE REDDITT MEMORIAL SCHOLARSHIP

American Business Women's Association-Pirate Charter Chapter
Attn: Scholarship Program
P.O. Box 20498
Greenville, NC 27858-0498
E-mail: pirateabwascholarship@yahoo.com

Summary To provide financial assistance to female residents of North Carolina interested in working on an undergraduate or graduate degree at a school in the state.

Eligibility This program is open to women who are residents of North Carolina and U.S. citizens. Applicants must be graduating high school seniors, undergraduates, or graduate students and have a GPA of 2.5 or higher. They must be attending or planning to attend an accredited college, university, community college, or vocational/technical school in North Carolina. Along with their application, they must submit a 2-page biographical sketch that includes information about their background, school activities, outside interests, honors and awards, work experience, community service, and long-term goals. Financial need is not considered in the selection process.

Financial data The stipend is $5,000.
Duration 1 year.

Additional information This program began in 1978.
Number awarded 2 each year.
Deadline May of each year.

[1044]
NORTH CAROLINA BUSINESS AND PROFESSIONAL WOMEN'S FOUNDATION SCHOLARSHIPS

Business and Professional Women of North Carolina
Attn: North Carolina Business and Professional Women's Foundation, Inc.
c/o Carol Ambrose, Scholarship Chair
2300 Cloister Drive
Charlotte, NC 28211
(704) 362-2066   E-mail: mcarolambrose65@gmail.com
Web: www.bpw-nc.org/Educational_Scholarship

Summary To provide financial assistance to women attending North Carolina colleges, community colleges, or graduate schools.

Eligibility This program is open to women who are currently enrolled in a community college, 4-year college, or graduate school in North Carolina. Applicants must be endorsed by a local BPW unit and have a GPA of 2.5 or higher. Along with their application, they must submit a 1-page statement that summarizes their career goals, previous honors, or community activities and justifies their need for this scholarship. U.S. citizenship is required.

Financial data The stipend is $1,000. Funds are paid directly to the recipient's school.
Duration 1 year; recipients may reapply.
Additional information This program began in 1996.
Number awarded 2 each year: 1 for an undergraduate and 1 for a graduate student.
Deadline April of each year.

[1045]
NWSA GRADUATE SCHOLARSHIP

National Women's Studies Association
11 East Mount Royal Avenue, Suite 100
Baltimore, MD 21202
(410) 528-0355   Fax: (410) 528-0357
E-mail: awards@nwsa.org
Web: www.nwsa.org/content.asp?admin=Y&contentid=16

Summary To provide funding to members of the National Women's Studies Association (NWSA) working on a graduate thesis in women's studies.

Eligibility This program is open to association members engaged in the research or writing stages of a master's thesis or Ph.D. dissertation in the interdisciplinary field of women's studies. The research project must focus on women and must enhance the NWSA mission. Applicants must submit brief statements on their financial need, feminist or community activities, and relevance of research to NWSA goals.

Financial data The grant is $1,000.
Duration 1 year.
Number awarded 1 each year.
Deadline May of each year.

[1046]
NYWICI FOUNDATION SCHOLARSHIPS

New York Women in Communications, Inc.
Attn: NYWICI Foundation
355 Lexington Avenue, 15th Floor
New York, NY 10017-6603
(212) 297-2133   Fax: (212) 370-9047
E-mail: nywicipr@nywici.org
Web: www.nywici.org/foundation/scholarships

Summary To provide financial assistance to female residents of designated eastern states who are interested in preparing for a career in communications at a college or graduate school in any state.

Eligibility This program is open to women who are seniors graduating from high schools in New York, New Jersey, Connecticut, or Pennsylvania or undergraduate or graduate students who are permanent residents of those states; they must be attending or planning to attend a college or university in any state. Graduate students must be members of New York Women in Communications, Inc. (NYWICI). Also eligible are women who reside outside the 4 states but are currently enrolled at a college or university within 1 of the 5 boroughs of New York City. All applicants must be working on a degree in a communications-related field (e.g., advertising, broadcasting, communications, digital media, English, film, journalism, marketing, public relations, publishing) and have a GPA of 3.2 or higher. Along with their application, they must submit a 2-page resume; a personal essay of 300 words on an assigned topic that changes annually; 2 letters of recommendation; and an official transcript. Selection is based on academic record, need, demonstrated leadership, participation in school and community activities, honors and other awards or recognition, work experience, goals and aspirations, and unusual personal and/or family circumstances. U.S. citizenship or permanent resident status is required.

Financial data The maximum stipend is $10,000.

Duration 1 year; recipients may reapply.

Number awarded Varies each year; recently, 10 were awarded.

Deadline January of each year.

[1047]
OACTA LAW STUDENT DIVERSITY SCHOLARSHIPS

Ohio Association of Civil Trial Attorneys
17 South High Street, Suite 200
Columbus, OH 43215
(614) 228-4727   E-mail: oacta@assnoffices.com
Web: www.oacta.org/About/diversity_scholarship.aspx

Summary To provide financial assistance to minorities and women who are enrolled at law schools in Ohio.

Eligibility This program is open to students entering their second or third year at a law school in Ohio. Applicants must be women or members of minority ethnic or racial groups (African American, Hispanic, Asian, Pan Asian, or Native American). Along with their application, they must submit a law school transcript and a cover letter that addresses their academic, personal, and professional accomplishments and why they should be selected as a recipient of this scholarship. Selection is based on academic achievement in law school,

professional interest in civil defense practice, service to community, and service to the cause of diversity.

Financial data The stipend is $1,250.

Duration 1 year.

Number awarded Up to 3 each year.

Deadline April of each year.

[1048]
OKLAHOMA CITY CHAPTER AWC SCHOLARSHIPS

Association for Women in Communications-Oklahoma
  City Chapter
c/o Tina Evans, Scholarship Committee Chair
1404 Fox View Court
Edmond, OK 73034
(405) 590-8466   E-mail: tina_evans@cox.net
Web: awcokc.org/scholarships

Summary To provide financial assistance to women from any state working on an undergraduate or graduate degree in communications or a related field at a school in Oklahoma.

Eligibility This program is open to women who are residents of any state working full time on an undergraduate or graduate degree in a communications-related field (e.g., public relations, journalism, advertising, photography, graphic design) at a 2- or 4-year college or university in Oklahoma. Applicants must submit a 250-word statement explaining why they are applying for the scholarship, why they chose to study communications, their goals after graduation, and related topics. Selection is based on aptitude, interest in a communications-related career, academic achievement, community service, and financial need.

Financial data Stipends range from $1,000 to $1,500.

Duration 1 year.

Additional information Recipients must enroll full time.

Number awarded Varies each year; recently, 5 were awarded: 1 at $1,500, 2 at $1,250, and 2 at $1,000.

Deadline February of each year.

[1049]
OLIVE LYNN SALEMBIER MEMORIAL REENTRY SCHOLARSHIP

Society of Women Engineers
Attn: Scholarship Selection Committee
203 North LaSalle Street, Suite 1675
Chicago, IL 60601-1269
(312) 596-5223   Toll Free: (877) SWE-INFO
Fax: (312) 644-8557   E-mail: scholarships@swe.org
Web: societyofwomenengineers.swe.org

Summary To provide financial assistance to women interested in returning to college or graduate school to study engineering or computer science.

Eligibility This program is open to women who are planning to enroll at an ABET-accredited 4-year college or university. Applicants must have been out of the engineering workforce and school for at least 2 years and must be planning to return as an undergraduate or graduate student to major in computer science, engineering technology, or engineering. Selection is based on merit.

Financial data The award is $1,500.

Duration 1 year; may be renewed up to 3 additional years, provided the recipient maintains a GPA of 3.0 or higher.

Additional information This program began in 1980.

Number awarded 1 each year.

Deadline February of each year.

[1050]
OLIVE WHITMAN MEMORIAL SCHOLARSHIP

Daughters of the American Revolution-New York State
Organization
c/o Nancy Goodnough
59 Susquehanna Avenue
Coopertown, NY 13326
(607) 547-8794   E-mail: ngoodnaugh@gmail.com
Web: www.nydar.org

Summary To provide financial assistance for college or graduate school to Native American women in New York.

Eligibility This program is open to women who are at least 50% Native American and residents of New York. Applicants must be graduating or have graduated from a high school in the state with a "B+" average. They must be attending or planning to attend an accredited college, university, or graduate school in the state.

Financial data The stipend is $1,000.

Duration 1 year.

Number awarded 1 each year.

Deadline April of each year.

[1051]
OMAHA CHAPTER AFWA SCHOLARSHIPS

Accounting and Financial Women's Alliance-Omaha
Chapter
c/o Natalya Walls, President
Bland & Associates, PC
450 Regency Parkway, Suite 120
Omaha, NE 68114
(402)397-8822   E-mail: omahaafwa@gmail.com
Web: www.omahaafwa.org

Summary To provide financial assistance to women from any state working on an undergraduate or graduate degree in accounting at a school in Nebraska.

Eligibility This program is open to women from any state enrolled part or full time in a bachelor's or master's degree program in accounting or finance at a college or university in Nebraska. Applicants must have completed at least 60 semester hours of a 4- or 5-year program. They must have a GPA of 3.0 or higher. Membership in the Accounting and Financial Women's Alliance (AFWA) is not required. Along with their application, they must submit an essay of 150 to 250 words on their career goals and objectives, the impact they want to have on the accounting or financial world, community involvement, and leadership examples. Selection is based on leadership, character, communication skills, scholastic average, and financial need.

Financial data The stipend is $1,000.

Duration 1 year.

Number awarded Varies each year; recently, 2 were awarded.

Deadline April of each year.

[1052]
OREGON BPW FOUNDATION SCHOLARSHIPS

Oregon Business and Professional Women's Foundation
Attn: Scholarship Program
P.O. Box 133
Roseburg, OR 97470
(541) 672-5820
Web: www.bpworegon.org

Summary To provide financial assistance to women in Oregon who are interested in returning to college.

Eligibility This program is open to women in Oregon who have been accepted into a program of study at an accredited U.S. institution. Applicants must be planning to work on a degree or certificate that will give them marketable skills to increase their economic security and enable them to enter the work force. They must be full-time students; part-time students may be eligible if they have completed at least 45 hours in their program of study. Along with their application, they must submit an essay on their short-term career goals, how this proposed training will help them to accomplish those goals, and how those apply to their long-range career goals. Financial need is considered in the selection process. U.S. citizenship is required.

Financial data A stipend is awarded (amount not specified). Funds are intended to cover tuition, fees, and other related expenses such as books.

Duration 1 year.

Number awarded Varies each year.

Deadline April of each year for summer and fall terms; September of each year for winter term; January of each year for spring term.

[1053]
OREGON EASTERN STAR TRAINING AWARDS FOR RELIGIOUS LEADERSHIP

Order of the Eastern Star-Grand Chapter of Oregon
c/o Holly Austin, ESTARL Scholarship Selection
Committee
14726 Albers Way N.E.
Aurora, OR 97002
(503) 678-1905   E-mail: hollydell@gmail.com
Web: www.oregonoes.org/Scholarships.html

Summary To provide financial assistance to female residents of Oregon who are attending college or seminary in any state to work on an undergraduate or graduate degree that will prepare them for a career in church service.

Eligibility This program is open to female residents of Oregon who are attending a school in any state that is accredited by the Accrediting Association of Bible Colleges, American Association of Schools of Religious Education, American Association of Theological School, National Association of Schools of Music, or similar association. Applicants must be working on an undergraduate or graduate degree that will prepare them for a full-time church vocation. They must submit a letter of reference from a denominational leader who can describe their relationship or prospect for full-time church service. Membership in the Order of the Eastern Star (OES) or other Masonic organization is not required, but applicants must be sponsored by an Oregon OES chapter. Financial need is considered in the selection process.

Financial data Stipends range from $500 to $5,000.

Duration 1 year.

Number awarded Varies each year; recently, 2 at $5,000, 1 at $1,500, and 2 at $500 were awarded.

Deadline April of each year.

[1054]
OUTPUTLINKS WOMAN OF DISTINCTION AWARD

Electronic Document Systems Foundation
Attn: EDSF Scholarship Awards
1845 Precinct Line Road, Suite 212
Hurst, TX 76054
(817) 849-1145   Fax: (817) 849-1185
E-mail: info@edsf.org
Web: www.edsf.org/what_we_do/scholarships/index.html

Summary To provide financial assistance to female undergraduate and graduate students from any country interested in preparing for a career in document management and graphic communications.

Eligibility This program is open to full-time female undergraduate and graduate students from any country who demonstrate a strong interest in preparing for a career in the document management and graphic communications industry, including computer science and engineering (e.g., web design, webmaster, software development, materials engineer, applications specialist, information technology designer, database manager); graphic and media communications (e.g., graphic designer, art director, illustrator, color scientist, print production, prepress imaging specialist, workflow specialist, document preparation, production and/or document distribution, content management, e-commerce, imaging science, printing, web authoring, electronic publishing, archiving, security); or business (e.g., sales, marketing, trade shows, customer service, project or product development, management). Preference is given to graduate students and upper-division undergraduates, but freshmen and sophomores who can show interest, experience, and/or commitment to the document management and graphic communication industry are encouraged to apply. Applicants must have a GPA of 3.0 or higher. Along with their application, they must submit 2 essays on assigned topics that change annually but relate to the document management and graphic communication industries. Selection is based on the essays, academic achievement, participation in school activities, community service, honors and organizational affiliations, education objectives, and recommendations; financial need is not considered.

Financial data The stipend is $5,000.

Duration 1 year.

Additional information This program is sponsored by OutputLinks Communications Group.

Number awarded 1 each year.

Deadline April of each year.

[1055]
PARSONS BRINCKERHOFF WOMEN IN LEADERSHIP SCHOLARSHIP

Conference of Minority Transportation Officials
Attn: National Scholarship Program
1875 I Street, N.W., Suite 500
Washington, DC 20006
(202) 857-8065   Fax: (202) 318-0364
Web: www.comto.org/?page=scholarshipapp

Summary To provide financial assistance to minority women who are working on a master's degree in civil engineering or other transportation-related field.

Eligibility This program is open to minority women who are working full time on a master's degree in civil engineering with intent to prepare for a leadership role in transportation. They must have a GPA of 3.0 or higher. Selection is based on academic achievement, honors and awards, demonstrated leadership skills, active commitment to community service and diversity, and a cover letter on their career goals. U.S. citizenship or legal resident status is required.

Financial data The stipend is $3,000. Funds are paid directly to the recipient's college or university.

Duration 1 year.

Additional information The Conference of Minority Transportation Officials (COMTO) was established in 1971 to promote, strengthen, and expand the roles of minorities in all aspects of transportation. This program is sponsored by Parsons Brinckerhoff, Inc. Recipients are required to become members of COMTO if they are not already members and attend the COMTO National Scholarship Luncheon.

Number awarded 1 each year.

Deadline May of each year.

[1056]
PAST PRESIDENTS SCHOLARSHIPS OF THE SOCIETY OF WOMEN ENGINEERS

Society of Women Engineers
Attn: Scholarship Selection Committee
203 North LaSalle Street, Suite 1675
Chicago, IL 60601-1269
(312) 596-5223   Toll Free: (877) SWE-INFO
Fax: (312) 644-8557   E-mail: scholarships@swe.org
Web: societyofwomenengineers.swe.org

Summary To provide financial assistance to women working on an undergraduate or graduate degree in engineering or computer science.

Eligibility This program is open to women who will be sophomores, juniors, seniors, or graduate students at ABET-accredited colleges and universities. Applicants must be U.S. citizens working full time on a degree in computer science or engineering. Along with their application, they must submit a 1-page essay on why they want to be an engineer or computer scientist, how they believe they will make a difference as an engineer or computer scientist, and what influenced them to study engineering or computer science. Selection is based on merit.

Financial data The stipend is $2,000.

Duration 1 year.

Additional information This program began in 1999 by an anonymous donor to honor the commitment and accomplishments of past presidents of the Society of Women Engineers (SWE).

Number awarded   2 each year.

Deadline   February of each year.

[1057]
PATSY TAKEMOTO MINK EDUCATION FOUNDATION EDUCATION SUPPORT AWARD

Patsy Takemoto Mink Education Foundation for Low-Income Women and Children
P.O. Box 769
Granby, MA 01033
Web: www.patsyminkfoundation.org/edsupport.html

Summary   To provide financial assistance for college or graduate school to low-income mothers.

Eligibility   This program is open to women who are at least 17 years of age and are from a low-income family (less than $20,000 annually for a family of 2, $24,000 for a family of 3, or $28,000 for a family of 4). Applicants must be mothers with minor children. They must be 1) enrolled in a skills training, ESL, or GED program; or 2) working on a vocational/technical, associate, bachelor's, master's, professional, or doctoral degree. Along with their application, they must submit brief essays on what this award will help them accomplish, the program in which they are or will be enrolled, how they decided on that educational pursuit, their educational goals, their educational experience, and their personal and educational history.

Financial data   The stipend is $5,000.

Duration   1 year.

Additional information   This program began in 2003.

Number awarded   Up to 5 each year.

Deadline   July of each year.

[1058]
PAYSCALE'S WOMEN IN STEM SCHOLARSHIP

Payscale, Inc.
1000 First Avenue South, Suite 500
Seattle, WA 98134
Web: www.payscale.com/education/scholarship

Summary   To provide financial assistance to women interested in working on an undergraduate or graduate degree in a field of science, technology, engineering, or mathematics (STEM).

Eligibility   This program is open to women enrolled or planning to enroll at an accredited college or university. Applicants must be interested in working on an associate, bachelor's, or graduate degree in a field of STEM. Selection is based primarily on an essay of 300 to 500 words on why they want to work on a STEM degree, what inspires them, and what they want to do with their degree.

Financial data   The stipend is $2,000.

Duration   1 year.

Additional information   This program began in 2016.

Number awarded   1 each year.

Deadline   February of each year.

[1059]
P.E.O. SCHOLAR AWARDS

P.E.O. Sisterhood
Attn: Scholar Awards Office
3700 Grand Avenue
Des Moines, IA 50312-2899
(515) 255-3153   Fax: (515) 255-3820
E-mail: psa@peodsm.org
Web: www.peointernational.org

Summary   To provide funding for doctoral study in any field to women in the United States or Canada.

Eligibility   This program is open to women who are working full time on a doctoral degree at universities in the United States or Canada. Students in master's degree, certificate, residency, specialization, or postdoctoral programs are not eligible. Applicants must be within 2 years of achieving their educational goal but have at least 1 full academic year remaining. They must be sponsored by a local P.E.O. chapter. Selection is based on academic record, academic awards and honors, scholarly activities, and recommendations; financial need is not considered. U.S. or Canadian citizenship is required.

Financial data   The stipend is $15,000.

Duration   1 year; nonrenewable.

Additional information   This program was established in 1991 by the Women's Philanthropic Educational Organization (P.E.O.).

Number awarded   Varies each year.

Deadline   November of each year.

[1060]
PETER B. WAGNER MEMORIAL AWARD FOR WOMEN IN ATMOSPHERIC SCIENCES

Desert Research Institute
Attn: Selection Committee, Wagner Award
2215 Raggio Parkway
Reno, NV 89512-1095
(775) 673-7300   Fax: (775) 673-7397
E-mail: vera.samburova@dri.edu
Web: www.dri.edu

Summary   To recognize and reward outstanding research papers written by women graduate students on atmospheric sciences.

Eligibility   Women working on a master's or doctoral degree in atmospheric sciences or a related field are invited to submit a research paper for consideration. The applicants may be enrolled at a university anywhere in the United States. They must submit a paper, up to 15 pages in length, based on original research directly related to the identification, clarification, and/or resolution of an atmospheric/climatic problem. Selection is based on the originality of ideas expressed, presentation of concept, how well the subject matter relates to real-world atmospheric/climatic problems or their resolution, and how well the research is defined by the introduction, methods, results, and conclusions of the manuscript.

Financial data   The award is $1,500.

Duration   The award is presented annually.

Additional information   This award was first presented in 1998.

Number awarded 1 each year.

Deadline March of each year.

[1061]
PHIPPS MEMORIAL SCHOLARSHIP

General Federation of Women's Clubs of Connecticut
c/o Joan Duffy, President
2 Quincy Close
Ridgefield, CT 06877
E-mail: duffy-gfwc@appsolutions.com
Web: www.gfwcct.org

Summary To provide financial assistance to women in Connecticut who are working on an undergraduate or graduate degree.

Eligibility This program is open to female residents of Connecticut who have completed at least 2 years of college. Applicants must have a GPA of 3.0 or higher and be working on a bachelor's or master's degree in any field. They must be U.S. citizens. Selection is based on academic ability, future promise, and financial need.

Financial data The stipend is $1,000.

Duration 1 year.

Number awarded 1 each year.

Deadline February of each year.

[1062]
PHOENIX SECTION SWE SCHOLARSHIPS

Society of Women Engineers-Phoenix Section
c/o Stephanie Kinsey, Scholarship Chair
Total Networks
4201 North 24th Street, Suite 230
Phoenix, AZ 85016
(602) 567-1910, ext. 121   E-mail: azkinsey@cox.net
Web: www.swephoenix.com/programs

Summary To provide financial assistance to women working on an undergraduate or graduate degree in engineering at designated colleges in Arizona.

Eligibility This program is open to women from any state currently enrolled at Arizona State University, DeVry, Northern Arizona University, or Embry Riddle University. Applicants must be working on an undergraduate or graduate degree in a field of engineering. Selection is based on an essay, academics, employment history, and participation in the Society of Women Engineers (SWE) and other activities.

Financial data The stipend is $1,000.

Duration 1 year.

Number awarded 2 or 3 each year.

Deadline Deadline not specified.

[1063]
PHYLLIS HUGHES MEMORIAL SCHOLARSHIP

General Federation of Women's Clubs of Iowa
Attn: Scholarship Chair
3839 Merle Hay Road, Suite 201
Des Moines, IA 50310-1321
(515) 276-0510   E-mail: gfwciowa@qwestoffice.net
Web: www.gfwciowa.org/id21.html

Summary To provide financial assistance to women from Iowa who are interested in attending designated law schools.

Eligibility This program is open to women from Iowa who are interested in attending the law school of the University of Iowa, Drake University, or Marquette University. Applicants must submit a personal letter about themselves and their family, reasons for applying, goals, and accomplishments; transcripts; letter of sponsorship from a local club member of the General Federation of Women's Clubs of Iowa; and information on their financial situation. Preference is given to students at Marquette.

Financial data The stipend is $1,500.

Duration 1 year.

Number awarded 1 each year.

Deadline February of each year.

[1064]
PHYLLIS V. ROBERTS SCHOLARSHIP

General Federation of Women's Clubs of Virginia
Attn: Scholarship Committee
513 Forest Avenue
P.O. Box 8750
Richmond, VA 23226
(804) 288-3724   Toll Free: (800) 699-8392
Fax: (804) 288-0341
E-mail: scholarships@gfwcvirginia.org
Web: www.gfwcvirginia.org/forms.htm

Summary To provide financial assistance to women residents of Virginia who are working on a graduate degree in a designated field.

Eligibility This program is open to women residents of Virginia who are working on a graduate degree at a college or university in the state. The field of study varies each year. Applicants must have an undergraduate GPA of 3.0 or higher. Along with their application, they must submit 1) a short statement of their reason for choosing a graduate degree in the designated field; and 2) a resume that includes educational and employment history, community service, and awards received.

Financial data The stipend is $1,000. Funds are paid directly to the recipient's college or university.

Duration 1 year.

Number awarded 3 each year.

Deadline March of each year.

[1065]
PI STATE NATIVE AMERICAN GRANTS-IN-AID

Delta Kappa Gamma Society International-Pi State Organization
c/o Arlene Ida, Native American Committee Chair
3 Sherwood Park Drive
Burnt Hills, NY 12027
E-mail: aiddski@nucap.rr.com
Web: www.deltakappagamma.org/NY

Summary To provide funding to Native American women from New York who plan to work in education or another service field.

Eligibility This program is open to Native American women from New York who are attending a 2- or 4-year college in the state. Applicants must be planning to work in education or another service field, but preference is given to those majoring in education. Both undergraduate and graduate students are eligible.

Financial data The grant is $500 per semester ($1,000 per year). Funds may be used for any career-related purpose, including purchase of textbooks.

Duration 1 semester; may be renewed for a total of 5 years and a total of $5,000 over a recipient's lifetime.

Number awarded Up to 5 each year.

Deadline May of each year for fall; January of each year for winter or spring.

[1066]
PRESBYTERIAN WOMEN OF COLOR GRANTS

Presbyterian Church (USA)
Attn: Office of Financial Aid for Service
100 Witherspoon Street
Louisville, KY 40202-1396
(502) 569-5224   Toll Free: (888) 728-7228, ext. 5224
Fax: (502) 569-8766   TDD: (800) 833-5955
E-mail: finaid@pcusa.org
Web: www.presbyterianmission.org

Summary To provide financial assistance to graduate students who are women of color and Presbyterian Church (USA) members interested in preparing for church occupations.

Eligibility This program is open to women of color who are full-time graduate students at a PCUSA seminary or accredited theological institution approved by their Committee on Preparation for Ministry. Applicants must be working on 1) an M.Div. degree and enrolled as an inquirer or candidate by a PCUSA presbytery; or 2) an M.A.C.E. degree and preparing for a church occupation. They must be PCUSA members, U.S. citizens or permanent residents, able to demonstrate financial need, and recommended by the financial aid officer at their theological institution. Along with their application, they must submit a 1,000-word essay on what they believe God is calling them to do in ministry.

Financial data Stipends range from $1,000 to $3,000 per year. Funds are intended as supplements to students who have been awarded a Presbyterian Study Grant but still demonstrate remaining financial need.

Duration 1 year; may be renewed up to 2 additional years.

Number awarded Varies each year; the sponsor awards approximately 130 grants for this and 3 related programs each year.

Deadline June of each year.

[1067]
PSBJ'S WOMEN OF INFLUENCE-LYTLE ENTERPRISES SCHOLARSHIP

Seattle Foundation
Attn: Scholarship Administrator
1200 Fifth Avenue, Suite 1300
Seattle, WA 98101-3151
(206) 515-2119   Fax: (206) 622-7673
E-mail: scholarships@seattlefoundation.org
Web: www.washboard.org

Summary To provide financial assistance to women from any state working on a graduate business degree at a university in Washington.

Eligibility This program is open to women from any state who are working on a master's degree in business at an accredited college or university in Washington. Applicants must be able to demonstrate financial need. Along with their application, they must submit a 250-word essay about themselves, their educational and career achievements, and their goals. Nontraditional students, including returning students and older adults, are strongly encouraged to apply.

Financial data The stipend is $7,500.

Duration 1 year; nonrenewable.

Additional information This program began in 2006 with support from the Puget Sound Business Journal (PSBJ) and Chuck and Karen Lytel. The recipient must attend the annual "Women of Influence" event in November.

Number awarded 3 each year.

Deadline March of each year.

[1068]
RACHEL ROYSTON PERMANENT SCHOLARSHIP

Delta Kappa Gamma Society International-Alpha Sigma
    State Organization
c/o Lydia Elsom, Chair
Royston Scholarship Foundation
47 West 40th Avenue
Spokane, WA 99203
E-mail: roystonscholarship@yahoo.com
Web: www.deltakappagamma.org/WA/rachel.html

Summary To provide financial assistance to women in Washington who are interested in working on a graduate degree in education at a university in any state.

Eligibility This program is open to women who are Washington residents doing graduate work in education at an approved institution of higher learning in any state, working on either a master's or doctoral degree or in a field of special interest. Applicants must submit 300-word essays on 1) their long-term professional goal and its significance to the field of education; 2) the steps toward their goal they will complete during the scholarship time period; and 3) anything else they wish the committee to know. Selection is based on scholarship, professional service, potential for future service in education, and promise of distinction. A personal interview is required of all finalists.

Financial data The amount of each award is set at the discretion of the foundation's board of trustees. Awards generally range from $500 to $2,000.

Duration Awards may be made for 1 quarter, semester, or academic year. A recipient may, upon fulfilling certain conditions, reapply for a second award.

Additional information This program became operational in 1967.

Number awarded Varies each year; recently, 6 of these scholarships, with a value of $10,000, were awarded. Since the program began, 285 scholarships worth $534,640 have been awarded.

Deadline November of each year.

[1069]
RALPH W. SHRADER DIVERSITY SCHOLARSHIPS

Armed Forces Communications and Electronics Association
Attn: AFCEA Educational Foundation
4400 Fair Lakes Court
Fairfax, VA 22033-3899
(703) 631-6138   Toll Free: (800) 336-4583, ext. 6138
Fax: (703) 631-4693   E-mail: scholarship@afcea.org
Web: www.afcea.org

Summary   To provide financial assistance to master's degree students in fields related to communications and electronics.

Eligibility   This program is open to U.S. citizens working on a master's degree at an accredited college or university in the United States. Applicants must be enrolled full time and studying computer science, engineering (chemical, electrical, electronic, communications, or systems), mathematics, physics, technology management, information technology, or other field directly related to the support of U.S. national security or intelligence enterprises. At least 1 of these scholarships is set aside for a woman or a minority. Selection is based primarily on academic excellence.

Financial data   The stipend is $3,000. Funds are paid directly to the recipient.

Duration   1 year.

Additional information   This program is sponsored by Booz Allen Hamilton.

Number awarded   Up to 5 each year, at least 1 of which is for a woman or minority candidate.

Deadline   May of each year.

[1070]
RANDY GERSON MEMORIAL GRANT

American Psychological Foundation
750 First Street, N.E.
Washington, DC 20002-4242
(202) 336-5843   Fax: (202) 336-5812
E-mail: foundation@apa.org
Web: www.apa.org/apf/funding/gerson.aspx

Summary   To provide funding to graduate students who are interested in conducting research in the psychology of couple and/or family dynamics and/or multi-generational processes.

Eligibility   This program is open to full-time graduate students in psychology. Applicants must be proposing a project that advances the systemic understanding of couple and/or family dynamics and/or multi-generational processes. Work that advances theory, assessment, or clinical practice in those areas is eligible. Preference is given to projects that use or contribute to the development of Bowen family systems. Selection is based on conformance with stated program goals, magnitude of incremental contribution, quality of proposed work, and applicant's competence to execute the project. The sponsor encourages applications from individuals who represent diversity in race, ethnicity, gender, age, disability, and sexual orientation.

Financial data   The grant is $6,000.

Duration   The grant is presented annually.

Additional information   This grant was first awarded in 1998.

Number awarded   1 each year.

Deadline   January of each year.

[1071]
RHODA D. HOOD MEMORIAL SCHOLARSHIP

Northwest Baptist Convention
Attn: Woman's Missionary Union
3200 N.E. 109th Avenue
Vancouver, WA 98682-7749
(360) 882-2101   Fax: (360) 882-2295
E-mail: linda@nwbaptist.org
Web: www.nwbaptist.org

Summary   To provide financial assistance to women from the Northwest who are attending college or seminary in any state to prepare for a career in vocational ministry, preferably with a Southern Baptist Convention church.

Eligibility   This program is open to women who have been active members of a church affiliated with the Northwest Baptist Convention and a member of the Woman's Missionary Union within their church. Special consideration is given to children of ministers from the Northwest. Applicants must be attending or planning to attend an accredited college, university, or Southern Baptist seminary in any state with the intention of serving in a vocational ministry position through a church or denomination; priority is given to applicants going into a mission vocation affiliated with the Southern Baptist Convention. Along with their application, they must submit 1) a written account of their conversion experience and their call to vocational ministry; and 2) a written endorsement from their church.

Financial data   A stipend is awarded (amount not specified).

Duration   1 year; may be renewed if the recipient maintains a GPA of 2.5 or higher.

Additional information   The Northwest Baptist Convention serves Oregon, Washington, and northern Idaho.

Number awarded   1 or more each year.

Deadline   May of each year for fall term; October of each year for spring term.

[1072]
RHONDA J.B. O'LEARY MEMORIAL SCHOLARSHIP

Educational Foundation for Women in Accounting
Attn: Foundation Administrator
136 South Keowee Street
Dayton, OH 45402
(937) 424-3391   Fax: (937) 222-5749
E-mail: info@efwa.org
Web: www.efwa.org/scholarships_graduate.php

Summary   To provide financial support to women who are enrolled in an undergraduate or graduate accounting degree program at a school in Washington.

Eligibility   This program is open to women from any state who are working on a bachelor's or master's degree in accounting at an accredited school in Washington. Selection is based on aptitude for accounting and business, commitment to the goal of working on a degree in accounting (including evidence of continued commitment after receiving this award), clear evidence that the candidate has established goals and a plan for achieving those goals (both personal and professional), and financial need. U.S. citizenship is required.

Financial data The stipend is $2,000 per year.

Duration 1 year; may be renewed 1 additional year if the recipient completes at least 12 hours each semester.

Additional information This program began in 2007 with funds provided by the Seattle Chapter of the American Society of Women Accountants (ASWA).

Number awarded 2 each year: 1 to an undergraduate and 1 to a graduate student.

Deadline April of each year.

[1073]
RITA MAE KELLY ENDOWMENT FELLOWSHIP

American Political Science Association
Attn: Centennial Center Visiting Scholars Program
1527 New Hampshire Avenue, N.W.
Washington, DC 20036-1206
(202) 483-2512   Fax: (202) 483-2657
E-mail: centennial@apsanet.org
Web: www.apsanet.org/centennial/grants

Summary To provide funding to members of the American Political Science Association (APSA) who are interested in conducting research on the intersection of gender, race, ethnicity, and political power at the Centennial Center for Political Science and Public Affairs.

Eligibility This program is open to members of the association who are interested in conducting research on the intersection of gender, race, ethnicity, and political power while in residence at the center. Support is available to pre-dissertation graduate students as well as for an award or public presentation. Non-resident scholars may also be eligible.

Financial data Grants normally range from $1,000 to $2,500.

Duration 2 weeks to 12 months.

Additional information This program was established in affiliation with the Women's Caucus for Political Science, the Latina Caucus for Political Science, the Committee for the Status of Latino/Latinas in the Profession, the Women and Politics Research Organized Section, and the Race, Ethnicity and Politics Organized Section.

Number awarded 1 or more each year.

Deadline February, June, or October of each year.

[1074]
RJOS MEDICAL STUDENT ACHIEVEMENT AWARDS

Ruth Jackson Orthopaedic Society
9400 West Higgins Road, Suite 500
Rosemont, IL 60018
(847) 698-1626   Fax: (847) 268-9461
E-mail: rjos@aaos.org
Web: www.rjos.org/category/research-grant-opportunities

Summary To recognize and reward female orthopedic students who demonstrate outstanding achievement.

Eligibility This award is available to women who are members of the Ruth Jackson Orthopaedic Society (RJOS) and attending medical school to prepare for a career in orthopedic surgery. Selection is based on achievements in research, leadership, mentoring, athletics, and community service/volunteerism.

Financial data The award provides up to $1,500 to assist with registration fees and travel expenses to attend the annual meeting of the American Academy of Orthopaedic Surgeons (AAOS).

Number awarded 1 each year.

Deadline October of each year.

[1075]
ROCHELLE NICOLETTE PERRY MEMORIAL SCHOLARSHIP

Society of Women Engineers
Attn: Scholarship Selection Committee
203 North LaSalle Street, Suite 1675
Chicago, IL 60601-1269
(312) 596-5223   Toll Free: (877) SWE-INFO
Fax: (312) 644-8557   E-mail: scholarships@swe.org
Web: societyofwomenengineers.swe.org

Summary To provide financial assistance to members of the Society of Women Engineers (SWE) who are working on an undergraduate or graduate degree in electrical engineering or engineering technology.

Eligibility This program is open to SWE members who are full-time sophomores, juniors, seniors, or graduate student at an ABET-accredited 4-year college or university. Applicants must be studying electrical engineering or engineering technology at schools in SWE Region E (Delaware, District of Columbia, eastern Pennsylvania, Maryland, New Jersey, New York, and Virginia) or Region H (Illinois, Indiana, Iowa, Michigan, Minnesota, North Dakota, South Dakota, and Wisconsin). Preference is given to applicants who can demonstrate a high level of dedication and passion for their own community, organizations, and engineering in general. Selection is based on merit.

Financial data The stipend is $1,000.

Duration 1 year.

Additional information This program began in 2014.

Number awarded 1 each year.

Deadline February of each year.

[1076]
ROCKY MOUNTAIN SECTION COLLEGE SCHOLARSHIPS

Society of Women Engineers-Rocky Mountain Section
c/o Christi Wisleder, College Scholarship Chair
Merrick & Company
5970 Greenwood Plaza Boulevard
Greenwood Village, CO 80111
(303) 751-0741   Toll Free: (800) 544-1714
Fax: (303) 751-2581   E-mail: christi.wisleder@gmail.com
Web: www.swe-rms.org/scholarships.html

Summary To provide financial assistance to women from any state who are working on an undergraduate or graduate degree in engineering or computer science at colleges and universities in Colorado and Wyoming.

Eligibility This program is open to women from any state who are enrolled as an undergraduate or graduate engineering student in an ABET-accredited engineering, computer science, or engineering technology program in Colorado or Wyoming (excluding zip codes 80800-81599). Applicants must have a GPA of 3.0 or higher. Along with their application, they must submit an essay on why they have chosen an engineering major, what they will accomplish or how they believe they will make a difference as an engineer, and who or what influenced them to study engineering. Selection is based on merit.

Financial data The stipend is at least $1,000.

Duration 1 year.

Additional information This program includes the following named scholarships: the Dorolyn Lines Scholarship, the Lottye Miner Scholarship, and the Rocky Mountain Section Pioneer Scholarship.

Number awarded 3 each year.

Deadline January of each year.

[1077]
ROSENFELD INJURY LAWYERS' SINGLE MOTHERS SCHOLARSHIPS

Rosenfeld Injury Lawyers
33 North Dearborn Street, Suite 1930
Chicago, IL 60602
(847) 835-8895
E-mail: jonathan@rosenfeldinjurylawyers.com
Web: www.rosenfeldinjurylawyers.com

Summary To recognize and reward, with funding for college or law school, single mothers who submit outstanding essays.

Eligibility This program is open to single mothers who are enrolled or planning to enroll at an accredited college, university, community college, or law school in any state. Applicants must have a GPA of 3.0 or higher. They must submit a 500-word essay on the advantages of going back to school while caring for their children as a mother. Staff at the sponsoring law firm select 5 finalists and post their essays on its website. The essays that receive the most support on social media are awarded the scholarships.

Financial data The award is a $1,000 scholarship.

Duration 1 year.

Number awarded 2 each year: 1 to an undergraduate student and 1 to a law student.

Deadline December of each year.

[1078]
ROY SCRIVNER MEMORIAL RESEARCH GRANTS

American Psychological Foundation
750 First Street, N.E.
Washington, DC 20002-4242
(202) 336-5843   Fax: (202) 336-5812
E-mail: foundation@apa.org
Web: www.apa.org/apf/funding/scrivner.aspx

Summary To provide funding to graduate students interested in conducting dissertation research on lesbian, gay, bisexual, and transgender (LGBT) family psychology and therapy.

Eligibility This program is open to doctoral candidates who are interested in conducting empirical research in all fields of the behavioral and social sciences that focus on LGBT family psychology and LGBT family therapy. Proposals are especially encouraged for empirical studies that address the following: problems faced by LGBT families such as those associated with cultural, racial, socioeconomic, and family structure diversity; successful coping mechanisms such as

sources of support and resilience for family members; and clinical issues and interventions in the domain of LGBT. Selection is based on conformance with stated program goals; quality of proposed work, including research plan and expected outcome; applicant's demonstrated scholarship and competence, and appropriateness of proposed budget. The sponsor encourages applications from individuals who represent diversity in race, ethnicity, gender, age, disability, and sexual orientation.

Financial data The grant is $15,000.

Duration 1 year.

Number awarded 1 each year.

Deadline October of each year.

[1079]
RUKMINI AND JOYCE VASUDEVAN SCHOLARSHIP

Wisconsin Medical Society
Attn: Wisconsin Medical Society Foundation
330 East Lakeside Street
Madison, WI 53715
(608) 442-3789   Toll Free: (866) 442-3800, ext. 3789
Fax: (608) 442-3851 E-mail: elizabeth.ringle@wismed.org
Web: www.wisconsinmedicalsociety.org

Summary To provide financial assistance to female students enrolled at medical schools in Wisconsin.

Eligibility This program is open to women who are entering their third or fourth year of full-time study at a medical school in Wisconsin. Applicants must submit a personal statement of 1 to 2 pages on their family background, achievements, current higher educational status, career goals, and financial need; their statement should include examples of their compassion, caring, and courage or hard work despite adversity or obstacles in life. Preference is given to residents of Wisconsin, those close to completing their degree, and those who demonstrate ties to their community and a desire to practice in Wisconsin. U.S. citizenship is required. Selection is based on financial need, academic achievement, personal qualities and strengths, and letters of recommendation.

Financial data The stipend is $5,000.

Duration 1 year.

Number awarded 1 each year.

Deadline January of each year.

[1080]
RUTH AND LINCOLN EKSTROM FELLOWSHIPS

Brown University
John Carter Brown Library
Attn: Fellowships Coordinator
P.O. Box 1894
Providence, RI 02912
(401) 863-5010   Fax: (401) 863-3477
E-mail: Valerie_Andrews@Brown.edu
Web: www.brown.edu

Summary To support scholars and graduate students interested in conducting research on the history of women at the John Carter Brown Library, which is renowned for its collection of historical sources pertaining to the Americas prior to 1830.

Eligibility This fellowship is open to U.S-based and foreign graduate students, scholars, and independent researchers. Graduate students must have passed their preliminary or general examinations. Applicants must be proposing to conduct research on the history of women and the family in the Americas prior to 1825, including the question of cultural influences on gender formation. Selection is based on the applicant's scholarly qualifications, the merits and significance of the project, and the particular need that the holdings of the John Carter Brown Library will fill in the development of the project.

Financial data The stipend is $2,100 per month.

Duration From 2 to 4 months.

Additional information Fellows are expected to be in regular residence at the library and to participate in the intellectual life of Brown University for the duration of the program.

Number awarded Varies each year; recently, 3 were awarded.

Deadline December of each year.

[1081]
RUTH G. WHITE P.E.O. SCHOLARSHIP

P.E.O. Foundation-California State Chapter
c/o Holly Harris, White Scholarship Fund
56 Cottage court
Sonora, CA 95370
E-mail: peoca.rgw@gmail.com
Web: www.peocalifornia.org

Summary To provide financial assistance to women from California who are interested in working on a medical-related degree at a graduate school in any state.

Eligibility This program is open to female residents of California who have completed their first year of graduate work in the field of medicine. Applicants may be studying in any state. They must submit a personal narrative that describes their background, interests, scholastic achievements, extracurricular activities, service, talents, and goals. Selection is based on character, integrity, academic excellence, and financial need. U.S. citizenship is required.

Financial data Stipends recently averaged $4,320.

Duration 1 year; recipients may reapply.

Additional information This fund was established in 1957.

Number awarded Varies each year; recently, 12 were awarded.

Deadline January of each year.

[1082]
RUTH H. BUFTON SCHOLARSHIP

American Business Women's Association
Attn: Stephen Bufton Memorial Educational Fund
9820 Metcalf Avenue, Suite 110
Overland Park, KS 66212
Toll Free: (800) 228-0007
Web: www.sbmef.org/National/index.cfm

Summary To provide financial assistance to female graduate students who are working on a degree in a specified field (the field changes each year).

Eligibility This program is open to women who are working on a graduate degree and have a cumulative GPA of 3.0 or higher. Applicants are not required to be members of the American Business Women's Association. Along with their application, they must submit a 250-word biographical sketch that includes information about their background, activities, honors, work experience, and long-term educational and professional goals. Financial need is not considered in the selection process. Annually, the trustees designate an academic discipline for which the scholarship will be presented that year. U.S. citizenship is required.

Financial data The stipend is $10,000 (paid over a 2-year period). Funds are paid directly to the recipient's institution to be used only for tuition, books, and fees.

Duration 2 years.

Additional information This program was created in 1986 as part of ABWA's Stephen Bufton Memorial Education Fund.

Number awarded 1 each odd-numbered year.

Deadline May of each odd-numbered year.

[1083]
RUTH R. AND ALYSON R. MILLER FELLOWSHIPS

Massachusetts Historical Society
Attn: Short-Term Fellowships
1154 Boylston Street
Boston, MA 02215-3695
(617) 646-0568   Fax: (617) 859-0074
E-mail: fellowships@masshist.org
Web: www.masshist.org/research/fellowships/short-term

Summary To fund research visits to the Massachusetts Historical Society for graduate students and other scholars interested in women's history.

Eligibility This program is open to advanced graduate students, postdoctorates, and independent scholars who are conducting research in women's history and need to use the resources of the Massachusetts Historical Society. Applicants must be U.S. citizens or foreign nationals holding appropriate U.S. government documents. Along with their application, they must submit a curriculum vitae and a proposal describing the project and indicating collections at the society to be consulted. Graduate students must also arrange for a letter of recommendation from a faculty member familiar with their work and with the project being proposed. Preference is given to candidates who live 50 or more miles from Boston.

Financial data The grant is $2,000.

Duration 4 weeks.

Additional information This fellowship was first awarded in 1998.

Number awarded 1 or more each year.

Deadline February of each year.

[1084]
RUTH WHITNEY SCHOLARSHIP

New York Women in Communications, Inc.
Attn: NYWICI Foundation
355 Lexington Avenue, 15th Floor
New York, NY 10017-6603
(212) 297-2133   Fax: (212) 370-9047
E-mail: nywicipr@nywici.org
Web: www.nywici.org/foundation/scholarships

Summary To provide financial assistance to female residents of designated eastern states who are interested in preparing for a career in magazine journalism or publishing at a college or graduate school in any state.

Eligibility This program is open to women who are residents of New York, New Jersey, Connecticut, or Pennsylvania and enrolled as undergraduate or graduate students at a college or university in any state. Graduate students must be members of New York Women in Communications, Inc. (NYWICI). Also eligible are women who reside outside the 4 states but are currently enrolled at a college or university within 1 of the 5 boroughs of New York City. Applicants must have some experience in writing, reporting, or design and be preparing for a career in magazine journalism or publishing. Along with their application, they must submit a 2-page resume; a personal essay of 300 words on an assigned topic that changes annually; 2 letters of recommendation; and an official transcript. Selection is based on academic record, need, demonstrated leadership, participation in school and community activities, honors and other awards or recognition, work experience, goals and aspirations, and unusual personal and/or family circumstances. U.S. citizenship or permanent resident status is required.

Financial data The stipend ranges up to $10,000.

Duration 1 year.

Additional information This program is sponsored by *Glamour* magazine, which invites the recipient to visit its offices and spend a week with its editorial team.

Number awarded 1 each year.

Deadline January of each year.

[1085]
S. EVELYN LEWIS MEMORIAL MEDICAL HEALTH SCIENCE SCHOLARSHIP

Zeta Phi Beta Sorority, Inc.
Attn: National Educational Foundation
1734 New Hampshire Avenue, N.W.
Washington, DC 20009
(202) 387-3103   Fax: (202) 232-4593
E-mail: info@zetaphibetasororityhq.org
Web: www.zpbnef1975.org/scholarships-and-descriptions

Summary To provide financial assistance to women interested in studying medicine or health sciences on the undergraduate or graduate school level.

Eligibility This program is open to women enrolled full time in a program on the undergraduate or graduate school level leading to a degree in medicine or health sciences. Proof of enrollment is required. Applicants need not be members of Zeta Phi Beta Sorority. Along with their application, they must submit a 150-word essay on their educational goals and professional aspirations, how this award will help them to achieve those goals, and why they should receive the award. Financial need is not considered in the selection process.

Financial data The stipend ranges from $500 to $1,000. Funds are paid directly to the college or university.

Duration 1 academic year.

Additional information Zeta Phi Beta is a traditionally African American sorority.

Number awarded 1 or more each year.

Deadline January of each year.

[1086]
SADIE T.M. ALEXANDER BOOK SCHOLARSHIPS

National Bar Association-Women Lawyers Division
Attn: Philadelphia Chapter
c/o Jacqueline Allen, Scholarship Committee Chair
P.O. Box 58004
Philadelphia, PA 19102-8004
(215) 686-7038   E-mail: scholarshipsfdnwldl@gmail.com
Web: www.nbawldphila.org

Summary To provide financial assistance to African American women who are enrolled at designated law schools in the Philadelphia region.

Eligibility This program is open to African American women entering their second or third year at the Thomas R. Kline School of Law at Drexel University, Beasley School of Law at Temple University, Rutgers (Camden) School of Law, University of Pennsylvania School of Law, Villanova School or Law, or Widener University School of Law. Applicants must submit essays on 1) their career aspirations, including how or why they chose a career in the law; and 2) an experience or personal/professional aspiration that would reflect the professional legacy of the scholarship's namesake. Selection is based on academic excellence, commitment to community service, and financial need.

Financial data The stipend ranges from $500 to $1,000. Funding is designed to help with the purchase of books.

Duration 1 year.

Number awarded Up to 6 each year.

Deadline June of each year.

[1087]
SAN DIEGO CHAPTER AWIS SCHOLARSHIP PROGRAM

Association for Women in Science-San Diego Chapter
Attn: Scholarship Committee
P.O. Box 178096
San Diego, CA 92177
E-mail: scholarship@awissd.org
Web: www.awissd.org/index.php/opportunities/scholarships

Summary To provide financial assistance to women who are working on an undergraduate or graduate degree in a field of science, technology, engineering, or mathematics (STEM) at a college in San Diego County, California.

Eligibility This program is open to women from any state currently enrolled at a college, university, or community college in San Diego County, California. Applicants must be working on an undergraduate or graduate degree in a field of STEM and have a GPA of 3.0 or higher. They must be U.S. citizens or permanent residents. Along with their application, they must submit a 750-word personal statement describing their career aspirations and scientific interests, including research experience and relevant extracurricular activities. Financial need is not considered in the selection process.

Financial data The stipend is $1,000.

Duration 1 year; nonrenewable.

Number awarded Varies each year; recently, 8 were awarded: 1 to a community college student, 3 to undergraduates, and 4 to graduate students.

Deadline February of each year.

[1088]
SARA EIKENBERRY VOICE SCHOLARSHIPS

Mu Phi Epsilon Fraternity
Attn: Mu Phi Epsilon Foundation
c/o Liana Sandin, Voice Scholarship Chair
6321 A Street
Lincoln, NE 68510-5010
(402) 560-7126   E-mail: liana.sandin@gmail.com
Web: www.mpefoundation.org

Summary To provide financial assistance to undergraduate or graduate student members of Mu Phi Epsilon who are studying mezzo-soprano or contralto voice.

Eligibility This program is open to undergraduate and graduate student members of Mu Phi Epsilon, a professional music fraternity, who are mezzo-sopranos or contraltos studying voice. Applicants must submit college transcripts; a current resume (including Mu Phi Epsilon participation); 2 letters of recommendation; a high quality compact disc recording that includes 3 art songs or arias of contrasting styles, 1 of which is in English; a list of the recorded repertoire with exact titles, opus numbers, composers' names, and timings; and recent reviews and programs.

Financial data The stipend is $1,000.

Duration 1 year.

Additional information The application submission fee is $25.

Number awarded 2 each year: 1 to an undergraduate and 1 to a graduate student.

Deadline February of each year.

[1089]
SARA OWEN ETHERIDGE STUDENT SCHOLARSHIP

Baptist Women in Ministry of Georgia
c/o Darlene Flaming, Scholarship Committee Chair
1400 Coleman Avenue
Macon, GA 31207
E-mail: bwimga@gmail.com

Summary To provide financial assistance to Baptist women from Georgia who are working on a graduate degree in theology at a seminary in any state.

Eligibility This program is open to women who are, or have been, residents of Georgia. Applicants must be Baptists who have completed at least 30 hours of study for a master's or doctoral degree at a seminary in any state. Along with their application, they must submit a brief narrative that includes a summary of their call to ministry, plans for carrying out their ministry, an autobiography, and a description of any ministry experience that illustrate their gifts for ministry.

Financial data The stipend is $1,500.

Duration 1 year.

Number awarded 1 or 2 each year.

Deadline March of each year.

[1090]
SARAH BRADLEY TYSON MEMORIAL FELLOWSHIP

Woman's National Farm and Garden Association, Inc.
c/o Mrs. Harold L. Matyn, Fellowship Committee Chair
3801 Riverview Terrace, South
East China Township, MI 48054
E-mail: matynjm@att.net
Web: www.wnfga.org/scholarships/fellowships

Summary To provide funding to women who have work experience and are interested in advanced study in agriculture, horticulture, and allied subjects.

Eligibility The fellowship is open to women interested in working on an advanced degree in the fields of agriculture, horticulture, or allied subjects at educational institutions of recognized standing within the United States. Applicants must have several years of experience. There are no application forms. Interested women should send a letter of application that contains an account of their educational training, a plan of study, references, samples of publishable papers, and a health certificate.

Financial data The fellowship award is $1,000 and is tenable at an American institution of higher learning chosen by the candidate with the approval of the fellowship committee.

Duration 1 year.

Additional information This program began in 1928. Students who accept the fellowships must agree to devote themselves to the study outlined in their application and to submit any proposed change in their plan to the committee for approval. They must send the committee at least 2 reports on their work, 1 at the end of the first semester and another upon completion of the year's work.

Number awarded Varies each year.

Deadline April of each year.

[1091]
SCHLESINGER LIBRARY DOCTORAL DISSERTATION GRANTS

Radcliffe Institute for Advanced Study at Harvard
   University
Attn: Arthur and Elizabeth Schlesinger Library
10 Garden Street
Cambridge, MA 02138
(617) 495-8647   Fax: (617) 496-8340
E-mail: slgrants@radcliffe.harvard.edu
Web: www.radcliffe.harvard.edu/schlesinger-library/grants

Summary To provide funding to doctoral students who need to use the holdings of the Arthur and Elizabeth Schlesinger Library on the History of Women in America to complete their dissertation.

Eligibility Applicants must be enrolled in a doctoral program in a relevant field, have completed their course work toward the doctoral degree, and have an approved dissertation topic by the time application is made. Priority is given to those whose projects require use of materials available nowhere else but the Schlesinger Library. The project description should indicate the purpose of the research, the Schlesinger Library holdings to be consulted, and the significance of those holdings to the project overall. Selection is based on the significance of the research, the project's potential contribution to the advancement of knowledge, and its creativity in using the library's holdings.

Financial data Grants range up to $3,000. Funds must be used to cover travel, living expenses, photocopying, and other incidental research expenses.

Duration Up to 1 year.

Additional information The Schlesinger Library is a non-circulating research library that documents the history of women in the United States during the 19th and 20th centuries. Recipients must present the results of their research in a colloquium at the library, give the library a copy of the completed dissertation, and acknowledge the program's support in the dissertation and any resulting publications.

Number awarded Varies each year; recently, 9 were awarded.

Deadline January of each year.

[1092]
SCHOLARSHIP PROGRAM FOR WIFLE MEMBERS ONLY

Women in Federal Law Enforcement
Attn: Scholarship Coordinator
2200 Wilson Boulevard, Suite 102
PMB 204
Arlington, VA 22201-3324
(301) 805-2180   Fax: (301) 560-8836
E-mail: WIFLE@comcast.net
Web: www.wifle.org/scholarshipprogram.htm

Summary To provide financial assistance for college or graduate school to women who are interested in preparing for a career in law enforcement and are members of Women in Federal Law Enforcement (WIFLE) or sponsored by a member.

Eligibility This program is open to women who are members of WIFLE or sponsored by a member and have completed at least 1 academic year of full-time study at an accredited 4-year college or university (or at a community college with the intention of transferring to a 4-year school). Applicants must be majoring in criminal justice or a related field (e.g., social sciences, public administration, computer science, finance, linguistic arts, chemistry, physics). They must have a GPA of 3.0 or higher. Students in graduate and postgraduate programs are also eligible, but those working on an associate degree are not. Along with their application, they must submit a letter demonstrating their financial need and describing their career objectives. U.S. citizenship is required.

Financial data The stipend is $1,500 per year.

Duration 1 year; may be renewed automatically for 1 additional year.

Number awarded 1 each year.

Deadline April of each year.

[1093]
SCHOLARSHIPS FOR WOMEN RESIDENTS OF THE STATE OF DELAWARE

American Association of University Women-Wilmington Branch
Attn: Scholarship Committee
1800 Fairfax Boulevard
Wilmington, DE 19803-3106
(302) 428-0939   E-mail: aauwwilm@gmail.com
Web: wilmington-de.aauw.net/scholarships

Summary To provide financial assistance to female residents of Delaware who plan to attend college in any state.

Eligibility This program is open to women who are U.S. citizens and 1) a Delaware resident and a high school graduate; 2) a Delaware resident and a senior at a high school in New Castle County; or 3) a resident of New Castle County, Delaware and a home-schooled student who can meet the admission requirements of the University of Delaware. Applicants must be attending or planning to attend a college or university in any state. Along with their application, they must submit a 150-word essay on what they plan to study and why. High school seniors must also submit a 150-word essay on either 1) what they would do and where they would do it if they had 4 hours to spend any place, either now or in history; or 2) the famous person, past or present, they would like to meet and why. Selection is based on scholastic standing, contributions to school and community, SAT or ACT scores, and financial need. An interview is required.

Financial data A stipend is awarded (amount not specified).

Duration 1 year.

Number awarded Varies each year; recently, 17 of these scholarships, worth $55,000, were awarded.

Deadline February of each year.

[1094]
SCHOLARSHIPS FOR WOMEN STUDYING INFORMATION SECURITY

Applied Computer Security Association
Attn: Director of Scholarship Programs
2906 Covington Road
Silver Spring, MD 20910
(703) 989-8907   E-mail: swsis@swsis.org
Web: swsis.wordpress.com/applying-for-scholarships

Summary To provide financial assistance to women who are working on an undergraduate or graduate degree in a field related to information security.

Eligibility This program is open to women who are entering their junior or senior year of undergraduate study or first year of a master's degree program. Applicants must be working on a degree in a field related to information security (e.g., network security, software security/assurance, operating systems security, database security, applications security, formal methods, forensics, cybersecurity, security usability). Along with their application, they must submit an essay describing their interest in the field, letters of reference, a resume or curriculum vitae, and transcripts. Preference is given to U.S. citizens and permanent residents.

Financial data Stipends range from $5,000 to $10,000 per year. Funds are paid directly to the recipient's institution.

Duration 1 year; may be renewed 1 additional year.

Additional information This program, which began in 2011, is managed by the Applied Computer Security Association (ACSA) and the Computing Research Association (CRA) Committee on the Status of Women in Computing Research. Additional funding is provided by Hewlett Packard.

Number awarded 16 each year.

Deadline January of each year.

[1095]
SCOTT AND PAUL PEARSALL SCHOLARSHIP

American Psychological Foundation
750 First Street, N.E.
Washington, DC 20002-4242
(202) 336-5843   Fax: (202) 336-5812
E-mail: foundation@apa.org
Web: www.apa.org/apf/funding/pearsall.aspx

Summary To provide funding to graduate students interested in conducting research on the psychological effect of stigma on people with disabilities.

Eligibility This program is open to full-time graduate students at accredited universities in the United States and Canada. Applicants must be interested in conducting research that seeks to increase the public's understanding of the psychological pain and stigma experiences by adults living with physical disabilities, such as cerebral palsy. Selection is based on conformance with stated program goals and the quality of proposed work. The sponsor encourages applications from individuals who represent diversity in race, ethnicity, gender, age, disability, and sexual orientation. Preference is given to proposals that contain a plan to disseminate findings to the public.

Financial data The grant is $10,000.

Duration 1 year.

Additional information This program began in 2013.

Number awarded 2 each year.

Deadline September of each year.

[1096]
SEATTLE PROFESSIONAL CHAPTER AWC SCHOLARSHIPS

Association for Women in Communications-Seattle
    Professional Chapter
Attn: Tina Christiansen, Vice-President, Finance
P.O. Box 60262
Shoreline, WA 98160
E-mail: tina@writeasrain.com
Web: www.seattleawc.org/scholarships-and-awards

Summary To provide financial assistance to female upper-division and graduate students in Washington who are preparing for a career in the communications industry.

Eligibility This program is open to female residents of any state who are enrolled at a 4-year college or university in Washington as a junior, senior, or graduate student. Applicants must be working on or planning to work on a degree in a communications program, including print and broadcast journalism, television and radio production, video or film, advertising, public relations, marketing, graphic or multimedia design, photography, speech communications, or technical communication. Selection is based on demonstrated excellence in communications, goals and progress toward a career in communications, contributions made to communications

on campus and/or in the community, scholastic achievement, and financial need.

Financial data The stipend is $1,500. Funds are paid directly to the recipient's school and must be used for tuition and fees.

Duration 1 year.

Number awarded 2 each year.

Deadline March of each year.

[1097]
SELECTED PROFESSIONS FELLOWSHIPS

American Association of University Women
Attn: AAUW Educational Foundation
1111 16th Street, N.W.
Washington, DC 20036-4873
(202) 785-7700   Toll Free: (800) 326-AAUW
Fax: (202) 872-1425   TDD: (202) 785-7777
E-mail: aauw@applyists.com
Web: www.aauw.org

Summary To aid women who are working on a master's degree in the fields of architecture, computer science, information science, engineering, mathematics, or statistics.

Eligibility This program is open to women who are U.S. citizens or permanent residents and who intend to pursue their professional careers in the United States. Applicants must be working full time on a master's degree in architecture, computer and information science, engineering, mathematics, or statistics. They must be students in an accredited U.S. institution of higher learning enrolled in any year of study. Special consideration is given to applicants who 1) demonstrate their intent to enter professional practice in disciplines in which women are underrepresented, to serve underserved populations and communities, or to pursue public interest areas; and 2) are nontraditional students. Selection is based on professional promise and personal attributes (50%), academic excellence and related academic success indicators (40%), and financial need (10%).

Financial data Stipends range from $5,000 to $18,000.

Duration 1 year, beginning in July.

Additional information The filing fee is $35.

Number awarded Varies each year; recently, a total of 25 Selected Professions Fellowships were awarded.

Deadline January of each year.

[1098]
SELECTED PROFESSIONS FELLOWSHIPS FOR WOMEN OF COLOR

American Association of University Women
Attn: AAUW Educational Foundation
1111 16th Street, N.W.
Washington, DC 20036-4873
(202) 785-7700   Toll Free: (800) 326-AAUW
Fax: (202) 872-1425   TDD: (202) 785-7777
E-mail: aauw@applyists.com
Web: www.aauw.org

Summary To aid women of color who are in their final year of graduate training in the fields of business administration, law, or medicine.

Eligibility This program is open to women who are working full time on a degree in fields in which women of color have been historically underrepresented: business administration

(M.B.A.), law (J.D.), or medicine (M.D., D.O.). They must be African Americans, Mexican Americans, Puerto Ricans and other Hispanics, Native Americans, Alaska Natives, Asian Americans, or Pacific Islanders. U.S. citizenship or permanent resident status is required. Applicants in business administration must be entering their second year of study; applicants in law must be entering their third year of study; applicants in medicine may be entering their third or fourth year of study. Special consideration is given to applicants who 1) demonstrate their intent to enter professional practice in disciplines in which women are underrepresented, to serve underserved populations and communities, or to pursue public interest areas; and 2) are nontraditional students. Selection is based on professional promise and personal attributes (50%), academic excellence and related academic success indicators (40%), and financial need (10%).

Financial data Stipends range from $5,000 to $18,000.

Duration 1 year, beginning in July.

Additional information The filing fee is $35.

Number awarded Varies each year; recently, a total of 25 Selected Professions Fellowships were awarded.

Deadline January of each year.

[1099]
SEMICONDUCTOR RESEARCH CORPORATION MASTER'S SCHOLARSHIP PROGRAM

Semiconductor Research Corporation
Attn: Global Research Collaboration
1101 Slater Road, Suite 120
P.O. Box 12053
Research Triangle Park, NC 27709-2053
(919) 941-9400   Fax: (919) 941-9450
E-mail: students@src.org
Web: www.src.org/student-center/fellowship/#tab2

Summary To provide financial assistance to minorities and women interested in working on a master's degree in a field of microelectronics relevant to the interests of the Semiconductor Research Corporation (SRC).

Eligibility This program is open to women and members of underrepresented minority groups (African Americans, Hispanics, and Native Americans). Applicants must be U.S. citizens or have permanent resident, refugee, or political asylum status in the United States. They must be admitted to an SRC participating university to work on a master's degree in a field relevant to microelectronics under the guidance of an SRC-sponsored faculty member and under an SRC-funded contract. Selection is based on academic achievement.

Financial data The fellowship provides full tuition and fee support, a competitive stipend (recently, $2,536 per month), an annual grant of $2,000 to the university department with which the student recipient is associated, and travel expenses to the Graduate Fellowship Program Annual Conference.

Duration Up to 2 years.

Additional information This program began in 1997 for underrepresented minorities and expanded to include women in 1999.

Number awarded Approximately 12 each year.

Deadline January of each year.

[1100]
SENATOR SCOTT WHITE MEMORIAL SCHOLARSHIP

Women's Transportation Seminar-Puget Sound Chapter
c/o Laurie Thomsen, Scholarship Co-Chair
Osborn Consulting, Inc.
1800 112th Avenue N.E.
Bellevue, WA 98004
(425) 451-4009   Fax: (888) 391-8517
E-mail: laurie@osbornconsulting.com
Web: www.wtsinternational.org

Summary To provide financial assistance to women undergraduate and graduate students from Washington working on a degree related to public policy or public administration in transportation.

Eligibility This program is open to women who are residents of Washington, studying at a college in the state, or working as an intern in the state. Applicants must be currently enrolled in an undergraduate or graduate degree program in public policy or public administration in a transportation-related field. They must have a GPA of 3.0 or higher and plans to prepare for a career in their field of study. Minority women are especially encouraged to apply. Along with their application, they must submit a 500-word statement about their career goals after graduation, how their goals are related to public policy or public administration, and why they think they should receive this scholarship award. Selection is based on that statement, academic record, financial need, and transportation-related activities or job skills.

Financial data The stipend is $2,500.

Duration 1 year.

Additional information This program began in 2012.

Number awarded 1 each year.

Deadline November of each year.

[1101]
SHARON JUNOD MCKIMPSON SCHOLARSHIP

Iowa United Methodist Foundation
2301 Rittenhouse Street
Des Moines, IA 50321
(515) 974-8927
Web: www.iumf.org/scholarships/general

Summary To provide financial assistance to female Methodists from Iowa, who are interested in working on a degree in mathematics or science at a college in any state.

Eligibility This program is open to women who are members of a United Methodist church in Iowa who are enrolled at a college or university in any state. Applicants must be working on an undergraduate or graduate degree in mathematics or science. They must submit transcripts, 3 letters of recommendation, ACT and/or SAT scores, and documentation of financial need.

Financial data Recently, the stipend was $1,650.

Duration 1 year.

Number awarded 1 each year.

Deadline February of each year.

[1102]
SIGMA ALPHA IOTA GRADUATE PERFORMANCE AWARDS

Sigma Alpha Iota Philanthropies, Inc.
One Tunnel Road
Asheville, NC 28805
(828) 251-0606   Fax: (828) 251-0644
E-mail: nh@sai-national.org
Web: www.sai-national.org

Summary To recognize and reward outstanding performances in vocal and instrumental categories by graduate student members of Sigma Alpha Iota (an organization of women musicians).

Eligibility This program is open to college and alumna members of the organization who are working on a graduate degree in the field of performance. Competitions are held in 4 categories: voice, piano or percussion, strings or harp, and woodwinds or brass.

Financial data Awards are $2,000 for first place or $1,500 for second place. Funds must be used for graduate study in the field of performance.

Duration The competition is held triennially.

Additional information The awards for piano or percussion and for woodwinds or brass are designated as the Mary Ann Starring Memorial Awards. The awards for strings or harp are designated as the Dorothy E. Morris Memorial Awards. The awards for vocalists are designated the Blanche Z. Hoffman Memorial Awards.

Number awarded 8 every 3 years: 1 first place and 1 second place in each of the 4 categories.

Deadline March of the year of the awards (2018, 2021, etc.).

[1103]
SIGMA ALPHA IOTA SUMMER MUSIC SCHOLARSHIPS

Sigma Alpha Iota Philanthropies, Inc.
One Tunnel Road
Asheville, NC 28805
(828) 251-0606   Fax: (828) 251-0644
E-mail: nh@sai-national.org
Web: app.smarterselect.com

Summary To provide financial assistance for summer study in music, in the United States or abroad, to members of Sigma Alpha Iota (an organization of women musicians).

Eligibility This program is open to undergraduate and graduate student members of the organization who are planning to study at a summer music program in the United States or abroad. Applicants must submit a complete resume (including musical studies and activities, academic GPA, community service record, and record of participation in Sigma Alpha Iota), supporting materials (recital and concert programs, reviews, repertoire list, etc.), a statement of why they chose this program and how it will aid their musical growth, a full brochure of information on the program (including cost and payment due dates), a copy of the completed summer school application and acceptance letter (when available), and a letter of recommendation from their major teacher.

Financial data The stipend is $1,000. Funds for study in the United States are applied directly to the recipient's tuition; funds for study abroad are mailed directly to the recipient.

Duration Summer months.

Number awarded 5 each year.

Deadline March of each year.

[1104]
SIGMA DELTA EPSILON FELLOWSHIPS

Sigma Delta Epsilon-Graduate Women in Science, Inc.
Attn: Fellowships Coordinator
P.O. Box 580140
Minneapolis, MN 55458
E-mail: fellowships@gwis.org
Web: www.gwis.org/?page=fellowship_program

Summary To provide funding to women interested in conducting research in the natural sciences anywhere in the world.

Eligibility This program is open to women from any country currently enrolled as a graduate student, engaged in post-doctoral research, or holding a junior faculty position. Applicants must be interested in conducting research anywhere in the world in the natural sciences (including physical, environmental, mathematical, computer, or life sciences), anthropology, psychology, or statistics. Membership in Sigma Delta Epsilon-Graduate Women in Science (SDE-GWIS) is encouraged.

Financial data The maximum grant is $10,000. Funds may be used for such research expenses as expendable supplies, small equipment, publication of research findings, travel and subsistence while performing field studies, or travel to another laboratory for collaborative research. They may not be used for salaries, tuition, child care, travel to professional meetings or to begin a new appointment, administrative overhead or indirect costs, personal computers, living allowances, or equipment for general use.

Duration 1 academic year.

Additional information This program includes the Adele Lewis Grant SDE Fellowship (awarded to the highest scoring applicant), the Hartley Corporation SDE Fellowship (awarded to the second highest scoring applicant), the Ethel K. Allen Fellowship, the Monique Braude Fellowship, the Eloise Gerry Fellowships, the Jean Langenheim Fellowship, the Nell I. Mondy Fellowship, and the Vessa Notchev Fellowship. Non-members of SDE-GWIS must pay an application fee of $50.

Number awarded Varies each year; recently, 6 were awarded.

Deadline January of each year.

[1105]
SIGMA GAMMA RHO SCHOLARSHIPS/ FELLOWSHIPS

Sigma Gamma Rho Sorority, Inc.
Attn: National Education Fund
1000 Southhill Drive, Suite 200
Cary, NC 27513
(919) 678-9720   Toll Free: (888) SGR-1922
Fax: (919) 678-9721
E-mail: customerservice@sgrho1922.org
Web: www.sgrho1922.org/nef

Summary To provide financial assistance for undergraduate or graduate study to applicants who can demonstrate financial need.

Eligibility This program is open to high school seniors, undergraduates, and graduate students who can demonstrate financial need. The sponsor is a traditionally African American sorority, but support is available to males and females of all races. Applicants must have a GPA of "C" or higher.

Financial data A stipend is awarded (amount not specified).

Duration 1 year.

Additional information This program includes the following named awards: the Lorraine A. Williams Scholarship, the Philo Sallie A. Williams Scholarship, the Cleo W. Higgins Scholarship (limited to doctoral students), the Lillie and Carnell VanLandingham Scholarship, the Minnie and William Blakely Book Scholarship, the Inez Colson Memorial Scholarship (limited to students majoring in education or mathematics at Savannah State University), and the Philo Geneva Young Scholarship. A processing fee of $20 is required.

Number awarded Varies each year.

Deadline April of each year.

[1106]
SIGNATURE FLIGHT SUPPORT CORPORATION SCHOLARSHIP

Women in Aviation International
Attn: Scholarships
Morningstar Airport
3647 State Route 503 South
West Alexandria, OH 45381-9354
(937) 839-4647 Fax: (937) 839-4645
E-mail: scholarships@wai.org
Web: www.wai.org

Summary To provide financial assistance for college to members of Women in Aviation International (WAI).

Eligibility This program is open to WAI members who are undergraduate or graduate students working on a degree in a field related to aviation, preferably FBO management. Applicants must have a GPA of 3.0 or higher and be a U.S. citizen. Along with their application, they must submit 1) a 500-word essay and professional resume that include their aviation history and goals, what they have done for themselves to achieve their goals, where they see themselves in 5 and 10 years, involvement in aviation activities, how the scholarship will help them achieve their objectives, and their present financial need; and 2) an essay of 500 to 1,000 words on their current educational status, why they chose a career in aviation, their experience in aviation, and their aspirations in the field.

Financial data The stipend is $1,500.

Duration 1 year.

Additional information This program was established in 2014 by Signature Flight Support Corporation.

Number awarded 1 each year.

Deadline November of each year.

[1107]
SOCIETY OF BIBLICAL LITERATURE REGIONAL SCHOLARS AWARDS

Society of Biblical Literature
c/o The Luce Center
825 Houston Mill Road, Suite 350
Atlanta, GA 30329
(404) 727-3100 Fax: (404) 727-3101
E-mail: sblexec@sbl-site.org
Web: www.sbl-site.org/membership/SBLAwards.aspx

Summary To provide funding for annual meeting attendance or professional development to members of the Society of Biblical Literature (SBL) at the doctoral or recent post-doctoral level.

Eligibility This award is available to SBL members who are Ph.D. candidates or who completed a Ph.D. within the past 4 years. Applicants must present at an SBL regional meeting an original work of their own scholarship and must submit a copy of the paper, along with a curriculum vitae, to the regional coordinator for their SBL region. Members of the selection committee attend the oral presentation and evaluate it on the basis of clear articulation of argument advanced, even and engaging delivery, clear pronunciation and style appropriate to oral presentation, and creative and appropriate use of presentation materials. The written papers are evaluated as oral presentations, not as research articles, on the basis of the following criteria: clarity of expression and argumentation, demonstrated knowledge and critical use of scholarly resources and publications, use and knowledge of the primary sources, and originality of ideas and solutions. Women and minorities are encouraged to apply.

Financial data The award is $1,000. funds may be used to support attendance at the SBL annual meeting or to promote future scholarship and professional development.

Duration The awards are presented annually.

Number awarded Up to 6 each year.

Deadline Each of the 11 SBL regions establishes its own deadline.

[1108]
SOCIETY OF WOMEN ENVIRONMENTAL PROFESSIONALS OF GREATER PHILADELPHIA SCHOLARSHIPS

Society of Women Environmental Professionals of
  Greater Philadelphia
c/o Joanna Waldron
411 Washington Lane
Fort Washington, PA 19034
(610) 757-7127 E-mail: swep.scholar.phila@gmail.com
Web: www.swepweb.com

Summary To provide financial assistance to women who live or attend school in the greater Philadelphia area and are working on a graduate or law degree in an environmental field.

Eligibility This program is open to women who are working on a graduate or law degree to prepare for a career in the environmental field. Applicants must reside in or attend college in southern New Jersey (Burlington, Camden, Cumberland, Gloucester, Mercer, Salem, or Sussex counties), eastern Pennsylvania (Bucks, Berks, Chester, Delaware, Lancaster, Lehigh, Montgomery, Northampton, or Philadelphia counties), or Delaware. They must have a GPA of 3.0 or higher. Along with their application, they must submit a 500-word essay on why they are interested in preparing for a career in an environmental field, including their educational plans and career objectives. Financial need is not considered in the selection process. U.S. citizenship or permanent resident status is required.

Financial data The stipend is $2,500.

Duration 1 year.

Number awarded 2 each year.

Deadline January of each year.

[1109]
SOROPTIMIST FOUNDER REGION FELLOWSHIPS

Soroptimist International of the Americas-Founder Region
c/o Bobbi Enderlin, President Founder Region Fellowship
P.O. Box 1876
Benicia, CA 94559
(707) 980-4356   E-mail: frfpresident@gmail.com
Web: www.founderregionfellowship.org

Summary To provide financial assistance to women from any state who are completing a doctoral degree at a university in the Founder Region of Soroptimist International of the Americas.

Eligibility This program is open to women from any state who are attending graduate school in the Founder Region of Soroptimist International of the Americas (which includes designated counties in northern California, the state of Hawaii, and the U.S. possessions of Guam and the Marianas). Applicants must have been advanced to candidacy for a doctoral degree and should be entering the final year of their program. Along with their application, they must submit a statement of purpose that includes how their area of study improves the lives of women and girls or contributes to the welfare of humanity. A personal interview is required.

Financial data Recently, stipends have been approximately $10,000.

Duration 1 year.

Additional information This program began in 1948. The designated northern California counties are Alameda, Contra Costa, Del Norte, Humboldt, Lake, Marin, Mendocino, Napa, Solano, and Sonoma.

Number awarded Varies each year; recently, 8 were awarded.

Deadline January of each year.

[1110]
SPACE COAST CHAPTER WOMEN IN DEFENSE SCHOLARSHIP PROGRAM

Women in Defense-Space Coast Chapter
Attn: Scholarship Program
P.O. Box 410832
Melbourne, FL 32941-0832
E-mail: stem@scwid.org
Web: www.scwid.org

Summary To provide financial assistance to women in Florida who are interested in working on an undergraduate or graduate degree in national security, defense, or a field related to science, technology, engineering, or mathematics (STEM) at a college in the state.

Eligibility This program is open to female residents of Florida who are graduating high school seniors, undergraduates, or graduate students enrolled or planning to enroll full or part time at an accredited college or university in the state. Applicants must be preparing for a career related to national security, defense, or a STEM-related field. They must be U.S. citizens and have a GPA of 3.0 or higher. Along with their application, they must submit an essay of 500 to 600 words that covers their career interest, prior accomplishments, and proposed program or course emphasis. Selection is based on that essay (25%), academic ability and field of study (15%), professional or academic recommendations (15%), defense and national security activities (15%), employment (10%), awards and honors (10%), and financial need (10%).

Financial data The stipend is $1,000.

Duration 1 year.

Number awarded At least 1 each year.

Deadline April of each year.

[1111]
SPP DIVERSITY RESEARCH GRANT

American Psychological Association
Attn: Division 54 (Society of Pediatric Psychology)
750 First Street, N.E.
Washington, DC 20002-4242
(202) 216-7602   Fax: (202) 336-5953
TDD: (202) 336-6123   E-mail: APAdiv54@gmail.com
Web: www.apadivisions.org

Summary To provide funding to graduate student and postdoctoral members of the Society of Pediatric Psychology (SPP) who are interested in conducting research on diversity aspects of pediatric psychology.

Eligibility This program is open to current members of the society who are graduate students, fellows, or early-career (within 3 years of appointment) faculty. Applicants must be interested in conducting pediatric psychology research that features diversity-related variables, such as race or ethnicity, gender, culture, sexual orientation, language differences, socioeconomic status, and/or religiosity. Along with their application, they must submit a 2,000-word description of the project, including its purpose, methodology, predictions, and implications; a detailed budget; a current curriculum vitae, and (for students) a curriculum vitae of the faculty research mentor and a letter of support from that mentor. Selection is based on relevance to diversity in child health (5 points), significance of the study (5 points), study methods and procedures (10 points), and investigator qualifications (10 points).

Financial data Grants up to $1,000 are available. Funds may not be used for convention or meeting travel, indirect costs, stipends of principal investigators, or costs associated with manuscript preparation.

Duration The grant is presented annually.

Additional information The Society of Pediatric Psychology is Division 54 of the American Psychological Association (APA). This grant was first presented in 2008.

Number awarded 1 each year.

Deadline September of each year.

[1112]
STANTON NUCLEAR SECURITY FELLOWSHIP

Stanford University
Center for International Security and Cooperation
Attn: Fellowships Coordinator
Encina Hall, Room C206-10
616 Serra Street
Stanford, CA 94305-6165
(650) 723-9625   Fax: (650) 724-5683
E-mail: CISACfellowship@stanford.edu
Web: cisac.fsi.stanford.edu/docs/cisac_fellowship_program

Summary To provide funding to doctoral candidates and junior scholars who are interested in conducting research on nuclear security issues at Stanford University's Center for International Security and Cooperation.

Eligibility This program is open to doctoral candidates, recent postdoctorates, and junior faculty. Applicants must be interested in conducting research on nuclear security issues while in residence at the center. The sponsor welcomes applications from women, minorities, and citizens of all countries.

Financial data The stipend ranges from $25,000 to $28,000 for doctoral candidates or from $48,000 to $66,000 for postdoctorates, depending on experience. Medical insurance is available for those who do not have coverage.

Duration 9 to 11 months.

Additional information Fellows are expected to write a dissertation chapter or chapters, publishable article or articles, and/or make significant progress on turning a thesis into a book manuscript. They should not plan to spend any time conducting research abroad or in other parts of the country.

Number awarded Varies each year; recently, 3 were awarded: 1 doctoral candidate, 1 recent postdoctorate, and 1 junior faculty member.

Deadline January of each year.

[1113]
STEPHEN BUFTON MEMORIAL EDUCATION FUND OUTRIGHT GRANTS PROGRAM

American Business Women's Association
Attn: Stephen Bufton Memorial Educational Fund
11050 Roe Avenue, Suite 200
Overland Park, KS 66211
Toll Free: (800) 228-0007
Web: www.sbmef.org/Opportunities.cfm

Summary To provide financial assistance to women undergraduate and graduate students in any field who are sponsored by a chapter of the American Business Women's Association (ABWA).

Eligibility This program is open to women who are at least juniors at an accredited college or university. Applicants must be working on an undergraduate or graduate degree and have a GPA of 2.5 or higher. They are not required to be ABWA members, but they must be sponsored by an ABWA chapter that has contributed to the fund in the previous chapter year. U.S. citizenship is required.

Financial data The maximum grant is $1,500. Funds are paid directly to the recipient's institution to be used only for tuition, books, and fees.

Duration 1 year. Grants are not automatically renewed, but recipients may reapply.

Additional information This program began in 1953. The ABWA does not provide the names and addresses of local chapters; it recommends that applicants check with their local Chamber of Commerce, library, or university to see if any chapter has registered a contact's name and number.

Number awarded Varies each year; since the inception of this program, it has awarded more than $14 million to more than 14,000 students.

Deadline May of each year.

[1114]
STUDENT FELLOWSHIP AWARDS FOR FEMALE SCHOLARS IN VISION RESEARCH

Prevent Blindness Ohio
Attn: Investigator Award
1500 West Third Avenue, Suite 200
Columbus, OH 43212
(614) 464-2020   Toll Free: (800) 301-2020, ext. 112
Fax: (614) 481-9670   E-mail: info@pbohio.org
Web: ohio.preventblindness.org

Summary To provide funding for research to women from any state working on a graduate degree in a field related to prevention of blindness at a university in Ohio.

Eligibility This program is open to women who are residents of any state working on a master's or doctoral degree at a recognized academic institution in Ohio. Applicants must be working on a biomedical, behavioral, or clinical degree and conducting research related to the prevention of blindness and preservation of sight. Preference is given to research topics that investigate public health issues related to the burden of eye-related health and safety topics. Appropriate fields in the health sciences include, but are not limited to, ophthalmology, optometry, nursing, genetics, public health, nutrition, gerontology, and bioengineering. U.S. citizenship or permanent resident status is required.

Financial data Grants range from $3,000 to $5,000.

Duration 1 year.

Additional information This program is supported by the Sarah E. Slack Prevention of Blindness Fund at the Muskingum County Community Foundation and The Levin Family Fund.

Number awarded 1 or more each year.

Deadline February of each year.

[1115]
SUSAN E. STUTZ-MCDONALD FOUNDATION SCHOLARSHIP

Society of Women Engineers
Attn: Scholarship Selection Committee
203 North LaSalle Street, Suite 1675
Chicago, IL 60601-1269
(312) 596-5223   Toll Free: (877) SWE-INFO
Fax: (312) 644-8557   E-mail: scholarships@swe.org
Web: societyofwomenengineers.swe.org

Summary To provide financial assistance to women who are members of the Society of Women Engineers (SWE) and working on a graduate degree in specified fields of engineering or computer science.

Eligibility This program is open to SWE members who will be full-time graduate students at ABET-accredited colleges and universities. Applicants must be working on a degree in computer science or civil or environmental engineering. Preference is given to students whose emphasis is on water or wastewater treatment. Selection is based on merit. U.S. citizenship or permanent status is required.

Financial data The stipend is $2,500, including $250 for travel to the SWE annual conference.

Duration 1 year.

Number awarded 2 each year.

Deadline February of each year.

[1116]
SUZANNE DOOLEY GRADUATE STUDENT TUITION SCHOLARSHIP

Women in Film Dallas
Attn: Scholarships and Grants
5930 Royal Lane, Suite E
PMB 236
Dallas, TX 75230
(214) 379-1171   Toll Free: (800) 724-0767
Fax: (214) 379-1172   E-mail: scholarships@wifdallas.org
Web: www.wifdallas.org/page-950618

Summary To provide financial assistance to women from any state who are working on a graduate degree in film, television, or video at colleges and universities in north Texas.

Eligibility This program is open to women who are residents of any state working full time on a graduate degree in film, television, or video at an accredited college or university in the following Texas counties: Collin, Dallas, Denton, Ellis, Kaufman, Rockwall, or Tarrant. Applicants must have consistently maintained a GPA of 3.0 or higher. Along with their application, they must submit a 1,000-word essay on their interest and experiences in motion picture arts and sciences, 2 letters of recommendation, and a short sample of their work. Financial need is not considered in the selection process.

Financial data The stipend is $1,000.

Duration 1 year.

Number awarded 1 each year.

Deadline June of each year.

[1117]
SWE CENTRAL NEW MEXICO RE-ENTRY SCHOLARSHIP

Society of Women Engineers
Attn: Scholarship Selection Committee
203 North LaSalle Street, Suite 1675
Chicago, IL 60601-1269
(312) 596-5223   Toll Free: (877) SWE-INFO
Fax: (312) 644-8557   E-mail: scholarships@swe.org
Web: societyofwomenengineers.swe.org

Summary To provide financial assistance to members of the Society of Women Engineers (SWE) from any state who are reentering college or graduate school in New Mexico to work on a degree in engineering or computer science.

Eligibility This program is open to members of the society who are sophomores, juniors, seniors, or graduate students at an ABET-accredited college, university, or 4-year engineering technology program in New Mexico. Applicants must be returning to college or graduate school after an absence of several years to work on a degree in computer science or

engineering. They must have a GPA of 3.0 or higher. Selection is based on merit. U.S. citizenship is required.

Financial data The stipend is $1,500 per year.

Duration 1 year; may be renewed up to 5 additional years.

Additional information This program, which began in 2005, is sponsored by the Central New Mexico section of SWE.

Number awarded 1 each year.

Deadline February of each year.

[1118]
SWE REGION E SCHOLARSHIP

Society of Women Engineers
Attn: Scholarship Selection Committee
203 North LaSalle Street, Suite 1675
Chicago, IL 60601-1269
(312) 596-5223   Toll Free: (877) SWE-INFO
Fax: (312) 644-8557   E-mail: scholarships@swe.org
Web: societyofwomenengineers.swe.org

Summary To provide financial assistance to members of the Society of Women Engineers (SWE) working on an undergraduate or graduate degree in engineering or computer science at a school in the mid-Atlantic (Region E).

Eligibility This program is open to members of the society who will be sophomores, juniors, seniors, or graduate students at ABET-accredited colleges and universities in Delaware, Maryland, New Jersey, New York, eastern Pennsylvania, Virginia, or Washington, D.C. Applicants must be working full time on a degree in computer science or engineering. Selection is based on merit.

Financial data The stipend is $1,500.

Duration 1 year.

Additional information This program began in 2014.

Number awarded 1 each year.

Deadline February of each year.

[1119]
SWE REGION G-JUDY SIMMONS MEMORIAL SCHOLARSHIP

Society of Women Engineers
Attn: Scholarship Selection Committee
203 North LaSalle Street, Suite 1675
Chicago, IL 60601-1269
(312) 596-5223   Toll Free: (877) SWE-INFO
Fax: (312) 644-8557   E-mail: scholarships@swe.org
Web: societyofwomenengineers.swe.org

Summary To provide financial assistance to members of the Society of Women Engineers (SWE) working on an undergraduate or graduate degree in engineering or computer science at a school in the Ohio Valley (Region G).

Eligibility This program is open to members of the society who will be sophomores, juniors, seniors, or graduate students at ABET-accredited colleges and universities in Kentucky, Ohio, western Pennsylvania, or West Virginia. Applicants must be working full time on a degree in computer science or engineering. Selection is based on merit.

Financial data The stipend is $1,250.

Duration 1 year.

Additional information This program, which began in 2014, is sponsored by Region G of SWE.

Number awarded 1 each year.

Deadline February of each year.

[1120]
SWE REGION H SCHOLARSHIP

Society of Women Engineers
Attn: Scholarship Selection Committee
203 North LaSalle Street, Suite 1675
Chicago, IL 60601-1269
(312) 596-5223   Toll Free: (877) SWE-INFO
Fax: (312) 644-8557   E-mail: scholarships@swe.org
Web: societyofwomenengineers.swe.org

Summary To provide financial assistance to members of the Society of Women Engineers (SWE) working on an undergraduate or graduate degree in engineering or computer science at a school in the upper Midwest (Region H).

Eligibility This program is open to members of the society who will be sophomores, juniors, seniors, or graduate students at ABET-accredited colleges and universities in Illinois, Indiana, Iowa, Michigan, Minnesota, North Dakota, South Dakota, or Wisconsin. Applicants must have a record of active involvement in SWE, based on the amount of time spent volunteering, level of commitment, and years of service. They must be working full time on a degree in computer science or engineering. Selection is based on merit and participation in SWE activities.

Financial data The stipend is $1,500 or $1,250.

Duration 1 year.

Additional information This program began in 2008.

Number awarded 2 each year: 1 at $1,500 and 1 at $1,250.

Deadline February of each year.

[1121]
SYLVA ASHWORTH SCHOLARSHIP

International Federation of Chiropractors and
   Organizations
Attn: Scholarships
2276 Wassergass Road
Hellertown, PA 18055
Toll Free: (800) 521-9856   Fax: (610) 838-3031
E-mail: ifcochiro@gmail.com
Web: www.ifcochiro.org

Summary To provide financial assistance to single mothers currently enrolled at a chiropractic college.

Eligibility This program is open to students currently enrolled at a chiropractic college who are single mothers. Applicants must be able to demonstrate financial need. Along with their application, they must submit a 2-page essay on their future practice of chiropractic as a single mother.

Financial data The stipend is $1,000.

Duration 1 year.

Additional information This program began in 1999.

Number awarded 1 each year.

Deadline March of each year.

[1122]
SYLVIA FORMAN PRIZE COMPETITION

American Anthropological Association
Attn: Association for Feminist Anthropology
2300 Clarendon Boulevard, Suite 1301
Arlington, VA 22201
(703) 528-1902   Fax: (703) 528-3546
Web: www.aaanet.org/sections/afa/sylvia-forman-prize

Summary To recognize and reward the best student essays in feminist anthropology.

Eligibility This award is available to graduate and undergraduate students who submit essays (up to 35 pages) in any subfield of anthropology that focus on such topics as feminist analysis of women's work, reproduction, sexuality, religion, language and expressive culture, family and kin relations, economic development, gender and material culture, gender and biology, women and development, globalization, or race and class. Essays that have been submitted for publication but have not yet been accepted may be eligible as entries. Already accepted or published articles may not be submitted. Only 1 submission per student is accepted. Selection is based on the use of feminist theory to analyze a particular issue; organization, quality, and clarity of writing; effective use of both theory and data; significance to feminist scholarship; timeliness and relevance of the topic; and originality of research topic.

Financial data The prize is $1,000 for a graduate student or $500 for an undergraduate.

Duration The competition is held annually.

Additional information The winning essays are published in the association's *Anthropology Newsletter*. This competition began in 1995.

Number awarded At least 2 each year: 1 for an undergraduate and 1 for a graduate student.

Deadline May of each year.

[1123]
SYLVIA LANE MENTOR FELLOWSHIP

Agricultural and Applied Economics Association
Attn: Trust Committee
555 East Wells Street, Suite 1100
Milwaukee, WI 53202
(414) 918-3190   Fax: (414) 276-3349
E-mail: info@aaea.org
Web: www.aaea.org

Summary To provide funding to young female scholars who are working on food, agricultural, or resource issues and interested in relocating in order to conduct research with an established expert at another university, institution, or firm.

Eligibility These fellowships are awarded to mentee/mentor pairs of individuals. Mentees must have completed at least 1 year in residence in an accredited American graduate degree program in agricultural economics or a closely-related discipline; women with Ph.D. degrees and advanced graduate students are encouraged to apply. Mentors must have a Ph.D. and established expertise in an area of food, agriculture, or natural resources. The goal is to enable female scholars to relocate in order to conduct research with an established expert at another university, institution, or firm, even though they may reside in different parts of the country. Selection is based on the relevance of the research problem, potential for generating output, synergy of the mentor/mentee pairing, and opportunity for advancing the mentee's research skills beyond her graduate studies and current position.

Financial data Awards range up to $2,500.

Duration Several weeks.

Additional information This program was established in 2008 by the Committee on Women in Agricultural Economics of the Agricultural and Applied Economics Association.

Number awarded 1 or more each year.

Deadline October of each year.

[1124]
SYMANTEC SCHOLARSHIP

Society of Women Engineers-Minnesota Section
Attn: Scholarship Committee
P.O. Box 18481
Minneapolis, MN 55418
E-mail: scholarships@swe-mn.org
Web: www.swe-mn.org/scholarships.html

Summary To provide financial assistance to women from any state working on an undergraduate or graduate degree in computer science or software engineering at colleges and universities in Minnesota, North Dakota, and South Dakota.

Eligibility This program is open to female undergraduate and graduate students at ABET-accredited engineering programs in Minnesota, North Dakota, or South Dakota. Applicants must be working full time on a degree in computer science or software engineering. Along with their application, they must submit a 250-word essay describing how they plan to utilize their engineering knowledge and skills after they graduate. Selection is based on potential to succeed as an engineer (20 points), communication skills (10 points), extracurricular or community involvement and leadership skills (10 points), demonstration of work experience and successes (10 points), and academic success (5 points).

Financial data The stipend is $1,500.

Duration 1 year.

Additional information This program is sponsored by Symantec Corporation.

Number awarded 1 each year.

Deadline March of each year.

[1125]
T & T HIKE SCHOLARSHIP

International Order of Job's Daughters
c/o Judy Burl, Supreme Scholarship Chair
121 Byrd Street
Hopewell, VA 23860
(804) 458-5552   E-mail: jgburl@aol.com
Web: www.jobsdaughtersinternational.org

Summary To provide financial assistance to members of Job's Daughters who are working on a degree related to speech disabilities.

Eligibility This program is open to Job's Daughters in good standing in their Bethels and unmarried majority members under 30 years of age. Applicants must be entering their junior year of college or higher in audiology, speech pathology, or deaf education. Selection is based on scholastic standing, Job's Daughters activities, recommendation by the Executive Bethel Guardian Council, faculty recommendations, and achievements outside Job's Daughters.

Financial data The stipend is $1,000.

Duration 1 year.

Number awarded 1 or more each year.

Deadline April of each year.

[1126]
TED AND RUTH NEWARD SCHOLARSHIPS

Society of Plastics Engineers
Attn: SPE Foundation
6 Berkshire Boulevard, Suite 306
Bethel, CT 06801
(203) 740-5457   Fax: (203) 775-8490
E-mail: foundation@4spe.org
Web: old.4spe.org/forms/spe-foundation-scholarship-form

Summary To provide financial assistance to undergraduate and graduate students, especially women, who have a career interest in the plastics industry.

Eligibility This program is open to full-time undergraduate students at 4-year colleges and 2-year technical programs and to graduate students. Preference is given to women for 1 of the scholarships. Applicants must be majoring in or taking courses that would be beneficial to a career in the plastics or polymer industry (e.g., plastics engineering, polymer sciences, chemistry, physics, chemical engineering, mechanical engineering, industrial engineering). Along with their application, they must submit 3 letters of recommendation; a high school and/or college transcript; a 1- to 2-page statement telling why they are applying for the scholarship, their qualifications, and their educational and career goals in the plastics industry; their employment history; and a list of current and past school activities and community activities and honors. Financial need is considered in the selection process. U.S. citizenship is required.

Financial data The stipend is $3,000. Funds are paid directly to the recipient's school.

Duration 1 year.

Number awarded 4 each year.

Deadline April of each year.

[1127]
TEXAS YOUNG LAWYERS ASSOCIATION DIVERSITY SCHOLARSHIP PROGRAM

Texas Young Lawyers Association
Attn: Diversity Committee
1414 Colorado, Fourth Floor
P.O. Box 12487
Austin, TX 78711-2487
(512) 427-1529   Toll Free: (800) 204-2222, ext. 1529
Fax: (512) 427-4117   E-mail: btrevino@texasbar.com
Web: www.tyla.org

Summary To provide financial assistance to residents of any state who are from diverse groups attending law school in Texas.

Eligibility This program is open to members of recognized diverse groups, including diversity based on gender, national origin, race, ethnicity, sexual orientation, gender identity, disability, socioeconomic status, and geography. Applicants must be attending an ABA-accredited law school in Texas. Along with their application, they must submit a brief essay on 1) why they believe diversity is important to the practice of law; and 2) what the Texas Young Lawyers Association and the State Bar of Texas can do to promote and support diversity in the legal profession. Selection is based on those essays, academic performance, demonstrated commitment to diversity, letters of recommendation, and financial need.

Financial data The stipend is $1,000.

Duration 1 year.

Number awarded At least 9 each year: at least 1 at each accredited law school in Texas.

Deadline October of each year.

[1128]
THE LEADERSHIP INSTITUTE SCHOLARSHIPS

The Leadership Institute for Women of Color Attorneys, Inc.
Attn: Scholarship Chair
1266 West Paces Ferry Road, N.W., Suite 263
Atlanta, GA 30327
(404) 443-5715   E-mail: hhorton@mcquirewoods.com
Web: www.leadingwomenofcolor.org

Summary To provide financial assistance to women of color who are attending law school.

Eligibility This program is open to women of color who have completed at least 1 year at an accredited law school and have a GPA of 3.0 or higher. Applicants must be U.S. citizens who can demonstrate a commitment to the legal profession. Along with their application, they must submit brief statements on their work experience, extracurricular activities, why they think it is important for women of color to serve in the legal profession, what they believe is necessary for success in the legal profession, and what they plan to do with their law degree.

Financial data The stipend is $3,000.

Duration 1 year.

Number awarded 5 each year.

Deadline December of each year.

[1129]
THOMPSON SCHOLARSHIP FOR WOMEN IN SAFETY

American Society of Safety Engineers
Attn: ASSE Foundation
Scholarship Award Program
520 North Northwest Highway
Park Ridge, IL 60068-2538
(847) 699-2929   Fax: (847) 296-3769
E-mail: assefoundation@asse.org
Web: foundation.asse.org/scholarships-and-grants

Summary To provide financial assistance to graduate students, especially women, working on a degree in safety-related fields.

Eligibility This program is open to students working on a graduate degree in occupational safety, health, environment, industrial hygiene, occupational health nursing, or a closely-related field (e.g., industrial or environmental engineering). Priority is given to women. Applicants must be full-time students who have completed at least 9 semester hours and have a GPA of 3.5 or higher. U.S. citizenship is not required. Membership in the American Society of Safety Engineers (ASSE) is not required, but preference is given to members.

Financial data The stipend is $1,500 per year.

Duration 1 year; recipients may reapply.

Number awarded 1 each year.

Deadline November of each year.

[1130]
TRAUB-DICKER RAINBOW SCHOLARSHIPS

Stonewall Community Foundation
Attn: Grants
446 West 33rd Street, Sixth Floor
New York, NY 10001
(212) 367-1155   Fax: (212) 367-1157
E-mail: grants@stonewallfoundation.org
Web: stonewallfoundation.org/grants/scholarships

Summary To provide financial assistance to undergraduate and graduate students who identify as lesbians.

Eligibility This program is open to lesbian-identified students who are 1) graduating high school seniors planning to attend a recognized college or university; 2) currently-enrolled undergraduates; and 3) graduate students. Applicants must submit 400-word essays on 1) their personal history, including a significant challenge or achievement in terms of community service, academic excellence, or dynamic leadership; 2) a particularly important experience they have had as a lesbian and how it has affected them; and 3) their plans or goals to give back to or focus on the lesbian, gay, bisexual, and transgender (LGBT) community while in school or after graduating. Selection is based on academic excellence, community service, and commitment to impacting LGBT issues. Financial need is not considered.

Financial data The stipend is $3,000. Funds are paid directly to the recipient's school to help pay for tuition, books, or room and board.

Duration 1 year.

Additional information This program began in 2004.

Number awarded 3 each year.

Deadline April of each year.

[1131]
UNITED AIRLINES PILOT SCHOLARSHIPS OF WOMEN IN AVIATION INTERNATIONAL

Women in Aviation International
Attn: Scholarships
Morningstar Airport
3647 State Route 503 South
West Alexandria, OH 45381-9354
(937) 839-4647   Fax: (937) 839-4645
E-mail: scholarships@wai.org
Web: www.wai.org

Summary To provide financial assistance to members of Women in Aviation International (WAI) who are working on an undergraduate or graduate degree to prepare for a career as a professional airline pilot.

Eligibility This program is open to WAI members who are currently enrolled as full-time juniors, seniors, or graduate students in an accredited collegiate aviation or aeronautical science program. Applicants must have a GPA of 3.0 or higher and an FAA instrument rating; preference is given to those with an FAA commercial certificate and/or an FAA multiengine rating. Along with their application, they must submit academic transcripts, copies of pilot and medical certificates, and an essay describing career aspirations and goals, achievements and honors, aviation development to date, involvement with WAI, volunteerism, leadership, and planned use of scholarship funds. Selection is based on merit, career aspirations, dedication, contributions to community, and service with WAI.

Financial data The stipend is $5,000. Funds are paid directly to the recipient's institution. The award includes round-trip airfare, accommodations, and registration to attend the WAI annual conference.

Duration Training must be completed within 1 year.

Additional information WAI is a nonprofit professional organization dedicated to encouraging women to consider an aviation career and to providing educational outreach activities and networking resources to women active in the industry. This program is sponsored by United Airlines.

Number awarded 2 each year.

Deadline November of each year.

[1132]
UNITED METHODIST WOMEN OF COLOR SCHOLARS PROGRAM

United Methodist Church
Attn: General Board of Higher Education and Ministry
Office of Loans and Scholarships
1001 19th Avenue South
P.O. Box 340007
Nashville, TN 37203-0007
(615) 340-7342   Fax: (615) 340-7367
E-mail: umscholar@gbhem.org
Web: www.gbhem.org

Summary To provide financial assistance to Methodist women of color who are working on a doctoral degree to prepare for a career as an educator at a United Methodist seminary.

Eligibility This program is open to women of color (have at least 1 parent who is African American, African, Hispanic, Asian, Native American, Alaska Native, or Pacific Islander) who have an M.Div. degree. Applicants must have been active, full members of a United Methodist Church for at least 3 years prior to applying. They must be enrolled full time in a degree program at the Ph.D. or Th.D. level to prepare for a career teaching at a United Methodist seminary.

Financial data The maximum stipend is $10,000 per year.

Duration 1 year; may be renewed up to 3 additional years.

Number awarded Varies each year; recently, 10 were awarded.

Deadline January of each year.

[1133]
UTC AEROSPACE SYSTEMS SCHOLARSHIP

Society of Women Engineers-Minnesota Section
Attn: Scholarship Committee
P.O. Box 18481
Minneapolis, MN 55418
E-mail: scholarships@swe-mn.org
Web: www.swe-mn.org/scholarships.html

Summary To provide financial assistance to women from any state working on an undergraduate or graduate degree in specified fields of engineering at colleges and universities in Minnesota, North Dakota, and South Dakota.

Eligibility This program is open to female undergraduate and graduate students at ABET-accredited engineering pro-

grams in Minnesota, North Dakota, or South Dakota. Applicants must be working full time on a degree in aerospace, electrical, industrial, manufacturing, or mechanical engineering. Along with their application, they must submit a 250-word essay describing how they plan to utilize their engineering knowledge and skills after they graduate. Selection is based on potential to succeed as an engineer (20 points), communication skills (10 points), extracurricular or community involvement and leadership skills (10 points), demonstration of work experience and successes (10 points), and academic success (5 points).

Financial data The stipend is $1,500.

Duration 1 year.

Additional information This program is sponsored by UTC Aerospace Systems.

Number awarded 1 each year.

Deadline March of each year.

[1134]
UTC/LCD DIVERSITY SCHOLARS PROGRAM

Lawyers Collaborative for Diversity
Attn: Program Coordinator
P.O. Box 230637
Hartford, CT 06123-0637
(860) 275-0668
E-mail: kdavis@lawyerscollaborativefordiversity.org
Web: www.lcdiversity.com/scholarships.htm

Summary To provide financial assistance and summer work experience to underrepresented students at law schools in Connecticut and western Massachusetts.

Eligibility This program is open to women and people of color from any state who are currently enrolled in the first year at a law school in Connecticut or western Massachusetts. Applicants must be available to work as an intern during the summer following their first year. Along with their application, they must submit 500-word essays on 1) why diversity is important to them and how the Connecticut legal community can improve diversity in the legal profession; and 2) why they should be selected for this program.

Financial data The program provides a stipend of $2,000 per year for the second and third years of law school, a paid internship during the summer after the first year at a member firm of the Lawyers Collaborative for Diversity (LCD), and an unpaid internship with a legal department of United Technologies Corporation during that same summer.

Duration The scholarship is for 2 years; the paid internship is for 5 weeks during the summer; the unpaid internship is for 3 weeks during the summer.

Additional information This program is sponsored by United Technologies Corporation (UTC).

Number awarded 2 each year.

Deadline January of each year.

[1135]
VALERIE RUSSELL SCHOLARSHIP

United Church of Christ
Attn: Associate Director, Grant and Scholarship
  Administration
700 Prospect Avenue East
Cleveland, OH 44115-1100
(216) 736-2166   Toll Free: (866) 822-8224, ext. 2166
Fax: (216) 736-3783   E-mail: scholarships@ucc.org
Web: www.ucc.org/russell_scholarship

Summary To provide financial assistance to African American laywomen who are members of a United Church of Christ (UCC) congregation and working on an undergraduate or graduate degree to advance the justice ministries of the denomination.

Eligibility This program is open to African American laywomen who have a strong theologically-grounded commitment to the justice ministries of the UCC but are not a member in discernment, licensed, commissioned, or ordained. Applicants must be 1) working on an undergraduate or graduate degree in a field that will affirm the values of the UCC and promote its justice commitments; or 2) already professionally engaged in justice work either in the church or in a secular organization and seeking funds for continuing education activities (e.g., classes, workshops, travel) that will assist in personal skill building.

Financial data Stipends range from $1,500 to $2,000 per year. Funds may be used for tuition for undergraduate or graduate study or for continuing education activities.

Duration 1 year; may be renewed.

Additional information This program began in 1997.

Number awarded 1 or more each year.

Deadline February of each year.

[1136]
VIOLET AND CYRIL FRANKS SCHOLARSHIP

American Psychological Foundation
750 First Street, N.E.
Washington, DC 20002-4242
(202) 336-5843   Fax: (202) 336-5812
E-mail: foundation@apa.org
Web: www.apa.org/apf/funding/franks.aspx

Summary To provide funding to doctoral students interested in conducting research related to mental illness.

Eligibility This program is open to full-time graduate students who are interested in conducting a research project that uses a psychological perspective to help understand and reduce stigma associated with mental illness. Applicants must identify the project's goal, the prior research that has been conducted in the area, whom the project will serve, the in intended outcomes and how the project will achieve those, and the total cost of the project. Selection is based on conformance with stated program goals, quality of proposed work, and applicant's demonstrated scholarship and competence. The sponsor encourages applications from individuals who represent diversity in race, ethnicity, gender, age, disability, and sexual orientation.

Financial data The grant is $5,000.

Duration 1 year.

Additional information This grant was first awarded in 2007.

Number awarded 1 each year.

Deadline May of each year.

[1137]
VIRGINIA A. POMEROY SCHOLARSHIP

Association for Women Lawyers
Attn: Foundation Scholarship Committee
3322 North 92nd Street
Milwaukee, WI 53222-3507
(414) 750-4404   Fax: (414) 255-3615
E-mail: dana@barefoot-marketing.com
Web: www.associationforwomenlawyers.org/scholarships

Summary To provide financial assistance to women enrolled at law schools in Wisconsin who are interested in service to the vulnerable or disadvantaged.

Eligibility This program is open to women who have completed the first or second year at a law school in Wisconsin. Applicants must be interested in preparing for a career of service to the vulnerable or disadvantaged through 1 or more of the following areas: civil rights law, public service, public policy, public interest law, or appellate practice.

Financial data The stipend varies; recently, awards averaged $2,500.

Duration 1 year.

Additional information This program began in 1998.

Number awarded Varies each year; recently, 2 were awarded.

Deadline June of each year.

[1138]
VIRGINIA M. WAGNER EDUCATIONAL GRANT

Soroptimist International of the Americas-Midwestern
  Region
c/o Kris Armstrong, Governor
607 West Hamilton Road
Bloomington, IL 61704-8616
E-mail: soroptimist@simwr.org
Web: www.simwr.org/virginia-wagner-award

Summary To provide financial assistance to women working on an undergraduate or graduate degree at a college or university in midwestern states.

Eligibility This program is open to women who reside in Illinois, Indiana, Kentucky, Michigan, Ohio, or Wisconsin and are attending college or graduate school in any state. Applicants must be working on a bachelor's, master's, or doctoral degree in the field of their choice. Awards are first presented at the club level, then in districts, and finally for the entire region. Selection is based on the effort toward education by the applicant and her family, cumulative GPA, extracurricular activities, general impression, and financial need.

Financial data Club level awards vary at the discretion of the club. District finalists receive a $500 award and are then judged at the regional level. The regional winner receives a $2,500 award.

Duration 1 year.

Additional information This program began in 1972 and given its current name in 2004.

Number awarded 4 district winners are selected each year; 1 of those receives the regional award.

Deadline January of each year.

[1139]
WALTER BYERS POSTGRADUATE SCHOLARSHIP PROGRAM

National Collegiate Athletic Association
Attn: Walter Byers Scholarship Committee Staff Liaison
700 West Washington Street
P.O. Box 6222
Indianapolis, IN 46206-6222
(317) 917-6683 Fax: (317) 917-6888
E-mail: lthomas@ncaa.org
Web: www.ncaa.org

Summary To provide financial assistance for graduate education in any field to student-athletes with outstanding academic records.

Eligibility This program is open to student-athletes who are seniors or already enrolled in graduate school while completing their final year of athletics eligibility at a member institution of the National Collegiate Athletic Association (NCAA). Men and women compete for scholarships separately. Applicants must be planning to work full time on a graduate degree or post-baccalaureate professional degree. They must have a GPA of 3.5 or higher, have evidenced superior character and leadership, and have demonstrated that participation in athletics and community service has been a positive influence on their personal and intellectual development. Candidates must be nominated by their institution's faculty athletic representative or chief academic officer. Financial need is not considered in the selection process.

Financial data The stipend is $24,000 per year.

Duration 2 years.

Additional information This program began in 1988 in honor of the former executive director of the NCAA.

Number awarded 2 each year: 1 is set aside for a female and 1 for a male.

Deadline January of each year.

[1140]
WANDA MUNN SCHOLARSHIP

Society of Women Engineers
Attn: Scholarship Selection Committee
203 North LaSalle Street, Suite 1675
Chicago, IL 60601-1269
(312) 596-5223 Toll Free: (877) SWE-INFO
Fax: (312) 644-8557 E-mail: scholarships@swe.org
Web: societyofwomenengineers.swe.org

Summary To provide financial assistance to women from selected northwestern states interested in returning to college or graduate school to study engineering or computer science.

Eligibility This program is open to women who are planning to enroll at an ABET-accredited 4-year college or university. Applicants must have been out of the engineering workforce and school for at least 2 years and must be planning to return as an undergraduate or graduate student to work on a degree in computer science or engineering. They must be residents of or attending school in Alaska, Idaho, Montana, Oregon, or Washington and have a GPA of 3.0 or higher. Selection is based on merit. Preference is given to engineers who already have a degree and are planning to reenter the engineering workforce after a period of temporary retirement.

Financial data The stipend is $1,500.

Duration 1 year.

Additional information This program is sponsored by the Eastern Washington Section of the Society of Women Engineers.

Number awarded 1 each year.

Deadline February of each year.

[1141]
WASHINGTON EPISCOPAL CHURCH WOMEN MEMORIAL SCHOLARSHIP FUND

Episcopal Diocese of Washington
Attn: Episcopal Church Women
Episcopal Church House
Mount St. Alban
Washington, DC 20016-5094
(202) 537-6530 Toll Free: (800) 642-4427
Fax: (202) 537-5784 E-mail: ecw.edow@gmail.com
Web: ecw-edow.org/outreach.html

Summary To provide financial assistance for graduate study of specified fields to women who are members of Episcopal churches in Washington, D.C.

Eligibility This program is open to women members of the Episcopal Church who have been a canonical member of the Diocese of Washington for at least 1 year prior to application. Priority is given to members who reside in the Diocese of Washington. Applicants must be enrolled in graduate or professional study and their course of study must be theology, counseling, social work, health administration, nursing, or medicine. Along with their application, they must submit a statement of purpose for working on a graduate degree and how they plan to use it, letters of recommendation (including 1 from their vicar or rector), financial information, and (if seeking ordination) a letter from their parish intern committee.

Financial data A stipend is awarded (amount not specified); funds are sent directly to the recipient's school.

Duration 1 year; may be renewed.

Additional information This program began in 1925. The Episcopal Diocese of Washington serves the District of Columbia and the Maryland counties of Charles, St. Mary's, Prince George's, and Montgomery.

Number awarded 1 or more each year.

Deadline May of each year.

[1142]
WAWH FOUNDERS DISSERTATION FELLOWSHIP

Western Association of Women Historians
c/o Cheryl Krasnick Warsh, Executive Director
Vancouver Island University
History Department
900 Fifth Street
Nanaimo, BC V9R 5S5
Canada
E-mail: ExecutiveDirector@wawh.org
Web: www.wawh.org

Summary To provide dissertation funding to graduate students who are members of the Western Association of Women Historians (WAWH).

Eligibility This program is open to graduate students who are members of WAWH, have advanced to candidacy, are writing their dissertation at the time of application, and are expecting to receive their Ph.D. no earlier than December of the calendar year in which the award is made. Selection is based on scholarly potential of the student, significance of the dissertation project for historical scholarship, and progress already made towards completing the necessary research.

Financial data The grant is $1,000. Funds may be used for any expenses related to the dissertation.

Duration 1 year.

Additional information This fellowship was first awarded in 1986.

Number awarded 1 each year.

Deadline January of each year.

[1143]
WAYNE F. PLACEK GRANTS

American Psychological Foundation
750 First Street, N.E.
Washington, DC 20002-4242
(202) 336-5843   Fax: (202) 336-5812
E-mail: foundation@apa.org
Web: www.apa.org/apf/funding/placek.aspx

Summary To provide funding to pre- and postdoctoral scholars interested in conducting research that will increase the general public's understanding of homosexuality and alleviate the stress experienced by gay men and lesbians.

Eligibility This program is open to scholars who have a doctoral degree (e.g., Ph.D., Psy.D., M.D.) and to graduate students in all fields of the behavioral and social sciences. Applicants must be interested in conducting empirical studies that address the following topics: prejudice, discrimination, and violence based on sexual orientation, including heterosexuals' attitudes and behaviors toward lesbian, gay, bisexual, and transgender (LGBT) people; family and workplace issues relevant to LGBT people; and subgroups of the LGBT population that have been historically underrepresented in scientific research. Selection is based on relevance to program goals, magnitude of incremental contribution, quality of proposed work, and applicant's demonstrated scholarship and research competence. The sponsor encourages applications from individuals who represent diversity in race, ethnicity, gender, age, disability, and sexual orientation.

Financial data The grant is $15,000.

Duration 1 year.

Additional information This program began in 1995.

Number awarded 1 or 2 each year.

Deadline February of each year.

[1144]
WBF SCHOLARSHIP AWARDS

Women's Bar Association of Illinois
Attn: Women's Bar Foundation
321 South Plymouth Court, Suite 4S
P.O. Box 641068
Chicago, IL 60664-1068
(312) 341-8530   E-mail: illinoiswbf@aol.com
Web: www.illinoiswbf.org

Summary To provide financial assistance to women from any state attending law school in Illinois.

Eligibility This program is open to female residents of any state enrolled at accredited law schools in Illinois.

Financial data The stipend is $10,000.

Duration 1 year.

Additional information This program began in 1966. It includes the Chief Justice Mary Ann G. McMorrow Scholarship, first presented in 2004, and the Esther Rothstein Scholarship, first awarded in 2002.

Number awarded Varies each year; recently, 9 were awarded. Since the program was established, it has awarded more than 280 scholarships worth more than $1.1 million.

Deadline Deadline not specified.

[1145]
WICHITA CHAPTER AFWA SCHOLARSHIPS

Accounting and Financial Women's Alliance-Wichita
   Chapter
c/o Kate Grant, Scholarship Chair
Kirkpatrick, Sprecker & Company, LLP
311 South Hillside Street
Wichita, KS 67211
(316) 685-1411, ext. 305   Toll Free: (877) 299-1532
Fax: (316) 685-4575   E-mail: ekgrant1215@gmail.com
Web: www.wichitaafwa.org/Scholarship_Requirements

Summary To provide financial assistance to women working on an undergraduate or graduate degree in accounting or finance at a college or university in Kansas.

Eligibility This program is open to women working full or part time on an associate, bachelor's, or master's degree in accounting or finance at a college or university in Kansas. Applicants must have completed at least 15 semester hours in a 2-year program or 60 semester hours in a 4-year program. They must have a cumulative GPA of 3.0 or higher. Membership in the Accounting and Financial Women's Alliance (AFWA) is not required. Along with their application, they must submit an essay of 150 to 250 words on their career goals and objectives, the impact they want to have on the accounting and financial world, community involvement, and leadership examples. Selection is based on leadership, character, communication skills, GPA, and financial need.

Financial data The stipend is $1,000.

Duration 1 year.

Additional information The highest-ranked recipient is entered into the national competition for scholarships that range from $1,500 to $4,500.

Number awarded Varies each year; recently, 3 were awarded.

Deadline February of each year.

[1146]
WIFLE ANNUAL SCHOLARSHIP PROGRAM

Women in Federal Law Enforcement
Attn: Scholarship Coordinator
2200 Wilson Boulevard, Suite 102
PMB 204
Arlington, VA 22201-3324
(301) 805-2180   Fax: (301) 560-8836
E-mail: WIFLE@comcast.net
Web: www.wifle.org/scholarshipprogram.htm

Summary To provide financial assistance for college or graduate school to women interested in preparing for a career in law enforcement.

Eligibility This program is open to women who have completed at least 1 academic year of full-time study at an accredited 4-year college or university (or at a community college with the intention of transferring to a 4-year school). Applicants must be majoring in criminal justice or a related field (e.g., social sciences, public administration, computer science, finance, linguistic arts, chemistry, physics). They must have a GPA of 3.0 or higher. Students in graduate and postgraduate programs are also eligible, but those working on an associate degree are not. Along with their application, they must submit a 500-word essay describing a community project in which they have been involved and the results or impact to the community. Selection is based on academic potential, achievement, and commitment to serving communities in the field of law enforcement. U.S. citizenship is required.

Financial data The stipend is $2,500.

Duration 1 year; may be renewed.

Number awarded Varies each year; recently, 6 were awarded.

Deadline April of each year.

[1147]
WILLIAM RUCKER GREENWOOD SCHOLARSHIP

Association for Women Geoscientists-Potomac Chapter
Attn: Scholarships
P.O. Box 6644
Arlington, VA 22206-0644
E-mail: awgpotomacschol@hotmail.com
Web: www.awg.org/members/po_scholarships.htm

Summary To provide financial assistance to minority women from any state working on an undergraduate or graduate degree in the geosciences at a college in the Potomac Bay region.

Eligibility This program is open to minority women who are residents of any state and currently enrolled as full-time undergraduate or graduate geoscience majors at an accredited, degree-granting college or university in Delaware, the District of Columbia, Maryland, Virginia, or West Virginia. Selection is based on the applicant's 1) participation in geoscience or earth science educational activities; and 2) potential for leadership as a future geoscience professional.

Financial data The stipend is $1,000. The recipient also is granted a 1-year membership in the Association for Women Geoscientists (AWG).

Duration 1 year.

Number awarded 1 each year.

Deadline April of each year.

[1148]
WISCONSIN WOMEN'S ALLIANCE FOUNDATION SCHOLARSHIP

Community Foundation for the Fox Valley Region, Inc.
Attn: Scholarships
4455 West Lawrence Street
Appleton, WI 54914
(920) 830-1290   Fax: (920) 830-1293
E-mail: scholarships@cffoxvalley.org
Web: www.cffoxvalley.org/page.aspx?pid=1313

Summary To provide financial assistance to mature women in Wisconsin who are working full time on an undergraduate or graduate degree at a school in any state.

Eligibility This program is open to Wisconsin women who are 25 years of age or older. Applicants must be attending an accredited 2- or 4-year college, university, or technical college to work on an undergraduate or graduate degree. Selection is based on career path and goals, employment history, volunteer activities, professional and community activities, and financial need.

Financial data The stipend ranges up to $1,000.

Duration 1 year.

Number awarded Normally, 3 each year.

Deadline March of each year.

[1149]
WLAM FOUNDATION SCHOLARS

Women Lawyers Association of Michigan Foundation
3150 Livernois, Suite 235
Troy, MI 48083
E-mail: wlamfmi@gmail.com
Web: www.wlamfoundation.org

Summary To provide financial assistance to women from any state enrolled at law schools in Michigan.

Eligibility This program is open to women from any state enrolled full or part time and in good academic standing at accredited law schools in Michigan. Applicants must be able to demonstrate leadership capabilities in advancing the position of women in society, including service in such areas as social justice, equality, family law, child advocacy, domestic violence, or work on behalf of underserved areas of populations. Along with their application, they must submit law school transcripts, a detailed letter of interest explaining how they meet the award criteria, a resume, and up to 3 letters of recommendation.

Financial data The stipend is $3,000.

Duration 1 year.

Additional information The accredited law schools are the University of Michigan Law School, Wayne State University Law School, University of Detroit Mercy School of Law, Western Michigan University Thomas M. Cooley Law School, and Michigan State University-Detroit College of Law. This program includes the Kimberly M. Cahill Scholarship (for a student at the University of Michigan Law School), the Dawn Van Hoek Scholarship (for a student at Wayne State University Law School), and the Dickinson Wright Women's Network Scholarship (for a student at Wayne State University Law School). Major support for the program is provided by General Motors.

Number awarded 10 each year: 2 at each participating law school.

Deadline October of each year.

[1150]
WOMAN'S MISSIONARY UNION OF VIRGINIA SEMINARY SCHOLARSHIP

Woman's Missionary Union of Virginia
2828 Emerywood Parkway
Richmond, VA 23294
(804) 915-5000, ext. 8267
Toll Free: (800) 255-2428 (within VA)
Fax: (804) 672-8008   E-mail: wmuv@wmuv.org
Web: www.wmuv.org

Summary To provide financial assistance to women from Virginia who are interested in attending a Baptist seminary.

Eligibility This program is open to women from Virginia who are interested in attending a seminary supported through the Baptist General Association of Virginia (BGAV). Applicants must be seeking career missions appointments and/or professional ministry positions in churches, associations, states, or the world. Along with their application, they must submit a 1,500-word essay that includes 1) their Christian testimony; 2) a brief biography of their life (church activities, study groups, awards, talents, sports, hobbies, mission projects and community service); and 3) how receiving this scholarship will impact their life and enable them to pursue the call of God in their life. An interview is required.

Financial data The stipend is $1,500 per year.

Duration 1 year; may be renewed up to 2 additional years.

Number awarded Up to 3 each year.

Deadline June of each year.

[1151]
WOMEN AND POLITICS FUND FELLOWSHIPS

American Political Science Association
Attn: Centennial Center Visiting Scholars Program
1527 New Hampshire Avenue, N.W.
Washington, DC 20036-1206
(202) 483-2512   Fax: (202) 483-2657
E-mail: centennial@apsanet.org
Web: www.apsanet.org/centennial/grants

Summary To provide funding to members of the American Political Science Association (APSA) who are interested in conducting research on women and politics at the Centennial Center for Political Science and Public Affairs.

Eligibility This program is open to members of the association who are interested in conducting research on women and politics while in residence at the center. Junior faculty members, postdoctoral fellows, and advanced graduate students are strongly encouraged to apply, but scholars at all stages of their careers are eligible. International applicants are also welcome if they have demonstrable command of spoken English. Non-resident scholars may also be eligible.

Financial data Grants normally range from $1,000 to $2,500.

Duration 2 weeks to 12 months.

Number awarded 1 or more each year.

Deadline February, June, or October of each year.

[1152]
WOMEN CHEFS AND RESTAURATEURS
SCHOLARSHIP PROGRAM

Women Chefs and Restaurateurs
Attn: Scholarship Program Coordinator
115 South Patrick Street, Suite 101
Alexandria, VA 22314
(630) 396-8339   Toll Free: (877) 927-7787
E-mail: Scholarship@womenchefs.org
Web: www.womenchefs.org/career-development

Summary To provide financial assistance to members of Women Chefs and Restaurateurs (WCR) who are interested in preparing for a culinary or related career.

Eligibility This program is open to women who are members of WCR, interested in attending a culinary or related school, and at least 18 years of age (21 for the wine scholarships). Recently, support was offered at the Italian culinary

experience, the classic culinary arts program, and the classic pastry arts program at the International Culinary Center (New York, New York); the Italian Culinary Experience, the classic pastry arts program, and the intensive sommelier program at the International Culinary Center (Campbell, California); the Barbara Lazaroff WCR Future Leader in Hospitality Scholarship; the Master the Art and Science of Sous-Vide Scholarship at the Culinary Research and Education Academy in Sterling, Virginia; the Trial Celebrity Chef Anita Lo Scholarship at Annisa in New York; a scholarship in the culinary program at Southern Alberta Institute of Technology (SAIT) in Calgary; and Ann Cooper's "Healthy School Lunch" Scholarship in Boulder, Colorado. Applicants must submit a 1-page essay about their food service career, their culinary interests, what inspires them professionally, and how the scholarship will contribute to their career.

Financial data In general, scholarships provide payment of full or partial tuition, or stipends of $5,000 to $7,500 per year.

Duration Program lengths vary; scholarships must be used during the calendar year in which they are awarded.

Additional information Students may apply for only 1 program on a single application; the fee is $25 for the first application $40 for multiple applications (to a maximum of 3).

Number awarded Varies each year.

Deadline July of each year.

[1153]
WOMEN DIVERS HALL OF FAME MARINE
CONSERVATION GRADUATE SCHOLARSHIPS

Women Divers Hall of Fame
43 MacKey Avenue
Port Washington, NY 11050-3628
E-mail: scholarships@wdhof.org
Web: www.wdhof.org/scholarships/scholarships.shtml

Summary To provide financial assistance to women who are working on a graduate degree in marine conservation.

Eligibility This program is open to women of any age who are enrolled in an accredited graduate academic or research program in the field of marine conservation. Applicants must be seeking funding to assist with college tuition and fees, to support independent research, or to support a research internship program at an accredited university.

Financial data Stipends are $2,000 or $1,000.

Duration 1 year.

Additional information This program includes scholarships supported by the Aggressor and Dancer Fleets and by the Sea of Change Foundation.

Number awarded 5 each year: 4 at $2,000 and 1 at $1,000.

Deadline November of each year.

[1154]
WOMEN IN FILM/DALLAS FINISHING FUNDS GRANT

Women in Film/Dallas
Attn: Scholarships and Grants
15110 Dallas Parkway, Suite 440
Dallas, TX 75248
(214) 379-1171   Toll Free: (800) 724-0767
Fax: (214) 379-1172   E-mail: scholarships@wifdallas.org
Web: www.wifdallas.org/page-986794

Summary To provide funding for completion of a film to women who are members of Women in Film/Dallas.

Eligibility This program is open to women who reside in Texas and are student, professional, associate, or corporate members of Women in Film/Dallas. Applicants must have a film project on which they have completed principal photography. Along with their application, they must submit a 5- to 10-minute sample of the work in progress; a 1-page description of the submitted footage; a 1,000-word personal statement that includes their interest and experiences in writing, directing, or producing films and the general aspects of their financial need; a treatment or synopsis of the film; and a plan for securing rights that still require clearance. Funding is available for short films (up to 35 minutes) and feature films (between 60 and 120 minutes).

Financial data Grants range up to $500 for short films or $3,000 for feature films.

Duration 1 year.

Number awarded At least 2 each year: 1 for a short film and 1 for a feature film.

Deadline March of each year.

[1155]
WOMEN IN LEADERSHIP SCHOLARSHIP OF BROWN AND CALDWELL

Brown and Caldwell
Attn: HR/Scholarship Program
1527 Cole Boulevard, Suite 300
Lakewood, CO 80401
(303) 239-5400   Fax: (303) 239-5454
E-mail: scholarships@brwncald.com
Web: www.brownandcaldwell.com/Scholarships.asp?id=4

Summary To provide financial assistance to female upper-division and graduate students working on a degree in an environmental or engineering field.

Eligibility This program is open to female U.S. citizens and permanent residents enrolled as full-time juniors, seniors, or graduate students at an accredited college or university. Applicants must identify as a woman who demonstrates leadership within the community. They must have a GPA of 3.0 or higher with a declared major in civil, chemical, or environmental engineering or an environmental science (e.g., biology, geology, hydrogeology, ecology). Along with their application, they must submit an essay (up to 250 words) on a topic that changes annually but relates to their personal development. Financial need is not considered in the selection process.

Financial data The stipend is $5,000.

Duration 1 year.

Additional information This program began in 1999.

Number awarded 1 each year.

Deadline May of each year.

[1156]
WOMEN IN MEDICINE LEADERSHIP SCHOLARSHIPS

Women in Medicine
P.O. Box 107
Colchester, VT 05446
E-mail: wim.doctors@gmail.com
Web: www.womeninmedicine.org

Summary To provide financial assistance to women who self-identify as LGBTQ and are currently enrolled in medical school.

Eligibility This program is open to LGBTQ women who are entering their second, third, or fourth year at an allopathic or osteopathic medical school in the United States or Canada. Applicants must submit a current curriculum vitae that includes involvement in LGBT-related organizations, participation in other college and medical school activities and organizations, research experience, part-time or full-time employment experience, additional awards or special recognitions, examples of their leadership within the LGBT community, and a statement of their future goals in medicine.

Financial data The stipend is $5,000.

Duration 1 year.

Number awarded 4 each year.

Deadline January of each year.

[1157]
WOMEN IN TOXICOLOGY SPECIAL INTEREST GROUP GRADUATE STUDENT ACHIEVEMENT AWARD

Society of Toxicology
Attn: Women in Toxicology Special Interest Group
1821 Michael Faraday Drive, Suite 300
Reston, VA 20190-5348
(703) 438-3115   Fax: (703) 438-3113
E-mail: sothq@toxicology.org
Web: www.toxicology.org/ai/af/awards_details.aspx?id=78

Summary To recognize and reward graduate student members of the Society of Toxicology (SOT), especially its Women in Toxicology Special Interest Group (WIT), who have demonstrated academic achievement.

Eligibility This program is open to graduate student members of the society who have demonstrated academic achievement in the field of toxicology and who have provided leadership and service in their chosen field and/or their community. Along with their application, they must submit a letter of recommendation from their adviser, a curriculum vitae and an abstract of a paper that has been accepted for presentation at the SOT annual meeting. Students who are not WIT members are strongly encouraged to join.

Financial data The winner receives a certificate and a monetary award.

Duration The award is presented annually.

Number awarded 1 each year.

Deadline December of each year.

[1158]
WOMEN IN TOXICOLOGY SPECIAL INTEREST GROUP VERA W. HUDSON AND ELIZABETH K. WEISBURGER SCHOLARSHIP FUND

Society of Toxicology
Attn: Women in Toxicology Special Interest Group
1821 Michael Faraday Drive, Suite 300
Reston, VA 20190-5348
(703) 438-3115   Fax: (703) 438-3113
E-mail: sothq@toxicology.org
Web: www.toxicology.org/ai/af/awards_details.aspx?id=122

Summary To provide funding to members of the Society of Toxicology (SOT), especially its Women in Toxicology Special Interest Group (WIT), who are conducting doctoral research in the field.

Eligibility This program is open to full-time graduate student members of the society who have been advanced to candidacy for a Ph.D. in toxicology. Students who are not WIT members are strongly encouraged to join. Along with their application, they must submit a narrative of 1 to 2 pages describing their graduate research hypothesis, background, and significance. Selection is based on relevance of the research to toxicology, scholastic achievement, demonstrated leadership (professionally and/or in the community), and letters of recommendation.

Financial data The grant is $2,000. Funds are paid to the recipient's university to be used for a tuition payment and/or other education and research-related expenses, including travel.

Duration 1 year.

Number awarded 1 each year.

Deadline December of each year.

[1159]
WOMEN OF THE ELCA SCHOLARSHIP PROGRAM

Women of the Evangelical Lutheran Church in America
Attn: Scholarships
8765 West Higgins Road
Chicago, IL 60631-4101
(773) 380-2741   Toll Free: (800) 638-3522, ext. 2741
Fax: (773) 380-2419   E-mail: valora.starr@elca.org
Web: www.womenoftheelca.org

Summary To provide financial assistance to lay women who are members of Evangelical Lutheran Church of America (ELCA) congregations and who wish to take classes on the undergraduate, graduate, professional, or vocational school level.

Eligibility This program is open to ELCA lay women who are at least 21 years of age and have experienced an interruption of at least 2 years in their education since high school. Applicants must have been admitted to an educational institution to prepare for a career in other than the ordained ministry. They may be working on an undergraduate, graduate, professional, or vocational school degree. U.S. citizenship is required.

Financial data The average stipend is $1,000 per year.

Duration 1 year; recipients may reapply for 1 additional year.

Additional information These scholarships are supported by several endowment funds: the Cronk Memorial Fund, the First Triennial Board Scholarship Fund, the General Scholarship Fund, the Mehring Fund, the Paepke Scholarship Fund, the Piero/Wade/Wade Fund, and the Edwin/Edna Robeck Scholarship.

Number awarded Varies each year; recently, 15 were awarded.

Deadline February of each year.

[1160]
WOMEN'S INDEPENDENCE SCHOLARSHIP PROGRAM

Women's Independence Scholarship Program, Inc.
Attn: WISP Program
4900 Randall Parkway, Suite H
Wilmington, NC 28403
(910) 397-7742   Toll Free: (866) 255-7742
Fax: (910) 397-0023   E-mail: nancy@wispinc.org
Web: www.wispinc.org/Scholarship/tabid/56/Default.aspx

Summary To provide financial assistance for college or graduate school to women who are victims of partner abuse.

Eligibility This program is open to women who are victims of partner abuse and have worked for at least 6 months with a nonprofit domestic violence victim services provider that is willing to sponsor them. Applicants must be interested in attending a vocational school, community college, 4-year college or university, or (in exceptional circumstances) graduate school as a full- or part-time student. They should have left an abusive partner at least 1 year previously; women who have been parted from their batterer for more than 5 years are also eligible, but funding for such applicants may be limited. Preference is given to single mothers with young children. Special consideration is given to applicants who plan to use their education to further the rights of, and options for, women and girls. Selection is based primarily on financial need. U.S. citizenship or permanent resident status is required.

Financial data Stipends depend on the need of the recipient, but they are at least $250 and average $2,000 per academic term. First priority is given to funding for direct educational expenses (tuition, books, and fees), which is paid directly to the educational institution. Second priority is for assistance in reducing indirect financial barriers to education (e.g., child care, transportation), which is paid directly to the sponsoring agency.

Duration 1 year; may be renewed if the recipient maintains a GPA of 2.75 or higher.

Additional information This program began in 1999 when the sponsor was known as the Sunshine Lady Foundation.

Number awarded Varies each year. Since the program began, it has awarded more than $16 million in scholarships to approximately 2,000 women.

Deadline Applications may be submitted at any time, but they must be received at least 2 months before the start of the intended program.

[1161]
WOMEN'S LEADERSHIP IN AGRICULTURE SCHOLARSHIP PROGRAM

Ohio Farm Bureau Federation
Attn: Foundation
280 North High Street, Sixth Floor
P.O. Box 182383
Columbus, OH 43218-2383
(614) 249-2400   Fax: (614) 249-2200
E-mail: foundation@ofbf.org
Web: www.ofbf.org/foundation/scholarships-and-grants

Summary To provide financial assistance to female residents of Ohio who are interested in attending college or graduate school in any state to prepare for a career related to agriculture.

Eligibility This program is open to female Ohio residents who are attending or planning to attend an accredited 2-year technical school, 2- or 4-year college or university, or graduate school in any state. Applicants do not need to be members of the Ohio Farm Bureau Federation, their respective county Farm Bureau, or any other club or organization directly related to vocational agriculture. Nor are they required to be working on a degree directly connected to a school and/or college of agriculture. However, they must submit an explanation of how their career plans involve an aspect of the field of agriculture (e.g., food production, scientific research, education or outreach, technical support, food processing, product distribution, marketing, policymaking, advocacy). Financial need is not considered in the selection process.

Financial data The stipend is at least $1,500.

Duration 1 year.

Additional information This program began in 2006 with a grant from the Charlotte R. Schmidlapp Fund.

Number awarded 1 or more each year.

Deadline February of each year.

[1162]
WOODROW WILSON DISSERTATION FELLOWSHIPS IN WOMEN'S STUDIES

Woodrow Wilson National Fellowship Foundation
5 Vaughn Drive, Suite 300
P.O. Box 5281
Princeton, NJ 08543-5281
(609) 452-7007, ext. 310   Fax: (609) 452-0066
E-mail: ws@woodrow.org
Web: www.woodrow.org/fellowships/womens-studies

Summary To provide funding to doctoral candidates in women's studies.

Eligibility This program is open to students in Ph.D. or Th.D. programs who have completed all pre-dissertation requirements in any field of study at graduate schools in the United States. Applicants must be in the final year of research on women that crosses disciplinary, regional, and cultural boundaries. Along with their application, they must include graduate school transcripts, letters of reference, a dissertation prospectus, a selected bibliography, a statement of interest in women's studies, and a time table for completion of the dissertation. Selection is based on originality and significance to women's studies, scholarly validity, applicant's academic preparation and ability to accomplish the work, and probabil-

ity that the dissertation will be completed within a reasonable time period.

Financial data Winners receive grants of $5,000 to be used for research expenses connected with the dissertation (e.g., travel, data collection, supplies).

Additional information Support for the program is provided by the Ford Foundation.

Number awarded Varies each year; recently, 10 were awarded.

Deadline October of each year.

[1163]
YOUNG LADIES' RADIO LEAGUE SCHOLARSHIPS

Foundation for Amateur Radio, Inc.
Attn: Scholarship Committee
P.O. Box 911
Columbia, MD 21044-0911
(410) 552-2652   Fax: (410) 981-5146
E-mail: farscholarships@gmail.com
Web: www.farweb.org

Summary To provide funding to female licensed radio amateurs who are interested in earning a bachelor's or graduate degree in the United States.

Eligibility This program is open to female radio amateurs who have at least an FCC Technician Class license or equivalent foreign authorization. Applicants must intend to work full or part time on a bachelor's or graduate degree at a college or university in the United States. There are no restrictions on the course of study or residency location. Non-U.S. amateurs are eligible. Preference is given to students working on a degree in communications, electronics, or related arts and sciences. Financial need is considered in the selection process.

Financial data The stipend is $2,000 or $1,000.

Duration 1 year.

Additional information This program, which is financed by the Young Ladies' Radio League and administered by the Foundation for Amateur Radio, includes the following named scholarships: the Ethel Smith, K4LMB, Memorial Scholarship (established in 2000 and restricted to full-time students), the Mary Lou Brown, NM7N, Memorial Scholarship (established in 2000 and restricted to full-time students), and the Martha "Marte" Wessel, K0EPE, Memorial Scholarship (established in 2014 and open to part-time students working full time).

Number awarded 3 each year: 2 at $2,000 and 1 at $1,000.

Deadline April of each year.

[1164]
YWAF HIGHER EDUCATION SCHOLARSHIPS

Young Women's Alliance
Attn: Foundation
P.O. Box 684612
Austin, TX 78701
(512) 553-6176
E-mail: development@youngwomensalliance.org
Web: www.youngwomensalliance.org/ywaf_scholarships

Summary To provide financial assistance to women from any state enrolled as upper-division or graduate students at a college or university in central Texas.

Eligibility This program is open to women from any state who are younger than 40 years of age. Applicants must have completed at least 60 undergraduate semester hours or be working on a graduate degree at an accredited institution of higher learning in central Texas. They must have devoted at least 40 hours of work on a Community Impact Project during the current semester. Along with their application, they must submit a description of their Community Impact Project and a personal statement about why they should be chosen to receive this scholarship. Selection is based on academic achievement, demonstrated leadership, commitment to both past community service and the Community Impact Project, and financial need.

Financial data The stipend is $2,500.

Duration 1 year.

Additional information This foundation was established in 1997.

Number awarded 1 or more each year.

Deadline March of each year.

[1165]
ZETA PHI BETA GENERAL GRADUATE FELLOWSHIPS

Zeta Phi Beta Sorority, Inc.
Attn: National Educational Foundation
1734 New Hampshire Avenue, N.W.
Washington, DC 20009
(202) 387-3103   Fax: (202) 232-4593
E-mail: info@zetaphibetasororityhq.org
Web: www.zpbnef1975.org/scholarships-and-descriptions

Summary To provide financial assistance to women who are working on a professional degree, master's degree, doctorate, or postdoctorate.

Eligibility Women graduate or postdoctoral students are eligible to apply if they have achieved distinction or shown promise of distinction in their chosen fields. Applicants need not be members of Zeta Phi Beta. They must be enrolled full time in a professional, graduate, or postdoctoral program. Along with their application, they must submit a 150-word essay on their educational goals and professional aspirations, how this award will help them to achieve those goals, and why they should receive the award. Financial need is not considered in the selection process.

Financial data The stipend ranges up to $2,500, paid directly to the recipient.

Duration 1 academic year; may be renewed.

Additional information Zeta Phi Beta is a traditionally African American sorority.

Number awarded 1 or more each year.

Deadline January of each year.

[1166]
ZORA NEALE HURSTON SCHOLARSHIP

Zeta Phi Beta Sorority, Inc.
Attn: National Educational Foundation
1734 New Hampshire Avenue, N.W.
Washington, DC 20009
(202) 387-3103   Fax: (202) 232-4593
E-mail: info@zetaphibetasororityhq.org
Web: www.zpbnef1975.org/scholarships-and-descriptions

Summary To provide financial assistance to graduate students working on a degree in anthropology or related fields.

Eligibility This program is open to full-time graduate students in anthropology or related fields. Applicants need not be members of Zeta Phi Beta. Along with their application, they must submit a 150-word essay on their educational goals and professional aspirations, how this award will help them to achieve those goals, and why they should receive the award. Financial need is not considered in the selection process.

Financial data The stipend ranges from $500 to $1,000.

Duration 1 academic year; may be renewed.

Additional information Zeta Phi Beta is a traditionally African American sorority.

Number awarded 1 each year.

Deadline January of each year.

Professionals/ Postdoctorates

Listed alphabetically by program title and described in detail here are 277 grants, awards, educational support programs, residencies, and other sources of "free money" available to women who are professionals and post-doctorates. This funding can be used to support research, creative activities, formal academic classes, training courses, and/or residencies in the United States.

[1167]
AAUW CAREER DEVELOPMENT GRANTS

American Association of University Women
Attn: AAUW Educational Foundation
1111 16th Street, N.W.
Washington, DC 20036-4873
(202) 785-7700   Toll Free: (800) 326-AAUW
Fax: (202) 872-1425   TDD: (202) 785-7777
E-mail: aauw@applyists.com
Web: www.aauw.org

Summary To provide financial assistance to women who are seeking career advancement, career change, or reentry into the workforce.

Eligibility This program is open to women who are U.S. citizens or permanent residents, have earned a bachelor's degree, received their most recent degree more than 4 years ago, and are making career changes, seeking to advance in current careers, or reentering the workforce. Applicants must be interested in working toward a master's degree, second bachelor's or associate degree, professional degree (e.g., M.D., J.D.), certification program, or technical school certificate. They must be planning to undertake course work at an accredited 2- or 4-year college or university (or a technical school that is licensed, accredited, or approved by the U.S. Department of Education). Primary consideration is given to women of color and women pursuing their first advanced degree or credentials in nontraditional fields. Support is not provided for prerequisite course work or for Ph.D. course work or dissertations. Selection is based on demonstrated commitment to education and equity for women and girls, reason for seeking higher education or technical training, degree to which study plan is consistent with career objectives, potential for success in chosen field, documentation of opportunities in chosen field, feasibility of study plans and proposed time schedule, validity of proposed budget and budget narrative (including sufficient outside support), and quality of written proposal.

Financial data Grants range from $2,000 to $12,000. Funds may be used for tuition, fees, books, supplies, local transportation, dependent child care, or purchase of a computer required for the study program.

Duration 1 year, beginning in July; nonrenewable.

Additional information The filing fee is $35.

Number awarded Varies each year; recently, 63 of these grants, with a value of $670,000, were awarded.

Deadline December of each year.

[1168]
ACM ATHENA LECTURER AWARD

Association for Computing Machinery
Attn: Awards Committee Liaison
2 Penn Plaza, Suite 701
New York, NY 10121-0701
(212) 626-0561   Toll Free: (800) 342-6626
Fax: (212) 944-1318   E-mail: acm-awards@acm.org
Web: awards.acm.org/athena/nominations.cfm

Summary To recognize and reward, with a lectureship, women researchers who have made outstanding contributions to computer science.

Eligibility This award is presented to women who have made outstanding contributions to research on computer sci-

ence. Nominees must be available to deliver a lecture at the Symposium on the Theory of Computing sponsored by the Special Interest Group on Algorithms and Computation Theory (SIGACT) of the Association for Computing Machinery (ACM).

Financial data The award is $24,500.

Duration The award is presented annually.

Additional information This award was established in 2006 and from then until 2016 was named the ACM-W Athena Lecturer Award. Financial support is provided by Google, Inc.

Number awarded 1 each year.

Deadline November of each year.

[1169]
AFRL/DAGSI OHIO STUDENT-FACULTY RESEARCH FELLOWSHIP PROGRAM

Dayton Area Graduate Studies Institute
3155 Research Boulevard, Suite 205
Kettering, OH 45420
(937) 781-4001   Fax: (937) 781-4005
E-mail: kelam@dagsi.org
Web: www.dagsi.org/pages/osrfp_proinforeq.html

Summary To provide funding to faculty and graduate students from any state who are enrolled at universities in Ohio that participate in the Dayton Area Graduate Studies Institute (DAGSI) and are interested in conducting research in aerospace technologies of interest to the U.S. Air Force.

Eligibility This program is open to research teams of full-time graduate students and faculty at 18 designated Ohio universities that participate in DAGSI. Applicants must be interested in conducting research that will utilize the facilities of the Air Force Research Laboratory (AFRL) at Wright-Patterson Air Force Base. All 4 directorates at the AFRL (sensors, materials and manufacturing, human effectiveness, and aerospace systems) participate in this program. Applications from Ph.D. candidates must be developed and written largely by the student, with support, guidance, and input as necessary from the faculty partner. For master's projects, the proposal can be developed and written jointly by the faculty member and the student. All participants (faculty and student) must be U.S. citizens. Underrepresented minorities, women, and persons with disabilities are strongly urged to apply.

Financial data Grants provide stipends of $23,500 for students who have a master's degree and are working on a Ph.D. or $18,500 for students who have a bachelor's degree and are working on a master's; student's tuition for 1 academic year; a faculty stipend of $11,000; student and faculty allowances of $3,000 each for program-related travel or other approved expenses; and overhead at a maximum off-campus rate of 26% of student and faculty stipends and miscellaneous allowances. The maximum DAGSI contribution is $51,000 for Ph.D. programs or $43,500 for master's programs; a cost-share commitment equal to one-third of the DAGSI contribution must be provided by the university, industry, AFRL, or other allowable government source.

Duration 1 year; master's awards are nonrenewable but Ph.D. awards may be renewed for 2 additional years. Students are expected to spend 8 consecutive weeks conducting research at AFRL and faculty members are expected to spend at least 3 weeks over the year conducting research at AFRL.

Additional information DAGSI was established in 1994 as a consortium of graduate engineering schools at the University of Dayton, Wright State University, and the Air Force Institute of Technology. The Ohio State University and the University of Cincinnati joined as affiliated members in 1996 and Miami University and Ohio University joined as associate members in 2001. Students from the following universities are also eligible to participate in this program: University of Akron, Bowling Green State University, Central State University, Cleveland State University, Kent State University, Shawnee State University, University of Toledo, Youngstown State University, Medical College of Ohio, Northeastern Ohio Universities College of Medicine, and Case Western Reserve University.

Number awarded At least 10 each year.

Deadline January of each year.

[1170]
ALEXANDER GRALNICK RESEARCH INVESTIGATOR PRIZE

American Psychological Foundation
750 First Street, N.E.
Washington, DC 20002-4242
(202) 336-5843   Fax: (202) 336-5812
E-mail: foundation@apa.org
Web: www.apa.org/apf/funding/gralnick.aspx

Summary To recognize and reward psychologists conducting exceptional research on serious mental illness.

Eligibility This program is open to psychologists who have a doctoral degree, have a record of significant research productivity, and are able to demonstrate evidence on continuing creativity in the area of research on serious mental illness (including, but not limited to, schizophrenia, bipolar disorder, and paranoia). Nominees must also have significant involvement in training and development of younger investigators. They must have an affiliation with an accredited college, university, or other treatment or research institution. The sponsor encourages nominations of individuals who represent diversity in race, ethnicity, gender, age, disability, and sexual orientation. Selection is based on the full breadth of research conducted and published to date, ongoing research productivity, and influence on a future generation of researchers.

Financial data The award is $20,000.

Duration The award is presented biennially, in even-numbered years.

Additional information This award was first presented in 2002.

Number awarded 1 each even-numbered year.

Deadline April of each even-numbered year.

[1171]
ALFRED P. SLOAN FOUNDATION RESEARCH FELLOWSHIPS

Alfred P. Sloan Foundation
630 Fifth Avenue, Suite 2200
New York, NY 10111-0242
(212) 649-1632   Fax: (212) 757-5117
E-mail: researchfellows@sloan.org
Web: www.sloan.org

Summary To provide funding for research in selected fields of science to recent doctorates.

Eligibility This program is open to scholars who are no more than 6 years from completion of the most recent Ph.D. or equivalent in chemistry, computational and evolutionary molecular biology, computer science, economics, mathematics, neuroscience, ocean sciences (including marine biology), physics, or a related interdisciplinary field. Applicants must have a tenure track position at a college or university in the United States or Canada. Direct applications are not accepted; candidates must be nominated by department heads or other senior scholars. Although fellows must be at an early stage of their research careers, they should give strong evidence of independent research accomplishments and creativity. The sponsor strongly encourages the participation of women and members of underrepresented minority groups.

Financial data The stipend is $30,000 per year. Funds are paid directly to the fellow's institution to be used by the fellow for equipment, technical assistance, professional travel, trainee support, or any other research-related expense; they may not be used to augment an existing full-time salary.

Duration 2 years; may be extended if unexpended funds still remain.

Additional information This program began in 1955, when it awarded $235,000 to 22 chemists, physicists, and pure mathematicians. Neuroscience was added in 1972, economics and applied mathematics in 1980, computer science in 1993, computational and evolutionary molecular biology in 2002, and ocean sciences in 2012. Currently, the program awards more than $5.5 million in grants annually.

Number awarded 126 each year: 23 in chemistry, 12 in computational and evolutionary molecular biology, 16 in computer science, 8 in economics, 20 in mathematics, 16 in neuroscience, 8 in ocean sciences, and 23 in physics.

Deadline September of each year.

[1172]
ALPHA DELTA KAPPA EXCELLENCE IN EDUCATION AWARD

Alpha Delta Kappa
Attn: Excellence in Education Award Program
1615 West 92nd Street
Kansas City, MO 64114
(816) 363-5525   Toll Free: (800) 247-2311
Fax: (816) 363-4010
E-mail: headquarters@alphadeltakappa.org
Web: www.alphadeltakappa.org

Summary To recognize and reward members of Alpha Delta Kappa, an honor society of women educators, who have made outstanding contributions to education.

Eligibility This award is available to Alpha Delta Kappa members who are actively involved in the education profession and are under contract in teaching, administration, or a specialized field of education. Members must be nominated by a colleague or parent. Nominees must demonstrate 1) exceptional professional dedication, knowledge, and skills; 2) recognition as an outstanding educator by colleagues, parents, and students; 3) exemplary contributions to education; 4) evidence of professional achievement and success; and 5) school and community collaboration.

Financial data The award is $2,500. The winner's school receives a grant of $2,500 to be used for professional development of its staff.

Duration The award is presented biennially, in even-numbered years.

Number awarded 1 each even-numbered year.

Deadline Nominations must be submitted by November of each odd-numbered year.

[1173]
ALPHA DELTA KAPPA REGIONAL PROFESSIONAL DEVELOPMENT SCHOLARSHIPS

Alpha Delta Kappa
Attn: Scholarships
1615 West 92nd Street
Kansas City, MO 64114
(816) 363-5525   Toll Free: (800) 247-2311
Fax: (816) 363-4010
E-mail: headquarters@alphadeltakappa.org
Web: www.alphadeltakappa.org

Summary To provide funding for advanced study or a project in connection with a degree program to members of Alpha Delta Kappa, an honor society of women educators.

Eligibility This program is open to Alpha Delta Kappa members who desire to pursue a planned program of study supportive of the purposes of the organization. Their proposed program may involve 1) meeting partial requirements for a degree, certification, or endorsements; 2) planning, research, or study through course work; or 3) setting up guidelines for evaluation. Applicants must submit a brief description of their professional development plan, a statement of the reasons for applying for this scholarship, and a description of how the scholarship will help them meet their professional goals and enrich the lives of their students.

Financial data Stipends average $1,500.

Duration The program normally should be completed within 1 year, although more time may be allowed through consultation between the recipient and her Regional Scholarship Programs committee.

Number awarded 14 each year: 2 in each Alpha Delta Kappa region.

Deadline Members must submit duplicate copies of their application to their Regional Scholarship Programs committee chair and to international headquarters by January of each year.

[1174]
AMBER GRANTS

WomensNet.Net
c/o Christina Lambert
7 Public Market
Rochester, NY 14609
E-mail: chrislambert@frontiernet.net
Web: www.ambergrantsforwomen.com/get-an-amber-grant

Summary To provide funding to women entrepreneurs who start a new business.

Eligibility This funding is available to women who are trying to start small businesses, home-based or online. Applicants must be seeking funds to upgrade equipment, pay for a web site, or meet other small but essential expenses necessary to get a new business off the ground. Selection is based on merit, potential success of the idea, and impact of the grant on the business; formal business plans are not

required. Each month, the organization awards a qualifying grant and posts it online. Open voting selects the annual grantee at the end of the calendar year.

Financial data Qualifying grants are $500. The annual grant is $1,000.

Duration These are 1-time grants.

Additional information This program began in 1998. The application fee is $7.

Number awarded 12 grants are awarded monthly, of which 1 is selected as the annual grantee.

Deadline Applications may be submitted at any time.

[1175]
AMELIA BEHRENS-FURNISS MEMORIAL HARDHAT DIVER TRAINING GRANTS

Women Divers Hall of Fame
43 MacKey Avenue
Port Washington, NY 11050-3628
E-mail: scholarships@wdhof.org
Web: www.wdhof.org/scholarships/scholarships.shtml

Summary To provide financial assistance to women divers who are interested in learning more about hardhat diving.

Eligibility This program is open to women divers of any age and background who wish to begin or further their training in hardhat diving through an approved hardhat dive training program. Applicants should be enrolled in or attending a commercial dive school.

Financial data The grant is $1,000. Funds are paid directly to the training facility.

Duration Training must be completed within 1 year.

Additional information Behrens-Furniss Memorial Hardhat Diver Training Grants.

Number awarded Varies each year; recently, 3 were awarded.

Deadline November of each year.

[1176]
AMELIA EARHART MEMORIAL SCHOLARSHIPS

Ninety-Nines, Inc.
4300 Amelia Earhart Road, Suite A
Oklahoma City, OK 73159
(405) 685-7969   Toll Free: (800) 994-1929
Fax: (405) 685-7985   E-mail: AEChair@ninety-nines.org
Web: www.ninety-nines.org/scholarships.htm

Summary To provide funding to members of the Ninety-Nines (an organization of women pilots) who are interested in advanced flight training or other technical study related to aviation.

Eligibility This program is open to women from any country who have been members of the organization for at least 1 year. They must be interested in 1 of the following 4 types of scholarships: 1) flight training, to complete an additional pilot certificate or rating or pilot training course; 2) jet type rating, to complete type rating certification in any jet; 3) technical training, to complete an aviation or aerospace technical training or certification course. Applicants for flight training scholarships must be a current pilot with the appropriate medical certification and approaching the flight time requirement for the rating or certificate. Applicants for jet type rating scholarships must be a current airline transport pilot with a first-class medical certificate and at least 100 hours of multi-engine flight time or combined multi-engine and turbine time. Applicants for technical training scholarships must be enrolled in a course (e.g., airframe and/or powerplant (A&P) mechanic certificate, dispatcher certificate, air traffic control training program, government or manufacturer's safety training) that is not part of a college degree program. All applicants must submit a 1-page essay about their activities in aviation, their participatin in the Ninety-Nines, their goals in aviation or aerospace, how they have financed their training and education so far, their financial need to complete their training, and how awarding them this scholarship will benefit the Ninety-Nines and the aviation community.

Financial data These scholarships provide payment of all costs to complete the appropriate rating or certificate.

Duration Support is provided until completion of the rating or certificate.

Additional information This program began in 1941.

Number awarded Varies each year; recently, 22 were awarded.

Deadline November of each year.

[1177]
AMELIA EARHART RESEARCH SCHOLAR GRANT

Ninety-Nines, Inc.
Attn: Chair, Research Scholar Grants
4300 Amelia Earhart Road, Suite A
Oklahoma City, OK 73159
(405) 685-7969   Toll Free: (800) 994-1929
Fax: (405) 685-7985   E-mail: AEChair@ninety-nines.org
Web: www.ninety-nines.org/scholarships.htm

Summary To provide funding to scholars interested in expanding knowledge about women in aviation and space.

Eligibility This program is open to scholars who are conducting research on the role of women in aviation and space. Disciplines may include, but are not limited to, biology, business administration, economics, ergonomics, history, human engineering, psychology, or sociology. Applicants may be seeking funding to be used in conjunction with other research activities, such as completion of requirements for an advanced degree or matching funds with other grants to support a program larger than either grant could sponsor independently.

Financial data The amount awarded varies; generally, the grant is at least $1,000.

Duration The grant is awarded periodically.

Number awarded 1 each granting period.

Deadline Deadline not specified.

[1178]
AMERICAN AIRLINES VETERAN'S INITIATIVE SCHOLARSHIP

Women in Aviation International
Attn: Scholarships
Morningstar Airport
3647 State Route 503 South
West Alexandria, OH 45381-9354
(937) 839-4647   Fax: (937) 839-4645
E-mail: scholarships@wai.org
Web: www.wai.org

Summary To provide financial assistance to members of Women in Aviation International (WAI) who are also veterans and interested in earning a degree or certificate in a field related to aviation maintenance.

Eligibility This program is open to WAI members who served honorably in the U.S. armed services and are interested in aviation or aeronautical education or training. Applicants must be enrolled or planning to enroll in an accredited flight school, institution, or college. Along with their application, they must submit a 500-word essay and professional resume that include their aviation history and goals, what they have done for themselves to achieve their goals, where they see themselves in 5 and 10 years, involvement in aviation activities, how the scholarship will help them achieve their objectives, and their present financial need. Selection is based on achievements, teamwork, leadership skills, motivation, and community service involvement.

Financial data The stipend is $5,000.

Duration Funds must be used within 1 year.

Additional information WAI is a nonprofit professional organization dedicated to encouraging women to consider an aviation career and to providing educational outreach activities and networking resources to women active in the industry. This program was established in 2012 by American Airlines.

Number awarded 1 each year.

Deadline November of each year.

[1179]
AMERICAN ASSOCIATION OF OBSTETRICIANS AND GYNECOLOGISTS FOUNDATION RESEARCH AND TRAINING SCHOLARSHIPS

American Association of Obstetricians and Gynecologists
  Foundation
9 Newport Drive, Suite 200
Forest Hill, MD 21050
(443) 640-1051   Fax: (443) 640-1031
E-mail: info@aaogf.org
Web: www.aaogf.org/scholarship.asp

Summary To provide funding to physicians interested in a program of research training in obstetrics and gynecology.

Eligibility Applicants must have an M.D. degree and be eligible for the certification process of the American Board of Obstetrics and Gynecology (ABOG). They must be interested in participating in research training conducted by 1 or more faculty mentors at an academic department of obstetrics and gynecology in the United States or Canada. The research training may be either laboratory-based or clinical, and should focus on fundamental biology, disease mechanisms, interventions or diagnostics, epidemiology, or translational research. Applicants for the scholarship co-sponsored by the Society for Maternal-Fetal Medicine (SMFM) must also be members or associate members of the SMFM. Women and minority candidates are strongly encouraged to apply. Selection is based on the scholarly, clinical, and research qualifications of the candidate; evidence of the candidate's commitment to an investigative career in academic obstetrics and gynecology in the United States or Canada; qualifications of the sponsoring department and mentor; overall quality of the mentoring plan; and quality of the research project.

Financial data The grant is $120,000 per year. Sufficient funds to support travel to the annual fellows' retreat must be set aside. The balance of the funds may be used for salary, technical support, and supplies.

Duration 1 year; may be renewed for 2 additional years, based on satisfactory progress of the scholar.

Additional information Scholars must devote at least 75% of their effort to the program of research training.

Number awarded 2 each year: 1 co-sponsored by ABOG and 1 co-sponsored by SMFM.

Deadline June of each year.

[1180]
AMERICAN ASSOCIATION OF UNIVERSITY WOMEN POSTDOCTORAL RESEARCH LEAVE FELLOWSHIPS

American Association of University Women
Attn: AAUW Educational Foundation
1111 16th Street, N.W.
Washington, DC 20036-4873
(202) 785-7700   Toll Free: (800) 326-AAUW
Fax: (202) 872-1425   TDD: (202) 785-7777
E-mail: aauw@applyists.com
Web: www.aauw.org

Summary To enable American women scholars who have achieved distinction or promise of distinction in their fields of scholarly work to engage in additional research.

Eligibility This program is open to women who have a research doctorate (e.g., Ph.D., Ed.D., D.B.A., D.M.) or an M.F.A. degree as of the application deadline. Applicants must be interested in conducting independent research; preference is given to projects that are not simply a revision of a doctoral dissertation. Fields of study include the arts and humanities, social sciences, and natural sciences. Selection is based on scholarly excellence, quality of project design, originality of project, scholarly significance of project to discipline, feasibility of project and proposed schedule, qualifications of applicant, potential of applicant to make a significant contribution to field, applicant's commitment to women's issues in profession and community, applicant's teaching experience, and applicant's mentoring of other women. U.S. citizenship or permanent resident status is required.

Financial data The stipend is $30,000. Funding is not provided for laboratory supplies and equipment, research assistants, publication costs, travel to professional meetings or seminars, tuition for additional course work, repayment of loans or other personal obligations, or tuition for a dependent's education.

Duration 1 year, beginning in July.

Additional information The filing fee is $45.

Number awarded Varies each year; recently, 12 were awarded.

Deadline November of each year.

[1181]
AMERICAN ASSOCIATION OF UNIVERSITY WOMEN SUMMER/SHORT-TERM RESEARCH PUBLICATION GRANTS

American Association of University Women
Attn: AAUW Educational Foundation
1111 16th Street, N.W.
Washington, DC 20036-4873
(202) 785-7700   Toll Free: (800) 326-AAUW
Fax: (202) 872-1425   TDD: (202) 785-7777
E-mail: aauw@applyists.com
Web: www.aauw.org

Summary To provide summer or short-term fellowships to women scholars interested in conducting postdoctoral research.

Eligibility This program is open to women who are interested in preparing research manuscripts for publication (but not to undertake new research). Applicants may be tenure-track, part-time, or temporary faculty or may be independent scholars or researchers, either new or established. They must have completed a doctoral or M.F.A. degree. U.S. citizenship or permanent resident status is required. Scholars with strong publishing records are discouraged from applying. Selection is based on scholarly excellence, quality of project design, originality of project, scholarly significance of project to discipline, feasibility of project and proposed schedule, qualifications of applicant, potential of applicant to make a significant contribution to field, applicant's commitment to women's issues in profession and community, applicant's teaching experience, and applicant's mentoring of other women.

Financial data The grant is $6,000. Funds may be used for stipends for recipient, clerical and technical support, research assistance related to verification (not basic research), supplies, and expenses. Grants do not cover travel, purchase of equipment, indirect costs, salary increase, or doctoral dissertation research or writing.

Duration 8 weeks; most recipients, especially full-time faculty, use the awards during the summer, but the research may be conducted at any time during the year.

Additional information The filing fee is $40.

Number awarded Varies each year; recently, 17 were awarded.

Deadline November of each year.

[1182]
AMERICAN EPILEPSY SOCIETY JUNIOR INVESTIGATOR RESEARCH AWARD

American Epilepsy Society
135 South LaSalle Street, Suite 2850
Chicago, IL 60603
(312) 883-3800   Fax: (312) 896-5784
E-mail: info@aesnet.org
Web: www.aesnet.org

Summary To provide funding to junior investigators who are interested in conducting research related to epilepsy.

Eligibility This program is open to recently independent investigators who have an M.D., Ph.D., Pharm.D., R.N., or equivalent degree and an academic appointment at the level of assistant professor or equivalent. Applicants must be interested in conducting basic, translational, or clinical epilepsy research, including studies of disease mechanisms or treatments, epidemiological or behavioral studies, the development of new technologies, or health services and outcomes research. Applications are especially encouraged from women, members of minority groups, and people with disabilities. U.S. citizenship is not required, but all research must be conducted in the United States.

Financial data The grant is $50,000 per year for direct costs of research.

Duration 1 year; nonrenewable.

Additional information In addition to the funding provided by the American Epilepsy Society, support is available from the TESS Research Foundation for applications focused on epilepsy due to SLC13A5 mutations; the LGS Foundation for applications focused on Lennox-Gastaut-Syndrome; the PCDH19 Alliance for applications focused on epilepsy due to PCDH19 mutations; the Dravet Syndrome Foundation for applications focused on Dravet Syndrome; Wishes for Elliott for applications focused on epilepsy due to SCN8A mutations; and the TS Alliance for applications focused on epilepsy associated with tuberous sclerosis complex (TSC).

Number awarded Varies each year.

Deadline Letters of intent must be submitted by October of each year; final proposals are due in January.

[1183]
AMERICAN EPILEPSY SOCIETY POSTDOCTORAL RESEARCH FELLOWSHIPS

American Epilepsy Society
135 South LaSalle Street, Suite 2850
Chicago, IL 60603
(312) 883-3800   Fax: (312) 896-5784
E-mail: info@aesnet.org
Web: www.aesnet.org

Summary To provide funding to postdoctoral fellows who are interested in conducting mentored research related to epilepsy.

Eligibility This program is open to postdoctoral fellows who have an M.D., Ph.D., Sc.D., Pharm.D., R.N., or equivalent degree. Applicants must be interested in conducting research with an epilepsy-related theme under the guidance of a mentor with expertise in epilepsy research. They must have a defined research plan and access to institutional resources to conduct the proposed project. Selection is based on the applicant's potential and commitment to develop as an independent and productive epilepsy researcher, academic record, and research experience; the mentor's research qualifications; the research training plan; and the quality of the research facilities, resources, and training opportunities. Applications are especially encouraged from women, members of minority groups, and people with disabilities. U.S. citizenship is not required, but all research must be conducted in the United States.

Financial data Grants range up $45,000, including $44,000 as stipend and $1,000 for travel support and complimentary registration to attend the sponsor's annual meeting.

Duration 1 year; nonrenewable.

Additional information In addition to the funding provided by the American Epilepsy Society, support is available from the TESS Research Foundation for applications focused on epilepsy due to SLC13A5 mutations; the LGS Foundation for applications focused on Lennox-Gastaut-Syndrome; the PCDH19 Alliance for applications focused on epilepsy due to

PCDH19 mutations; the Dravet Syndrome Foundation for applications focused on Dravet Syndrome; Wishes for Elliott for applications focused on epilepsy due to SCN8A mutations; and the TS Alliance for applications focused on epilepsy associated with tuberous sclerosis complex (TSC).

Number awarded Varies each year.

Deadline Letters of intent must be submitted by October of each year; final proposals are due in January.

[1184]
AMERICAN LEGION AUXILIARY EMERGENCY FUND

American Legion Auxiliary
Attn: AEF Program Case Manager
8945 North Meridian Street
Indianapolis, IN 46260
(317) 569-4544   Fax: (317) 569-4502
E-mail: aef@alaforveterans.org
Web: www.alaforveterans.org

Summary To provide funding to members of the American Legion Auxiliary who are facing temporary emergency needs.

Eligibility This program is open to members of the American Legion Auxiliary who have maintained their membership for the immediate past 2 consecutive years and have paid their dues for the current year. Applicants must need emergency assistance for the following purposes: 1) food, shelter, and utilities during a time of financial crisis; 2) food and shelter because of weather-related emergencies and natural disasters; or 3) educational training for eligible members who lack the necessary skills for employment or to upgrade competitive workforce skills. They must have exhausted all other sources of financial assistance, including funds and/or services available through the local Post and/or Unit, appropriate community welfare agencies, or state and federal financial aid for education. Grants are not available to settle already existing or accumulated debts, handle catastrophic illness, resettle disaster victims, or other similar problems.

Financial data The maximum grant is $2,400. Payments may be made directly to the member or to the mortgage company or utility. Educational grants may be paid directly to the educational institution.

Duration Grants are expended over no more than 3 months.

Additional information This program began in 1969. In 1981, it was expanded to include the Displaced Homemaker Fund (although that title is no longer used).

Number awarded Varies each year.

Deadline Applications may be submitted at any time.

[1185]
ANN E. KAMMER MEMORIAL FELLOWSHIP FUND

Marine Biological Laboratory
Attn: Division of Research
7 MBL Street
Woods Hole, MA 02543-1015
(508) 289-7173   Fax: (508) 457-1924
E-mail: research@mbl.edu
Web: www.mbl.edu/research/whitman-awards

Summary To provide funding to women who have faculty positions and wish to conduct summer research at the Marine Biological Laboratory (MBL) in Woods Hole, Massachusetts.

Eligibility This program is open to female faculty members who are interested in conducting summer research at the MBL. Applicants must submit a statement of the potential impact of this award on their career development. Preference is given to investigators working in the neurosciences.

Financial data Grants range from $5,000 to $25,000, typically to cover laboratory rental and/or housing costs. Awardees are responsible for other costs, such as supplies, shared resource usage, affiliated staff who accompany them, or travel.

Duration 4 to 10 weeks during the summer.

Number awarded 1 each year.

Deadline December of each year.

[1186]
ANN WOOD-KELLY MEMORIAL SCHOLARSHIP

Ninety-Nines, Inc.-Eastern New England Chapter
c/o Vanessa Blakeley, Scholarship Chair
77 Corey Street
West Roxbury, MA 02132
E-mail: blakeley.vanessa@gmail.com
Web: www.womenpilotsene.org/scholarships.htm

Summary To provide financial assistance to female residents of New England who are interested in preparing for a career in aviation.

Eligibility This program is open to women who are at least of high school age and reside or study in 1 of the following states: Maine, New Hampshire, Rhode Island, Vermont, Massachusetts, or Connecticut. Applicants must be studying or planning to study in an area of aviation at an accredited college or university, at a college or other flight school, or with a private instructor. They must have at least a private pilot certificate. Along with their application, they must submit a personal letter describing their aviation-related goals, including descriptions of all their aviation-related activities. Selection is based on academic achievement, interest and dedication to a career in aviation, recommendations, involvement in aviation activities (e.g., flying, aviation employment, model airplane building, science fair projects), and financial need.

Financial data The stipend is $1,500.

Duration 1 year.

Number awarded 1 each year.

Deadline January of each year.

[1187]
ANNE BRIDGE BADDOUR AVIATION SCHOLARSHIP

Women in Aviation International
Attn: Scholarships
Morningstar Airport
3647 State Route 503 South
West Alexandria, OH 45381-9354
(937) 839-4647   Fax: (937) 839-4645
E-mail: scholarships@wai.org
Web: www.wai.org

Summary To provide funding to members of Women in Aviation International (WAI) who are interested in completing an Airline Transport Pilot (ATP) certificate, instrument rating, or multiengine rating.

Eligibility This program is open to women who are WAI members and have at least a private pilot certificate with 150 hours of flying time. Applicants must be able to demonstrate "a burning desire to become a professional pilot" and be on track towards an instrument rating, multiengine rating, or the ATP. Along with their application, they must submit a 500-word essay and professional resume that include their aviation history and goals, what they have done for themselves to achieve their goals, where they see themselves in 5 and 10 years, involvement in aviation activities, how the scholarship will help them achieve their objectives, and their present financial need.

Financial data The stipend is $2,000.

Duration Training must be completed within 1 year.

Additional information WAI is a nonprofit professional organization dedicated to encouraging women to consider an aviation career and to providing educational outreach activities and networking resources to women active in the industry.

Number awarded 1 each year.

Deadline November of each year.

[1188]
ANNE FIROR SCOTT MID-CAREER FELLOWSHIP

Southern Association for Women Historians
c/o Michelle Haberland, Executive Secretary
Georgia Southern University
Department of History
1208 Forest Building
P.O. Box 8054
Statesboro, GA 30460-8054
(912) 478-1867   Fax: (912) 478-0377
E-mail: mah@georgiasouthern.edu
Web: www.thesawh.org

Summary To provide funding to mid-career women historians who are working on a second book or equivalent project in southern and/or gender history.

Eligibility This program is open to women who have achieved associate professor status, those who have taught at least 5 years, established public historians, and published independent scholars. Applicants must be members of the Southern Association for Women Historians (SAWH) who have received the Ph.D. or equivalent terminal degree within the past 10 years. They must be seeking funding for a second book or equivalent project that focuses on southern or gender history that will make a significant contribution to either or both of those fields. The fellowship cannot be used to revise a dissertation for publication. Historians working at colleges and universities, particularly teaching institutions, independent scholars, and public historians are especially encouraged to apply.

Financial data The grant is $2,000.

Duration The grant is awarded biennially, in even-numbered years.

Number awarded 1 each even-numbered year.

Deadline April of each even-numbered year.

[1189]
ANNIE JUMP CANNON AWARD IN ASTRONOMY

American Astronomical Society
Attn: Prizes and Awards
2000 Florida Avenue, N.W., Suite 400
Washington, DC 20009-1231
(202) 328-2010   Fax: (202) 234-2560
E-mail: aas@aas.org
Web: www.aas.org

Summary To recognize and reward female postdoctoral scholars for significant research in astronomy.

Eligibility This award is available to North American female astronomers who completed their Ph.D. within the past 5 years. Self-nominations are allowed. Selection is based on completed research and promise for future research.

Financial data The award is $1,500.

Duration The award is presented annually.

Additional information This award was established in 1934 by the American Astronomical Society (AAS). From 1974 through 2004, it was awarded by the American Association of University Women (AAUW) Educational Foundation with the advice of the AAS. Effective in 2005, the AAS resumed administration of the award.

Number awarded 1 each year.

Deadline June of each year.

[1190]
APA/DIVISION 39 GRANT

American Psychological Foundation
750 First Street, N.E.
Washington, DC 20002-4242
(202) 336-5843   Fax: (202) 336-5812
E-mail: foundation@apa.org
Web: www.apa.org/apf/funding/division-39.aspx

Summary To provide funding to psychologists who wish to conduct psychoanalytical research related to underserved populations.

Eligibility This program is open to psychologists who have a demonstrated knowledge of psychoanalytical principles. Applicants may be, but are not required to be, practicing psychoanalytic therapists. Preference is given to graduate students involved in dissertation research, early-career professionals, and/or those who demonstrate a long-term interest in research related to underserved populations. The research may be of an empirical, theoretical, or clinical nature. Selection is based on conformance with stated program goals and qualifications; quality and potential impact of both previous and proposed research projects; originality, innovation, and contribution to the field with both previous and proposed research projects; and applicant's demonstrated interest in research related to underserved populations. The sponsor encourages applications from individuals who represent diversity in race, ethnicity, gender, age, disability, and sexual orientation.

Financial data The grant is $4,000.

Duration 1 year.

Additional information This program, which began in 2014, is sponsored by the American Psychological Association's Division 39 (Psychoanalysis).

Number awarded 1 each year.

Deadline July of each year.

[1191]
APF/DIVISION 29 EARLY CAREER AWARD

American Psychological Foundation
750 First Street, N.E.
Washington, DC 20002-4242
(202) 336-5843   Fax: (202) 336-5812
E-mail: foundation@apa.org
Web: www.apa.org/apf/funding/div-29.aspx

Summary To recognize and reward young psychologists who have made outstanding contributions to psychotherapy.

Eligibility This award is available to psychologists who are no more than 10 years past completion of their doctoral degree. Nominees must have demonstrated promising professional achievement related to psychotherapy theory, practice, research, or training. They must be members of Division 29 (Psychotherapy) of the American Psychological Association. Self-nominations are not accepted. Selection is based on conformance with stated program goals and qualifications and applicant's demonstrated accomplishments and promise. The sponsor encourages nominations of individuals who represent diversity in race, ethnicity, gender, age, disability, and sexual orientation.

Financial data The award is $2,500.

Duration The award is presented annually.

Additional information This award was established in 1981 and named the Jack D. Krasner Memorial Award. It was renamed in 2007.

Number awarded 1 each year.

Deadline Nominations must be submitted by December of each year.

[1192]
APF/DIVISION 37 DIANE J. WILLIS EARLY CAREER AWARD

American Psychological Foundation
750 First Street, N.E.
Washington, DC 20002-4242
(202) 336-5843   Fax: (202) 336-5812
E-mail: foundation@apa.org
Web: www.apa.org/apf/funding/div-37-willis.aspx

Summary To provide funding to young psychologists interested in conducting research or other projects related to children and families.

Eligibility This program is open to young psychologists who completed a doctoral degree (Ed.D., Psy.D., Ph.D.) within the past 10 years. Applicants must be interested in conducting research or other projects that inform, advocate for, and improve the mental health and well-being of children and families, particularly through public policy. The sponsor encourages applications from individuals who represent diversity in race, ethnicity, gender, age, disability, and sexual orientation.

Financial data The grant is $2,000.

Duration 1 year.

Additional information This program, sponsored by Division 37 (Child and Family Policy and Practice) of the American Psychological Association (APA), began in 2013.

Number awarded 1 each year.

Deadline January of each year.

[1193]
APF/F.I.S.H. FOUNDATION VISIONARY GRANT TO DECREASE ETHNIC AND RACIAL DISCRIMINATION IN EDUCATION

American Psychological Foundation
750 First Street, N.E.
Washington, DC 20002-4242
(202) 336-5843   Fax: (202) 336-5812
E-mail: foundation@apa.org
Web: www.apa.org/apf/funding/fish.aspx

Summary To provide funding to psychologists who wish to conduct projects to reduce disparities in education and achievement that result from discrimination.

Eligibility This program is open to early-career (within 10 years of completion of postdoctoral work) psychologists who wish to conduct research, education, and intervention efforts that aim to reduce discrimination in education and achievement that result from discrimination and help minority students achieve their maximum potential. Preference is given to 1) pilot projects that, if successful, would be strong candidates for support from major federal and foundation funding agencies; and 2) "demonstration projects" that promise to generalize broadly to similar settings in other geographical areas and/or to other settings. Selection is based on innovative and potential impact qualities; quality, viability, and promise of proposed work; criticality of proposed funding for proposed work; and clear and comprehensive methodology. The sponsor encourages applications from individuals who represent diversity in race, ethnicity, gender, age, disability, and sexual orientation.

Financial data The grant is $20,000.

Duration 1 year.

Additional information This program is sponsored by the F.I.S.H. (Funding Individual Spiritual Health) Foundation.

Number awarded 1 each year.

Deadline September of each year.

[1194]
ART MEETS ACTIVISM GRANT PROGRAM

Kentucky Foundation for Women
Heyburn Building
332 West Broadway, Suite 1215-A
Louisville, KY 40202-2184
(502) 562-0045   Toll Free: (866) 654-7564
Fax: (502) 561-0420   E-mail: team@kfw.org
Web: www.kfw.org/grants/art-meets-activism

Summary To support women and organizations in Kentucky wishing to conduct artistic activities that will benefit women and girls in the state.

Eligibility This program is open to women artists who have resided in Kentucky for at least 1 year and whose work is feminist in nature and is intentionally focused on social change outcomes. Nonprofit organizations are also eligible if their proposed project is artist driven. Applicants may be seeking funding for a range of artistic activities, including arts education programs focused on women or girls, community participation in the creation of new art forms, community based projects involving new partnerships between artists and activists, and arts-based community projects with social change themes or contents. In the selection process, the following criteria are considered: art work in the sample is strong, highly original, and reflects feminism and social change; the proposed activities will directly benefit women and girls in Kentucky; application and work sample demonstrate applicant's understanding and practice of feminism; application and work sample demonstrate a clear understanding of the relationship between art and social change; work plan, timeline, and budget are clear, detailed, and realistic; and applicant's ability to complete the proposed activities is clearly shown. If applications are of equal artistic merit, priority is given to first-time applicants and those from underrepresented demographic populations (such as lesbians, African Americans, and women with disabilities).

Financial data Grants may range from $1,000 to $7,500, but most average between $3,000 and $5,000.

Duration Up to 1 year.

Additional information The foundation was established in 1985. Funding is not provided for general operating costs for organizations; for-profit organizations; tuition costs or living expenses while working toward a degree; endowment or capital campaigns; activities that do not focus on changing the lives of women in Kentucky; the promotion of religious doctrines; non-art related expenses, such as overdue bills or taxes; or work conducted by artists or organizations that have not resided in Kentucky for at least 1 year.

Number awarded Varies each year; recently, 28 were awarded. A total of $100,000 is available annually.

Deadline February of each year.

[1195]
ART-IN-ED ARTIST'S BOOK RESIDENCY GRANTS

Women's Studio Workshop
722 Binnewater Lane
P.O. Box 489
Rosendale, NY 12472
(845) 658-9133   Fax: (845) 658-9031
E-mail: info@wsworkshop.org
Web: www.wsworkshop.org

Summary To provide a residency and financial support to women interested in producing a limited edition artist's book and working with young people.

Eligibility This program is open to emerging artists who come from different regions of the country and/or diverse cultural backgrounds. Applicants must be interested in spending half their time involved with the design and production of a limited edition artist's book, and the other half working with young people in an arts-in-education program. Along with their application, they must submit a 1-page description of the proposed project, including the media and studio needed; a CD or flash drive with up to 10 images of recent work; a 1-page history of their relevant experience working with youth; a structural dummy of the project; a materials budget; and a resume.

Financial data The program provides a stipend of $350 per week, a $750 materials grant, travel costs up to $250 within the continental United States, and housing while in residence.

Duration 8 to 10 weeks (between February and May with elementary school students or between October and December with high school students).

Number awarded 2 each year.

Deadline November of each year.

[1196]
ARTIST ENRICHMENT GRANT PROGRAM

Kentucky Foundation for Women
Heyburn Building
332 West Broadway, Suite 1215-A
Louisville, KY 40202-2184
(502) 562-0045   Toll Free: (866) 654-7564
Fax: (502) 561-0420   E-mail: team@kfw.org
Web: www.kfw.org/grants/artist-enrichment

Summary To support women in Kentucky who wish to promote positive social change through feminist expression in the arts.

Eligibility This program is open to women who have resided in Kentucky for at least 1 year and are artists at any stage in their career able to demonstrate potential in terms of quality of work and an understanding of the power of art for social change. Applicants must be seeking funding for a range of activities, including artistic development, artist residencies, the exploration of new areas or techniques, or building a body of work. In the selection process, the following criteria are considered: art work in the sample is strong, highly original, and reflects feminism and social change; the proposed activities will further the applicant's development as a feminist social change artist; application and work sample demonstrate applicant's understanding and practice of feminism; application and work sample demonstrate a clear understanding of the relationship between art and social change; work plan, timeline, and budget are clear, detailed, and realistic; and applicant's ability to complete the proposed activities is clearly shown. If applications are of equal artistic merit, priority is given to first-time applicants and those from underrepresented demographic populations (such as lesbians, African Americans, and women with disabilities).

Financial data Grants may range from $1,000 to $5,000, but most average between $2,000 and $4,000.

Duration Up to 1 year.

Additional information The foundation was established in 1985. Funding is not provided for general operating costs for organizations; for-profit organizations; tuition costs or living expenses while working toward a degree; endowment or capital campaigns; projects that do not focus on changing the lives of women in Kentucky; the promotion of religious doctrines; non-art related expenses, such as overdue bills or taxes; or work conducted by artists or organizations that have not resided in Kentucky for at least 1 year.

Number awarded Varies each year; recently, 41 were awarded. A total of $100,000 is available annually.

Deadline August of each year.

[1197]
ARTIST'S BOOK RESIDENCY GRANTS

Women's Studio Workshop
722 Binnewater Lane
P.O. Box 489
Rosendale, NY 12472
(845) 658-9133   Fax: (845) 658-9031
E-mail: info@wsworkshop.org
Web: www.wsworkshop.org

Summary To provide funding and a residency at the Women's Studio Workshop (WSW) to female artists who are interested in producing a book.

Eligibility This program is open to female artists who are interested in producing new books that will have a press run of 50 to 100 copies. Applicants must submit a 1-page description of the proposed project, a description of the media/studios they will need to print the book, a structural dummy, a materials budget, a resume, and 10 images of recent work.

Financial data The program provides a stipend of $350 per week, a $750 materials grant, travel costs up to $250 within the continental United States, and housing while in residence.

Duration 6 to 8 weeks.

Additional information This program provides an opportunity for book artists to come and work in residency at WSW in Rosendale, New York. Selected artists are involved in all aspects of the design and production of their new books. The studio provides technical advice and, when possible, help with editing. Assistance with marketing is also available. The contract requires that 20% of the published books go to the sponsor for archives, exhibition, and display copies; 20% to the artist; and 60% for general marketing.

Number awarded Varies each year.

Deadline November of each year.

[1198]
ARTTABLE MENTORED INTERNSHIPS FOR DIVERSITY IN THE VISUAL ARTS PROFESSIONS

ArtTable Inc.
1 East 53rd Street, Fifth Floor
New York, NY 10022
(212) 343-1735   Fax: (866) 363-4188
E-mail: info@arttable.org
Web: www.arttable.org/summermentoredinternship

Summary To provide an opportunity for women who are from diverse backgrounds to gain mentored work experience during the summer and to prepare for a career as an art professional.

Eligibility This program is open to women who are college seniors, recent graduates, or graduate students and interested in preparing for a career as a visual arts professional (including administrative director, art adviser, art appraiser, art critic, art dealer, art librarian, arts funder, arts lawyer, conservator, curator, editor, educator, fundraiser, management consultant, public relations consultant, writer). Applicants must be from a cultural or ethnic background that is underrepresented in the field. They must be interested in working during the summer with a mentor at an art museum or similar facility. U.S. citizenship or permanent resident status is required.

Financial data The stipend is $3,000. The hosting institution or mentor receives $500 for administrative and other costs.

Duration 8 weeks during the summer.

Additional information This program began in 2000. Support is provided by the Samuel H. Kress Foundation.

Number awarded Varies each year; recently, 5 of these internships were awarded.

Deadline February of each year.

[1199]
ASBMR YOUNG INVESTIGATOR AWARD IN HONOR OF NICOLA C. PARTRIDGE

American Society for Bone and Mineral Research
Attn: Executive Director
2025 M Street, N.W., Suite 800
Washington, DC 20036-3309
(202) 367-1161   Fax: (202) 367-2161
E-mail: asbmr@asbmr.org
Web: www.asbmr.org/young-investigator-awards

Summary To recognize and reward outstanding abstracts submitted by young female investigators to the annual meeting program committee of the American Society for Bone and Mineral Research (ASBMR).

Eligibility This program is open to female investigators who are the first and presenting author of the highest-ranked abstracts within each category for the ASBMR annual meeting. Applicants must have completed a Ph.D. or residency training for an M.D., D.D.S., or equivalent within the past 5 years. Nominations are not accepted; all abstracts submitted to the program committee for presentation at the annual meeting are automatically considered.

Financial data The award is $1,000.

Duration The award is presented annually.

Additional information This program began in 2014.

Number awarded 1 each year.

Deadline April of each year.

[1200]
ASECS WOMEN'S CAUCUS EDITING AND TRANSLATION FELLOWSHIP

American Society for Eighteenth-Century Studies
c/o Wake Forest University
P.O. Box 7867
Winston-Salem, NC 27109
(336) 727-4694   Fax: (336) 727-4697
E-mail: asecs@wfu.edu
Web: asecs.press.jhu.edu

Summary To provide funding to postdoctoral scholars working on an editing or translating project that deals with women's issues in the 18th century.

Eligibility This program is open to members of the American Society for Eighteenth-Century Studies (ASECS) who are working on an editing or translating project. Applicants must have a Ph.D. or be an emeritae/i faculty who does not already have professional support for the project. The project must translate and/or edit works by 18th century women writers or works that significantly advance understanding of women's experiences in the 18th century or offer a feminist analysis of an aspect of 18th-century culture and/or society.

Financial data The grant is $1,000.

Duration The grant is offered annually.

Additional information This award, offered by the Women's Caucus of the ASECS, was first presented in 2004. The recipient is asked to submit a brief written report on the progress of the project 1 year after receiving the award and, wherever possible, will serve on the award committee in the following year.

Number awarded 1 each year.

Deadline January of each year.

[1201]
ASM CAREER DEVELOPMENT GRANTS FOR POSTDOCTORAL WOMEN

American Society for Microbiology
Attn: Membership Board
1752 N Street, N.W.
Washington, DC 20036-2804
(202) 942-9253   Fax: (202) 942-9346
E-mail: adempsey@asmusa.org
Web: www.asm.org

Summary To provide funding for career development activities to postdoctoral female members of the American Society for Microbiology (ASM).

Eligibility This program is open to women who have a doctoral degree, are currently performing postdoctoral work in microbiology at an institution in the United States, have no more than 5 years of relevant research experience since completing their doctorate, and are ASM members. Applicants must be seeking funding to travel to a meeting, visit another laboratory, take a course in a geographically distant place, or other purpose to advance their career. Along with their application, they must submit a statement that describes their academic accomplishments, career goals, and intended use of the grant to aid their career.

Financial data The grant is $1,500.

Duration Grants are awarded annually.

Additional information This program began in 2006.

Number awarded 3 each year.

Deadline January of each year.

[1202]
ASSOCIATION FOR WOMEN IN SPORTS MEDIA MID-CAREER GRANT

Association for Women in Sports Media
Attn: Vice President of Professional Development
7742 Spalding Drive, Suite 377
Norcross, GA 30092
E-mail: midcareergrant@awsmonline.org
Web: www.awsmonline.org

Summary To provide funding to members of the Association for Women in Sports Media (AWSM) who are interested in additional training.

Eligibility This program is open to AWSM members who are interested in obtaining additional training, as through on online journalism seminar or video production class. Applicants must submit a resume that includes their professional experience, formal education, professional development seminars or workshops, or other relevant training experiences; a 500-word statement on how this grant would help them; and a description of how the grant would be used.

Financial data Grants range from $500 to $1,500.

Duration These are 1-time grants.

Additional information This program began in 2008 with funding from the Ethics and Excellence in Journalism Foundation.

Number awarded 2 each year.

Deadline November of each year.

[1203]
ASTRONOMY AND ASTROPHYSICS POSTDOCTORAL FELLOWSHIPS

National Science Foundation
Directorate for Mathematical and Physical Sciences
Attn: Division of Astronomical Sciences
4201 Wilson Boulevard, Room 1080n
Arlington, VA 22230
(703) 292-5039   Fax: (703) 292-9034
TDD: (800) 281-8749   E-mail: hgupta@nsf.gov
Web: www.nsf.gov

Summary To provide funding to recent doctoral recipients in astronomy or astrophysics who are interested in pursuing a program of research and education in the United States or at eligible foreign sites.

Eligibility This program is open to U.S. citizens, nationals, and permanent residents who completed a Ph.D. in astronomy or astrophysics during the previous 5 years. Applicants must be interested in a program of research of an observational, instrumental, or theoretical nature, especially research that is facilitated or enabled by new ground-based capability in radio, optical/IR, or solar astrophysics. Research may be conducted at a U.S. institution of higher education; a national center, facility, or institute funded by the National Science Foundation (NSF), such as the Kavli Institute for Theoretical Physics; a U.S. nonprofit organization with research and educational missions; and/or an international site operated by a U.S. organization eligible for NSF funding, such as Cerro Tololo InterAmerican Observatory. The proposal must include a coherent program of educational activities, such as teaching a course each year at the host institution or an academic institution with ties to the host institution, developing educational materials, or engaging in a significant program of outreach or general education. In the selection process, consideration is given to the achievement of societally relevant outcomes, including full participation of women, persons with disabilities, and underrepresented minorities.

Financial data Grants up to $100,000 per year are available, including a stipend of $69,000 per year paid directly to the fellow and an allowance of $31,000 per year to cover expenses directly related to the research, facilities and other institutional resources, and fringe benefits.

Duration Up to 3 years.

Number awarded 8 to 9 each year.

Deadline October of each year.

[1204]
ATMOSPHERIC AND GEOSPACE SCIENCES POSTDOCTORAL RESEARCH FELLOWSHIPS

National Science Foundation
Directorate for Geosciences
Attn: Division of Atmospheric and Geospace Sciences
4201 Wilson Boulevard, Room 775S
Arlington, VA 22230
(703) 292-8520   Fax: (703) 292-9022
TDD: (800) 281-8749   E-mail: amadams@nsf.gov
Web: www.nsf.gov

Summary To provide funding to postdoctoral scientists interested in conducting research in the United States or any other country related to activities of the National Science Foundation (NSF) Division of Atmospheric and Geospace Sciences.

Eligibility This program is open to U.S. citizens, nationals, and permanent residents who received a Ph.D. within the past 3 years. Applicants must be interested in conducting a research project that is relevant to the activities of NSF Division of Atmospheric and Geospace Sciences: studies of the physics, chemistry, and dynamics of Earth's upper and lower atmosphere and its space environment; research on climate processes and variations; or studies to understand the natural global cycles of gases and particles in Earth's atmosphere. The project should be conducted at an institution (college or university, private nonprofit institute or museum, government installation, or laboratory) in the United States or abroad other than the applicant's Ph.D.-granting institution. In the selection process, consideration is given to the achievement of societally relevant outcomes, including full participation of women, persons with disabilities, and underrepresented minorities.

Financial data Grants are $86,000 per year, including a stipend of $58,000 per year, a research allowance of $19,000 per year, and a fringe benefit allowance of $9,000 per year. For fellows who wish to conduct research abroad, an additional supplement of $10,000 is provided.

Duration 2 years.

Number awarded 10 each year.

Deadline January of each year.

[1205]
ATMOSPHERIC SCIENCES ASCENT AWARD

American Geophysical Union
Attn: Atmospheric Sciences Section
2000 Florida Avenue, N.W.
Washington, DC 20009-1277
(202) 462-6900   Toll Free: (800) 966-2481
Fax: (202) 328-0566   E-mail: leadership@agu.org
Web: atmospheres.agu.org/awards/ascent-award

Summary To recognize and reward mid-career members of the American Geophysical Union (AGU) who have conducted outstanding research in atmospheric sciences.

Eligibility This award is available to AGU members who completed their Ph.D. between 8 and 20 years previously and are employed in academic, government, or the private sector. Nominees must demonstrate excellence in research and leadership in the field of atmospheric sciences. Nominations of women and underrepresented minorities are encouraged.

Financial data The award consists of $1,000, a certificate, and dinner during the annual meeting of the Atmospheric Sciences Section of the AGU.

Duration The award is presented annually.

Additional information These awards were first presented in 2012.

Number awarded Up to 4 each year.

Deadline April of each year.

[1206]
AWHONN NOVICE RESEARCHER AWARD

Association of Women's Health, Obstetric and Neonatal
 Nurses
Attn: Research Grants Program
1800 M Street, N.W., Suite 740S
Washington, DC 20036
(202) 261-2402   Toll Free: (800) 673-8499, ext. 2402
Fax: (202) 728-0575
E-mail: researchprograms@awhonn.org
Web: www.awhonn.org/?AvailableGrants

Summary To provide funding for small research projects to members of the Association of Women's Health, Obstetric and Neonatal Nurses (AWHONN) who qualify as novice researchers.

Eligibility This program is open to members of the association who have at least a master's degree or are currently enrolled in a master's program and completing a thesis or clinical research project. Applicants must be interested in beginning areas of study, investigating clinical issues, and/or launching a pilot study. They must identify a senior researcher who has agreed to serve as mentor and who submits a letter of support describing the role he or she will be implementing.

Financial data The grant is $5,000. Funds may not be used for indirect costs, tuition, computer hardware or printers, conference attendance, or salary for the principal investigator or other investigators.

Duration 1 year.

Number awarded 1 each year.

Deadline November of each year.

[1207]
B. JUNE WEST RECRUITMENT GRANT

Delta Kappa Gamma Society International-Theta State
 Organization
c/o Sharron Stepro, Committee on Professional Affairs
 Chair
10038 San Marcos Court
Las Cruces, NM 88007-8954
(575) 541-8922   E-mail: jsrhett@comcast.net
Web: thetastatenmdkg.weebly.com

Summary To provide financial assistance to women in New Mexico who are interested in preparing for a career as a teacher.

Eligibility This program is open to women residents of New Mexico who are 1) graduating high school seniors planning to go into education; 2) college students majoring in education; or 3) teachers needing educational assistance. Applicants must submit a list of activities in which they are involved, 3 letters of recommendation, a list of achievements and awards, and a statement of their educational goal and

how this grant would be of assistance to them. Financial need is not considered in the selection process.

Financial data A stipend is awarded (amount not specified).

Duration 1 year.

Number awarded 1 or more each year.

Deadline February of each year.

[1208]
BAILEY'S WOMEN'S PRIZE FOR FICTION

Booktrust
45 East Hill
London SW18 2QZ
England
44 20 8516 2977   Fax: 44 20 8516 2978
E-mail: baileyswomensprize@booktrust.org.uk
Web: www.womensprizeforfiction.co.uk

Summary To recognize and reward the most outstanding novels by women from any country that are written in English and published in the United Kingdom.

Eligibility Eligible to be considered for this prize are novels written by women (of any nationality) in English and published in the United Kingdom during the 12 months prior to March 31 of the year of the award. Submissions may also have been published in other countries, including the United States, as long as its first U.K. publication was within the prescribed time period. Ineligible works include books of short stories, novellas (stories between 12,000 and 30,000 words), and translations of books originally written in other languages.

Financial data The prize is 30,000 pounds and a bronze figurine known as the "Bessie."

Duration The prize is awarded annually.

Additional information This prize, first awarded in 1996, is the United Kingdom's largest annual literary award for a single novel. It was formerly known as the Orange Broadband Prize for Fiction but since 2014 has been sponsored by Bailey's.

Number awarded 1 each year.

Deadline Deadline not specified.

[1209]
BARNARD WOMEN POETS PRIZE

Barnard College
Attn: Department of English
417 Barnard Hall
3009 Broadway
New York, NY 10027-6598
(212) 854-2116   Fax: (212) 854-9498
E-mail: english@barnard.edu
Web: english.barnard.edu/women-poets/contest

Summary To recognize and reward outstanding unpublished poetry written by American women.

Eligibility This program is open to women writers who have already published 1 book of poetry (in an edition of 500 copies or more) and are seeking a publisher for a second collection. Manuscripts that are under option to another publisher are not eligible. Applicants should submit 3 copies of a book-length manuscript (the page limit is not specified).

Financial data The prize is $1,500 and publication of the manuscript.

Duration The prize is awarded biennially.

Additional information This prize was first awarded in 2003. Winning submissions are published by W.W. Norton & Co. The entry fee is $20.

Number awarded 1 each odd-numbered year.

Deadline October of each even-numbered year.

[1210]
BECKY TOPELSON SCHOLARSHIPS

JEWISHcolorado
Attn: Women's Philanthropy Director
300 South Dahlia Street, Suite 300
Denver, CO 80246-8118
(303) 316-6459 Fax: (303) 322-8328
E-mail: slangert@JEWISHcolorado.org
Web: www.jewishcolorado.org/scholarships

Summary To provide funding for professional development activities in Colorado or Israel to young Jewish women.

Eligibility This program is open to female residents of Colorado between 21 and 45 years of age. Applicants must have been identified as a leader or someone with leadership potential in the Jewish community. They must be interested in attending nonprofit Jewish conferences, missions to Israel, young adult programs, or any other Jewish program. The focus of the program must be on leadership development, not professional development.

Financial data Grants range up to $1,000. Funds may be used only to subsidize registration fees for the conference, not the hotel or airfare.

Duration These are 1-time grants.

Additional information This sponsor was formerly named the Allied Jewish Federation of Colorado.

Number awarded 1 or more each year.

Deadline August of each year.

[1211]
BEE WINKLER WEINSTEIN FUND

Stonewall Community Foundation
Attn: Grants
446 West 33rd Street, Sixth Floor
New York, NY 10001
(212) 367-1155 Fax: (212) 367-1157
E-mail: grants@stonewallfoundation.org
Web: www.stonewallfoundation.org/grants/scholarships

Summary To provide funding to lesbians and other women who wish to become self-sufficient but face obstacles because of their sexual identity.

Eligibility This program is open to lesbians, female bisexuals, and transgender individuals (male to female). Applicants must be between 18 and 25 years of age and able to demonstrate financial need. They must be striving to become self-sufficient but lack funding and other support from their family because of sexual or gender identity. Examples of eligible needs include GED tutoring, work uniforms, legal name changes, college application fees, domestic needs (e.g., bedding, rental security deposits), and licensing and testing fees. Support for tuition for vocational or technical training is available, but the cost of academic tuition for college or graduate school is not covered.

Financial data Grants have ranged from $35 to $1,500. Funds are made payable to 501(C)3 organizations.

Duration These are 1-time grants.

Number awarded Varies each year.

Deadline Applications may be submitted at any time.

[1212]
BERKSHIRE CONFERENCE FIRST BOOK PRIZES

Berkshire Conference of Women Historians
c/o Terri Snyder
California State University at Fullerton
University Hall 416
800 North State College Boulevard
P.O. Box 34080
Fullerton, CA 92834-9480
(657) 278-3748 E-mail: snyder@fullerton.edu
Web: www.berksconference.org/prizes

Summary To recognize and reward women who have written outstanding first books in history.

Eligibility This prize is awarded for the best first book written by a woman normally resident in North America during the preceding year. Prizes are awarded in 2 categories: 1) books in any historical field; and 2) books that deal substantially with the history of women, gender, and/or sexuality. Textbooks, juveniles, fiction, poetry, collections of essays, and documentary collections are not eligible.

Financial data The prize is $1,000.

Duration The prize is awarded annually.

Number awarded 2 each year: 1 in each category.

Deadline October of each year.

[1213]
BILL WHITEHEAD AWARD FOR LIFETIME ACHIEVEMENT

Publishing Triangle
332 Bleecker Street, D36
New York, NY 10014
E-mail: publishingtriangle@gmail.com
Web: www.publishingtriangle.org/awards.asp

Summary To recognize and reward writers who have dealt openly with gay or lesbian issues.

Eligibility This is a lifetime achievement award. It is presented to writers whose body of work makes a significant contribution to gay and lesbian literature. The award alternates between women (in even-numbered years) and men (in odd-numbered years). Only members of the Publishing Triangle may nominate candidates for the award.

Financial data The award is $3,000.

Duration The award is presented annually.

Additional information The Publishing Triangle is an association of lesbians and gay men in publishing. This award was first presented in 1989.

Number awarded 1 each year.

Deadline November of each year.

[1214]
BIRDELLA ROSS SCHOLARSHIP

Delta Kappa Gamma Society International-Tau State
  Organization
c/o Mary Kay Feltes, Scholarship Committee Chair
P.O. Box 51
Owatonna, MN 55060
Web: dkgmn.weebly.com/forms.html

Summary To provide financial assistance to members of
Delta Kappa Gamma Society International in Minnesota who
are interested in pursuing advanced study or training.

Eligibility This program is open to residents of Minnesota
who have been members of Delta Kappa Gamma (an honorary society of women educators) for at least 2 years. Applicants must be interested in working on a graduate degree,
obtaining licensure, or attending a special workshop. Along
with their application, they must submit a 100-word essay
describing their short- and long-term goals and a short outline of the proposed program for which they are seeking this
scholarship.

Financial data The stipend is $4,000. Funds are paid
directly to the college or university.

Duration 1 year.

Number awarded 1 each odd-numbered year.

Deadline February of each odd-numbered year.

[1215]
B.K. KRENZER MEMORIAL REENTRY SCHOLARSHIP

Society of Women Engineers
Attn: Scholarship Selection Committee
203 North LaSalle Street, Suite 1675
Chicago, IL 60601-1269
(312) 596-5223   Toll Free: (877) SWE-INFO
Fax: (312) 644-8557   E-mail: scholarships@swe.org
Web: societyofwomenengineers.swe.org

Summary To provide financial assistance to women interested in returning to college or graduate school to study engineering or computer science.

Eligibility This program is open to women who are planning to enroll at an ABET-accredited 4-year college or university. Applicants must have been out of the engineering workforce and school for at least 2 years and must be planning to
return as an undergraduate or graduate student to work on a
degree in computer science or engineering. Selection is
based on merit. Preference is given to engineers who already
have a degree and are planning to reenter the engineering
workforce after a period of temporary retirement.

Financial data The stipend is $2,500.

Duration 1 year.

Additional information This program began in 1996.

Number awarded 1 each year.

Deadline February of each year.

[1216]
BOEING COMPANY CAREER ENHANCEMENT SCHOLARSHIP

Women in Aviation International
Attn: Scholarships
Morningstar Airport
3647 State Route 503 South
West Alexandria, OH 45381-9354
(937) 839-4647   Fax: (937) 839-4645
E-mail: scholarships@wai.org
Web: www.wai.org

Summary To provide financial assistance to members of
Women in Aviation International (WAI) who are active in aerospace and need financial support to advance their career.

Eligibility This program is open to WAI members who wish
to advance their career in the aerospace industry in the fields
of engineering, technology development, or management.
Applicants may be 1) full-time or part-time employees working in the aerospace industry or a related field; or 2) students
working on an aviation-related degree who are at least sophomores and have a GPA of 2.5 or higher. Along with their
application, they must submit a 500-word essay and professional resume that include their aviation history and goals,
what they have done for themselves to achieve their goals,
where they see themselves in 5 and 10 years, involvement in
aviation activities, how the scholarship will help them achieve
their objectives, and their present financial need.

Financial data The stipend is $2,500.

Duration 1 year.

Additional information WAI is a nonprofit professional
organization dedicated to encouraging women to consider an
aviation career and to providing educational outreach activities and networking resources to women active in the industry. This program is sponsored by the Boeing Company.

Number awarded 2 each year.

Deadline November of each year.

[1217]
BRUCE AND JANE WALSH GRANT IN MEMORY OF JOHN HOLLAND

American Psychological Foundation
750 First Street, N.E.
Washington, DC 20002-4242
(202) 336-5843   Fax: (202) 336-5812
E-mail: foundation@apa.org
Web: www.apa.org/apf/funding/walsh.aspx

Summary To provide funding to psychologists who wish to
investigate how personality, culture, and environment influence work behavior and health.

Eligibility This program is open to early-career (within 10
years of completion of postdoctoral work) psychologists who
wish to conduct scholarly or applied research and/or educational activities investigating how personality, culture, and
environment influence work behavior and health (mental and
physical. Preference is given to 1) pilot projects that, if successful, would be strong candidates for support from major
federal and foundation funding agencies; and 2) "demonstration projects" that promise to generalize broadly to similar settings in other geographical areas and/or to other settings.
Selection is based on the applicant's demonstrated competence and capability to execute the proposed work. The spon-

sor encourages applications from individuals who represent diversity in race, ethnicity, gender, age, disability, and sexual orientation.

Financial data The grant is $13,000.

Duration 1 year.

Additional information This program began in 2015.

Number awarded 1 each year.

Deadline September of each year.

[1218]
BYRD FELLOWSHIP PROGRAM

Ohio State University
Byrd Polar and Climate Research Center
Attn: Fellowship Committee
Scott Hall Room 108
1090 Carmack Road
Columbus, OH 43210-1002
(614) 292-6531   Fax: (614) 292-4697
E-mail: contact@bpcrc.osu.edu
Web: bpcrc.osu.edu/byrdfellow

Summary To provide funding to postdoctorates interested in conducting research on the Arctic or Antarctic areas at Ohio State University.

Eligibility This program is open to postdoctorates of superior academic background who are interested in conducting advanced research on either Arctic or Antarctic problems at the Byrd Polar and Climate Research Center at Ohio State University. Applicants must have received their doctorates within the past 5 years. Along with their application, they must submit a description of the specific research to be conducted during the fellowship and a curriculum vitae. Women, minorities, Vietnam-era veterans, disabled veterans, and individuals with disabilities are particularly encouraged to apply.

Financial data The stipend is $44,000 per year; an allowance of $5,000 for research and travel is also provided.

Duration 18 months.

Additional information This program was established by a major gift from the Byrd Foundation in memory of Rear Admiral Richard Evelyn Byrd and Marie Ames Byrd, his wife. Except for field work or other research activities requiring absence from campus, fellows are expected to be in residence at the university for the duration of the program.

Number awarded 1 each year.

Deadline March of each year.

[1219]
CAREER AWARDS FOR MEDICAL SCIENTISTS

Burroughs Wellcome Fund
21 T.W. Alexander Drive, Suite 100
P.O. Box 13901
Research Triangle Park, NC 27709-3901
(919) 991-5100   Fax: (919) 991-5160
E-mail: info@bwfund.org
Web: www.bwfund.org

Summary To provide funding to biomedical scientists in the United States and Canada who require assistance to make the transition from postdoctoral training to faculty appointment.

Eligibility This program is open to citizens, permanent residents, and temporary residents of the United States and Canada who are authorized to work in the country and have

an M.D., D.D.S., D.O., or D.V.M. degree and from 2 to 11 years of postdoctoral research experience. Candidates who work in reproductive science are encouraged to apply. Applicants must be interested in a program of research training in the area of basic biomedical, disease-oriented, or translational research. Training must take place at a degree-granting medical school, graduate school, hospital, or research institute in the United States or Canada. The sponsor encourages applications from women and underrepresented minorities (Blacks or African Americans, Hispanics or Latinos, Native Americans, Native Hawaiians, or Alaskan Natives).

Financial data The stipend is $140,000 per year.

Duration 5 years.

Additional information This program began in 1995 as Career Awards in the Biomedical Sciences (CABS). It was revised to its current format in 2006 as a result of the NIH K99/R00 Pathway to Independence program. As the CABS, the program provided more than $100 million in support to 241 U.S. and Canadian scientists. Awardees are required to devote at least 75% of their time to research-related activities.

Number awarded Varies each year: recently, 10 were granted.

Deadline September of each year.

[1220]
CAREER DEVELOPMENT AWARDS IN DIABETES RESEARCH

Juvenile Diabetes Research Foundation International
Attn: Senior Director, Research Administration
26 Broadway, 14th Floor
New York, NY 10004
(212) 479-7519   Toll Free: (800) 533-CURE
Fax: (212) 785-9595   E-mail: emilligan@jdrf.org
Web: grantcenter.jdrf.org

Summary To assist young scientists of any nationality to develop into independent investigators in diabetes-related research.

Eligibility This program is open to postdoctorates early in their faculty careers who show promise as diabetes researchers. Applicants must have received their first doctoral (M.D., Ph.D., D.M.D., D.V.M., or equivalent) degree at least 3 but not more than 7 years previously. They may not have an academic position at the associate professor, professor, or equivalent level, but they must be a faculty member (instructor or assistant professor) at a university, health science center, or comparable institution with strong, well-established research and training programs. The proposed research must relate to Type 1 diabetes, but it may be basic or clinical. There are no citizenship requirements. Applications are encouraged from women, members of minority groups underrepresented in the sciences, and people with disabilities. The proposed research may be conducted at foreign or domestic, for-profit or non-profit, or public or private institutions, including universities, colleges, hospitals, laboratories, units of state or local government, or eligible agencies of the federal government. Selection is based on the applicant's perceived ability and potential for a career in Type 1 diabetes research, the caliber of the proposed research, and the quality and commitment of the host institution.

Financial data The total award may be up to $150,000 each year. Indirect costs cannot exceed 10%.

Duration Up to 5 years.

Additional information Fellows must spend up to 75% of their time in research.

Number awarded Varies each year; recently, 2 were awarded.

Deadline July of each year.

[1221]
CAROL TYLER AWARD

International Precious Metals Institute
5101 North 12th Avenue, Suite C
Pensacola, FL 32504
(850) 476-1156   Fax: (850) 476-1548
E-mail: mail@ipmi.org
Web: www.ipmi.org/awards/index.cfm

Summary To recognize and reward women who have a record of outstanding achievement in the science and technology of precious metals.

Eligibility This award is available to women who are graduate students or currently employed in industry or academia. Nominees must have made outstanding theoretical and experimental contributions to the science and technology of precious metals. They may be residents of any country.

Financial data The award is $5,000 and a certificate.

Duration The award is presented annually.

Additional information This award was first presented in 2011.

Number awarded 1 each year.

Deadline January of each year.

[1222]
CAROLINE CRAIG AUGUSTYN AND DAMIAN AUGUSTYN AWARD IN DIGESTIVE CANCER

American Gastroenterological Association
Attn: AGA Research Foundation
Research Awards Manager
4930 Del Ray Avenue
Bethesda, MD 20814-2512
(301) 222-4012   Fax: (301) 654-5920
E-mail: awards@gastro.org
Web: www.gastro.org

Summary To provide funding to junior investigators interested in conducting research related to digestive cancer.

Eligibility Applicants must have an M.D., Ph.D., or equivalent degree and a full-time faculty position at an accredited North American institution. They must have received an NIH K series or other federal or non-federal career development award of at least 4 years duration, but may not have received an R01 or equivalent award. For M.D. applicants, no more than 7 years may have elapsed following the completion of clinical training, and for Ph.D. applicants no more than 7 years may have elapsed since the completion of their degree. Individual membership in the American Gastroenterology Association (AGA) is required. The proposal must relate to the pathogenesis, prevention, diagnosis, or treatment of digestive cancer. Women and underrepresented minority investigators are strongly encouraged to apply. Selection is based on the qualifications of the candidate; the novelty, feasibility, and significance of their research; and their potential for an independent research career.

Financial data The grant is $40,000. Funds may be used for salary, supplies, or equipment. Indirect costs are not allowed.

Duration 1 year.

Number awarded 1 each year.

Deadline January of each year.

[1223]
CARRIE CHAPMAN CATT PRIZE FOR RESEARCH ON WOMEN AND POLITICS

Iowa State University
Attn: Carrie Chapman Catt Center for Women and Politics
309 Carrie Chapman Catt Hall
2224 Osborn Drive
Ames, IA 50011-4009
(515) 294-3181   Fax: (515) 294-3741
E-mail: cattcntr@iastate.edu
Web: cattcenter.las.iastate.edu

Summary To recognize and reward outstanding research in the area of women and politics.

Eligibility This competition is open to scholars at all levels, including graduate students and junior faculty, who are planning to conduct research in the area of women and politics. Applicants must submit a detailed description of their research project, including 1) its purpose and content; 2) a discussion of relevant theory, contributions to literature in the field, and methodology; 3) a statement on how this prize will contribute to the research project; 4) a timetable for completion of the project; and 5) a bibliography. They also must submit a 1-page biographical statement. Research projects can address the annual conference theme or any other topic related to women and politics.

Financial data Prizes are $2,000 for winners or $1,000 for honorable mention. All prize-winners may also receive travel expenses to Des Moines, Iowa where awards are presented at the annual conference of the Carrie Chapman Catt Center for Women and Politics.

Duration The prizes are awarded annually.

Number awarded Up to 4 winners and up to 2 honorable mentions are selected each year.

Deadline November of each year.

[1224]
CATHARINE STIMPSON PRIZE FOR OUTSTANDING FEMINIST SCHOLARSHIP

Signs: Journal of Women in Culture and Society
Northeastern University
c/o Suzanna Walter
263 Holmes Hall
360 Huntington Avenue
Boston, M 02115
(617) 373-5837   Fax: (617) 373-4373
E-mail: signs@neu.edu
Web: www.journals.uchicago.edu

Summary To recognize and reward authors of outstanding papers in feminist scholarship.

Eligibility This competition is open to feminist scholars who are less than 7 years since receipt of their terminal degree. Applicants must submit a paper, up to 10,000 words in length, on a topic in the field of interdisciplinary feminist scholarship.

Financial data The prize is $1,000.

Duration The prize is presented biennially, in odd-numbered years.

Number awarded 1 each odd-numbered year.

Deadline February of each even-numbered year.

[1225]
CATHERINE PRELINGER AWARD

Coordinating Council for Women in History
c/o Sandra Dawson, Executive Director
Northern Illinois University
Department of History and Women's Studies
715 Zulauf Hall
DeKalb, IL 60115
(815) 895-2624   E-mail: Prelingeraward@theccwh.org
Web: www.theccwh.org

Summary To provide funding to members of the Coordinating Council for Women in History (CCWH) for a project that focuses on women's roles in history.

Eligibility This program is open to members of CCWH whose academic path has not followed the traditional pattern of uninterrupted study. Applicants must hold either A.B.D. status or a Ph.D. and be engaged in scholarship that is historical in nature, although their degree may be in related fields. They must submit a description of a project they propose to undertake with this award, including the work they intend to complete, the schedule they have developed, the sources they intend to use, and the contribution the work will make to women in history. Independent and non-academic scholars are encouraged to apply.

Financial data The grant is $20,000.

Duration 1 year.

Additional information This program began in 1998.

Number awarded 1 each year.

Deadline May of each year.

[1226]
CELIA M. HOWARD FELLOWSHIP

Illinois Federation of Business Women's Clubs
c/o Fayrene Wright, Howard Fellowship Fund Committee
  Chair
804 East Locust Street
Robinson, IL 62454
(618) 546-1233   E-mail: fayrene26@gmail.com
Web: www.celiamhowardfellowship.com

Summary To provide funding to women in Illinois who are interested in working on a graduate degree in specified fields at eligible universities.

Eligibility This program is open to Illinois women who are U.S. citizens; have been Illinois residents for at least the past 2 years; have earned a bachelor's degree with at least 12 hours of undergraduate work in economics, history, and/or political science; and have a GPA of 3.0 or higher. A personal interview may be required. Applicants must be planning to study for a master's degree in administration of justice at Southern Illinois University at Carbondale or Edwardsville; a J.D. degree at the University of Illinois College of Law at Urbana-Champaign; a master's degree in diplomacy at the Fletcher School of Law and Diplomacy in Medford, Massachusetts; or a master's degree in international studies, modern languages, or world business at the Garvin School of

International Management in Glendale, Arizona. Selection is based on financial need, previous graduate study, practical business experience in government, and leadership experience.

Financial data Awards normally pay full tuition and recently averaged $16,250 per year. Funds are paid directly to the recipient's school.

Duration 1 year; renewable.

Additional information This program began in 1948.

Number awarded Varies each year; recently, 8 were awarded.

Deadline November of each year.

[1227]
CENTER FOR ADVANCED STUDY IN THE BEHAVIORAL SCIENCES FELLOWSHIPS

Center for Advanced Study in the Behavioral Sciences
Attn: Secretary and Program Coordinator
75 Alta Road
Stanford, CA 94305-8090
(650) 736-0100   Fax: (650) 736-0221
E-mail: casbs-info@casbs.org
Web: casbs.stanford.edu/fellowships

Summary To provide funding to behavioral scientists who are interested in conducting research at Stanford University's Center for Advanced Study in the Behavioral Sciences.

Eligibility Eligible to be nominated for this fellowship are scientists and scholars from this country or abroad who show exceptional accomplishment or promise in the core social and behavioral disciplines: anthropology, economics, history, political science, psychology, or sociology; applications are also accepted from scholars in a wide range of humanistic disciplines, communications, education, linguistics, and the biological, computer, health, and natural sciences. Selection is based on standing in the field rather than on the merit of a particular project under way at a given time. A special effort is made to promote diversity among the scholars by encouraging participation from groups that often have been overlooked in academia: women, minorities, international scholars, and scholars from a wide variety of colleges and universities.

Financial data The stipend is based on the fellow's regular salary for the preceding year, with a cap of $73,000. In most cases, the fellow contributes to the cost of the stipend with support from sabbatical or other funding source.

Duration From 9 to 11 months.

Additional information This program partners with the Berggruen Institute to select fellows whose work focuses on understanding technological, social, and cultural changes that may radically transform humanity; the American Council of Learned Societies to participate in the Frederick Burkhardt Residential Fellowship Program; the William T. Grant Foundation to select scholars whose work emphasizes reducing inequality; the Mindset Scholars Network which hosts a fellow who is interested in interdisciplinary scholarship on mindsets and serving in a leadership role in the Mindset research community; the Presence-CASBS Fellowship that addresses focus areas of harnessing technology for the human experience in medicine, studying and advocating for the patient-physician relationship, and reducing medical errors; the Stanford Cyber Initiative which selects a fellow who will be engaged in producing policy-relevant research on the integration of cyber technologies in our ways of life and informing debate about urgent cyber issues; and the National Applied Research Laboratories of Taiwan which selects a fellow in the behavioral and social sciences from Taiwan. Fellows must be in residence in a community within 10 miles of the center for the duration of the program (that requirement excludes San Francisco, Berkeley, and San Jose, for example).

Number awarded Approximately 45 each year.

Deadline November of each year.

[1228]
CENTER FOR THE EDUCATION OF WOMEN VISITING SCHOLAR PROGRAM

University of Michigan
Attn: Center for the Education of Women
330 East Liberty Street
Ann Arbor, MI 48104-2289
(734) 764-6343   Fax: (734) 998-6203
E-mail: bsulliva@umich.edu
Web: www.cew.umich.edu/research/vs

Summary To provide funding to scholars from any country interested in conducting research on women at the University of Michigan's Center for the Education of Women.

Eligibility This program is open to scholars from the United States and abroad who have a Ph.D. or equivalent degree. Applicants must be interested in utilizing the resources of the center to explore the following or related issues: women in nontraditional fields, leadership, women and work, gender and poverty, women in higher education, women of color in the academy, or gender equity in education and employment.

Financial data Scholars receive office space, full access to University of Michigan facilities and programs (including library and computing resources), and stipends up to $7,500. An additional $1,000 is paid upon receipt of the scholar's paper.

Duration From 2 to 12 months.

Additional information Visiting scholars must be in residence at the center for the duration of the program. They are expected to prepare a working paper on the basis of their research.

Number awarded Varies each year.

Deadline February of each year.

[1229]
CHARLES L. BREWER DISTINGUISHED TEACHING OF PSYCHOLOGY AWARD

American Psychological Foundation
750 First Street, N.E.
Washington, DC 20002-4242
(202) 336-5843   Fax: (202) 336-5812
E-mail: foundation@apa.org
Web: www.apa.org/apf/funding/brewer.aspx

Summary To recognize and reward distinguished career contributions to the teaching of psychology.

Eligibility This award is available to psychologists who demonstrate outstanding teaching. Selection is based on evidence of influence as a teacher of students who become psychologists, research on teaching, development of effective teaching methods and/or materials, development of innovation curricula and courses, performance as a classroom teacher, demonstrated training of teachers of psychology,

teaching of advanced research methods and practice in psychology, and/or administrative facilitation of teaching. Nominators must complete an application form, write a letter of support, and submit the nominee's current vitae and bibliography. The sponsor encourages nominations of individuals who represent diversity in race, ethnicity, gender, age, disability, and sexual orientation.

Financial data Awardees receive a plaque, a $2,000 honorarium, and an all-expense paid trip to the annual convention where the award is presented.

Duration The award is presented annually.

Additional information This award, originally named the Distinguished Teaching in Psychology Award, was first presented in 1970.

Number awarded 1 each year.

Deadline Nominations must be submitted by November of each year.

[1230]
CHEST DIVERSITY COMMITTEE MINORITY INVESTIGATOR RESEARCH GRANT

American College of Chest Physicians
Attn: The CHEST Foundation
2595 Patriot Boulevard
Glenview, IL 60026
(224) 521-9527   Toll Free: (800) 343-2227
Fax: (224) 521-9801   E-mail: grants@chestnet.org
Web: www.chestnet.org

Summary To provide funding to minority physicians who are interested in conducting clinical or translational research on topics of interest to the American College of Chest Physicians (ACCP).

Eligibility This program is open to members of the ACCP who are members of an underrepresented group (African American, Latin American, Hispanic American, Asian/Pacific Island American, Native American, women). Applicants must be interested in conducting a clinical or translational research project that contributes to the understanding of the pathophysiology or treatment of conditions or diseases related to pulmonary, cardiovascular, critical care, or sleep medicine. They may be at later career stages, but special consideration is given to those within 5 years of completing an advanced training program.

Financial data The grant is $25,000.

Duration 1 year, beginning in July.

Additional information This program is supported in part by AstraZeneca.

Number awarded 1 each year.

Deadline April of each year.

[1231]
CHURCH TRAINING AND DEACONESS HOUSE SCHOLARSHIP

Episcopal Diocese of Pennsylvania
Attn: Church Training and Deaconess House Scholarship Fund
3717 Chestnut Street, Suite 300
Philadelphia, PA 19104
(215) 627-6434, ext. 101   Fax: (267) 900-2928
E-mail: nevin-field@stpetersphila.org
Web: www.diopa.org/deaconess-training

Summary To provide financial assistance for graduate school to women preparing for a career in religious or benevolent work for the Episcopal Church.

Eligibility This program is open to women who are seeking to be ordained to the ministry of the Episcopal Church or to work on a graduate degree that would further their lay ministry. Preference is given to women in the Diocese of Pennsylvania. Applicants must submit a 250-word essay on how they expect to use this graduate educational training to advance their ordained or lay ministry within the Episcopal Church or the church at large. Selection is based on the quality of the essay, academic record, and financial need.

Financial data Stipends range from $2,000 to $3,000.

Duration 1 year; may be renewed up to 2 additional years.

Number awarded 1 or more each year.

Deadline March of each year.

[1232]
COMMUNITY ACTION GRANTS

American Association of University Women
Attn: AAUW Educational Foundation
1111 16th Street, N.W.
Washington, DC 20036-4873
(202) 785-7700   Toll Free: (800) 326-AAUW
Fax: (202) 872-1425   TDD: (202) 785-7777
E-mail: aauw@applyists.com
Web: www.aauw.org

Summary To provide seed money to branches or divisions of the American Association of University Women (AAUW) or to individual women for projects or non-degree research that promote education and equity for women and girls.

Eligibility This program is open to individual women who are U.S. citizens or permanent residents, AAUW branches, AAUW state organizations, and local community-based non-profit organizations. Applicants must be proposing projects that have direct public impact, are non-partisan, and take place within the United States or its territories. Grants for 1 year provide seed money for new projects; topic areas are unrestricted but should include a clearly defined activity that promotes education and equity for women and girls. Grants for 2 years provide start-up funds for longer-term programs that address the particular needs of the community and develop girls' sense of efficacy through leadership or advocacy opportunities; funds support planning activities, coalition building, implementation, and evaluation. Special consideration is given to 1) AAUW branch and state projects that seek community partners (e.g., local schools or school districts, businesses, other community-based organizations); and 2) projects focused on K-14 girls' achievement in mathematics, science, and/or technology. Selection is based on relevance of the proposed project to education and equity for women and girls, strength of the project rationale, clarity and creativity of the project design, feasibility of the project, strength of the evaluation plan, strength of the dissemination plan, impact of the project, overall quality of the proposal, and potential for and/or commitment of additional funds and involvement from community organizations and/or businesses.

Financial data Grants for 1 year range from $2,000 to $7,000. Grants for 2 years range from $5,000 to $10,000. Funds are to be used for such project-related expenses as office supplies, mailing, photocopying, honoraria, and transportation. Funds cannot cover salaries for project directors or regular, ongoing overhead costs for any organization.

Duration 1 or 2 years, beginning in July.

Additional information The filing fee is $35.

Number awarded Varies each year; recently, 15 1-year grants and 17 2-year grants, with a total value of $258,561, were awarded.

Deadline March of each year.

[1233]
COSROW SCHOLARSHIP

United Methodist Church-Oklahoma Conference
Attn: Commission on the Status and Role of Women
1501 N.W. 24th Street
Oklahoma, OK 73106-3635
(405) 530-2000   Toll Free: (800) 231-4166
Fax: (405) 525-4164
Web: www.okumc.org/awards

Summary To provide financial assistance to Methodist women from Oklahoma interested in preparing for full-time ministry.

Eligibility This program is open to women who are members of the Oklahoma Conference of the United Methodist Church (UMC). Applicants must be interested in full-time ministry in the UMC as a seminary student, by taking pre-seminary courses, or by pursuing ministerial education through the Course of Study program.

Financial data A stipend is awarded (amount not specified).

Duration 1 year.

Number awarded 1 or more each year.

Deadline August of each year.

[1234]
COVIDIEN RESEARCH AND DEVELOPMENT PILOT AWARD IN TECHNOLOGY

American Gastroenterological Association
Attn: AGA Research Foundation
Research Awards Manager
4930 Del Ray Avenue
Bethesda, MD 20814-2512
(301) 222-4012   Fax: (301) 654-5920
E-mail: awards@gastro.org
Web: www.gastro.org

Summary To provide funding to investigators interested in conducting research and development of devices or technologies that may impact the diagnosis or treatment of digestive disease.

Eligibility This program is open to investigators interested in researching and developing new devices, designing and testing a significant improvement to an existing technology, developing a new diagnostic, developing a novel research method technology, and/or investigating the application of nanotechnology or methodologies such as computational biology to the field of gastroenterology. Applicants must have an M.D. or Ph.D. degree and a full-time faculty position at a North American educational institution. Membership in the American Gastroenterological Association (AGA) is required. Selection is based primarily on the potential impact of the study on diagnosing or treating digestive disease. Women and minorities are strongly encouraged to apply.

Financial data The grant is $30,000. Funds are to be used for project costs, including salary, supplies, and equipment but excluding travel. Indirect costs are not allowed. An additional $1,000 is provided as a travel stipend to attend the AGA Technology Summit.

Duration 1 year.

Number awarded 1 each year.

Deadline January of each year.

[1235]
CYNOSURE SCREENWRITING AWARDS

BroadMind Entertainment
3699 Wilshire Boulevard, Suite 850
Los Angeles, CA 90010
(310) 855-8730   E-mail: cynosure@broadmindent.com
Web: www.broadmindent.com/id10.html

Summary To recognize and reward outstanding unpublished screenplays with compelling female protagonists or that showcase diversity.

Eligibility Writers in any country are eligible to submit unpublished feature-length scripts (90-130 pages) with either a female protagonist or with a protagonist (either male or female) from a diverse background. Scripts may be submitted under 1 category only. Scripts by multiple authors are acceptable. More than 1 script may be submitted, provided the signed entry/release form and an application fee accompany each submission. Scripts must be registered with the WGA or with the U.S. Copyright Office. Screenplays must be in English and may be of any genre.

Financial data The prize is $5,000 for the best script from either category. The first runner-up from each category receives $1,000 and the second runner-up from each category receives $250.

Duration The competition is held annually.

Additional information This competition began in 1999. The fee is $50 for early entries, $65 for regular entries, or $75 for late entries.

Number awarded 5 each year: 1 for the best script from either category and 2 runners-up from each category.

Deadline Deadlines are March of each year for early, May of each year for regular, or September of each year for late entries.

[1236]
DARE TO DREAM SCHOLARSHIP

Women in Aviation International
Attn: Scholarships
Morningstar Airport
3647 State Route 503 South
West Alexandria, OH 45381-9354
(937) 839-4647   Fax: (937) 839-4645
E-mail: scholarships@wai.org
Web: www.wai.org

Summary To provide funding to members of Women in Aviation International (WAI) who are interested in obtaining an additional rating or certificate.

Eligibility This program is open to women who are WAI members and interested in furthering their career in aviation. Applicants must be interested in working on an instrument or multiengine rating, a commercial license, or certified flight instructor (CFI) certificate. Along with their application, they

must submit a 500-word essay and professional resume that include their aviation history and goals, what they have done for themselves to achieve their goals, where they see themselves in 5 and 10 years, involvement in aviation activities, how the scholarship will help them achieve their objectives, and their present financial need.

Financial data The stipend is $3,000. Funds are paid directly to the flight school.

Duration Training must be completed within 1 year.

Additional information WAI is a nonprofit professional organization dedicated to encouraging women to consider an aviation career and to providing educational outreach activities and networking resources to women active in the industry.

Number awarded 1 each year.

Deadline November of each year.

[1237]
DARLENE CLARK HINE AWARD

Organization of American Historians
Attn: Award and Committee Coordinator
112 North Bryan Street
Bloomington, IN 47408-4141
(812) 855-7311   Fax: (812) 855-0696
E-mail: khamm@oah.org
Web: www.oah.org

Summary To recognize and reward authors of outstanding books dealing with African American women's and gender history.

Eligibility This award is presented to the author of the outstanding book in African American women's and gender history. Entries must have been published during the current calendar year.

Financial data The award is $1,000.

Duration The award is presented annually.

Additional information This award was first presented in 2010.

Number awarded 1 each year.

Deadline September of each year.

[1238]
DAVID H. AND BEVERLY A. BARLOW GRANT

American Psychological Foundation
750 First Street, N.E.
Washington, DC 20002-4242
(202) 336-5843   Fax: (202) 336-5812
E-mail: foundation@apa.org
Web: www.apa.org/apf/funding/barlow.aspx

Summary To provide funding to psychologists who wish to conduct research or other activities related to the connection between behavior and health.

Eligibility This program is open to psychologists who wish to engage in innovative research, education, or intervention efforts that advance psychological knowledge and application in understanding and fostering the connection between behavior and health. Preference is given 1) early-career psychologists (no more than 10 years of postdoctoral experience); 2) pilot projects that, if successful, would be strong candidates for support from major federal and foundation funding agencies; and 3) "demonstration projects" that promise to generalize broadly to similar settings in other geographical areas and/or to other settings. Applicants must demonstrate competence and capability to execute the proposed work. The sponsor encourages applications from individuals who represent diversity in race, ethnicity, gender, age, disability, and sexual orientation.

Financial data The grant ranges up to $9,000.

Duration 1 year.

Additional information This program began in 2014.

Number awarded 1 each year.

Deadline September of each year.

[1239]
DAVID WECHSLER EARLY CAREER GRANT FOR INNOVATIVE WORK IN COGNITION

American Psychological Foundation
750 First Street, N.E.
Washington, DC 20002-4242
(202) 336-5843   Fax: (202) 336-5812
E-mail: foundation@apa.org
Web: www.apa.org/apf/funding/wechsler.aspx

Summary To provide funding to early-career psychologists who wish to conduct research related to cognition.

Eligibility This program is open to psychologists who have an Ed.D., Psy.D., or Ph.D. degree from an accredited university and no more than 10 years of postdoctoral experience. Applicants must be interested in conducting innovative research in neuropsychology, intelligence, and/or the assessment aspects of cognition. Selection is based on conformance with stated program goals and qualifications; quality and potential impact of proposed work; originality, innovation, and contribution to the field with both proposed project; and applicant's demonstrated competence and capability to execute the proposed work. The sponsor encourages applications from individuals who represent diversity in race, ethnicity, gender, age, disability, and sexual orientation.

Financial data The grant ranges up to $25,000.

Duration 1 year.

Additional information This program began in 2014.

Number awarded 1 each year.

Deadline June of each year.

[1240]
DENHAM FELLOWSHIP

Stage Directors and Choreographers Society
Attn: Stage Directors and Choreographers Foundation
321 West 44th Street, Suite 804
New York, NY 10036-5477
(646) 524-2226   Fax: (212) 302-6195
E-mail: Foundation@SDCweb.org
Web: www.sdcfoundation.org/opportunities/fellowships

Summary To provide an opportunity for aspiring young directors, especially women, to develop their directing skills.

Eligibility This program is open to young directors, especially women, who are interested in developing a program to improve their skills. Applicants may be proposing either 1) fee enhancement, for which they are seeking funding to augment a fee offered by a theater or director; or 2) self-producing, for which they are seeking funding for a directorial project they will develop themselves. Along with their application, they must submit 1) a 1-page resume; 2) 2 letters of recommendation (including 1 from the producing theater's artistic or pro-

ducing director for a fee enhancement award); 3) for applicants for self-producing awards, verification that the production will occur (e.g., agreement with theater); and 4) a 2-page letter of intent, including the challenges posed by the proposed project, their goals and how they will achieve them, and the potential impact of both the project and the fellowship on their craft and career.

Financial data The stipend is $2,500.

Duration 1 year.

Additional information This program began in 2006.

Number awarded 1 each year.

Deadline July of each year.

[1241]
DIVISION 17 COUNSELING PSYCHOLOGY GRANTS

American Psychological Foundation
750 First Street, N.E.
Washington, DC 20002-4242
(202) 336-5843   Fax: (202) 336-5812
E-mail: foundation@apa.org
Web: www.apa.org/apf/funding/counseling.aspx

Summary To provide funding to psychologists who wish to conduct a project related to counseling psychology.

Eligibility This program is open to psychologists who wish to conduct a project to enhance the science and practice of counseling psychology, including basic and applied research, literary, and educational activities. Applicants must be members of Division 17 (Society of Counseling Psychotherapy) of the American Psychological Association with 10 years or less of postdoctoral experience. Selection is based on conformance with stated program goals, magnitude of incremental contribution in specified activity area, quality of proposed work, and applicant's demonstrated competence and capability to execute the proposed work. The sponsor encourages applications from individuals who represent diversity in race, ethnicity, gender, age, disability, and sexual orientation.

Financial data Grants range up to $7,000.

Duration 1 year.

Additional information These grants were first awarded in 2007.

Number awarded Varies each year; recently, 4 were awarded.

Deadline March of each year.

[1242]
DOROTHY BRACY/JANICE JOSEPH MINORITY AND WOMEN NEW SCHOLAR AWARD

Academy of Criminal Justice Sciences
7339A Hanover Parkway
P.O. Box 960
Greenbelt, MD 20768-0960
(301) 446-6300   Toll Free: (800) 757-ACJS
Fax: (301) 446-2819   E-mail: info@acjs.org
Web: www.acjs.org/Awards

Summary To recognize and reward minority and women junior scholars who have made outstanding contributions to the field of criminal justice.

Eligibility This award is available to members of the Academy of Criminal Justice Sciences (ACJS) who are members of a group that has experienced historical discrimination, including minorities and women. Applicants must have obtained a Ph.D. in a field of criminal justice within the past 7 years and be able to demonstrate a strong record as a new scholar in the areas of research, teaching, and service.

Financial data The award is $1,000.

Duration The award is presented annually.

Number awarded 1 each year.

Deadline October of each year.

[1243]
DR. BESSIE ELIZABETH DELANEY FELLOWSHIP

National Dental Association
Attn: National Dental Association Foundation, Inc.
3517 16th Street, N.W.
Washington, DC 20010
(734) 544-1336   E-mail: admin@ndaonline.org
Web: www.ndafoundation.org

Summary To provide financial assistance to women who are members of minority groups and interested in working on a postdoctoral degree in fields related to dentistry.

Eligibility This program is open to female members of minority groups who are working on a postdoctoral degree in an area related to dentistry, such as public health, administration, pediatrics, research, or law. Students working on a master's degree beyond their residency may be considered. Applicants must be members of the National Dental Association (NDA) and U.S. citizens or permanent residents. Along with their application, they must submit a letter explaining why they should be considered for this scholarship, 2 letters of recommendation, a curriculum vitae, a description of the program, nomination by their program director, and documentation of financial need.

Financial data The stipend is $10,000.

Duration 1 year.

Additional information This program, established in 1990, is supported by the Colgate-Palmolive Company.

Number awarded 1 each year.

Deadline May of each year.

[1244]
DRS. ROSALEE G. AND RAYMOND A. WEISS RESEARCH AND PROGRAM INNOVATION GRANT

American Psychological Foundation
750 First Street, N.E.
Washington, DC 20002-4242
(202) 336-5843   Fax: (202) 336-5812
E-mail: foundation@apa.org
Web: www.apa.org/apf/funding/weiss.aspx

Summary To provide funding to professionals interested in conducting projects that use psychology to solve social problems related to the priorities of the American Psychological Foundation (APF).

Eligibility This program is open to professionals at nonprofit organizations engaged in research, education, and intervention projects and programs. Applicants must be interested in conducting an activity that uses psychology to solve social problems in the following priority areas: understanding and fostering the connection between mental and physical health; reducing stigma and prejudice; understanding and preventing violence to create a safer, more humane world; or

addressing the long-term psychological needs of individuals and communities in the aftermath of disaster. Preference is given to psychologists within 10 years of completion of their doctorate; pilot projects that, if successful, would be strong candidates for support from major federal and foundation funding agencies; and "demonstration projects" that promise to generalize broadly to similar settings in other geographical areas and/or to other settings. Selection is based on the criticality of the proposed funding for the proposed work; clarity and comprehensiveness of methodology; innovative and potential impact qualities; and quality, viability, and promise of proposed work. The sponsor encourages applications from individuals who represent diversity in race, ethnicity, gender, age, disability, and sexual orientation.

Financial data The grant is $1,000.

Duration 1 year; nonrenewable.

Additional information This program began in 2003.

Number awarded 1 each year.

Deadline September of each year.

[1245]
E. GAIL DE PLANQUE NATIONAL AWARD

American Nuclear Society
Attn: Honors and Awards
555 North Kensington Avenue
La Grange Park, IL 60526-5535
(708) 352-6611   Toll Free: (800) 323-3044
Fax: (708) 352-0499   E-mail: honors@ans.org
Web: www.ans.org/honors/va-planque

Summary To recognize and reward women who have made outstanding contributions to the field of nuclear science and engineering.

Eligibility Nominees for this award must be women who have made outstanding contributions to the field of nuclear science and engineering. They are not required to be members of the American Nuclear Society, but they must be affiliated with the nuclear community in some manner. Their work may involve outstanding lifetime or singular achievements in 1) technical leadership for work performed in their subject area; 2) leadership of a major research, design, construction, or operations effort; or 3) accomplishment in the field of public policy affecting nuclear science and technology.

Financial data The award consists of $5,000 and a bronze medallion.

Duration The award is presented annually.

Additional information This award was first presented in 2014.

Number awarded 1 each year.

Deadline July of each year.

[1246]
EARLY CAREER PATIENT-ORIENTED DIABETES RESEARCH AWARD

Juvenile Diabetes Research Foundation International
Attn: Senior Director, Research Administration
26 Broadway, 14th Floor
New York, NY 10004
(212) 479-7519   Toll Free: (800) 533-CURE
Fax: (212) 785-9595   E-mail: emilligan@jdrf.org
Web: grantcenter.jdrf.org

Summary To provide funding to physician scientists (particularly women, minorities, and persons with disabilities) who are interested in pursuing a program of clinical diabetes-related research training.

Eligibility This program is open to investigators in diabetes-related research who have an M.D. or M.D./Ph.D. degree and a faculty appointment at the late training or assistant professor level. Applicants must be sponsored by an investigator who is affiliated full time with an accredited institution, who pursues patient-oriented clinical research, and who agrees to supervise the applicant's training. There are no citizenship requirements. Applications are encouraged from women, members of minority groups underrepresented in the sciences, and people with disabilities. Areas of relevant research can include: mechanisms of human disease, therapeutic interventions, clinical trials, and the development of new technologies. The proposed research may be conducted at foreign or domestic, for-profit or nonprofit, or public or private institutions, including universities, colleges, hospitals, laboratories, units of state or local government, or eligible agencies of the federal government.

Financial data The total award may be up to $150,000 each year, up to $75,000 of which may be requested for research (including a technician, supplies, equipment, and travel). The salary request must be consistent with the established salary structure of the applicant's institution. Equipment purchases in years other than the first must be strongly justified. Indirect costs may not exceed 10%.

Duration The award is for 5 years and is generally nonrenewable.

Number awarded Varies each year.

Deadline July of each year.

[1247]
EARTH SCIENCES POSTDOCTORAL FELLOWSHIPS

National Science Foundation
Directorate for Geosciences
Attn: Division of Earth Sciences
4201 Wilson Boulevard, Room 785S
Arlington, VA 22230
(703) 292-5047   Fax: (703) 292-9025
TDD: (800) 281-8749   E-mail: lpatino@nsf.gov
Web: www.nsf.gov

Summary To provide funding to postdoctoral scientists interested in participating in a program of research training and education, in the United States or abroad, in a field relevant to the work of the Division of Earth Sciences of the National Science Foundation (NSF).

Eligibility This program is open to U.S. citizens, nationals, and permanent residents who received a Ph.D. within the past 18 months. Applicants must be interested in a program of research training in any of the disciplines supported by the NSF Division of Earth Sciences: geobiology and low temperature geochemistry, geomorphology and land use dynamics, geophysics, hydrologic sciences, petrology and geochemistry, sedimentary geology and paleobiology, and tectonics. The project should be conducted at an institution in the United States or abroad other than the applicant's Ph.D.-granting institution. The application must include a plan to broaden the participation of groups underrepresented in earth sciences (women, persons with disabilities, African

Americans, Hispanics, Native Americans, Alaska Natives, and Pacific Islanders).

Financial data Grants are $87,000 per year, including a stipend of $62,000 per year and an annual fellowship allowance of $25,000 that is intended to cover direct research expenses, facilities and other institutional resources, and fringe benefits. For fellows who wish to conduct research abroad, an additional supplement of $10,000 is provided.

Duration 2 years.

Number awarded 10 each year.

Deadline January of each year.

[1248]
EDUCATOR'S AWARD

Delta Kappa Gamma Society International
Attn: Educator's Award Committee
416 West 12th Street
P.O. Box 1589
Austin, TX 78767-1589
(512) 478-5748   Toll Free: (888) 762-4685
Fax: (512) 478-3961   E-mail: soceditr@dkg.org
Web: www.dkg.org/category/committee/educators-award

Summary To recognize women's contributions to education that may influence future directions in the profession; these contributions may be in research, philosophy, or any other area of learning that is stimulating and creative.

Eligibility Any published book in research, philosophy, or another area of learning that stimulates the intellect and imagination may be submitted for consideration if it is written by 1 or 2 women in Canada, Costa Rica, Denmark, El Salvador, Estonia, Finland, Germany, Guatemala, Iceland, Mexico, the Netherlands, Norway, Panama, Puerto Rico, Sweden, the United Kingdom, or the United States and copyrighted (in its first edition or the first English translation) during the preceding calendar year. Contributions should possess excellence in style, be well-edited and attractive in format, and be of more than local interest. Ineligible are methods books, skill books, textbooks, and unpublished manuscripts.

Financial data The award is $2,500. In the case of dual authorship, the prize is divided in the same manner as royalties are divided by the awardees' publisher.

Duration The award is granted annually.

Additional information This award was first presented in 1946.

Number awarded 1 each year.

Deadline January of each year.

[1249]
EINSTEIN POSTDOCTORAL FELLOWSHIP PROGRAM

Smithsonian Astrophysical Observatory
Attn: Chandra X-Ray Center
Einstein Fellowship Program Office
60 Garden Street, MS4
Cambridge, MA 02138
(617) 496-7941   Fax: (617) 495-7356
E-mail: fellows@head.cfa.harvard.edu
Web: cxc.harvard.edu/fellows

Summary To provide funding to recent postdoctoral scientists who are interested in conducting research related to high energy astrophysics missions of the National Aeronautics and Space Administration (NASA).

Eligibility This program is open to postdoctoral scientists who completed their Ph.D., Sc.D., or equivalent doctoral degree within the past 3 years in astronomy, physics, or related disciplines. Applicants must be interested in conducting research related to NASA Physics of the Cosmos program missions: Chandra, Fermi, XMM-Newton and International X-Ray Observatory, cosmological investigations relevant to the Planck and JDEM missions, and gravitational astrophysics relevant to the LISA mission. They must be citizens of the United States or English-speaking citizens of other countries who have valid visas. Women and minorities are strongly encouraged to apply.

Financial data Stipends are approximately $66,500 per year. Fellows may also receive health insurance, relocation costs, and moderate support (up to $16,000 per year) for research-related travel, computing services, publications, and other direct costs.

Duration 3 years (depending on a review of scientific activity).

Additional information This program, which began in 2009 with funding from NASA, incorporates the former Chandra and GLAST Fellowship programs.

Number awarded Varies each year; recently, 13 were awarded.

Deadline November of each year.

[1250]
ELEANOR ROOSEVELT FUND AWARD

American Association of University Women
Attn: AAUW Educational Foundation
1111 16th Street, N.W.
Washington, DC 20036-4873
(202) 785-7624   Toll Free: (800) 326-AAUW
Fax: (202) 872-1425   TDD: (202) 785-7777
E-mail: fellowships@aauw.org
Web: www.aauw.org

Summary To recognize and reward individuals, organizations, institutions, or projects that provide an equitable school environment for women and girls.

Eligibility Nominations for this award are not solicited from the general public. The goals of the Eleanor Roosevelt Fund are to 1) remove barriers to women's and girls' participation in education; 2) promote the value of diversity and cross-cultural communication; and 3) develop greater understanding of the ways women learn, think, work, and play. Individuals, organizations, institutions, or projects that work for those goals are eligible to be nominated for this award. Their activities may include classroom teaching, educational and research contributions, or legal and legislative work that contributes to equity for women and girls. Although the award focuses on education, the nominee need not be an educator.

Financial data The award is $5,000.

Duration The award is presented biennially.

Additional information This award was established in 1989.

Number awarded 1 each odd-numbered year.

Deadline Nominations must be submitted by October of even-numbered years.

[1251]
ELSEVIER GUT MICROBIOME PILOT RESEARCH AWARD

American Gastroenterological Association
Attn: AGA Research Foundation
Research Awards Manager
4930 Del Ray Avenue
Bethesda, MD 20814-2512
(301) 222-4012   Fax: (301) 654-5920
E-mail: awards@gastro.org
Web: www.gastro.org

Summary To provide funding to new or established gastroenterologists for pilot research projects in areas related to the gut microbiome.

Eligibility Applicants must have an M.D., Ph.D., or equivalent degree and a full-time faculty position at an accredited North American institution. They may not hold grants for projects on a similar topic from other agencies. Individual membership in the American Gastroenterology Association (AGA) is required. The proposal must enable investigators to obtain new data on the relationships of the gut microbiota to digestive health and disease that can ultimately lead to subsequent grant applications for more substantial funding and duration. Women and minority investigators are strongly encouraged to apply. Selection is based on novelty, importance, feasibility, environment, and overall likelihood that the project will lead to more substantial grants in gut microbiome research.

Financial data The grant is $25,000. Funds may be used for salary, supplies, or equipment. Indirect costs are not allowed.

Duration 1 year.

Additional information This award is sponsored by Elsevier Science.

Number awarded 1 each year.

Deadline January of each year.

[1252]
ELSEVIER PILOT RESEARCH AWARDS

American Gastroenterological Association
Attn: AGA Research Foundation
Research Awards Manager
4930 Del Ray Avenue
Bethesda, MD 20814-2512
(301) 222-4012   Fax: (301) 654-5920
E-mail: awards@gastro.org
Web: www.gastro.org

Summary To provide funding to new or established investigators for pilot research projects in areas related to gastroenterology or hepatology.

Eligibility Applicants must have an M.D., Ph.D., or equivalent degree and a full-time faculty position at an accredited North American institution. They may not hold grants for projects on a similar topic from other agencies. Individual membership in the American Gastroenterology Association (AGA) is required. The proposal must involve obtaining new data that can ultimately provide the basis for subsequent grant applications for more substantial funding and duration in gastroenterology- or hepatology-related areas. Women and minority investigators are strongly encouraged to apply. Selection is based on novelty, importance, feasibility, environment, institutional commitment, and overall likelihood that the project will lead to more substantial grants.

Financial data The grant is $25,000. Funds may be used for salary, supplies, or equipment. Indirect costs are not allowed.

Duration 1 year.

Additional information This award is sponsored by Elsevier Science.

Number awarded 2 each year.

Deadline January of each year.

[1253]
ENID A. NEIDLE SCHOLAR-IN-RESIDENCE PROGRAM

American Dental Education Association
Attn: ADEA Access, Diversity, and Inclusion
655 K Street, N.W., Suite 800
Washington, DC 20001
(202) 289-7201, ext. 197   Fax: (202) 289-7204
E-mail: dabreuk@adea.org
Web: www.adea.org

Summary To provide funding to women dental faculty members who are interested in a residency at the American Dental Education Association (ADEA) in Washington, D.C.

Eligibility This program is open to full-time female faculty with primary teaching appointments in predoctoral and advanced dental education programs at ADEA-member institutions; female junior dental and dental hygiene faculty members are particularly encouraged to apply. Candidates must belong to ADEA. They must be interested in concentrating on issues that affect women faculty during a residency at ADEA in Washington, D.C. Interested faculty members should submit the following: a completed application form, a personal statement on their general interests and expectations for the residency, a letter of recommendation from their dean or chief administrative officer, a current curriculum vitae, and a formal letter of support from a colleague or mentor.

Financial data Scholars receive a $15,000 stipend to cover travel and living expenses while at the residency in Washington, D.C. It is a requirement of the program that the fellow's institution continue to provide salary support and fringe benefits for the duration of the experience.

Duration 2 to 3 months.

Additional information This program, established in 1994, is sponsored by the ADEA and Johnson & Johnson Healthcare Products. While in Washington, D.C., it is expected that the scholar will gain perspectives on issues facing women faculty, including promotion, advancement, and tenure policies; entry and reentry into the workforce; child care and elder care; women's health; work patterns; advanced education and research opportunities; and other gender-related issues. The scholar is assigned to a senior ADEA staff member and will have the opportunity to be involved in a range of activities there, in addition to her own project.

Number awarded 1 each year.

Deadline October of each year.

[1254]
ENVIRONMENT AND NATURAL RESOURCES FELLOWSHIPS

Harvard University
John F. Kennedy School of Government
Belfer Center for Science and International Affairs
Attn: STPP Fellowship Coordinator
79 John F. Kennedy Street, Mailbox 53
Cambridge, MA 02138
(617) 495-1498   Fax: (617) 495-8963
E-mail: patricia_mclaughlin@hks.harvard.edu
Web: belfercenter.ksg.harvard.edu

Summary To provide funding to professionals, postdoctorates, and doctoral students interested in conducting research on environmental and natural resource issues at the Belfer Center for Science and International Affairs at Harvard University in Cambridge, Massachusetts.

Eligibility The postdoctoral fellowship is open to recent recipients of the Ph.D. or equivalent degree, university faculty members, and employees of government, military, international, humanitarian, and private research institutions who have appropriate professional experience. Applicants for predoctoral fellowships must have passed their general examinations. Scholars from a wide range of disciplinary and multi-disciplinary fields and those holding a Ph.D. in engineering or in the natural sciences are strongly encouraged to apply. The program especially encourages applications from women, minorities, and citizens of all countries. All applicants must be interested in conducting research on projects of the Environment and Natural Resources (ENRP) Program. Recently, those included projects on energy technology innovation, sustainable energy development in China, managing the atom, and the geopolitics of energy.

Financial data The stipend is $37,500 for postdoctoral research fellows or $25,000 for predoctoral research fellows. Fellows who renew their grant receive a monthly stipend of $3,750 for postdoctoral fellows or $2,500 for predoctoral fellows. Stipends for advanced research fellows vary. Health insurance is also provided.

Duration 10 months; may be renewed on a month-by-month basis.

Additional information Fellows are expected to devoted some portion of their time to collaborative endeavors, as arranged by the appropriate program or project director. Predoctoral fellows are expected to contribute to the program's research activities, as well as work on (and ideally complete) their dissertations. Postdoctoral research fellows are also expected to complete a book, monograph, or other significant publication during their period of residence.

Number awarded A limited number each year.

Deadline January of each year.

[1255]
EPILEPSY FOUNDATION CLINICAL RESEARCH APPRENTICESHIP

American Epilepsy Society
135 South LaSalle Street, Suite 2850
Chicago, IL 60603
(312) 883-3800   Fax: (312) 896-5784
E-mail: info@aesnet.org
Web: www.aesnet.org

Summary To provide funding to clinical health care professionals interested in a mentored clinical research training apprenticeship.

Eligibility This program is open to clinicians who have a doctoral degree and have been accepted into an epilepsy fellowship at a level 3 or 4 epilepsy center in the United States. Applicants must identify a mentor at the center who will agree to work with them and be able to identify their role in the project that will leader to a publication or independent scholarship related to the project. The individualized training program may consist of both didactic training and a supervised research experience that is designed to develop the necessary knowledge and skills in the chosen area of research and foster their career goals. Selection is based on the quality of the proposed research training program, the applicant's qualifications, the preceptor's qualifications, and the adequacy of clinical training, research facilities, and other epilepsy-related programs at the institution. Applications are especially encouraged from women, members of minority groups, and people with disabilities. U.S. citizenship is not required, but all research must be conducted in the United States.

Financial data The grant provides $25,000 per year for salary plus $10,000 per year for class work and travel to appropriate meetings.

Duration 1 year, either the first or second year of fellowship.

Additional information Support for this program is provided by the Epilepsy Foundation.

Number awarded 2 each year.

Deadline Letters of intent must be submitted by October of each year; final proposals are due in January.

[1256]
EPILEPSY RESEARCH RECOGNITION AWARDS PROGRAM

American Epilepsy Society
135 South LaSalle Street, Suite 2850
Chicago, IL 60603
(312) 883-3800 Fax: (312) 896-5784
E-mail: info@aesnet.org
Web: www.aesnet.org

Summary To recognize and reward investigators anywhere in the world who have conducted outstanding research related to epilepsy.

Eligibility This award is available to active scientists and clinicians working in any aspect of epilepsy. Candidates must be nominated by their home institution and be at the level of associate professor or professor. There are no geographic restrictions; nominations from outside the United States and North America are welcome. Awards are presented for basic science and clinical science. Selection is based on pioneering research, quality of publications, research productivity, training activities, other contributions in epilepsy, and anticipated productivity over the next decade.

Financial data The award includes an honorarium of $10,000, 2 nights free lodging at the annual conference, round-trip economy airfare, and free registration for the scientific program.

Additional information This program began in 1991.

Number awarded 2 each year: 1 for basic science and 1 for clinical science.

Deadline August of each year.

[1257]
ERIC AND BARBARA DOBKIN NATIVE ARTIST FELLOWSHIP FOR WOMEN

School for Advanced Research
Attn: Indian Arts Research Center
660 Garcia Street
P.O. Box 2188
Santa Fe, NM 87504-2188
(505) 954-7205 Fax: (505) 954-7207
E-mail: iarc@sarsf.org
Web: www.sarweb.org/index.php?artists

Summary To provide an opportunity for Native American women artists to improve their skills through a spring residency at the Indian Arts Research Center in Santa Fe, New Mexico.

Eligibility This program is open to Native American women who excel in the arts, including sculpture, performance, basketry, painting, printmaking, digital art, mixed media, photography, pottery, writing, and filmmaking. Applicants should be attempting to explore new avenues of creativity, grapple with new ideas to advance their work, and strengthen existing talents. Along with their application, they must submit a current resume, examples of their current work, and a 2-page statement that explains why they are applying for this fellowship, how it will help them realize their professional and/or personal goals as an artist, and the scope of the project they plan to complete during the residency.

Financial data The fellowship provides a stipend of $3,000 per month, housing, studio space, supplies allowance, and travel reimbursement to and from the center.

Duration 3 months, beginning in March.

Additional information Fellows work with the staff and research curators at the Indian Arts Research Center, an academic division of the School of American Research that is devoted solely to Native American art scholarship. The center has a significant collection of Pueblo pottery, Navajo and Pueblo Indian textiles, and early 20th-century Indian paintings, as well as holdings of jewelry and silverwork, basketry, clothing, and other ethnological materials. This fellowship was established in 2001.

Number awarded 1 each year.

Deadline January of each year.

[1258]
ESTHER KATZ ROSEN FUND GRANTS

American Psychological Foundation
750 First Street, N.E.
Washington, DC 20002-4242
(202) 336-5843 Fax: (202) 336-5812
E-mail: foundation@apa.org
Web: www.apa.org/apf/funding/rosen.aspx

Summary To provide funding to graduate students and early-career psychologists interested in conducting research or other projects on psychological issues relevant to giftedness in children.

Eligibility This program is open to 1) graduate students at universities in the United States and Canada who have advanced to candidacy; and 2) psychologists who completed their doctoral degree within the past 10 years. Applicants must be interested in engaging in activities related to identified gifted and talented children and adolescents, including research, pilot projects, research-based programs, or projects aimed at improving the quality of education in psychological science and its application in secondary schools for high ability students. Selection is based on conformance with stated program goals and qualifications, quality and impact of proposed work, innovation and contribution to the field, and applicant's demonstrated competence and capability to execute the proposed work. The sponsor encourages applications from individuals who represent diversity in race, ethnicity, gender, age, disability, and sexual orientation.

Financial data Grants range from $1,000 to $50,000.

Duration 1 year.

Additional information The Esther Katz Rosen Fund was established in 1974. In 2013, the sponsor combined the Rosen Graduate Student Fellowship, the Rosen Early Career Research Grant, and the Pre-College Grant program into this single program.

Number awarded Varies each year; recently, 2 were awarded.

Deadline February of each year.

[1259]
EUDORA WELTY PRIZE

Mississippi University for Women
Attn: Department of Languages, Literature, and
  Philosophy
Painter Hall, Room 111
P.O. Box MUW-1634
Columbus, MS 39701
(662) 329-7386   Fax: (662) 329-7387
E-mail: info@humanities.muw.edu
Web: www.muw.edu/welty/weltyprize

Summary To recognize and reward original works of interpretive scholarship from disciplines within the humanities and related to women's studies, Southern studies, or modern letters.

Eligibility Eligible to be submitted are unpublished book-length manuscripts (80,000 to 100,000 words) complete at the time of submission and not under consideration by any other press. Submissions must be original works of interpretive scholarship and from disciplines within the humanities related to women's studies, Southern studies, or modern literature. Collections of essays, bibliographies, translations, and unrevised theses or dissertations are not eligible.

Financial data The prize consists of a cash award of $2,000 and publication of the winning manuscript by the University Press of Mississippi.

Duration The prize is presented annually.

Additional information This prize, established in 1989, is jointly sponsored by Mississippi University for Women and the University Press of Mississippi.

Number awarded 1 each year.

Deadline April of each year.

[1260]
FACULTY EARLY CAREER DEVELOPMENT PROGRAM

National Science Foundation
Directorate for Education and Human Resources
Senior Staff Associate for Cross Directorate Programs
4201 Wilson Boulevard, Room 805
Arlington, VA 22230
(703) 292-8600   TDD: (800) 281-8749
E-mail: info@nsf.gov
Web: www.nsf.gov

Summary To provide funding to outstanding new faculty in science and engineering fields of interest to the National Science Foundation (NSF) who intend to develop academic careers involving both research and education.

Eligibility This program, identified as the CAREER program, is open to faculty members who meet all of the following requirements: 1) be employed in a tenure-track (or equivalent) position at an institution in the United States, its territories or possessions, or the Commonwealth of Puerto Rico that awards degrees in a field supported by NSF or that is a nonprofit, non-degree granting organization, such as a museum, observatory, or research laboratory; 2) have a doctoral degree in a field of science or engineering supported by NSF: 3) not have competed more than 3 times in this program; 4) be untenured; and 5) not be a current or former recipient of a Presidential Early Career Award for Scientists and Engineers (PECASE) or CAREER award. Applicants are not required to be U.S. citizens or permanent residents. They must submit a career development plan that indicates a description of the proposed research project, including preliminary supporting data (if appropriate), specific objectives, methods, procedures to be used, and expected significance of the results; a description of the proposed educational activities, including plans to evaluate their impact; a description of how the research and educational activities are integrated with each other; and results of prior NSF support (if applicable). Proposals from women, underrepresented minorities, and persons with disabilities are especially encouraged.

Financial data The grant is at least $80,000 per year (or $100,000 per year for the Directorate of Biological Sciences or the Office of Polar Programs), including indirect costs or overhead.

Duration 5 years.

Additional information This program is operated by various disciplinary divisions within the NSF; for a list of the participating divisions and their telephone numbers, contact the sponsor. Outstanding recipients of these grants are nominated for the NSF component of the PECASE awards, which are awarded to 20 recipients of these grants as an honorary award.

Number awarded Approximately 400, with a value of $222,000,000, are awarded each year.

Deadline July of each year.

[1261]
FASEB EXCELLENCE IN SCIENCE AWARD

Federation of American Societies for Experimental Biology
Attn: Excellence in Science Award
9650 Rockville Pike
Bethesda, MD 20814-3998
(301) 634-7092   Fax: (301) 634-7049
E-mail: info@faseb.org
Web: www.faseb.org

Summary To recognize and reward women whose research in experimental biology has contributed significantly to our understanding of their discipline.

Eligibility Nominations for this award may be submitted by members of the component societies of the Federation of American Societies for Experimental Biology (FASEB). Nominees must be women who are senior in their field and have a national reputation for outstanding contributions in research, leadership, and mentorship. They must also be members of 1 or more of the 30 societies of FASEB. Letters of nomination should identify the nominee's contributions to the field that represents her outstanding achievement in science, leadership and mentorship, evidence of national recognition, honors and awards, and a selected bibliography. Self-nominations are not accepted.

Financial data The award consists of a $10,000 unrestricted research grant, travel expenses to the annual meeting, complimentary registration at the meeting, and a plaque.

Duration This award is presented annually.

Additional information This award was first presented in 1989. Member societies of FASEB include the American Physiological Society (APS), American Society for Biochemistry and Molecular Biology (ASBMB), American Society for Pharmacology and Experimental Therapeutics (ASPET), American Society for Investigative Pathology (ASIP), American Society for Nutrition (ASN), American Association of Immunologists (AAI), American Association of Anatomists (AAA), The Protein Society, American Society for Bone and Mineral Research (ASBMR), American Society for Clinical Investigation (ASCI), The Endocrine Society, American Society of Human Genetics (ASHG), Society for Developmental Biology (SDB), American Peptide Society (APEPS), Association of Biomolecular Resource Facilities (ABRF), Society for the Study of Reproduction (SSR), Teratology Society, International Society for Computational Biology (ISCB), American College of Sports Medicine (ACSM), Biomedical Engineering Society (BMES), Genetics Society of America, American Federation for Medical Research (AFMR), The Histochemical Society (HCS) Society for Pediatric Research (SPR), Society for Glycobiology (SFG), Association for Molecular Pathology (AMP), Society for Redox Biology and Medicine (SFRBM), Society for Experimental Biology and Medicine (SEBM), American Aging Association, and the U.S. Human Proteome Organization (US HUPO).

Number awarded 1 each year.

Deadline Nominations must be submitted by February of each year.

[1262]
FEMINIST ACTIVISM AWARD

Sociologists for Women in Society
Attn: Administrative Officer
University of Kansas
Department of Sociology
1415 Jayhawk Boulevard, Room 716
Lawrence, KS 66045
(785) 864-9405   E-mail: swsao@outlook.com
Web: www.socwomen.org/feminist-activism-award-2

Summary To recognize and reward members of Sociologists for Women in Society (SWS) who have used sociology to improve conditions for women in society.

Eligibility This program is open to SWS members who have notably and consistently used sociology to better the lives of women. Nominees may be volunteers, non-volunteers, academicians, or private/public sector employees. Selection is based on advocacy and outreach efforts.

Financial data The award includes an honorarium of $1,000 and up to $500 for travel expenses to the organization's summer meeting where the recipient presents a lecture.

Duration The award is presented annually.

Additional information This award was first presented in 1995.

Number awarded 1 each year.

Deadline Nominations must be submitted by February of each year.

[1263]
F.J. MCGUIGAN EARLY CAREER INVESTIGATOR RESEARCH PRIZE ON UNDERSTANDING THE HUMAN MIND

American Psychological Foundation
750 First Street, N.E.
Washington, DC 20002-4242
(202) 336-5843   Fax: (202) 336-5812
E-mail: foundation@apa.org
Web: www.apa.org/apf/funding/mcguigan-prize.aspx

Summary To provide funding to young psychologists interested in conducting research related to the human mind.

Eligibility This program is open to investigators who have earned a doctoral degree in psychology or in a related field within the past 7 years. Nominees must have an affiliation with an accredited college, university, or other research institution. They must be engaged in research that seeks to explicate the concept of the human mind. The approach must be materialistic and should be primarily psychophysiological, but physiological and behavioral research may also qualify. Self-nominations are not accepted; candidates must be nominated by a senior colleague. The sponsor encourages nominations of individuals who represent diversity in race, ethnicity, gender, age, disability, and sexual orientation.

Financial data The grant is $25,000.

Duration These grants are awarded biennially, in even-numbered years.

Additional information The first grant under this program was awarded in 2002.

Number awarded 1 every other year.

Deadline February of even-numbered years.

[1264]
FLORENCE NIGHTINGALE DAVID AWARD

Committee of Presidents of Statistical Societies
c/o Jianwen Cai, David Award Committee Chair
University of North Carolina at Chapel Hill
Department of Biostatistics
McGavran-Greenberg Hall, CB 7420
Chapel Hill, NC 27599-7420
(919) 966-7788   E-mail: cai@bios.unc.edu
Web: community.amstat.org/copss/awards/fn-david

Summary To recognize and reward female statisticians who have made notable contributions to the field.

Eligibility This program is open to women who have demonstrated excellence as a role model to women in statistical research, leadership of multidisciplinary collaborative groups, statistics education, or leadership in the profession. Nominees may be of any age, race, sexual orientation, nationality, or citizenship, but they must be living at the time of their nomination.

Financial data The award consists of a plaque and a cash honorarium of $1,000.

Duration The award is presented biennially, in odd-numbered years.

Additional information The award was established in 2001.

Number awarded 1 every other year.

Deadline January of odd-numbered years.

[1265]
FLORIDA GOLDCOAST CHAPTER 75TH ANNIVERSARY SCHOLARSHIP

Ninety-Nines, Inc.-Florida Goldcoast Chapter
c/o Kimberley Lowe
100 Edgewater Drive, Unit 342
Coral Gables, FL 33133-6980
(305) 984-0561   E-mail: flynlowe@comcast.net
Web: www.flgoldcoast99s.org/scholarships.html

Summary To provide financial assistance to female pilots in Florida who are interested in an aviation training program at a college or flight school in the state.

Eligibility This program is open to women who have a private pilot's certificate and are either residents of Florida or students currently enrolled in an aviation training program in the state. Applicants must be interested in acquiring an additional rating or certificate, attending a college program, or engaging in another aviation endeavor. Along with their application, they must submit a statement describing their education, aviation training and experience, aviation organizations, and employment history; another statement covering their educational purpose and/or aviation goals, their goals, why they chose aviation, and the pilot certificate or rating, college degree, or other goal they plan to attain using this scholarship; and 2 letters of reference. Selection is based on financial need, desire to prepare for a career in aviation, ability to represent women in aviation, likelihood of success in reaching goals, and neatness and completeness of application package.

Financial data The stipend is $2,000.

Duration 1 year.

Number awarded 1 or more each year.

Deadline November of each year.

[1266]
FLYING MONTAGUES SCHOLARSHIP

Women Soaring Pilots Association
c/o Phyllis Wells
P.O. Box 278
Aguila, AZ 85320
(719) 429-4999   E-mail: pwells634@aol.com
Web: www.womensoaring.org/?p=info

Summary To provide financial assistance to women interested in obtaining a commercial rating in gliders and/or a certified instructor rating.

Eligibility This program is open to women who are members of the Women Soaring Pilots Association (WSPA) and interested in obtaining a commercial rating in gliders and/or a certified instructor rating in gliders. Applicants for a commercial rating must have at least 15 hours flight time in gliders and at least 50 flights in a glider while acting as PIC. Applicants for an instructor rating in gliders must already have a commercial rating and have passed both FAA written examinations. They must attend the Women Soaring Seminar. Along with their application, they must submit a 500-word essay explaining their goals and previous experiences as they relate to gliders and how this scholarship will help them meet their goals.

Financial data The scholarship provides $500 for the recipient to complete a commercial or instructor rating and $1,000 to attend the Women Soaring Seminar, including seminar registration and glider flight instruction, rental, and tow fees during the seminar. Recipients who obtain an instructor rating and give at least 10 hours of flight instruction receive an additional $500.

Duration The rating must be completed within 1 year.

Number awarded 1 each year.

Deadline May of each year.

[1267]
FOUNDATION FOR THE HISTORY OF WOMEN IN MEDICINE FELLOWSHIPS

Foundation for the History of Women in Medicine
c/o Archives for Women in Medicine
Francis A. Countway Library of Medicine
10 Shattuck Street
Boston, MA 02115
(617) 432-2170   E-mail: chm@hms.harvard.edu
Web: www.fhwim.org/fellowships/foundation-fellowships

Summary To provide funding to students and scholars interested in short-term use of resources in the Boston area to conduct research on the history of women and medicine.

Eligibility This program is open to doctoral candidates and other advanced scholars interested in using the Archives for Women in Medicine at the Countway Library's Center for the History of Medicine in Boston. Applicants must be interested in conducting research on the history of women in medicine. Preference is given to projects that deal specifically with women as physicians, health workers, or medical scientists, but proposals dealing with the history of women's health issues are also considered. Preference is given to applicants who live beyond commuting distance of the Countway.

Financial data The grant is $5,000.

Duration Recipients may conduct research on a flexible schedule during 1 academic year.

Additional information The Francis A. Countway Library of Medicine, the largest academic medical library in the United States, was established in 1960 as the result of an alliance between the Boston Medical Library and the Harvard Medical School Library.

Number awarded 1 or 2 each year.

Deadline March of each year.

[1268]
FRAMELINE COMPLETION FUND

Frameline
Attn: Completion Fund
145 Ninth Street, Suite 300
San Francisco, CA 94103
(415) 703-8650   Fax: (415) 861-1404
E-mail: info@frameline.org
Web: frameline.org

Summary To provide funding to lesbian, gay, bisexual, and transgender (LGBT) film/video artists.

Eligibility This program is open to LGBT artists who are in the last stages of the production of documentary, educational, narrative, animated, or experimental projects about or of interest to LGBT people and their communities. Applicants may be independent artists, students, producers, or nonprofit corporations. They must be interested in completion work and must have 90% of the production completed; projects in development, script-development, pre-production, or production are not eligible. Student projects are eligible only if the student maintains artistic and financial control of the project. Women and people of color are especially encouraged to apply. Selection is based on financial need, the contribution the grant will make to completing the project, assurances that the project will be completed, and the statement the project makes about LGBT people and/or issues of concern to them and their communities.

Financial data Grants range from $1,000 to $5,000.

Duration These are 1-time grants.

Additional information This program began in 1990.

Number awarded Varies each year; recently, 5 were awarded. Since this program was established, it has provided $464,200 in support to 136 films.

Deadline October of each year.

[1269]
FRAMELINE40 AT&T AUDIENCE AWARDS

Frameline
Attn: Festival
145 Ninth Street, Suite 300
San Francisco, CA 94103
(415) 703-8650   Fax: (415) 861-1404
E-mail: info@frameline.org
Web: ticketing.frameline.org/festival/about/awards.aspx

Summary To recognize and reward outstanding films of interest to the lesbian, gay, bisexual, and transgender (LGBT) audience.

Eligibility This competition is open to directors of films by, about, and of interest to LGBT people. Applicants must submit previews of their work on DVD or VHS in the following categories: narrative feature films (40 minutes and longer), documentary feature films (40 minutes and longer), and shorts (all films less than 40 minutes in length). The program actively seeks out work by women and people of color. Recently, awards have been presented for best feature film, best documentary film, and best short film.

Financial data Awards are $1,000 for best feature and best documentary and $500 for best short film.

Duration The awards are presented annually.

Additional information No fees are charged for the early deadline. Standard fees are $35 for the regular deadline, $50 for the late deadline, or $55 for the extended deadline. Student fees are $15 for regular, late, and extended deadlines. Fees are waived for youth up to 18 years of age.

Number awarded 3 each year.

Deadline December of each year for the early deadline; January of each year for the regular deadline; mid-February for the late deadline; and the end of February for the extended deadline.

[1270]
FRAN SARGENT SCHOLARSHIP

Ninety-Nines, Inc.-Florida Goldcoast Chapter
c/o Kimberley Lowe
100 Edgewater Drive, Unit 342
Coral Gables, FL 33133-6980
(305) 984-0561   E-mail: flynlowe@comcast.net
Web: www.flgoldcoast99s.org/scholarships.html

Summary To provide financial assistance to female pilots in Florida who are interested in an aviation training program at a college or flight school in the state.

Eligibility This program is open to women who have a private pilot's certificate and are either residents of Florida or students currently enrolled in an aviation training program in the state. Applicants must be interested in acquiring an additional rating or certificate, attending a college program, or engaging in another aviation endeavor. Along with their application, they must submit a statement describing their education, aviation training and experience, aviation organizations, and employment and/or educational history; another statement covering their educational purpose and/or aviation goals, their goals, why they chose aviation, and the pilot certificate or rating, college degree, or other goal they plan to attain using this scholarship; and 2 letters of reference. Selection is based on financial need, desire to prepare for a career in aviation, ability to represent women in aviation, likelihood of success in reaching goals, and neatness and completeness of application package.

Financial data The stipend is $2,500.

Duration 1 year.

Number awarded 1 or more each year.

Deadline October of each year.

[1271]
FRANCES LEWIS FELLOWSHIPS IN GENDER AND WOMEN'S STUDIES

Virginia Historical Society
Attn: Chair, Research Fellowships and Awards Committee
428 North Boulevard
P.O. Box 7311
Richmond, VA 23221-0311
(804) 342-9686   Fax: (804) 355-2399
E-mail: fpollard@vahistorical.org
Web: www.vahistorical.org/research/fellowships.htm

Summary To offer short-term financial assistance to pre- and postdoctoral scholars interested in conducting research in women's studies at the Virginia Historical Society.

Eligibility This program is open to doctoral candidates, faculty, or independent scholars interested in conducting research in women's studies. Applicants whose research promises to result in a significant publication, such as in the society's documents series of edited texts or in the *Virginia Magazine of History and Biography,* receive primary consideration. Along with their application, they must submit a resume, 2 letters of recommendation, a description of the research project (up to 2 pages), and a cover letter. Because the program is designed to help defray research travel expenses, residents of the Richmond metropolitan area are not eligible. Also ineligible are undergraduates, master's students, and graduate students not yet admitted to Ph.D. candidacy. Selection is based on the applicants' scholarly qualifications, the merits of their research proposals, and the appropriateness of their topics to the holdings of the Virginia Historical Society.

Financial data A few small grants (up to $150 per week) are awarded for mileage to researchers who live at least 50 miles from Richmond. The majority of the awards are $500 per week and go to researchers who live further away and thus incur greater expenses.

Duration Up to 3 weeks a year. Recipients may reapply in following years up to these limits: a maximum of 3 weeks in a 5-year period for doctoral candidates; a maximum of 6 weeks in a 5-year period for faculty or independent scholars.

Additional information The society's library contains 7 million manuscripts and thousands of books, maps, broadsides, newspapers, and historical objects. This program was formerly known as the Sydney and Frances Lewis Fellowships. Recipients are expected to work on a regular basis in the society's reading room during the period of the award.

Number awarded Varies each year; recently, the society awarded a total of 20 research fellowships.

Deadline January of each year.

[1272]
FRANK NELSON DOUBLEDAY MEMORIAL AWARD

Wyoming Arts Council
2301 Central Avenue, Second Floor
Cheyenne, WY 82002
(307) 777-7742   Fax: (307) 777-5499
TDD: (307) 777-5964   E-mail: rachel.clifton@wyo.gov
Web: wyoarts.state.wy.us

Summary To recognize and reward outstanding female writers (in any genre) who live in Wyoming.

Eligibility This program is open to female writers who live in Wyoming for at least 10 months of the year, are older than 18 years of age, and are not full-time students or faculty members. Writers are eligible if they have never published a book; if they have published only 1 full-length book of fiction, poetry, or nonfiction; of if they have published no more than 1 book of poetry, 1 of fiction, and 1 of nonfiction. They are invited to submit manuscripts of poetry (up to 10 printed pages with no more than 1 poem per page), fiction or creative nonfiction (up to 25 pages), or drama and screenplays (up to 25 pages).

Financial data The award is $1,000.

Duration The award is presented annually.

Number awarded 1 each year.

Deadline October of each year.

[1273]
GAIUS CHARLES BOLIN DISSERTATION AND POST-MFA FELLOWSHIPS

Williams College
Attn: Dean of the Faculty
880 Main Street
Hopkins Hall, Third Floor
P.O. Box 141
Williamstown, MA 01267
(413) 597-4351   Fax: (413) 597-3553
E-mail: gburda@williams.edu
Web: faculty.williams.edu

Summary To provide financial assistance to members of underrepresented groups who are interested in teaching courses at Williams College while working on their doctoral dissertation or building their post-M.F.A. professional portfolio.

Eligibility This program is open to members of underrepresented groups, including ethnic minorities, first-generation college students, women in predominantly male fields, and scholars with disabilities. Applicants must be 1) doctoral candidates in any field who have completed all work for a Ph.D. except for the dissertation; or 2) artists who completed an M.F.A. degree within the past 2 years and are building their professional portfolio. They must be willing to teach a course at Williams College. Along with their application, they must submit a full curriculum vitae, a graduate school transcript, 3 letters of recommendation, a copy of their dissertation prospectus or samples of their artistic work, and a description of their teaching interests within a department or program at Williams College. U.S. citizenship or permanent resident status is required.

Financial data Fellows receive $38,000 for the academic year, plus housing assistance, office space, computer and library privileges, and a research allowance of up to $4,000.

Duration 2 years.

Additional information Bolin fellows are assigned a faculty adviser in the appropriate department. This program was established in 1985. Fellows are expected to teach a 1-semester course each year. They must be in residence at Williams College for the duration of the fellowship.

Number awarded 2 each year.

Deadline November of each year.

[1274]
GEOPHYSICAL FLUID DYNAMICS FELLOWSHIPS

Woods Hole Oceanographic Institution
Attn: Academic Programs Office
Clark Laboratory, MS 31
266 Woods Hole Road
Woods Hole, MA 02543-1541
(508) 289-2950   Fax: (508) 457-2188
E-mail: gfd@whoi.edu
Web: www.whoi.edu/main/gfd/fellowships

Summary To provide summer research and study opportunities at Woods Hole Oceanographic Institution (WHOI) to pre- and postdoctoral scholars interested in geophysical fluid dynamics.

Eligibility This program is open to pre- and postdoctorates who are interested in pursuing research or study opportunities in a field that involves non-linear dynamics of rotating, stratified fluids. Fields of specialization include classical fluid dynamics, physical oceanography, meteorology, geophysical fluid dynamics, astrophysics, planetary atmospheres, hydromagnetics, physics, and applied mathematics. Applications from women and members of underrepresented groups are particularly encouraged.

Financial data Participants receive a stipend of $6,284 and an allowance for travel expenses within the United States.

Duration 10 weeks during the summer.

Additional information Each summer, the program at WHOI revolves around a central theme. A recent theme related to shear turbulence. The main components of the summer program are a series of principal lectures, a set of supplementary research seminars, and research projects conducted by the student fellows with the active support of the staff. Funding for this program, which began in 1959, is provided by the National Science Foundation and Office of Naval Research.

Number awarded Up to 10 graduate students are supported each year.

Deadline February of each year.

[1275]
GEORGIA BABLADELIS BEST PWQ PAPER AWARD

American Psychological Association
Attn: Division 35 (Psychology of Women)
750 First Street, N.E.
Washington, DC 20002-4242
(202) 216-7602   Fax: (202) 336-5953
TDD: (202) 336-6123 E-mail: martha.bergen@gmail.com
Web: www.apadivisions.org

Summary To recognize and reward authors of outstanding articles published in *Psychology of Women Quarterly* (PWQ).

Eligibility This award is presented to the author of the article published in PWQ during the preceding year. All accepted papers are considered.

Financial data The award is $1,000.

Duration This award is presented annually.

Additional information This award was first presented in 2011.

Number awarded 1 each year.

Deadline Deadline not specified.

[1276]
GERTRUDE AND MAURICE GOLDHABER DISTINGUISHED FELLOWSHIPS

Brookhaven National Laboratory
Attn: Bill Bookless
Building 460
40 Brookhaven Avenue
Upton, NY 11973
(631) 344-5734   E-mail: barkigia@bnl.gov
Web: www.bnl.gov/HR/goldhaber

Summary To provide funding to postdoctoral scientists interested in conducting research at Brookhaven National Laboratory (BNL).

Eligibility This program is open to scholars who are no more than 3 years past receipt of the Ph.D. and are interested in working at BNL. Candidates must be interested in working in close collaboration with a member of the BNL scientific staff and qualifying for a scientific staff position at BNL upon completion of the appointment. The sponsoring scientist must have an opening and be able to support the candidate at the standard starting salary for postdoctoral research associates. The program especially encourages applications from minorities and women.

Financial data The program provides additional funds to bring the salary to $81,200 per year.

Duration 3 years.

Additional information This program is funded by Battelle Memorial Institute and the State University of New York at Stony Brook.

Number awarded Up to 2 each year.

Deadline June of each year.

[1277]
GILDA MURRAY SCHOLARSHIPS

Texas Business Women
Attn: Texas Business and Professional Women's
  Foundation
P.O. Box 70
Round Rock, TX 78680-0070
E-mail: info@tbwconnect.com
Web: www.texasbpwfoundation.org/scholarships.php

Summary To provide financial assistance to members of Texas Business Women (TBW) who are interested in career advancement.

Eligibility This program is open to members of TBW who are interested in pursuing education or training necessary to prepare for employment or to advance in a business or profession. Applicants must be at least 25 years of age and have a record of active participation in the association. Along with their application, they must submit a 1-page description of the course and its benefits to them. Selection is based on merit and need.

Financial data Funding covers 50% of the cost of the training, to a maximum of $1,000 per year.

Duration 1 year; may be renewed.

Additional information This program began in 1998 when Texas Business Women was named Texas Federation of Business and Professional Women's Clubs.

Number awarded 1 or more each year.

Deadline Applications may be submitted at any time.

[1278]
GITA CHUADHURI PRIZE

Western Association of Women Historians
c/o Cheryl Krasnick Warsh, Executive Director
Vancouver Island University
History Department
900 Fifth Street
Nanaimo, BC V9R 5S5
Canada
E-mail: ExecutiveDirector@wawh.org
Web: www.wawh.org/awards/gita-chaudhuri-prize

Summary   To recognize and reward outstanding books on rural women published by members of the Western Association of Women Historians (WAWH).

Eligibility   Members of the WAWH are eligible to submit their books for consideration if they were published any time during the preceding 3 years. The entry must be a single-authored monograph based on original research that relates to rural women, from any era and any place in the world. Anthologies and edited works are not eligible for consideration.

Financial data   The award is $1,000.

Duration   The award is presented annually.

Additional information   This award was first presented in 2009.

Number awarded   1 each year.

Deadline   January of each year.

[1279]
GLORIA E. ANZALDUA BOOK PRIZE

National Women's Studies Association
Attn: Book Prizes
11 East Mount Royal Avenue, Suite 100
Baltimore, MD 21202
(410) 528-0355   Fax: (410) 528-0357
E-mail: awards@nwsa.org
Web: www.nwsa.org

Summary   To recognize and reward members of the National Women's Studies Association (NWSA) who have written outstanding books on women of color and transnational issues.

Eligibility   This award is available to NWSA members who submit a book that was published during the preceding year. Entries must present groundbreaking scholarship in women's studies and make a significant multicultural feminist contribution to women of color and/or transnational studies.

Financial data   The award provides an honorarium of $1,000 and lifetime membership in NWSA.

Duration   The award is presented annually.

Additional information   This award was first presented in 2008.

Number awarded   1 each year.

Deadline   April of each year.

[1280]
HADASSAH-BRANDEIS INSTITUTE ARTIST-IN-RESIDENCE PROGRAM

Brandeis University
Hadassah-Brandeis Institute
Attn: Program Manager
515 South Street
Mailstop 079
Waltham, MA 02454-9110
(781) 736-8113   Fax: (781) 736-2078
E-mail: dolins@brandeis.edu
Web: www.brandeis.edu/hirjw/residencies/artist.html

Summary   To provide an opportunity for artists to work on a significant project in the field of Jewish women's studies while in residence at the Hadassah-Brandeis Institute (HBI) of Brandeis University.

Eligibility   This program is open to artists who are working in the area of Jewish women's and gender studies. Applicants must be interested in working on a significant artistic project while in residence at the institute and in producing an exhibit for the Kniznick Gallery at the Brandeis University Women's Studies Research Center (WSRC). Preference is given to artists who create a site-specific exhibit that 1) is visually and artistically impressive and original; 2) is related to fresh ways of thinking about Jews and gender; 3) is international in nature; 4) asks important questions and provokes dialogue; 5) is related to research being produced and promoted by the HBI; 6) provides a context for education; 7) is appropriate in scale for the Kniznick Gallery; and 8) includes new work produced during the residency. Applications (in English) from outside the United States are welcome.

Financial data   Artists receive a stipend of $3,000 ($750 per week), a materials subsidy of $250, and studio space at the WSRC.

Duration   4 to 6 weeks, beginning in March.

Additional information   The Hadassah-Brandeis Institute was formerly the Hadassah International Research Institute on Jewish Women at Brandeis University. This program began in 2008.

Number awarded   1 or more each year.

Deadline   September of each year.

[1281]
HADASSAH-BRANDEIS INSTITUTE RESEARCH AWARDS

Brandeis University
Hadassah-Brandeis Institute
Attn: Program Manager
515 South Street
Mailstop 079
Waltham, MA 02454-9110
(781) 736-8113   Fax: (781) 736-2078
E-mail: dolins@brandeis.edu
Web: www.brandeis.edu/hbi/grants/research.html

Summary   To provide funding to scholars, graduate students, writers, activists, and artists conducting research in the field of Jewish women's studies.

Eligibility   This program offers senior grants (for established scholars and professionals) and junior grants (for graduate students and scholars within 3 years of receiving a Ph.D.). All applicants must be interested in conducting interdisciplinary research on Jewish women and gender issues, although there are no gender or religious limitations. Graduate students in recognized master's and Ph.D. programs are encouraged to apply. Applications from outside the United States are welcome. Grants are awarded in 10 categories: history; the Yishuv and Israel; Diaspora studies; families, children, and the Holocaust; gender, culture, religion, and the law; women's health; Judaism; biography; the arts (performance arts, visual arts, creative writing); and film and video. Applications must specify the category and may be for only 1 category. Selection is based on excellence.

Financial data Senior grants are $5,000 and junior grants are $2,000.

Duration 1 year.

Additional information The Hadassah-Brandeis Institute was formerly the Hadassah International Research Institute on Jewish Women at Brandeis University.

Number awarded Between 20 and 30 each year.

Deadline September of each year.

[1282]
HEATHER WESTPHAL MEMORIAL SCHOLARSHIP AWARD

International Association of Fire Chiefs
Attn: IAFC Foundation
4025 Fair Ridge Drive, Suite 300
Fairfax, VA 22033-2868
(703) 896-4822   Fax: (703) 273-9363
E-mail: Sbaroncelli@iafc.org
Web: www.iafcf.org/Scholarship.htm

Summary To provide financial assistance to female firefighters, especially members of the International Association of Fire Chiefs, who wish to further their academic education.

Eligibility This program is open to women who are active members of state, county, provincial, municipal, community, industrial, or federal fire departments in the United States or Canada and have demonstrated proficiency as members for at least 2 years of paid or 3 years of volunteer service. Dependents of members are not eligible. Applicants must be planning to work on an associate or bachelor's degree at a recognized institution of higher education. Along with their application, they must submit a 250-word essay that includes a brief description of the course work, how the course work will benefit their fire service career and department and improve the fire service, and their financial need. Preference is given to members of the International Association of Fire Chiefs (IAFC).

Financial data A stipend is awarded (amount not specified).

Duration Up to 1 year.

Additional information This program began in 2009 with support from the International Association of Women in Fire and Emergency Service.

Number awarded 1 each year.

Deadline April of each year.

[1283]
HECKSEL-SUTHERLAND SCHOLARSHIP

Ninety-Nines, Inc.-Michigan Chapter
c/o Rosemary Sieracki, Administrator
41490 Hanford Road
Canton, MI 48187-3512
(734) 981-4787   E-mail: sierackr@att.net
Web: www.michigan99s.info/node/6

Summary To provide financial assistance to women in Michigan who are interested in attending a school in any state to prepare for a career in aviation.

Eligibility This program is open to women who live in Michigan and are interested in preparing for a career in aviation or aeronautics. Applicants must be enrolled or planning to enroll in private pilot training, additional pilot certificate or rating, college education in aviation, technical training in aviation, or other aviation-related training. Along with their application, they must submit 1) a 1-page essay on how the money will be used; 2) documentation from the training or academic institution verifying the cost of the training; 3) copies of all aviation and medical certificates and the last 3 pages of the pilot logbook (if applicable); and 4) an essay that covers their aviation history, short- and long-term goals, how the scholarship will help them achieve those goals, any educational awards and honors they have received, their significant or unique achievements, where training would be received and the costs involved, their involvement in aviation activities, and their community involvement. Selection is based on motivation, willingness to accept responsibility, reliability, and commitment to success.

Financial data The stipend is $2,000.

Duration 1 year.

Additional information This program began in 2012.

Number awarded 1 each year.

Deadline October of each year.

[1284]
HELEN GARTNER HAMMER SCHOLAR-IN-RESIDENCE PROGRAM

Brandeis University
Hadassah-Brandeis Institute
Attn: Program Manager
515 South Street
Mailstop 079
Waltham, MA 02454-9110
(781) 736-8113   Fax: (781) 736-2078
E-mail: dolins@brandeis.edu
Web: www.brandeis.edu

Summary To provide an opportunity for scholars, artists, writers, and communal professionals to conduct research in the field of Jewish women's studies while in residence at the Hadassah-Brandeis Institute of Brandeis University.

Eligibility This program is open to scholars, artists, writers, and communal professionals who are working in the area of Jewish women's and gender studies. Applicants must be interested in taking time from their regular institutional duties to work at the institute. Scholars outside the United States and those with an international research focus are especially encouraged to apply.

Financial data Scholars receive a stipend of $3,000 per month and office space at the Brandeis University Women's Studies Research Center.

Duration 1 month to 1 semester.

Additional information The Hadassah-Brandeis Institute was formerly the Hadassah International Research Institute on Jewish Women at Brandeis University.

Number awarded Varies each year; recently, 12 of these residencies were awarded.

Deadline January of each year.

[1285]
HELEN HAMMER TRANSLATION PRIZE

Brandeis University
Hadassah-Brandeis Institute
Attn: Program Manager
515 South Street
Mailstop 079
Waltham, MA 02454-9110
(781) 736-8113   Fax: (781) 736-2078
E-mail: dolins@brandeis.edu
Web: www.brandeis.edu/hirjw/grants/translation.html

Summary To provide funding for the translation of books that deal with Jewish women's studies, generally from another language into English.

Eligibility This program is open to authors of books that deal in a significant way with Jews and gender and to potential translators who have the author's permission to translate the book. The book to be translated must already have been published in another language and may be fiction, academic scholarship, or a trade book with general public interest. Preference is given to books to be translated from another language into English.

Financial data Grant amounts vary, and may be used only for payment of actual translation costs.

Duration Grants are awarded annually.

Additional information The Hadassah-Brandeis Institute was formerly the Hadassah International Research Institute on Jewish Women at Brandeis University. This program began in 2009.

Number awarded 1 or more each year.

Deadline November of each year.

[1286]
HENRY P. DAVID GRANTS FOR RESEARCH AND INTERNATIONAL TRAVEL IN HUMAN REPRODUCTIVE BEHAVIOR AND POPULATION STUDIES

American Psychological Foundation
750 First Street, N.E.
Washington, DC 20002-4242
(202) 336-5843   Fax: (202) 336-5812
E-mail: foundation@apa.org
Web: www.apa.org/apf/funding/david.aspx

Summary To provide funding to young psychologists who are interested in conducting research on reproductive behavior.

Eligibility This program is open to doctoral students in psychology working on a dissertation and young psychologists who have no more than 10 years of postgraduate experience. Applicants must be interested in conducting research on

human reproductive behavior or an area related to population concerns. Along with their application, they must submit a current curriculum vitae, 2 letters of recommendation, and an essay of 1 to 2 pages on their interest in human reproductive behavior or in population studies. The sponsor encourages applications from individuals who represent diversity in race, ethnicity, gender, age, disability, and sexual orientation.

Financial data The grant is $1,500.

Duration The grant is presented annually.

Additional information Every third year (2017, 1020), the program also provides support for a non-U.S. reproductive health/population science professional to travel to and participate in the Psychosocial Workshop, held in conjunction with the Population Association of America annual meeting.

Number awarded 2 in the years when the program offers support to a non-U.S. professional to travel to the United States; 1 in other years.

Deadline November of each year.

[1287]
HERBERT AND BETTY CARNES FUND

American Ornithologists' Union
c/o Brian D. Peer, Research Awards Chair
Western Illinois University
Department of Biological Sciences
Waggoner Hall 333
Macomb, IL 61455
(309) 298-2336   E-mail: BD_peer@wiu-edu
Web: www.americanornithology.org

Summary To provide funding to female graduate students and scholars who are members of the American Ornithologists' Union (AOU) and interested in conducting research on avian biology.

Eligibility This program is open to female AOU members who are graduate students, postdoctorates, or other researchers without access to major funding agencies. Applicants must be interested in conducting research on avian biology. They must be nonsmokers (have not smoked in at least the previous 6 months). Along with their application, they should send a cover letter (about 5 pages) describing their proposed project, a budget, and 1 letter of reference. Selection is based on significance and originality of the research question, clarity of the objectives, feasibility of the plan of research, and appropriateness of the budget.

Financial data The maximum award is $2,500 per year.

Duration 1 year; recipients may reapply for 1 additional award.

Number awarded The sponsor awards a total of 28 to 30 grants each year.

Deadline January of each year.

[1288]
HEWLETT-PACKARD HARRIETT B. RIGAS AWARD

Institute of Electrical and Electronics Engineers
Attn: IEEE Education Society
c/o Edwin C. Jones, Jr., Awards Committee Chair
University of St. Thomas
School of Engineering
OSS111
2115 Summit Avenue
St. Paul, MN 55105
(651) 962-5750   E-mail: e.c.jones@ieee.org
Web: www.ieee-edusociety.org

Summary To recognize and reward women who have made significant contributions to electrical and/or computer engineering education.

Eligibility This award is available to women who are tenured or tenure-track faculty in an ABET-accredited engineering program with teaching and/or research specialization in electrical and/or computer engineering. Nominees must have demonstrated excellence in undergraduate and/or graduate teaching, commitment to electrical/computer engineering education, active participation in encouraging and supporting increased participation of women in electrical/computer engineering, demonstrated scholarship and research, evidence of the development of educational technology that enhances student learning, and serving to the engineering profession.

Financial data The award includes an honorarium of $2,000, a plaque, a certificate, registration fees for the Frontiers in Education (FIE) Conference, and reimbursement of expenses for attendance at that conference to accept the award.

Duration The award is presented annually.

Additional information This award, first presented in 1995, is sponsored by Hewlett-Packard.

Number awarded 1 each year.

Deadline April of each year.

[1289]
HORIZONS FOUNDATION SCHOLARSHIP PROGRAM

Women in Defense
c/o National Defense Industrial Association
2111 Wilson Boulevard, Suite 400
Arlington, VA 22201-3061
(703) 522-1820   Fax: (703) 522-1885
E-mail: wid@ndia.org
Web: www.womenindefense.net

Summary To provide financial assistance to members of Women in Defense (WID) who are upper-division or graduate students engaged in or planning careers related to the national security interests of the United States.

Eligibility This program is open to WID members who are already working in national security fields as well as women planning such careers. Applicants must 1) be currently enrolled at an accredited college or university, either full or part time, as graduate students or upper-division undergraduates; 2) demonstrate financial need; 3) be U.S. citizens; 4) have a GPA of 3.25 or higher; and 5) demonstrate interest in preparing for a career related to national security or defense. The preferred fields of study include business (as it relates to

national security or defense), computer science, cyber security, economics, engineering, government relations, international relations, law (as it relates to national security or defense), mathematics, military history, political science, physics, and security studies; others are considered if the applicant can demonstrate relevance to a career in national security or defense. Selection is based on academic achievement, participation in defense and national security activities, field of study, work experience, statements of objectives, recommendations, and financial need.

Financial data The stipend ranges up to $10,000.

Duration 1 year; renewable.

Additional information This program began in 1988.

Number awarded Varies each year; recently, 3 worth $16,000 were awarded.

Deadline July of each year.

[1290]
HUBBLE FELLOWSHIPS

Space Telescope Science Institute
Attn: Hubble Fellowship Program Office
3700 San Martin Drive
Baltimore, MD 21218
(410) 338-2474   Fax: (410) 338-4211
E-mail: hfinquiry@stsci.edu
Web: www.stsci.edu

Summary To provide funding to recent postdoctoral scientists who are interested in conducting research related to the Hubble Space Telescope or related missions of the National Aeronautics and Space Administration (NASA).

Eligibility This program is open to postdoctoral scientists who completed their doctoral degree within the past 3 years in astronomy, physics, or related disciplines. Applicants must be interested in conducting research related to NASA Cosmic Origins missions: the Hubble Space Telescope, Herschel Space Observatory, James Webb Space Telescope, Stratospheric Observatory for Infrared Astronomy, or the Spitzer Space Telescope. They may U.S. citizens or English-speaking citizens of other countries with valid visas. Research may be theoretical, observational, or instrumental. Women and members of minority groups are strongly encouraged to apply.

Financial data Stipends are approximately $66,500 per year. Other benefits may include health insurance, relocation costs, and support for travel, equipment, and other direct costs of research.

Duration 3 years: an initial 1-year appointment and 2 annual renewals, contingent on satisfactory performance and availability of funds.

Additional information This program, funded by NASA, began in 1990 and was limited to work with the Hubble Space Telescope. A parallel program, called the Spitzer Fellowship, began in 2002 and was limited to work with the Spitzer Space Telescope. In 2009, those programs were combined into this single program, which was also broadened to include the other NASA Cosmic Origins missions. Fellows are required to be in residence at their host institution engaged in full-time research for the duration of the grant.

Number awarded Varies each year; recently, 17 were awarded.

Deadline October of each year.

[1291]
INTERNATIONAL SECURITY AND COOPERATION POSTDOCTORAL FELLOWSHIPS

Stanford University
Center for International Security and Cooperation
Attn: Fellowships Coordinator
Encina Hall, Room C206-10
616 Serra Street
Stanford, CA 94305-6165
(650) 723-9625   Fax: (650) 724-5683
E-mail: CISACfellowship@stanford.edu
Web: cisac.fsi.stanford.edu/docs/cisac_fellowship_program

Summary To provide funding to postdoctorates who are interested in conducting research on international security problems at Stanford University's Center for International Security and Cooperation.

Eligibility This program is open to scholars who have a Ph.D. or equivalent degree from the United States or abroad and would benefit from using the resources of the center. Applicants may be working in any discipline of the social sciences, humanities, natural sciences, law, or engineering that relates to international security problems. Relevant topics include nuclear weapons policy and nonproliferation; nuclear energy; cybersecurity, cyberwarfare, and the future of the Internet; war and civil conflict; global governance, migration and transnational flows, from norms to criminal trafficking; biosecurity and global health; implications of geostrategic shifts; insurgency, terrorism, and homeland security; and consolidating peace after conflict. The sponsor welcomes applications from women, minorities, and citizens of all countries.

Financial data The stipend ranges from $48,000 to $66,000, depending on experience. Medical insurance is available for those who do not have coverage.

Duration 9 to 11 months.

Additional information Fellows are expected to write a publishable article or articles and/or make significant progress on turning a thesis into a book manuscript. They should not plan to spend any time conducting research abroad or in other parts of the country.

Number awarded Varies each year; recently, 7 were awarded.

Deadline January of each year.

[1292]
INTERNATIONAL WOMEN'S FILM FESTIVAL PRIZES

Festival International de Films de Femmes
c/o Maison des Arts de Créteil
Place Salvador Allende
94000 Créteil
France
33 1 49 80 38 98   Fax: 33 1 43 99 04 10
E-mail: filmsfemmes@wanadoo.fr
Web: www.filmsdefemmes.com

Summary To recognize and reward outstanding films directed by women at a competition in France.

Eligibility Recent films directed by women from any country may be considered for this competition. There are 3 sections: full-length feature films, full-length documentaries, and short-length feature and documentary films. Entries must be submitted in 16mm, 35mm, or video. They must have been completed within the previous 21 months and not yet shown or broadcast in France. Each year, different prizes are available; recently, the Grand Jury Prize was offered for the best full-length feature film; Audience Awards were offered for the best feature film, the best documentary, the best French short film, and the best foreign short film; the "Graine de Ciné-phage" Jury Award was presented for the best short documentary; the University Paris Créteil Jury Award was presented for the best European short film; the Anna Politkovskaya Jury Prize was awarded for the best documentary feature; and the FranceTV Feminine Prize was presented to the outstanding director in the musical section.

Financial data Recently, the Grand Jury Prize was 3,000 Euros; the Audience Awards were 2,000 Euros for the best feature film and the best documentary, 500 Euros for the best foreign short film, and purchase of broadcasting rights for the best French short film; the "Graine de Cinéphage" Jury Award was 1,000 Euros; the University Paris Créteil Jury Award was 1,500 Euros; the Anna Politkovskaya Jury Prize (created in 2009) was 4,000 Euros; and the FranceTV Feminine Prize (created in 2015) was 5,000 Euros.

Duration The prizes are awarded annually.

Additional information The competition, which began in 1978, is held at the Festival in Créteil, a suburb in the south of Paris.

Number awarded The number of prizes varies each year.

Deadline November of each year.

[1293]
IOTA SIGMA PI NATIONAL HONORARY MEMBER

Iota Sigma Pi
c/o Lily M. Ng, National Director for Professional Awards
Cleveland State University
Department of Chemistry
3077 Euclid Avenue
Cleveland, OH 44115-2516
(612) 455-9354   E-mail: lilymsng@gmail.com
Web: www.iotasigmapi.info

Summary To recognize exceptional and significant achievement by women working in chemistry or allied fields.

Eligibility Nominees for the award must be outstanding women chemists. They may be from any country and need not be members of Iota Sigma Pi. Each active chapter is entitled to make only 1 nomination, but individual members, individual chemists, or groups of chemists may make independent nominations if properly documented. The nomination dossier must contain the candidate's name and address, educational and professional background, membership in professional societies, area of specialization or research, honors, awards, citations, publications, and letters of recommendation.

Financial data The award consists of $1,500, a certificate, and a lifetime waiver of Iota Sigma Pi dues.

Duration The award is granted triennially (2020, 2023, etc.).

Additional information This award was first presented in 1921.

Number awarded 1 every 3 years.

Deadline Nominations must be submitted by February of the year of award.

[1294]
ISA FINANCIAL SCHOLARSHIPS

International Society of Women Airline Pilots
Attn: Scholarships
723 South Casino Center Boulevard, Second Floor
Las Vegas, NV 89101-6716
E-mail: Scholarship@iswap.org
Web: www.iswap.org

Summary To help women from any country who are working on their pilot certificates and ratings and are interested in preparing for a career as an airline pilot or instructor.

Eligibility This program is open to women who are working to acquire an Airline Transport Pilot (ATP) license or a Certified Flight Instructor (CFI) Multi-Engine Certificate. Applicants must submit a 500-word essay that covers their aviation history and goals; what they have done for themselves to achieve their goals; where they see themselves in 5 and 10 years; how the scholarship will help them achieve their objective, and their present financial need. Selection is based on achievements, attitude, commitment, dedication, motivation, reliability, responsibility, teamwork, and financial need.

Financial data The stipend is $3,500.

Duration Training must be completed within 1 year.

Additional information This program began in 1988.

Number awarded 4 each year.

Deadline November of each year.

[1295]
J. CORDELL BREED AWARD FOR WOMEN LEADERS

Society of Automotive Engineers
Attn: Award Program Staff
400 Commonwealth Drive
Warrendale, PA 15096-0001
(724) 776-4970   Toll Free: (877) 606-7323
Fax: (724) 776-0790   E-mail: awards@sae.org
Web: awards.sae.org/wec

Summary To recognize and reward female members of the Society of Automotive Engineering (SAE) who have been active in the mobility industry.

Eligibility This award is presented to women who participate in and are involved in SAE activities. Nominees must 1) exhibit outstanding service to their company and community; 2) demonstrate excellent leadership as a supervisor, manager, or member in a team environment; 3) display innovation and uniqueness in achieving corporate and personal goals; 4) provide important engineering or technical contributions to the mobility industry; 5) demonstrate strong interpersonal skills; and 6) have overcome adversity.

Financial data The award consists of an engraved plaque and an honorarium of $2,000.

Duration The award is presented annually.

Additional information This award was established in 1999 by the SAE Women Engineers Committee (WEC).

Number awarded 1 each year.

Deadline Nominations must be submitted by July of each year.

[1296]
JANE CHAMBERS PLAYWRITING AWARD

Association for Theatre in Higher Education
Attn: Women and Theatre Program
P.O. Box 1290
Boulder, CO 80306-1290
(303) 530-2167   Toll Free: (888) 284-3737
Fax: (303) 530-2168   E-mail: vpawards@athe.org
Web: www.womenandtheatreprogram.com

Summary To recognize and reward outstanding plays and performance texts that were created by women and have a majority of parts for women performers.

Eligibility Women are invited to submit plays and performance texts that reflect a feminist perspective and contain significant opportunities for women performers. Scripts may be produced or unproduced. There is no limitation on length, style, or subject. Current undergraduate and graduate students may enter the student category of the competition.

Financial data The general award consists of $1,000, free registration to attend the Women and Theatre Conference (early August), and a rehearsed reading of the winning piece at that conference. The student award is $150 and a year's membership in Women and Theatre.

Duration The competition is held annually.

Number awarded 1 general award and 1 student award are presented each year.

Deadline February of each year.

[1297]
JOAN AND JOSEPH BIRMAN RESEARCH PRIZE IN TOPOLOGY AND GEOMETRY

Association for Women in Mathematics
11240 Waples Mill Road, Suite 200
Fairfax, VA 22030
(703) 934-0163   Fax: (703) 359-7562
E-mail: awm@awm-math.org
Web: sites.google.com

Summary To recognize and reward women who are early in their research careers and have made outstanding contributions in topology or geometry.

Eligibility This award is available to women who are faculty members at U.S. institutions and within 10 years of receiving their Ph.D. or have not yet received tenure. Nominees must have conducted exceptional research in topology or geometry, interpreted broadly to include geometric group theory and related areas.

Financial data The award includes a cash prize and honorary plaque.

Duration The award is presented biennially, in odd-numbered years.

Additional information This award was first presented in 2015.

Number awarded 1 each year.

Deadline Nominations must be submitted by February of each even-numbered year.

[1298]
JOAN F. GIAMBALVO FUND FOR THE ADVANCEMENT OF WOMEN

American Medical Association
Attn: AMA Foundation
330 North Wabash Avenue, Suite 39300
Chicago, IL 60611-5885
(312) 464-4743　　　　　Fax: (312) 464-4142
E-mail: wpc@ama-assn.org
Web: www.ama-assn.org

Summary To provide funding to physicians and medical students who are interested in conducting a research project related to women in the medical profession.

Eligibility This program is open to investigators or teams of investigators of whom at least 1 member is a medical student or physician. Applicants must be interested in conducting a research project that will advance the progress of women in the medical profession and strengthen the ability of the American Medical Association (AMA) to identify and address the needs of women physicians and medical students.

Financial data The grant is $10,000.

Duration 1 year.

Additional information This program, which began in 2006, is offered by the AMA Foundation in collaboration with the AMA Women Physicians Section (WPS) and with support from Pfizer.

Number awarded 2 each year.

Deadline July of each year.

[1299]
JOAN KELLY MEMORIAL PRIZE IN WOMEN'S HISTORY

American Historical Association
Attn: Book Prize Administrator
400 A Street, S.E.
Washington, DC 20003-3889
(202) 544-2422　　　　　Fax: (202) 544-8307
E-mail: awards@historians.org
Web: www.historians.org

Summary To recognize and reward outstanding works in women's history and/or feminist theory that were published during the previous year.

Eligibility The prize is open to works in any chronological period, any geographical location, or any area of feminist theory that incorporate an historical perspective. Preference is given to books that demonstrate originality of research, creativity of insight, graceful stylistic presentation, analytical skills, and recognition of the important role of sex and gender in the historical process.

Financial data The prize is $1,000.

Duration The award is granted annually.

Additional information This prize was established in 1984 by the Coordinating Committee on Women in the Historical Profession and the Conference Group on Women's History (now the Coordinating Council for Women in History) and is administered by the American Historical Association.

Number awarded 1 each year.

Deadline May of each year.

[1300]
JOHN AND POLLY SPARKS EARLY CAREER GRANT FOR PSYCHOLOGISTS INVESTIGATING SERIOUS EMOTIONAL DISTURBANCE (SED)

American Psychological Foundation
750 First Street, N.E.
Washington, DC 20002-4242
(202) 336-5843　　　　　Fax: (202) 336-5812
E-mail: foundation@apa.org
Web: www.apa.org/apf/funding/sparks-early-career.aspx

Summary To provide funding to early-career psychologists interested in conducting research on serious emotional disturbance in children.

Eligibility This program is open to young psychologists who completed a doctoral degree (Ed.D., Psy.D., Ph.D.) within the past 10 years. Applicants must be interested in conducting research in the area of early intervention and treatment for serious emotional disturbance in children. Selection is based on conformance with stated program goals and qualifications, quality and impact of proposed work, innovation and contribution to the field with proposed project, and applicant's demonstrated competence and capability to execute the proposed work. The sponsor encourages applications from individuals who represent diversity in race, ethnicity, gender, age, disability, and sexual orientation.

Financial data The grant is $17,000.

Duration 1 year.

Additional information This program began in 2013.

Number awarded 1 each year.

Deadline May of each year.

[1301]
JONATHAN REICHERT AND BARBARA WOLFF-REICHERT AWARD FOR EXCELLENCE IN ADVANCED LABORATORY INSTRUCTION

American Physical Society
Attn: Honors Program
One Physics Ellipse
College Park, MD 20740-3844
(301) 209-3268　　　　　Fax: (301) 209-0865
E-mail: honors@aps.org
Web: www.aps.org/programs/honors/awards/lab.cfm

Summary To recognize and reward physicists who have made outstanding achievements in teaching undergraduate laboratory courses.

Eligibility This award is available to individuals or teams of individuals who have taught, developed, and sustained advanced undergraduate physics laboratory courses for at least 4 years at an institution in the United States. Nominations should present evidence of the dissemination of the laboratory work to the broader physics community. Nominations of qualified women and members of underrepresented minority groups are especially encouraged.

Financial data The award consists of $5,000 as an honorarium, a certificate citing the accomplishments of the recipient, and an allowance up to $2,000 for travel expenses to the meeting where the award is presented.

Duration The award is presented annually.

Additional information This award was established in 2012.

Number awarded 1 each year.
Deadline June of each year.

[1302]
JOSEPH B. GITTLER AWARD OF THE AMERICAN PSYCHOLOGICAL FOUNDATION

American Psychological Foundation
750 First Street, N.E.
Washington, DC 20002-4242
(202) 336-5843   Fax: (202) 336-5812
E-mail: foundation@apa.org
Web: www.apa.org/apf/funding/gittler.aspx

Summary To recognize and reward scholars in psychology who have made outstanding contributions to the philosophical foundations of the discipline.

Eligibility This award is available to psychologists who have an Ed.D., Psy.D., or Ph.D. degree and who are making and will continue to make scholarly contributions to the philosophical foundations of psychological knowledge. Self-nominations are welcome. Selection is based on conformance with stated program goals and magnitude of contributions The sponsor encourages nominations of individuals who represent diversity in race, ethnicity, gender, age, disability, and sexual orientation.

Financial data The award is $7,500.

Duration The award is presented annually.

Additional information This award was first presented in 2008.

Number awarded 1 each year.

Deadline Nominations must be submitted by May of each year.

[1303]
JOSEPH H. FICHTER RESEARCH GRANT COMPETITION

Association for the Sociology of Religion
Attn: Executive Officer
University of South Florida
Department of Sociology
4202 East Fowler Avenue, CPR 107
Tampa, FL 33620
(813) 974-2633   Fax: (813) 974-6455
E-mail: jcavendi@usf.edu
Web: www.sociologyofreligion.com

Summary To provide funding to scholars interested in conducting research on women and religion.

Eligibility This program is open to scholars involved in research on women and religion or on the intersection between religion and gender or religion and sexualities. Scholars at the beginning of their careers are particularly encouraged to apply; dissertation research qualifies for funding. Applicants must be members of the association at the time the application is submitted. The proposal should outline the rationale and plan of the research, previous research, methodology proposed, timeline, and budget; a curriculum vitae should also be included. Simultaneous submissions to other grant competitions are permissible if the applicant is explicit about which budget items in the Fichter grant proposal do not overlap items in other submitted proposals.

Financial data Each year, a total of $24,000 is available to be awarded.

Duration 1 year.
Number awarded Varies each year; recently, 6 were awarded.
Deadline April of each year.

[1304]
JUDY GRAHN AWARD FOR LESBIAN NONFICTION

Publishing Triangle
332 Bleecker Street, D36
New York, NY 10014
E-mail: publishingtriangle@gmail.com
Web: www.publishingtriangle.org/awards.asp

Summary To recognize and reward outstanding lesbian nonfiction writers or writings.

Eligibility This award is presented to authors of books that have had significant influence on lesbians. For the purposes of this award, "lesbian nonfiction" is defined as nonfiction affecting lesbian lives. The book may be written by a lesbian, or about lesbians or lesbian culture, or both. It must have been published in the United States or Canada.

Financial data The award is $1,000.

Duration The award is presented annually.

Additional information The Publishing Triangle is an association of lesbians and gay men in publishing. This award was first presented in 1997. Current members of the Publishing Triangle may nominate authors for free; all others must pay a $35 fee.

Number awarded 1 each year.

Deadline November of each year.

[1305]
JUVENILE DIABETES RESEARCH FOUNDATION INNOVATIVE GRANTS

Juvenile Diabetes Research Foundation International
Attn: Senior Director, Research Administration
26 Broadway, 14th Floor
New York, NY 10004
(212) 479-7519   Toll Free: (800) 533-CURE
Fax: (212) 785-9595   E-mail: emilligan@jdrf.org
Web: grantcenter.jdrf.org

Summary To provide funding to scientists who are interested in conducting innovative diabetes-related research.

Eligibility Applicants must have an M.D., D.M.D., D.V.M., Ph.D., or equivalent degree and have a full-time faculty position or equivalent at a college, university, medical school, or other research facility. They must be seeking "seed" money for investigative work based on a sound hypothesis for which preliminary data are insufficient for a regular research grant but that are likely to lead to important results for the treatment of diabetes and its complications. Applicants must specifically explain how the proposal is innovative. Selection is based on 1) innovation, potential impact, and relevance to the goals of the sponsor; 2) feasibility of experimental approach and completion in 1 year; 3) clarity of proposed objectives; 4) qualifications and research experience of the principal investigators and collaborators; 5) availability of resources and facilities necessary for the project; and 6) appropriateness of the proposed budget in relation to the proposed research. There are no citizenship requirements. Applications are encouraged from women, members of minority groups underrepresented in the sciences, and people with disabilities. The proposed research may be conducted at foreign or domestic, for-profit or nonprofit, or public or private institutions, including universities, colleges, hospitals, laboratories, units of state or local government, or eligible agencies of the federal government.

Financial data Awards are limited to $100,000 plus 10% indirect costs.

Duration 1 year; nonrenewable.

Number awarded Varies each year; recently, 5 were awarded.

Deadline July of each year.

[1306]
JUVENILE DIABETES RESEARCH FOUNDATION STRATEGIC RESEARCH AGREEMENTS

Juvenile Diabetes Research Foundation International
Attn: Senior Director, Research Administration
26 Broadway, 14th Floor
New York, NY 10004
(212) 479-7519   Toll Free: (800) 533-CURE
Fax: (212) 785-9595   E-mail: emilligan@jdrf.org
Web: grantcenter.jdrf.org

Summary To provide funding to scientists who are interested in conducting diabetes-related research that addresses critical gaps and challenges.

Eligibility Applicants must have an M.D., D.M.D., D.V.M., Ph.D., or equivalent degree and have a full-time faculty position or equivalent at a college, university, medical school, or other research facility. They must be seeking funding to address critical gaps and challenges and potential breakthroughs in Type 1 diabetes research. Selection is based on potential to prove principle of new approaches to unsolved problems of Type 1 diabetes; relevance to the objectives of the sponsor; scientific, technical, or medical significant of the research proposal; innovative quality of the proposed study; soundness of the clinical study design; availability of sufficient pre-clinical data to justify the proposed clinical study; qualifications and research experience of the principal investigators and collaborators; potential benefits and risks to patients who will be involved in the research, plans to limit risks, and other ethical considerations; availability of resources and facilities necessary for the study; and appropriateness of the proposed budget in relation to the proposed research. There are no citizenship requirements. Applications are encouraged from women, members of minority groups underrepresented in the sciences, and people with disabilities. The proposed research may be conducted at foreign or domestic, for-profit or non-profit, or public or private institutions, including universities, colleges, hospitals, laboratories, units of state or local government, or eligible agencies of the federal government.

Financial data Awards depend on the availability of funds.

Duration Up to 3 years.

Number awarded Varies each year.

Deadline February, August, or November of each year.

[1307]
KATE GLEASON AWARD

ASME International
Attn: Committee on Honors
Two Park Avenue
New York, NY 10016-5990
(212) 591-7094   Toll Free: (800) THE-ASME
Fax: (212) 591-8080   E-mail: mckivorf@asme.org
Web: www.asme.org

Summary To recognize and reward distinguished female leaders in engineering.

Eligibility This award is available to women who are highly successful entrepreneurs in a field of engineering or who had a lifetime of achievement in the engineering profession.

Financial data The award consists of $10,000, travel support to attend the meeting where the award is presented, a bronze medal, and a certificate.

Duration The award is presented annually.

Additional information This award was established in 2011.

Number awarded 1 each year.

Deadline January of each year.

[1308]
KATHERINE E. WEIMER AWARD

American Physical Society
Attn: Division of Plasma Physics
One Physics Ellipse
College Park, MD 20740-3844
(301) 209-3200   Fax: (301) 209-0865
Web: www.aps.org

Summary To recognize and reward women who have made outstanding contributions to plasma science research.

Eligibility This award is available to female plasma scientists who received their Ph.D. within the previous 10 years. Nominees must have made outstanding achievements in plasma science research.

Financial data The award consists of $2,000, a certificate citing the contributions of the recipient, and an allowance for travel to the meeting of the American Physical Society (APS) at which the award is presented.

Duration The award is presented triennially (2017, 2020, etc.).

Additional information This prize was established in 2001.

Number awarded 1 every 3 years.

Deadline March of the year of the award.

[1309]
KENNEDY CENTER SUMMER INTERNSHIP

Sigma Alpha Iota Philanthropies, Inc.
One Tunnel Road
Asheville, NC 28805
(828) 251-0606   Fax: (828) 251-0644
E-mail: nh@sai-national.org
Web: app.smarterselect.com

Summary To provide summer internships at the Kennedy Center to members of Sigma Alpha Iota (an organization of women musicians).

Eligibility This program is open to student members of the organization who are interested in a summer internship at the DeVos Institute for Arts Management at the John F. Kennedy Center for the Performing Arts in Washington, D.C. Applicants must be juniors, seniors, graduate students, or graduates out of school for less than 2 years.

Financial data The stipend is $2,400.

Duration 10 weeks during the summer.

Additional information Assignments are full time, with possible college credit available.

Number awarded 1 or more each year.

Deadline February of each year.

[1310]
KENNETH B. AND MARNIE P. CLARK FUND

American Psychological Foundation
750 First Street, N.E.
Washington, DC 20002-4242
(202) 336-5843   Fax: (202) 336-5812
E-mail: foundation@apa.org
Web: www.apa.org/apf/funding/clark-fund.aspx

Summary To provide funding to psychologists who wish to conduct a project related to academic achievement in children.

Eligibility This program is open to psychologists who wish to conduct research or development activities that promote the understanding of the relationship between self-identity and academic achievement with an emphasis on children in grade levels K-8. Eligibility alternates between graduate students in odd-numbered years and early-career (within 10 years of completion of postdoctoral work) psychologists. Selection is based on conformance with stated program goals and qualifications; quality and potential impact of proposed work; originality, innovation, and contribution to the field with the proposed project; and applicant's demonstrated competence and capability to execute the proposed work. The sponsor encourages applications from individuals who represent diversity in race, ethnicity, gender, age, disability, and sexual orientation.

Financial data The grant is $10,000.

Duration 1 year.

Additional information This program began in 2012.

Number awarded 1 each year.

Deadline June of each year.

[1311]
KENTUCKY UNIVERSITY RESEARCH POSTDOCTORAL FELLOWSHIP

University of Kentucky
Attn: Vice President for Research
311 Main Building, 0032
Lexington, KY 40506-0032
(859) 257-5090   Fax: (859) 323-2800
E-mail: vprgrants@uky.edu
Web: www.research.uky.edu

Summary To provide an opportunity for recent postdoctorates, especially women, to conduct research at the University of Kentucky (UK).

Eligibility This program is open to U.S. citizens and permanent residents who have completed a doctoral degree within the past 2 years. Applicants must be interested in conducting an individualized research program under the mentorship of 1 or more U.K. professors. Special consideration is given to women interested in conducting research in fields in which they can contribute to diversity at U.K., including, but not limited to, engineering, life sciences, and physical sciences. Selection is based on evidence of scholarship with competitive potential for a tenure-track faculty appointment at a research university, compatibility of specific research interests with those in doctorate-granting units at U.K., quality of the research proposal, support from mentor and references, and effect of the appointment on the educational benefit of diversity within the research or professional area.

Financial data The fellowship provides a stipend of $35,000 plus $5,000 for support of research activities.

Duration Up to 2 years.

Additional information Fellows actively participate in research and teaching as well as service to the university, their profession, and the community. This program began in 1992.

Number awarded 2 each year.

Deadline October of each year.

[1312]
KPMG BEST PAPER AWARD GENDER SECTION

American Accounting Association
Attn: Gender Issues and Worklife Balance Section
5717 Bessie Drive
Sarasota, FL 34233-2399
(941) 921-7747   Fax: (941) 923-4093
E-mail: awards@aaahq.org
Web: www.aaahq.org

Summary To recognize and reward outstanding papers on gender issues presented at the annual meeting of the American Accounting Association (AAA).

Eligibility This competition is open to authors of papers presented at the AAA annual meeting. At least 1 of the authors must be a member of the Gender Issues and Worklife Balance section.

Financial data The award is $1,000.

Duration The award is presented annually.

Additional information This award is supported by the KPMG Foundation.

Number awarded 1 each year.

Deadline February of each year.

[1313]
KPMG OUTSTANDING DISSERTATION AWARD GENDER SECTION

American Accounting Association
Attn: Gender Issues and Worklife Balance Section
5717 Bessie Drive
Sarasota, FL 34233-2399
(941) 921-7747   Fax: (941) 923-4093
E-mail: awards@aaahq.org
Web: www.aaahq.org

Summary To recognize and reward outstanding dissertations on gender issues in accounting.

Eligibility This competition is open to authors of dissertations completed in the prior calendar year. Manuscripts need not be focused solely on gender issues and worklife balance, but they must include some consideration of those topics.

Financial data The award is $1,000.

Duration The award is presented annually.

Additional information This award is supported by the KPMG Foundation.

Number awarded 1 each year.

Deadline February of each year.

[1314]
KPMG OUTSTANDING PUBLISHED MANUSCRIPT AWARD GENDER SECTION

American Accounting Association
Attn: Gender Issues and Worklife Balance Section
5717 Bessie Drive
Sarasota, FL 34233-2399
(941) 921-7747   Fax: (941) 923-4093
E-mail: awards@aaahq.org
Web: www.aaahq.org

Summary To recognize and reward outstanding research publications on gender issues in accounting.

Eligibility This competition is open to authors of articles published in the prior calendar year. Manuscripts need not be focused solely on gender issues and worklife balance, but they must include some consideration of those topics. At least 1 of the authors must be a member of the Gender Issues and Worklife Balance section of the American Accounting Association.

Financial data The award is $1,000.

Duration The award is presented annually.

Additional information This award is supported by the KPMG Foundation.

Number awarded 1 each year.

Deadline February of each year.

[1315]
LABORATORY ASTROPHYSICS PRIZE

American Astronomical Society
Attn: Laboratory Astrophysics Division
2000 Florida Avenue, N.W., Suite 400
Washington, DC 20009-1231
(202) 328-2010   Fax: (202) 234-2560
E-mail: aas@aas.org
Web: lad.aas.org/prizes/lab_astro_prize

Summary To recognize and reward outstanding contributions to laboratory astrophysics.

Eligibility Nominees for this award must have made outstanding contributions to laboratory physics over an extended period of time. Full consideration is given to qualified women, members of underrepresented minority groups, and scientists from outside the United States.

Financial data The prize includes a cash award, a framed certificate, and reimbursement of travel expenses to attend a meeting where an invited is presented.

Duration The prize is presented annually.

Additional information This prize was first presented in 2015.

Number awarded 1 each year.

Deadline September of each year.

[1316]
LAD EARLY CAREER AWARD

American Astronomical Society
Attn: Laboratory Astrophysics Division
2000 Florida Avenue, N.W., Suite 400
Washington, DC 20009-1231
(202) 328-2010   Fax: (202) 234-2560
E-mail: aas@aas.org
Web: lad.aas.org/prizes/lab_astro_prize

Summary To recognize and reward outstanding contributions to laboratory astrophysics by early-career scientists.

Eligibility Nominees for this award must have made outstanding contributions to laboratory physics early in their professional career. They must have no more than 10 years of professional experience since their Ph.D. or equivalent degree. Full consideration is given to qualified women, members of underrepresented minority groups, and scientists from outside the United States.

Financial data The prize includes a cash award, a framed certificate, and reimbursement of travel expenses to attend a meeting where an invited is presented.

Duration The prize is presented annually.

Additional information This prize was first presented in 2016.

Number awarded 1 each year.

Deadline September of each year.

[1317]
LEGACY ARTISTS RESIDENCY GRANT

Women's Studio Workshop
722 Binnewater Lane
P.O. Box 489
Rosendale, NY 12472
(845) 658-9133   Fax: (845) 658-9031
E-mail: info@wsworkshop.org
Web: www.wsworkshop.org

Summary To provide a residency and financial support at the Women's Studio Workshop (WSW) to women interested in printmaking or papermaking.

Eligibility This program is open to women who are interested in working in the printmaking or hand papermaking studios while in residence at the WSW. They must provide a 1-page summary of their proposed project, a resume, and a CD with 10 images of their recent work.

Financial data The program provides a stipend of $2,100, a $250 travel stipend, a materials budget of $500, unlimited studio use, and housing while in residence.

Duration 6 weeks.

Number awarded 1 each year.

Deadline January of each year.

[1318]
LEO GOLDBERG FELLOWSHIPS

National Optical Astronomy Observatories
Attn: Human Resources Office
950 North Cherry Avenue
P.O. Box 26732
Tucson, AZ 85726-6732
(520) 318-8000   Fax: (520) 318-8360
E-mail: hrnoao@noao.edu
Web: ast.noao.edu/opportunities/post-doc-programs

Summary To provide an opportunity for postdoctorates in astronomy to conduct research at the facilities of the National Optical Astronomy Observatories (NOAO) in Arizona or Chile.

Eligibility This program is open to recent Ph.D. recipients in observational astronomy, astronomical instrumentation, or theoretical astrophysics. Applicants must be interested in conducting a research program of their own choosing or participating in a current NOAO initiative at Kitt Peak National Observatory (KPNO) near Tucson, Arizona or Cerro Tololo Inter-American Observatory (CTIO) in La Serena, Chile. Women and candidates from underrepresented minorities are particularly encouraged to apply. Preference is given to Native Americans living on or near the Tohono O'Odham Reservation in Arizona. Selection is based on the applicant's promise for an outstanding career in astronomy, their proposed use of KPNO or CTIO facilities, the relationship of their research to a proposed interaction with NOAO programs to develop community facilities, and the relationship of their research to programs conducted by NOAO staff.

Financial data A competitive salary is paid. Additional support is provided to fellows and their families in Chile.

Duration 5 years. The first 4 years are spent either at Kitt Peak or in La Serena; the final year is spent at a U.S. university or astronomical institute willing to host the fellow.

Additional information NOAO is supported under a contract between the National Science Foundation and the Association of Universities for Research in Astronomy, Inc. This program, which began in 2002, was formerly known as the NOAO 5-Year Science Fellowship.

Number awarded 1 each year.

Deadline November of each year.

[1319]
LEO SZILARD LECTURESHIP AWARD

American Physical Society
Attn: Honors Program
One Physics Ellipse
College Park, MD 20740-3844
(301) 209-3268   Fax: (301) 209-0865
E-mail: honors@aps.org
Web: www.aps.org/programs/honors/awards/szilard.cfm

Summary To recognize and reward physicists for their work in areas of benefit to society.

Eligibility This program is open to living physicists who have promoted the use of physics for the benefit of society in such areas as the environment, arms control, and science policy. Nominations of qualified women, members of underrepresented minority groups, and scientists from outside the United States are especially encouraged.

Financial data The award consists of $3,000, a certificate citing the contributions of the recipient, and a $2,000 allowance to pay for travel expenses for lectures given by the recipient at an American Physical Society meeting and at 2 or more educational institutions or research laboratories in the year following the award.

Duration The award is presented annually.

Additional information This award was established in 1974. Since 1998 it has been supported by donations from the John D. and Catherine T. MacArthur Foundation, the Energy Foundation, the David and Lucile Packard Foundation, and individuals.

Number awarded 1 each year.

Deadline June of each year.

[1320]
LILLA JEWEL AWARD FOR WOMEN ARTISTS

McKenzie River Gathering Foundation
Attn: Office Manager
1235 S.E. Morrison Street, Suite A
Portland, OR 97214
(503) 289-1517   Toll Free: (800) 489-6743
Fax: (503) 232-1731   E-mail: info@mrgfoundation.org
Web: www.mrgfoundation.org

Summary To recognize and reward women performance artists in Oregon who utilize the spoken word.

Eligibility Eligible to apply for this award are women artists in Oregon whose work relies on the spoken word and performance. Applicants must have demonstrated success as a spoken word artist and experience performing spoken word in front of a large audience. They must be interested in developing a work for presentation at the sponsoring organization's annual fundraising party. The performance may include music and mixed media. It should address progressive social, racial, economic, and/or environmental justice issues. Priority is given to women of color and those who identify as LGBT.

Financial data The award is $2,500.

Duration The award is presented annually.

Number awarded 1 each year.

Deadline November of each year.

[1321]
LINDA FENNER SCHOLARSHIP

JEWISHcolorado
Attn: Women's Philanthropy Director
300 South Dahlia Street, Suite 300
Denver, CO 80246-8118
(303) 316-6459   Fax: (303) 322-8328
E-mail: slangert@JEWISHcolorado.org
Web: www.jewishcolorado.org/scholarships

Summary To provide funding for professional development activities in Colorado or Israel to young Jewish women.

Eligibility This program is open to female residents of Colorado between 21 and 45 years of age. Applicants must have been identified as a leader or someone with leadership potential in the Jewish community. They must be interested in attending nonprofit Jewish conferences, missions to Israel, young adult programs, or any other Jewish program. The focus of the program must be on leadership development, not professional development.

Financial data The maximum grant for each individual is $2,500. Funds may be used only to subsidize registration fees for the conference, not the hotel or airfare.

Duration These are 1-time grants.

Additional information This sponsor was formerly named the Allied Jewish Federation of Colorado.

Number awarded Varies each year; a total of $5,000 is available for this program each year.

Deadline August of each year.

[1322]
LIZETTE PETERSON-HOMER INJURY PREVENTION GRANT AWARD

American Psychological Foundation
750 First Street, N.E.
Washington, DC 20002-4242
(202) 336-5843   Fax: (202) 336-5812
E-mail: foundation@apa.org
Web: www.apa.org/apf/funding/peterson-homer.aspx

Summary To provide funding to graduate students and faculty interested in conducting research related to the prevention of injuries in children.

Eligibility This program is open to graduate students and faculty interested in conducting research that focuses on the prevention of physical injury in children and young adults through accidents, violence, abuse, or suicide. Applicants must submit a 100-word abstract, description of the project, detailed budget, curriculum vitae, and letter from the supporting faculty supervisor (if the applicant is a student). Selection is based on conformance with stated program goals, magnitude of incremental contribution, quality of proposed work, and applicant's demonstrated scholarship and research competence. The sponsor encourages applications from individuals who represent diversity in race, ethnicity, gender, age, disability, and sexual orientation.

Financial data Grants up to $5,000 are available.

Additional information This program began in 1999 as the Rebecca Routh Coon Injury Research Award. The current name was adopted in 2003. It is supported by Division 54 (Society of Pediatric Psychology) of the American Psychological Association and the American Psychological Foundation.

Number awarded 1 each year.

Deadline September of each year.

[1323]
LONE STAR RISING CAREER SCHOLARSHIP

Association for Women Geoscientists
Attn: AWG Foundation
12000 North Washington Street, Suite 285
Thornton, CO 80241
(303) 412-6219   Fax: (303) 253-9220
E-mail: AWGLoneStar@gmail.com
Web: www.awg.org/eas/scholarships.htm

Summary To provide assistance to female geoscientists who have been out of the workforce and need funding to resume their career.

Eligibility This program is open to women in the geoscience profession who wish to resume their career after having been out of the workforce. Applicants must be seeking funding for such professional development costs as enrollment in geoscience training courses or workshops, fees for certifications and licensing, professional membership fees, or any other costs to help them reenter the workforce. Along with their application, they must submit a 1-page personal statement describing their academic qualifications, professional work history, and any recent volunteer or home activities relevant to their area of expertise.

Financial data Grants range up to $3,000.

Duration 1 year.

Additional information This program is sponsored by the Lone Star Chapter of the Association for Women Geoscien-

tists (AWG), but neither Texas residency nor AWG membership are required.

Number awarded 1 or more each year.

Deadline October of each year.

[1324]
L'OREAL USA FELLOWSHIPS FOR WOMEN IN SCIENCE

L'Oréal USA
c/o American Association for the Advancement of Science
Education and Human Resources
1200 New York Avenue, Sixth Floor
Washington, DC 20005
(202) 326-6677   E-mail: lorealusafellowships@aaas.org
Web: www.aaas.org

Summary To provide research funding to postdoctoral women scientists.

Eligibility This program is open to women who have a Ph.D. in the life sciences, physical or material sciences, engineering, technology, computer science, or mathematics. Additional areas of study include immunology, all areas of chemistry, earth science, and medical research. Women who have an M.D. or whose work is in psychology, science education, or social science are not eligible. Applicants must be full-time postdoctoral associates and may not hold a faculty position. They must be planning to conduct a research project in their field of specialization at an institution in the United States or Puerto Rico. They must be U.S. citizens or permanent residents.

Financial data The grant is $60,000.

Duration 1 year.

Additional information This program, established in 2003, is sponsored by L'Oréal USA and administered by the American Association for the Advancement of Science (AAAS).

Number awarded 5 each year.

Deadline February of each year.

[1325]
LOREEN ARBUS DISABILITY AWARENESS GRANTS

New York Women in Film & Television
Attn: Fund for Women Filmmakers
6 East 39th Street, Suite 1200
New York, NY 10016-0112
(212) 679-0870, ext. 39   Fax: (212) 679-0899
E-mail: grants@nywift.org
Web: www.nywift.org/article.aspx?ID=3626

Summary To provide funding to women filmmakers who are interested in making a film on disability issues.

Eligibility This program is open to women who are interested in making a film on physical or developmental disability issues. The film must be work-in-progress of any length or genre but may not be a finished film. Applicants must submit a 2- to 4-page description of the project, a budget indicating amount raised to date, a list of key creative personnel with 1-paragraph bios, and an online link to the work-in-progress.

Financial data The grant is $7,500. Funds may be used only for completion work.

Duration These grants are provided annually.

Number awarded 1 or more each year.

Deadline May of each year.

[1326]
LOT SHAFAI MID-CAREER DISTINGUISHED ACHIEVEMENT AWARD

Institute of Electrical and Electronics Engineers
Attn: Antennas and Propagation Society
445 Hoes Lane
P.O. Box 1331
Piscataway, NJ 08855-1331
(732) 562-3900   Fax: (732) 981-1769
E-mail: webeditor@ieeeaps.org
Web: www.ieeeaps.org

Summary To recognize and reward women of mid-career status who have demonstrated outstanding achievement in the field of antennas and propagation.

Eligibility This award is presented to women who are members of the Institute of Electrical and Electronics Engineers (IEEE), younger than 41 years of age, and working in the field of antennas and propagation. Selection is based on a demonstration of prior technical accomplishments and future potential that earmark them as current and future leaders in the field as well as role models for future generations of women.

Financial data The award includes an honorarium of $1,000 and a plaque.

Duration The award is presented annually.

Additional information This program began in 2012.

Number awarded 1 each year.

Deadline December of each year.

[1327]
LOUISE EISENHARDT RESIDENT TRAVEL SCHOLARSHIP

American Association of Neurological Surgeons
Attn: Women in Neuroscience
5550 Meadowbrook Drive
Rolling Meadows, IL 60008-3852
(847) 378-0500   Toll Free: (888) 566-AANS
Fax: (847) 378-0600   E-mail: kny@aans.org
Web: www.neurosurgerywins.org

Summary To recognize and reward female neurosurgical residents who submit outstanding abstracts for presentation at the annual meeting of the American Association of Neurological Surgeons (AANS).

Eligibility This program is open to female neurosurgical residents who submit outstanding pioneering clinical or laboratory research abstracts for presentation at the AANS annual meeting.

Financial data The award consists of $1,000. Funds are to be used to cover travel expenses.

Duration The award is presented annually.

Additional information This award, first presented in 2000, is sponsored by Women in Neurosurgery.

Number awarded 1 each year.

Deadline Deadline not specified.

[1328]
M. HILDRED BLEWETT SCHOLARSHIP

American Physical Society
Attn: Committee on the Status of Women in Physics
One Physics Ellipse, Fourth Floor
College Park, MD 20740-3844
(301) 209-3231   Fax: (301) 209-0865
E-mail: blewett@aps.org
Web: www.aps.org

Summary To provide funding to early-career women interested in returning to physics research after interrupting those careers for family reasons.

Eligibility This program is open to women who have completed work toward a Ph.D. in physics and currently have an affiliation with a research-active educational institution or national laboratory in Canada or the United States. Applicants must be interested in conducting a research project after interrupting their career for family reasons. They must currently reside in the United States or Canada and be citizens or legal residents of those countries. No matching contribution from the institution is required, but institutional support is considered as evidence of support for the applicant.

Financial data The grant is $45,000. Funds may be used for dependent care (limited to 50% of the award), salary, travel, equipment, and tuition and fees.

Duration 1 year.

Additional information This program began in 2005.

Number awarded Varies each year; recently, 4 were awarded.

Deadline May of each year.

[1329]
M. LOUISE CARPENTER GLOECKNER, M.D. SUMMER RESEARCH FELLOWSHIP

Drexel University College of Medicine
Attn: Archives and Special Collections
2900 West Queen Lane
Philadelphia, PA 19129
(215) 991-8340   Fax: (215) 991-8172
E-mail: archives@drexelmed.edu
Web: archives.drexelmed.edu/fellowship.php

Summary To provide funding to scholars and students interested in conducting research during the summer on the history of women in medicine at the Archives and Special Collections on Women in Medicine at Drexel University in Philadelphia.

Eligibility This program is open to students at all levels, scholars, and general researchers. Applicants must be interested in conducting research utilizing the archives, which emphasize the history of women in medicine, nursing, medical missionaries, the American Medical Women's Association, American Women's Hospital Service, and other women in medical organizations. Selection is based on research background of the applicant, relevance of the proposed research project to the goals of the applicant, overall quality and clarity of the proposal, appropriateness of the proposal to the holdings of the collection, and commitment of the applicant to the project.

Financial data The grant is $4,000.

Duration 4 to 6 weeks during the summer.

Number awarded   1 each year.

Deadline   March of each year.

[1330]
MARA CRAWFORD PERSONAL DEVELOPMENT SCHOLARSHIP

Kansas Federation of Business & Professional Women's Clubs, Inc.
Attn: Kansas BPW Educational Foundation, Inc.
c/o Kathy Niehoff, Executive Secretary
605 East 15th
Ottawa, KS 66067
(785) 242-9319   Fax: (785) 242-1047
E-mail: kathyniehoff@sbcglobal.net
Web: kansasbpw.memberlodge.org/page-450103?

Summary   To provide financial assistance to women in Kansas who are already in the workforce but are interested in pursuing additional education.

Eligibility   This program is open to women residents of Kansas who graduated from high school more than 5 years previously and are already in the workforce. Applicants may be seeking a degree in any field of study and may be attending a 2-year, 4-year, vocational, or technological program. They must submit a 3-page personal biography in which they express their career goals, the direction they want to take in the future, their proposed field of study, their reason for selecting that field, the institutions they plan to attend and why, their circumstances for reentering school (if a factor), and what makes them uniquely qualified for this scholarship. Preference is given to applicants who demonstrate they have serious family responsibilities and obligations. Applications must be submitted through a local unit of the sponsor.

Financial data   A stipend is awarded (amount not specified).

Duration   1 year.

Number awarded   1 or more each year.

Deadline   December of each year.

[1331]
MARCIA FEINBERG AWARD

Association of Jewish Women Publishers
13730 Loumont Street
Whittier, CA 90601

Summary   To recognize and reward Jewish women who have made outstanding contributions to careers in library science and publishing.

Eligibility   This award is presented to Jewish women who received a library science doctoral degree from a university in the upper Midwest (Montana, South Dakota, North Dakota, or Minnesota). Nominees must have spent a portion of their career working as a librarian, and then changed careers to enter the field of publishing. They may currently reside in any state except Nebraska or Rhode Island. Selection is based on service to the library profession, awards received for librarianship, innovativeness, and loyalty to colleagues.

Financial data   The award includes an honorarium of $10,000 and a gold engraved plaque.

Duration   The award is presented annually.

Additional information   This award, named in honor of a well-known 19th-century Jewish woman librarian and publisher, has been presented annually since 1923. Self-nomina-

tions are not accepted. Only professional colleagues may nominate a candidate.

Number awarded   1 each year.

Deadline   August of each year.

[1332]
MARGARET FULLER AWARDS PROGRAM

Unitarian Universalist Association
Attn: UU Women's Federation
258 Harvard Street
Brookline, MA 02446
(617) 838-6989   E-mail: uuwf@uua.org
Web: www.uuwf.org/margaret-fuller-grants-program

Summary   To provide funding to Unitarian Universalists working on projects that promote feminist theology.

Eligibility   This program is open to Unitarian Universalist (UU) women interested in working on a scholarly project that relates to any of the thematic strands of UU feminist theology. The project should result in a product that can be shared widely with UU women, such as a book, curriculum materials, program outlines or descriptions, DVDs, audio-tapes, workshop templates, or publishable articles. Examples of appropriate projects include poetry, drama, ritual, song, curricula for youth or adults, historical or theological analyses of the lives and writings of early feminists, or scholarly descriptions of feminist theories and theologies. Grants are generally made to individuals, although group projects may be eligible.

Financial data   Grants range from $500 to $5,000.

Duration   Proposed projects should take not more than 1 to 2 years to complete.

Additional information   This program originated as the Feminist Theology Award program in 1989. That program ended in 1997 and was succeeded by this in 2002. Funds are not available for graduate school or to support dissertations. Funding is no longer available for computer hardware.

Number awarded   1 or more each year.

Deadline   March of each year.

[1333]
MARGARET OAKLEY DAYHOFF AWARD

Biophysical Society
Attn: Awards Committee
11400 Rockville Pike, Suite 800
Rockville, MD 20852
(240) 290-5600   Fax: (240) 290-5555
E-mail: society@biophysics.org
Web: www.biophysics.org

Summary   To recognize and reward outstanding junior women scientists in fields of interest to the Biophysical Society.

Eligibility   This program is open to junior women scientists whose writings have made substantial contributions to scientific fields within the range of interest of the society but who have not yet attained university tenure. Candidates who have a Ph.D. or equivalent degree remain eligible until they have completed 10 years of full-time work following the degree. Candidates with a baccalaureate degree but without a Ph.D. have 12 years of eligibility. Time taken off for child rearing is not counted. Candidates who work in non-academic environments are eligible if their work is published and meets academic standards, and if they do not have tenure equivalency.

Membership is the society is required. Nominations may be submitted by any member of the society in good standing, but self-nominations are not accepted.

Financial data The award is $2,000.

Duration The award is presented annually.

Additional information This award was established in 1984.

Number awarded 1 each year.

Deadline April of each year.

[1334]
MARGARET S. PETERSEN AWARD

American Society of Civil Engineers
Attn: Honors and Awards Program
1801 Alexander Bell Drive
Reston, VA 20191-4400
(703) 295-6000　　　　Toll Free: (800) 548-ASCE
Fax: (703) 295-6222　　　　E-mail: awards@asce.org
Web: www.asce.org/templates/award-detail.aspx?id=1625

Summary To recognize and reward female members of the Environmental and Water Resources Institute (EWRI) of the American Society of Civil Engineers (ASCE) who have demonstrated outstanding service to the work of that institute.

Eligibility This award is women who are members of EWRI or ASCE (except student members) who have demonstrate exemplary service to the water resources and environmental science and engineering community. Criteria include EWRI leadership through standing or task committee participation and university or industry excellence in the water resource, hydraulics, or environmental-related science and engineering profession.

Financial data The award consists of a crystal vase and a cash prize determined annually, based on the income from the award endowment.

Duration The award is presented annually.

Number awarded 1 each year.

Deadline Nominations are due by the end of September of each year.

[1335]
MARGARET W. ROSSITER HISTORY OF WOMEN IN SCIENCE PRIZE

History of Science Society
Attn: Nominations
University of Notre Dame
440 Geddes Hall
Notre Dame, IN 46556
(574) 631-1194　　　　Fax: (574) 631-1533
E-mail: prizes@hssonline.org
Web: www.hssonline.org

Summary To recognize and reward scholars who publish outstanding work in the specialty field of women in the history of science.

Eligibility Books and articles published during the last 4 years are eligible for consideration, provided they deal with a topic related to women in science, including discussions of women's activities in science, analyses of past scientific practices that deal explicitly with gender, and investigations regarding women as viewed by scientists. Entries may take a biographical, institutional, theoretical, or other approach to the topic. They may relate to medicine, technology, and the social sciences as well as the natural sciences.

Financial data The prize is $1,000.

Duration This is an annual award, presented in alternate years to the most outstanding article (even-numbered years) and the most outstanding book (odd-numbered years).

Additional information This award was established in 1987 and given its current name in 2004.

Number awarded 1 each year.

Deadline March of each year.

[1336]
MARGO HARRIS HAMMERSCHLAG BIENNIAL AWARD

National Association of Women Artists, Inc.
80 Fifth Avenue, Suite 1405
New York, NY 10011-8002
(212) 675-1616　　　　E-mail: office@thenawa.org
Web: thenawa.org/content/catalog-awards

Summary To provide funding to women artists whose medium is direct carving.

Eligibility This program is open to female U.S. citizens and permanent residents who are artists working in direct carving. Applicants must submit 20 slides of directly carved sculpture or 20 images on CD-R or in JPEG format for PC. Slides or images must depict at least 10 works. At least 75% of the applicant's individual work must have been produced by direct carving.

Financial data The grant is $5,000.

Duration The grant is awarded biennially, in odd-numbered years.

Additional information The application fee is $35.

Number awarded 1 every other year.

Deadline November of even-numbered years.

[1337]
MARIA GOEPPERT-MAYER AWARD

American Physical Society
Attn: Honors Program
One Physics Ellipse
College Park, MD 20740-3844
(301) 209-3268　　　　Fax: (301) 209-0865
E-mail: honors@aps.org
Web: www.aps.org

Summary To recognize the achievements of outstanding female physicists and to offer them an opportunity to share these achievements by delivering public lectures.

Eligibility This award is available to women who are working in a field of physics and are in the early stages of their careers. They must have received their doctorates no more than 10 years ago. Nominations of members of underrepresented minority groups and scientists from outside the United States are especially encouraged.

Financial data The award is $2,500 plus a $4,000 travel allowance to cover the costs of providing lectures at 4 institutions of the recipient's choice.

Duration The lectures must be given within 2 years after the award is presented.

Additional information The lectures may be given at 4 institutions of the recipient's choice within the United States or its possessions, and at the meeting of the American Physical Society at which the award is presented. The award was established by the General Electric Foundation (now the GE Fund) in 1985.

Number awarded   1 each year.

Deadline   June of each year.

[1338]
MARIAM K. CHAMBERLAIN FELLOWSHIP IN WOMEN AND PUBLIC POLICY

Institute for Women's Policy Research
Attn: Fellowship Coordinator
1200 18th Street, N.W., Suite 301
Washington, DC 20036
(202) 785-5100   Fax: (202) 833-4362
E-mail: MKCfellowship@iwpr.org
Web: www.iwpr.org/about/fellowships

Summary   To provide work experience at the Institute for Women's Policy Research (IWPR) to college graduates and graduate students who are interested in economic justice for women.

Eligibility   This program is open to scholars interested in conducting research projects on policies that affect women. Current topics of interest include the quality of women's jobs, including wages, paid sick leave, paid family leave, and workplace flexibility; increasing access to higher education and non-traditional jobs for low-income women and women with children; examining socioeconomic supports for women in job training programs, and for college students with children; the economic status of women and girls, women of color, and immigrant women across the United States. Applicants should have at least a bachelor's degree in social science (e.g., psychology, education, sociology, public policy), statistics, economics, mathematics, or women's studies. Graduate work is desirable but not required. They should have strong quantitative and library research skills and knowledge of women's issues. Familiarity with Microsoft Word and Excel is required; knowledge of STATA, SPSS, SAS, or graphics software is a plus. Members of underrepresented groups, based on race, color, religion, gender, national origin, age, disability, marital or veteran status, sexual orientation, or any other legally protected status, are especially encouraged to apply.

Financial data   The stipend is $31,000 and includes health insurance and a public transportation stipend.

Duration   9 months, beginning in September.

Additional information   The institute is a nonprofit, scientific research organization that works primarily on issues related to equal opportunity and economic and social justice for women. Research topics vary each year but relate to women and public policy.

Number awarded   1 each year.

Deadline   February of each year.

[1339]
MARIE CURIE DISTINGUISHED POSTDOCTORAL FELLOWSHIP

Los Alamos National Laboratory
Attn: Postdoctoral Program Office
HR-5, MS-P290
P.O. Box 1663
Los Alamos, NM 87545
(505) 665-5306   Fax: (505) 665-4562
E-mail: postdocprogram@lanl.gov
Web: www.lanl.gov

Summary   To provide an opportunity for outstanding female postdoctoral scholars to pursue independent research at the Los Alamos National Laboratory (LANL).

Eligibility   This program is open to women who received a doctoral degree within the past 3 years in any area of research related to the mission of the LANL. Candidates must be nominated and sponsored by a member of the laboratory's technical staff. Nominees must display extraordinary ability and show clear and definite promise of becoming outstanding leaders in scientific research. There are no citizenship requirements.

Financial data   The annual stipend is $108,000 in the first year, $109,600 in the second year, and $111,000 in the third year. A comprehensive benefits package includes incoming relocation reimbursement.

Duration   3 years.

Additional information   Core competencies of LANL include theory, modeling, and high-performance computing; complex experimentation and measurement; nuclear and advanced materials; nuclear weapons science and technology; analysis and assessment; earth and environmental systems; bioscience and biotechnology; and nuclear science, plasmas, and beams.

Number awarded   Up to 2 each year.

Deadline   October of each year.

[1340]
MARINE BIOLOGICAL LABORATORY RESEARCH FELLOWSHIPS

Marine Biological Laboratory
Attn: Division of Research
7 MBL Street
Woods Hole, MA 02543-1015
(508) 289-7173   Fax: (508) 457-1924
E-mail: research@mbl.edu
Web: www.mbl.edu/research/whitman-awards

Summary   To provide funding to scientists who wish to conduct summer research at the Marine Biological Laboratory (MBL) in Woods Hole, Massachusetts.

Eligibility   This program is open to faculty members who are interested in conducting summer research at the MBL. Applicants must submit a statement of the potential impact of this award on their career development. The program encourages applications focused on 1) evolutionary, genetic, and genomic approaches in regenerative and developmental biology and neuroscience with an emphasis on novel marine organisms; and 2) integrated imaging and computational approaches to illuminate cellular function and biology emerging from the study of marine and other organisms. Preference is given to early stage investigators, those new to the MBL, women, and minorities.

Financial data Grants range from $5,000 to $25,000, typically to cover laboratory rental and/or housing costs. Awardees are responsible for other costs, such as supplies, shared resource usage, affiliated staff who accompany them, or travel.

Duration 4 to 10 weeks during the summer.

Additional information This program is funded by many different endowments, some of which impose additional requirements.

Number awarded Varies each year; recently, 18 scientists received support from this program.

Deadline December of each year.

[1341]
MARJORIE C. ADAMS WOMEN'S CAREER DEVELOPMENT AWARDS

Foundation Fighting Blindness
Attn: Director, Grants and Awards Programs
7168 Columbia Gateway Drive, Suite 100
Columbia, MD 21046
(410) 423-0600   Toll Free: (800) 683-5555
TDD: (800) 683-5551 E-mail: grants@FightBlindness.org
Web: www.blindness.org

Summary To enable women who are junior faculty members to obtain research training related to retinal degenerative diseases (RDDs).

Eligibility This program is open to female junior investigators at nonprofit institutions who have an M.D., D.O., or equivalent foreign degree and are in their first, second, or third year of a junior faculty appointment. Applicants must be clinicians who currently care for patients with RDDs. They must be interested in engaging in a program of mentored research training directed toward providing therapies for RDDs. The training program may be clinical or laboratory based and must address 1 of the sponsor's priority research program areas: gene therapy, regenerative medicine, novel medical therapies, genetics, cellular and molecular mechanisms of disease, or clinical structure and function studies.

Financial data The grant is $75,000 per year. No indirect costs are paid.

Duration 5 years.

Number awarded Varies each year; recently, 3 were awarded.

Deadline March of each year.

[1342]
MARY ISABEL SIBLEY FELLOWSHIP FOR FRENCH STUDIES

Phi Beta Kappa Society
Attn: Director of Society Affairs
1606 New Hampshire Avenue, N.W.
Washington, DC 20009
(202) 745-3287   Fax: (202) 986-1601
E-mail: awards@pbk.org
Web: www.pbk.org

Summary To provide funding to women interested in conducting dissertation or advanced research on French studies in the United States or any other country.

Eligibility This program is open to unmarried women between 25 and 35 years of age who have demonstrated their ability to conduct original research. Applicants must be planning to conduct a research project dealing with French language or literature. They must hold the doctorate or have fulfilled all the requirements for the doctorate except the dissertation, and they must be planning to devote full time to their research during the fellowship year. Along with their application, they must submit a statement that includes a description of the project, the present state of the project, where the study would be carried out, and expectations regarding publication of the results of the study. Eligibility is not restricted to members of Phi Beta Kappa or to U.S. citizens.

Financial data The stipend is $20,000.

Duration 1 year (the fellowship is offered in even-numbered years only).

Additional information Periodic progress reports are not required, but they are welcomed. It is the hope of the committee that the results of the year of research will be made available in some form, although no pressure for publication will be put on the recipient.

Number awarded 1 every other year.

Deadline January of even-numbered years.

[1343]
MARY ISABEL SIBLEY FELLOWSHIP FOR GREEK STUDIES

Phi Beta Kappa Society
Attn: Director of Society Affairs
1606 New Hampshire Avenue, N.W.
Washington, DC 20009
(202) 745-3287   Fax: (202) 986-1601
E-mail: awards@pbk.org
Web: www.pbk.org

Summary To provide funding to women interested in conducting dissertation or advanced research on Greek studies in the United States or any other country.

Eligibility This program is open to unmarried women between 25 and 35 years of age who have demonstrated their ability to conduct original research. Applicants must be planning to conduct a research project dealing with Greek language, literature, history, or archaeology. They must hold the doctorate or have fulfilled all the requirements for the doctorate except the dissertation, and they must be planning to devote full time to their research during the fellowship year. Along with their application, they must submit a statement that includes a description of the project, the present state of the project, where the study would be carried out, and expectations regarding publication of the results of the study. Eligibility is not restricted to members of Phi Beta Kappa or to U.S. citizens.

Financial data The stipend is $20,000.

Duration 1 year (the fellowship is offered in odd-numbered years only).

Additional information Periodic progress reports are not required, but they are welcomed. It is the hope of the committee that the results of the year of research will be made available in some form, although no pressure for publication will be put on the recipient.

Number awarded 1 every other year.

Deadline January of odd-numbered years.

[1344]
MARY JANE OESTMANN PROFESSIONAL WOMEN'S ACHIEVEMENT AWARD

American Nuclear Society
Attn: Honors and Awards
555 North Kensington Avenue
La Grange Park, IL 60526-5535
(708) 352-6611   Toll Free: (800) 323-3044
Fax: (708) 352-0499   E-mail: honors@ans.org
Web: www.ans.org/honors/va-oestmann

Summary To recognize and reward women who have made outstanding contributions to the field of nuclear science.

Eligibility This award is presented to women who have contributed outstanding personal dedication and technical achievement in the fields of nuclear science, engineering, research, or education. Nominees need not be a member of the American Nuclear Society (ANS), but they should be affiliated with the nuclear community in some manner. The award may be given for lifetime achievement or for a singular outstanding contribution to the technical community.

Financial data The award consists of an honorarium of $1,000 and an engraved plaque.

Duration The award is presented annually.

Additional information This award was first presented in 1991.

Number awarded 1 each year.

Deadline July of each year.

[1345]
MARY LILY RESEARCH GRANTS

Duke University
David M. Rubenstein Rare Book and Manuscript Library
Attn: Sallie Bingham Center for Women's History and
   Culture
P.O. Box 90185
Durham, NC 27708-0185
(919) 660-5828   Fax: (919) 660-5934
E-mail: cwhc@duke.edu
Web: library.duke.edu/rubenstein/bingham/grants

Summary To provide funding to scholars at all levels who wish to use the resources of the Sallie Bingham Center for Women's History and Culture in the Special Collections Library at Duke University.

Eligibility This program is open to undergraduates, graduate students, faculty members, and independent scholars in any academic field who wish to use the resources of the center for their research in women's studies. Writers, creative and performing artists, filmmakers, and journalists are also eligible. Applicants must reside outside a 100-mile radius of Durham, North Carolina. Undergraduate and graduate students must be currently enrolled, be working on a degree, and enclose a letter of recommendation from their adviser or thesis director. Faculty members must be working on a research project and enclose a curriculum vitae. Independent scholars must be working on a nonprofit project and enclose a curriculum vitae. Research topics should be strongly supported by the collections of the center.

Financial data Grants up to $1,000 are available; funds may be used for travel, accommodations, meals, and photocopying and reproduction expenses.

Additional information The library's collections are especially strong in the history of feminist activism and theory, prescriptive literature, girls' literature, artists' books by women, lay and ordained church women, gender expression, women's sexuality, and the history and culture of women in the South. A number of prominent women writers have placed their personal and professional papers in the collections.

Number awarded Varies each year; recently, 11 were awarded.

Deadline January of each year.

[1346]
MATHEMATICAL SCIENCES POSTDOCTORAL RESEARCH FELLOWSHIPS

National Science Foundation
Directorate for Mathematical and Physical Sciences
Attn: Division of Mathematical Sciences
4201 Wilson Boulevard, Room 1025N
Arlington, VA 22230
(703) 292-4856   Fax: (703) 292-9032
TDD: (800) 281-8749   E-mail: bpalka@nsf.gov
Web: www.nsf.gov

Summary To provide financial assistance to postdoctorates interested in pursuing research training in mathematics in the United States or any other country.

Eligibility Applicants for these fellowships must 1) be U.S. citizens, nationals, or permanent residents; 2) have earned a Ph.D. in a mathematical science or have had equivalent research training and experience; 3) have held the Ph.D. for no more than 2 years; and 4) have not previously held any other postdoctoral fellowship from the National Science Foundation (NSF) or been offered an award from this program. They must be proposing to conduct a program of postdoctoral research training at an appropriate nonprofit U.S. institution, including government laboratories, national laboratories, and privately sponsored nonprofit institutes, as well as institutions of higher education in any country. A senior scientist at the institution must indicate availability for consultation and agreement to work with the fellow. In the selection process, consideration is given to the achievement of societally relevant outcomes, including full participation of women, persons with disabilities, and underrepresented minorities.

Financial data The total grant is $150,000, consisting of 3 components: 1) a monthly stipend of $5,000 for full-time support or $2,500 for half-time support, paid directly to the fellow; 2) a research allowance of $12,000, also paid directly to the fellow; and 3) an institutional allowance of $9,000, paid to the host institution for fringe benefits (including health insurance payments for the fellow) and expenses incurred in support of the fellow, such as space, equipment, and general purpose supplies. Fellows who wish to conduct their training at an international host institution may apply for an additional allowance of up to $10,000.

Duration Fellows may select either of 2 options: the research fellowship option provides full-time support for any 18 academic-year months in a 3-year period, in intervals not shorter than 3 consecutive months; the research instructorship option provides a combination of full-time and half-time support over a period of 3 academic years. Both options include 6 summer months.

Number awarded 30 to 33 each year. A total of $5.0 million is available for this program annually.

Deadline October of each year.

[1347]
MICROSOFT RESEARCH PRIZE IN ALGEBRA AND NUMBER THEORY

Association for Women in Mathematics
11240 Waples Mill Road, Suite 200
Fairfax, VA 22030
(703) 934-0163   Fax: (703) 359-7562
E-mail: awm@awm-math.org
Web: sites.google.com

Summary To recognize and reward women who are early in their research careers and have made outstanding contributions in algebra.

Eligibility This award is available to women who are faculty members at U.S. institutions and within 10 years of receiving their Ph.D. or have not yet received tenure. Nominees must have conducted exceptional research in an area of algebra, interpreted broadly to include number theory, cryptography, combinatorics, or other applications, as well as more traditional areas of algebra.

Financial data The award includes a cash prize and honorary plaque.

Duration The award is presented biennially, in even-numbered years.

Additional information This award, first presented in 2014, is sponsored by Microsoft Research.

Number awarded 1 each year.

Deadline Nominations must be submitted by February of each odd-numbered year.

[1348]
MID KOLSTAD SCHOLARSHIP

Women Soaring Pilots Association
c/o Phyllis Wells
P.O. Box 278
Aguila, AZ 85320
(719) 429-4999   E-mail: pwells634@aol.com
Web: www.womensoaring.org/?p=info

Summary To provide financial assistance to mature women interested in obtaining their private glider license.

Eligibility This program is open to women over 25 years of age who are student glider pilots, have soloed in a glider, and have taken and passed the required FAA Knowledge Test. Applicants must be members of the Women Soaring Pilots Association (WSPA). They must be interested in a program of training for a private glider certificate or add-on rating. Along with their application, they must submit a 500-word essay explaining their goals and previous experiences as they relate to gliders and how this scholarship will help them meet their goals.

Financial data The stipend is $1,500.

Duration 1 year.

Number awarded 1 or more each year.

Deadline May of each year.

[1349]
MINISTRY TO WOMEN AWARD

Unitarian Universalist Association
Attn: UU Women's Federation
258 Harvard Street
Brookline, MA 02446
(617) 838-6989   E-mail: uuwf@uua.org
Web: www.uuwf.org/ministry-to-women-award

Summary To recognize and reward significant actions that have improved the lot of women.

Eligibility Individuals or organizations that have ministered to women in an outstanding manner are considered for this award. Originally, only non-Unitarian Universalists were eligible, but currently women who are UU members may be nominated.

Financial data The prize is a $1,000 honorarium, a citation, and travel expenses to the awards presentation.

Duration The award is presented annually.

Additional information This award was established in 1974.

Number awarded 1 or more each year.

Deadline Deadline not specified.

[1350]
MINNIE L. MAFFETT FELLOWSHIPS

Texas Business Women
Attn: Texas Business and Professional Women's
    Foundation
P.O. Box 70
Round Rock, TX 78680-0070
E-mail: info@tbwconnect.com
Web: www.texasbpwfoundation.org/scholarships.php

Summary To provide financial assistance to women in Texas interested in studying or conducting research in a medical field.

Eligibility This program is open to 1) female graduates of Texas medical schools interested in postgraduate or research work; 2) women who have been awarded a graduate degree in health science or medical science from a Texas university and are seeking certification as a physician assistant or nurse practitioner; 3) women who need financial aid for the first year in establishing a family practice in a rural area of Texas with a population of less than 5,000; and 4) fourth-year female medical students who are completing an M.D. or D.O. degree at an accredited medical school in Texas.

Financial data The stipend recently was $5,000.

Duration 1 year; nonrenewable.

Additional information This program began in 1948 when Texas Business Women was named Texas Federation of Business and Professional Women's Clubs.

Number awarded Varies each year; recently, 3 were awarded.

Deadline December of each year.

[1351]
MISS AMERICA'S OUTSTANDING TEEN SCHOLARSHIPS

Miss America's Outstanding Teen, Inc.
Attn: Business and Scholarship Manager
12718 DuPont Circle, Suite A5B
Tampa, FL 33626
(813) 510-3237   E-mail: amanda@maoteen.org
Web: www.maoteen.org/scholarships

Summary To recognize and reward, with college scholarships, girls who are selected for the national finals of the Miss America's Outstanding Teen competition.

Eligibility These awards are presented to the girls who participate in the national finals of the Miss America's Outstanding Teen competition. Girls must be U.S. citizens between 13 and 17 years of age. They first enter a competition in their home state. Selection of scholarship winners is based on academic merit and civic and social achievement. Awards are also presented for Preliminary Evening Wear/On State Question, Preliminary Talent, Outstanding Vocal Talent, Outstanding Dance Talent, Outstanding Instrumental Talent, Outstanding Dance Talent, Scholastic Excellence, Outstanding Achievement in Academic Life, and First, Second, and Third Place Ad Sales.

Financial data Stipends are $25,000 for Miss America's Outstanding Teen, $10,000 for first runner-up, $7,500 for second runner-up, $5,000 for third runner-up, and $2,000 for fourth runner-up. Each of the 5 semi-finalists wins a $1,500 scholarship and all non-finalists win $1,000 scholarships. Other scholarships range from $500 to $2,000.

Duration The competition is held annually.

Number awarded All 52 girls (1 from each state plus 1 from the District of Columbia and 1 from the Virgin Islands) who compete in the Miss America's Outstanding Teen National Pageant receive at least 1 scholarship. A total of 76 scholarships is awarded each year.

Deadline Each state organization sets its own deadline; check with the national organization to learn the date in your state.

[1352]
MONIGUE'S SCHOLARSHIP

Women Soaring Pilots Association
c/o Phyllis Wells
P.O. Box 278
Aguila, AZ 85320
(719) 429-4999   E-mail: pwells634@aol.com
Web: www.womensoaring.org/?p=info

Summary To provide financial assistance to women interested in obtaining a certified instructor rating in gliders.

Eligibility This program is open to women who are members of the Women Soaring Pilots Association (WSPA) and interested in obtaining a certified instructor rating in gliders. Applicants must already have a commercial rating for gliders. Along with their application, they must submit a 500-word essay explaining their goals and previous experiences as they relate to gliders and how this scholarship will help them meet their goals. Selection is based on realism of goals, dedication to those goals, and commitment to encourage other women to be involved in soaring.

Financial data The scholarship provides $500 for the recipient to complete a commercial or instructor rating and $1,000 to attend the Women Soaring Seminar, including seminar registration and glider flight instruction, rental, and tow fees during the seminar. Recipients who obtain an instructor rating and give at least 10 hours of flight instruction receive an additional $500.

Duration The rating must be completed within 1 year.

Number awarded 1 each year.

Deadline May of each year.

[1353]
MONTICELLO COLLEGE FOUNDATION FELLOWSHIP FOR WOMEN

Newberry Library
Attn: Committee on Awards
60 West Walton Street
Chicago, IL 60610-3305
(312) 255-3666   Fax: (312) 255-3513
E-mail: research@newberry.org
Web: www.newberry.org/long-term-fellowships

Summary To provide funding to women who wish to conduct postdoctoral research at the Newberry Library.

Eligibility This program is open to women at the early stages (pre-tenure) of their academic career. Applicants must be interested in conducting research in a field appropriate to the collections of the library. Preference is given to proposals particularly concerned with the study of women.

Financial data The maximum stipend is $4,200 per month.

Duration 4 to 6 months.

Additional information Nearly all of the Newberry's 1 million volumes and 5 million manuscripts relate to the history of western Europe and the Americas. Fellows are expected to participate actively in the Newberry's scholarly community.

Number awarded 1 or more each year.

Deadline November of each year.

[1354]
MORGAN/O'NEILL UNDERWATER PHOTOGRAPHY GRANT

Women Divers Hall of Fame
43 MacKey Avenue
Port Washington, NY 11050-3628
E-mail: scholarships@wdhof.org
Web: www.wdhof.org/scholarships/scholarships.shtml

Summary To provide financial assistance to women photographers who are interested in continuing their professional development in the field of underwater photography.

Eligibility This program is open to qualified women photographers of any age who are also certified divers with significant dive experience. Applicants must be serious, career-minded women with the intent to continue to develop their career in underwater photography. They must submit a photographic portfolio and an essay.

Financial data The grant is $2,000; funds may be used for master digital workshops or other developmental classes in underwater photography, but not to purchase equipment.

Duration 1 year.

Number awarded 1 each year.

Deadline November of each year.

[1355]
MYRNA F. BERNATH BOOK AWARD

Society for Historians of American Foreign Relations
Attn: Amy Sayward, Executive Director
Middle Tennessee State University
Department of History
MTSU Box 23
Peck Hall, Room 279
Murfreesboro, TN 37132
(615) 898-2569   E-mail: amy.sayward@mtsu.edu
Web: www.shafr.org/content/myrna-f-bernath-book-award

Summary To recognize and reward outstanding books written by women on U.S. foreign relations.

Eligibility Eligible to be considered for this award are books written by women on U.S. foreign relations, transnational history, international history, peace studies, cultural interchange, and defense or strategic studies that were published during the previous 2 years. Authors or publishers should submit 5 copies of books that meet these requirements. Nominees must be members of the Society for Historians of American Foreign Relations. Selection is based on the book's contribution to scholarship.

Financial data The award is $2,500.

Duration The award is offered biennially.

Additional information This award was first presented in 1991.

Number awarded 1 each even-numbered year.

Deadline January of each even-numbered year.

[1356]
MYRNA F. BERNATH FELLOWSHIP AWARD

Society for Historians of American Foreign Relations
Attn: Amy Sayward, Executive Director
Middle Tennessee State University
Department of History
MTSU Box 23
Peck Hall, Room 279
Murfreesboro, TN 37132
(615) 898-2569   E-mail: amy.sayward@mtsu.edu
Web: www.shafr.org

Summary To provide funding to women who are members of the Society for Historians of American Foreign Relations (SHAFR) and interested in conducting research on the history of U.S. foreign relations in the United States or any other country.

Eligibility This program is open to women at U.S. universities who wish to conduct historically-based research in the United States or abroad and to women from other countries who wish to conduct research in the United States. The proposed study should focus on U.S. foreign relations, transnational history, international history, peace studies, cultural interchange, or defense or strategic studies. Preference is given to applications from graduate students and those who completed their Ph.D. within the past 5 years. Applicants must submit a project narrative that includes the purpose of the study, significance and scholarly contribution, sources and methods, and timeline for completion.

Financial data The grant is $5,000.

Duration The grant is presented biennially, in odd-numbered years.

Additional information This grant was first presented in 1992.

Number awarded 1 each odd-numbered year.

Deadline September of each even-numbered year.

[1357]
NANCY MALONE MARKETING AND PROMOTION GRANT

New York Women in Film & Television
Attn: Fund for Women Filmmakers
6 East 39th Street, Suite 1200
New York, NY 10016-0112
(212) 679-0870, ext. 39   Fax: (212) 679-0899
E-mail: grants@nywift.org
Web: www.nywift.org/article.aspx?ID=4827

Summary To provide funding to help emerging woman directors get their film recognized and ready for distribution.

Eligibility This program is open to women directors who have completed or are completing a dramatic feature film. Films may be first- or second-time works by their director. Films co-directed by a woman and a man are not eligible. Applicants must be seeking funding for festival entry fees, marketing materials, video duplication, publicists, promotion at the film's opening, or other approved marketing and promotional expenses. They must submit a marketing plan with proposed expenses.

Financial data The grant is $5,000.

Duration This grant is awarded annually.

Number awarded 1 or more each year.

Deadline May of each year.

[1358]
NANCY WEISS MALKIEL JUNIOR FACULTY FELLOWSHIPS

Woodrow Wilson National Fellowship Foundation
Attn: Junior Faculty Fellowship Program
5 Vaughn Drive, Suite 300
P.O. Box 5281
Princeton, NJ 08543-5281
(609) 452-7007, ext. 141   Fax: (609) 452-0066
E-mail: NWMFellows@woodrow.org
Web: www.woodrow.org/fellowships/nwmfellowship

Summary To provide funding for research to junior faculty in the humanities or social sciences, especially those whose work relates to themes emphasized by the program's namesake.

Eligibility This program is open to assistant professors in tenure-track appointments who have successfully passed their institution's standard tenure review and are currently in the fourth or fifth year of their appointment. Applicants may be working in any field of the humanities or social sciences, but preference is given to those whose work involves African American issues, women's issues, and/or higher education. They must be seeking funding for preparation of a final tenure dossier.

Financial data The grant is $10,000. Funds may be used for research, research assistance, acquisition of research materials, transcription, travel, or publication related to projects presented as part of the tenure dossier.

Duration 1 year.
Number awarded 5 each year.
Deadline January of each year.

[1359]
NATALIE HOPKINS AWARDS

California Native Plant Society
Attn: Educational Grants Committee
2707 K Street, Suite 1
Sacramento, CA 95816-5113
(916) 447-2677 Fax: (916) 447-2727
E-mail: cnps@cnps.org
Web: www.cnps.org/cnps/education/grants.php

Summary To provide funding to female graduate students and scholars interested in conducting research on California's native plants.

Eligibility This program is open to women who are graduate students or other researchers interested in conducting a project related to California native plant studies. There is no standardized application form. Applicants should submit a proposal that contains the following information: title of the project, description of the project (e.g., purpose, objectives, hypotheses, methodology, significance), estimated date of completion, description of the final project, budget, academic status, and personal qualifications.

Financial data Grants recently have ranged from $300 to $1,000.

Additional information This program began in 2007.

Number awarded Varies each year; recently, 6 were awarded.

Deadline September of each year.

[1360]
NATIONAL CENTER FOR ATMOSPHERIC RESEARCH POSTDOCTORAL FELLOWSHIPS

National Center for Atmospheric Research
Attn: Advanced Study Program
3090 Center Green Drive
P.O. Box 3000
Boulder, CO 80307-3000
(303) 497-1601 Fax: (303) 497-1646
E-mail: asp-apply@asp.ucar.edu
Web: www.asp.ucar.edu/pdfp/pd_announcement.php

Summary To provide funding to recent doctorates who wish to conduct research at the National Center for Atmospheric Research (NCAR) in Boulder, Colorado.

Eligibility This program is open to recent Ph.D.s and Sc.D.s in atmospheric sciences as well as specialists from such disciplines as applied mathematics, biology, chemistry, computer science, economics, engineering, geography, geology, physics, and science education. Applicants must be interested in conducting research at the center in atmospheric sciences and global change. Selection is based on the applicant's scientific capability and potential, originality and independence, and the match between their interests and the research opportunities at the center. Applications from women and minorities are encouraged.

Financial data The stipend is $60,500 in the first year and $62,000 in the second year. Fellows also receive life and health insurance, a relocation allowance, an allowance of $750 for moving and storing personal belongings, and scien-

tific travel and registration fee reimbursement up to $3,500 per year.

Duration 2 years.

Additional information NCAR is operated by the University Corporation for Atmospheric Research (a consortium of universities and research institutes) and sponsored by the National Science Foundation.

Number awarded Varies; currently, up to 9 each year.

Deadline January of each year.

[1361]
NATIONAL LEAGUE OF AMERICAN PEN WOMEN BIENNIAL MUSIC COMPETITION

National League of American Pen Women
1300 17th Street, N.W.
Washington, DC 20036-1973
(202) 785-1997 Fax: (202) 452-8868
E-mail: musicchair@nlapw.org
Web: www.nlapw.org/music-competitions

Summary To recognize and reward members of the National League of American Pen Women (NLAPW) who have composed outstanding works of music.

Eligibility This competition is open to NLAPW members who compose works of music between 3 and 15 minutes in length. Compositions may be orchestral, vocal, electronic, small ensemble, choral, and/or solo instrument. Applicants must submit 2 scores of the music and 2 CDs of its performance.

Financial data Awards are $1,000 for first, $500 for second, and $250 for third.

Duration The awards are granted biennially, in even-numbered years.

Additional information An entry fee of $50 must accompany each application.

Number awarded 3 each even-numbered year.

Deadline October of odd-numbered years.

[1362]
NATIONAL URBAN FELLOWS PROGRAM

National Urban Fellows, Inc.
Attn: Program Director
1120 Avenue of the Americas, Fourth Floor
New York, NY 10036
(212) 730-1700 Fax: (212) 730-1823
E-mail: info@nuf.org
Web: www.nuf.org/fellows-overview

Summary To provide mid-career public sector professionals, especially people of color and women, with an opportunity to strengthen leadership skills through a master's degree program coupled with a mentorship.

Eligibility This program is open to U.S. citizens who have a bachelor's degree, have at 5 to 7 years of professional work experience with 2 years in a management capacity, have demonstrated leadership capacity with potential for further growth, have a GPA of 3.0 or higher, and can demonstrate a commitment to public service. Applicants must submit a 1-page autobiographical statement, a 2-page personal statement, and a 2-page statement on their career goals. They may be of any racial or ethnic background, but the program's goal is to increase the number of competent administrators from underrepresented ethnic and cultural groups at all levels of public and private urban management organizations. Semifinalists are interviewed.

Financial data The stipend is $25,000. Fellows are required to pay a $500 registration fee and a $7,500 co-investment tuition payment upon acceptance and enrollment in the program.

Duration 14 months.

Additional information The program begins with a summer semester of study at Bernard M. Baruch College of the City University of New York. Following this, fellows spend 9 months in mentorship assignments with a senior administrator in a government agency, a major nonprofit, or a foundation. The final summer is spent in another semester of study at Baruch College. Fellows who successfully complete all requirements are granted a master's of public administration from that college. A $150 processing fee must accompany each application.

Number awarded Approximately 40 to 50 each year.

Deadline December of each year.

[1363]
NUPUR CHAUDHURI FIRST ARTICLE PRIZE

Coordinating Council for Women in History
c/o Sandra Dawson, Executive Director
Northern Illinois University
Department of History and Women's Studies
715 Zulauf Hall
DeKalb, IL 60115
(815) 895-2624   E-mail: chaudhuriaward@theccwh.org
Web: www.theccwh.org

Summary To recognize and reward members of the Coordinating Council for Women in History (CCWH) who have published outstanding first articles in an historical journal.

Eligibility This award is available to CCWH members who have published an article in a refereed journal during the preceding 2 years. The article must be the first published by the candidate and must have full scholarly apparatus. All fields of history are eligible.

Financial data The award is $1,000.

Duration The award is presented annually.

Additional information This award was established in 2010.

Number awarded 1 each year.

Deadline May of each year.

[1364]
NWSA/UNIVERSITY OF ILLINOIS PRESS FIRST BOOK PRIZE

National Women's Studies Association
Attn: Book Prizes
11 East Mount Royal Avenue, Suite 100
Baltimore, MD 21202
(410) 528-0355   Fax: (410) 528-0357
E-mail: awards@nwsa.org
Web: www.nwsa.org

Summary To recognize and reward members of the National Women's Studies Association (NWSA) who submit outstanding manuscripts in the field of women's and gender studies.

Eligibility This award is available to NWSA members who submit a manuscript of a dissertation or first book. Entries

should reflect cutting-edge intersectional feminist scholarship, whether historical or contemporary.

Financial data The award includes publication by the University of Illinois Press and a $1,000 advance against royalties.

Duration The award is presented annually.

Additional information This award was first presented in 2011.

Number awarded 1 each year.

Deadline May of each year.

[1365]
NYWIFT RAVENAL FOUNDATION FEATURE FILM GRANT

New York Women in Film & Television
Attn: Fund for Women Filmmakers
6 East 39th Street, Suite 1200
New York, NY 10016-0112
(212) 679-0870, ext. 39   Fax: (212) 679-0899
E-mail: grants@nywift.org
Web: www.nywift.org/article.aspx?ID=4827

Summary To provide funding to woman film directors for work on their second film.

Eligibility This program is open to women directors older than 40 years of age who have previously directed a dramatic feature film or feature documentary that was released theatrically in the United States or included in a major film festival, or a feature-length television movie shown on a national TV platform. Applicants must be seeking funding for pre-production, production, or post-production expenses for their second film. They must submit a description of the project, budget, list of key creative personnel, and online link to the work-in-progress.

Financial data The grant is $7,500.

Duration This grant is awarded annually.

Number awarded 1 or more each year.

Deadline May of each year.

[1366]
ORTHOPAEDIC RESEARCH AND EDUCATION FOUNDATION NEW INVESTIGATOR GRANT

Orthopaedic Research and Education Foundation
Attn: Grants Manager
9400 West Higgins Road, Suite 215
Rosemont, IL 60018
(847) 430-5108   Fax: (847) 823-8125
E-mail: communications@oref.org
Web: www.oref.org

Summary To provide funding to residents, fellows, and junior orthopedic surgeons who are interested in conducting seed research.

Eligibility This program is open to orthopedic surgeons who have completed their formal training within the past 4 years, residents, and fellows. Applicants must be seeking seed and start-up funding for promising research grants. The clinical relevance of the project must be clearly noted in the abstract and statement of specific aims and be obvious from the title and study design. The program includes awards reserved for women and underrepresented minorities.

Financial data The grant is $50,000.

Duration 1 year.

Number awarded 8 each year, of which 1 is reserved for a woman who is a member of the Ruth Jackson Orthopaedic Society and 1 is reserved for an underrepresented minority member of the J. Robert Gladden Orthopaedic Society.

Deadline August of each year.

[1367]
PAULA DE MERIEUX RHEUMATOLOGY FELLOWSHIP AWARD

American College of Rheumatology
Attn: Rheumatology Research Foundation
2200 Lake Boulevard N.E.
Atlanta, GA 30319
(404) 633-3777   Fax: (404) 633-1870
E-mail: foundation@rheumatology.org
Web: rheumresearch.org/Awards/Education_Training

Summary To provide funding to women and underrepresented minorities interested in a program of training for a career providing clinical care to people affected by rheumatic diseases.

Eligibility This program is open to trainees at ACGME-accredited institutions. Applications must be submitted by the training program director at the institution who is responsible for selection and appointment of trainees. The program must train and prepare fellows to provide clinical care to those affected by rheumatic diseases. Trainees must be women or members of underrepresented minority groups, defined as Black Americans, Hispanics, and Native Americans (Native Hawaiians, Alaska Natives, and American Indians). They must be U.S. citizens, nationals, or permanent residents. Selection is based on the institution's pass rate of rheumatology fellows, publication history of staff and previous fellows, current positions of previous fellows, and status of clinical faculty.

Financial data The grant is $50,000, to be used as salary for the trainee. Other trainee costs (e.g., fees, health insurance, travel, attendance at scientific meetings) are to be incurred by the recipient's institutional program. Supplemental or additional support to offset the cost of living may be provided by the grantee institution.

Duration Up to 1 year.

Additional information This fellowship was first awarded in 2005.

Number awarded 1 each year.

Deadline July of each year.

[1368]
PAULA STERN ACHIEVEMENT AWARD

American Society for Bone and Mineral Research
Attn: Executive Director
2025 M Street, N.W., Suite 800
Washington, DC 20036-3309
(202) 367-1161   Fax: (202) 367-2161
E-mail: asbmr@asbmr.org
Web: www.asbmr.org

Summary To recognize and reward women who have made outstanding scientific contributions in the area of bone and mineral research.

Eligibility This award is presented to a woman who has made significant scientific achievements in the field of bone

and mineral research and has promoted the professional development and advancement of women in the field.

Financial data The award consists of a $2,000 honorarium and a plaque.

Duration The award is presented annually.

Additional information This award was first presented in 2010.

Number awarded 1 each year.

Deadline April of each year.

[1369]
PEARSON EARLY CAREER GRANT

American Psychological Foundation
750 First Street, N.E.
Washington, DC 20002-4242
(202) 336-5843   Fax: (202) 336-5812
E-mail: foundation@apa.org
Web: www.apa.org/apf/funding/pearson.aspx

Summary To provide funding to early-career psychologists interested in conducting a project in an area of critical society need.

Eligibility This program is open to psychologists who have an Ed.D., Psy.D., or Ph.D. from an accredited experience and no more than 10 years of postdoctoral experience. Applicants must be interested in conducting a project to improve areas of critical need in society, including (but not limited to) innovative scientifically-based clinical work with serious mental illness, serious emotional disturbance, incarcerated or homeless individuals, children with serious emotional disturbance (SED), or adults with serious mental illness (SMI). Selection is based on conformance with stated program goals and qualifications, quality and impact of proposed work, innovation and contribution to the field with proposed project, applicant's demonstrated competence and capability to execute the proposed work. The sponsor encourages applications from individuals who represent diversity in race, ethnicity, gender, age, disability, and sexual orientation.

Financial data The grant is $12,000.

Duration 1 year.

Additional information This grant, supported by Pearson Education, was first awarded in 2010.

Number awarded 1 each year.

Deadline December of each year.

[1370]
PEMBROKE CENTER POSTDOCTORAL FELLOWSHIPS

Brown University
Attn: Pembroke Center for Teaching and Research on Women
172 Meeting Street
Box 1958
Providence, RI 02912
(401) 863-2643   Fax: (401) 863-1298
E-mail: Pembroke_Center@brown.edu
Web: www.brown.edu

Summary To provide funding to postdoctoral scholars interested in conducting research at Brown University's Pembroke Center for Teaching and Research on Women on the cross-cultural study of gender.

Eligibility Fellowships are open to scholars in relevant fields who have completed their Ph.D. but do not have a tenured position at an American college or university. Applicants must be willing to spend a year in residence at the Pembroke Center for Teaching and Research on Women and participate in a research project related to gender and/or sexuality. The project focuses on a theme that changes annually (recently: "Aesthetics and the Question of Beauty"). The center encourages underrepresented minority and international scholars to apply.

Financial data The stipend is $50,000 plus $1,500 for research expenses.

Duration 1 academic year.

Additional information Postdoctoral fellows in residence participate in weekly seminars and present at least 2 public papers during the year, as well as conduct an individual research project. Supplementary funds are available for assistance with travel expenses from abroad. This program includes the following named fellowships: the Nancy L. Buc Postdoctoral Fellowship, the Artemis A.W. and Martha Joukowsky Postdoctoral Fellowship, and the Carol G. Lederer Postdoctoral Fellowship.

Number awarded 3 or 4 each year.

Deadline December of each year.

[1371]
P.E.O. PROGRAM FOR CONTINUING EDUCATION

P.E.O. Sisterhood
Attn: Scholar Awards Office
3700 Grand Avenue
Des Moines, IA 50312-2899
(515) 255-3153   Fax: (515) 255-3820
E-mail: psa@peodsm.org
Web: www.peointernational.org

Summary To provide financial assistance to mature women interested in resuming or continuing their academic or technical education.

Eligibility This program is open to mature women who are citizens of the United States or Canada and have experienced an interruption in their education that has lasted at least 24 consecutive months during their adult life. Applicants are frequently single parents who must acquire marketable skills to support their families. They must be within 2 years of completing an academic or technical course of study and be sponsored by a local P.E.O. chapter. Students enrolled in a doctoral degree program are not eligible.

Financial data The maximum stipend is $3,000.

Duration 1 year; nonrenewable.

Additional information This program was established in 1973 by the Women's Philanthropic Educational Organization (P.E.O.).

Number awarded Varies each year; for a recent biennium, 3,242 of these awards, with a total value of nearly $4.3 million, were granted.

Deadline Applications may be submitted at any time.

[1372]
POSTDOCTORAL FELLOWSHIPS IN DIABETES RESEARCH

Juvenile Diabetes Research Foundation International
Attn: Senior Director, Research Administration
26 Broadway, 14th Floor
New York, NY 10004
(212) 479-7519   Toll Free: (800) 533-CURE
Fax: (212) 785-9595   E-mail: emilligan@jdrf.org
Web: grantcenter.jdrf.org

Summary To provide research training to scientists who are beginning their professional careers and are interested in participating in research training on the causes, treatment, prevention, or cure of diabetes or its complications.

Eligibility This program is open to postdoctorates who are interested in a career in Type 1 diabetes-relevant research. Applicants must have received their first doctoral degree (M.D., Ph.D., D.M.D., or D.V.M.) within the past 5 years and may not have a faculty appointment. There are no citizenship requirements. Applications are encouraged from women, members of minority groups underrepresented in the sciences, and people with disabilities. The proposed research training may be conducted at foreign or domestic, for-profit or nonprofit, or public or private institutions, including universities, colleges, hospitals, laboratories, units of state or local government, or eligible agencies of the federal government. Applicants must be sponsored by an investigator who is affiliated full time with an accredited institution and who agrees to supervise the applicant's training. Selection is based on the applicant's previous experience and academic record; the caliber of the proposed research; and the quality of the mentor, training program, and environment.

Financial data Stipends range from $42,840 to $56,376 per year (depending upon years of experience). In any case, the award may not exceed the salary the recipient is currently earning. Fellows also receive a research allowance of $5,500 per year.

Duration 3 years.

Additional information Fellows must devote 100% of their effort to the fellowship project.

Number awarded Varies each year; recently, 8 were awarded.

Deadline July of each year.

[1373]
PRIZE FOR A FACULTY MEMBER FOR RESEARCH IN AN UNDERGRADUATE INSTITUTION

American Physical Society
Attn: Honors Program
One Physics Ellipse
College Park, MD 20740-3844
(301) 209-3268   Fax: (301) 209-0865
E-mail: honors@aps.org
Web: www.aps.org

Summary To recognize and reward physics faculty members at undergraduate institutions.

Eligibility Nominees for this prize must be members of the physics faculty at undergraduate institutions. They must have contributed substantially to physics research and provided inspirational guidance and encouragement to undergraduate students participating in that research. Nominations of qualified women and members of underrepresented minority groups are especially encouraged.

Financial data The prize consists of a stipend of $5,000 to the recipient, a grant of $5,000 to the recipient's institution for research, a certificate citing the accomplishments of the recipient, and an allowance for travel expenses to the meeting of the American Physical Society (APS) at which the prize is presented.

Duration The prize is presented annually.

Additional information This prize was established in 1984 by a grant from the Research Corporation.

Number awarded 1 each year.

Deadline June of each year.

[1374]
PROFESSIONAL ASSOCIATES PROGRAM FOR WOMEN AND MINORITIES AT BROOKHAVEN NATIONAL LABORATORY

Brookhaven National Laboratory
Attn: Diversity Office, Human Resources Division
Building 400B
P.O. Box 5000
Upton, New York 11973-5000
(631) 344-2703   Fax: (631) 344-5305
E-mail: palmore@bnl.gov
Web: www.bnl.gov/diversity/programs.asp

Summary To provide professional experience in scientific areas at Brookhaven National Laboratory (BNL) to members of underrepresented groups.

Eligibility This program is open to underrepresented minorities (African Americans, Hispanics, or Native Americans), people with disabilities, and women. Applicants must have earned at least a bachelor's degree and be seeking professional experience in fields of science, engineering, or administration. They must plan to attend a graduate or professional school and express an interest in long-term employment at BNL. U.S. citizenship or permanent resident status is required.

Financial data Participants receive a competitive salary.

Duration 1 year.

Additional information Interns work in a goal-oriented on-the-job training program under the supervision of employees who are experienced in their areas of interest.

Number awarded Varies each year.

Deadline Applications may be submitted at any time.

[1375]
PUBLIC ART RESIDENCY GRANT

Women's Studio Workshop
722 Binnewater Lane
P.O. Box 489
Rosendale, NY 12472
(845) 658-9133   Fax: (845) 658-9031
E-mail: info@wsworkshop.org
Web: www.wsworkshop.org

Summary To provide funding to female artists who are interested in creating new public art projects along the Walkill Valley Rail Trail in Ulster County, New York.

Eligibility This program is open to female artists who are interested in creating public art along the Walkill Valley Rail

Trail, which runs from near the Women's Studio Workshop in Kingston to New Paltz in Ulster County. Applicants must agree to be in residence at the Workshop while working on the project. They must submit a description of the proposed project including the studio in which they wish to work, an image script, a resume, and 10 images of recent work.

Financial data The program provides a stipend of $350 per week, a travel subsidy, studio access, and housing while in residence.

Duration 4 weeks, between April and July.

Additional information This program is supported by the National Endowment for the Arts.

Number awarded 1 each year.

Deadline September of each year.

[1376]
R. ROBERT & SALLY FUNDERBURG RESEARCH AWARD IN GASTRIC CANCER

American Gastroenterological Association
Attn: AGA Research Foundation
Research Awards Manager
4930 Del Ray Avenue
Bethesda, MD 20814-2512
(301) 222-4012   Fax: (301) 654-5920
E-mail: awards@gastro.org
Web: www.gastro.org

Summary To provide funding to established investigators who are working on research that enhances fundamental understanding of gastric cancer pathobiology.

Eligibility This program is open to faculty at accredited North American institutions who have established themselves as independent investigators in the field of gastric biology, pursuing novel approaches to gastric mucosal cell biology, including the fields of gastric mucosal cell biology, regeneration and regulation of cell growth, inflammation as precancerous lesions, genetics of gastric carcinoma, oncogenes in gastric epithelial malignancies, epidemiology of gastric cancer, etiology of gastric epithelial malignancies, or clinical research in diagnosis or treatment of gastric carcinoma. Applicants must be individual members of the American Gastroenterological Association (AGA). Women and minority investigators are strongly encouraged to apply. Selection is based on the novelty, feasibility, and significance of the proposal. Preference is given to novel approaches.

Financial data The grant is $50,000 per year. Funds are to be used for the salary of the investigator. Indirect costs are not allowed.

Duration 2 years.

Number awarded 1 each year.

Deadline August of each year.

[1377]
RESEARCH SCHOLAR AWARDS OF THE AMERICAN GASTROENTEROLOGICAL ASSOCIATION

American Gastroenterological Association
Attn: AGA Research Foundation
Research Awards Manager
4930 Del Ray Avenue
Bethesda, MD 20814-2512
(301) 222-4012   Fax: (301) 654-5920
E-mail: awards@gastro.org
Web: www.gastro.org/grants/research-scholar-award-rsa

Summary To provide research funding to young investigators developing an independent career in an area of gastroenterology, hepatology, or related fields.

Eligibility Applicants must hold full-time faculty positions at North American universities or professional institutes at the time of application. They should be early in their careers (fellows and established investigators are not appropriate candidates). Candidates with an M.D. degree must have completed clinical training within the past 7 years and those with a Ph.D. must have completed their degree within the past 7 years. Membership in the American Gastroenterological Association (AGA) is required. Selection is based on significance, investigator, innovation, approach, environment, relevance to AGA mission, and evidence of institutional commitment. Women, minorities, and physician/scientist investigators are strongly encouraged to apply.

Financial data The grant is $90,000 per year. Funds are to be used for project costs, including salary, supplies, and equipment but excluding travel. Indirect costs are not allowed.

Duration 3 years.

Additional information At least 70% of the recipient's research effort should relate to the gastrointestinal tract or liver.

Number awarded Varies each year; recently, 5 were awarded.

Deadline August of each year.

[1378]
RITA MAE KELLY ENDOWMENT FELLOWSHIP

American Political Science Association
Attn: Centennial Center Visiting Scholars Program
1527 New Hampshire Avenue, N.W.
Washington, DC 20036-1206
(202) 483-2512   Fax: (202) 483-2657
E-mail: centennial@apsanet.org
Web: www.apsanet.org/centennial/grants

Summary To provide funding to members of the American Political Science Association (APSA) who are interested in conducting research on the intersection of gender, race, ethnicity, and political power at the Centennial Center for Political Science and Public Affairs.

Eligibility This program is open to members of the association who are interested in conducting research on the intersection of gender, race, ethnicity, and political power while in residence at the center. Support is available to pre-dissertation graduate students as well as for an award or public presentation. Non-resident scholars may also be eligible.

Financial data Grants normally range from $1,000 to $2,500.

Duration 2 weeks to 12 months.

Additional information This program was established in affiliation with the Women's Caucus for Political Science, the Latina Caucus for Political Science, the Committee for the Status of Latino/Latinas in the Profession, the Women and Politics Research Organized Section, and the Race, Ethnicity and Politics Organized Section.

Number awarded 1 or more each year.

Deadline February, June, or October of each year.

[1379]
RJOS/OREF/DEPUY RESEARCH GRANT IN WOMEN'S MUSCULOSKELETAL HEALTH

Ruth Jackson Orthopaedic Society
9400 West Higgins Road, Suite 500
Rosemont, IL 60018
(847) 698-1626   Fax: (847) 268-9461
E-mail: rjos@aaos.org
Web: www.rjos.org/category/research-grant-opportunities

Summary To provide funding to new orthopedic surgeons who are interested in conducting research in women's musculoskeletal health.

Eligibility This program is open to new orthopedic surgeons who are interested in conducting research that enhances knowledge in the area of women's musculoskeletal health and our understanding of how gender and diversity differences affect the outcomes of orthopedic procedures. The research may be basic, translational, clinical, and/or health services.

Financial data The grant is $15,000.

Duration 1 year.

Additional information This program is jointly sponsored by the Ruth Jackson Orthopaedic Society (RJOS) and the Orthopaedic Research and Education Foundation (OREF). Funding is provided by DePuy Orthopaedics.

Number awarded 1 each year.

Deadline September of each year.

[1380]
RJOS/ZIMMER RESEARCH GRANT

Ruth Jackson Orthopaedic Society
9400 West Higgins Road, Suite 500
Rosemont, IL 60018
(847) 698-1626   Fax: (847) 268-9461
E-mail: rjos@aaos.org
Web: www.rjos.org/category/research-grant-opportunities

Summary To provide funding to members of the Ruth Jackson Orthopaedic Society (RJOS) who are interested in conducting pilot research.

Eligibility This program is open to women who are board certified or board eligible orthopaedic surgeons and RJOS members. Applicants must be seeking seed and start-up funding for promising research projects. Clinical or basic science projects are encouraged. Preference is given to grants with a focus on women's musculoskeletal health.

Financial data The grant is a $30,000.

Duration 1 year; nonrenewable.

Additional information Funding for this program is provided by Zimmer, Inc.

Number awarded 2 each year.
Deadline October of each year.

[1381]
ROBERT AND DAYLE WALDEN MEMORIAL SCHOLARSHIP

Whirly-Girls International
c/o Colleen Chen, Vice President Scholarships
P.O. Box 437
Franconia, NH 03580
(603) 505-4668   Fax: (603) 505-4667
E-mail: wgvpsch@whirlygirls.org
Web: www.whirlygirls.org/wg-scholarships

Summary To provide financial assistance to members of Whirly-Girls International who are interested in upgrading their current helicopter rating.

Eligibility This program is open to women who have been members of Whirly-Girls International for at least 1 year. Applicants must be interested in upgrading their current helicopter rating, through commercial, instrument, instructor, ATP, or turbine transition training. Along with their application, they must submit brief statements on how they intend to utilize this scholarship, their career goals in the helicopter industry, and how this scholarship will help them achieve those goals.

Financial data The stipend is $6,000.

Duration Training must be completed within 1 year.

Additional information This program began in 2015. Completed applications must include $45 to cover the cost of processing and mailing.

Number awarded 1 each year.

Deadline September of each year.

[1382]
ROBERT L. FANTZ MEMORIAL AWARD FOR YOUNG PSYCHOLOGISTS

American Psychological Foundation
750 First Street, N.E.
Washington, DC 20002-4242
(202) 336-5843   Fax: (202) 336-5812
E-mail: foundation@apa.org
Web: www.apa.org/apf/funding/fantz.aspx

Summary To provide funding to promising young investigators in psychology.

Eligibility This program is open to young investigators in psychology or related disciplines. Candidates must show 1) evidence of basic scientific research or scholarly writing in perceptual-cognitive development and the development of selection attention; and 2) research and writing on the development of individuality, creativity, and free-choice of behavior. The sponsor encourages applications from individuals who represent diversity in race, ethnicity, gender, age, disability, and sexual orientation.

Financial data The award is $2,000. Funds are paid directly to the recipient's institution for equipment purchases, travel, computer resources, or other expenses related to the work recognized by the award.

Duration The award is presented annually.

Additional information This award was first presented in 1992.

Number awarded 1 each year.
Deadline Deadline not specified.

[1383]
ROME FOUNDATION FUNCTIONAL GI AND MOTILITY DISORDERS PILOT RESEARCH AWARD

American Gastroenterological Association
Attn: AGA Research Foundation
Research Awards Manager
4930 Del Ray Avenue
Bethesda, MD 20814-2512
(301) 222-4012   Fax: (301) 654-5920
E-mail: awards@gastro.org
Web: www.gastro.org

Summary To provide funding to investigators at all levels interested in conducting pilot research related to functional gastrointestinal and motility disorders.

Eligibility This program is open to early stage and established investigators, postdoctoral research fellows, and combined research and clinical fellows. Applicants must be interested in conducting pilot research on the pathophysiology, diagnosis, and/or treatment of functional gastrointestinal or motility disorders. They must have an M.D. or Ph.D. degree and a full-time faculty position at a North American educational institution. Membership in the American Gastroenterological Association (AGA) is required. Selection is based on novelty, importance, feasibility, environment, and the overall likelihood that the project will lead to subsequent, more substantial grants in the areas of functional gastrointestinal and motility disorders research. Women and minorities are strongly encouraged to apply.

Financial data The grant is $50,000. Funds are to be used for project costs, including salary, supplies, and equipment but excluding travel. Indirect costs are not allowed.

Duration 1 year.

Additional information This program is sponsored by the Rome Foundation.

Number awarded Varies each year; recently, 2 were awarded.

Deadline January of each year.

[1384]
RONA JAFFE FOUNDATION FELLOWSHIP

Vermont Studio Center
80 Pearl Street
P.O. Box 613
Johnson, VT 05656
(802) 635-2727   Fax: (802) 635-2730
E-mail: info@vermontstudiocenter.org
Web: www.vermontstudiocenter.org/fellowships

Summary To provide funding to emerging women writers who are interested in a residency at the Vermont Studio Center in Johnson, Vermont.

Eligibility This program is open to women writers of fiction, poetry, or creative nonfiction who are unpublished, or have begun publishing in literary journals, or are just completing their first book. Applicants must be interested in a first-time residency at the center in Johnson, Vermont. Poets must submit up to 10 pages or their work and other writers must submit

10 to 15 pages. Selection is based on artistic merit. U.S. citizenship or permanent resident status is required.

Financial data The award pays $3,950, which covers all residency fees. An additional stipend of $1,250 is designed to help cover expenses associated with taking the residency, including (but not limited to) travel, rent, child care, or the replacement of lost income.

Duration 4 weeks.

Additional information This award is sponsored by the Rona Jaffe Foundation. The application fee is $25.

Number awarded 1 each year.

Deadline February, June, or September of each year.

[1385]
RONA JAFFE FOUNDATION WRITERS' AWARDS

Rona Jaffe Foundation
c/o Beth McCabe
Digitas New York
355 Park Avenue South
New York, NY 10010
(212) 610-5000   E-mail: Jaffemedia@fairpoint.net
Web: www.ronajaffefoundation.org

Summary To recognize and reward outstanding women writers.

Eligibility These awards are presented to women who have written outstanding fiction, poetry, and creative nonfiction. Authors are normally in the early stages of their writing careers and awards are intended to make writing time available and provide assistance for such specific purposes as child care, research, and related travel activities. Application and nominations are not accepted; the foundation identifies writers through its internal processes.

Financial data The awards are $30,000.

Duration The awards are presented annually.

Additional information This program began in 1995.

Number awarded 6 each year.

Deadline Deadline not specified.

[1386]
ROSALIND FRANKLIN YOUNG INVESTIGATOR AWARD

Genetics Society of America
9650 Rockville Pike
Bethesda, MD 20814-3998
(301) 634-7300   E-mail: society@genetics-gsa.org
Web: www.genetics-gsa.org/awards/rosalind.shtml

Summary To provide funding to young women from any country conducting advanced research in genetics.

Eligibility This program is open to women who have recently completed a doctoral degree in genetics within the past 1 to 3 years. Applicants may be citizens of any country, but they must have an independent faculty position and must be listed as the principal investigator on all research published from their laboratory. In the selection process, consideration is given to questions as to whether the nominee is clearly building on her experience through the years, does she show scientific creativity and leadership, has she demonstrated independence in developing her scientific research, and has she made seminal discoveries on her own.

Financial data The grant is $25,000 per year. Funds may be used only for direct costs of research, not for the recipient's salary or overhead expenses.

Duration 3 years.

Additional information This program was established in 2004 by The Gruber Foundation, then named the Peter and Patricia Gruber Foundation.

Number awarded 2 are awarded every 3 years (2019, 2022, etc.).

Deadline March of the year of the award.

[1387]
ROSE MARY CRAWSHAY PRIZES

British Academy
Attn: Chief Executive and Secretary
10-11 Carlton House Terrace
London SW1Y 5AH
England
44 20 7969 5255   Fax: 44 20 7969 5300
E-mail: chiefexec@britac.ac.uk
Web: www.britac.ac.uk/rose-mary-crawshay-prize

Summary To recognize and reward women who have written or published outstanding historical or critical works on any subject connected with English literature.

Eligibility Women of any nationality are eligible to be nominated if within the preceding 3 years they have written an historical or critical work on any subject connected with English literature. Preference is given to works on Byron, Shelley, or Keats. Submissions are invited from publishing houses only.

Financial data The prize is 500 pounds.

Duration The prize is awarded each year.

Additional information The prize was established by Rose Mary Crawshay in 1888.

Number awarded 1 or 2 each year.

Deadline December of each year.

[1388]
RUSTY KANOKOGI FUND FOR THE ADVANCEMENT OF U.S. JUDO

Women's Sports Foundation
Attn: Award and Grant Programs Manager
Eisenhower Park
1899 Hempstead Turnpike, Suite 400
East Meadow, NY 11554-1000
(516) 307-3915   Toll Free: (800) 227-3988
E-mail: lflores@womenssportsfoundation.org
Web: www.womenssportsfoundation.org

Summary To provide funding for training activities to women judo athletes.

Eligibility This program is open to women who are amateur judo athletes eligible to compete for a U.S. national team and U.S. citizens or legal residents. Applicants must have successful competitive records and the potential to achieve even higher performance levels and rankings. They must be seeking funding for coaching, specialized training, and/or travel. Selection is based on present and potential level and ranking, lack of support from traditional sources, role of award in continued participation and advancement, potential impact of grant on advancing women in sports, contribution to greater visibility of female athletes, and financial need. Priority is given to applicants who present a plan for reimbursing the grant in the future, whether financially or otherwise contributing to women's sports.

Financial data A total of $5,000 is available for this program each year.

Duration Individuals may receive only 1 grant per calendar year and 3 grants in a lifetime.

Additional information This program began in 2009.

Number awarded Up to 3 each year.

Deadline March of each year.

[1389]
RUTH AND LINCOLN EKSTROM FELLOWSHIPS

Brown University
John Carter Brown Library
Attn: Fellowships Coordinator
P.O. Box 1894
Providence, RI 02912
(401) 863-5010   Fax: (401) 863-3477
E-mail: Valerie_Andrews@Brown.edu
Web: www.brown.edu

Summary To support scholars and graduate students interested in conducting research on the history of women at the John Carter Brown Library, which is renowned for its collection of historical sources pertaining to the Americas prior to 1830.

Eligibility This fellowship is open to U.S-based and foreign graduate students, scholars, and independent researchers. Graduate students must have passed their preliminary or general examinations. Applicants must be proposing to conduct research on the history of women and the family in the Americas prior to 1825, including the question of cultural influences on gender formation. Selection is based on the applicant's scholarly qualifications, the merits and significance of the project, and the particular need that the holdings of the John Carter Brown Library will fill in the development of the project.

Financial data The stipend is $2,100 per month.

Duration From 2 to 4 months.

Additional information Fellows are expected to be in regular residence at the library and to participate in the intellectual life of Brown University for the duration of the program.

Number awarded Varies each year; recently, 3 were awarded.

Deadline December of each year.

[1390]
RUTH ANDERSON COMMISSION PRIZE

International Alliance for Women in Music
c/o Susan Borwick, President
Wake Forest University
Department of Music
M319 Scales Fine Arts Center
P.O. Box 7345
Winston-Salem, NC 27109-7345
(336) 758-5953   E-mail: president@iawm.org
Web: www.iawm.org/competitions/search-for-new-music

Summary To recognize and reward members of the International Alliance for Women (IAWM) who are commissioned to compose a new sound installation for electro-acoustic music.

Eligibility This award is presented to an IAWM member who is commissioned to compose a new sound installation for electro-acoustic music. Applicants must submit a detailed proposal of the sound installation. The location of the installation may be, but is not restricted to, an IAWM annual concert or congress.

Financial data The prize is $1,000. The prize is presented to the recipient after submitting a report to IAWM following the public showing of the completed installation.

Duration The project must be completed within 12 months.

Number awarded 1 each year.

Deadline May of each year.

[1391]
RUTH I. MICHLER MEMORIAL PRIZE

Association for Women in Mathematics
11240 Waples Mill Road, Suite 200
Fairfax, VA 22030
(703) 934-0163   Fax: (703) 359-7562
E-mail: michlerprize@awm-math.org
Web: sites.google.com

Summary To recognize and reward, with a fellowship at Cornell University, outstanding women mathematicians.

Eligibility This prize is available to women recently promoted to associate professor or equivalent position in the mathematical sciences at an institution of higher learning other than Cornell University. Applicants may be of any nationality and hold a position in any country. They must submit a proposal describing a research or book project to be undertaken during the fellowship period and explaining how the semester in the mathematics department at Cornell University will enhance their project or research career. Selection is based on the excellence of the applicant's research and the potential benefit to her of a semester in the mathematics department at Cornell.

Financial data The prize is $47,000. A supplemental housing and subsistence award of $3,000 is also provided.

Duration The prize is presented annually. The recipient may spend a semester of her choice in residence at Cornell.

Additional information This prize was first presented in 2007.

Number awarded 1 each year.

Deadline October of each year.

[1392]
RUTH LYTTLE SATTER PRIZE IN MATHEMATICS

American Mathematical Society
Attn: Prizes and Awards
201 Charles Street
Providence, RI 02904-2294
(401) 455-4107   Toll Free: (800) 321-4AMS
Fax: (401) 455-4046
Web: www.ams.org

Summary To recognize and reward women who have made outstanding contributions to mathematics.

Eligibility This program is open to female mathematicians who have made outstanding contributions to research in the field. The work must have been completed within the past 6 years.

Financial data The prize is $5,000.

Duration The prize is awarded biennially, in odd-numbered years.

Additional information This prize was first awarded in 1991.

Number awarded 1 every other year.

Deadline June of each even-numbered year.

[1393]
RUTH P. MORGAN GRANTS

Southern Methodist University
William P. Clements Center for Southwest Studies
Dallas Hall 356
P.O. Box 750176
Dallas, TX 75275-0176
(214) 768-3684   Fax: (214) 768-4129
E-mail: swcenter@smu.edu
Web: www.smu.edu

Summary To provide funding to advanced scholars interested in using the Archives of Women of the Southwest at DeGolyer Library, Southern Methodist University (Dallas, Texas).

Eligibility This program is open to advanced scholars interested in conducting research at the DeGolyer Library using the Archives of Women of the Southwest. Applicants must live outside the Dallas and Fort Worth metropolitan areas. They should submit an outline of the project, an explanation of how work in the DeGolyer Library collections will enhance it, length of time expected to be spent there, a curriculum vitae, and 2 letters of reference.

Financial data The grant is $700 per week. Funds are intended to help pay the costs of travel, lodging, and research materials.

Duration From 1 to 2 weeks.

Additional information The Archives of Women of the Southwest includes papers of leaders in women's organizations and social and political reform movements, papers of outstanding women in the professions, the arts, and voluntary service; papers of families and of women in private life; records of women's organizations and organizations concerned with women's issues; and oral history interviews.

Number awarded 1 or more each year.

Deadline May of each year for use between June and November; November of each year for use between December and May.

[1394]
RUTH R. AND ALYSON R. MILLER FELLOWSHIPS

Massachusetts Historical Society
Attn: Short-Term Fellowships
1154 Boylston Street
Boston, MA 02215-3695
(617) 646-0568   Fax: (617) 859-0074
E-mail: fellowships@masshist.org
Web: www.masshist.org/research/fellowships/short-term

Summary To fund research visits to the Massachusetts Historical Society for graduate students and other scholars interested in women's history.

Eligibility This program is open to advanced graduate students, postdoctorates, and independent scholars who are conducting research in women's history and need to use the resources of the Massachusetts Historical Society. Applicants

must be U.S. citizens or foreign nationals holding appropriate U.S. government documents. Along with their application, they must submit a curriculum vitae and a proposal describing the project and indicating collections at the society to be consulted. Graduate students must also arrange for a letter of recommendation from a faculty member familiar with their work and with the project being proposed. Preference is given to candidates who live 50 or more miles from Boston.

Financial data The grant is $2,000.

Duration 4 weeks.

Additional information This fellowship was first awarded in 1998.

Number awarded 1 or more each year.

Deadline February of each year.

[1395]
SADOSKY RESEARCH PRIZE IN ANALYSIS

Association for Women in Mathematics
11240 Waples Mill Road, Suite 200
Fairfax, VA 22030
(703) 934-0163   Fax: (703) 359-7562
E-mail: awm@awm-math.org
Web: sites.google.com

Summary To recognize and reward women who are early in their research careers and have made outstanding contributions in mathematical analysis.

Eligibility This award is available to women who are faculty members at U.S. institutions and within 10 years of receiving their Ph.D. or have not yet received tenure. Nominees must have conducted exceptional research in any area of mathematical analysis.

Financial data The award includes a cash prize and honorary plaque.

Duration The award is presented biennially, in even-numbered years.

Additional information This award was first presented in 2014.

Number awarded 1 each year.

Deadline Nominations must be submitted by February of each odd-numbered year.

[1396]
SARA A. WHALEY BOOK PRIZE

National Women's Studies Association
Attn: Book Prizes
11 East Mount Royal Avenue, Suite 100
Baltimore, MD 21202
(410) 528-0355   Fax: (410) 528-0357
E-mail: awards@nwsa.org
Web: www.nwsa.org

Summary To recognize and reward members of the National Women's Studies Association (NWSA) who have written outstanding books on topics related to women and labor.

Eligibility This award is available to NWSA members who submit a book manuscript that relates to women and labor, including migration and women's paid jobs, illegal immigration and women's work, impact of AIDS on women's employment, trafficking of women and women's employment, women and domestic work, or impact of race on women's work. Both senior scholars (who have issued at least 2 books and published the entry within the past year) and junior scholars (who have a publication contract or a book in production) are eligible. Women of color of U.S. or international origin are encouraged to apply.

Financial data The award is $2,000.

Duration The awards are presented annually.

Additional information This award was first presented in 2008.

Number awarded 2 each year: 1 to a senior scholar and 1 to a junior scholar.

Deadline April of each year.

[1397]
SARAH BRADLEY TYSON MEMORIAL FELLOWSHIP

Woman's National Farm and Garden Association, Inc.
c/o Mrs. Harold L. Matyn, Fellowship Committee Chair
3801 Riverview Terrace, South
East China Township, MI 48054
E-mail: matynjm@att.net
Web: www.wnfga.org/scholarships/fellowships

Summary To provide funding to women who have work experience and are interested in advanced study in agriculture, horticulture, and allied subjects.

Eligibility The fellowship is open to women interested in working on an advanced degree in the fields of agriculture, horticulture, or allied subjects at educational institutions of recognized standing within the United States. Applicants must have several years of experience. There are no application forms. Interested women should send a letter of application that contains an account of their educational training, a plan of study, references, samples of publishable papers, and a health certificate.

Financial data The fellowship award is $1,000 and is tenable at an American institution of higher learning chosen by the candidate with the approval of the fellowship committee.

Duration 1 year.

Additional information This program began in 1928. Students who accept the fellowships must agree to devote themselves to the study outlined in their application and to submit any proposed change in their plan to the committee for approval. They must send the committee at least 2 reports on their work, 1 at the end of the first semester and another upon completion of the year's work.

Number awarded Varies each year.

Deadline April of each year.

[1398]
SARAH STANLEY GORDON EDWARDS AND ARCHIBALD CASON EDWARDS ENDOWMENT FOR FELLOWSHIPS

Virginia Center for the Creative Arts
Attn: Admissions Committee
154 San Angelo Drive
Amherst, VA 24521
(434) 946-7236   Fax: (434) 946-7239
E-mail: vcca@vcca.com
Web: www.vcca.com

Summary To provide support to female painters, especially Native Americans, who are interested in a residency at the Virginia Center for the Creative Arts in Sweet Briar, Virginia.

Eligibility This program is open to female painters older than 25 years of age who are interested in a residency at the center so they can concentrate solely on their creative work. Preference is given to Native American painters. Applicants must submit samples of their work completed within the past 4 years.

Financial data The fellowship provides payment of all residency costs, including a private bedroom, separate studio, and 3 prepared meals a day.

Duration 2 weeks.

Additional information This program began in 2016. The application fee is $40.

Number awarded 1 each year.

Deadline January of each year for June to September residencies; May of each year for October to January residencies; September of each year for February to May residencies.

[1399]
SCHLESINGER LIBRARY ORAL HISTORY GRANTS

Radcliffe Institute for Advanced Study at Harvard University
Attn: Arthur and Elizabeth Schlesinger Library
10 Garden Street
Cambridge, MA 02138
(617) 495-8647   Fax: (617) 496-8340
E-mail: slgrants@radcliffe.harvard.edu
Web: www.radcliffe.harvard.edu/schlesinger-library/grants

Summary To provide funding to scholars who are conducting oral history interviews related to the history of women.

Eligibility This program is open to scholars who are conducting oral history interviews relevant to the history of women or gender in the United States. The interviews must take place in accordance with guidelines of the Oral History Association, that consent is obtained from interviewees for their words to be viewed by researchers worldwide, and that copies or transcripts of the interviews be deposited in the Schlesinger Library. Selection is based on the significance of the research and the project's potential contribution to the advancement of knowledge.

Financial data Grants range up to $3,000. Funds must be used to cover travel, living expenses, photocopying, and other incidental research expenses.

Duration This are 1-time grants.

Additional information The Schlesinger Library is a non-circulating research library that documents the history of women in the United States during the 19th and 20th centuries. These grants were first awarded in 2012.

Number awarded Varies each year; recently, 4 were awarded.

Deadline January of each year.

[1400]
SCHLESINGER LIBRARY RESEARCH SUPPORT GRANTS

Radcliffe Institute for Advanced Study at Harvard
  University
Attn: Arthur and Elizabeth Schlesinger Library
10 Garden Street
Cambridge, MA 02138
(617) 495-8647   Fax: (617) 496-8340
E-mail: slgrants@radcliffe.harvard.edu
Web: www.radcliffe.harvard.edu/schlesinger-library/grants

Summary To provide funding to faculty and unaffiliated scholars who are actively pursuing research that requires or will benefit from access to the holdings of the Schlesinger Library on the History of Women in America.

Eligibility Eligible to apply are scholars who have a doctoral degree or equivalent research and writing experience. Priority is given to those whose projects require use of materials available nowhere else but the Schlesinger Library. The project description should indicate the purpose of the research, the Schlesinger Library holdings to be consulted, and the significance of those holdings to the project overall. Selection is based on the significance of the research, the project's potential contribution to the advancement of knowledge, and its creativity in using the library's holdings.

Financial data Grants range up to $3,000. Funds must be used to cover travel, living expenses, photocopying, and other incidental research expenses.

Duration Summer months or the academic year.

Additional information The Schlesinger Library is a non-circulating research library that documents the history of women in the United States during the 19th and 20th centuries.

Number awarded Varies each year; recently, 9 were awarded.

Deadline January of each year.

[1401]
SCHMIEDER LEADERSHIP SCHOLARSHIP FOR WOMEN FACULTY AT ELCA COLLEGES AND SEMINARIES

Women of the Evangelical Lutheran Church in America
Attn: Scholarships
8765 West Higgins Road
Chicago, IL 60631-4101
(773) 380-2741   Toll Free: (800) 638-3522, ext. 2741
Fax: (773) 380-2419   E-mail: valora.starr@elca.org
Web: www.womenoftheelca.org

Summary To provide financial assistance to female faculty members at Evangelical Lutheran Church of America (ELCA) institutions who wish to participate in a leadership and management summer training institute.

Eligibility This program is open to female faculty at ELCA colleges, universities, and seminaries. Applicants must be interested in enrolled at a summer institute of their choice, provided that the program includes work in governance, financial management, administration, and professional development. They must be nominated by the president of their institution, which also must agree to provide partial assistance for the program.

Financial data The program provides a grant of $2,000 to $4,000; additional funding must be provided by the recipient's institution.

Duration Recipients are eligible for support for a maximum of 2 years.

Additional information Recipients are expected to submit an evaluation of the institute experience to the sponsor within 3 months of the training and to share learning experiences with colleagues at their home institution and, if requested, at Women of the ELCA events.

Number awarded Varies each year, depending upon the funds available. Since the program was established, it has awarded scholarships to 22 women.

Deadline February of each year.

[1402]
SHARON KEILLOR AWARD FOR WOMEN IN ENGINEERING EDUCATION

American Society for Engineering Education
Attn: Awards Administration
1818 N Street, N.W., Suite 600
Washington, DC 20036-2479
(202) 331-3550   Fax: (202) 265-8504
E-mail: board@asee.org
Web: www.asee.org

Summary To recognize and reward outstanding women engineering educators.

Eligibility This award is presented to a woman engineering educator who has an outstanding record in teaching engineering students and reasonable performance histories of research and service within an engineering school. Nominees must have an earned doctoral degree in an engineering discipline and have at least 5 years of teaching experience in an engineering school.

Financial data The award consists of a $2,000 honorarium and an inscribed plaque.

Duration The award is granted annually.

Number awarded 1 each year.

Deadline January of each year.

[1403]
SHOOTING STAR GRANTS

Montana Federation of Business and Professional
  Women's Organizations
Attn: Montana BPW Foundation, Inc.
P.O. Box 303
Great Falls, MT 59403
E-mail: mtbpwfoundation@gmail.com
Web: sites.google.com

Summary To provide funding to Montana women interested in personal or professional development.

Eligibility This program is open to women in Montana seeking funding for self-sufficiency, professional development, acquisition of skills, or business start-up and expansion. Funding is not available for scholarships, religious purposes, veteran or fraternal organizations, general endowment funds, or fundraising. Applicants must submit brief statements that 1) describe the project, business, or professional opportunity for which they are requesting funds; 2) describe how the opportunity will help them in their professional development; 3) identify the timeline for the project; 4) list other programs or funding they have requested for this project; 5) describe the projected outcomes of the project and the methods that will be used to measure those; and 6) discuss their goals and objectives once this project is completed.

Financial data   Grants up to $1,000 are available.

Number awarded   Varies each year; recently, 5 were awarded.

Deadline   January of each year.

[1404]
SIGMA DELTA EPSILON FELLOWSHIPS

Sigma Delta Epsilon-Graduate Women in Science, Inc.
Attn: Fellowships Coordinator
P.O. Box 580140
Minneapolis, MN 55458
E-mail: fellowships@gwis.org
Web: www.gwis.org/?page=fellowship_program

Summary   To provide funding to women interested in conducting research in the natural sciences anywhere in the world.

Eligibility   This program is open to women from any country currently enrolled as a graduate student, engaged in postdoctoral research, or holding a junior faculty position. Applicants must be interested in conducting research anywhere in the world in the natural sciences (including physical, environmental, mathematical, computer, or life sciences), anthropology, psychology, or statistics. Membership in Sigma Delta Epsilon-Graduate Women in Science (SDE-GWIS) is encouraged.

Financial data   The maximum grant is $10,000. Funds may be used for such research expenses as expendable supplies, small equipment, publication of research findings, travel and subsistence while performing field studies, or travel to another laboratory for collaborative research. They may not be used for salaries, tuition, child care, travel to professional meetings or to begin a new appointment, administrative overhead or indirect costs, personal computers, living allowances, or equipment for general use.

Duration   1 academic year.

Additional information   This program includes the Adele Lewis Grant SDE Fellowship (awarded to the highest scoring applicant), the Hartley Corporation SDE Fellowship (awarded to the second highest scoring applicant), the Ethel K. Allen Fellowship, the Monique Braude Fellowship, the Eloise Gerry Fellowships, the Jean Langenheim Fellowship, the Nell I. Mondy Fellowship, and the Vessa Notchev Fellowship. Nonmembers of SDE-GWIS must pay an application fee of $50.

Number awarded   Varies each year; recently, 6 were awarded.

Deadline   January of each year.

[1405]
SOCIETY OF BIBLICAL LITERATURE REGIONAL SCHOLARS AWARDS

Society of Biblical Literature
c/o The Luce Center
825 Houston Mill Road, Suite 350
Atlanta, GA 30329
(404) 727-3100   Fax: (404) 727-3101
E-mail: sblexec@sbl-site.org
Web: www.sbl-site.org/membership/SBLAwards.aspx

Summary   To provide funding for annual meeting attendance or professional development to members of the Society of Biblical Literature (SBL) at the doctoral or recent postdoctoral level.

Eligibility   This award is available to SBL members who are Ph.D. candidates or who completed a Ph.D. within the past 4 years. Applicants must present at an SBL regional meeting an original work of their own scholarship and must submit a copy of the paper, along with a curriculum vitae, to the regional coordinator for their SBL region. Members of the selection committee attend the oral presentation and evaluate it on the basis of clear articulation of argument advanced, even and engaging delivery, clear pronunciation and style appropriate to oral presentation, and creative and appropriate use of presentation materials. The written papers are evaluated as oral presentations, not as research articles, on the basis of the following criteria: clarity of expression and argumentation, demonstrated knowledge and critical use of scholarly resources and publications, use and knowledge of the primary sources, and originality of ideas and solutions. Women and minorities are encouraged to apply.

Financial data   The award is $1,000. funds may be used to support attendance at the SBL annual meeting or to promote future scholarship and professional development.

Duration   The awards are presented annually.

Number awarded   Up to 6 each year.

Deadline   Each of the 11 SBL regions establishes its own deadline.

[1406]
SPP DIVERSITY RESEARCH GRANT

American Psychological Association
Attn: Division 54 (Society of Pediatric Psychology)
750 First Street, N.E.
Washington, DC 20002-4242
(202) 216-7602   Fax: (202) 336-5953
TDD: (202) 336-6123   E-mail: APAdiv54@gmail.com
Web: www.apadivisions.org

Summary   To provide funding to graduate student and postdoctoral members of the Society of Pediatric Psychology (SPP) who are interested in conducting research on diversity aspects of pediatric psychology.

Eligibility   This program is open to current members of the society who are graduate students, fellows, or early-career (within 3 years of appointment) faculty. Applicants must be interested in conducting pediatric psychology research that features diversity-related variables, such as race or ethnicity, gender, culture, sexual orientation, language differences, socioeconomic status, and/or religiosity. Along with their application, they must submit a 2,000-word description of the project, including its purpose, methodology, predictions, and implications; a detailed budget; a current curriculum vitae, and (for students) a curriculum vitae of the faculty research mentor and a letter of support from that mentor. Selection is based on relevance to diversity in child health (5 points), significance of the study (5 points), study methods and procedures (10 points), and investigator qualifications (10 points).

Financial data Grants up to $1,000 are available. Funds may not be used for convention or meeting travel, indirect costs, stipends of principal investigators, or costs associated with manuscript preparation.

Duration The grant is presented annually.

Additional information The Society of Pediatric Psychology is Division 54 of the American Psychological Association (APA). This grant was first presented in 2008.

Number awarded 1 each year.

Deadline September of each year.

[1407]
STANTON NUCLEAR SECURITY FELLOWSHIP

Stanford University
Center for International Security and Cooperation
Attn: Fellowships Coordinator
Encina Hall, Room C206-10
616 Serra Street
Stanford, CA 94305-6165
(650) 723-9625   Fax: (650) 724-5683
E-mail: CISACfellowship@stanford.edu
Web: cisac.fsi.stanford.edu/docs/cisac_fellowship_program

Summary To provide funding to doctoral candidates and junior scholars who are interested in conducting research on nuclear security issues at Stanford University's Center for International Security and Cooperation.

Eligibility This program is open to doctoral candidates, recent postdoctorates, and junior faculty. Applicants must be interested in conducting research on nuclear security issues while in residence at the center. The sponsor welcomes applications from women, minorities, and citizens of all countries.

Financial data The stipend ranges from $25,000 to $28,000 for doctoral candidates or from $48,000 to $66,000 for postdoctorates, depending on experience. Medical insurance is available for those who do not have coverage.

Duration 9 to 11 months.

Additional information Fellows are expected to write a dissertation chapter or chapters, publishable article or articles, and/or make significant progress on turning a thesis into a book manuscript. They should not plan to spend any time conducting research abroad or in other parts of the country.

Number awarded Varies each year; recently, 3 were awarded: 1 doctoral candidate, 1 recent postdoctorate, and 1 junior faculty member.

Deadline January of each year.

[1408]
SUSAN SMITH BLACKBURN PRIZE

Susan Smith Blackburn Prize, Inc.
c/o Leslie Swackhamer, Chair
Sam Houston State University
Department of Theatre and Musical Theatre
UTC 112
Huntsville, TX 77341-2297
(936) 294-1333   Fax: (936) 294-3898
E-mail: susansmithblackburn@gmail.com
Web: www.blackburnprize.org

Summary To recognize and reward women who have written works of outstanding quality for the English-speaking theater.

Eligibility This award is available to women who have written a full-length play in English. Playwrights may not submit their work directly. Each year, prominent professionals (directors or literary managers) are asked to nominate plays from the United States, United Kingdom, Ireland, Canada, South Africa, Australia, and New Zealand for consideration. Plays are eligible whether or not they have been produced, but any premier production must have taken place within the preceding 12 months. Each script is read by at least 3 members of a screening committee in order to select 10 finalists. All final nominations are read by all 6 judges.

Financial data The prizes are $25,000 to the winner, $10,000 for special commendation, and $5,000 to each of the other finalists.

Duration The prizes are awarded annually.

Additional information The prizes are administered in Houston, London, and New York by a board of directors who choose 6 judges each year, 3 in the United States and 3 in the United Kingdom. The prize was established in 1978 by the friends and family of Susan Smith Blackburn, the American writer/actress who spent the last 15 years of her life in London.

Number awarded 1 winner, 1 special commendation recipient, and 8 other finalists are chosen each year.

Deadline September of each year.

[1409]
SWS FEMINIST LECTURER AWARD

Sociologists for Women in Society
Attn: Administrative Officer
University of Kansas
Department of Sociology
1415 Jayhawk Boulevard, Room 716
Lawrence, KS 66045
(785) 864-9405   E-mail: swsao@outlook.com
Web: www.socwomen.org/feminist-lecturer-award-2

Summary To provide funding to enable distinguished feminist scholars to deliver guest lectures at campuses that might otherwise not have access to major work in the field.

Eligibility Feminist scholars (with advanced degrees or the equivalent experience) are eligible to be nominated. They must be interested in delivering a lecture at 2 college campuses that are rural, isolated, or not located in or near major metropolitan centers.

Financial data The society pays the recipient $1,000 as an honorarium.

Duration The award is presented annually.

Additional information This program began in 1985. The lecture may be published in the association's journal, *Gender and Society*.

Number awarded 1 lecturer is selected each year; 2 institutions are selected to host her.

Deadline Nominations for the lecturer and applications from institutions interested in serving as a host are due by February of each year.

[1410]
SYLVIA LANE MENTOR FELLOWSHIP

Agricultural and Applied Economics Association
Attn: Trust Committee
555 East Wells Street, Suite 1100
Milwaukee, WI 53202
(414) 918-3190   Fax: (414) 276-3349
E-mail: info@aaea.org
Web: www.aaea.org

Summary To provide funding to young female scholars who are working on food, agricultural, or resource issues and interested in relocating in order to conduct research with an established expert at another university, institution, or firm.

Eligibility These fellowships are awarded to mentee/mentor pairs of individuals. Mentees must have completed at least 1 year in residence in an accredited American graduate degree program in agricultural economics or a closely-related discipline; women with Ph.D. degrees and advanced graduate students are encouraged to apply. Mentors must have a Ph.D. and established expertise in an area of food, agriculture, or natural resources. The goal is to enable female scholars to relocate in order to conduct research with an established expert at another university, institution, or firm, even though they may reside in different parts of the country. Selection is based on the relevance of the research problem, potential for generating output, synergy of the mentor/mentee pairing, and opportunity for advancing the mentee's research skills beyond her graduate studies and current position.

Financial data Awards range up to $2,500.

Duration Several weeks.

Additional information This program was established in 2008 by the Committee on Women in Agricultural Economics of the Agricultural and Applied Economics Association.

Number awarded 1 or more each year.

Deadline October of each year.

[1411]
THEODORE BLAU EARLY CAREER AWARD FOR OUTSTANDING CONTRIBUTION TO PROFESSIONAL CLINICAL PSYCHOLOGY

American Psychological Foundation
750 First Street, N.E.
Washington, DC 20002-4242
(202) 336-5843   Fax: (202) 336-5812
E-mail: foundation@apa.org
Web: www.apa.org/apf/funding/blau.aspx

Summary To recognize and reward early-career clinical psychologists who have made outstanding professional accomplishments.

Eligibility This award is available to clinical psychologists who are no more than 10 years past completion of their doctoral degree. Nominees must have a record of accomplish-

ments that may include promoting the practice of clinical psychology through professional service; innovation in service delivery; novel application of applied research methodologies to professional practice; positive impact on health delivery systems; development of creative educational programs for practice; or other novel or creative activities advancing the service of the profession. Self-nominations are accepted. The sponsor encourages nominations of individuals who represent diversity in race, ethnicity, gender, age, disability, and sexual orientation.

Financial data The award is $4,000.

Duration The award is presented annually.

Additional information This award, first presented in 1998, is sponsored by Division 12 (Society of Clinical Psychology) of the American Psychological Association.

Number awarded 1 each year.

Deadline Nominations must be submitted by October of each year.

[1412]
THEODORE MILLON AWARD IN PERSONALITY PSYCHOLOGY

American Psychological Foundation
750 First Street, N.E.
Washington, DC 20002-4242
(202) 336-5843   Fax: (202) 336-5812
E-mail: foundation@apa.org
Web: www.apa.org/apf/funding/millon.aspx

Summary To recognize and reward psychologists who have made outstanding contributions to the science of personality psychology.

Eligibility This award is available to psychologists engaged in advancing the science of personality psychology, including the areas of personology, personality theory, personality disorders, and personality measurement. Nominees should be between 8 and 20 years past completion of their doctoral degree. The sponsor encourages nominations of individuals who represent diversity in race, ethnicity, gender, age, disability, and sexual orientation.

Financial data The award is $1,000.

Duration The award is presented annually.

Additional information This award, established in 2004, is sponsored by Division 12 (Society of Clinical Psychology) of the American Psychological Association.

Number awarded 1 each year.

Deadline Nominations must be submitted by October of each year.

[1413]
UCAR VISITING SCIENTIST PROGRAMS

University Corporation for Atmospheric Research
Attn: Visiting Scientist Programs
3090 Center Green Drive
P.O. Box 3000
Boulder, CO 80307-3000
(303) 497-1605   Fax: (303) 497-8668
E-mail: vspapply@ucar.edu
Web: www.vsp.ucar.edu

Summary To provide funding to recent postdoctorates in atmospheric sciences who wish to participate in designated research programs.

Eligibility This program is open to postdoctorates (preferably those who received their Ph.D. within the preceding 3 years) who wish to conduct research with experienced scientists at designated facilities. Applicants must submit a cover letter stating the name of the program, potential host and institution, and where they learned of this opportunity; their curriculum vitae; names and addresses of at least 4 professional references; an abstract of their Ph.D. dissertation; and a description of the research they wish to conduct at the relevant facility. Women and minorities are encouraged to apply. U.S. citizenship is not required, although the research must be conducted at a U.S. institution.

Financial data The salary is $60,000 for the first year and $62,000 for the second year. A moving allowance of $750, an allowance of $5,000 per year for scientific travel, and a $3,000 publication allowance for the term of the award are also provided. Benefits include health and dental insurance, sick and annual leave, paid holidays, participation in a retirement fund, and life insurance.

Duration 2 years.

Additional information Recently, positions were available through 3 programs: 1) the NOAA Climate and Global Change Postdoctoral Fellowship Program (sponsored by the National Oceanic and Atmospheric Administration; 2) the Postdocs Applying Climate Expertise (PACE) Fellowship Program; and 3) the Jack Eddy Postdoctoral Program in heliophysics (defined as all science common to the field of Sun-Earth connections).

Number awarded Recently, 8 fellowships for the NOAA Climate and Global Change Postdoctoral Fellowship Program, 2 for the PACE Fellowship Program, and 4 for the Jack Eddy Postdoctoral Program were awarded.

Deadline January of each year for the NOAA Climate and Global Change Postdoctoral Fellowship Program and the Jack Eddy Postdoctoral Program; May of each year for the PACE Fellowship Program.

[1414]
VALERIE RUSSELL SCHOLARSHIP

United Church of Christ
Attn: Associate Director, Grant and Scholarship
  Administration
700 Prospect Avenue East
Cleveland, OH 44115-1100
(216) 736-2166   Toll Free: (866) 822-8224, ext. 2166
Fax: (216) 736-3783   E-mail: scholarships@ucc.org
Web: www.ucc.org/russell_scholarship

Summary To provide financial assistance to African American laywomen who are members of a United Church of Christ (UCC) congregation and working on an undergraduate or graduate degree to advance the justice ministries of the denomination.

Eligibility This program is open to African American laywomen who have a strong theologically-grounded commitment to the justice ministries of the UCC but are not a member in discernment, licensed, commissioned, or ordained. Applicants must be 1) working on an undergraduate or graduate degree in a field that will affirm the values of the UCC and promote its justice commitments; or 2) already professionally engaged in justice work either in the church or in a secular organization and seeking funds for continuing educa-

tion activities (e.g., classes, workshops, travel) that will assist in personal skill building.

Financial data Stipends range from $1,500 to $2,000 per year. Funds may be used for tuition for undergraduate or graduate study or for continuing education activities.

Duration 1 year; may be renewed.

Additional information This program began in 1997.

Number awarded 1 or more each year.

Deadline February of each year.

[1415]
VERNA ROSS ORNDORFF CAREER
PERFORMANCE GRANT

Sigma Alpha Iota Philanthropies, Inc.
One Tunnel Road
Asheville, NC 28805
(828) 251-0606   Fax: (828) 251-0644
E-mail: nh@sai-national.org
Web: app.smarterselect.com

Summary To provide funding for advanced study, coaching, or other activities directly related to the development of a musical career to members of Sigma Alpha Iota (an organization of women musicians).

Eligibility This program is open to members of the organization who are preparing for a concert career. Singers may not be older than 35 years of age and instrumentalists may not be older than 32. Applicants may not have professional management, but they must have had considerable performing experience outside the academic environment.

Financial data The grant is $5,000; funds must be used for advanced study, coaching, or other purposes directly related to the development of a professional performing career.

Duration 1 year.

Additional information The area supported rotates annually among strings, woodwinds, and brass (2017); piano, harpsichord, organ, and percussion (2018); and voice (2019).

Number awarded 1 each year.

Deadline March of each year.

[1416]
VICTORIA SCHUCK AWARD

American Political Science Association
1527 New Hampshire Avenue, N.W.
Washington, DC 20036-1206
(202) 483-2512   Fax: (202) 483-2657
E-mail: apsa@apsanet.org
Web: www.apsanet.org

Summary To recognize and rewar authors of outstanding scholarly books on women and politics.

Eligibility Eligible to be nominated (by publishers or individuals) are scholarly political science books issued the previous year on women and politics.

Financial data The award is $1,000.

Duration The award is presented annually.

Additional information This award was first presented in 1988.

Number awarded 1 each year.

Deadline February of each year.

[1417]
VIOLET DILLER PROFESSIONAL EXCELLENCE AWARD

Iota Sigma Pi
c/o Lily M. Ng, National Director for Professional Awards
Cleveland State University
Department of Chemistry
3077 Euclid Avenue
Cleveland, OH 44115-2516
(612) 455-9354   E-mail: lilymsng@gmail.com
Web: www.iotasigmapi.info

Summary To recognize exceptional and significant achievement by women working in chemistry or allied fields.

Eligibility Nominees for the award must be women chemists who have made significant contributions to academic, governmental, or industrial chemistry; in education; in administration; or in a combination of those areas. They may be from any country and need not be members of Iota Sigma Pi. Each active chapter is entitled to make only 1 nomination, but individual members, individual chemists, or groups of chemists may make independent nominations if properly documented. Contributions may include innovation design, development, application, or promotion of a principle or practice that has widespread significance to the scientific community or society on a national level.

Financial data The award consists of $1,000, a certificate, and a lifetime waiver of Iota Sigma Pi dues.

Duration The award is granted triennially (2020, 2023, etc.).

Additional information This award was first presented in 1984.

Number awarded 1 every 3 years.

Deadline Nominations must be submitted by February of the year of award.

[1418]
WANDA MUNN SCHOLARSHIP

Society of Women Engineers
Attn: Scholarship Selection Committee
203 North LaSalle Street, Suite 1675
Chicago, IL 60601-1269
(312) 596-5223   Toll Free: (877) SWE-INFO
Fax: (312) 644-8557   E-mail: scholarships@swe.org
Web: societyofwomenengineers.swe.org

Summary To provide financial assistance to women from selected northwestern states interested in returning to college or graduate school to study engineering or computer science.

Eligibility This program is open to women who are planning to enroll at an ABET-accredited 4-year college or university. Applicants must have been out of the engineering workforce and school for at least 2 years and must be planning to return as an undergraduate or graduate student to work on a degree in computer science or engineering. They must be residents of or attending school in Alaska, Idaho, Montana, Oregon, or Washington and have a GPA of 3.0 or higher. Selection is based on merit. Preference is given to engineers who already have a degree and are planning to reenter the engineering workforce after a period of temporary retirement.

Financial data The stipend is $1,500.

Duration 1 year.

Additional information This program is sponsored by the Eastern Washington Section of the Society of Women Engineers.

Number awarded 1 each year.

Deadline February of each year.

[1419]
WANDA REDER PIONEER IN POWER AWARD

Institute of Electrical and Electronics Engineers
Attn: Power and Energy Society
445 Hoes Lane
P.O. Box 1331
Piscataway, NJ 08855-1331
(732) 562-3883   Fax: (732) 562-3881
E-mail: pes-awardsadmin@ieee.org
Web: www.ieee-pes.org

Summary To recognize and reward women who are members of the Power and Energy Society (PES) of the Institute of Electrical and Electronics Engineers (IEEE) and have made outstanding contributions to the field.

Eligibility This award is available to senior female PES members who have demonstrated a high level of influence is technical development, infrastructure enhancement, entrepreneurial or management practices, or education within the field of electric power and energy engineering. Selection is based on efforts, accomplishments, and future potential to be an inspiration and role model for other women in the industry.

Financial data The award consists of an honorarium of $1,500 and a plaque.

Duration The award is presented annually.

Additional information The Power and Energy Society was formerly known as the Power Engineering Society.

Number awarded 1 each year.

Deadline January of each year.

[1420]
WASHINGTON STATE BUSINESS AND PROFESSIONAL WOMEN'S FOUNDATION MATURE WOMAN EDUCATIONAL SCHOLARSHIP

Washington State Business and Professional Women's Foundation
Attn: Sue Tellock, Scholarship Committee Chair
1914 N.W. 87th Circle
Vancouver, WA 98665
Web: www.bpwwafoundation.org/scholarships

Summary To provide financial assistance to mature women from Washington interested in attending postsecondary school in the state for retraining or continuing education.

Eligibility This program is open to women over 30 years of age who have been residents of Washington for at least 2 years. Applicants must be planning to enroll at a college or university in the state for a program of retraining or continuing education. Along with their application, they must submit a 500-word essay on their specific short-term goals and how the proposed training will help them accomplish those goals and make a difference in their professional career. Financial need is considered in the selection process. U.S. citizenship is required.

Financial data The stipend is $1,000.

Duration 1 year.

Number awarded Varies each year; recently, 3 were awarded.

Deadline May of each year.

[1421]
WAYNE F. PLACEK GRANTS

American Psychological Foundation
750 First Street, N.E.
Washington, DC 20002-4242
(202) 336-5843 Fax: (202) 336-5812
E-mail: foundation@apa.org
Web: www.apa.org/apf/funding/placek.aspx

Summary To provide funding to pre- and postdoctoral scholars interested in conducting research that will increase the general public's understanding of homosexuality and alleviate the stress experienced by gay men and lesbians.

Eligibility This program is open to scholars who have a doctoral degree (e.g., Ph.D., Psy.D., M.D.) and to graduate students in all fields of the behavioral and social sciences. Applicants must be interested in conducting empirical studies that address the following topics: prejudice, discrimination, and violence based on sexual orientation, including heterosexuals' attitudes and behaviors toward lesbian, gay, bisexual, and transgender (LGBT) people; family and workplace issues relevant to LGBT people; and subgroups of the LGBT population that have been historically underrepresented in scientific research. Selection is based on relevance to program goals, magnitude of incremental contribution, quality of proposed work, and applicant's demonstrated scholarship and research competence. The sponsor encourages applications from individuals who represent diversity in race, ethnicity, gender, age, disability, and sexual orientation.

Financial data The grant is $15,000.

Duration 1 year.

Additional information This program began in 1995.

Number awarded 1 or 2 each year.

Deadline February of each year.

[1422]
WDHOF ADVANCED DIVE TRAINING GRANTS

Women Divers Hall of Fame
43 MacKey Avenue
Port Washington, NY 11050-3628
E-mail: scholarships@wdhof.org
Web: www.wdhof.org/scholarships/scholarships.shtml

Summary To provide financial assistance to women divers who are interested in participating in a program of advanced dive training.

Eligibility This program is open to women divers of any age who are interested in advanced training programs in the areas of 1) recreational diving; 2) technical or cave driving; or 3) any type of diving needed for the applicant's profession (e.g., scientific diving). Applicants must be interested in participating in an approved scuba diving program beyond the basic certification level.

Financial data The grant is $1,000, including $500 for the training and $500 for equipment.

Duration 1 year.

Number awarded 3 each year: 1 for each type of training.

Deadline November of each year.

[1423]
WDHOF SCHOLARSHIP IN MARINE OR UNDERWATER EDUCATION

Women Divers Hall of Fame
43 MacKey Avenue
Port Washington, NY 11050-3628
E-mail: scholarships@wdhof.org
Web: www.wdhof.org/scholarships/scholarships.shtml

Summary To provide financial assistance to women who wish to conduct research or develop a K-12 education project in a field related to underwater science, technology, engineering, or mathematics (STEM).

Eligibility This program is open to women of any age who are interested in 1) planning and conducting an education project in marine or underwater STEM for students in grades K-12; or 2) conducting independent research in any underwater STEM area. Applicants must have a degree in education, museum studies, or other relevant area and have experience teaching marine science, technology, or engineering at any K-12 level.

Financial data The grant is $2,000.

Duration 1 year.

Number awarded 1 each year.

Deadline November of each year.

[1424]
W.E.B. DUBOIS FELLOWSHIP FOR RESEARCH ON RACE AND CRIME

Department of Justice
National Institute of Justice
Attn: W.E.B. DuBois Fellowship Program
810 Seventh Street, N.W.
Washington, DC 20531
Toll Free: (800) 851-3420 Fax: (301) 240-5830
TDD: (301) 240-6310 E-mail: grants@ncjrs.gov
Web: www.nij.gov

Summary To provide funding to junior investigators interested in conducting research on "crime, justice, and culture in various societal contexts."

Eligibility This program is open to investigators who have a Ph.D. or other doctoral-level degree (including a legal degree of J.D. or higher). Applicants should be early in their careers and not have been awarded tenure. They must be interested in conducting research that relates to specific areas that change annually but relate to criminal justice policy and practice in the United States. The sponsor strongly encourages applications from women and minorities. Selection is based on understanding of the problem and its importance (10%); quality and technical merit (40%); potential for a significant scientific or technical advance that will improve criminal/juvenile justice in the United states (20%); capabilities, demonstrated productivity, and experience of the principal investigator and the institution (15%); and dissemination strategy to broader audiences (15%).

Financial data Grants range up to $100,000 for fellows who propose to conduct secondary data analysis or up to $150,000 for fellows who proposed to conduct primary data collection. Funds may be used for salary, fringe benefits, reasonable costs of relocation, travel essential to the project, and office expenses not provided by the sponsor. Indirect costs are limited to 20%.

Duration Up to 24 months; residency at the National Institute of Justice (NIJ) is not required but it is available.

Number awarded Up to 3 each year.

Deadline May of each year.

[1425]
WEBBER GROUP CAREER ADVANCEMENT SCHOLARSHIP

Maine Federation of Business and Professional Women's Clubs
Attn: BPW/Maine Futurama Foundation
c/o Marilyn V. Ladd, Office Manager
103 County Road
Oakland, ME 04963
Web: www.bpwmefoundation.org/scholarship-program

Summary To provide financial assistance to Maine women over 30 years of age who are continuing a program of higher education.

Eligibility This program is open to women who are older than 30 years of age and residents of Maine. Applicants must be continuing in, or returning to, an accredited program of higher education or job-related training, either full or part time. They must have a definite plan to use the desired training in a practical and immediate way to improve chances for advancement, train for a new career field, or enter or reenter the job market. Along with their application, they must submit a statement describing their educational, personal, and career goals, including financial need, expectations of training, and future plans for using this educational program.

Financial data The stipend is $1,200. Funds are paid directly to the school.

Duration 1 year.

Number awarded 1 or more each year.

Deadline April of each year.

[1426]
WHIRLY-GIRLS HELICOPTER ADD-ON FLIGHT TRAINING SCHOLARSHIP

Whirly-Girls International
c/o Colleen Chen, Vice President Scholarships
P.O. Box 437
Franconia, NH 03580
(603) 505-4668   Fax: (603) 505-4667
E-mail: wgvpsch@whirlygirls.org
Web: www.whirlygirls.org/wg-scholarships

Summary To provide financial assistance to women pilots interested in obtaining an additional helicopter rating.

Eligibility This program is open to certificated female pilots who do not currently have a helicopter rating but desire to add that on to their certificate. Along with their application, they must submit brief statements on how they intend to utilize this scholarship, their career goals in the helicopter industry, and how this scholarship will help them achieve those goals.

Financial data The stipend is $8,000.

Duration Training must be completed within 1 year.

Additional information Completed applications must include $45 to cover the cost of processing and mailing.

Number awarded 1 each year.

Deadline September of each year.

[1427]
WHIRLY-GIRLS MEMORIAL FLIGHT TRAINING SCHOLARSHIP

Whirly-Girls International
c/o Colleen Chen, Vice President Scholarships
P.O. Box 437
Franconia, NH 03580
(603) 505-4668   Fax: (603) 505-4667
E-mail: wgvpsch@whirlygirls.org
Web: www.whirlygirls.org/wg-scholarships

Summary To provide financial assistance to members of Whirly-Girls International who are interested in obtaining an additional helicopter rating.

Eligibility This program is open to women who have been members of Whirly-Girls International for at least 1 year. Applicants must be interested in advanced helicopter flight training to upgrade their current rating (typically toward commercial, instrument, instructor, ATP, long line or turbine transition training). Along with their application, they must submit brief statements on how they intend to utilize this scholarship, their career goals in the helicopter industry, and how this scholarship will help them achieve those goals.

Financial data The stipend is $8,000.

Duration Training must be completed within 1 year.

Additional information This program combines the former Phelan International Flight Training Scholarship and Doris Mullen Flight Training Scholarship. Completed applications must include $45 to cover the cost of processing and mailing.

Number awarded 1 each year.

Deadline September of each year.

[1428]
WOMEN AND POLITICS FUND FELLOWSHIPS

American Political Science Association
Attn: Centennial Center Visiting Scholars Program
1527 New Hampshire Avenue, N.W.
Washington, DC 20036-1206
(202) 483-2512   Fax: (202) 483-2657
E-mail: centennial@apsanet.org
Web: www.apsanet.org/centennial/grants

Summary To provide funding to members of the American Political Science Association (APSA) who are interested in conducting research on women and politics at the Centennial Center for Political Science and Public Affairs.

Eligibility This program is open to members of the association who are interested in conducting research on women and politics while in residence at the center. Junior faculty members, postdoctoral fellows, and advanced graduate students are strongly encouraged to apply, but scholars at all stages of their careers are eligible. International applicants are also welcome if they have demonstrable command of spoken English. Non-resident scholars may also be eligible.

Financial data Grants normally range from $1,000 to $2,500.

Duration 2 weeks to 12 months.

Number awarded 1 or more each year.

Deadline February, June, or October of each year.

[1429]
WOMEN IN AVIATION MANAGEMENT SCHOLARSHIP

Women in Aviation International
Attn: Scholarships
Morningstar Airport
3647 State Route 503 South
West Alexandria, OH 45381-9354
(937) 839-4647   Fax: (937) 839-4645
E-mail: scholarships@wai.org
Web: www.wai.org

Summary To provide financial assistance to members of Women in Aviation International (WAI) who are in an aviation management field and interested in attending leadership-related courses or seminars.

Eligibility This program is open to WAI members in an aviation management field who have exemplified the traits of leadership, community spirit, and volunteerism. Applicants must be interested in attending a leadership-related course or seminar or participating in some other means of advancing their managerial position. Along with their application, they must submit a 500-word essay and professional resume that include their aviation history and goals, what they have done for themselves to achieve their goals, where they see themselves in 5 and 10 years, involvement in aviation activities, how the scholarship will help them achieve their objectives, and their present financial need.

Financial data The stipend is $1,000.

Additional information WAI is a nonprofit professional organization dedicated to encouraging women to consider an aviation career and to providing educational outreach activities and networking resources to women active in the industry.

Number awarded 1 each year.

Deadline November of each year.

[1430]
WOMEN IN CORPORATE AVIATION LEADERSHIP SCHOLARSHIP

Women in Corporate Aviation
c/o Stacey Kotria, Scholarship Committee Co-Chair
Yum Brands Inc.
1441 Gardiner Lane
Louisville, KY 40213
E-mail: scholarships-wca@wca-intl.org
Web: www.wca-intl.org/scholarships

Summary To provide financial assistance to members of Women in Corporate Aviation (WCA) who are interested in professional development activities toward a career in aviation management.

Eligibility This program is open to WCA members who are currently employed in the corporate aviation industry and are interested in preparing for a career in aviation management. Applicants must be interested in participating in such programs as the National Business Aviation Association (NBAA) Certified Aviation Manager Certification, NBAA leadership conference, or NBAA PDP courses. They must possess relevant certifications such as pilot certification, A&P, dispatcher's license, or ATC certification.

Financial data The stipend is $3,000. Funds may be used only for program fees and examination fees.

Duration Up to 1 year.

Additional information This program is co-sponsored by Home Depot.

Number awarded 1 each year.

Deadline August of each year.

[1431]
WOMEN IN FILM/DALLAS FINISHING FUNDS GRANT

Women in Film/Dallas
Attn: Scholarships and Grants
15110 Dallas Parkway, Suite 440
Dallas, TX 75248
(214) 379-1171   Toll Free: (800) 724-0767
Fax: (214) 379-1172   E-mail: scholarships@wifdallas.org
Web: www.wifdallas.org/page-986794

Summary To provide funding for completion of a film to women who are members of Women in Film/Dallas.

Eligibility This program is open to women who reside in Texas and are student, professional, associate, or corporate members of Women in Film/Dallas. Applicants must have a film project on which they have completed principal photography. Along with their application, they must submit a 5- to 10-minute sample of the work in progress; a 1-page description of the submitted footage; a 1,000-word personal statement that includes their interest and experiences in writing, directing, or producing films and the general aspects of their financial need; a treatment or synopsis of the film; and a plan for securing rights that still require clearance. Funding is available for short films (up to 35 minutes) and feature films (between 60 and 120 minutes).

Financial data Grants range up to $500 for short films or $3,000 for feature films.

Duration 1 year.

Number awarded At least 2 each year: 1 for a short film and 1 for a feature film.

Deadline March of each year.

[1432]
WOMEN IN TOXICOLOGY SPECIAL INTEREST GROUP POSTDOCTORAL FELLOW ACHIEVEMENT AWARD

Society of Toxicology
Attn: Women in Toxicology Special Interest Group
1821 Michael Faraday Drive, Suite 300
Reston, VA 20190-5348
(703) 438-3115   Fax: (703) 438-3113
E-mail: sothq@toxicology.org
Web: www.toxicology.org/ai/af/awards_details.aspx?id=148

Summary To recognize and reward postdoctoral members of the Society of Toxicology (SOT), especially its Women in Toxicology Special Interest Group (WIT), who have demonstrated academic achievement.

Eligibility This program is open to postdoctoral members of the society who have demonstrated academic achievement in the field of toxicology and who have provided leadership and service in their chosen field and/or their community. Along with their application, they must submit a letter of recommendation from their adviser, a curriculum vitae, and an abstract of a paper that has been accepted for presentation at the SOT annual meeting. Students who are not WIT members are strongly encouraged to join.

Financial data   The winner receives a certificate and a monetary award.

Duration   The award is presented annually.

Number awarded   1 each year.

Deadline   December of each year.

[1433]
WOMEN IN UNITED METHODIST HISTORY RESEARCH GRANT

United Methodist Church
General Commission on Archives and History
Attn: General Secretary
36 Madison Avenue
P.O. Box 127
Madison, NJ 07940
(973) 408-3189   Fax: (973) 408-3909
E-mail: gcah@gcah.org
Web: www.gcah.org

Summary   To support research related to the history of women in the United Methodist Church.

Eligibility   Proposed research projects must deal specifically with the history of women in the United Methodist Church or its antecedents. Proposals on women of color and on history at the grassroots level are especially encouraged. Applicants must submit a description of the project, including its significance, format, timetable, budget, and how the results will be disseminated.

Financial data   The grant is at least $1,000. Grant funds are not to be used for equipment, publication costs, or researcher's salary.

Duration   These grants are awarded annually.

Number awarded   Varies each year. A total of $2,500 is available for this program annually.

Deadline   December of each year.

[1434]
WOMEN MILITARY AVIATORS DREAM OF FLIGHT SCHOLARSHIP

Women in Aviation International
Attn: Scholarships
Morningstar Airport
3647 State Route 503 South
West Alexandria, OH 45381-9354
(937) 839-4647   Fax: (937) 839-4645
E-mail: scholarships@wai.org
Web: www.wai.org

Summary   To provide financial assistance to members of Women in Aviation International (WAI) who have military experience and are interested in flight training or academic study.

Eligibility   This program is open to WAI members who have military experience and are enrolled at an accredited academic institution or an FAA Part 141 approved flight school. Applicants must be seeking flight ratings in order to pursue opportunities in aviation. Along with their application, they must submit 1) a 500-word essay and professional resume that include their aviation history and goals, what they have done for themselves to achieve their goals, where they see themselves in 5 and 10 years, involvement in aviation activi-

ties, how the scholarship will help them achieve their objectives, and their present financial need; and 2) a narrative addressing their demonstrated persistence and determination to fly, ability to complete their current training program with 1 year, and their interest and/or participation in military aviation.

Financial data   The stipend is $2,500. A 1-year membership in Women Military Aviators (WMA) is also provided.

Duration   Recipients must be able to complete training within 1 year.

Additional information   WAI is a nonprofit professional organization dedicated to encouraging women to consider an aviation career and to providing educational outreach activities and networking resources to women active in the industry. WMA established this program in 2005 to honor the women aviators who were serving or had served in Iraq and Afghanistan.

Number awarded   1 each year.

Deadline   November of each year.

[1435]
WOMEN WRITERS FELLOWSHIPS OF OREGON LITERARY FELLOWSHIPS

Literary Arts, Inc.
Attn: Oregon Book Awards and Fellowships Program
   Coordinator
925 S.W. Washington Street
Portland, OR 97205
(503) 227-2583   Fax: (503) 243-1167
E-mail: susan@literary-arts.org
Web: www.literary-arts.org

Summary   To provide funding to women writers in Oregon interested in working on a literary project.

Eligibility   This program is open to women who have been residents of Oregon for at least 1 year and are interested in initiating, developing, or completing a literary project in the areas of poetry, fiction, literary nonfiction, drama, or young readers' literature. Priority is given to women whose writing explores race, ethnicity, class, physical disability, and/or sexual orientation. Writers in the early stages of their careers are especially encouraged to apply. Selection is based primarily on literary merit.

Financial data   Grants are at least $2,500.

Duration   The grants are presented annually.

Additional information   Funding for this program is provided by the Ralph L. Smith Foundation.

Number awarded   1 each year.

Deadline   June of each year.

[1436]
WOMEN'S FILM PRESERVATION FUND GRANTS

New York Women in Film & Television
Attn: Women's Film Preservation Fund
6 East 39th Street, Suite 1200
New York, NY 10016-0112
(212) 679-0870   Fax: (212) 679-0899
E-mail: info@nywift.org
Web: www.nywift.org/article.aspx?id=22

Summary   To provide funding to restore and preserve films in which women have had significant creative roles.

Eligibility Eligible to apply for this funding are individuals and nonprofit organizations who are interested in preserving films in which women had key creative roles, as directors, writers, producers, editors, or performers. Films may be from any era, of any length, on any subject matter, and in any film format or base. Selection is based on the artistic, historic, cultural, and/or educational importance of the film, especially in relation to the role of women in film history; significance of the key creative women in the production; evidence of the artistic and technical expertise of those planning and executing the project; urgency of the need to preserve the film; appropriateness of the budget for the proposed work; and realism of the plan for making the film available to professionals, scholars, and interested audiences.

Financial data The maximum grant is $10,000. Funds may be used only for actual costs connected with restoration and preservation, not for salaries or general administrative costs. In addition to cash grants, the fund also awards approximately $25,000 worth of in-kind post-production services for films created by or related to women.

Duration These grants are provided annually.

Number awarded Varies each year; recently, 3 were awarded.

Deadline May of each year.

[1437]
WOMEN'S LAW AND PUBLIC POLICY FELLOWSHIP PROGRAM

Georgetown University Law Center
Attn: Women's Law and Public Policy Fellowship Program
600 New Jersey Avenue, N.W., H5024A
Washington, DC 20001
(202) 662-9650   Fax: (202) 662-9117
E-mail: wlppfp@law.georgetown.edu
Web: www.law.georgetown.edu

Summary To provide an opportunity for recently-graduated public interest lawyers in the Washington D.C. area to work on women's rights issues.

Eligibility This program is open to recent graduates of law schools accredited by the American Bar Association. Applicants must be interested in working on women's rights issues in the Washington, D.C. area (e.g., at the Georgetown University School of Law, the National Partnership for Women and Families, the National Women's Law Center).

Financial data The stipend is approximately $41,000 per year.

Duration The fellowships at Georgetown Law are 2-year teaching assignments; other fellowships are for 1 year.

Additional information This program includes several named fellowships, including the Rita Charmatz Davidson Fellowship (to work on issues primarily affecting poor women), the Harriet R. Burg Fellowship (to work primarily on issues affecting women with disabilities), and Ford Foundation Fellowships (to focus on issues concerning women and AIDS/HIV). Fellows are supervised by attorneys at the participating organizations.

Number awarded Approximately 6 each year.

Deadline November of each year.

[1438]
WOMEN'S LEADERSHIP TRAINING GRANT

Society for Vascular Surgery
Attn: Diversity and Inclusion Committee
633 North St. Clair Street, 22nd Floor
Chicago, IL 60611
(312) 334-2300   Toll Free: (800) 258-7188
Fax: (312) 334-2320
E-mail: vascular@vascularsociety.org
Web: www.vascularweb.org

Summary To provide financial assistance for leadership training to female members of the Society for Vascular Surgery (SVS).

Eligibility This program is open to women who have completed training in vascular surgery and are SVS members. Applicants must be interested in participating in a leadership training program (e.g., personal leadership coaching, traveling to meet women leaders, or specific programs targeted for leaders in medicine, higher education, or health care). Preference is given to applications that clearly describe how the grant will advance the leadership goals of the candidate and that include a clear action plan.

Financial data The grant is $5,000.

Duration Up to 1 year.

Additional information This program began in 2007.

Number awarded 3 each year: 1 to a women 0-5 years out of training, 1 to a woman 6-10 years out of training, and 1 to a woman more than 10 years out of training.

Deadline April of each year.

[1439]
WOMEN'S SPORTS FOUNDATION TRAVEL AND TRAINING FUND

Women's Sports Foundation
Attn: Award and Grant Programs Manager
Eisenhower Park
1899 Hempstead Turnpike, Suite 400
East Meadow, NY 11554-1000
(516) 307-3915   Toll Free: (800) 227-3988
E-mail: lflores@womenssportsfoundation.org
Web: www.womenssportsfoundation.org

Summary To provide funding for travel and training activities to women athletes (both individuals and teams).

Eligibility This program is open to women who are amateur athletes and U.S. citizens or legal residents. Applicants must demonstrate the ability, based on competitive record and years in training, to reach and compete at an elite level; they should have competed regionally (outside their state), nationally, or internationally and/or be ranked by a national governing body. Athletes may apply as individuals or as a team consisting of 2 or more women. High school, college, university, and community recreation sports teams are not eligible.

Financial data Grants range from $2,500 to $10,000.

Duration Individuals and teams may receive only 1 grant per calendar year and 3 grants in a lifetime.

Additional information This program, established in 1984, is currently funded by the Gatorade Company.

Number awarded Varies each year; recently, 33 of these grants (30 to individuals and 3 to teams) with a total value of $100,000 were awarded. Since the program was established, it has awarded grants to more than 1,400 individuals and teams.

Deadline   March of each year.

[1440]
WOMEN'S STUDIES IN RELIGION PROGRAM RESEARCH ASSOCIATES

Harvard Divinity School
Attn: Director of Women's Studies in Religion Program
45 Francis Avenue
Cambridge, MA 02138
(617) 495-5705   Fax: (617) 496-8564
E-mail: wsrp@hds.harvard.edu
Web: wsrp.hds.harvard.edu/research-associates

Summary   To encourage and support research on the relationship between religion, gender, and culture.

Eligibility   This program is open to scholars who have a Ph.D. in the field of religion. Candidates with primary competence in other humanities, social sciences, and public policy fields who have a serious interest in religion and religious professionals with equivalent achievements are also eligible. Applicants should be proposing to conduct research projects at Harvard Divinity School's Women's Studies in Religion Program (WSRP) on topics related to the history and function of gender in religious traditions, the institutionalization of gender roles in religious communities, or the interaction between religion and the personal, social, and cultural situations of women. Appropriate topics include feminist theology, biblical studies, ethics, women's history, and interdisciplinary scholarship on women in world religions. Selection is based on the quality of the applicant's research prospectus, outlining objectives and methods; its fit with the program's research priorities; the significance of the contribution of the proposed research to the study of religion, gender, and culture, and to its field; and agreement to produce a publishable piece of work by the end of the appointment.

Financial data   The stipend is $60,000; health insurance and reimbursement of some expenses are also provided.

Duration   1 academic year, from September to June.

Additional information   This program was founded in 1973. Fellows at the WSRP devote the majority of their appointments to individual research projects in preparation for publication, meeting together regularly for discussion of research in process. They also design and teach new courses related to their research projects and offer a series of lectures in the spring. Recipients are required to be in full-time residence at the school while carrying out their research project.

Number awarded   5 each year. The group each year usually includes at least 1 international scholar, 1 scholar working on a non-western tradition, 1 scholar of Judaism, and 1 minority scholar.

Deadline   October of each year.

[1441]
WOMEN'S STUDIO WORKSHOP PARENT RESIDENCY GRANT

Women's Studio Workshop
722 Binnewater Lane
P.O. Box 489
Rosendale, NY 12472
(845) 658-9133   Fax: (845) 658-9031
E-mail: info@wsworkshop.org
Web: www.wsworkshop.org

Summary   To provide funding to female artists who have dependent children and are interested in creating new art work in 1 of the studios of the Women's Studio Workshop (WSW).

Eligibility   This program is open to female artists who have dependent children under 15 years of age. Applicants must be interested in working in 1 of the WSW studios: intaglio, letterpress, papermaking, screenprinting, photography, or ceramics. They must submit a childcare plan that includes proposed use of the stipend, a description of the proposed project including the studio in which they wish to work, an image script, a resume, and 10 images of recent work.

Financial data   The program provides a childcare stipend of $1,000, up to $250 for travel costs, studio access, and housing while in residence. The childcare subsidy may be used to bring a caregiver or partner to stay for the residency period, finding a childcare facility in the area, locating individuals in the area who can provide childcare, or paying for childcare at their family's home base.

Duration   4 weeks.

Additional information   This program is supported by the Sustainable Arts Foundation. Children are not allowed to accompany the artist into the studio.

Number awarded   1 each year.

Deadline   October of each year.

[1442]
ZETA ORIONIS FELLOWSHIP

Vermont Studio Center
80 Pearl Street
P.O. Box 613
Johnson, VT 05656
(802) 635-2727   Fax: (802) 635-2730
E-mail: info@vermontstudiocenter.org
Web: www.vermontstudiocenter.org/fellowships

Summary   To provide funding to mature female painters who are interested in a residency at the Vermont Studio Center in Johnson, Vermont.

Eligibility   Eligible to apply for this support are female painters who are 45 years of age or older. Applicants must be interested in a residency at the center in Johnson, Vermont. They must submit up to 20 slides or visual images of their work. Selection is based on artistic merit and financial need.

Financial data   The fellowship provides for payment of the residency fee of $3,950, which covers studio space, room, board, lectures, and studio visits.

Duration   4 weeks.

Number awarded   2 each year.

Deadline   February, June, or September of each year.

[1443]
ZETA PHI BETA GENERAL GRADUATE FELLOWSHIPS

Zeta Phi Beta Sorority, Inc.
Attn: National Educational Foundation
1734 New Hampshire Avenue, N.W.
Washington, DC 20009
(202) 387-3103   Fax: (202) 232-4593
E-mail: info@zetaphibetasororityhq.org
Web: www.zpbnef1975.org/scholarships-and-descriptions

Summary To provide financial assistance to women who are working on a professional degree, master's degree, doctorate, or postdoctorate.

Eligibility Women graduate or postdoctoral students are eligible to apply if they have achieved distinction or shown promise of distinction in their chosen fields. Applicants need not be members of Zeta Phi Beta. They must be enrolled full time in a professional, graduate, or postdoctoral program. Along with their application, they must submit a 150-word essay on their educational goals and professional aspirations, how this award will help them to achieve those goals, and why they should receive the award. Financial need is not considered in the selection process.

Financial data The stipend ranges up to $2,500, paid directly to the recipient.

Duration 1 academic year; may be renewed.

Additional information Zeta Phi Beta is a traditionally African American sorority.

Number awarded 1 or more each year.

Deadline January of each year.

Indexes

Program Title Index

If you know the name of a particular funding program open to women and want to find out where it is covered in the directory, use the Program Title Index. Here, program titles are arranged alphabetically, word by word. To assist you in your search, every program is listed by all its known names or abbreviations. In addition, we've used an alphabetical code (within parentheses) to help you determine if the program is aimed at you: U = Undergraduates; G = Graduate Students; P = Professionals/Postdoctorates. Here's how the code works: if a program is followed by (U) 241, the program is described in the Undergraduates chapter, in entry 241. If the same program title is followed by another entry number—for example, (P) 1370—the program is also described in the Professionals/Postdoctorates chapter, in entry 1370. Remember: the numbers cited here refer to program entry numbers, not to page numbers in the book.

Aircraft Technical Publishers General Aviation Maintenance Scholarship. *See* ATP General Aviation Maintenance Scholarship, entry (U) 80

Airport Minority Advisory Council Member Award. *See* AMAC Member Award, entry (U) 29

Alabama Golf Association Women's Scholarship Fund, (U) 21

Alberta E. Crowe Star of Tomorrow Award, (U) 22

Alcoa Chuck McLane Scholarship, (U) 23

Alexander Book Scholarships. *See* Sadie T.M. Alexander Book Scholarships, entry (G) 1086

Alexander Gralnick Research Investigator Prize, (P) 1170

Alexander Memorial Scholarship. *See* Daughters of Penelope Undergraduate Scholarships, entry (U) 178

Alexandra Apostolides Sonenfeld Scholarship. *See* Daughters of Penelope Undergraduate Scholarships, entry (U) 178

Alexandra Kirkley, MD Traveling Fellowship, (G) 728

Alfred P. Sloan Foundation Research Fellowships, (P) 1171

Alice Ayer Music Scholarship. *See* Waldo and Alice Ayer Music Scholarship, entry (U) 659

Alice T. Schafer Mathematics Prize, (U) 24

Alice Wilkey Poynter Scholarship, (G) 729

Alida W. Parker Scholarship. *See* Delta Kappa Gamma Scholarship Program, entry (G) 826

Allen Fellowship. *See* Sigma Delta Epsilon Fellowships, entries (G) 1104, (P) 1404

Allen Fellowships. *See* Frances C. Allen Fellowships, entry (G) 879

Allen Scholarship. *See* Delta Kappa Gamma Scholarship Program, entry (G) 826

Allen Scholarship Award. *See* J. Frances Allen Scholarship Award, entry (G) 937

Allen Scholarships. *See* Florence Allen Scholarships, entry (U) 250

Alliance for Women in Media Joint Scholarship. *See* NCTA/AWM Joint Scholarship, entries (U) 492, (G) 1037

Allman Medical Scholarships. *See* Dr. David B. Allman Medical Scholarships, entry (G) 839

Alpha Delta Kappa Excellence in Education Award, (P) 1172

Alpha Delta Kappa Regional Professional Development Scholarships, (G) 730, (P) 1173

Alpha Kappa Alpha Endowment Awards, (U) 25, (G) 731

Alpha Kappa Alpha Graduate Scholarships, (G) 732

Alpha Kappa Alpha Undergraduate Scholarships, (U) 26

Alpha Phi/Betty Mullins Jones Scholarship, (U) 27

Alpha State Aspiring Educator Awards, (U) 28

Alyson R. Miller Fellowships. *See* Ruth R. and Alyson R. Miller Fellowships, entries (G) 1083, (P) 1394

AMAC Member Award, (U) 29

Amber Grants, (P) 1174

Amelia Behrens-Furniss Memorial Hardhat Diver Training Grants, (P) 1175

Amelia Earhart Fellowship Awards, (G) 733

Amelia Earhart Memorial Academic Scholarships, (U) 30, (G) 734

Amelia Earhart Memorial Scholarships, (U) 31, (P) 1176

Amelia Earhart Research Scholar Grant, (G) 735, (P) 1177

Amelia Kemp Memorial Scholarship, (U) 32, (G) 736

American Airlines Aircraft Maintenance Technician Scholarship, (U) 33

American Airlines Engineering Scholarship, (U) 34

American Airlines Veteran's Initiative Scholarship, (U) 35, (P) 1178

American Association of Japanese University Women Scholarship Program, (U) 36, (G) 737

American Association of Obstetricians and Gynecologists Foundation Research and Training Scholarships, (P) 1179

American Association of University Women Career Development Grants. *See* AAUW Career Development Grants, entries (U) 4, (G) 717, (P) 1167

American Association of University Women Dissertation Fellowships, (G) 738

American Association of University Women Postdoctoral Research Leave Fellowships, (P) 1180

American Association of University Women Summer/Short-Term Research Publication Grants, (P) 1181

American Baptist Churches of Wisconsin Adult Women in Seminary Education Scholarships, (U) 37, (G) 739

American Baptist Churches of Wisconsin Continuing Education for Adult Women Scholarships, (U) 38

American Baptist Women's Ministries of New York State Scholarships, (U) 39, (G) 740

American Baptist Women's Ministries of Wisconsin Adult Women Seminary Scholarship, (G) 741

American Baptist Women's Ministries of Wisconsin Continuing Education for Adult Women Scholarship, (U) 40

American Business Women's Association President's Scholarship, (U) 41

American Epilepsy Society Junior Investigator Research Award, (P) 1182

American Epilepsy Society Postdoctoral Research Fellowships, (P) 1183

American Epilepsy Society Predoctoral Research Fellowships, (G) 742

American Health Information Management Association Foundation Diversity Scholarships. *See* AHIMA Foundation Diversity Scholarships, entries (U) 16, (G) 727

American Legion Auxiliary Emergency Fund, (U) 42, (P) 1184

American Legion Auxiliary Spirit of Youth Scholarship for Junior Members. *See* Spirit of Youth Scholarship for Junior Members, entry (U) 607

American Medical Women's Association Medical Education Scholarships. *See* AMWA Medical Education Scholarships, entry (G) 746

American Meteorological Society Freshman Undergraduate Scholarships. *See* AMS Freshman Undergraduate Scholarships, entry (U) 46

American Meteorological Society Graduate Fellowship in the History of Science, (G) 743

American Meteorological Society Graduate Fellowships. *See* AMS Graduate Fellowships, entry (G) 745

American Meteorological Society Named Scholarships, (U) 43

American Museum of Natural History Graduate Student Fellowship Program, (G) 744

American Psychological Association/Division 39 Grant. *See* APA/Division 39 Grant, entries (G) 755, (P) 1190

American Psychological Foundation/Division 29 Early Career Award. *See* APF/Division 29 Early Career Award, entry (P) 1191

American Psychological Foundation/Division 37 Diane J. Willis Early Career Award. *See* APF/Division 37 Diane J. Willis Early Career Award, entry (P) 1192

American Psychological Foundation/F.I.S.H. Foundation Visionary Grant to Decrease Ethnic and Racial Discrimination in Education. *See* APF/F.I.S.H. Foundation Visionary Grant to Decrease Ethnic and Racial Discrimination in Education, entry (P) 1193

American Psychological Foundation Graduate Student Scholarships. *See* APF Graduate Student Scholarships, entry (G) 756

U–Undergraduates   **G–Graduate Students**   **P–Professionals/Postdoctorates**

U–Undergraduates　　　**G–Graduate Students**　　　**P–Professionals/Postdoctorates**

U–Undergraduates   G–Graduate Students   P–Professionals/Postdoctorates

U–Undergraduates   **G–Graduate Students**   **P–Professionals/Postdoctorates**

Gail Burns-Smith "Dare to Dream" Scholarships, (U) 266

Gaius Charles Bolin Dissertation and Post-MFA Fellowships, (G) 883, (P) 1273

Galloway Scholarship. *See* June P. Galloway Undergraduate Scholarship, entry (U) 358

Gamers in Real Life Scholarship Program. *See* G.I.R.L. Scholarship Program, entry (U) 275

Garber Scholarship. *See* Association for Women in Sports Media Scholarship/Internship Program, entries (U) 77, (G) 766

Gardner PEO Scholarship. *See* Ethel O. Gardner PEO Scholarship, entries (U) 239, (G) 864

Gavrila Scholarship for Women. *See* ARFORA/Martha Gavrila Scholarship for Women, entry (G) 758

Gaynor Award. *See* Florence Gaynor Award, entry (G) 871

GE Women's Network Engineering Scholarship, (U) 267, (G) 884

GE Women's Network Scholarships, (U) 268

Geis Memorial Award, (G) 885

General Federation of Women's Clubs Rhode Island Arts Scholarship Program. *See* GFWC RI Arts Scholarship Program, entry (U) 273

Generation Google Scholarships for High School Seniors, (U) 269

Geneva Young Scholarship. *See* Sigma Gamma Rho Scholarships/Fellowships, entries (U) 594, (G) 1105

Geography and Spatial Sciences Doctoral Dissertation Research Improvement Awards, (G) 886

Geological Society of America Graduate Student Research Grants, (G) 887

Geophysical Fluid Dynamics Fellowships, (G) 888, (P) 1274

George D. Matthews, Sr. Memorial Scholarship. *See* Dixie Softball Scholarships, entry (U) 197

George Michael Memorial HPC Fellowships. *See* ACM/IEEE-CS George Michael Memorial HPC Fellowships, entry (G) 720

George Shaver Family Scholarship. *See* Luella and George Shaver Family Scholarship, entry (U) 404

Georgia Association for Women Lawyers Scholarships, (G) 889

Georgia Association of Black Women Attorneys Foundation Scholarships. *See* GABWA Foundation Scholarships, entry (G) 882

Georgia Babladelis Best PWQ Paper Award, (P) 1275

Georgia Harkness Scholarship Awards, (G) 890

Gerrish Scholarships. *See* Doris M. Gerrish Scholarships, entry (U) 202

Gerry Fellowships. *See* Sigma Delta Epsilon Fellowships, entries (G) 1104, (P) 1404

Gerson Memorial Grant. *See* Randy Gerson Memorial Grant, entry (G) 1070

Gertrude and Maurice Goldhaber Distinguished Fellowships, (P) 1276

Gertrude Boyd Crane Scholarship, (G) 891

Gertrude M. Cox Scholarship in Statistics, (G) 892

GET IT Girl College Technology Scholarship Program, (U) 270

Getsoyan Scholarship. *See* Armenian International Women's Association Scholarships, entries (U) 68, (G) 759

GFWC/MFWC Hebron Memorial Scholarship, (U) 271, (G) 893

GFWC/Ohio Federation of Women's Clubs Clubwoman Scholarship, (U) 272

GFWC RI Arts Scholarship Program, (U) 273

Ghawi Scholarship. *See* Jessica Redfield Ghawi Scholarship, entry (U) 346

Giambalvo Fund for the Advancement of Women. *See* Joan F. Giambalvo Fund for the Advancement of Women, entries (G) 945, (P) 1298

Giambalvo Memorial Scholarship. *See* Joan F. Giambalvo Fund for the Advancement of Women, entries (G) 945, (P) 1298

Gilbreth Memorial Scholarship. *See* Lillian Moller Gilbreth Memorial Scholarship, entry (U) 390

Gilda Murray Scholarships, (U) 274, (G) 894, (P) 1277

Giles Scholarship. *See* Delta Kappa Gamma Scholarship Program, entry (G) 826

Gillette Scholarships. *See* R.L. Gillette Scholarships, entry (U) 556

Giraffe Fund Emergency Grants for Undergraduates. *See* Cheryl Kraff-Cooper, M.D. Giraffe Fund Emergency Grants for Undergraduates, entry (U) 152

G.I.R.L. Scholarship Program, (U) 275

Girl Scouts Nation's Capital Gold Award Scholarships, (U) 276

Girl Scouts of New Mexico Trails Gold Award Scholarship, (U) 277

Gita Chuadhuri Prize, (P) 1278

Gittler Award. *See* Joseph B. Gittler Award of the American Psychological Foundation, entries (G) 947, (P) 1302

Gladys Anderson Emerson Scholarship, (U) 278

Gladys Bales Scholarship for Mature Women, (U) 279

Gladys C. Anderson Memorial Scholarship, (U) 280, (G) 895

Gladys K. and John K. Simpson Scholarship Fund. *See* Society of Daughters of the United States Army Scholarships, entry (U) 600

Gladys L. Mersereau Grants-in-Aid, (U) 281

Glamour's Top Ten College Women Competition, (U) 282

GLAST Fellowships. *See* Einstein Postdoctoral Fellowship Program, entry (P) 1249

Gleason Award. *See* Kate Gleason Award, entry (P) 1307

Gleason Scholarship. *See* Kate Gleason Scholarship, entries (U) 363, (G) 954

Gleiter—Engineering Endeavor Scholarship. *See* Roberta Banaszak Gleiter—Engineering Endeavor Scholarship, entry (U) 559

Gloeckner, M.D. Summer Research Fellowship. *See* M. Louise Carpenter Gloeckner, M.D. Summer Research Fellowship, entries (U) 410, (G) 976, (P) 1329

Gloria E. Anzaldúa Book Prize, (P) 1279

Glorine Tuohey Memorial Scholarship, (G) 896

Go On Girl Aspiring Writer Scholarship, (U) 283

Go Red Multicultural Scholarship Fund, (U) 284, (G) 897

Goeppert-Mayer Award. *See* Maria Goeppert-Mayer Award, entry (P) 1337

Gold Award Scholarship in Honor of Marilynn Carr. *See* Girl Scouts Nation's Capital Gold Award Scholarships, entry (U) 276

Goldberg Fellowships. *See* Leo Goldberg Fellowships, entry (P) 1318

Goldhaber Distinguished Fellowships. *See* Gertrude and Maurice Goldhaber Distinguished Fellowships, entry (P) 1276

Goldie B. Wolfe Miller Women Leaders in Real Estate Initiative Scholarship. *See* CREW Network Foundation Scholarship Program, entries (U) 170, (G) 818

Goldman Education Awards. *See* Rhode Island Commission on Women/Freda H. Goldman Education Awards, entry (U) 554

Gonzalez Memorial Scholarships. *See* Millie Gonzalez Memorial Scholarships, entry (U) 448

Goodman Memorial Scholarship. *See* Arthur H. Goodman Memorial Scholarship, entry (U) 70

Google Anita Borg Memorial Scholarships, (U) 285, (G) 898

Gower Scholarship. *See* California P.E.O. Selected Scholarships, entries (U) 137, (G) 794

Grace Murray Hopper Memorial Scholarships. *See* Admiral Grace Murray Hopper Memorial Scholarships, entry (U) 8

Kirkley, MD Traveling Fellowship. *See* Alexandra Kirkley, MD Traveling Fellowship, entry (G) 728

Kirsten R. Lorentzen Award, (U) 374

Klausman Women in Business Scholarships. *See* Jane M. Klausman Women in Business Scholarships, entries (U) 332, (G) 939

Knudstrup Scholarship. *See* Irene Drinkall Franke/Mary Seeley Knudstrup Scholarship, entry (G) 933

Koch Discovery Scholarships, (U) 375

Kohring Women in Transition Scholarship. *See* Business Women of Missouri Scholarships, entry (U) 131

Kolstad Scholarship. *See* Mid Kolstad Scholarship, entry (P) 1348

Koppitz Child Psychology Graduate Fellowships. *See* Elizabeth Munsterberg Koppitz Child Psychology Graduate Fellowships, entry (G) 851

Kottis Family Scholarship. *See* Daughters of Penelope Undergraduate Scholarships, entry (U) 178

KPMG Best Paper Award Gender Section, (P) 1312

KPMG Future Leaders Program, (U) 376

KPMG Outstanding Dissertation Award Gender Section, (P) 1313

KPMG Outstanding Published Manuscript Award Gender Section, (P) 1314

Kraff-Cooper, M.D. Giraffe Fund Emergency Grants for Undergraduates. *See* Cheryl Kraff-Cooper, M.D. Giraffe Fund Emergency Grants for Undergraduates, entry (U) 152

Krasner Memorial Award. *See* APF/Division 29 Early Career Award, entry (P) 1191

Krenzer Memorial Reentry Scholarship. *See* B.K. Krenzer Memorial Reentry Scholarship, entries (U) 114, (G) 789, (P) 1215

Kuhn Scholarship. *See* Heloise Werthan Kuhn Scholarship, entry (U) 299

Kuriansky Scholarship. *See* APF Graduate Student Scholarships, entry (G) 756

L

LA FRA Scholarship, (U) 377

La Jolla Lasik National Scholarship, (U) 378

Laboratory Astrophysics Division Early Career Award. *See* LAD Early Career Award, entry (P) 1316

Laboratory Astrophysics Prize, (P) 1315

LAD Early Career Award, (P) 1316

Ladies Auxiliary of the Fleet Reserve Association Scholarship. *See* LA FRA Scholarship, entry (U) 377

Lambda Kappa Sigma Grants, (G) 962

Landreth Scholarship. *See* Missouri Women's Golf Education Association Scholarships, entry (U) 464

Lane Mentor Fellowship. *See* Sylvia Lane Mentor Fellowship, entries (G) 1123, (P) 1410

Langenheim Fellowship,. *See* Sigma Delta Epsilon Fellowships, entries (G) 1104, (P) 1404

Lao American Women Association of Washington D.C. Metropolitan Area Vocational Training/GED Scholarship Fund, (U) 379

Laughlin AM Mode Memorial Scholarship. *See* Helen Laughlin AM Mode Memorial Scholarship, entry (U) 297

Laurels Fund Scholarships, (G) 963

Lauren Love Memorial Scholarship, (U) 380, (G) 964

Lauretta M. Michael Scholarship. *See* Edwin G. and Lauretta M. Michael Scholarship, entry (U) 224

Law and Social Sciences Doctoral Dissertation Research Improvement Grants, (G) 965

Law Scholarship. *See* Honolulu Alumnae Panhellenic Association Collegiate Scholarships, entry (U) 304

Lazaroff WCR Future Leader in Hospitality Scholarship. *See* Women Chefs and Restaurateurs Scholarship Program, entries (U) 679, (G) 1152

LCDR Eiffert Foster Student Scholarship, (U) 381

LCDR Janet Cochran and CDR Connie Greene Scholarship, (U) 382

The Leadership Institute Scholarships, (G) 1128

Leadership Legacy Scholarship for Graduates, (G) 966

Leah J. Dickstein, M.D. Award, (G) 967

Leah Rowland Scholarship. *See* Honolulu Alumnae Panhellenic Association Collegiate Scholarships, entry (U) 304

Leah Siegel Scholarship. *See* Association for Women in Sports Media Scholarship/Internship Program, entries (U) 77, (G) 766

Leanna Dorworth Memorial Scholarship, (U) 383

Leatrice Gregory Pendray Scholarship, (U) 384

Lederer Postdoctoral Fellowship. *See* Pembroke Center Postdoctoral Fellowships, entry (P) 1370

Leeta Wagy Memorial Scholarship. *See* Irene and Leeta Wagy Memorial Scholarship, entry (U) 325

Legacy Artists Residency Grant, (P) 1317

Legacy Scholarship in Memory of Beloved ABWA Good Guy, Jack Marlett, (U) 385

Legacy Scholarship in Memory of Beloved Member, Caroline Vaclav, (U) 386

LeGendre Fellowship for Advanced Graduate Study. *See* New York Grace LeGendre Endowment Fund Fellowships, entry (G) 1042

Lemieux-Lovejoy Youth Scholarship, (U) 387

Leo Goldberg Fellowships, (P) 1318

Leo Szilard Lectureship Award, (P) 1319

Leppe Hawai'i Scholarship Fund. *See* Barbara Leppe Hawai'i Scholarship Fund, entry (U) 92

Leslie S. Parker Memorial Scholarship, (U) 388, (G) 968

Leta Andrews Scholarship, (U) 389

Letti P. Trefz Scholarship. *See* Delta Kappa Gamma Scholarship Program, entry (G) 826

Levinson Scholarship. *See* APF Graduate Student Scholarships, entry (G) 756

Lewis Fellowships in Gender and Women's Studies. *See* Frances Lewis Fellowships in Gender and Women's Studies, entries (G) 880, (P) 1271

Lewis Grant SDE Fellowship. *See* Sigma Delta Epsilon Fellowships, entries (G) 1104, (P) 1404

Lewis Memorial Scholarship in Medical Health Sciences. *See* S. Evelyn Lewis Memorial Medical Health Science Scholarship, entries (U) 569, (G) 1085

Lichtenberg Graduate Fellowship. *See* Carolyn Helman Lichtenberg Graduate Fellowship, entry (G) 798

Liguori Foundation Sports Media Scholarship. *See* Ann Liguori Foundation Sports Media Scholarship, entry (U) 49

Lilla Jewel Award for Women Artists, (P) 1320

Lillian Moller Gilbreth Memorial Scholarship, (U) 390

Lillian Wall Scholarship, (U) 391

Lillie and Carnell VanLandingham Scholarship. *See* Sigma Gamma Rho Scholarships/Fellowships, entries (U) 594, (G) 1105

Lily Research Grants. *See* Mary Lily Research Grants, entries (U) 430, (G) 998, (P) 1345

Lincoln Ekstrom Fellowship. *See* Ruth and Lincoln Ekstrom Fellowships, entries (G) 1080, (P) 1389

Linda Fenner Scholarship, (P) 1321

U–Undergraduates   **G–Graduate Students**   **P–Professionals/Postdoctorates**

McBride Memorial Endowed Scholarship Fund. *See* Barbara McBride Memorial Endowed Scholarship Fund, entries (U) 93, (G) 776

McCallum Memorial Scholarship. *See* Bobbi McCallum Memorial Scholarship, entry (U) 117

McCarthy Memorial Academic Scholarship for Women with Bleeding Disorders. *See* Doreen McMullan McCarthy Memorial Academic Scholarship for Women with Bleeding Disorders, entries (U) 200, (G) 830

McConnel Family Scholarship, (G) 1004

McDonald P.E.O. Scholarship. *See* California P.E.O. Selected Scholarships, entries (U) 137, (G) 794

McDonald Scholarship. *See* Michele L. McDonald Scholarship, entry (U) 445

McDonnell Memorial Scholarship. *See* Cady McDonnell Memorial Scholarship, entry (U) 134

McGuigan Dissertation Award. *See* F.J. McGuigan Dissertation Award, entry (G) 870

McGuigan Early Career Investigator Research Prize on Understanding the Human Mind. *See* F.J. McGuigan Early Career Investigator Research Prize on Understanding the Human Mind, entry (P) 1263

McGuire Scholarship. *See* Mary Macon McGuire Scholarship, entry (U) 431

McKay Scholarship Program. *See* Jim McKay Scholarship Program, entry (G) 944

McKern Scholarship. *See* Betty McKern Scholarship, entry (U) 106

Mckimpson Scholarship. *See* Sharon Junod Mckimpson Scholarship, entries (U) 588, (G) 1101

McLane Scholarship. *See* Alcoa Chuck McLane Scholarship, entry (U) 23

McLean Memorial Scholarship. *See* Elizabeth McLean Memorial Scholarship, entry (U) 228

McMorrow Scholarship. *See* WBF Scholarship Awards, entry (G) 1144

Medical Research Fellows Program, (G) 1005

Medtronic SWEnet Scholarship, (U) 441, (G) 1006

Meekins Scholarship. *See* Phyllis G. Meekins Scholarship, entry (U) 539

Meier Scholarship. *See* Benton-Meier Scholarships, entry (G) 779

Memorial Education Fund Fellowships, (G) 1007

Men's Auxiliary of the Society of Women Engineers Scholarships. *See* MASWE Scholarships, entry (U) 440

Meredith Corporation Scholarship, (U) 442, (G) 1008

Meredith Thoms Memorial Scholarships, (U) 443

Mersereau Grants-in-Aid. *See* Gladys L. Mersereau Grants-in-Aid, entry (U) 281

Mgrdichian Scholarship. *See* Hasmik Mgrdichian Scholarship, entry (U) 291

Michael A. Anderson, Sr. Memorial Scholarship, (G) 1009

Michael Baker Scholarship for Diversity in Engineering, (U) 444

Michael Memorial HPC Fellowships. *See* ACM/IEEE-CS George Michael Memorial HPC Fellowships, entry (G) 720

Michael P. Johnson Scholarship. *See* Cuba Wadlington, Jr. and Michael P. Johnson Scholarship, entry (U) 171

Michael Scholarship. *See* Edwin G. and Lauretta M. Michael Scholarship, entry (U) 224

Michele L. McDonald Scholarship, (U) 445

Michelle Jackson Scholarship Fund, (G) 1010

Michigan Council of Women in Technology Foundation Scholarships, (U) 446, (G) 1011

Michigan Job's Daughters Scholarships, (U) 447

Michler Memorial Prize. *See* Ruth I. Michler Memorial Prize, entry (P) 1391

Microsoft Research Prize in Algebra and Number Theory, (P) 1347

Mid Kolstad Scholarship, (P) 1348

Mike Eidson Scholarship, (G) 1012

Mike Roberts Memorial Scholarship. *See* Association for Women in Sports Media Scholarship/Internship Program, entries (U) 77, (G) 766

Milam Scholarships. *See* Delta Kappa Gamma Scholarship Program, entry (G) 826

Mildred A. Butler Career Development Award. *See* Voice of Working Women Career Development Awards, entry (U) 658

Mildred Richards Taylor Memorial Scholarship, (G) 1013

Mileti Scholarship. *See* Junior Girls' Golf Scholarship Foundation Scholarships, entry (U) 359

Miller Fellowships. *See* Ruth R. and Alyson R. Miller Fellowships, entries (G) 1083, (P) 1394

Miller Synchronized Swimming Scholarship. *See* Kim Miller Synchronized Swimming Scholarship, entry (U) 373

Miller Women Leaders in Real Estate Initiative Scholarship. *See* CREW Network Foundation Scholarship Program, entries (U) 170, (G) 818

Millie Gonzalez Memorial Scholarships, (U) 448

Millon Award. *See* Theodore Millon Award in Personality Psychology, entry (P) 1412

Milwaukee Chapter AFWA Scholarships, (U) 449

Miner Scholarship. *See* Rocky Mountain Section College Scholarships, entries (U) 563, (G) 1076

Minerva National Scholarship, (U) 450

Ministry to Women Award, (P) 1349

Mink Education Foundation Scholarships. *See* Patsy Takemoto Mink Education Foundation Education Support Award, entries (U) 527, (G) 1057

Minkwitz Scholarship. *See* Delta Kappa Gamma Scholarship Program, entry (G) 826

Minnesota Child Care Grant Program, (U) 451

Minnesota Legion Auxiliary Past Presidents Parley Health Care Scholarship, (U) 452

Minnesota Section SWE Boston Scientific Scholarship, (U) 453, (G) 1014

Minnesota Section SWE Scholarship, (U) 454

Minnesota Women's Golf Association Scholarship, (U) 455

Minnie and William Blakely Book Scholarship. *See* Sigma Gamma Rho Scholarships/Fellowships, entries (U) 594, (G) 1105

Minnie L. Maffett Fellowships, (G) 1015, (P) 1350

Miriam Levinson Scholarship. *See* APF Graduate Student Scholarships, entry (G) 756

Miss America Academic Achievement Awards, (U) 456

Miss America Community Service Awards, (U) 457

Miss America Competition Awards, (U) 458

Miss America STEM Scholarships, (U) 459

Miss America's Outstanding Teen Scholarships, (U) 460, (P) 1351

Miss Congeniality Award. *See* Miss America Competition Awards, entry (U) 458

Miss Teen of America Scholarships, (U) 461

Missirian Scholarship. *See* Armenian International Women's Association Scholarships, entries (U) 68, (G) 759

Missouri Angus Auxiliary Queen Program, (U) 462

Missouri Job's Daughters Scholarships, (U) 463

Missouri Women's Golf Education Association Scholarships, (U) 464

U–Undergraduates   **G–Graduate Students**   **P–Professionals/Postdoctorates**

U–Undergraduates   G–Graduate Students   P–Professionals/Postdoctorates

U–Undergraduates   **G–Graduate Students**   **P–Professionals/Postdoctorates**

U–Undergraduates   **G–Graduate Students**   **P–Professionals/Postdoctorates**

U–Undergraduates   G–Graduate Students   P–Professionals/Postdoctorates

Sponsoring Organization Index

The Sponsoring Organization Index makes it easy to identify agencies that offer financial aid primarily or exclusively to women. In this index, the sponsoring organizations are listed alphabetically, word by word. In addition, we've used an alphabetical code (within parentheses) to help you identify the intended recipients of the funding offered by the organizations: U = Undergraduates;   G = Graduate Students;   P = Professionals/Postdoctorates. For example, if the name of a sponsoring organization is followed by (U) 241, a program sponsored by that organization is described in the Undergraduates chapter, in entry 241. If that sponsoring organization's name is followed by another entry number—for example, (G) 1370—the same or a different program sponsored by that organization is described in the Professionals/Postdoctorates chapter, in entry 1370. Remember: the numbers cited here refer to program entry numbers, not to page numbers in the book.

A

Abaris Training Resources, Inc., (U) 76

Academy of Criminal Justice Sciences, (P) 1242

Accounting and Financial Women's Alliance, (G) 843

Accounting and Financial Women's Alliance. Billings Chapter, (U) 111

Accounting and Financial Women's Alliance. Denver Chapter, (U) 191

Accounting and Financial Women's Alliance. District of Columbia Area Chapter, (U) 196

Accounting and Financial Women's Alliance. Huntsville Chapter, (U) 313, (G) 921

Accounting and Financial Women's Alliance. Milwaukee Chapter, (U) 449

Accounting and Financial Women's Alliance. Omaha Chapter, (U) 513, (G) 1051

Accounting and Financial Women's Alliance. Richmond Chapter, (U) 479

Accounting and Financial Women's Alliance. Tulsa Chapter, (U) 642

Accounting and Financial Women's Alliance. Wichita Chapter, (U) 669, (G) 1145

Acxiom Corporation, (U) 6, (G) 722

Advanced Laboratory Physics Association, (U) 2

Adventure Science Center, (U) 645

Aggressor and Dancer Fleets, (G) 1153

Agricultural and Applied Economics Association. Committee on Women in Agricultural Economics, (G) 1123, (P) 1410

Agriculture Future of America, (U) 98

Air Products and Chemicals, Inc., (U) 18

Airbus Helicopters, (U) 76

Aircraft Owners and Pilots Association, (U) 57

Aircraft Technical Publishers, (U) 80

Airport Minority Advisory Council, (U) 29, 85

Alabama Golf Association, (U) 21

Alabama Law Foundation, (G) 953

Alaska Community Foundation, (U) 589

Albuquerque Community Foundation, (U) 551

Alcoa Foundation, (U) 23

Alfred P. Sloan Foundation, (P) 1171

The Allen Endowment, (U) 250

Alliance for Women in Media, (U) 255-256, 397, 492, (G) 874-875, 971, 1037

Alpha Chi Omega Foundation, (G) 813

Alpha Delta Kappa, (G) 730, (P) 1172-1173

Alpha Delta Kappa. Florida Chapter, (U) 251, (G) 872

Alpha Delta Kappa. North Carolina Chapter, (U) 241

Alpha Epsilon Phi, (U) 152

Alpha Kappa Alpha Sorority, Inc., (U) 25-26, (G) 731-732, 840

Alpha Kappa Alpha Sorority, Inc. Xi Psi Omega Chapter, (U) 705

Amateur Athletic Union of the United States, (U) 3

American Academy of Physician Assistants, (U) 380, (G) 964

American Accounting Association, (P) 1312-1314

American Agri-Women, (U) 341, 598

American Airlines, (U) 33-35, (P) 1178

American Anthropological Association, (U) 627, (G) 725, 1122

American Association for Justice, (G) 1012

American Association for the Advancement of Science, (P) 1324

American Association of Japanese University Women, (U) 36, (G) 737

American Association of Neurological Surgeons, (P) 1327

American Association of Obstetricians and Gynecologists Foundation, (P) 1179

American Association of Petroleum Geologists Foundation, (G) 934

American Association of Physics Teachers, (U) 2

American Association of University Women, (U) 4, (G) 717, 738, 1097-1098, (P) 1167, 1180-1181, 1232, 1250

American Association of University Women. Honolulu Branch, (U) 306, 644, (G) 916

U–Undergraduates   **G–Graduate Students**   **P–Professionals/Postdoctorates**

U–Undergraduates   **G–Graduate Students**   **P–Professionals/Postdoctorates**

U–Undergraduates　　　　**G–Graduate Students**　　　　**P–Professionals/Postdoctorates**

U–Undergraduates   **G–Graduate Students**   **P–Professionals/Postdoctorates**

Residency Index

Some programs listed in this book are set aside for women who are residents of a particular state, region, or other geographic location. Others are open to applicants wherever they may live. The Residency Index will help you pinpoint programs available in your area as well as programs that have no residency restrictions at all (these are listed under the term "United States"). To use this index, look up the geographic areas that apply to you (always check the listings under "United States"), jot down the entry numbers listed for the recipient level that applies to you (Undergraduates, Graduate Students, or Professionals/Postdoctorates), and use those numbers to find the program descriptions in the directory. To help you in your search, we've provided some "see" and "see also" references in the index entries. Remember: the numbers cited here refer to program entry numbers, not to page numbers in the book.

Tenability Index

Some programs listed in this book can be used only in specific cities, counties, states, or regions. Others may be used anywhere in the United States. The Tenability Index will help you locate funding that is restricted to a specific area as well as funding that has no tenability restrictions (these are listed under the term "United States"). To use this index, look up the geographic areas where you'd like to go (always check the listings under "United States"), jot down the entry numbers listed for the recipient group that represents you (Undergraduates, Graduate Students, Professionals/Postdoctorates), and use those numbers to find the program descriptions in the directory. To help you in your search, we've provided some "see" and "see also" references in the index entries. Remember: the numbers cited here refer to program entry numbers, not to page numbers in the book.

Subject Index

There are hundreds of specific subject fields covered in this directory. Use the Subject Index to identify these topics, as well as the recipient level supported (Undergraduates, Graduate Students, or Professionals/Postdoctorates) by the available funding programs. To help you pinpoint your search, we've included many "see" and "see also" references. Since a large number of programs are not restricted by subject, be sure to check the references listed under the "General programs" heading in the subject index (in addition to the specific terms that directly relate to your interest areas); hundreds of funding opportunities are listed there that can be used to support activities in any subject area (although the programs may be restricted in other ways). Remember: the numbers cited in this index refer to program entry numbers, not to page numbers in the book.

A

Accounting: **Undergraduates,** 11, 29, 85, 111, 129, 150, 157, 171, 191, 196, 223, 313, 319, 445, 449, 466, 469, 479, 513, 555, 568, 642, 669, 684, 686; **Graduate Students,** 724, 808, 843, 849, 921, 963, 1017-1018, 1051, 1072, 1145; **Professionals/ Postdoctorates,** 1312-1314. *See also* Finance; General programs

Acting. *See* Performing arts

Administration. *See* Business administration; Education, administration; Management; Personnel administration; Public administration

Advertising: **Undergraduates,** 144, 237, 255-256, 323, 397, 492, 508, 510, 550, 583; **Graduate Students,** 859, 874-875, 971, 1037, 1046, 1048, 1096. *See also* Communications; General programs; Marketing; Public relations

Aeronautical engineering. *See* Engineering, aeronautical

Aeronautics: **Undergraduates,** 384; **Graduate Students,** 726, 1024; **Professionals/Postdoctorates,** 1169. *See also* Aviation; Engineering, aeronautical; General programs; Physical sciences

Aerospace engineering. *See* Engineering, aerospace

Aerospace sciences. *See* Space sciences

African American studies: **Professionals/Postdoctorates,** 1237, 1358. *See also* General programs; Minority studies

Aged and aging: **Graduate Students,** 863, 1114. *See also* General programs; Social sciences

Agribusiness: **Undergraduates,** 341, 541, 598, 696; **Graduate Students,** 1161. *See also* Agriculture and agricultural sciences; Business administration; General programs

Agricultural communications: **Undergraduates,** 341, 598. *See also* Agriculture and agricultural sciences; Communications; General programs

Agricultural economics. *See* Economics, agricultural

Agricultural education. *See* Education, agricultural

Agricultural engineering. *See* Engineering, agricultural

Agricultural technology: **Undergraduates,** 341, 598. *See also* Agriculture and agricultural sciences; General programs; Technology

Agriculture and agricultural sciences: **Undergraduates,** 98, 101, 341, 372, 412, 598, 630, 638, 696; **Graduate Students,** 961, 1090, 1123, 1161; **Professionals/Postdoctorates,** 1397, 1410. *See also* Biological sciences; General programs

Agrimarketing and sales. *See* Agribusiness

Air conditioning engineering. *See* Engineering, refrigerating and air conditioning

American history. *See* History, American

American Indian studies. *See* Native American studies

American studies: **Graduate Students,** 1000. *See also* General programs; Humanities

Animation: **Undergraduates,** 275. *See also* Filmmaking; General programs

Anthropology: **Undergraduates,** 627; **Graduate Students,** 725, 744, 777, 1104, 1122, 1166; **Professionals/Postdoctorates,** 1227, 1404. *See also* General programs; Social sciences

Applied arts. *See* Arts and crafts

Aquatic sciences. *See* Oceanography

Archaeology: **Undergraduates,** 148; **Graduate Students,** 803, 996; **Professionals/Postdoctorates,** 1343. *See also* General programs; History; Social sciences

Architectural engineering. *See* Engineering, architectural

Architecture: **Undergraduates,** 29, 75, 78, 85, 244, 287, 396, 403, 478, 646; **Graduate Students,** 974, 1097. *See also* Fine arts; General programs

Architecture, naval. *See* Naval architecture

Arithmetic. *See* Mathematics

Armament and disarmament: **Professionals/Postdoctorates,** 1319. *See also* General programs; Military affairs; Peace studies

Armed services. *See* Military affairs

Art: **Undergraduates,** 273, 286, 292, 298, 414; **Graduate Students,** 831; **Professionals/Postdoctorates,** 1194-1196, 1257, 1280, 1375. *See also* Education, art; Fine arts; General programs; Illustrators and illustrations; names of specific art forms

Italian studies: **Undergraduates,** 14, 485; **Graduate Students,** 1029. See also General programs; Humanities

J

Jazz. See Music, jazz

Jewelry: **Undergraduates,** 695. See also Arts and crafts; General programs

Jewish history. See History, Jewish

Jewish studies: **Graduate Students,** 902; **Professionals/ Postdoctorates,** 1280-1281, 1284-1285. See also General programs; Religion and religious activities

Jobs. See Employment

Journalism: **Undergraduates,** 14, 55, 110, 117, 144, 217, 226, 237, 255-256, 283, 294, 342, 348, 397, 492, 508, 510, 567, 583; **Graduate Students,** 729, 859, 874-875, 971, 1037, 1046, 1048, 1084, 1096. See also Broadcasting; Communications; General programs; names of specific types of journalism

Journalism, broadcast: **Undergraduates,** 346, 583; **Graduate Students,** 1096. See also Communications; General programs; Radio; Television

Journalism, online: **Undergraduates,** 255-256, 294, 397, 492; **Graduate Students,** 874-875, 971, 1037. See also General programs; Journalism

Journalism, agriculture. See Agricultural communications

Journalism, sports. See Sports reporting

Junior colleges. See Education, higher

Jurisprudence. See Law, general

L

Labor unions and members: **Undergraduates,** 129; **Professionals/Postdoctorates,** 1396. See also General programs; Industrial relations

Landscape architecture: **Undergraduates,** 75, 78. See also Botany; General programs; Horticulture

Language and linguistics: **Undergraduates,** 168, 577, 670; **Graduate Students,** 804, 1092, 1146; **Professionals/ Postdoctorates,** 1226-1227. See also General programs; Humanities; names of specific languages

Language, English: **Undergraduates,** 14, 55, 144, 237, 283, 502, 508; **Graduate Students,** 859, 1046. See also General programs; Language and linguistics

Language, French: **Graduate Students,** 995; **Professionals/ Postdoctorates,** 1342. See also General programs; Language and linguistics

Language, Greek: **Graduate Students,** 996; **Professionals/ Postdoctorates,** 1343. See also General programs; Language and linguistics

Language, Italian: **Undergraduates,** 485; **Graduate Students,** 1029. See also General programs; Language and linguistics

Latin American history. See History, Latin American

Law enforcement. See Criminal justice

Law, general: **Undergraduates,** 208, 301, 319, 427, 544, 565, 685; **Graduate Students,** 719, 760, 767-768, 778, 804, 806, 835-836, 853, 857, 882, 889, 912, 930, 953, 965, 969, 989, 991, 994, 1047, 1077, 1086, 1098, 1127-1128, 1134, 1144, 1149; **Professionals/Postdoctorates,** 1226, 1291. See also Criminal justice; General programs; Paralegal studies; Social sciences; names of legal specialties

Lawyers. See Law, general

Leadership: **Undergraduates,** 72, 341, 598; **Graduate Students,** 831; **Professionals/Postdoctorates,** 1210, 1228, 1321. See also General programs; Management

Legal assistants. See Paralegal studies

Legal studies and services. See Law, general

Lesbianism. See Homosexuality

Librarians. See Library and information services, general

Libraries and librarianship, art: **Undergraduates,** 71; **Graduate Students,** 762; **Professionals/Postdoctorates,** 1198. See also General programs

Library and information services, general: **Professionals/ Postdoctorates,** 1331. See also General programs; Social sciences; names of specific types of librarianship

Life sciences. See Biological sciences

Linguistics. See Language and linguistics

Literature: **Undergraduates,** 14, 283, 502, 556; **Graduate Students,** 848, 1000; **Professionals/Postdoctorates,** 1259. See also General programs; Humanities; names of specific types of literature

Literature, English: **Undergraduates,** 14, 55, 283; **Graduate Students,** 905; **Professionals/Postdoctorates,** 1387. See also General programs; Literature

Literature, French: **Graduate Students,** 995; **Professionals/ Postdoctorates,** 1342. See also General programs; Literature

Literature, Greek: **Graduate Students,** 996; **Professionals/ Postdoctorates,** 1343. See also General programs; Literature

Litigation: **Graduate Students,** 965, 1012. See also General programs; Law, general

Logistics: **Undergraduates,** 129, 399, 587, 701, 704; **Graduate Students,** 805, 812, 908, 966. See also Business administration; General programs; Transportation

Lung disease: **Professionals/Postdoctorates,** 1230. See also Disabilities; General programs; Health and health care; Medical sciences

M

Magazines. See Journalism; Literature

Management: **Undergraduates,** 30, 118, 129, 188, 206, 259, 522, 541, 595; **Graduate Students,** 734, 792, 833, 876, 924, 1036, 1054, 1106; **Professionals/Postdoctorates,** 1216, 1401, 1429. See also General programs; Social sciences

Management, construction: **Undergraduates,** 78, 263, 287, 396, 478, 643; **Graduate Students,** 881. See also Construction industry; General programs; Management

Manufacturing engineering. See Engineering, manufacturing

Maps and mapmaking. See Cartography

Marine sciences: **Undergraduates,** 680-681; **Graduate Students,** 844, 888, 1153; **Professionals/Postdoctorates,** 1171, 1274, 1340, 1423. See also General programs; Sciences; names of specific marine sciences

Marketing: **Undergraduates,** 129, 144, 206, 237, 259, 364, 442, 508, 522, 541, 550, 583; **Graduate Students,** 833, 859, 876, 1008, 1046, 1054, 1096. See also Advertising; General programs; Public relations; Sales

Mass communications. See Communications

Materials engineering. See Engineering, materials

Materials sciences: **Undergraduates,** 5, 59, 302, 433, 672; **Graduate Students,** 924, 1002, 1024, 1028, 1031; **Professionals/Postdoctorates,** 1339. See also General programs; Physical sciences

Calendar Index

Since most funding programs have specific deadline dates, some may have already closed by the time you begin to look for money. You can use the Calendar Index to identify which programs are still open. To do that, go to the recipient category (Undergraduates, Graduate Students, or Professionals/Postdoctorates) that interests you, think about when you'll be able to complete your application forms, go to the appropriate months, jot down the entry numbers listed there, and use those numbers to find the program descriptions in the directory. Keep in mind that the numbers cited here refer to program entry numbers, not to page numbers in the book.

Professionals/Postdoctorates:

Made in the USA
Middletown, DE
10 January 2018